# EX-LIBRIS



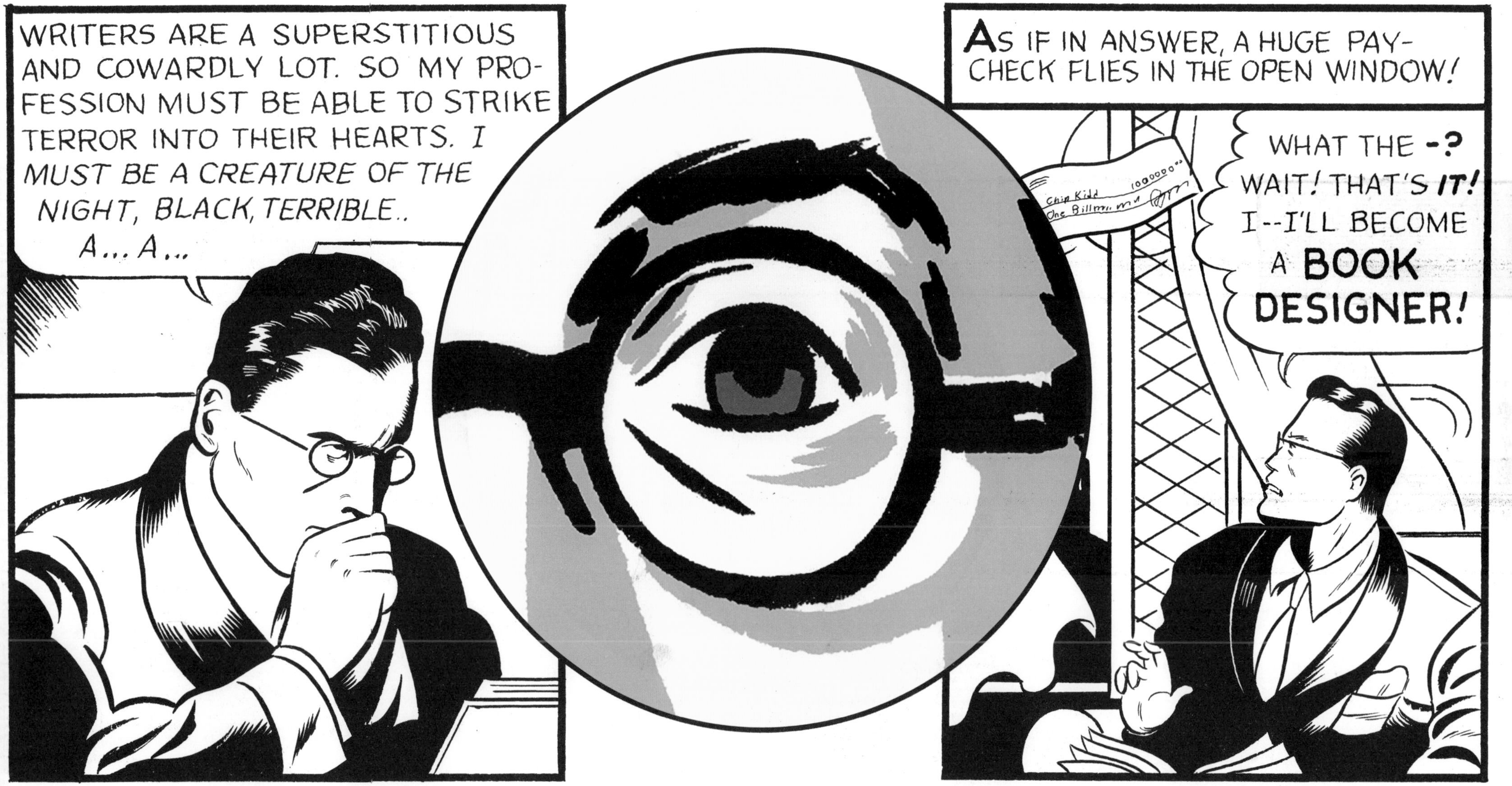
WRITERS ARE A SUPERSTITIOUS AND COWARDLY LOT. SO MY PROFESSION MUST BE ABLE TO STRIKE TERROR INTO THEIR HEARTS. I MUST BE A CREATURE OF THE NIGHT, BLACK, TERRIBLE.. A... A...
AS IF IN ANSWER, A HUGE PAYCHECK FLIES IN THE OPEN WINDOW!
WHAT THE -? WAIT! THAT'S *IT*! I--I'LL BECOME A **BOOK DESIGNER!**

# CHAS. I. KIDD.

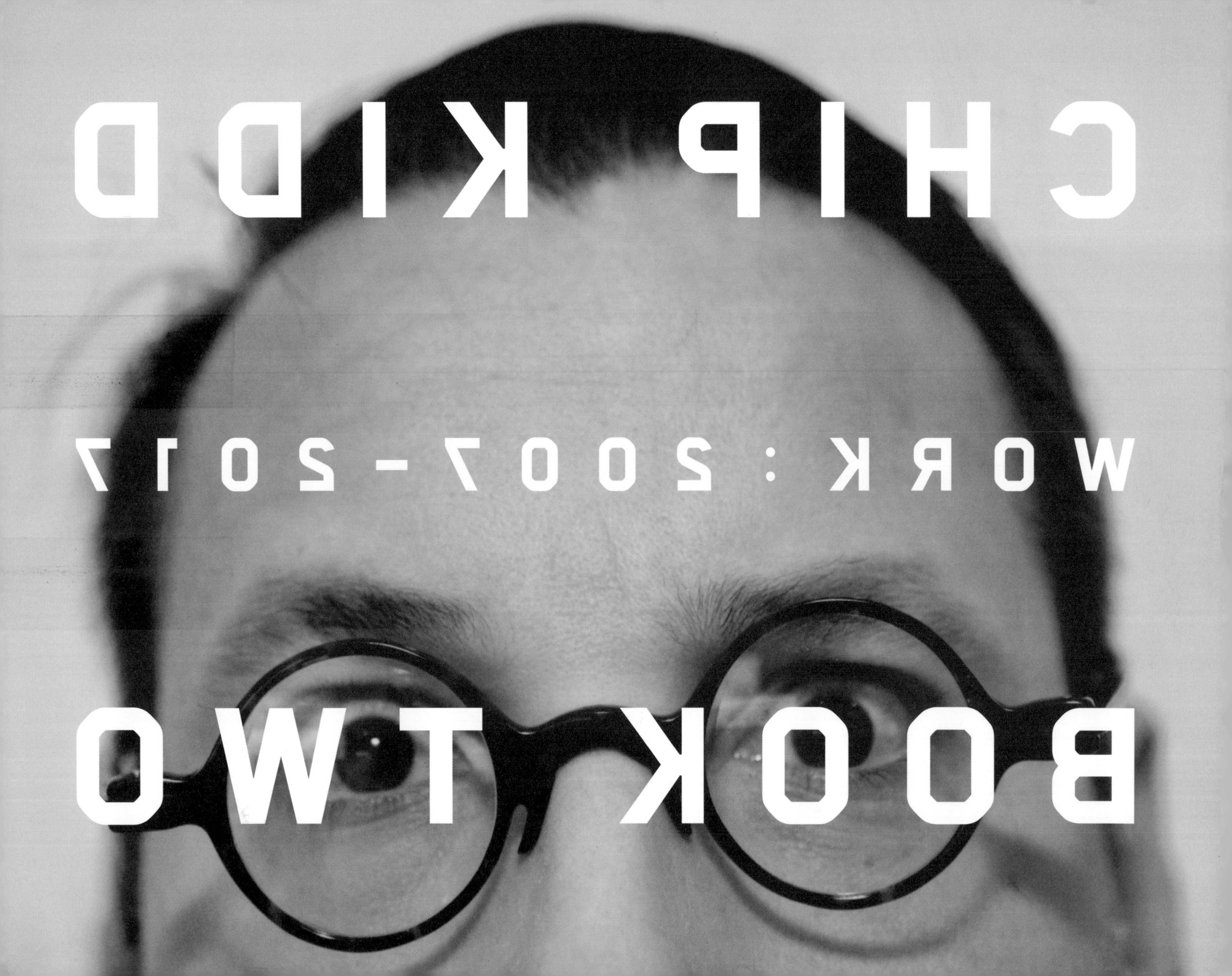
CHIP KIDD
WORK: 2007-2017
BOOK TWO

# CHIP KIDD

INTRODUCTIONS BY    HARUKI MURAKAMI    NEIL GAIMAN    ORHAN PAMUK

## WORK : 2007 - 2017

DESIGN BY MARK MELNICK    PHOTOGRAPHY BY GEOFF SPEAR

# BOOK TWO

RIZZOLI
NEW YORK

New York · Paris · London · Milan

*For J. D. McClatchy*

First published in the United States of America
by Rizzoli International Publications, Inc.
300 Park Avenue South, New York, NY 10010
*www.rizzoliusa.com*

*Chip Kidd Book Two*


2017 2018 2019 2020 2021 / 10 9 8 7 6 5 4 3 2 1
ISBN: 9780847860081

Library of Congress Control Number:
2017934352

Printed in China



Editor: Ian Luna
Project Editors: Monica Davis & Meaghan McGovern
Copy Editor: Mary Ellen Wilson
Editorial Management: Lynn Scrabis
Production: Maria Pia Gramaglia & Susan Lynch

Publisher: Charles Miers

Cover Design: Chip Kidd
Book Design: Mark Melnick
Author portrait (spine & endpaper): Michael Cho
"Ex Libris" endpaper art: Chris Ware
Author photograph (endpaper & title page): Martin Parr

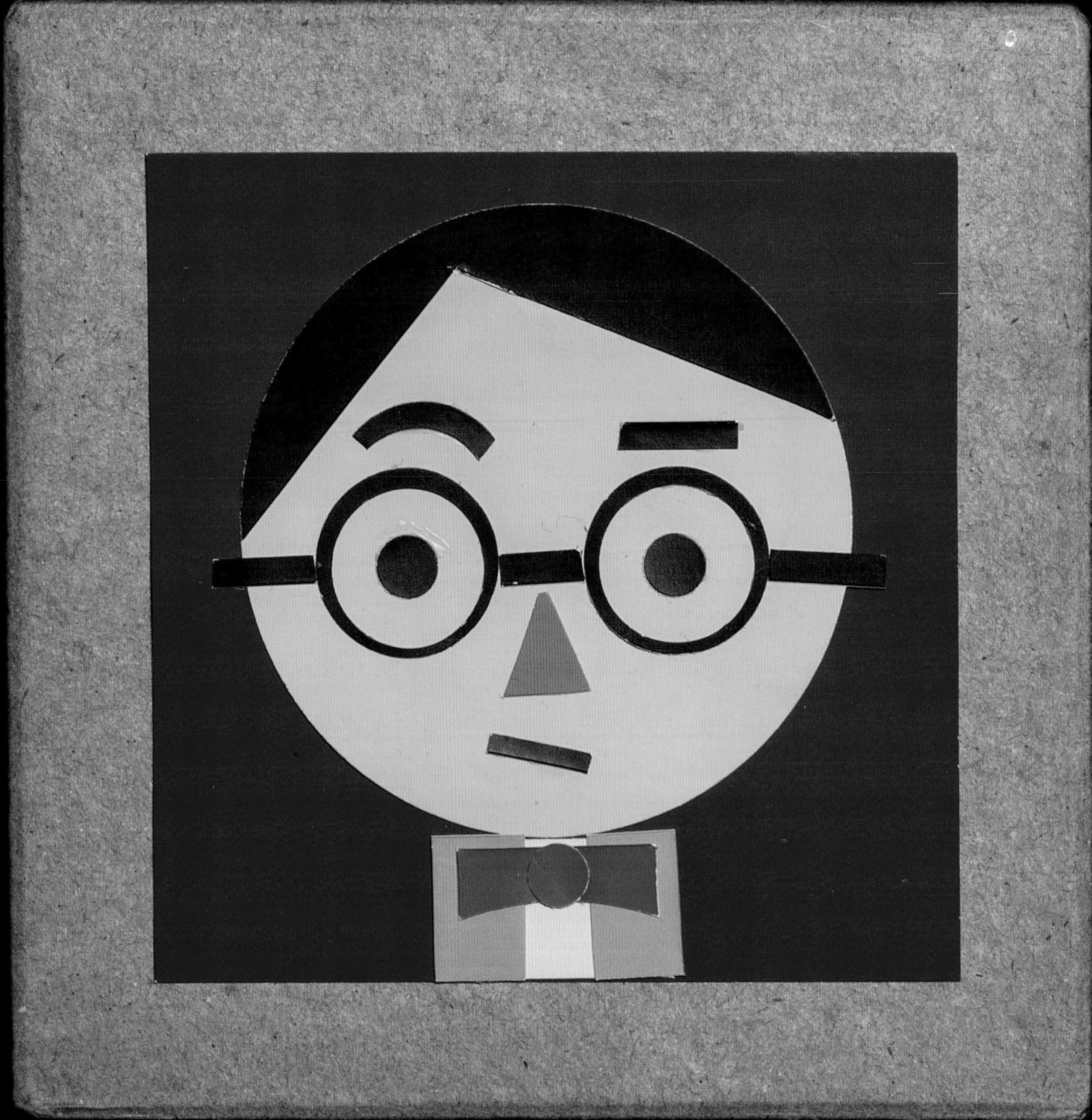

**RIGHT & PAGE 5:** Shadow box lid art and

# Chip Kidd in dialogue with Chip Kidd

SUMMER 2016

**Q:** Regarding your work: really, why should anyone care?

**A:** Gee, thanks a lot.

**Q:** Sorry. Little joke. But you know you actually feel that way.

**A:** At times. Thus this book, I suppose.

**Q:** So, what's happened in the last ten years, since the release of *Book One*?

**A:** A lot. Not much. Everything. Nothing.

**Q:** What an utterly pretentious, meaningless answer.

**A:** True. But you know you actually feel that way.

**Q:** Touché. Let's start over—with your favorite question of the last decade: Has the introduction of e-books changed the way you design?

**A:** Not favorite question, but the most frequently asked. It used to be that the first query I would get after giv-ing a talk would be the inevitable "Do you really read the books before you design them?" Now it's "How have e-books affected your design process?" Quickly followed by "What's the future of publishing?"

As for the first question, the answer is "Not at all." I will get into that later. As for the second, "I have absolutely no idea. I honestly don't and never have."

**Q:** But you must think about it all the time.

**A:** You know I do, but that isn't the same as pretending to know what's going to happen. And more to the point, that has little bearing on how I go about creating a cover, which is what I really should be thinking about.

As we know, the fate of book publishing has been in flux ever since the business has existed. Change has been the only thing that's never changed about it. Yet I feel the archival nature of the hardcover book solidly argues against its going away—it's permanent, it will be kept and shelved and referred to, it will outlast us all. And when the lights go out, you can fire up a candle and open the book to read and it will work just fine.

One thing I have understood again and again in the last 30 years (and counting) since I've been doing this work is that, no matter what form a book takes, its author wants the work visually represented—in as interesting and memorable a way as possible. I truly believe that won't change. Globally we are a visual culture, and we want to look at a *thing*, even if that thing represents a text that we are meant to more than just look at—that we're meant to read and absorb.

**Q:** I can't help but notice that this book contains a lot of selfies with some of the better-known authors and clients you've worked with.

**A:** Correct. And that is not a question.

**Q:** Ok. Why?

**A:** Oh, it's totally self-indulgent, of course. But if this book is a record of my existence on Earth and what I've done with it (and that is definitely how I view it, however self-important that sounds), then I think those pictures are a valid component of same. Part of what I've loved so much about what I do is the remarkable number and vari-ety of extraordinary people I've had the honor to work for, and with. Why not show some of that?

**Q:** And how much longer do you see yourself doing this kind of work?

**A:** For as long as I can, and for as long as people want me to do it. And pay me to do it, that's very important. One thing that does worry me in the abstract: if we're not careful as a profession to focus on ideas, graphic design could devolve into something like a computer algorithm anyone can buy and plug their problem into. Several online self-publishing programs have already offered this (six "Crime Thriller" cover options to choose from, all of them ghastly, in the worst possible way). That's not design, that's decoration.

**Q:** Getting back to the "Not at all." How have e-books not changed the cover design process?

**A:** Because that process is about ideas, not the medium in which they're received. What really has changed exponentially during the time I've been working is the speed with which something can get done. And that of course means computers. That will never, ever cease to amaze me, because I was lucky enough to be part of the last generation of designers who learned the craft by hand, before the arrival of Apple.

Yes, lucky. Because I can appreciate how difficult it used to be to make something, how painstaking and labor-intensive. And I believe that made you really think long and hard about what you wanted to do before plunging in and taking a week or more with the typesetting, the paste-up, ordering the color prints to the right size, etc. I don't miss that drudgery, at all, but I do think it made me hone my conceptual-thinking skills. This will make me sound like an old crab, but nowadays you do a design workshop at a school and once you give the assignment the kids instantly head right to the web. That's the start of their process. It's a shame.

**Q:** You do sound like an old crab. Why a shame?

**A:** Because the web is not going to think for them. They

**Q:** How do you know that's not what they're doing?

**A:** Because I see what they come up with. Look, I'm certainly not saying they're all mindless lemmings (there are plenty of talented students, there always will be), and it's not a new problem—I remember a student in our design curriculum at Penn State in the early '80s who had a fancy airbrush kit so all of his projects had a kind of slick, smooth sheen that caught you off guard for just a moment, until you realized that there wasn't much—if any—substance or thought behind them. But they looked pretty. If this sounds interesting, trust me, it wasn't—and the teacher was smart enough to see right through it and call him on it.

**Q:** That was Lanny Sommese?

**A:** Yes, and Bill Kinser, our other genius graphic design professor, who was of the same temperament. They were both sharp as tacks. You didn't need to just work hard in their classes; you needed to work smart.

**Q:** Switching gears, why no Instagram account?

**A:** Because there's only so much social media one can deal with and get any work done. I post on Twitter and Facebook, occasionally, and that has to suffice. I'm sure I could be smarter about it, but any image or message about (or aside from) my work I want to share with the public is covered by those outlets, and my website, at least for now.

**Q:** Do you enjoy writing?

**A:** No, I hate it. I'm terrible at it, and this "interview" is

**Q:** Then why do you do it?

**A:** Because I think it's an important part of growing as a designer, especially one who is in the book business. Learning how to write is learning how to articulate the message you want to send in the most effective way possible, and that is what designers are supposed to do. The problem is that I work with some of the best writers in the world, and when I read their work I think, "Why am I even bothering?" But you have to, you have to keep trying.

**Q:** What's the best question you've ever been asked?

**A:** Hmmmm. I guess "What's the dumbest way you almost died?"

**Q:** And the answer?

**A:** Giving a talk at Weiden and Kennedy in the East End of London on a morning in June of 2006.

**Q:** Oh, yeah. God. What the hell happened anyway?

**A:** You know all too well. And I'm NOT going into the details here. Maybe I'll write about it in a book someday.

**Q:** You've said over the years that third-rate writers are the hardest to work with because they subconsciously want the jacket to make up for the mediocrity of their text. Yes?

**A:** WHAT? I have *never* said that and you know it.

**Q:** Not publicly. But you've thought it?

**A:** I'm NOT answering that. And anyway we've run out of space.

"Talent?

*You* wouldn't know talent if it sat in your lap and painted the Sistine Chapel ceiling on the roof of your mouth."

—**David & Amy Sedaris,**

***One Woman Shoe***

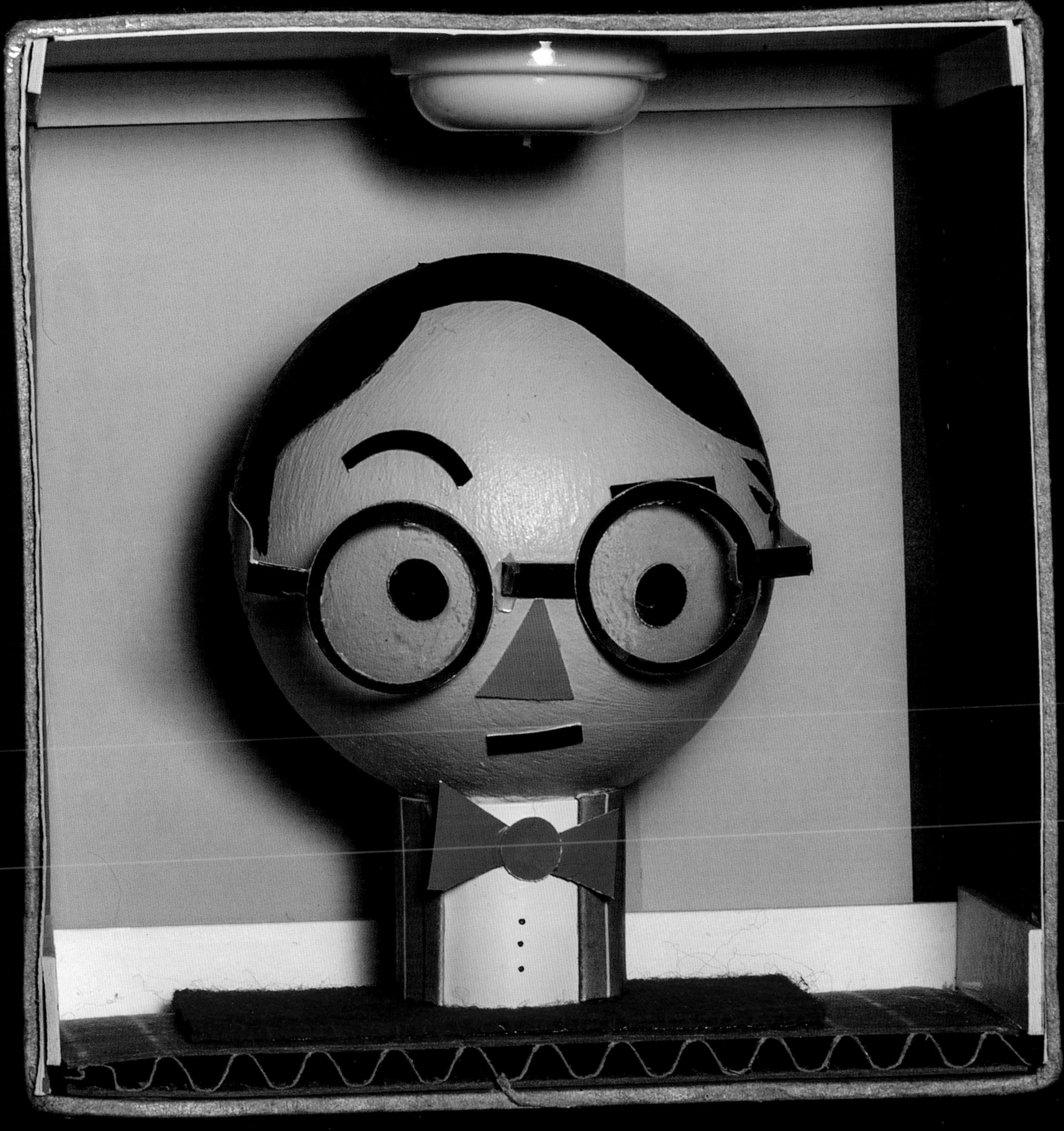

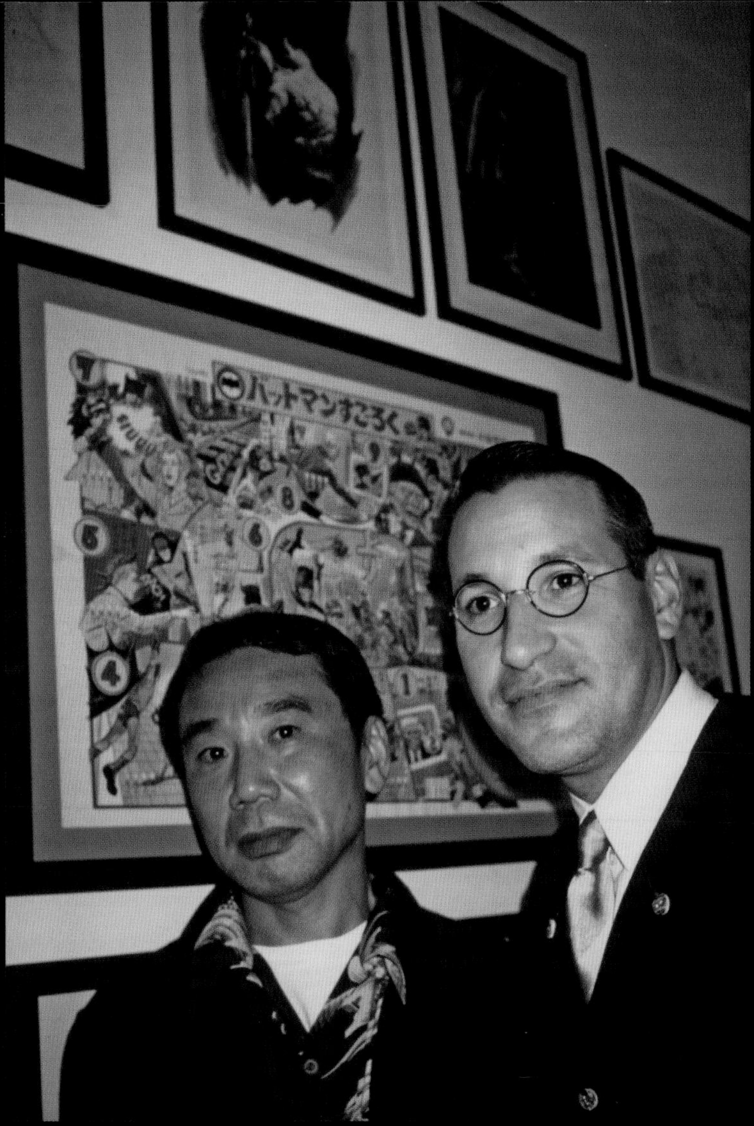
バットマンすごろく

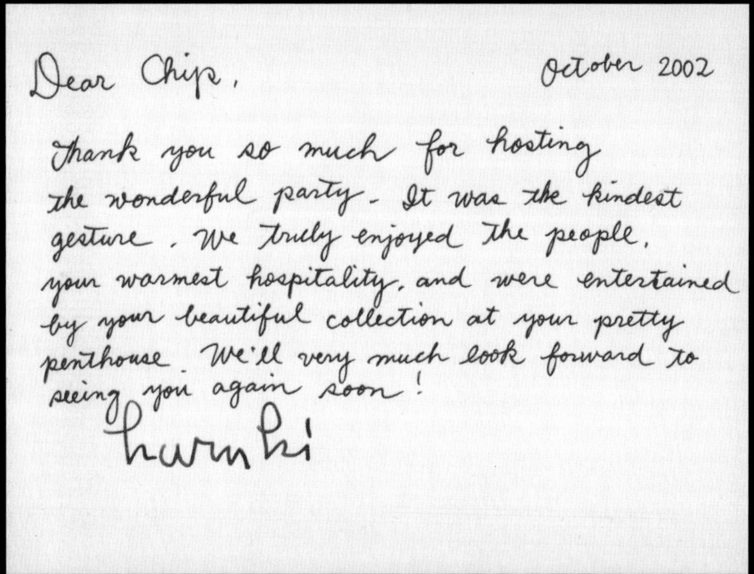
Dear Chip, October 2002

Thank you so much for hosting the wonderful party. It was the kindest gesture. We truly enjoyed the people, your warmest hospitality, and were entertained by your beautiful collection at your pretty penthouse. We'll very much look forward to seeing you again soon!

Haruki

ESSAY

# Haruki Murakami

## WHAT'S IN A NAME?

The first time I met Chip Kidd was at the Knopf offices in New York in the early 1990s. Chip was—and to my surprise still is—an employee of Knopf.

When I was introduced to him my first thought was, "Chip Kidd? What a unique name." I don't know what image springs to mind for most Americans, but for me, as a Japanese, the name Chip Kidd evoked a gunman in one of those old-time, silent-era Westerns or a cartoon film. A beautiful heroine is tied to the railroad tracks by an evil villain, a locomotive steams full speed towards them, when suddenly Chip Kidd, the dashing hero with his blazing pair of six-shooters, gallops to the rescue astride his trusty white stallion.

At that point I should have asked him straight up, "Is that your real name? Or a nickname you use for business?" but I figured since I'd just met him that would have been kind of rude. Ever since then, whenever we meet I mean to ask, but I somehow never have. So which is it?

Be that as it may, the real-life Chip Kidd isn't the type of person who would look good with a pair of six-shooters (or an AK 47 or M16 for that matter). And I can't picture him on a white stallion either. (This is entirely conjecture, but I wonder: has Chip even once in his life been on a horse of any color?)

The city landscape is what suits Chip. What I mean is, since the only time I see Chip is in either New York or Tokyo, I can only picture him walking down city streets. Whenever he comes to Tokyo the two of us always down prodigious amounts of saké. And if he has the time, he wanders all over Tokyo, like he's lived here all his life, indulging an appetite for unusual Japanese toys or old picture books. Always on the move. No time to spare, it would seem, to jump astride a white stallion and rescue a heroine.

But strangely enough, the more I look at the countless book designs he's created, the more I feel that Chip Kidd is the perfect name for him. The boundlessly inventive ideas, the out-of-the-box perspective, the sly sense of humor, the carefully calculated anachronisms, the occasional glimpse of the lyrical. The name "Chip Kidd" resonates with a combination of all these elements.

And to me, at least, what wafts up from that name is a sense of the visionary. An exquisite, clear visionary sense, yet one slightly estranged from reality—one that can only exist in the streets of the city, or perhaps in old silent movies or animated films. And that inimitable, cozy alienation that hangs over both the name Chip Kidd and each one of the book covers he's designed is something I cannot help but adore.

It goes without my saying, but what makes his book designs so amazing is the deep love and respect he (no doubt) feels towards the form of books themselves. Plus his amazing ability to grasp the content and voice of a book and channel that essence into his design. It's that combination of affection, respect, and deep understanding that makes his designs so captivating to so many people.

As they say, you can't judge a book by its cover. How many people pick up books in bookstores because of his designs is something only God knows. Not being God, I have no idea how much his designs have helped boost sales of my own books. But what I do know is that Chip has continued to be an invaluable partner. Which is why, whenever he stops by Tokyo, the least I can do is treat him to as much saké as he likes.

Even if Chip wouldn't look good riding a white stallion and brandishing a pair of silver six-shooters, in keeping with his name he does stride off, a legendary hero, into a book cover sunset. A wonderful, perfectly Chip Kidd–like, visionary sunset. —H.M.

*Translated by Philip Gabriel*

**OPPOSITE:** Photo from a party that I threw for Haruki at my apartment way back in 2002. Such a thrill for me, I was eager to show him all of my Japanese Batman stuff from the 1960s. Haruki's thoughtful thank-you note is below.

**RIGHT:** A photograph showing the process behind the design of Haruki's short story collection, *Men Without Women* (Knopf, 2017). In the upper left is a photo of us at dinner in Tokyo, April 2016. I laid a sheet of vellum over the photograph and used a grease pencil to draw his silhouette. Next, I took the Japanese kanji for "woman" and morphed it into a puzzle piece. Finally, I cut that piece out of his heart. If you read the book, this makes perfect sense, trust me. Happily, the pain and suffering implied is all fiction.

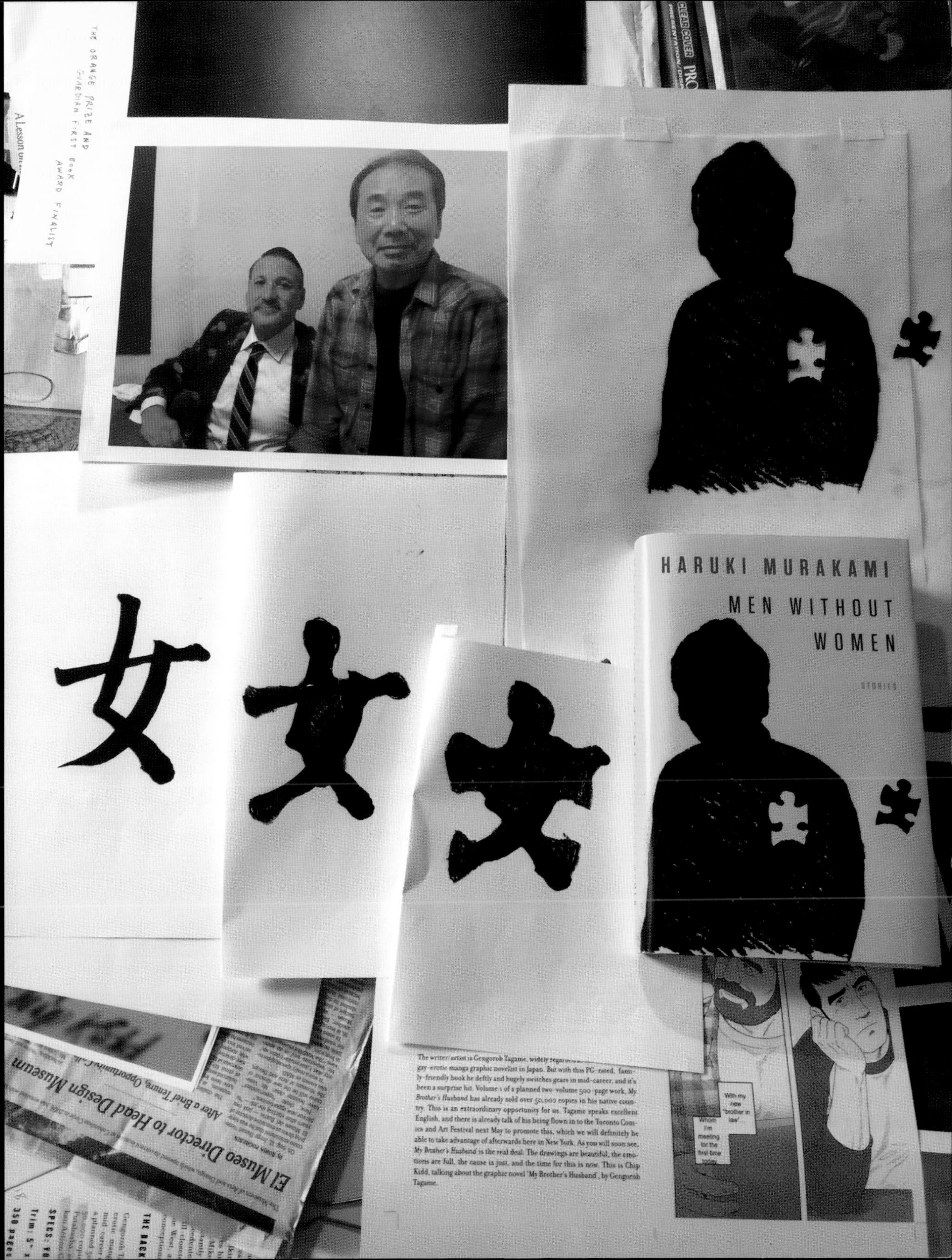
THE ORANGE PRIZE AND GUARDIAN FIRST BOOK AWARD FINALIST
女
HARUKI MURAKAMI
MEN WITHOUT WOMEN
STORIES
El Museo Director to Head Design Museum

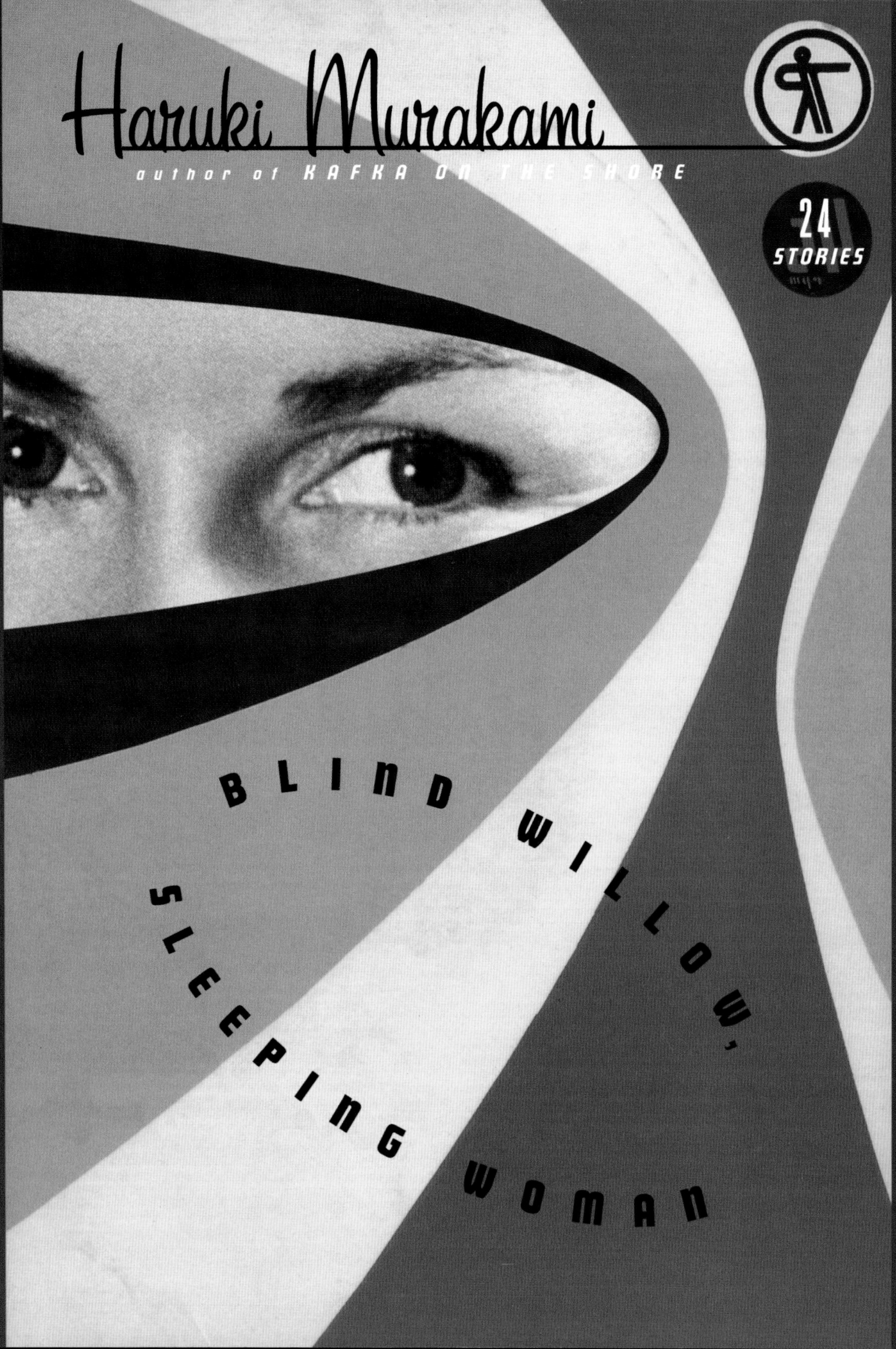
Haruki Murakami
author of KAFKA ON THE SHORE
24 STORIES
BLIND WILLOW,
SLEEPING WOMAN



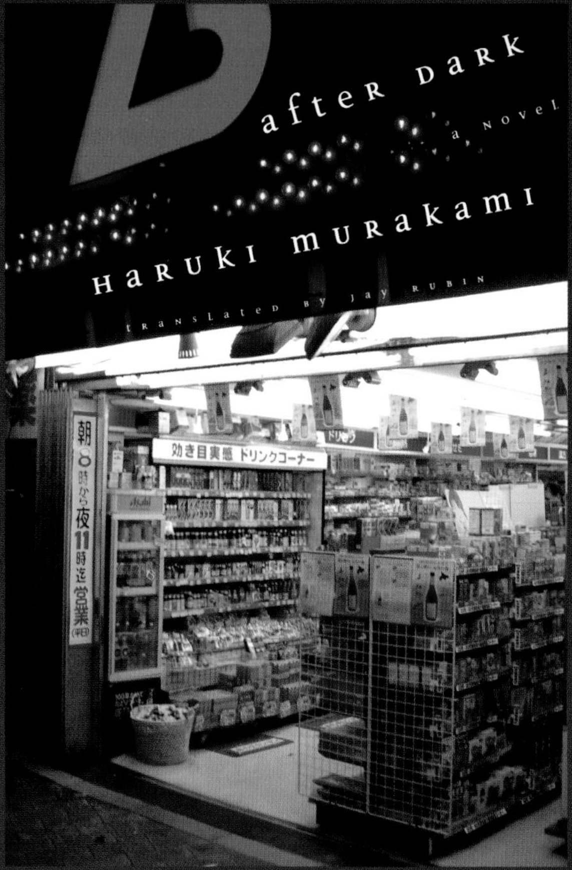
after DARK
a novel
HARUKI MURAKAMI
TRANSLATED BY JAY RUBIN

## Portfolio · Haruki Murakami

The title of Haruki Murakami's novella *After Dark* is literal—it's a story that takes place in Tokyo in the middle of a single night. As luck would have it, I was attending a design conference in that wonderful city during the time I was working on the jacket, so I just wandered around one evening between the hours of 10 p.m. and 3 a.m. and took a lot of pictures. This was not as exhausting as it may sound because when you travel to Japan from the West (especially the East Coast), your daytime and nighttime inner clocks are switched until they slowly repair themselves. So I was wide awake. This was in 2006, so

**LEFT:** I used the iconography of vintage Japanese jazz records for this collection of Haruki's stories. He is a great jazz aficionado and constantly refers to music in his work. Knopf, 2006. **ABOVE:** One of the many convenience stores in Tokyo that is open all hours. Worth trying for the *After Dark* jacket, but too pedestrian; doesn't feel like fiction to me.

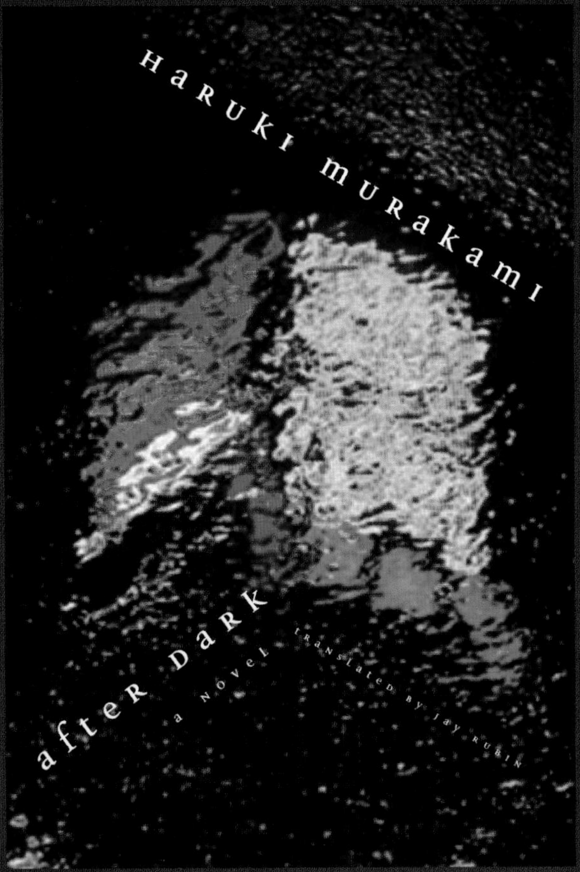
HARUKI MURAKAMI
after DARK
a NOVEL
TRANSLATED BY JAY RUBIN

I did not yet have a cellphone that had any kind of quality camera. I used a high-resolution Panasonic Lumix point-and-shoot that I have to this day, which does a terrific job with candid shots. Tokyo is like New York in that there are plenty of places that are open 24/7. One that caught my eye was a pachinko parlor, a sort of arcade that features Japanese pinball machines, and it was strikingly lit in bright pink and yellow. Just as I was about to take a picture of it from the sidewalk, two huge glass doors with frosted vertical stripes slid shut. *Click!* I thought "Damn!" and waited for them to open again. Only the next day did I realize that this was the shot—it perfectly captured the book's sense of mystery and disorientation. Even though you probably don't know what you're looking at, it's formally intriguing.

**ABOVE:** A reflection in the rain of a neon-lit building in the Ginza. Nice picture, but too abstract. **RIGHT:** Bingo. Or, rather, pachinko! Knopf, 2007.

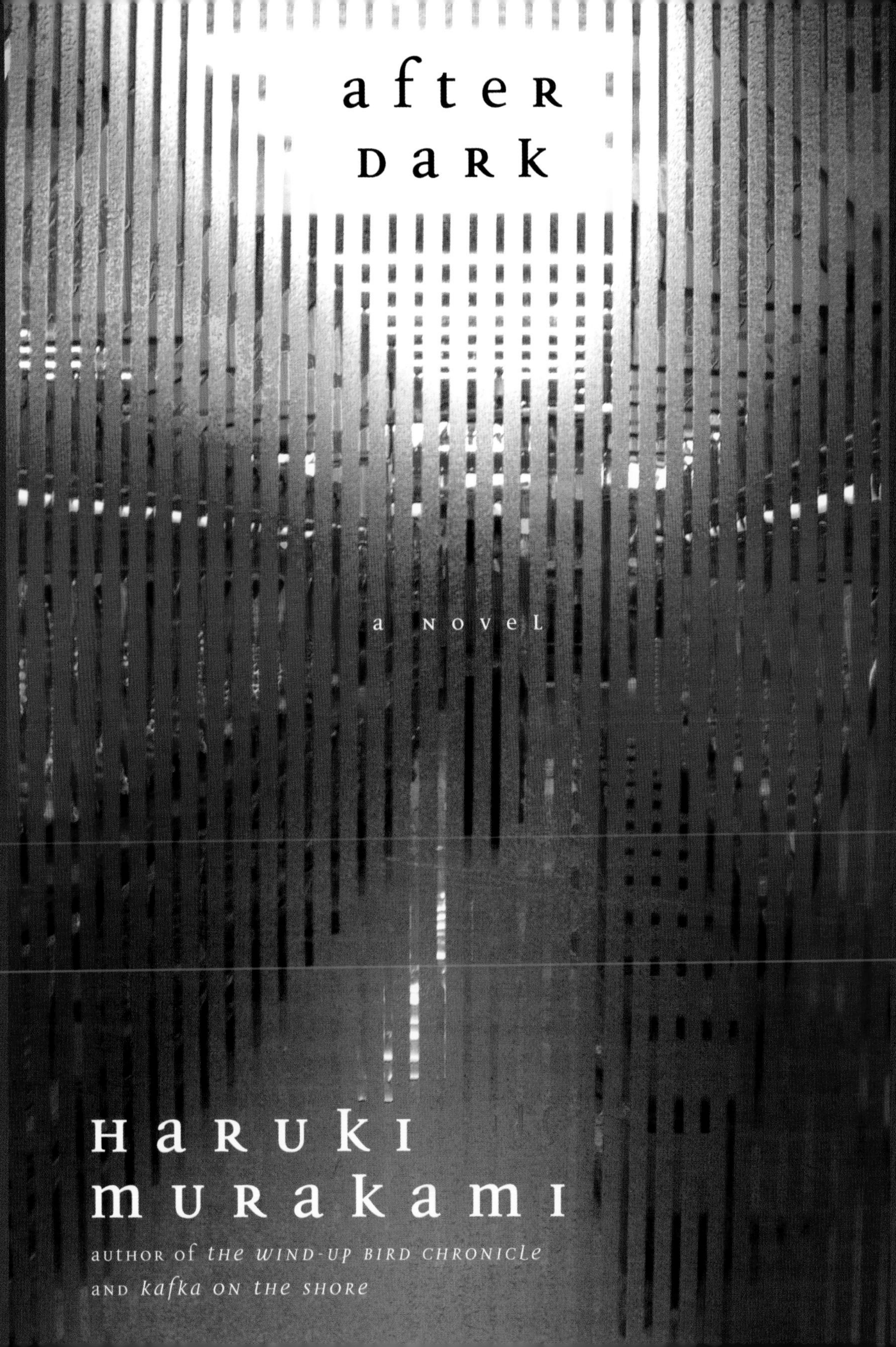
after
DARK
a NOVEL
HARUKI
MURAKAMI
author of the wind-up bird chronicle
and kafka on the shore

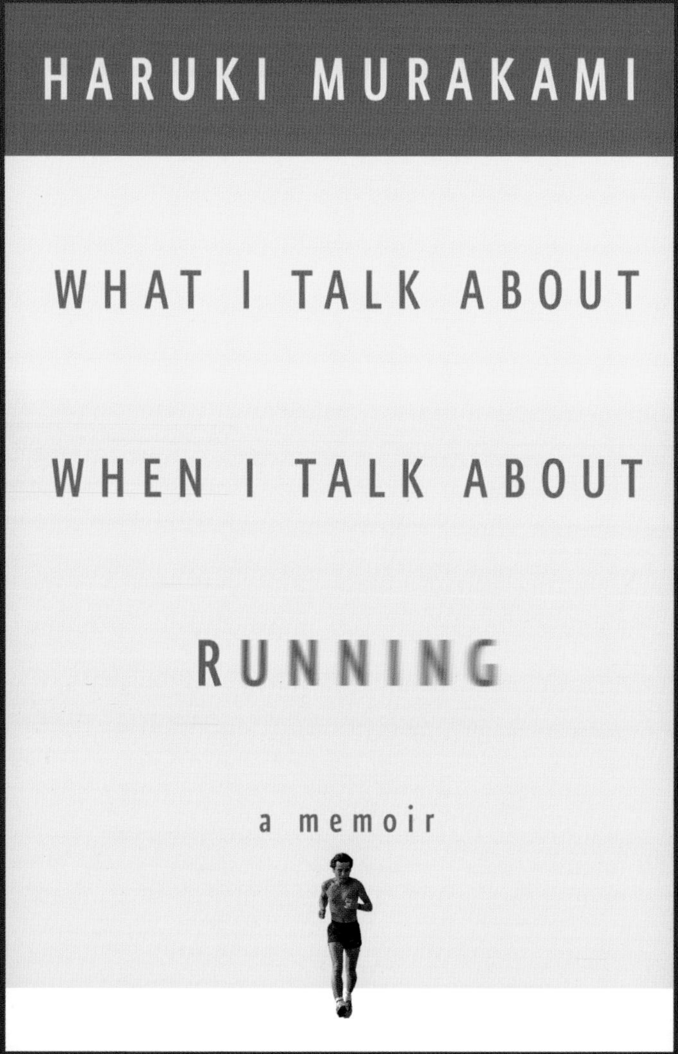
HARUKI MURAKAMI
WHAT I TALK ABOUT
WHEN I TALK ABOUT
RUNNING
a memoir

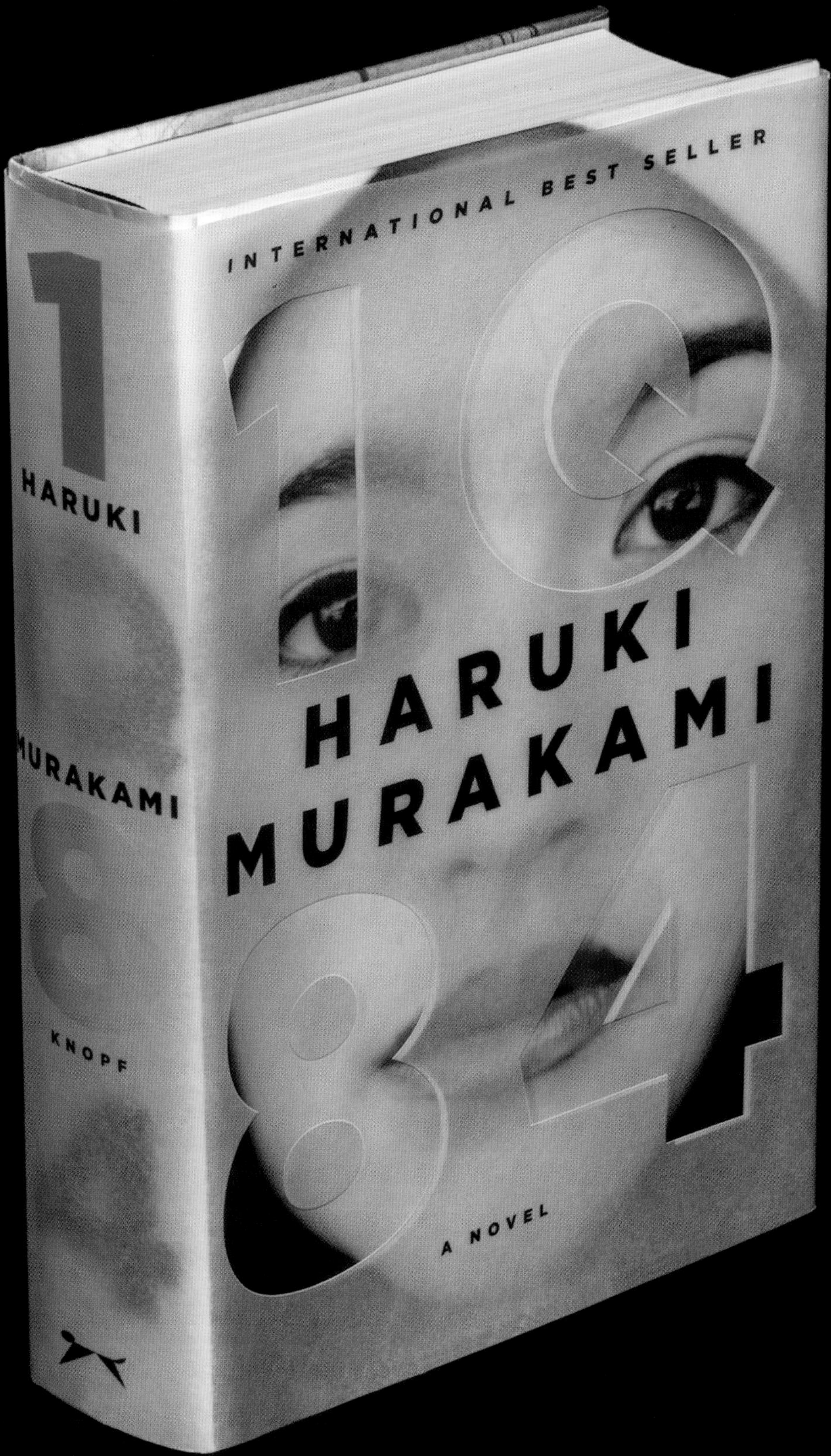
INTERNATIONAL BEST SELLER
HARUKI MURAKAMI
A NOVEL
1
HARUKI
MURAKAMI
KNOPF

Haruki never ceases to amaze me with his prolificity and variety. In that respect he reminds me a lot of John Updike, who would take time out from writing fiction to publish books on art, Ted Williams (see p. 75), and a meditation on golf. For Haruki, in this case it was his love of running. I wanted to keep the design simple, with somewhat playful typography gently huffing and puffing towards the end of the title. The photo of the author becomes an icon rather than a portrait; this is Haruki, after all, not Jim Fixx. (Yes, that's a good thing.)

**ABOVE:** Knopf, 2008. **RIGHT & OPPOSITE:** Knopf, 2011.

*1Q84* is an epic story that deftly weaves many complex themes: the notion of identity, totalitarian authority, existential duality, vigilante justice, what it means to be a reclusive genius, and literary ambition itself—just to name a few. What binds it all together is Haruki's own brand of magic realism, chiefly the idea of parallel planes of existence.

I wanted to exploit this concept by stretching the physical relationship of a book's jacket to its binding/cover in a way that I hadn't yet seen, and which the narrative completely suggested. Specifically, making the two become one. They need each other. I had scratched the surface of this idea with co-designer Barbara deWilde way back in 1992 with the presentation of Donna Tartt's *The Secret History*, but this was going to be different. The earlier design used clear acetate for the cover and separated the type on that surface from the image on the binding. Now I was going to use semi-transparent vellum, and print four-color process on it, so that the jacket and binding would create a unified perception of type and image that can be effectively experienced only when they are together.

The manufacturing challenges were considerable, and our head of production, the genius/magician/saint Andy Hughes, figured it out in his usual rabbit-out-of-a-hat style. But it was nail-biting down to the wire because just as we were about to go to press, the bindery refused to take the job. I don't blame them, but let me back up and explain: in most trade book publishing, book jackets and bindings are produced by two different companies. Once the jackets are printed, they are shipped to the bindery to be wrapped around the books.

The problem was this: because the vellum jacket material was unusually thin and slick (though extremely tear-resistant, very important), the bindery foreman said there was no way to guarantee that the jacket image would line up exactly with the binding image, and the printer (the venerable R. R. Donnelley, God bless them) couldn't be held responsible for any misalignment. What Andy negotiated was that there would be an allowance for a quarter-inch slippage either to the right or left, and was that okay with me?

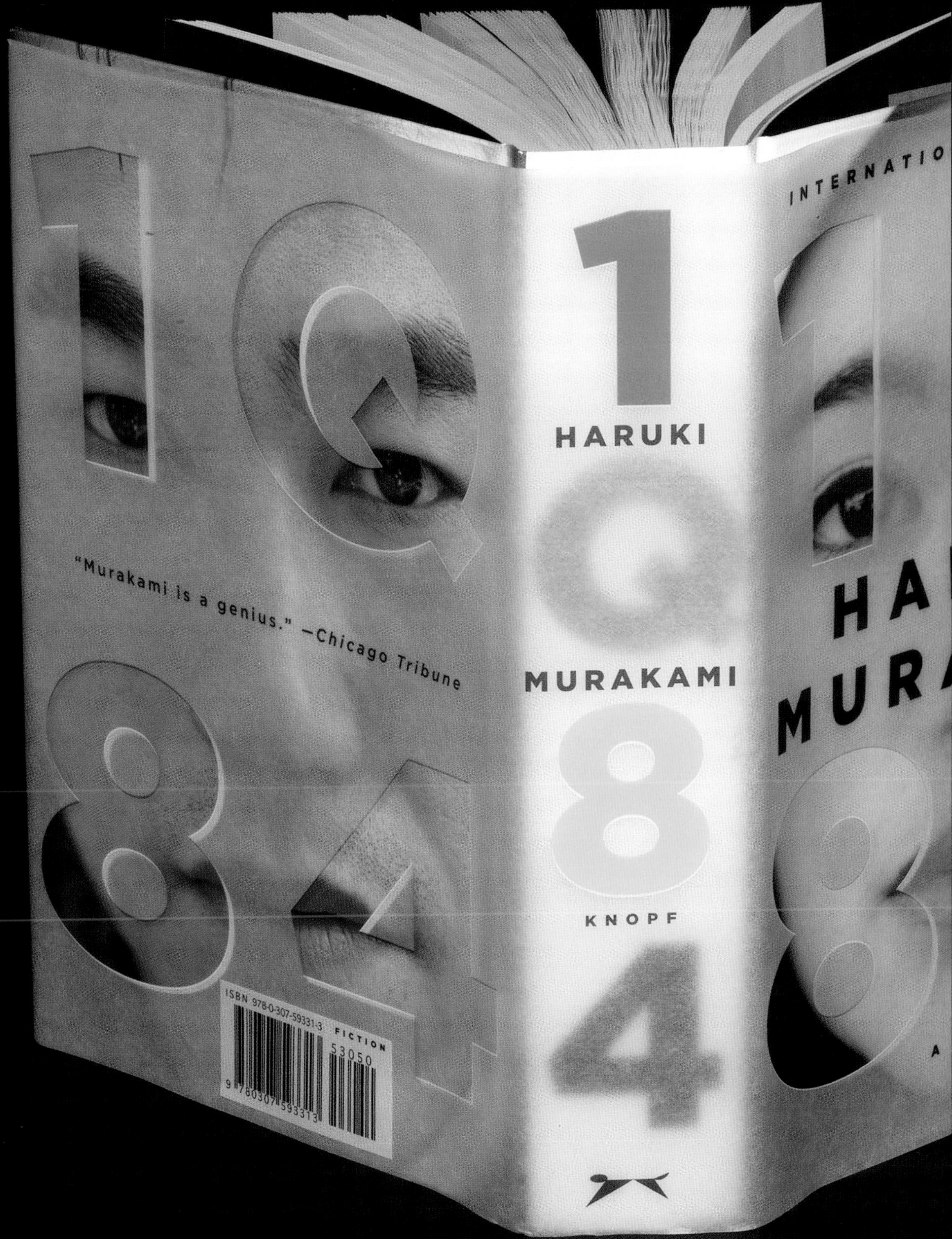

1Q84
"Murakami is a genius." —Chicago Tribune
ISBN 978-0-307-59331-3
FICTION
53050
1
HARUKI
Q
MURAKAMI
8
KNOPF
4
INTERNATIO

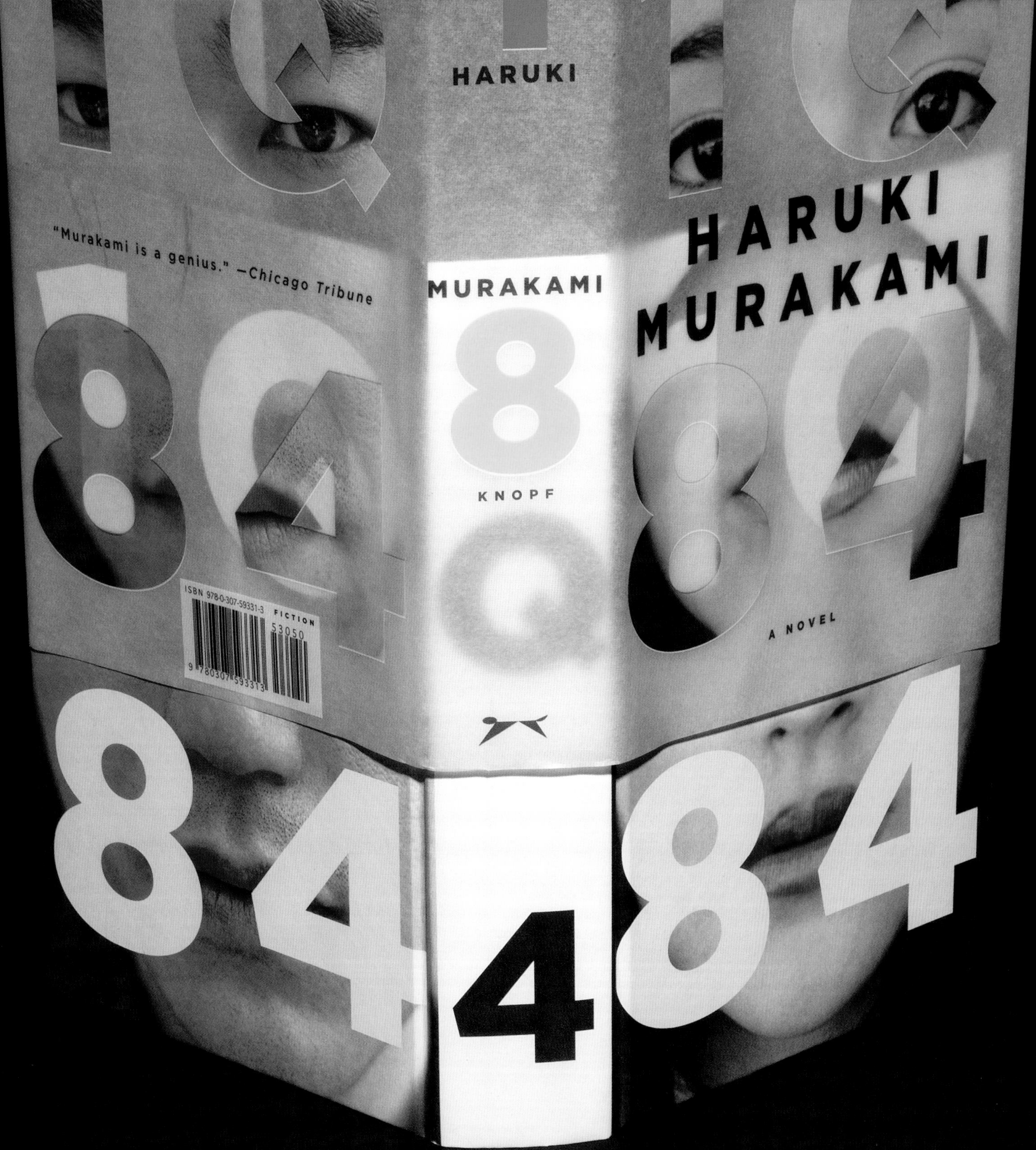
HARUKI
"Murakami is a genius." —Chicago Tribune
MURAKAMI
8
KNOPF
HARUKI
MURAKAMI
A NOVEL
ISBN 978-0-307-59331-3
FICTION
53050
84
4
84

Indeed it was, and I only retroactively realized that the design could thoroughly withstand that variance and not seem like a mistake. Full speed ahead, and Donnelley proceeded.

It was interesting to see various versions of the cover in bookstores: some were perfectly aligned, some had white drop shadows either left or right, but they all worked. Had it been more than a quarter inch, that might have seemed too extreme, but Donnelley really came through.

I coordinated the interior book design with the intrepid and brilliant Maggie Hinders on our staff, whom I have so loved working with on all of Murakami's books, as well as a certain *City on Fire* (pp. 248–53). She is grace, talent, and patience personified.

This book signified Murakami's first appearance on the *New York Times* hardcover fiction best-seller list, and it debuted at #2, which was extraordinary (just like him!).

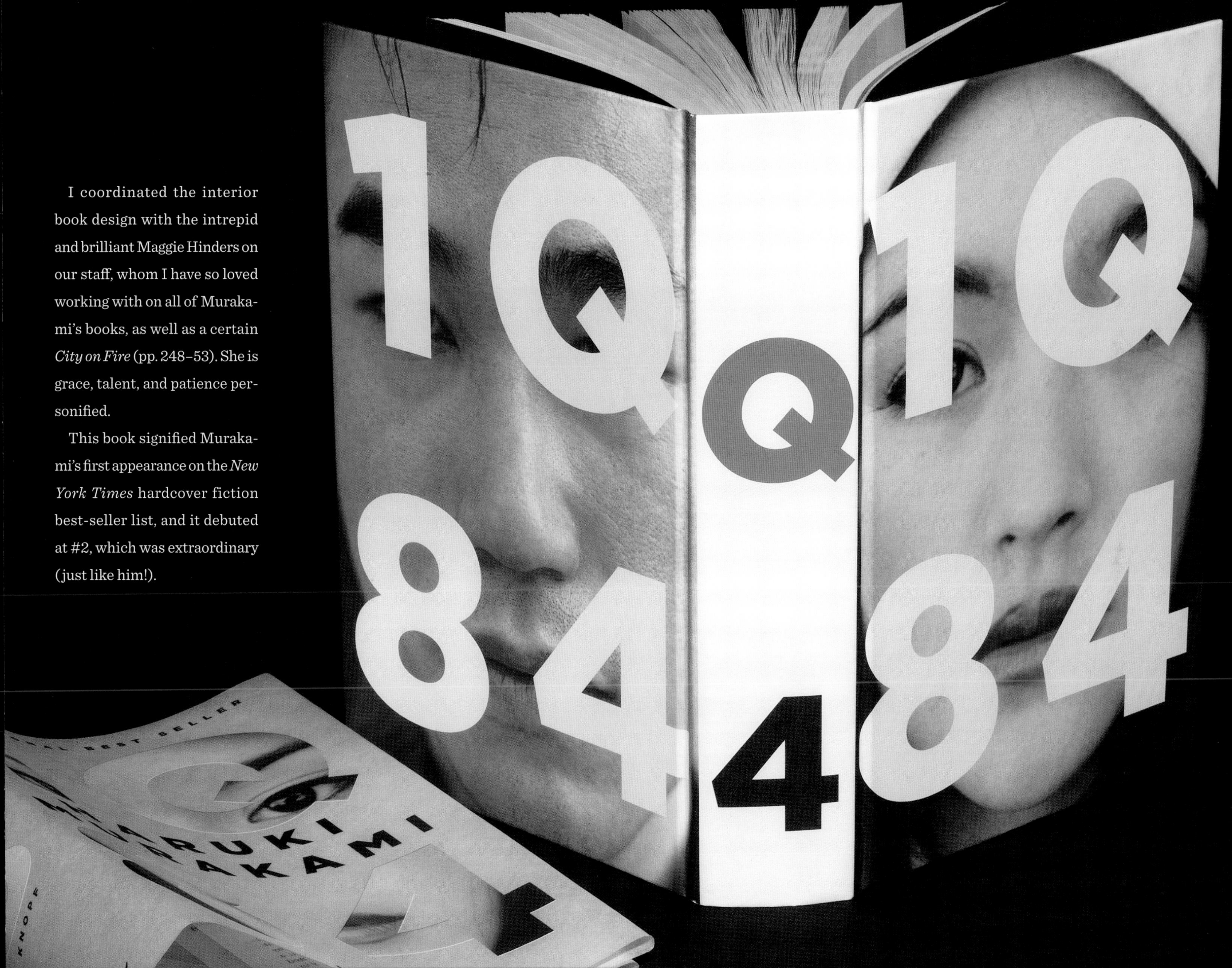
1Q
84
Q
4
1Q
84
BEST SELLER
RUKI
AKAMI
KNOPF

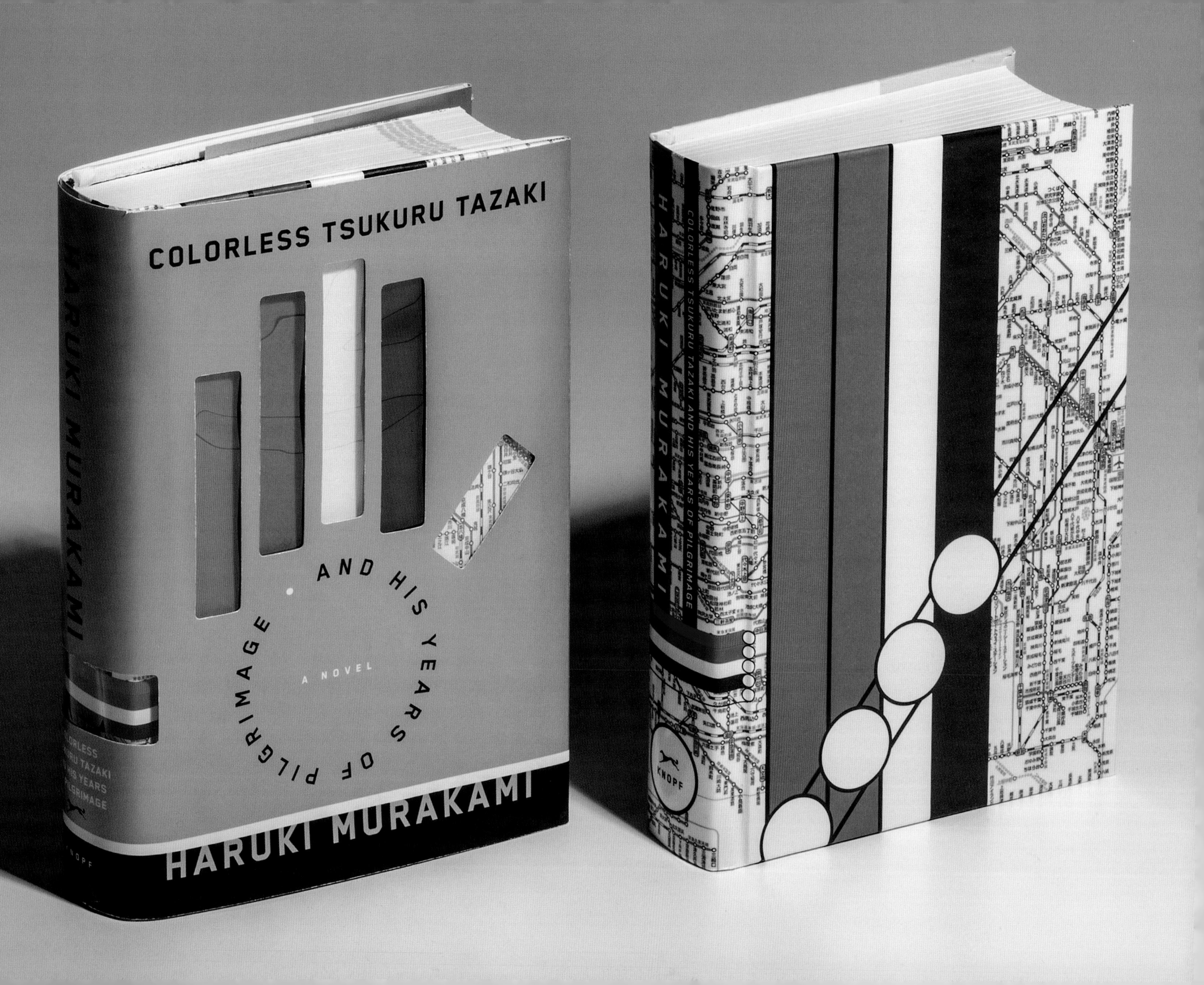
COLORLESS TSUKURU TAZAKI
AND HIS YEARS OF PILGRIMAGE
A NOVEL
HARUKI MURAKAMI
COLORLESS TSUKURU TAZAKI AND HIS YEARS OF PILGRIMAGE
HARUKI MURAKAMI
KNOPF

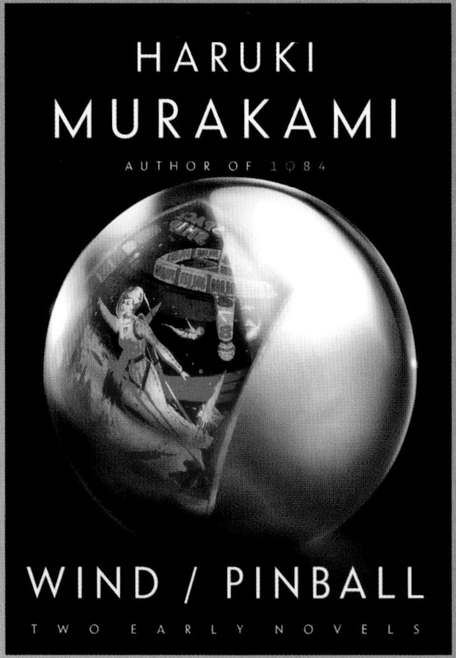
HARUKI
MURAKAMI
AUTHOR OF 1Q84
WIND / PINBALL
TWO EARLY NOVELS

**OPPOSITE:** Knopf, 2014.

**LEFT:** Murakami's first two novels in one volume; image by Geoff Spear. Knopf, 2015.

**RIGHT:** A conversation in book form about music with maestro Seiji Ozawa. Illustration by Eric Hanson. The music notation refers to the first bars of Beethoven's second piano concerto. Knopf, 2016.

To go from a book with a title as terse and emblematic as *1Q84* to one that's called *Colorless Tsukuru Takami and His Years of Pilgrimage* is almost as perverse as it is challenging to a designer. But all the ingredients were there in the text to guide the design: five friends in high school in Japan, four of whose names translated to colors—Mr. Red, Mr. Blue, Miss Black, and Miss White. The fifth, the narrator of the story, has no color to his name, thus the title. From the first few pages we learn that he is in despair because his friends have disowned him without warning the summer after their freshman year at college. He spends the rest of the book picking himself up off the floor and then slowly discovering why they abandoned him. At one point during his quest, one of the friends reflects that "we were like five fingers on a hand," so that suggested the configuration on the jacket. For the case, I used a detail from a map of the Tokyo subway system, which Colorless goes to work for upon graduation. His "transparent" subway line is intersecting with stops at each of the others, representing his journey in the story.

This design was even more complicated and abstract than that of *1Q84*, and yet the book debuted at #1 on the *New York Times* Best-Seller List and stayed there for four weeks. I think that was a testament to both Murakami's ever-increasing popularity with readers and the Knopf publishing team's dedication, commitment, and support for his work, now for over two decades and counting.

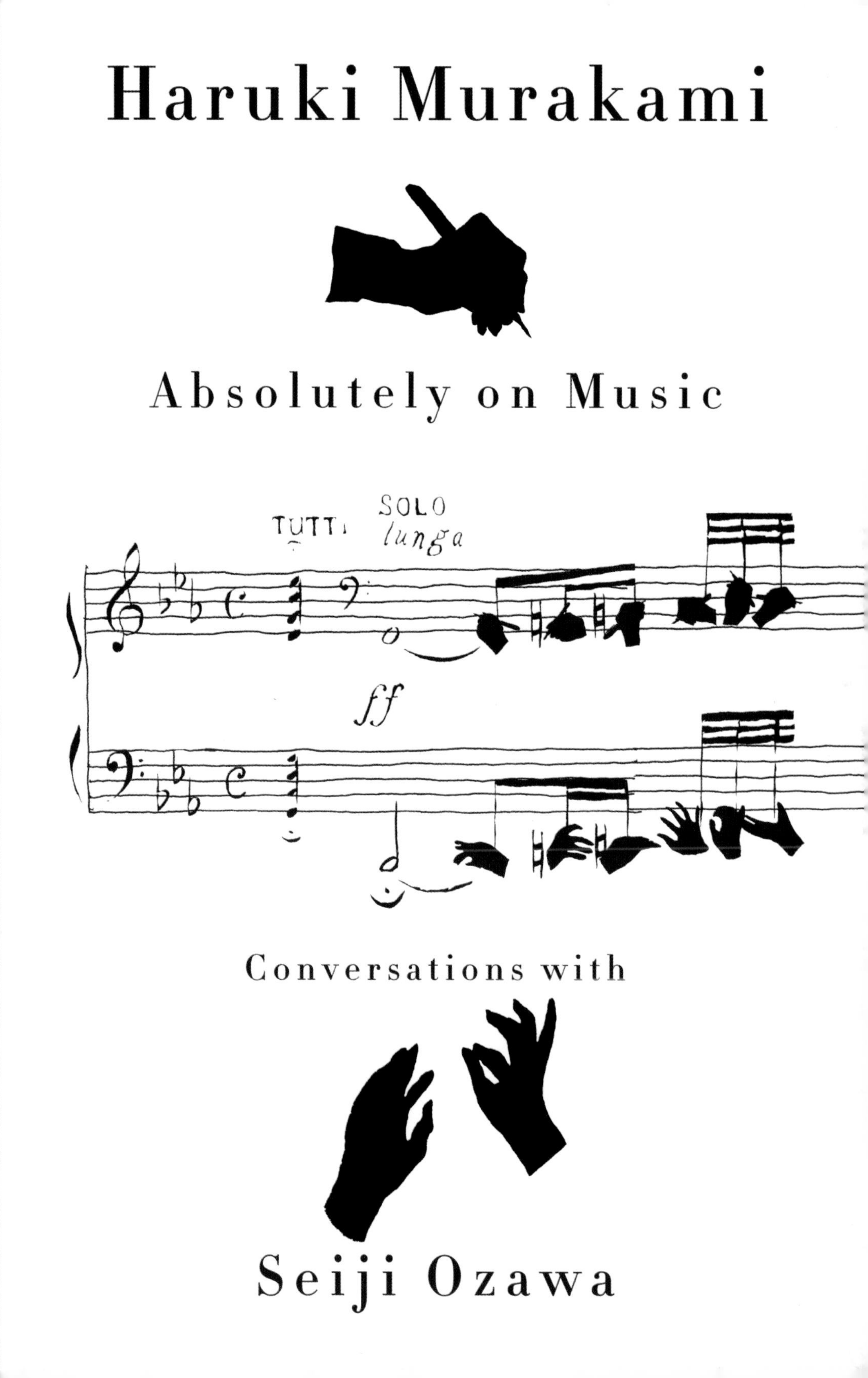
Haruki Murakami
Absolutely on Music
TUTTI
SOLO
lunga
ff
Conversations with
Seiji Ozawa

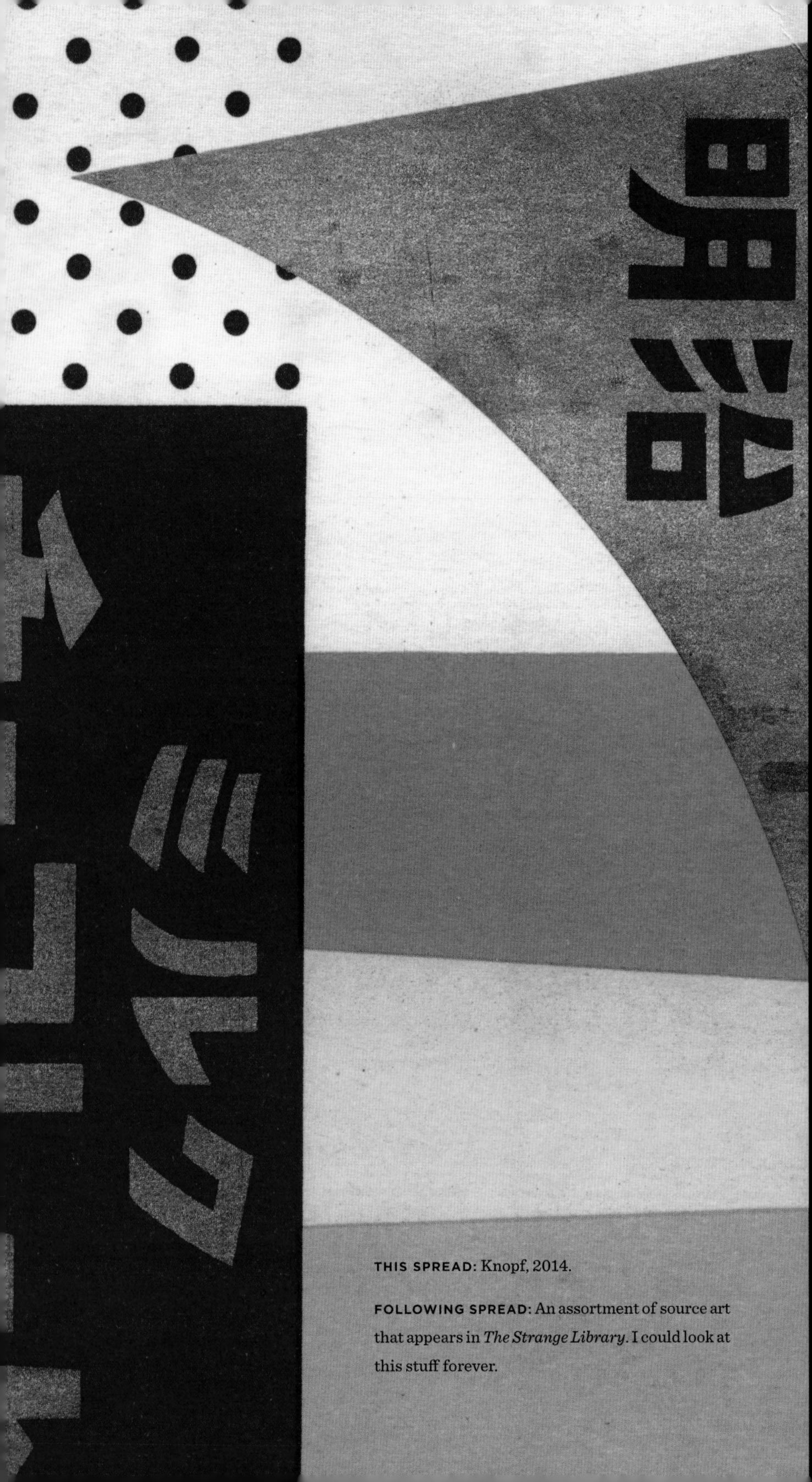

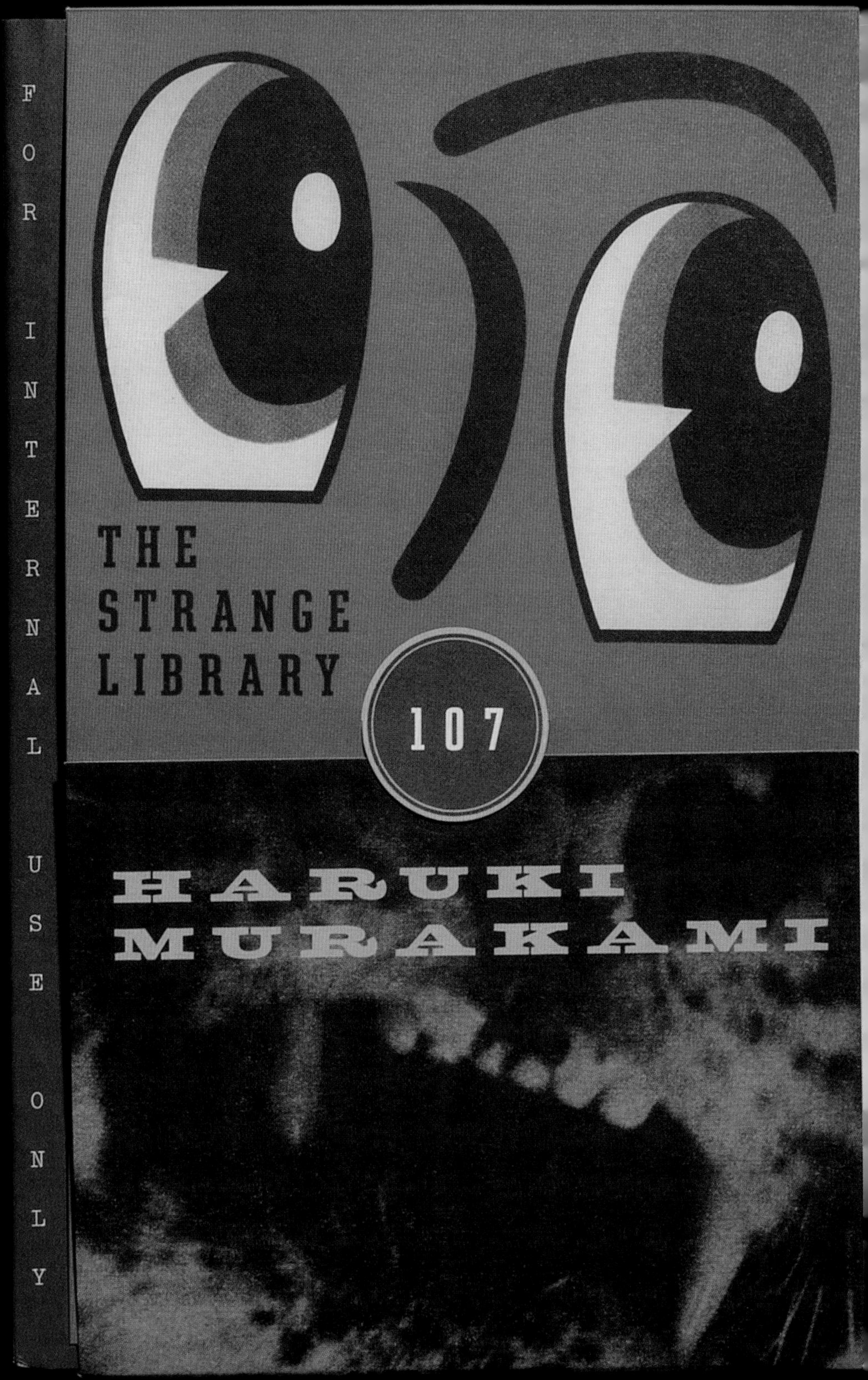
FOR INTERNAL USE ONLY
THE STRANGE LIBRARY
107
HARUKI MURAKAMI

**THIS SPREAD:** Knopf, 2014.

**FOLLOWING SPREAD:** An assortment of source art that appears in *The Strange Library*. I could look at this stuff forever.

*The Strange Library* was a dream job in several senses of the word. The story is just twenty-odd pages of manuscript—a dark fantasy about a little boy trapped in his local library and alternately tormented and saved by the supernatural spirits therein. Intrepid Knopf editor-in-chief Sonny Mehta gave me a totally free brief to "make it into a visual book."

However I wanted to do that was up to me. Wow.

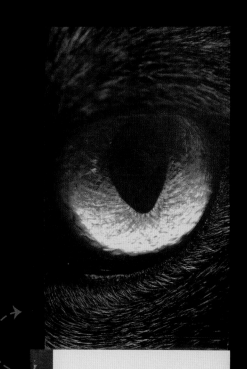

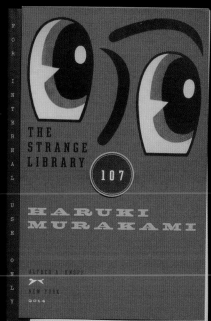

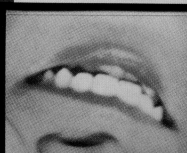

FOR INTERNAL USE ONLY
THE STRANGE LIBRARY
107
HARUKI MURAKAMI
ALFRED A. KNOPF
NEW YORK
2014

FOR INTERNAL USE ONLY
(1)
The library was even more hushed than usual.
My new leather shoes clacked against the gray linoleum. Their hard, dry sound was unlike my normal footsteps. Every time I get

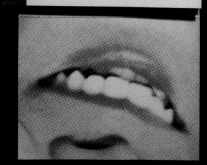

**THIS SPREAD:** There was already a European edition of this book, which used commissioned illustration to accompany the text, and a British version that relied heavily on the visual vernacular of libraries (card catalogues, dusty old tomes, yellowed pages, etc.). They were fine, but for me they took any similar approach off the table and freed me to go into weirder, more emblematic territory. For the past decade-plus I had been collecting vintage paper ephemera during my trips to Japan (see next spread), and that seemed to me the way to go. For the format, I thought of a matchbook (there is one inside) and a kind of puzzle that you have to figure out in order to open it.

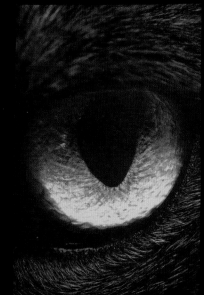

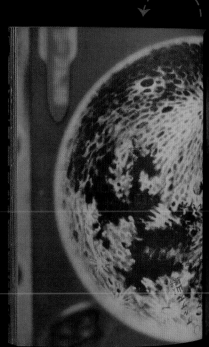

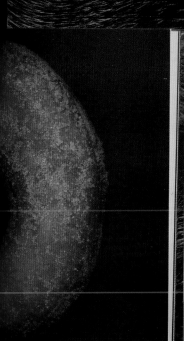

Once you do and start reading, you are "trapped" inside it (and constantly watched by a fearsome green-eyed dog, as the boy is) until you close it again and "escape" to the real world. I figured these objects would suggest some of the reference materials that the boy might encounter during his internment in the library.

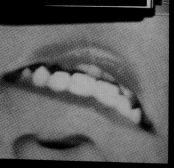

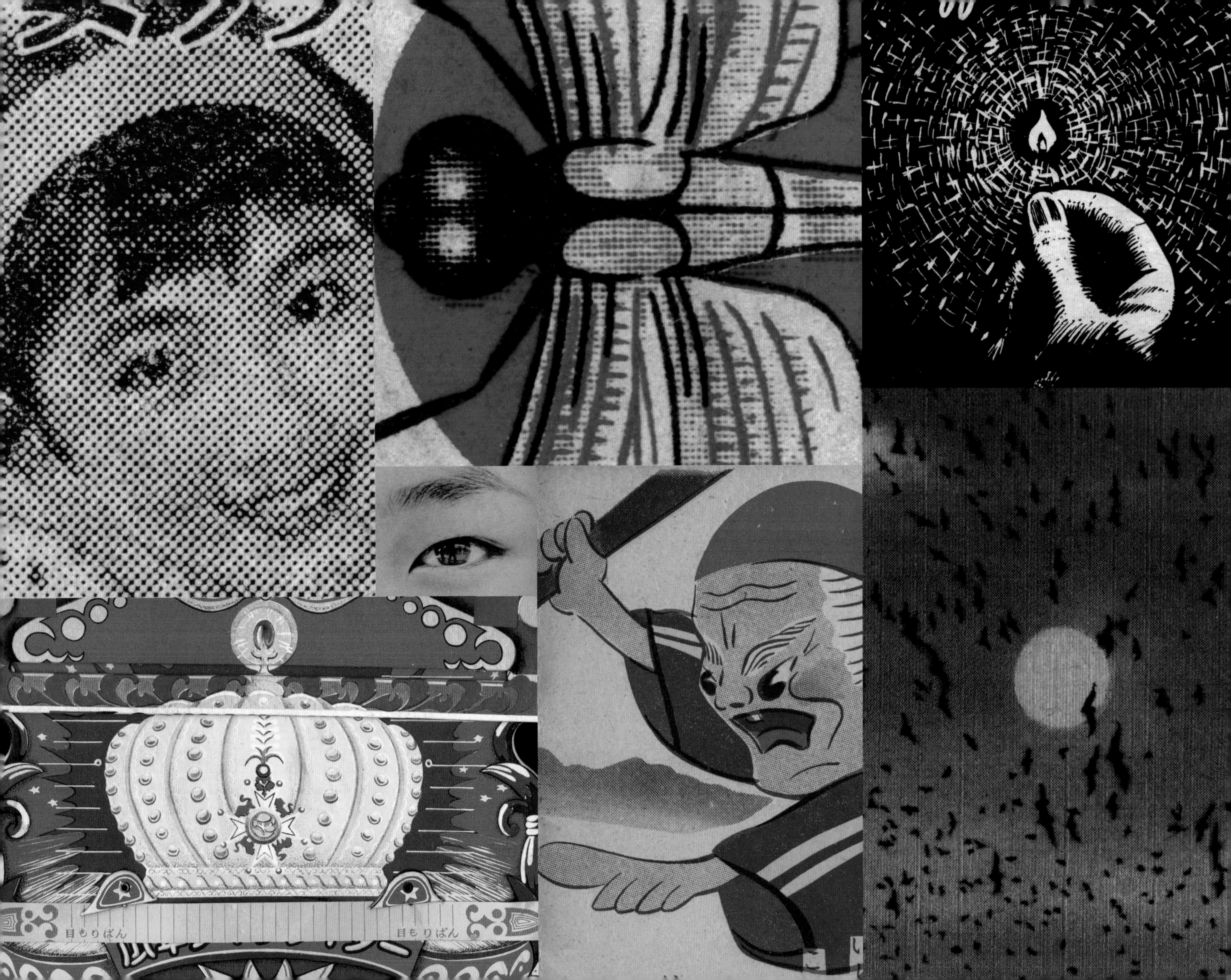
目もりばん
目もりばん

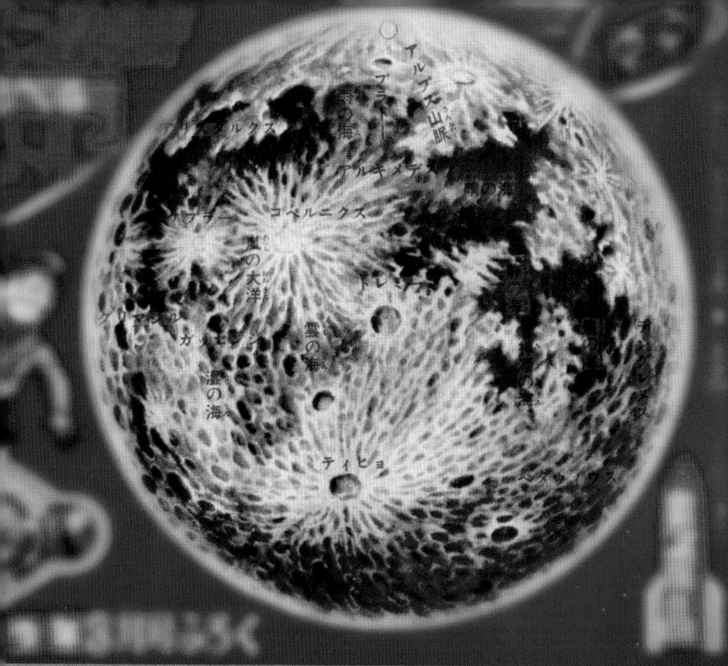

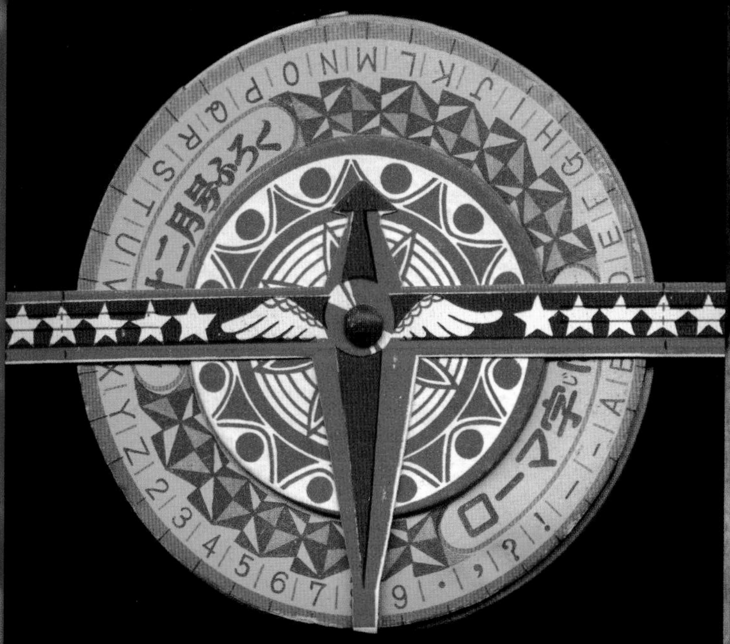

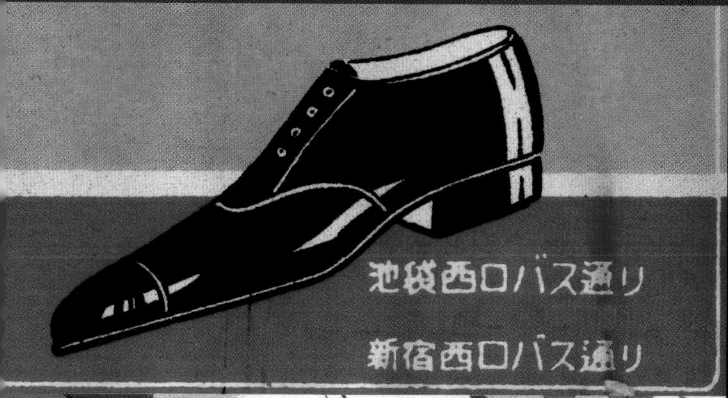
池袋西口バス通り
新宿西口バス通り

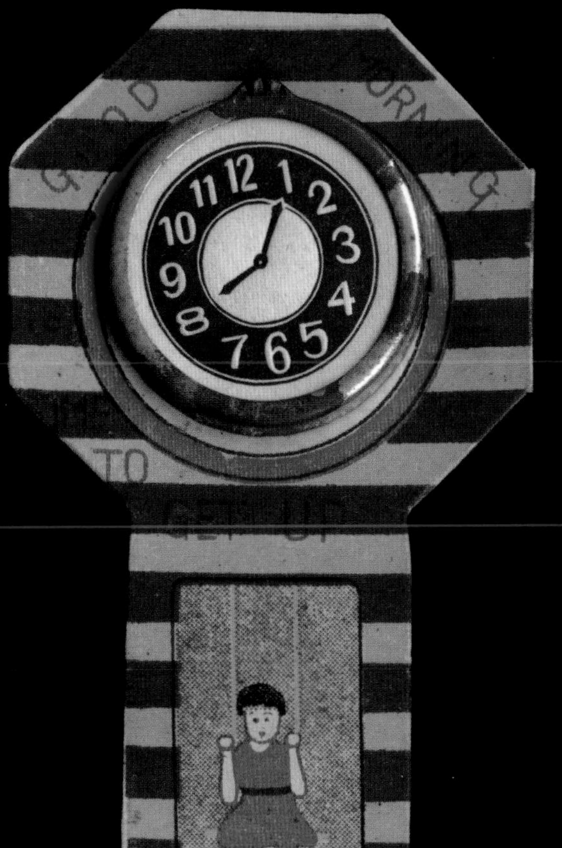
GOOD
TO

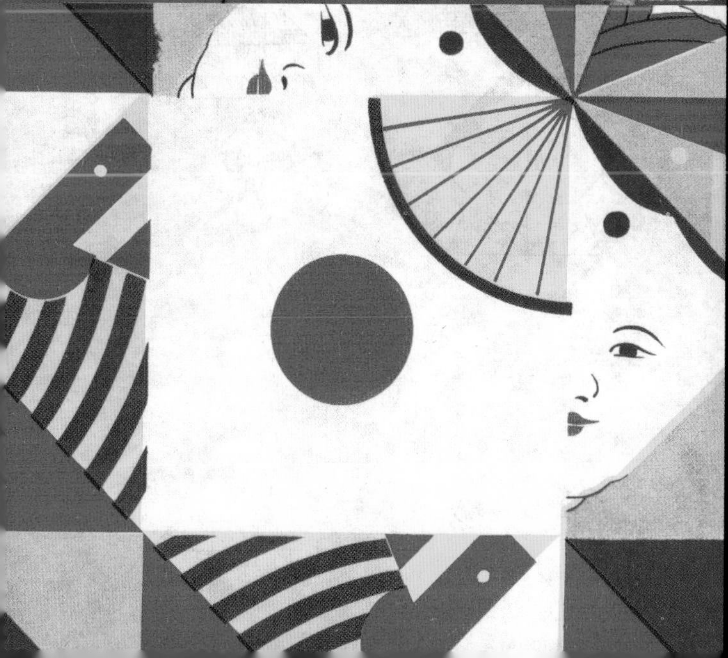

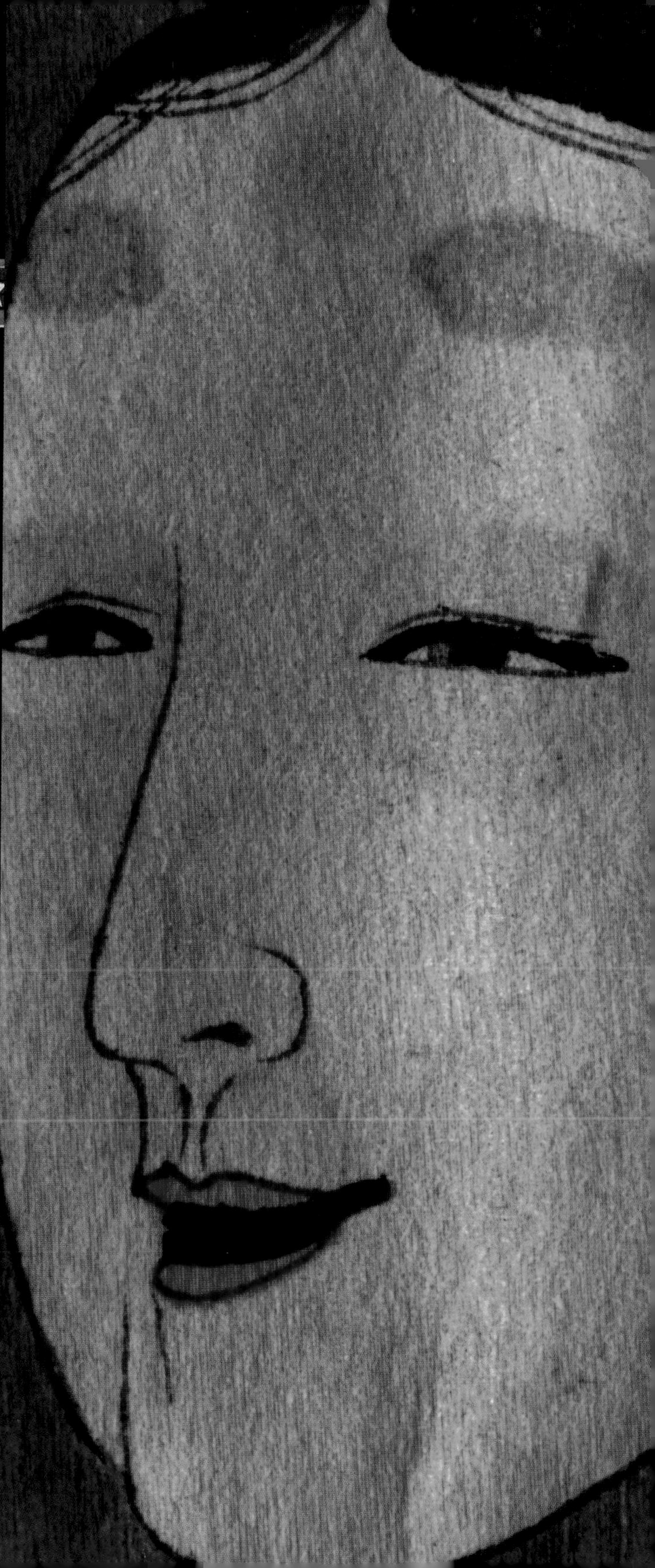

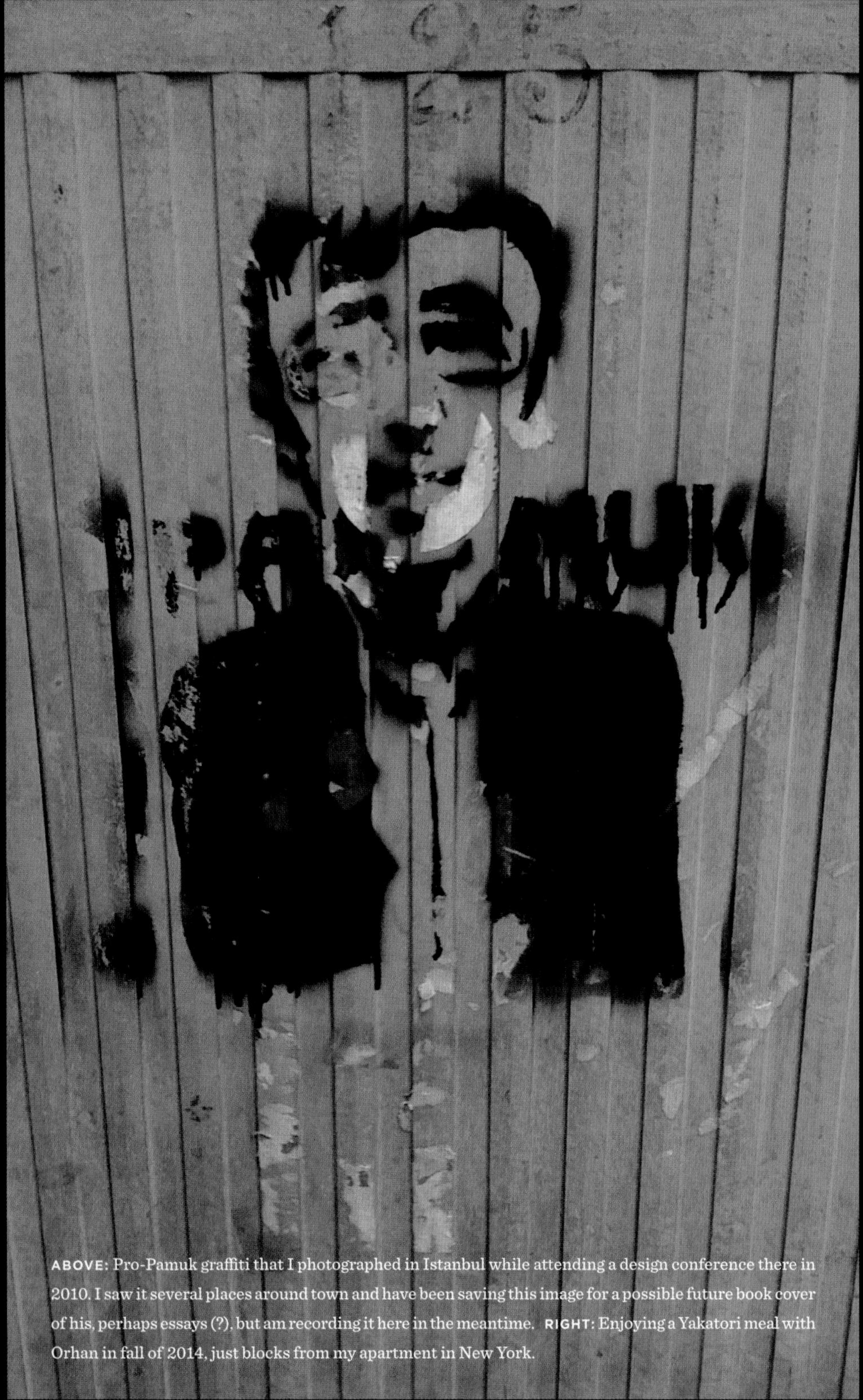

**ABOVE:** Pro-Pamuk graffiti that I photographed in Istanbul while attending a design conference there in 2010. I saw it several places around town and have been saving this image for a possible future book cover of his, perhaps essays (?), but am recording it here in the meantime. **RIGHT:** Enjoying a Yakatori meal with Orhan in fall of 2014, just blocks from my apartment in New York.

ESSAY

# Orhan Pamuk

## FURTHER NOTES ON BOOK COVERS

Why is the sight of an eye staring out at me from the cover or the spine of a book so perplexing? Perhaps because for me, the cover of a book is a symbol that lets us "see" the whole of what's inside.

A friend of mine, a lover of literature, told me that his new job at a small academic press wasn't too difficult. But there was one thing that bothered him: the people who worked there were thoroughly unenthusiastic about the books they published. The house had a standard cover design, and they used this template for all the books they published; they never designed new covers.

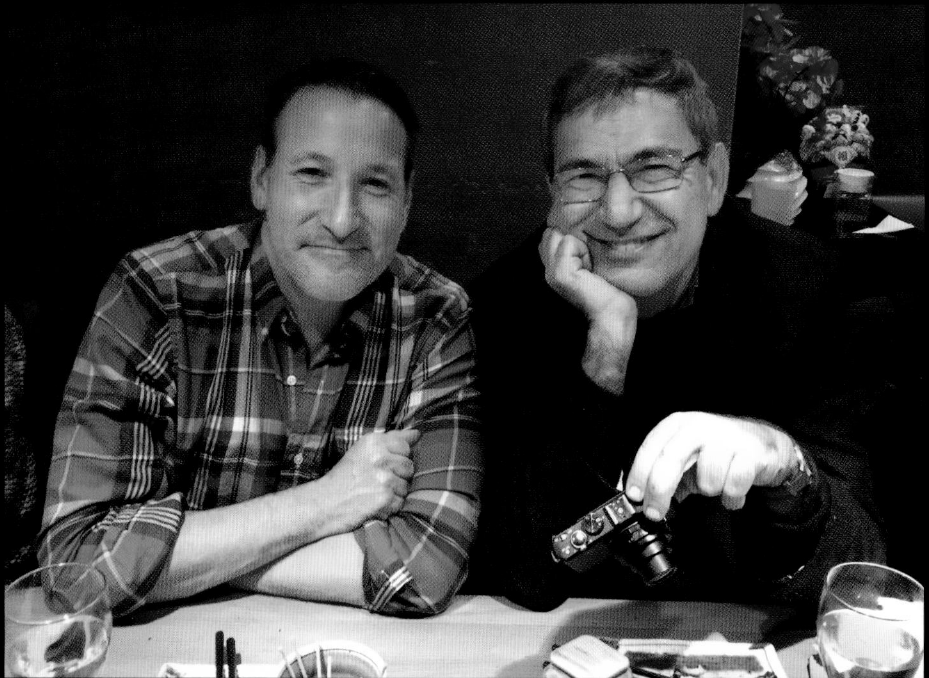

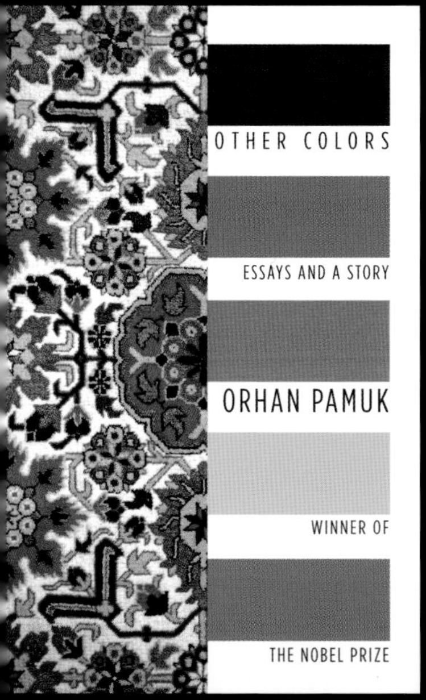
OTHER COLORS
ESSAYS AND A STORY
ORHAN PAMUK
WINNER OF
THE NOBEL PRIZE

The sign of a good cover is when you are able to recognize the book it belongs to just by looking at the image, the colors, and the design, without needing to look at the title of the book or the name of the author.

When I buy a new edition of a book I love, I like to tell myself I'm doing it because there have been updates and corrections to the text, or there's a new introduction . . . But in truth, I'm only buying it because I really want that new cover.

I like leafing through my library with friends, talking about books and their authors. The best part is when someone says: "I've got this book, too. But mine has a different cover."

It is always a surprise and a thrill to see a book that's held a special place in our lives, a book we've read over and over again and truly believed in, published years later with a completely different cover design. Our youthful dreams and the books that inspired them will always endure! But soon we begin to think that this new cover offers a strange and curious insight into a book we thought we knew well, bringing to light new sides to it that we hadn't paid much attention to all those years ago. Are we the ones to have changed, or is it the book? Or are today's readers just different? A new cover design on a book we used to love can end up feeling like a betrayal.

I've met many writers who've said that if their book hasn't done well, "it's because of the cover!" And perhaps some of these writers have a point. But I have yet to meet a single writer who'll tell me that the success of their book is "thanks to the cover." —O.P.

**ABOVE:** My first design for *Other Colors*, deemed by Orhan's agent as "shrieking of Islam," and not in a good way. Hard to disagree with that. **RIGHT:** The final design—no, that's not the author, but it is the Galata Bridge over the Bosporus. I'm employing the tried-and-true "juxtaposition of black-and-white next to color" approach. Knopf, 2007.

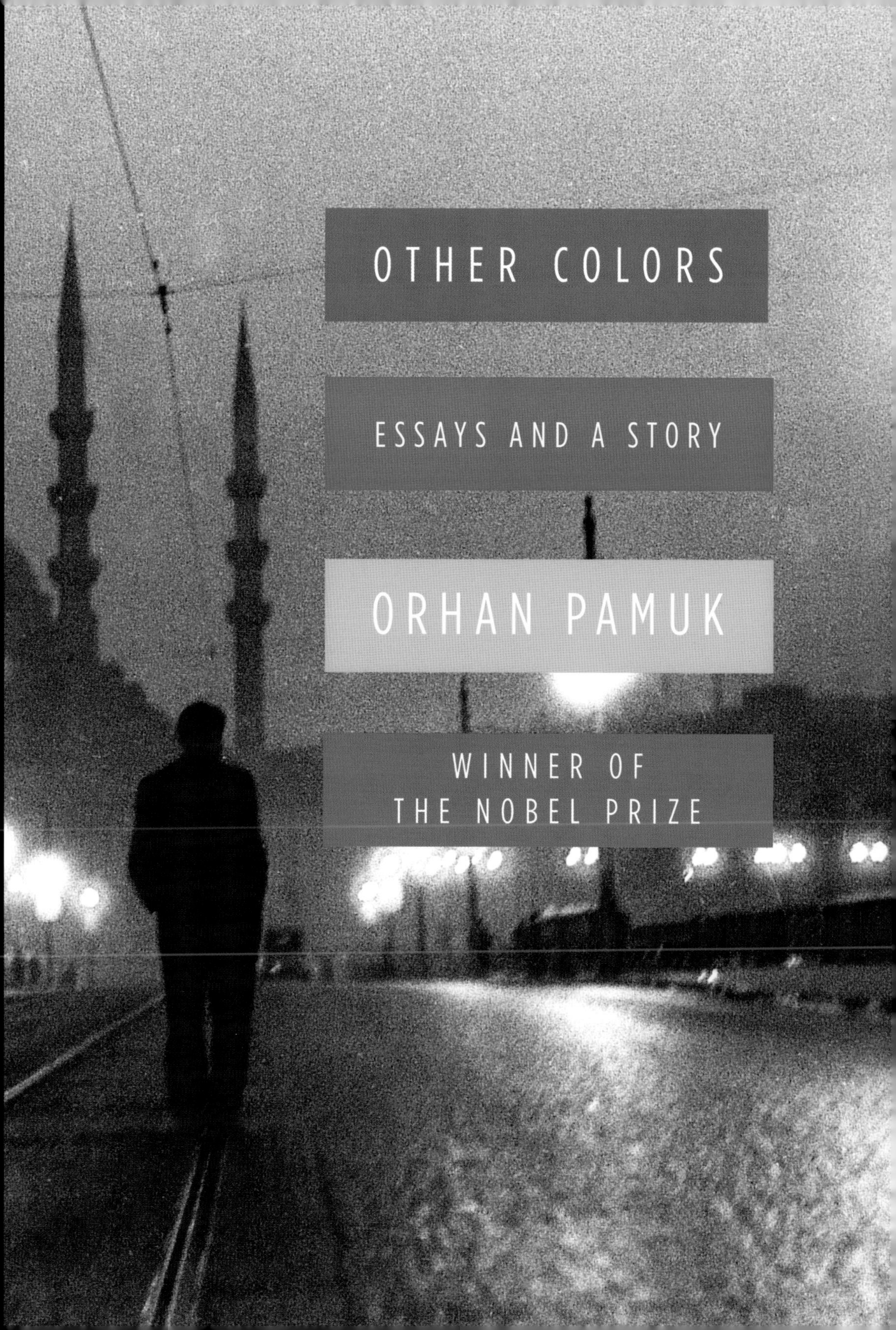
OTHER COLORS
ESSAYS AND A STORY
ORHAN PAMUK
WINNER OF
THE NOBEL PRIZE

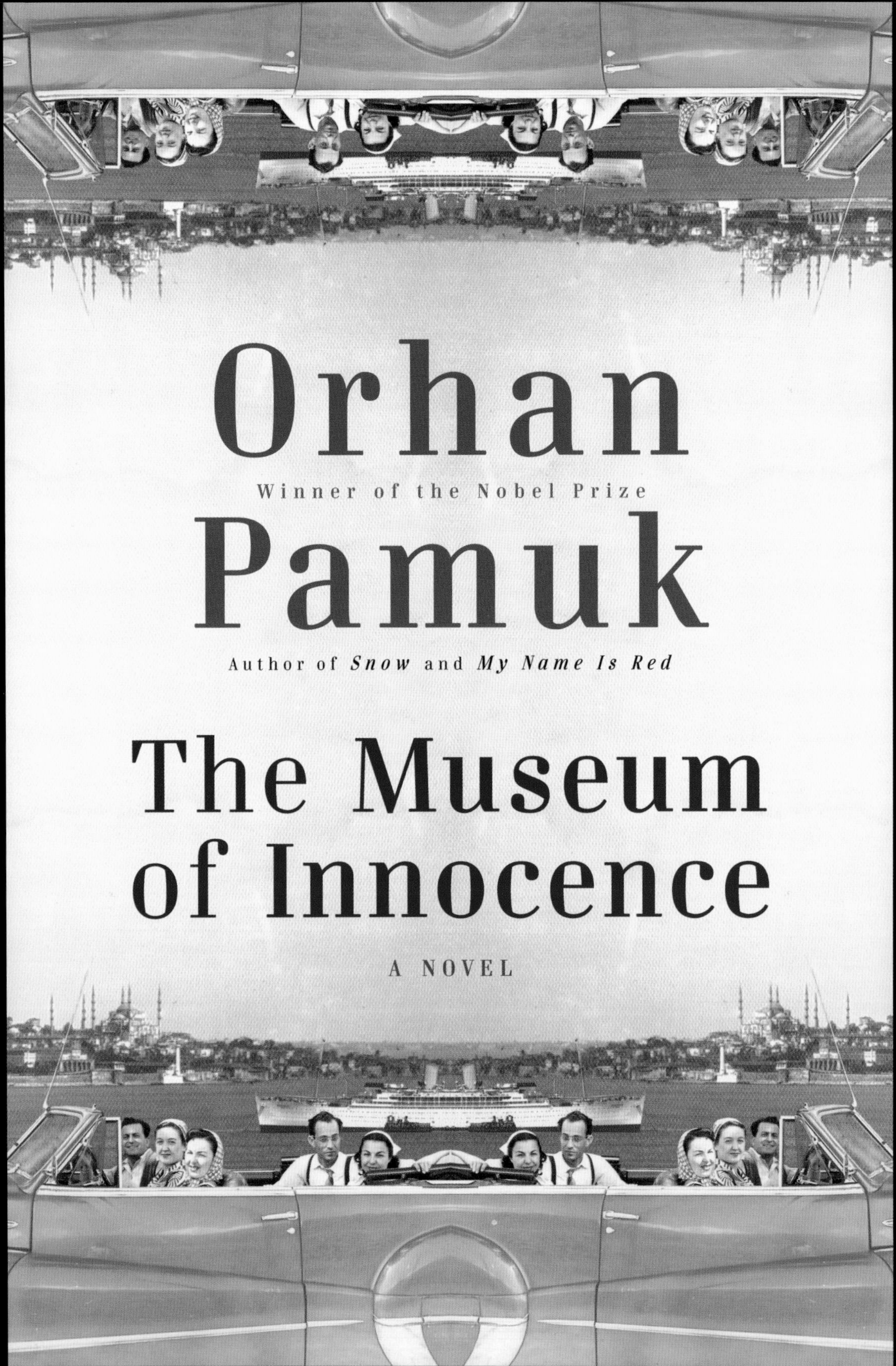
Orhan
Winner of the Nobel Prize
Pamuk
Author of Snow and My Name Is Red
The Museum of Innocence
A NOVEL

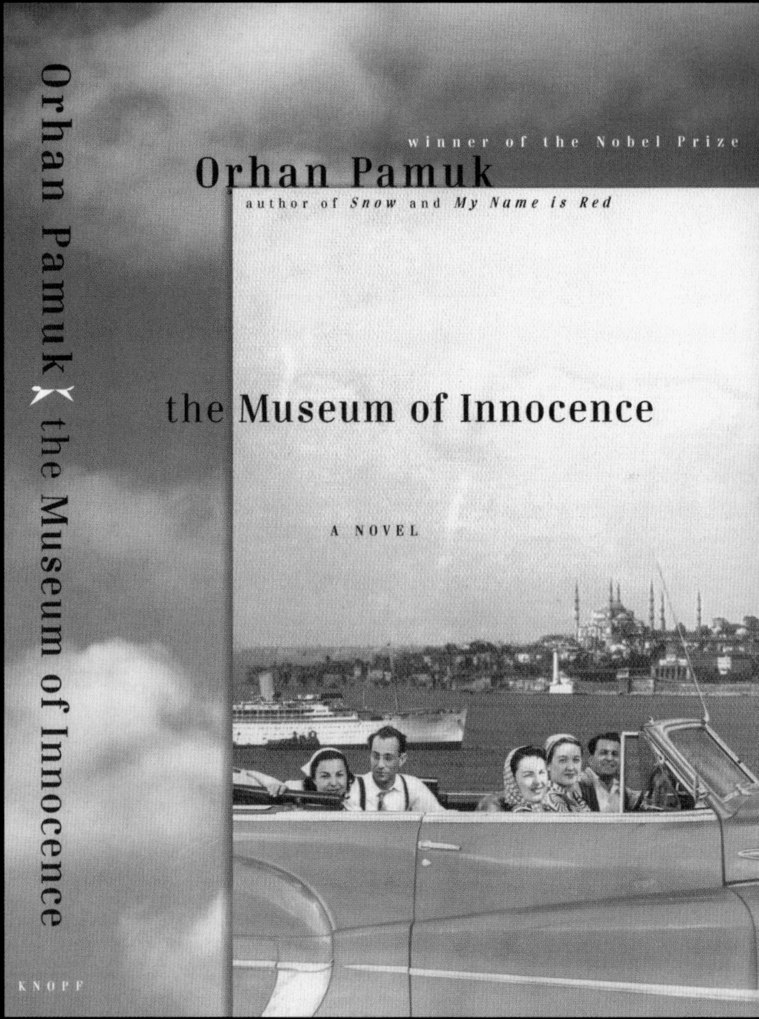
Orhan Pamuk the Museum of Innocence
KNOPF
winner of the Nobel Prize
Orhan Pamuk
author of Snow and My Name is Red
the Museum of Innocence
A NOVEL

## Portfolio · Orhan Pamuk

Orhan Pamuk is one of the most courageous people I know. He spoke out publicly in Turkey in 2005 about the Armenian genocide and deaths of Kurds during the Ottoman Empire, at his own peril (it is very much illegal there to do so). By then he was far and away the most popular Turkish living writer; regardless, he faced trial for "crimes against Turkish honor." Ultimately the charges were overruled, though with a stiff fine and an ominous warning. This whole event raised—and continues to shine the spotlight on—serious freedom of speech issues in his country. A country that, despite all of this, he still dearly loves.

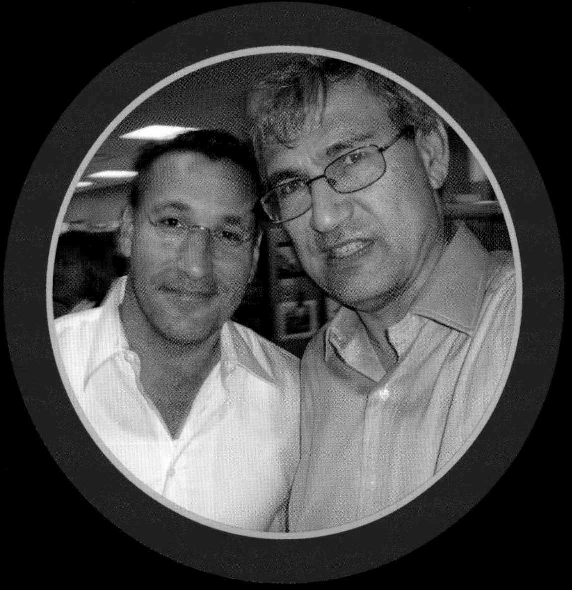

It has been an honor to know and work with him for 15 years, since *My Name Is Red* appeared in 2001. After that there was *Snow* and *Other Colors*, but it was with *The Museum of Innocence* that I truly began to eel a kinship with his passion for collecting, preserving, and enshrining he objects and ephemera that have come to signify things and people hat enthrall us. In the novel, a wealthy businessman named Kemal is engaged to Sibel, but then suddenly meets Füsun—a shopgirl—while ourchasing a handbag for his intended. A passionate, illicit romance (with Füsun) ensues, and when it abruptly and heartbreakingly ends, Kemal creates an exhibition of objects that chronicle every moment he can scavenge from the relationship. It becomes his museum of his life with her, his way of keeping his joy with her alive.

And the crazy, wonderful thing is that Orhan created just such a place; t is housed in a building in the Çukurcuma neighborhood of Beyoğlu, stanbul, and displays a collection evocative of everyday life and culture of Istanbul during the period in which the novel is set.

**PPOSITE, RIGHT:** Orhan provided this collage to use on *Museum*, and this was my first try at he jacket, but... **OPPOSITE, LEFT:** This was the final jacket. I wanted to provide a more inter-esting, almost kaleidoscopic use of the image, to mimic Kemal's obsessive frame of mind. Knopf, 2009. **ABOVE:** Orhan and I at the impromptu celebration of his winning the Nobel Prize for Literature in the halls of Knopf, October 12, 2006. **RIGHT:** My cover for Orhan's second novel, *Silent House*, finally translated into English in 2012. It depicts a traditional Turkish tea service.

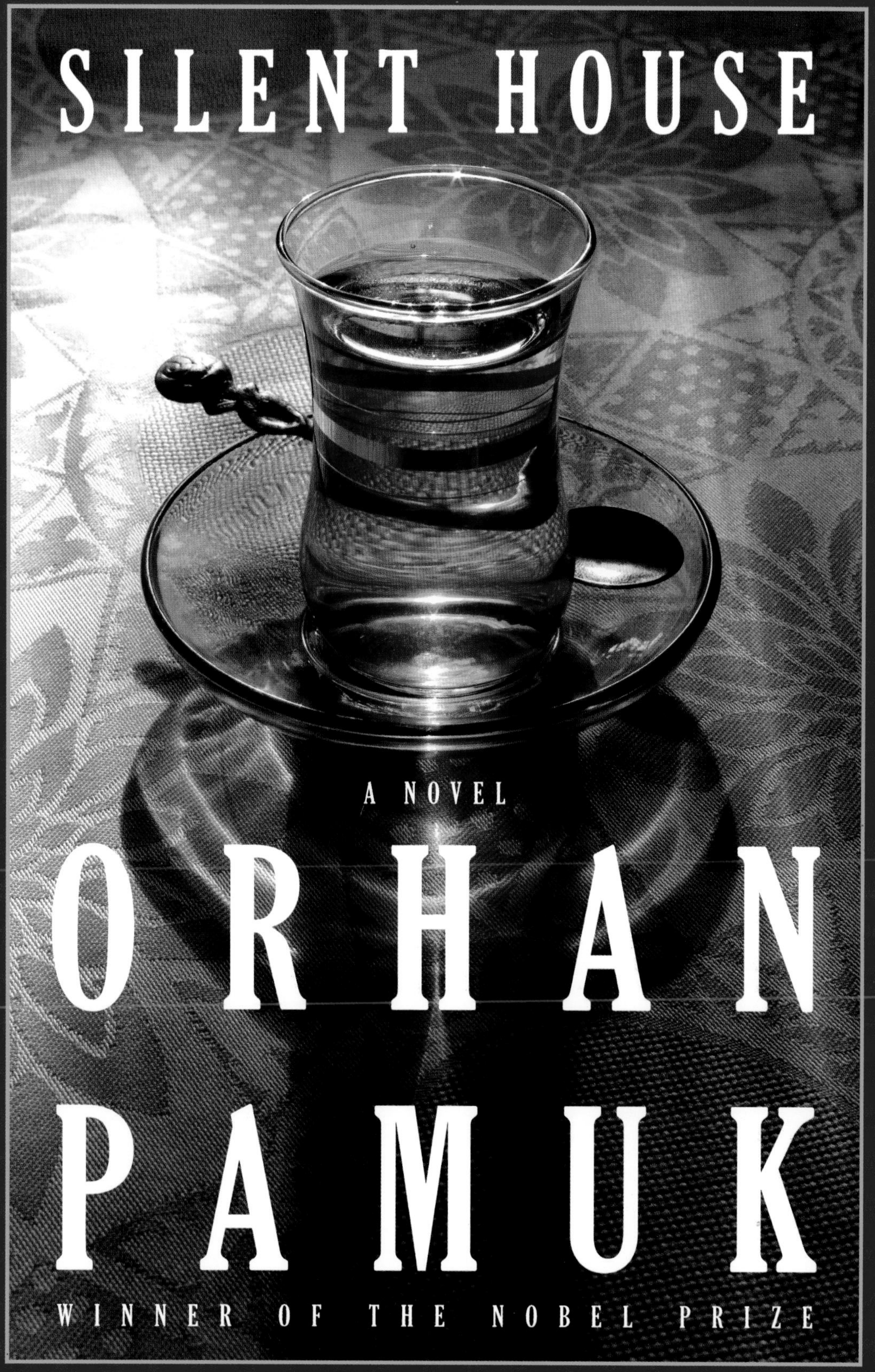

SILENT HOUSE
A NOVEL
ORHAN PAMUK
WINNER OF THE NOBEL PRIZE

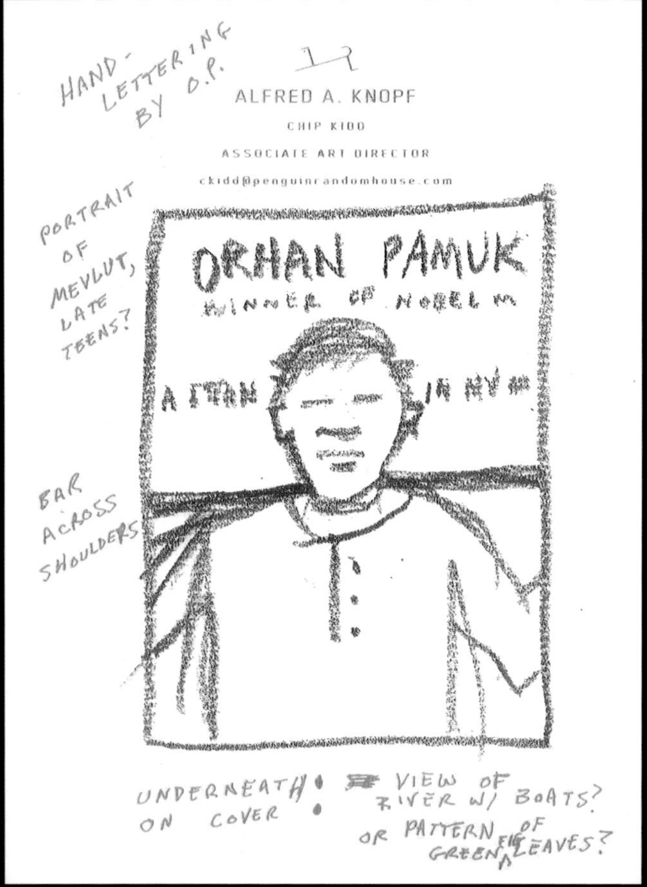
HAND-LETTERING BY O.P.
ALFRED A. KNOPF
CHIP KIDD
ASSOCIATE ART DIRECTOR
ckidd@penguinrandomhouse.com
PORTRAIT OF MEVLUT, LATE TEENS?
ORHAN PAMUK
BAR ACROSS SHOULDERS
UNDERNEATH ON COVER
VIEW OF RIVER W/ BOATS?
OR PATTERN OF GREEN LEAVES?

*A Strangeness in My Mind* tells an altogether different kind of story, about a street vendor named Mevlut who sells yogurt and boza—a traditional, mildly alcoholic Turkish malted beverage. The book chronicles Mevlut's life, loves, and travails and thereby paints a portrait of Istanbul and how it has evolved over the last fifty years.

While working on this design, I was invited over to Orhan's Columbia University apartment in New York after a dinner at the American Academy of Arts and Letters and saw for the first time in our working relationship that: 1) He loves to draw. 2) He does it constantly. And most important, 3) He's really good at it. I was embarrassed that I didn't know, but this was definitely the perfect direction for *Strangeness*.

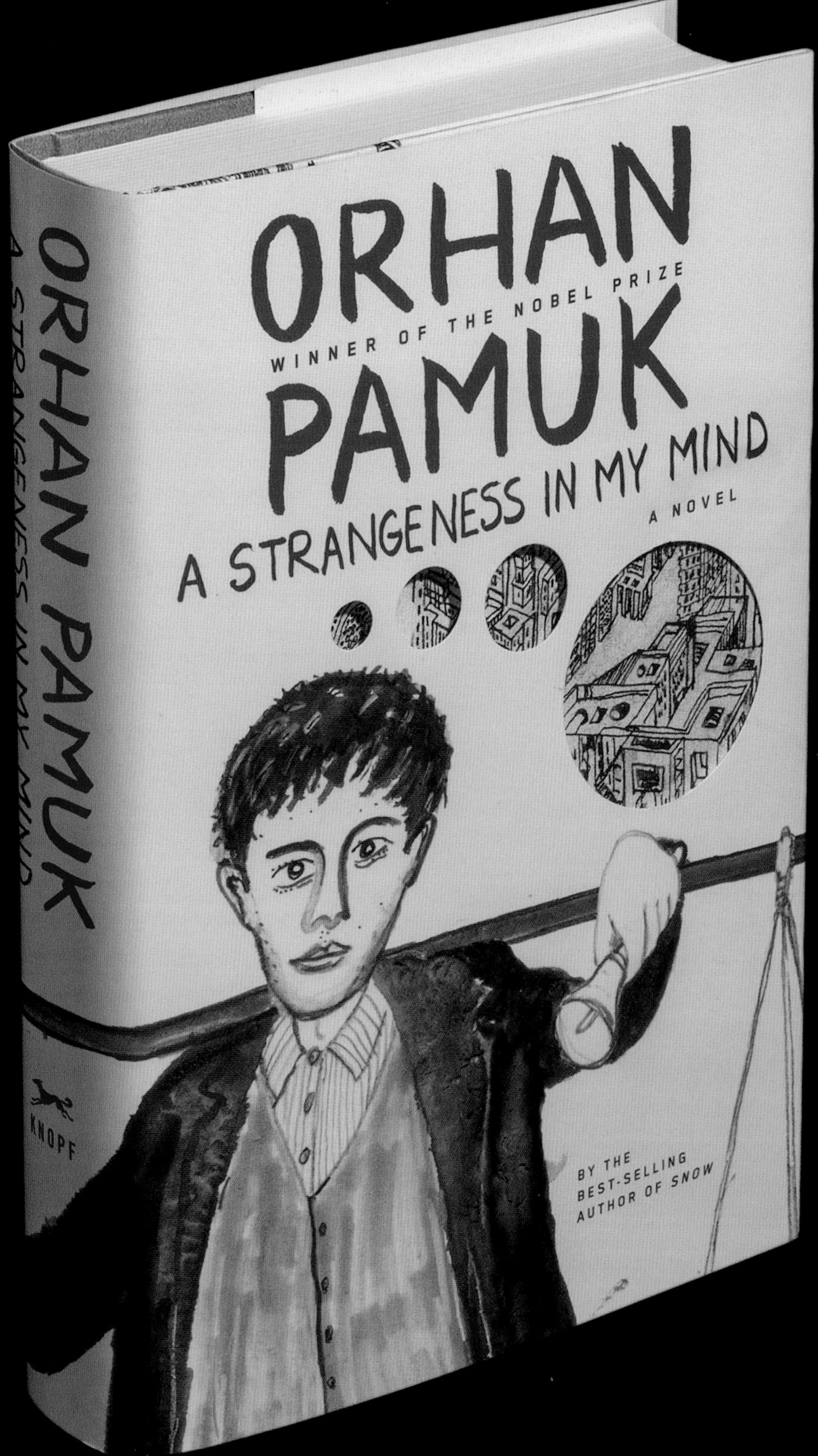
ORHAN PAMUK
WINNER OF THE NOBEL PRIZE
A STRANGENESS IN MY MIND
A NOVEL
BY THE BEST-SELLING AUTHOR OF SNOW
ORHAN PAMUK A STRANGENESS IN MY MIND
KNOPF

**ABOVE:** My sketch for the direction of the cover. **RIGHT & OPPOSITE:** Orhan's deft interpretation of it. The thought bubbles are die-cut holes that give way to the panorama of Istanbul and the Bosporus beneath. Knopf, 2015. All drawings and lettering by Orhan Pamuk.

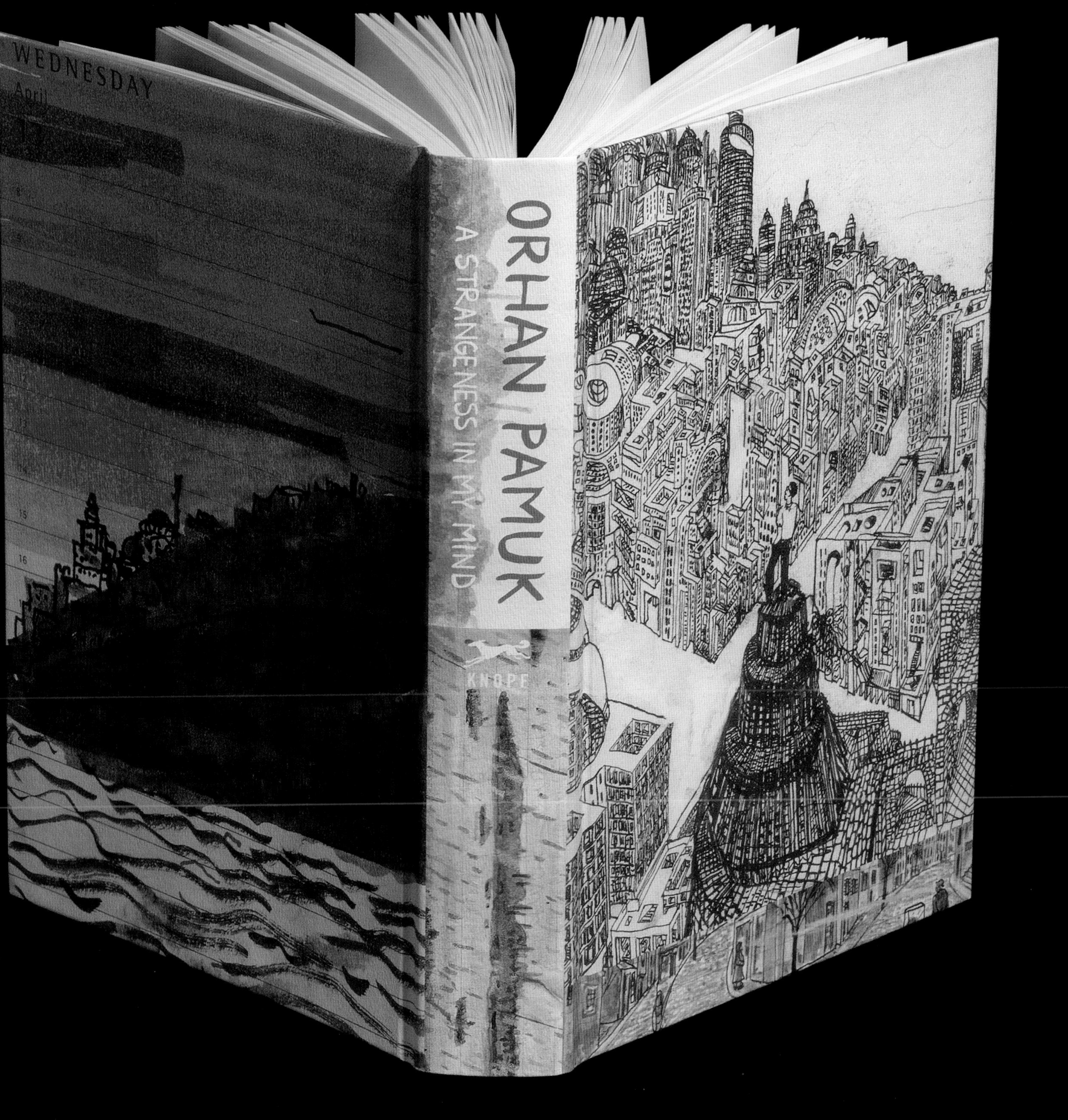
WEDNESDAY
April
ORHAN PAMUK
A STRANGENESS IN MY MIND
KNOPF

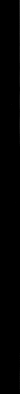

# Neil Gaiman

Trying and failing to remember when I first became aware of Chip Kidd. I knew his covers before I knew him, that's for sure, but which covers? *Geek Love* perhaps? The first of the beloved books. As I became aware of him as a designer, I became aware how many of the book covers of books I loved were his. And were *smart*.

Sooner or later we met. We discussed Sandman and Batman in front of an audience. He is a snappy dresser and an enthusiast: he loves things, and he wants other people to love the things he loves.

We have worked together only once: he took a speech by me on making mistakes and making art, both of them, and he made the speech into a poem, a piece of red and greeny-blue concrete poetry, like something that fell here from a 3D world, a little book of how to fail right and how to adventure and how to dream.

He broke every rule in publishing to make it, including some that the publishers didn't realize were rules until Chip did it differently.

I was so proud of him.

Once, at an awards ceremony, carried away by the glory of the moment, on stage in front of thousands, he became the only gentleman ever to French-kiss me.

I bask in reflected glory.

—N.G.

MAKE GOOD ART

Husband runs off with a politician?

Leg crushed and then eaten by a mutated boa constrictor?

IRS on your trail?

Cat exploded?

ISBN 978-0-307-96184-6
52000
9 780307 961846

COVER DESIGN BY CHIP KIDD

TWO OUT OF THREE IS FINE.

Neil Gaiman's 'Make Good Art' speech.

HarperCollins

FAN-TASTIC MIS-TAKES

Neil Gaiman's 'Make Good Art' speech.

# Portfolio · Neil Gaiman

It's difficult to put into words how valuable it is what Neil Gaiman does, and how much sheer pleasure he's given his huge base of devoted and dreamy readers. Or at least it is for me; it would not be difficult for Neil Gaiman, because he can articulate just about anything more beautifully and with more feeling than most mortals.

I first took notice of his work when he wrote a comic book series in 1987 for DC Comics based on a totally obscure character named Black Orchid. It was illustrated by someone named Dave McKean. Being the geek that I proudly am, I knew who Black Orchid was, but I was not exactly a fan—she was a kind of third-rate Batwoman from the 1970s. Yet this new series made me pay attention anew. Now she had nuance and an origin story and an actual inner life. Amazing. Who was this guy?

Then *Sandman* happened. Again, Neil had taken a DC Comics character who had no right to be interesting and made it utterly fascinating. I say "it" because in Neil's hands the Sandman was no longer a person but a sort of god, a sibling of the Endless, a family of disparate deities whose names all began with "D": Dream, Despair, Destiny, Destruction, Desire, and Death. It was mesmerizing.

So, what was Neil doing?

He was making good art.

Neil's "Make Good Art" project started out as a commencement address he gave at the University of the Arts in Philadelphia in 2012. Which went viral. Then I was contacted by an editor at HarperCollins to make the speech into a book. I watched Neil present it onscreen and as I listened I could start to see how the text could look on the page. It was bizarre, thrilling, and frankly not un-dreamlike.

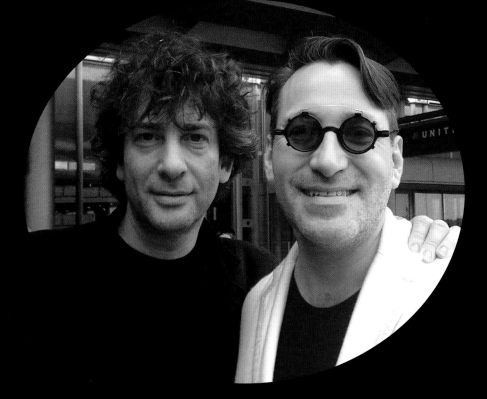

Here was the opportunity to design *Make Good Art* as the ultimate Typography 401 assignment: how do you design and set a text to look like what it is saying? Or more to the point, how do you make the reading experience of the book unique from watching the speech? (Which, by the way, anyone could do for free, and had already done to the tune of over a million views). So this project, to me, was emblematic of a crucial crossroads that no less than the entire book-making process had come to: can I still make you want this information as ink on paper, something that you want to literally grab onto and hold? Is seeing it on YouTube enough, or do you need it embodied, arranged graphically on the page, the form enhancing the content? In short, do you need my visual interpretation of it? That question was impossible to answer until I gave it a shot, so I plunged in (see opposite & following spread).

• • •

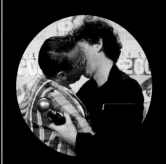

Okay, the whole "kiss at the Eisner Awards" thing. This was semi-spontaneous, but the night before we had had dinner in San Diego during ComicCon 2013, and it came up that comedian host Jonathan Ross wanted to kiss Neil onstage at the Eisners ceremony, but Mr. Gaiman was demurring. Cut to the next night at the awards; I was to be accepting on behalf of Chris Ware's *Building Stories*, which was up for something like five honors. He won them all, and the ultimate was the last one for the night, for Best Graphic Album, Original Work, the equivalent of the Oscars' Best Picture. And Neil was presenting.

And I was receiving, and how could we not?

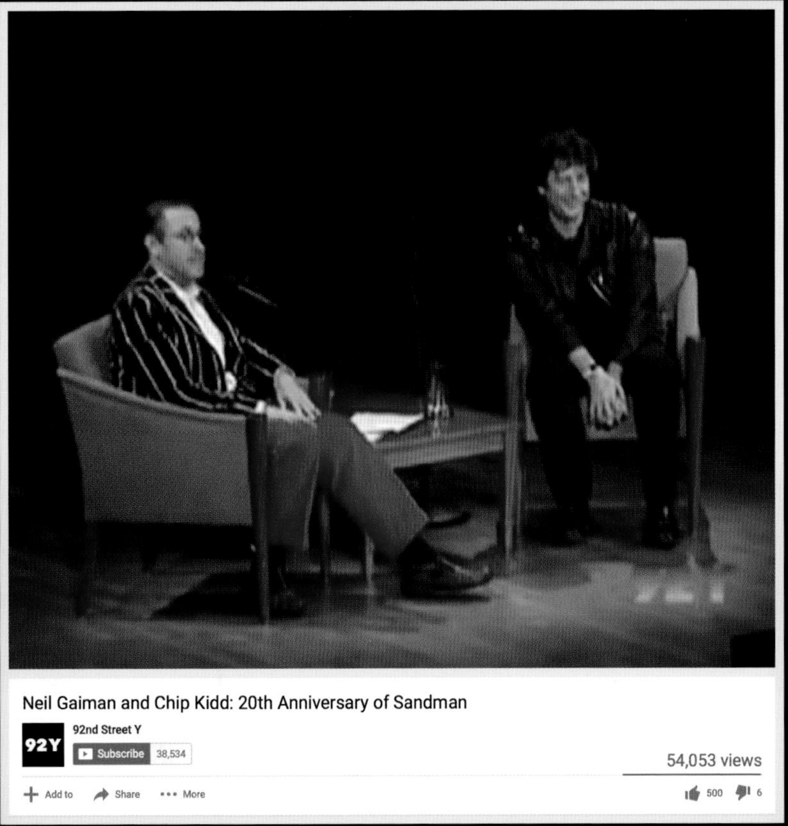
Neil Gaiman and Chip Kidd: 20th Anniversary of Sandman
92Y
92nd Street Y
Subscribe 38,534
54,053 views
Add to
Share
More
500
6

In the midst of all this, I was invited by the 92nd Street Y in New York City to interview Neil onstage about the 20th anniversary of *Sandman* (above). It was fanboy glee for me, and I held an informal contest on my website weeks ahead to reach out to other fans and have them submit potential questions. One of the most interesting suggestions was: "Get him to do his impressions of William Shatner and Harlan Ellison, they are priceless." And sure enough, I eventually brought that up, and he seemed delighted and delivered dead-on mimics of both of them, with hilarious contexts for each. And then the subject changed to a Batman story that he was working on for Detective Comics (#686 & #853), and I was entranced, and we started geeking out on Batman, which ultimately led to my writing a Batman graphic novel (see pp. 296–314).

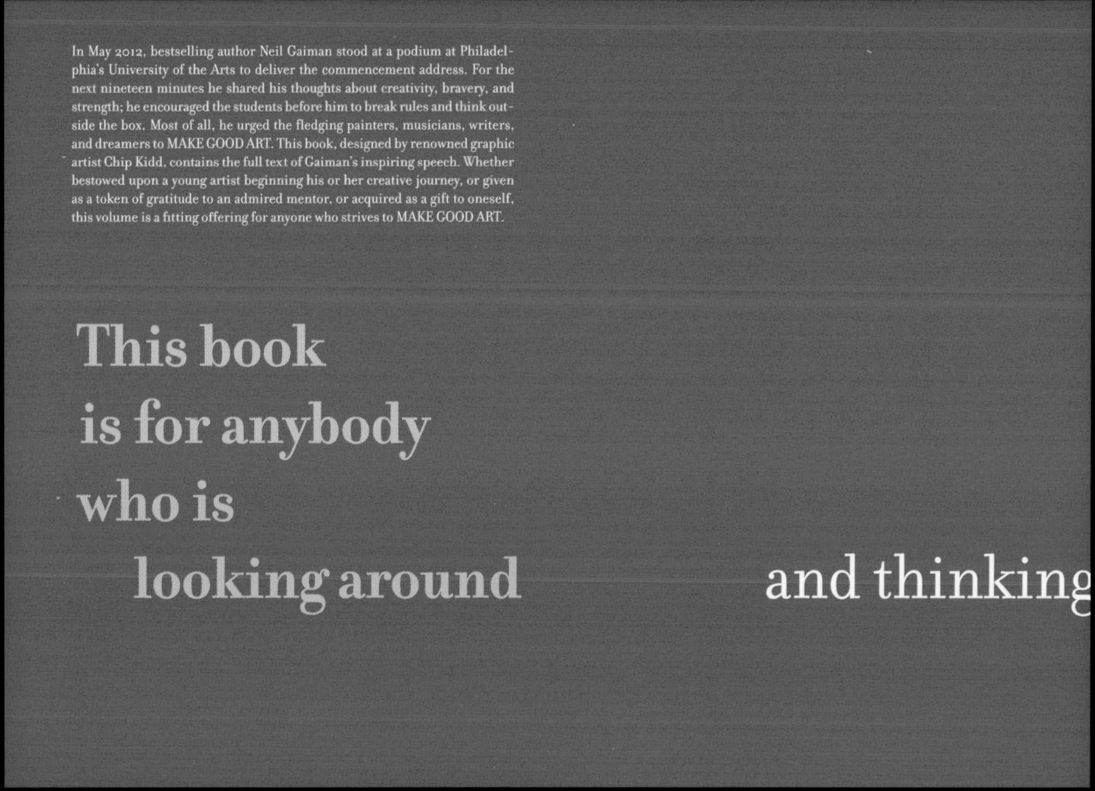
In May 2012, bestselling author Neil Gaiman stood at a podium at Philadelphia's University of the Arts to deliver the commencement address. For the next nineteen minutes he shared his thoughts about creativity, bravery, and strength; he encouraged the students before him to break rules and think outside the box. Most of all, he urged the fledging painters, musicians, writers, and dreamers to MAKE GOOD ART. This book, designed by renowned graphic artist Chip Kidd, contains the full text of Gaiman's inspiring speech. Whether bestowed upon a young artist beginning his or her creative journey, or given as a token of gratitude to an admired mentor, or acquired as a gift to oneself, this volume is a fitting offering for anyone who strives to MAKE GOOD ART.
This book
is for anybody
who is
looking around
and thinking



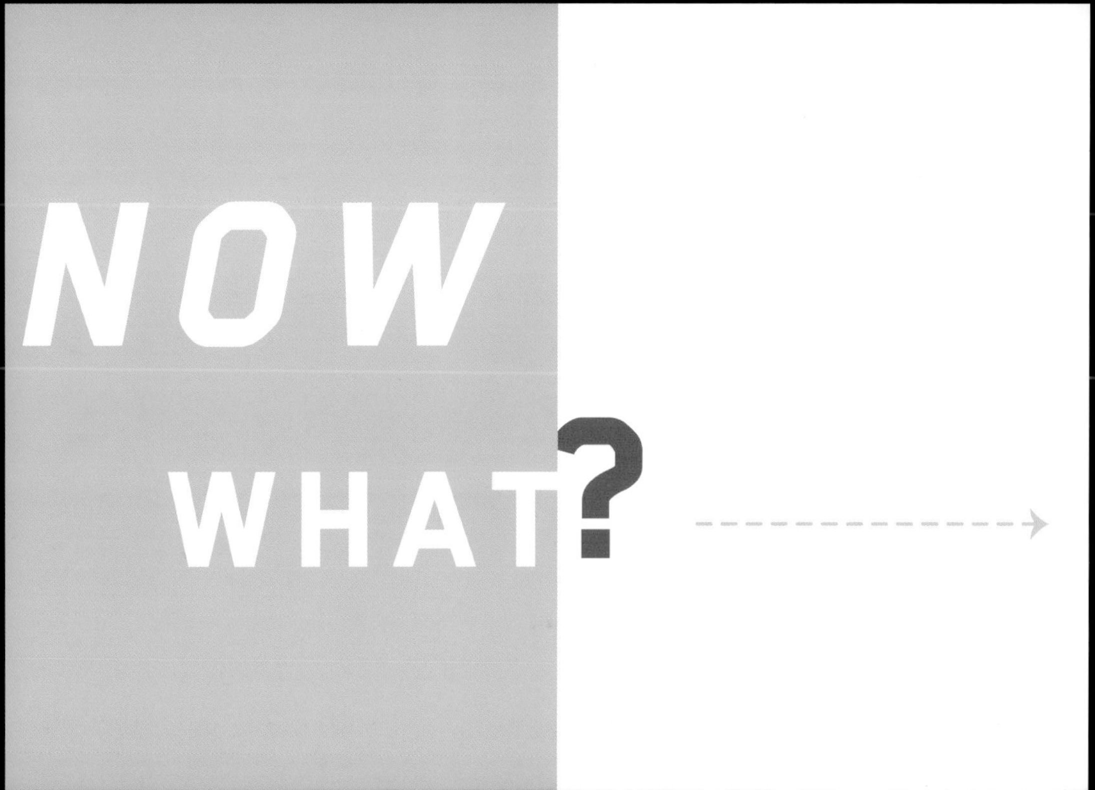
NOW
WHAT?

**RIGHT & FOLLOWING SPREAD:** This kind of typographic storytelling has its roots in both the works of Lewis Carroll (one of Neil's favorites, naturally) and what became known as concrete poetry of the Dada and Russian Constructivist movements in the early 20th century.

17. May 2012

## school

"I never really expected to find myself giving advice to people graduating from an establishment of higher education. I never graduated from any such establishment. I never even started at one. I **escaped** from

as soon as I could, when the prospect of

four

more

years

of

enforced learning before I'd become the writer I wanted to be was stifling.

never did. The nearest thing I had was a list I made when I was 15 of everything I wanted to do:

to write an adult novel,

a children's book,

a comic,

a movie,

record an audiobook,

write an episode of Doctor Who

. . . and so on.

**I DIDN'T HAVE A CAREER.**

I just did the next thing on the list.

So I thought I'd tell you

everything I wish I'd known

starting out, and a few things that,

looking back on it, I suppose that I did

know. And that I would also give you

the best piece of advice I'd ever got,

which I completely

failed to

follow.

I got out into the world, I wrote, and I became a better writer the more I wrote, and I wrote some more, and nobody ever seemed to mind that I was making it up as I went along, they just read what I wrote and they paid for it. **or they didn't.** and often they commissioned me to write something else for them.

Which has left me with a healthy respect

and fondness for higher education

that those of my friends and family,

# WHO

# ATTENDED

# UNIVERSITIES,

were cured of long ago.

Looking back,

I've had a remarkable ride.

I'm not sure I can call it a **CAREER**,

because a **CAREER** implies that I had

some kind of **CAREER** plan, and I

→

→

→

**1**irst of all:

When you start out on a career in the arts you have no idea what you are doing.

THIS

IS GREAT.

PEOPLE WHO

know what they are doing

know the rules,

and know what is

possible and

impossible.

You do not.

AND YOU SHOULD NOT.

The rules on what is possible and impossible in the arts were made by people who had not tested the bounds of the possible by going beyond them.

AND YOU CAN.

6D · THURSDAY, JULY 22, 2004 · USA TODAY

# Kidd covers design, murder in 'Learners'

Though Chip Kidd may be best known for his book covers – his designs have graced titles by David Sedaris, Michael Crichton and hundreds of other authors – occasionally he likes to work between them.

Kidd's new piece of fiction, *The Learners*, makes its debut today as part of USATODAY.com's Open Book series. A new chapter of his exclusive, seven-part novella will be published online each Thursday at open book.usatoday.com.

*The Learners* serves as a sequel of sorts to Kidd's first novel, 2001's *The Cheese Monkeys* (Perennial, $13.95). Set in the early 1960s, *The Learners* follows a young graphic designer who decides to answer the first newspaper ad he creates.

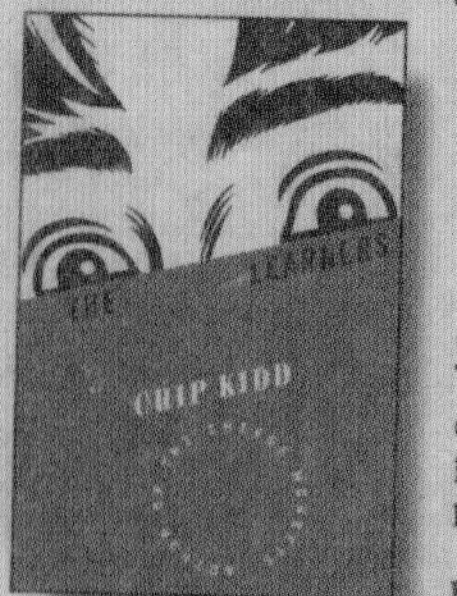
CHIP KIDD

What follows is "a murder mystery about a killing that may never have taken place," Kidd says.

Not only does Kidd draw on his graphic-design background for the narrative, but he also incorporates it into the text. Typography plays a crucial role in *The Learners*; font size and design pull readers into the action.

A few lessons from Kidd's college psychology classes also are thrown in: A central character in *The Learners* is real-life social psychologist Stanley Milgram, whose experiments during the 1960s still incite controversy.

Kidd plans to expand his novella into a full-length book, tentatively set for release in 2006.

"This really is the story I've been wanting to tell all along," says the author, who took a month-long break from his design job at Knopf to write *The Learners* at Bogliasco, Italy's Liguria Study Center.

Kidd also is working with book publisher Rizzoli to develop "a definitive coffee table book" of his designs. He also is an editor at large for Pantheon's graphic novels division. And then, of course, there are more book covers: "Designing is so rewarding in a way that writing isn't."

Look for Kidd's work on titles by Augusten Burroughs and John Updike in coming months – and, a couple years from now, on Kidd's next novel.

Read the first chapter of *The Learners* at open book.usatoday.com

By Whitney Matheson

USA TODAY .com For more reviews, book news and a searchable archive of USA TODAY's Best-Selling Books list, visit us on the Web at books.usatoday.com

## About this list

USA TOD... 'culates a list of 300 best-selling books. The first 50 are listed ... SA TODAY's list is based on a computer analysis of re... eek. Included are more than 1.5 milli... dependent, chain, discount a... Davis Kidd ... eth Book ... e.). ...

Hardcov...

| This wk. | Last wk. | |
|---|---|---|
| 1 | 1 | |
| 2 | 4 | |
| 3 | New | |
| 4 | 8 | |
| 5 | 3 | B |
| 6 | 5 | Th |
| 7 | 2 | My |
| 8 | New | Slo |
| 9 | 9 | The |
| 10 | 6 | Blin |
| 11 | 10 | The Guid |
| 12 | 7 | Sam's |
| 13 | 12 | The P |
| 14 | 16 | The Be |
| 15 | 11 | The Ru |
| 16 | 14 | The Fiv Mitch Al |
| 17 | 17 | Decepti |
| 18 | 22 | The Sec |
| 19 | 24 | Shadow |
| 20 | 23 | The Curi in the Ni |
| 21 | 18 | Dress You David Seda |
| 22 | 25 | Digital Fo |
| 23 | 26 | The Lovely |
| 24 | 240 | The Ultima Phil McGraw |
| 25 | New | Kiss Me Wh |
| 26 | 19 | Ten Big Ones |
| 27 | 15 | When He Wa |
| 28 | 21 | The Vanished |
| 29 | 28 | Eats, Shoots a |
| 30 | 27 | Weekend Wa |
| 31 | 20 | Sense of Evil |
| 32 | 32 | The Time Tr |
| 33 | 13 | Dark Destin |
| 34 | 33 | Life of Pi/Ya |
| 35 | 38 | The Devil W |
| 36 | 37 | Reading Lo |
| 37 | 29 | The Dark T |
| 38 | 44 | I, Robot/Is |
| 39 | 39 | The Sou |
| 40 | 31 | Anna K by Rich |
| 41 | 34 | Dark |
| 42 | | |

"Q: And babies?

A: And babies."

– *The New York Times,*

Nov. 25, 1969

Chapter 1

## AND NOW A WORD FROM OUR SPONSOR.

Sorry to interrupt, but something just occurred to me, something helpful: If you're anything like me, the very first time you murder someone is always the hardest. The most difficult to accept, to absorb, to understand. And I was thinking, just now, that it probably gets easier with practice. Look at Bonnie and Clyde – after that bank teller in Tuskarora (*so* uncooperative) it just didn't matter anymore. I mean, by the third or the fourth or the 10th, you're most likely not brooding over the first, because by then (logic tells us) you have a lot more on your mind. Heck, by then you've evolved into a whole other species, right?

But I never had a third or a fourth, see. Or even a second. It was just the one. Which is probably why things went the way they did.

And yes, I think we all, whether or not we admit it (or realize it), are well versed in the daily, casual torture of those around us – strangers, loved ones, waiters, the elderly – to every degree of discomfort. But that's one thing. Taking a life is another. Actual, physical killing. Now *that's* shocking.

At least it was to me.

• • •

In the spring of 1961 I was ready. After four years of studying graphic design at State U., I had my portfolio in hand and one goal – to work at the advertising agency of Spear, Rakoff & Ware. Why? Easy: That's where my idol Winter Sorbeck started, long ago.

Now, of course Winter is a whole other story, but suffice it to say that if S, R & W was good enough for him, then for me it was mandatory. Winter had been my freshman design teacher, and though he left the school soon after that – vanished, actually – I learned enough from him to know I wanted to *be* him. Without the psychosis.

Spear, Rakoff & Ware was located in New Haven, Conn., a place I'd never been. I knew it was the home of Yale University, but other than that it might as well have been on Pluto. This would take some doing.

"Could I have the art department, please?" I've come to realize I don't possess many virtues, but Focus is one of them. Once I know I want something, something big, then I construct a plan and follow it through 'til it's either finally mine or outlawed by the sciences. That is, after all, what designers do, isn't it? Step 1: Look up information, phone.

"Who's calling, please?" I asked if Mr. Milburn "Sketchy" Spear was still the head art director. A heavy sigh, then: "Hold please."

Finally, "Spear." It was him! I explained my intentions. The years had not changed his enthusiasm.

"Oh, you don't want to work here." The voice: experienced, kind and exhausted. Santa Claus on the afternoon of Dec. 25.

"Um, yes, I do."

"Really?"

"Yes, sir."

Silence.

"Hello?"

"Sorry, I'm inking. Mind's a porch screen when I'm inking. I'm trying to do a crowd scene with a No. 5 Pedigree pen tip. Should be using a Radio 914. Doesn't really matter – can't draw anymore anyway, never could. God,. I *stink*. Wouldn't you rather work someplace else?"

Hmmm. "No, sir, I'd like to work for your firm. You know, to sort of get my feet wet." Dreadful. Why did I say that?

"Heh." He sounded like a lawnmower trying to start. "Heh. That's what I thought. I mean, that's what *I* thought when I started here. You know when that was?"

"No. I – "

"You know dirt?"

"Dirt?"

"Dirt."

"Um, yes. Dirt."

"Well, I started here the year before they discovered it."

"I see."

"Heh."

"At least ... it must have been spotless when you arrived."

"Heh-heh. Can you airbrush?"

"Yes, but – "

"Operate a photostat machine?"

"Well, I – "

"Do you know what I'm doing right now?"

"Uh, drawing a crowd scene with a ... No. 5 Pedigree pen tip?"

"No, that's done. Now I'm trying to decide what kind of face the potato chip should have. That's always a problem. Problems, problems."

"Pardon?"

"For this newspaper ad. A half-pager, due by five. Everyone signed off on it yesterday – the crowd, see, they've all filed out into the street to worship a giant potato chip."

"I see."

"Because it's a Krinkle Kut. One of our biggest accounts."

"Right."

"Six stories tall." His tone was casually conversational, as if he was describing his brother-in-law. "So, exactly what sort of expression should he have on his face? Because obviously, he's a very happy potato chip, to be a Krinkly Kolossus, and in the thrall of all these tiny people, who adore him so."

"Well ... it's obvious to me."

"That right?"

"He should look ***chipper***."

"Heh."

"So to speak. But not so smug. He doesn't want to frighten everyone. I mean, *I'd* be wary of a jagged slab of tuber towering over my fellow citizens, our fate in his many, many eyes. Especially if he's been fried in lard. Which he has, I hope?"

"Heh. You still want to work here?"

"Definitely."

# The Experiment Requires You to Continue . . .

When *The Cheese Monkeys* first came out in the fall of 2001 and I went on the book tour, the first question I'd get during the Q & A would be, "Why is it set in 1957?" The real answer was, "Because the sequel, *The Learners*, will be set in 1961, so I started four years backwards from that." But of course that wouldn't have made sense to anybody but me, and it would have been premature to declare it anyway. So I said instead, "I like that time period for the themes of this book, because it was just before Pop Art happened and confused everything. And Penn State when I was there in the '80s was not so different from the late '50s." Which was also true, but not the whole story, as it were.

I had been obsessed with Stanley Milgram's "obedience to authority" experiments at Yale in 1961 since I first learned of them during my Psych 101 class at Penn State in 1983. Milgram, at the tender age of 27, had the genius idea of how one might re-create Nazi Germany of the late 1930s in a laboratory and quantifiably study what made it possible. He did so by placing ads in the local New Haven paper soliciting paid volunteers for an experiment concerning "learning and memory." Once someone responded and agreed to participate, they were ushered into the lab with another volunteer, and the two of them were told to draw lots to determine who would be the Learner and who would be the Teacher. At this point they would be told by the lab technician that it wasn't just about memory and learning, but also about the role of punishment in the process. The Learner would be seated on the other side of a wall in the lab, so the Teacher could hear him but not see him. The Learner would be hooked up to an apparatus/machine attached to his arm that would allow the Teacher to administer electric shocks to the Learner that ranged from 5 volts up to 500. It was explained that the Teacher would read (into a microphone, broadcast to the Learner on the other side of the wall) a series of word pairs: "x, x; x, x; x, x." Then he would go back and read the first word, and the Learner would have to select which was the second via an electronic switch on the apparatus/machine. If the Learner got it right, they would continue. If not, the Teacher would shock the Learner. With each wrong response, the shocks would increase in voltage. Both participants were assured that the shocks would be painful but not fatal. All of this would be overseen by a Yale psych lab technician with a clipboard who was, even though this detail was not articulated at this stage, the presiding figure of authority.

**OPPOSITE, LEFT:** An announcement in *USA Today* that the book would be happening. The cover image is a placeholder I put together using a swipe from Charles Burns.

**OPPOSITE, RIGHT:** Teaser excerpt from the book that was accessible via *USA Today*'s website.

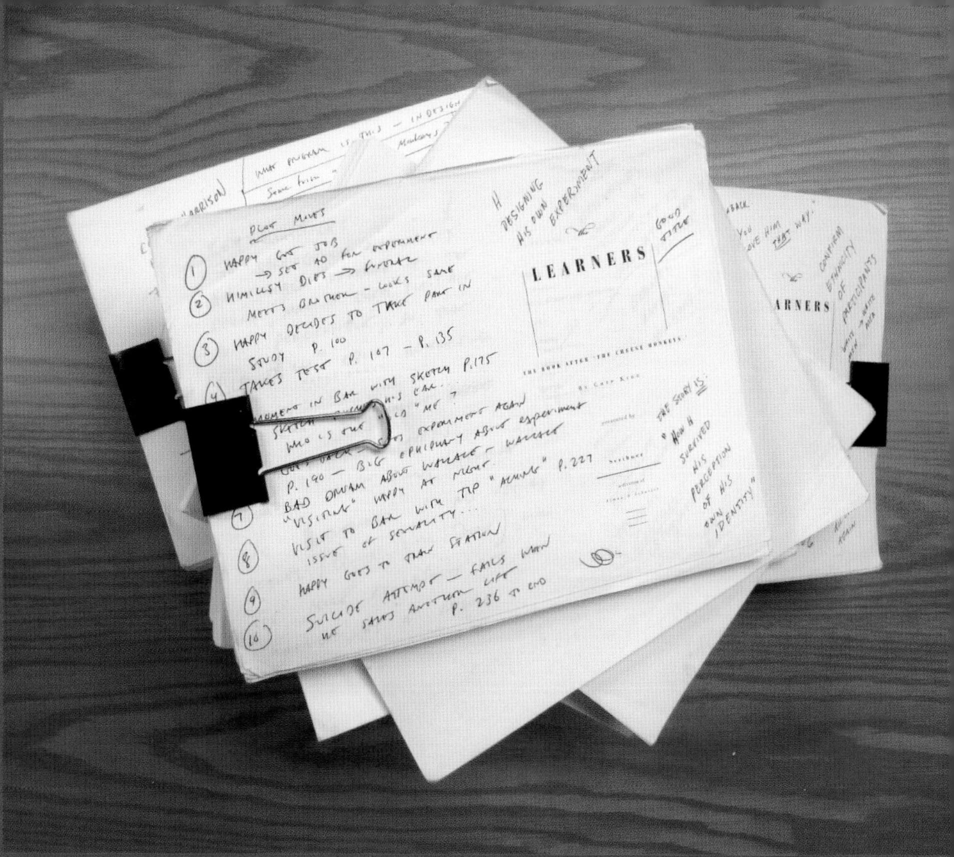
LEARNERS

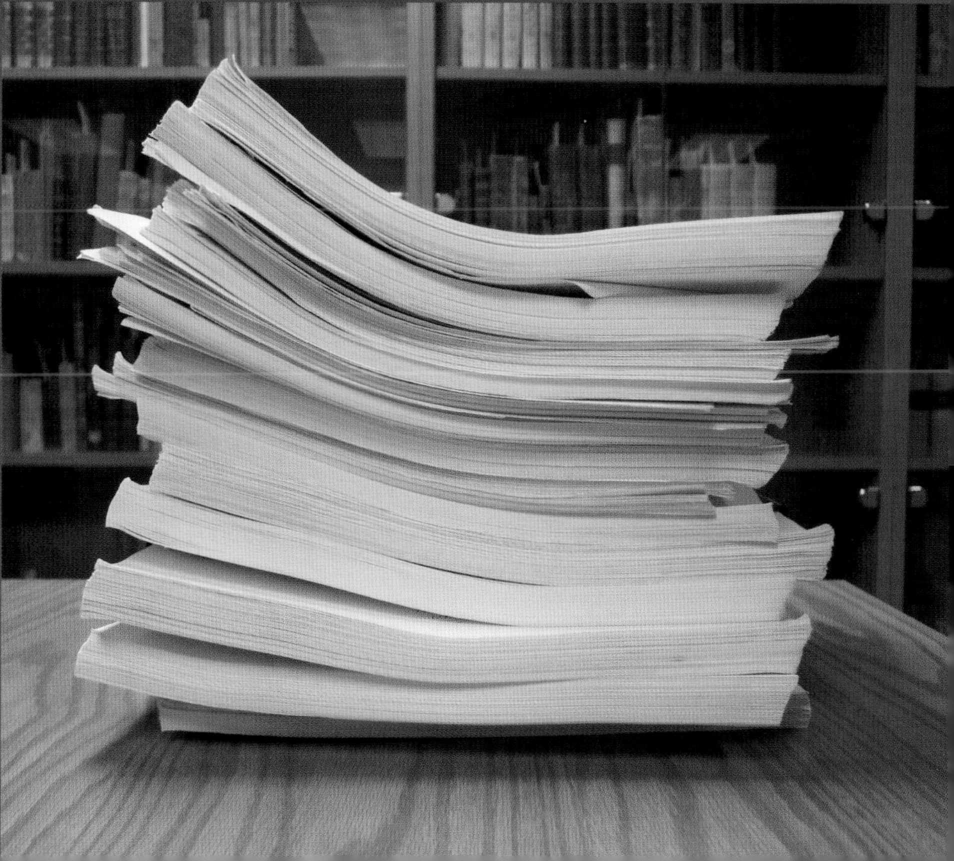

**RIGHT:** Revise, revise, revise.

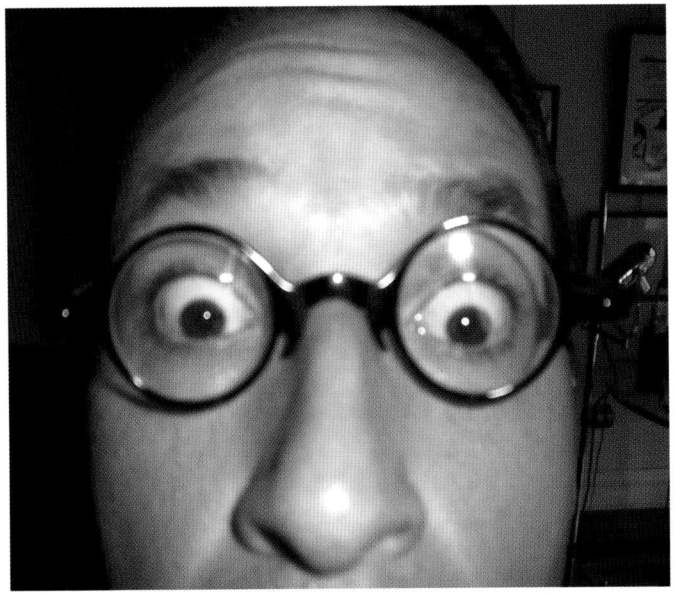

My idea was that you'd be seeing my character (Happy) in the middle of participating in the experiment and totally freaking out. I knew that Charles Burns would be perfect to draw this and he graciously agreed to do it.

**LEFT:** Bad but effective selfie to show Charles how I wanted to look on the cover and give him decent photo reference for my glasses, especially the hinges.

**BELOW:** My pathetic drawing of same, with notes to underline what I was going for. This was likely not necessary, as Charles is a pro and a genius draftsman, but I know in my own work that more information is better than less, as long as it's not so much that you want to leave the project.

**RIGHT:** Charles's pencil-rendering for approval. Wow!

**OPPOSITE:** Chris Ware hand-lettered the title.

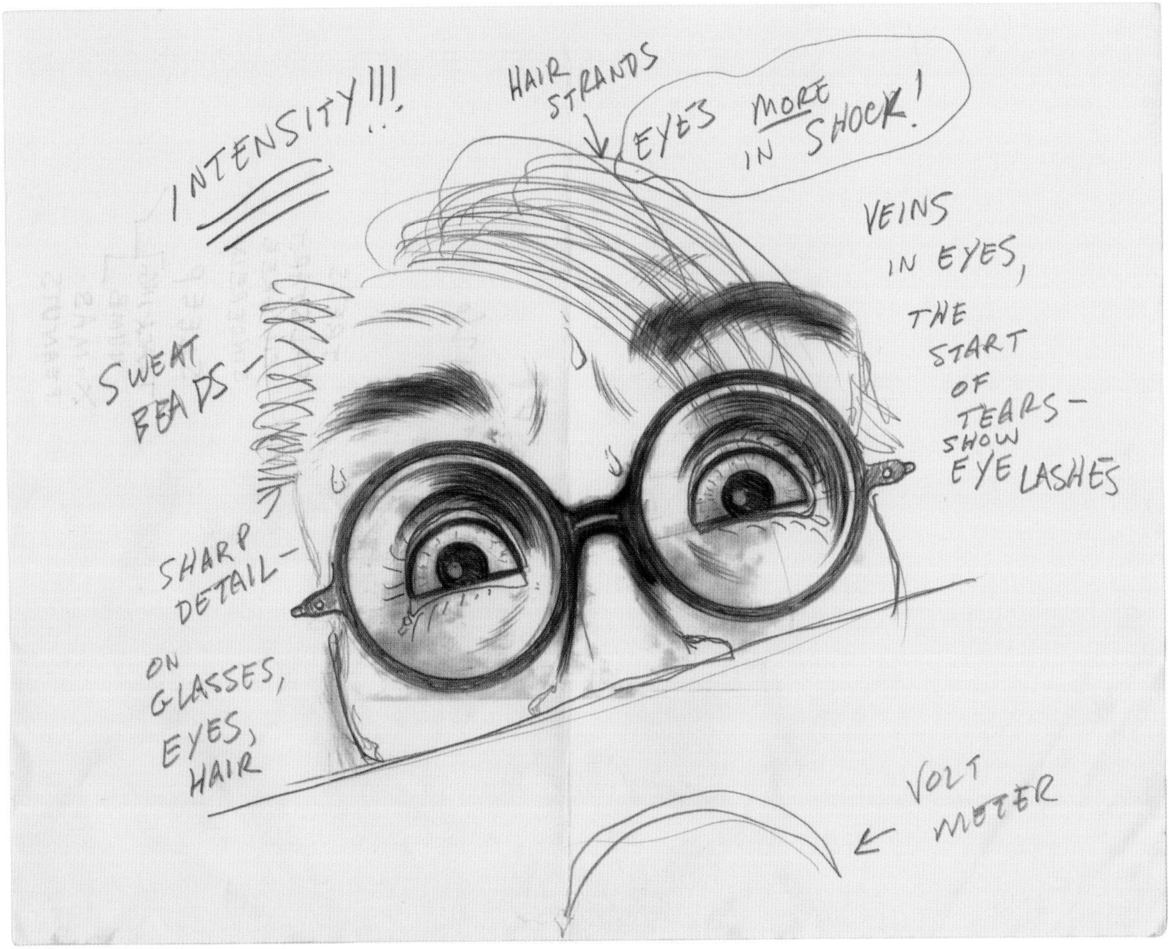
INTENSITY!!!
HAIR STRANDS
EYES MORE IN SHOCK!
VEINS IN EYES,
THE START OF TEARS-
SHOW EYE LASHES
SWEAT BEADS
SHARP DETAIL-
ON GLASSES, EYES, HAIR
VOLT METER



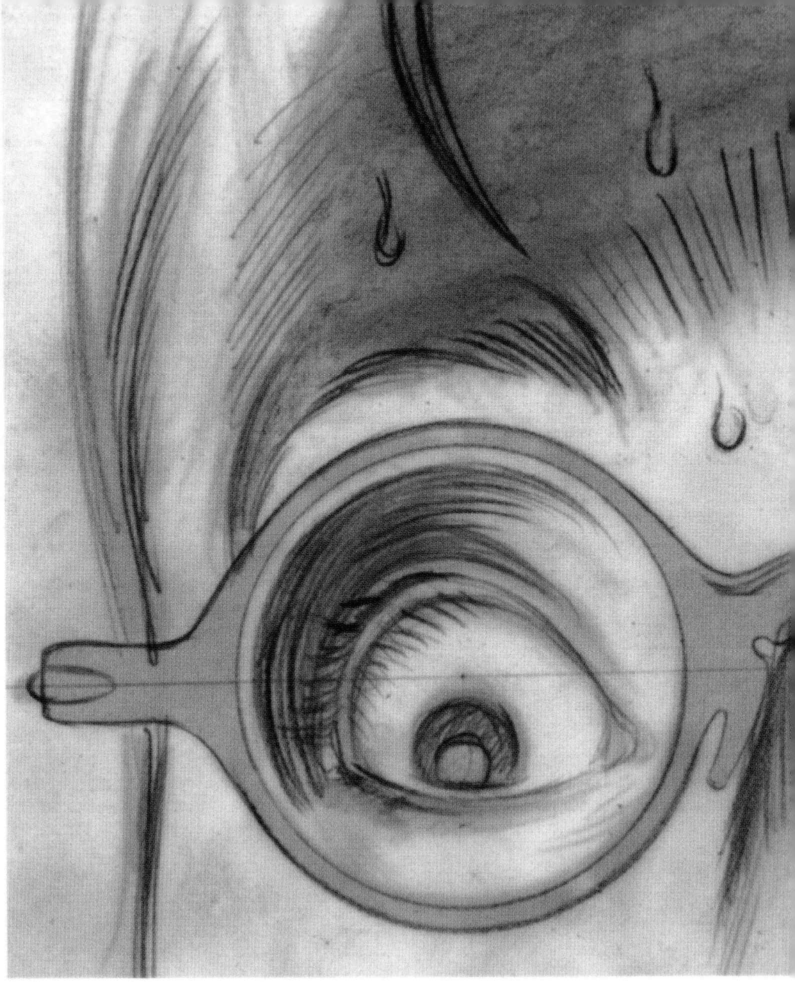

The whole thing is a setup in order to test the only person who isn't in on it—the one volunteer who is marked the Teacher from the outset—and to see how far he will go on the shock board to "teach" the Learner. The other "volunteer" is a plant, an actor who always draws the lot to be the Learner and follows that part through. He is a mild-mannered man in his late 50s who "has a heart condition" and is wary of the shocks. The lab technician "reassures" him that Yale is responsible for everything that happens here, reiterating that the shocks "may be painful but not fatal." Regardless of how this information assuages any participants, the experiment begins. At first the Learner gets the word pairs right, but then he doesn't. And the Teacher has to administer the shocks, in succession of intensity, until the Learner denotes the correct answer. But

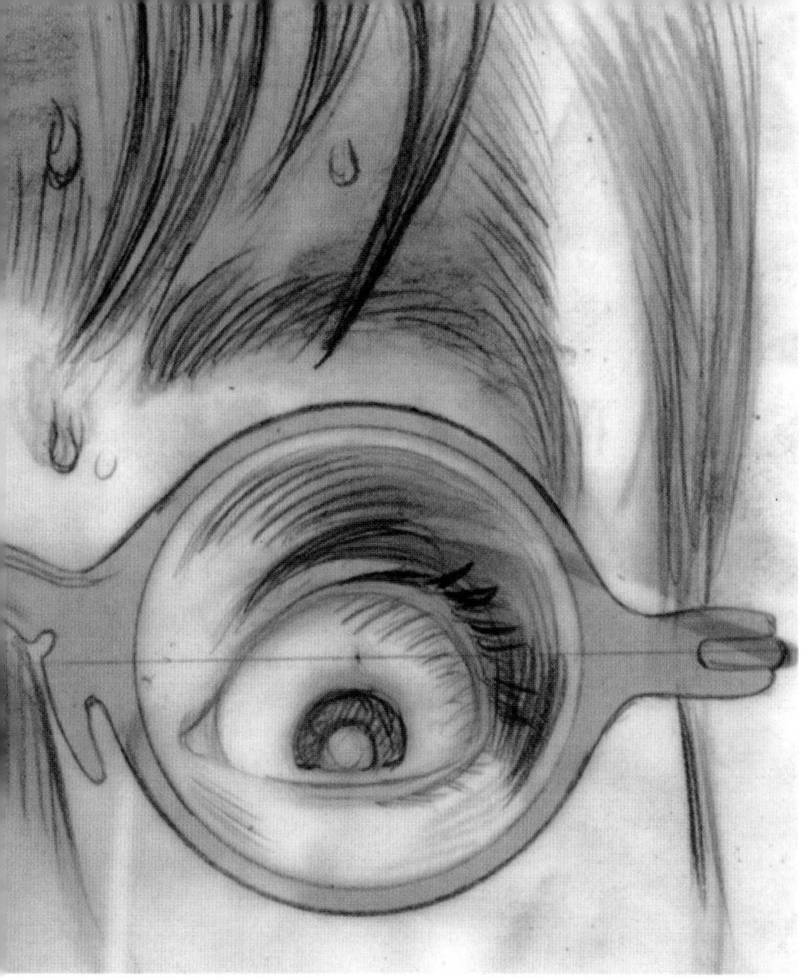

he doesn't, and the question then becomes one of how far up on the shock board the Teacher is willing to go. Milgram's faculty advisors, who had to approve the experiment and its funding, nearly nixed it in the nest because they didn't believe that anyone would fall for such a ploy. But Milgram prevailed, and after three years, hundreds of participants, and multiple controls (including moving the experiment off-campus to remove the intimidated-by-Yale factor), a full 60% of the participants went to the full end of the shock board, in theory killing the Learner. All of this hearkens back to the "I was only just following orders" defense used at Nazi war crimes trials. But what most intrigued me about the experiment was that it was such a brilliant piece of design, and that's what I really wanted to write a novel about.

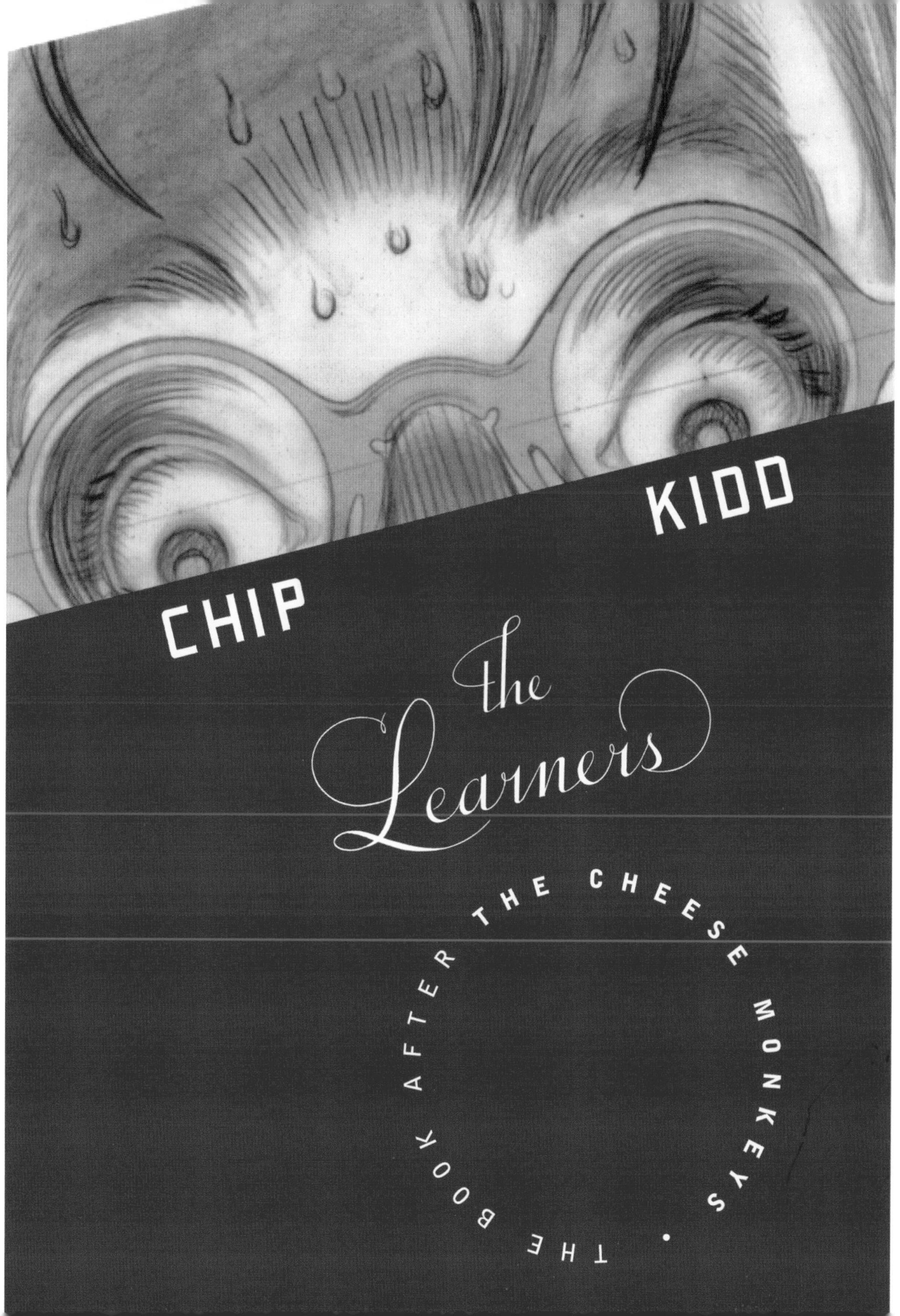
CHIP KIDD
the Learners
THE BOOK AFTER THE CHEESE MONKEYS

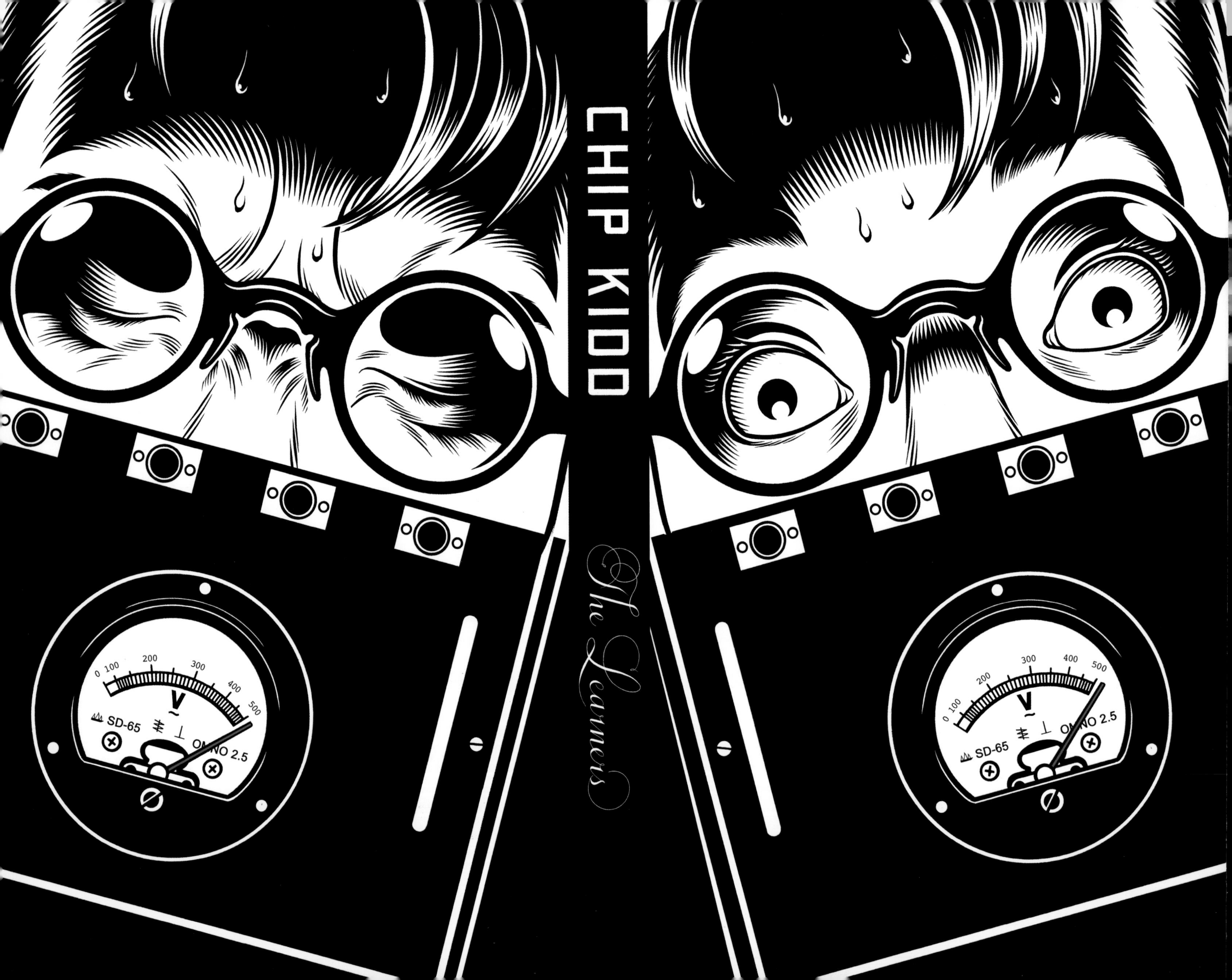
CHIP KIDD
The Learners
0 100 200 300 400 500
V
SD-65
0 100 200 300 400 500
V
SD-65

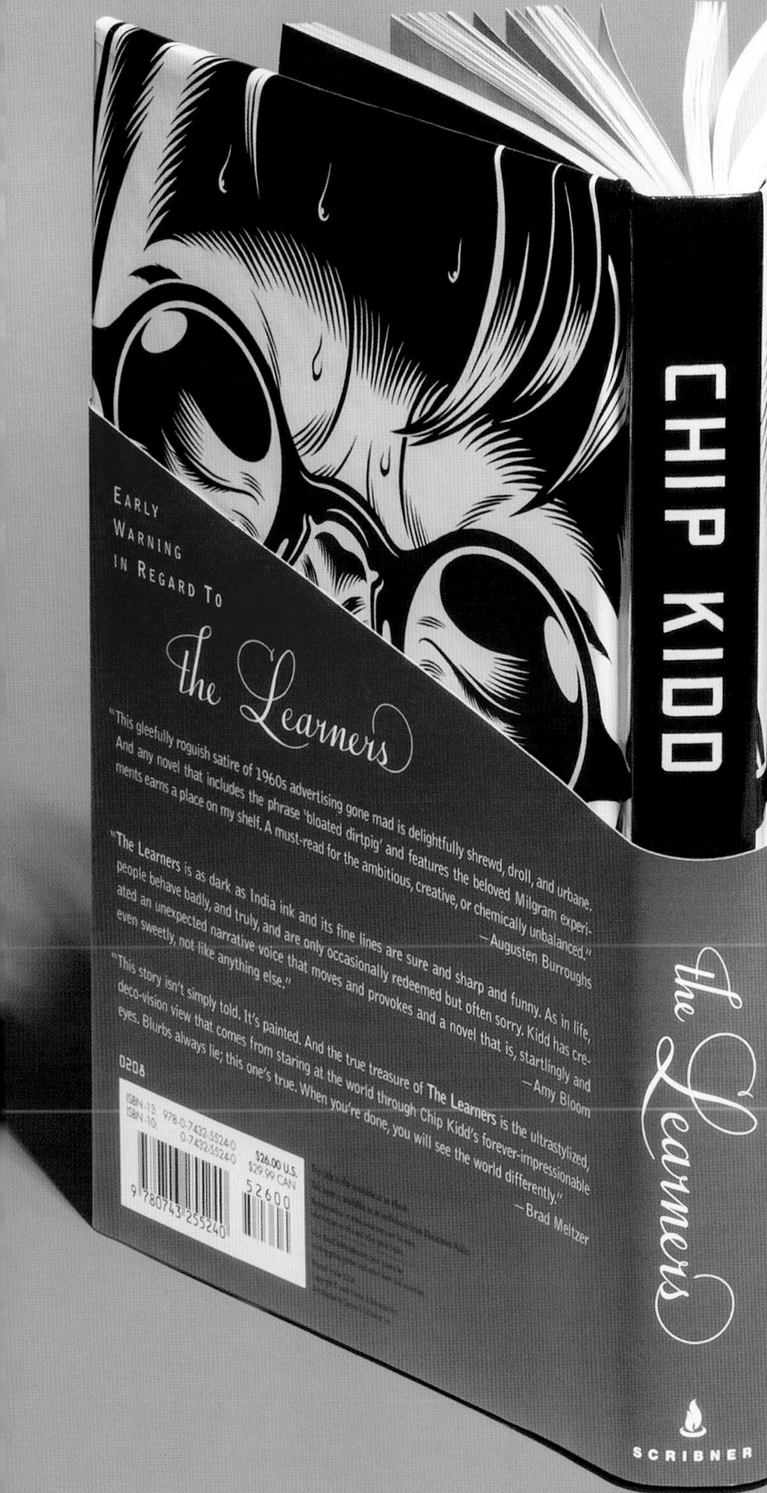
EARLY WARNING IN REGARD TO
the Learners
“This gleefully roguish satire of 1960s advertising gone mad is delightfully shrewd, droll, and urbane. And any novel that includes the phrase ‘bloated dirtpig’ and features the beloved Milgram experiments earns a place on my shelf. A must-read for the ambitious, creative, or chemically unbalanced.”
—Augusten Burroughs
“The Learners is as dark as India ink and its fine lines are sure and sharp and funny. As in life, people behave badly, and truly, and are only occasionally redeemed but often sorry. Kidd has created an unexpected narrative voice that moves and provokes and a novel that is, startlingly and even sweetly, not like anything else.”
—Amy Bloom
“This story isn't simply told. It's painted. And the true treasure of The Learners is the ultrastylized, deco-vision view that comes from staring at the world through Chip Kidd's forever-impressionable eyes. Blurbs always lie; this one's true. When you're done, you will see the world differently.”
—Brad Meltzer
0208
ISBN-13 978-0-7432-5524-0
ISBN-10 0-7432-5524-0
$26.00 U.S.
$29.99 CAN
CHIP KIDD
the Learners
SCRIBNER
CHIP KIDD
the Learners
THE BOOK AFTER THE CHEESE MONKEYS

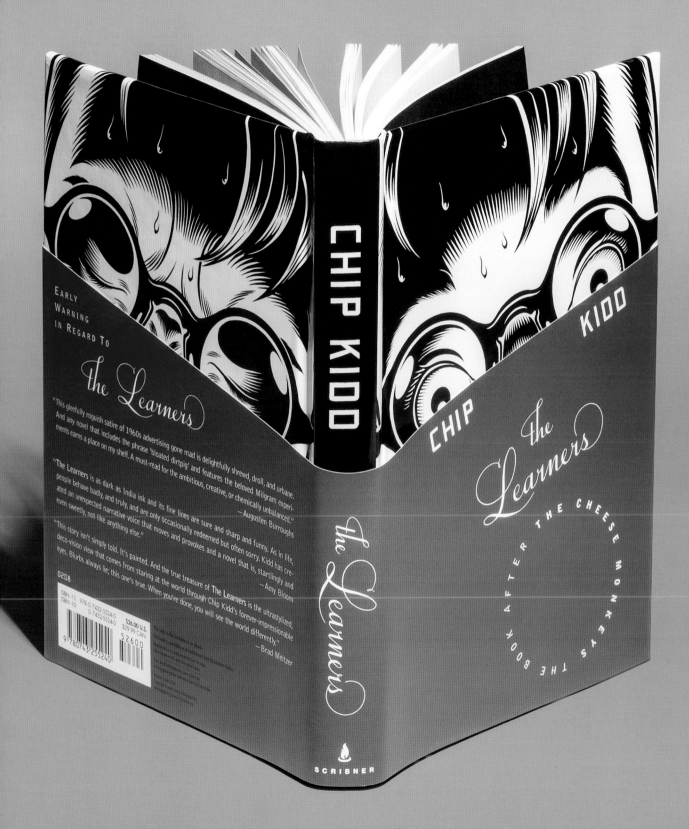

But how would all of this fit into a sequel to *The Cheese Monkeys*? Because Happy (narrator of *Monkeys*, basically me) has now (1961) graduated from State U with a major in graphic design and lands an entry-level position at the advertising agency of Spear, Rakoff and Ware (I know, I know). Among his first assignments is to typeset an advertisement to run daily in the *New Haven Register*. The client? One professor Stanley Milgram. I had pondered for quite some time what I might have done during the experiment, and my theory—in all honesty—was that I probably would have done as instructed, however great the duress, because the designer mentality is to see a problem through to the end. The only way to "solve" the situation that Milgram set up was to quit it, and Happy is not a quitter. But all of this has tremendous consequences for him, and that plays out dramatically (at least I hope) in the last third of the book.

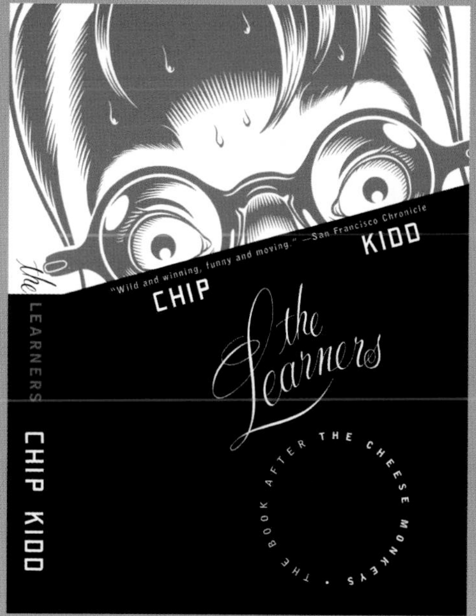
"Wild and winning, funny and moving." —San Francisco Chronicle
CHIP KIDD
the Learners
THE BOOK AFTER THE CHEESE MONKEYS
the LEARNERS CHIP KIDD



**OPPOSITE:** Press proof of the binding/cover of *The Learners*, featuring Charles's finished art of the face and voltage meter of the shock machine. **LEFT:** Finished book package, the jacket a sort of "gag" at a slant. Scribner, 2008. **ABOVE:** The paperback adaptation. Chris wanted to redraw the title lettering, and I changed up the colors while keeping the basic design. HarperPerennial, 2009.

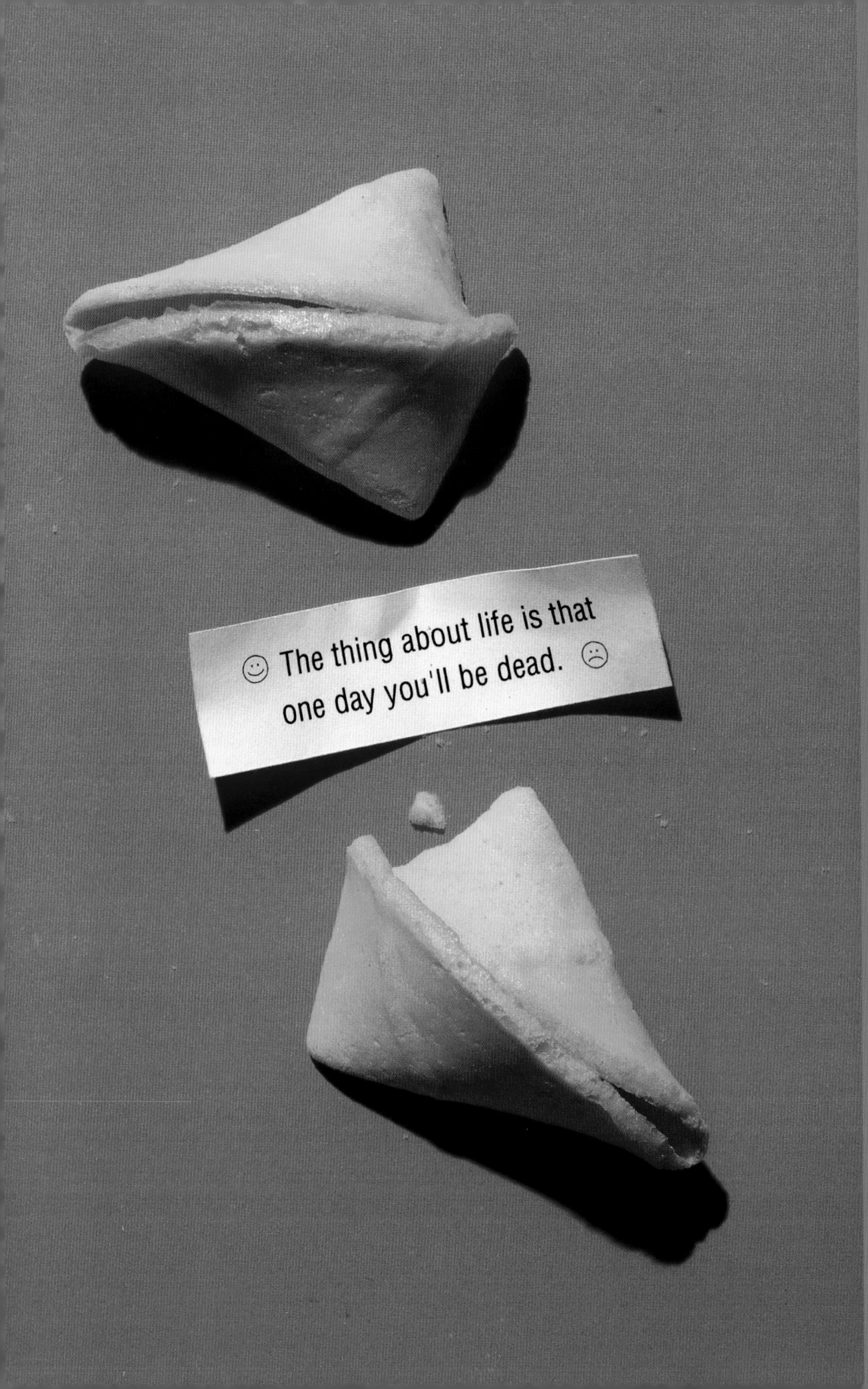
The thing about life is that
one day you'll be dead.

# The thing about life is that one day you'll be dead

David Shields

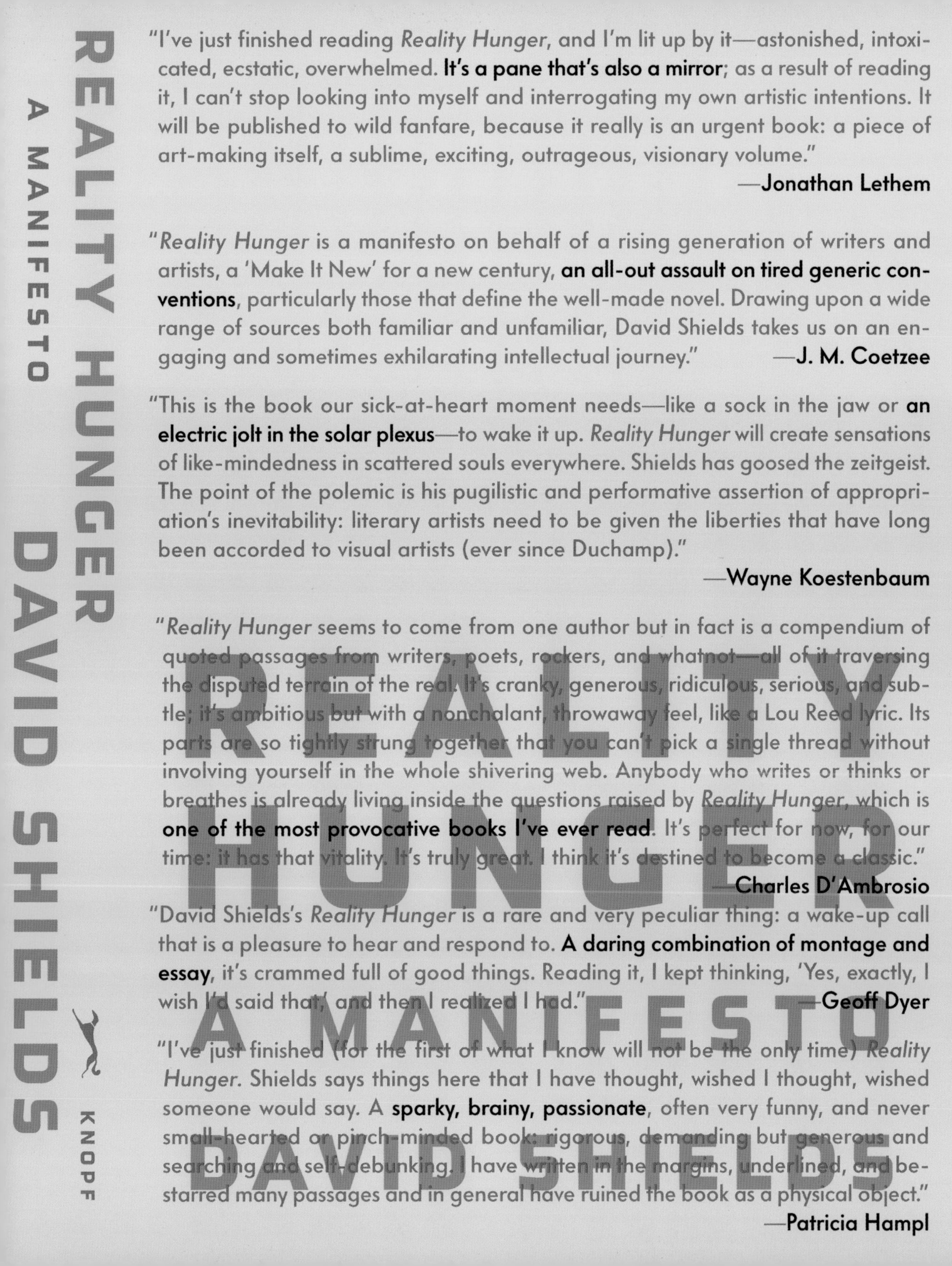
REALITY HUNGER
A MANIFESTO
DAVID SHIELDS
KNOPF
"I've just finished reading Reality Hunger, and I'm lit up by it—astonished, intoxicated, ecstatic, overwhelmed. It's a pane that's also a mirror; as a result of reading it, I can't stop looking into myself and interrogating my own artistic intentions. It will be published to wild fanfare, because it really is an urgent book: a piece of art-making itself, a sublime, exciting, outrageous, visionary volume."
—Jonathan Lethem
"Reality Hunger is a manifesto on behalf of a rising generation of writers and artists, a 'Make It New' for a new century, an all-out assault on tired generic conventions, particularly those that define the well-made novel. Drawing upon a wide range of sources both familiar and unfamiliar, David Shields takes us on an engaging and sometimes exhilarating intellectual journey."
—J. M. Coetzee
"This is the book our sick-at-heart moment needs—like a sock in the jaw or an electric jolt in the solar plexus—to wake it up. Reality Hunger will create sensations of like-mindedness in scattered souls everywhere. Shields has goosed the zeitgeist. The point of the polemic is his pugilistic and performative assertion of appropriation's inevitability: literary artists need to be given the liberties that have long been accorded to visual artists (ever since Duchamp)."
—Wayne Koestenbaum
"Reality Hunger seems to come from one author but in fact is a compendium of quoted passages from writers, poets, rockers, and whatnot—all of it traversing the disputed terrain of the real. It's cranky, generous, ridiculous, serious, and subtle; it's ambitious but with a nonchalant, throwaway feel, like a Lou Reed lyric. Its parts are so tightly strung together that you can't pick a single thread without involving yourself in the whole shivering web. Anybody who writes or thinks or breathes is already living inside the questions raised by Reality Hunger, which is one of the most provocative books I've ever read. It's perfect for now, for our time: it has that vitality. It's truly great. I think it's destined to become a classic."
—Charles D'Ambrosio
"David Shields's Reality Hunger is a rare and very peculiar thing: a wake-up call that is a pleasure to hear and respond to. A daring combination of montage and essay, it's crammed full of good things. Reading it, I kept thinking, 'Yes, exactly, I wish I'd said that,' and then I realized I had."
—Geoff Dyer
"I've just finished (for the first of what I know will not be the only time) Reality Hunger. Shields says things here that I have thought, wished I thought, wished someone would say. A sparky, brainy, passionate, often very funny, and never small-hearted or pinch-minded book: rigorous, demanding but generous and searching and self-debunking. I have written in the margins, underlined, and be-starred many passages and in general have ruined the book as a physical object."
—Patricia Hampl

## Being and Nothingness

I have been designing book jackets for David Shields from very early on in my (and his) career, since I designed his first collection of essays, *Remote*. With *The Thing about Life Is That One Day You'll Be Dead*, he delves into the considerable issue of what it means to be aware of one's mortality. My big idea was to read the title in a fortune cookie (opposite, left), which seemed like a natural to me but was deemed too trivial. I later tried to repurpose this concept for David Sedaris (see p. 91) with the same results. As per Winter Sorbeck's warning in *The Cheese Monkeys*, I had fallen in love with the idea and needed to break it off.

The final answer was just to render it straightforwardly in type, with a pleasant sky-blue background to juxtapose the frankly blunt message of the title (opposite, right).

*Reality Hunger* is a different sort of undertaking. As billed, it is indeed a manifesto—on the nature of art and the blurring of the line between fiction and nonfiction. The advance reviews were so abundant, immediate, and positive that I thought they should make up the background/foundation of the cover.

**OPPOSITE, RIGHT:** Knopf, 2007. **LEFT:** Knopf, 2010.

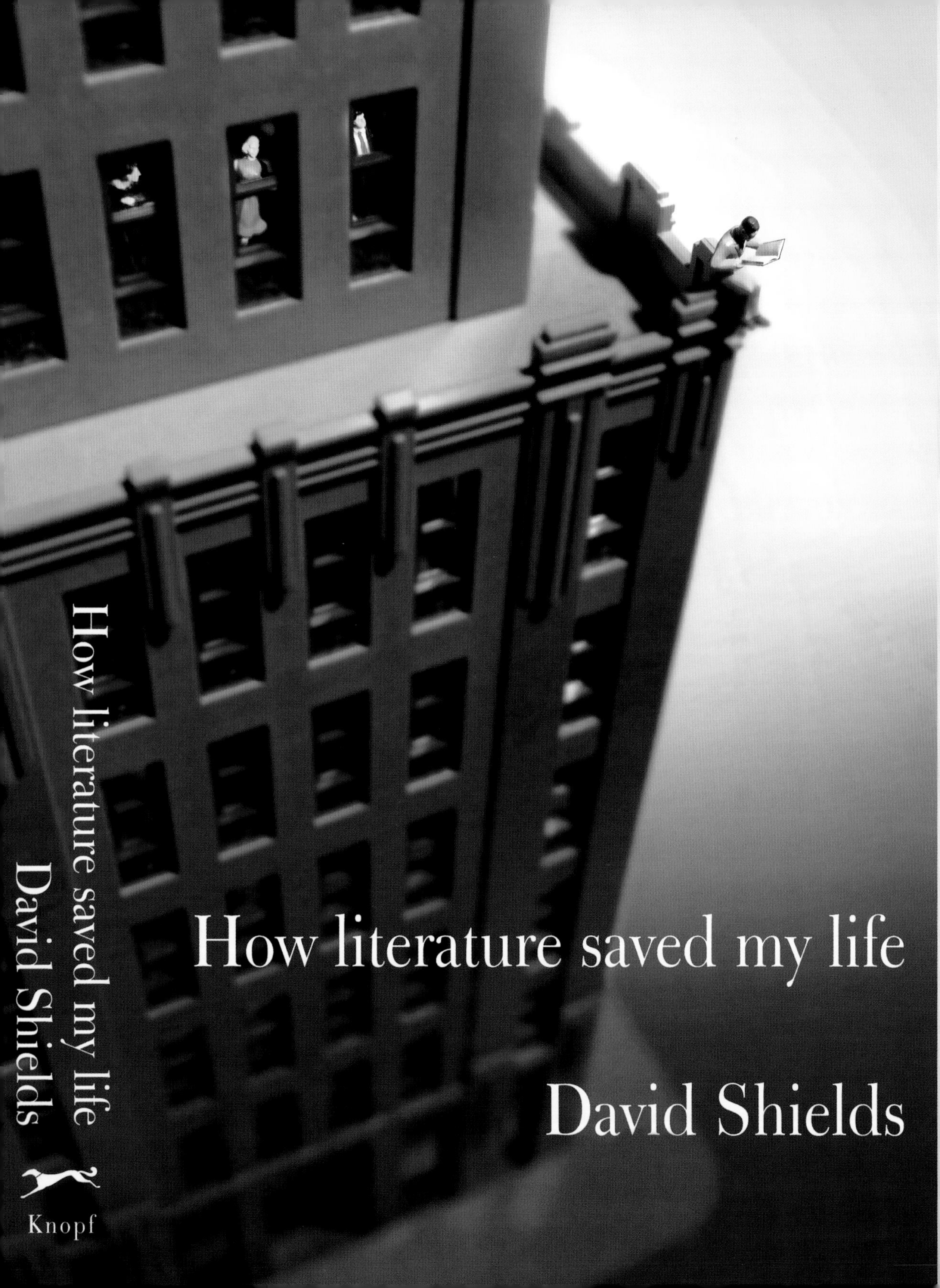
How literature saved my life
David Shields
Knopf
How literature saved my life
David Shields

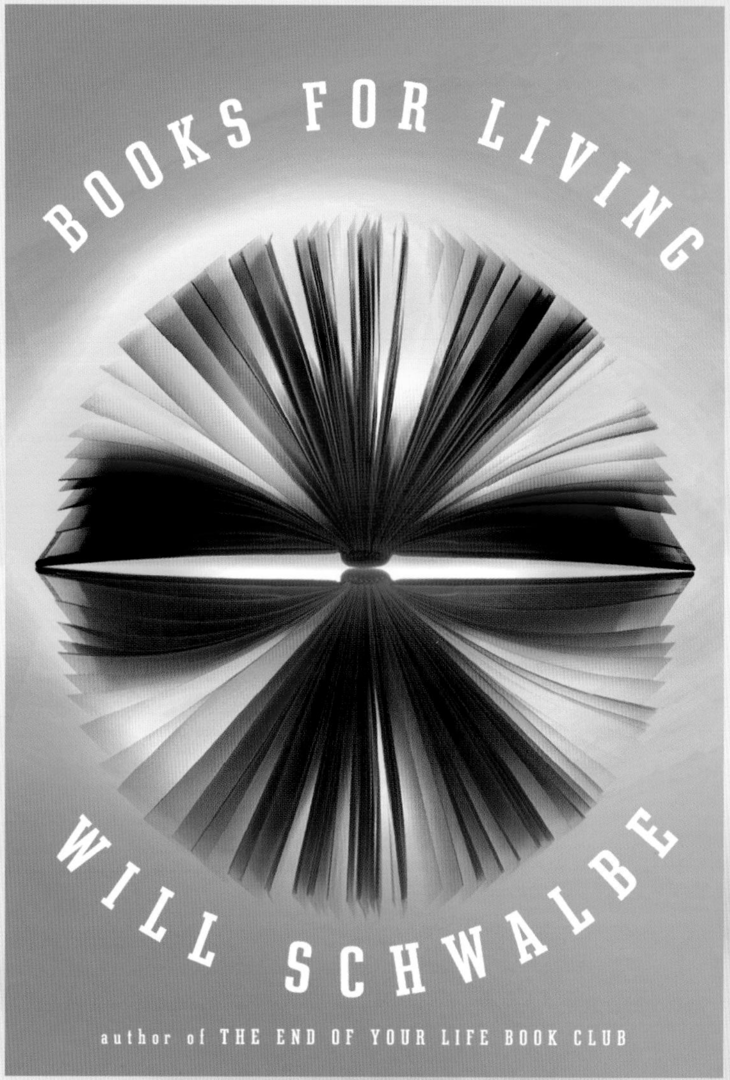
BOOKS FOR LIVING
WILL SCHWALBE
author of THE END OF YOUR LIFE BOOK CLUB

## Illuminating Manuscripts

Books about books are their own genre, and as always it takes resourceful thinking to avoid clichés. For *How Literature Saved My Life,* I thought about trying to stage this scenario with real people (which would have been tremendously complicated), but photographer Geoff Spear's suggestion to build a set with plastic figures (left) proved to be so effective that we didn't have to. Plus, with an idea like this, it's important that it look interesting yet not horrifying. If that was an actual person just inches away from a death-plunge, it would change the point that I felt the author was trying to make—that literature saved him in a philosophical way, rather than a physical one. At the same time, how do you show that? This concept gets the idea across with just enough whimsy.

Will Schwalbe's *The End of Your Life Book Club* was a lovely, poignant, and very unlikely best seller. A bibliographical memoir of reading books with his mother as she was facing a terminal illness, it explored similar themes to those in David Shields's book, but in a totally different way. His follow-up, *Books for Living*, is the yin to the former's yang, a meditation on a group of books that inspire his life as he is living it now.

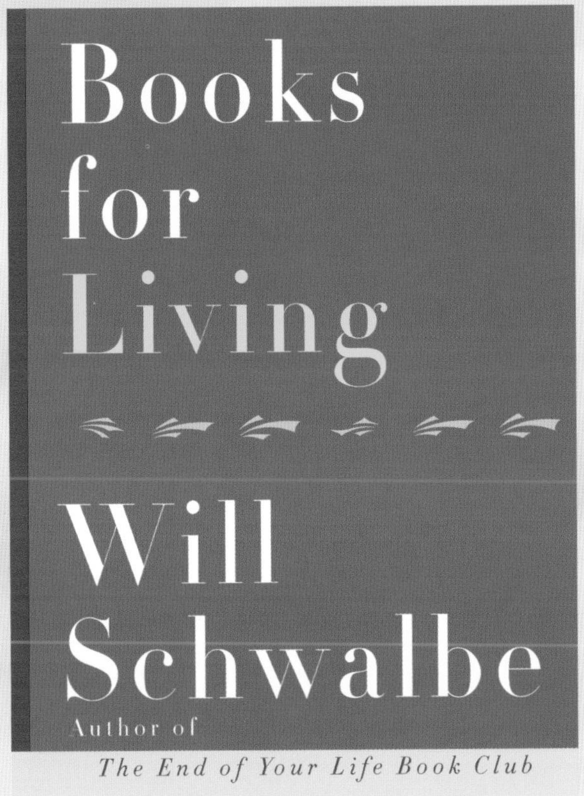
Books
for
Living
Will
Schwalbe
Author of
The End of Your Life Book Club

**OPPOSITE, LEFT:** Knopf, 2013. **OPPOSITE, RIGHT:** My first idea, shot by Geoff, was to depict a book as a light source; paired with its reflection, it starts to resemble an eye. Very colorful and joyous. However, it was then decided in-house that we should follow the design scheme of the previous book, which was created by Carol Devine Carson (the fabulous VP art director of the Knopf imprint and my infinitely patient boss of 29 years, as of this writing). So that is exactly what I did. **ABOVE:** Knopf, 2016. **RIGHT:** The "city reflected in a puddle" idea worked here for *A Hand Reached Down to Guide Me,* as it did not for *The Great Inversion* (p. 121).

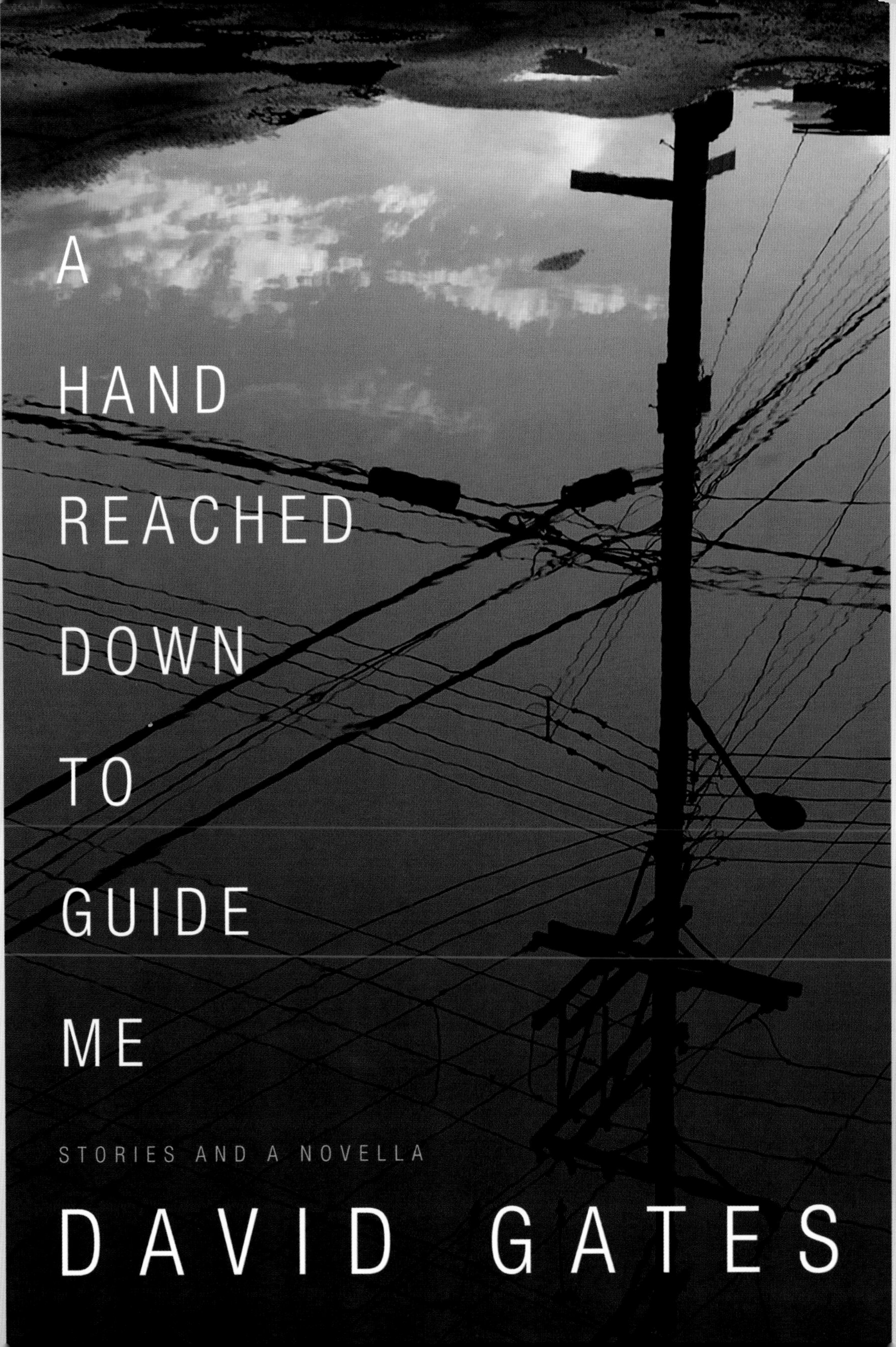
A
HAND
REACHED
DOWN
TO
GUIDE
ME
STORIES AND A NOVELLA
DAVID GATES

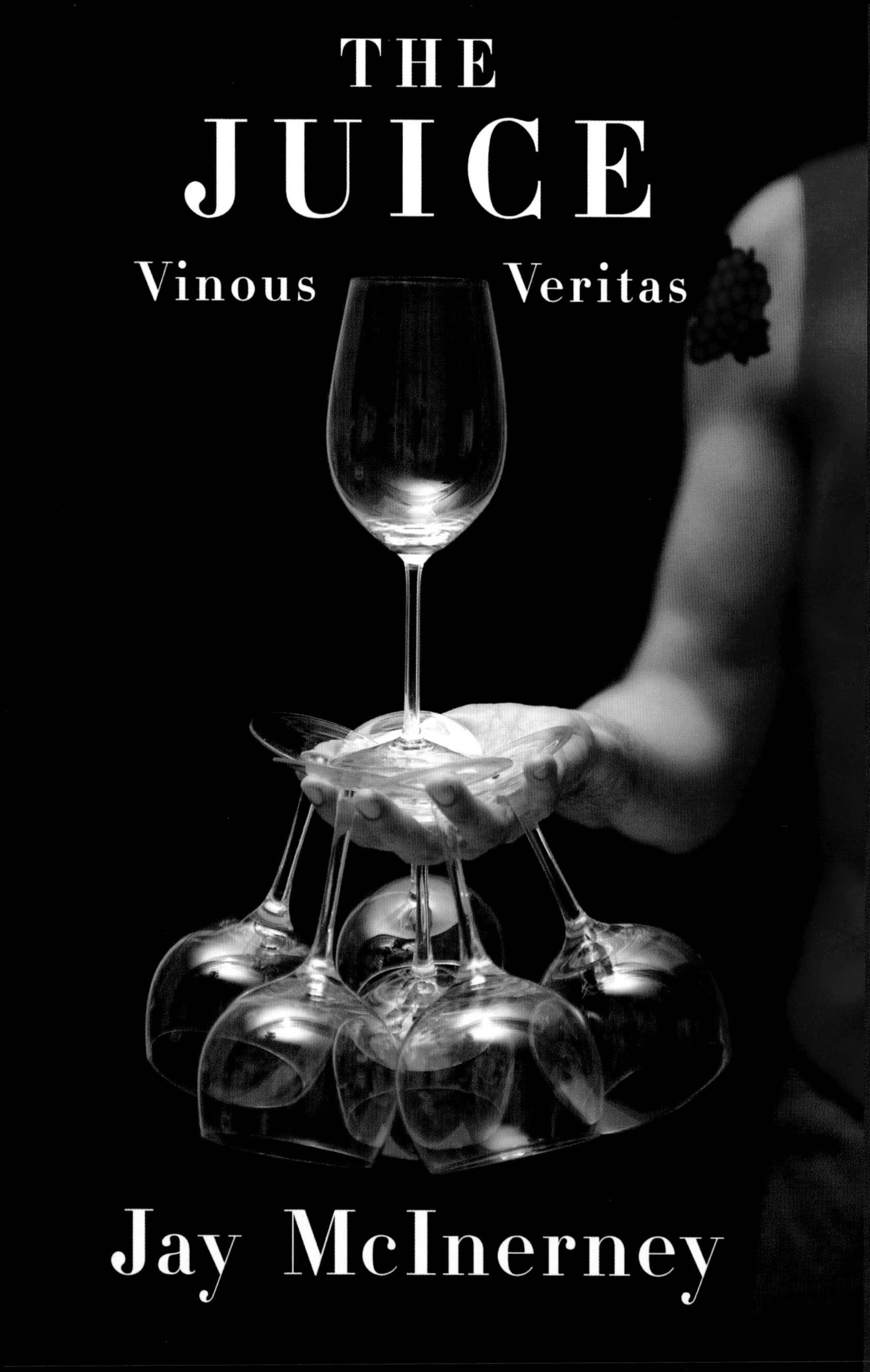
THE
JUICE
Vinous Veritas
Jay McInerney

## Purple Prose

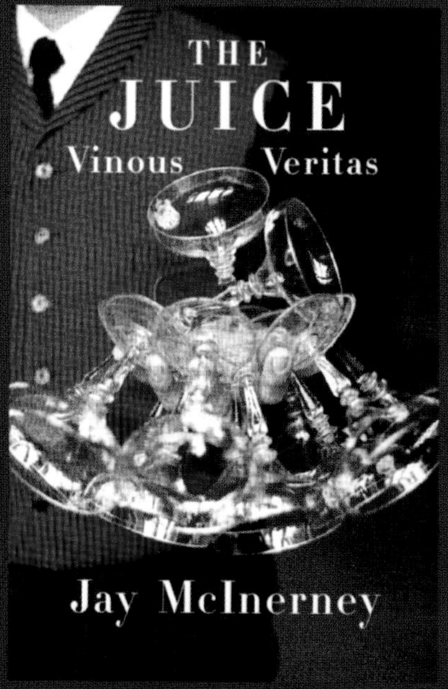
THE
JUICE
Vinous Veritas
Jay McInerney

I probably love wine as much as Jay McInerney does, I just don't know how to write about it. After a few glasses, I can scarcely write my own name. But his take on it is as intoxicating as the subject, and I have loved working on jackets for Jay's wine writing—they present delicious visual opportunities. The first one was for *The Hedonist in the Cellar*, and it was fairly obvious to me to make it look like a menu from a venerable old Parisian restaurant that never replaces the menus, not only because their classic bill of fare will never change, but because the accumulation of wine stains thereon only confirms how much the food was enjoyed.

But for *The Juice* I wanted to present a more authentic "diner experience" type of image, and then I saw a Parisian waiter carrying a zillion wineglasses in one hand. I found a good existing image (above, by Ralph Gibson) that served (sorry) the purpose. But then Jay pointed out that technically those glasses are for champagne, not wine. So we would need to re-create it properly ourselves. With our budgets shrinking as they always do, I was the model (near left) and Geoff Spear photographed the shot, but Jay wanted an edgier version and asked if the waiter could be shirtless under his vest and have a tattoo on his shoulder. I am ink-free and intend to remain so for the rest of eternity, but that's why they created Photoshop.

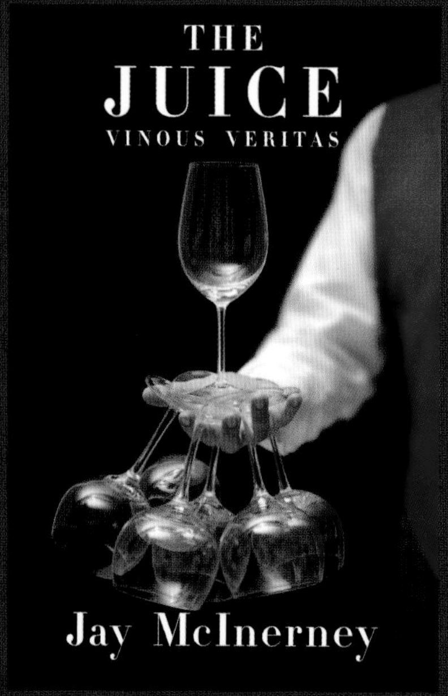
THE
JUICE
VINOUS VERITAS
Jay McInerney

**FAR LEFT:** Knopf, 2012. Photography by Geoff Spear.

**OPPOSITE:** Knopf, 2006. Geoff shot this one, too, to get that great texture, as ever.

ACCLAIM FOR

*Bacchus & Me*

ey has become the best wine writer in America."
—*Salon*

ey's wine judgments are sound, his anecdotes witty, literary references impeccable. Not many wine e good reads; this one is." —*The New York Times*

ing a menu at a great restaurant, *Bacchus and Me* with small courses and surprising and exotic fla- ıcational and delicious at the same time . . . I'll ıse for the holidays." —Mario Batali

ıity, buttery world of wine writing, there's nothing it." —*The Atlanta Journal-Constitution*

prisoners approach in musing over the pleasures ape." —*The Miami Herald*

this book is like eating sushi or tapas—there is ıy bite there, but what a mouthful of flavor."
—*Richmond Times-Dispatch*

ɾtunate that Jay McInerney has chosen to shower ense gifts on a new source of pleasure: the grape. *hus and Me,* his informed, conversational tone ıe reader on a whirlwind tour of the wine world. ʋry companion who is clearly at home with and the subject." —Danny Meyer

ISBN 1-4000-4482-0

COOKING

52400

9 781400 044825

A HEDONIST IN THE CELLAR

Jay McInerney

Knopf

# *A Hedonist in the Cellar*

## ADVENTURES IN WINE

**Jay McInerney**

"[He] provides some of the finest writing on the subject of wine . . . Brilliant, witty, comical, and often shamelessly provocative." —Robert M. Parker, Jr.

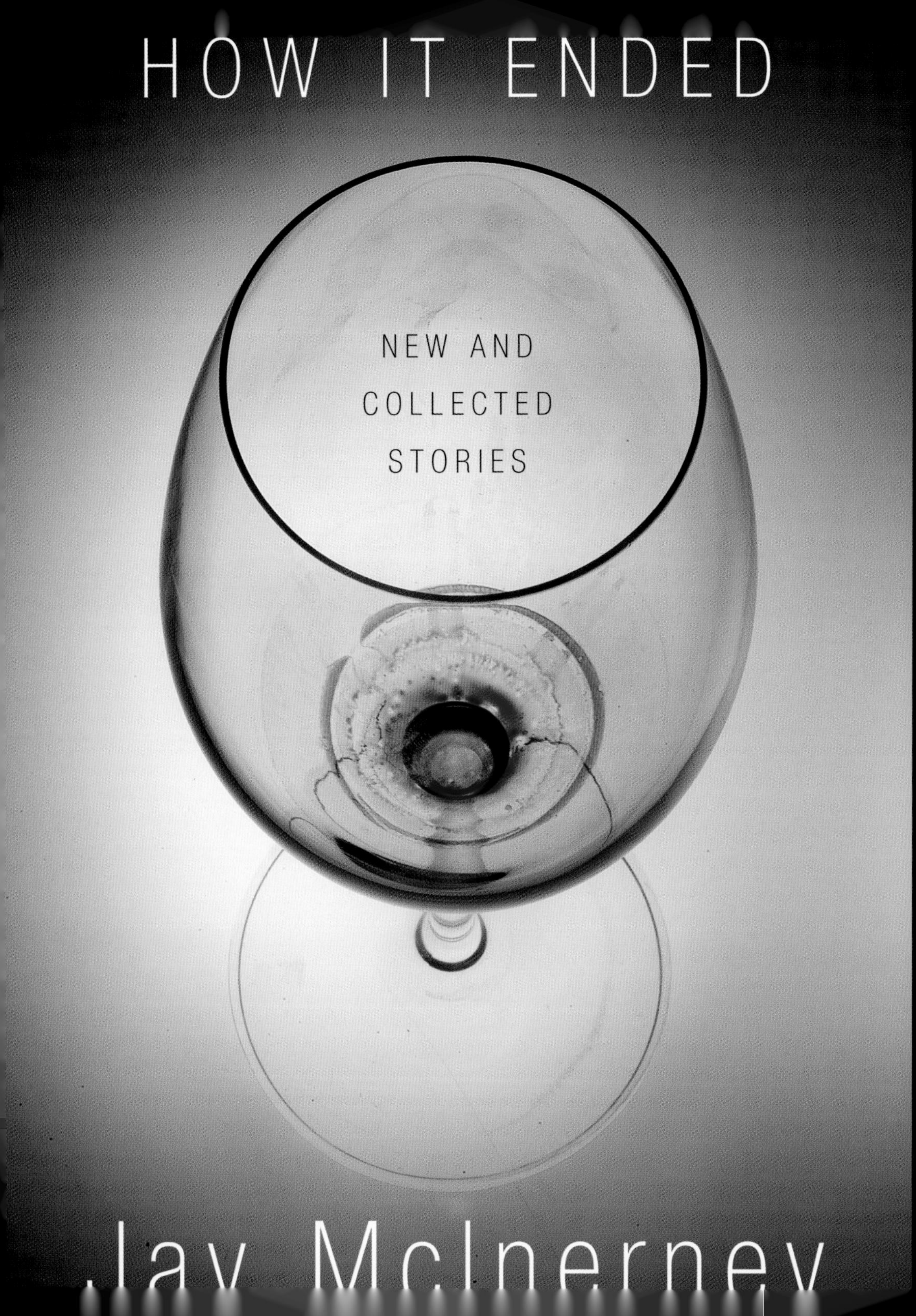
HOW IT ENDED
NEW AND
COLLECTED
STORIES
Jay McInerney

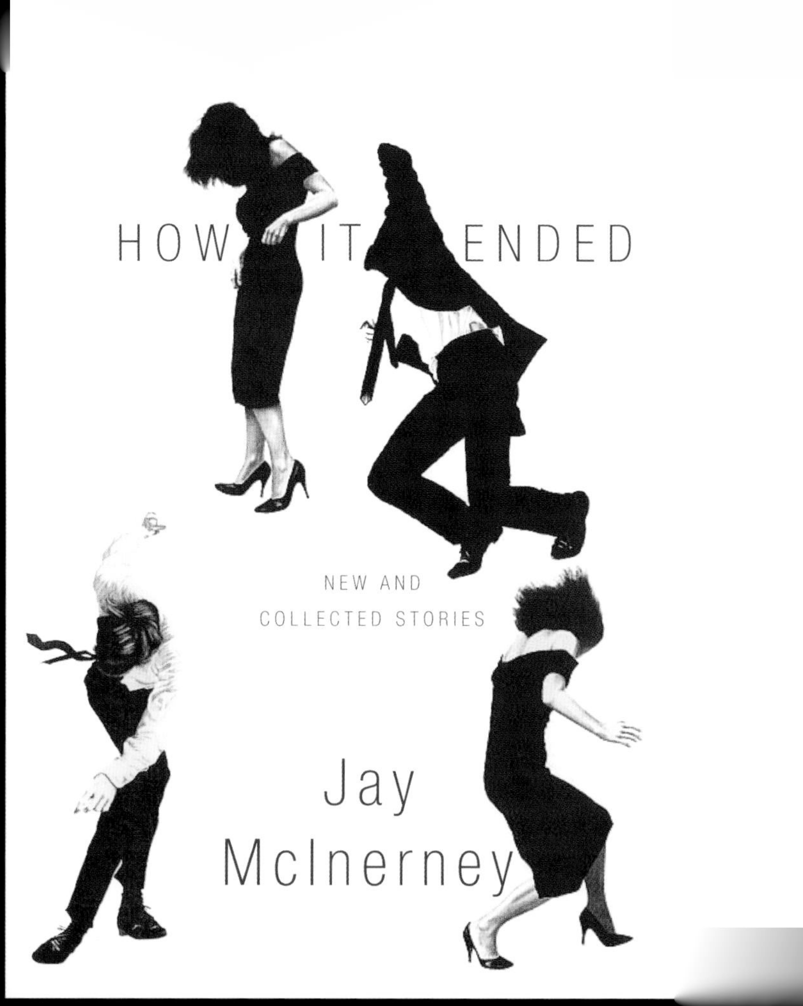
HOW IT ENDED
NEW AND
COLLECTED STORIES
Jay
McInerney

*How It Ended* appeared in the time between Jay's two wine book was a collection of short stories featuring his stylish and suprer distressed members of the upper-class New York demimonde. years I had wanted to pair the *Men in the Cities* drawings by Ro Longo with Jay's work, and this finally seemed like the right fit (abc The artist's representatives wouldn't allow it. Next idea: I tried concept at left, but Jay felt that it could be perceived as another b about his writing on vino. Fair enough. So I turned to the inimit photographer of New York City society Patrick McMullan. Of co this was the right choice (opposite; Knopf, 2009). Initially I wa quite sure what I was looking for, but when I found it, bingo. The image on the front cover shows a fashion show catwalk before models appear. Below that, presumably, the morning after. Ouch

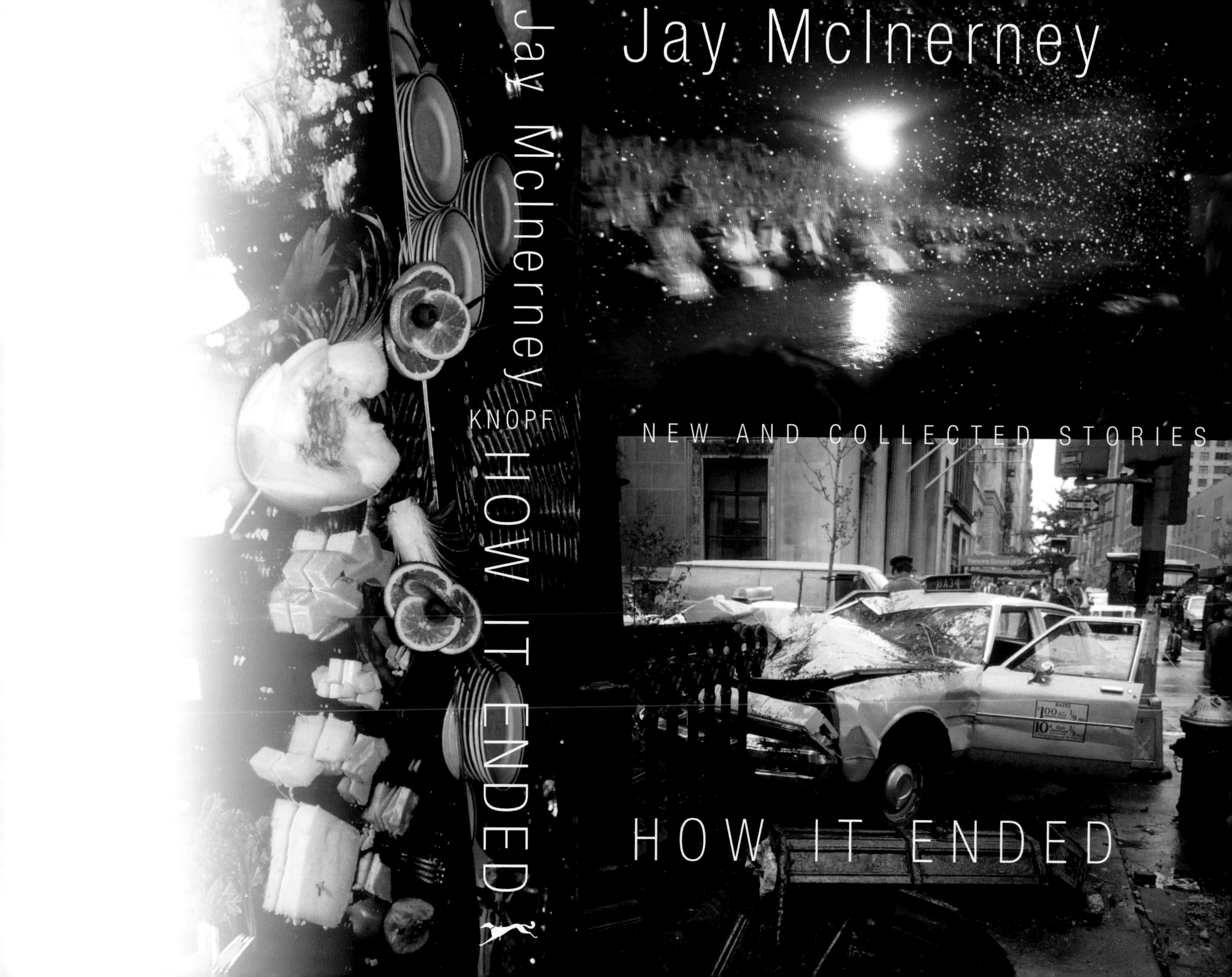
Jay McInerney
KNOPF
HOW IT ENDED
Jay McInerney
NEW AND COLLECTED STORIES
HOW IT ENDED

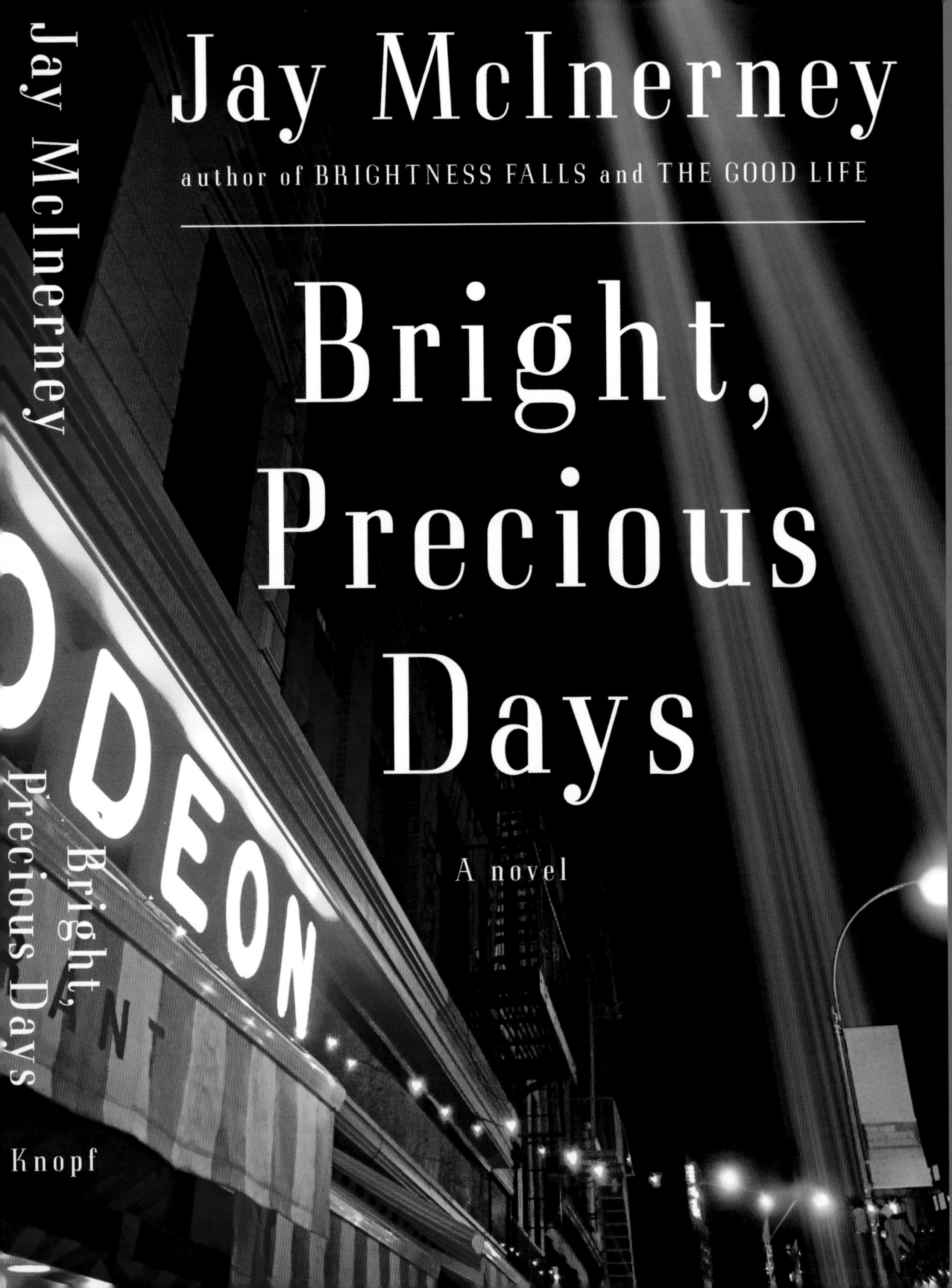
Jay McInerney
Bright, Precious Days
Knopf
Jay McInerney
author of BRIGHTNESS FALLS and THE GOOD LIFE
Bright, Precious Days
A novel
ODEON

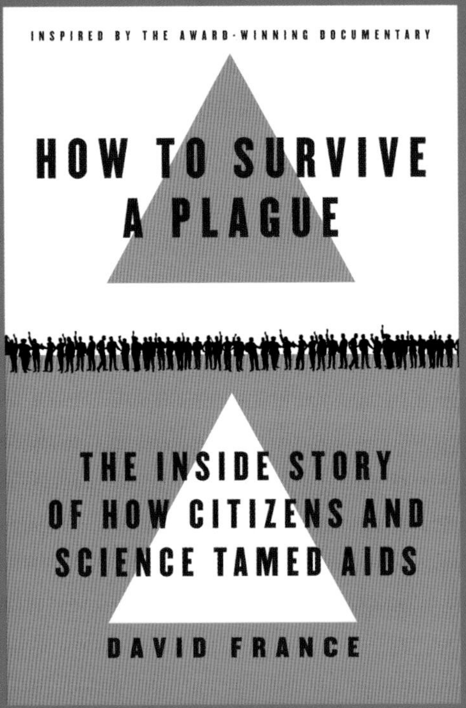
INSPIRED BY THE AWARD-WINNING DOCUMENTARY
HOW TO SURVIVE A PLAGUE
THE INSIDE STORY OF HOW CITIZENS AND SCIENCE TAMED AIDS
DAVID FRANCE

## Light Years

*Bright, Precious Days* is Jay's third novel in a trilogy chronicling the lives of a New York City couple named Corrine and Russell Calloway. Starting with *Brightness Falls* and continuing with *The Good Life*, the books create a Fitzgeraldian portrait of contemporary Manhattan life, both pre- and post-9/11. For this jacket (left), I went back to the scene of the crime—as in, the iconic cover of Jay's breakthrough debut, *Bright Lights, Big City*, which featured this storefront. I took this photo myself in front of the Odeon restaurant in Tribeca but now the view on 9/11 included the "Towers of Light" (added by photographer Terry Sanders) to commemorate the attacks. Jay had some reservations about this image, because the trilogy was not technically related to the debut, and that was understandable. But Corrine and Russell live in this neighborhood, so I thought it was appropriate, plus it spoke to the theme of the terrorist attacks that resonates throughout the book. Jay ultimately agreed.

David France's documentary *How to Survive a Plague* is the most devastating, spot-on chronicle of the AIDS crisis ever committed to film. In 2016 he put the final touches on a book version, and he wanted to start anew concerning the graphics. My initial idea was to mimic an ACT UP poster, like the ones I'd seen all over the city in the late '80s when I first arrived (opposite, right). But it didn't adequately convey the sense of humanity involved. However, a photograph of a "die-in" in 1992 on Fifth Avenue during the annual Gay Pride Parade sure did (below). I will never forget participating in one, and the agreed-upon pact of silence that accompanied it, conveyed to us by, well, word of mouth. We'd lay there inert on the street for perhaps five minutes (which seemed like an eternity), and then, coming up from downtown, an unstoppable wave of defiant screaming, rising up and enveloping us all. It was cathartic, shocking, and—at the time—all that we had.

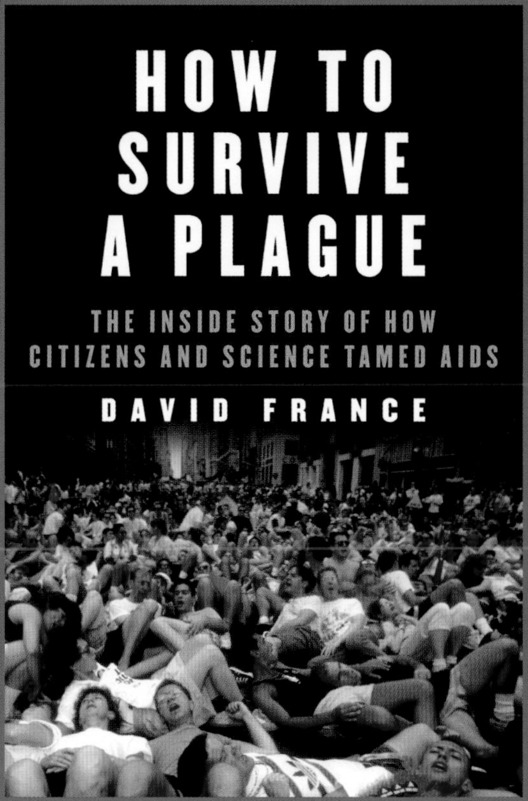
HOW TO
SURVIVE
A PLAGUE
THE INSIDE STORY OF HOW
CITIZENS AND SCIENCE TAMED AIDS
DAVID FRANCE

**OPPOSITE, LEFT:** Knopf, 2016. **RIGHT:** I've been a Bob Mould fan since college, when Hüsker Dü first bloomed. This cover for his memoir is a white-fade riff on the Nabokov *Original of Laura* jacket (see p. 185). Little, Brown, 2011.

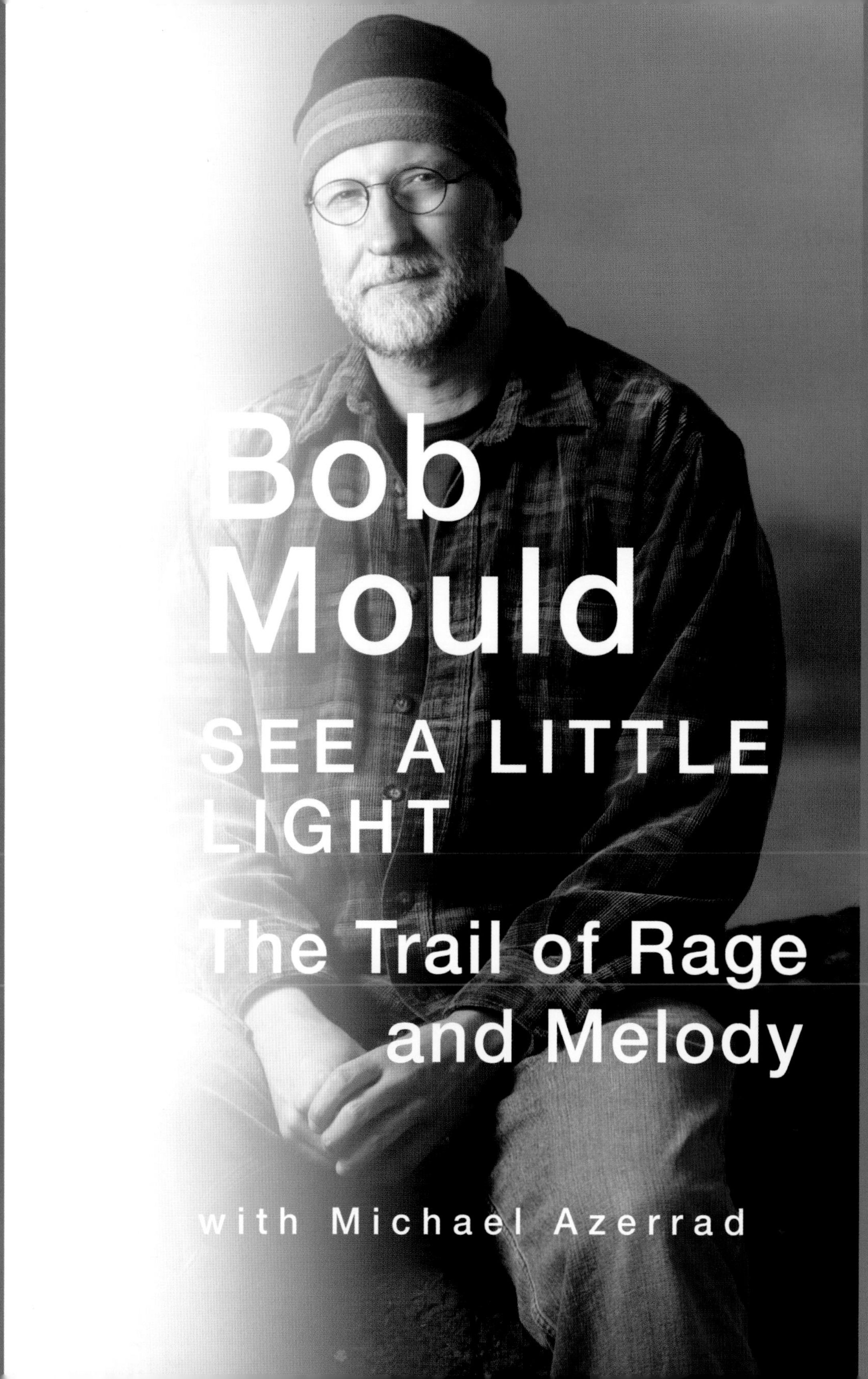
Bob
Mould
SEE A LITTLE
LIGHT
The Trail of Rage
and Melody
with Michael Azerrad

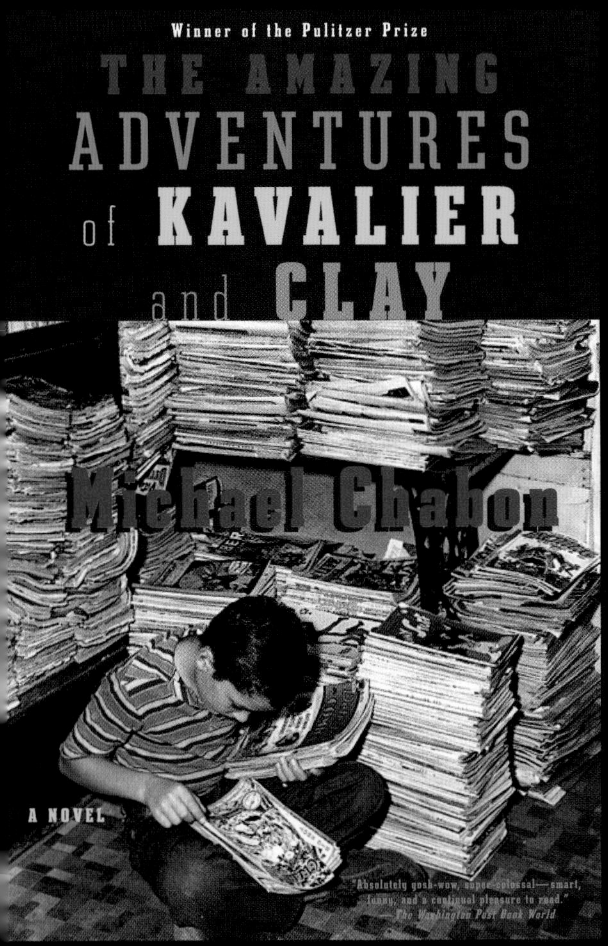
Winner of the Pulitzer Prize
THE AMAZING ADVENTURES of KAVALIER and CLAY
Michael Chabon
A NOVEL
"Absolutely gosh-wow, super-colossal—smart, funny, and a continual pleasure to read." — The Washington Post Book World

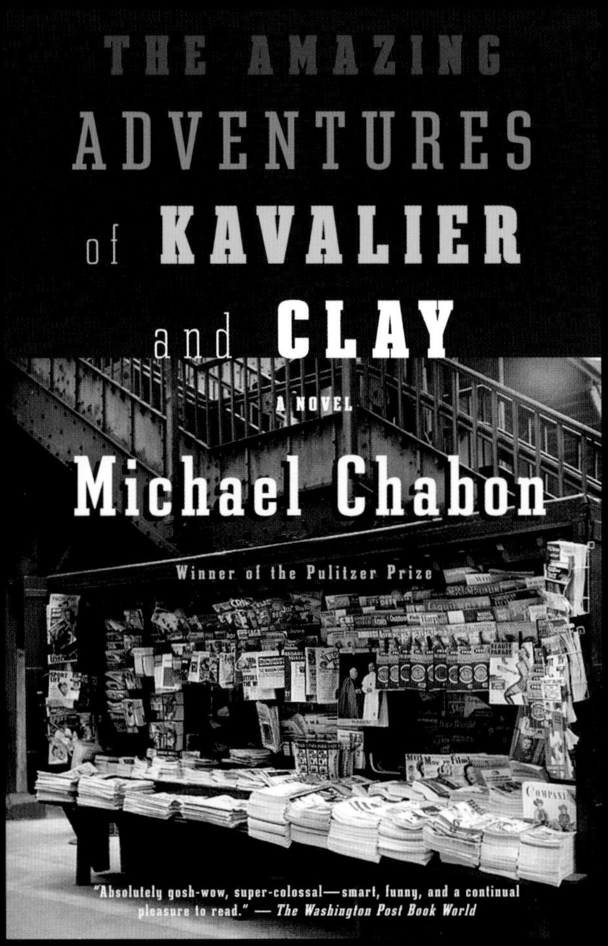
THE AMAZING ADVENTURES of KAVALIER and CLAY
A NOVEL
Michael Chabon
Winner of the Pulitzer Prize
"Absolutely gosh-wow, super-colossal—smart, funny, and a continual pleasure to read." — The Washington Post Book World

## Challah if you need us . . .

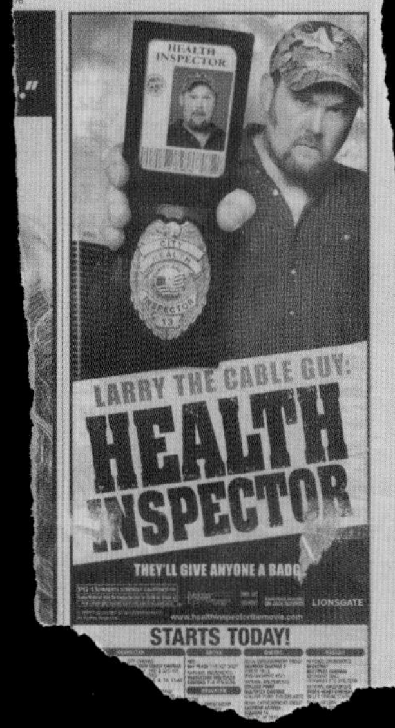
HEALTH INSPECTOR
LARRY THE CABLE GUY:
HEALTH INSPECTOR
THEY'LL GIVE ANYONE A BADGE
LIONSGATE
STARTS TODAY!

*The Yiddish Policemen's Union* is such an uncannily persuasive bit of storytelling that at fifty pages in, it had me thinking, "Wow, I never realized there was such a vital postwar Orthodox Jewish enclave in Sitka, Alaska!" Of course there never was—but as Michael Chabon creates it, you believe it. When a murder takes place in said milieu, that community's own Sam Spade takes over the investigation, and considerable complications set in about how to do that among such a closed, tight-lipped group. It is absolutely riveting. Michael asked me to design the cover, and I was thrilled at the prospect of finally working with him. I got hooked on the concept of a police badge represented as a Star of David, and how that would be presented to potential suspects. This is one of the few cover ideas for which I personally made the drawings (see *The Orenda*, p. 190).

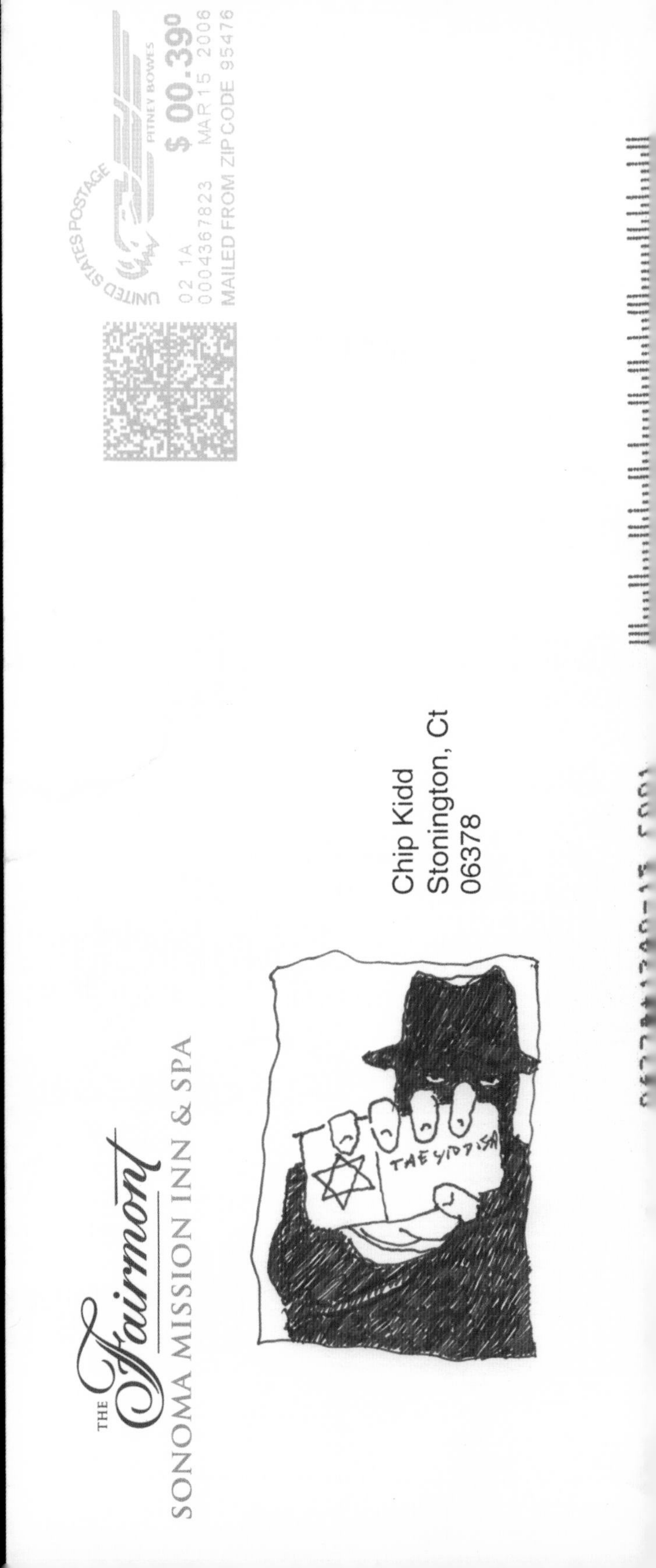
UNITED STATES POSTAGE
PITNEY BOWES
$ 00.39⁰
02 1A
0004367823 MAR 15 2006
MAILED FROM ZIP CODE 95476
Chip Kidd
Stonington, Ct
06378
THE YIDDISH
THE Fairmont
SONOMA MISSION INN & SPA

**RIGHT:** I am channeling my inner Frank Miller here, and Michael loved it. Alas, the publisher—HarperCollins—did not, saying it looked too much like a graphic novel. (Doh!)

**OPPOSITE, LEFT:** Michael also asked me to come up with some ideas for a new paperback release of his Pulitzer Prize–winning novel *The Amazing Adventures of Kavalier and Clay*, and my thought was to try delicious vintage photos of newsstands from the early 1940s featuring the first comic books. This, too, was a no-go (thank you again, HarperCollins!) because it "didn't look like fiction." Well, damn. The story's supposed to be about funny-books in the real world and I thought they worked here for that purpose. Oh, well . . . So far, I can't get arrested in Chabon-Town. Seriously, I adore him and his work, and I hope it can happen some day.

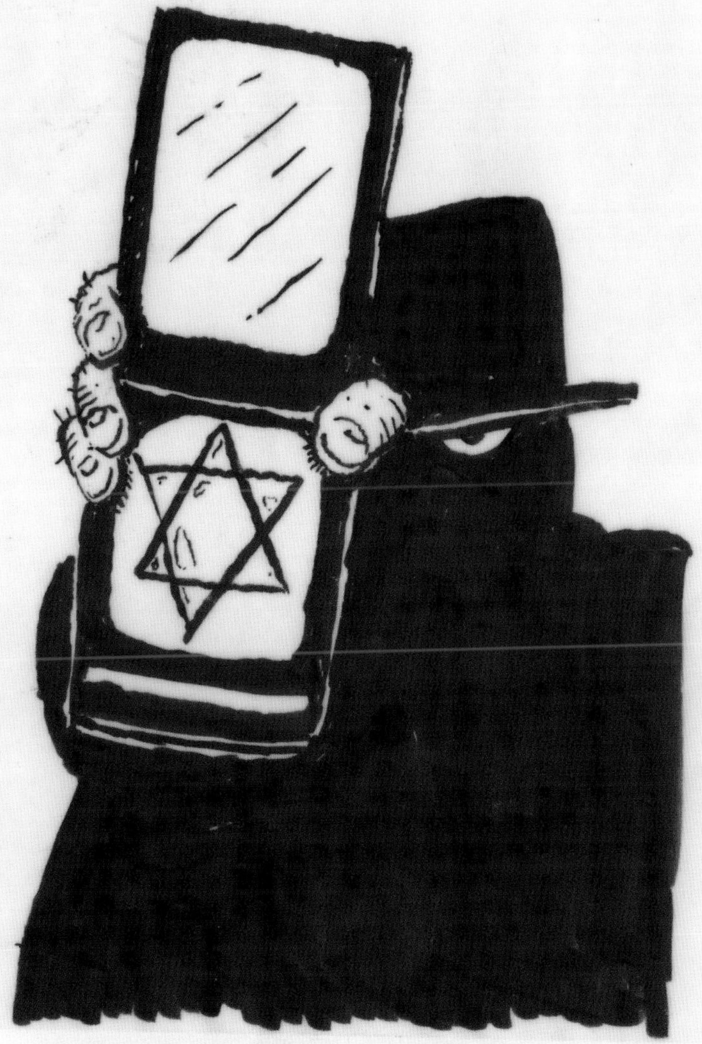

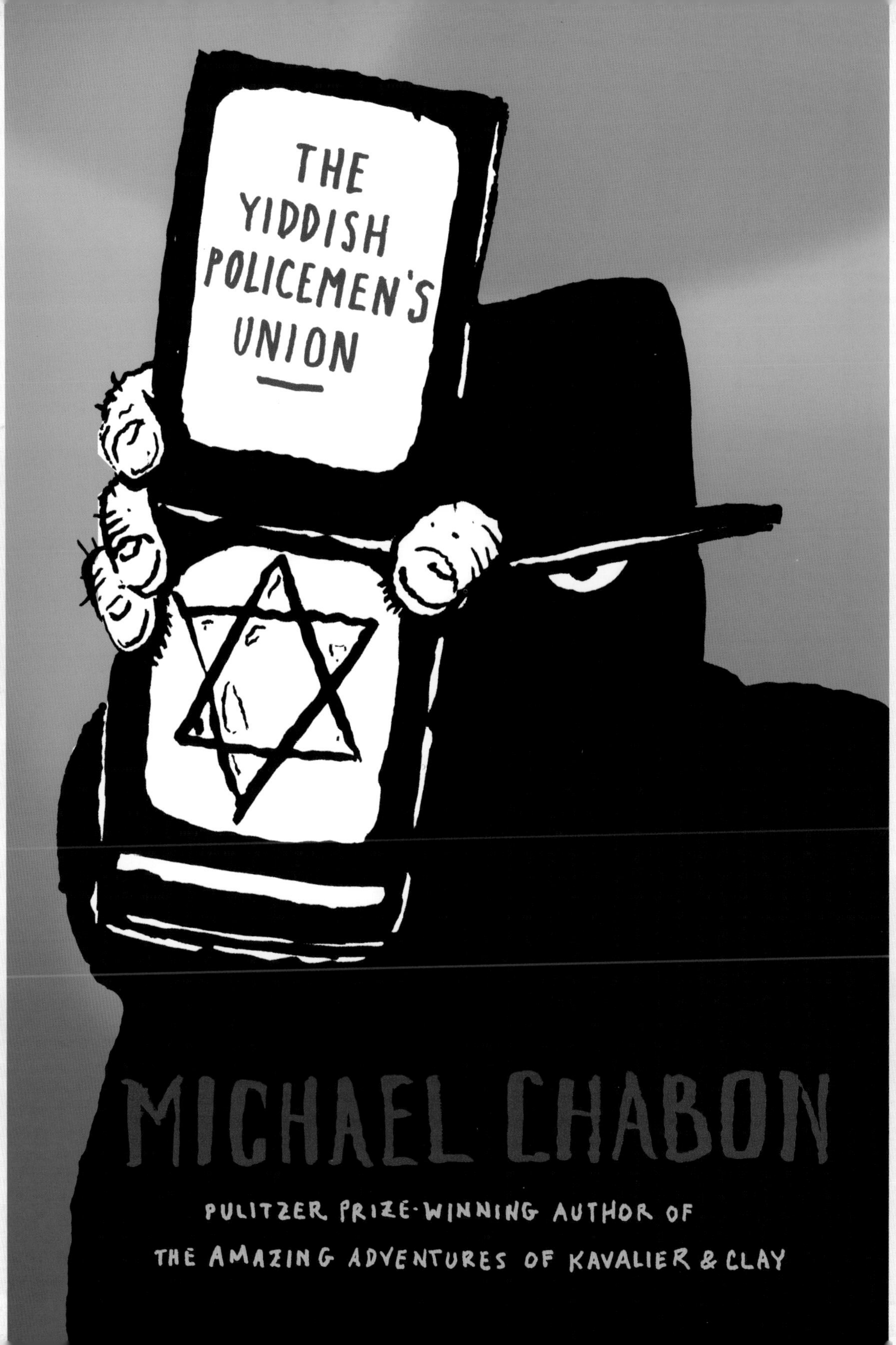
THE YIDDISH POLICEMEN'S UNION
MICHAEL CHABON
PULITZER PRIZE-WINNING AUTHOR OF
THE AMAZING ADVENTURES OF KAVALIER & CLAY

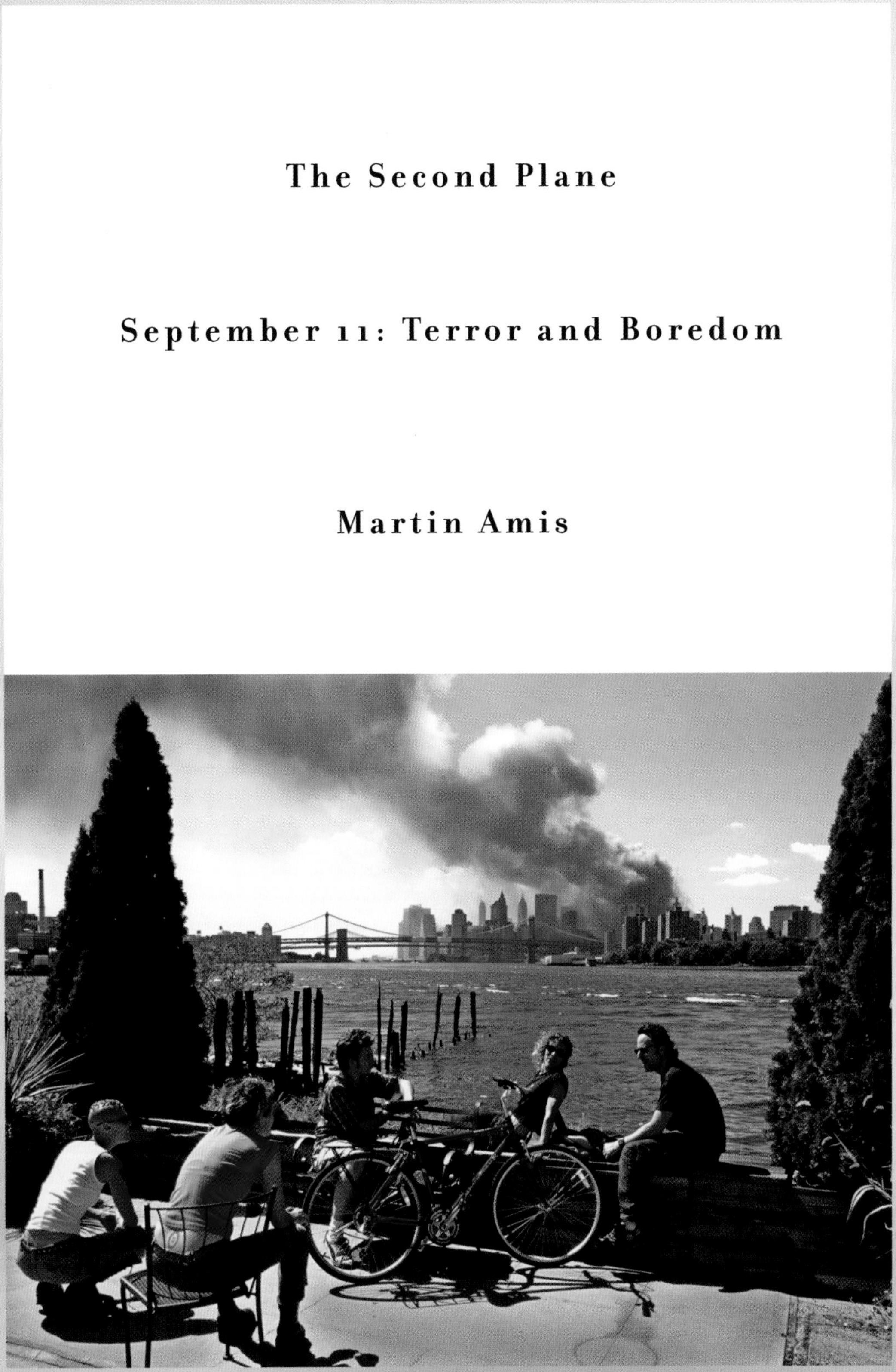
The Second Plane
September 11: Terror and Boredom
Martin Amis

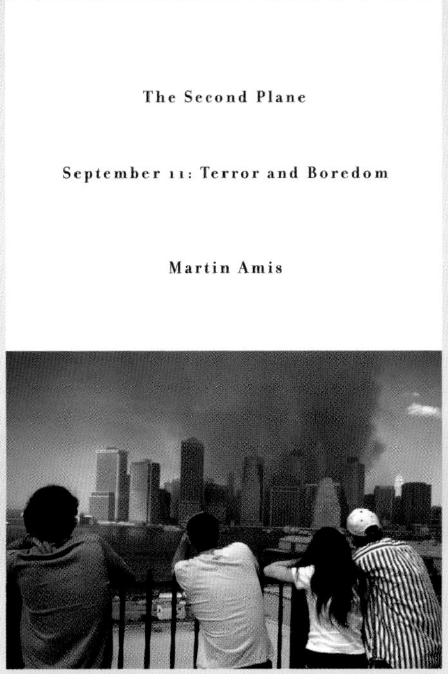
The Second Plane
September 11: Terror and Boredom
Martin Amis

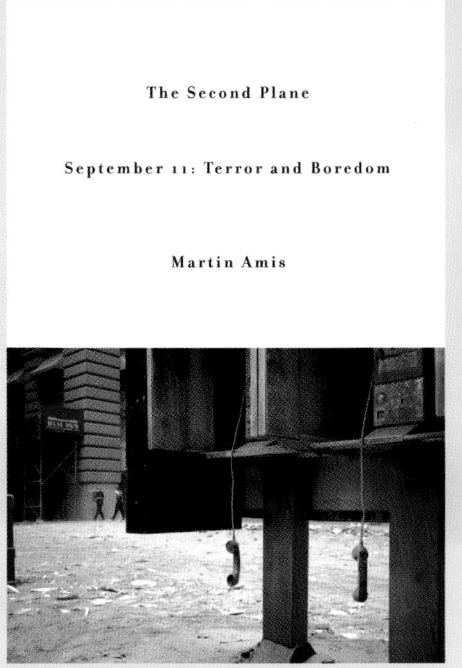
The Second Plane
September 11: Terror and Boredom
Martin Amis

# Darkness on the Edge of Town

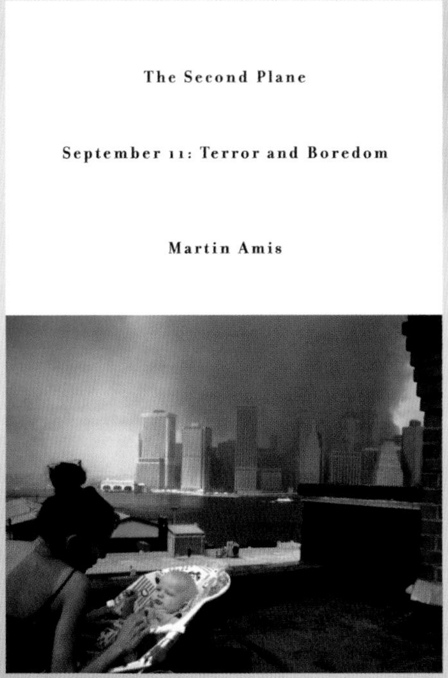
The Second Plane
September 11: Terror and Boredom
Martin Amis

Martin Amis's *The Second Plane* is his take on the events of 9/11 centering on the point of how deliberate and coldly calculated it all was, and that the moment the second plane went into the other World Trade Tower, it signified a plan, one confirmed that morning that nothing that was going on was an accident. I started researching and found an extraordinary group of photographs (this page) from a licensed photo stock agency depicting people going about their daily lives that morning before anyone really understood what was hap-

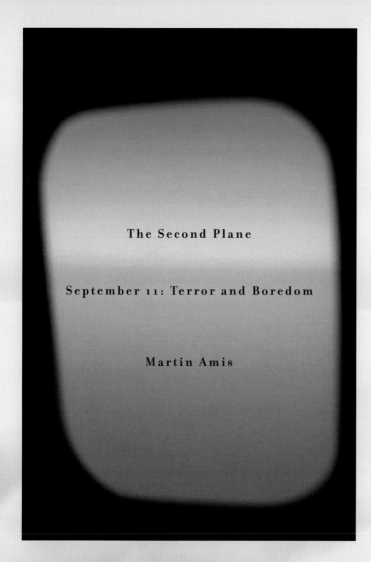

The Second Plane

September 11: Terror and Boredom

Martin Amis

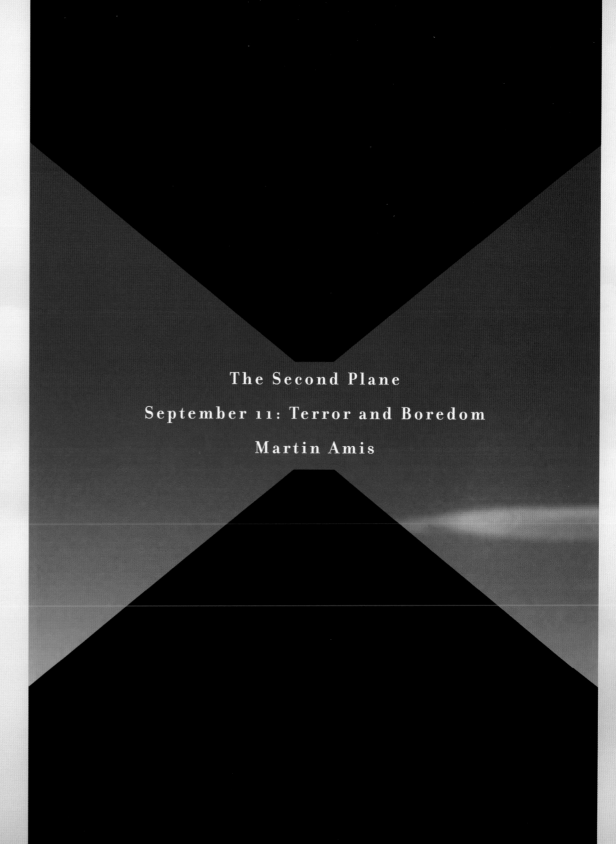

The Second Plane

September 11: Terror and Boredom

Martin Amis

pening. I thought these perfectly captured what Amis was describing. However, it turned out that there were no model releases for these images, nor would they be forthcoming, thus we couldn't use them. (So why were they available on the photo-stock site in the first place? I have no idea, and no reason was ever given.)

I then recruited my brilliant colleague Peter Mendelsund to help me rethink the approach, and we ended up with the final design seen at right (Knopf, 2008). This works well both graphically and conceptually and puts the reader directly in the middle of what's about to happen—even if they can't tell right away. Which is sadly and heart-breakingly the point.

AMTRAK

B Ticket Coupon C
01 of 01

I acknowledge receipt of ticket(s) and agree to accept billing to the credit card identified below.

X

Date of Issue 30OCT09 Place of Issue NLC Res. # 95675

SIGN HERE - ID REQD ON-BOARD

Name of Passenger: KIDD/CHARLES

Riders 1 Type Rider 1F Status OK

From NEW LONDON,CT

To NEW YORK PENN,NY

Carrier 2V Train 171 Date 30NOV09 Time 0949A

Not Valid Before/After 30NOV/29NOV10

Accom YD RESERVD COACH

VALID PHOTO ID REQUIRED

Endorsement/Restrictions

ONE-WAY SPECIAL FARE -- NO STOPOVERS

REFUND FEE MAY APPLY

Form of Payment IK43.00 2115

Rail Fare $43.00

Accom Charge $.00

Total Charge $43.00

Fare Plans DOF1

Pricing Pts NLC-NYP

Tkt. Ptr. VQ59

0980520019500

3039191620025

NRPT 97 STOCK CONTROL NO. TKT NO.– DO NOT MARK OR STAMP IN WHITE AREA

REV. 9-07

PRINTED IN U.S.A. BY MAGNETIC TICKET & LABEL CORP., DALLAS, TX

Riders 1 AMTRAK Baggage

Name of Passenger KIDD/CHARLES

From NEW LONDON,CT

To NEW YORK PENN,NY

Carrier 2V Train 171 Date 30NOV09

Accom YD Space/Car RESERVD COACH

Form of Payment IK43.00 2115

Rail Fare $43.00 Accom Charge $.00

Fare Plans DOF1 Total $43.00

Ticket Number 3039191620025 No. of 01 01

Date of Issue 30OCT09 Reservation # 95675

PASSENGER RECEIPT

AMTRAK

MONDAY, NOVEMBER 30, 2009

CHARLES KIDD IS ON TRAIN #171

LEAVING NEW LONDON, CT 9:49 am

ARRIVING NEW YORK, PENN STATION 12:40 pm

RESERVED COACH

$43.00

3039191620025

AMTRAK

MON 11/30/09

CHARLES KIDD

TRAIN #171

NEW LONDON, CT

NEW YORK, PENN STA

RESERVED COACH

$43.00

# Design and ReDesign

Rethinking the typical train ticket, perhaps the planet's most confusing use of paper.

There's graphic design, and then there's graphic design. I consider myself lucky to make a living producing the second, italicized version. That is to say, more often than not my job is to create graphic design that generates mystery, suggesting possibilities as opposed to providing them.

In my case that means book covers, which I've been designing for over 23 years. I'm often asked if I have a 'formula' or set stylistic approach to creating them, and I certainly don't, but there is one very simple principle I try and hold myself to every time, no matter what the book is: a good book cover should make a potential reader want to read the book. Period.

I've found that one of the best ways to do this is to make something that looks, frankly, odd. Hopefully in an intriguing way, rather than in an "Oh my God, your left breast is three times the size of the right one" kind of way. What a good cover designer aims to do is not only get your attention, but get you to investigate. And then buy.

Okay, so that's the second, italicized version. But this column isn't really about that. It's about the first.

Graphic design—as we defined it in school—is purposeful planning and the form that it takes. Now we're talking about the things you actually have to use in your daily life which must be clear, concise and direct. One of the best examples that comes quickly to mind is the stop sign. Even if you can't read it you know exactly what it wants you to do. There is no extemporaneous information involved, or needed. (I could take this a step further and add that the speed-bump is an even more effective piece of design to convince drivers to slow down, but I digress).

It is common sense to say that everything in a man-made society must be designed by someone, and yet you can see this imperative abused and taken for granted everywhere and all of the time.

Take Amtrak. Now, for the record, I love Amtrak. In theory.

But let's look at practice. I'm going to go out on a limb here and say that two qualities one does not want in a train ticket are Mystery and Oddness, and yet that is exactly what Amtrak gives us.

Let's say you are me, and you are taking a train from one place to another. Look at the actual ticket at the top of the next page, and see if you can figure out:

1. When you are leaving, date and time.
2. Where you are leaving from.
3. Where you are going to.
4. When you are scheduled to arrive.
5. What the assigned ID number of the train is.

These are not unimportant things to understand at a glance, and I should know. I do a LOT of train travel on Amtrak, on average once a week, and it's easy to lose track (so to speak). When they introduced the high-speed Acela train in 2000, this Manhattanite jumped for joy, because it meant that I'd never have to fly to Boston, Philadelphia, Baltimore or Washington, D.C. ever again. And I'm extremely grateful for that.

But while Amtrak will allow you to book a trip online, they will not allow you to print out your ticket (the way airlines do) and that's only the start of the problem. You have to go to one of their ATM-like Kwik-Trak machines (or God forbid, a ticket counter) and print it out there. And once you have, look at what you get. I have often stood in the middle of Penn Station (another design disaster) momentarily seized by panic as the numbers on the departure board shift like tumbling dominoes and I look to my ticket for confirmation of my departure details, only to be met by what appears to be a sudoku puzzle of letters. Travel itself—at least for me—creates in the traveler a state of perpetual uncertainty, and there can't be enough direction concerning where one needs to be and when, and what is happening in the meantime. (The trains are often delayed. Ahem.)

So I think this ticket demands a redesign, and this is what I propose. It needs to be as straight-forward as possible, a simple statement that can't be misunderstood, like good advice. I'm not talking about making something "beautiful" here, I'm proposing something that *works*—legible and easily comprehended—and can be produced using the ink-jet technology currently in place.

I have made an effort to include all the information that exists on the original, minus the redundancies and bureaucratic weirdness, which may be unavoidable (yet should be). But even if you can't avoid it, you can definitely give it a more coherent order.

So all aboard, Amtrak. The Simplicity station should be your next destination.

Originally appeared in *McSweeney's*, No. 33, January 19, 2010.

POST-SCRIPT: Since this article appeared (and not because of it, I have no doubt), Amtrak has changed up its system so that now you can get your ticket downloaded to your smartphone (like everything else, but it took a while), and you get a QR code for the conductor to scan. You can also print out the ticket yourself, and it is indeed much easier to parse. But this whole idea was one that I expanded upon for my second TED talk concerning clarity in public transportation instruction (see p. 285).

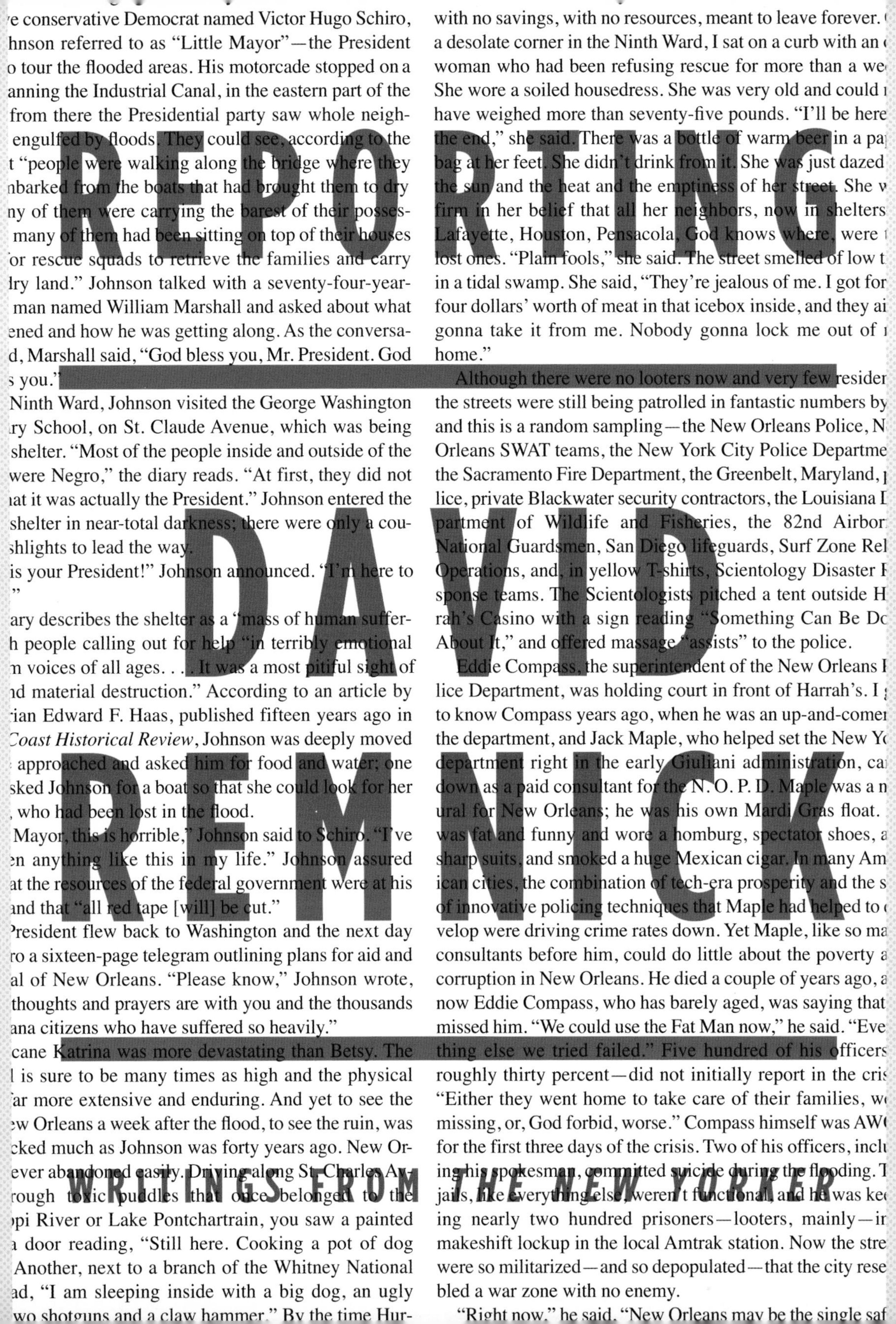

e conservative Democrat named Victor Hugo Schiro, ̶hnson referred to as "Little Mayor"—the President ̶o tour the flooded areas. His motorcade stopped on a ̶anning the Industrial Canal, in the eastern part of the ̶from there the Presidential party saw whole neigh- ̶engulfed by floods. They could see, according to the ̶t "people were walking along the bridge where they ̶nbarked from the boats that had brought them to dry ̶ny of them were carrying the barest of their posses- ̶many of them had been sitting on top of their houses ̶or rescue squads to retrieve the families and carry ̶lry land." Johnson talked with a seventy-four-year- ̶man named William Marshall and asked about what ̶ened and how he was getting along. As the conversa- ̶d, Marshall said, "God bless you, Mr. President. God ̶s you."

Ninth Ward, Johnson visited the George Washington ̶ry School, on St. Claude Avenue, which was being ̶shelter. "Most of the people inside and outside of the ̶were Negro," the diary reads. "At first, they did not ̶at it was actually the President." Johnson entered the ̶shelter in near-total darkness; there were only a cou- ̶shlights to lead the way.

̶is your President!" Johnson announced. "I'm here to ̶"

̶ary describes the shelter as a "mass of human suffer- ̶h people calling out for help "in terribly emotional ̶n voices of all ages. . . . It was a most pitiful sight of ̶d material destruction." According to an article by ̶rian Edward F. Haas, published fifteen years ago in ̶*Coast Historical Review*, Johnson was deeply moved ̶approached and asked him for food and water; one ̶sked Johnson for a boat so that she could look for her ̶, who had been lost in the flood.

̶Mayor, this is horrible," Johnson said to Schiro. "I've ̶en anything like this in my life." Johnson assured ̶at the resources of the federal government were at his ̶and that "all red tape [will] be cut."

̶President flew back to Washington and the next day ̶ro a sixteen-page telegram outlining plans for aid and ̶al of New Orleans. "Please know," Johnson wrote, ̶thoughts and prayers are with you and the thousands ̶ana citizens who have suffered so heavily."

̶cane Katrina was more devastating than Betsy. The ̶l is sure to be many times as high and the physical ̶ar more extensive and enduring. And yet to see the ̶ew Orleans a week after the flood, to see the ruin, was ̶cked much as Johnson was forty years ago. New Or- ̶ever abandoned easily. Driving along St. Charles Av- ̶rough toxic puddles that once belonged to the ̶pi River or Lake Pontchartrain, you saw a painted ̶a door reading, "Still here. Cooking a pot of dog ̶Another, next to a branch of the Whitney National ̶ad, "I am sleeping inside with a big dog, an ugly ̶wo shotguns and a claw hammer." By the time Hur-

with no savings, with no resources, meant to leave forever. ̶a desolate corner in the Ninth Ward, I sat on a curb with an ̶woman who had been refusing rescue for more than a wee̶ She wore a soiled housedress. She was very old and could ̶ have weighed more than seventy-five pounds. "I'll be here̶ the end," she said. There was a bottle of warm beer in a pa̶ bag at her feet. She didn't drink from it. She was just dazed ̶ the sun and the heat and the emptiness of her street. She w̶ firm in her belief that all her neighbors, now in shelters ̶ Lafayette, Houston, Pensacola, God knows where, were ̶ lost ones. "Plain fools," she said. The street smelled of low t̶ in a tidal swamp. She said, "They're jealous of me. I got for̶ four dollars' worth of meat in that icebox inside, and they ai̶ gonna take it from me. Nobody gonna lock me out of ̶ home."

Although there were no looters now and very few resider̶ the streets were still being patrolled in fantastic numbers by ̶ and this is a random sampling—the New Orleans Police, N̶ Orleans SWAT teams, the New York City Police Departme̶ the Sacramento Fire Department, the Greenbelt, Maryland, ̶ lice, private Blackwater security contractors, the Louisiana ̶ partment of Wildlife and Fisheries, the 82nd Airbor̶ National Guardsmen, San Diego lifeguards, Surf Zone Rel̶ Operations, and, in yellow T-shirts, Scientology Disaster ̶ sponse teams. The Scientologists pitched a tent outside H̶ rah's Casino with a sign reading "Something Can Be Do̶ About It," and offered massage "assists" to the police.

Eddie Compass, the superintendent of the New Orleans ̶ lice Department, was holding court in front of Harrah's. I ̶ to know Compass years ago, when he was an up-and-comer̶ the department, and Jack Maple, who helped set the New Yo̶ department right in the early Giuliani administration, ca̶ down as a paid consultant for the N.O.P.D. Maple was a n̶ ural for New Orleans; he was his own Mardi Gras float. ̶ was fat and funny and wore a homburg, spectator shoes, a̶ sharp suits, and smoked a huge Mexican cigar. In many Am̶ ican cities, the combination of tech-era prosperity and the s̶ of innovative policing techniques that Maple had helped to ̶ velop were driving crime rates down. Yet Maple, like so ma̶ consultants before him, could do little about the poverty a̶ corruption in New Orleans. He died a couple of years ago, a̶ now Eddie Compass, who has barely aged, was saying that ̶ missed him. "We could use the Fat Man now," he said. "Eve̶ thing else we tried failed." Five hundred of his officers ̶ roughly thirty percent—did not initially report in the cris̶ "Either they went home to take care of their families, we̶ missing, or, God forbid, worse." Compass himself was AWO̶ for the first three days of the crisis. Two of his officers, inclu̶ ing his spokesman, committed suicide during the flooding. T̶ jails, like everything else, weren't functional, and he was kee̶ ing nearly two hundred prisoners—looters, mainly—in ̶ makeshift lockup in the local Amtrak station. Now the stre̶ were so militarized—and so depopulated—that the city rese̶ bled a war zone with no enemy.

"Right now," he said. "New Orleans may be the single saf̶

---

**DAVID REMNICK**

**REPORTING**

WRITINGS FROM *THE NEW YORKER*

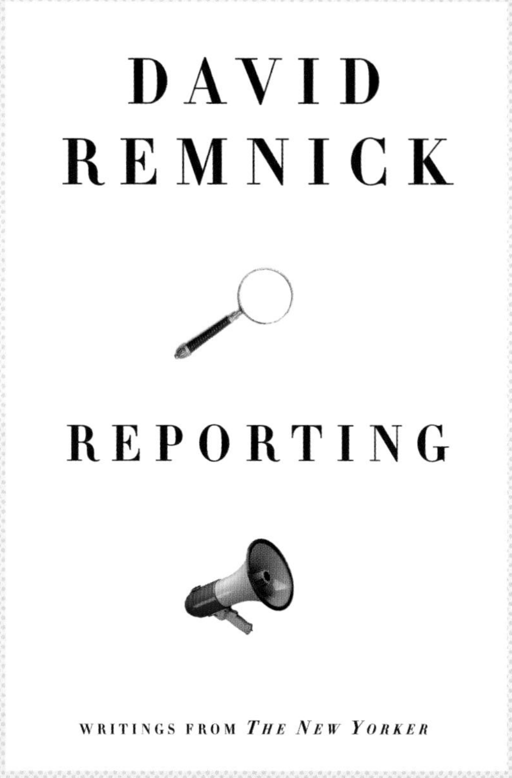

RIGHT: An early comp for David Remnick's collection of pieces called *Reporting*. I wanted the jacket icons to say "investigate, then announce," but reporting is about writing, not shouting into a megaphone.

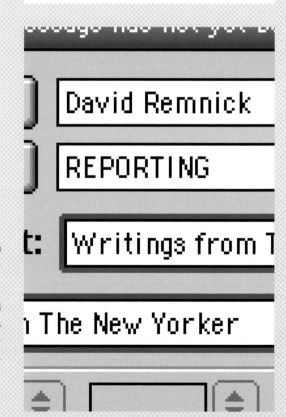

David Remnick

REPORTING

t: Writings from T

n The New Yorker

RIGHT: A second attempt, this time using the visual vernacular of e-mail at the time.

LEFT: The final jacket, inspired by Italian Futurist fliers from the '20s and '30s, which surprinted red art over the text. Knopf, 2006.

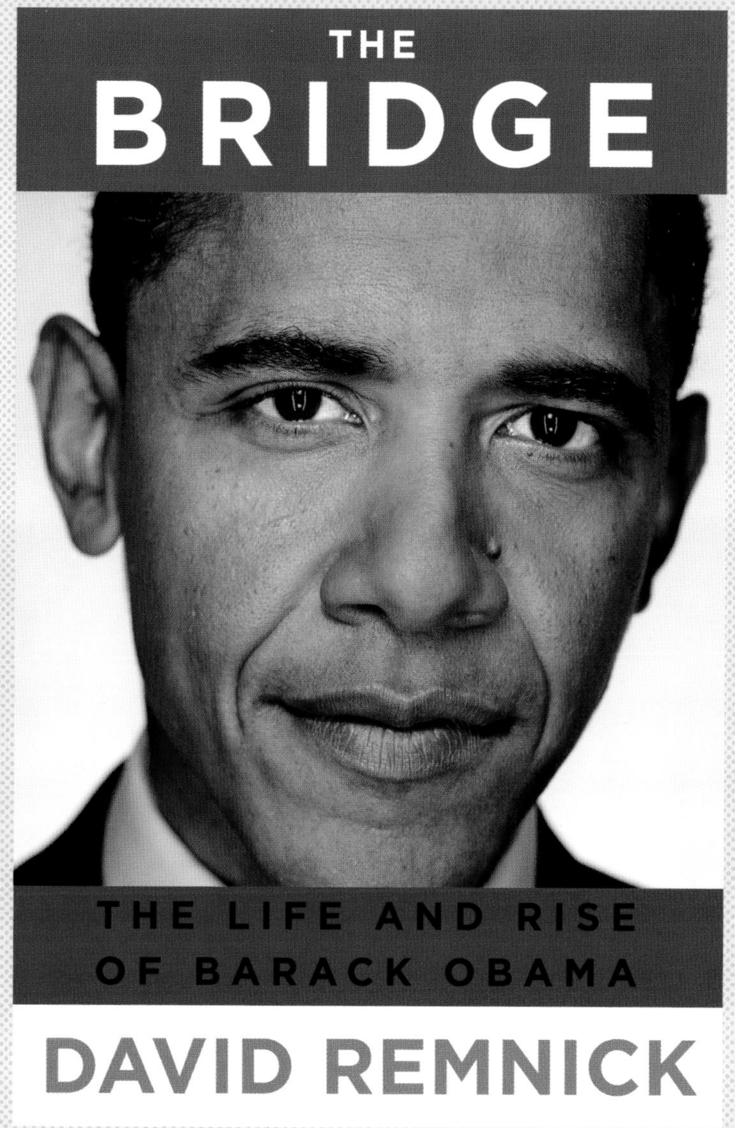
THE
BRIDGE
THE LIFE AND RISE
OF BARACK OBAMA
DAVID REMNICK

## Crossing That Bridge

David Remnick is a phenomenon as the editor of the most venerable magazine in the country, as well as the author of his own books and reporting covering everything from the Kremlin to his seminal studies of the success of Barack Obama and Muhammad Ali.

**RIGHT:** The original title of what became *The Bridge*. I loved the drama of this image, but it was determined that we needed his face. **ABOVE:** Photographer Martin Schoeler generously obliged. Knopf, 2010.

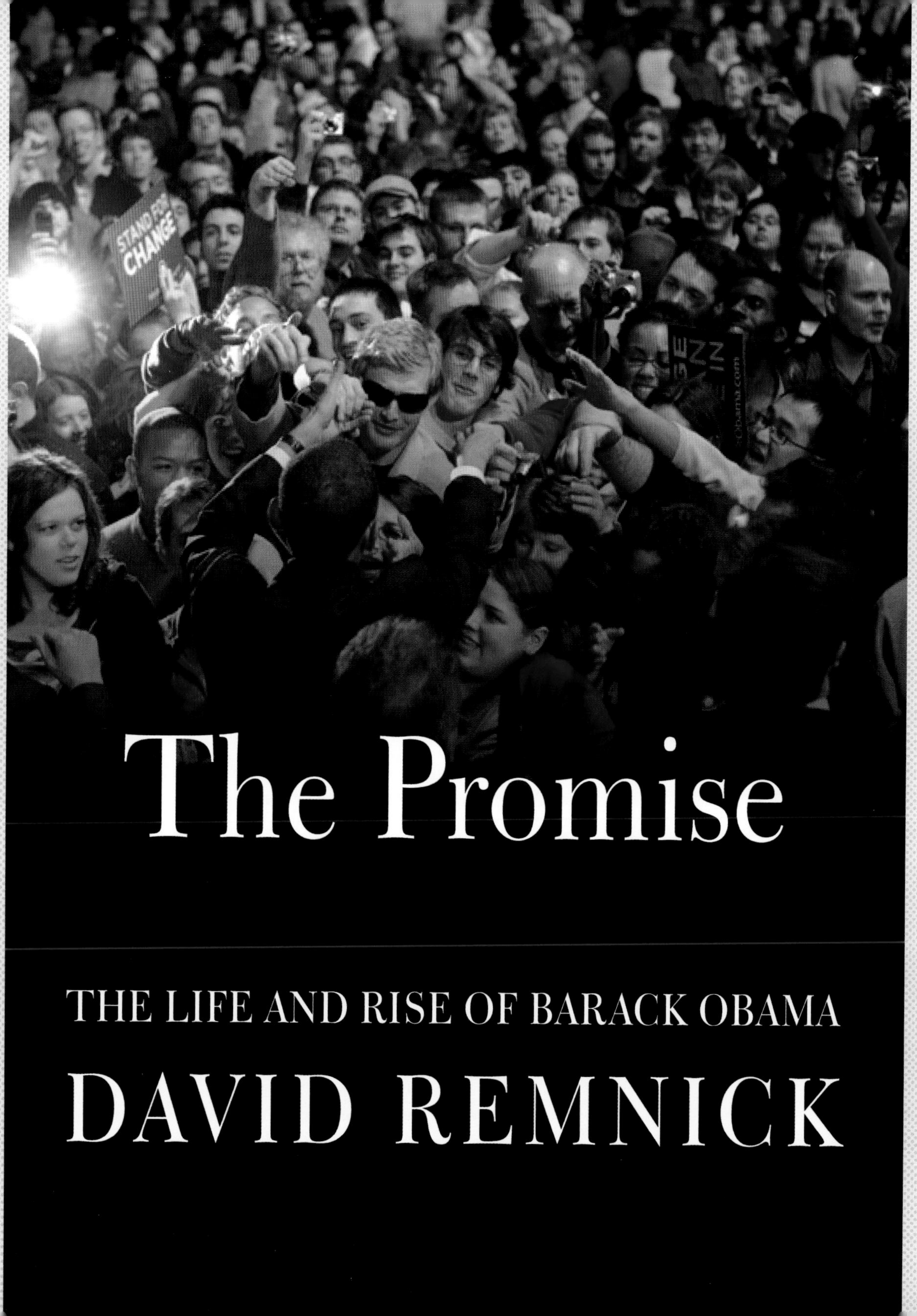
STAND FOR
CHANGE
The Promise
THE LIFE AND RISE OF BARACK OBAMA
DAVID REMNICK

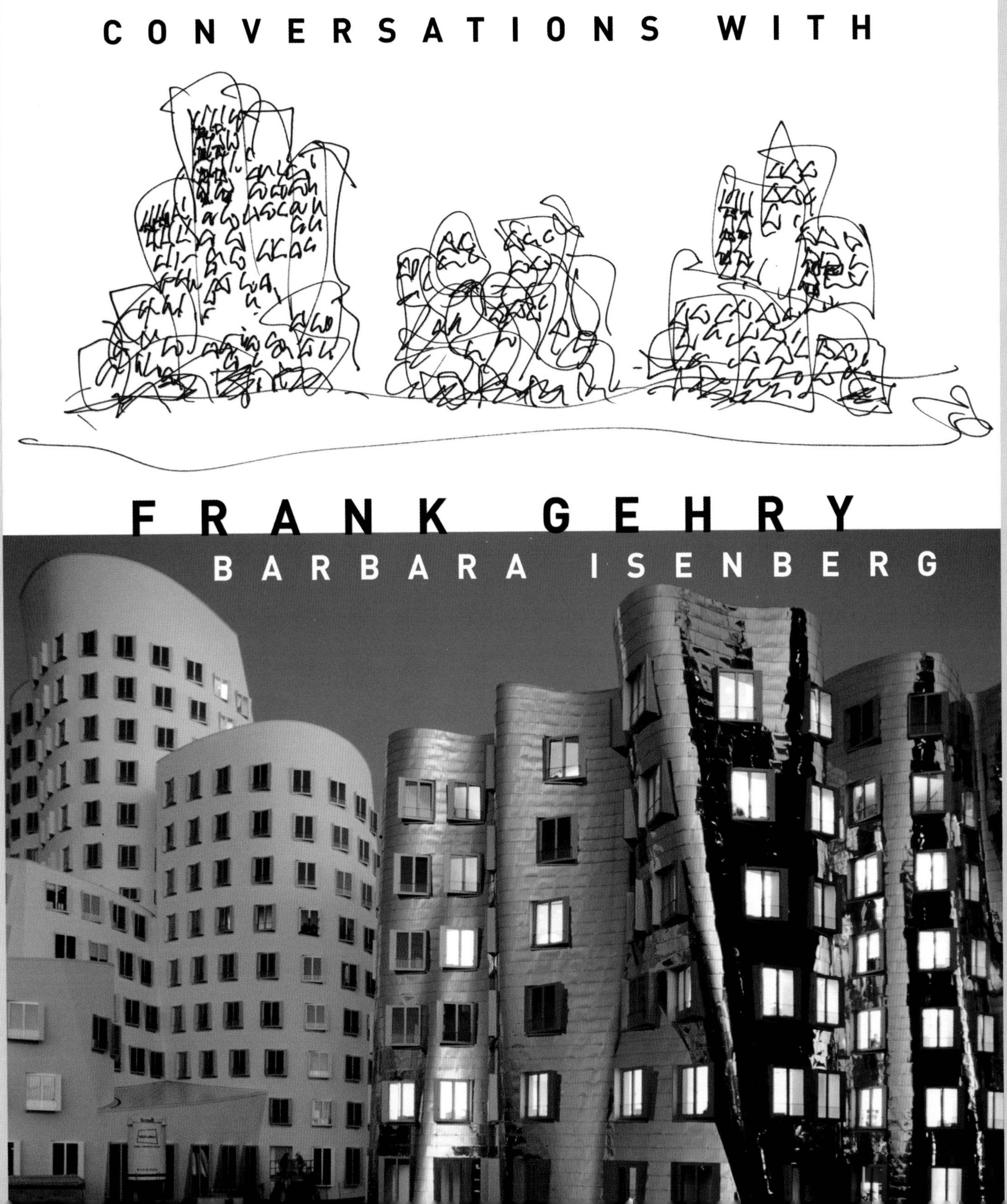
CONVERSATIONS WITH
FRANK GEHRY
BARBARA ISENBERG

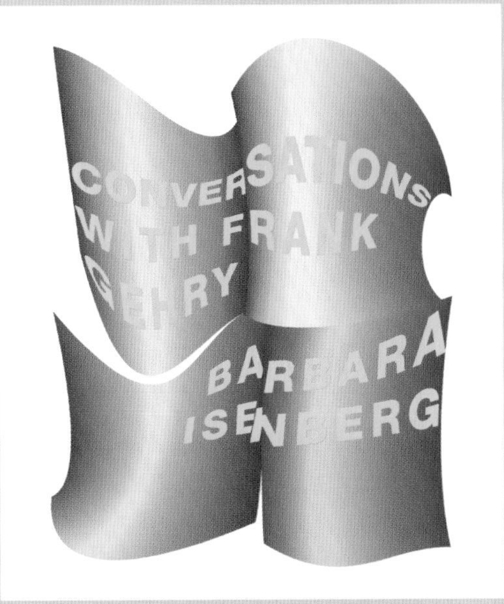
CONVERSATIONS WITH FRANK GEHRY
BARBARA ISENBERG

## Frank Discussions

I have not had the pleasure of meeting genius architect Frank Gehry, but I am an enormous fan and was more than happy to design the cover of Barbara Isenberg's collection of conversations she's had with him regarding his work.

My first attempt (above) was purely a creation of my own, a sort of appreciation of his aesthetic. Gehry, however, did not appreciate it, and I totally understood.

I started over by showing an oversimplified but totally accurate "before and after" juxtaposition (left) of one of his drawings for a housing complex in Germany and the resulting structure. How you get from one to the other is an utter mystery to me, and that's what the discussions in the book are all about.

**LEFT:** Knopf, 2009. **OPPOSITE, LEFT:** Knopf, 2006.

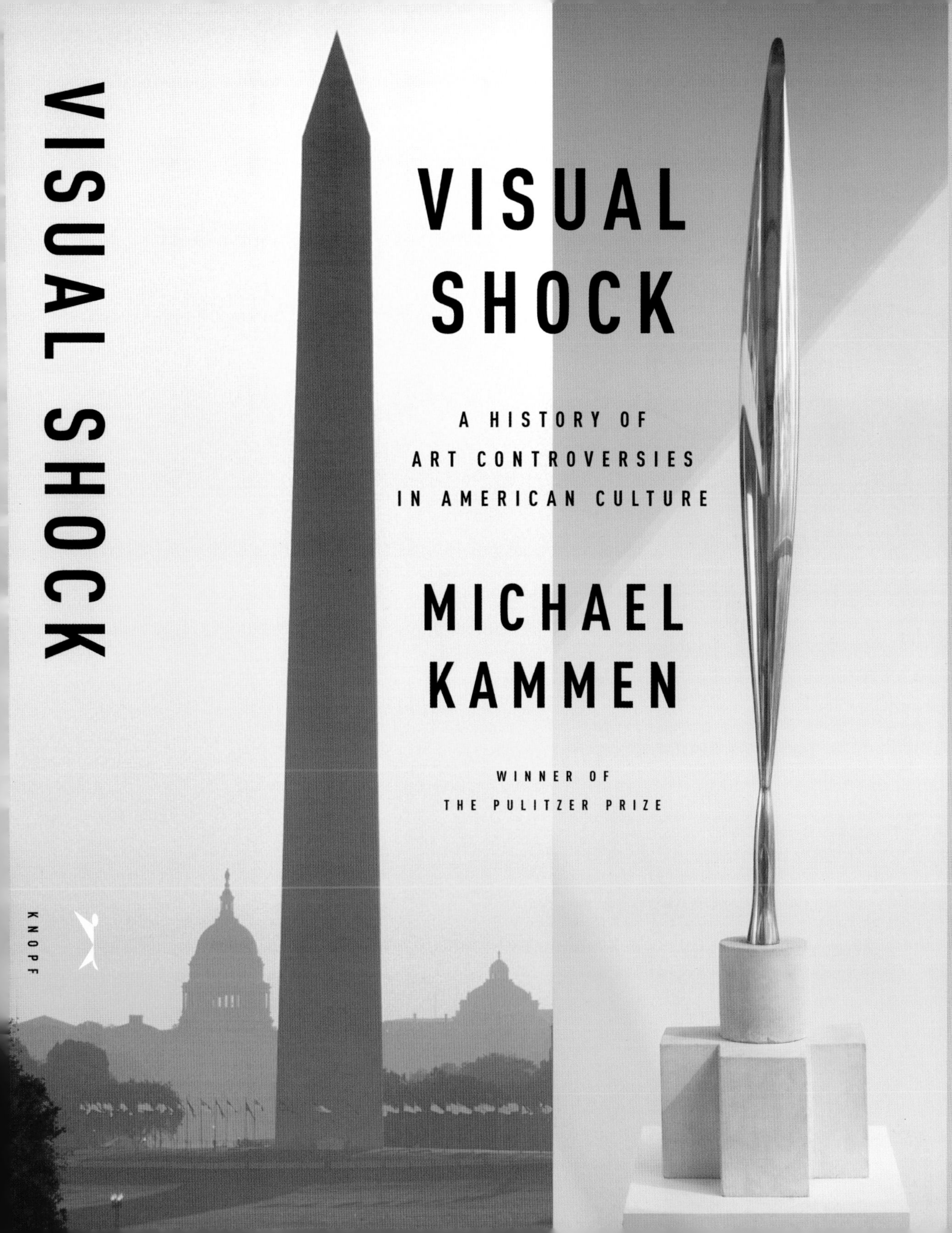
VISUAL SHOCK
KNOPF
VISUAL SHOCK
A HISTORY OF
ART CONTROVERSIES
IN AMERICAN CULTURE
MICHAEL KAMMEN
WINNER OF
THE PULITZER PRIZE

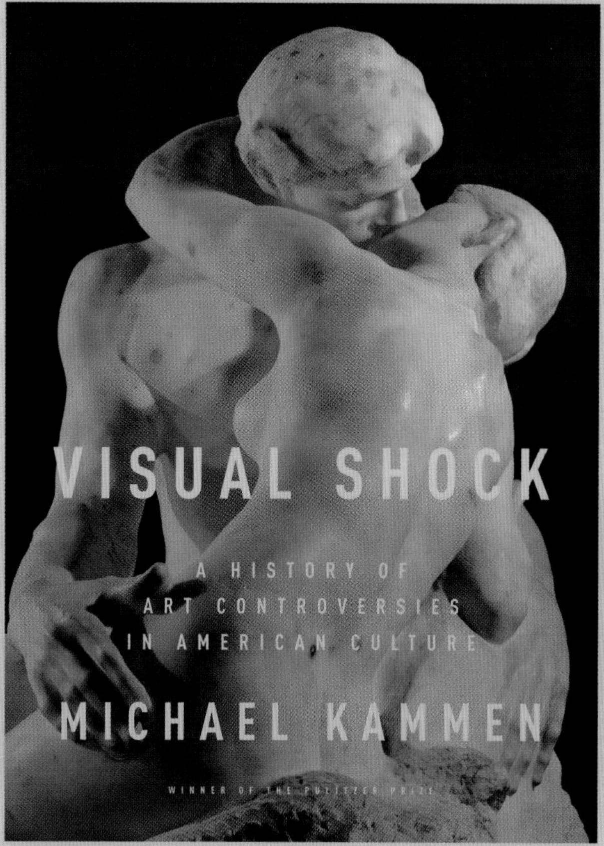
VISUAL SHOCK
A HISTORY OF
ART CONTROVERSIES
IN AMERICAN CULTURE
MICHAEL KAMMEN

## Shock Me

Michael Kammen's exploration of how art has provoked outrage in the general culture provided multiple choices for what to show on the cover. For instance, who doesn't love Rodin, and what could be better than *The Kiss* (above)? The thing is, though, this gorgeous statue was controversial at the time, but certainly isn't now. When I went through the rest of the art in the book, I couldn't help pairing the Washington Monument with Brancusi's *Bird in Space* (left). It's just the way my head works: the difference in scale and context, coupled with the undeniable similarity in form, inspires instant evaluation in the mind. Plus, on a superficial but undeniable level, the colors work great together.

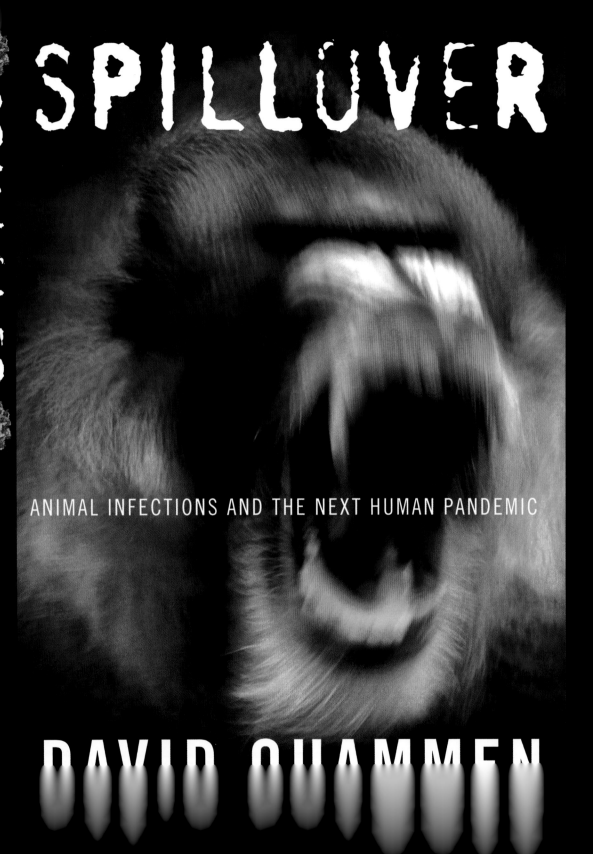

# SPILLOVER

ANIMAL INFECTIONS AND THE NEXT HUMAN PANDEMIC

## DAVID QUAMMEN

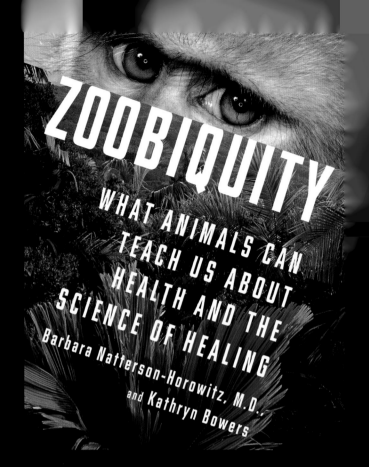

# ZOOBIQUITY

WHAT ANIMALS CAN
TEACH US ABOUT
HEALTH AND THE
SCIENCE OF HEALING

Barbara Natterson-Horowitz, M.D.,
and Kathryn Bowers

## You're an Animal

David Quammen's *Spillover* (left), with its thorough and reasoned explanation of how the next pandemic for human-kind will be born of African wildlife, is just plain scary, and the cover needed to be, too.

*Zoobiquity* (above) was on the opposite end of the same scale, theorizing that the study of disease and healing in animals can inform effective treatments in humans. My first idea was a peek-a-boo cover (opposite) using a newly popular selfie of a primate taken at the time of publication. Budgetary constraints nipped this direction in the bud, but

# ZOOBIQUITY

## Redefining the Boundaries of Human Medicine

Dr. Barbara Natterson Horowitz and Kathryn Bowers

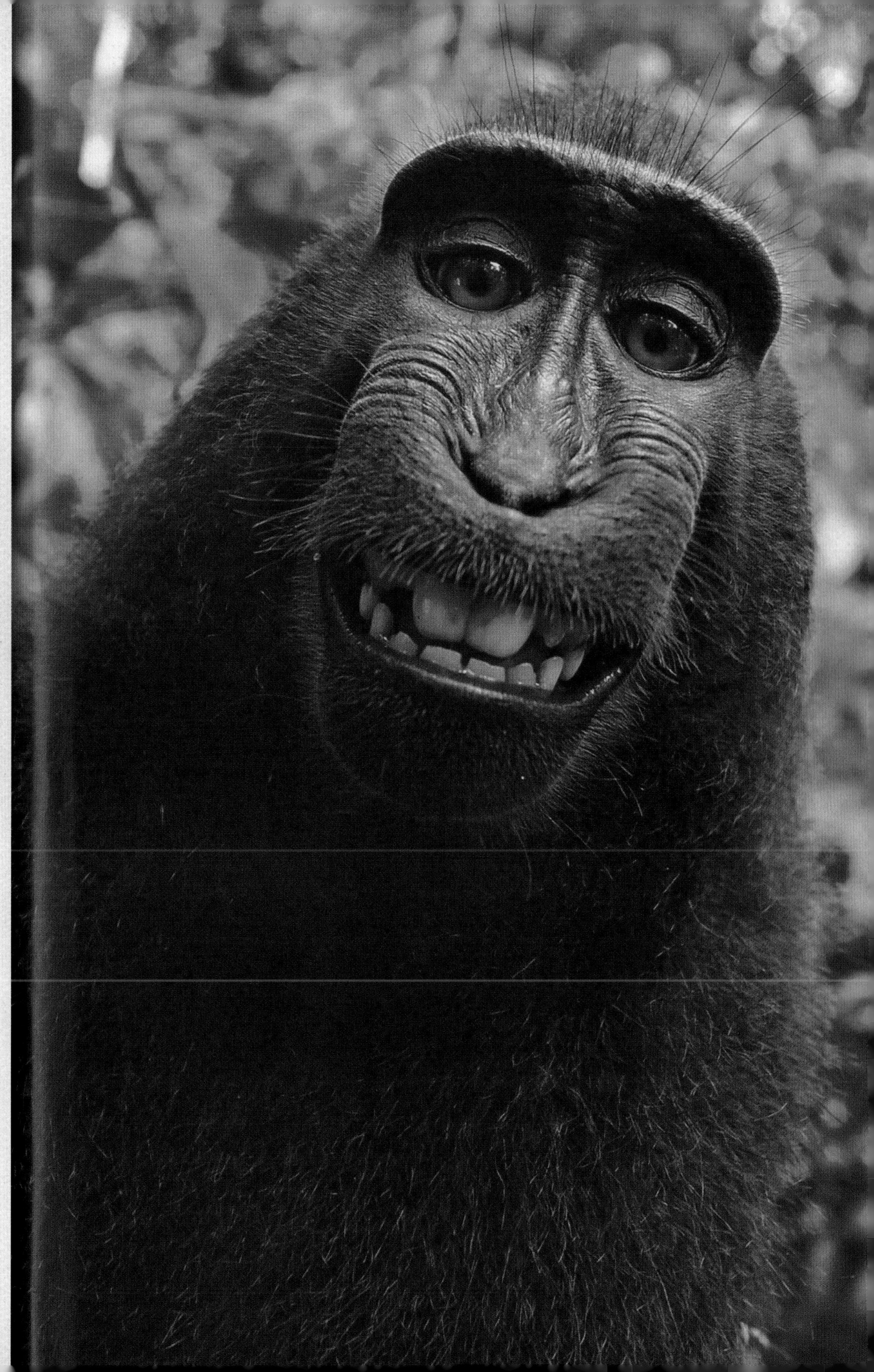

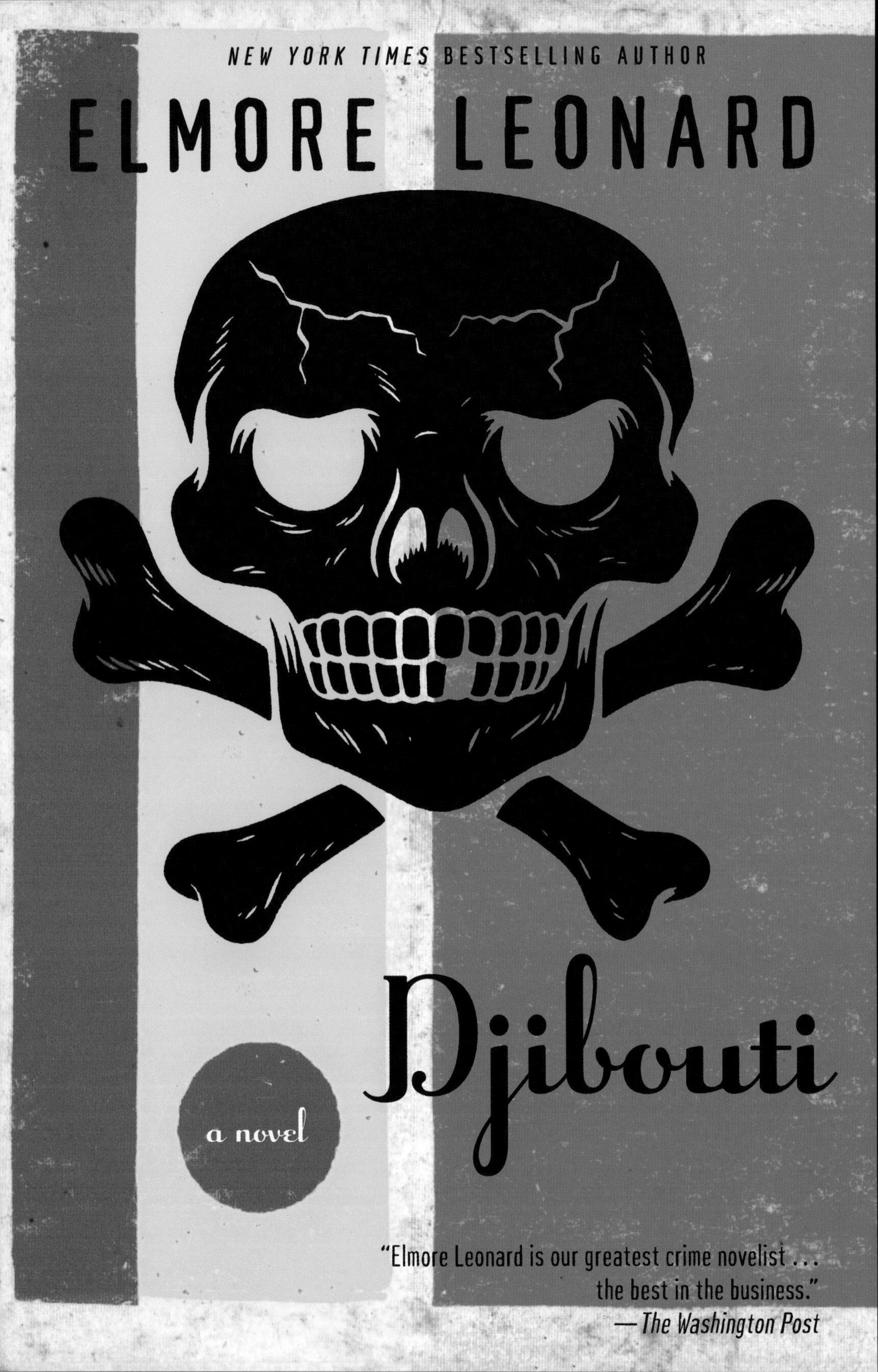
NEW YORK TIMES BESTSELLING AUTHOR
ELMORE LEONARD
Djibouti
a novel
"Elmore Leonard is our greatest crime novelist . . . the best in the business."
—The Washington Post

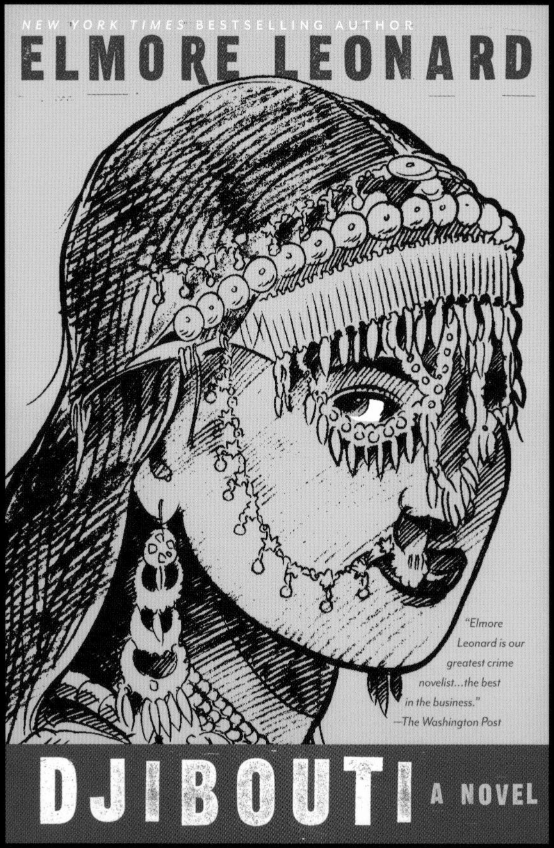
NEW YORK TIMES BESTSELLING AUTHOR
ELMORE LEONARD
"Elmore Leonard is our greatest crime novelist...the best in the business."
—The Washington Post
DJIBOUTI A NOVEL

## Hearts of Darkness

The last Elmore Leonard title I worked on was *Djibouti*. It was a bittersweet experience because nothing I came up with saw print, and he died shortly after publication. But as with everything "Dutch" wrote, it was interesting to work on, and the illustrator Mark Matcho more than rose to the challenge of sketching a young African princess and her elaborate bejeweled countenance (above). A version of this image eventually became the cover, though long after it was taken out of my hands and further abstracted.

I also thought about tapping into the book's theme of Somali pirates, so I tried using an African-accented skull and crossbones motif (left) which I loved. Alas, it didn't seem to excite anyone else involved. My role in the project pretty much ended there; sad, because we had done so much great work in the past on his previous titles. Hey, we'll always have *Cuba Libre*. Seriously, what a great writer, and I was thrilled he wanted to work with me in the first place. Here's to Chilly Palmer!

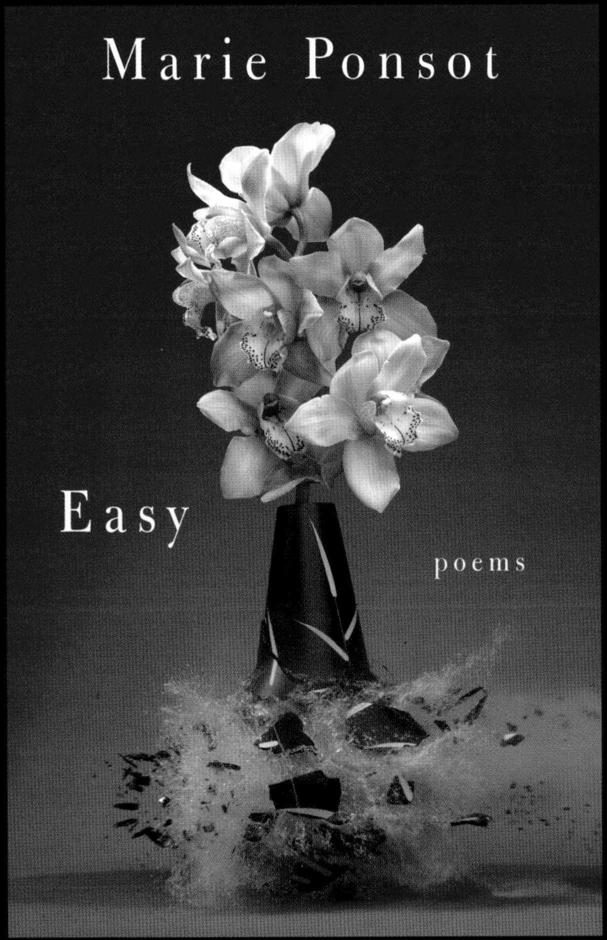
Marie Ponsot
Easy
poems

## Make It Look Easy

I have had the pleasure of working with the poet Marie Ponsot for many years, and *Easy* was as much fun to read and interpret as her earlier works, *The Green Dark* and *Springing*.

Stop-motion photographer Martin Klima's extraordinary shots of exploding bud vases seemed the perfect metaphor for Ponsot's explorations of trying to age gracefully amidst life's mounting indignities. While everything at the surface looks perfectly composed, underneath it is quite another story. I think anyone with a taste of life can relate. The question of what would be the final cover was all that remained, and the tulip at right (Knopf, 2009) was deemed the most effective. I suppose red flowers will do that every time.

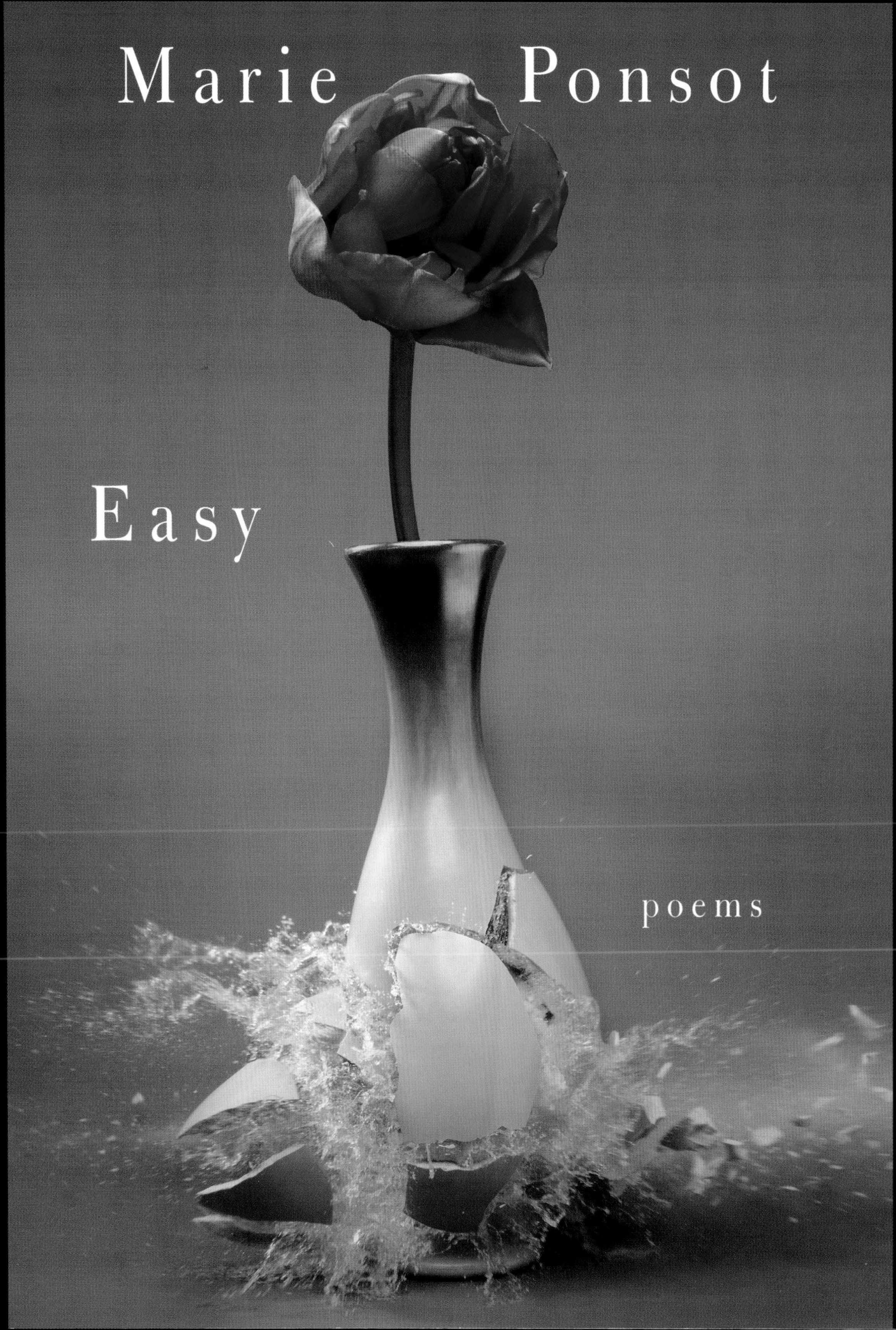
Marie Ponsot
Easy
poems

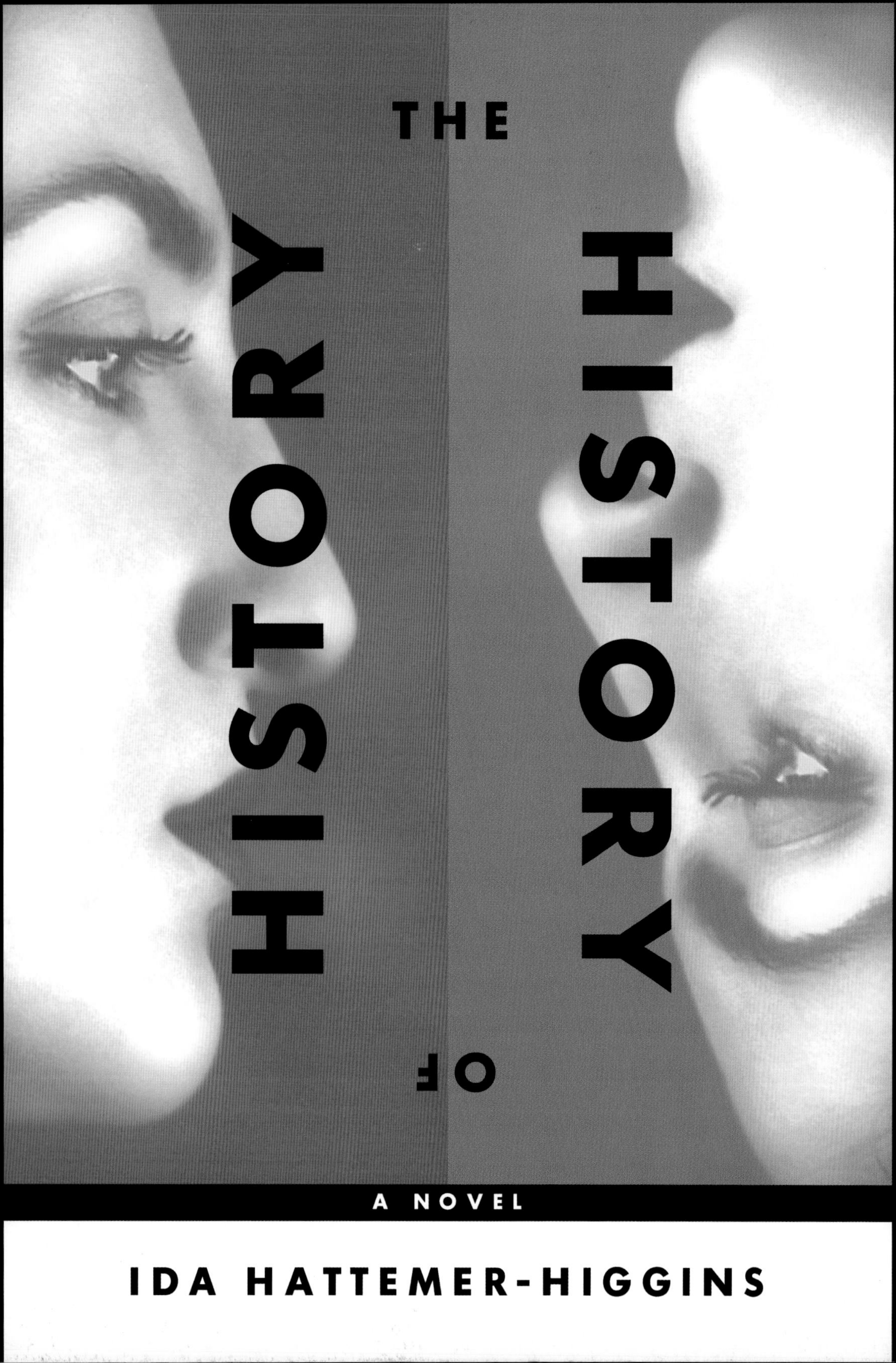
THE
HISTORY
OF
HISTORY
A NOVEL
IDA HATTEMER-HIGGINS

# Revolutions

True story, swear to God: this is how the *New York Times* arrived at my doorstep on Thursday May 8, 2008 (below and opposite left). If ever there was an omen to heed, this was it. With Dmitri Medvedev announced on the front page as the new president of Russia, a small flap of the paper had ripped away (from his crotch!) to reveal a tiny headline on a section of page 3 that reads "Trickery," from a totally unrelated story on the table of contents. This apparently happened in transit. Weird, eerie, prescient forces at work.

**LEFT:** Knopf, 2011. **OPPOSITE, RIGHT:** Knopf, 2015.

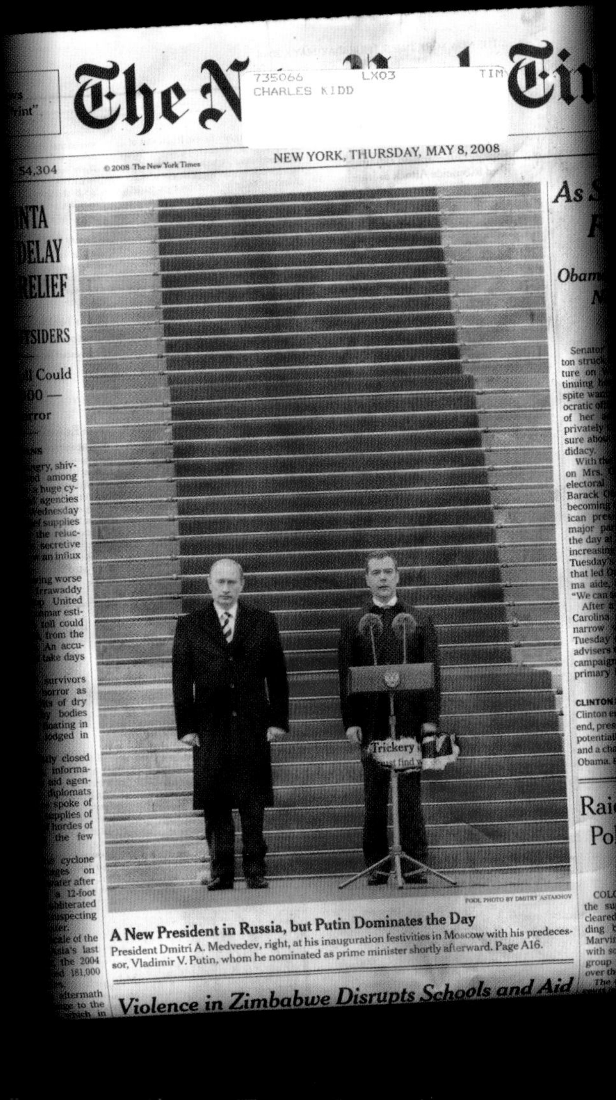
735066 LX03
CHARLES KIDD
NEW YORK, THURSDAY, MAY 8, 2008
A New President in Russia, but Putin Dominates the Day
President Dmitri A. Medvedev, right, at his inauguration festivities in Moscow with his predecessor, Vladimir V. Putin, whom he nominated as prime minister shortly afterward. Page A16.
Trickery
Violence in Zimbabwe Disrupts Schools and Aid

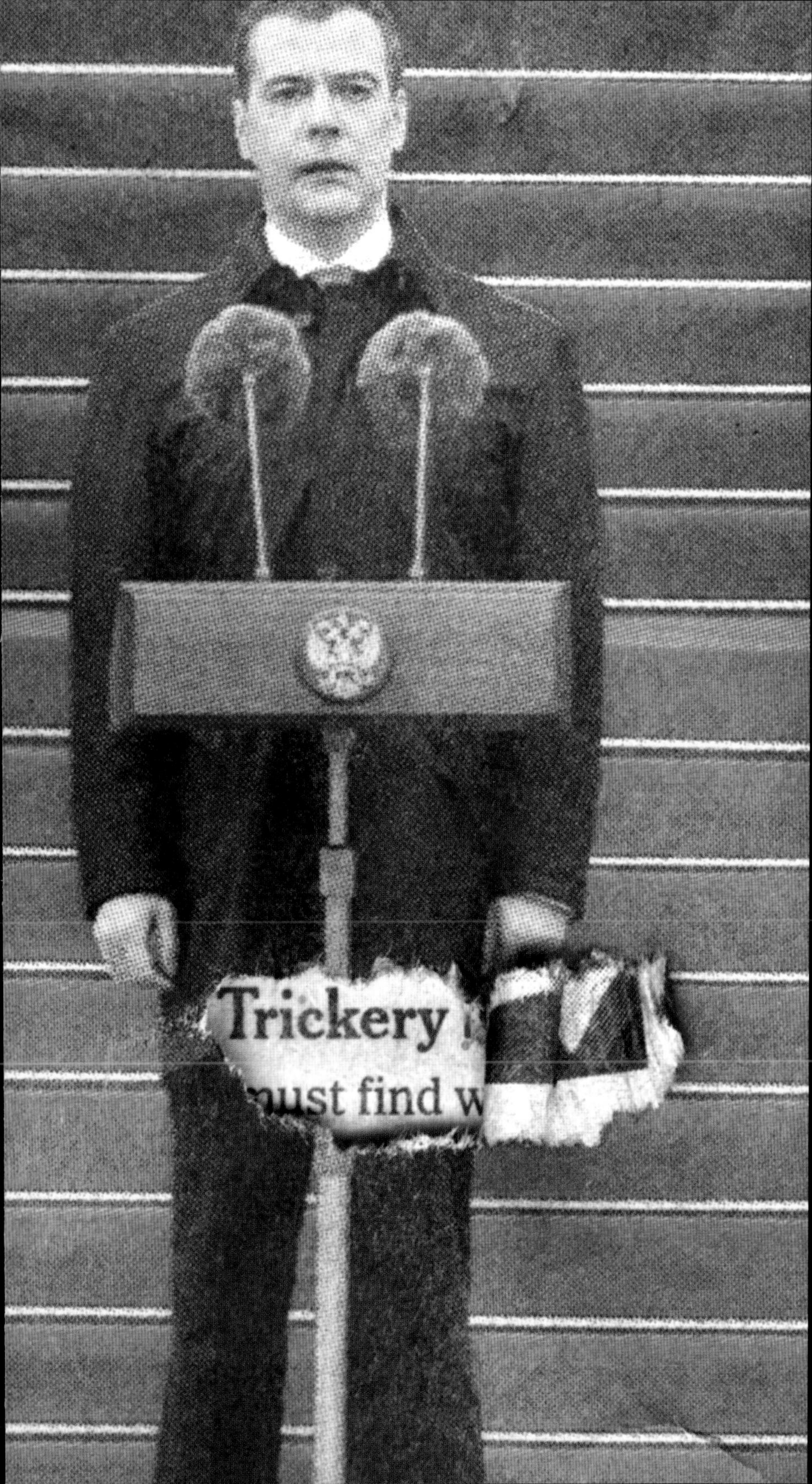
Trickery
must find

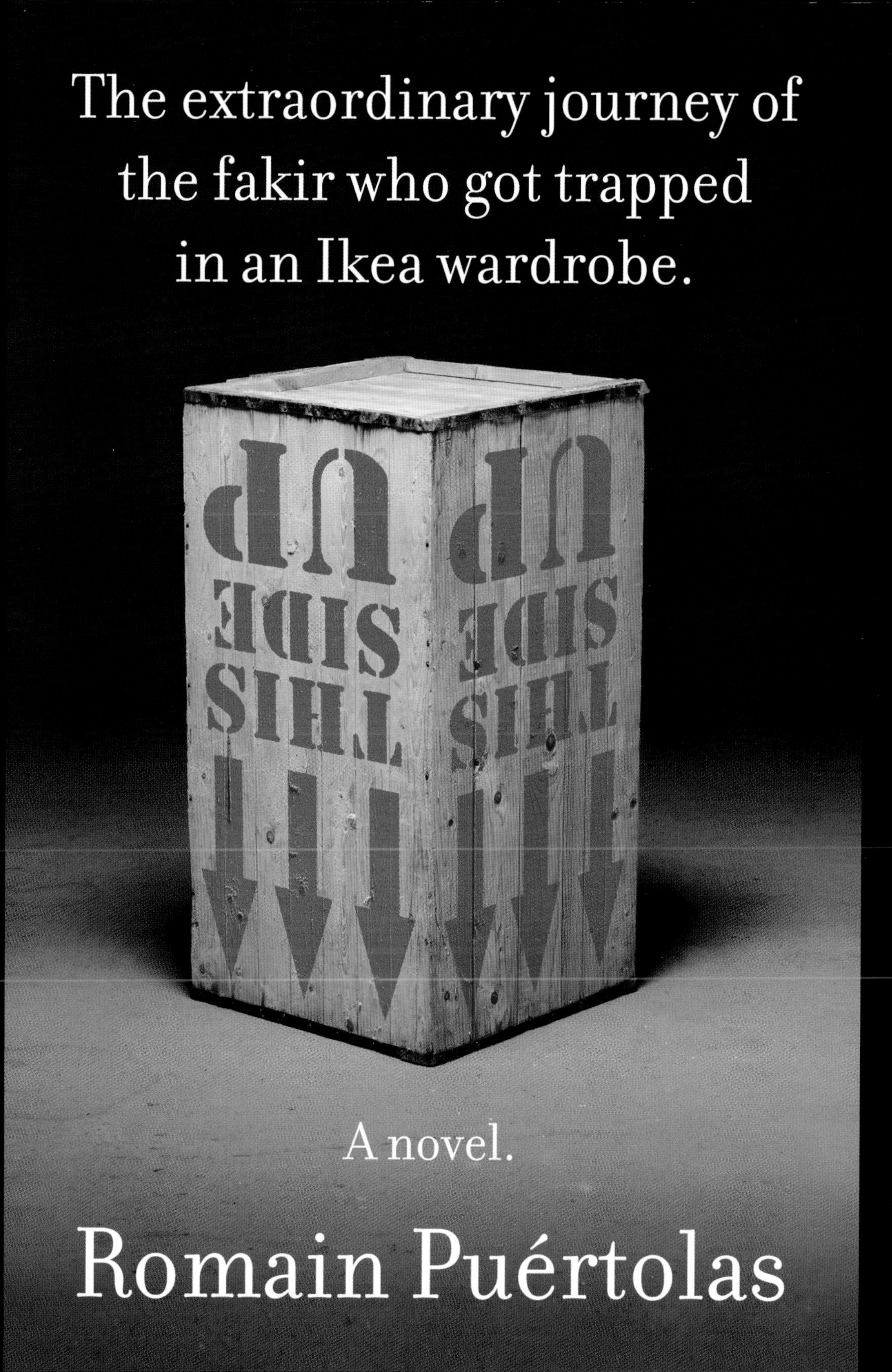
The extraordinary journey of
the fakir who got trapped
in an Ikea wardrobe.
THIS SIDE UP
THIS SIDE UP
A novel.
Romain Puértolas

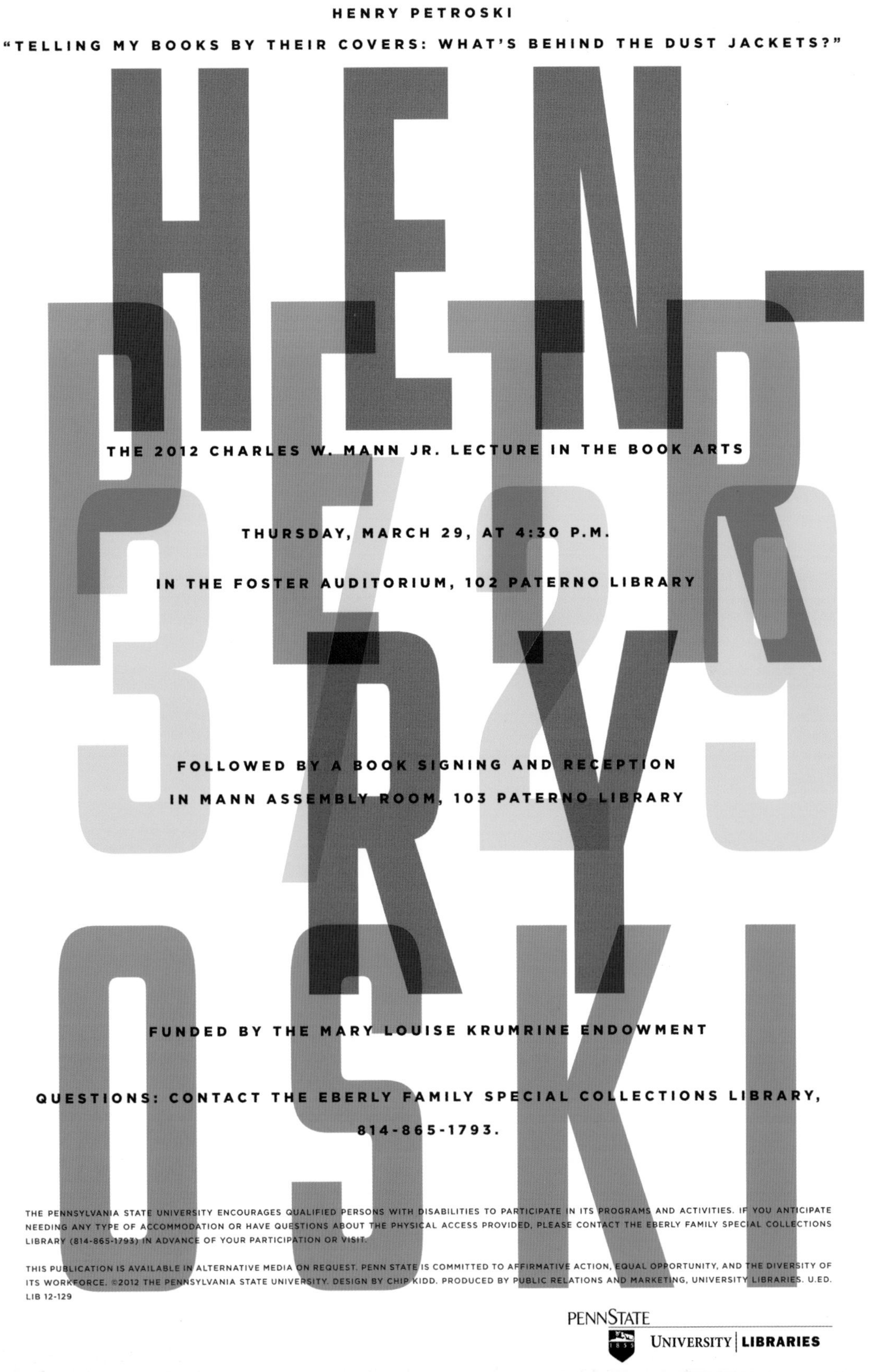
HENRY PETROSKI
"TELLING MY BOOKS BY THEIR COVERS: WHAT'S BEHIND THE DUST JACKETS?"
HEN-
PETR-
OSKI
3/29
THE 2012 CHARLES W. MANN JR. LECTURE IN THE BOOK ARTS
THURSDAY, MARCH 29, AT 4:30 P.M.
IN THE FOSTER AUDITORIUM, 102 PATERNO LIBRARY
FOLLOWED BY A BOOK SIGNING AND RECEPTION
IN MANN ASSEMBLY ROOM, 103 PATERNO LIBRARY
FUNDED BY THE MARY LOUISE KRUMRINE ENDOWMENT
QUESTIONS: CONTACT THE EBERLY FAMILY SPECIAL COLLECTIONS LIBRARY, 814-865-1793.
THE PENNSYLVANIA STATE UNIVERSITY ENCOURAGES QUALIFIED PERSONS WITH DISABILITIES TO PARTICIPATE IN ITS PROGRAMS AND ACTIVITIES. IF YOU ANTICIPATE NEEDING ANY TYPE OF ACCOMMODATION OR HAVE QUESTIONS ABOUT THE PHYSICAL ACCESS PROVIDED, PLEASE CONTACT THE EBERLY FAMILY SPECIAL COLLECTIONS LIBRARY (814-865-1793) IN ADVANCE OF YOUR PARTICIPATION OR VISIT.
THIS PUBLICATION IS AVAILABLE IN ALTERNATIVE MEDIA ON REQUEST. PENN STATE IS COMMITTED TO AFFIRMATIVE ACTION, EQUAL OPPORTUNITY, AND THE DIVERSITY OF ITS WORKFORCE. ©2012 THE PENNSYLVANIA STATE UNIVERSITY. DESIGN BY CHIP KIDD. PRODUCED BY PUBLIC RELATIONS AND MARKETING, UNIVERSITY LIBRARIES. U.ED. LIB 12-129
PENNSTATE
UNIVERSITY | LIBRARIES



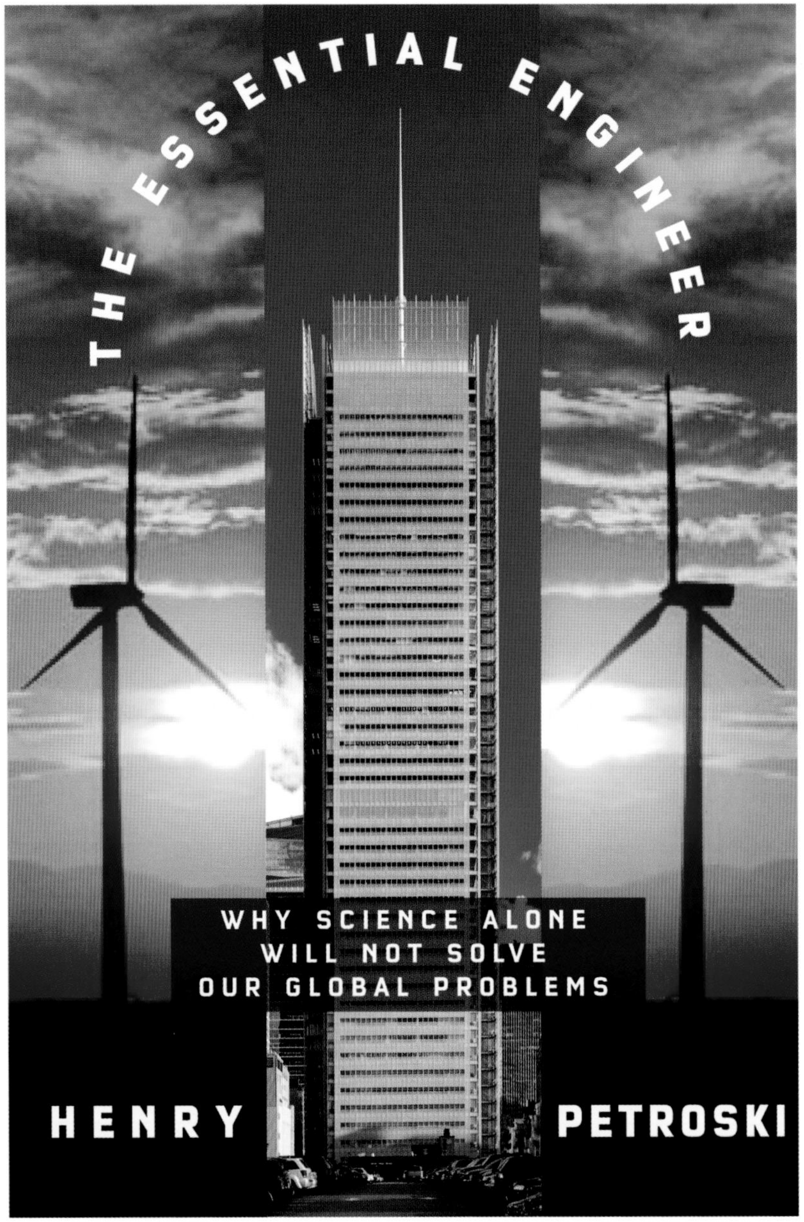
THE ESSENTIAL ENGINEER
WHY SCIENCE ALONE
WILL NOT SOLVE
OUR GLOBAL PROBLEMS
HENRY
PETROSKI

## Petroski-ite

I have designed engineer/writer Henry Petroski's jackets for years, and when he gave a lecture at my alma mater, Penn State, I was delighted to design the poster (left). Only Henry could write a scholarly history of the toothpick (opposite). Here, I couldn't resist turning the jacket into a typical suburban hors d'oeuvre from my childhood. Sonny Mehta, Knopf's

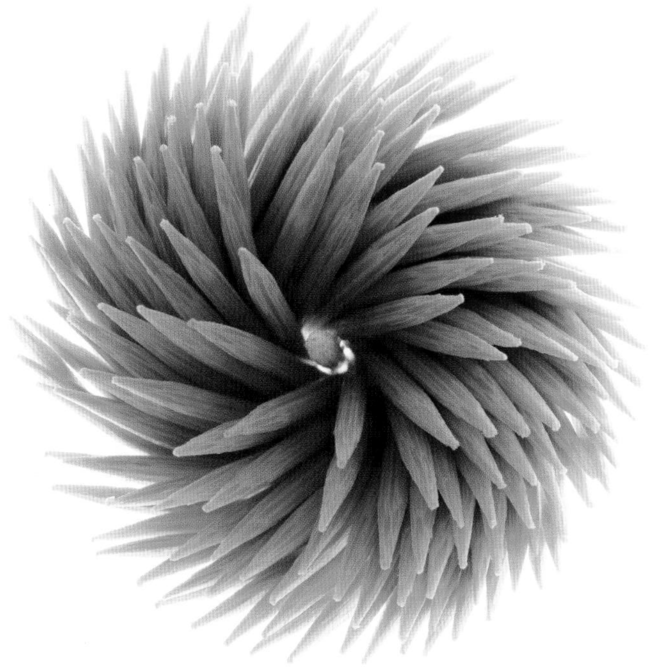

editor-in-chief, was (to my total amusement) baffled by this concoction, and I had to not only explain it but also convince him that it was, in fact, an actual thing people ate at cocktail parties.

**ABOVE & BELOW:** Various unused toothpick studies by Geoff Spear.
**OPPOSITE, RIGHT:** Knopf, 2010. **RIGHT:** Knopf, 2007. Photograph by Geoff Spear.

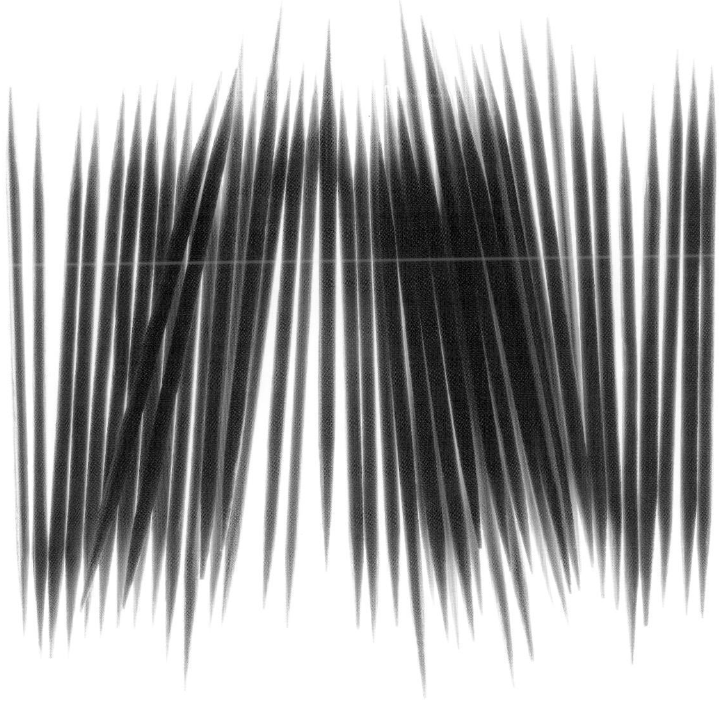

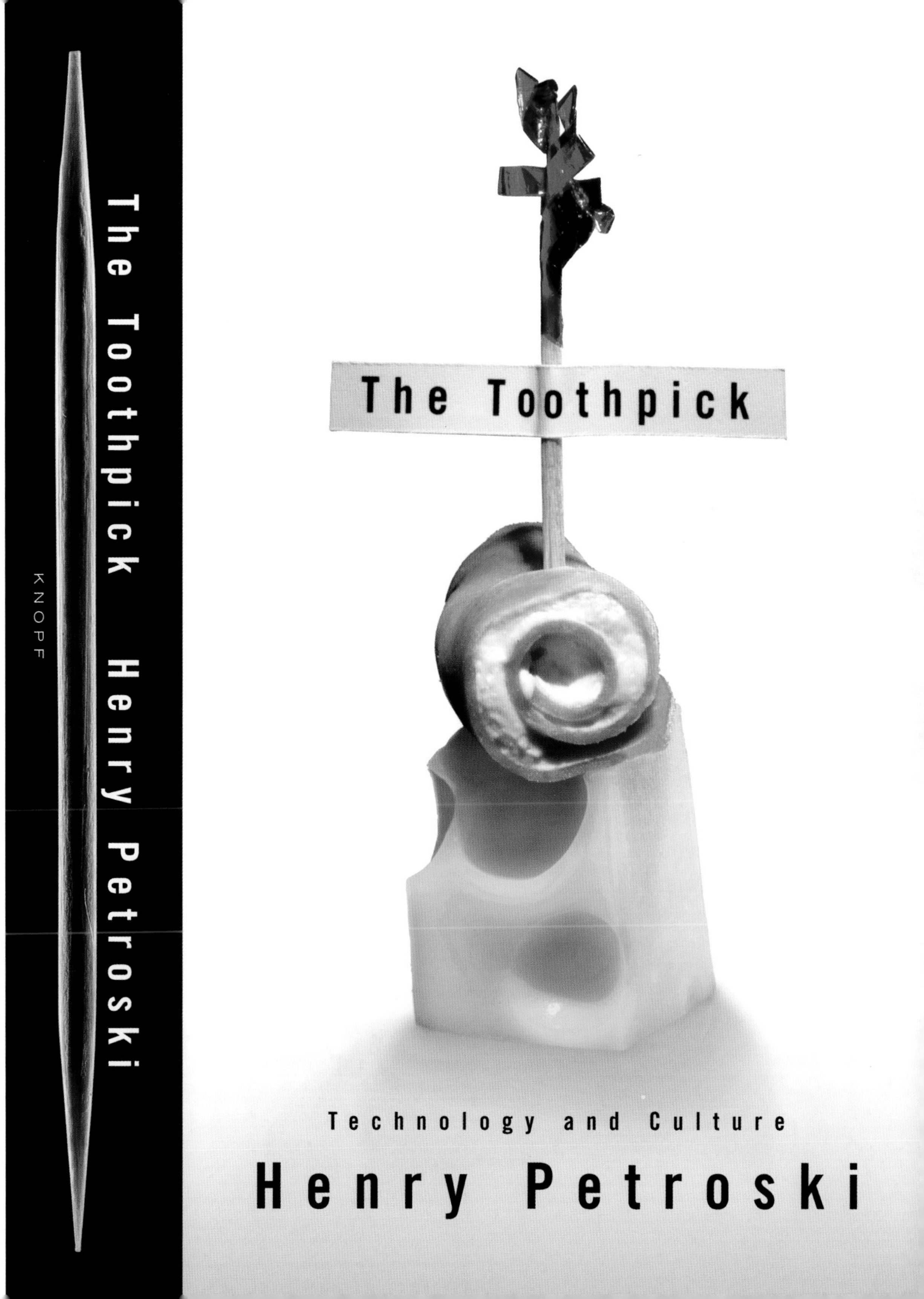
The Toothpick Henry Petroski
KNOPF
The Toothpick
Technology and Culture
Henry Petroski

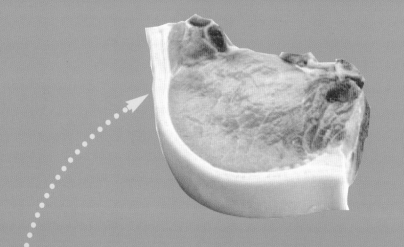

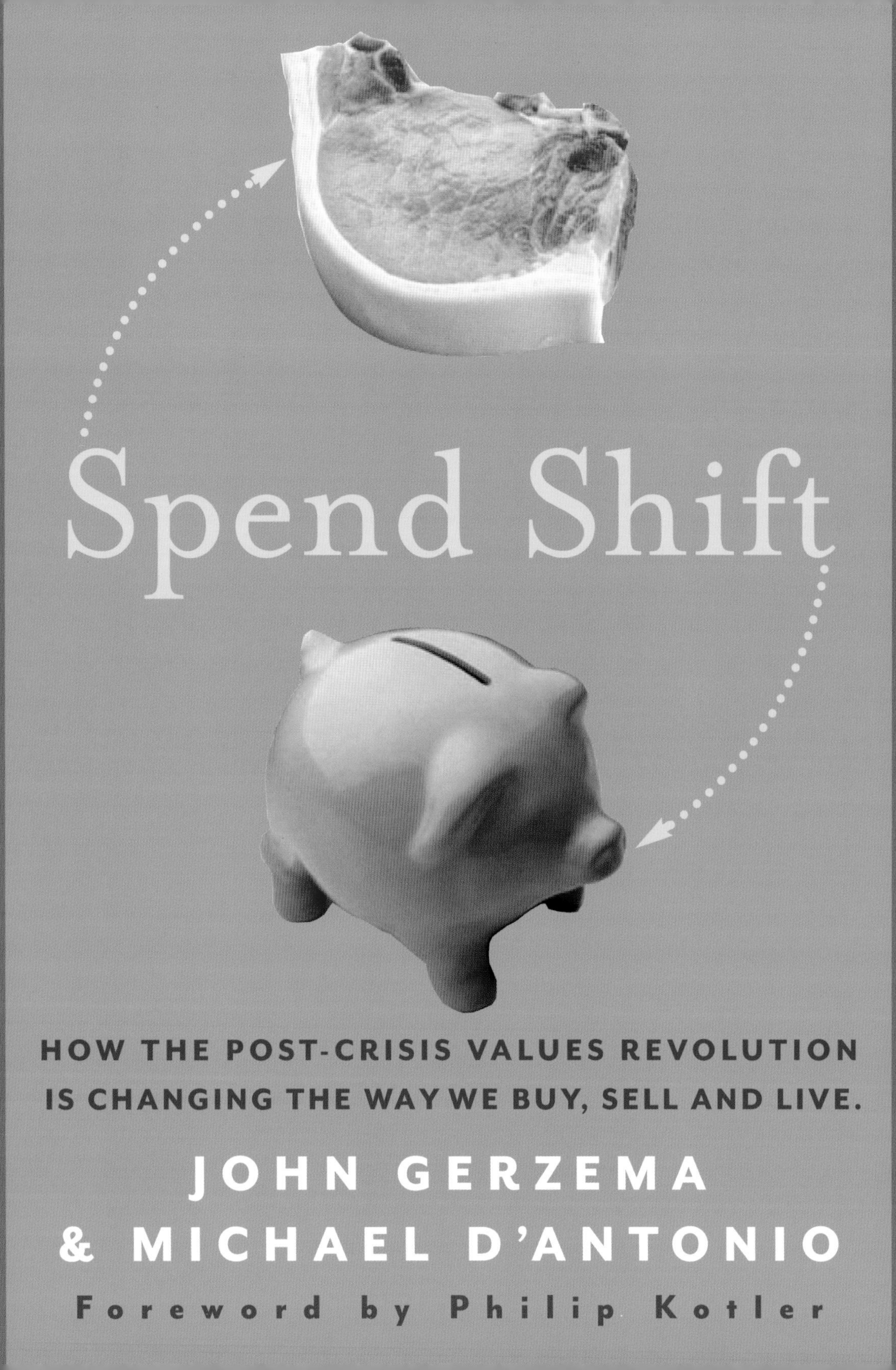

# Spend Shift

## HOW THE POST-CRISIS VALUES REVOLUTION IS CHANGING THE WAY WE BUY, SELL AND LIVE.

## JOHN GERZEMA & MICHAEL D'ANTONIO

Foreword by Philip Kotler

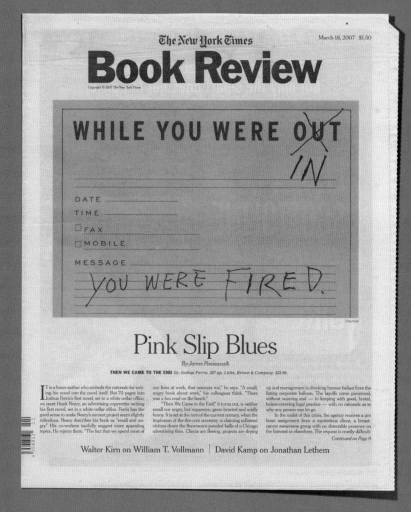

The New York Times — March 18, 2007 $1.50

# Book Review

Copyright © 2007 The New York Times

**WHILE YOU WERE OUT** ~~OUT~~ *IN*

DATE
TIME
☐ FAX
☐ MOBILE
MESSAGE
YOU WERE FIRED.

Chip Kidd

## Pink Slip Blues

*By James Poniewozik*

THEN WE CAME TO THE END *By Joshua Ferris. 387 pp. Little, Brown & Company. $23.99.*

IT is a brave author who embeds the rationale for writing his novel into the novel itself. But 70 pages into Joshua Ferris's first novel, set in a white-collar office, we meet Hank Neary, an advertising copywriter writing his first novel, set in a white-collar office. Ferris has the good sense to make Neary's earnest project seem slightly ridiculous. Neary describes his book as "small and angry." His co-workers tactfully suggest more appealing topics. He rejects them. "The fact that we spend most of our lives at work, that interests me," he says. "A small, angry book about work," his colleagues think. "There was a fun read on the beach."

"Then We Came to the End," it turns out, is neither small nor angry, but expansive, great-hearted and acidly funny. It is set at the turn of the current century, when the implosion of the dot-com economy is claiming collateral victims down the fluorescent-paneled halls of a Chicago advertising firm. Clients are fleeing, projects are drying up and management is chucking human ballast from the listing corporate balloon. The layoffs come piecemeal, without warning and — in keeping with good, brutal, heinie-covering legal practice — with no rationale as to why any person was let go.

In the midst of this crisis, the agency receives a pro bono assignment from a mysterious client, a breast-cancer awareness group with no detectable presence on the Internet or elsewhere. The request is cruelly difficult:

Continued on Page 9

Walter Kirn on William T. Vollmann | David Kamp on Jonathan Lethem

## Saving for a Rainy Day

I am not great with designing covers about the financial world because it's very difficult (for me, anyway) to make that material look interesting. But I try to rise to the challenge. For *Spend Shift* (left), a meditation on lessons to be learned from the terrible monetary crisis of 2008, the idea of frivolous "pork" spending contrasted with the age-old concept of a piggy bank to save your pennies (whoever came up with that idea in the first place?) was too tempting not to try. It seemed to get the point across, and the authors agreed.

Joshua Ferris's brilliant novel about the dysfunctions of a Chicago advertising agency at the end of the 1990s, *And Then We Came to the*

*End*, was to be featured on the cover of the *New York Times Book Review* and they asked me to illustrate it (opposite, right). Anyone who is familiar with corporate office life at that time knows of the "While You Were Out" slips that assistants used to take messages regarding missed calls for their bosses. They were bright pink, as were firing notices, aka "pink slips."

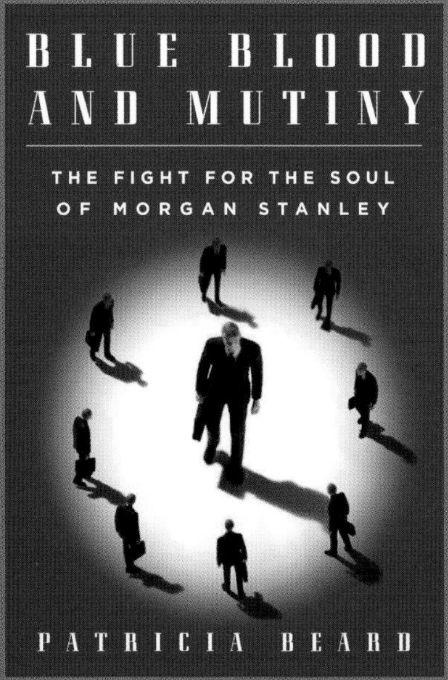
BLUE BLOOD AND MUTINY
THE FIGHT FOR THE SOUL OF MORGAN STANLEY
PATRICIA BEARD

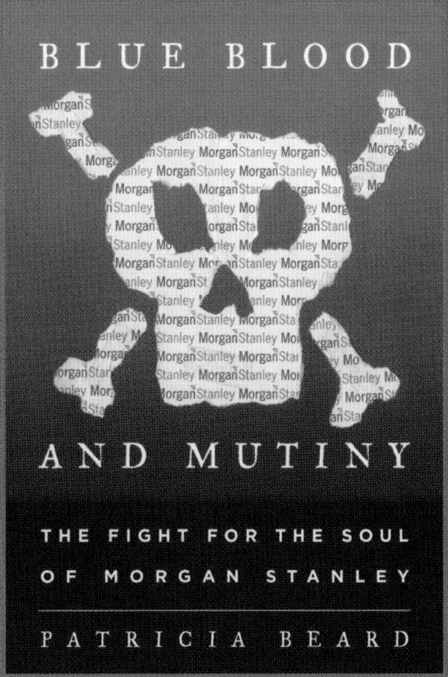
BLUE BLOOD
AND MUTINY
THE FIGHT FOR THE SOUL OF MORGAN STANLEY
PATRICIA BEARD

**ABOVE LEFT:** The author came to me personally to explain this saga of the CEO of Morgan Stanley (Phillip J. Purcell) being ousted by a cabal of eight of his own retired executives. I thought this design (with a photograph by Geoff Spear) conveyed that rather dramatically. But the author disagreed. **ABOVE RIGHT:** One final attempt, but it, too, was nixed. **OPPOSITE, LEFT:** Jossey-Bass, 2010. **RIGHT:** Simon & Schuster, 2009.

Then there is Beth Kobliner (right), who deserves some kind of award for being a financial guru with the heart and soul of a saint. She just wants to give young people an urgent sense of what they need to be thinking about in terms of their financial future, at a time in their lives when they are thinking about anything but. Although the book and cover are from 2009, the issues they address could not be more relevant today, and will only become more so with each generation. Geoff Spear did the photo composite, with my ever-present thumb. Can you imagine if your ATM slip* actually said this?

*If you don't know what an ATM slip is, presumably because you do all your banking now by smartphone, you really need to read this book more than EVER.

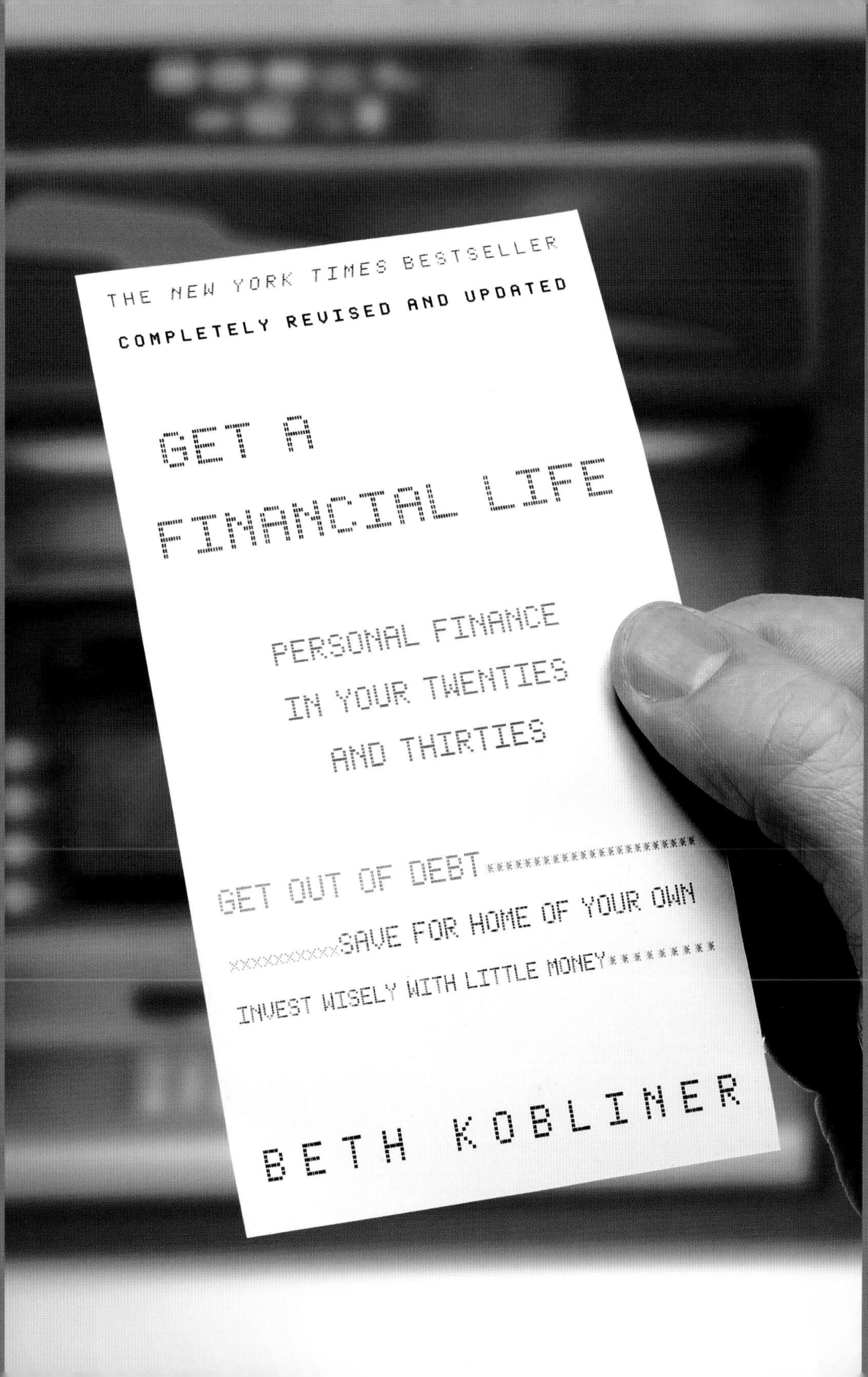
THE NEW YORK TIMES BESTSELLER
COMPLETELY REVISED AND UPDATED
GET A
FINANCIAL LIFE
PERSONAL FINANCE
IN YOUR TWENTIES
AND THIRTIES
GET OUT OF DEBT
SAVE FOR HOME OF YOUR OWN
INVEST WISELY WITH LITTLE MONEY
BETH KOBLINER

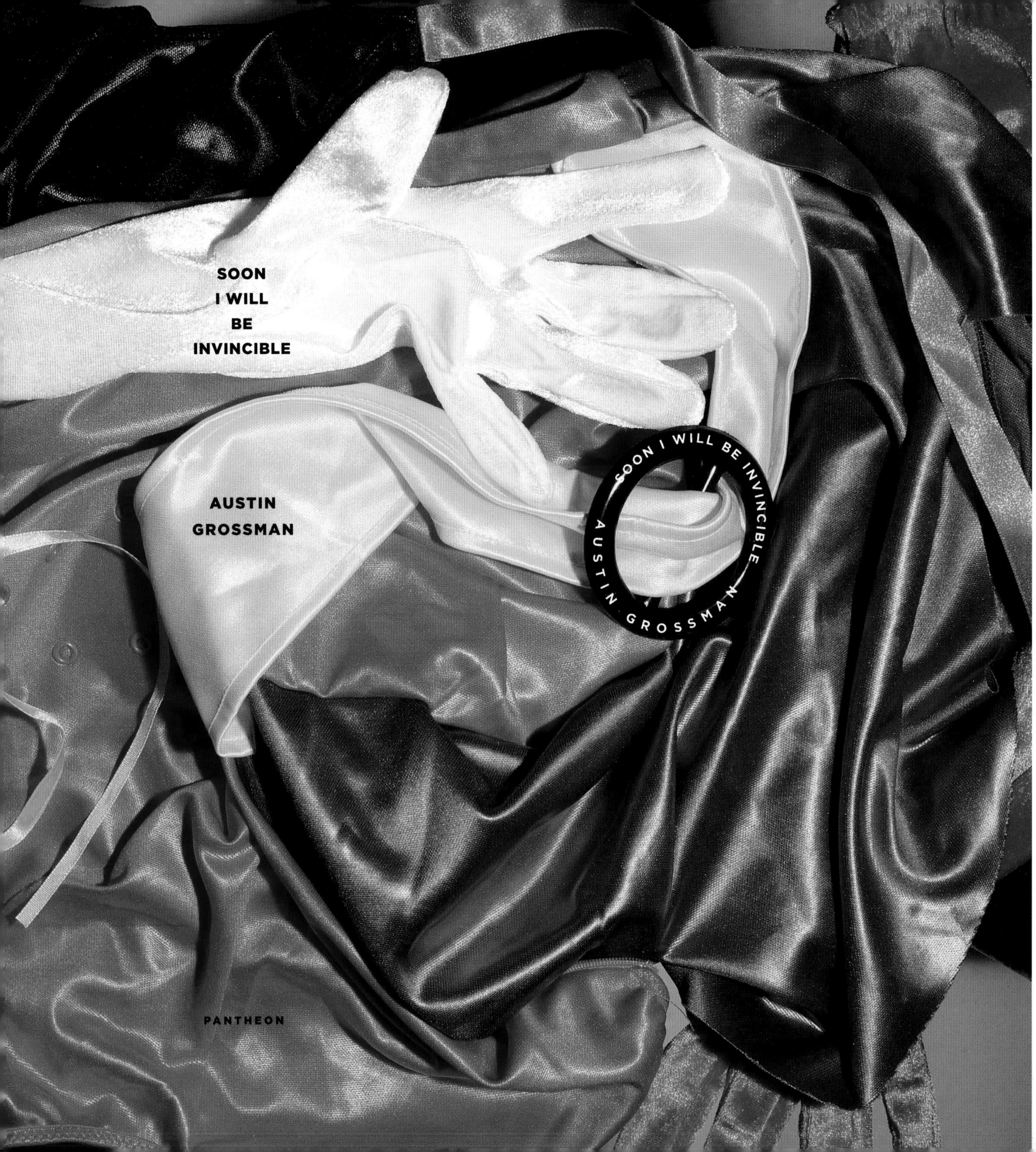
SOON I WILL BE INVINCIBLE
AUSTIN GROSSMAN
SOON I WILL BE INVINCIBLE · AUSTIN GROSSMAN
PANTHEON

# Nerd Patrol

Ah, now these are my people, the superheroes and villains and all those who love (and love to hate) them. Austin Grossman knows this breed (especially the latter) all too well, and in his novel *Soon I Will Be Invincible*, he foresaw what would make films like *Despicable Me* and *Suicide Squad* such huge hits: namely, aligning the audience's viewpoint and sympathy with the bad guys, who have backstories and motivations that humanize them and give their actions depth beyond just wanting to take over the world (though that's still on the agenda, don't you worry).

Since this book wasn't a graphic novel, I wanted to make the visual component about the preliminaries: suiting up for the big battles, instead of any kind of conventional "heroic" character shots. It's all about the process of getting into costume and putting on the helmet that will broadcast your brainwaves to the minds of the unsuspecting masses.

**THIS SPREAD:** Pantheon, 2007. All styling and photography by my secret weapon, Geoff Spear.

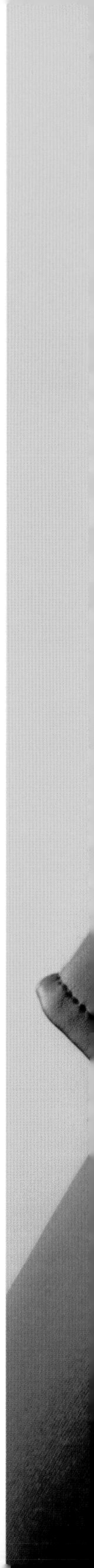

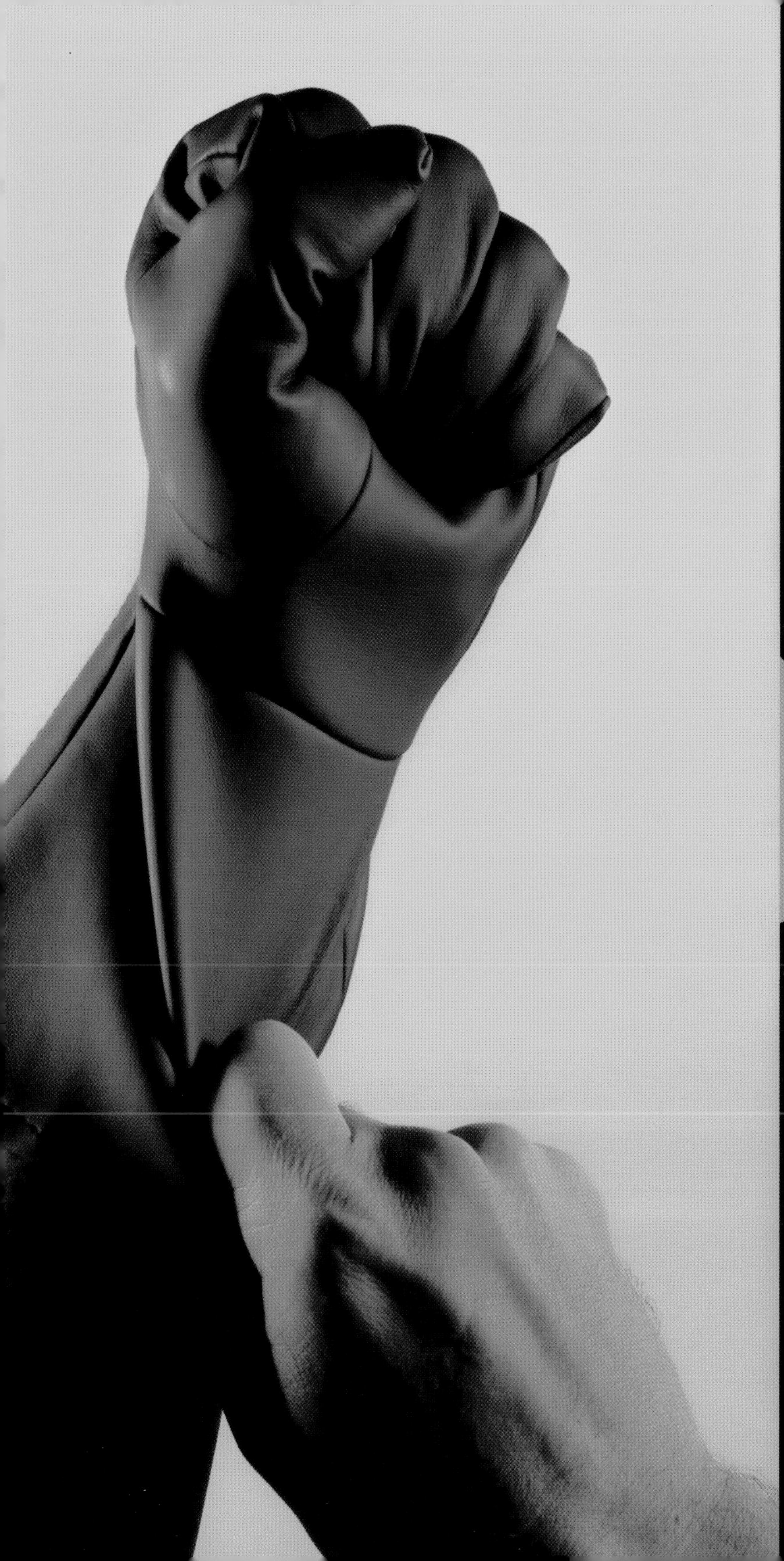

SOON I WILL BE INVINCIBLE

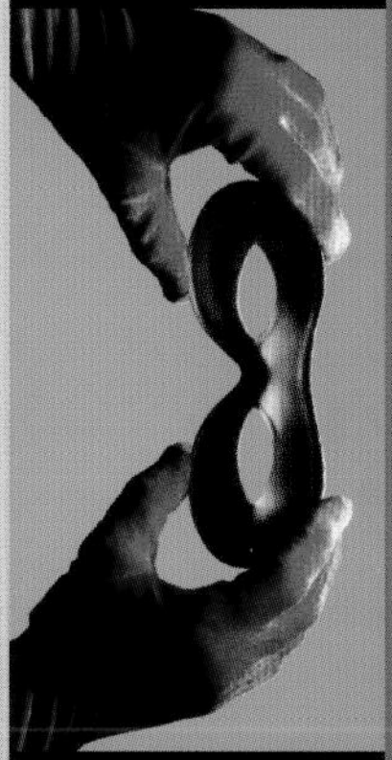

AUSTIN GROSSMAN

PANTHEON

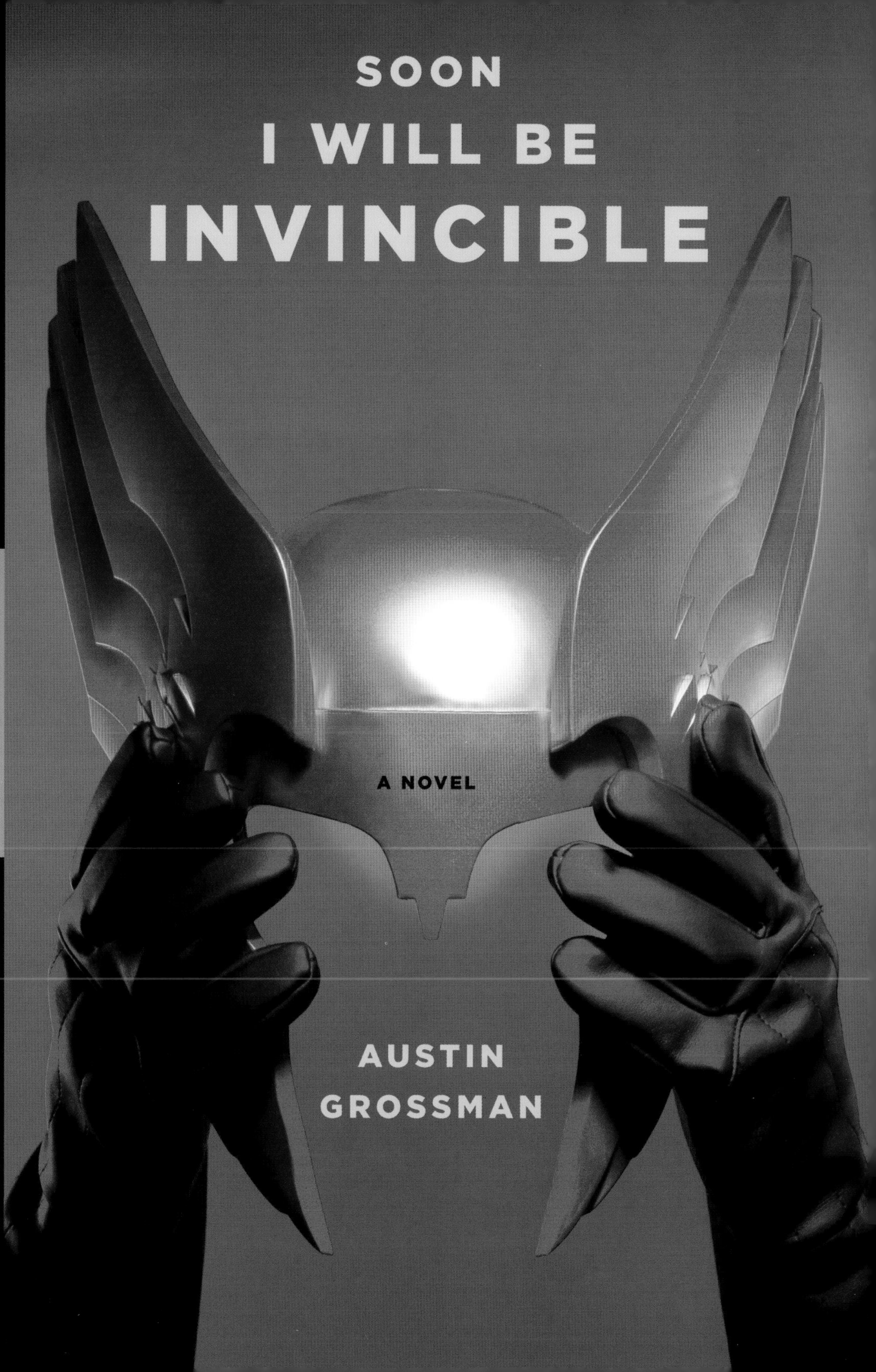

# SOON I WILL BE INVINCIBLE

A NOVEL

AUSTIN GROSSMAN

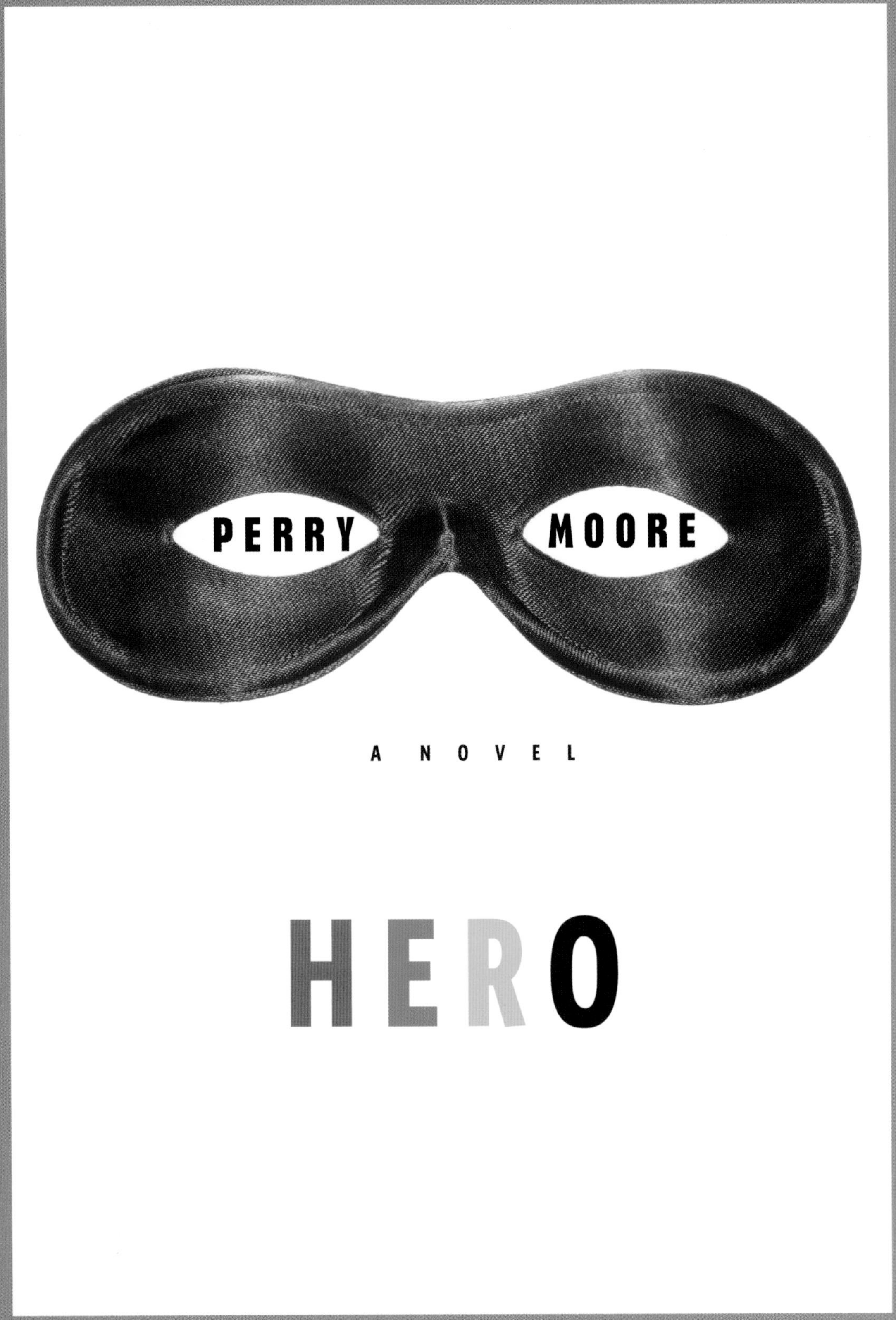
PERRY
MOORE
A NOVEL
HERO

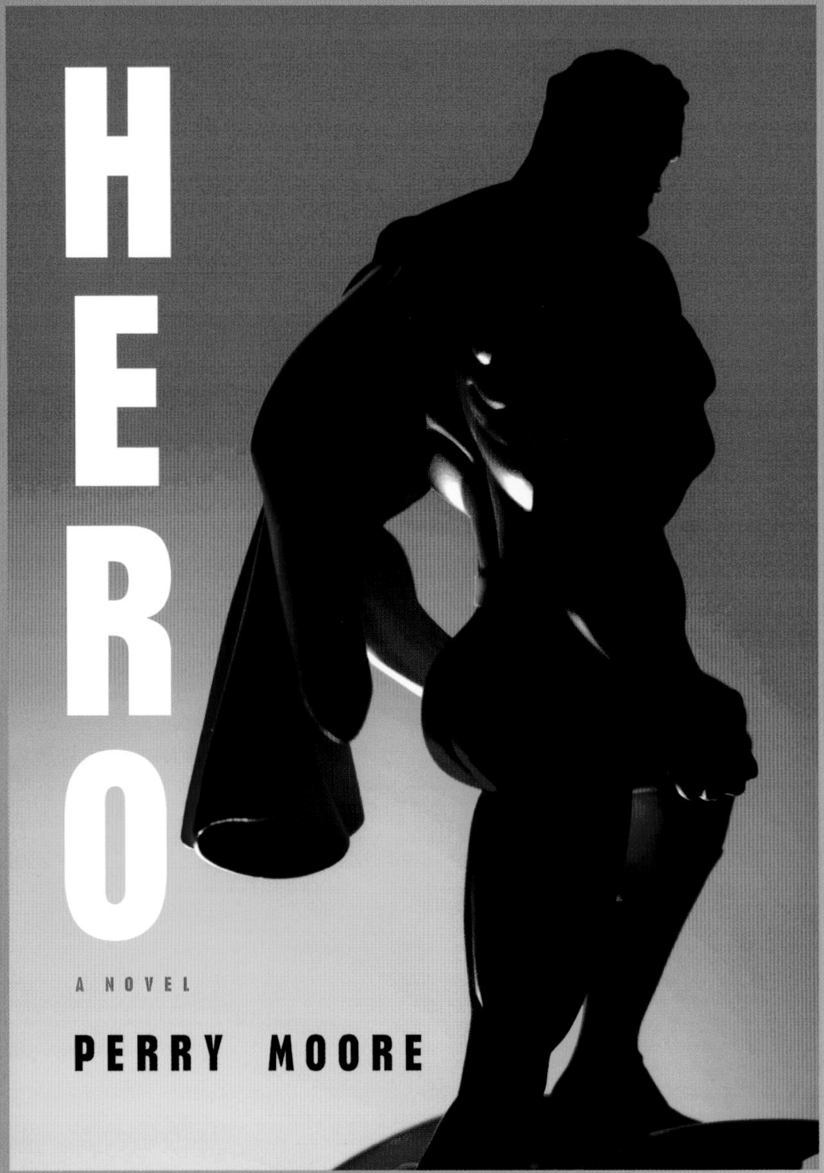
HERO
A NOVEL
PERRY MOORE

## Well-Drawn Characters

*Hero*, by Perry Moore, uses the superhero trope in a different way—with the goal of acceptance towards same-sex desire and orientation within the genre. My first thought was to photograph an officially licensed Superman statue (above) and have Geoff light it so that it could be any caped hero, while highlighting his—*ahem*—assets. Talk about buns of steel! This was a little too much for the publisher, so I went with a more iconic take on the

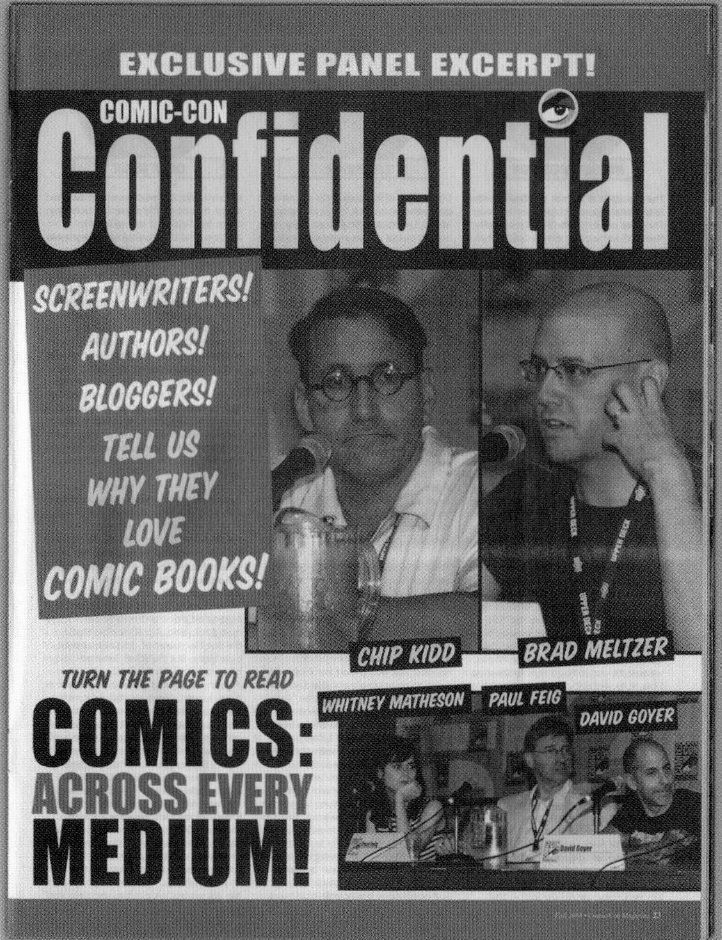
EXCLUSIVE PANEL EXCERPT!
COMIC-CON
Confidential
SCREENWRITERS! AUTHORS! BLOGGERS! TELL US WHY THEY LOVE COMIC BOOKS!
CHIP KIDD
BRAD MELTZER
TURN THE PAGE TO READ
COMICS: ACROSS EVERY MEDIUM!
WHITNEY MATHESON
PAUL FEIG
DAVID GOYER

classic "Robin-type" mask (opposite, left). Perry's first and last name each had five letters, so they balanced perfectly in the eyeholes. And since there were four letters in the title, I was able to use the color scheme of CMYK printing (cyan, magenta, yellow, black)—which I've incorporated into many designs (see the spine of *1Q84,* p. 11, and the logo for Abrams ComicArts, p. 218, just to name two).

**OPPOSITE, LEFT:** Hyperion, 2007. **ABOVE:** A parody tabloid page from the good old San Diego ComicCon program book, circa 2007. This panel holds amazing memories for me, as the other panelists are so incredibly accomplished. (I remember Paul Feig turning to me beforehand to say he was a fan [!!] and when I asked him what he was working on he replied with something along the lines of, "This movie called *Bridesmaids,* I'm so excited about it!" Now we all know why.) **RIGHT:** The MoCCA fest is the scrappy indie counterpoint to ComicCon's industry juggernaut, and I love it just as much. In 2006 they asked me to design the poster, and I in turn asked my friend the genius Charles Burns if I could use his art. As you can see, he said yes.

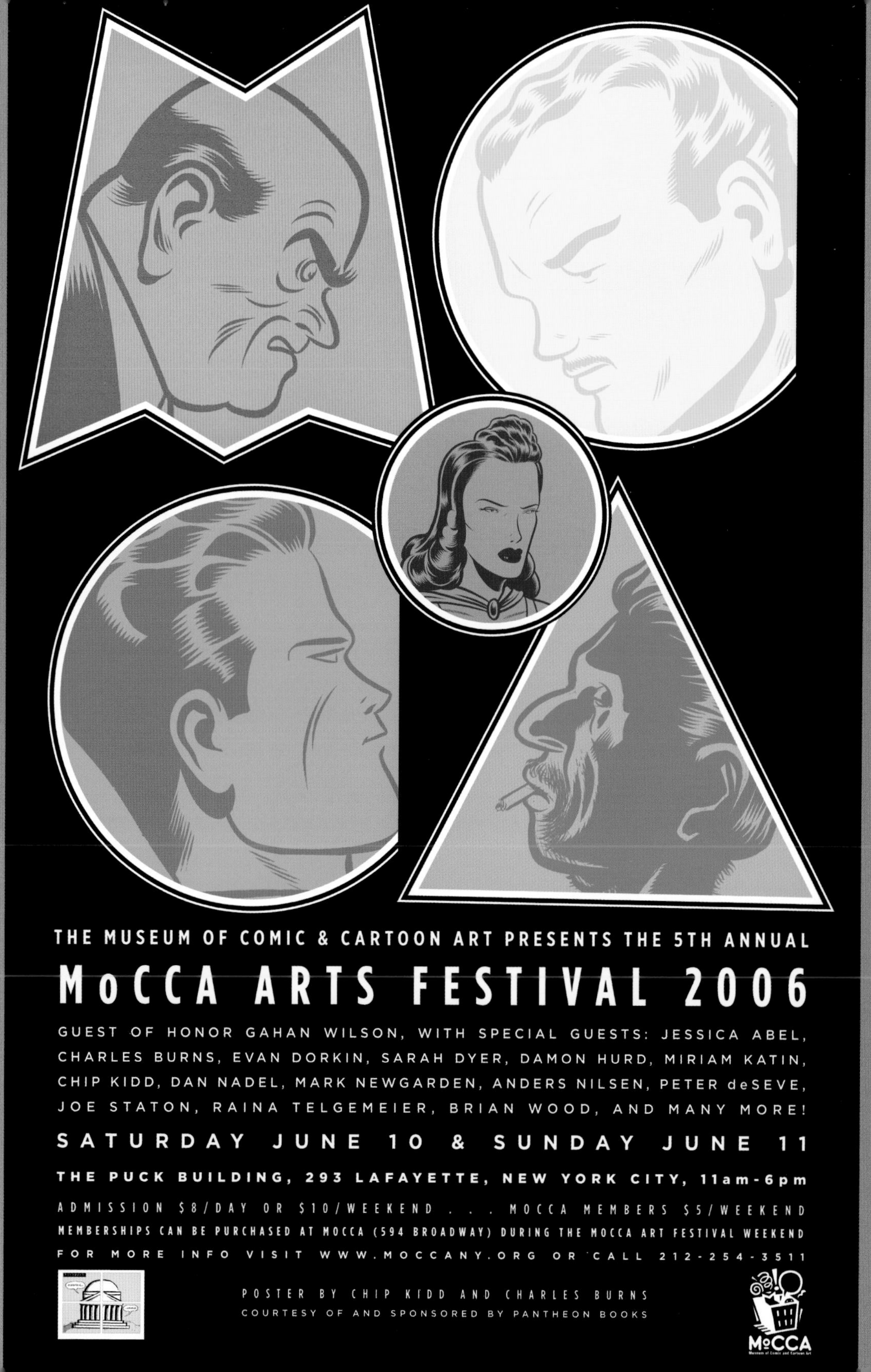
THE MUSEUM OF COMIC & CARTOON ART PRESENTS THE 5TH ANNUAL
MoCCA ARTS FESTIVAL 2006
GUEST OF HONOR GAHAN WILSON, WITH SPECIAL GUESTS: JESSICA ABEL, CHARLES BURNS, EVAN DORKIN, SARAH DYER, DAMON HURD, MIRIAM KATIN, CHIP KIDD, DAN NADEL, MARK NEWGARDEN, ANDERS NILSEN, PETER deSEVE, JOE STATON, RAINA TELGEMEIER, BRIAN WOOD, AND MANY MORE!
SATURDAY JUNE 10 & SUNDAY JUNE 11
THE PUCK BUILDING, 293 LAFAYETTE, NEW YORK CITY, 11am-6pm
ADMISSION $8/DAY OR $10/WEEKEND . . . MOCCA MEMBERS $5/WEEKEND
MEMBERSHIPS CAN BE PURCHASED AT MOCCA (594 BROADWAY) DURING THE MOCCA ART FESTIVAL WEEKEND
FOR MORE INFO VISIT WWW.MOCCANY.ORG OR CALL 212-254-3511
POSTER BY CHIP KIDD AND CHARLES BURNS
COURTESY OF AND SPONSORED BY PANTHEON BOOKS
MoCCA

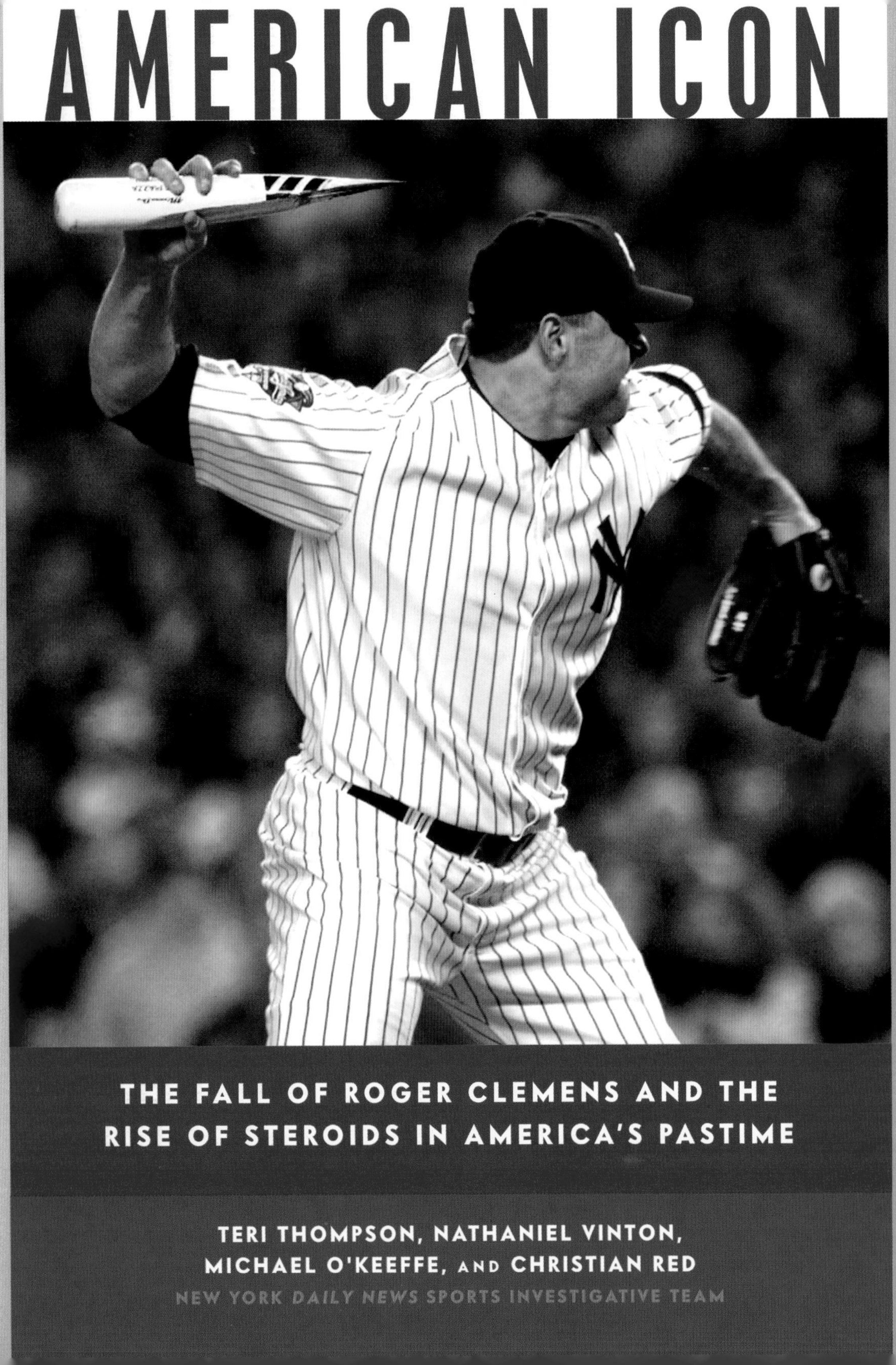
AMERICAN ICON
THE FALL OF ROGER CLEMENS AND THE RISE OF STEROIDS IN AMERICA'S PASTIME
TERI THOMPSON, NATHANIEL VINTON, MICHAEL O'KEEFFE, AND CHRISTIAN RED
NEW YORK DAILY NEWS SPORTS INVESTIGATIVE TEAM

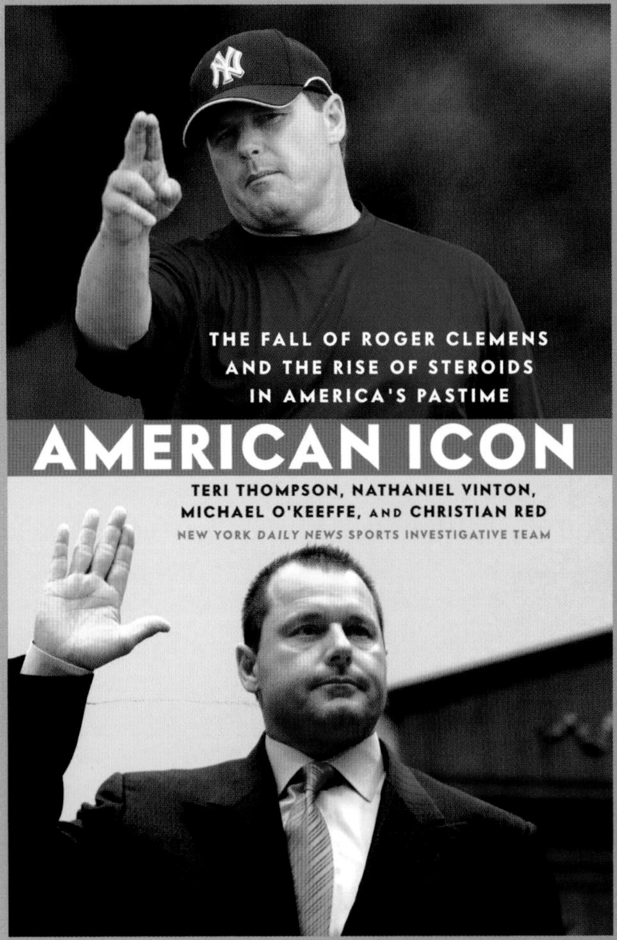
THE FALL OF ROGER CLEMENS AND THE RISE OF STEROIDS IN AMERICA'S PASTIME
AMERICAN ICON
TERI THOMPSON, NATHANIEL VINTON, MICHAEL O'KEEFFE, AND CHRISTIAN RED
NEW YORK DAILY NEWS SPORTS INVESTIGATIVE TEAM

## Sporting Chances

In case it comes as a surprise, I am not exactly a sports fan. Okay, that's the understatement of the century. But I think a good designer should be able to solve problems based on a wide range of subjects, even if said subjects might not be of particular interest to them. (This is not the same as creating design to promote something you are morally against, there is a huge difference, more on that later.) But I certainly knew who Roger Clemens was, and what he had done, because I am a New Yorker of more than three decades. As such, it is pretty much impossible not to hear, read, and see everything about the Mets and the Yankees and all of their shenanigans, whether you want to or not. (I resent this, as I do with reality TV: onerous celebrities and everything else the media

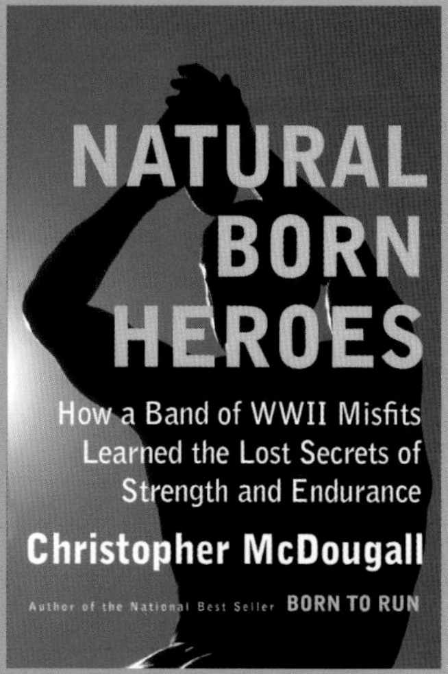
NATURAL
BORN
HEROES
How a Band of WWII Misfits
Learned the Lost Secrets of
Strength and Endurance
Christopher McDougall
Author of the National Best Seller BORN TO RUN

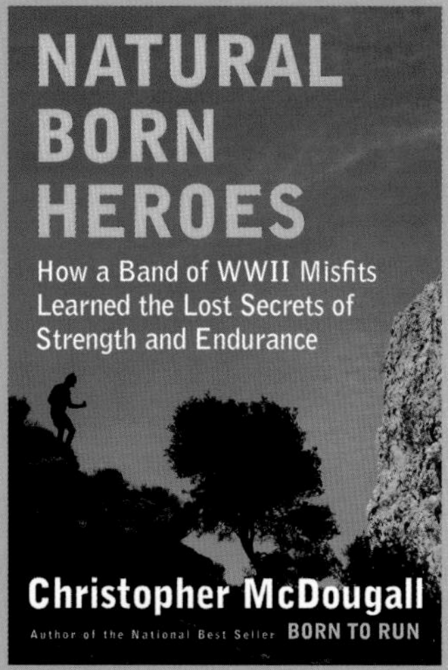
NATURAL
BORN
HEROES
How a Band of WWII Misfits
Learned the Lost Secrets of
Strength and Endurance
Christopher McDougall
Author of the National Best Seller BORN TO RUN

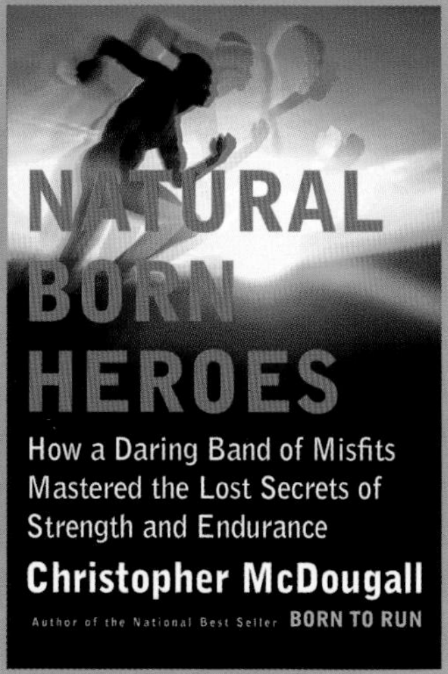
NATURAL
BORN
HEROES
How a Daring Band of Misfits
Mastered the Lost Secrets of
Strength and Endurance
Christopher McDougall
Author of the National Best Seller BORN TO RUN

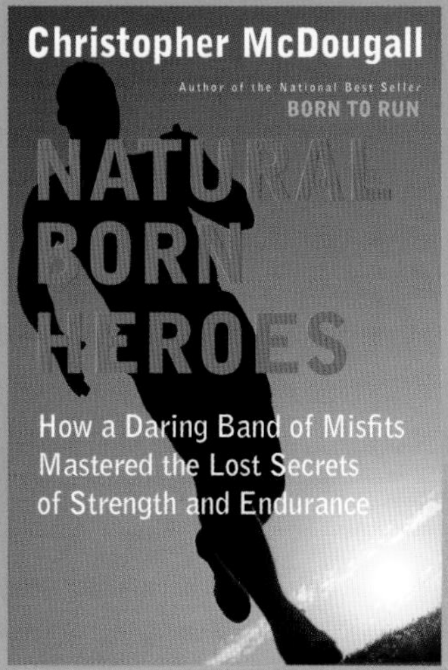
Christopher McDougall
Author of the National Best Seller
BORN TO RUN
NATURAL
BORN
HEROES
How a Daring Band of Misfits
Mastered the Lost Secrets
of Strength and Endurance

will not let us ignore, no matter how much we want to. But mea culpa, I'm part of the media, so I am guilty, too.) Anyway, I loved the juxtaposition of the photograph of Clemens making a signal on the field and then swearing under oath that he didn't use steroids (opposite, right). Ultimately, this design didn't have the power of the unforgettable image of Clemens wielding a broken bat like a hunting knife or battle spear (opposite, left).

**OPPOSITE:** Knopf, 2009. **ABOVE:** Even though Christopher McDougall's book is a WWII period piece, I first experimented with the visual vernacular of contemporary ads for sports events and gear. **RIGHT:** The final image is not as stylized and shows that much of the action takes place at night (it is a composite image). Knopf, 2015.

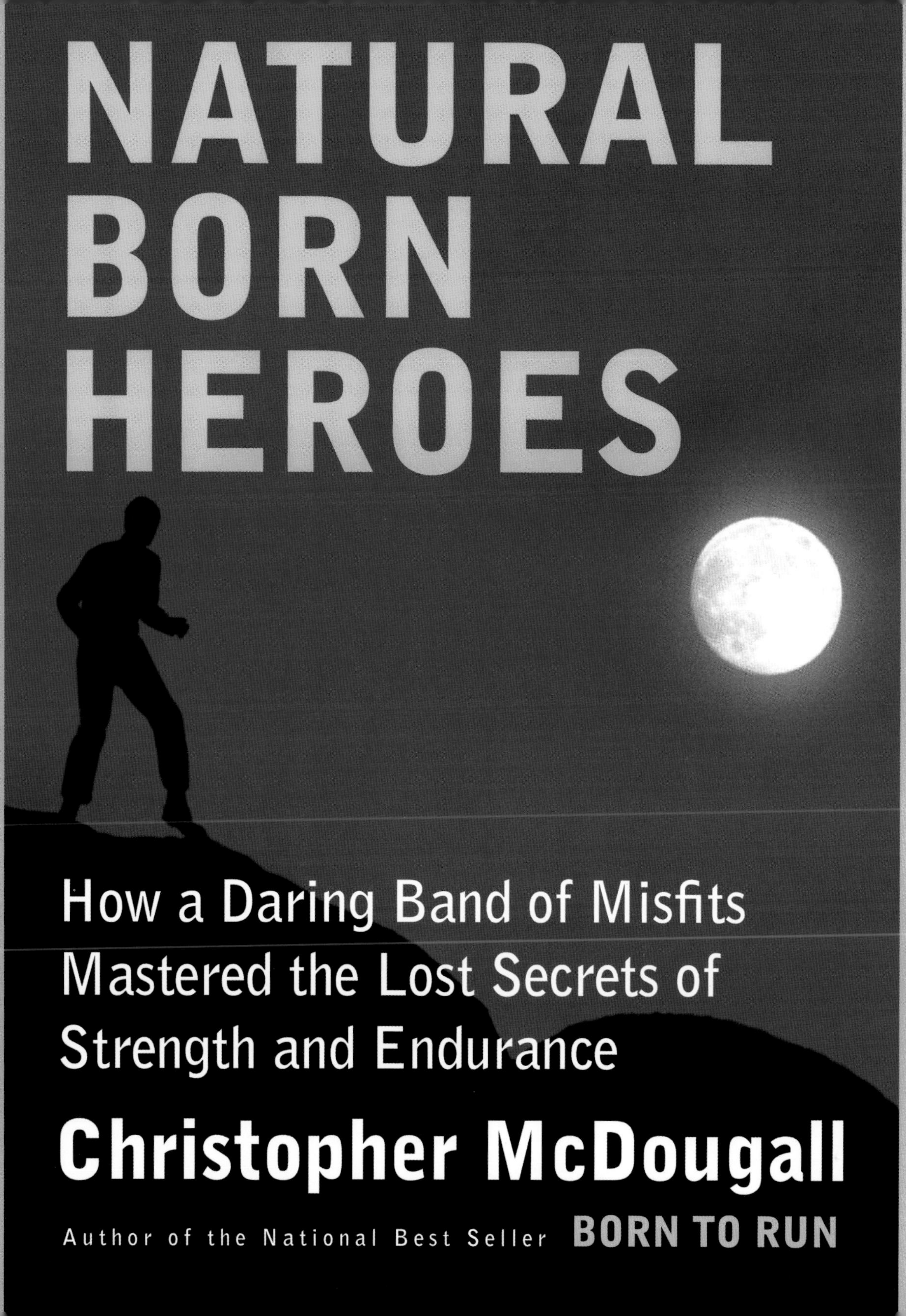
NATURAL
BORN
HEROES
How a Daring Band of Misfits
Mastered the Lost Secrets of
Strength and Endurance
Christopher McDougall
Author of the National Best Seller BORN TO RUN

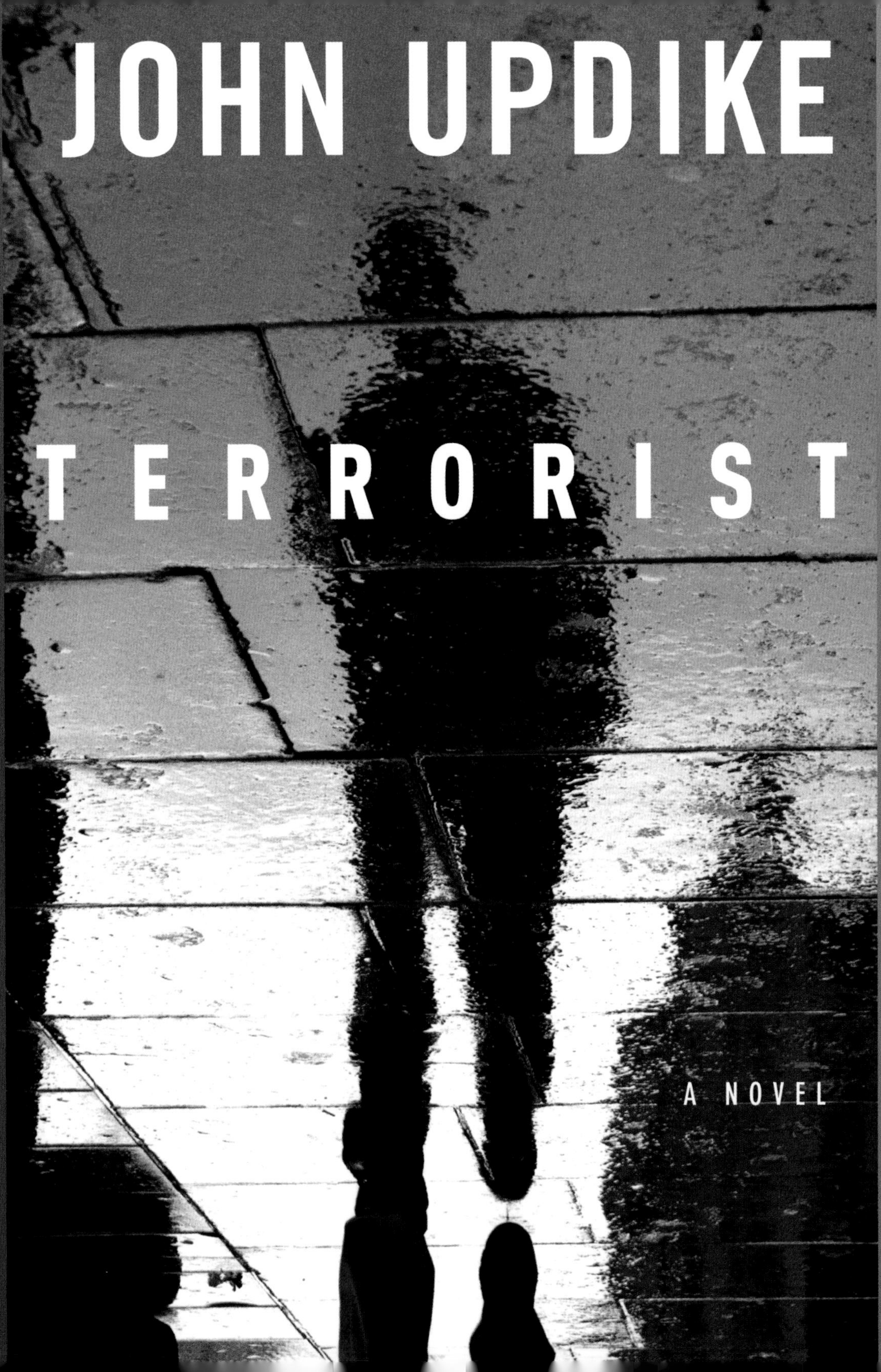
JOHN UPDIKE
TERRORIST
A NOVEL

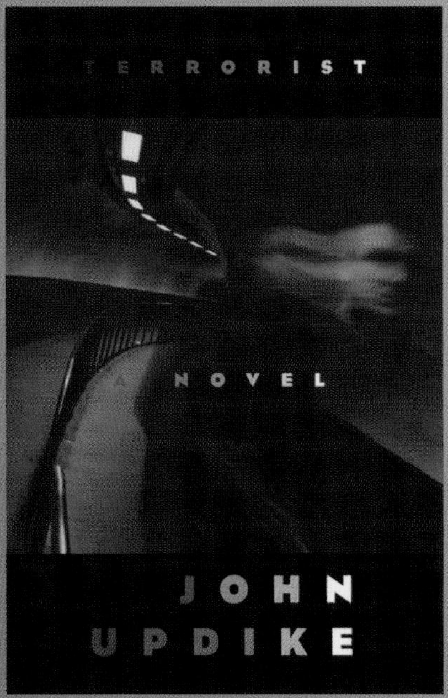
TERRORIST
A NOVEL
JOHN
UPDIKE

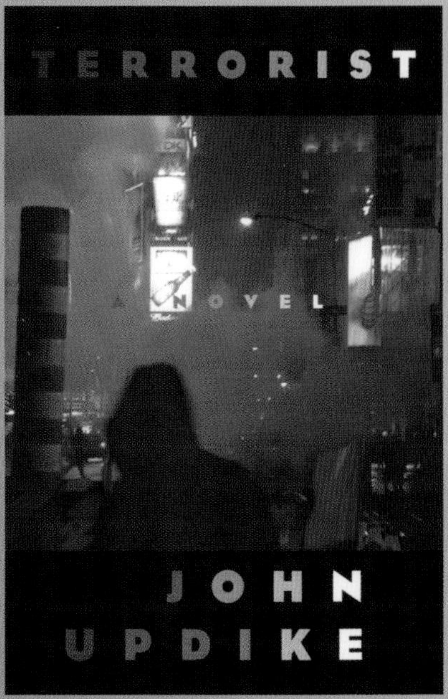
TERRORIST
A NOVEL
JOHN
UPDIKE

Nov. 9. 2005

Dear Chip:

Your jacket is terrific, brilliant, masterly, worthy of the Chip Kidd I keep reading about in the papers.

It wasn't what I expected when I came into Judith's office -- I thought I'd see a version of my newspaper idea -- so I did a double-take, like everybody else, and then laughed. *Seek My Face* was meant to cause a double-take, but it always looked a bit too much like a face, and Ballantine's paperback even more so. But this is a real fooler, and when you turn the thing upside you realize not only that it is a reflection but that the man is walking *toward* you, whereas his reflection seems definitely to be walking *away*. I was worried that you had cut off too much of the (real) feet at the bottom, and on looking at the original I see you snipped off only a miniscule amount, and I'll assume you know what you're doing and did the best cropping possible.

Then I underwent a little qualm that the author and title look too much as if *I'm* the terrorist; but no, the size and spacing are such that only a moron, who had never seen a jacket before, would misread. And "A Novel" is clear enough, and perfectly placed.

The whole thing is perfect, in fact, including the purple. Don't change a thing. This was an impossible book to put a jacket on, and you've done it.

And during a period, I know, when you're busy with your own amazing book. A writer, so called, gave the sermon in the local Episcopal church last Sunday, and when I shook his hand at the door he congratulated me on the foreword for "Chip's book." His name is Michael Malone -- do you know him? What *I* dote upon is, of course, the photos of our two fathers, and long-razed SHS, and the hopeful little urchin behind his mimeograph stencil.

Congratulations, and many thanks for that scary upside-down jacket.

John

# Bidding Adieu

The letter opposite is the single most touching and meaningful from an author I have ever received, for several reasons. First, I think the jacket for *Terrorist* is the best I was ever able to create for Mr. Updike, and he seems to agree. Full disclosure: he provided the art, but I was the one who turned it upside-down (opposite, left) and ignored the author's suggestion of placing it within a newspaper front-page context. That would've been too busy, and if you invert the book and look at the image, it suddenly becomes too mundane. This was presumptuous on my part, but I thought it was the right thing to try—if he didn't like it, then I'd change it. I didn't have to. Second, this project came along as I was putting the finishing touches on *Book One,* for which he had—with great grace and attention to detail—written the foreword, and he notes that here. I do indeed know the writer Michael Malone, who is a dear friend for whom I designed several covers (that were featured in *Book One*). I had no idea he preached (!!). Third, there was always the special bond Mr. Updike and I shared via our fathers: Wesley Updike was Thomas Kidd's math teacher at Shillington (Pennsylvania) High School from 1944 to 1946. John was perpetually touched by this connection, as was I. It seemed fated—in the best way—that we would eventually work together.

**OPPOSITE, FAR LEFT:** Knopf, 2006.

**OPPOSITE, TOP RIGHT:** Some preliminary design sketches for *Terrorist*.

**NEAR RIGHT & RIGHT:** John's meditation on the career of Ted Williams, designed soon after the author's death. I first looked at baseball card art (how can you not?), but a photo was more effective—look at the hope in those eyes! Plus, the title is so potentially befuddling, I wanted your eyes to hit the author's name first. Many thanks to Martha Updike, John's widow, for her support on this project. Library of America, 2010.

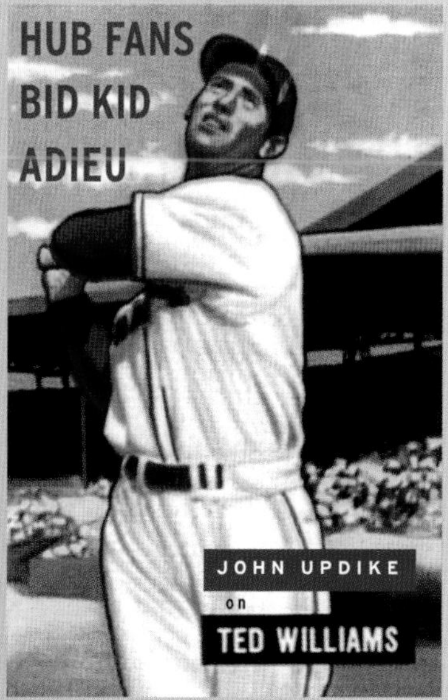
HUB FANS
BID KID
ADIEU
JOHN UPDIKE
on
TED WILLIAMS

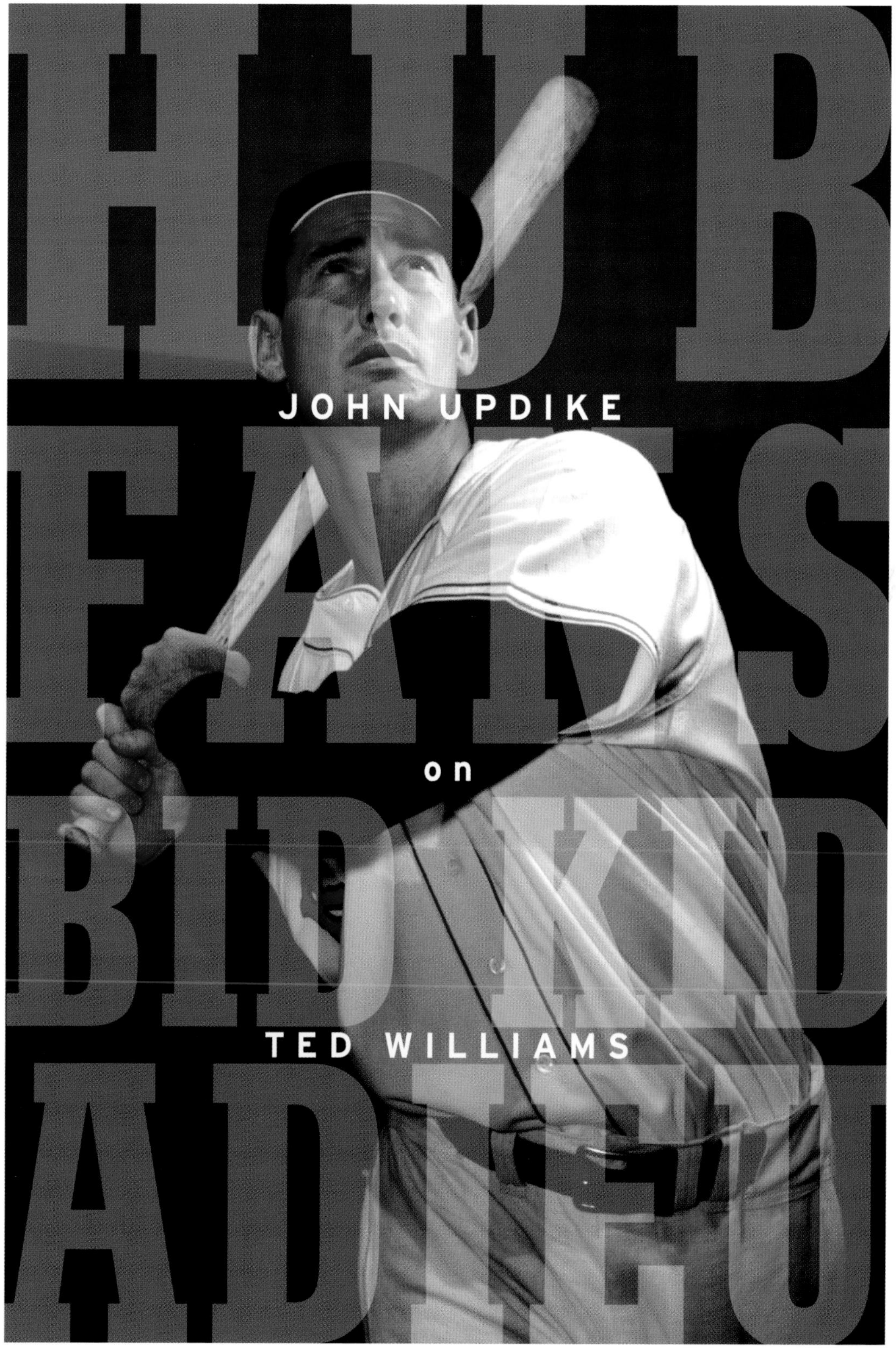
HUB
FANS
BID KID
ADIEU
JOHN UPDIKE
on
TED WILLIAMS

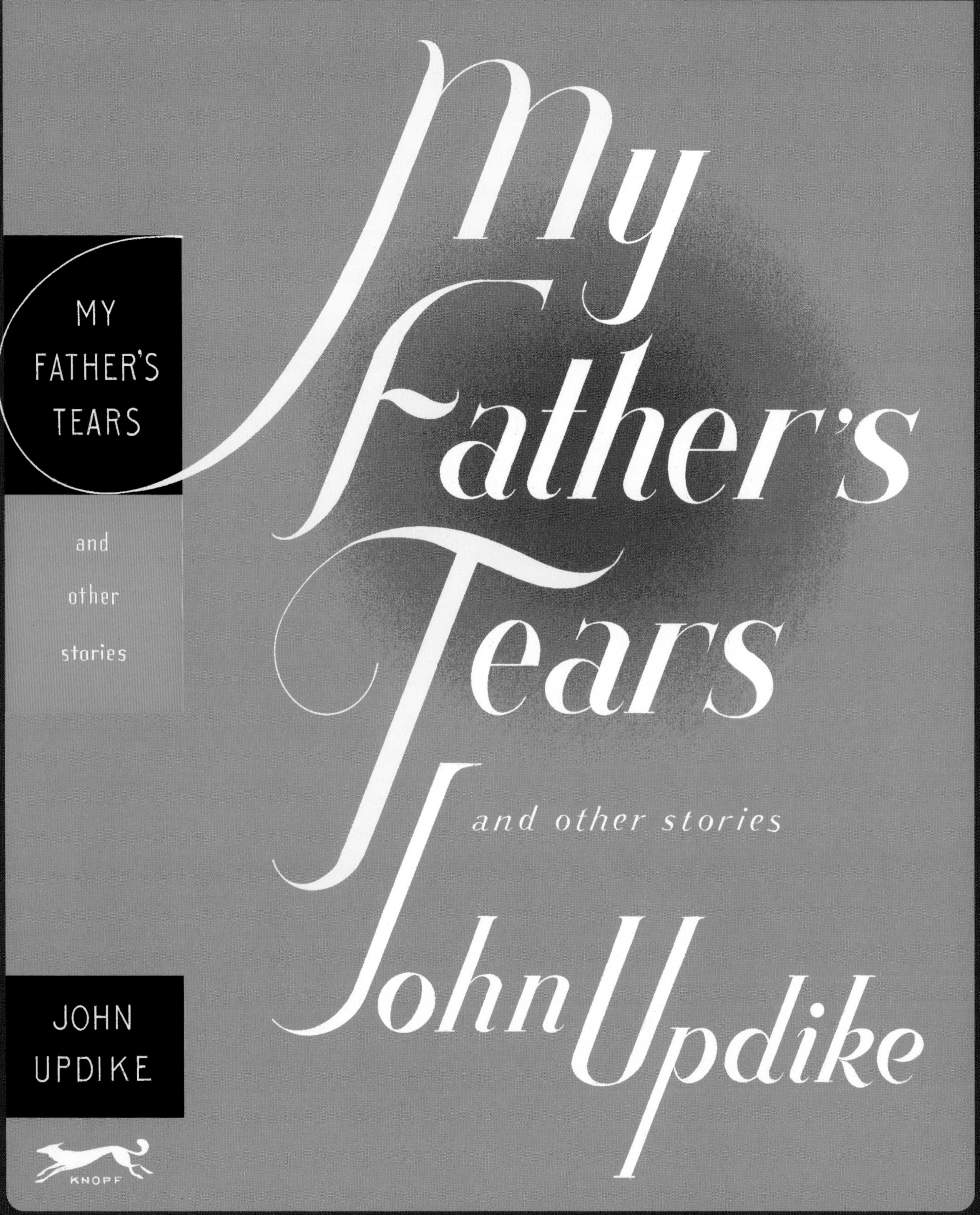
My Father's Tears
and other stories
John Updike
MY FATHER'S TEARS
and other stories
JOHN UPDIKE
KNOPF

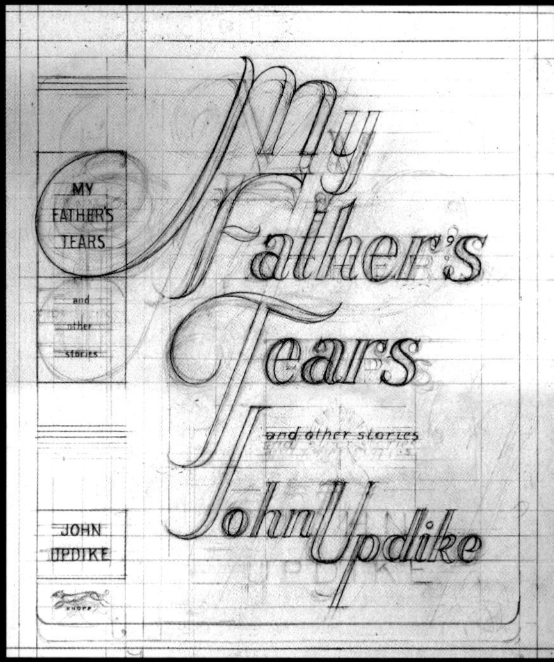
My Father's Tears
and other stories
John Updike
MY FATHER'S TEARS
and other stories
JOHN UPDIKE

I felt Chris Ware (p. 161) was the best person to design what was to be Mr. Updike's last book of stories, *My Father's Tears*, because he was such a fan. I thought the jacket needed to be hand-lettered—and there's no one better for that than Chris. Heartbreakingly, John didn't agree (below) . . .

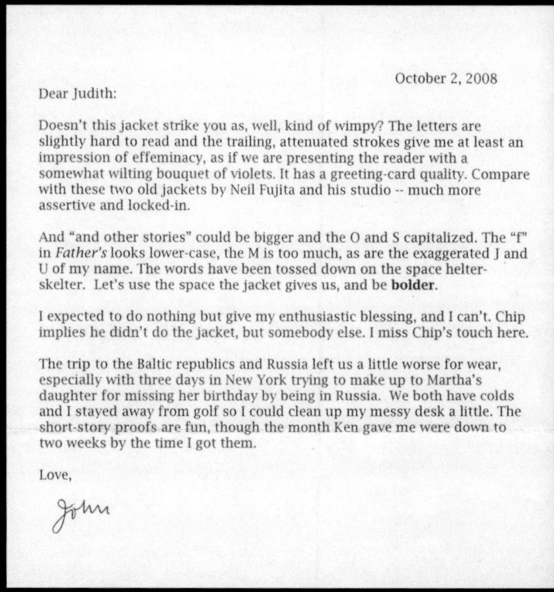

October 2, 2008

Dear Judith:

Doesn't this jacket strike you as, well, kind of wimpy? The letters are slightly hard to read and the trailing, attenuated strokes give me at least an impression of effeminacy, as if we are presenting the reader with a somewhat wilting bouquet of violets. It has a greeting-card quality. Compare with these two old jackets by Neil Fujita and his studio -- much more assertive and locked-in.

And "and other stories" could be bigger and the O and S capitalized. The "f" in *Father's* looks lower-case, the M is too much, as are the exaggerated J and U of my name. The words have been tossed down on the space helter-skelter. Let's use the space the jacket gives us, and be **bolder**.

I expected to do nothing but give my enthusiastic blessing, and I can't. Chip implies he didn't do the jacket, but somebody else. I miss Chip's touch here.

The trip to the Baltic republics and Russia left us a little worse for wear, especially with three days in New York trying to make up to Martha's daughter for missing her birthday by being in Russia. We both have colds and I stayed away from golf so I could clean up my messy desk a little. The short-story proofs are fun, though the month Ken gave me were down to two weeks by the time I got them.

Love,

John

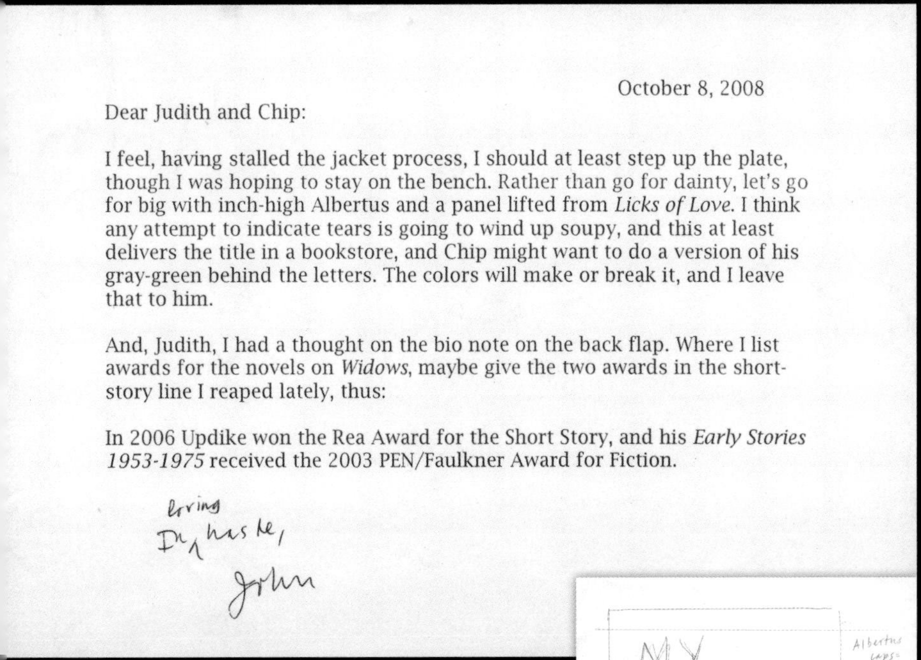
October 8, 2008

Dear Judith and Chip:

I feel, having stalled the jacket process, I should at least step up the plate, though I was hoping to stay on the bench. Rather than go for dainty, let's go for big with inch-high Albertus and a panel lifted from *Licks of Love*. I think any attempt to indicate tears is going to wind up soupy, and this at least delivers the title in a bookstore, and Chip might want to do a version of his gray-green behind the letters. The colors will make or break it, and I leave that to him.

And, Judith, I had a thought on the bio note on the back flap. Where I list awards for the novels on *Widows*, maybe give the two awards in the short-story line I reaped lately, thus:

In 2006 Updike won the Rea Award for the Short Story, and his *Early Stories 1953-1975* received the 2003 PEN/Faulkner Award for Fiction.

Loving
In haste,

John

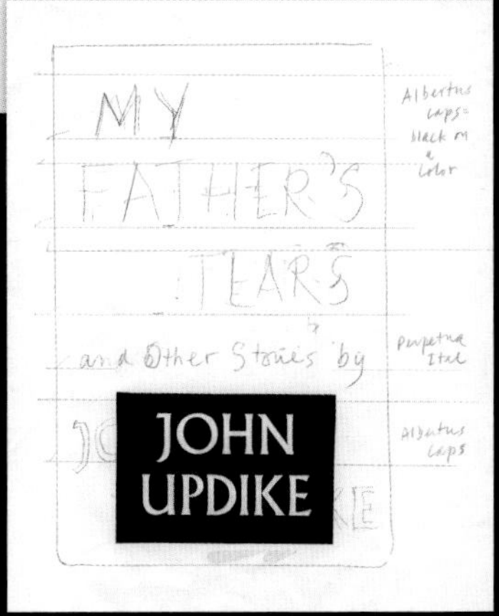
MY
FATHER'S
TEARS
and Other Stories by
JOHN
UPDIKE

. . and so he took it upon himself to go back to the heavy Albertus lettering that made the "Rabbit" books so distinctive (right). We had never argued with him on matters like this, and we weren't going to start. My boss and friend Carol Devine Carson took on the design duties from there and did an admirably handsome job.

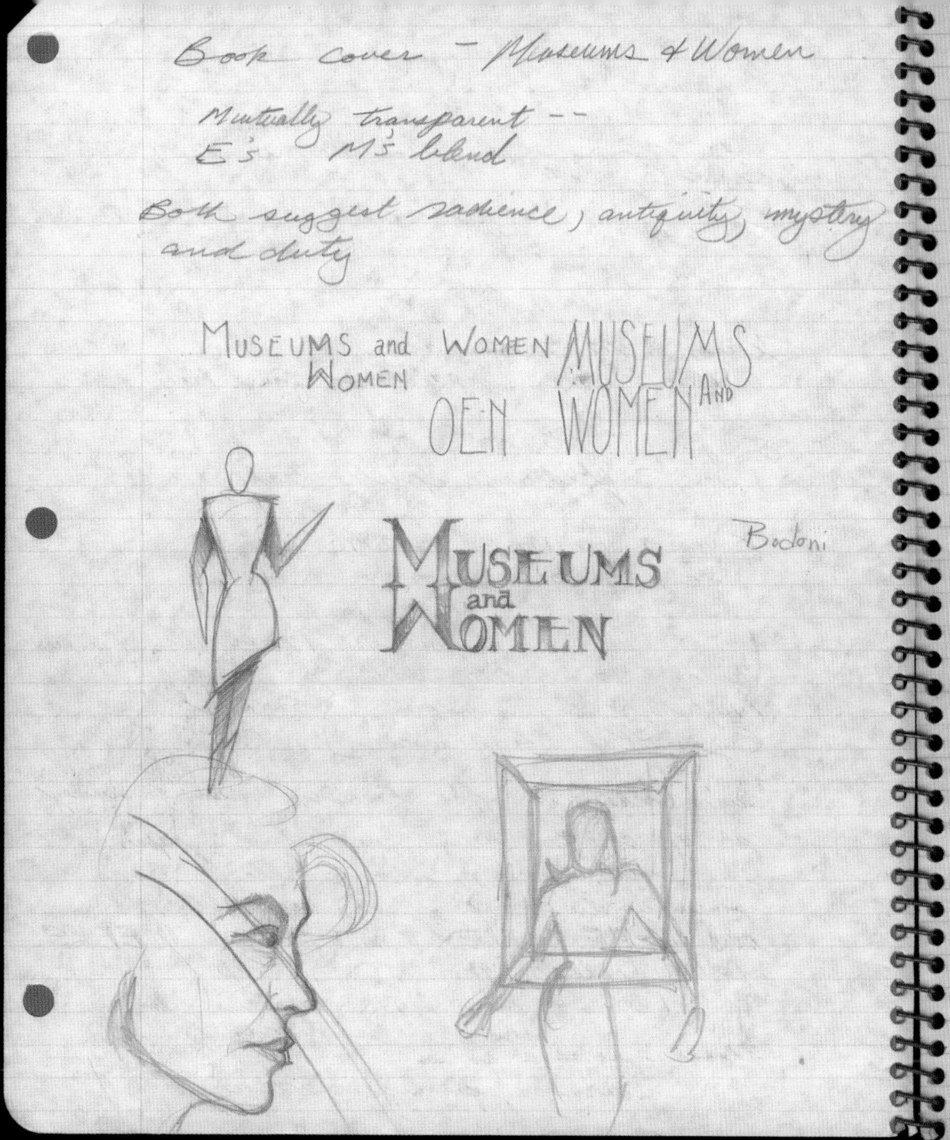
Book cover – Museums & Women
Mutually transparent --
E's M's blend
Both suggest sadness, antiquity, mystery and duty
MUSEUMS and WOMEN
MUSEUMS AND WOMEN
Bodoni
MUSEUMS and WOMEN

In the spring of 2015 I transferred the entire archive of my work to the Special Collections Library at my alma mater, Penn State. This was, for me, a momentous and moving occasion (both emotionally and literally) and a young archivist named Alyssa Carver was assigned to organize and tabulate all 300+ boxes of material (right) that ranged from my scratchings as a child, through my college projects, and including all of my professional work. She's done an amazing job, and one of the things she managed to unearth was something I'd been unable to find for *Book One*: a page of sketches I had done as a college sophomore for my first

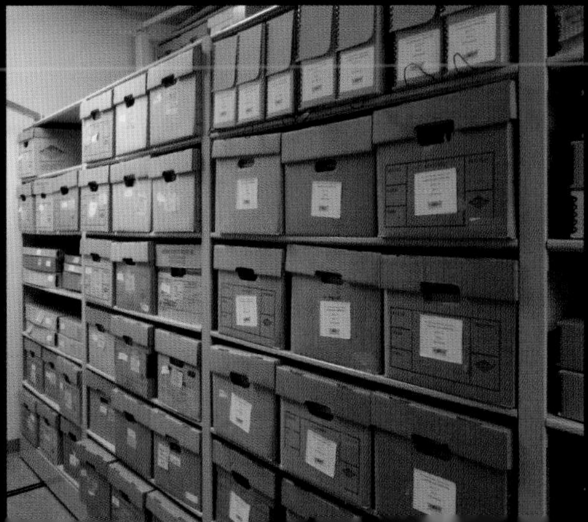

graphic design assignment, which was to create a cover for John Updike's collection of stories titled *Museums and Women*. I have told the tale of what a terrible job I did many times (see *Book One*, p. 24), but could never find the visuals to back it up (I must have destroyed the piece out of embarrassed rage). But here's the proof: bad drawings and totally misconceived typography. It was a good thing I had three more years in school to learn, along with great teachers and fellow students to help me do it. And the astonishing professional relationship that I eventually enjoyed with the author is so ironic, it will forever boggle my mind.

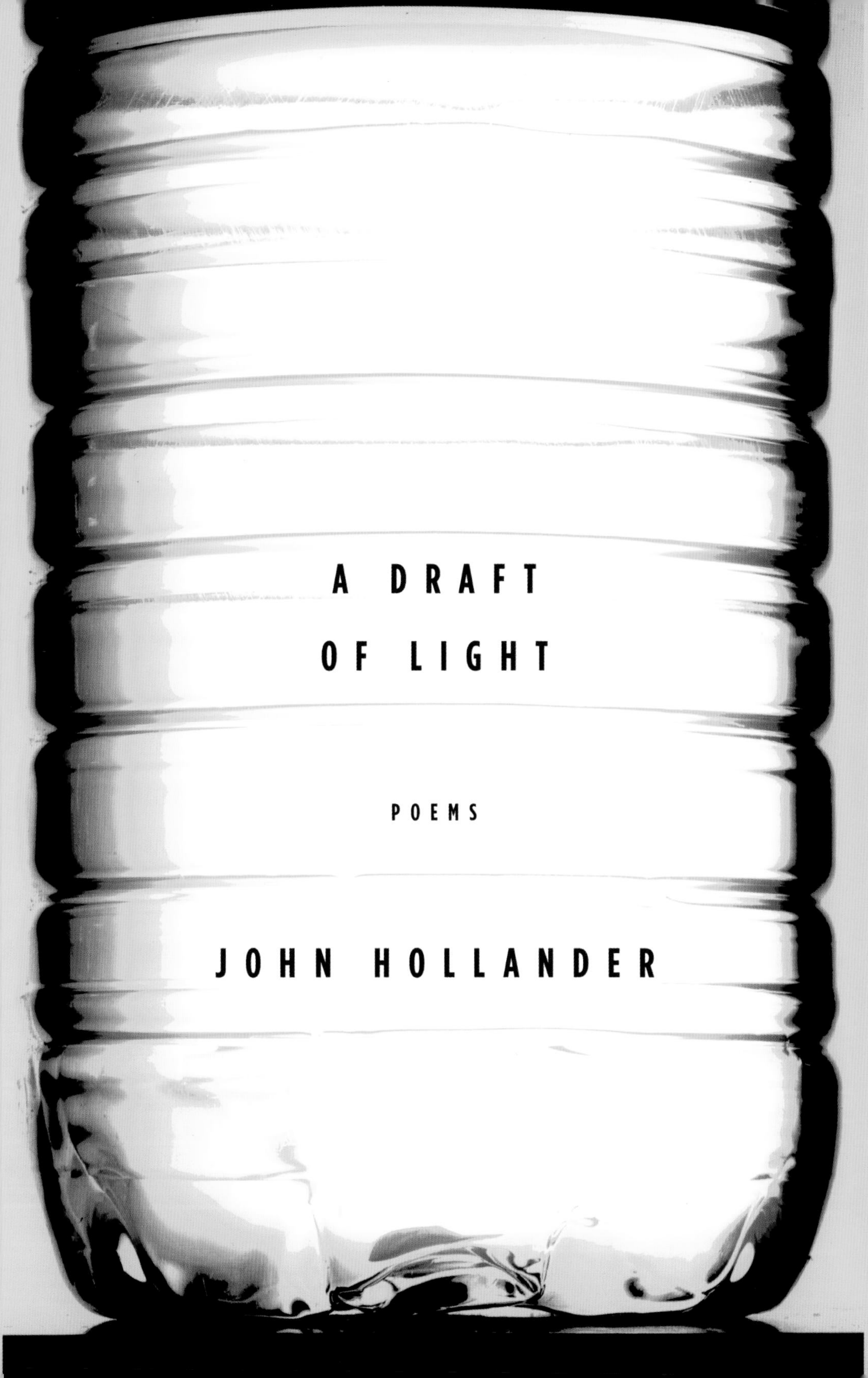
A DRAFT
OF LIGHT
POEMS
JOHN HOLLANDER



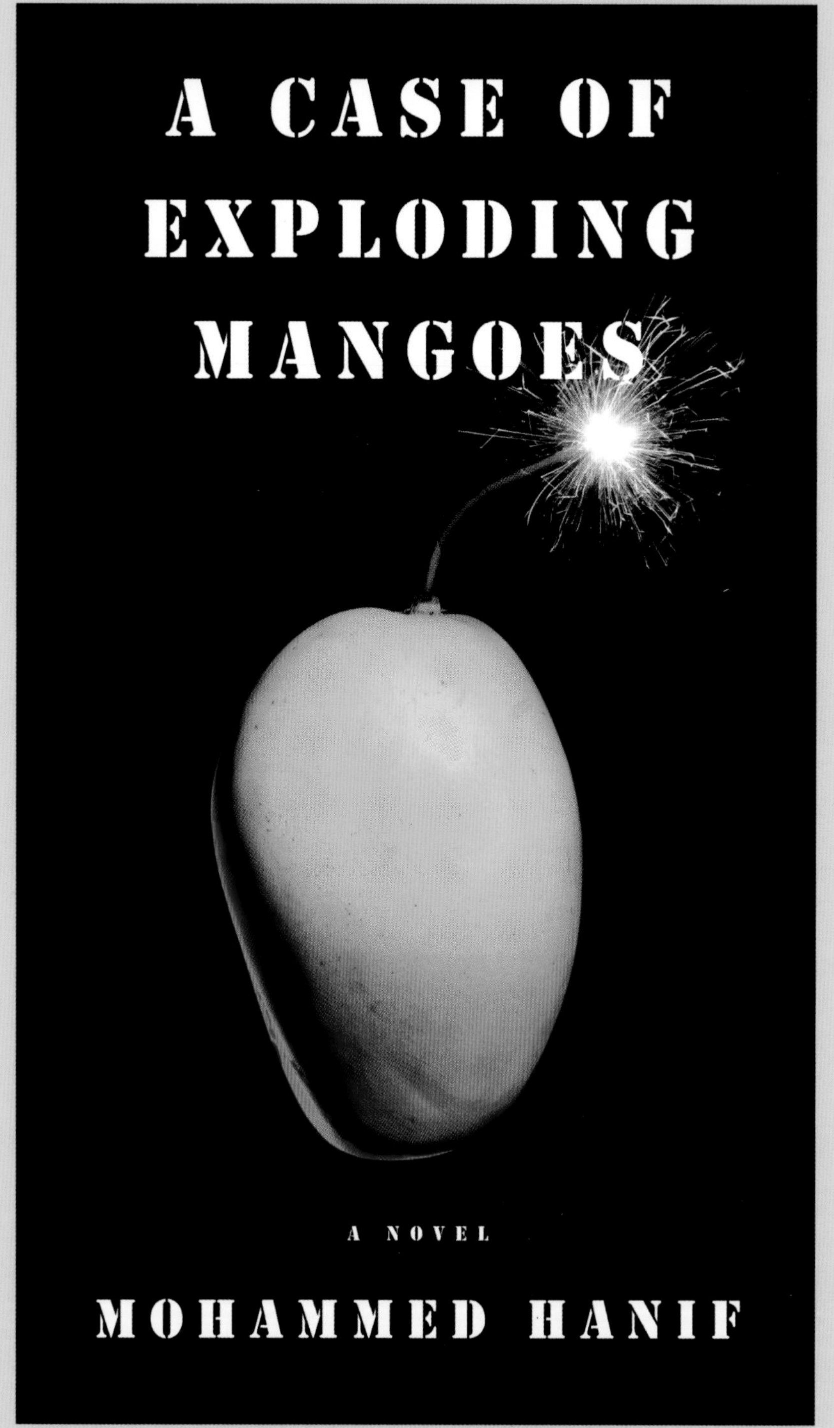
A CASE OF
EXPLODING
MANGOES
A NOVEL
MOHAMMED HANIF

**LEFT:** Knopf, 2008. Photography by Geoff Spear.
**ABOVE:** Knopf, 2008. Photography by Geoff Spear. **OPPOSITE, LEFT:** Knopf, 2013.
**OPPOSITE, RIGHT:** Knopf, 2007.

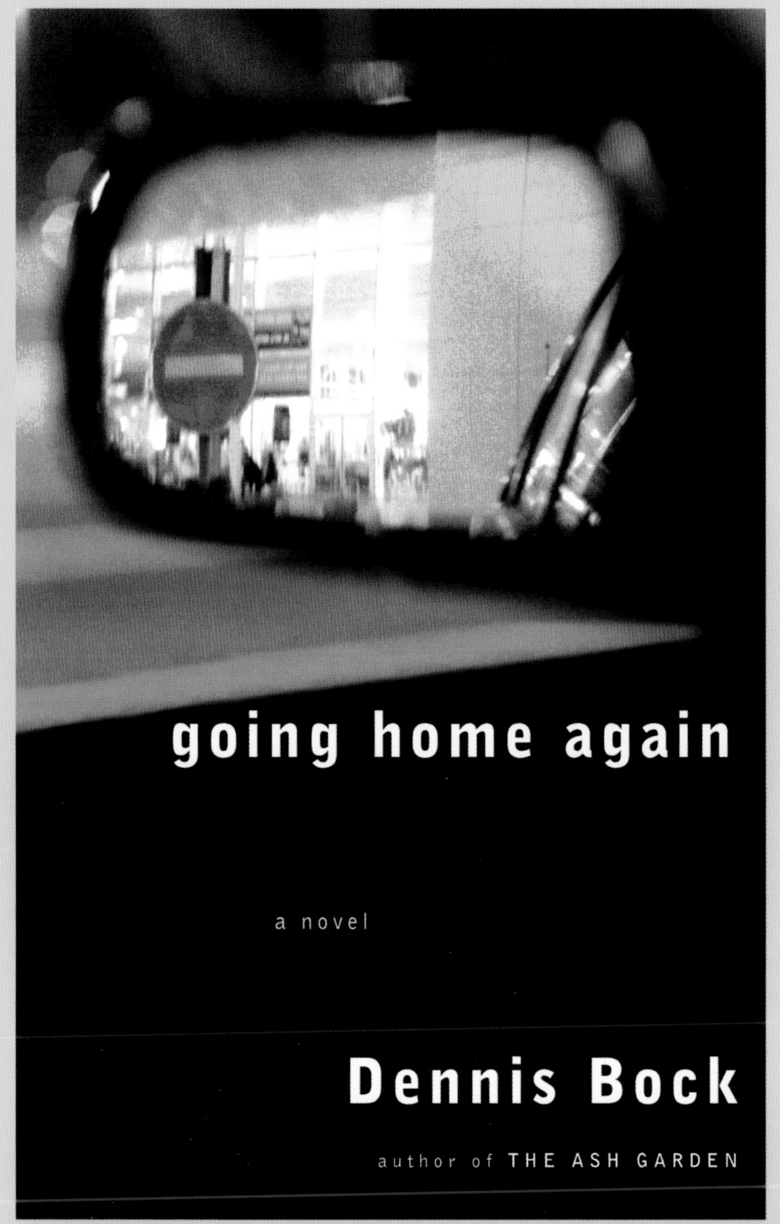
going home again
a novel
Dennis Bock
author of THE ASH GARDEN

## Gold Rush

As I write this, there has been a recent trend in book cover design (pointed out by no less than the *Wall Street Journal,* in a visual feature) concerning the use of golden yellow. I have been as guilty of using this color as everyone else, and I think the reasons are clear: it's warm, it's inviting, it's visual comfort food.

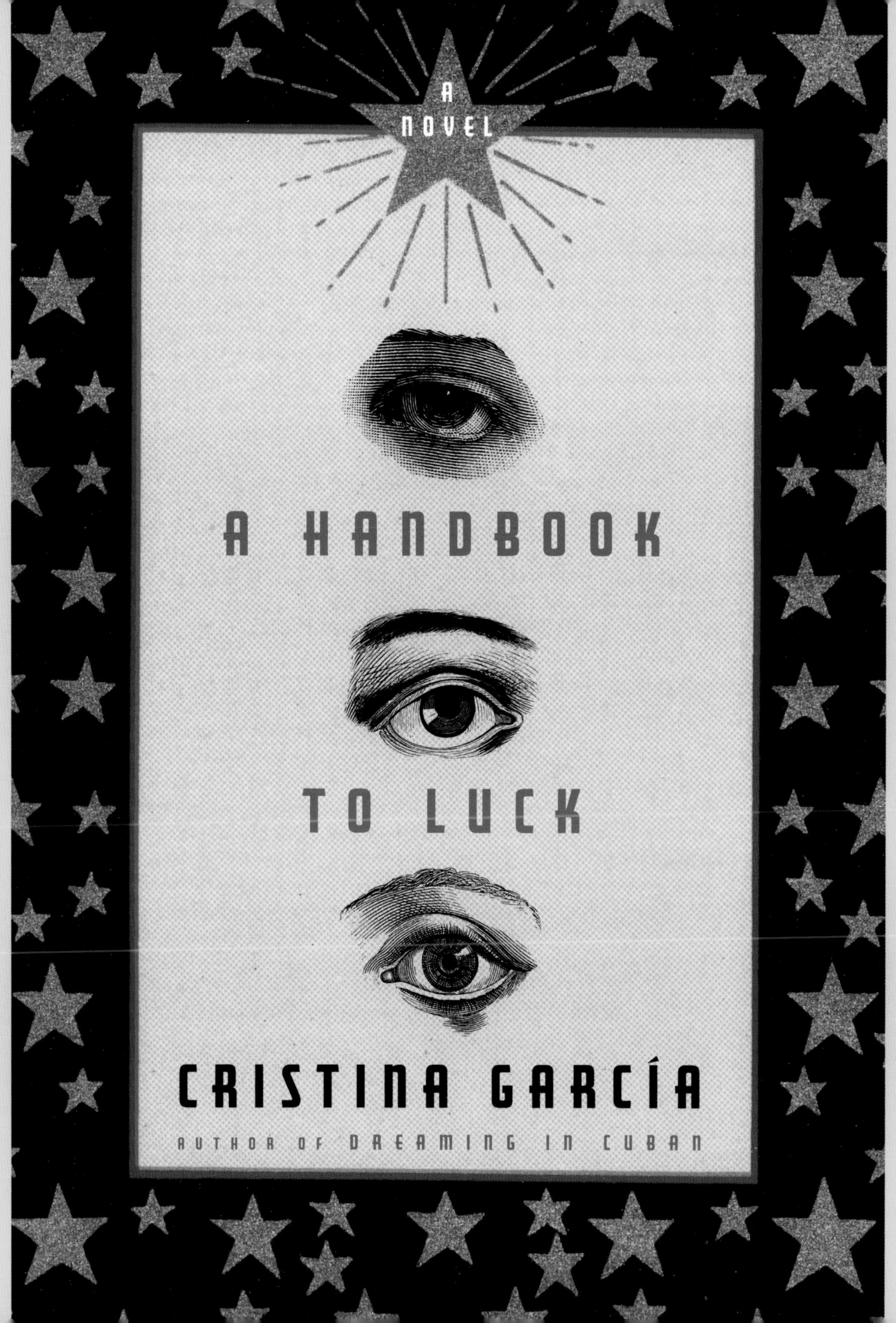
A NOVEL
A HANDBOOK
TO LUCK
CRISTINA GARCÍA
AUTHOR OF DREAMING IN CUBAN

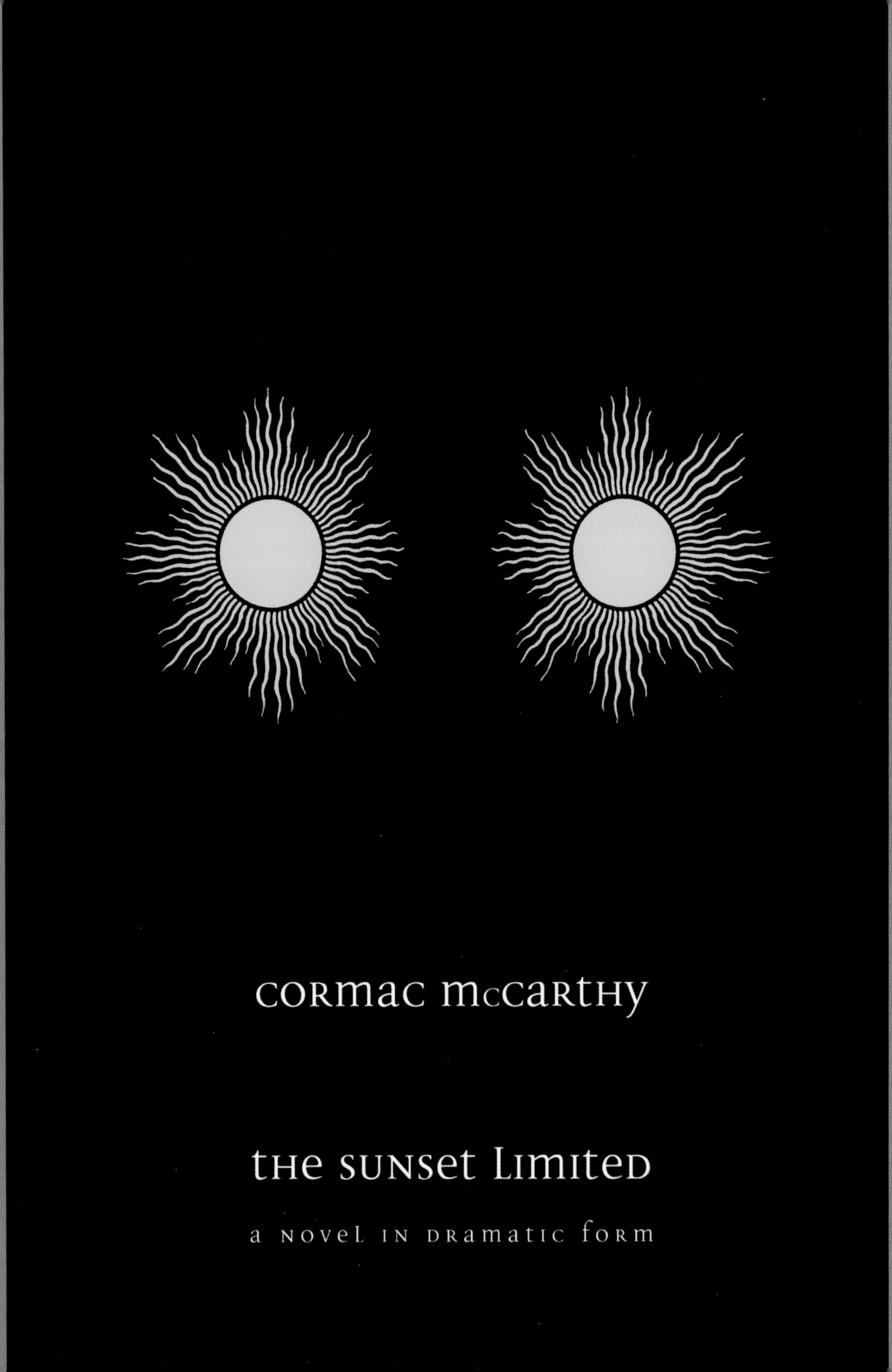
cormac mccarthy
the sunset limited
a novel in dramatic form

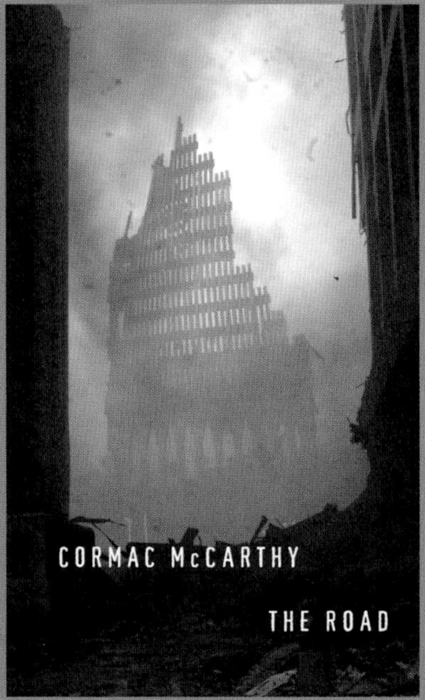
CORMAC McCARTHY
THE ROAD

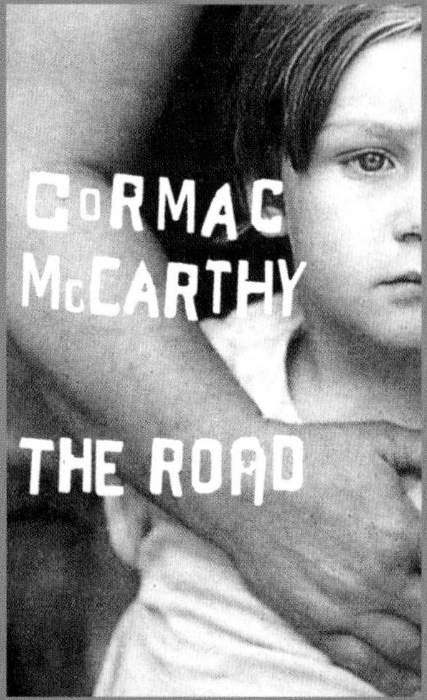
CORMAC McCARTHY
THE ROAD

## Road Warriors

Reading Cormac McCarthy's *The Road* in manuscript form was thrilling, devastating, and yet another reminder of how privileged I am to have my job at Knopf and to work with this author. In the office, as the manuscript was slowly circulating, very soon something like the phrase "A Classic Greek Tragedy for the Millennial Age" was being respectfully whispered in the halls by those lucky enough to read it first—and it wasn't hyperbole. I thought this was by far the most affecting and brilliantly controlled work from this artist I had ever read, and in retrospect it preceded Robert Kirkman's *The Walking Dead* by several years while drawing on many of the same themes as that international phenomenon: a mysterious global catastrophe that brings the world as we know it to a stop—and then for those who survive, the sheer daily trial of trying to stay alive without knowing exactly what the rules are. Of course the difference is that *The Road* dials back the sci-fi quotient by not going so far as to add zombies to the mix, but that only makes it

**LEFT:** *The Sunset Limited*, a play about a man who tries to throw himself in front of a train, the man who saves him, and their ensuing conversation. Knopf, 2006. **ABOVE:** Early comps.

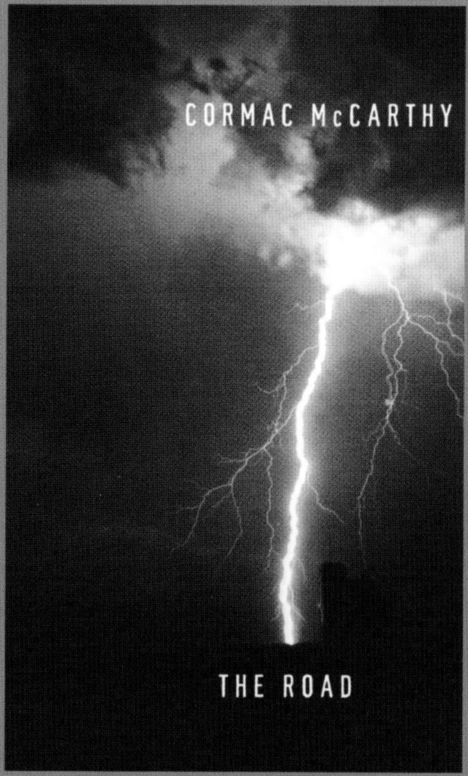
CORMAC McCARTHY
THE ROAD

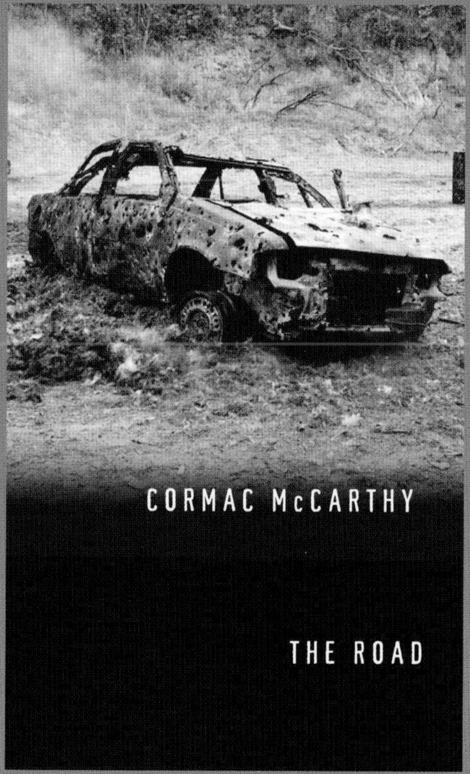
CORMAC McCARTHY
THE ROAD

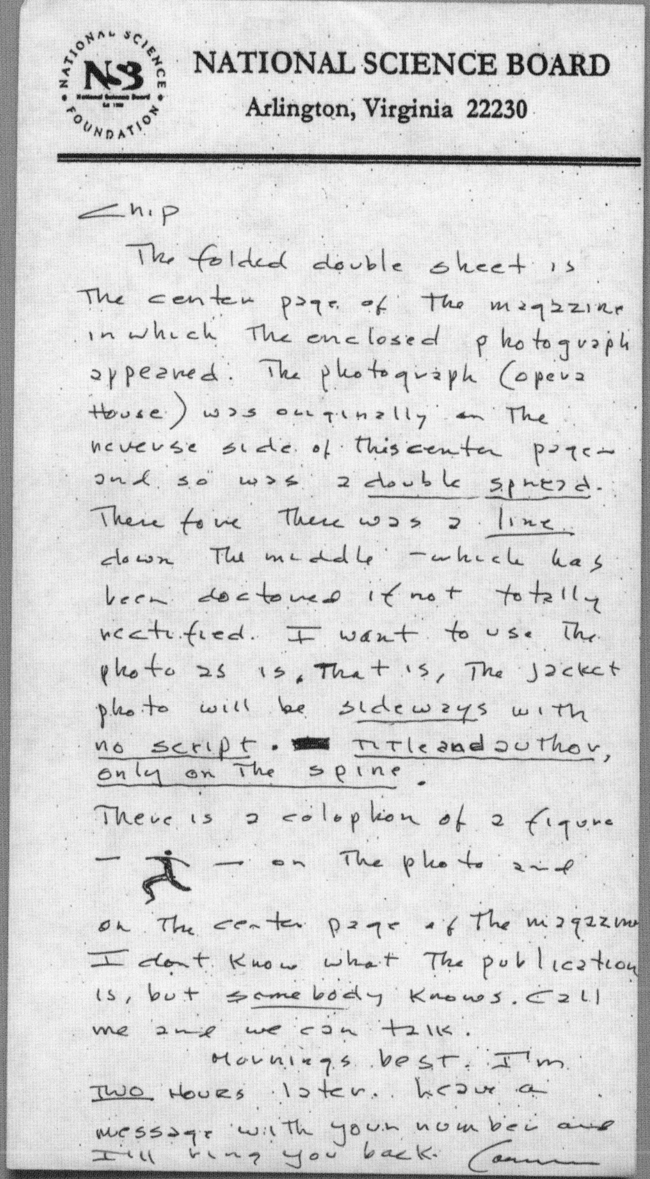

NATIONAL SCIENCE BOARD
Arlington, Virginia 22230

Chip

The folded double sheet is the center page of the magazine in which the enclosed photograph appeared. The photograph (opera house) was originally on the reverse side of this center page and so was a double spread. Therefore there was a line down the middle—which has been doctored if not totally rectified. I want to use the photo as is. That is, the jacket photo will be sideways with no script. [redacted] Title and author, only on the spine.

There is a colophon of a figure — — on the photo and on the center page of the magazine. I don't know what the publication is, but somebody knows. Call me and we can talk.

Mornings best. I'm two hours later. Leave a message with your number and I'll ring you back. Cormac

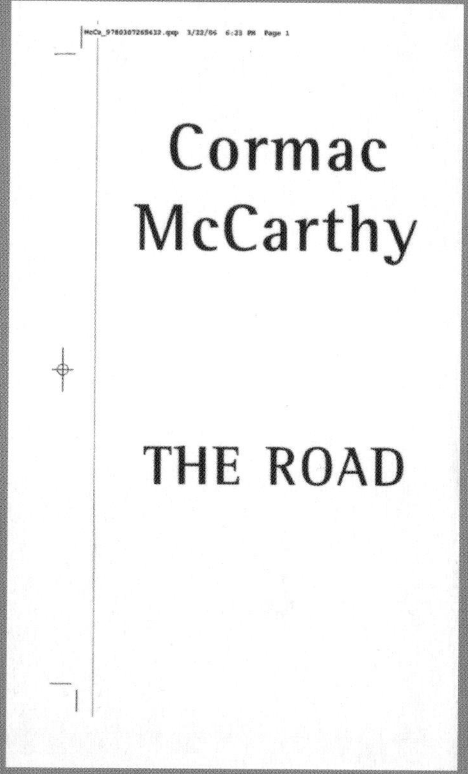
Cormac
McCarthy
THE ROAD



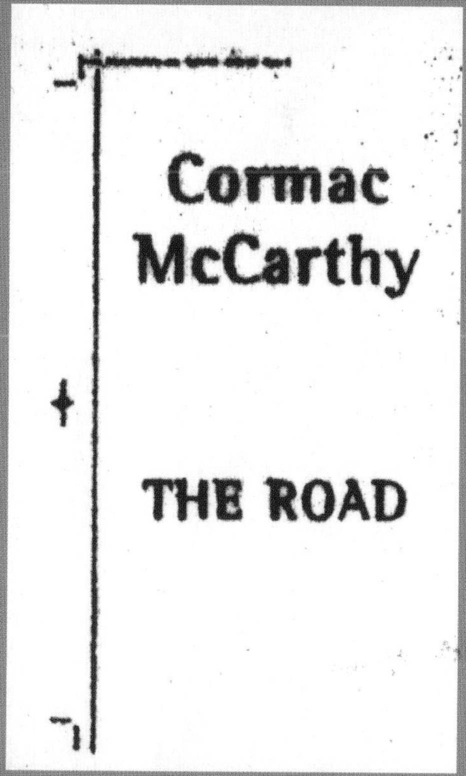
Cormac
McCarthy
THE ROAD

even more terrifying. These are people pushed to the edge of their humanity to do anything to stay alive, which frankly makes them more dangerous and monstrous than mindless wandering flesh-eaters. The focus is on a father (the narrator) and his young son, whom he will do anything to defend and protect, at any cost.

**LEFT, TOP:** An early comp. **LEFT, BOTTOM:** I really thought I nailed it here, using a photo by Jason Fulford. Cormac disagreed. **ABOVE:** A letter from Cormac detailing his design requests. Also included was a photo he discovered, showing a dilapidated theater in Havana (overleaf). **RIGHT:** Lettering I distressed on our copy machine, which was eventually used for the final jacket.

rmac
arthy

ROAD

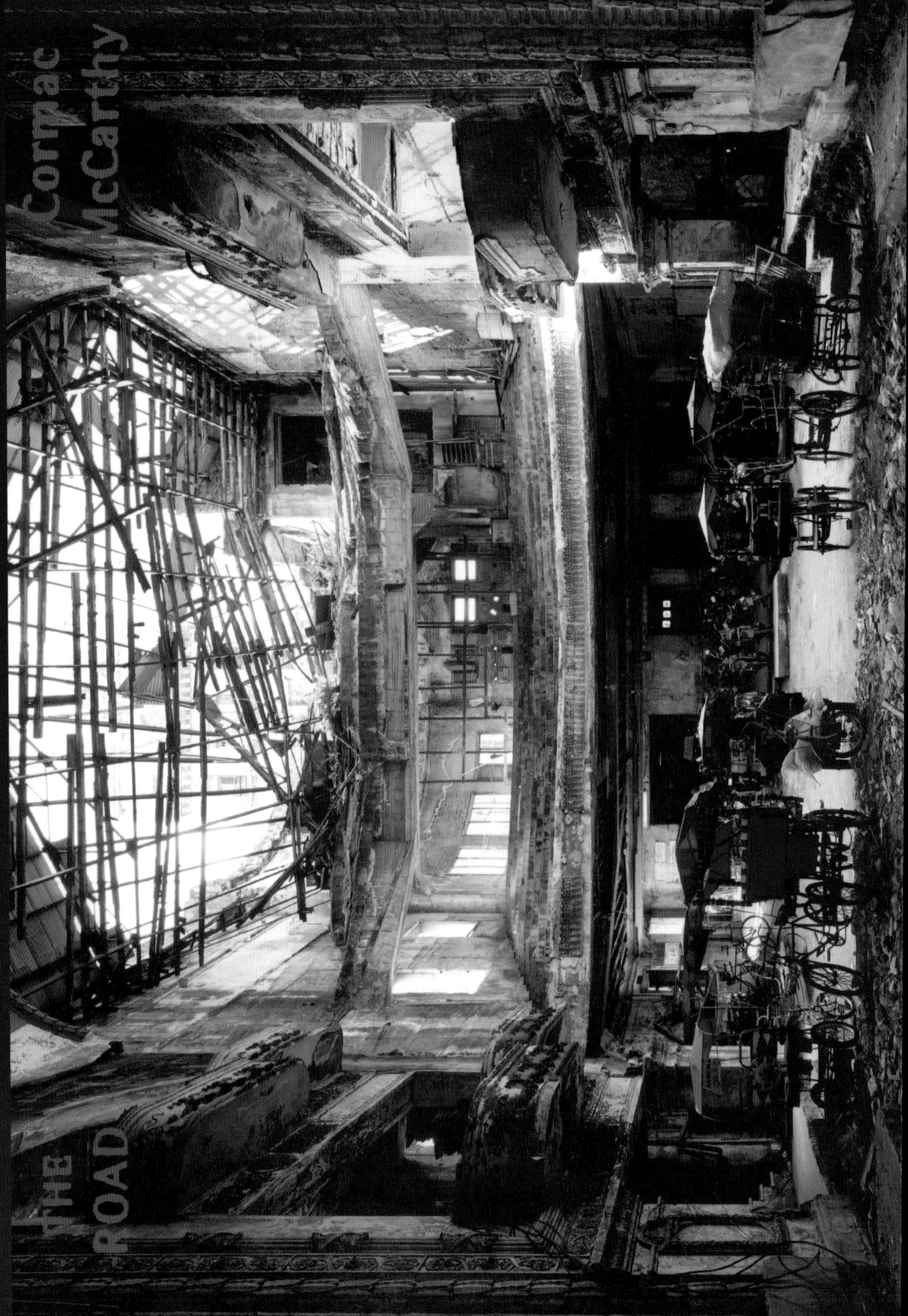
Cormac
McCarthy
THE
ROAD

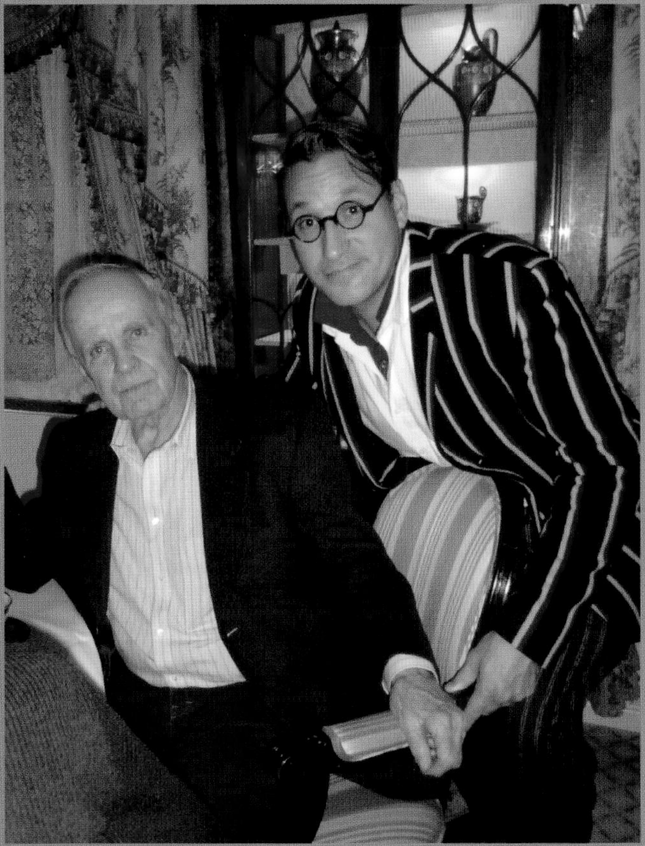

As described in his letter, Cormac wanted Andrew Moore's photograph of the collapsed theater (opposite) to be set on its side to accommodate the format. He also wanted something (or didn't want it, to be more specific) that made our marketing and sales department very concerned: his name and the title nowhere on the front cover, only the spine. As a designer, I thought this request was really ballsy and cool, but the reality was that it would have been recklessly counterproductive. That approach just didn't prepare you for what the book really was: an extremely dark and spare meditation on what would happen if all the basic conventions of modern civilization were suddenly removed, and we as a people were rendered savages again. Everyone involved finally agreed on the design at right, soon to be adorned with an "Oprah's Book Club" sticker, which allowed any remaining doubts of success to instantly evaporate. Bless you, Oprah. I mean that in all sincerity.

**ABOVE:** With Cormac at a private dinner to celebrate the premiere of HBO's production of *The Sunset Limited*, starring Tommy Lee Jones and Samuel L. Jackson. **RIGHT:** Knopf, 2006.

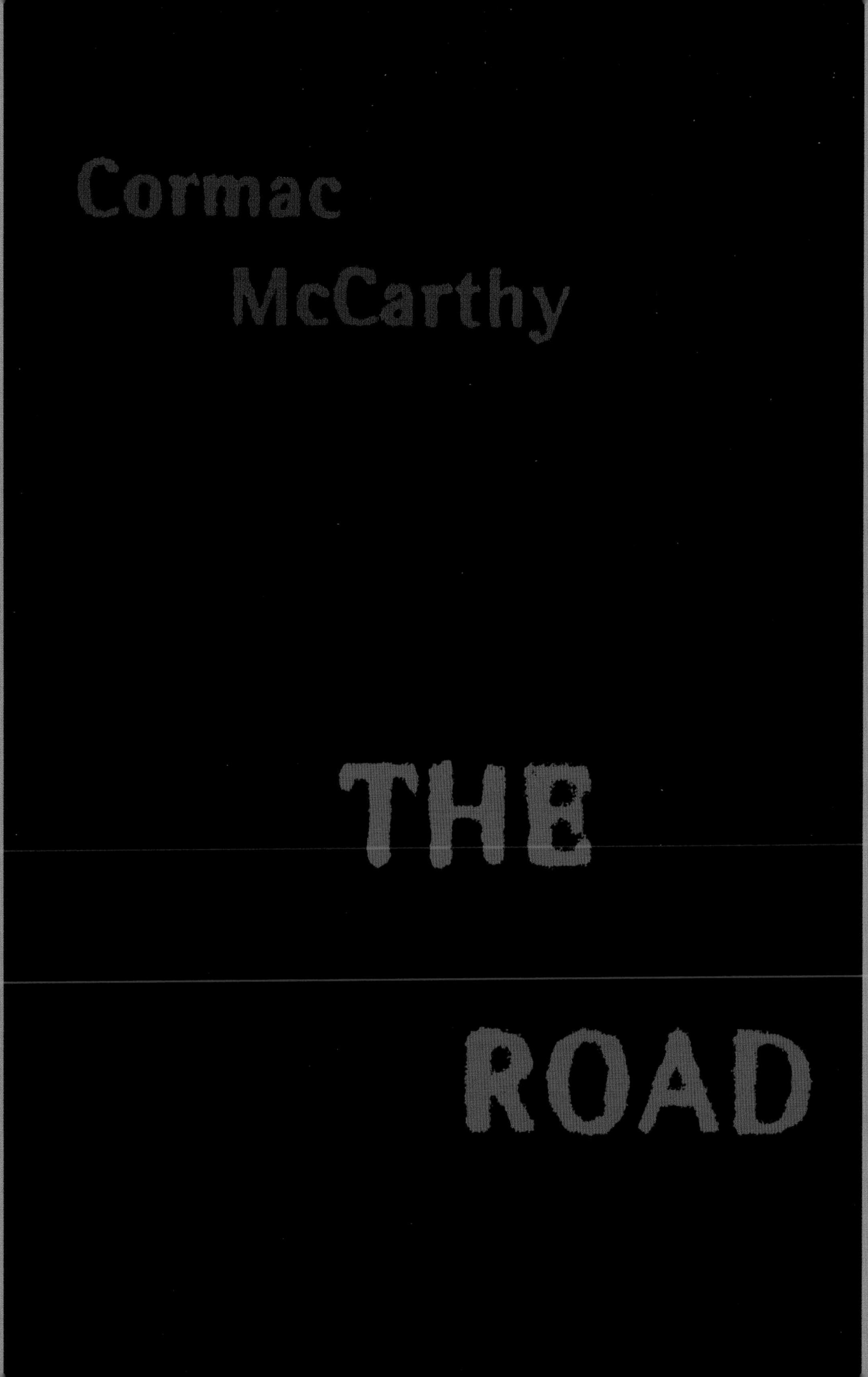
Cormac
McCarthy
THE
ROAD

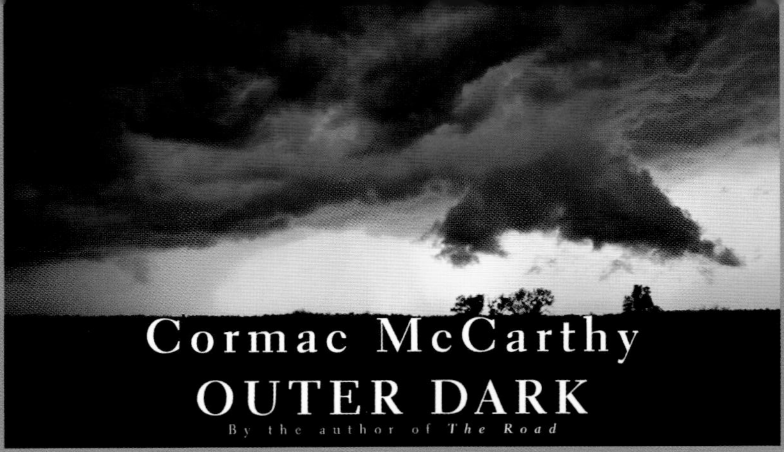
Cormac McCarthy
OUTER DARK
By the author of The Road

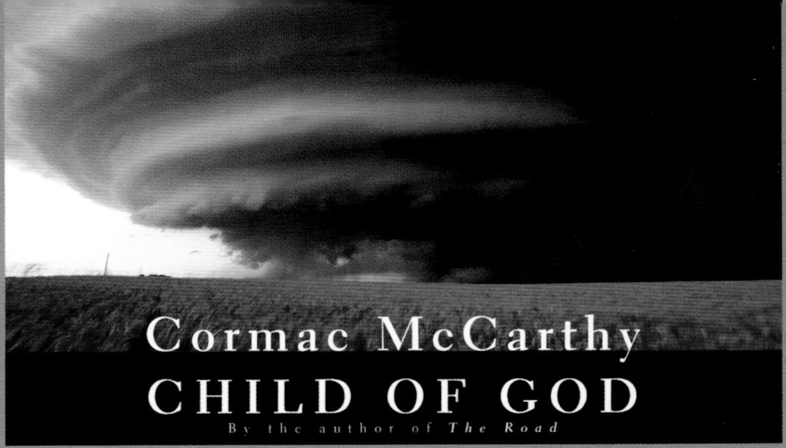
Cormac McCarthy
CHILD OF GOD
By the author of The Road

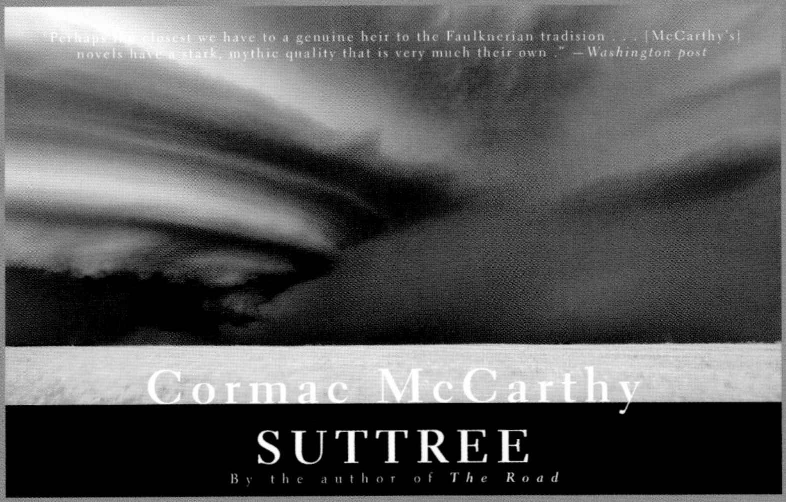
"Perhaps the closest we have to a genuine heir to the Faulknerian tradision . . . [McCarthy's] novels have a stark, mythic quality that is very much their own ." —Washington post
Cormac McCarthy
SUTTREE
By the author of The Road

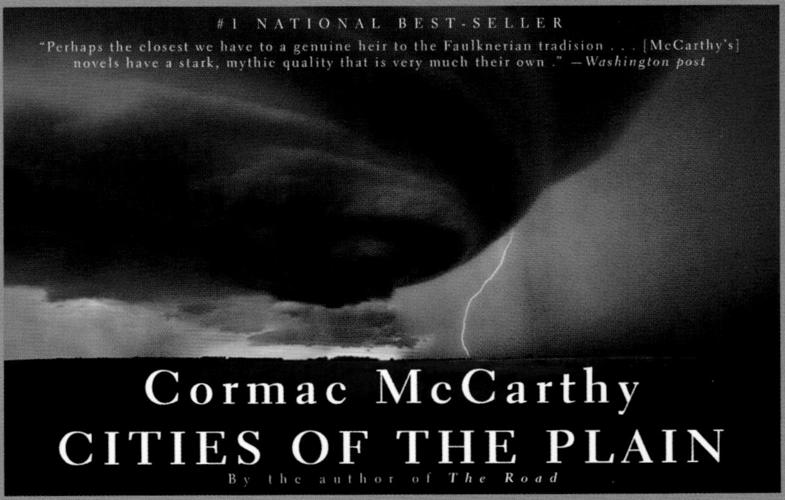
#1 NATIONAL BEST-SELLER
"Perhaps the closest we have to a genuine heir to the Faulknerian tradision . . . [McCarthy's] novels have a stark, mythic quality that is very much their own ." —Washington post
Cormac McCarthy
CITIES OF THE PLAIN
By the author of The Road

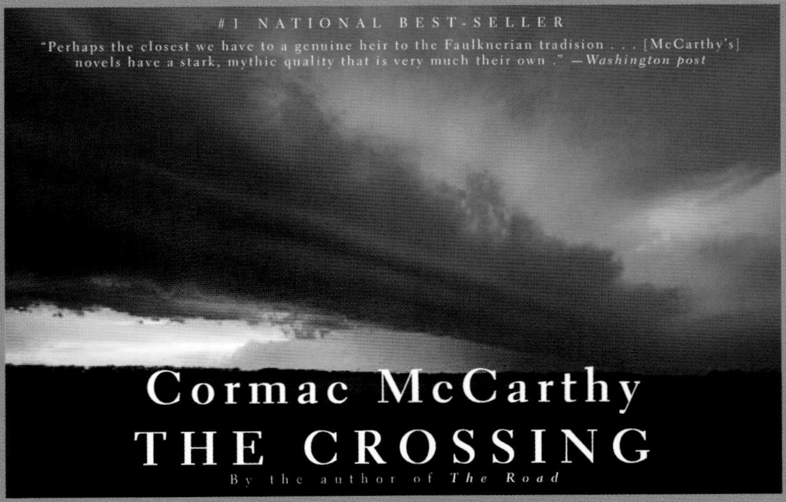
#1 NATIONAL BEST-SELLER
"Perhaps the closest we have to a genuine heir to the Faulknerian tradision . . . [McCarthy's] novels have a stark, mythic quality that is very much their own ." —Washington post
Cormac McCarthy
THE CROSSING
By the author of The Road

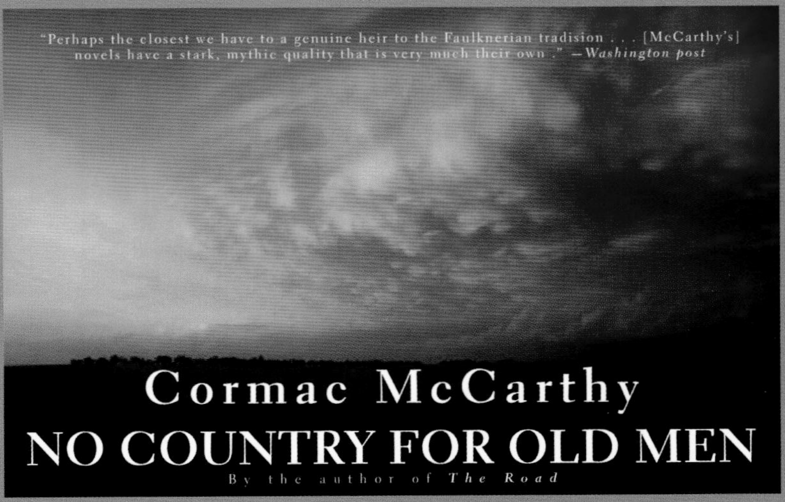
"Perhaps the closest we have to a genuine heir to the Faulknerian tradision . . . [McCarthy's] novels have a stark, mythic quality that is very much their own ." —Washington post
Cormac McCarthy
NO COUNTRY FOR OLD MEN
By the author of The Road

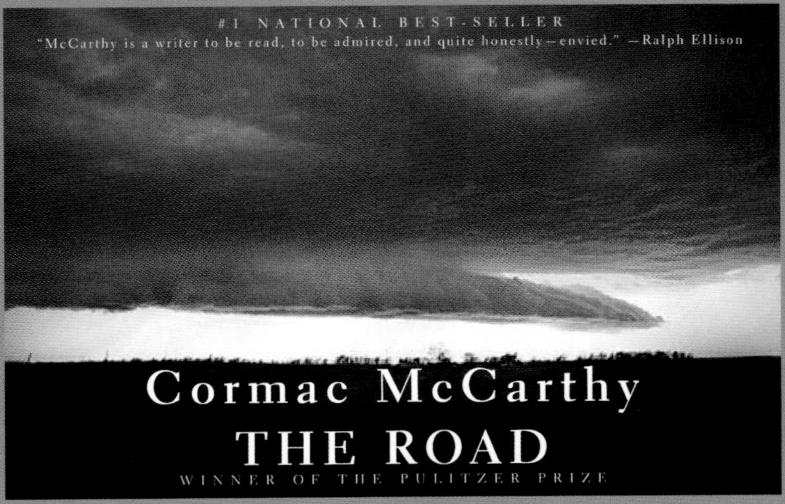
#1 NATIONAL BEST-SELLER
"McCarthy is a writer to be read, to be admired, and quite honestly—envied." —Ralph Ellison
Cormac McCarthy
THE ROAD
WINNER OF THE PULITZER PRIZE

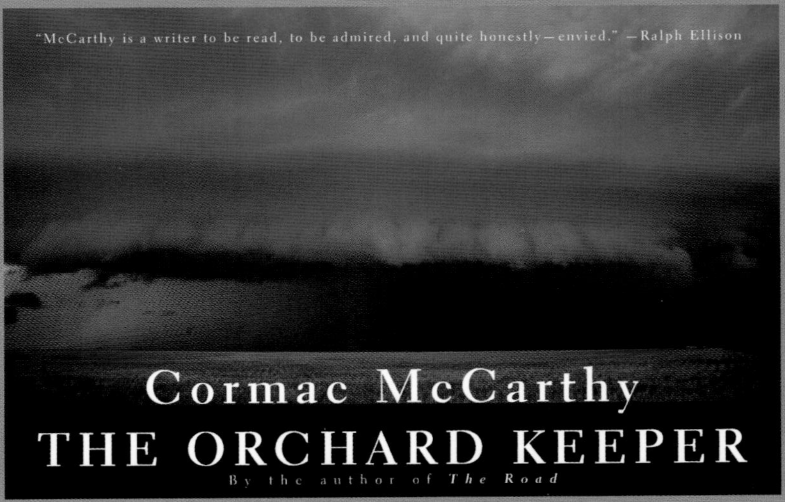
"McCarthy is a writer to be read, to be admired, and quite honestly—envied." —Ralph Ellison
Cormac McCarthy
THE ORCHARD KEEPER
By the author of The Road

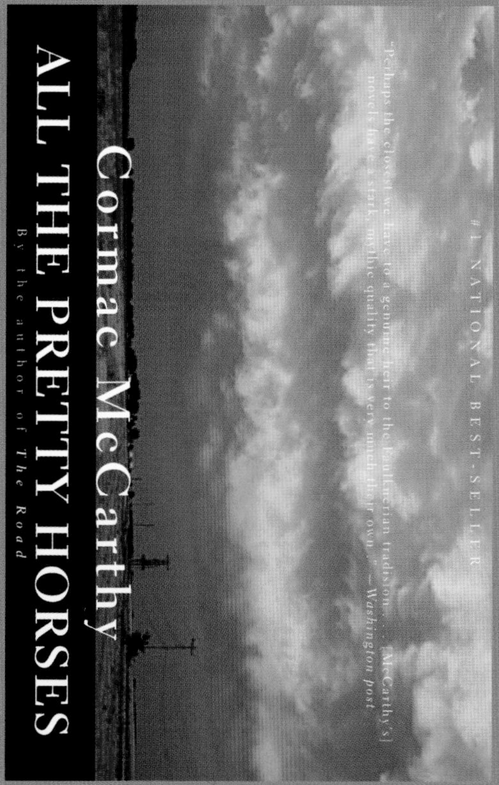
#1 NATIONAL BEST-SELLER
Cormac McCarthy
ALL THE PRETTY HORSES
By the author of The Road

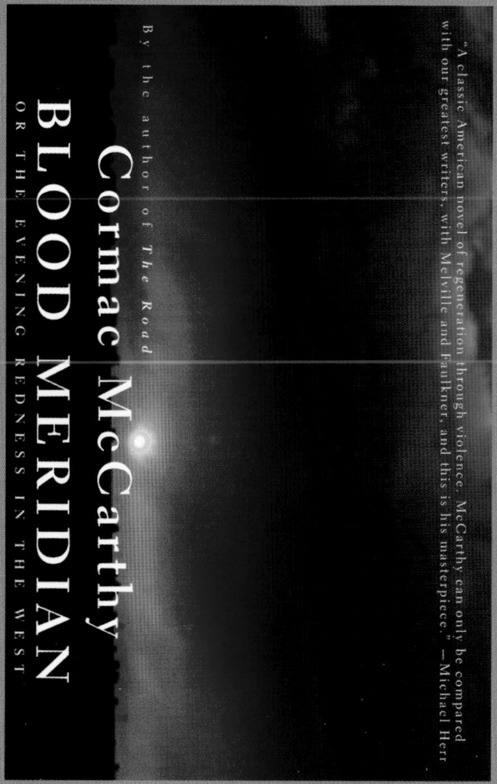
"A classic American novel of regeneration through violence. McCarthy can only be compared with our greatest writers, with Melville and Faulkner, and this is his masterpiece." —Michael Herr
By the author of The Road
Cormac McCarthy
BLOOD MERIDIAN
OR THE EVENING REDNESS IN THE WEST

Shortly after *The Road* was released, Sonny Mehta asked me to do some exploratory work on how I might redesign Cormac's backlist for Vintage Paperbacks. I was thrilled at the prospect and started to think about basic visual themes that united the work: wide-open landscapes, peril, savagery, the American West, and . . . storms. McCarthy's descriptions of epic weather systems across the vast deserts and plains are jaw-dropping, and I knew there were extreme-weather pictures to match. The thing was, images like these naturally work better horizontally (thus the term "landscape format") than vertically. So I really went from the gut and decided that all the covers would be rotated onto their sides (much like Cormac had initially wanted on *The Road*) and I mocked them up (this spread). This approach, sadly, was nipped in the bud, with potential confusion about how booksellers would display the books becoming the concern that led to their doom. The one design from this series that did get produced is shown at right, featuring a photo of a crop fire by Larry Schwarm, who provided the image for *Cities of the Plain*.

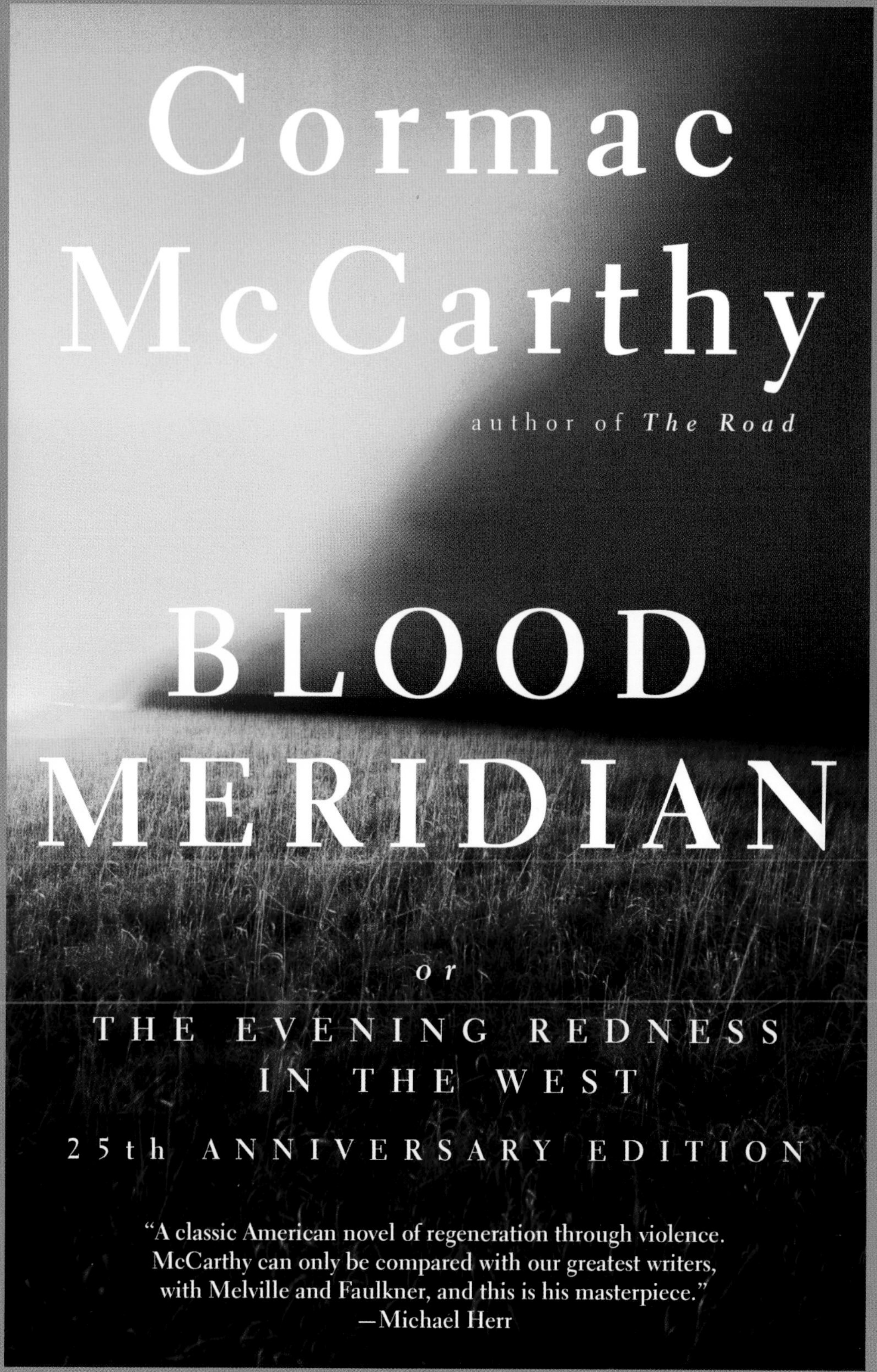
Cormac McCarthy
author of The Road
BLOOD MERIDIAN
or
THE EVENING REDNESS IN THE WEST
25th ANNIVERSARY EDITION
"A classic American novel of regeneration through violence. McCarthy can only be compared with our greatest writers, with Melville and Faulkner, and this is his masterpiece."
—Michael Herr

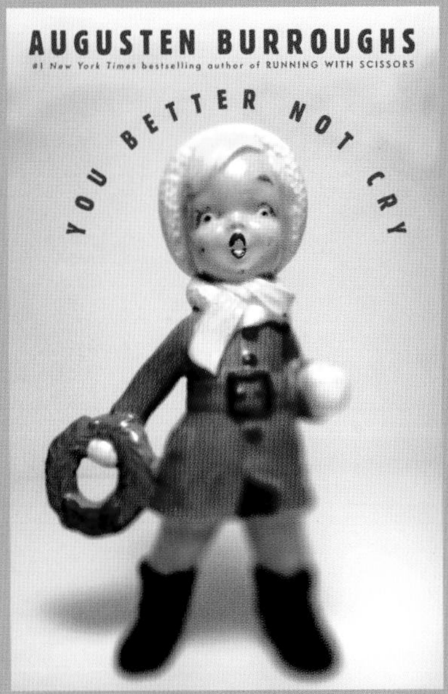
AUGUSTEN BURROUGHS
YOU BETTER NOT CRY

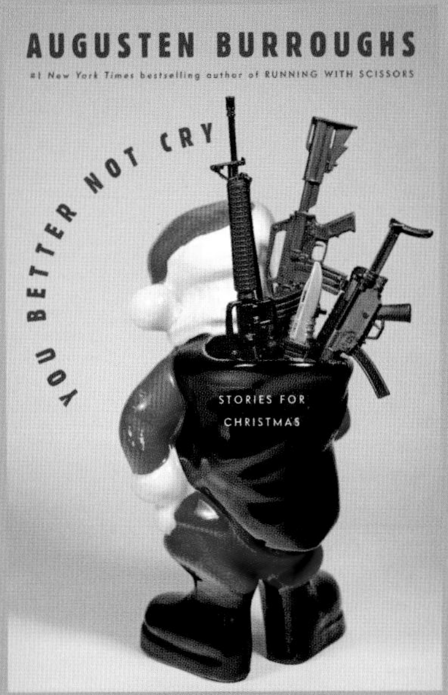
AUGUSTEN BURROUGHS
YOU BETTER NOT CRY
STORIES FOR CHRISTMAS

## Sadomasochristmas

What a great assignment: Augusten Burroughs writes about the absurdity and stifling forced-family "happiness" of Christmas. And it was to be called *You Better Not Cry*. This job should have been so, so easy. And at first, it was. At the time I got the call, photographer Tom Allen (see *Zoetrope* magazine, pp. 188–89) was doing a hilarious blog called something like *The Twelve Tawdry Days of X-Mas*, going into local Goodwills near his hometown in Wisconsin and photographing (then posting) sad, vintage cast-offs of the season. I definitely thought this would do. I started with the little third-rate Hummel figurine of the girl holding the Christmas wreath in her right hand and, well, freaking out (above left). Why, we don't know; doesn't matter. I liked this image and sent it to Augusten, who appreciated it but said it wasn't mean enough. So I went back to Tom and suggested the ceramic Santa candy holder, and putting an arsenal of miniature weapons in his sack (above right). That looked good, but why not then bring the two together (right), so now we know why she's freaking out. Okay, done, right? Then a week of silence goes by, never a good sign, and the art director finally calls and says, for real: "We had a marketing meeting this morning and spent fifteen minutes



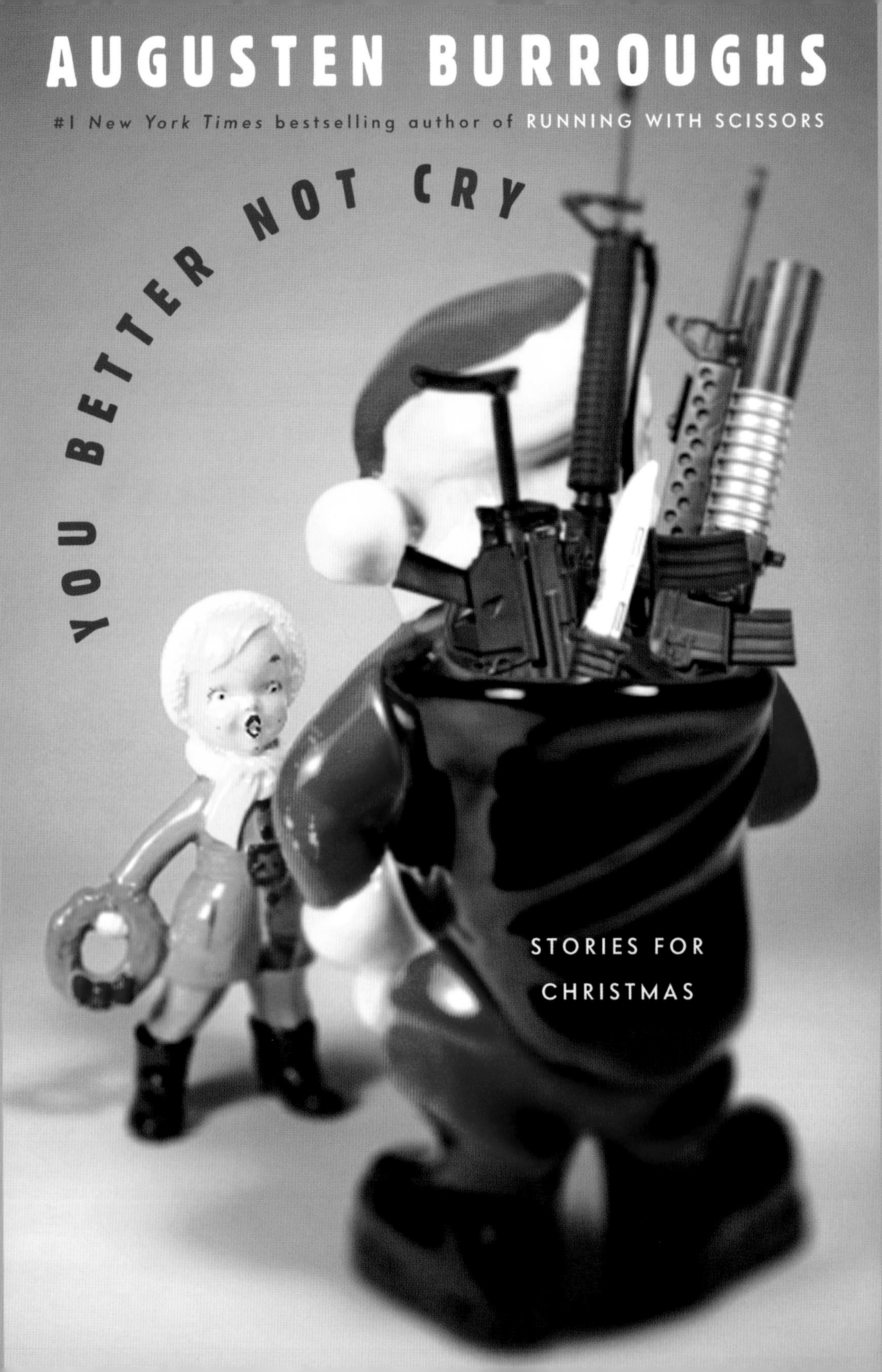
AUGUSTEN BURROUGHS
#1 New York Times bestselling author of RUNNING WITH SCISSORS
YOU BETTER NOT CRY
STORIES FOR CHRISTMAS

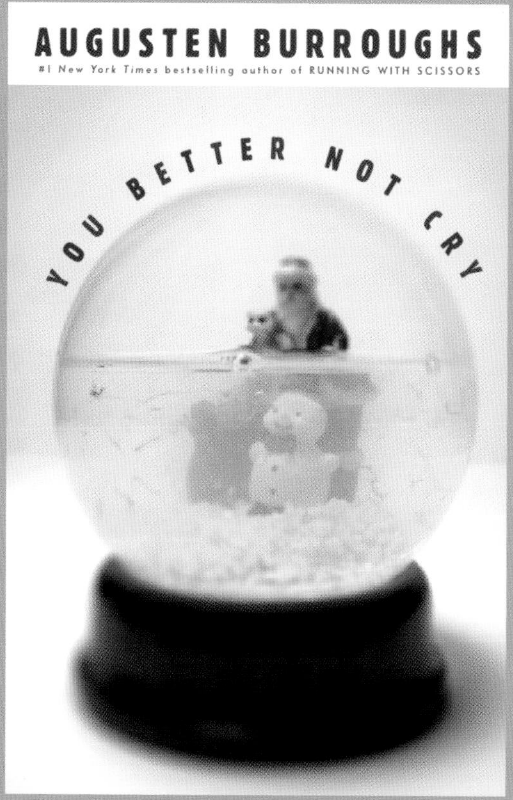
AUGUSTEN BURROUGHS
#1 New York Times bestselling author of RUNNING WITH SCISSORS
YOU BETTER NOT CRY

arguing about whether or not Santa is showing the little girl his penis." And I'm thinking, "So, the guns aren't enough for you?" But what I'll admit I said instead was, "Do they want him to?" Which was quickly rejoindered by "No! They don't!"

To which I responded, "Okay, so now what?" The answer was either start over or bail. I couldn't bear the thought of the latter—why wasn't I nailing this? A shot of a leaking snow globe was suitably pathetic (above) but didn't cut it, and then I had an idea-gasm: pets! People do all sorts of appalling things to their animals for the holidays, and I knew Augusten had a pit bull. I found this stock photo (right) and really thought I'd finally crossed the finish line. Not! Somehow even this image wasn't blowing everyone's dress up, and the plug was pulled. The dreaded kill fee. Adding insult to injury was what they finally came up with. You'll have to google it, and you won't believe it. Suffice it to say they decided that Father Christmas needed to show his junk after all. *Ahem.*

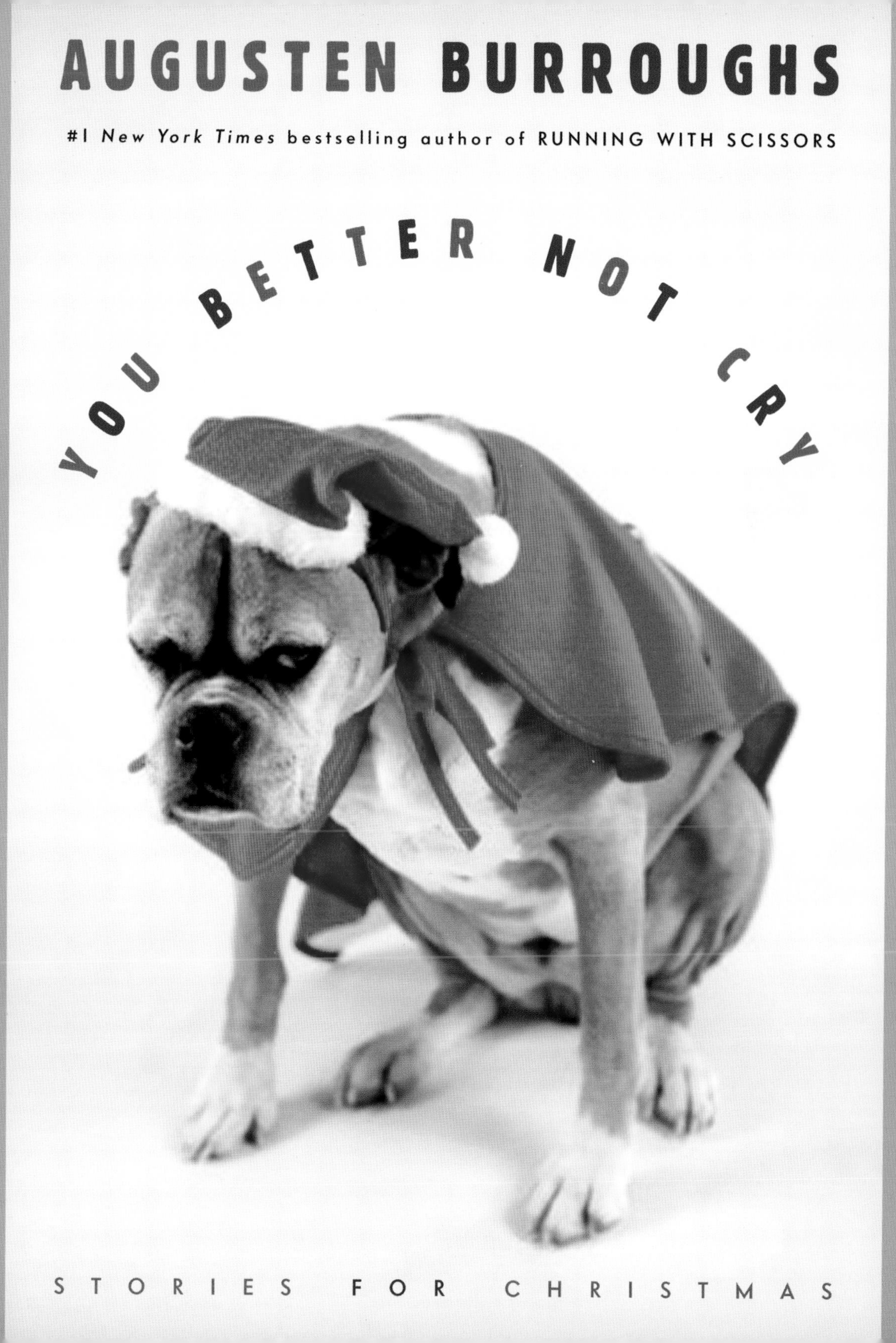
AUGUSTEN BURROUGHS
#1 New York Times bestselling author of RUNNING WITH SCISSORS
YOU BETTER NOT CRY
STORIES FOR CHRISTMAS

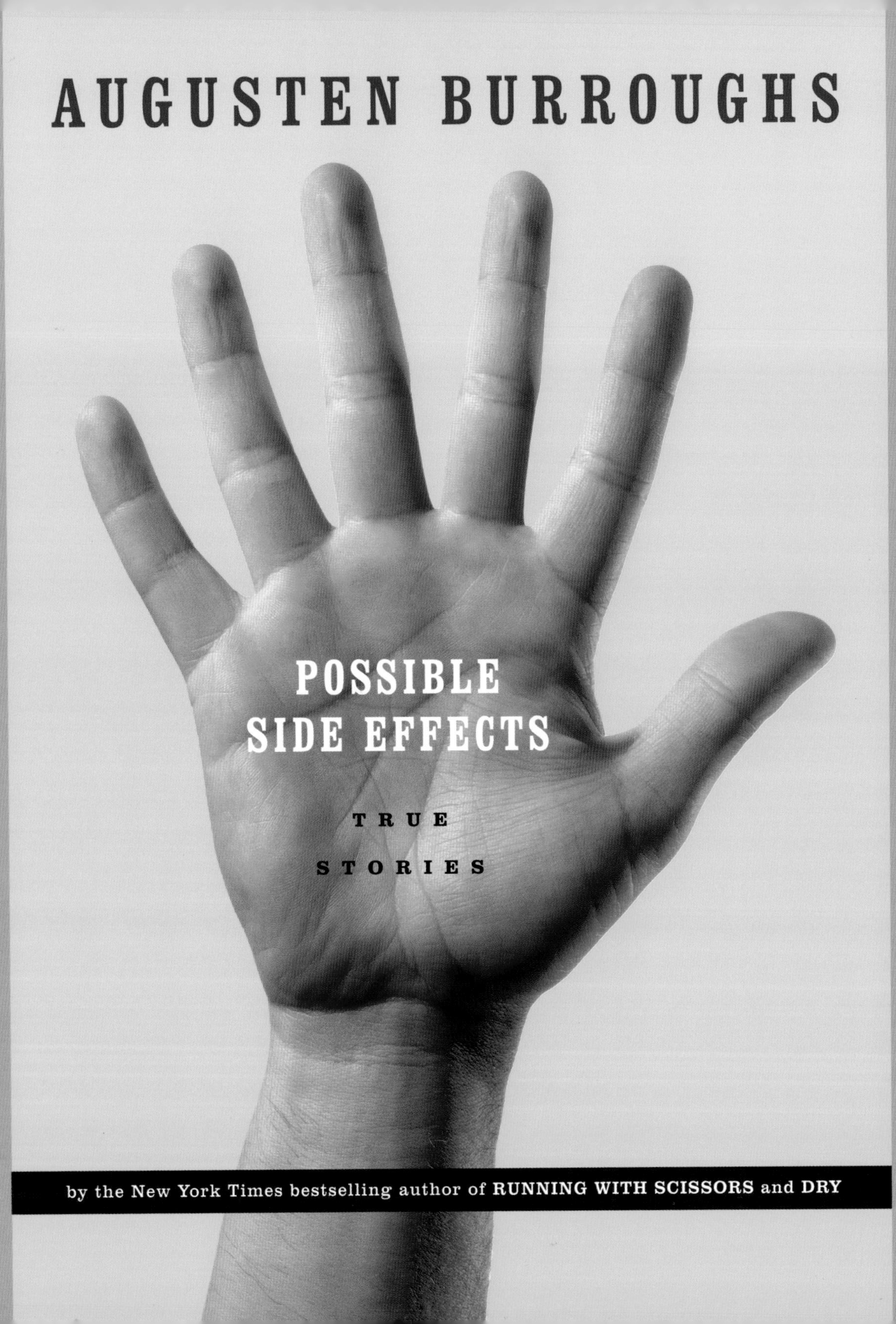
AUGUSTEN BURROUGHS
POSSIBLE SIDE EFFECTS
TRUE STORIES
by the New York Times bestselling author of RUNNING WITH SCISSORS and DRY

88

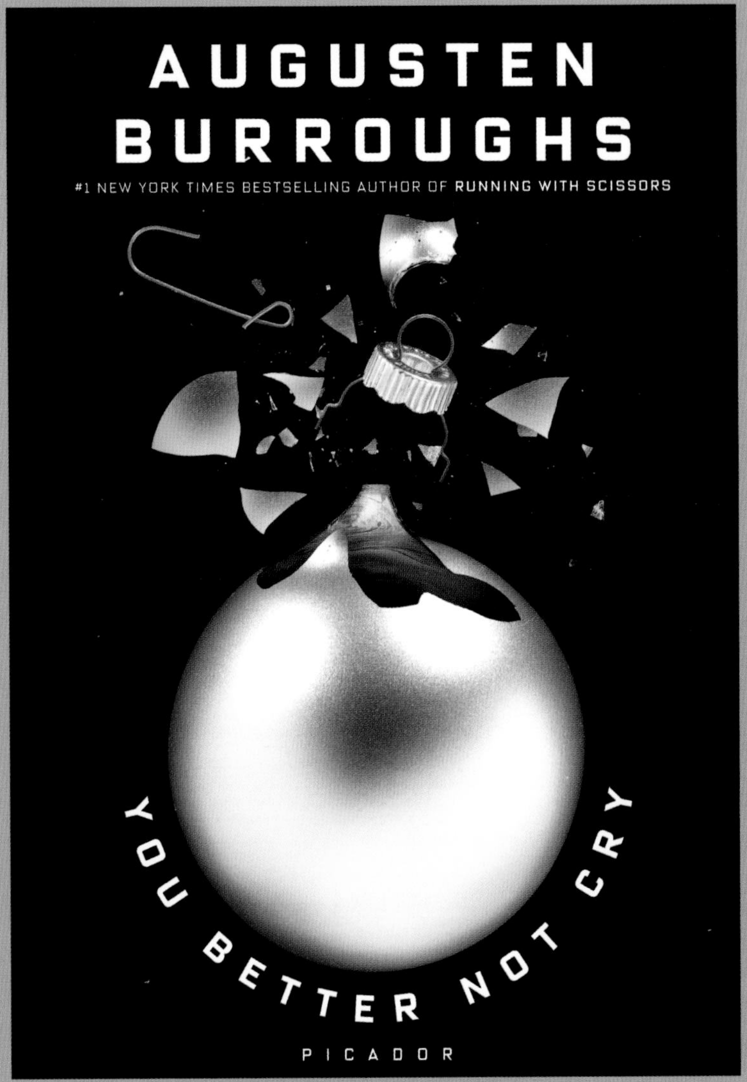
AUGUSTEN BURROUGHS
#1 NEW YORK TIMES BESTSELLING AUTHOR OF RUNNING WITH SCISSORS
YOU BETTER NOT CRY
PICADOR

For the Picador paperback (above) they decided to give me another try. It needed to be dialed back, so this time I decided Geoff Spear should create the image, and we caught an ornament midshatter. Not so loaded with baggage, but it got the point across successfully. We applied a similar sensibility to Augusten's often-neglected first novel, *Sellevision* (opposite, left), to mimic early on-air motion graphics of mid-1970s commercial TV.

The very moment Augusten told me the title of the book *Possible Side Effects* (left) over the phone I knew what it should be. But I didn't tell him; instead I called Geoff and explained my idea and he

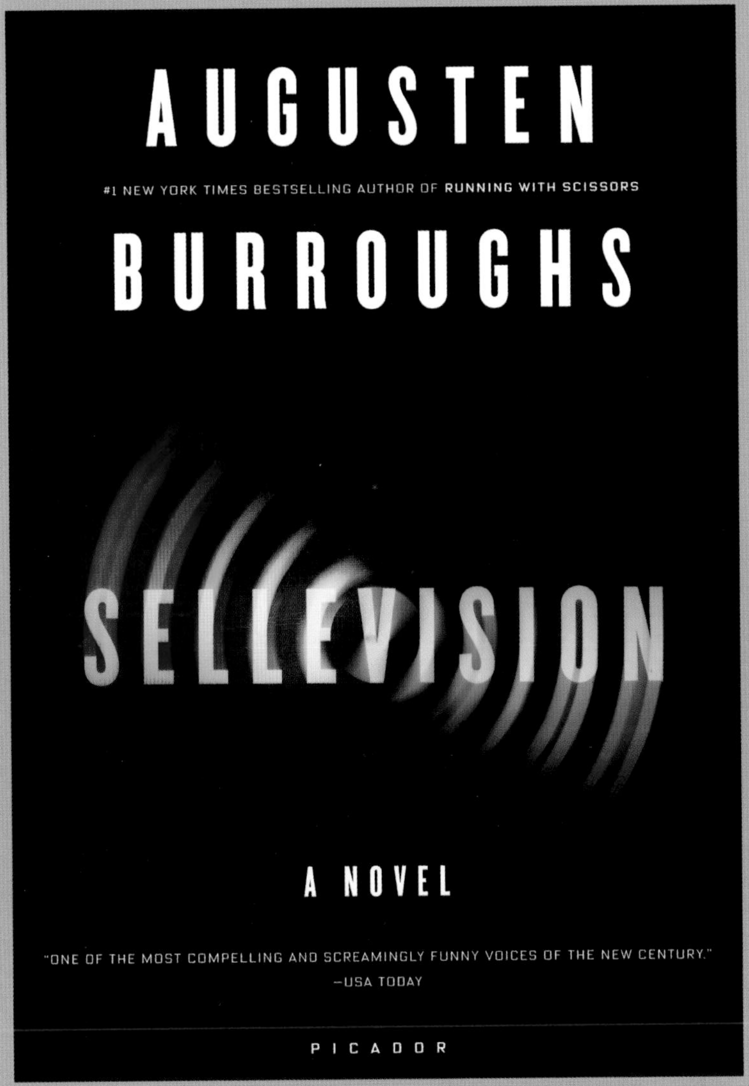
AUGUSTEN
#1 NEW YORK TIMES BESTSELLING AUTHOR OF RUNNING WITH SCISSORS
BURROUGHS
SELLEVISION
A NOVEL
"ONE OF THE MOST COMPELLING AND SCREAMINGLY FUNNY VOICES OF THE NEW CENTURY."
—USA TODAY
PICADOR

totally pulled it off (or stuck it on, as the case may be) by shooting my hand and then seamlessly adding a sixth finger.

Augusten's memoir of his father, *A Wolf at the Table* (right), was a much darker book about his abusive father. The psoriasis on his hands at its worst turned them into red claws. We achieved this shot very simply, with a bent fork and a red gel over the light, no computer trickery involved. I hadn't thought of these jackets as a yin-yang diptych (they are years apart), but that's what they became.

**OPPOSITE, LEFT:** St. Martin's Press, 2006. **OPPOSITE, RIGHT:** Picador, 2010. **ABOVE:** Picador, 2010. **RIGHT:** St. Martin's Press, 2008.

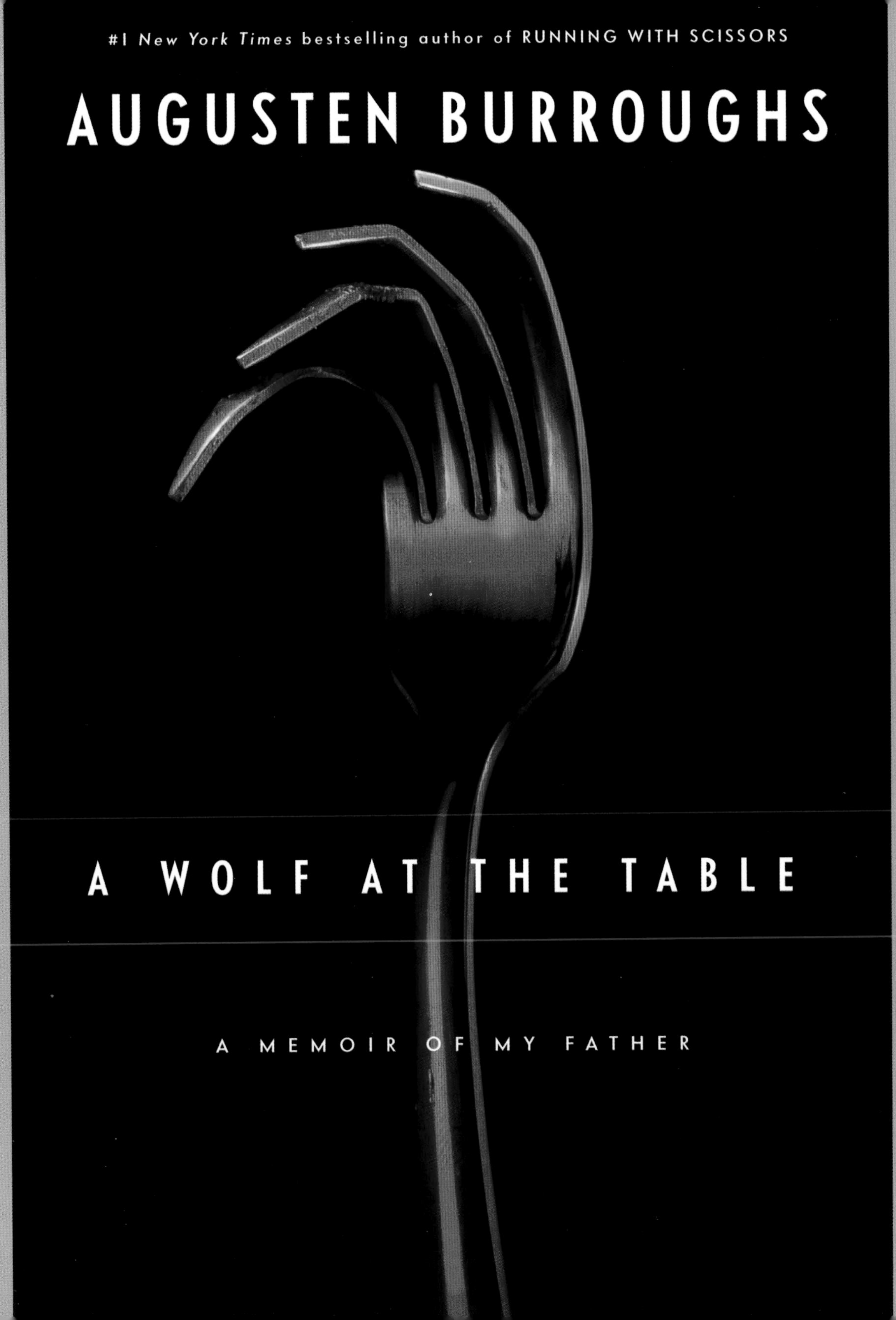
#1 New York Times bestselling author of RUNNING WITH SCISSORS
AUGUSTEN BURROUGHS
A WOLF AT THE TABLE
A MEMOIR OF MY FATHER

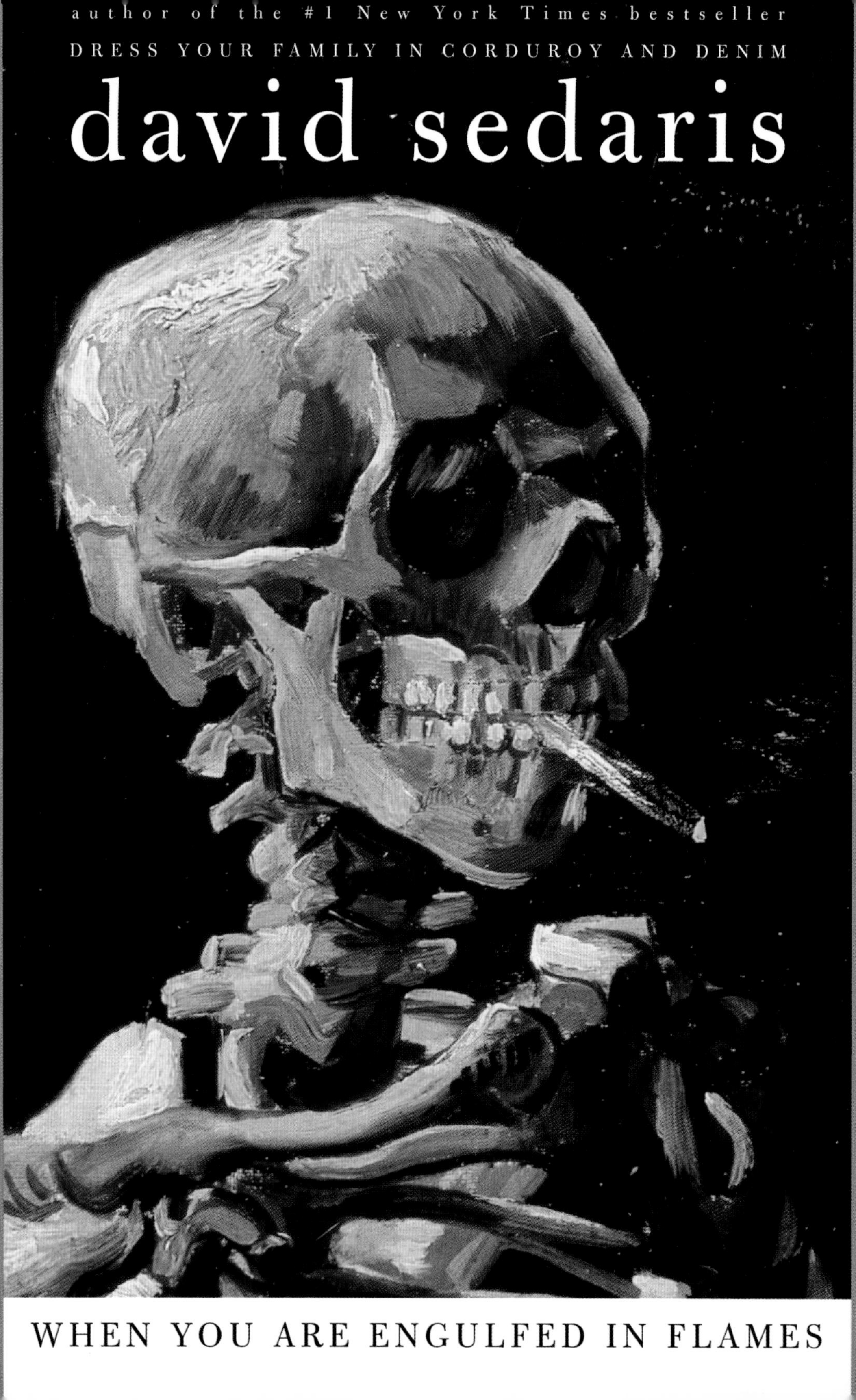
author of the #1 New York Times bestseller
DRESS YOUR FAMILY IN CORDUROY AND DENIM
david sedaris
WHEN YOU ARE ENGULFED IN FLAMES



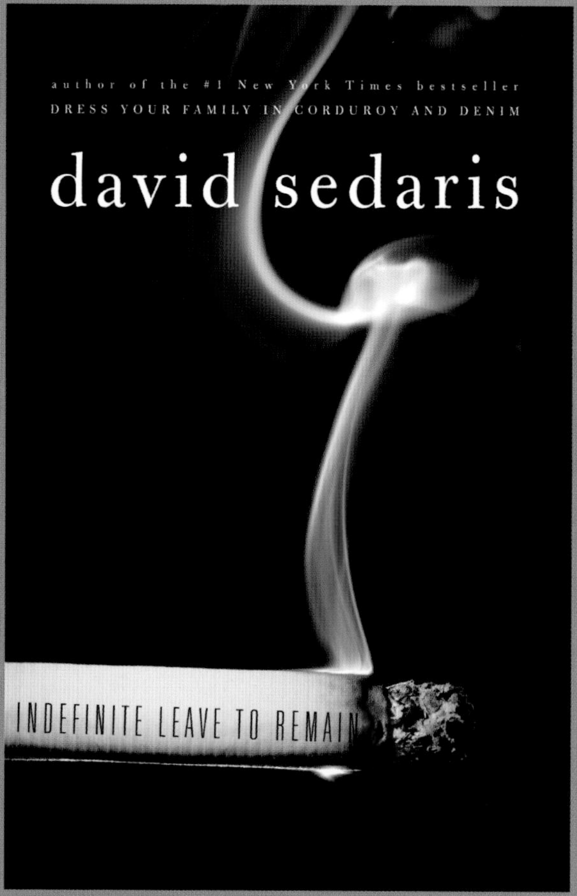
author of the #1 New York Times bestseller
DRESS YOUR FAMILY IN CORDUROY AND DENIM
david sedaris
INDEFINITE LEAVE TO REMAIN

## Where There's Smoke . . .

The title of David Sedaris's *When You Are Engulfed in Flames* (left) went through two previous incarnations, each requiring (to my mind) completely different visual approaches. The first title was *All the Beauty You Will Ever Need* (opposite, left), which I thought was lovely and for which I repurposed the fortune cookie idea I initially tried for David Shields (see p. 38). Little, Brown (the publisher) liked this concept very much and used it for a promotional sampler, but soon after, David was going through Customs at Heathrow and his passport was stamped "Indefinite Leave To Remain," which he apparently saw as both hilarious and a sign to change the name of the book. To me, this new title would not have enough visual connect to the fortune cookie concept, but could be applied to a burning cigarette, a motif that occurs in several of the essays. So Geoff and I did a shot thereof and I applied the type. I thought

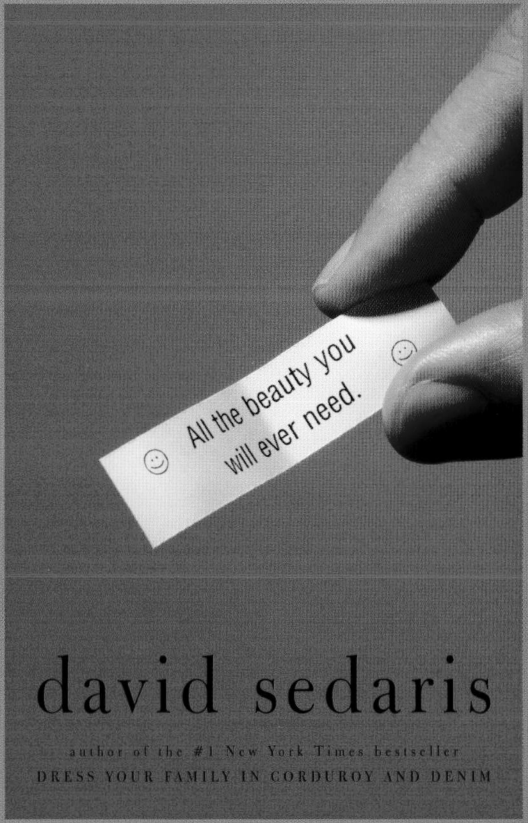
All the beauty you
will ever need.
david sedaris
author of the #1 New York Times bestseller
DRESS YOUR FAMILY IN CORDUROY AND DENIM

it looked great—it's hard to lose with a beautiful wisp of smoke. But then word came down that David had found a piece of art he liked better, a painting by no less than Vincent van Gogh of a skeleton smoking (opposite, left), which led to yet another title change, *When You Are Engulfed in Flames*. The art looked great, actually; I was just dubious they'd get the rights to use it, but that didn't seem to be a problem. So, I thought: just treat the typography very straightforwardly, and it would be done. And it was.

*Holidays on Ice* was much more fun. In an amazing coincidence, my friend Stephen Webster—a photography teacher in Columbus, Ohio, and a huge Sedaris fan—assigned the book to his class, asking them to create new cover imagery. He sent the results to me, not knowing that the book was about to be reissued and that I was working, at the time, on a new cover. This photograph by student Marshall Troy was perfect, and we used it. How often does that happen? As often as you-know-where freezes over.

**OPPOSITE, LEFT:** Little, Brown, 2008. **RIGHT:** Little, Brown, 2008.

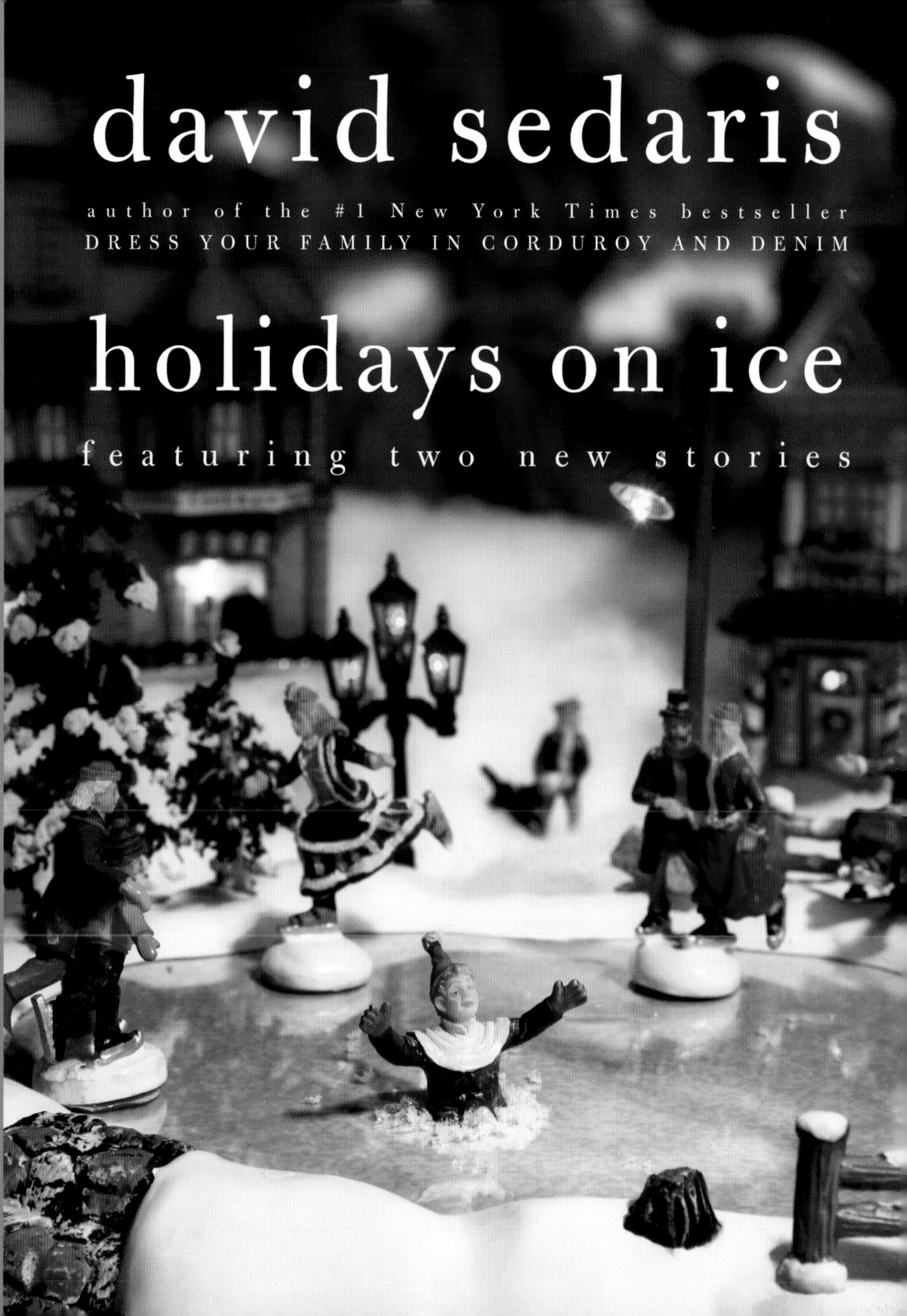
david sedaris
author of the #1 New York Times bestseller
DRESS YOUR FAMILY IN CORDUROY AND DENIM
holidays on ice
featuring two new stories

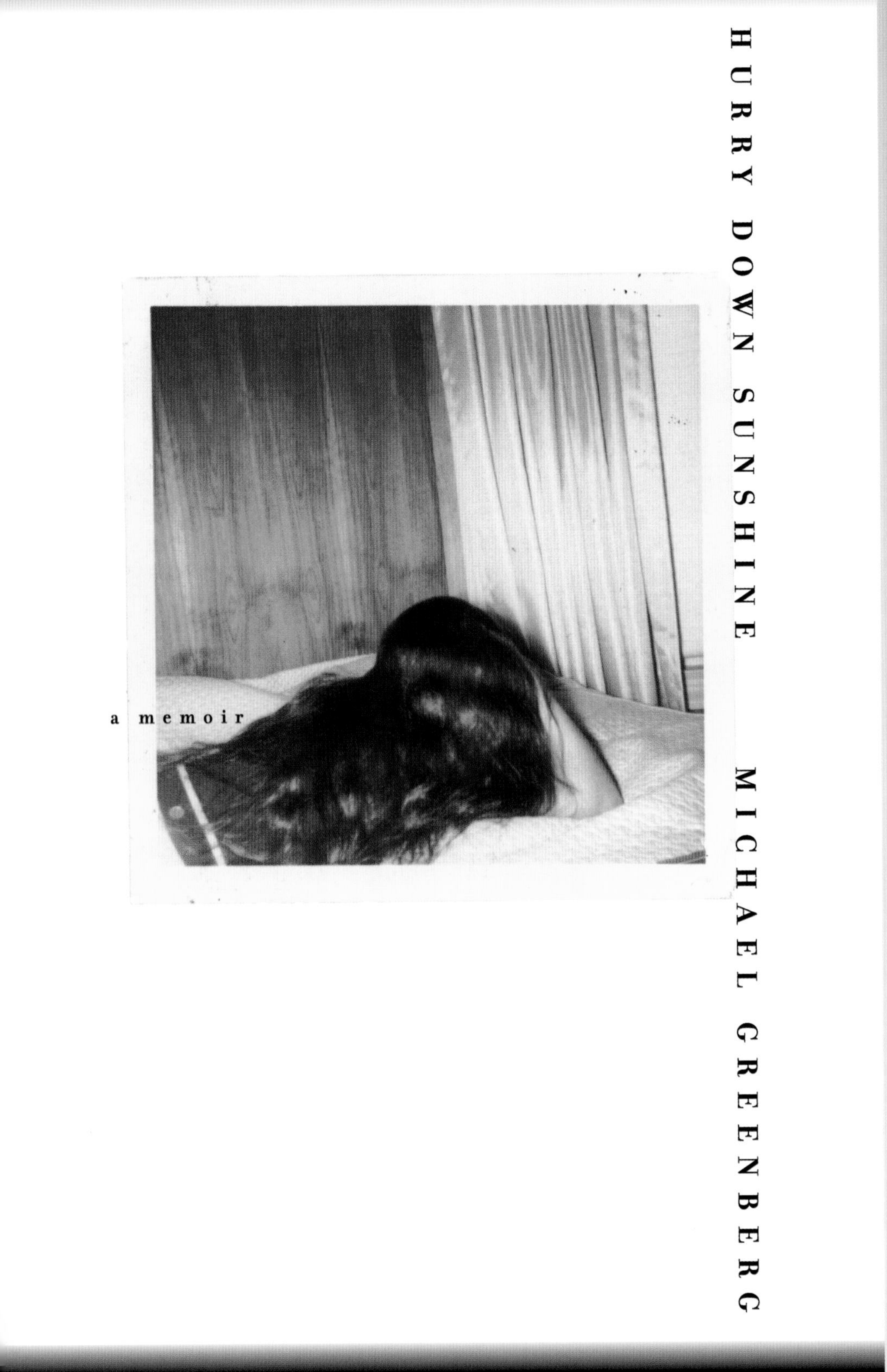
HURRY DOWN SUNSHINE
a memoir
MICHAEL GREENBERG

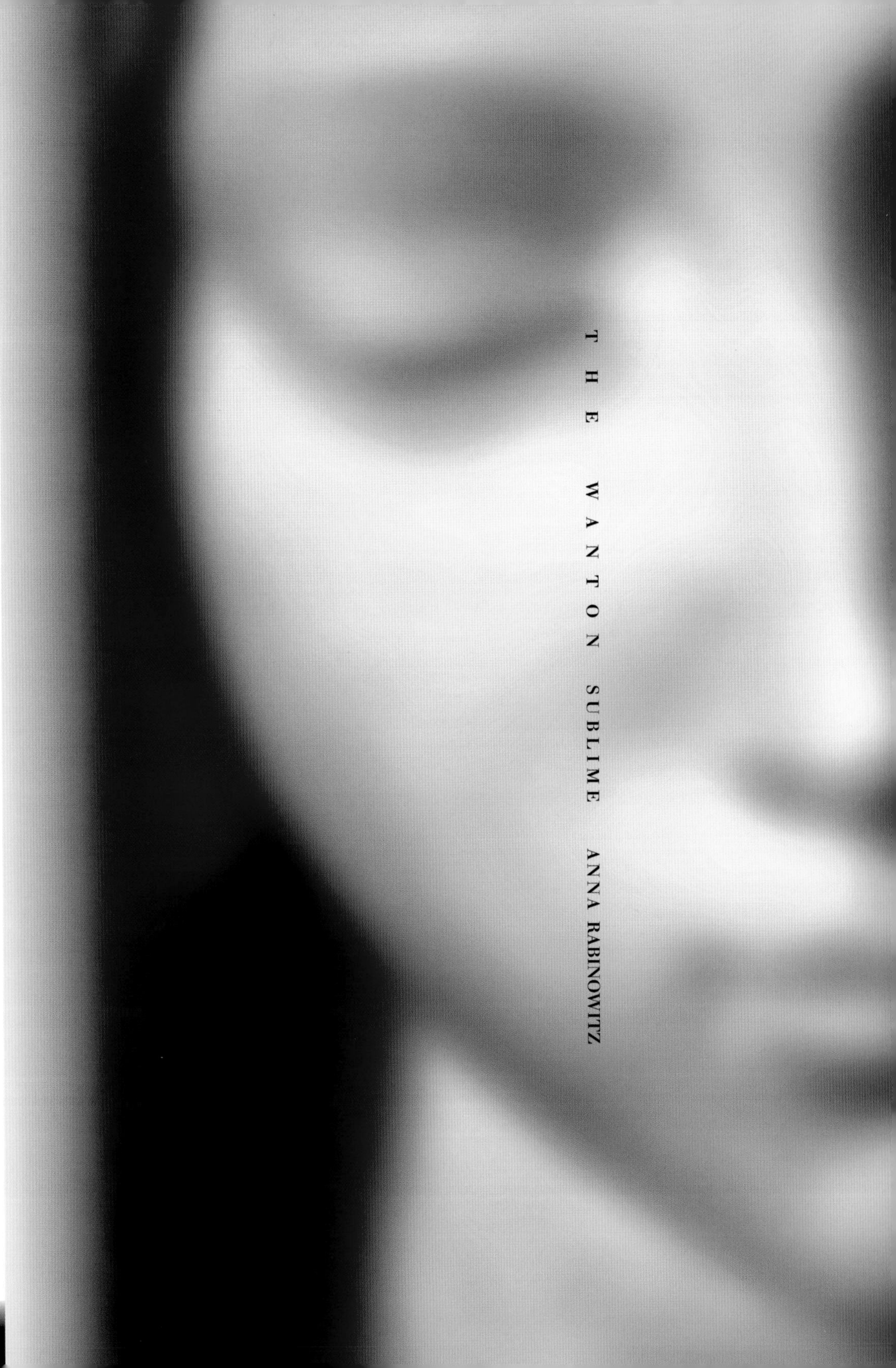
THE WANTON SUBLIME
ANNA RABINOWITZ

# Photographic Memories

*Hurry Down Sunshine* (opposite, left) and *The Wanton Sublime* (left) are very different books (the former is a memoir, the latter a series of impressionistic poems), but both convey a searing sense of lament and suffering that I thought required a compelling image to evoke instant empathy from the reader, to make them want to help. Michael Greenberg writes movingly about his teenaged daughter's struggle with mental illness; Anna Rabinowitz cuts through pieties and myths to get at the essential humanity of the Virgin Mary and, ultimately, of all women.

Donald Justice provided these slides of his paintings for use as possible cover art (right). They are shown exactly as I looked at them on a light box at the office—they are collected, they are poetic, they are in the perfect context for this cover.

OPPOSITE, LEFT: Other Press, 2008. LEFT: Tupelo Press, 2006. RIGHT: Knopf, 2004.

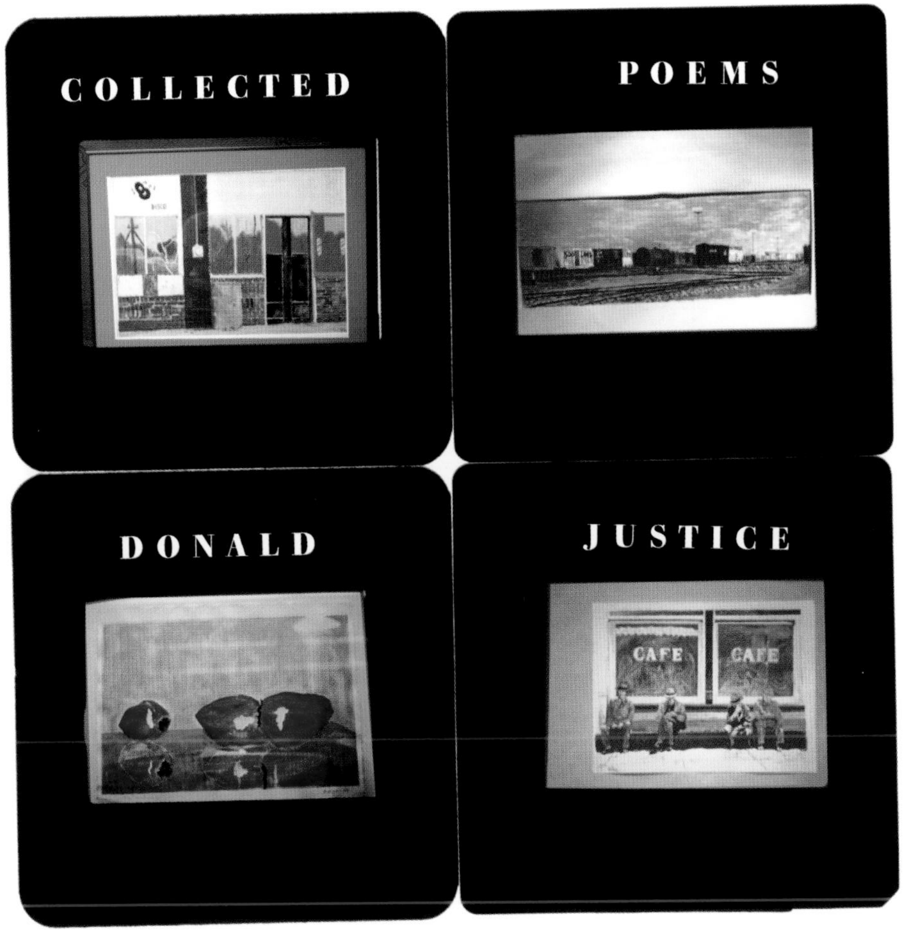

COLLECTED

POEMS

DONALD

JUSTICE

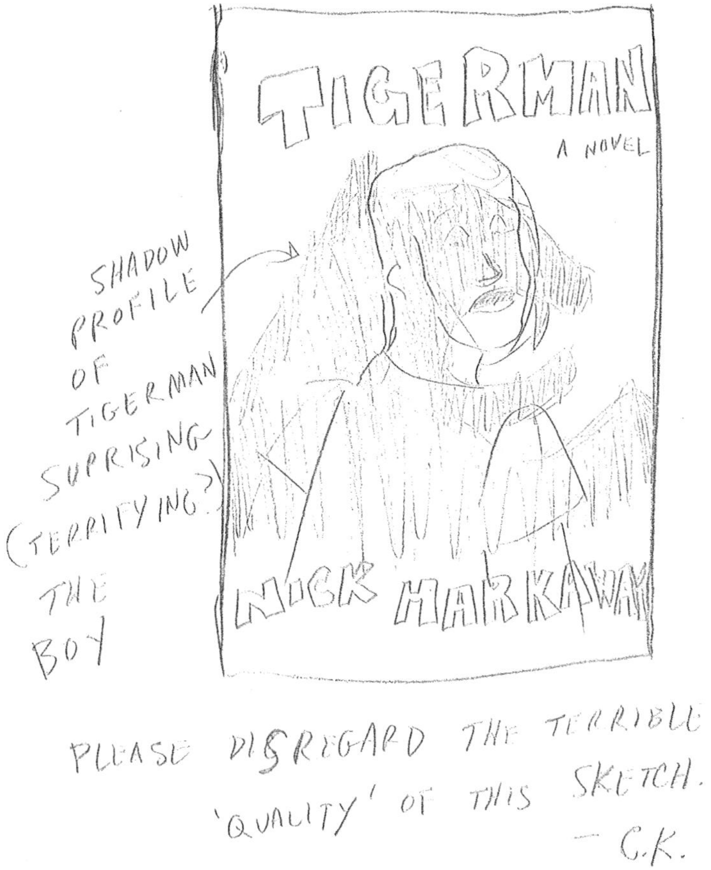
TIGERMAN
A NOVEL
SHADOW PROFILE OF TIGERMAN SUPRISING (TERRIFYING?) THE BOY
NICK HARKAWAY
PLEASE DISREGARD THE TERRIBLE 'QUALITY' OF THIS SKETCH.
— C.K.

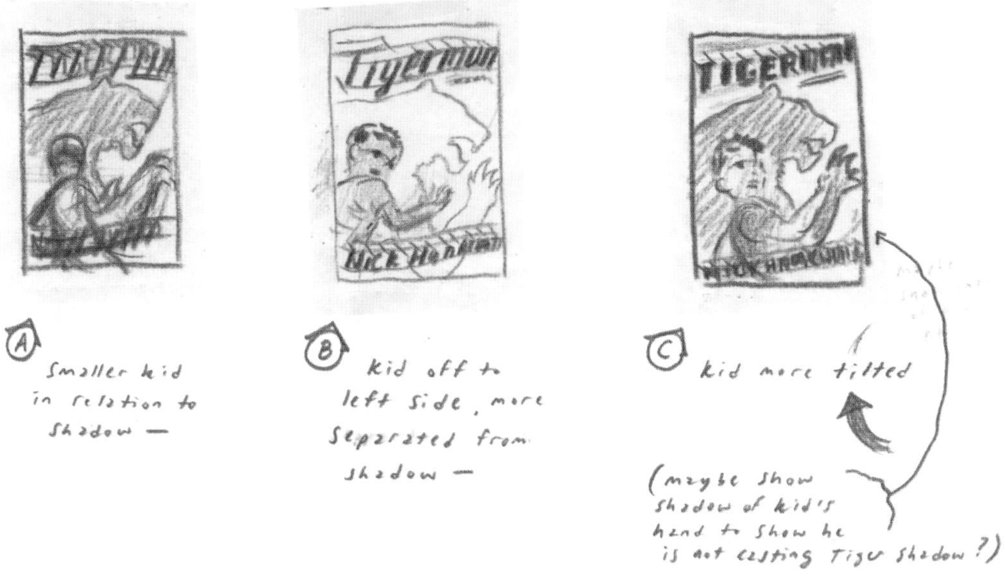
Tigerman
TIGERMAN
A
Smaller kid in relation to shadow —
B
Kid off to left side, more separated from shadow —
C
kid more tilted
(maybe show shadow of kid's hand to show he is not casting Tiger shadow?)

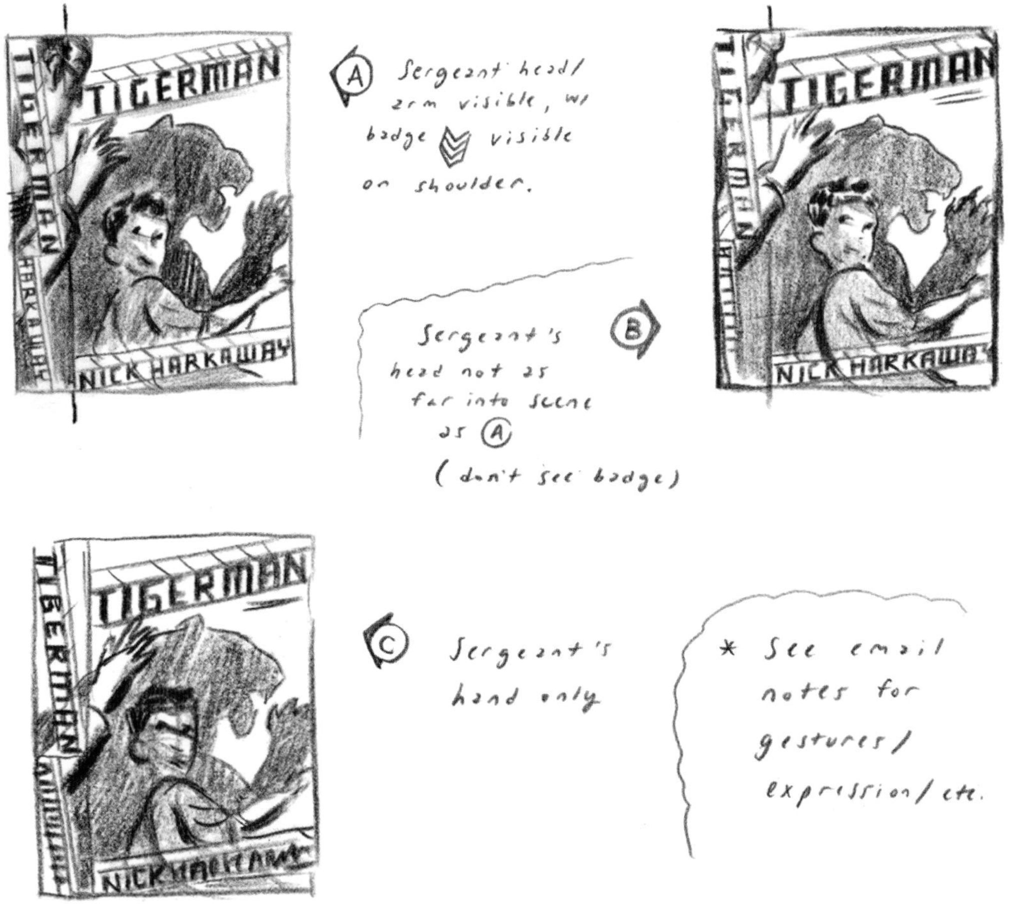
TIGERMAN
NICK HARKAWAY
A
Sergeant head/arm visible, w/ badge visible on shoulder.
Sergeant's head not as far into scene as A (don't see badge)
B
C
Sergeant's hand only
* See email notes for gestures/expression/etc.



## Hear Me Roar

I had been a fan of Vancouver-based illustrator and painter Ryan Heshka for years, and Nick Harkaway's novel *Tigerman* (Knopf, 2014) provided the perfect opportunity to finally work with him. It's the story of Sergeant Lester Ferris, a good man in need of a rest. After a long career of being shot at, he's about to retire, and the backwater island of Mancreu, a former British colony in legal limbo—belching toxic clouds of waste and facing imminent destruction by an international community afraid for their own safety—is the ideal place to serve out his time. There is an illicit Black Fleet lurking in the bay: spy stations, arms dealers, offshore hospitals, drug factories, and torture centers. Lester's brief, however, is to sit tight and turn a blind eye, so he drinks tea and befriends a brilliant, internet-addled street kid with a comic-book fixation. When Mancreu's fragile society erupts in violence, Lester must be more than just an observer: he has no choice but to rediscover the man of action he once was and find out what kind of hero the island—and the boy—will need. Which is, *ahem*, Tigerman.

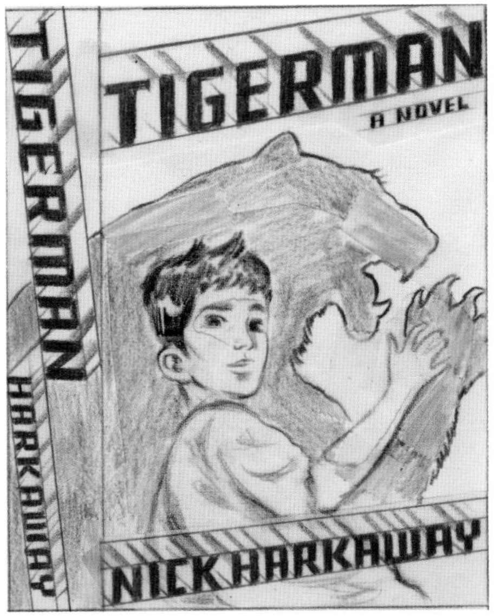
TIGERMAN
A NOVEL
TIGERMAN
HARKAWAY
NICK HARKAWAY

I thought of a shadow immediately—that Ferris was casting the silhouette of Tigerman over the boy and catching him by surprise. Ryan totally got this, and it then became a matter of nuance: at first I thought the lad should be terrified, but eventually we all agreed that he should look more empowered than afraid. Nick was in on this direction every step of the way, and he had some vital suggestions about details like Ferris's uniform. We honestly didn't intend it, but there is definitely a shout-out to the *Jurassic Park* image here.

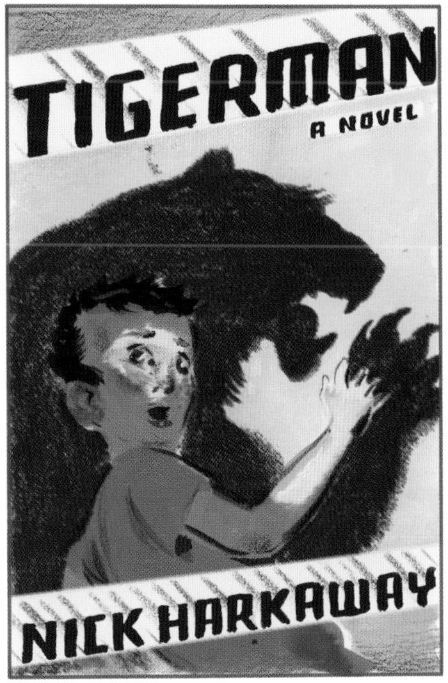
TIGERMAN
A NOVEL
NICK HARKAWAY

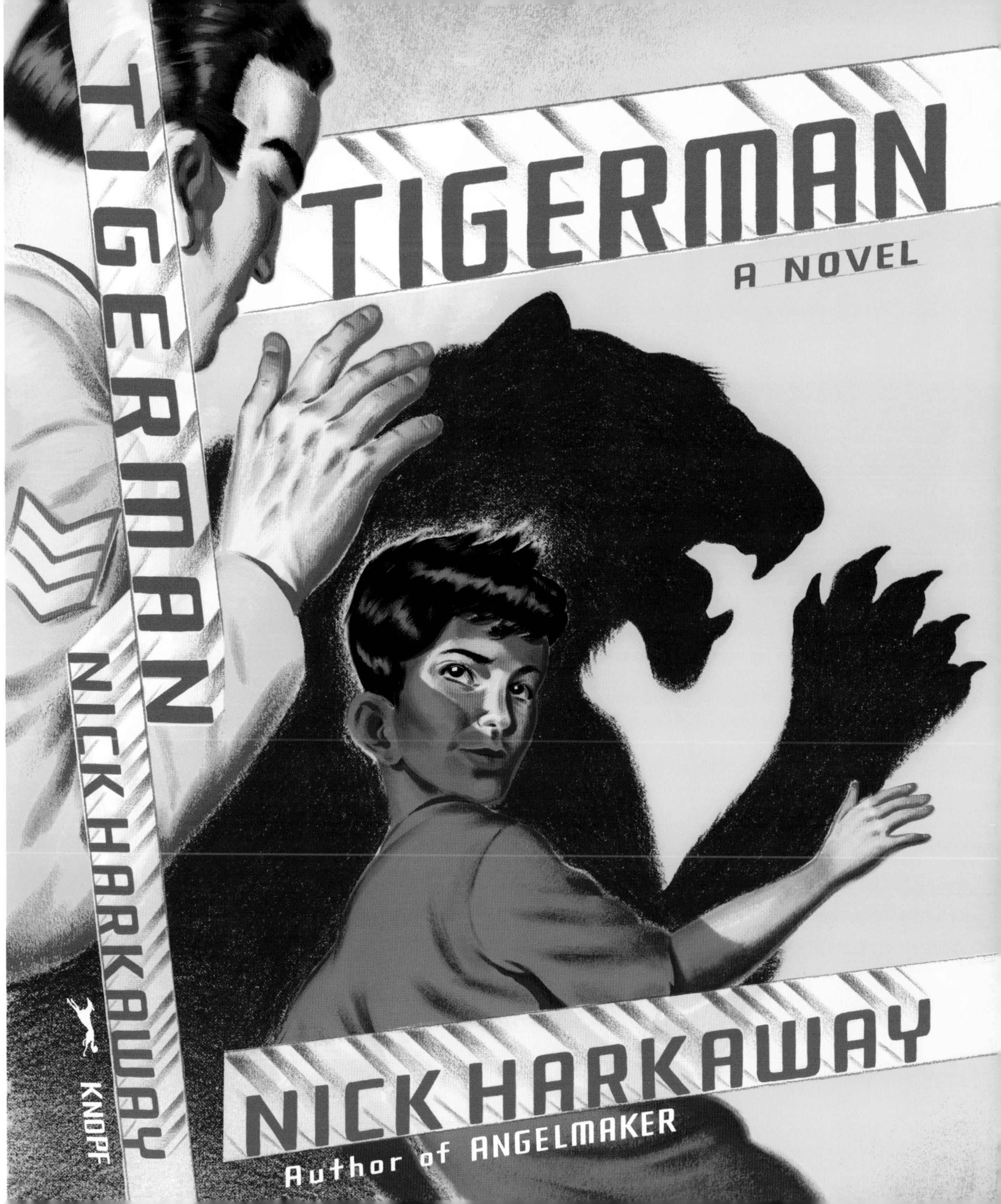
TIGERMAN
NICK HARKAWAY
KNOPF
TIGERMAN
A NOVEL
NICK HARKAWAY
Author of ANGELMAKER

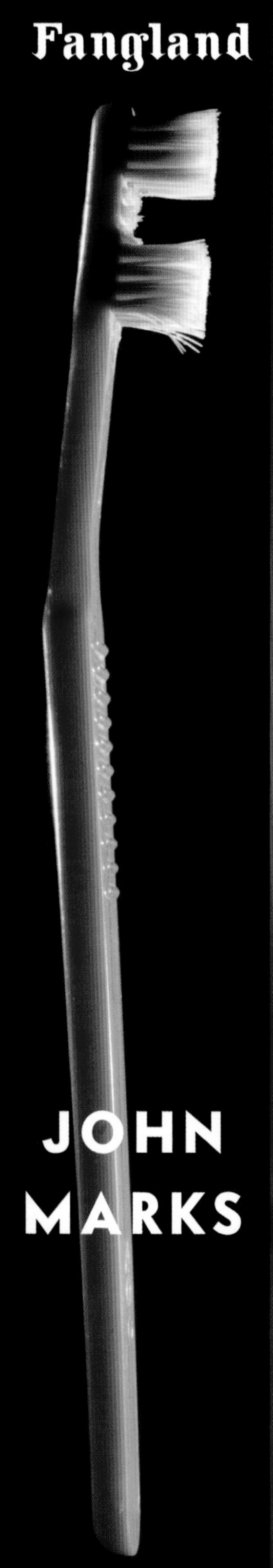
Fangland
JOHN
MARKS



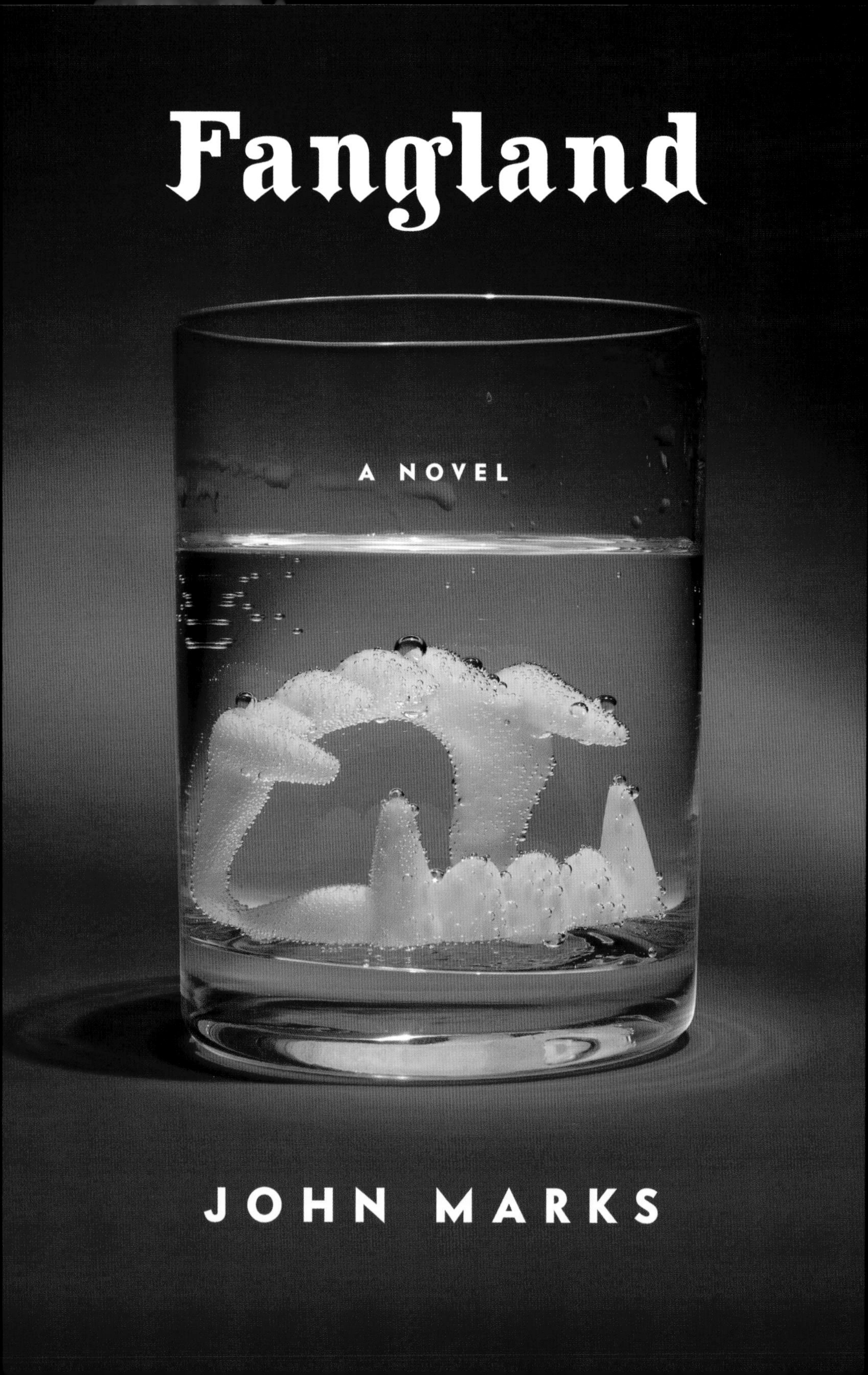
Fangland
A NOVEL
JOHN MARKS

## Use Your Teeth

The plot of *Fangland* is a little too ridiculous to bear dignified elaboration, but it involves vampires of a certain age (hey, they're immortal) and in love. And really, really horny. Maybe because it was a freelance job, and thus relatively little at stake (sorry!), but I couldn't resist the idea of fangs in a bedside glass of water (left) and a customized toothbrush. But boy, the publisher sure could (resist, that is)—I wasn't even given a second shot at this one. Killed in the coffin. (Thank you, Geoff, for trying, as always.)

Karen Russell's fascinating *Sleep Donation*—an e-book original for Francis Coady's sadly short-lived Atavist Books digital imprint—gave me my single chance so far to create an interactive book cover that incorporated sound, touch, and image transition into the experience (opposite, left). Kevin Tong provided the illustrations for a story about an alternate future in which a life-threatening sleep-deprivation disease has descended on humanity, and only a few qualified donors can provide relief.

When you first "open" the book you see the eyeball on the screen, which grows increasingly bloodshot and the sound of buzzing starts to build. Then you have to poke the eyeball and the scene shifts to night, the eye becomes the moon, the buzzing is replaced by crickets, and you see the full title. I loved this experience, but it also bolstered why I like traditional printed books—they can't be turned off with a switch.

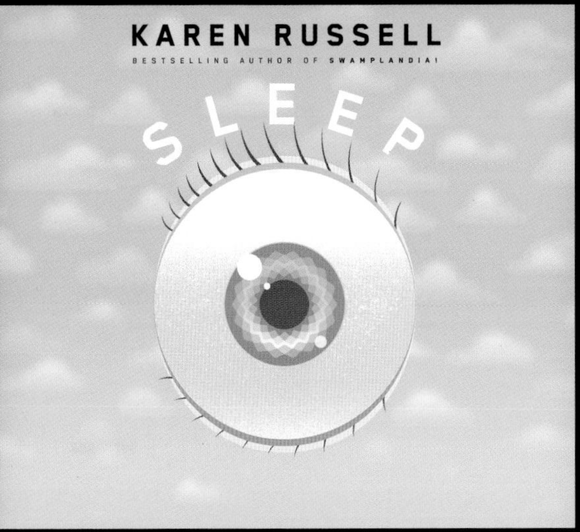
KAREN RUSSELL
BESTSELLING AUTHOR OF SWAMPLANDIA!
SLEEP

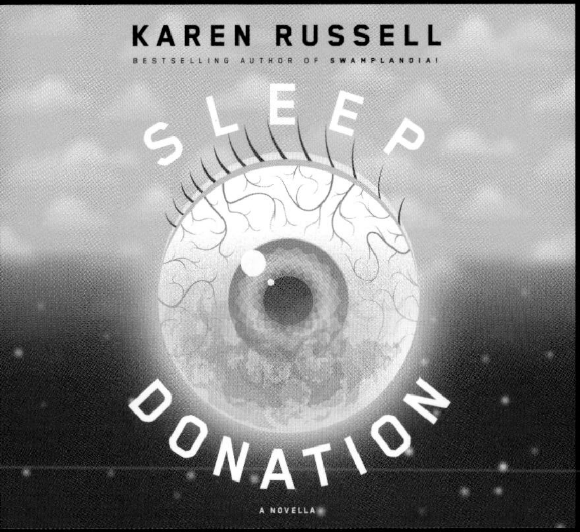
KAREN RUSSELL
BESTSELLING AUTHOR OF SWAMPLANDIA!
SLEEP
DONATION
A NOVELLA

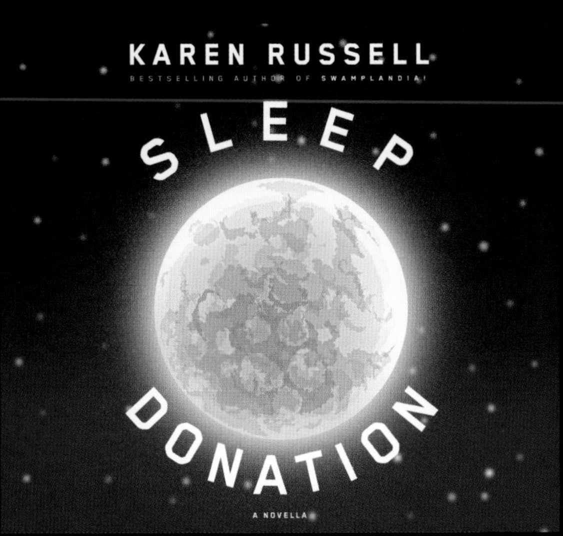
KAREN RUSSELL
BESTSELLING AUTHOR OF SWAMPLANDIA!
SLEEP
DONATION
A NOVELLA

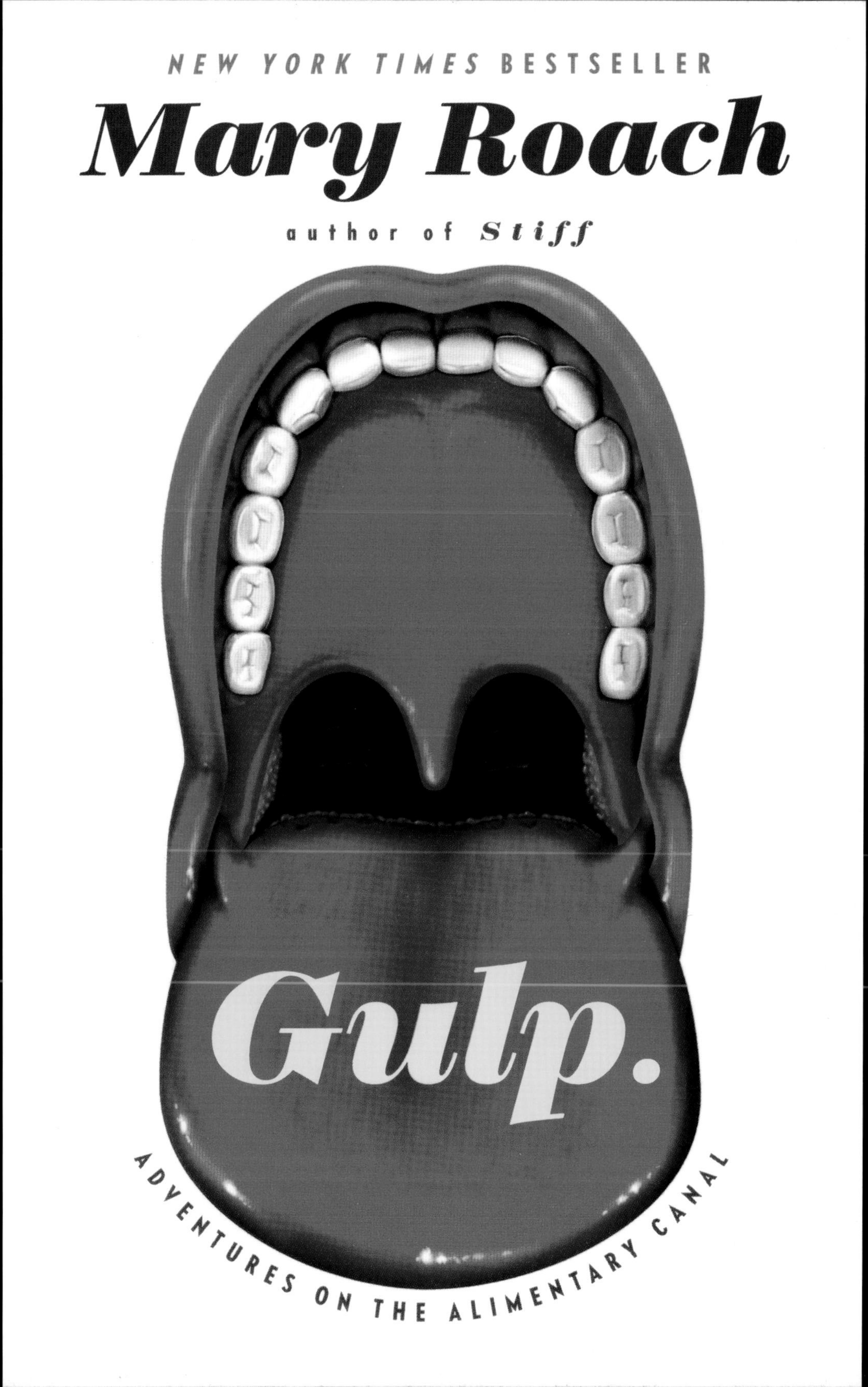
NEW YORK TIMES BESTSELLER
Mary Roach
author of Stiff
Gulp.
ADVENTURES ON THE ALIMENTARY CANAL

**RIGHT:** Mary Roach is the best high-school science teacher you always wanted and never had. She makes subjects like human cadavers and animal sex seem like the coolest things in the world. Likewise the human digestive system, the subject of *Gulp* (W. W. Norton, 2013). I realized I need to show the start of the process in as palatable a way as possible, as opposed to the end of said system. *Ahem.* This book—and cover—was a big hit. My work on the follow-up, *Grunt* (overleaf), sadly, was not.

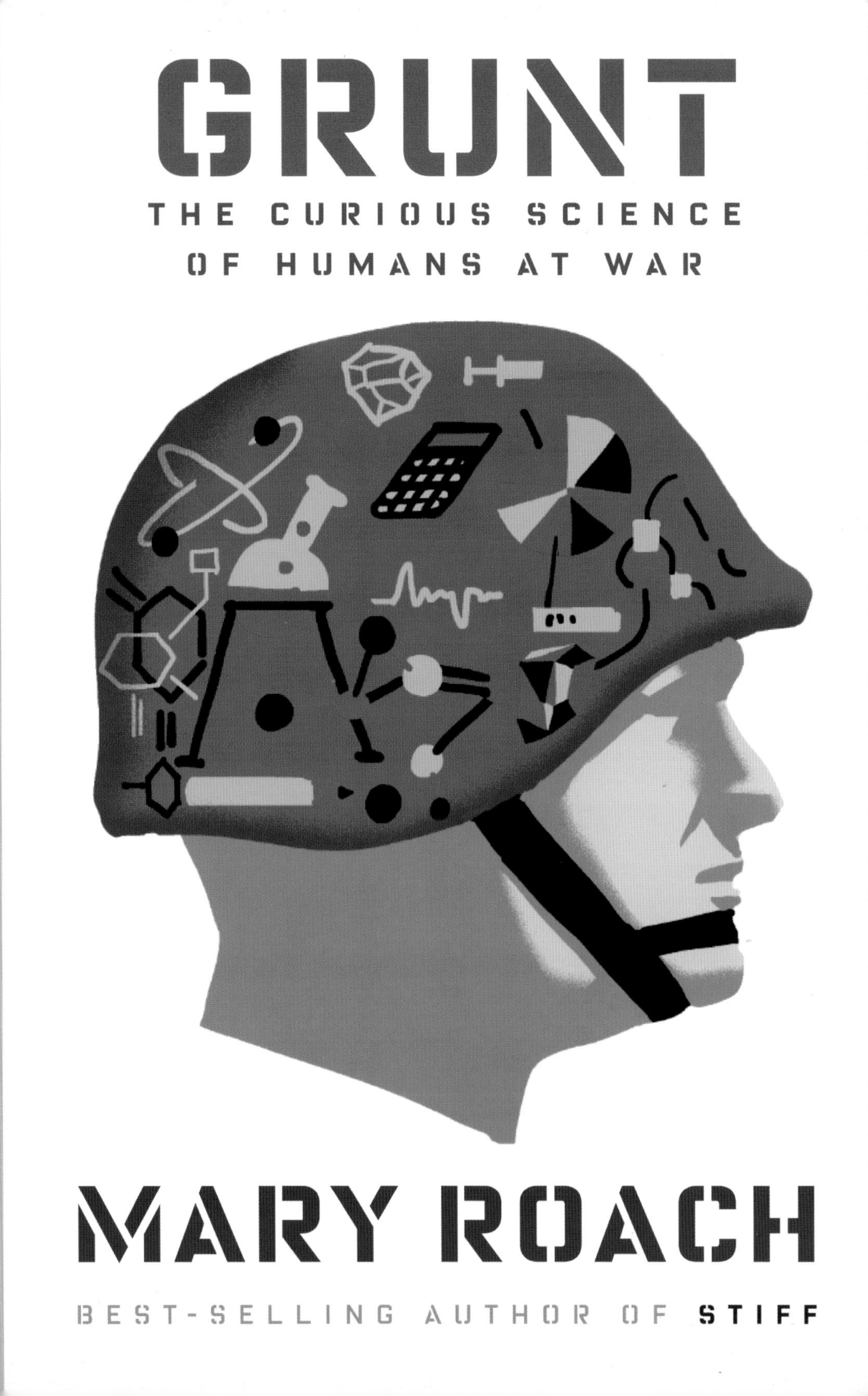
GRUNT
THE CURIOUS SCIENCE
OF HUMANS AT WAR
MARY ROACH
BEST-SELLING AUTHOR OF STIFF



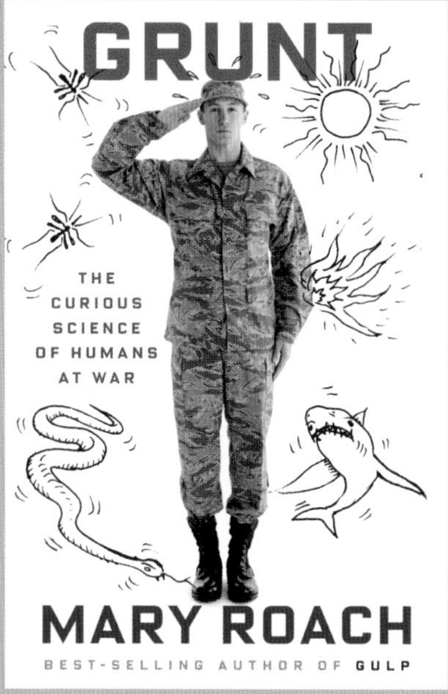
GRUNT
THE CURIOUS SCIENCE OF HUMANS AT WAR
MARY ROACH
BEST-SELLING AUTHOR OF GULP

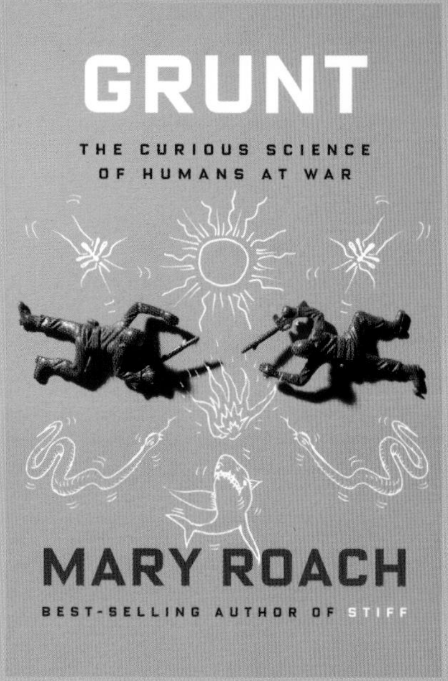
GRUNT
THE CURIOUS SCIENCE
OF HUMANS AT WAR
MARY ROACH
BEST-SELLING AUTHOR OF STIFF

I was excited by the chance to work on *Grunt*, Mary Roach's examination of "the curious science of humans at war." This book wasn't about politics; it was about how best to serve our military through science and technology. It had everything to do with how efforts in the lab could mitigate the struggles on the battlefield. For the jacket, I was told that it had to look amusing, which kept throwing me off—to me, there was nothing that inspired a whimsical take on our troops engaging in battle. I asked good friend and brilliant conceptual illustrator Christoph Niemann to get involved, and these efforts (left & lower left) were deemed too retro/WWII. They asked me to work with real images of soldiers (above left), but that didn't achieve the desired effect, and neither did toy soldiers. I was sorry the project ended there. I really thought we were on the right path.

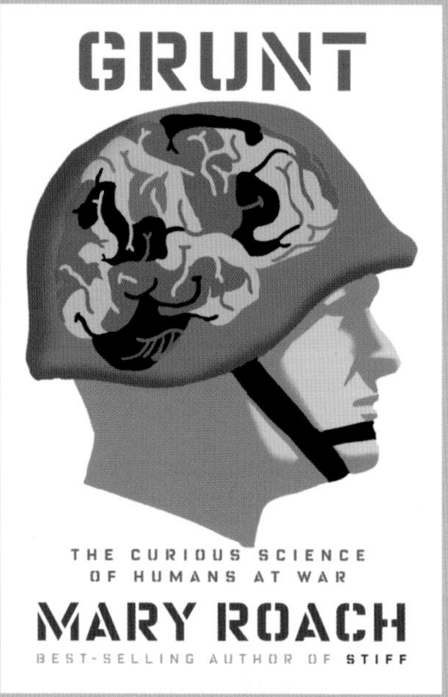
GRUNT
THE CURIOUS SCIENCE
OF HUMANS AT WAR
MARY ROACH
BEST-SELLING AUTHOR OF STIFF

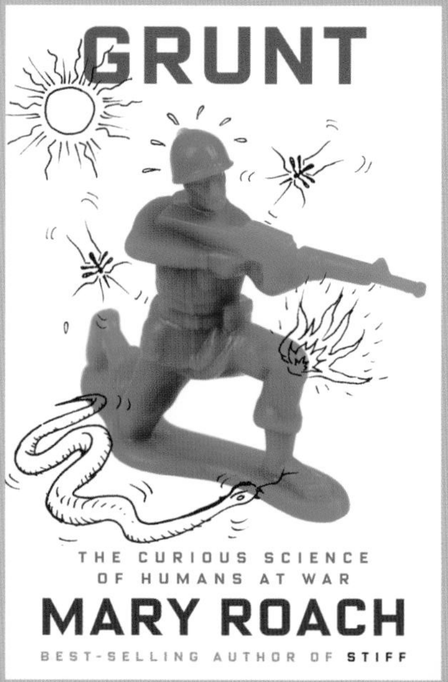
GRUNT
THE CURIOUS SCIENCE
OF HUMANS AT WAR
MARY ROACH
BEST-SELLING AUTHOR OF STIFF

## Profiles in Courage

*Duty* is Robert M. Gates's memoir of his time as U.S. Secretary of Defense under three very different administrations. It was the perfect title—declarative, clear without being overfamiliar, and to the point. Part of the challenge was that the manuscript was embargoed; no one in-house other than the editor Jonathan Segal and Sonny Mehta were allowed to read it until publication. The reason was the considerable revelations that the recently retired Gates was going to make; in the meantime all I had to go on were discussions with Jonathan about the tone and essence of the book, which was about balancing the ultimate military command with a tremendous sense of compassion. We discussed doing our own photo shoot, but a search of existing photography led to a recent *Time* magazine cover from February 15, 2010, shot by the wonderful portrait photographer Platon. The *Time* cover had clearly been Photoshopped, but Platon's rep had outtakes: stark full-color headshots that I felt were much more powerful than the black-and-white full-figure image the magazine ran. Even better, permissions were not a problem. So there it is at right: just the perfect mix of power and vulnerability that is so touchingly conveyed in the text (once we got a chance to read it!). The book was a huge hit, and the front page of the *New York Times Book Review* declared it "probably one of the best Washington memoirs ever." Gates's follow-up was a book on leadership (below), for which I used a shot of him on the tarmac about to address a phalanx of reporters in China.

**RIGHT:** Knopf, 2014. **BELOW:** Knopf, 2016. Photo courtesy of Stephen Salpukas/William & Mary.

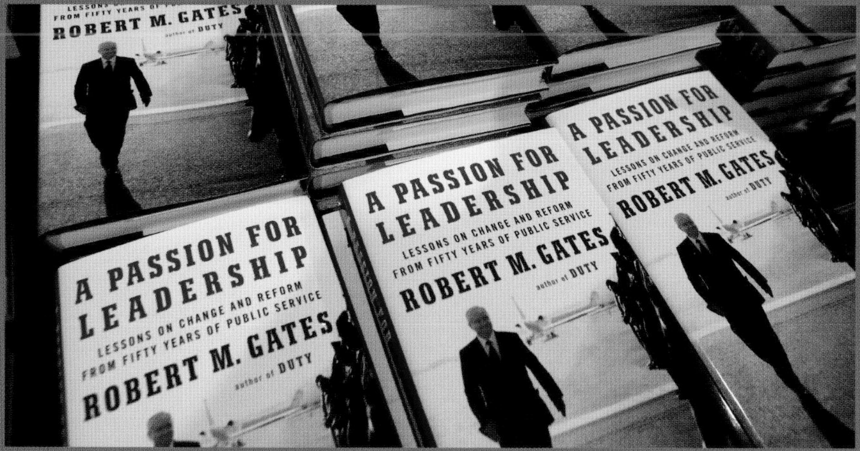
A PASSION FOR LEADERSHIP
LESSONS ON CHANGE AND REFORM FROM FIFTY YEARS OF PUBLIC SERVICE
ROBERT M. GATES
author of DUTY

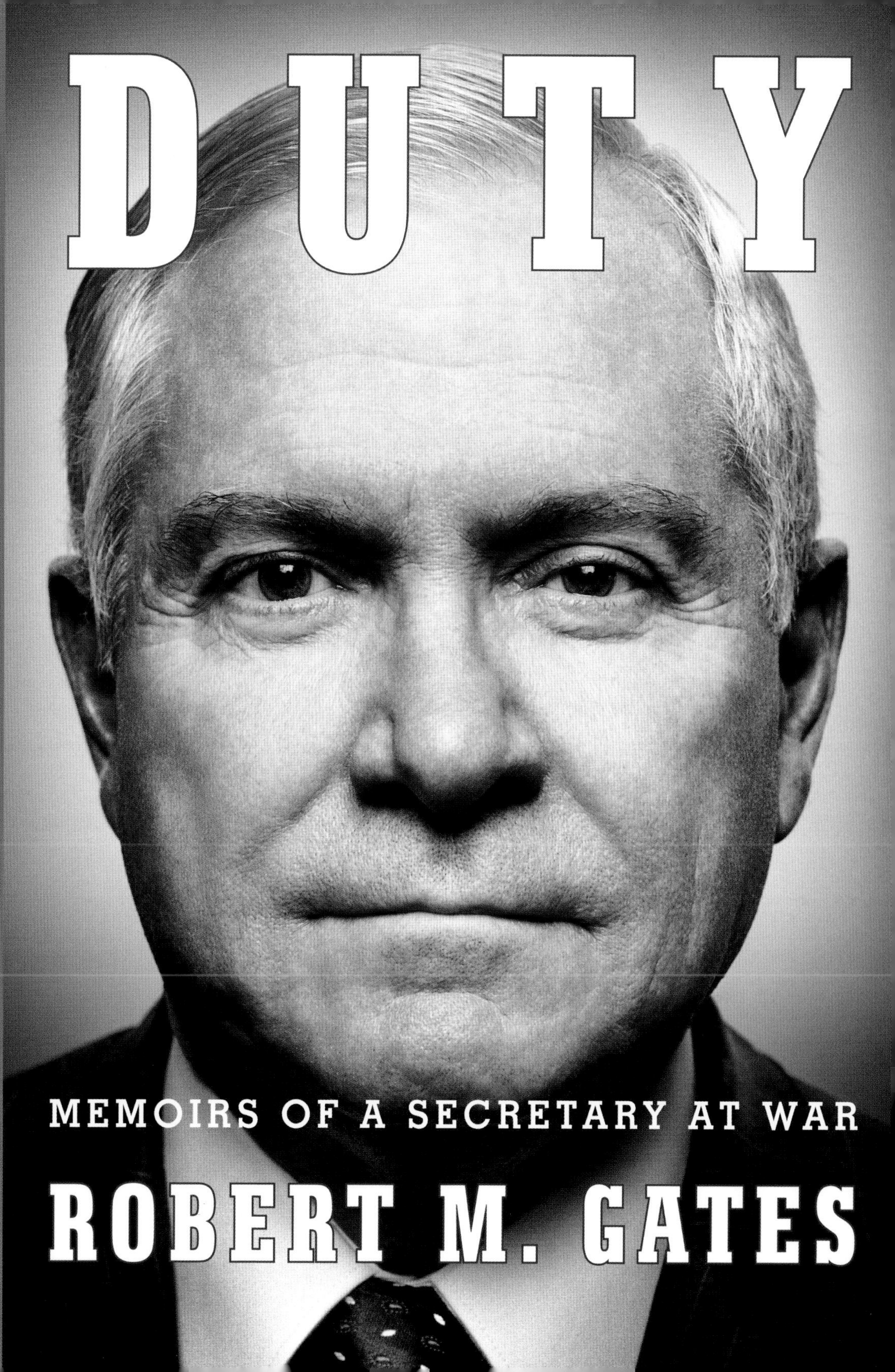
DUTY
MEMOIRS OF A SECRETARY AT WAR
ROBERT M. GATES

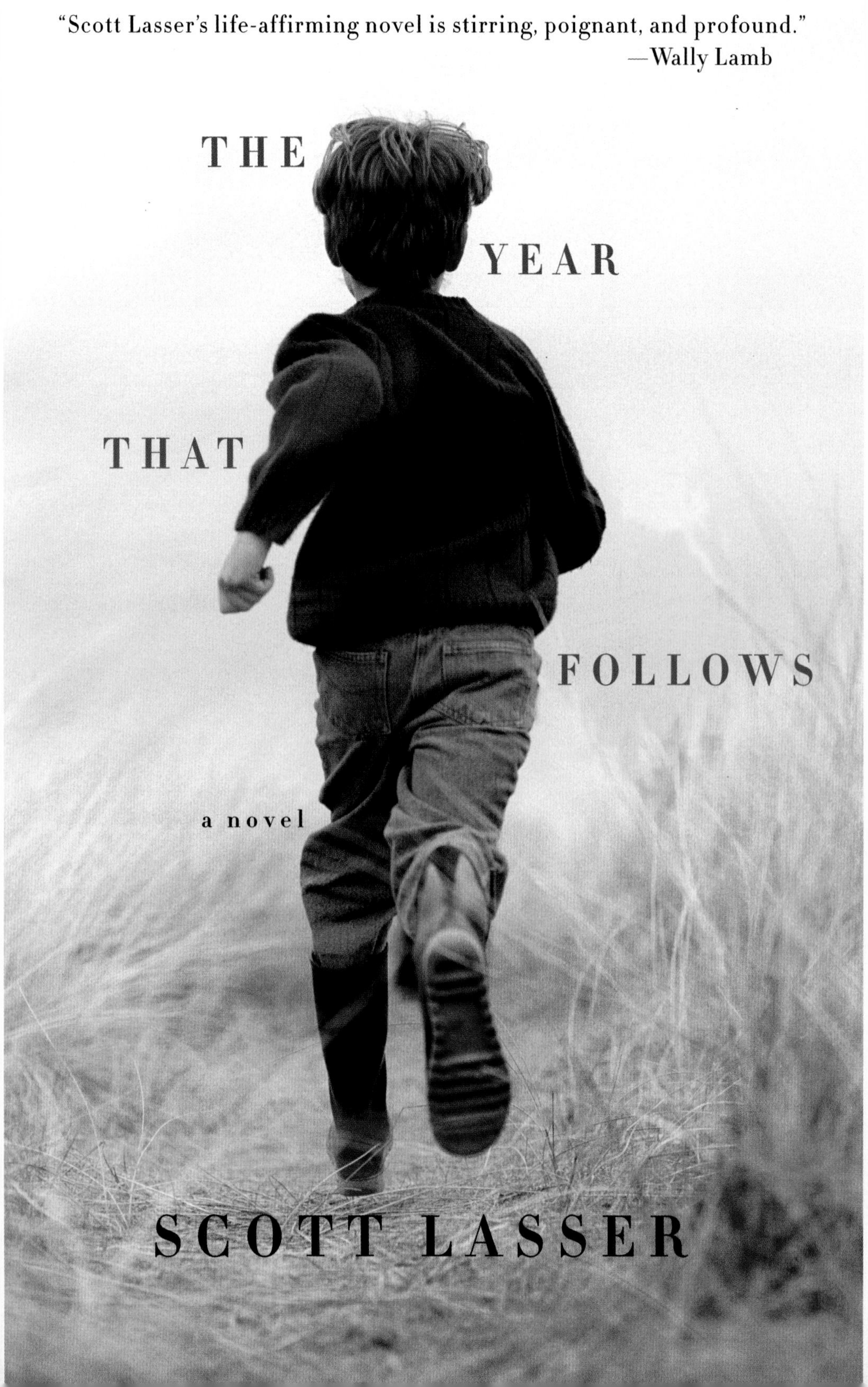
"Scott Lasser's life-affirming novel is stirring, poignant, and profound."
—Wally Lamb
THE
YEAR
THAT
FOLLOWS
a novel
SCOTT LASSER



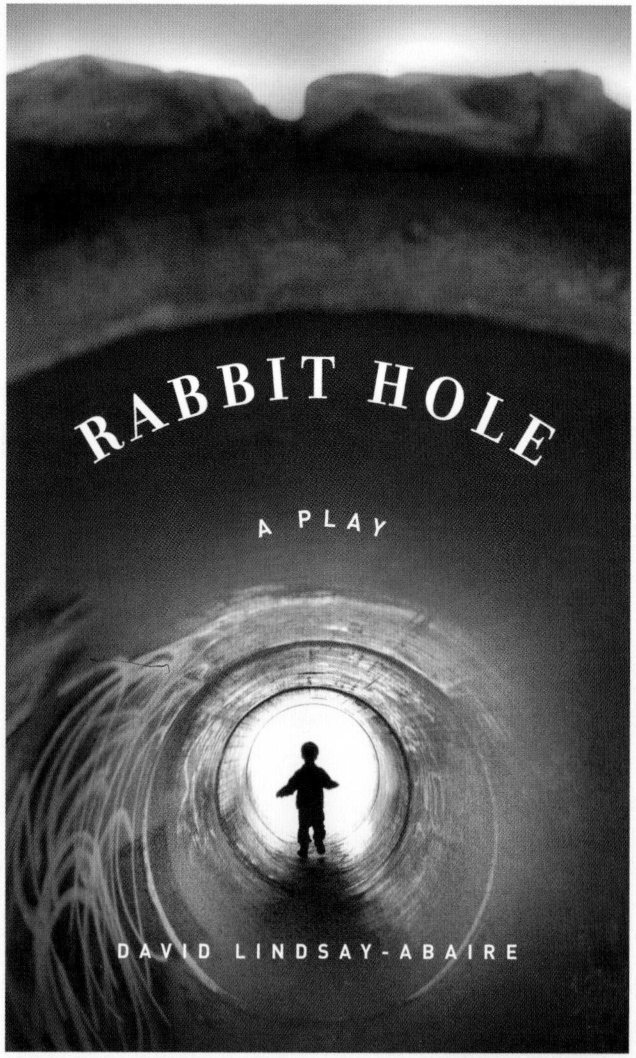
RABBIT HOLE
A PLAY
DAVID LINDSAY-ABAIRE

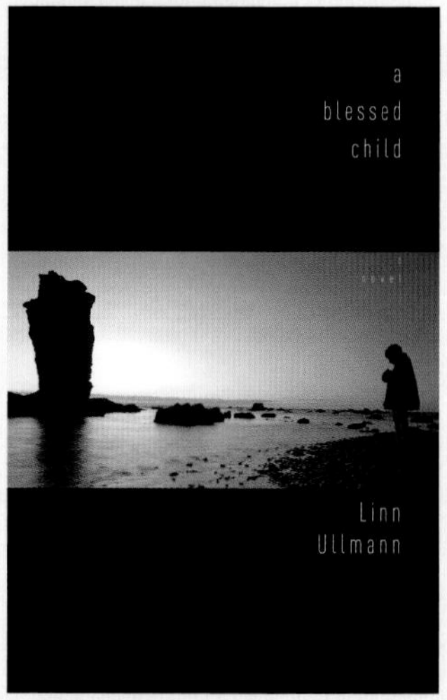
a
blessed
child
Linn
Ullmann

**LEFT:** Knopf, 2009.

**ABOVE:** Theatre Communications Group, 2006.

**RIGHT:** Linn Ullmann—daughter of Ingmar Bergman and Liv Ullmann—explores themes of familial loyalty despite turbulent emotions among a group of three sisters with the same father but different mothers in *A Blessed Child*. The story takes place on the tiny Baltic island of Hammerso. Monolithic rock formations on the beach are common there. Knopf, 2008.

# Child's Play

The title of Scott Lasser's novel (opposite, left) refers to the year that follows 9/11, as well as a young woman's quest to find the orphaned child of her brother, who died in the towers.

*Rabbit Hole* (opposite, right) by David Lindsay-Abaire is a play that hinges on the tragic loss of a young boy who runs into street traffic and is mowed down by a car driven by an unwitting teenager. All those who survive the victim—his parents, grandparents, and the young driver—are forced to deal with the consequences of this tragedy and figure out how to go on in the wake of it. On Broadway, the mother was played by Cynthia Nixon, who brought the audience to tears every night. For the book jacket I wanted to present a starker idea of the child transitioning from our realm of existence to another.

*Death of a Murderer* (right) by Rupert Thomson is a parable about the crimes of the notorious real-life British serial child-sex "Moors-murderer" Myra Hindley, as seen through the eyes of Billy Tyler, an underachieving, unambitious policeman who gets the night shift guarding the killer's body, which is lying in a hospital morgue before cremation.

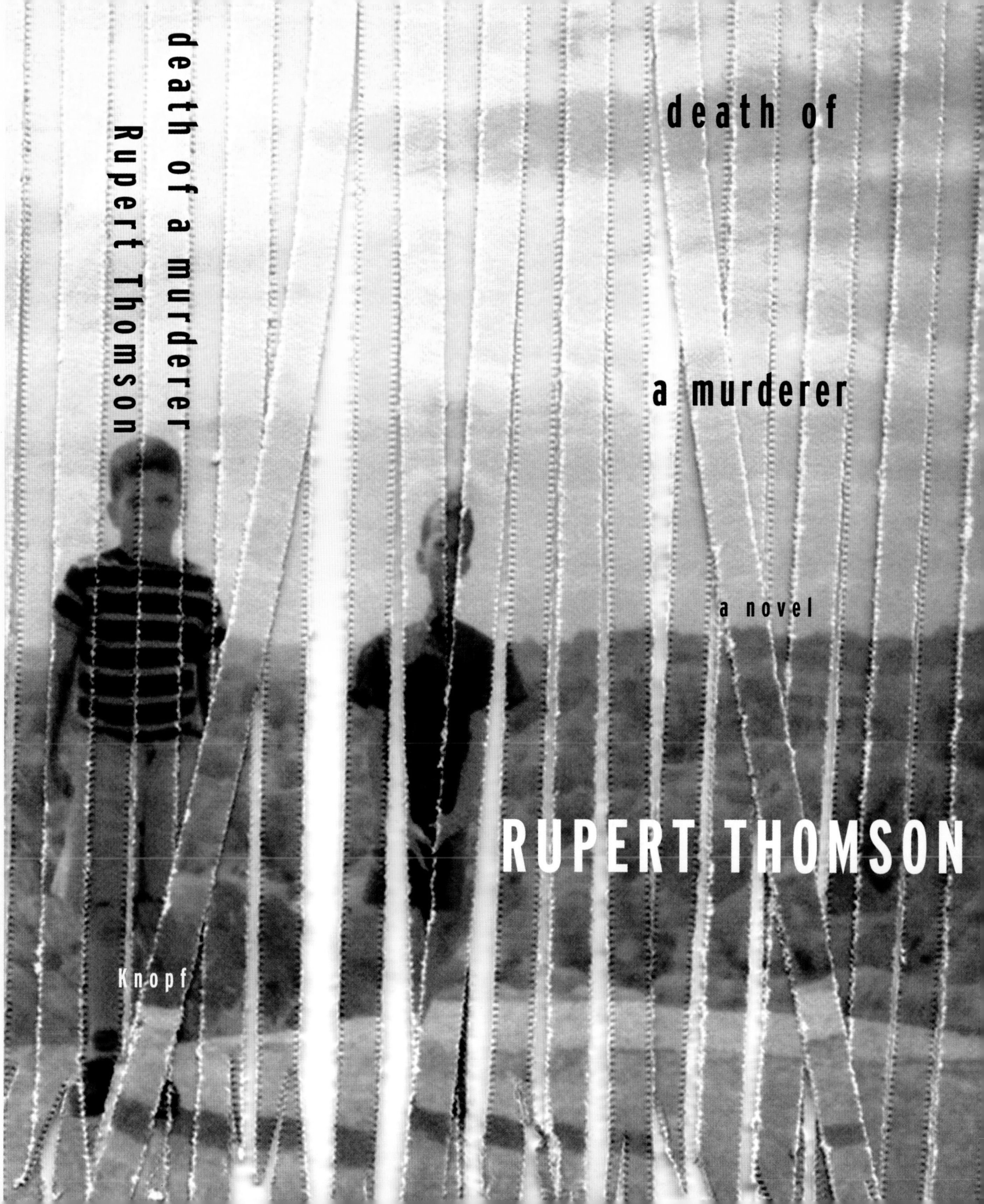
death of a murderer
Rupert Thomson
Knopf
death of
a murderer
a novel
RUPERT THOMSON

ROBERT
HUGHES

THINGS
I
DIDN'T
KNOW

KNOPF

# ROBERT HUGHES

# THINGS I DIDN'T KNOW

## A MEMOIR

by the author of THE FATAL SHORE

## Signature Style

The design of Robert Hughes's memoir of his early years before he became the most acclaimed art critic of the late 20th century, *Things I Didn't Know* (left), is a riff on the cover I created for a revised and updated edition of his seminal book *The Shock of the New*. It's a visual tweak on the idea of personal revisionist history, with a nod to the confessional, rather than the cover-up.

For the cover of *The Spectacle of Skill* (right), a posthumous collection of Hughes's collected writings that included the beginnings of what was to be the follow-up to *Things I Didn't Know*, I went all sentimental and used the background of a stretched canvas and Bob's signature of the dedication that he wrote in my copy of *American Visions: The Epic History of Art in America*.

**OPPOSITE:** Knopf, 2006.
**RIGHT:** Knopf, 2015.

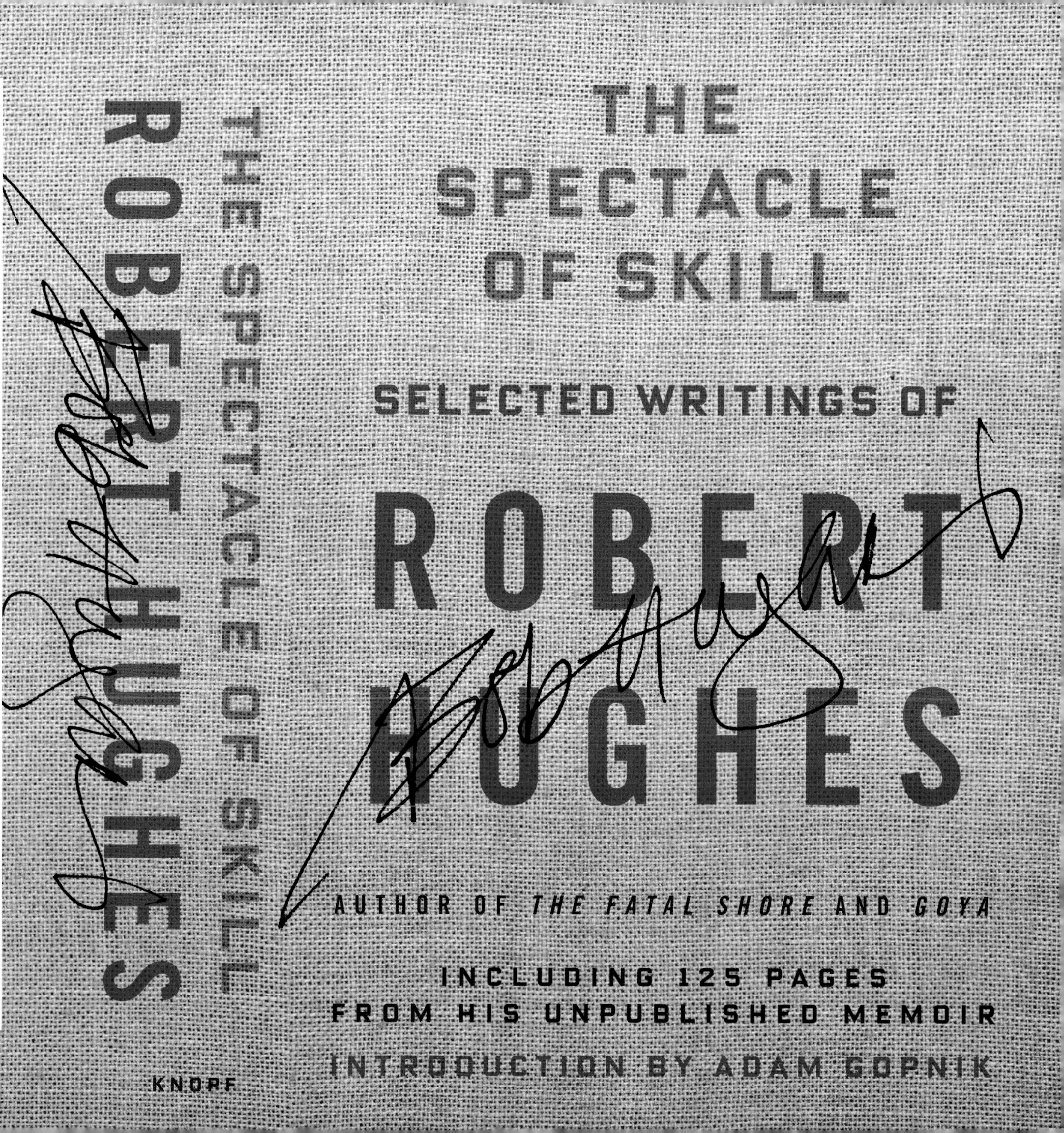
ROBERT HUGHES
THE SPECTACLE OF SKILL
KNOPF
THE SPECTACLE OF SKILL
SELECTED WRITINGS OF
ROBERT HUGHES
AUTHOR OF THE FATAL SHORE AND GOYA
INCLUDING 125 PAGES FROM HIS UNPUBLISHED MEMOIR
INTRODUCTION BY ADAM GOPNIK

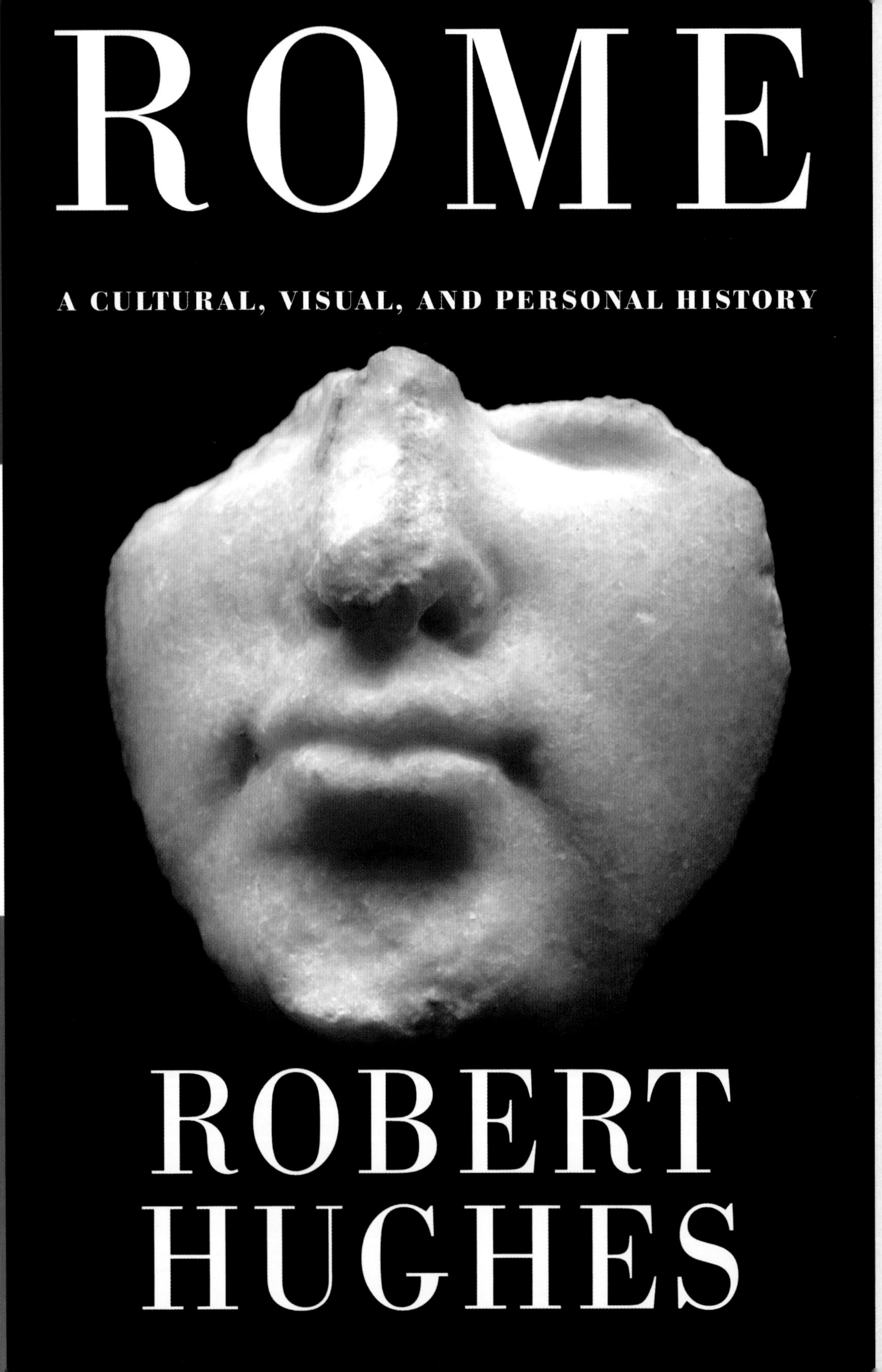
ROME
A CULTURAL, VISUAL, AND PERSONAL HISTORY
ROBERT
HUGHES

**RIGHT, TOP & BOTTOM:** I was able to design Hughes's *Rome* while he was still alive and I struggled with using the Sistine ceiling or Bernini's *Ecstasy of Saint Teresa.* But both were too busy for the stark look I thought was necessary; the type didn't read well.

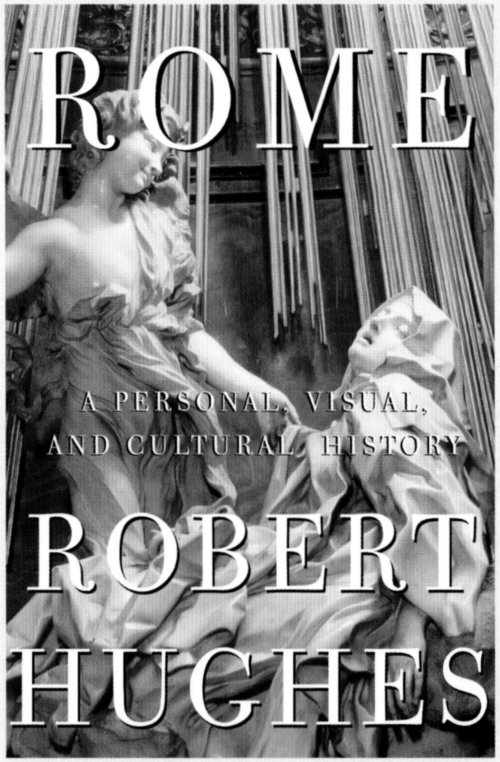
ROME
A PERSONAL, VISUAL,
AND CULTURAL HISTORY
ROBERT
HUGHES

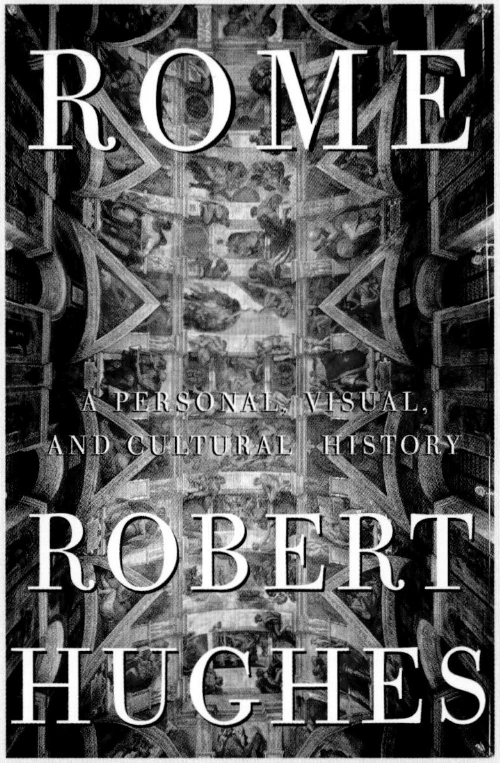
ROME
A PERSONAL, VISUAL,
AND CULTURAL HISTORY
ROBERT
HUGHES

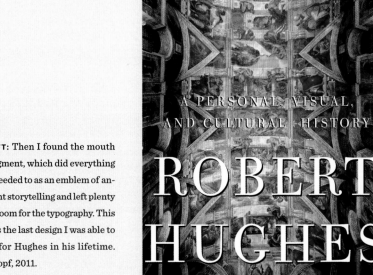

**LEFT:** Then I found the mouth fragment, which did everything it needed to as an emblem of ancient storytelling and left plenty of room for the typography. This was the last design I was able to do for Hughes in his lifetime. Knopf, 2011.

## Body Politic

Yes, that's his real hat. Or one of them, anyway. There are so many wonderful images of Abraham Lincoln in this book, but it was the hat that really got me. Plus, how many historic figures are so iconic that you can read the name and see that image and totally get it? The authors were true sports for trusting me on this. Lincoln is everyone's hero, for every good reason; the greatness of all that he said and did still resonates with us today, and it will for generations to come.

**RIGHT:** Knopf, 2008.

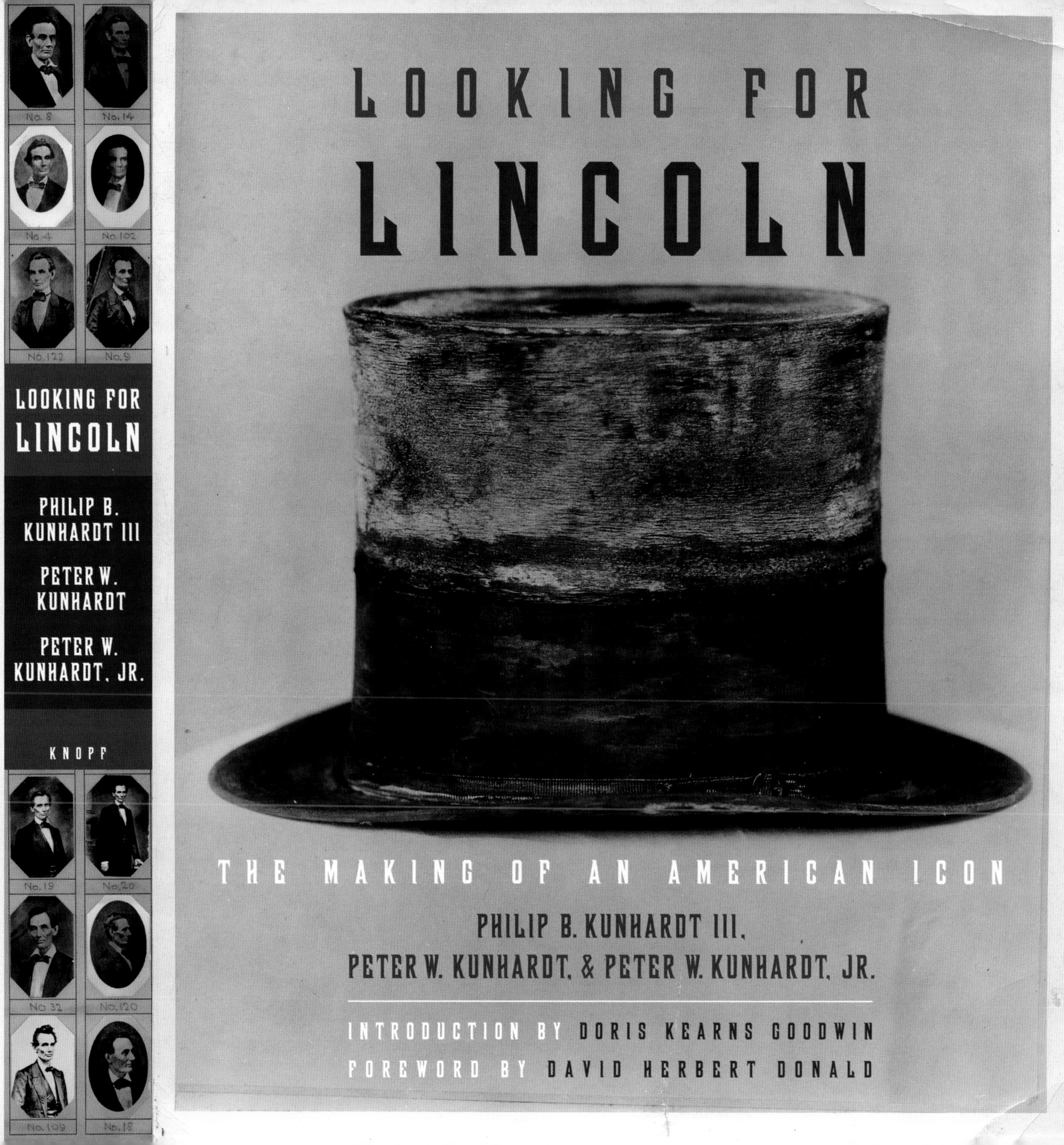
No. 8
No. 14
No. 4
No. 102
No. 122
No. 9
LOOKING FOR LINCOLN
PHILIP B. KUNHARDT III
PETER W. KUNHARDT
PETER W. KUNHARDT, JR.
KNOPF
No. 19
No. 20
No. 32
No. 120
No. 109
No. 18
LOOKING FOR LINCOLN
THE MAKING OF AN AMERICAN ICON
PHILIP B. KUNHARDT III,
PETER W. KUNHARDT, & PETER W. KUNHARDT, JR.
INTRODUCTION BY DORIS KEARNS GOODWIN
FOREWORD BY DAVID HERBERT DONALD

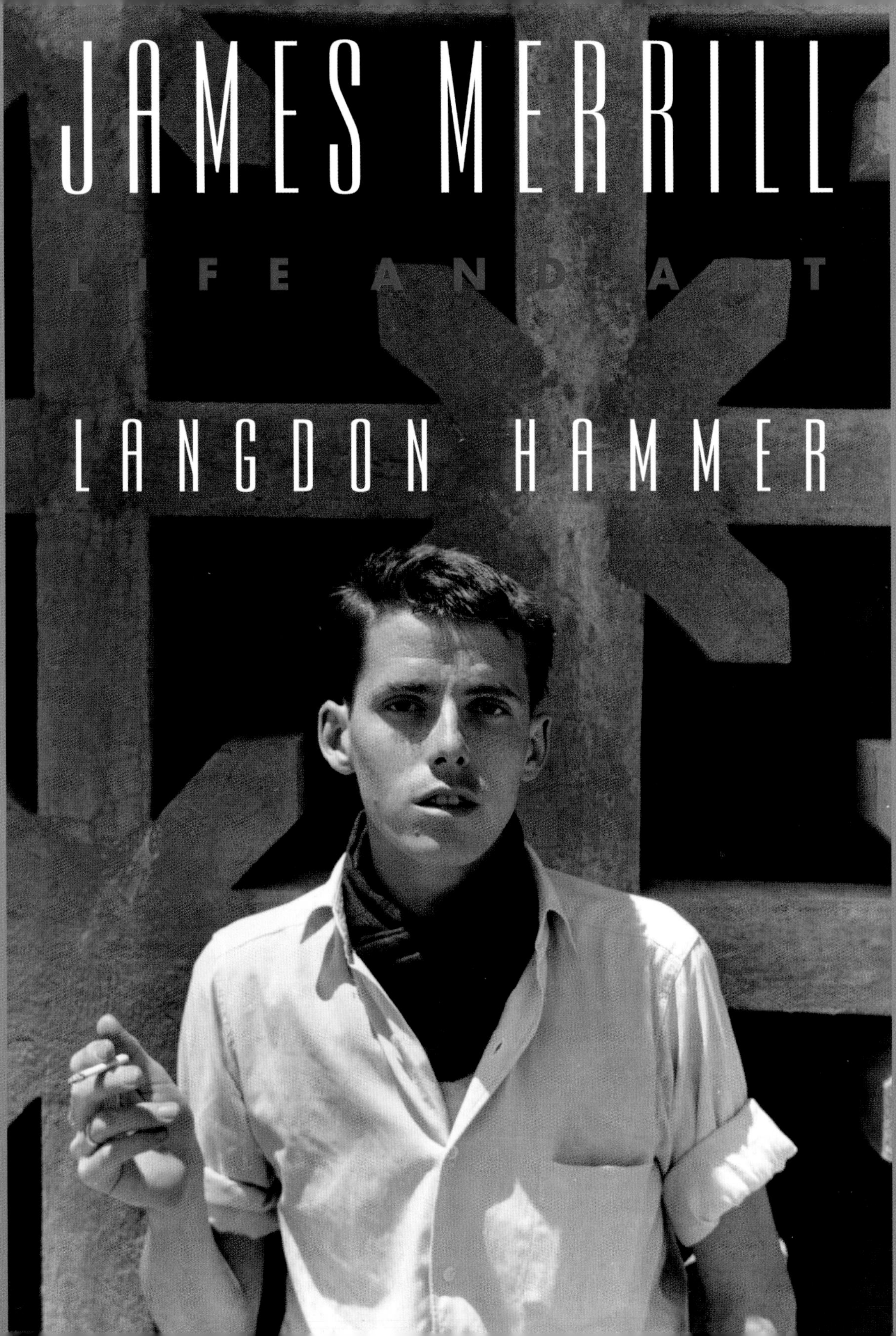
JAMES MERRILL
LIFE AND ART
LANGDON HAMMER



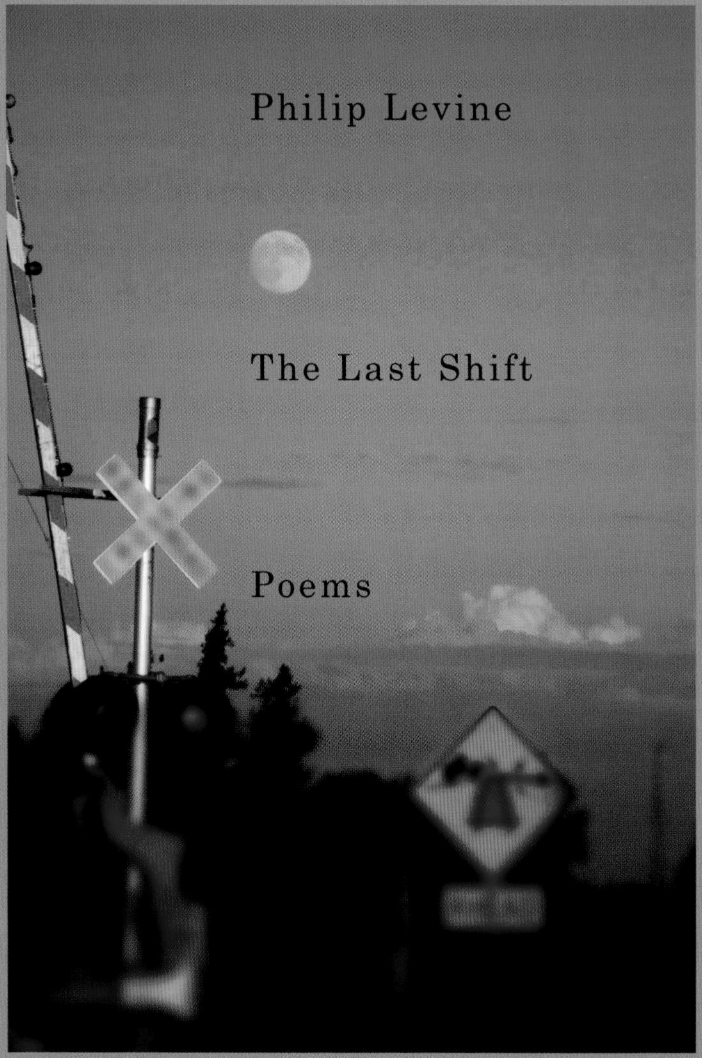
Philip Levine
The Last Shift
Poems

## Lettermen Jackets

Prior to this biography of James Merrill (left), I had designed half a dozen collections of his oeuvre (poems, plays, novels) using photos of him later in life, but this jacket had to be different. The author, Lanny Hammer, found this image of the young poet on the cusp of becoming the artist he would become, and it was just so right. The sense of promise, passion, and the career to come are all there.

This book (above) is the wonderful poet Philip Levine's "last shift" in more ways than one. It was published posthumously in late fall of 2016.

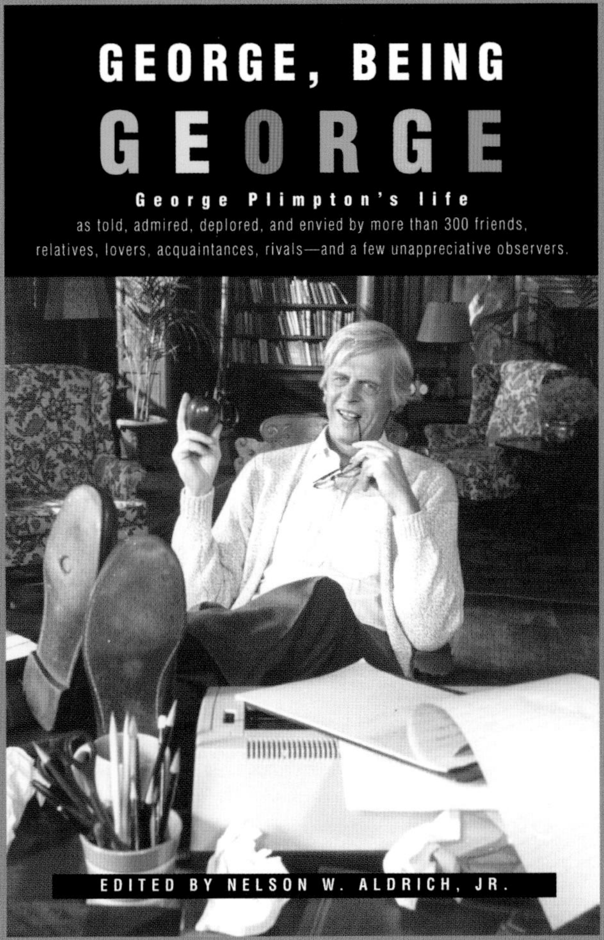
GEORGE, BEING
GEORGE
George Plimpton's life
as told, admired, deplored, and envied by more than 300 friends,
relatives, lovers, acquaintances, rivals—and a few unappreciative observers.
EDITED BY NELSON W. ALDRICH, JR.

It is hard to put into words all that George Plimpton meant to me, to say nothing of his importance to his many fans, or his contribution to immersive journalism. He tapped me to be the cover art director for *The Paris Review* from 1995 to his death in 2003. In that time he threw not one but two book parties for me in his Upper East Side apartment, and I will be forever grateful.

When it came time to do the cover for his biography by friend Nelson Aldrich, we just had to go with the fireworks (right), one of his many delightful passions. The coloring of the letters of his first name is a reference to the binding design of his ground-breaking book *Edie*. Obscure, I know, but it still looks good if the reader doesn't get that.

**OPPOSITE, LEFT:** Knopf, 2015. **OPPOSITE, RIGHT:** Knopf, 2016.
**RIGHT:** Random House, 2008.

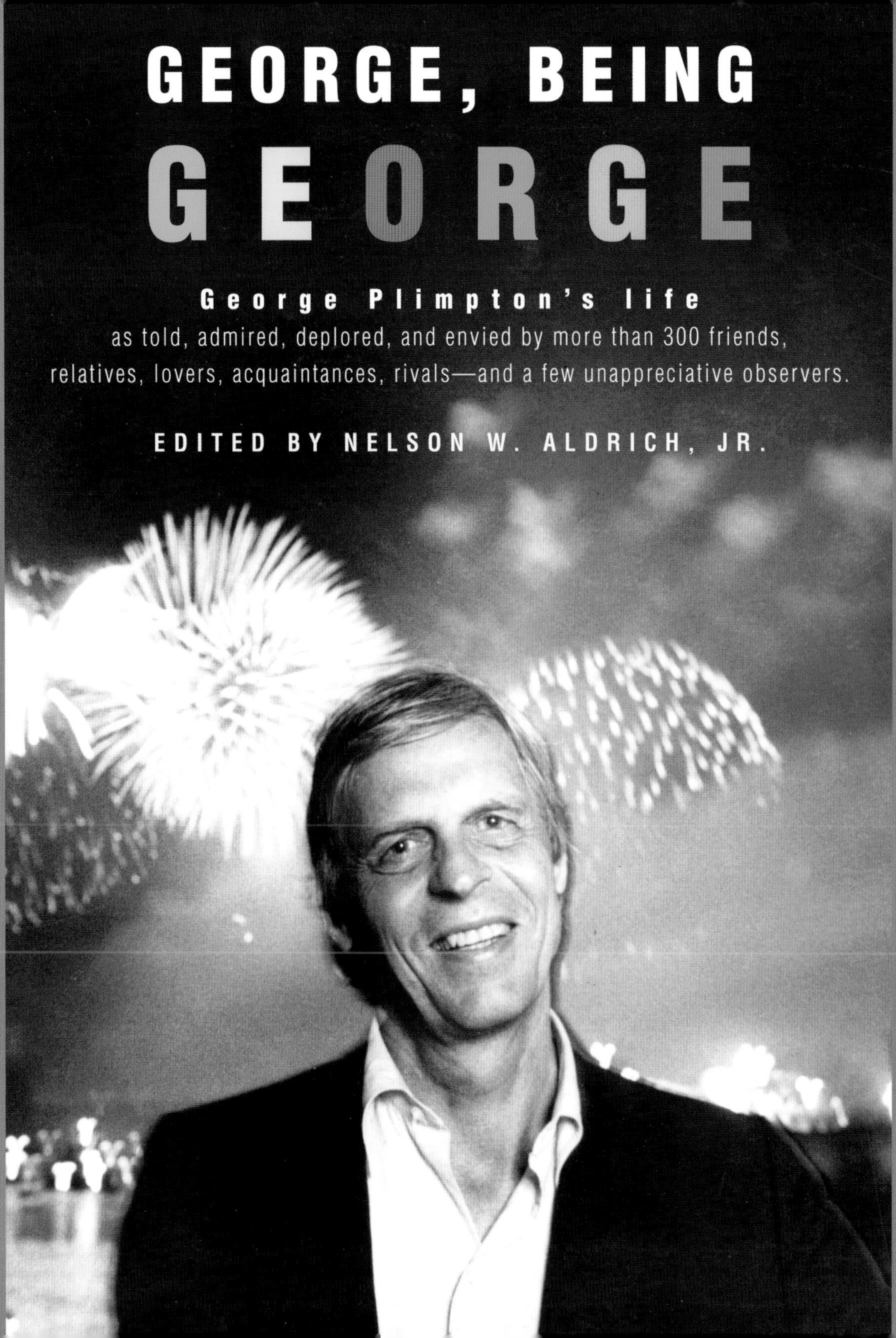
GEORGE, BEING
GEORGE
George Plimpton's life
as told, admired, deplored, and envied by more than 300 friends,
relatives, lovers, acquaintances, rivals—and a few unappreciative observers.
EDITED BY NELSON W. ALDRICH, JR.

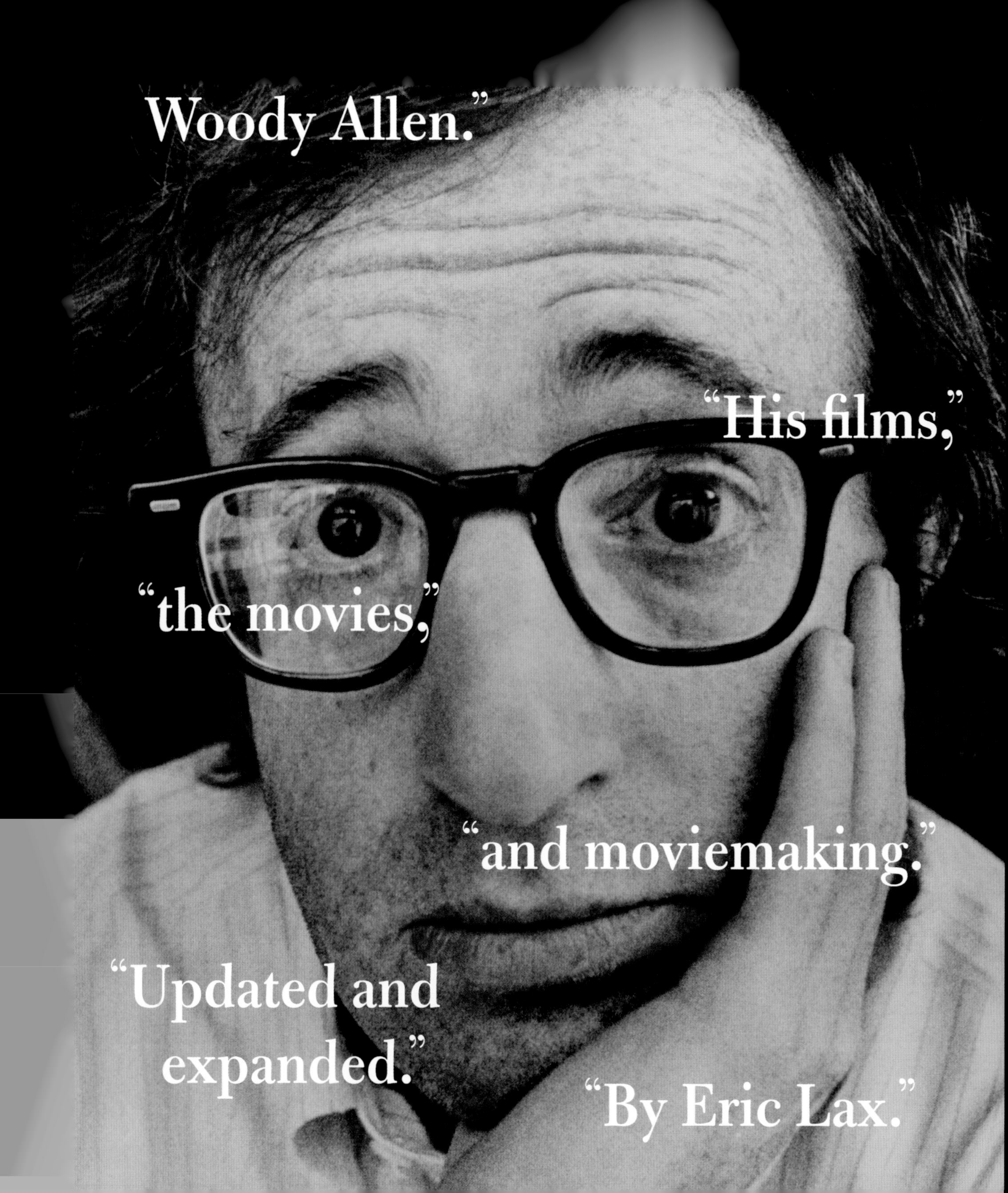
"Woody Allen."
"His films,"
"the movies,"
"and moviemaking."
"Updated and expanded."
"By Eric Lax."

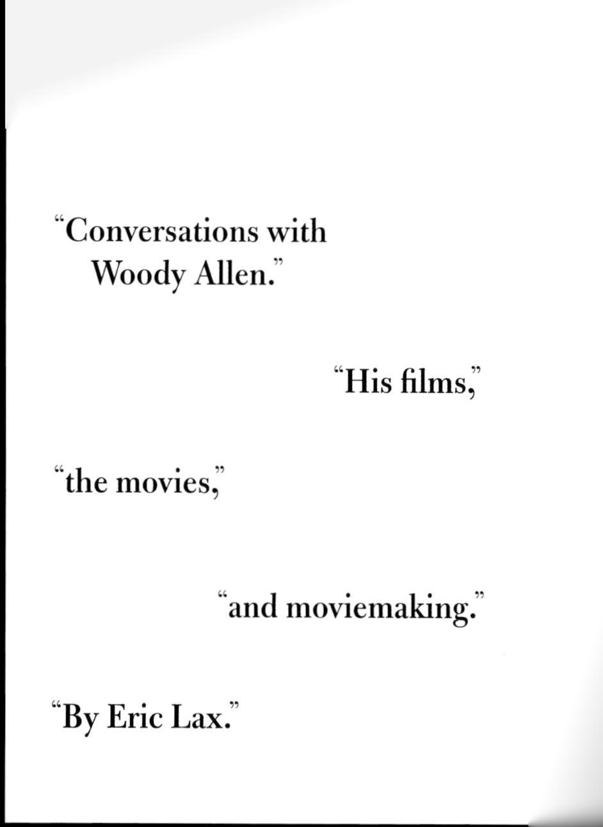
"Conversations with Woody Allen."
"His films,"
"the movies,"
"and moviemaking."
"By Eric Lax."

## I'm sorry, what?

Shown above is the jacket for the original hardcover edition of this book. To me, it was so "Woody" in its reliance on the volley of discussion, and at the time everyone agreed. It became part of the permanent collection of the National Design Museum and won numerous other awards. However, for the paperback (left), it was decided that the cover needed his face, and I was more than willing to oblige. The concept still works, especially since his mouth is not moving—you look into his eyes and just hear it all.

**LEFT:** Knopf, 2009.
**ABOVE:** Knopf, 2007. **OPPOSITE, LEFT:** Knopf, 1993.
**OPPOSITE, RIGHT:** Knopf, 2010.

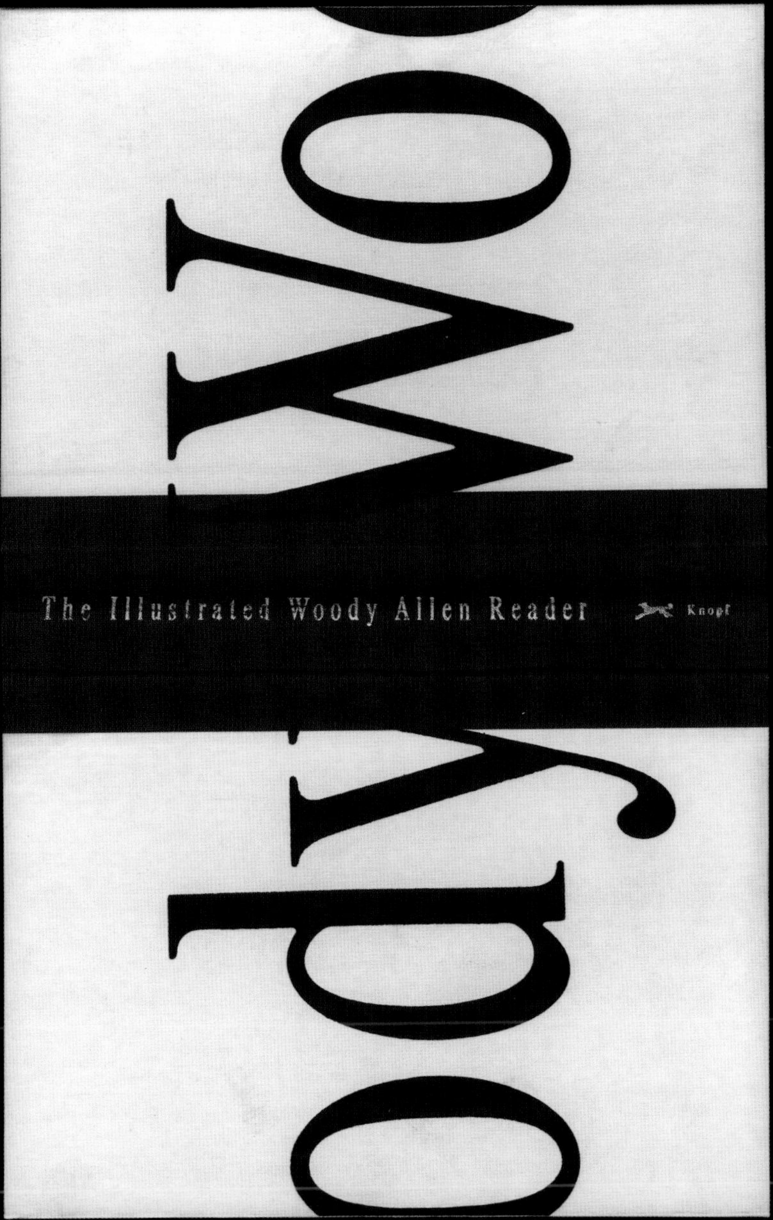
The Illustrated Woody Allen Reader
Knopf

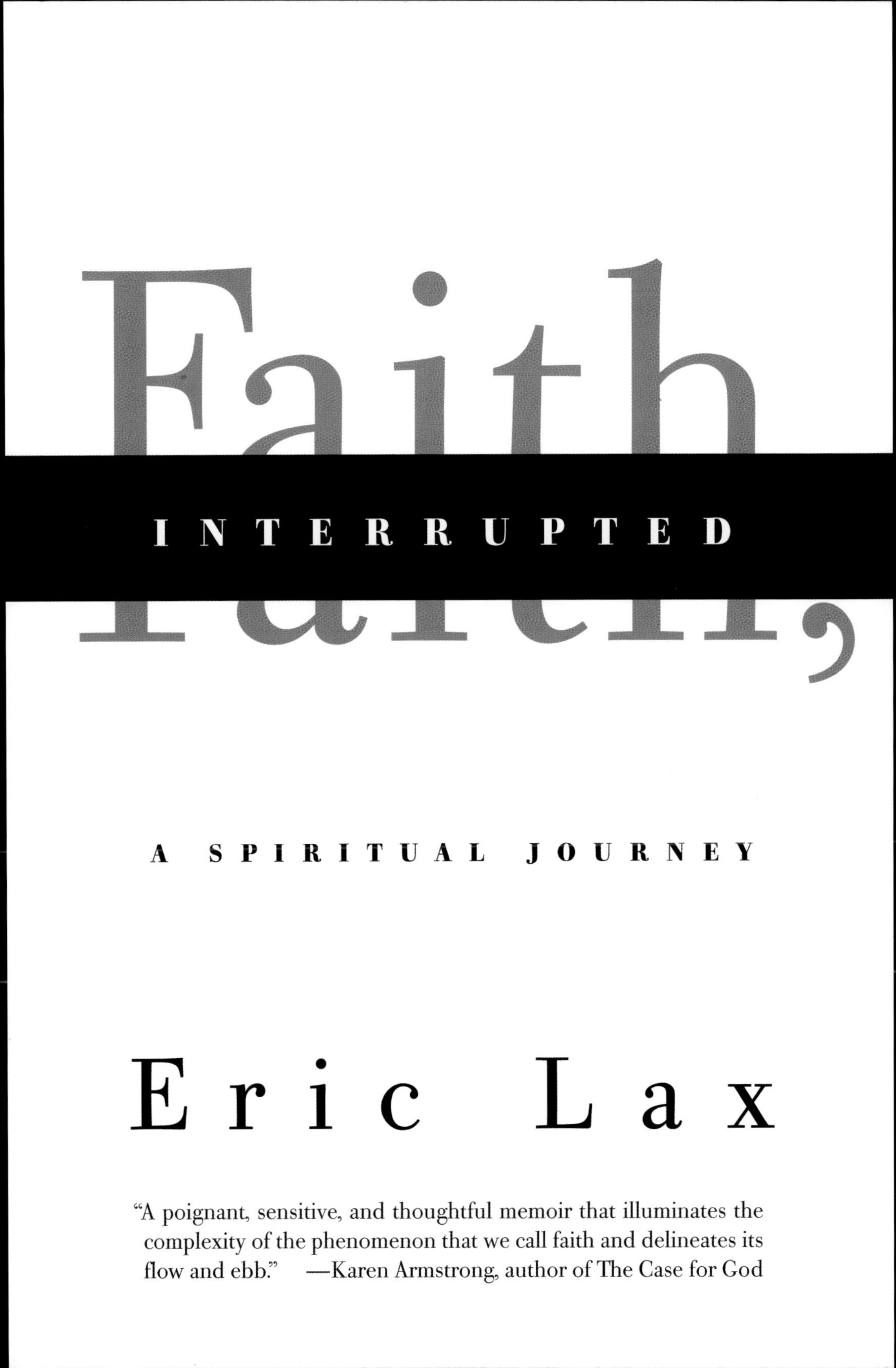
Faith,
INTERRUPTED
A SPIRITUAL JOURNEY
Eric Lax
"A poignant, sensitive, and thoughtful memoir that illuminates the complexity of the phenomenon that we call faith and delineates its flow and ebb." —Karen Armstrong, author of The Case for God

The binding cover of *The Illustrated Woody Allen Reader* is shown above; it played with the breaking up of his name as in film frames.

For Allen chronicler Eric Lax's memoir on faith (right), I wanted to use the same formal visual vocabulary as for the Allen books while giving it Lax's own identity.

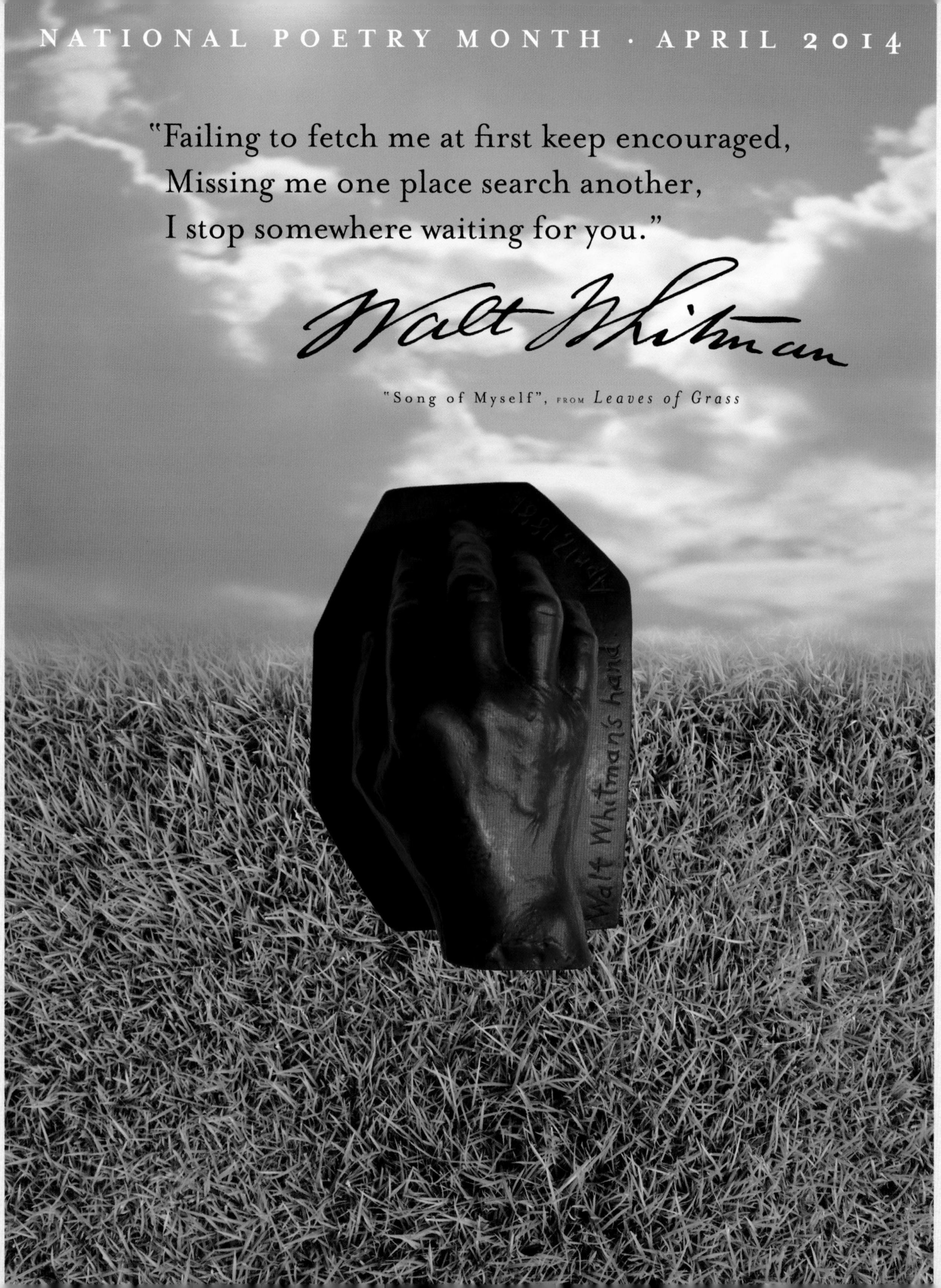
NATIONAL POETRY MONTH · APRIL 2014
"Failing to fetch me at first keep encouraged,
Missing me one place search another,
I stop somewhere waiting for you."
Walt Whitman
"Song of Myself", FROM Leaves of Grass
Walt Whitman's hand

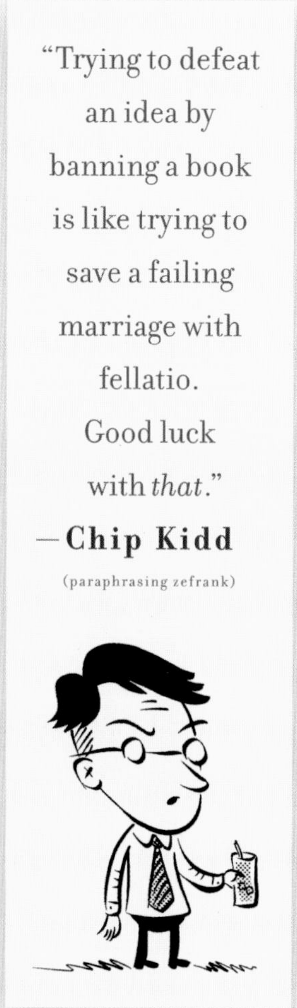
"Trying to defeat an idea by banning a book is like trying to save a failing marriage with fellatio. Good luck with that."
—Chip Kidd
(paraphrasing zefrank)

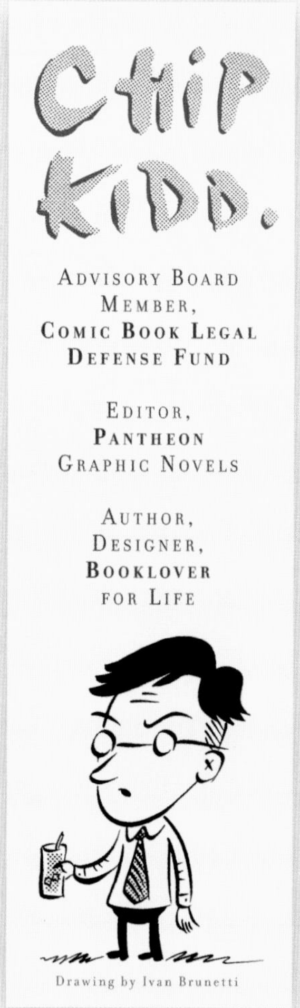
Chip Kidd.
Advisory Board Member, Comic Book Legal Defense Fund
Editor, Pantheon Graphic Novels
Author, Designer, Booklover for Life
Drawing by Ivan Brunetti

## Keep Encouraged

I've been overseeing the poster for National Poetry Month for the Academy of American Poets since 2005, designing two of them myself. In 2014 I used a Walt Whitman theme (left), depicting an actual-size image of a life cast of Whitman's hand. These posters go out to thousands of schools across the country, so I wanted kids to be able to put their hands on his to compare and, hopefully, connect.

Pantheon issued a series of giveaway bookmarks featuring quotes about banning books (above). Here, I'm paraphrasing pioneering video blogger Ze Frank.

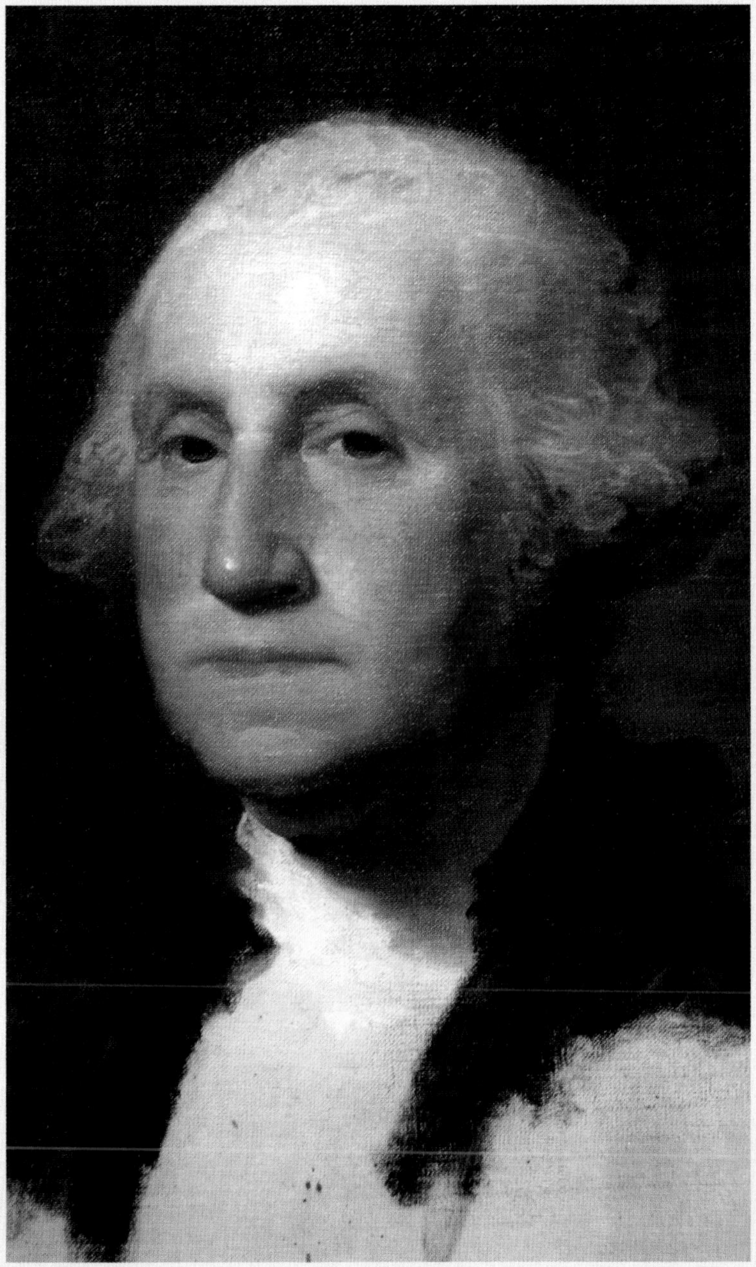

Larry Kramer can be a polarizing figure, but no one can deny that he has fearlessly made a seismic difference in the lives of gay men and women. Besides his activism, he is an excellent writer, and I was thrilled that he asked me to work on *The American People* (right; Farrar, Straus and Giroux, 2015), his epic, years-in-the-making retelling of a vital era in the history of the United States.

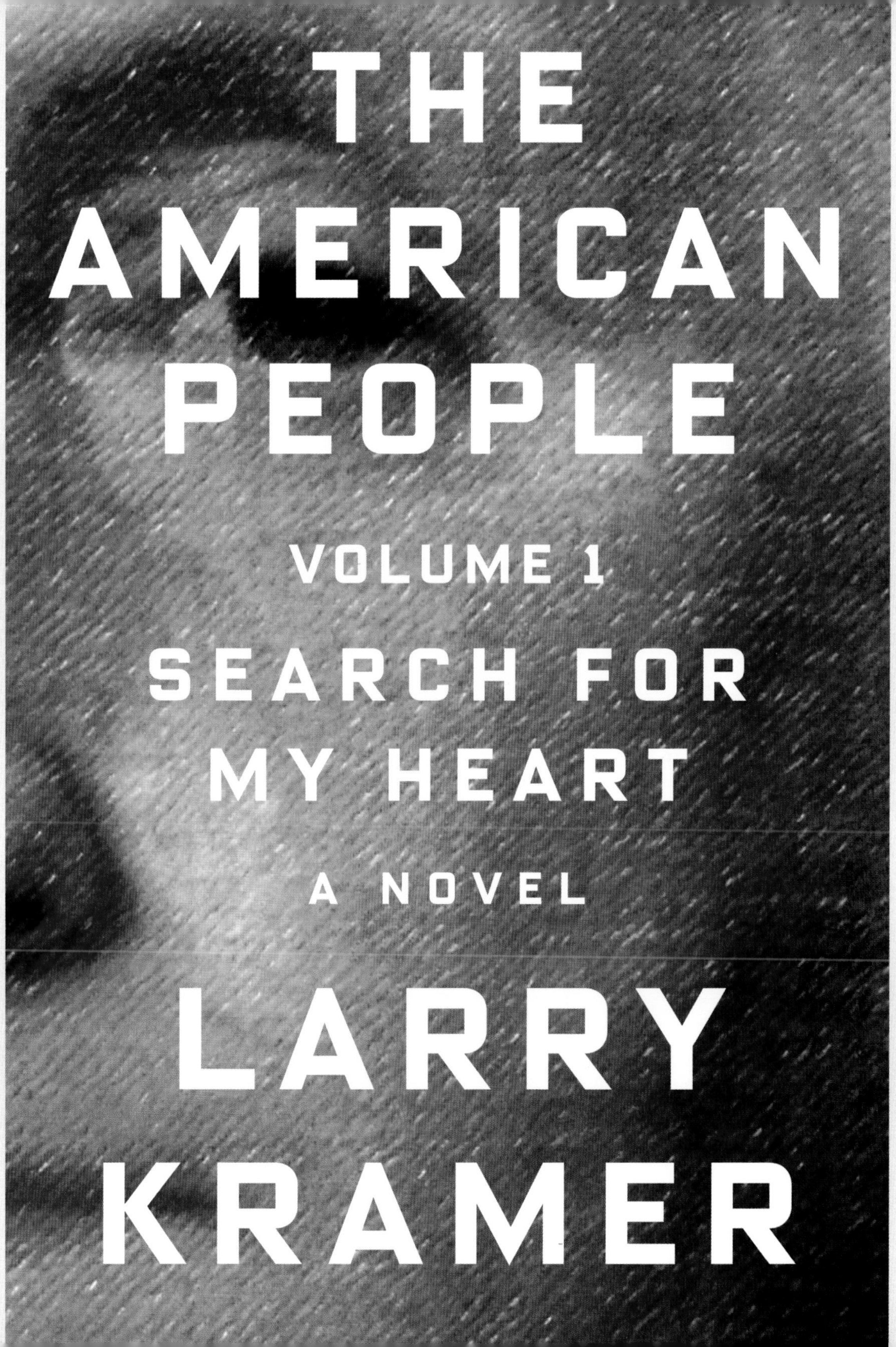
THE AMERICAN PEOPLE
VOLUME 1
SEARCH FOR MY HEART
A NOVEL
LARRY KRAMER

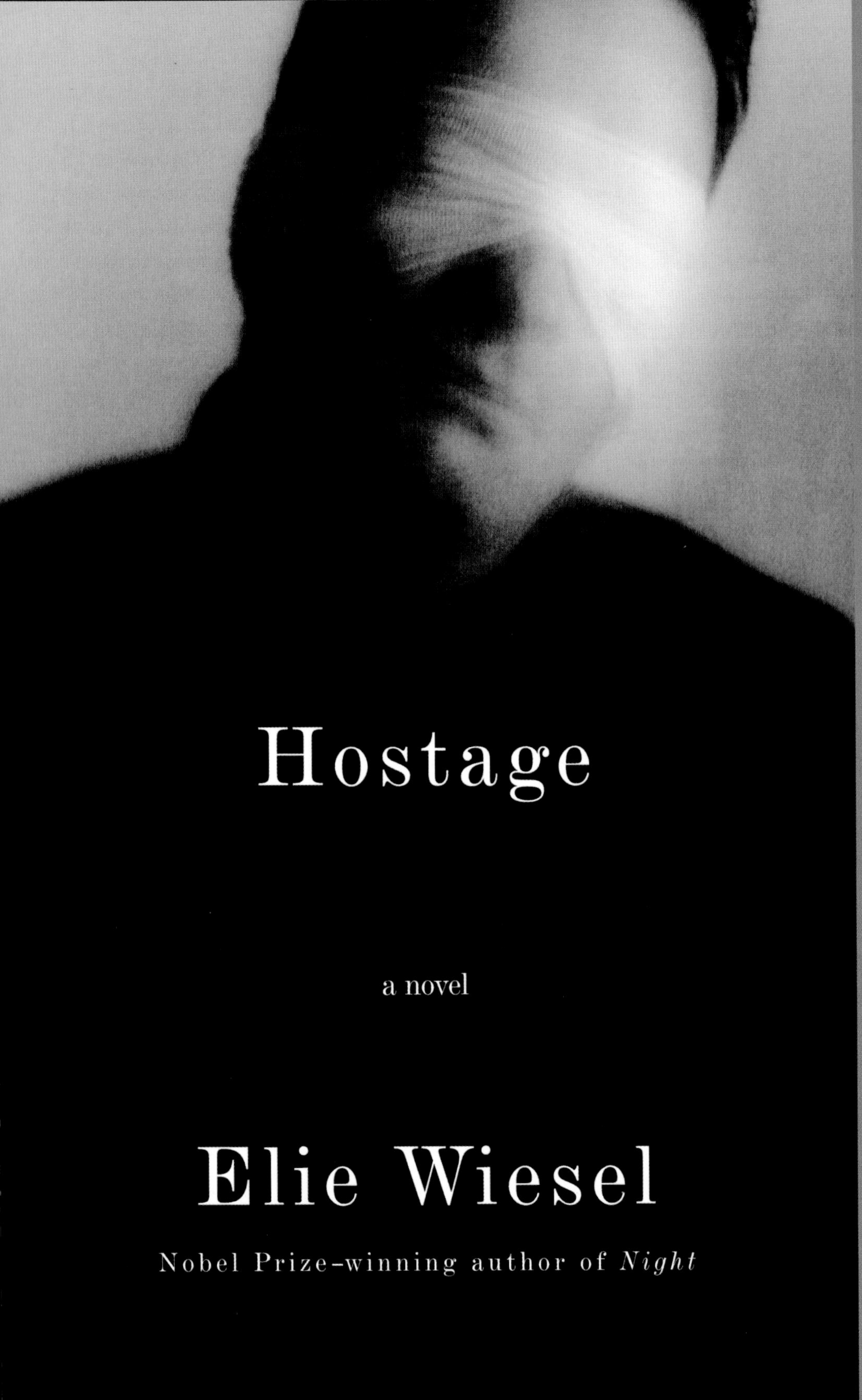
Hostage
a novel
Elie Wiesel
Nobel Prize-winning author of *Night*

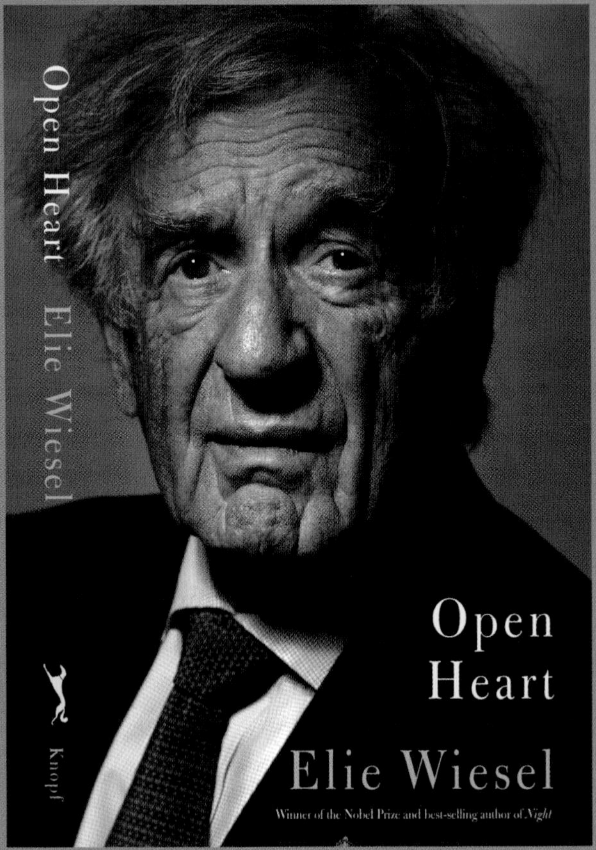
Open Heart Elie Wiesel
Knopf
Open Heart
Elie Wiesel
Winner of the Nobel Prize and best-selling author of *Night*

## Soul Survivor

For Elie Wiesel's memoir about undergoing open heart surgery in his 80s (above; Knopf, 2012), we wanted to commission a unique, contemporary photographic portrait. My first choice was the magnificent Albert Watson. We couldn't afford what he would normally charge, but Albert and I knew each other slightly, and I suspected that if he had time in his schedule, he wouldn't be able to resist the chance to do a sitting with the Nobel Prize–winning author of *Night*. I contacted him, and he had the time, and indeed he couldn't resist. He shot the photo at Mr. Wiesel's offices in Manhattan. It would be the last time the author had his portrait taken, for what would be his last book.

Wiesel's penultimate work, a novel called *Hostage* (left; Knopf, 2012), combines elements of Kafka and Scheherazade, as an innocent man named Shaltiel Feigenberg—a writer—has been taken hostage, blindfolded and tied to a chair in a dark basement. His captors, an Arab and an Italian, don't explain why the innocent Shaltiel has been chosen, just that his life will be bartered for the freedom of three Palestinian prisoners. As his days of waiting commence, Shaltiel resorts to what he does best, telling stories—to himself and to the men who hold his fate in their hands.

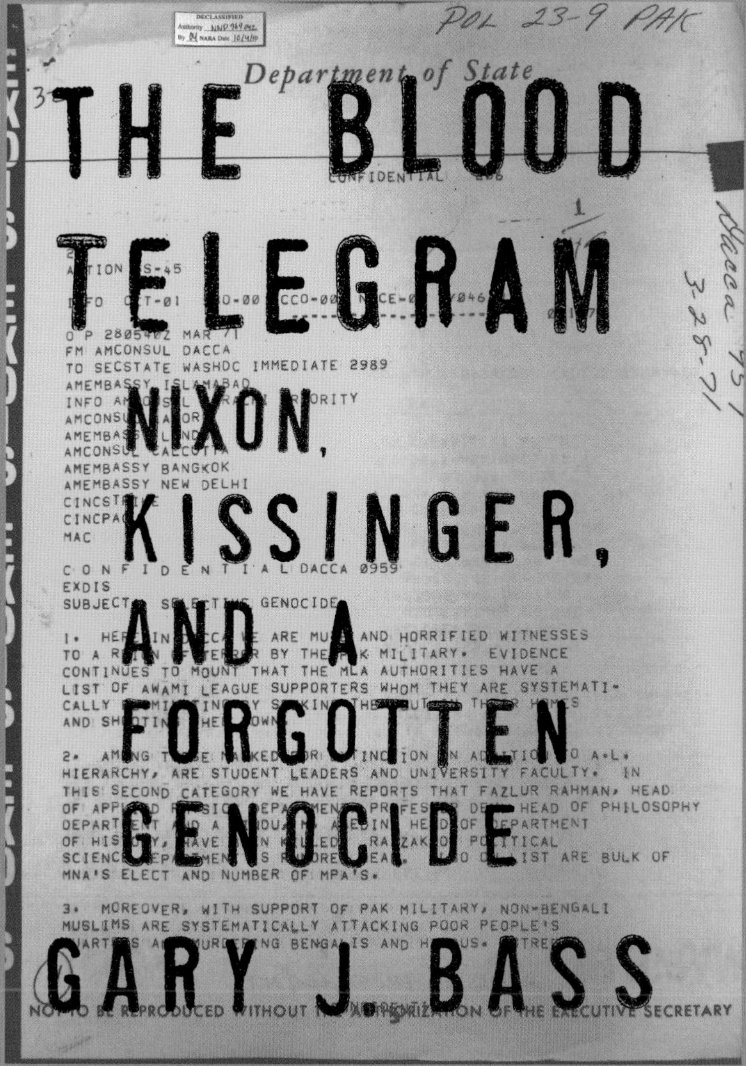
POL 23-9 PAK
Department of State
THE BLOOD TELEGRAM
NIXON, KISSINGER, AND A FORGOTTEN GENOCIDE
GARY J. BASS

**ABOVE:** Gary J. Bass obtained access to documents which prove that in 1971 Richard Nixon and Henry Kissinger played a significant role in the genocidal cleansing of East Pakistan's Bengali/Hindu population. I used one of said documents as a background and colored it blood red. Knopf, 2013.

**RIGHT:** Jay Cantor imagined four fictions about the life of Kafka as told by some of his closest friends and lovers. I did the portrait myself with crayon, but another direction was chosen.

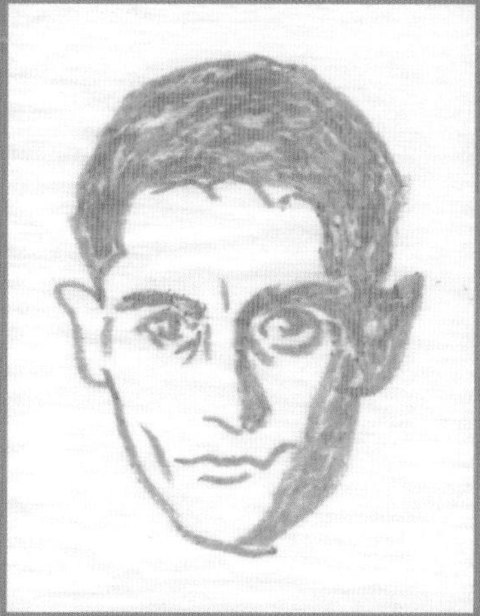

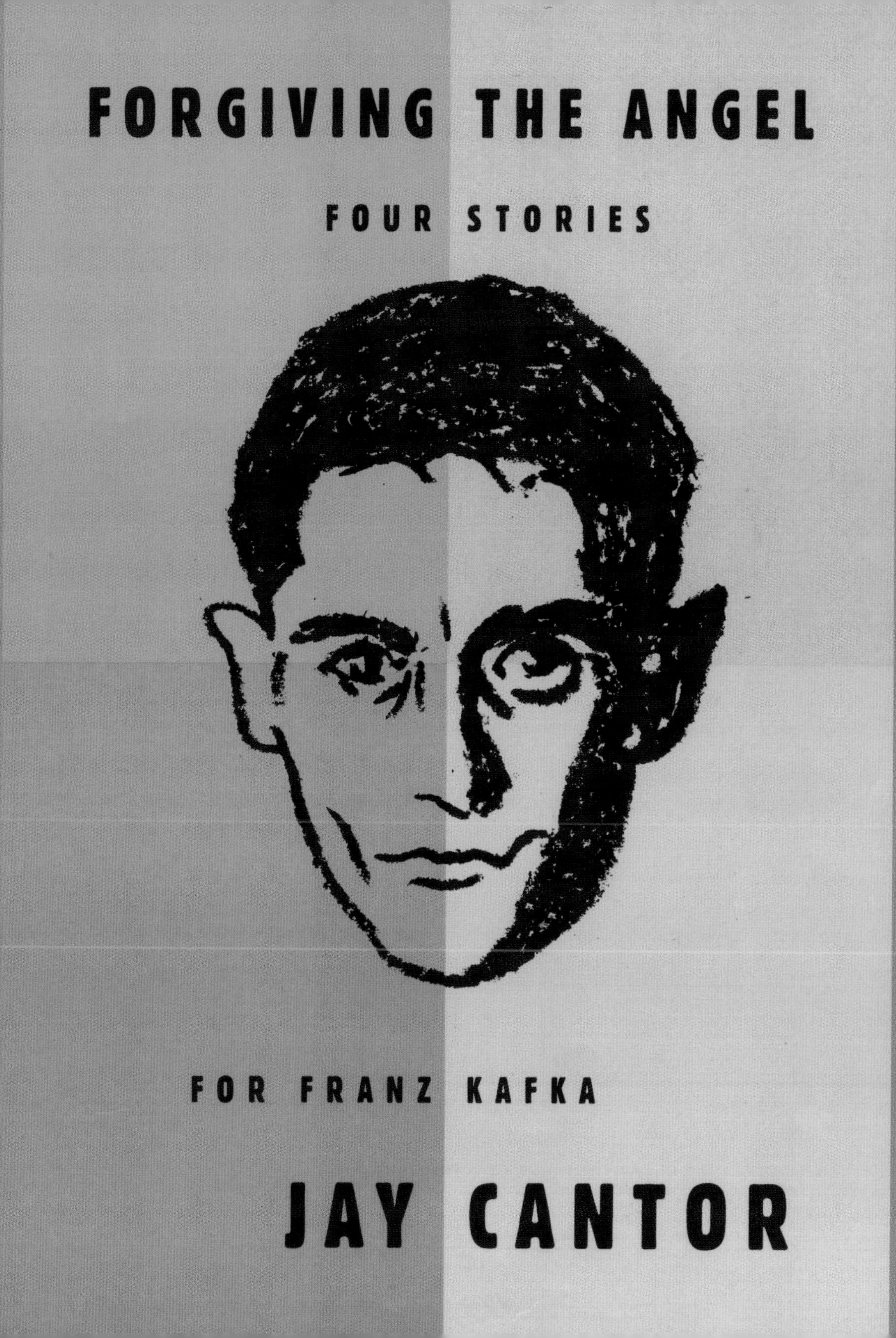
FORGIVING THE ANGEL
FOUR STORIES
FOR FRANZ KAFKA
JAY CANTOR

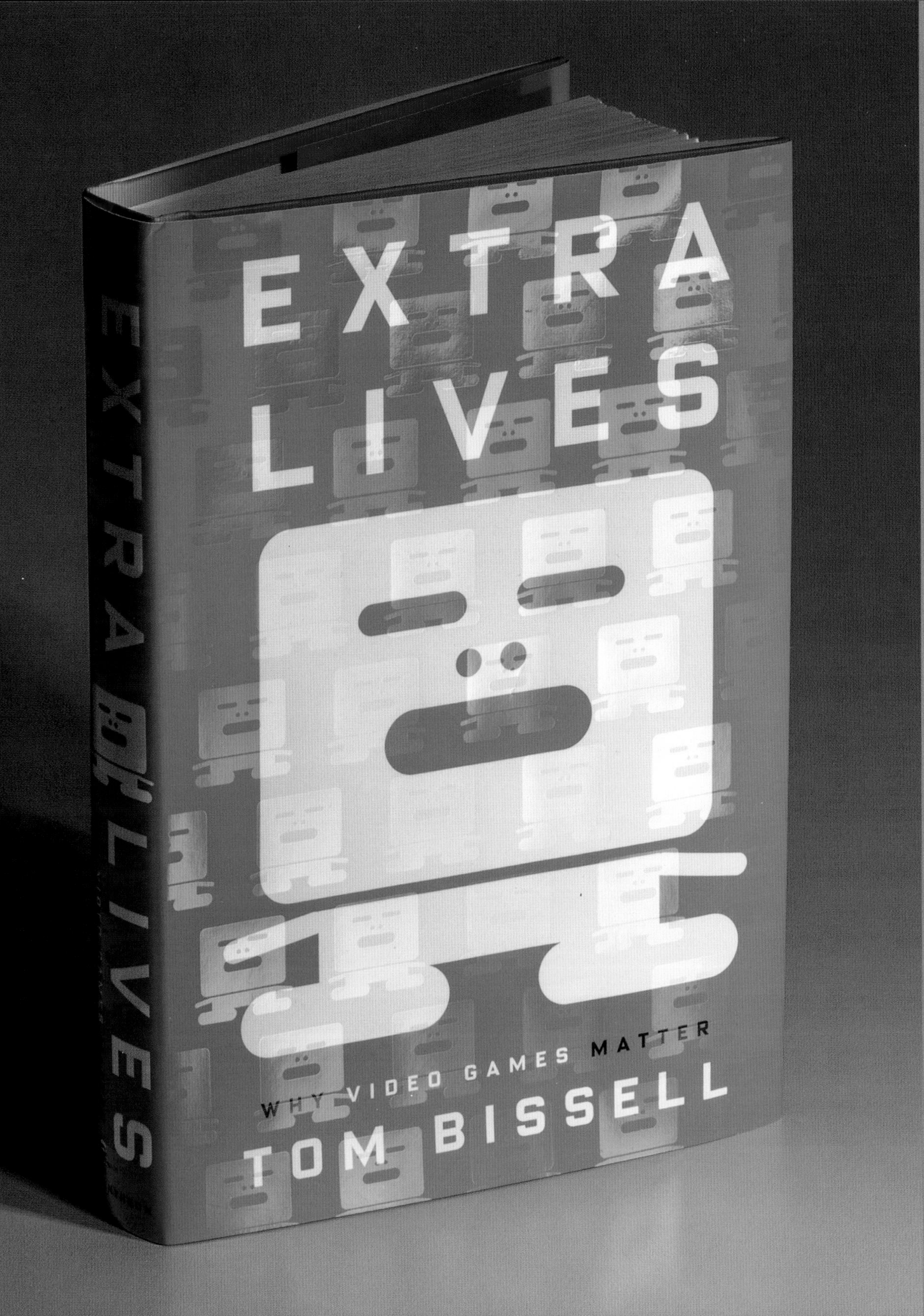
EXTRA LIVES
WHY VIDEO GAMES MATTER
TOM BISSELL
EXTRA LIVES

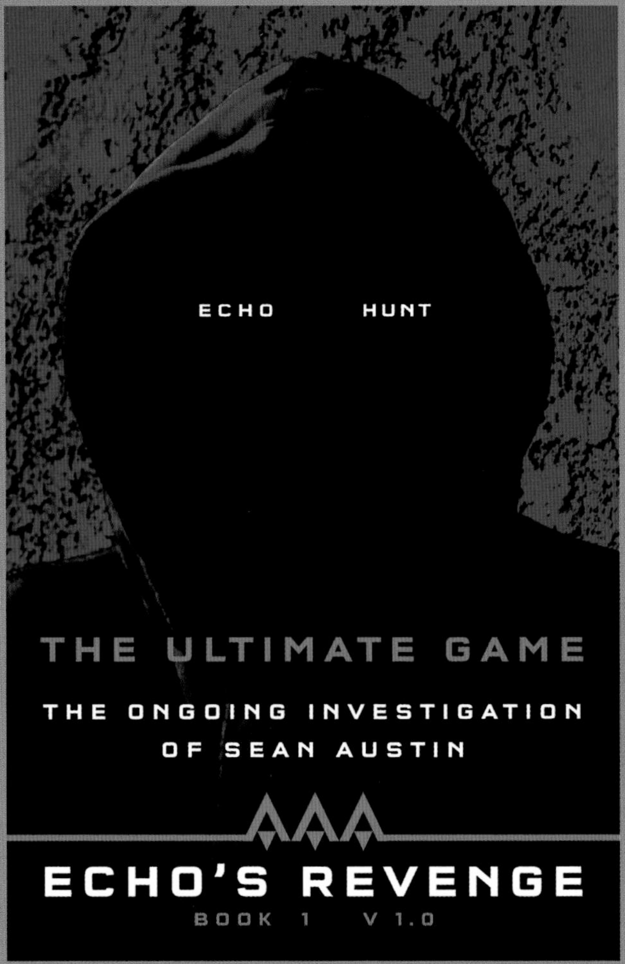
ECHO HUNT
THE ULTIMATE GAME
THE ONGOING INVESTIGATION OF SEAN AUSTIN
ECHO'S REVENGE
BOOK 1 V 1.0

## Ready Player One

Despite being a big comic book and superhero nerd, I am not a video gamer. But I certainly understand the mentality. Tom Bissell writes passionately and knowledgeably about video gaming culture (left) and his marathon binge session with Grand Theft Auto and the like. Given the title, I created an avatar character of his voracious gaming appetite and then gave him an army of extra lives in a pattern that was spot-glossed onto the jacket.

*Echo Hunt* (above) was designed years ago and I scarcely remember the story line, though it looks like it would fit right in with the current USA series *Mr. Robot*, of which I am a huge fan.

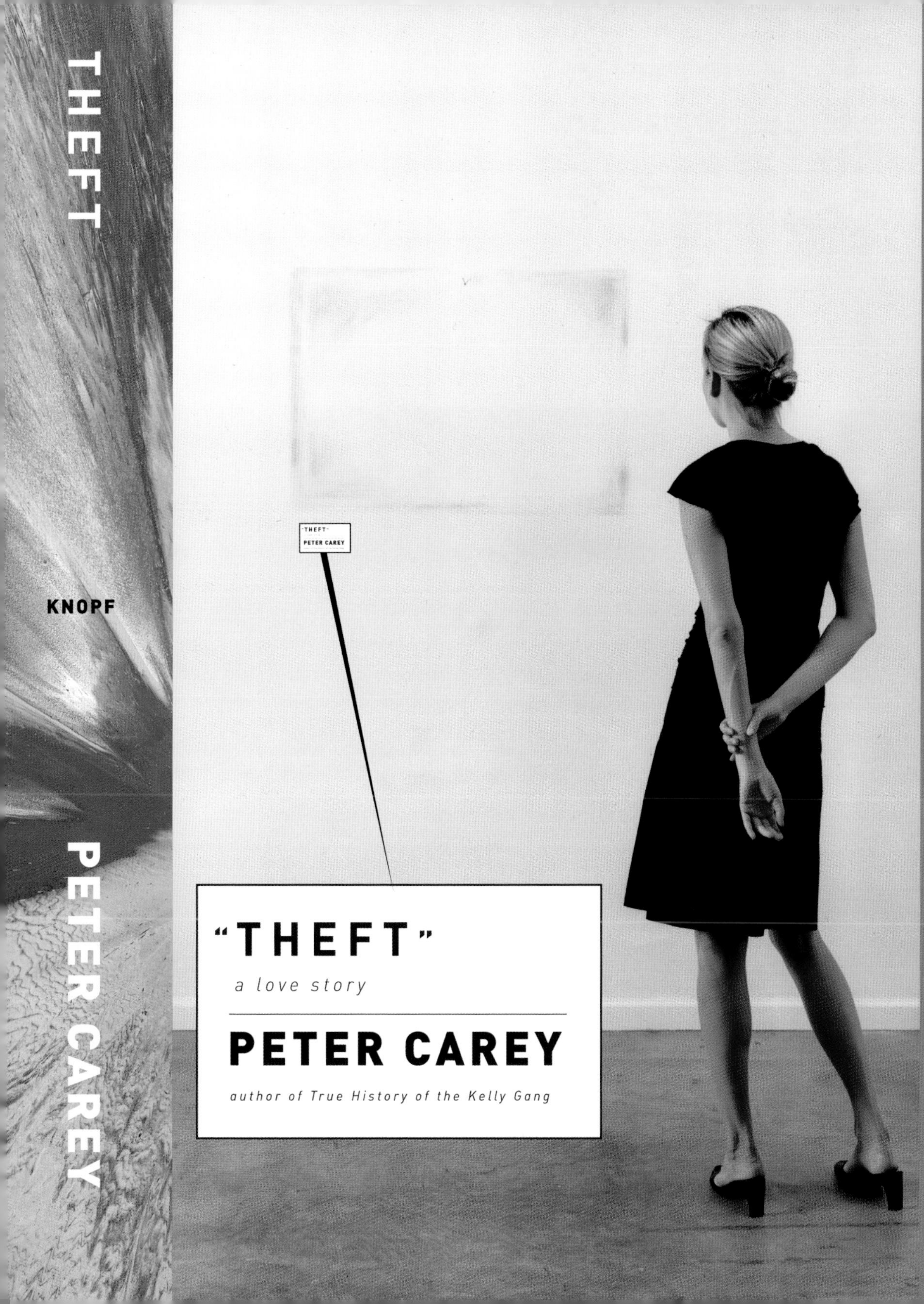
THEFT
KNOPF
PETER CAREY
"THEFT"
a love story
PETER CAREY
author of True History of the Kelly Gang

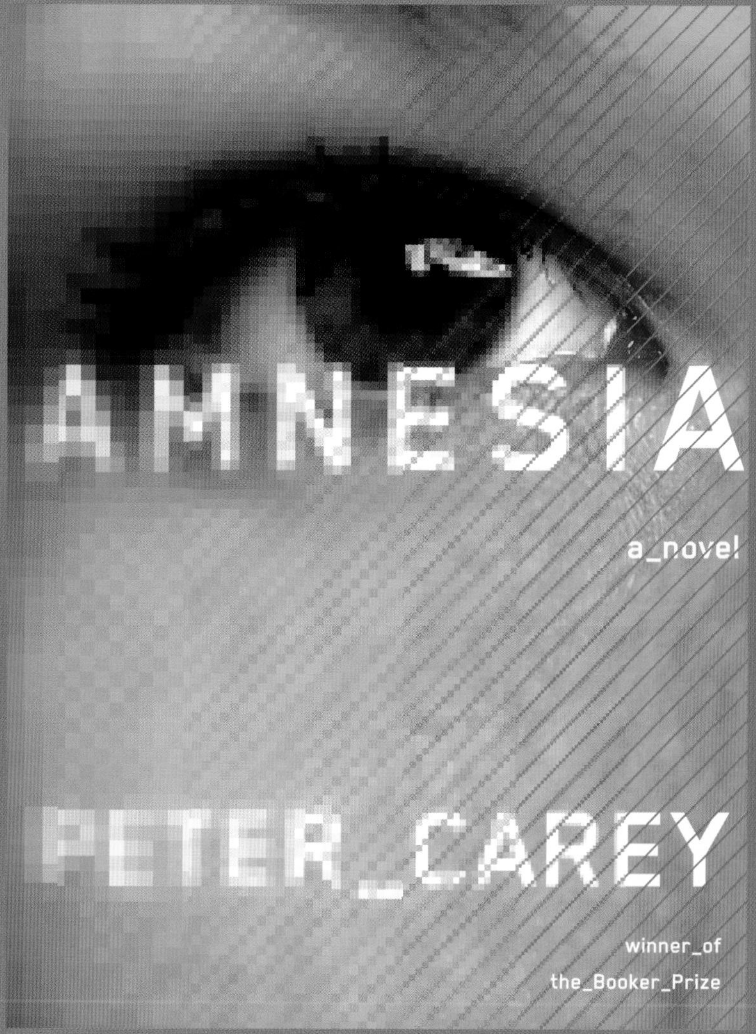
AMNESIA
a_novel
PETER_CAREY
winner_of
the_Booker_Prize

I have been working on Peter Carey's books since 1992, and I am delighted by his writing and the seemingly endless supply of captivating puzzles he sets up for himself and, subsequently, for me. No two stories or novels are remotely alike, and for that I bow to him. *Theft* (left) is about an art thief and forger, and the photographer Jason Fulford expertly set up and shot this image at my instruction.

*Amnesia* (above) was more complicated. It's about a computer virus that threatens to disrupt the world, and the cover needed a visual metaphor of it gradually doing so. Always: left to right, left to right . . .

**OPPOSITE, RIGHT:** Pantheon, 2010. **OPPOSITE, LEFT:** Reality Games, 2012. **LEFT:** Knopf, 2006. **ABOVE:** Knopf, 2015.

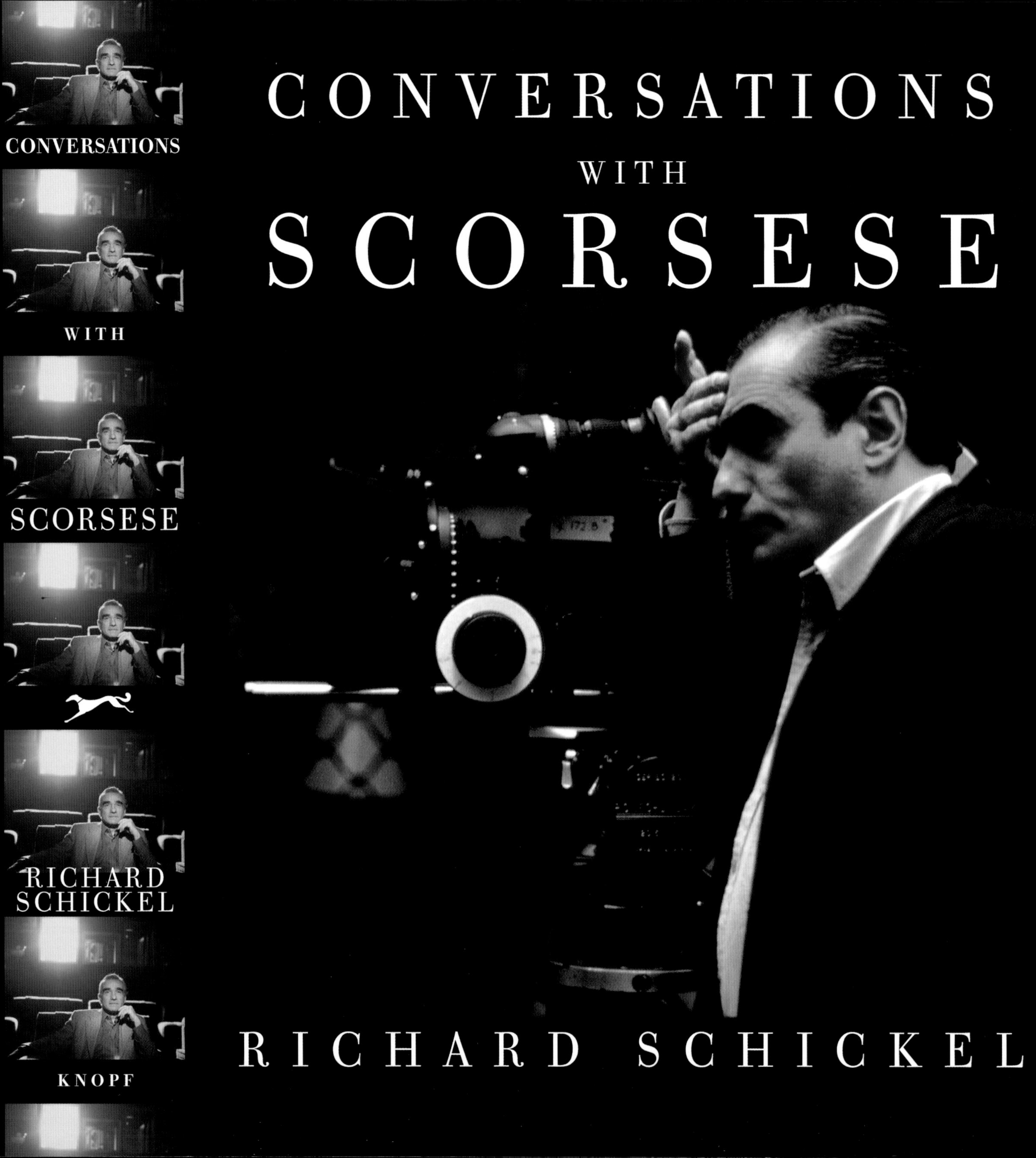
CONVERSATIONS
WITH
SCORSESE
RICHARD SCHICKEL
KNOPF
CONVERSATIONS
WITH
SCORSESE
RICHARD SCHICKEL



## Method Men

Books about movies and the people who make, star in, and review them provide their own opportunities to represent one of the most influential and complex art forms of the last hundred years. The jacket for Richard Schickel's *Conversations with Scorsese* (left) was more standard, with an iconic portrait of the great director next to a massive movie camera on the front, and then a frame-by-frame sequence of him in the screening room on the spine.

But Schickel's *Keepers* (opposite, left), a collection and reflection of his favorite films from a lifetime of reviews for *Time* magazine, allowed for much more creative license. I wanted to re-create the experience of sitting in the theater and watching the opening credits roll, thus my nod to the classic opening of *Star Wars*, with the typography gently and wistfully evaporating away from you.

There are so many books on Marlon Brando, the key to designing Stefan Kanfer's *Somebody* (opposite, right) was finding an image that wasn't overly familiar and then cropping it dramatically.

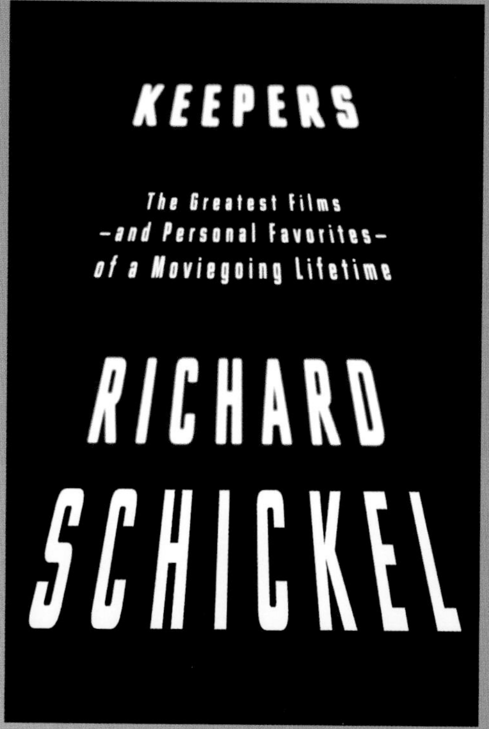
KEEPERS
The Greatest Films
—and Personal Favorites—
of a Moviegoing Lifetime
RICHARD
SCHICKEL

**OPPOSITE:** Knopf, 2011.
**ABOVE & BELOW:** Knopf, 2015. **RIGHT:** Knopf, 2008.

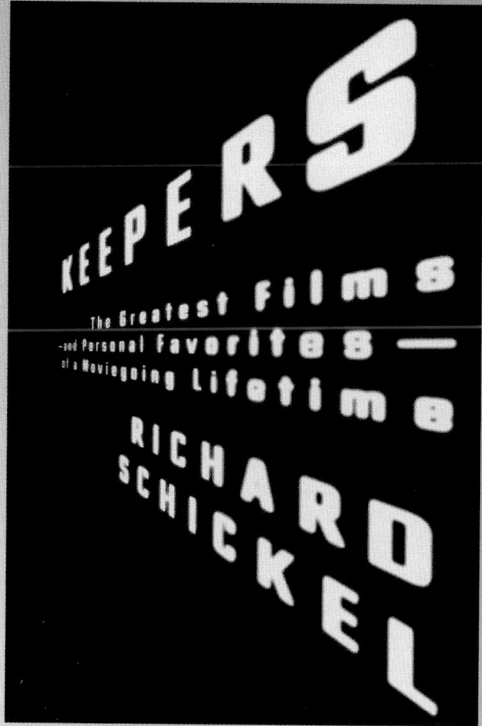
KEEPERS
The Greatest Films
—and Personal Favorites—
of a Moviegoing Lifetime
RICHARD
SCHICKEL

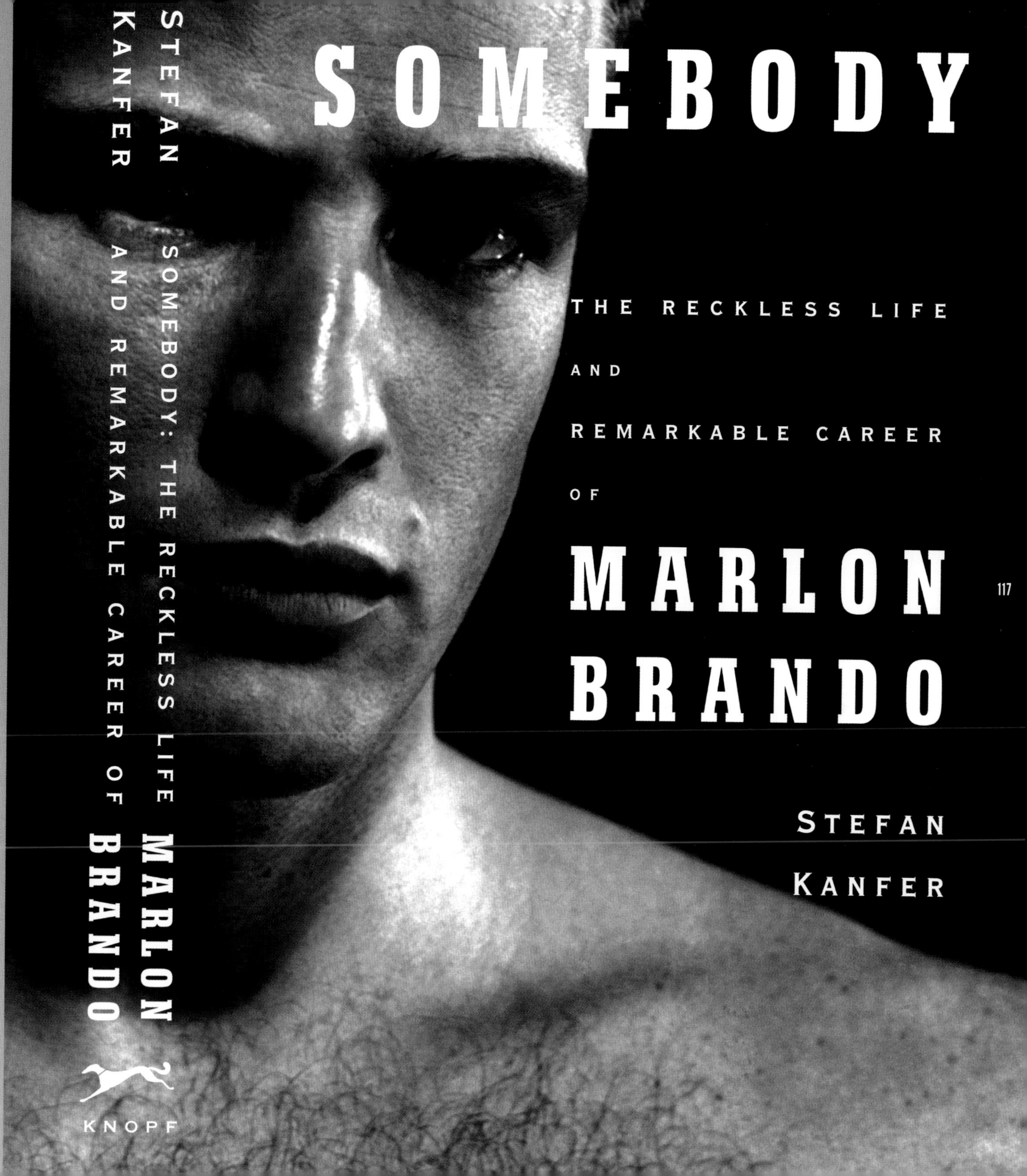
STEFAN KANFER
SOMEBODY: THE RECKLESS LIFE AND REMARKABLE CAREER OF MARLON BRANDO
KNOPF
SOMEBODY
THE RECKLESS LIFE
AND
REMARKABLE CAREER
OF
MARLON
BRANDO
STEFAN
KANFER

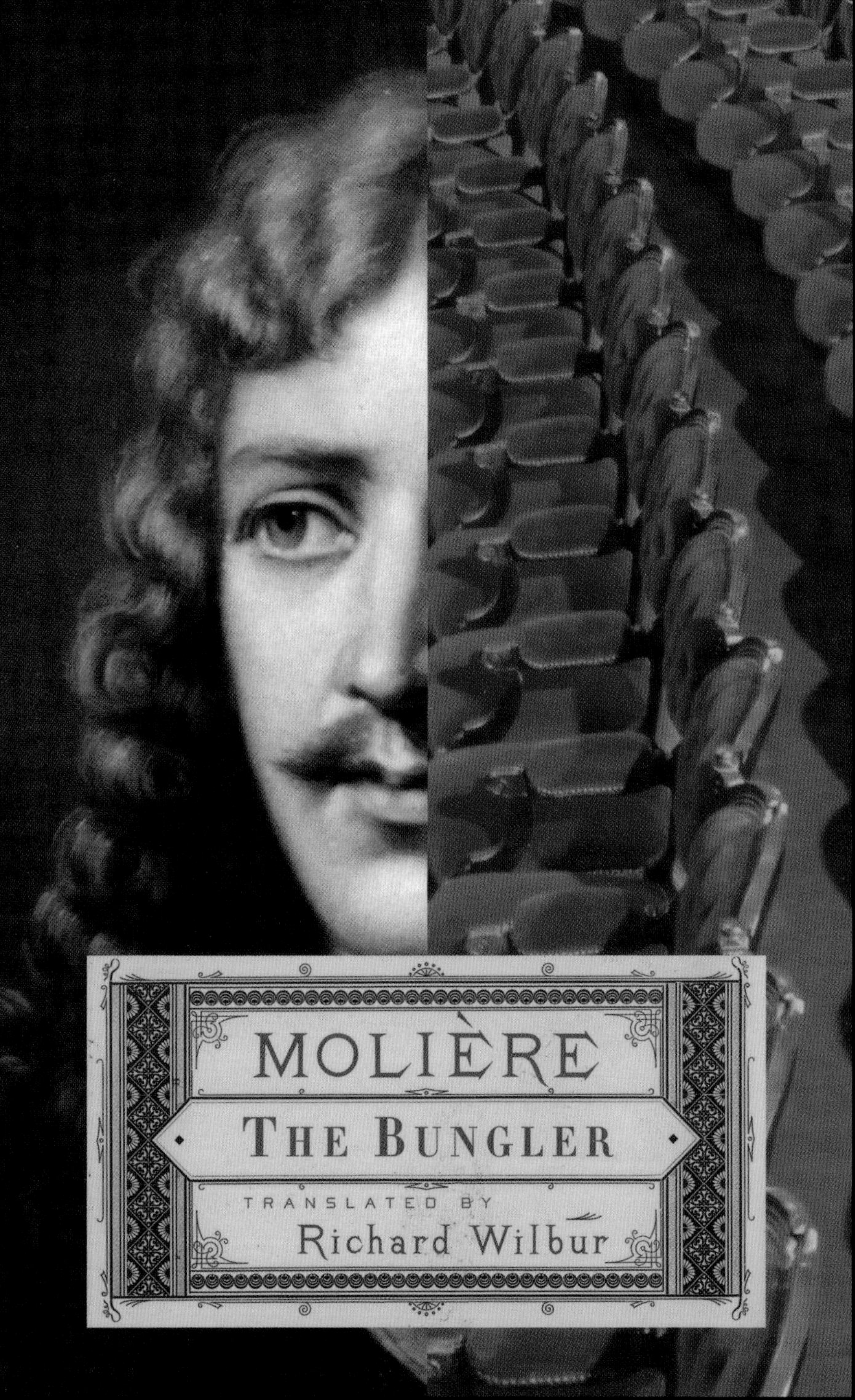
MOLIÈRE
THE BUNGLER
TRANSLATED BY
Richard Wilbur

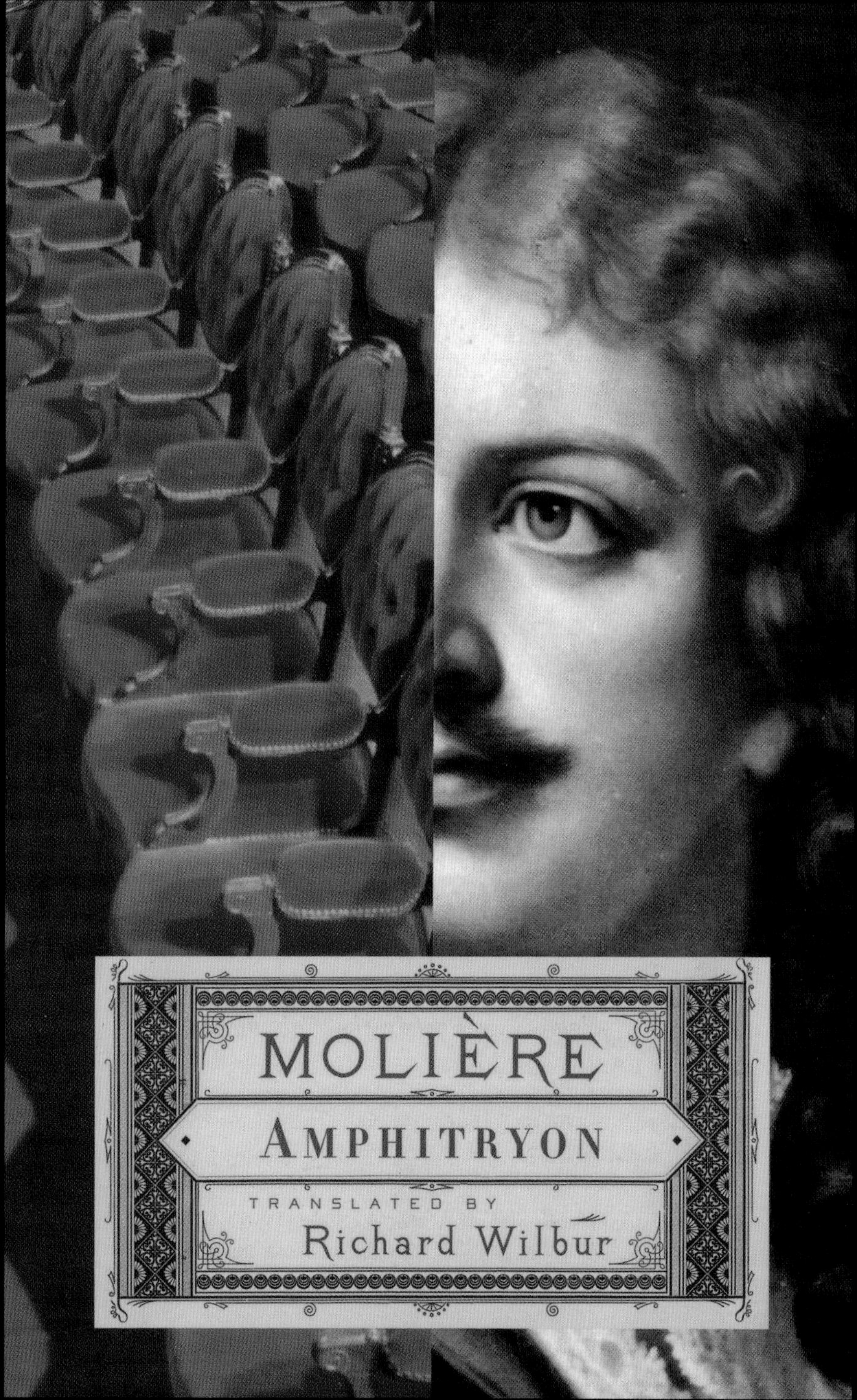
MOLIÈRE
AMPHITRYON
TRANSLATED BY
Richard Wilbur

## The Four Faces of French Farce

Okay, here's a confession: Personally, I put the 17th-century French playwright Molière into the same category as Hayden, Bob Dylan, Robert Crumb, Allen Ginsberg, Matisse, Thomas Pynchon, and Jimi Hendrix. Which is to say—

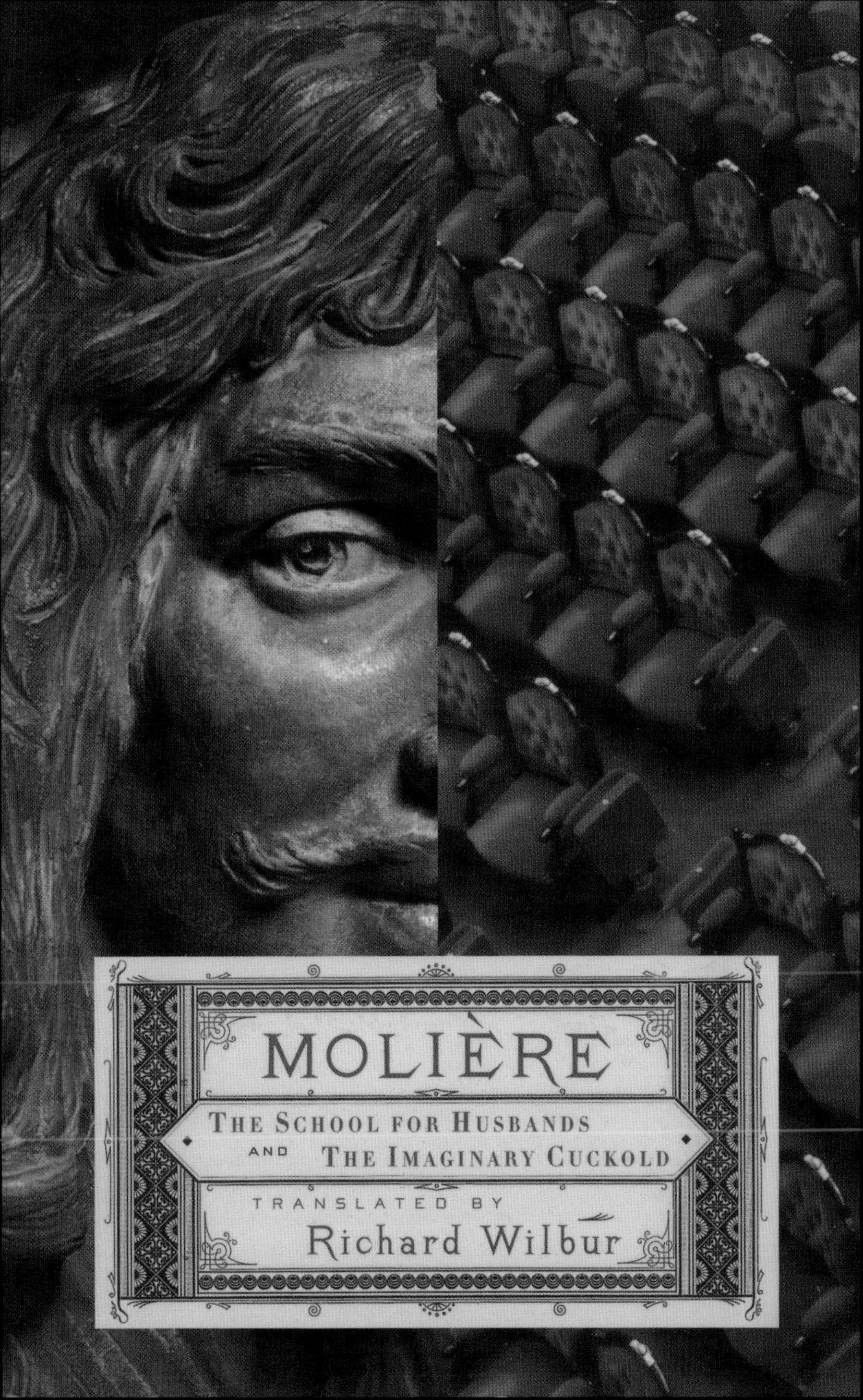
MOLIÈRE
THE SCHOOL FOR HUSBANDS
AND THE IMAGINARY CUCKOLD
TRANSLATED BY
Richard Wilbur

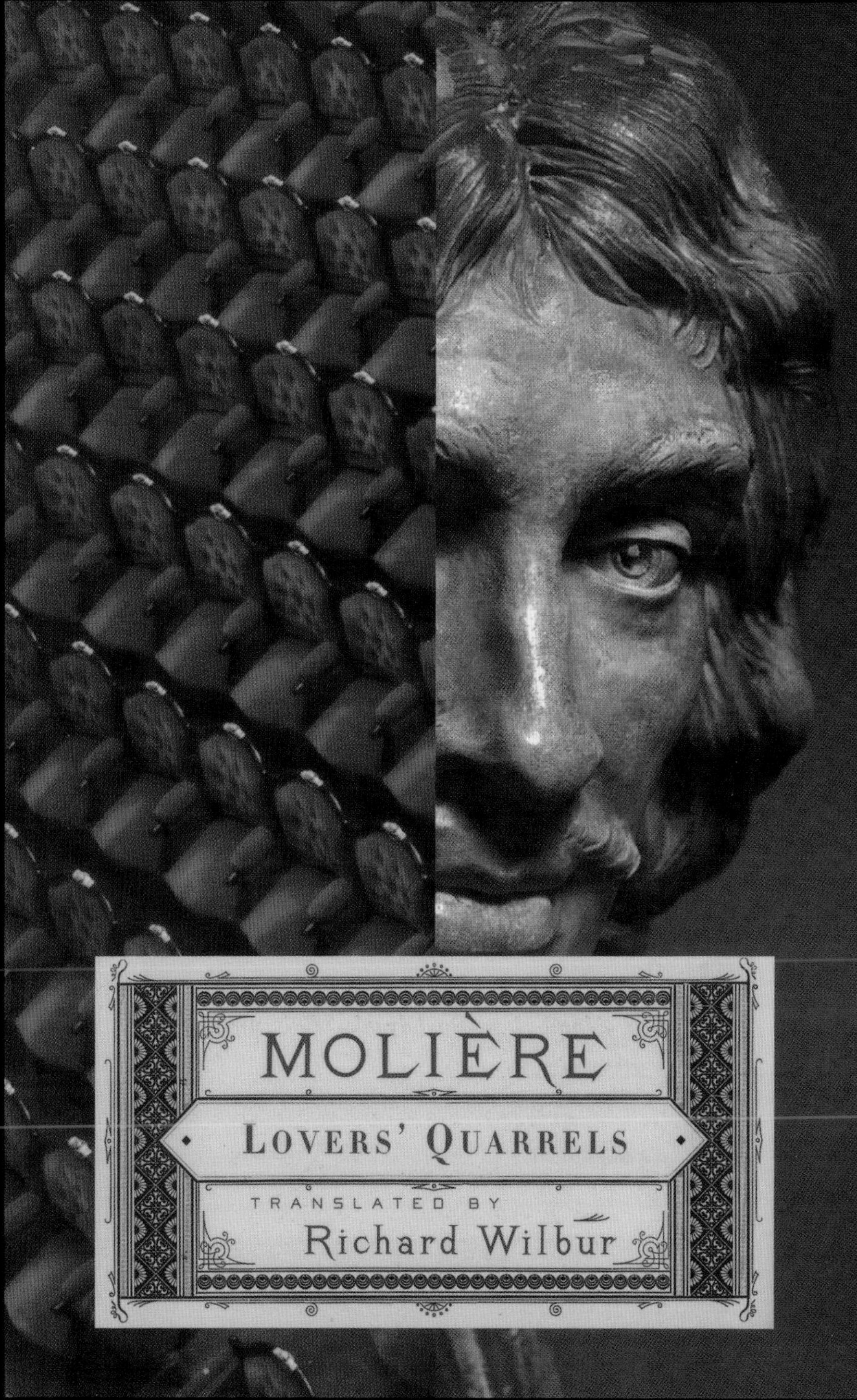
MOLIÈRE
LOVERS' QUARRELS
TRANSLATED BY
Richard Wilbur

I respect them all, but I am not really a fan of any of them. But in my job, representing someone's art doesn't mean you have to like it; you just have to understand it and do right by it. And of course respecting it helps, too. In this case, translator Richard Wilbur definitely thought I did. (Theatre Communications Group, 2010; 2010; 2009; 2009)

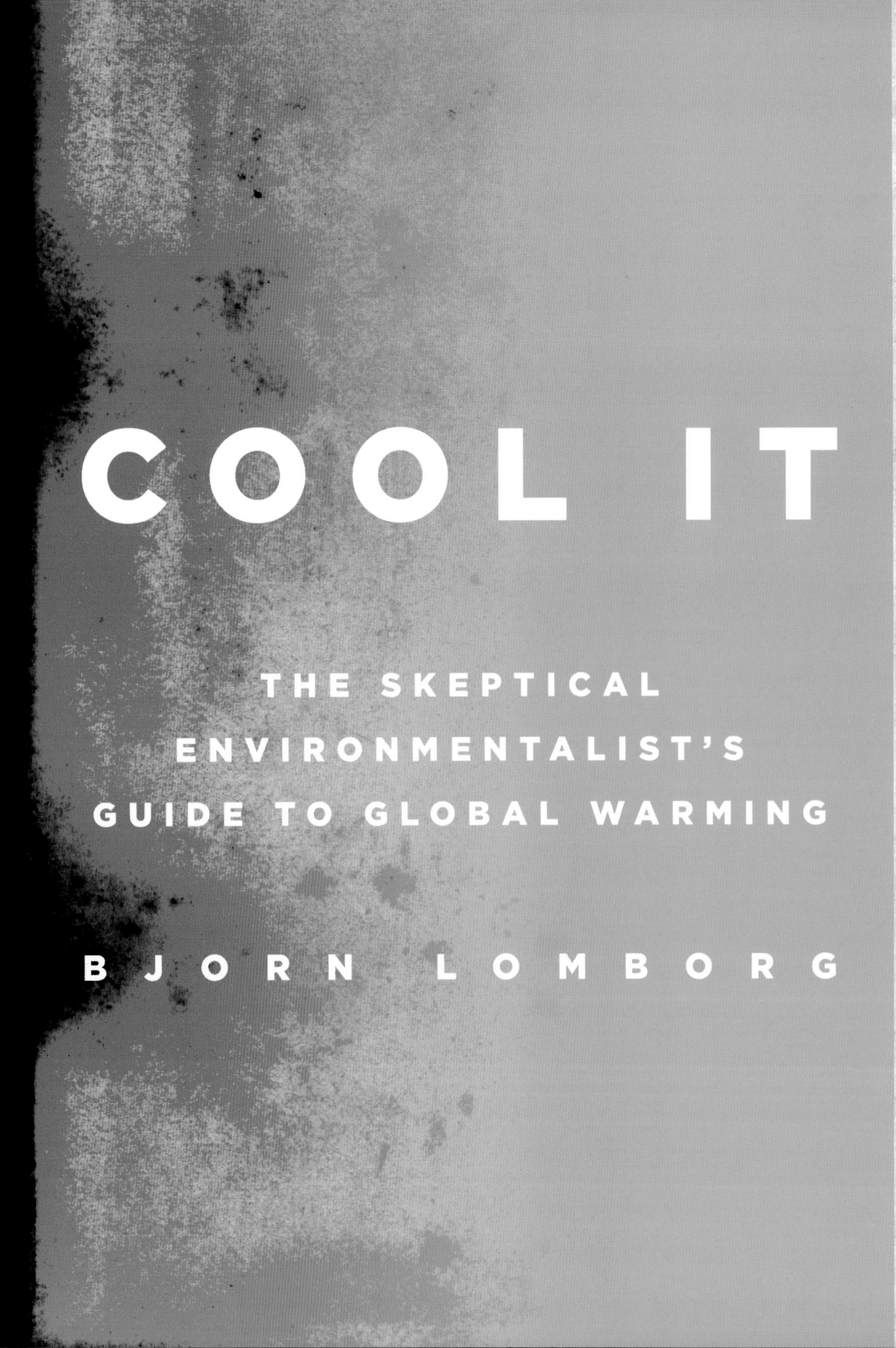
COOL IT
THE SKEPTICAL ENVIRONMENTALIST'S GUIDE TO GLOBAL WARMING
BJORN LOMBORG

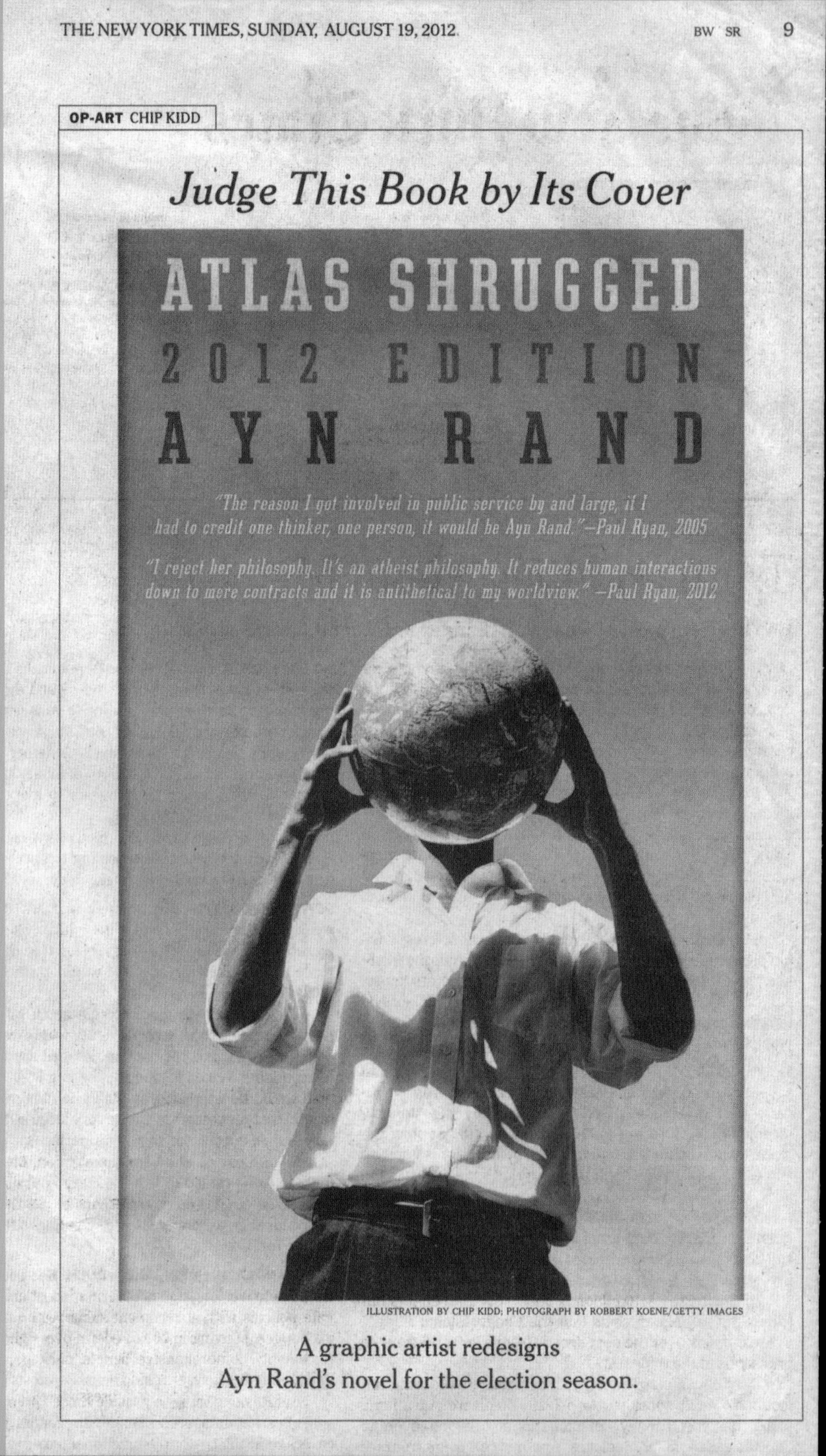
THE NEW YORK TIMES, SUNDAY, AUGUST 19, 2012. BW SR 9

**OP-ART** CHIP KIDD

*Judge This Book by Its Cover*

ATLAS SHRUGGED
2012 EDITION
AYN RAND
"The reason I got involved in public service by and large, if I had to credit one thinker, one person, it would be Ayn Rand."—Paul Ryan, 2005
"I reject her philosophy. It's an atheist philosophy. It reduces human interactions down to mere contracts and it is antithetical to my worldview." —Paul Ryan, 2012

ILLUSTRATION BY CHIP KIDD; PHOTOGRAPH BY ROBBERT KOENE/GETTY IMAGES

A graphic artist redesigns
Ayn Rand's novel for the election season.

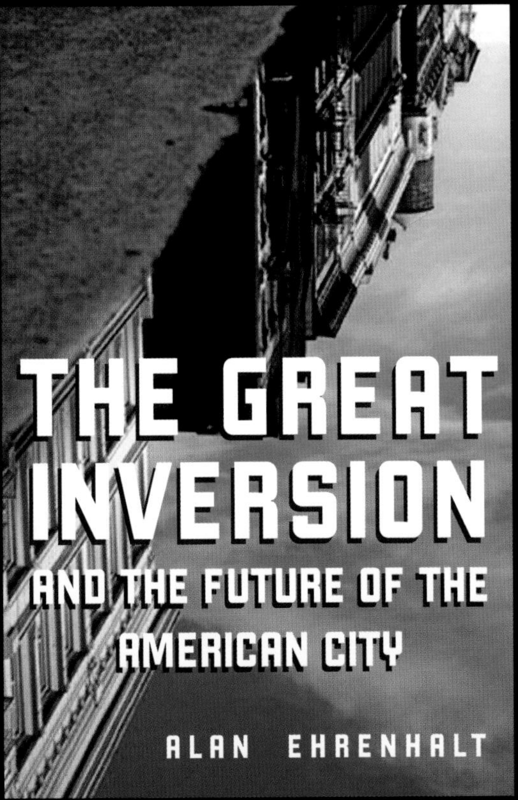
THE GREAT INVERSION
AND THE FUTURE OF THE AMERICAN CITY
ALAN EHRENHALT

## Hot Topic

In *Cool It* (opposite, left; Knopf, 2007), scientist Bjorn Lomborg makes a case for how economically wasteful most plans are for combating global warming. I wanted the cover to go from hot to cool as you scan it left to right.

An op-ed illustration for the *New York Times* (opposite, right) commenting on Paul Ryan's flip-flopping regarding his Ayn Rand worship.

My first attempt at the cover of Alan Ehrenhalt's examination of the phenomenon of reverse migration of people back into densely populated urban areas is shown above. The author responded better to an image via Google Maps of Bushwick, Brooklyn (right; Knopf, 2012), which provides one of the case studies for the book.

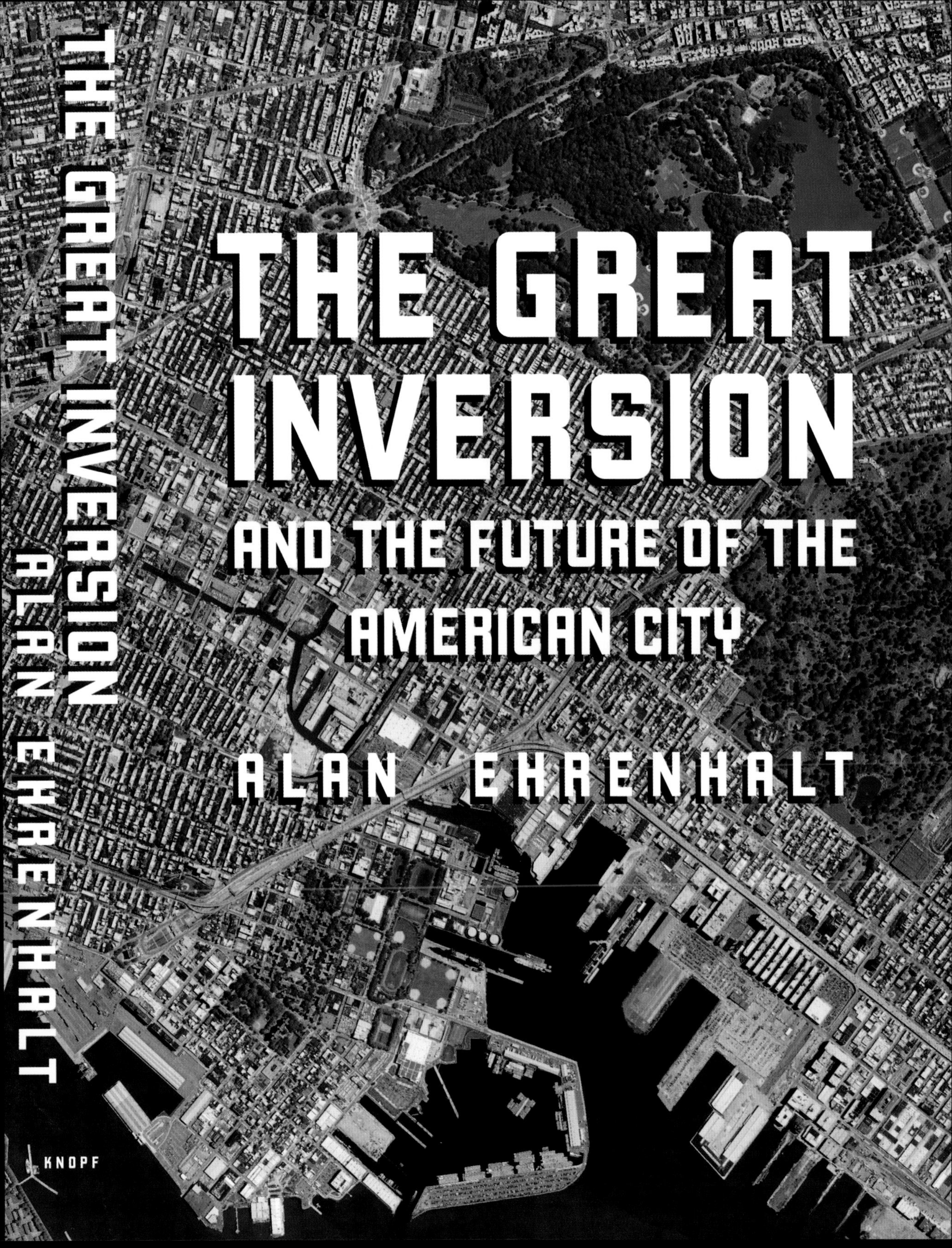
THE GREAT INVERSION
ALAN EHRENHALT
THE GREAT INVERSION
AND THE FUTURE OF THE AMERICAN CITY
ALAN EHRENHALT
KNOPF

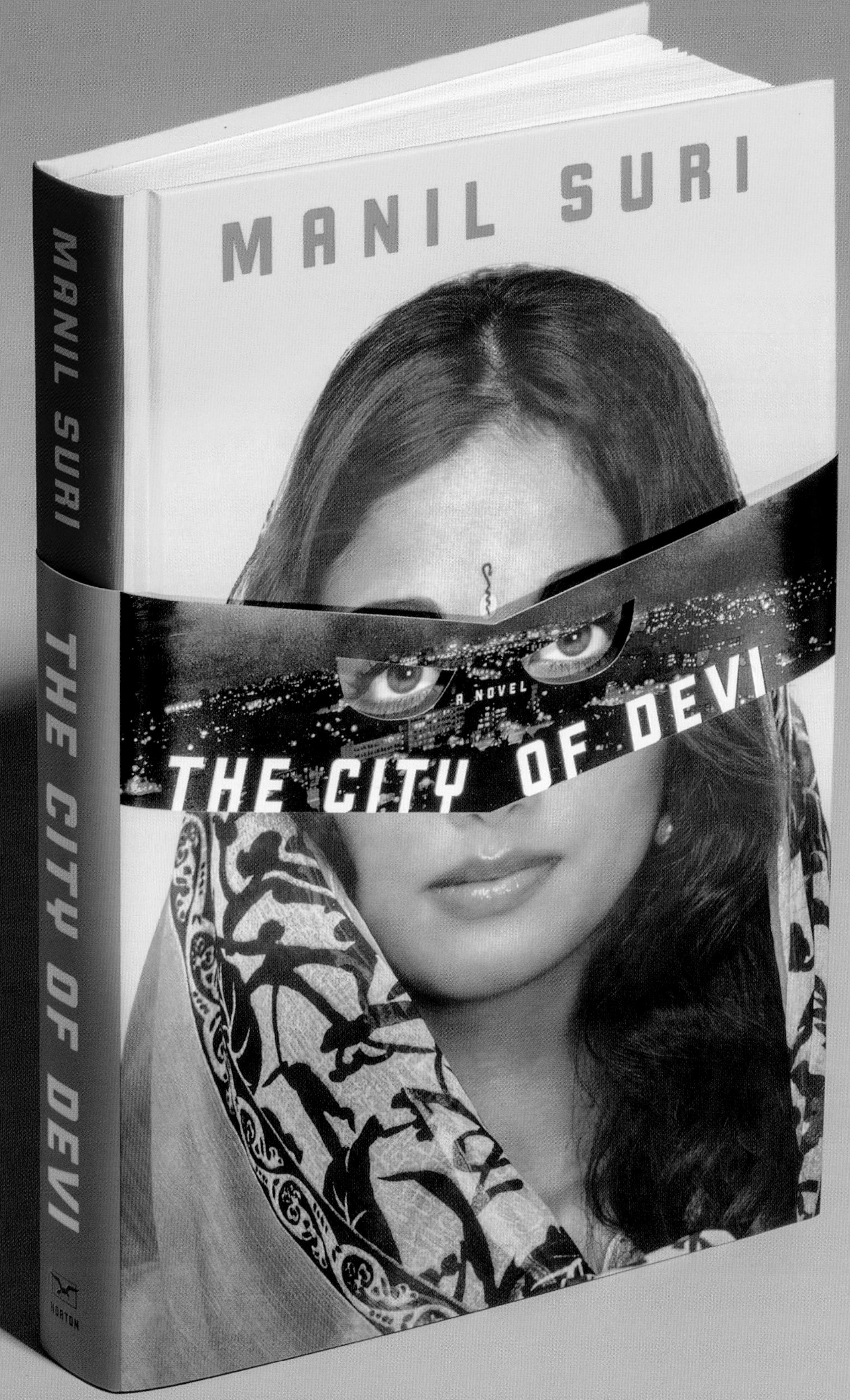
MANIL SURI
MANIL SURI
A NOVEL
THE CITY OF DEVI
THE CITY OF DEVI
NORTON

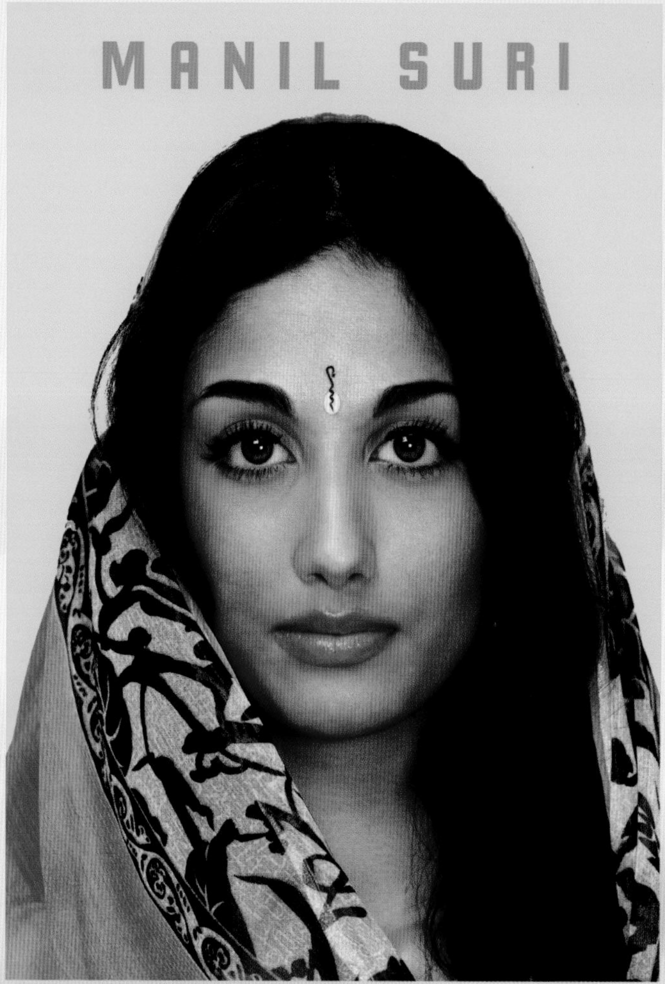
MANIL SURI

## Revealing Story

In the novel *The City of Devi* (left; Norton, 2013), Manil Suri weaves a tale of dystopian Mumbai on the brink of nuclear annihilation. Two disparate souls, Sarita and Jaz, are thrown together in the chaos. Narrowly evading danger at every step, both are inexorably drawn to Devi Maa, the patron goddess who has reputedly appeared in person to save her city.

I thought of Devi as a superheroine, and turned the city itself into her disguise (left), with her true identity underneath (above). This goes back to the cover design for *Batman Collected*—the idea that the jacket itself is a mask for the book.

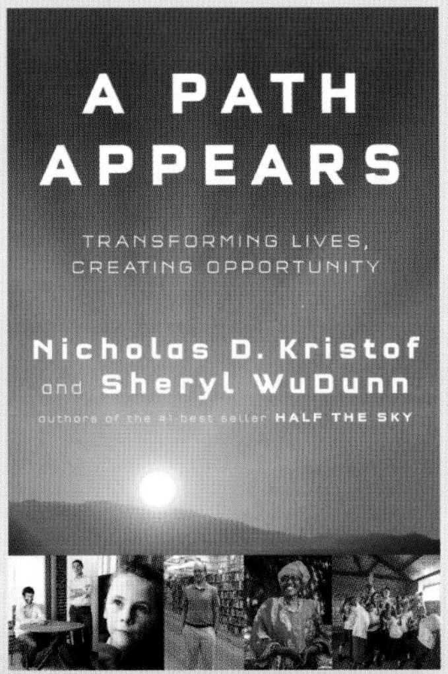
A PATH APPEARS
TRANSFORMING LIVES, CREATING OPPORTUNITY
Nicholas D. Kristof
and Sheryl WuDunn
authors of the #1 best seller HALF THE SKY

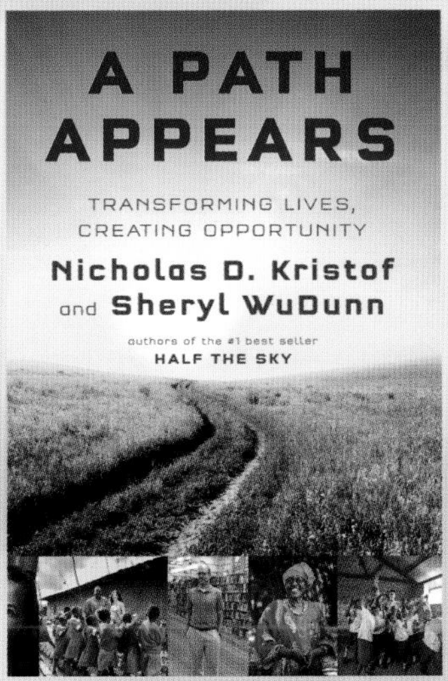
A PATH APPEARS
TRANSFORMING LIVES, CREATING OPPORTUNITY
Nicholas D. Kristof
and Sheryl WuDunn
authors of the #1 best seller
HALF THE SKY

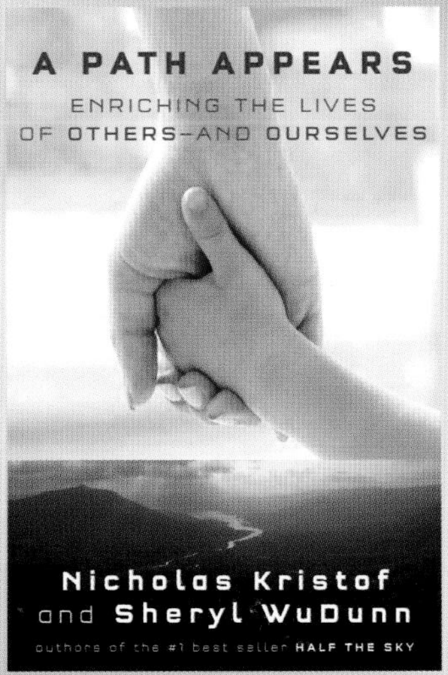
A PATH APPEARS
ENRICHING THE LIVES OF OTHERS—AND OURSELVES
Nicholas Kristof
and Sheryl WuDunn
authors of the #1 best seller HALF THE SKY

# Unseen. Unheard. Until Now.

Nicholas Kristof and Sheryl WuDunn really want to change the world for the better, and through their humanitarian investigative journalism and best-selling books about how altruism can positively affect us and the people we help, they are actually doing it. I was lucky enough to design their third and fourth books, *Half the Sky* (Knopf, 2009) and *A Path Appears* (Knopf, 2014), and in both cases they made the job easier by providing a lot of their own photography.

The design for *Half the Sky* is admittedly literal, but it is the bisected faces of the women that make it memorable. These are the actual people Nicholas and Sheryl report on in the book, and they had the portraits shot themselves. In most cases, the women have no voice, so that is symbolically depicted. The implication is that by opening the book you will hear their stories and learn how you can help.

For *A Path Appears*, I tried several directions, and the final one (left, center) refers to the idea that the authors are advocating a grass-roots approach to community and global activism. As on the previous jacket, the photographs along the bottom show the people who are chronicled in the text.

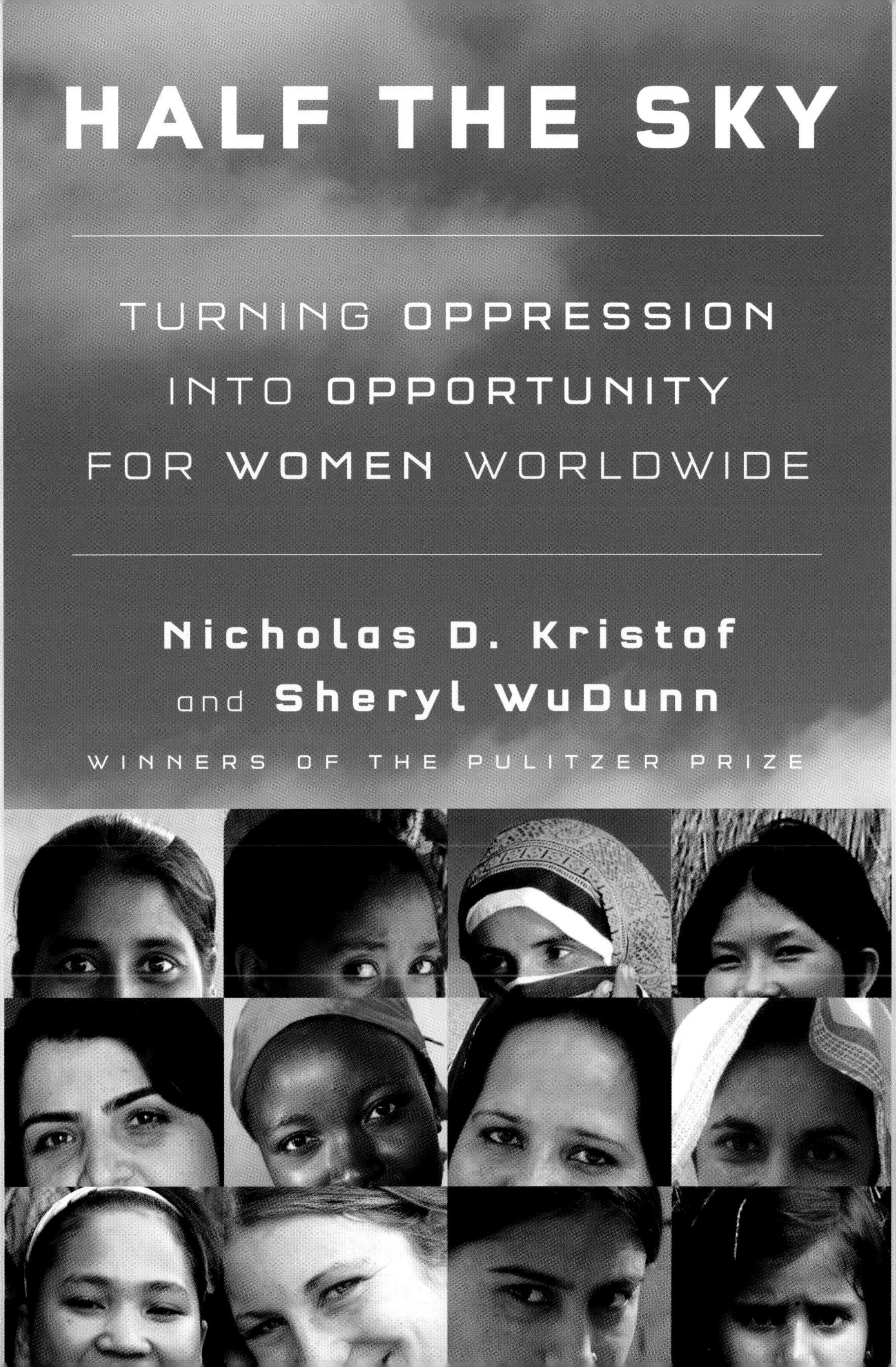
HALF THE SKY
TURNING OPPRESSION INTO OPPORTUNITY FOR WOMEN WORLDWIDE
Nicholas D. Kristof
and Sheryl WuDunn
WINNERS OF THE PULITZER PRIZE

FREEDOM ISN'T FREE
THIS IS ABUSE OF THE
## FREEDOM OF
# SPEECH

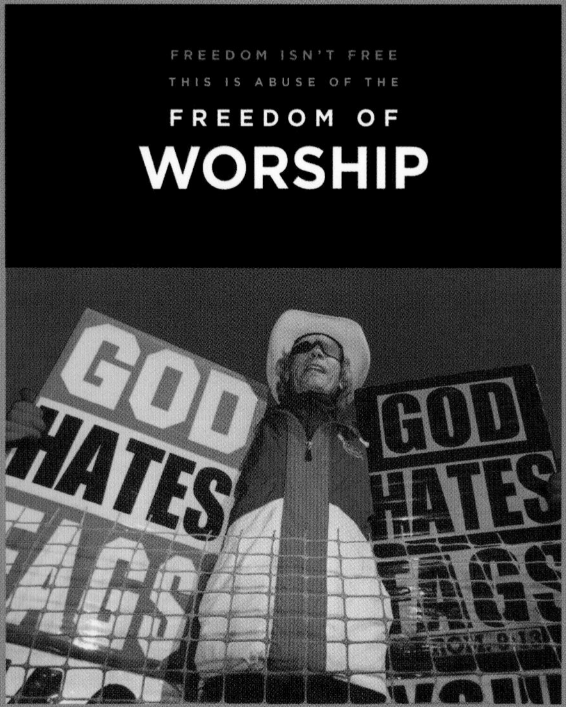

FREEDOM ISN'T FREE
THIS IS ABUSE OF THE
## FREEDOM OF
# WORSHIP

## Better Angels

In 2003, the Wolfsonian Museum in South Beach, Miami (one of the very best and underrecognized design museums in the country—go there now) created the Thoughts on Democracy invitational, inviting designers from all over the US to reinterpret Norman Rockwell's "Four Freedoms" posters from 1943, originally created to help sell war bonds, ultimately raising $132 million. The paintings—*Freedom of Speech, Freedom of Worship, Freedom from Want,* and *Freedom from Fear*—are now in the Norman Rockwell Museum in Stockbridge, Massachusetts. The four freedoms refer to President Franklin D. Roosevelt's January 1941 Four Freedoms State of the Union address in which he identified essential human rights that should be universally protected. The theme was incorporated into the Atlantic Charter and became part of the charter of the United Nations.

Sixty years later, the Wolfsonian asked a contemporary group of designers to think about what these freedoms mean now. Are they the same? Different? Changed?

I decided to recast them under the rubric of "Freedom Isn't Free," suggesting they are now not only taken for granted but also routinely abused. How? Take a look: "Freedom of Speech" means you can burn the flag, but to what end? That strikes me as something that people who hate America would do. Yes, you have the right to do it, but what message are you sending? "Freedom of Worship" means you can morally condemn any group or individual whose values you don't agree with, in the name of whatever god you want. And we're all supposed to take it seriously. "Freedom from Fear" has come to mean that you can shoot/kill anyone you think is threatening you, under whatever circumstances, and let the courts sort it out. As we have seen, this is devastating from both sides of the law. "Freedom from Want" has led to an epidemic of obesity in America that affects everyone and that we all ultimately pay for. We are only left to imagine what FDR or Rockwell would make of the present state of affairs.

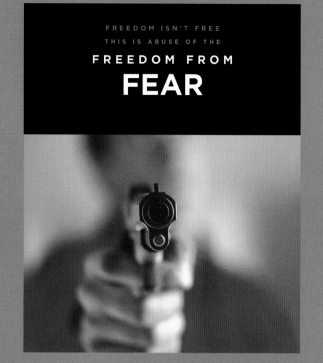

FREEDOM ISN'T FREE
THIS IS ABUSE OF THE
## FREEDOM FROM
# FEAR

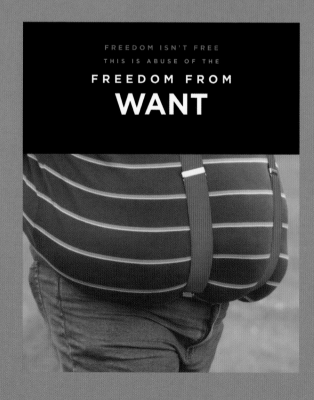

FREEDOM ISN'T FREE
THIS IS ABUSE OF THE
## FREEDOM FROM
# WANT

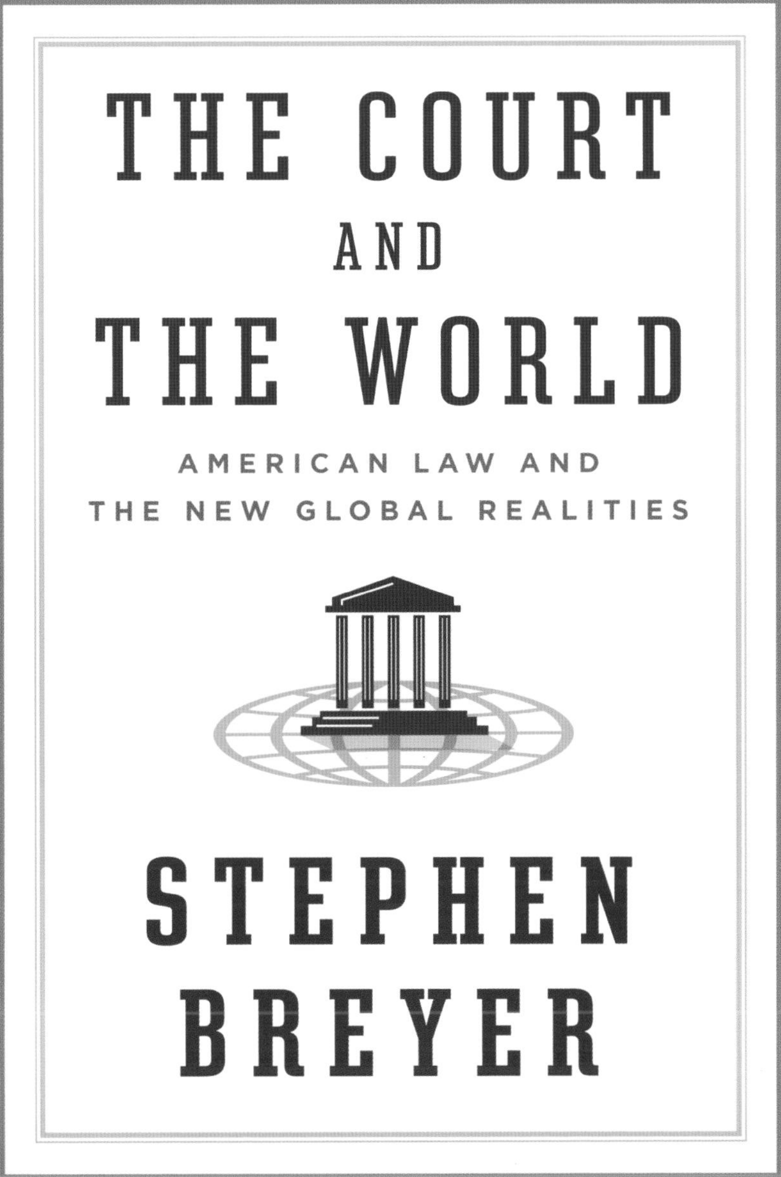
THE COURT
AND
THE WORLD
AMERICAN LAW AND
THE NEW GLOBAL REALITIES
STEPHEN
BREYER

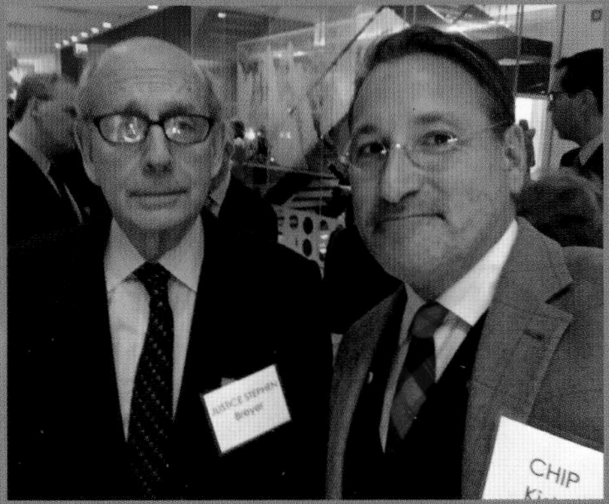

I have been honored to design not one but two books for Supreme Court Justice Stephen Breyer (left), who is a real gent. And, fun fact: he listens to French poetry in the original language when he jogs in the morning.

**ABOVE:** Knopf, 2015. Illustration by Oliver Munday.
**RIGHT:** Knopf, 2010.

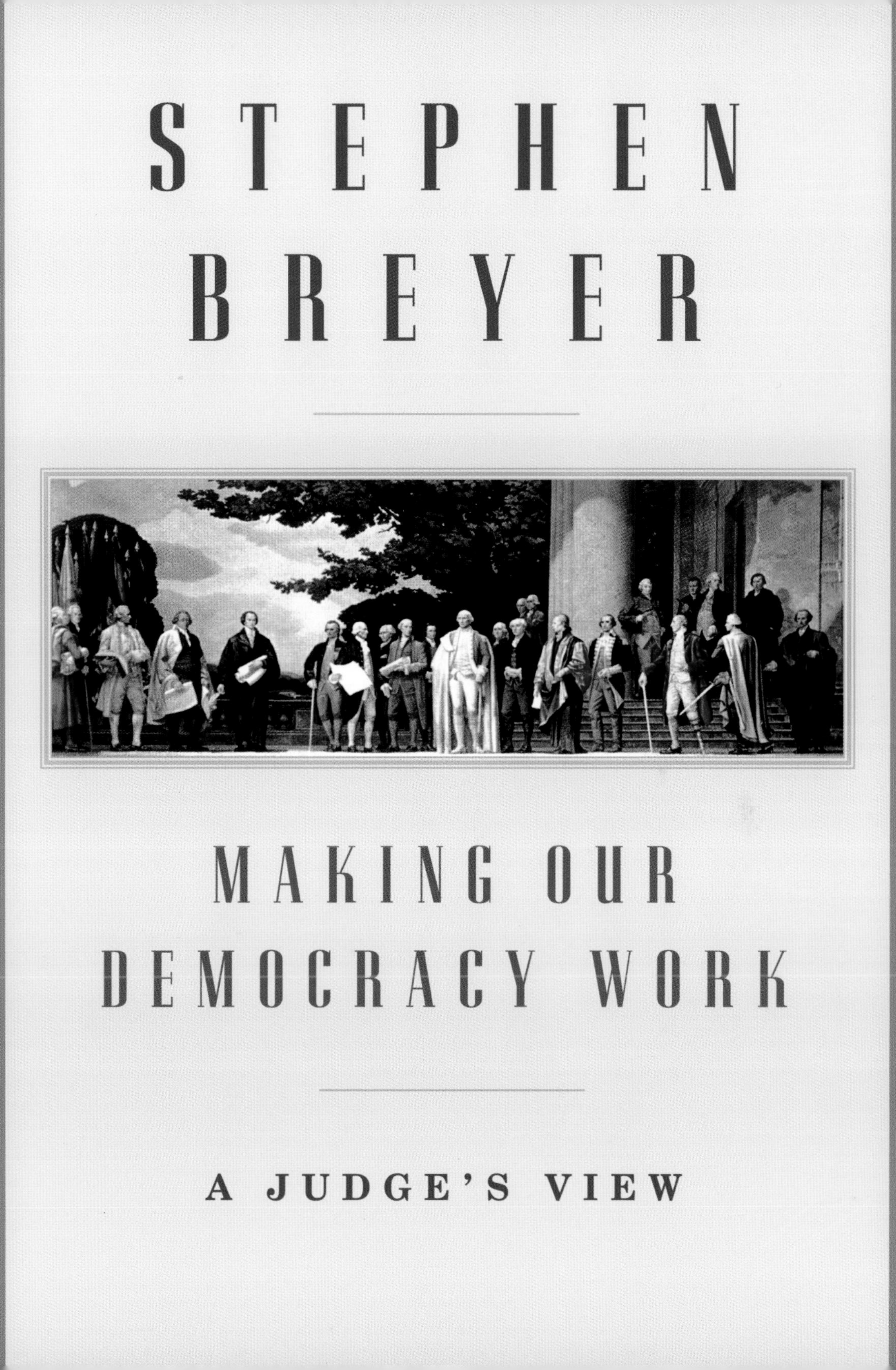
STEPHEN
BREYER
MAKING OUR
DEMOCRACY WORK
A JUDGE'S VIEW

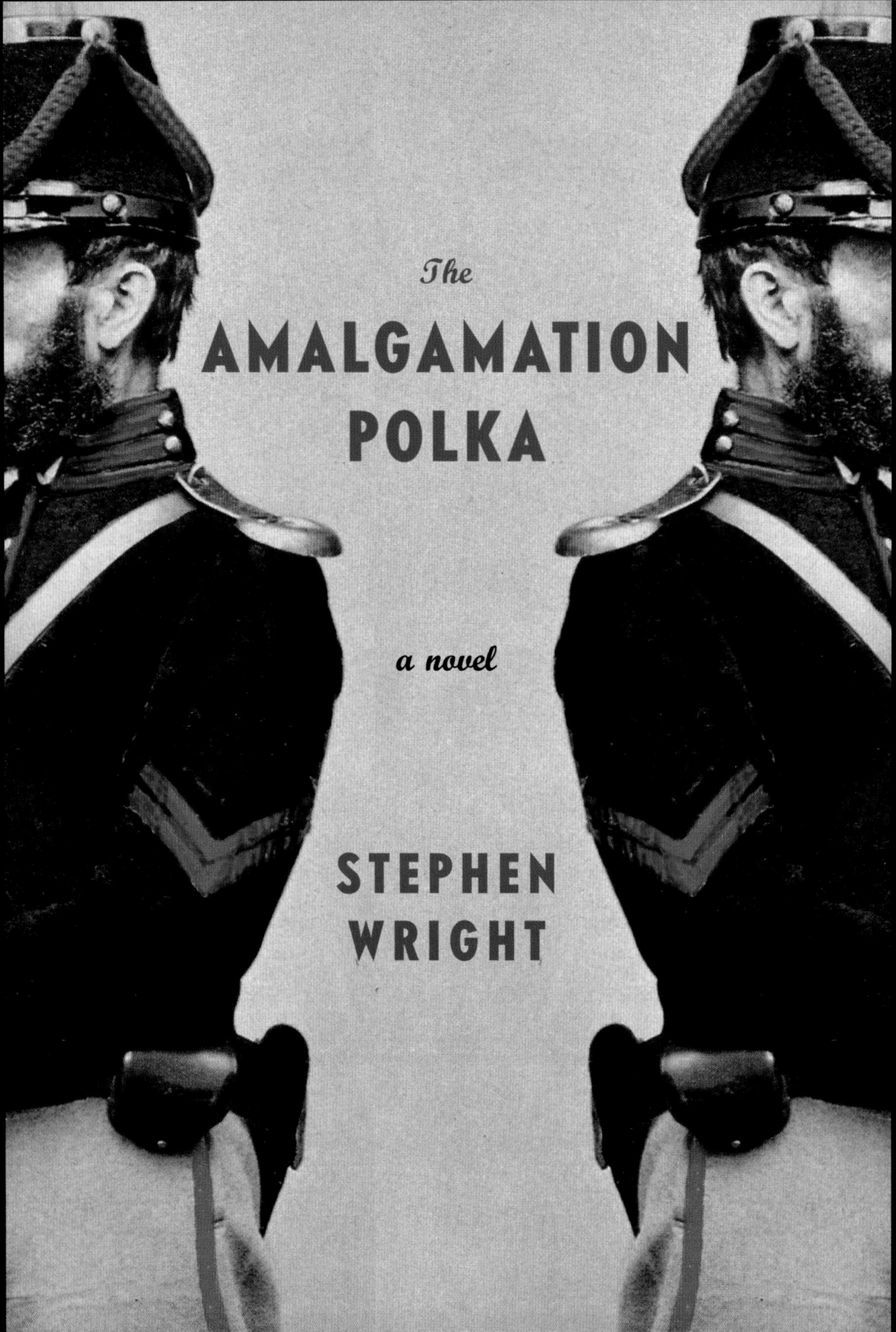
The
AMALGAMATION
POLKA
a novel
STEPHEN
WRIGHT

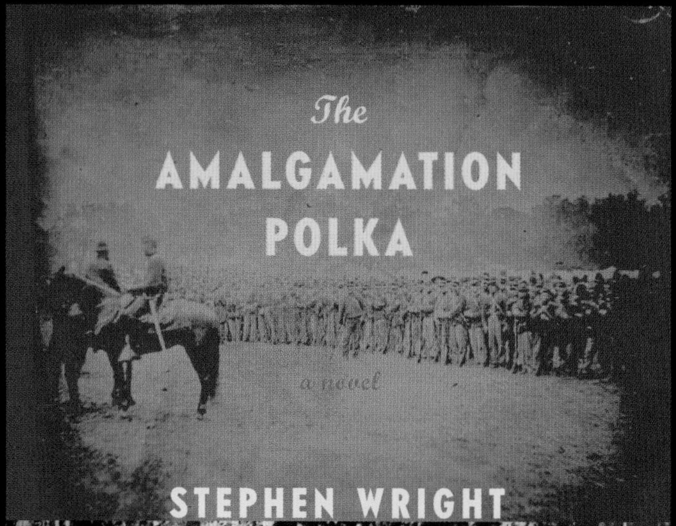
The
AMALGAMATION
POLKA
a novel
STEPHEN WRIGHT

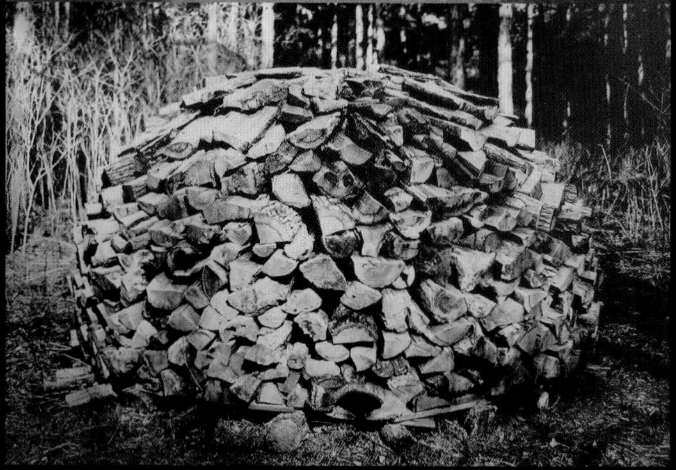

## Stacked Like Cordwood

A novel of the American Civil War, *The Amalgamation Polka* by Stephen Wright is about a vengeful Union soldier named Liberty Fish. The plot ventures into the realm of the surreal to convey the madness that takes hold during the protagonist's quest to find his grandparents, who were cruel slaveholders. I first tried using historical photography (above) in an attempt at a bloodless yet ghoulish if/then metaphor. The better solution (left) lay in the absurdly perfectly symmetrical placement of the soldiers. This shot was also genuinely of the time period, but indicates that something "novelistic" and weirder is going on.

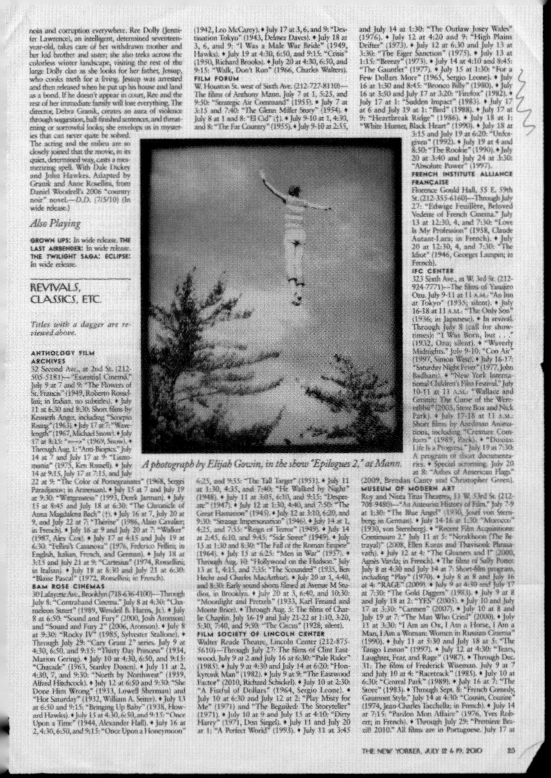
Also Playing
REVIVALS, CLASSICS, ETC.
THE NEW YORKER, JULY 12 & 19, 2010
*A photograph by Elijah Gowin, in the show "Epilogues 2," at Mann.*

**OPPOSITE, LEFT:** Knopf, 2006.

**RIGHT:** Knopf, 2011.

*Daughters of the Revolution* is best summarized by our own in-house description: "In 1968, a clerical mistake threatens the prestigious but cash-strapped Goode School in the small New England town of Cape Wilde. After a century of all-male, old-boy education, the school accidentally admits its first female student: Carole Faust, a brilliant, outspoken, fifteen-year-old black girl whose arrival will have both an immediate and long-term effect on the prep school and everyone in its orbit. There's the school's philandering headmaster, Goddard 'God' Byrd, who had promised co-education 'over his dead body;' there's EV, the daughter of God's widowed mistress who watches Carole's actions as she grows older with wide eyes and admiration; and there's Carole herself, who bears the singular challenge of being the First Girl in a world that's not quite ready to embrace her."

I was thinking of EV when I saw this photo in the *New Yorker* by Elijah Gowin. It really seemed to embody the spirit of educational emancipation in the book.

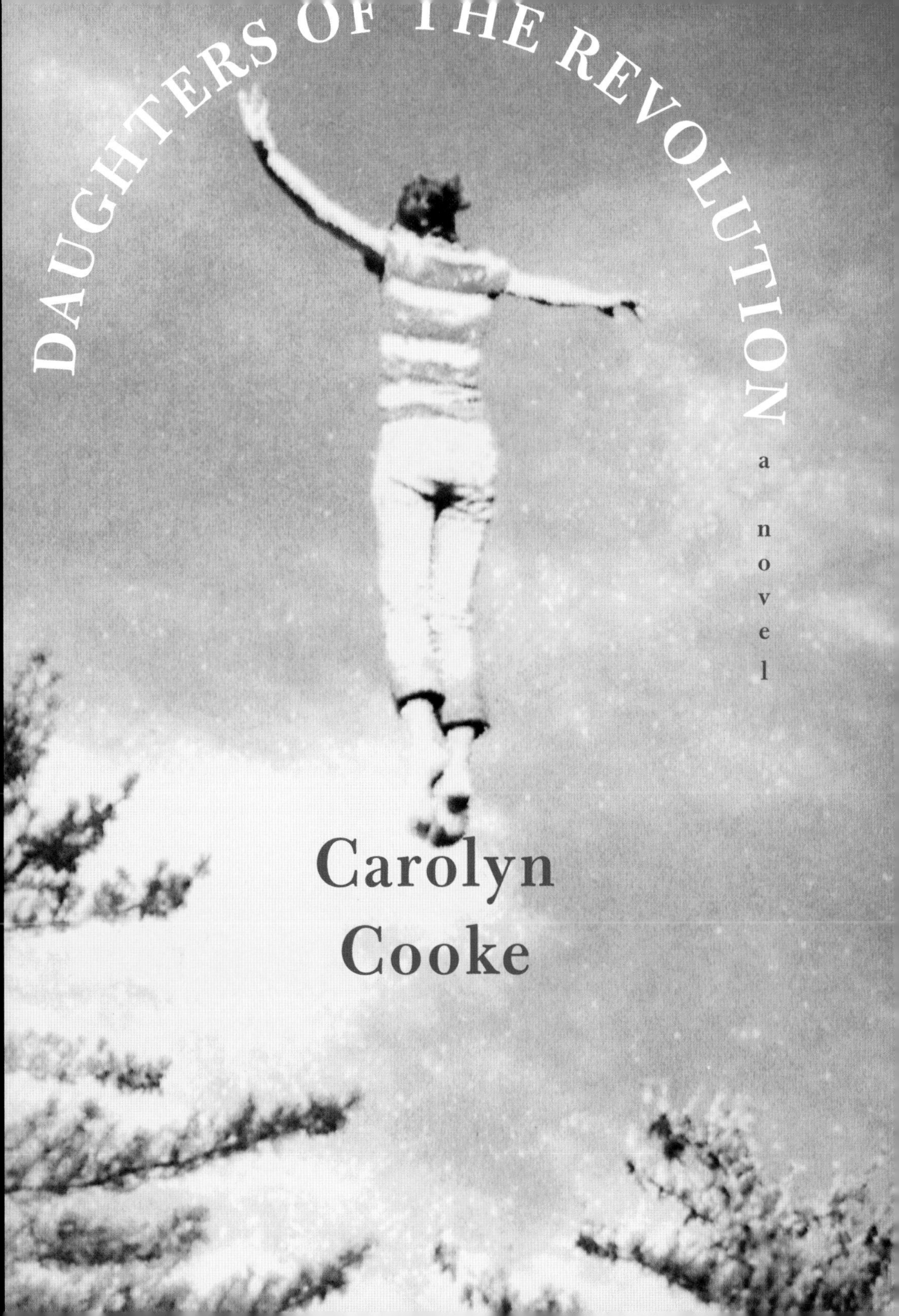
DAUGHTERS OF THE REVOLUTION
a novel
Carolyn Cooke

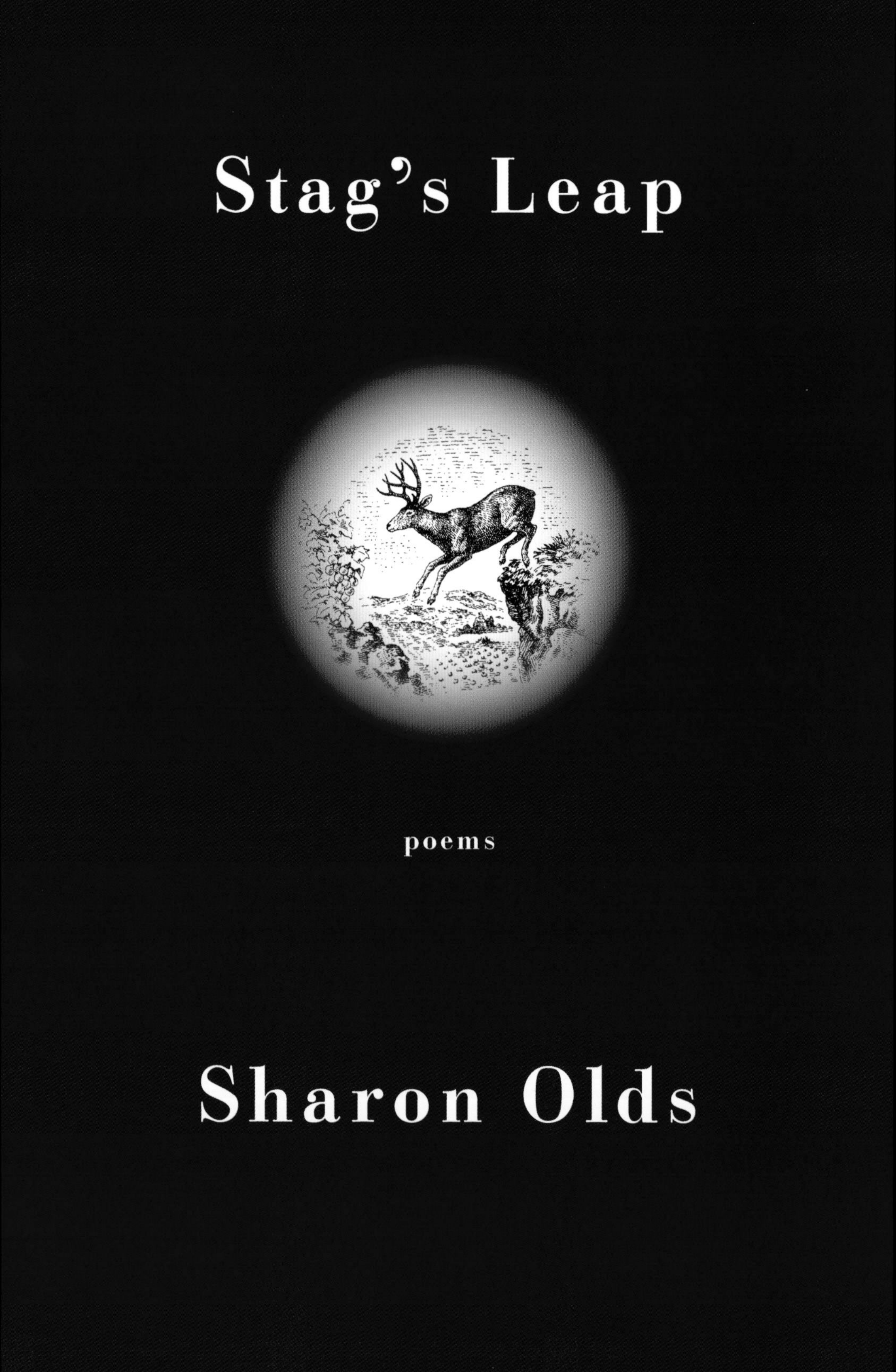
Stag's Leap
poems
Sharon Olds

# Man, Verses, Nature

*"Then the drawing on the label of our favorite red wine*
*looks like my husband, casting himself off a*
*cliff in his fervor to get free of me."*

This bravely written collection of poems is about the dissolution of Sharon Olds's marriage, the loss of her beloved to someone else. The metaphors are obvious here, and I just had to step back and stage the jacket as straightforwardly as possible, according to her wishes below, sent to her editor Deb Garrisson. The book went on to win the 2013 Pulitzer Prize for poetry.

---

Dear Deb,

I have here somewhere . . . the image from the old label of Stag's Leap. They have a streamlined leaping stag on their bottles now, I think, but this old one was the label I was looking at when I wrote the title poem.

I think I should write Robert Britain . . . the good news that the book will come out in Sept., and that I'm hoping to use something like the image of the deer on his label (he owns the vineyard). I don't know if I should be asking for permission . . . or just telling him the good news?

What I picture is a book cover the color of Cabernet Sauvignon, that dark almost blackish(ish) magenta, with the deer image in the middle—in white? I love black, but would it show up?

Above, the title, Stag's Leap—again I'd love black but would it show up—in plain old letters with serifs. Below, my name, in the same type face but smaller. And I'm hoping Carol, or whoever it is, your great art dept., can make a few possible drafts without going to a lot of expense. I hate to waste Knopf's money doing many mock-ups to get it feeling right!

I think I'd be happy with a cover just "burgundy" & black or white—I have recovered over the years from wanting some of it in bright gold!!!!!

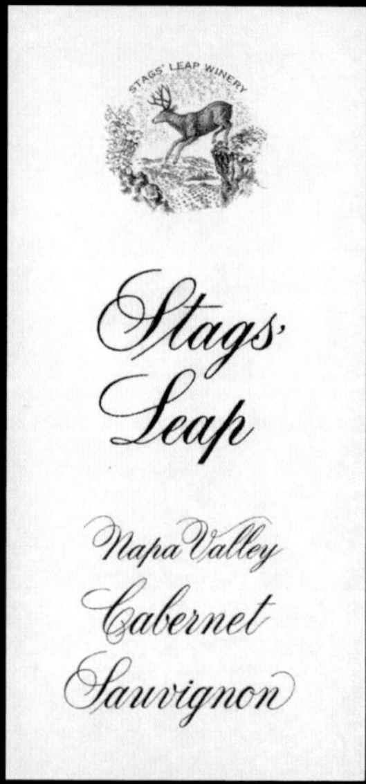
STAGS' LEAP WINERY
Stags' Leap
Napa Valley
Cabernet
Sauvignon

Love,
Sharon

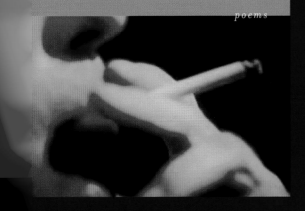

Winner of the Pulitzer Prize

MARK STRAND

MAN AND CAMEL

*poems*

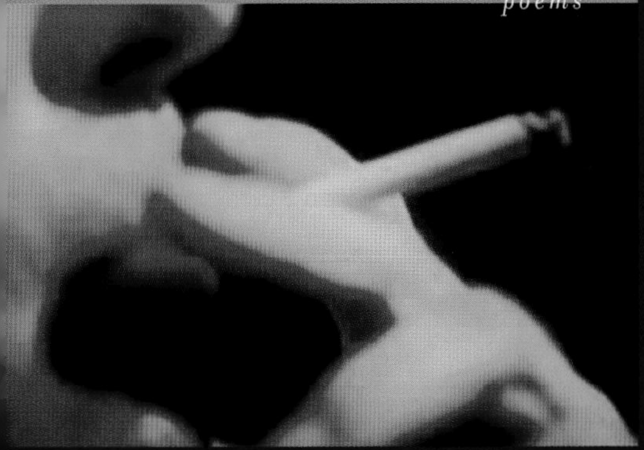

MARK STRAND

MAN AND CAMEL

*poems*

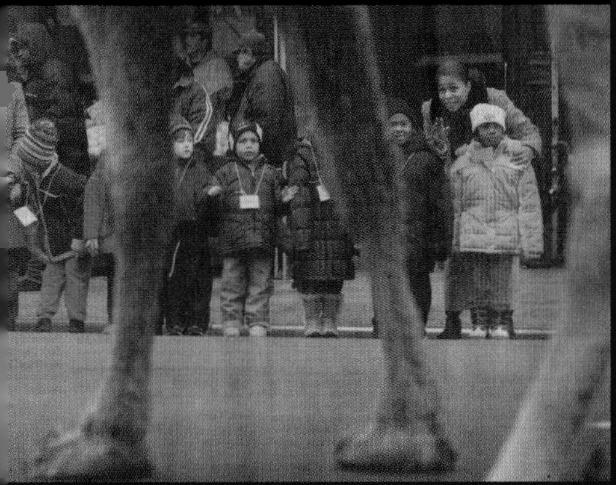

MARK STRAND

Winner of the Pulitzer Prize

# Man and Camel

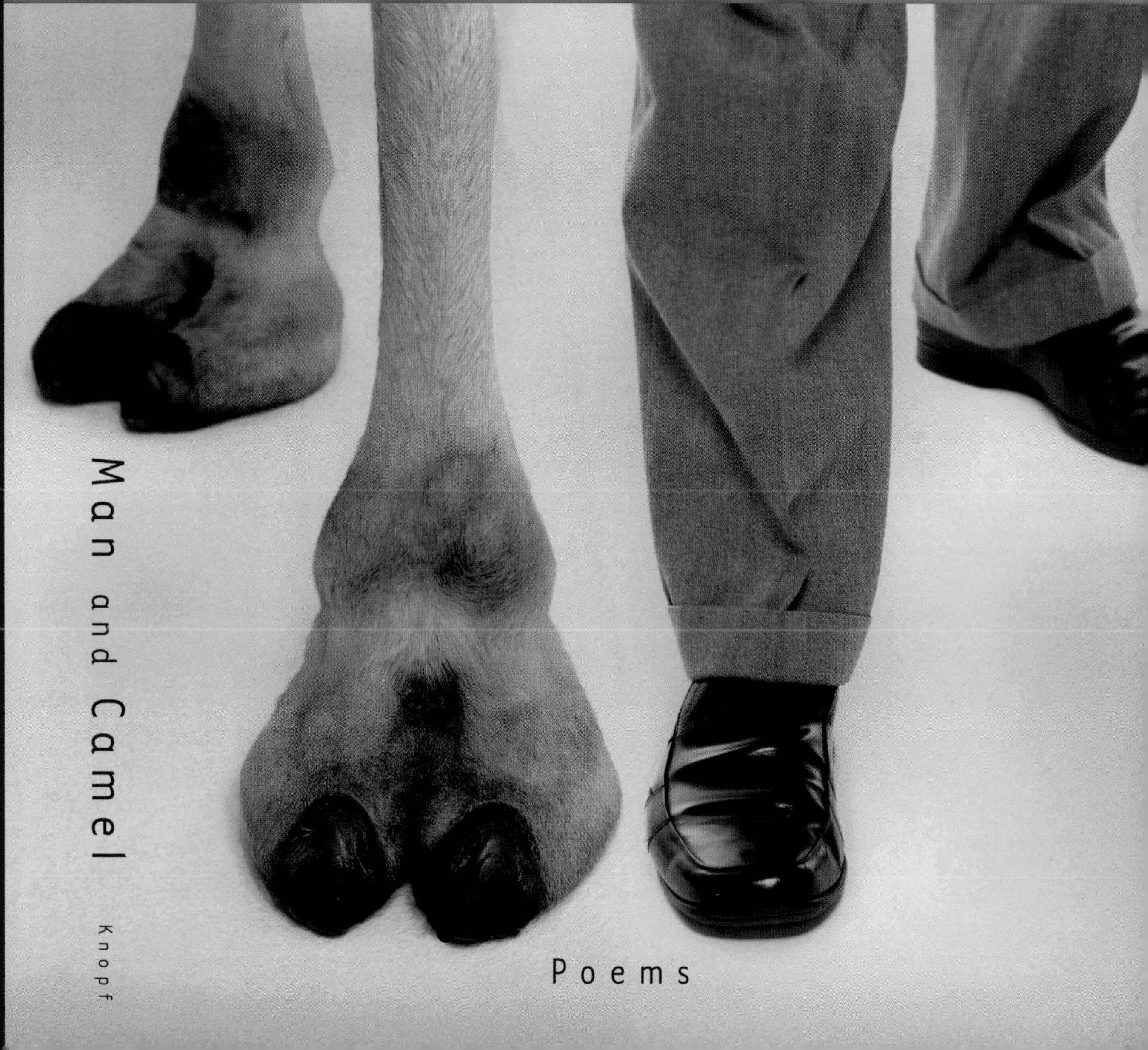

Man and Camel
Knopf
Poems

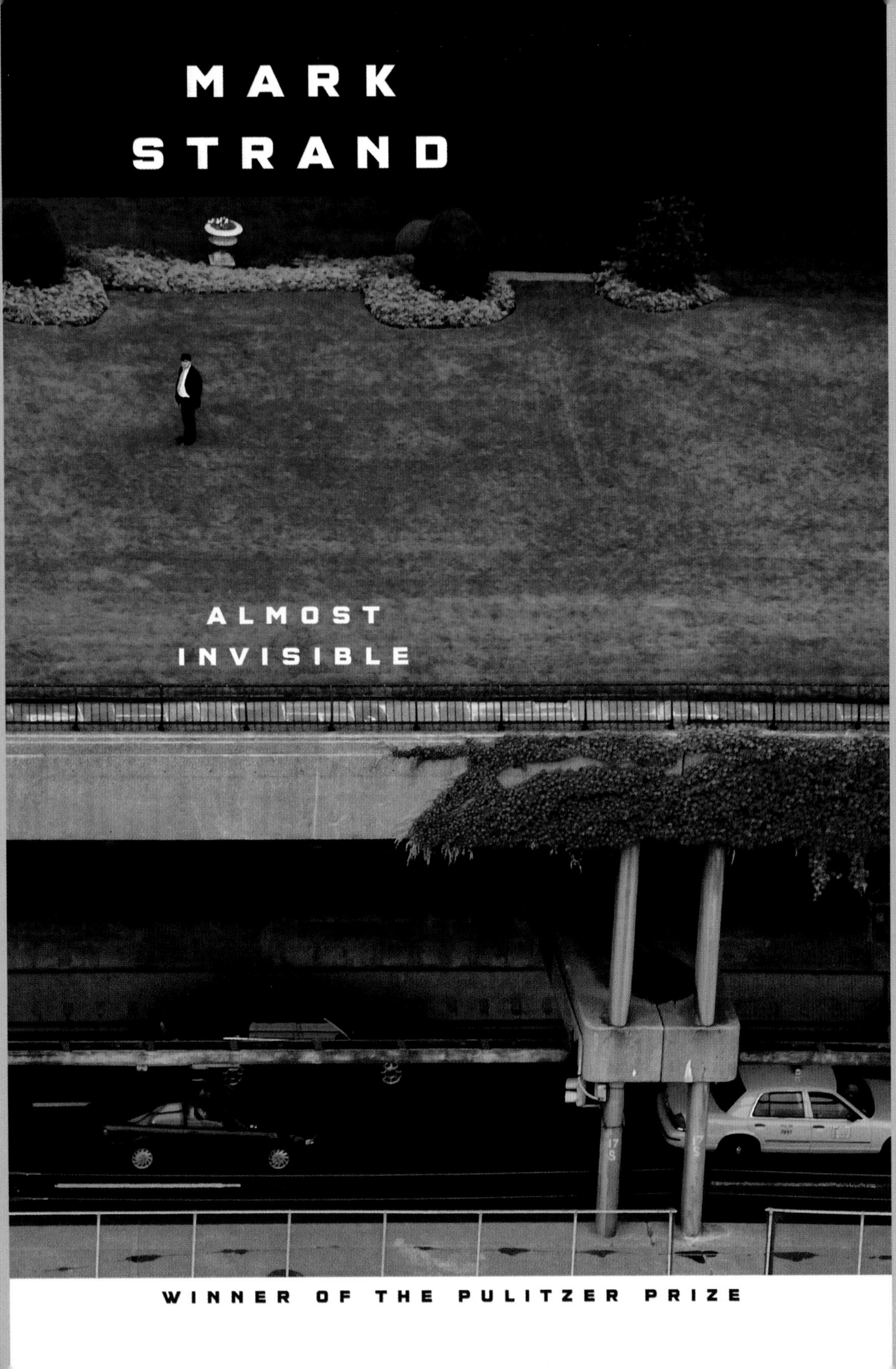
MARK
STRAND
ALMOST
INVISIBLE
WINNER OF THE PULITZER PRIZE

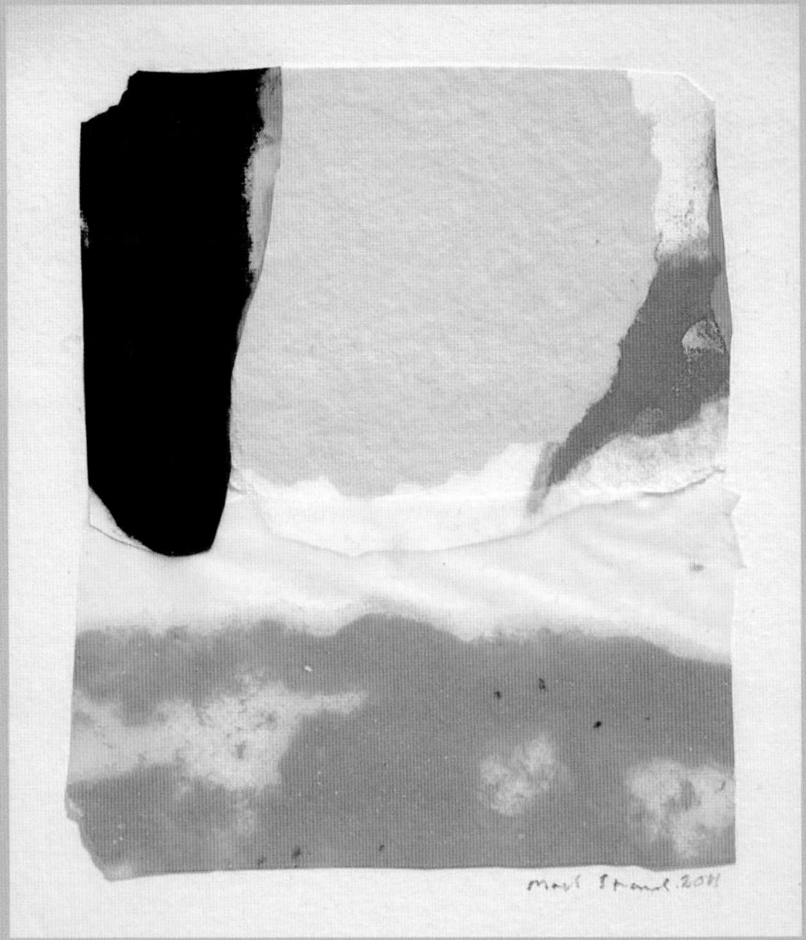

## Multiple Strands

I got to know the poet Mark Strand through his writing and his friendship with Sandy (McClatchy, my husband), and of course because Knopf published him. *Man and Camel* (previous page) was the first book I worked on for him, and my urge to avoid the inevitable frankly lost. That's actually my foot in the photograph (the one on the right, thank you!). I liked the one with the cigarette best, but the poem wasn't really about that. Oh well.

For *Almost Invisible* (left) I started with one of Mark's own paper montages (above) and further abstracted it (opposite, upper left), but he wasn't thrilled with the result. Then I fell in love with the aerial photos of Vincent Laforet, and this one single shot of two very different levels of the FDR drive on the upper-eastern rim of Manhattan did the trick.

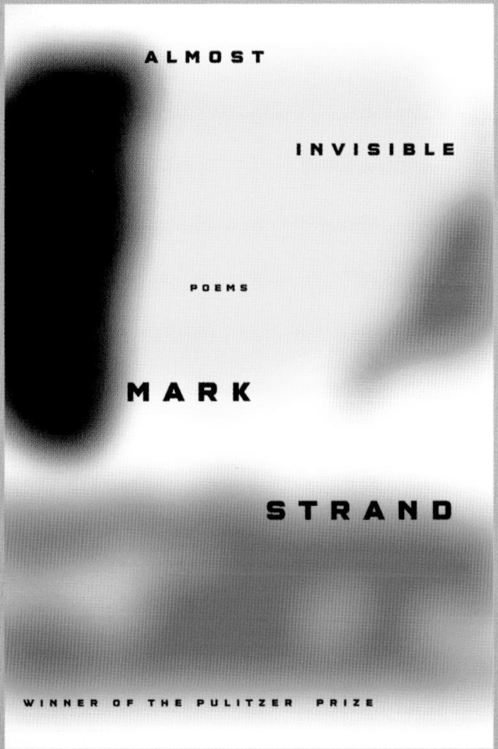
ALMOST
INVISIBLE
POEMS
MARK
STRAND
WINNER OF THE PULITZER PRIZE

For the *Collected Poems* I tried a few ideas (below), but Mark really wanted *Yes, But* by Saul Steinberg, and was able to get the rights, and that was fine with us. It was to be his last book published in his lifetime.

**PAGE 129:** Knopf, 2006. **OPPOSITE, LEFT:** Knopf, 2012. **RIGHT:** Knopf, 2014.

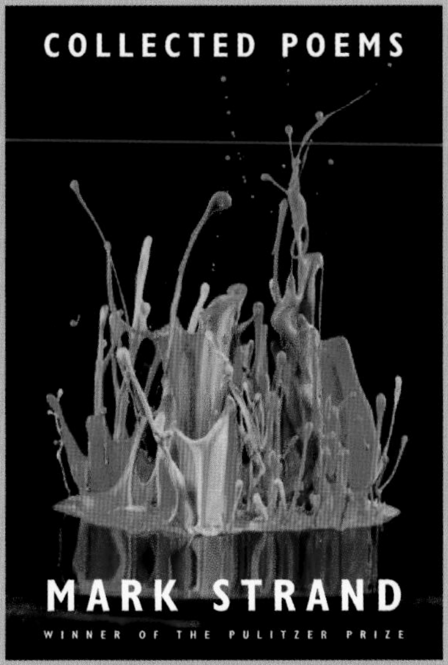
COLLECTED POEMS
MARK STRAND
WINNER OF THE PULITZER PRIZE

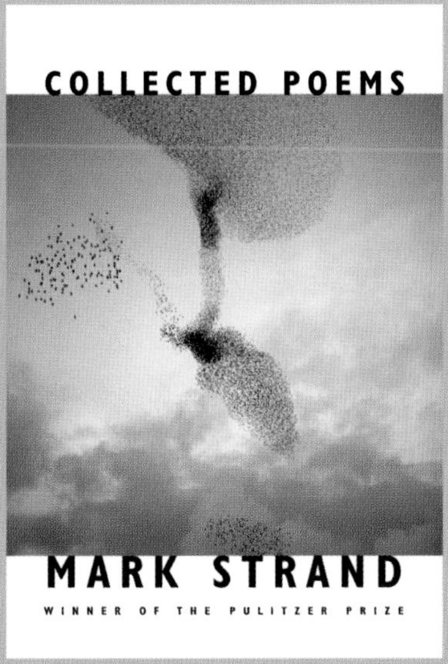
COLLECTED POEMS
MARK STRAND
WINNER OF THE PULITZER PRIZE

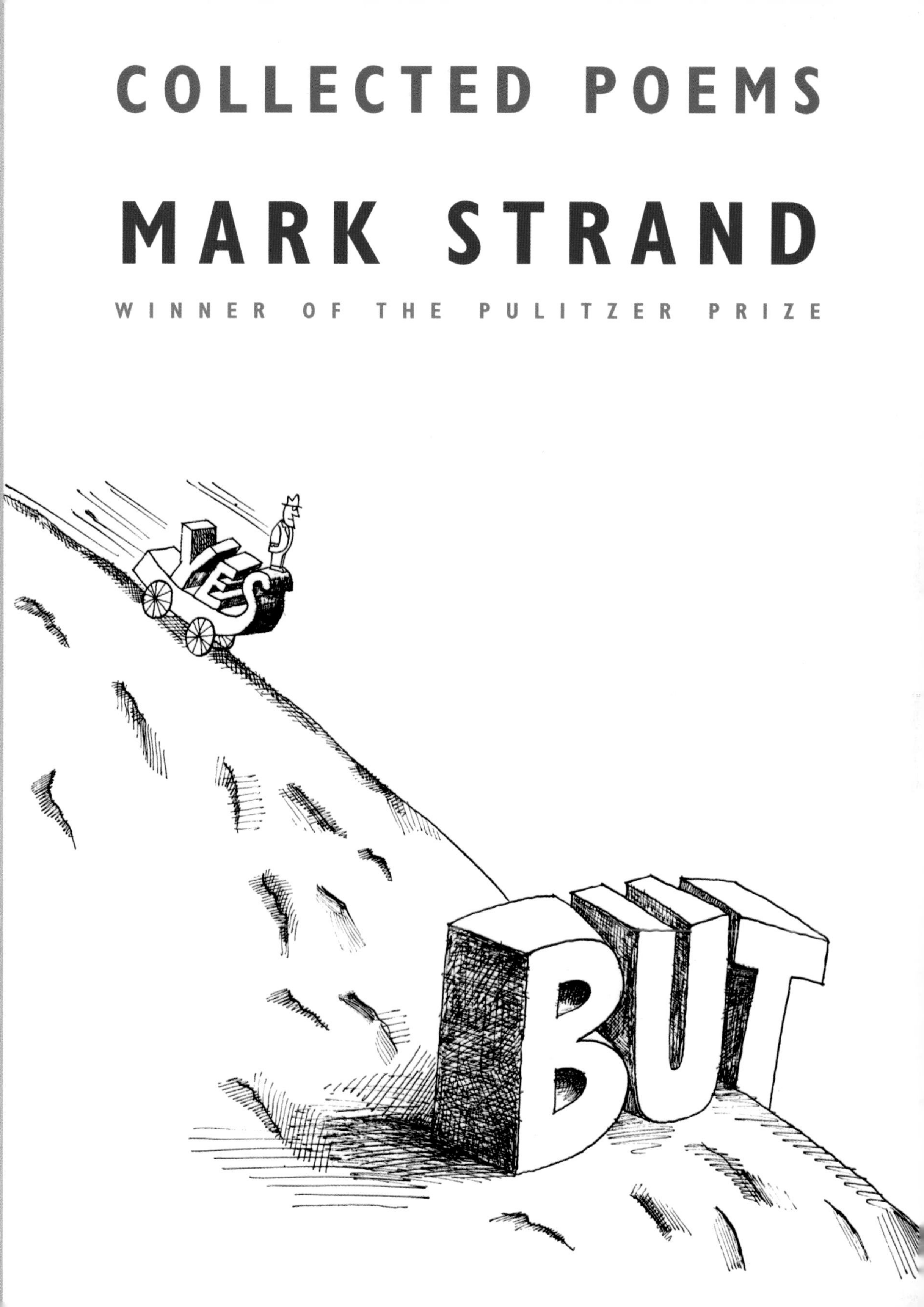
COLLECTED POEMS
MARK STRAND
WINNER OF THE PULITZER PRIZE
YES
BUT

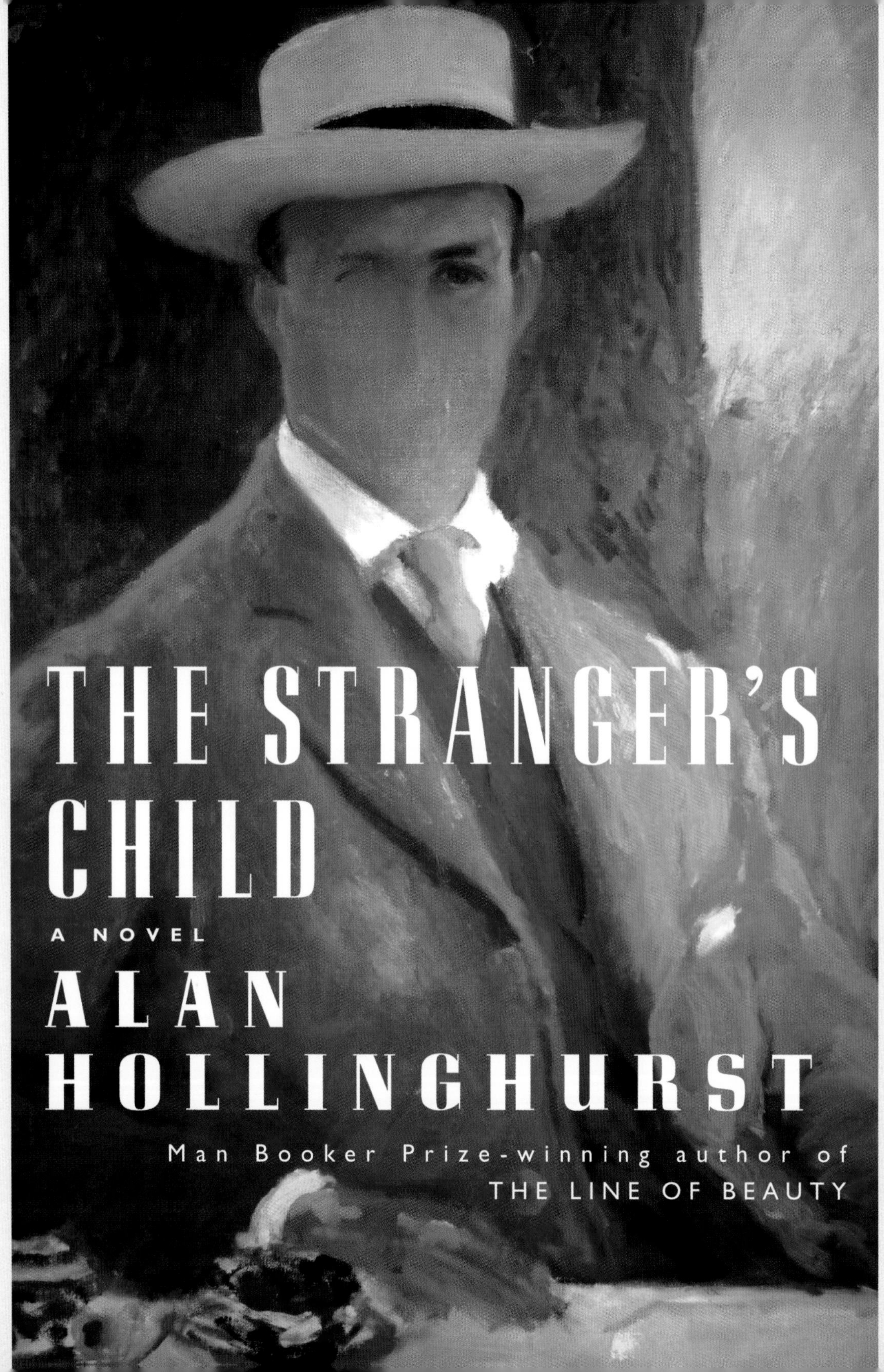
THE STRANGER'S CHILD
A NOVEL
ALAN HOLLINGHURST
Man Booker Prize-winning author of
THE LINE OF BEAUTY

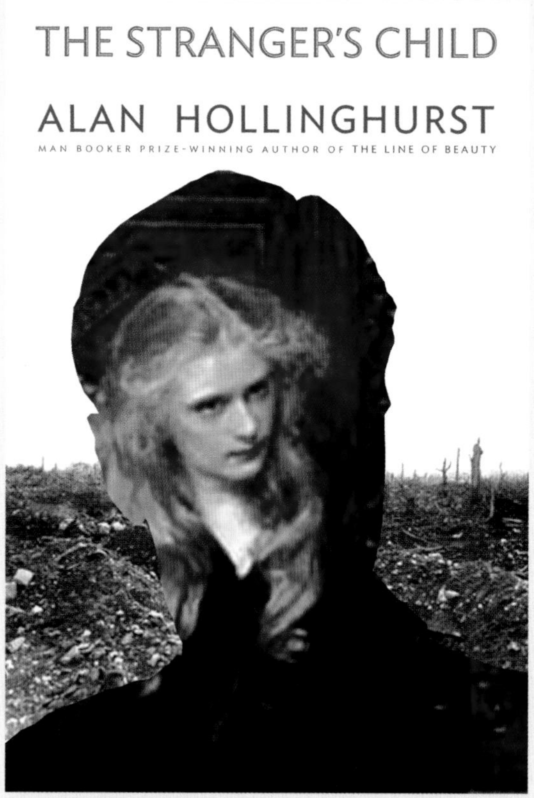
THE STRANGER'S CHILD
ALAN HOLLINGHURST
MAN BOOKER PRIZE-WINNING AUTHOR OF THE LINE OF BEAUTY

## Strangers in Town

Alan Hollinghurst's period novel *The Stranger's Child* is about a young British writer named Cecil Valance who creates a poem that captivates his country's populace, just before he goes off to fight and die in World War I. His survivors, Daphne Sawle and her brother George, who both believed themselves to be his romantic interest (George is more on the mark there, actually), are left to pick up the pieces and make sense of his legacy.

The first design I tried (above) was too ambitious, using a silhouette of a figure meant to be Cecil, filled with an image of Daphne and set against a WWI trench scene. The colors were nice, but there is too much going on.

This unfinished painting by Eugene Speicher (left) had been hanging in Sandy's apartment for years when one evening while I was pondering this cover I looked over at it during dinner and realized, "Wait, it's Cecil!" The author and editor agreed: it was perfect for this book, the genteel sense of a beguiling but ultimately unknowable figure.

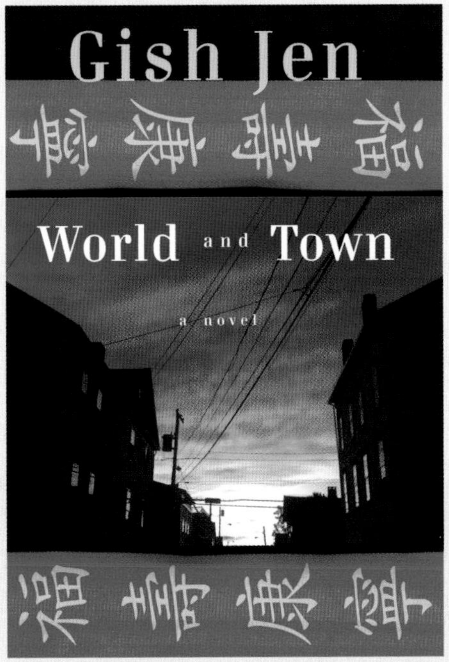
Gish Jen
World and Town
a novel

**OPPOSITE, LEFT:** Knopf, 2011.

**RIGHT:** Knopf, 2010.

Gish Jen continues her work of writing novels about how first-generation Asian Americans adapt to their new lives in the US. *World and Town* takes place in a sleepy New England village named Riverlake and explores its reaction to a family who has arrived from Cambodia. I took the photo (above) in my own small town of Stonington, Connecticut, during a particularly glorious sunset. The final cover (right) inserts a symbol of the one culture within the context of the other.

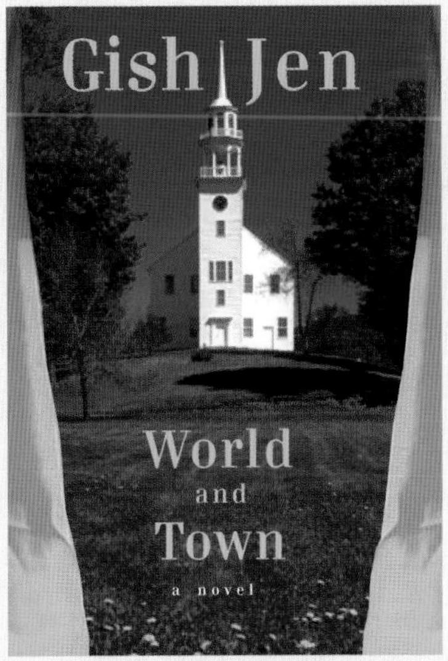
Gish Jen
World
and
Town
a novel

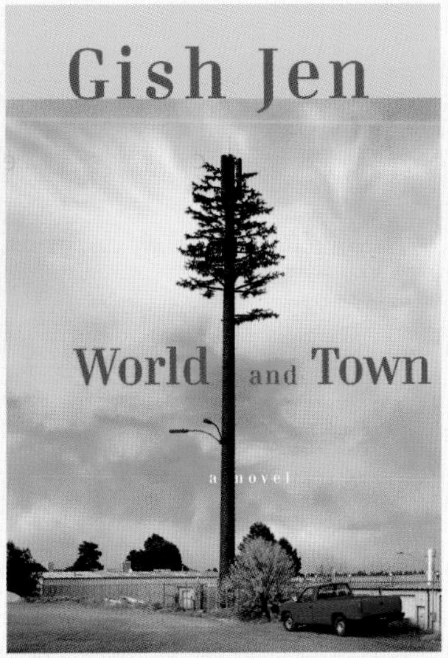
Gish Jen
World and Town
a novel

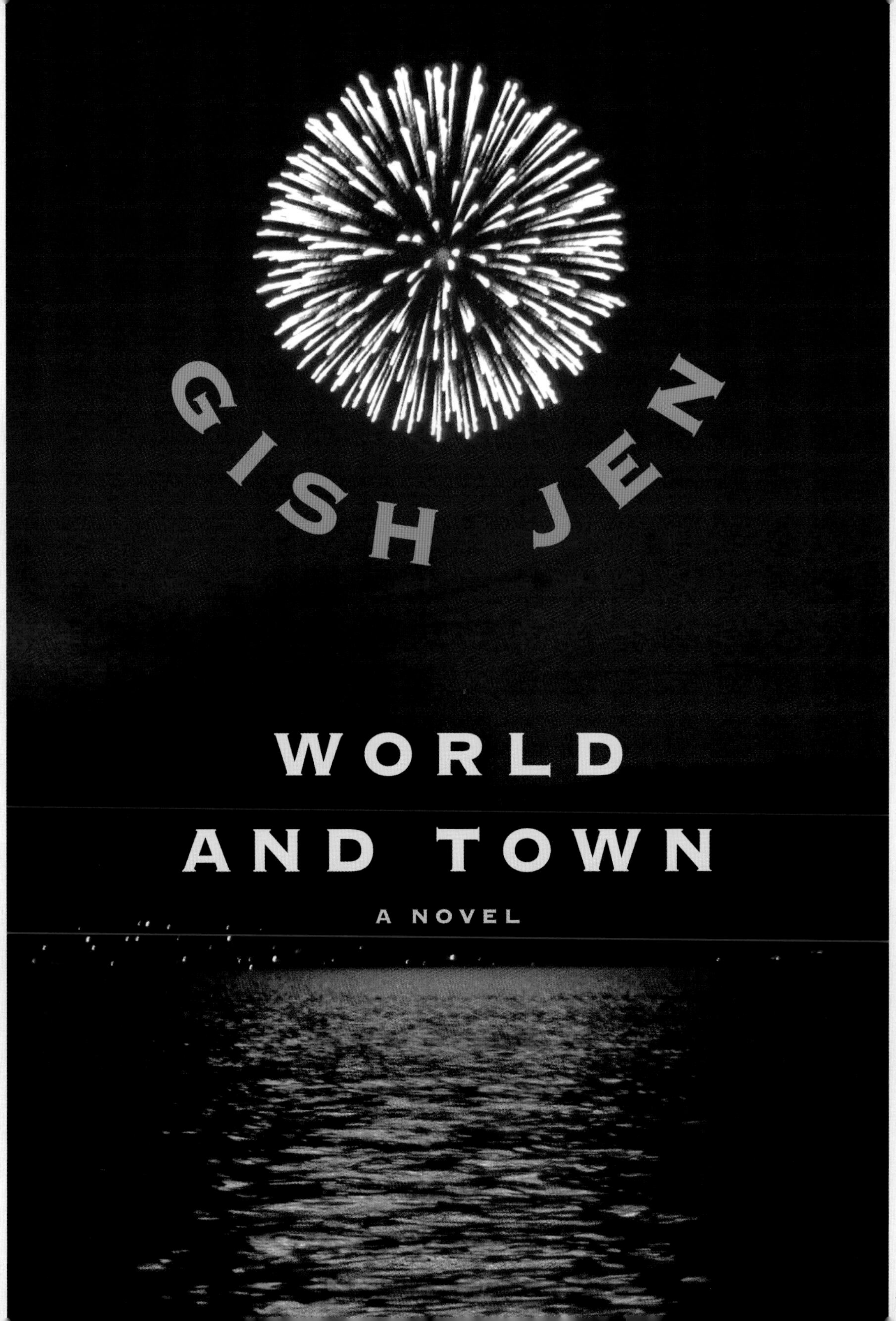
GISH JEN
WORLD
AND TOWN
A NOVEL

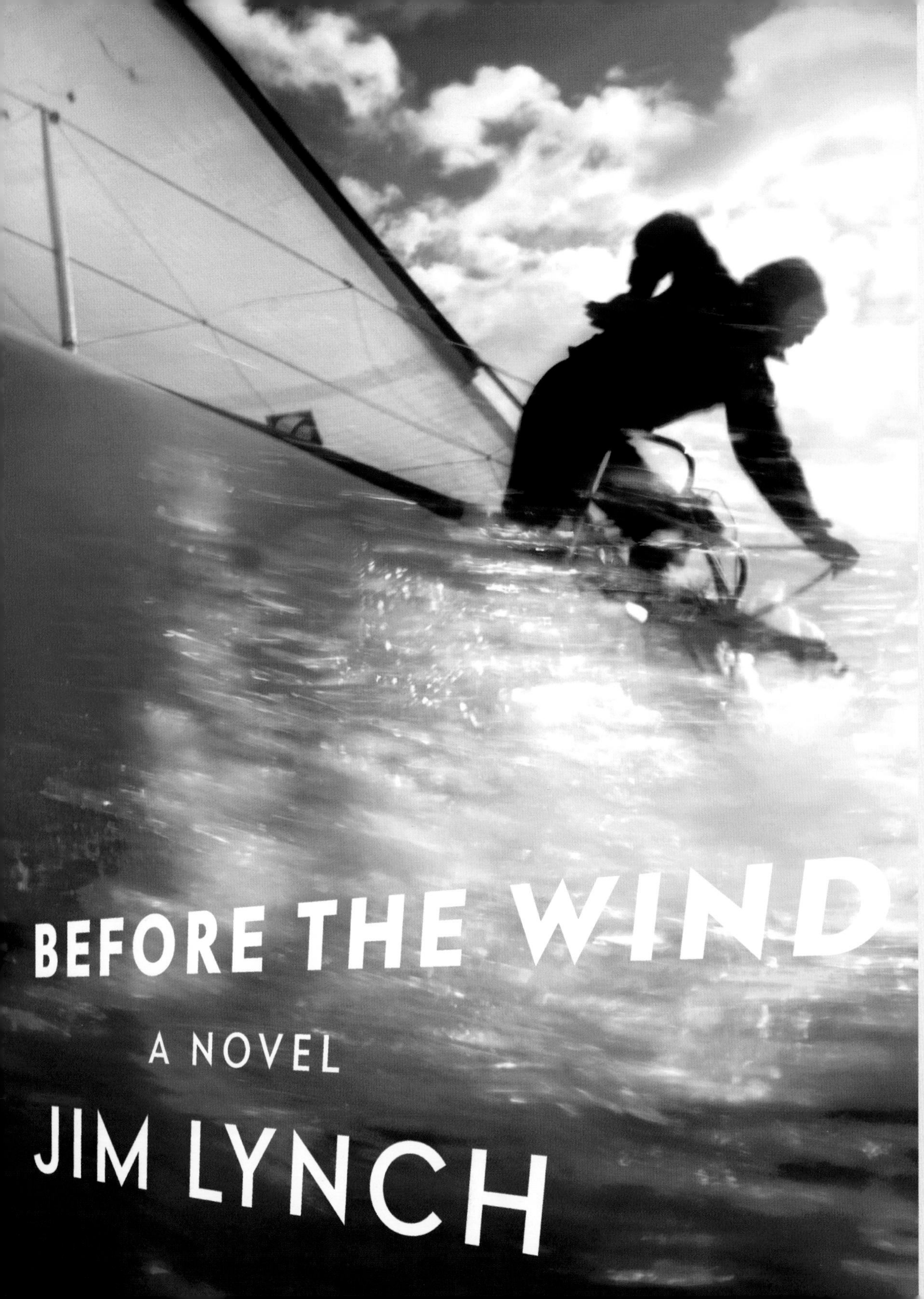
BEFORE THE WIND
A NOVEL
JIM LYNCH

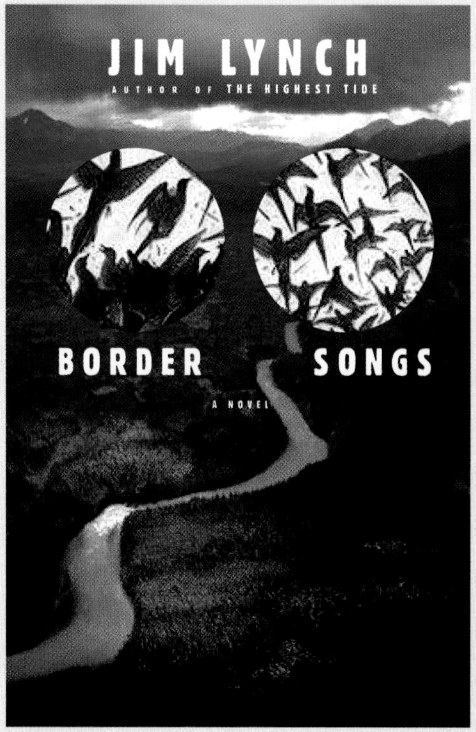
JIM LYNCH
AUTHOR OF THE HIGHEST TIDE
BORDER
SONGS
A NOVEL

## Surf & Turf

Jim Lynch's novel *Border Songs*, in which a hyper-obsessive form of bird-watching plays a central role, afforded me the opportunity to ask the artist Walton Ford if we could use one of his magnificent nature-gone-berserk paintings on the cover. He graciously obliged (opposite). We in the Knopf art department had known Walton for years, since we assigned him the cover artwork for Tatyana Tolstaya's 1989 novel, *On the Golden Porch*, when he was an illustrator pursuing freelance work.

**LEFT:** Lynch's most recent novel revolves around a family with a history in competitive sailboating. Knopf, 2016. **ABOVE:** An early idea I had to use the painting as seen through two die-cut holes in the jacket to mimic the idea of bird-watching through binoculars. **RIGHT:** Knopf, 2009.

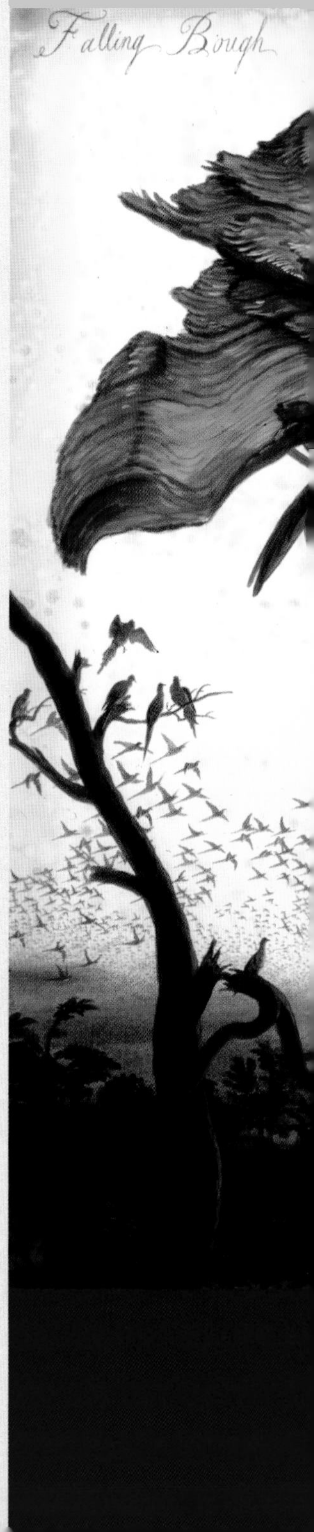
Falling Bough

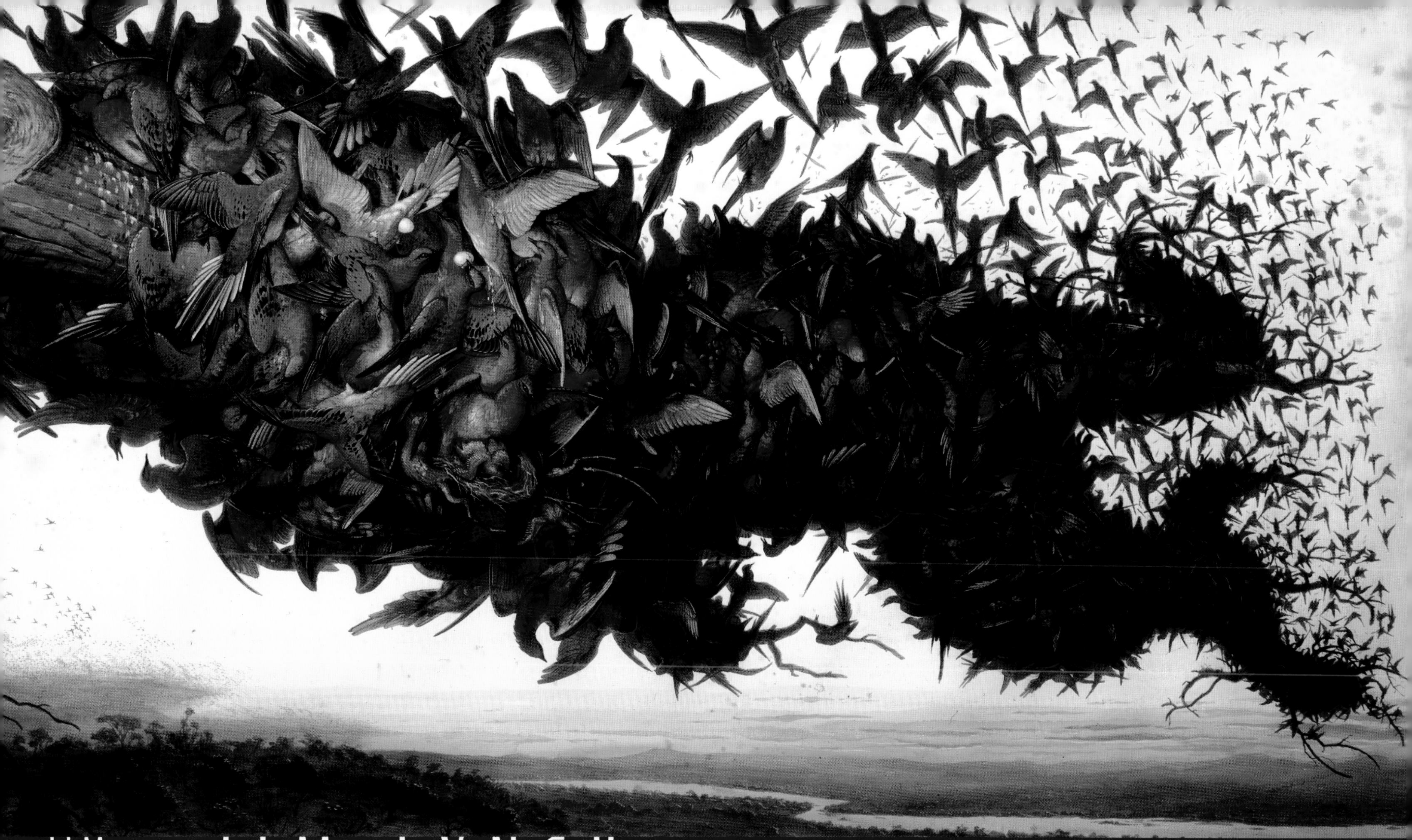

JIM
LYNCH

KNOPF

# JIM LYNCH

AUTHOR OF THE HIGHEST TIDE

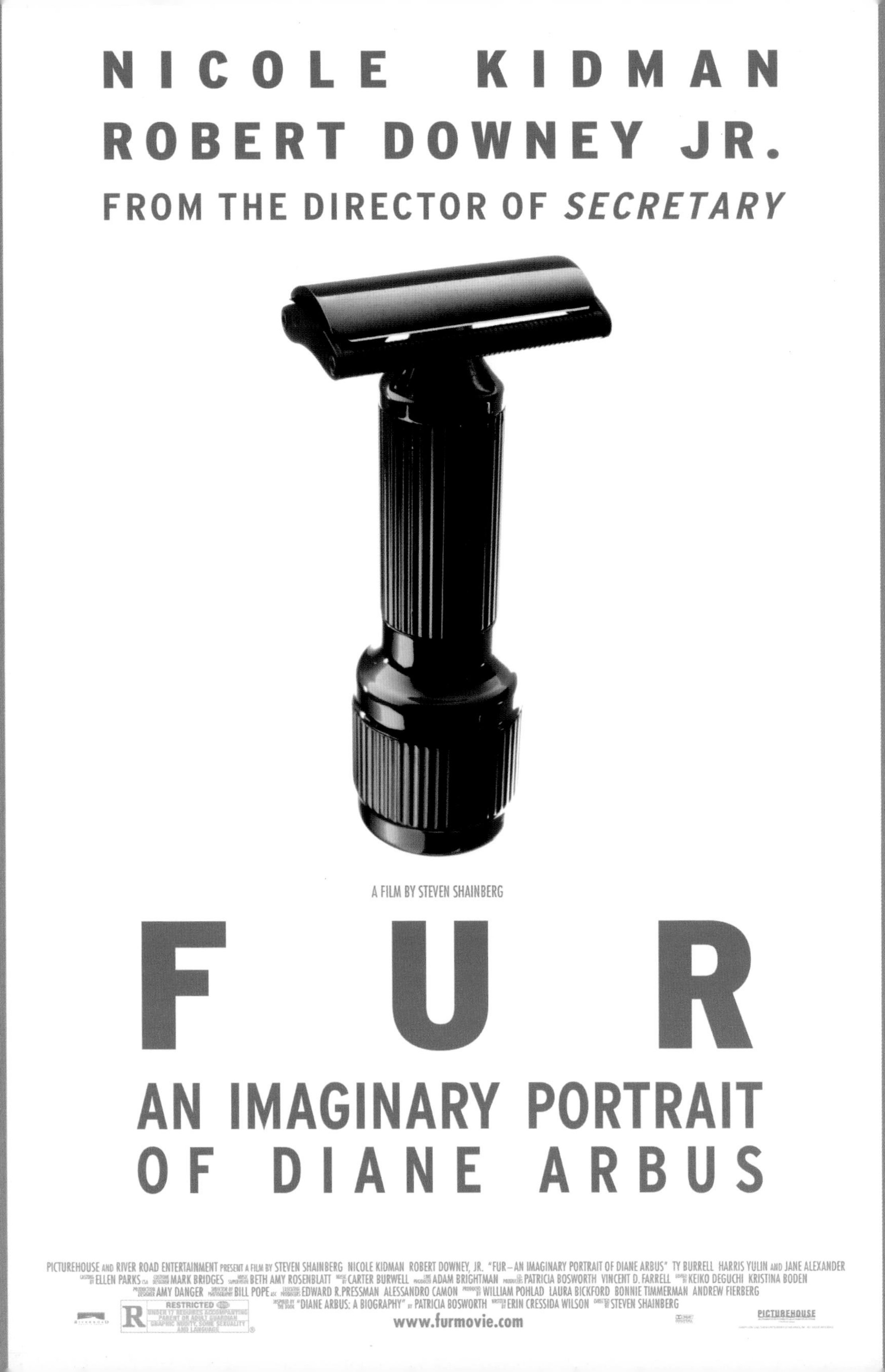
NICOLE KIDMAN
ROBERT DOWNEY JR.
FROM THE DIRECTOR OF *SECRETARY*
A FILM BY STEVEN SHAINBERG
FUR
AN IMAGINARY PORTRAIT
OF DIANE ARBUS
RESTRICTED
www.furmovie.com
PICTUREHOUSE

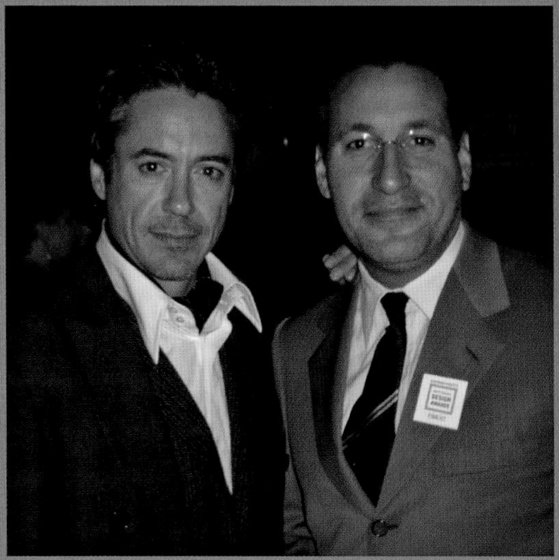

**LEFT:** With Robert Downey Jr. at the first screening of the film. He was super cool and had already been signed to be Iron Man.

**OPPOSITE:** For the briefest moment, the teaser posters were up in New York City. It really pops well, especially in this context.

## Fuzzy Portrait

The 2006 film *Fur* has the distinction of being the only movie starring the two A-list actors Nicole Kidman and Robert Downey Jr., and it barely even opened. It is based on a crucial period in the life of the photographer Diane Arbus, except—because the Arbus estate refused to grant access to her images or lend any other official support—it's an imagined idea of that life. And a really, really weird one.

It starts in 1958 with Diane (Kidman) living a fairly conventional New York City life with her husband, Allan Arbus (Ty Burrell), the son of a wealthy furrier clan. An incident with a clogged drain in their apartment (it's filled with fur!) leads her to a relationship with a neighbor downstairs, Lionel Sweeney (Downey Jr.), who has hypertrichosis (look it up). She subsequently enters into a netherworld populated by transvestites, dwarves, and other freakish outcasts living on the fringes of society. She soon decides to photograph them, and a career is born. Except that's not at all how it happened in real life. But hey, it's a movie—with the word "imaginary" figuring prominently in the subtitle.

In something of a climactic scene, Lionel asks Diane to shave off all of his body hair (don't ask) and she obliges, using a razor of the period. I chose this object from my own collection as a symbol for the teaser poster (left), shot by Geoff Spear.

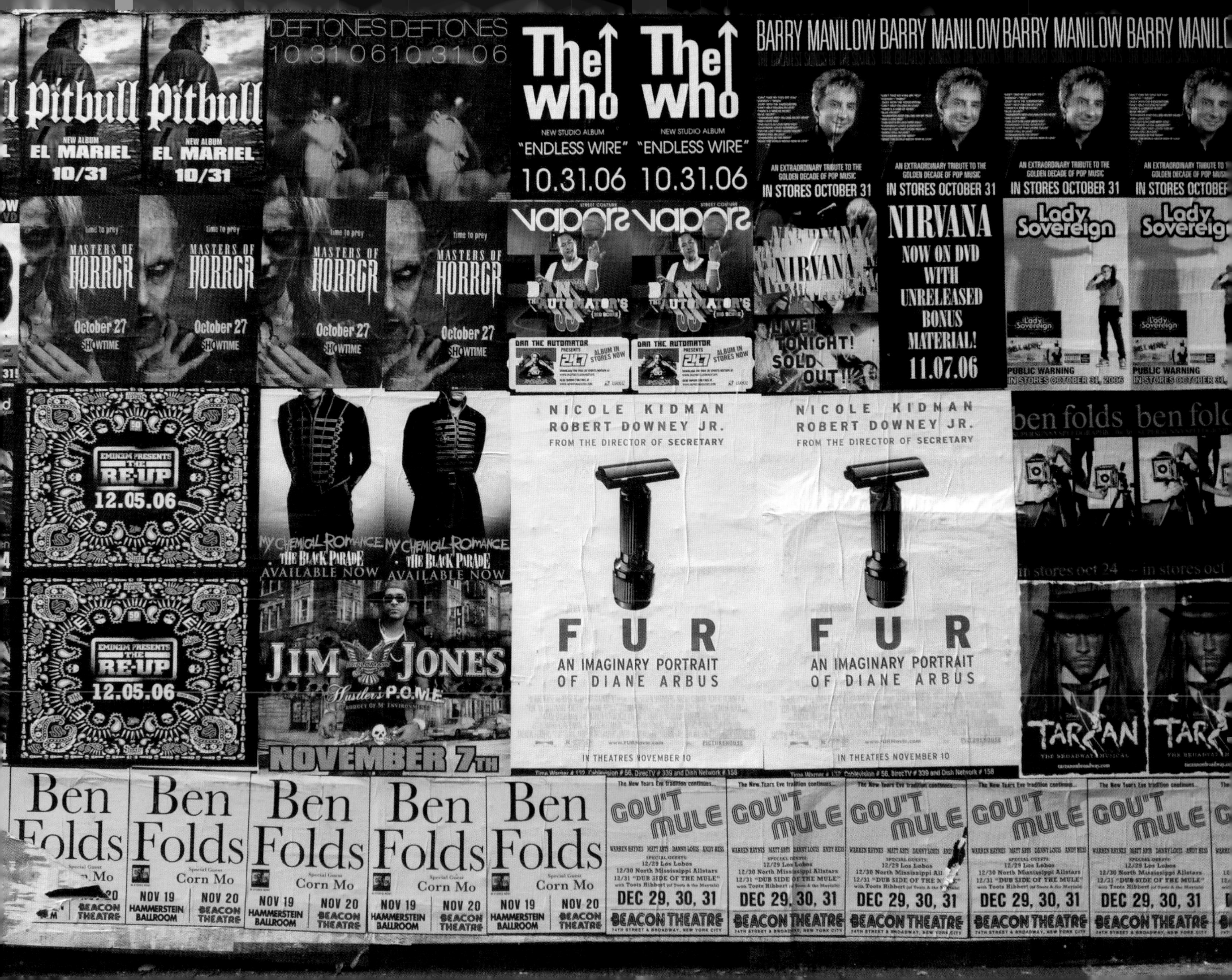
Pitbull
NEW ALBUM
EL MARIEL
10/31
Pitbull
NEW ALBUM
EL MARIEL
10/31
DEFTONES DEFTONES
10.31.06 10.31.06
The who
NEW STUDIO ALBUM
"ENDLESS WIRE"
10.31.06
The who
NEW STUDIO ALBUM
"ENDLESS WIRE"
10.31.06
BARRY MANILOW BARRY MANILOW BARRY MANILOW BARRY MANILO
AN EXTRAORDINARY TRIBUTE TO THE GOLDEN DECADE OF POP MUSIC
IN STORES OCTOBER 31
AN EXTRAORDINARY TRIBUTE TO THE GOLDEN DECADE OF POP MUSIC
IN STORES OCTOBER 31
AN EXTRAORDINARY TRIBUTE TO THE GOLDEN DECADE OF POP MUSIC
IN STORES OCTOBER 31
AN EXTRAORDINARY TRIBUTE TO THE GOLDEN DECADE OF POP MUSIC
IN STORES OCTOBER
time to prey
MASTERS OF HORROR
October 27
SHOWTIME
time to prey
MASTERS OF HORROR
October 27
SHOWTIME
time to prey
MASTERS OF HORROR
October 27
SHOWTIME
time to prey
MASTERS OF HORROR
October 27
SHOWTIME
STREET COUTURE
vapors
DAN THE AUTOMATOR'S
DAN THE AUTOMATOR
PRESENTS
2K7
ALBUM IN STORES NOW
STREET COUTURE
vapors
DAN THE AUTOMATOR'S
DAN THE AUTOMATOR
PRESENTS
2K7
ALBUM IN STORES NOW
NIRVANA
LIVE! TONIGHT! SOLD OUT!!
NIRVANA
NOW ON DVD WITH UNRELEASED BONUS MATERIAL!
11.07.06
Lady Sovereign
PUBLIC WARNING
IN STORES OCTOBER 31, 2006
Lady Sovereign
PUBLIC WARNING
IN STORES OCTOBER 31,
EMINEM PRESENTS THE RE-UP
12.05.06
EMINEM PRESENTS THE RE-UP
12.05.06
MY CHEMICAL ROMANCE
THE BLACK PARADE
AVAILABLE NOW
MY CHEMICAL ROMANCE
THE BLACK PARADE
AVAILABLE NOW
JIM JONES
Hustler's P.O.M.E.
NOVEMBER 7TH
NICOLE KIDMAN
ROBERT DOWNEY JR.
FROM THE DIRECTOR OF SECRETARY
FUR
AN IMAGINARY PORTRAIT OF DIANE ARBUS
www.FURmovie.com
IN THEATRES NOVEMBER 10
NICOLE KIDMAN
ROBERT DOWNEY JR.
FROM THE DIRECTOR OF SECRETARY
FUR
AN IMAGINARY PORTRAIT OF DIANE ARBUS
IN THEATRES NOVEMBER 10
Time Warner # 132 Cablevision # 56, DirecTV # 339 and Dish Network # 158
ben folds ben folds
in stores oct 24 – in stores oct
TARZAN
THE BROADWAY MUSICAL
Ben Folds
Special Guest
Corn Mo
NOV 19
HAMMERSTEIN BALLROOM
NOV 20
BEACON THEATRE
The New Years Eve tradition continues...
GOV'T MULE
WARREN HAYNES MATT ABTS DANNY LOUIS ANDY HESS
SPECIAL GUESTS:
12/29 Los Lobos
12/30 North Mississippi Allstars
12/31 "DUB SIDE OF THE MULE"
DEC 29, 30, 31
BEACON THEATRE
74TH STREET & BROADWAY, NEW YORK CITY

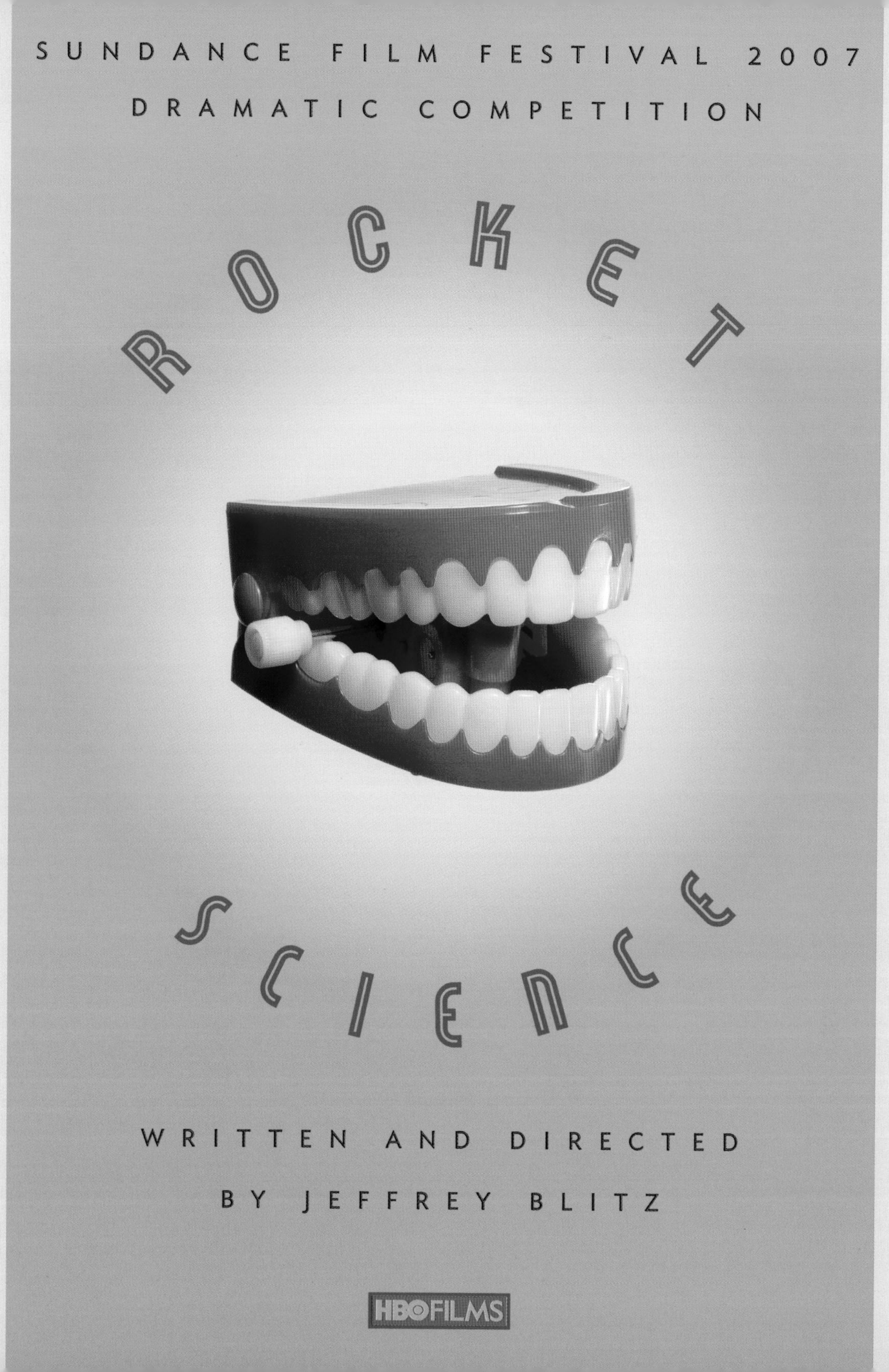
SUNDANCE FILM FESTIVAL 2007
DRAMATIC COMPETITION
ROCKET
SCIENCE
WRITTEN AND DIRECTED
BY JEFFREY BLITZ
HBOFILMS

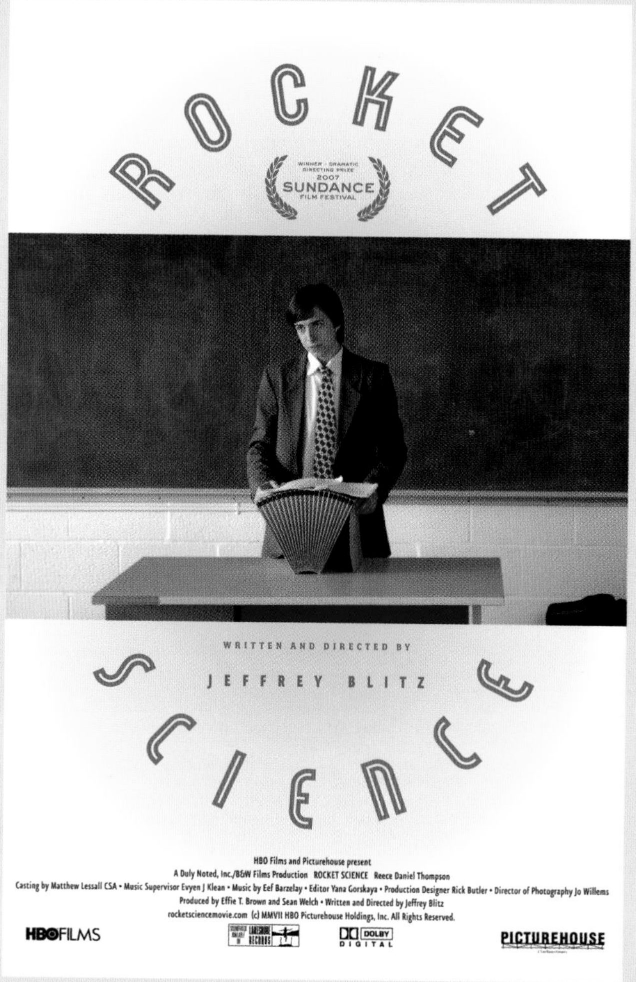
ROCKET
WINNER - DRAMATIC DIRECTING PRIZE 2007 SUNDANCE FILM FESTIVAL
WRITTEN AND DIRECTED BY
JEFFREY BLITZ
SCIENCE
HBO Films and Picturehouse present
A Duly Noted, Inc./B&W Films Production ROCKET SCIENCE Reece Daniel Thompson
Casting by Matthew Lessall CSA • Music Supervisor Evyen J Klean • Music by Eef Barzelay • Editor Yana Gorskaya • Production Designer Rick Butler • Director of Photography Jo Willems
Produced by Effie T. Brown and Sean Welch • Written and Directed by Jeffrey Blitz
rocketsciencemovie.com (c) MMVII HBO Picturehouse Holdings, Inc. All Rights Reserved.
HBOFILMS
DOLBY DIGITAL
PICTUREHOUSE

# Pitch Imperfect

Though we couldn't have known it at the time, the significance of the 2007 indie film *Rocket Science* was that it introduced Anna Kendrick to the world. But she wasn't the star, so for the poster I used images of the lead, Reece Thompson. He plays Hal Hefner, a shy fifteen-year-old student at Plainsboro High School in New Jersey, who has a stuttering problem and wants to join the class debate team. I used a pair of chattering teeth for the teaser (left), shot by Geoff Spear, and they went for it.

**ABOVE:** The final poster for the film, using none of the conceptual ideas I came up with about stuttering or speech. **OPPOSITE:** Unused poster ideas. Kendrick is great in it, by the way, as Hefner's initial debate partner and then turncoat femme fatale.

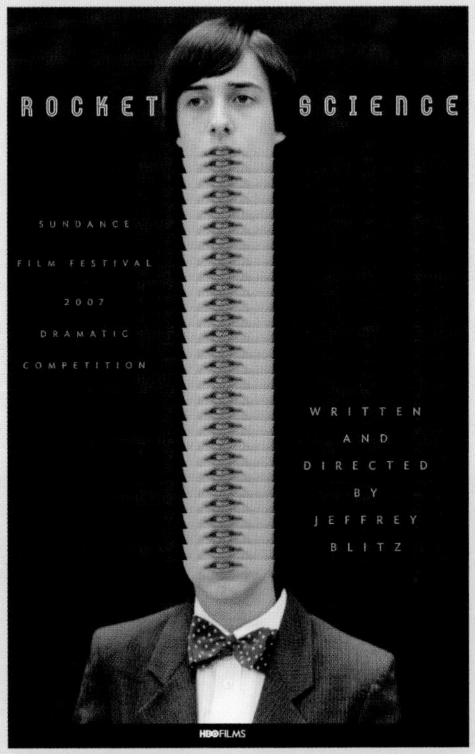
ROCKET SCIENCE
SUNDANCE
FILM FESTIVAL
2007
DRAMATIC
COMPETITION
WRITTEN
AND
DIRECTED
BY
JEFFREY
BLITZ
HBO FILMS

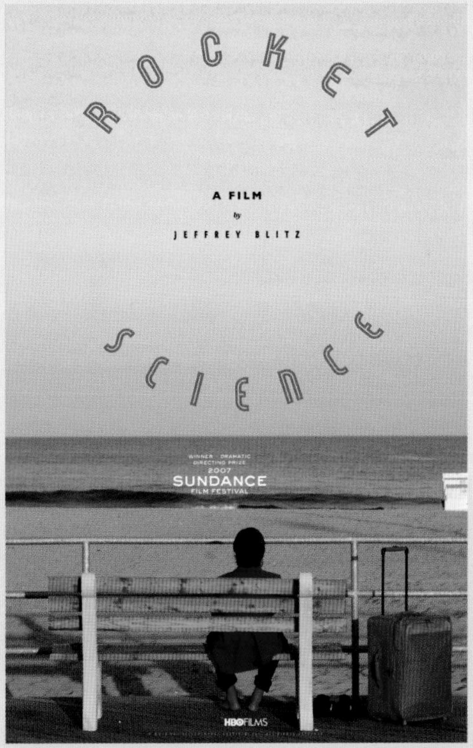
ROCKET
A FILM
by
JEFFREY BLITZ
SCIENCE
WINNER · DRAMATIC
DIRECTING PRIZE
2007
SUNDANCE
FILM FESTIVAL
HBO FILMS

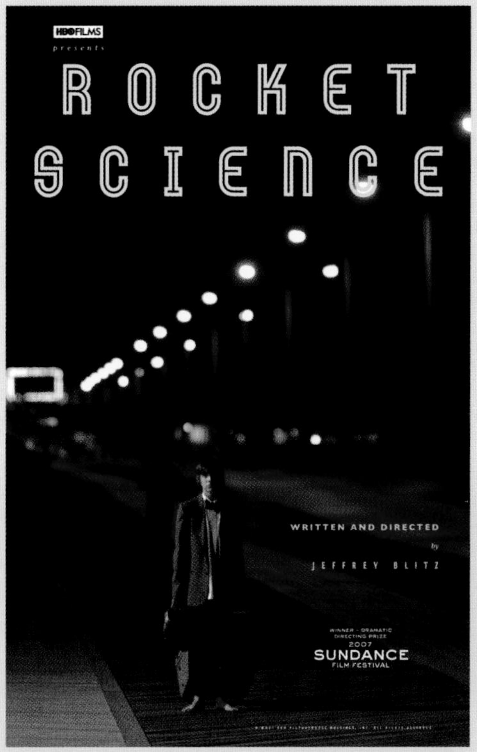
HBO FILMS
presents
ROCKET
SCIENCE
WRITTEN AND DIRECTED
by
JEFFREY BLITZ
WINNER · DRAMATIC
DIRECTING PRIZE
2007
SUNDANCE
FILM FESTIVAL

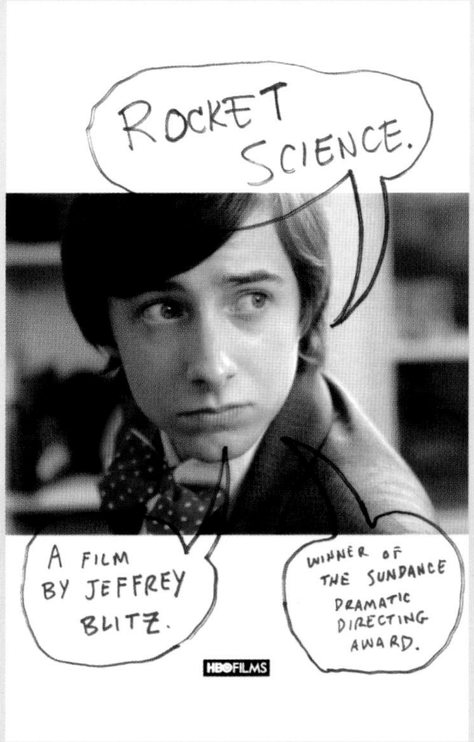
ROCKET SCIENCE.
A FILM BY JEFFREY BLITZ.
WINNER OF THE SUNDANCE DRAMATIC DIRECTING AWARD.
HBO FILMS



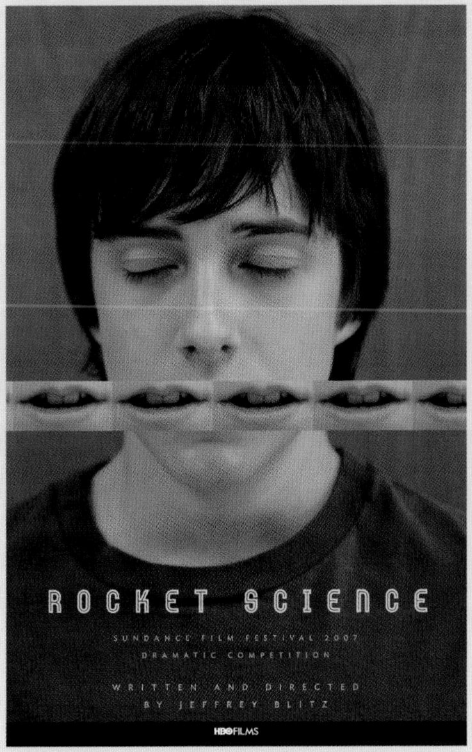
ROCKET SCIENCE
SUNDANCE FILM FESTIVAL 2007
DRAMATIC COMPETITION
WRITTEN AND DIRECTED
BY JEFFREY BLITZ
HBO FILMS

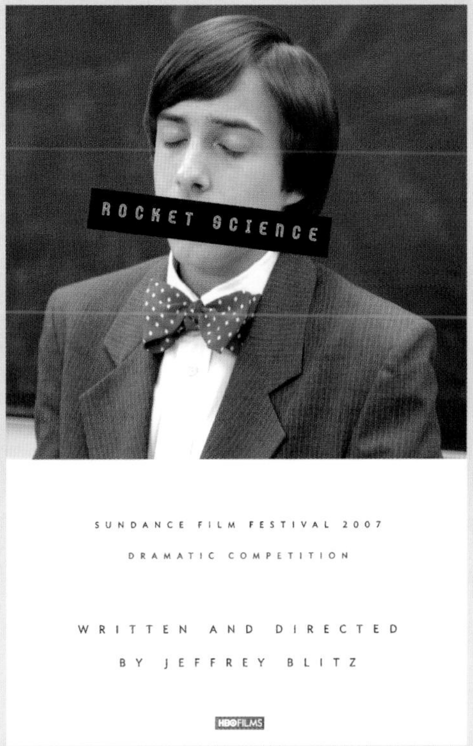
ROCKET SCIENCE
SUNDANCE FILM FESTIVAL 2007
DRAMATIC COMPETITION
WRITTEN AND DIRECTED
BY JEFFREY BLITZ
HBO FILMS

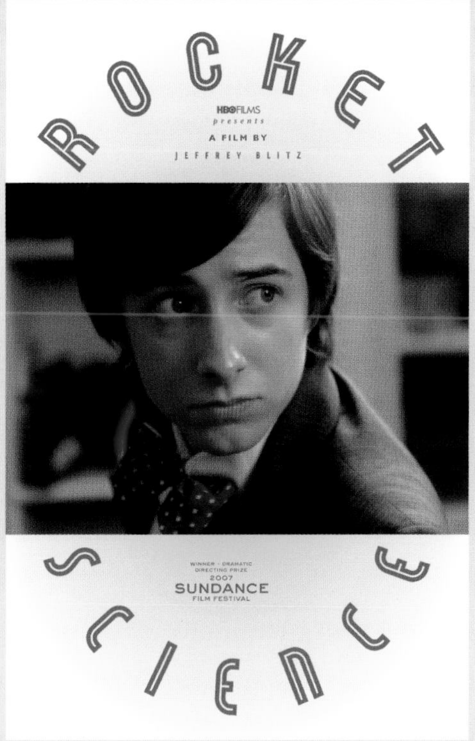
ROCKET
HBO FILMS
presents
A FILM BY
JEFFREY BLITZ
WINNER · DRAMATIC
DIRECTING PRIZE
2007
SUNDANCE
FILM FESTIVAL
SCIENCE

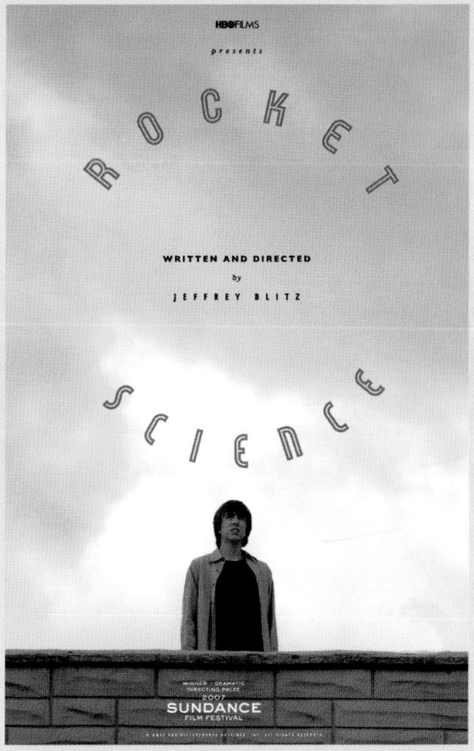
HBO FILMS
presents
ROCKET
WRITTEN AND DIRECTED
by
JEFFREY BLITZ
SCIENCE
WINNER · DRAMATIC
DIRECTING PRIZE
2007
SUNDANCE
FILM FESTIVAL

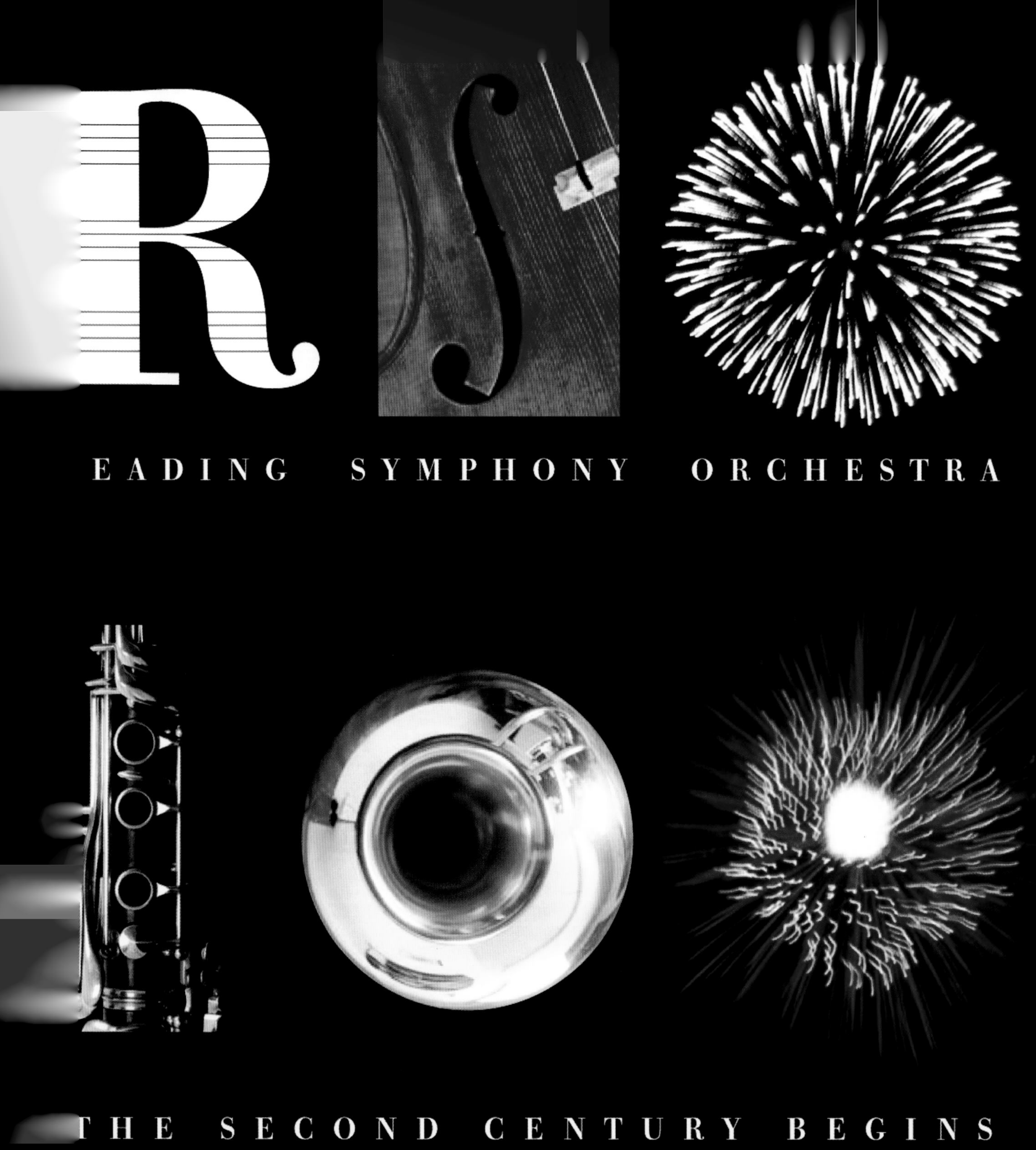
EADING SYMPHONY ORCHESTRA
THE SECOND CENTURY BEGINS

## Super Sonics

The fun here is to compare a job for the Reading Symphony Orchestra (left), from my hometown in Pennsylvania, with one for the director of the Metropolitan Opera in New York (opposite; Knopf, 2006). For the RSO, the assignmen was to create a logo and poster to celebrate th 100th anniversary of the institution. Rather tha focusing on the past, I thought it would be bette to look ahead.

The cover for the memoir of Joseph Volpe provided me with the once-in-a-lifetime (sc far, anyway) opportunity to work with the legendary photographer Annie Leibovitz. Or, more accurately, to observe her in action. Editor Shelley Wanger knows the artist well, and Annie respected Mr. Volpe and really wanted to shoo at the Met, so she cheerfully agreed to do it (Goc knows we couldn't afford her day rate). Thus ensued a fascinating afternoon whereupon I go to sit back at the great house and watch her work It was a much freer and looser process than I was expecting—Annie let the stage be all the backdro she needed, no other props or production necessary. It was just Annie and her camera, with one assistant. She was efficient and cheerful and energetic—no attitude at all—and tried several locations within the context of the hall. She had wha she needed within a few hours, and in the fina shot there is enough of the sense of being back stage to cue viewers to the insider's view of wha they will experience upon reading the book

THE
TOUGHEST
SHOW
ON EARTH

JOSEPH
VOLPE

KNOPF

THE
TOUGHEST
SHOW ON EARTH
MY RISE AND REIGN AT
THE METROPOLITAN OPERA
JOSEPH VOLPE

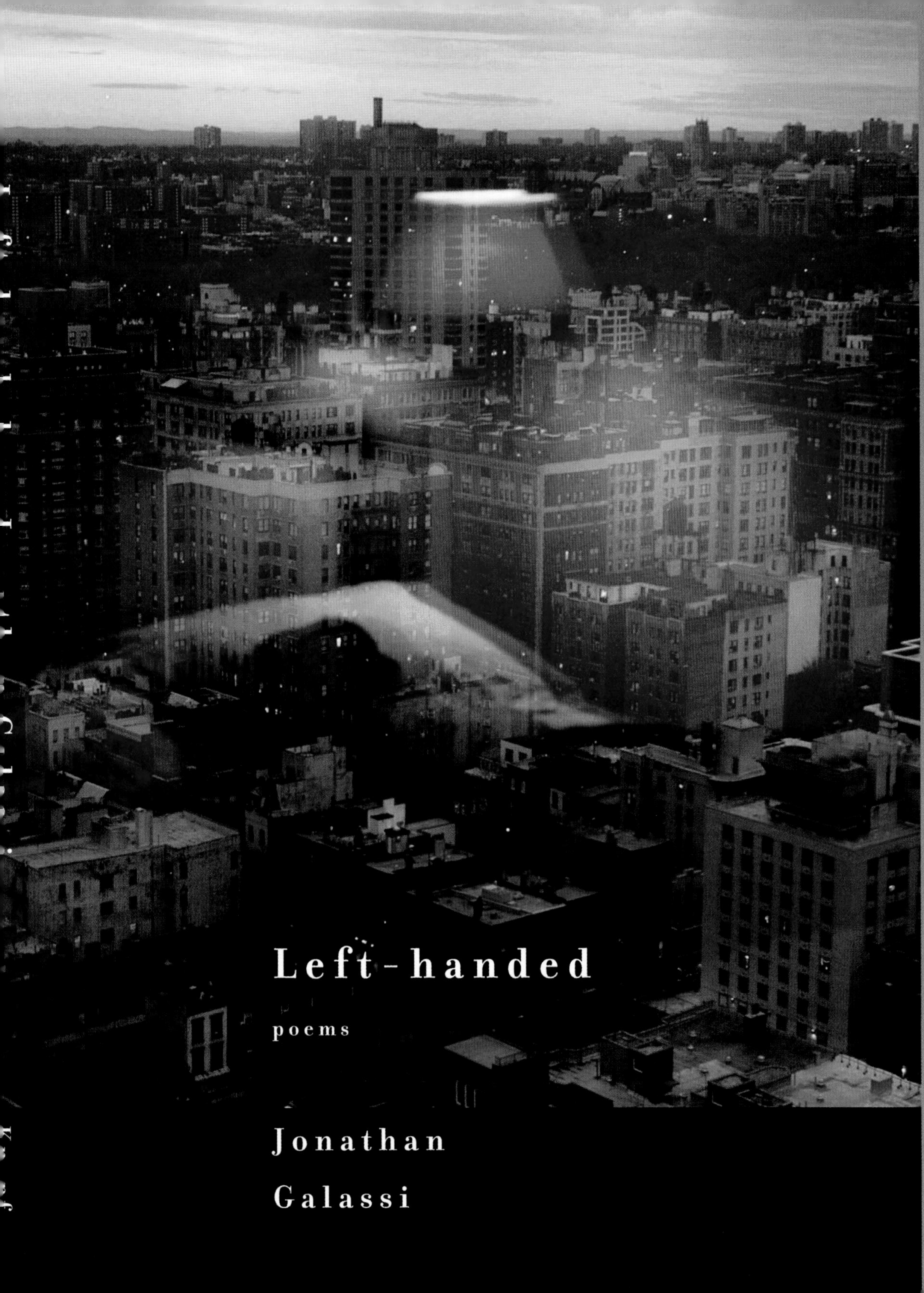
Left-handed
poems
Jonathan
Galassi

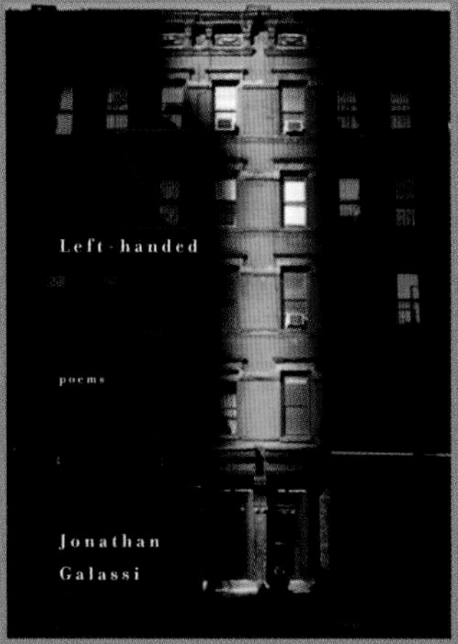
Left-handed
Jonathan
Galassi

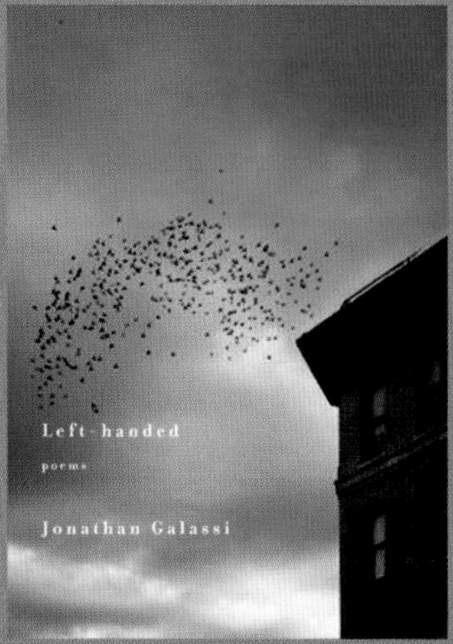
Left-handed
Jonathan Galassi

## Glossy Galassi

Jonathan Galassi is not only a friend and a Knopf author, he also happens to be the editor-in-chief of Farrar, Straus and Giroux, Knopf's primary competitor for literary fiction. Such situations are not uncommon in the genteel world of publishing, but that doesn't make them any less tricky. Mr. Galassi came out as gay relatively late in life, and that is what much of his poetry collection, *Left-Handed*, is about. Now, I am left-handed and gay myself, but that didn't seem to help me figure out the cover of this book—I did many designs, all incorporating (however subtly) the idea of things coming in from the left (above), which Jonathan thought were all too literal. This image I finally found (left) was the answer, a reflection in a window of someone lounging in bed, with the possibilities, hopes, determinations, and probable pitfalls of the Great City lying before him.

**LEFT:** Knopf, 2012. **OPPOSITE, LEFT:** Omnidawn, 2010.

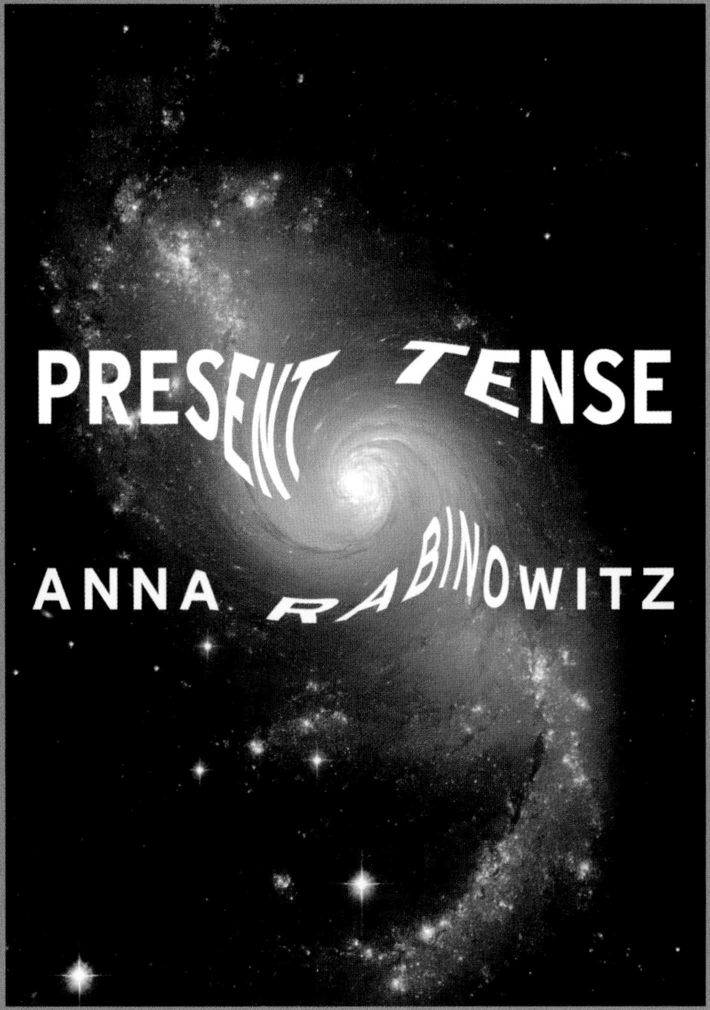
PRESENT TENSE
ANNA RABINOWITZ

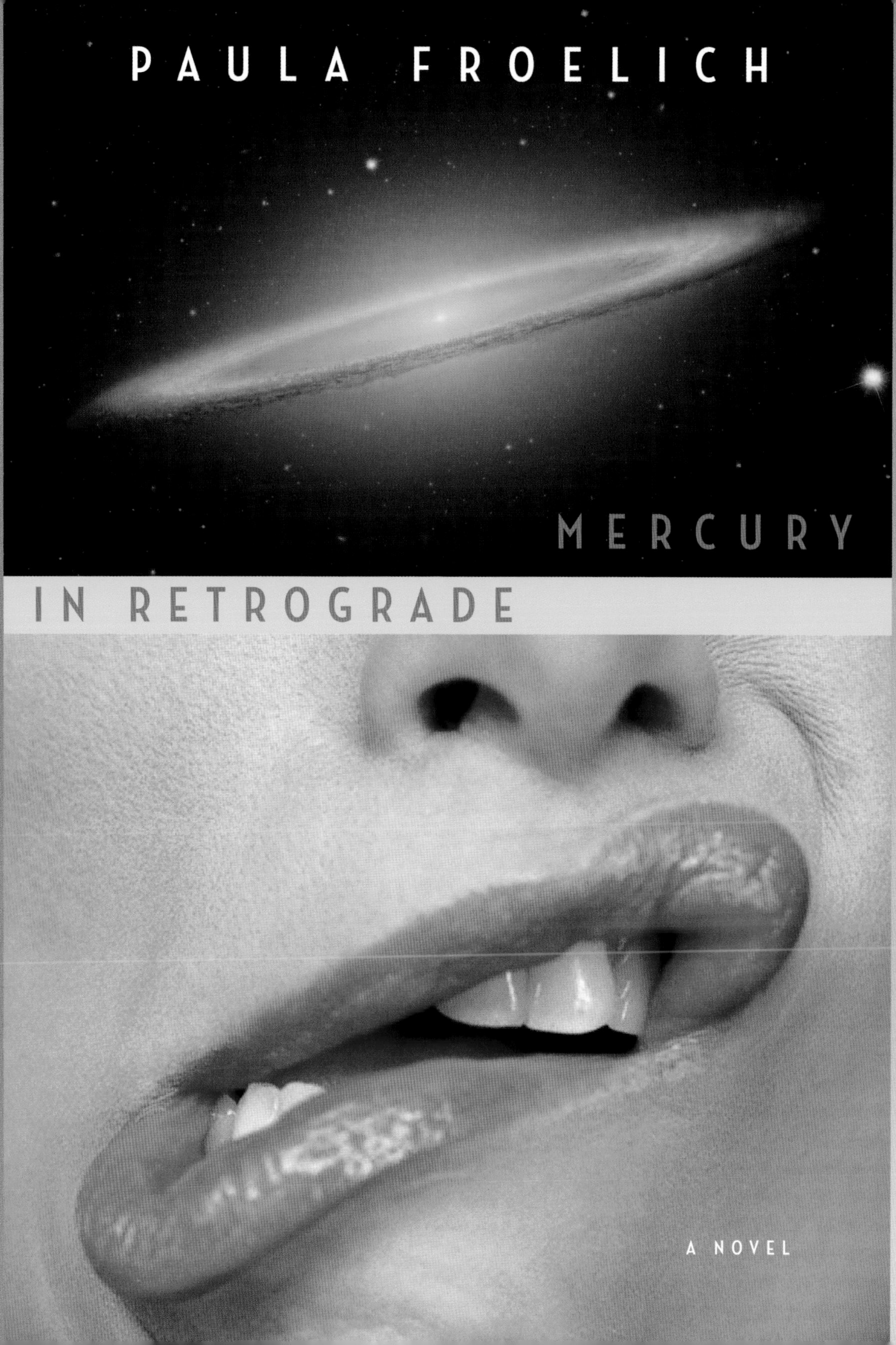
PAULA FROELICH
MERCURY
IN RETROGRADE
A NOVEL

## Cosmic Disturbance

I represented Anna Rabinowitz's apocalypse-centric poetry collection, *Present Tense* (above), with a Hubble telescope shot integrated with the typography, creating the illusion of a cosmic spiral.

For Paula Froelich's novel *Mercury in Retrograde* (right), her concerns were somewhat more earthbound (a young NYC career journalist taking on an early midlife crisis), but I couldn't resist trying another view from the Hubble, juxtaposed with a similar shape that could be created by one of her character's many frustrating situations. I found myself making the same face when this was rejected.

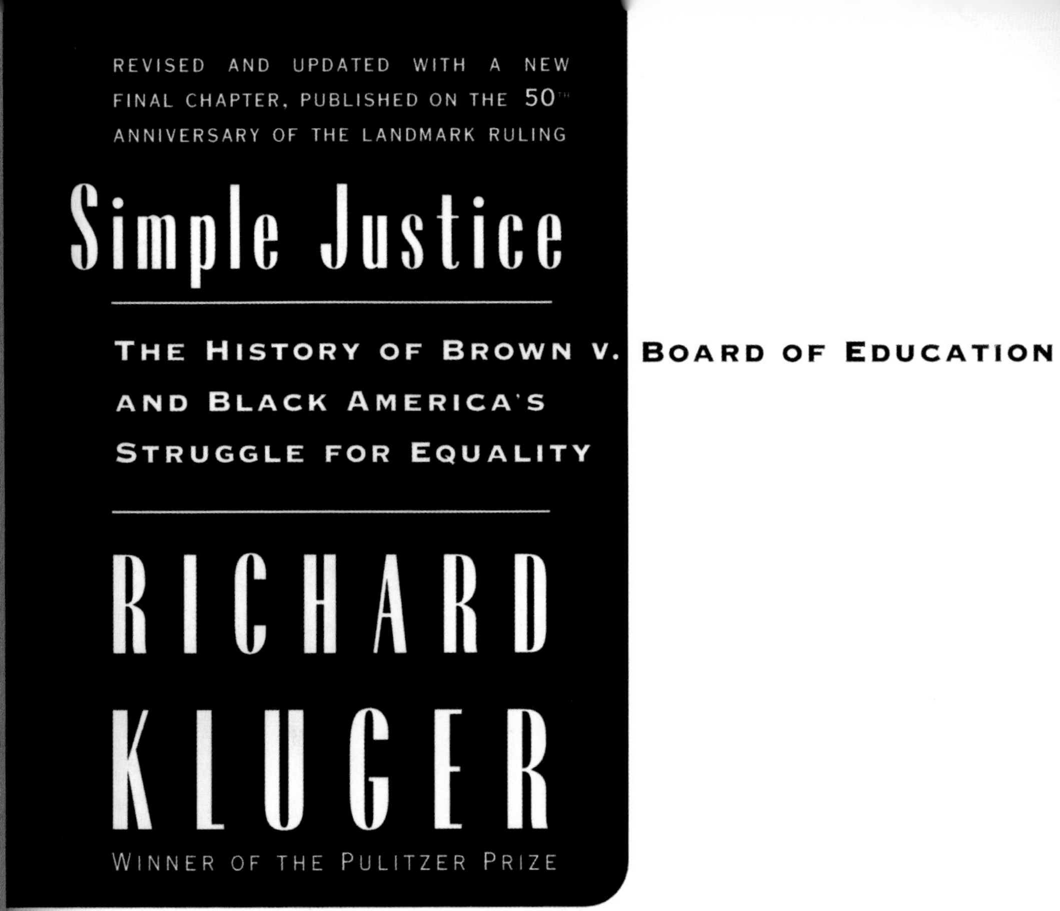

REVISED AND UPDATED WITH A NEW FINAL CHAPTER, PUBLISHED ON THE 50TH ANNIVERSARY OF THE LANDMARK RULING
Simple Justice
THE HISTORY OF BROWN V. BOARD OF EDUCATION AND BLACK AMERICA'S STRUGGLE FOR EQUALITY
RICHARD KLUGER
WINNER OF THE PULITZER PRIZE

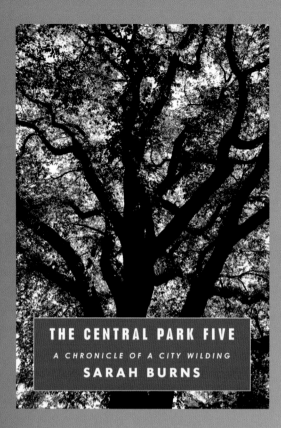

THE CENTRAL PARK FIVE
A CHRONICLE OF A CITY WILDING
SARAH BURNS

**NEAR LEFT:**
Knopf, 2011.

**OPPOSITE, RIGHT:**
Knopf, 2011.

# Their Lives Matter

Books based on racially charged themes and subjects require an especially well-considered visual approach, today more than ever. My design for *Simple Justice* (left) was rejected, much to my dismay, as being too "overthought" and not looking "big" enough. Maybe they were right, but I wanted to convey a sense of "Us" vs. "Them" using visual compartmentalization, with a vast white majority of the cover space trying to overpower a smaller black "stronghold" of information. No go.

I had better luck with this account (above) of the notorious "Central Park Jogger" rape case from the early 1990s, and the five black and Hispanic men who were convicted of the crime but then ultimately exonerated. I had recently seen photographer Nathan Harger's stunning black-and-white pictures in *New York* magazine of trees in Central Park, and they seemed perfect for this concept: they could be perceived literally as what the victim was looking at during the attack, or figuratively as a tremendously complex symbol of the criminal justice system that convicted the wrong people.

Henry "Skip" Gates's *Life on These Shores*—an epic scholarly illustrated book on the African American experience in the United States—presented its own challenge, though not one that any of us at Knopf expected. Everyone liked the first version of the jacket I created (below left), and that's what we presented at sales conference and posted on Amazon.

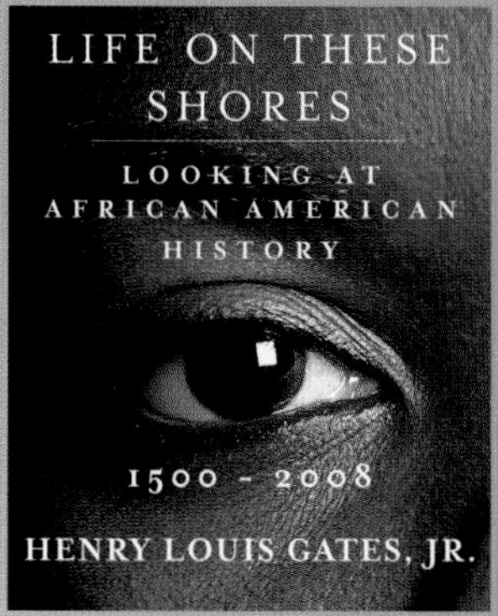
LIFE ON THESE SHORES
LOOKING AT AFRICAN AMERICAN HISTORY
1500 - 2008
HENRY LOUIS GATES, JR.

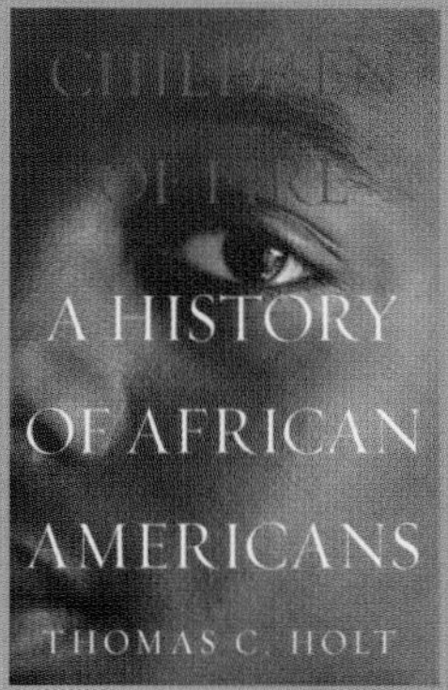
A HISTORY OF AFRICAN AMERICANS
THOMAS C. HOLT

Several months later, just as we were getting ready to go to press, Skip's assistant found something remarkably similar online (above right) for a book that dealt with pretty much the same subject (by an acquaintance of Skip's, no less) and that was going to be published a month before ours. It was something we'd have to deal with quickly, at the last minute. I decided that two eyes to witness history were better than one, and then the big idea that no one seemed to notice or comment on: changing the colors of the country from red, white, and blue to red, black, and blue (right). I'm not sure that anyone got it, or if they did, no one raised any concerns. Which is inspiring, I suppose—booksellers and readers alike seemed color-blind to it.

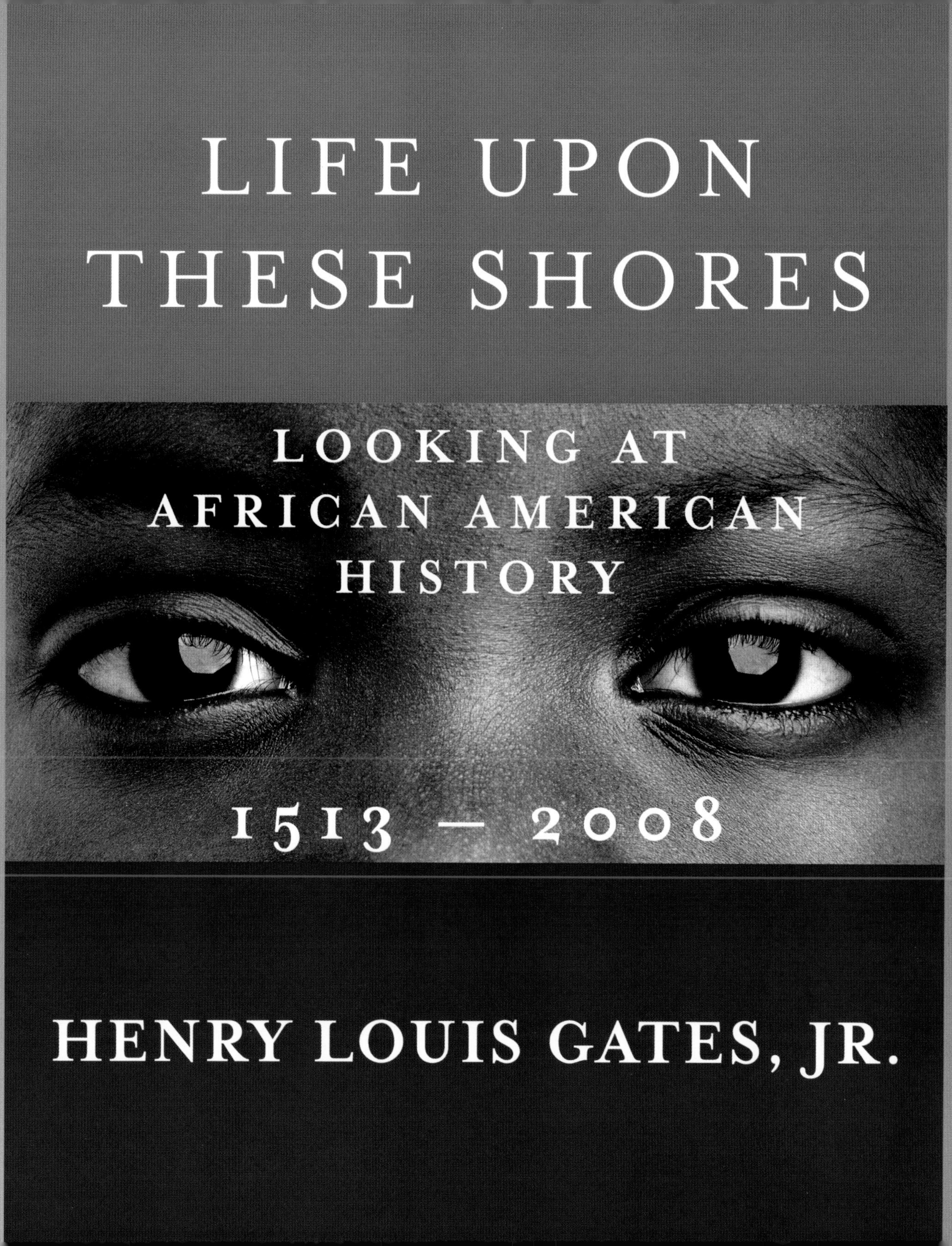
LIFE UPON THESE SHORES
LOOKING AT AFRICAN AMERICAN HISTORY
1513 — 2008
HENRY LOUIS GATES, JR.

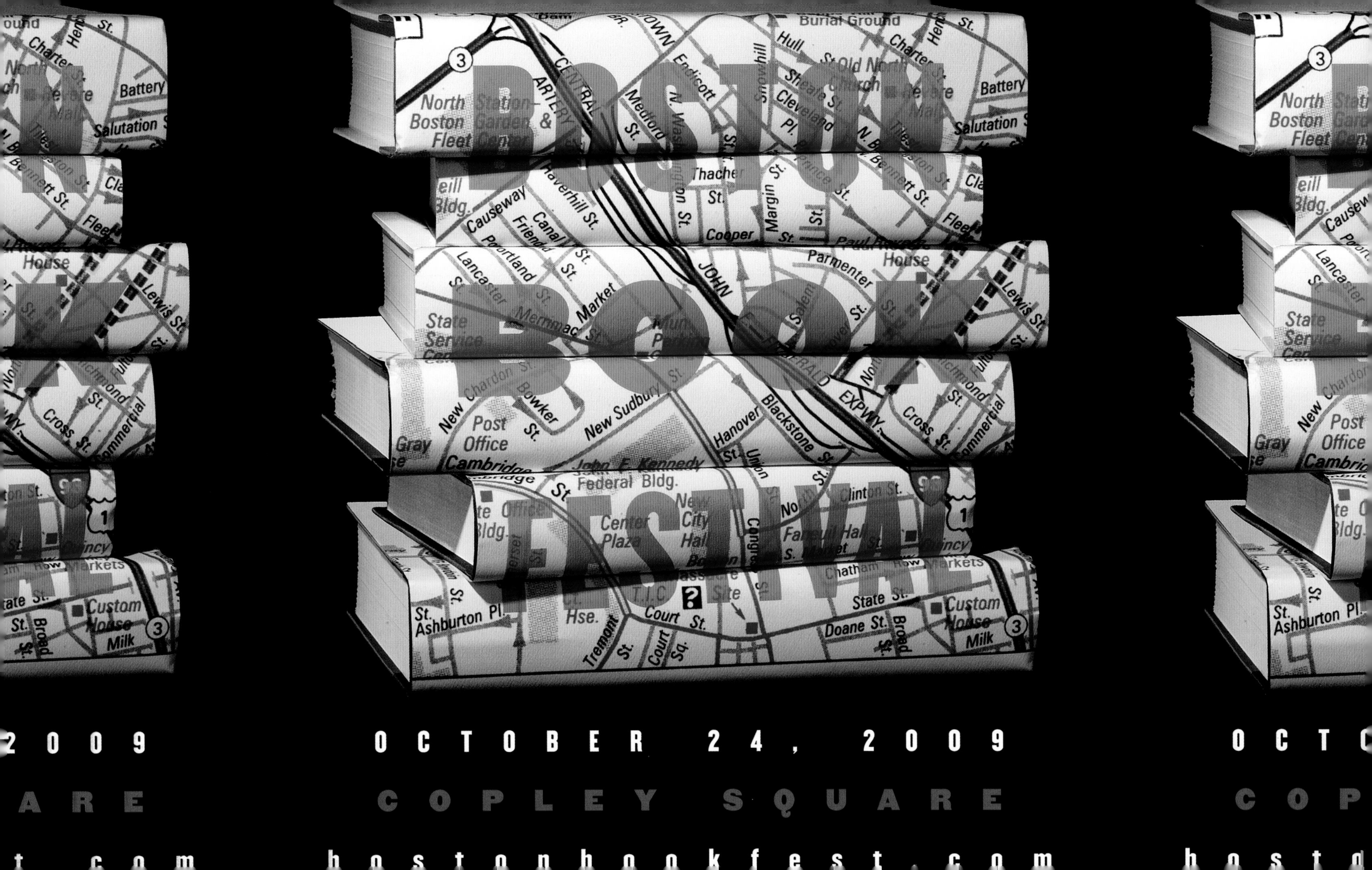
BOSTON BOOK FESTIVAL
OCTOBER 24, 2009
COPLEY SQUARE
bostonbookfest.com

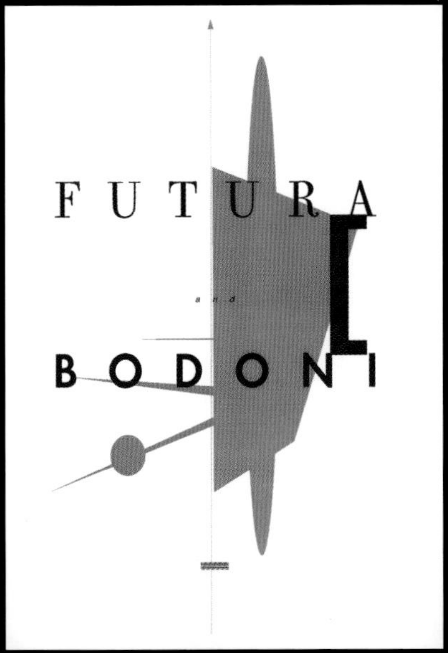
FUTURA
BODONI

## Poster Conventions

Posters are supposed to basically do the same thing as book covers—get your attention and direct it at something you may not have previously considered, whether it's an event or an idea. Sometimes they just have to look cool, and that's fine, as long as they serve a specific purpose in an interesting way.

In 2009, Deborah Porter was putting together the first Boston Book Festival and asked me to create the accompanying poster. I'd seen many regional book fair graphics over the years, but none that integrated the physicality of books with a map of where the event was going to take place. I created the props, Geoff shot it. I didn't want to use any Boston clichés, like beans or tri-corner hats; I just wanted it to be about the idea of books in that city.

The poster for my appearance at the AIGA Dallas chapter (right) was a much more open brief; it was to be an "art poster," and there would be a silkscreened limited edition. I hearkened back to a very early computer sketch of mine (above), where I made Futura and Bodoni fonts trade places. This is an extremely type-nerdy joke, but I think it looked cool, even if the viewer didn't get it.

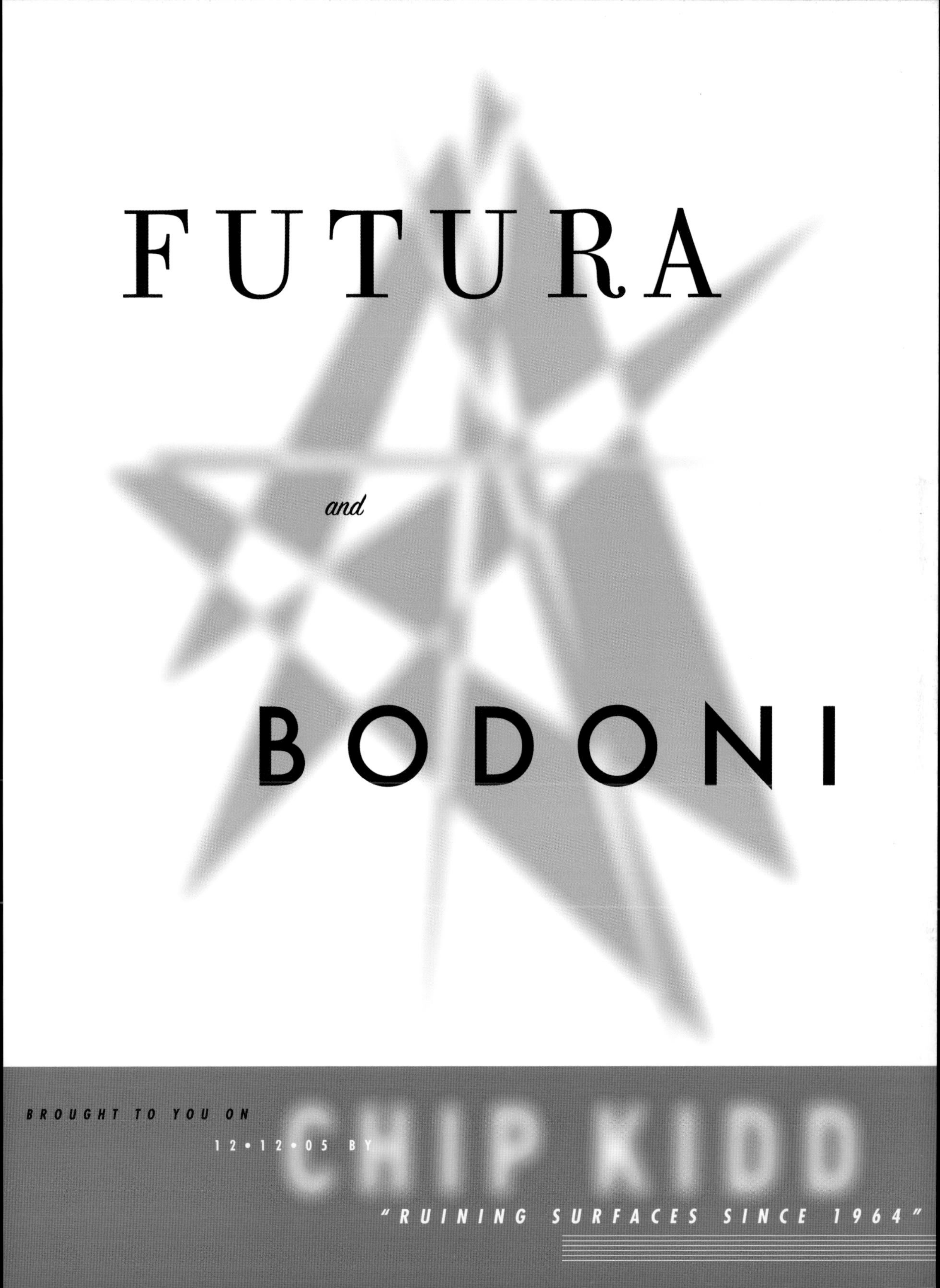
FUTURA
and
BODONI
BROUGHT TO YOU ON
12•12•05 BY
CHIP KIDD
"RUINING SURFACES SINCE 1964"

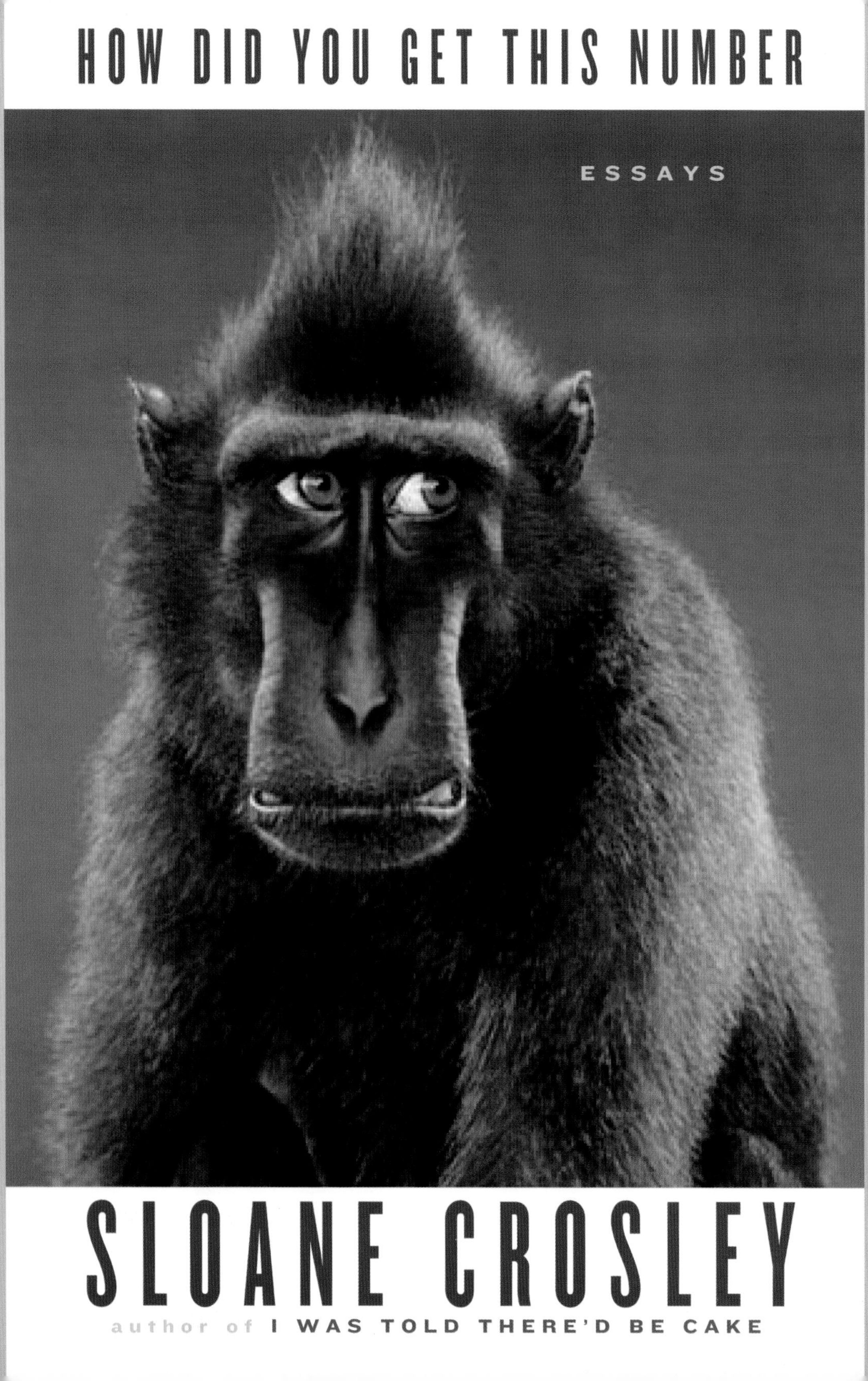
HOW DID YOU GET THIS NUMBER
ESSAYS
SLOANE CROSLEY
author of I WAS TOLD THERE'D BE CAKE



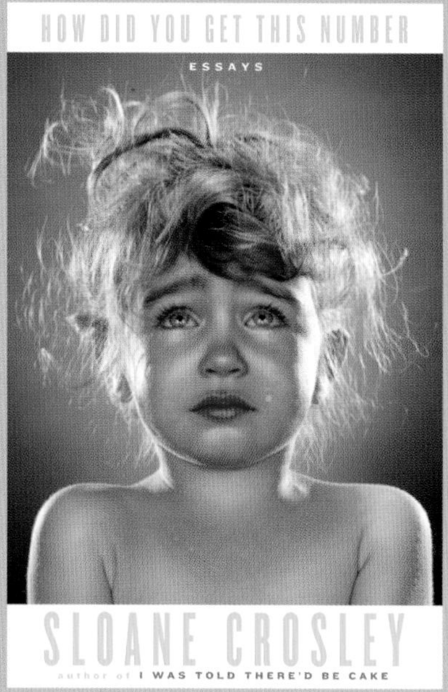
HOW DID YOU GET THIS NUMBER
ESSAYS
SLOANE CROSLEY
author of I WAS TOLD THERE'D BE CAKE

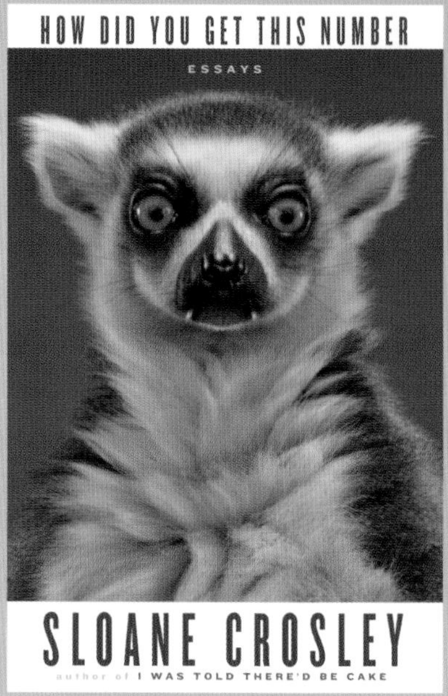
HOW DID YOU GET THIS NUMBER
ESSAYS
SLOANE CROSLEY
author of I WAS TOLD THERE'D BE CAKE

I think photographer Jill Greenberg is a genius, especially her portraits of children and animals (left and above), and felt she was a perfect fit for the hilarious essays of my beloved former Knopf Group colleague Sloane Crosley. Sloane agreed, but went with a bear by Jill that was not of my choosing. That was fine with me, as long as everyone was happy, but I liked these better. How did we get this number, anyway?

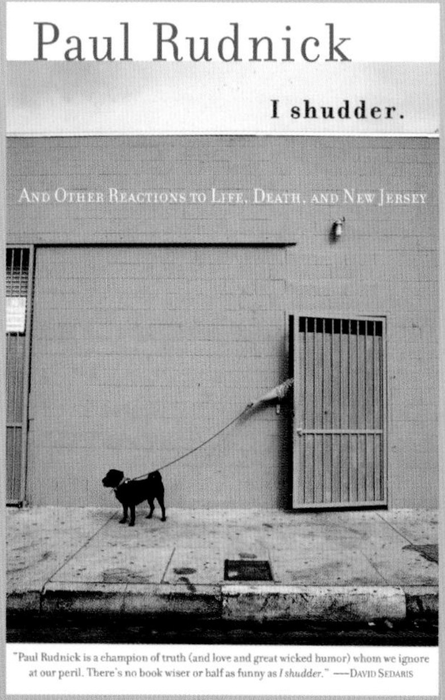
Paul Rudnick
I shudder.
AND OTHER REACTIONS TO LIFE, DEATH, AND NEW JERSEY
"Paul Rudnick is a champion of truth (and love and great wicked humor) whom we ignore at our peril. There's no book wiser or half as funny as I shudder." —DAVID SEDARIS

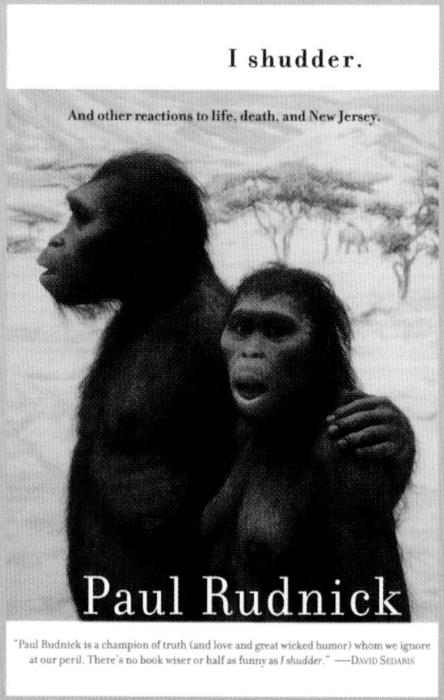
I shudder.
And other reactions to life, death, and New Jersey.
Paul Rudnick
"Paul Rudnick is a champion of truth (and love and great wicked humor) whom we ignore at our peril. There's no book wiser or half as funny as I shudder." —DAVID SEDARIS

## Chick Lit

Paul Rudnick, along with David Sedaris and Augusten Burroughs, is among the funniest writers I've had the great luck to work with. The title of his collection of essays *I Shudder* is based on an expression used by his relatives to comment on things that are repellent and fearful for them. One of Paul's quirks is that he only likes to eat candy (there is an essay about it), with a special fondness for marshmallow Peeps. So I bought a package of them and set up a photo shoot with Geoff. As you may or may not know, these sugared chemical gobs of goo are molded into rows to look like abstract chicks aligned next to one another. My initial thought was to shoot a complete phalanx of them, but before we were able to set up the shot, Geoff's son (and my godson), Jet, aged five, had gone and eaten one of them while we weren't looking. Sneaky. But perfect, as it provided context: the "birds" looked pretty paranoid anyway, and now the implicit message was, "Whoa, so who's next?" Another happy accident. *Burp*.

**OPPOSITE, BOTTOM:** Two earlier unused ideas. I dearly loved that couple of Neanderthals from the Natural History Museum on the right, and they (along with Jet!) eventually were featured in the graphics for Paul Simon's *Surprise* album. **THIS PAGE:** Harper, 2009.

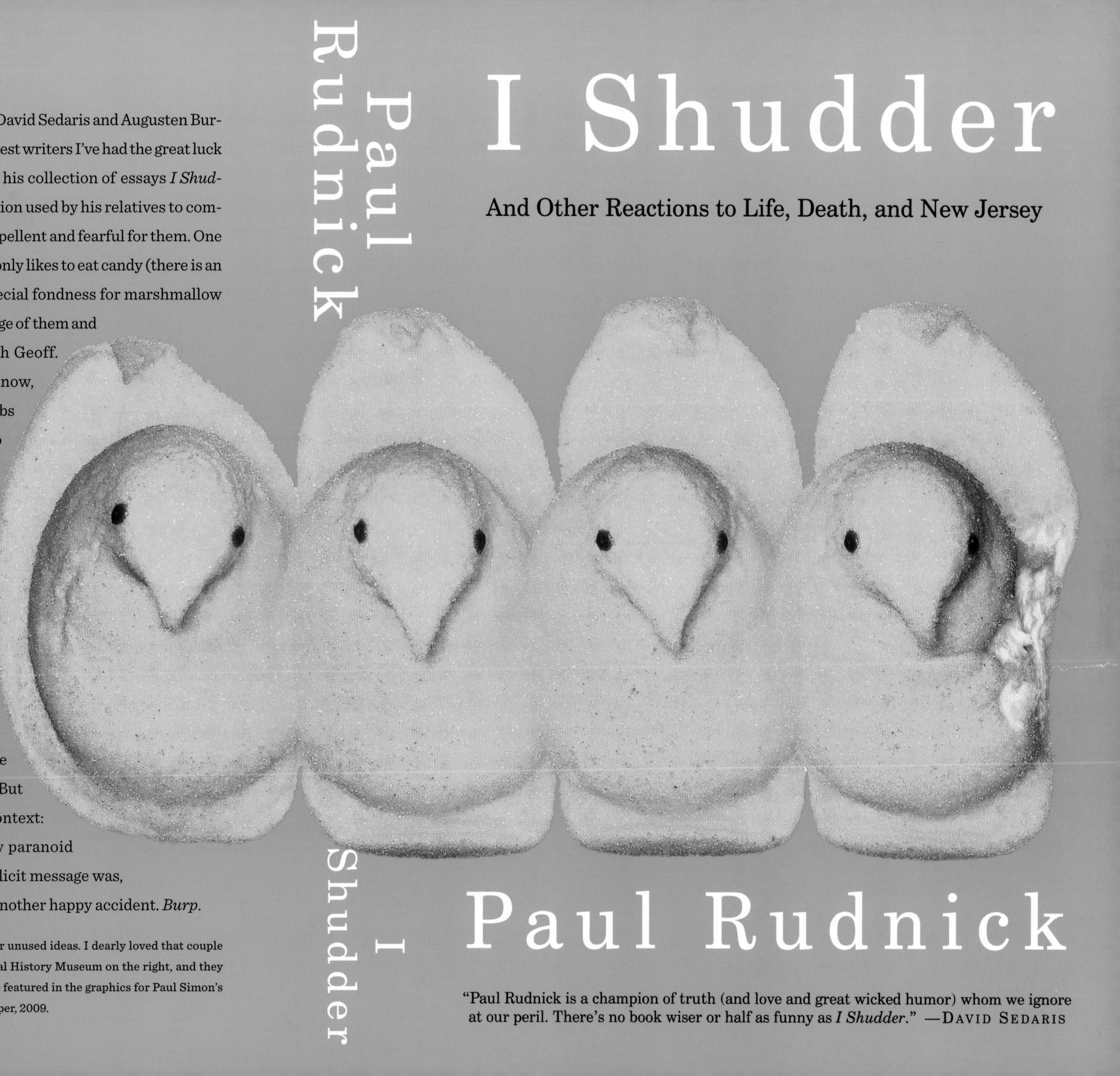
Paul Rudnick
I Shudder
I Shudder
And Other Reactions to Life, Death, and New Jersey
Paul Rudnick
"Paul Rudnick is a champion of truth (and love and great wicked humor) whom we ignore at our peril. There's no book wiser or half as funny as I Shudder." —DAVID SEDARIS

# "What's the story?"

www.morningglory.com



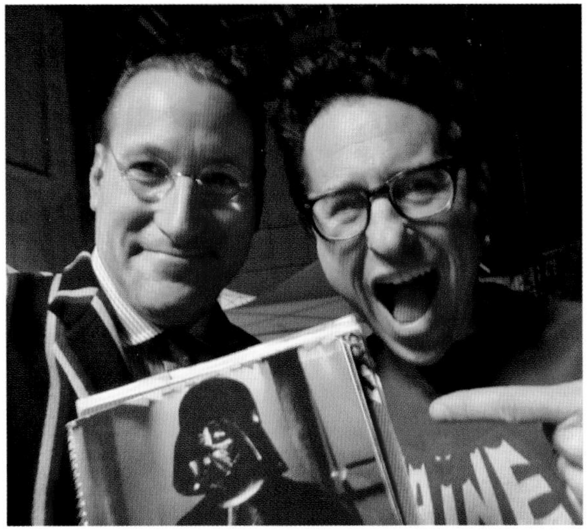

**LEFT:** Me on the set of *The Force Awakens*, September 19, 2014, Pinewood Studios, London. I am presenting J. J. with a Star Wars scrapbook that I made as a 13-year-old.

## Morning, J. J.

In August of 2010 a woman from Paramount Pictures phoned me. She sounded British, polite, and a little annoyed. "You're a difficult man to get a hold of." What she meant was there was no phone number or e-mail address on my website or Facebook page. This was quite true, and my theory, however arrogant, was that if someone really needed to get a hold of me, they'd figure it out (I'm listed, after all). And sure enough she did. "How can I help you?" I asked.

What followed led to my friendship with no less than J. J. Abrams, but I am getting ahead of myself. The immediate problem at hand was that his production company Bad Robot was producing its first romantic comedy called *Morning Glory* with Paramount, and J. J. had suggested that they contact me to help with the marketing. This was incredibly flattering, but I was totally intimidated by talent that was way out of my league. Besides J. J. producing, the film starred Rachel McAdams, Harrison Ford, and Diane Keaton. *Gulp*. My previous experiences with movie posters was slim and strictly limited to indies (*Rocket Science*, pp. 138–39; *Fur*, pp. 136–37). But if J. J. liked my work and wanted me to give it a shot, I wasn't going to say no. However, it also became apparent that I was brought in at the eleventh hour. The movie was set to open that November and there was already a trailer online. Double *gulp*. I was brought in to Paramount's New York City offices to screen the movie

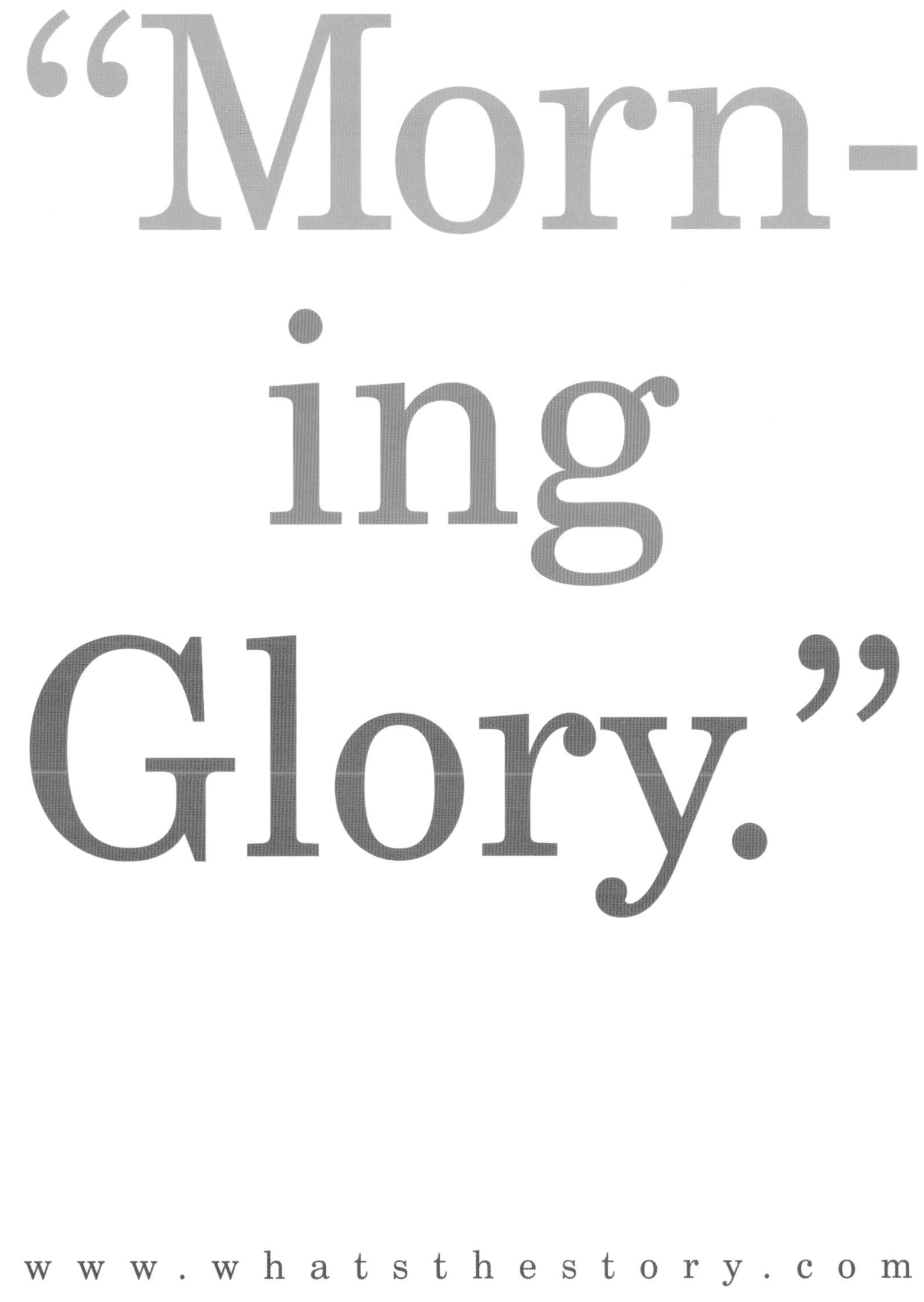
"Morn-
ing
Glory."
www.whatsthestory.com

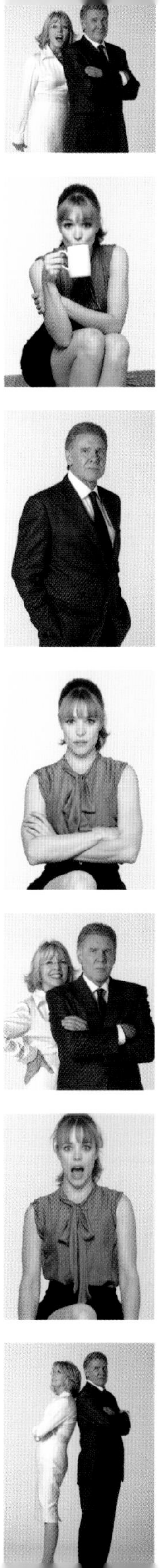

and was sent tons of digital files of on-set photography and studio photo sessions with the stars. I was completely overwhelmed, but took a deep breath and decided to start from a theoretical beginning. As in, a teaser campaign.

I kept hearing the Oasis lyric in my head: "What's the story morning glory?" So that led to two all-type posters, the color of the letters suggesting a sunrise. I texted them to J. J., who responded immediately. He loved them. I kept going.

**LEFT:** A small sampling of the studio photography done for the movie. I felt these were usable, with one change: convert them to black and white, and put only the typography in color. Below is an early test, with fictitious blurbs I composed.

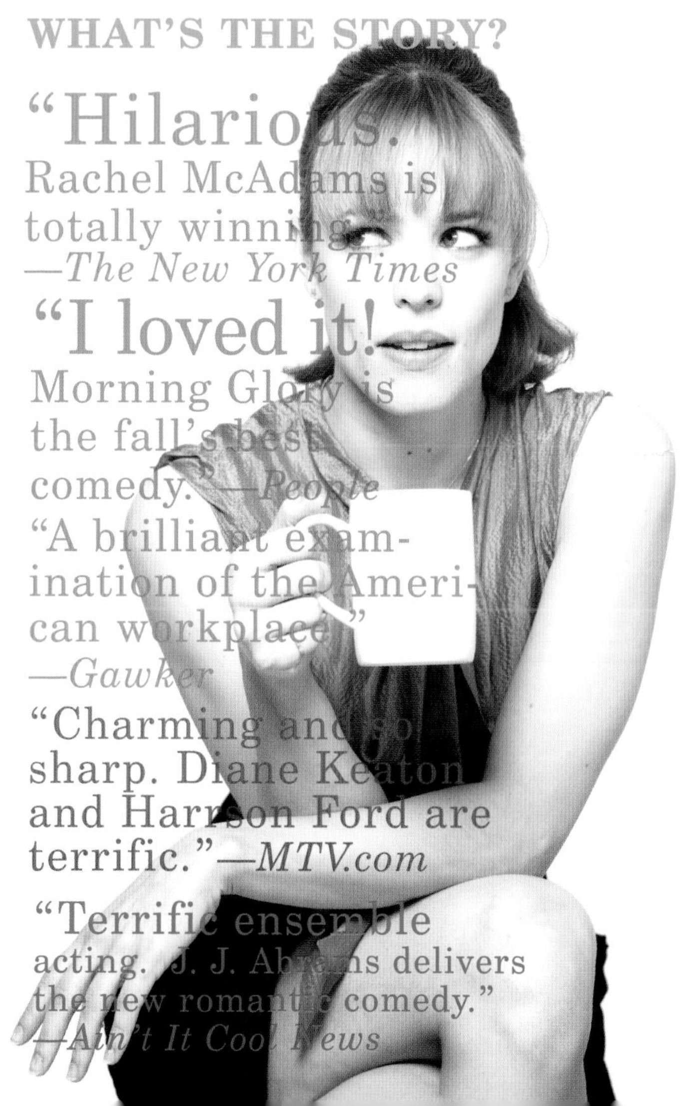
WHAT'S THE STORY?
"Hilarious. Rachel McAdams is totally winning." —The New York Times
"I loved it! Morning Glory is the fall's best comedy." —People
"A brilliant examination of the American workplace." —Gawker
"Charming and so sharp. Diane Keaton and Harrison Ford are terrific." —MTV.com
"Terrific ensemble acting. J. J. Abrams delivers the new romantic comedy." —Ain't It Cool News

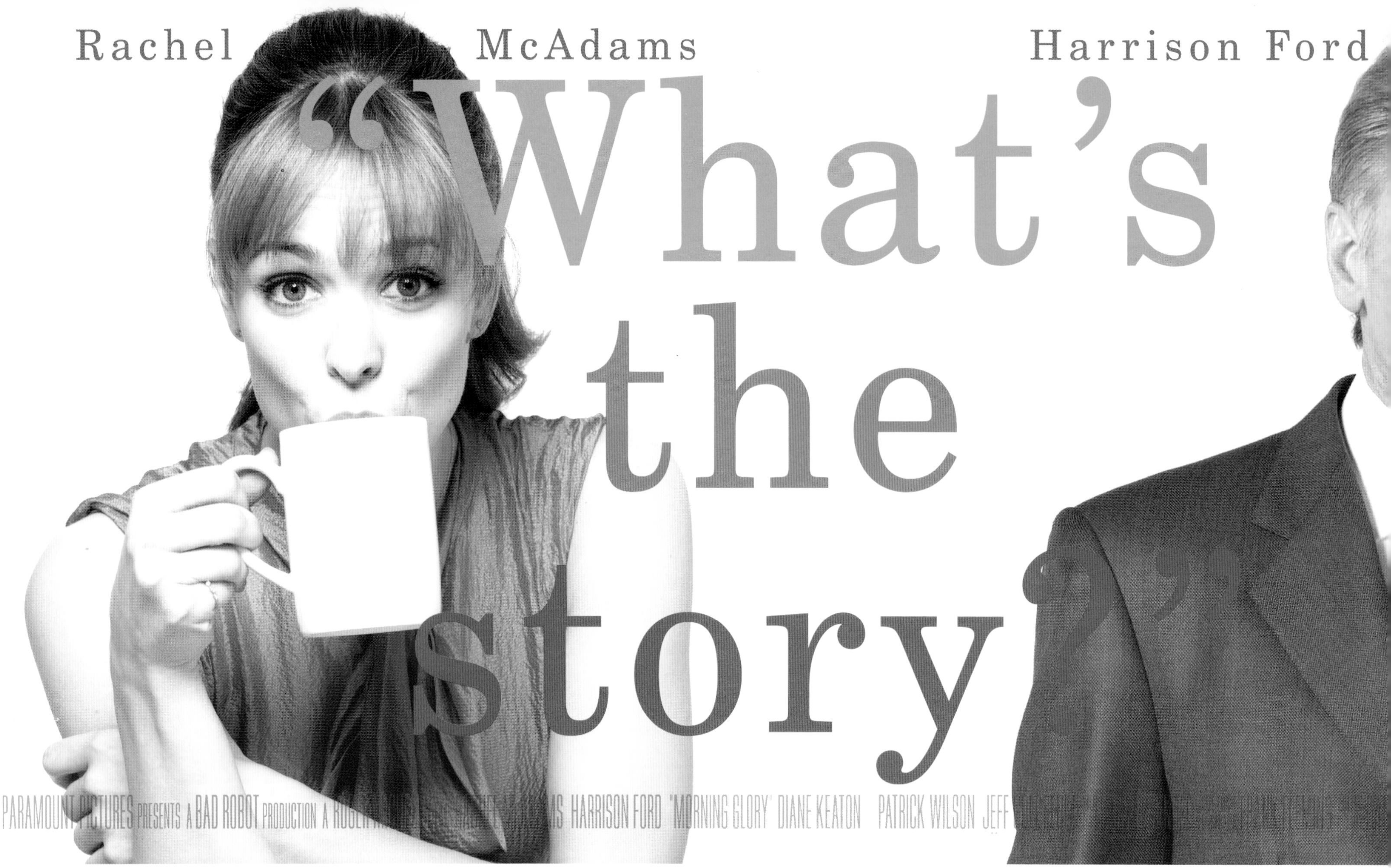
Rachel McAdams
Harrison Ford
PARAMOUNT PICTURES PRESENTS A BAD ROBOT PRODUCTION
HARRISON FORD "MORNING GLORY" DIANE KEATON PATRICK WILSON

# "What's the story?"



The story of the film is a mash-up of *The Mary Tyler Moore Show*, *Broadcast News*, and *Working Girl*. Rachel McAdams plays Becky Fuller, a young producer of a local newscast called "Good Morning New Jersey." At the beginning of the movie, she is unceremoniously laid off. After sending out dozens of résumés, to her amazement she lands an interview at a big broadcast network in New York City called IBS, to be an executive producer at its struggling morning show, "Daybreak." The head of the network, Jerry Barnes (Jeff Goldblum), reluctantly hires her, telling her that she will fail. Thanks a lot, Jerry!

The show, it turns out, is in a terrible downward spiral, perpetually a distant fourth place in the ratings. One of the first things Becky does is fire its insufferable lead male co-anchor, much to the relief and thanks of his female counterpart, Colleen Peck, deliciously played by Diane Keaton. Quickly needing a replacement, Becky accidentally discovers that the legendary newsman Mike Pomery (Harrison Ford) is still under contract to the network and getting a full salary, essentially to do nothing. Becky decides to change that. Mike will have none of it, until Becky makes him understand that legally he has to.

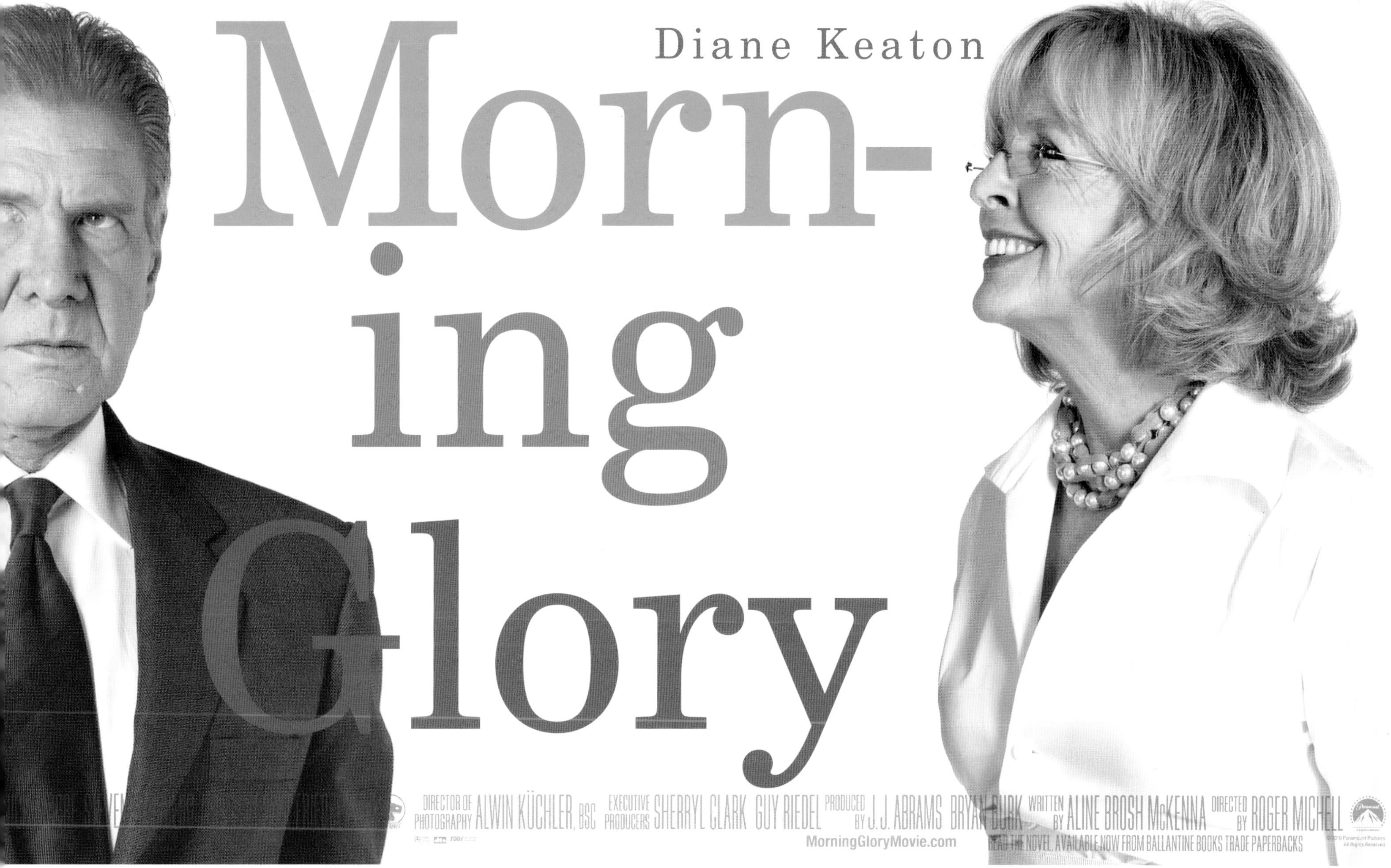
Diane Keaton
Morning Glory
DIRECTOR OF PHOTOGRAPHY ALWIN KÜCHLER, BSC EXECUTIVE PRODUCERS SHERRYL CLARK GUY RIEDEL PRODUCED BY J.J. ABRAMS WRITTEN BY ALINE BROSH McKENNA DIRECTED BY ROGER MICHELL
MorningGloryMovie.com
THE NOVEL, AVAILABLE NOW FROM BALLANTINE BOOKS TRADE PAPERBACKS



He is not happy. Nor is Colleen, who despises his pretension. Cue the live on-air hijinks, which are a lot of fun (watch the trailer on YouTube to see if you agree). There's a running gag with the weatherman that is priceless, among many other comic gems. But what I most like about the movie is that it's really about all of the concepts that Becky has to keep coming up with to try and save the show. She has to just keep thinking of idea after idea. Some of them don't work, but a lot of them do, and it starts to turn things around. That aspect of the story was fascinating to me; the life of a graphic designer is quite similar.

**ABOVE:** Once the basic scheme of the campaign was approved, it had to be adaptable to multiple formats, including billboards, of course.

**RIGHT:** One of the many final incarnations. Sunset Boulevard, baby!

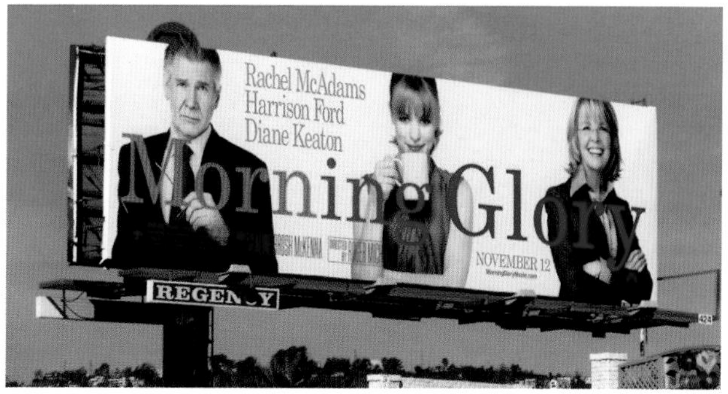
Rachel McAdams
Harrison Ford
Diane Keaton
Morning Glory
NOVEMBER 12

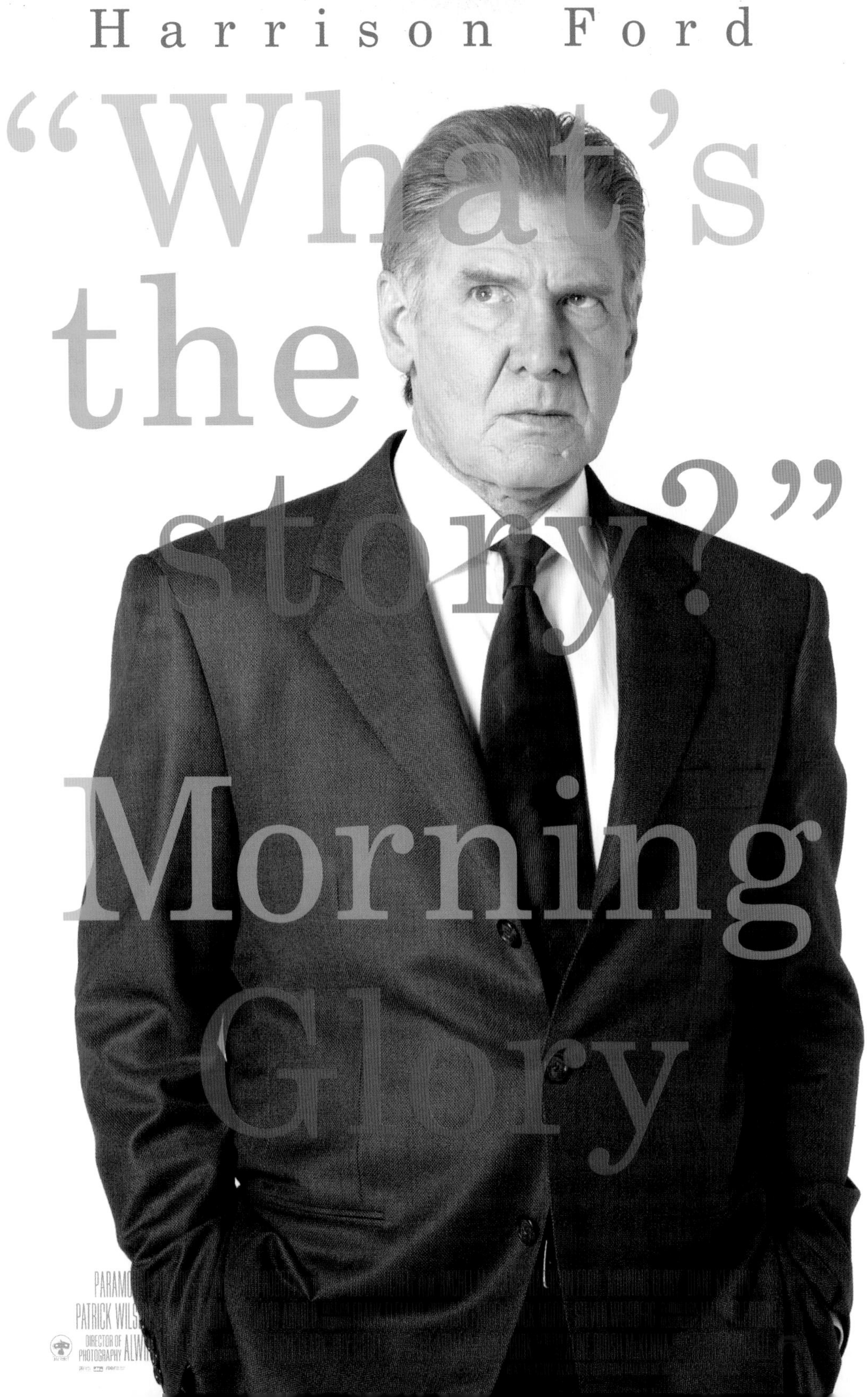
Harrison Ford
“What’s the story?”
Morning Glory



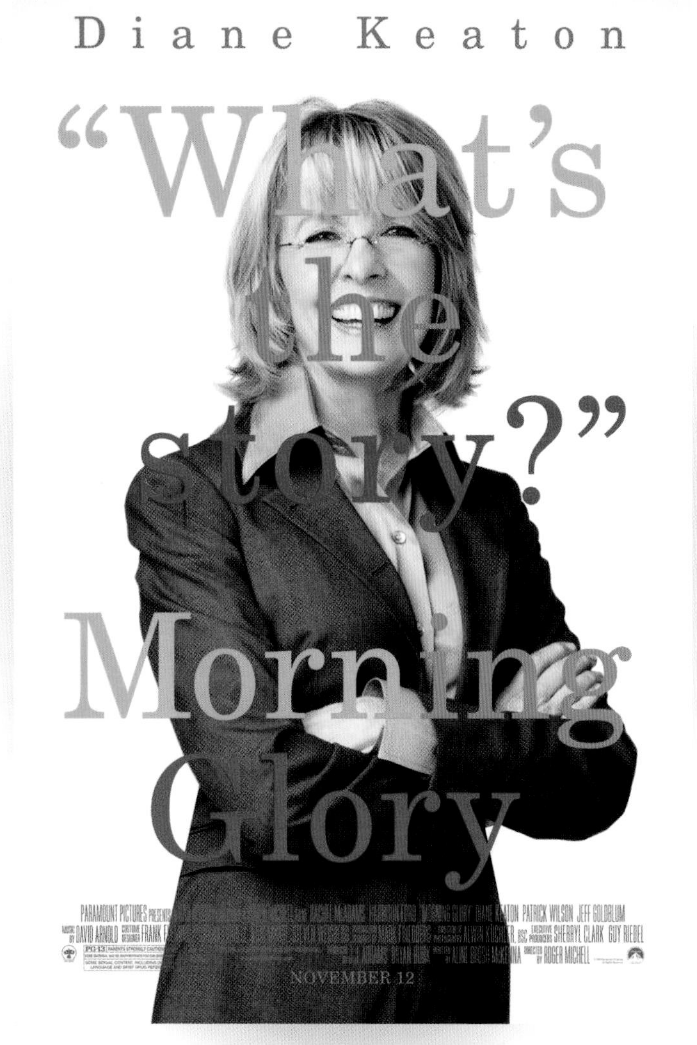
Diane Keaton
“What’s the story?”
Morning Glory
NOVEMBER 12

My approach was to make the posters for *Morning Glory* look like they could conceivably be advertisements for “Daybreak” itself, even if you didn’t know what the movie was about. In retrospect, the entire process went amazingly smoothly, given everything at stake and the relatively little time involved. Paramount went with my initial presentation without altering or compromising it, and that is thanks to J. J.’s involvement. Best of all, we became friends as a result of the experience.

**OPPOSITE:** J. J. has been trying his hand at commercial lettering (don’t ask me why, I have no idea, but look at how good he is with a brush!) and tried multiple versions of my name in his practice book. He also took this photo and sent it to me for use here. I’d say he definitely has a fallback if the movie thing dries up.

Chip Kidd

Chip Kidd

Chip Kidd

Chip Kidd

Chip Kidd

Chip Kidd

Chip Kidd

Chip Kidd

Chip Kidd

CHIP

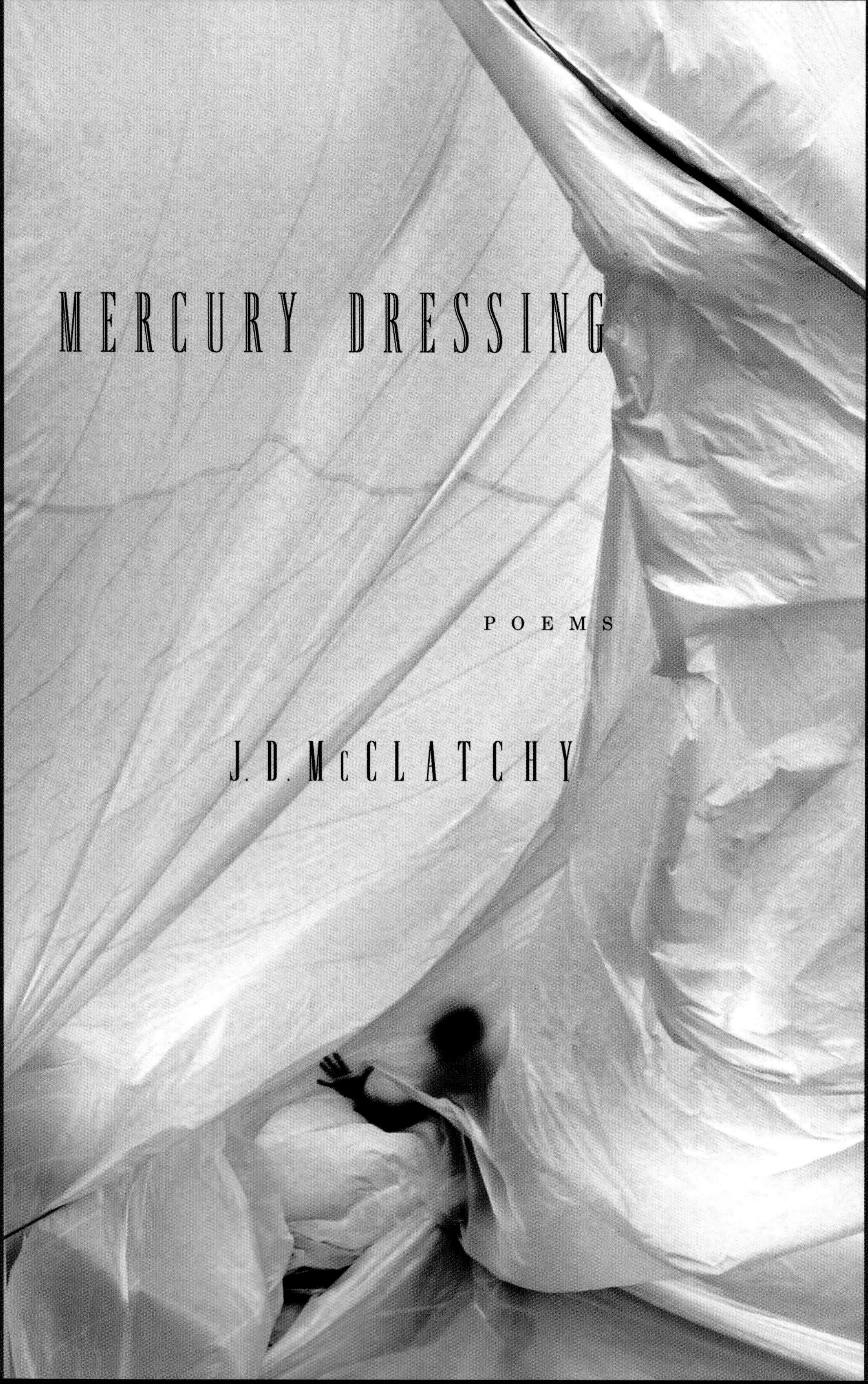
MERCURY DRESSING
POEMS
J.D. McCLATCHY

**RIGHT:** Portrait of Sandy in his study in Stonington, CT, by Stone Roberts, 2013.

**LEFT:** Knopf, 2009.

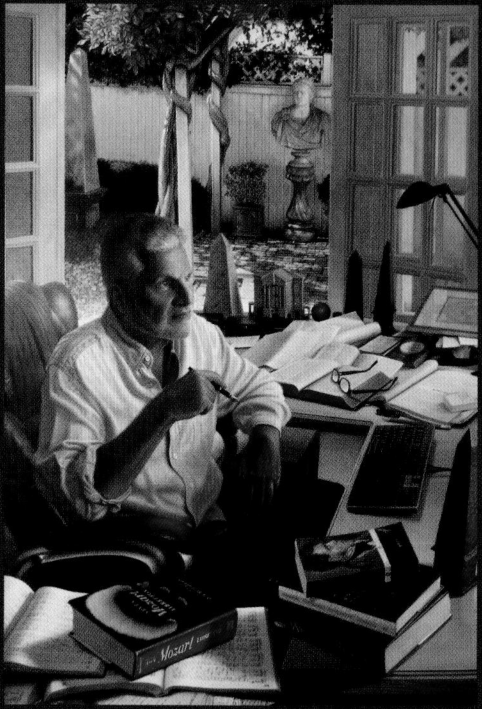

## Plundered Art

It has been over 21 years since we're together now, and I suppose the fact that designing the covers for my husband J. D. (Sandy) McClatchy's books is still something of, well, an adventure is a good sign. Hey, easy is boring, right? Trust me, it is not boring.

The title of *Mercury Dressing* (left) is literal; for better or worse, it's about the god Mercury putting on clothes. On a weekend stay at my pal the photo dealer Paul Amador's house in East Hampton, I spied a book of sports photography lying on his coffee table. In it I found this extraordinary depiction of a crew member changing a sail on a ship during the America's Cup boat race. Bingo—it was gorgeous, available, and ambiguous in all the right ways.

The cover of *Plundered Hearts* (opposite, left), Sandy's volume of new and selected poems, has developed into a very interesting story. Sandy co-taught with the painter Vincent Desiderio during a stint at the Vermont Studio Center in the early 1990s and they became great friends. Sandy had always loved Vincent's work, especially his epic mural *Sleep*, which shows a vast array of seemingly unrelated adults in various states of undress in the world's widest bed. It was Sandy's idea to ask to use this art, and Vincent's gallery gave us permission . . .

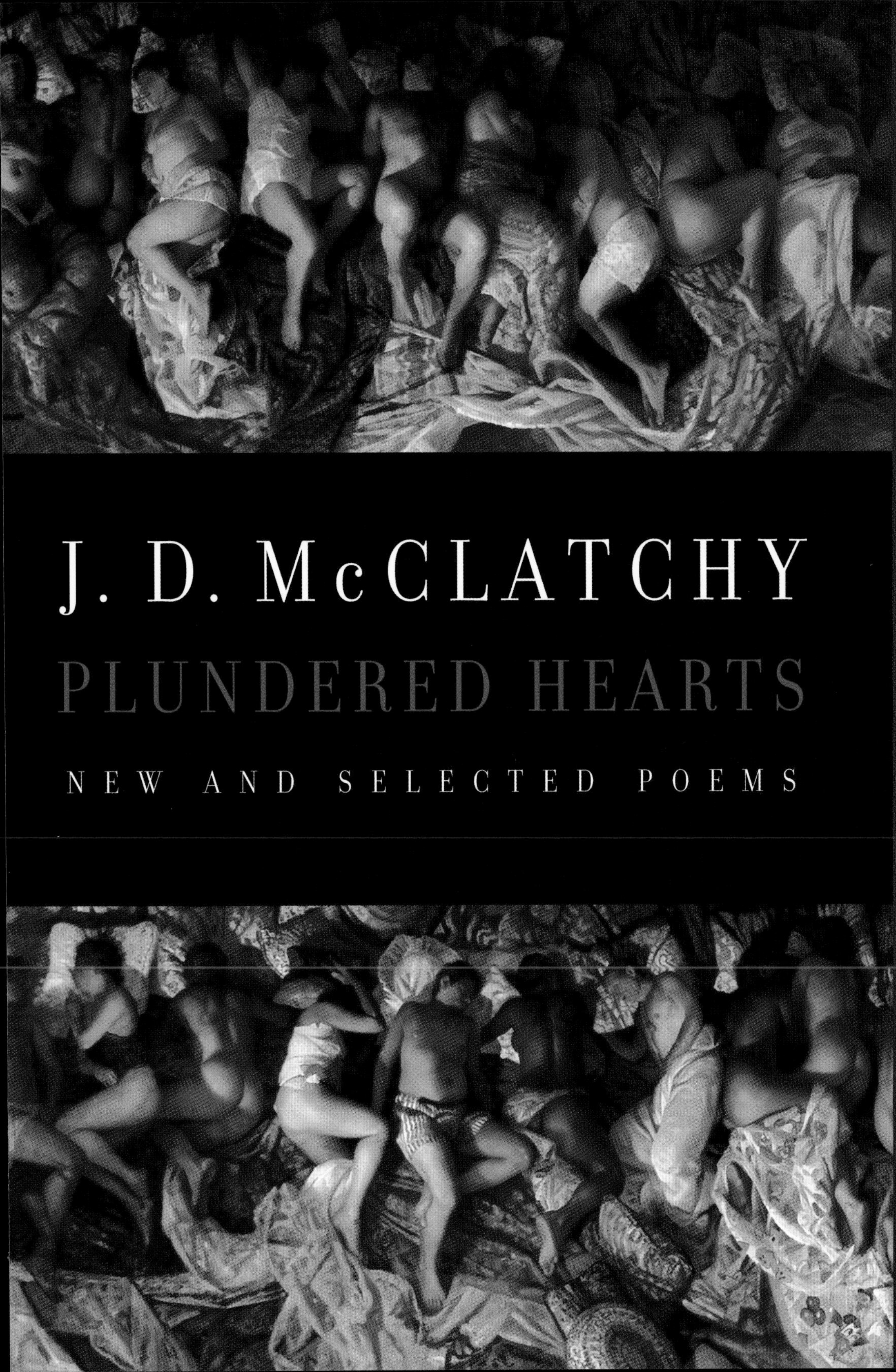
J. D. McCLATCHY
PLUNDERED HEARTS
NEW AND SELECTED POEMS

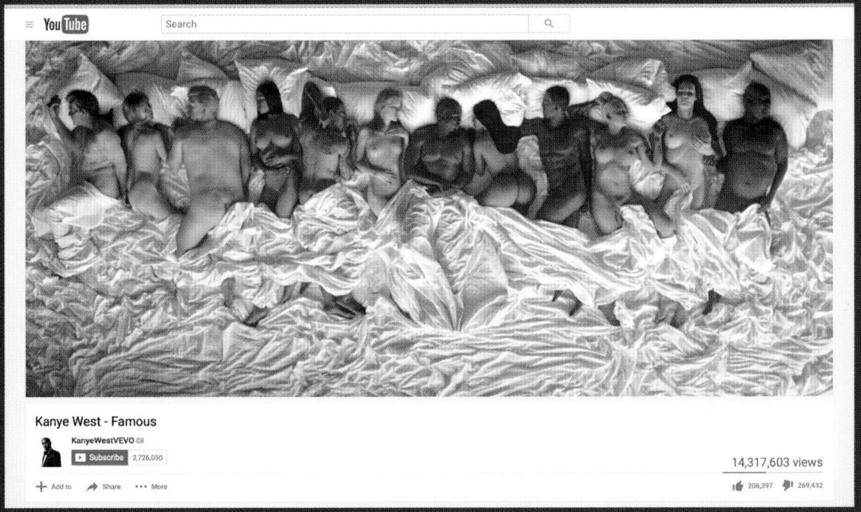
Search
Kanye West - Famous
KanyeWestVEVO
Subscribe
14,317,603 views

. . . then two years later Kanye West decided that he liked the painting as well, and he adapted it for the video for his song "Famous" (opening shot, above). Vincent generously approved the usage and declined any financial compensation.

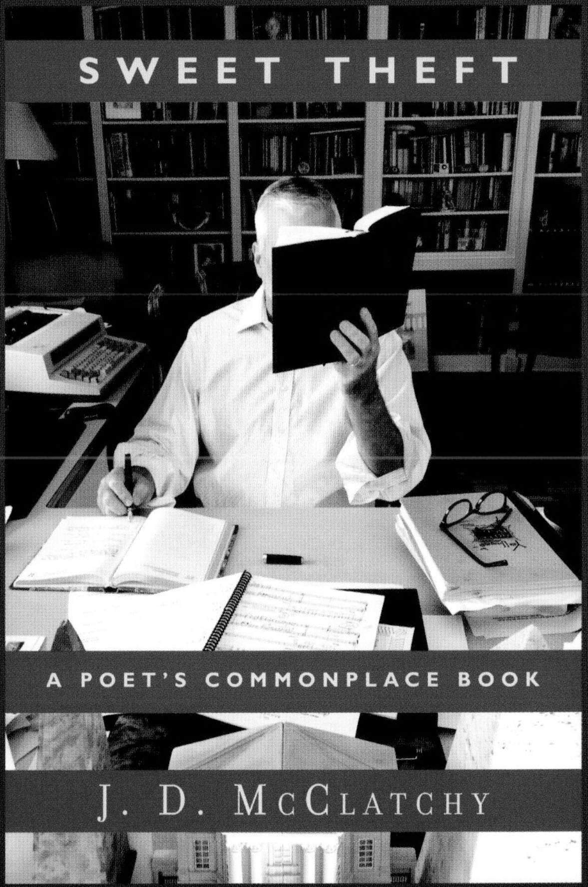
SWEET THEFT
A POET'S COMMONPLACE BOOK
J. D. McCLATCHY

**LEFT:** Knopf, 2014.

**RIGHT:** Sandy's next book, *Sweet Theft* (Counterpoint, 2016). I photographed the cover myself. So far, no word from Yeezy about a buyout, but hope springs eternal.

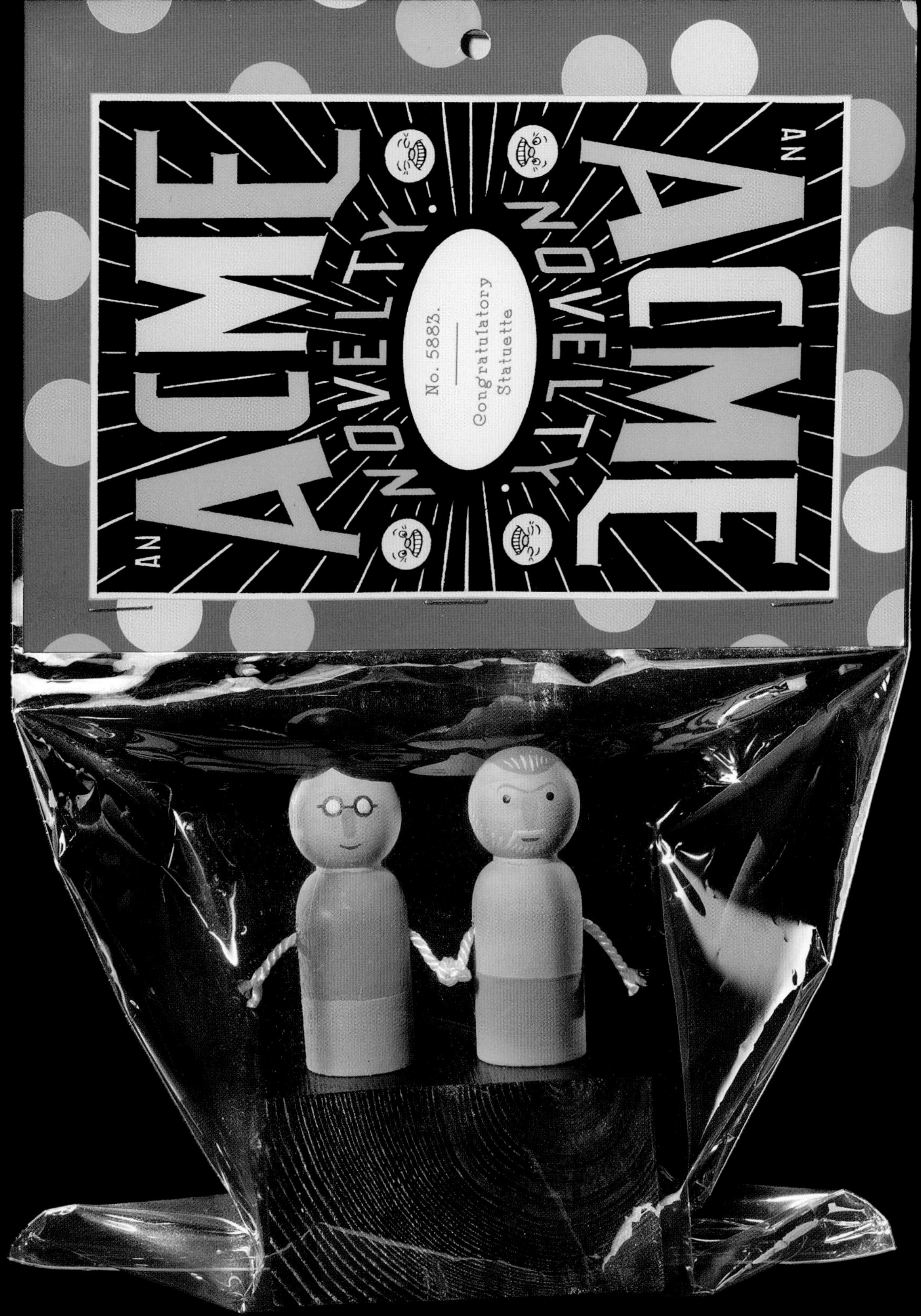

AN ACME NOVELTY
AN ACME NOVELTY
No. 5883.
Congratulatory Statuette


# Tying the Knot

Although we were definitely supporters of marriage-equality rights, for many years Sandy and I also didn't think it was something that we personally needed. We were quite committed to each other for close to two decades, our families were totally accepting, why bother?

Then our minds were changed by the legalization of same-sex marriage in New York, a slight tax advantage, and—most crucially—a health scare. In November of 2013 we made it official in a small civil ceremony at City Hall. Chris Ware commemorated the event by immortalizing us in captivating painted wood and knotted string (left).

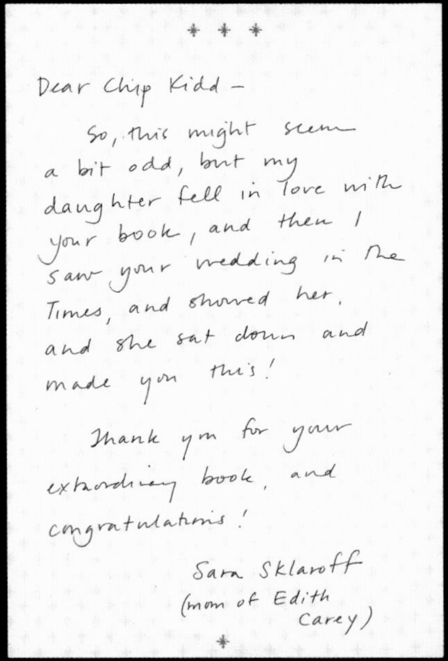

Dear Chip Kidd –

So, this might seem a bit odd, but my daughter fell in love with your book, and then I saw your wedding in the Times, and showed her, and she sat down and made you this!

Thank you for your extraordinary book, and congratulations!

Sara Sklaroff
(mom of Edith Carey)

And then something truly amazing happened. We had the wedding announced in the *New York Times*, which was read to an 8-year-old girl named Edith Carey by her mother, Sara Sklaroff. Edith had studied my book *Go* (pp. 279–81) and was a fan, and then she sent me the letter you see opposite. I don't know quite else what to say, except that if there were any questions in my mind about hope for the next generation of humanity (and there were, frankly), with this she gloriously erased them.

Thank you, Edith.

HAPPY WEDDING TO fight

KERNING

# ☺ HAPPY WEDDING!!!!!!!!!!!!!!!!!

Chip Kidd  +  J.D. Mcclatchy

Dear Chip Kidd and J.D. Mcclatchy,    11-12-13

When I heard about your wedding I thought is was AWESOME!!! want to know why?

Because I think being gay is AWESOME!!!!!!

Also because my BFF (Buddie for forever) has two moms who are AWESOME!!!!

I know about you guys because I read "Go" (even though I'm 8!) (Don't tell the publisher). From,

Edith Carey ☺

P.S. I did a report on your book!

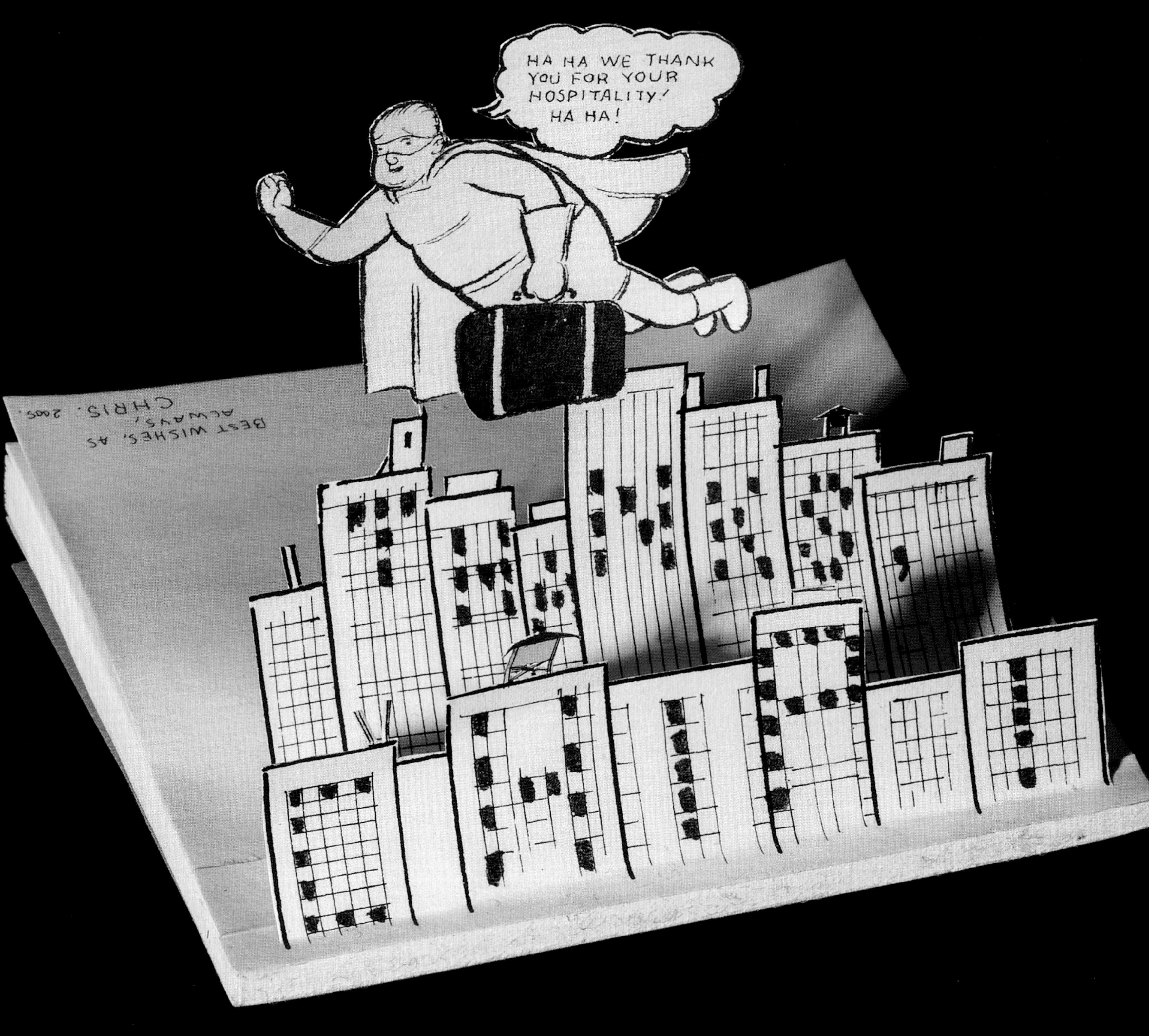
HA HA WE THANK YOU FOR YOUR HOSPITALITY! HA HA!
BEST WISHES, AS ALWAYS, CHRIS. 2005.

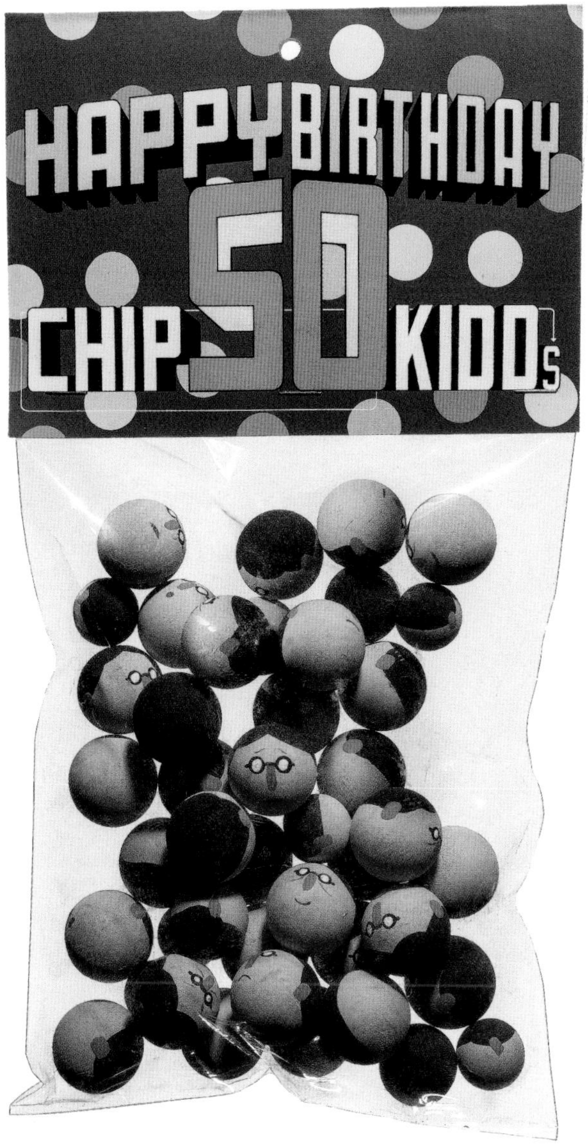
HAPPY BIRTHDAY
CHIP 50 KIDD's

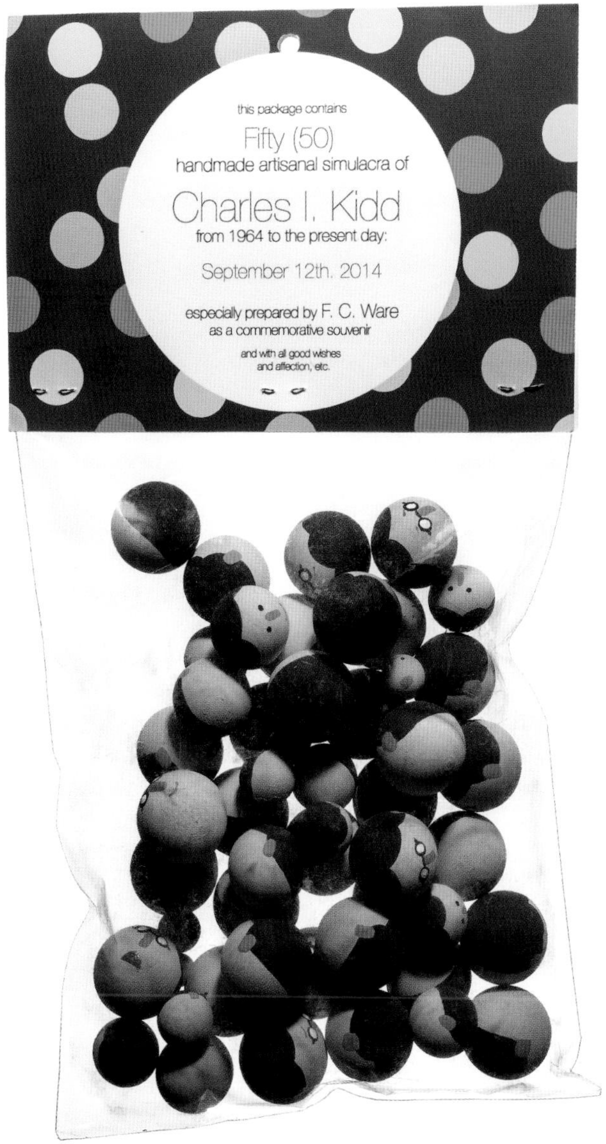
this package contains
Fifty (50)
handmade artisanal simulacra of
Charles I. Kidd
from 1964 to the present day:
September 12th, 2014
especially prepared by F. C. Ware
as a commemorative souvenir
and with all good wishes
and affection, etc.

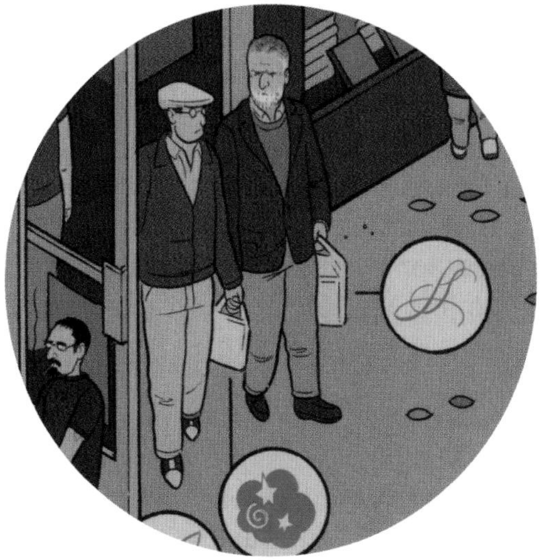

**LEFT:** To commemorate my 50th birthday, Chris did what anyone else would do: he carved and painted 50 versions of my head out of wood, one for each year of my life, and packaged them like lemon drops. **ABOVE & BELOW:** Sandy and I make a cameo in the upper left of this page for *Time* magazine about reading.

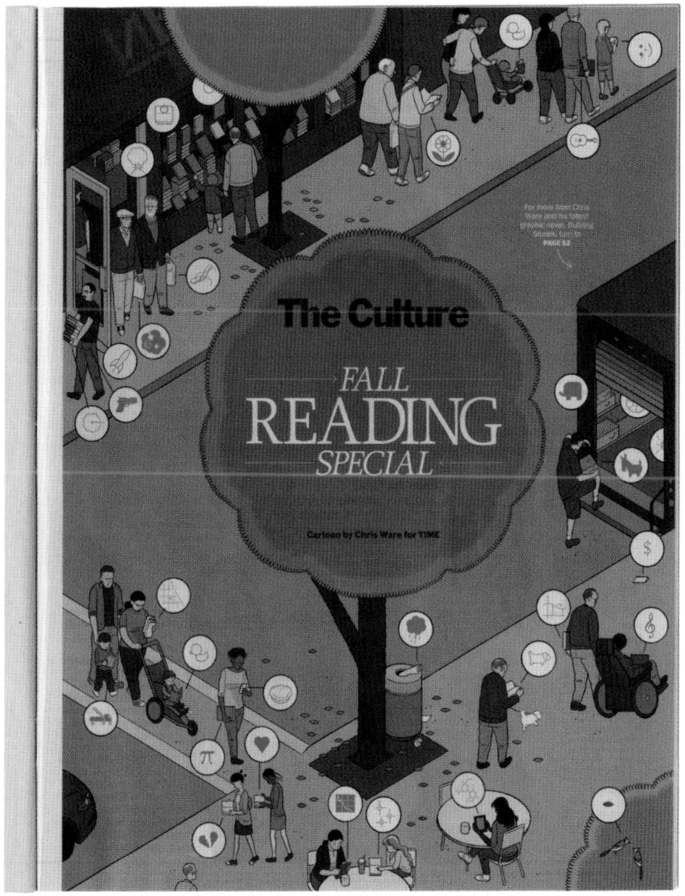
The Culture
FALL
READING
SPECIAL

# The Nicest Guy on Earth

Speaking of Chris Ware, please don't hate me (as he is wont to say) for showing a few more personal pieces he has created over the years. Opposite is a little item that never ceases to amaze me and makes me seriously question if he really is a mere mortal. It is a standard Post-it pad, 3 × 3 in., that has been inked and meticulously cut into a diorama of his Super-Man character flying over the city as a thank-you note for staying at my apartment in 2005. It is fragile as a bee's wings, but I keep it in a glass case for protection. It took me well over a year to notice that the blacked-in windows of the buildings spell out "THANKS, CHIP!"

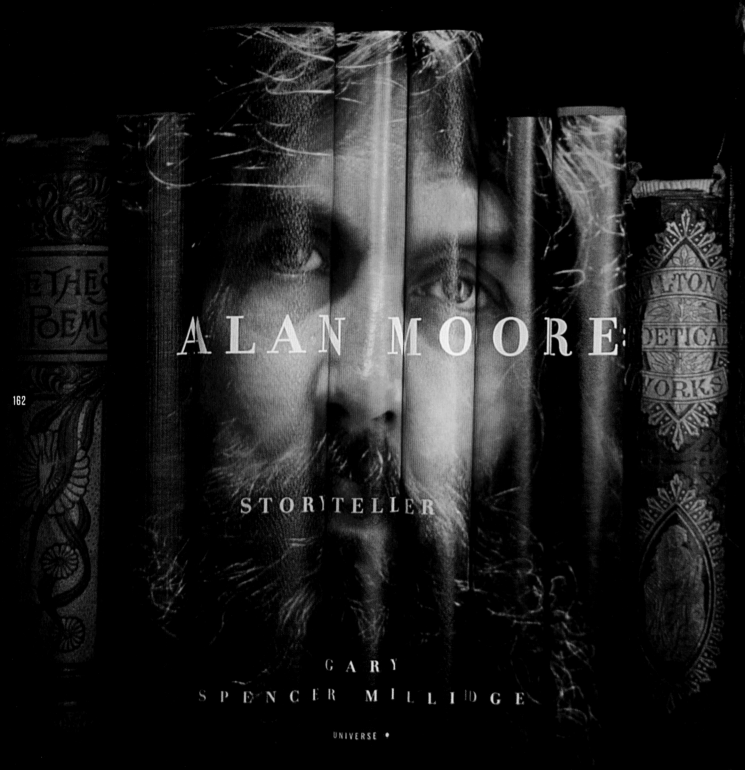

ALAN MOORE:

STORYTELLER

GARY
SPENCER MILLIDGE

UNIVERSE •

## Watch It

If Alan Moore is the Leo Tolstoy of comics, then *Watchmen* (1986) is his *War and Peace*, as millions of fans including the filmmaker Terry Gilliam (who tried for years to turn the comic book into a movie) regard it. Add me to that list.

And yet Moore has long since turned his back on his own epic feat of graphic novel storytelling, having fallen out with his publisher, DC Comics, in the late 1980s, seemingly over creators' rights. Problems apparently involved innocuous yet minimally profitable related products like official Watchmen badges and a Watchmen wristwatch, from whose sales Moore and co-creator and illustrator Dave Gibbons saw no income. If that is indeed the truth, it is certainly one of the saddest and most needless cases of misuse of the classic work-for-hire clause in modern comics history, and DC would be to blame. But it doesn't speak well of Moore either—it's as if he were searching for a jumping-off point to escape the superhero genre and what he saw as the yoke of corporate culture.

Again, this is all speculation on my part, but when Dave Gibbons approached me in 2007 to design the definitive coffee-table art book about creating the Watchmen comics series, I was not going to say no. But the key question in any such project was: is there

**LEFT:** Portrait of Alan Moore on book spines that I created for a biography of the writer. Photographed by José Villarubia. Universe, 2011.

really a book's worth of stuff here? The answer was soon revealed as Yes: Dave had saved every scrap of paper—scripts and notes from Alan, sketches, color tests, costume designs, influences, thumbnails of all the pages—basically everything but any examples of finished, original art used for printing. Which was okay—I felt we had a book without needing that—but I had to know: would Alan be freaked out or otherwise upset by this book? Dave swore he wouldn't, but noted that Alan also wasn't going to contribute anything other than what he had originally supplied. I was in, and recruited my friend and co-designer Mike Essl to do the heavy lifting on the project. And that became *Watching the Watchmen*, published in 2008 by Titan Books.

At right is a first try at the cover, replicating the hand of the Rorschach character holding up the bloodied smiley-face button in the opening scene of the story. This was one of the original "official" badges that ticked Alan off in the first place, so it was nixed. Also, Titan cut Geoff Spear from the project, which I was not happy about. The reason was that all the artwork was in the UK, and the insurance costs made bringing it to the US out of the question, so a UK photographer had to shoot it all. I thought the results were subpar and said so, but my complaint fell on deaf ears. We had to work with what we got, but if you compare it to, say, any of Geoff's work on our Peanuts books, well, the difference is clear.

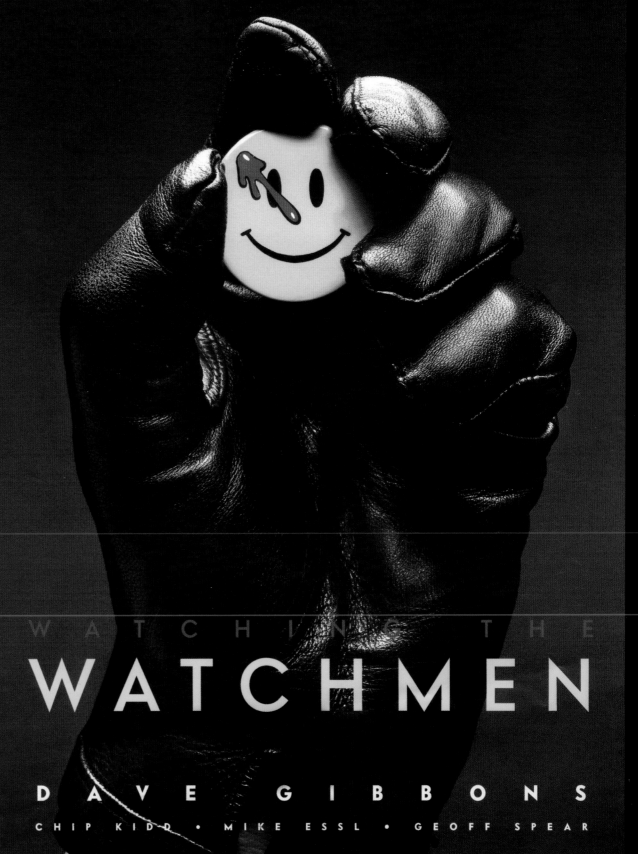

WATCHING THE
WATCHMEN
DAVE GIBBONS
CHIP KIDD • MIKE ESSL • GEOFF SPEAR

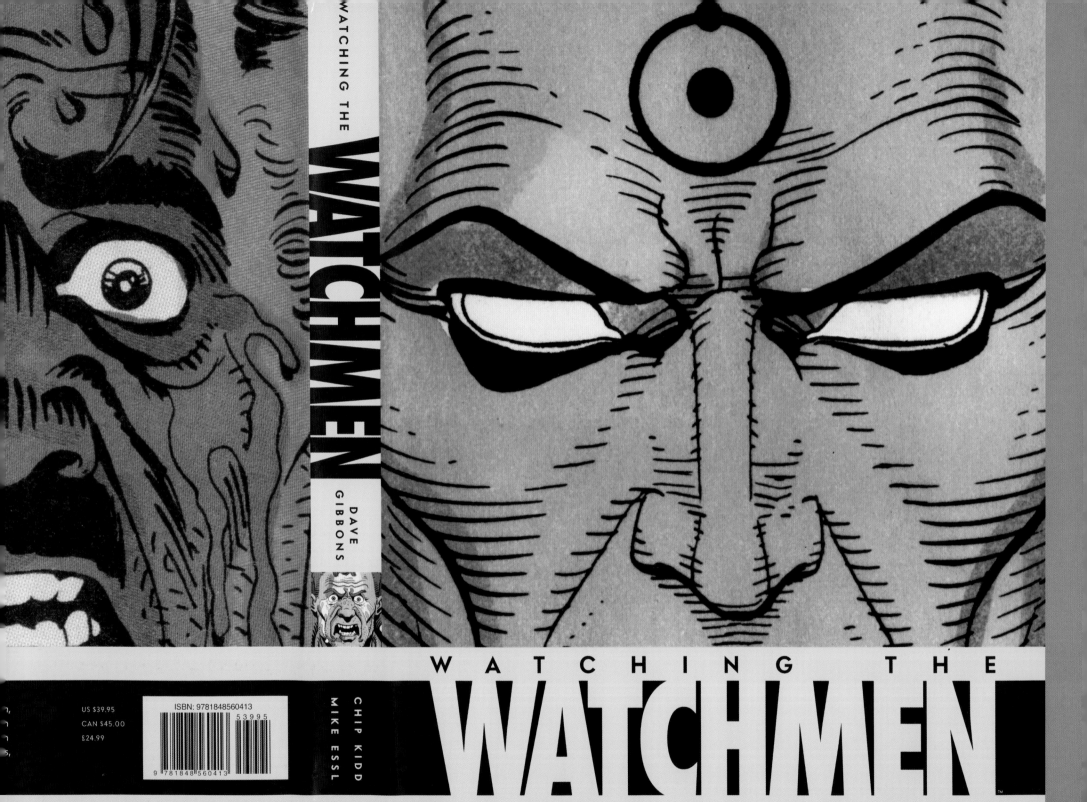

US $39.95
CAN $45.00
£24.99

ISBN: 9781848560413

WATCHING THE WATCHMEN

DAVE GIBBONS

CHIP KIDD
MIKE ESSL

TITAN BOOKS

# WATCHING THE WATCHMEN™

**DAVE GIBBONS**

**CHIP KIDD · MIKE ESSL**

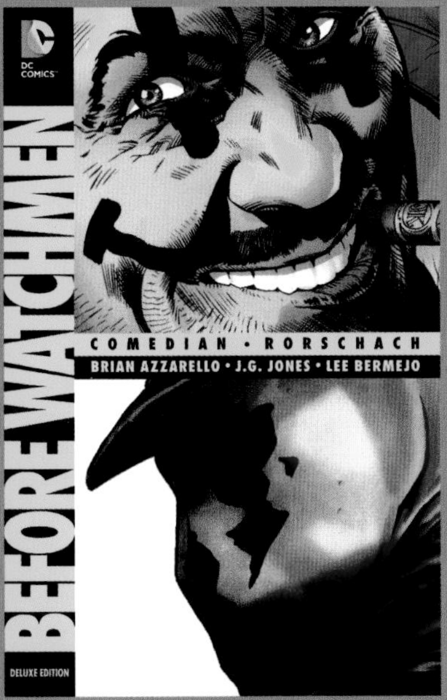
DC COMICS
BEFORE WATCHMEN
COMEDIAN • RORSCHACH
BRIAN AZZARELLO • J.G. JONES • LEE BERMEJO
DELUXE EDITION

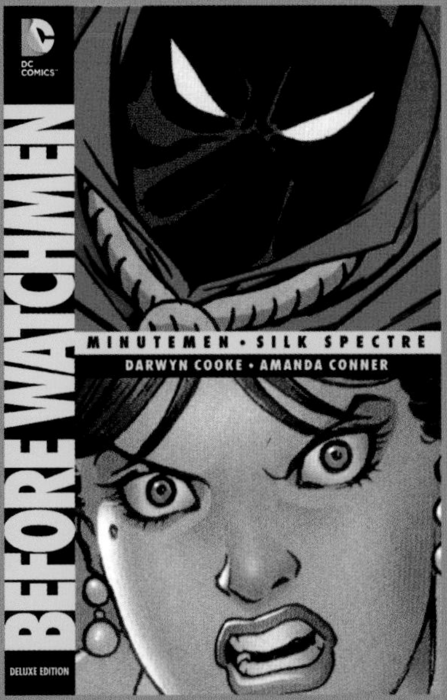
DC COMICS
BEFORE WATCHMEN
MINUTEMEN • SILK SPECTRE
DARWYN COOKE • AMANDA CONNER
DELUXE EDITION

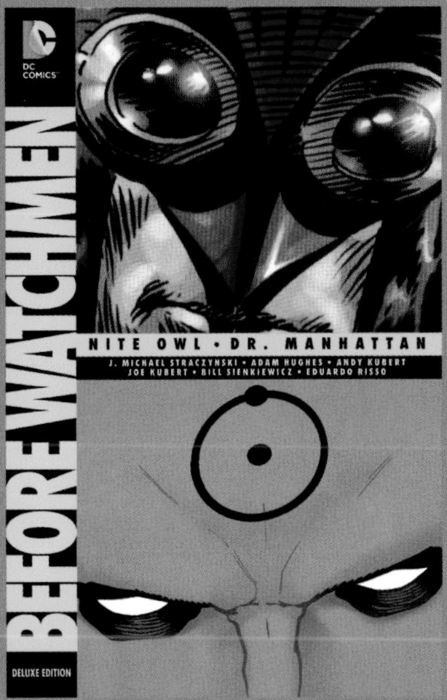
DC COMICS
BEFORE WATCHMEN
NITE OWL • DR. MANHATTAN
J. MICHAEL STRACZYNSKI • ADAM HUGHES • ANDY KUBERT
JOE KUBERT • BILL SIENKIEWICZ • EDUARDO RISSO
DELUXE EDITION

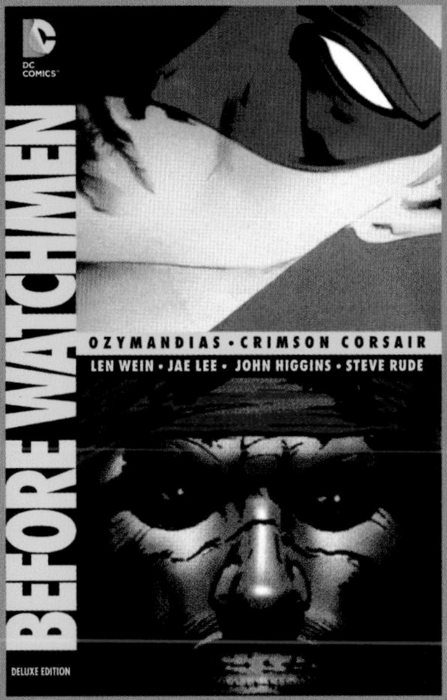
DC COMICS
BEFORE WATCHMEN
OZYMANDIAS • CRIMSON CORSAIR
LEN WEIN • JAE LEE • JOHN HIGGINS • STEVE RUDE
DELUXE EDITION

**OPPOSITE:** Final cover, spine, and partial back cover of *Watching the Watchmen*, using an inked sketch of Dr. Manhattan on the front, an unmasked Rorschach on the spine, and a despairing Comedian on the back, all by Dave Gibbons. Titan, 2008. **ABOVE:** If I didn't earn Alan Moore's scorn on *Watching the Watchmen*, I probably did by designing the covers of the trade editions of *Before Watchmen* in 2014, the controversial miniseries that speculated on the lives of the characters before the events of the original Watchmen book. **RIGHT:** *Before Watchmen* had variant covers (boy did it, as any popular series would; see my *Convergence* covers on pp. 264–67), and I was asked to make one for Rorschach #3. This was crazy fun. Geoff shot it, and that's my hand in the glove grabbing my own freaking-out face. All through a window of a Rorschach blot that he would be seeing through his mask as he scares the bejesus out of a baddie (me!).

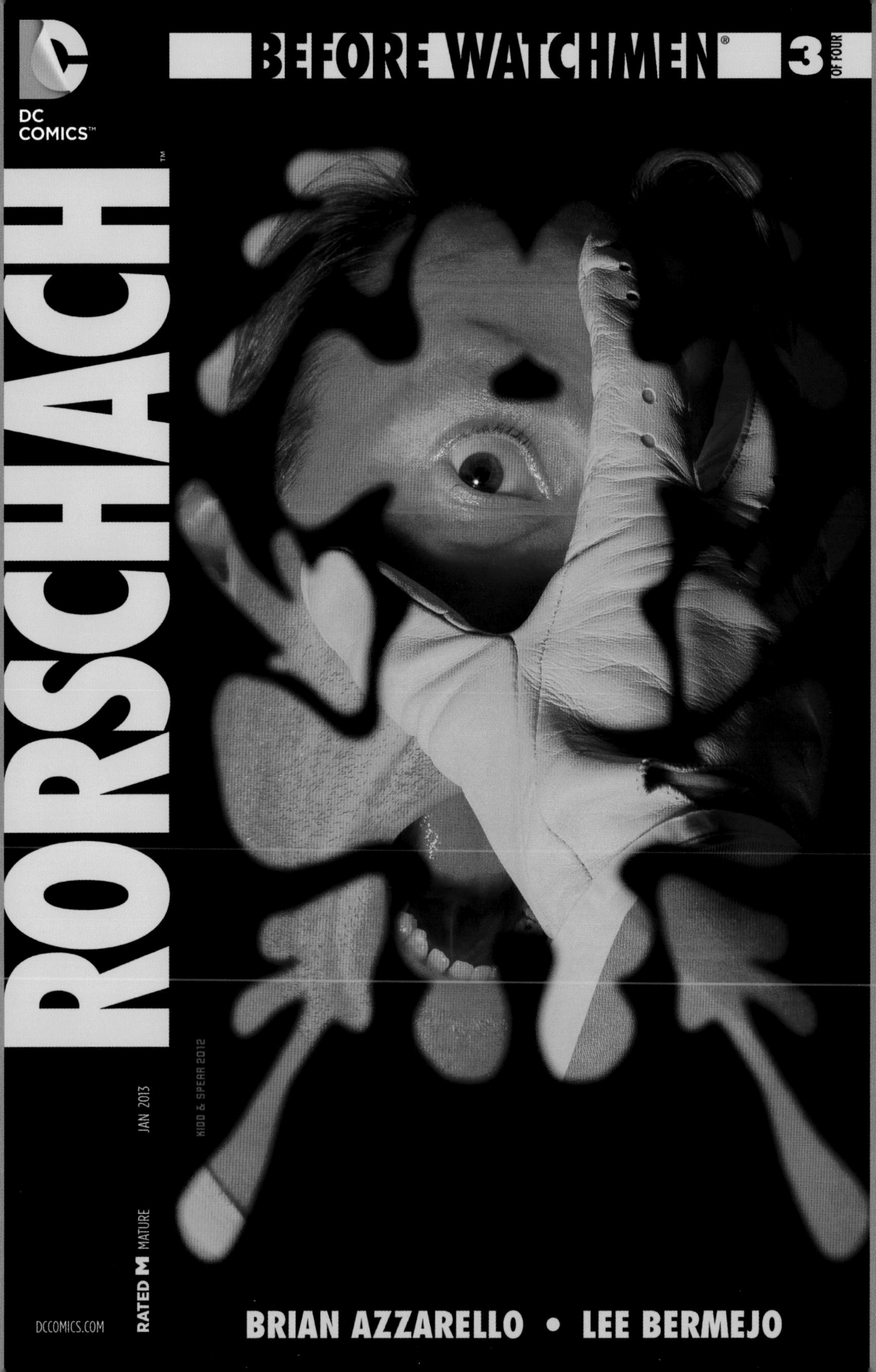
DC COMICS
BEFORE WATCHMEN
3 OF FOUR
RORSCHACH
JAN 2013
KIDD & SPEAR 2012
RATED M MATURE
DCCOMICS.COM
BRIAN AZZARELLO • LEE BERMEJO

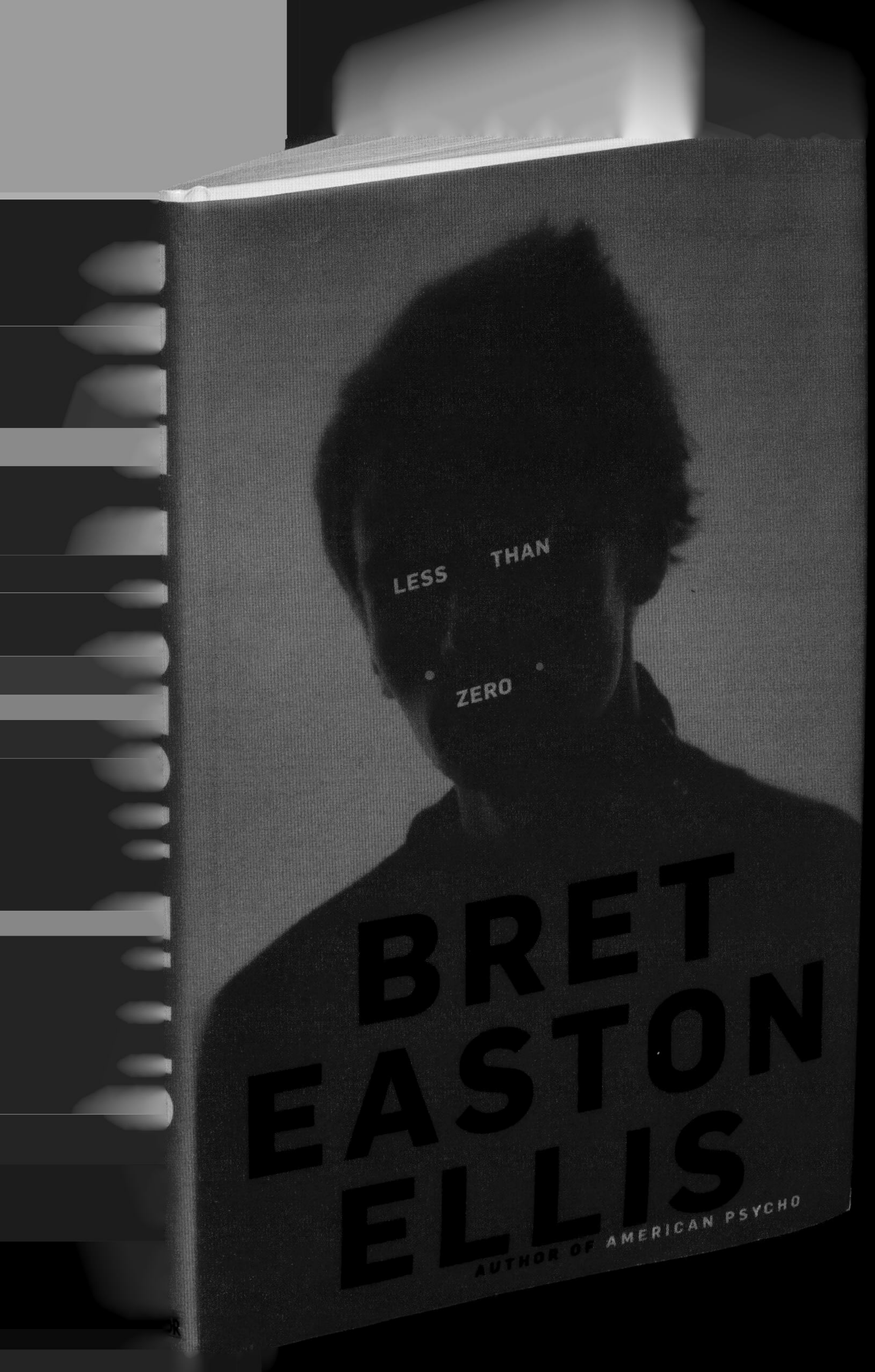
LESS THAN
ZERO
BRET
EASTON
ELLIS
AUTHOR OF AMERICAN PSYCHO

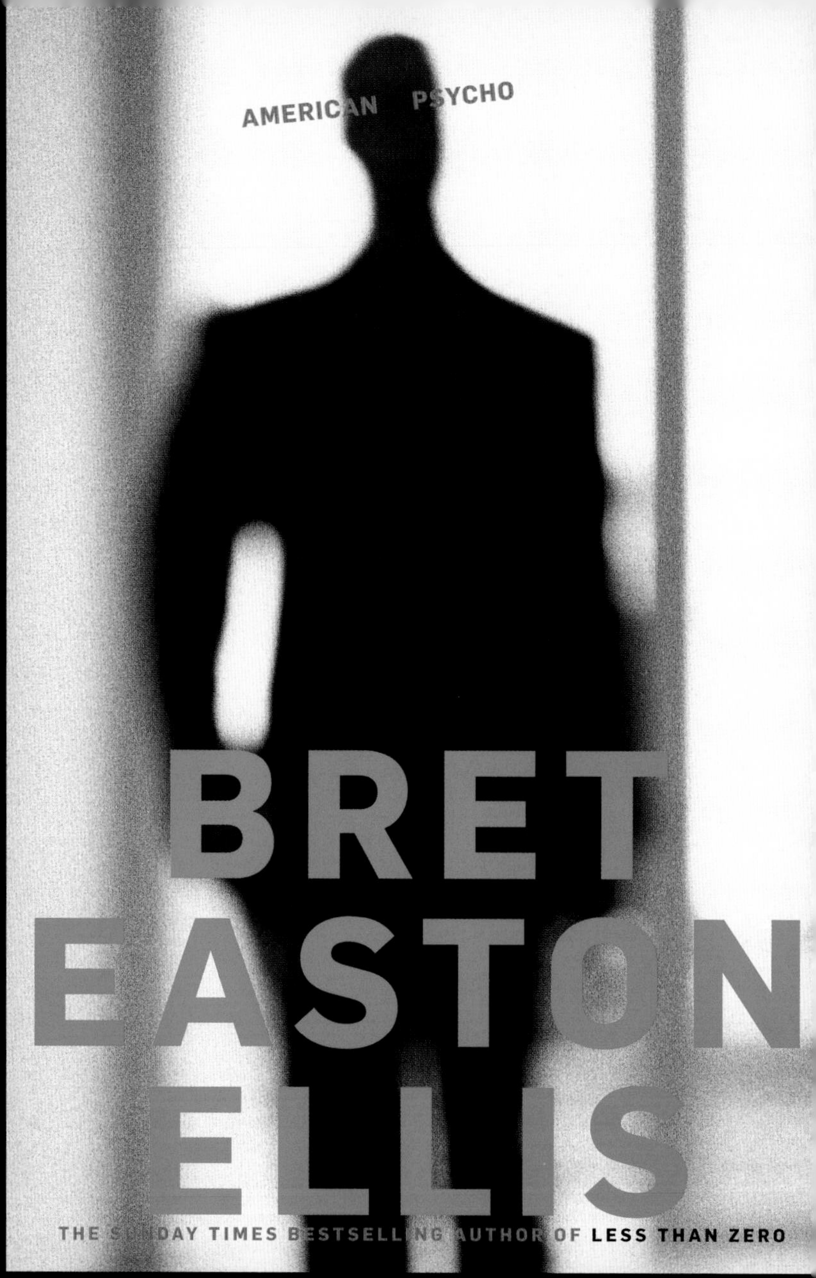
AMERICAN PSYCHO
BRET
EASTON
ELLIS
THE SUNDAY TIMES BESTSELLING AUTHOR OF LESS THAN ZERO

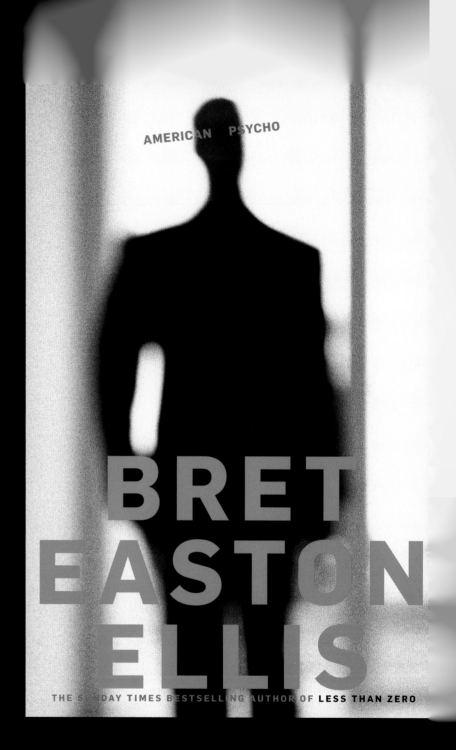

**LEFT:** My 2010 redesign of *Less Than Zero* as adapted by Picador in the UK, which added a red vellum jacket, I thought to very cool effect. **ABOVE:** I had always wanted to do my take on *American Psycho*, and with the series redesign, I finally got my chance. Aside from the red typography, I wanted to avoid any hint of blood anywhere on the cover. Picador, 2011. **OPPOSITE, RIGHT:** Knopf, 2010

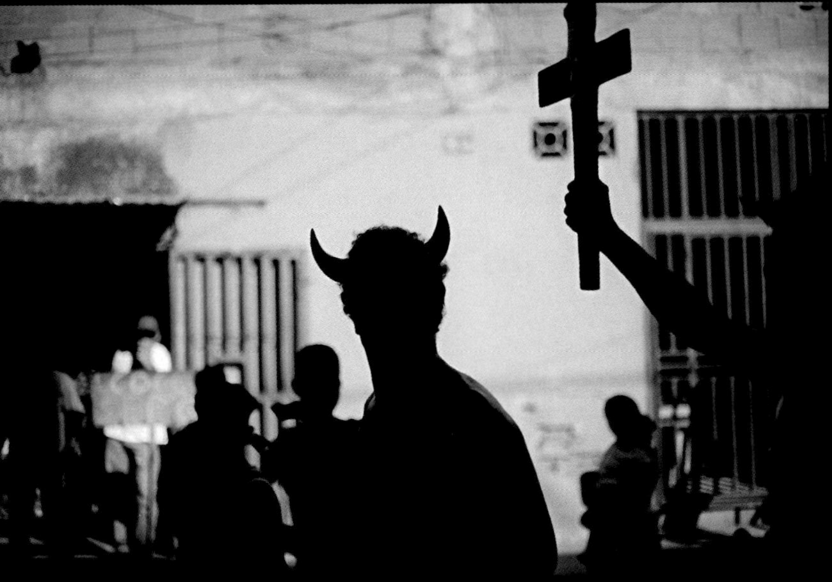

# Bedroom Eyes

*Imperial Bedrooms*, Bret Easton Ellis's sequel to his career-making iconic novel *Less Than Zero*, takes its title from yet another work by Elvis Costello. The story revisits the characters from the first book 25 years later, and the protagonist is once again Clay, who is now a writer and film producer in Los Angeles. During one particularly debauched weekend in Palm Springs, someone off-handedly likens Clay to Satan himself, and when I chanced upon this amazing photo by Christopher Anderson (above) of a mock exorcism ritual in South America, it seemed perfect. I was given permission by the artist to crop it, in order to isolate the main figure, and I felt that if I made the author name relatively huge I could get away with reducing the title to 12 points and yet strategically place it for legibility. This approach caught the eyes of Bret's publisher in the UK, and they commissioned me to adapt his backlist in this scheme (opposite, right).

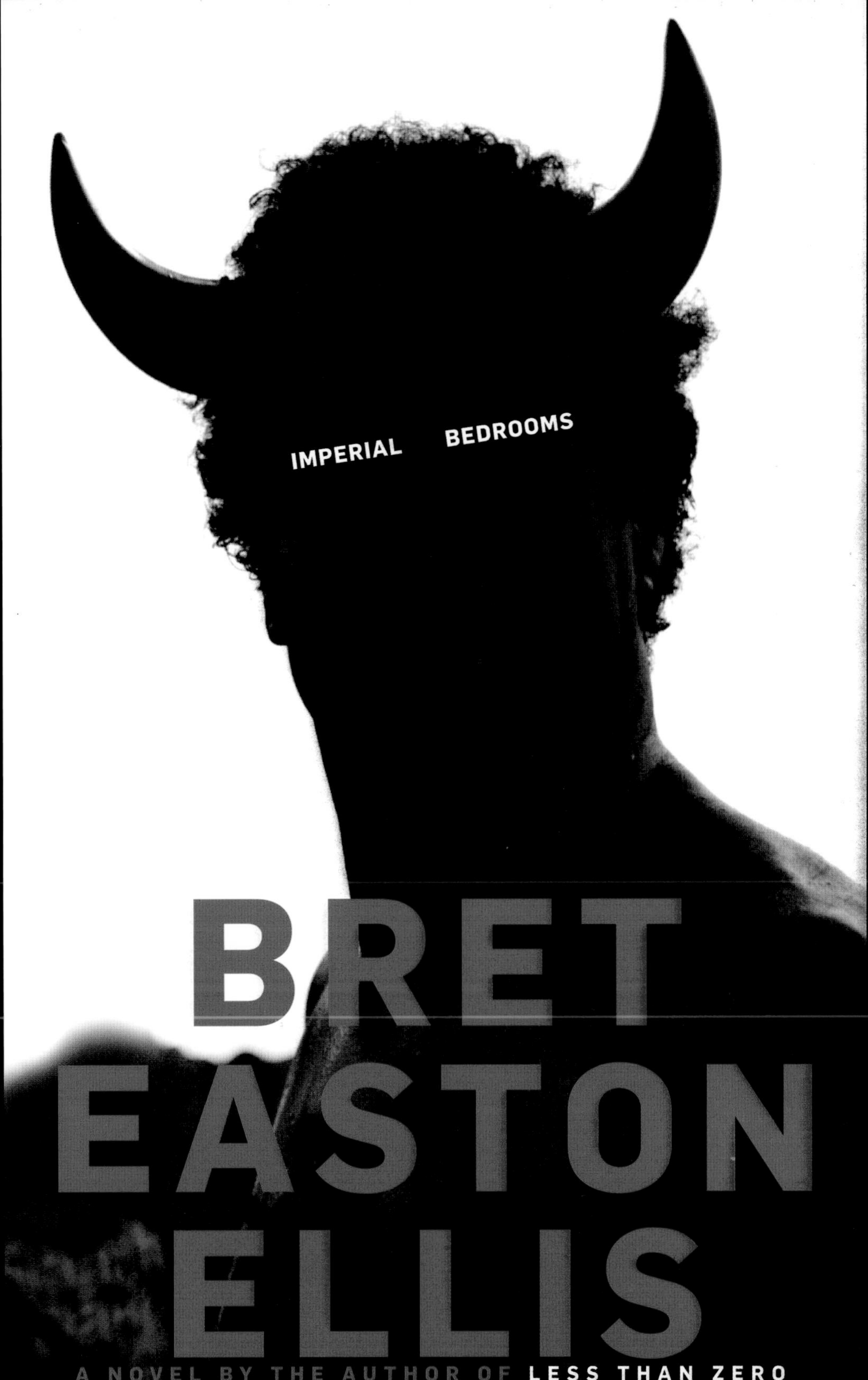

IMPERIAL BEDROOMS
BRET EASTON ELLIS
A NOVEL BY THE AUTHOR OF LESS THAN ZERO

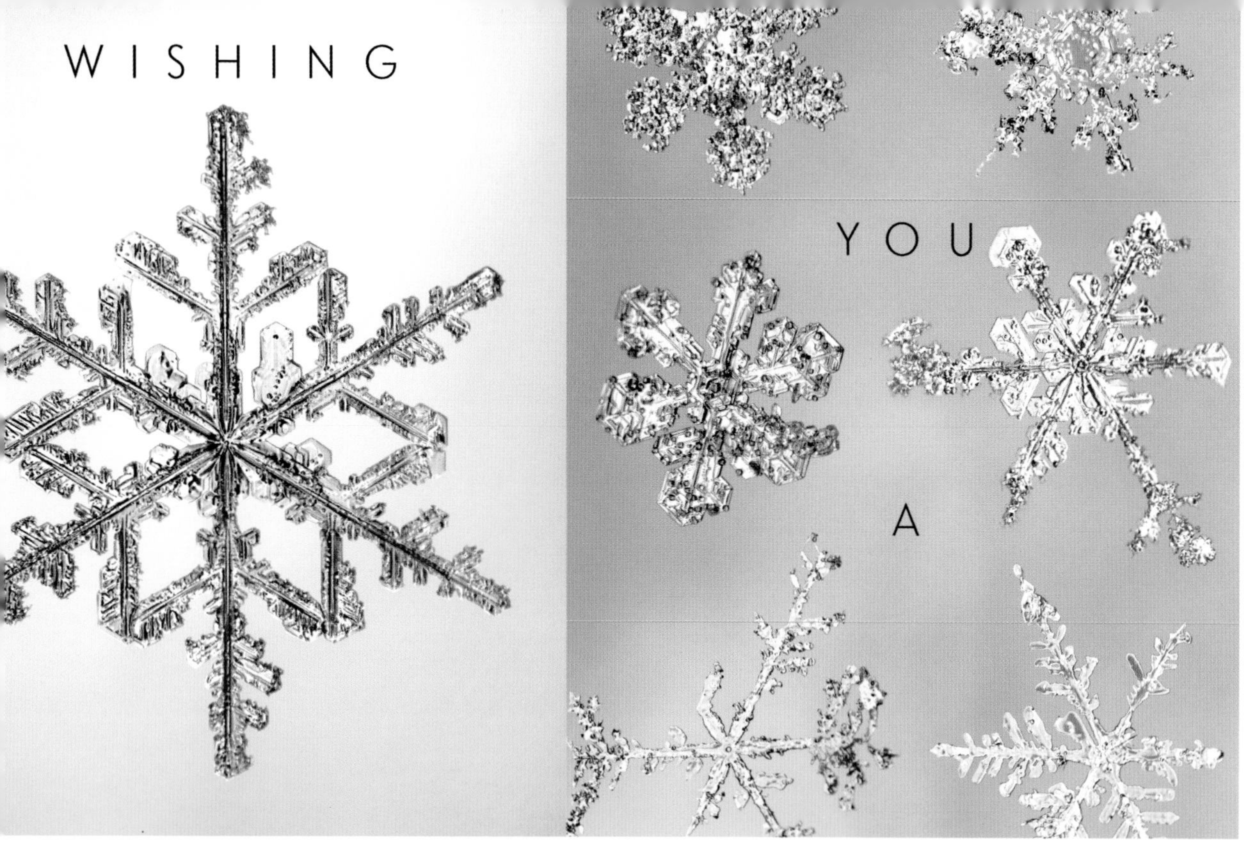
WISHING
YOU
A

## No Two Alike

One of the duties you are charged with when you win the National Design Award for Communications (pp. 214–15) is designing the annual holiday card for the Cooper-Hewitt, a branch of the Smithsonian in New York City. At the time (2008) I'd become quite taken with the remarkable photographs that artists Mike and Doug Starn were taking of snowflakes.

As you can imagine, it's not an easy thing to do, and to this day I have no idea how they made them, but the results are stunning—perfect examples of what can only be called natural design. I had admired the Starns' work for decades, but this was a whole new side of their talent, and they graciously donated the use of these images for the National Design Museum.

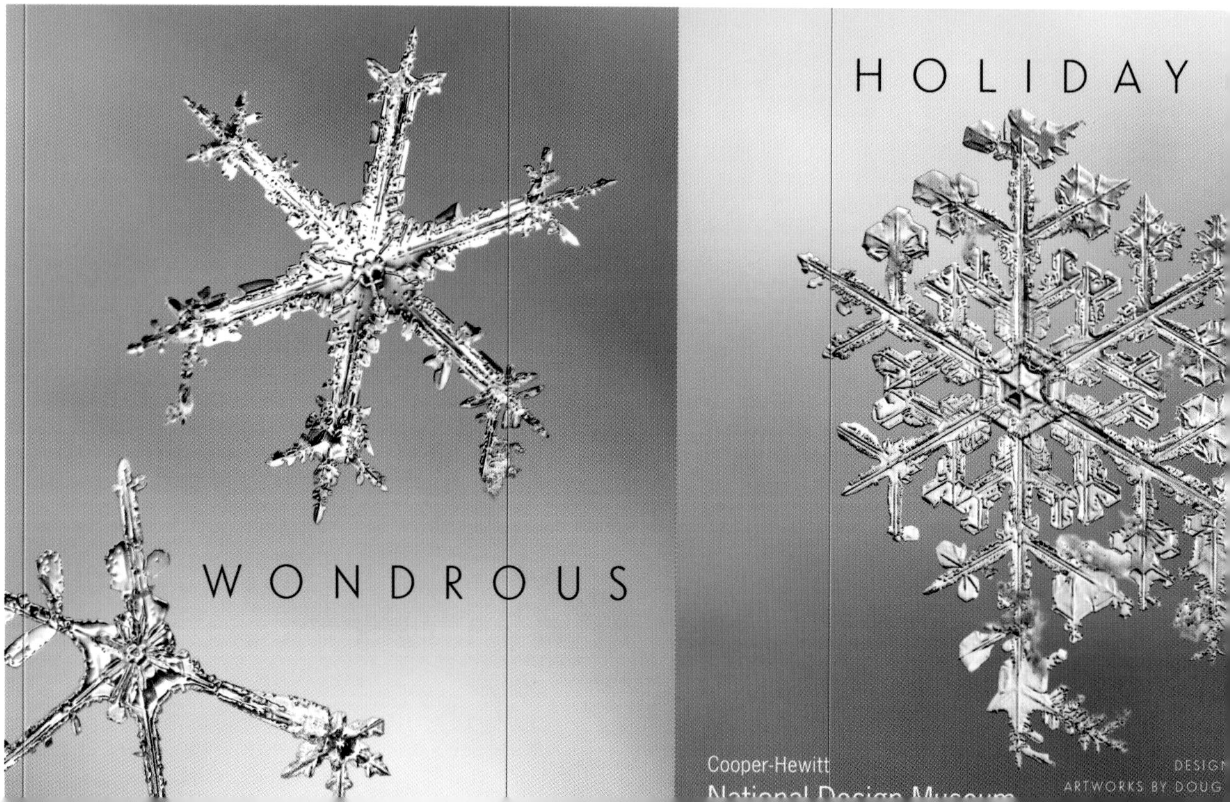
HOLIDAY
WONDROUS
Cooper-Hewitt
ARTWORKS BY DOUG

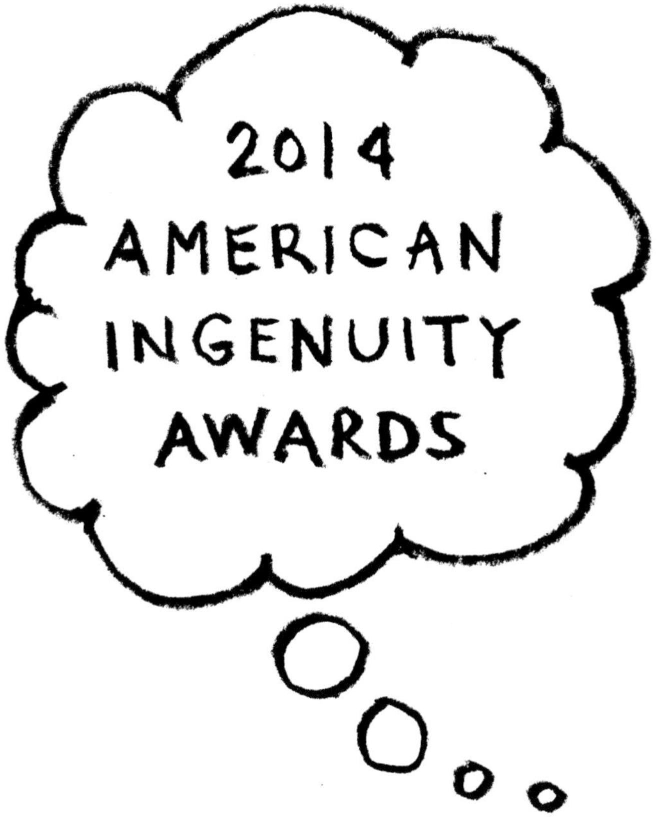
2014
AMERICAN
INGENUITY
AWARDS

## Think Something Up!

Speaking of the Smithsonian, the museum wanted a cover design for its magazine to honor the American Ingenuity Awards, a celebration of the year's great ideas.

Now, I know using a glowing light bulb to represent an idea is a total cliché, but I'd hoped that making the filament into a special custom shape would help the resulting image transcend the ordinary. Geoff Spear came to the rescue, as always. Back in my flea-market-haunting days, I used to see vintage light bulbs from the '20s and '30s that had these fantastic novelty filaments shaped like all sorts of things, from licensed characters like Mickey Mouse to flowers, stars, animals, and so on. I'd never seen one in the outline of the United States of America, but that was definitely called for here.

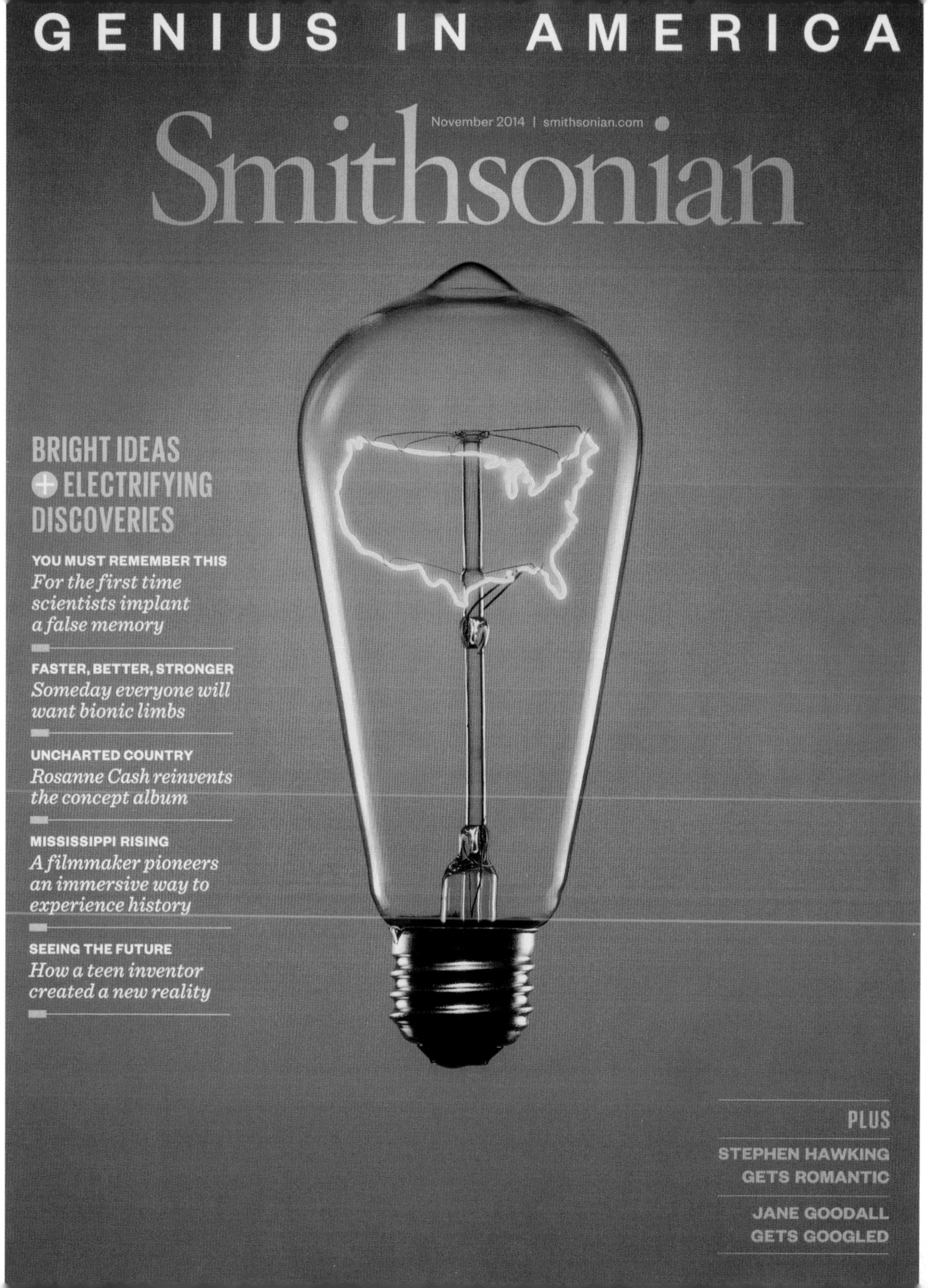
GENIUS IN AMERICA
November 2014 | smithsonian.com
Smithsonian
BRIGHT IDEAS
+ ELECTRIFYING
DISCOVERIES
YOU MUST REMEMBER THIS
For the first time scientists implant a false memory
FASTER, BETTER, STRONGER
Someday everyone will want bionic limbs
UNCHARTED COUNTRY
Rosanne Cash reinvents the concept album
MISSISSIPPI RISING
A filmmaker pioneers an immersive way to experience history
SEEING THE FUTURE
How a teen inventor created a new reality
PLUS
STEPHEN HAWKING GETS ROMANTIC
JANE GOODALL GETS GOOGLED

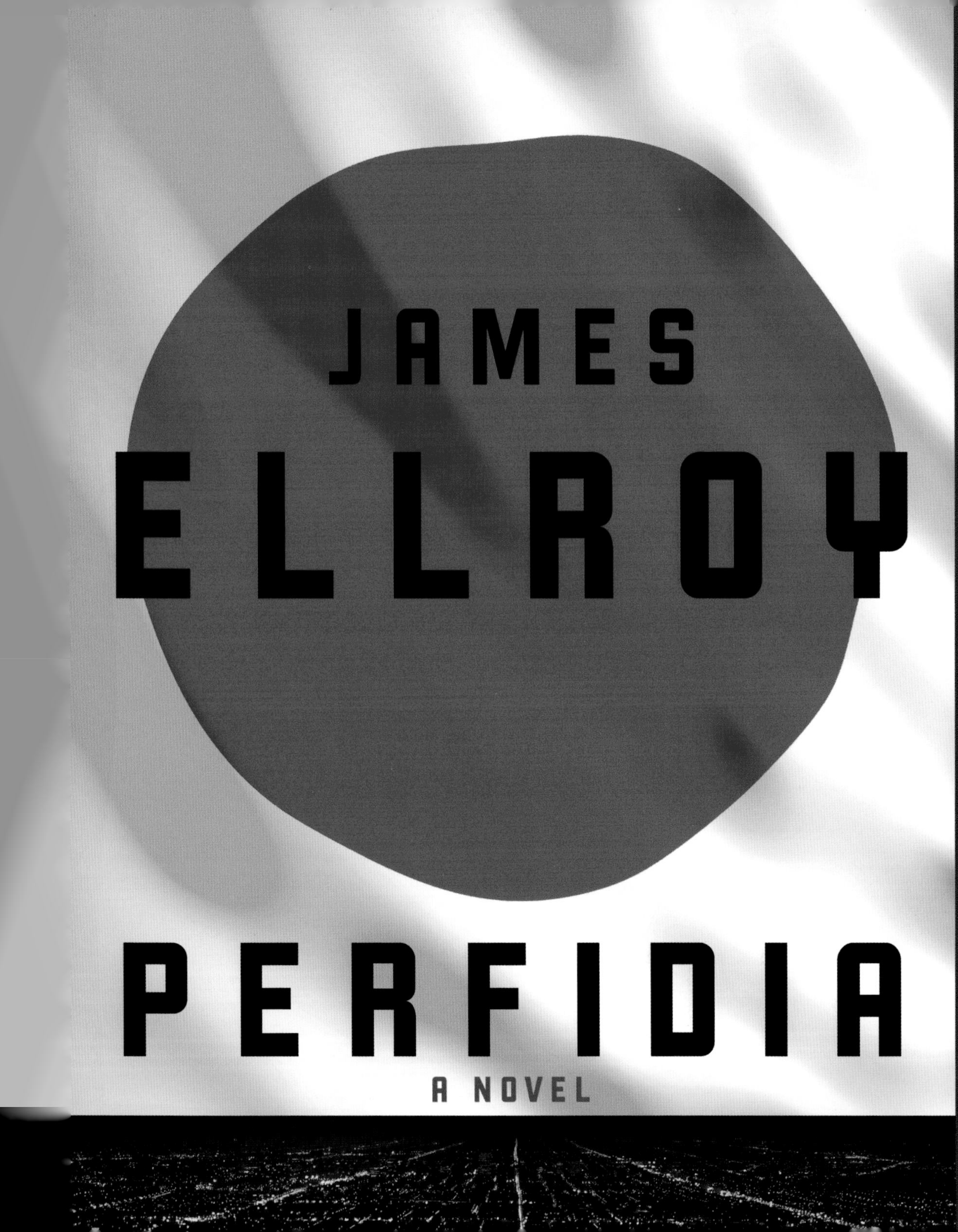
JAMES
ELLROY
PERFIDIA
A NOVEL

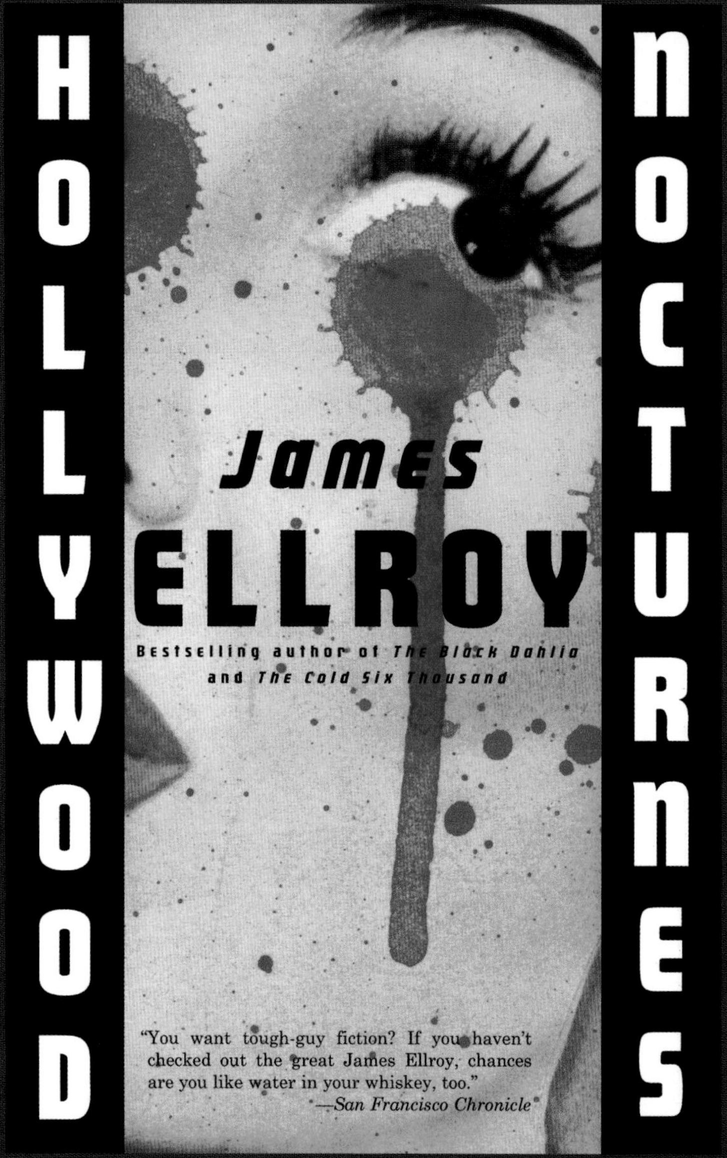
HOLLYWOOD
NOCTURNES
James
ELLROY
Bestselling author of The Black Dahlia
and The Cold Six Thousand
"You want tough-guy fiction? If you haven't checked out the great James Ellroy, chances are you like water in your whiskey, too."
—San Francisco Chronicle

## Blood, Simple

Novelist James Ellroy, as ever, remains a friend and colleague. His 2004 book, *Perfidia* (left), is about the effect that the events of Pearl Harbor on December 7, 1941, had on the Japanese American community in Los Angeles. All wrapped around a murder investigation, of course, which happens to be conducted by a Japanese American detective in the LAPD. It gets complicated

For the redesign of the Vintage paperback edition of James's short story collection *Hollywood Nocturnes* (opposite, right), I broke my "no splattered blood" rule. But at least the viscera in question has landed onto a movie poster from the '50s (not telling which one) and thus is taken out of context.

*Blood's a Rover* (right) is one of James's epic L.A. period novels, and since "Blood" was in the title, that freed me from having to show any. This became a classic case of a photographer (Jean Nathan) coming into the office at just the right time to show me her portfolio during a cold call, and me paying attention. This stop-motion image of a car turning onto an intersection in downtown L.A. had just the right feel, those red tail lights a great metaphor for moving blood. It was perfect—we just had to retouch a few details so that it would suit the time period of the novel. James, of course, knew exactly which intersection this was and how it had changed. For example, the name of the hotel is now obscured, but not in a casually noticeable way.

**OPPOSITE, LEFT:** Knopf, 2014.
**OPPOSITE, RIGHT:** Vintage, 2007.
**RIGHT:** Knopf, 2009.

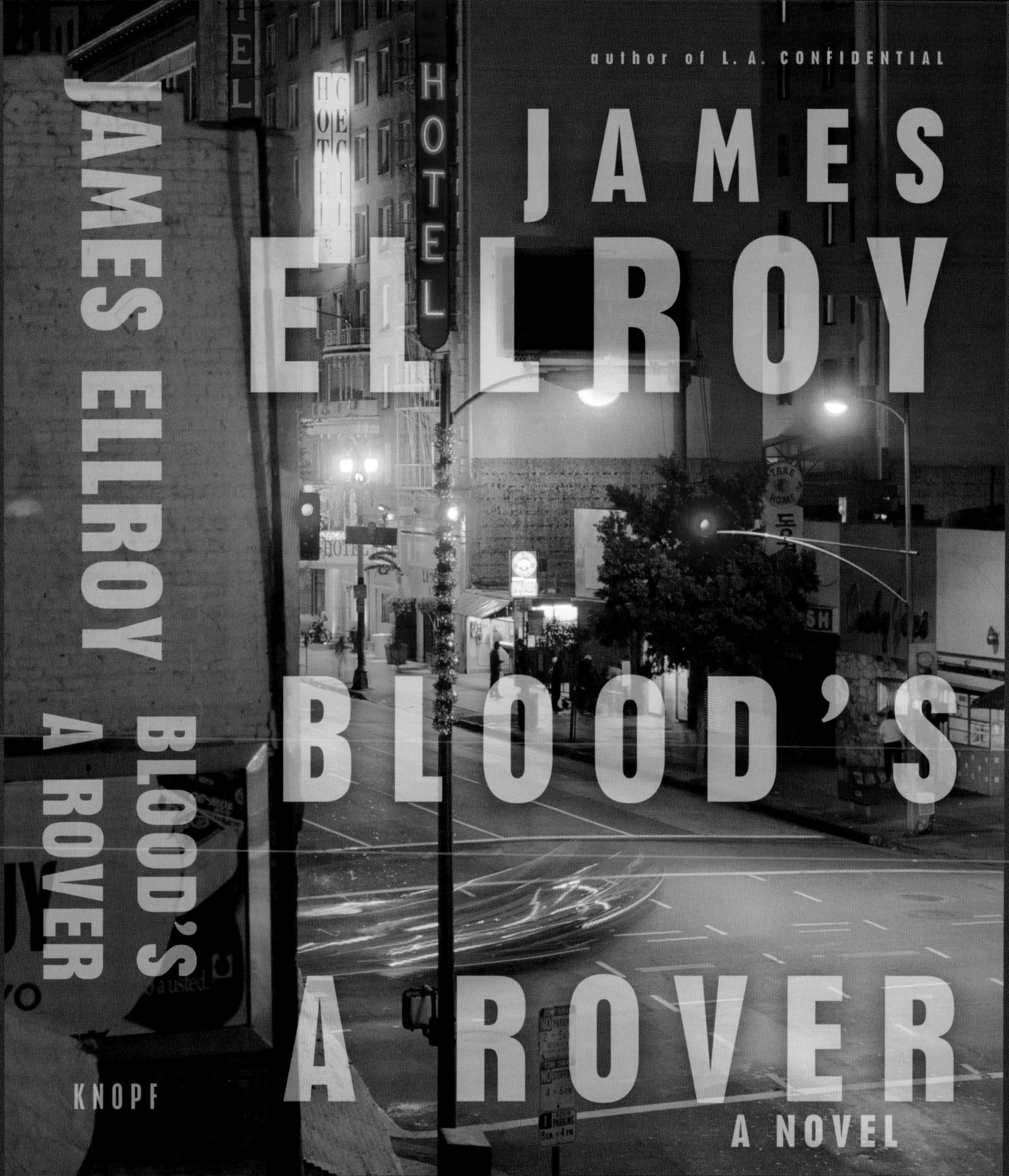
JAMES ELLROY
BLOOD'S A ROVER
KNOPF
author of L.A. CONFIDENTIAL
JAMES
ELLROY
BLOOD'S
A ROVER
A NOVEL

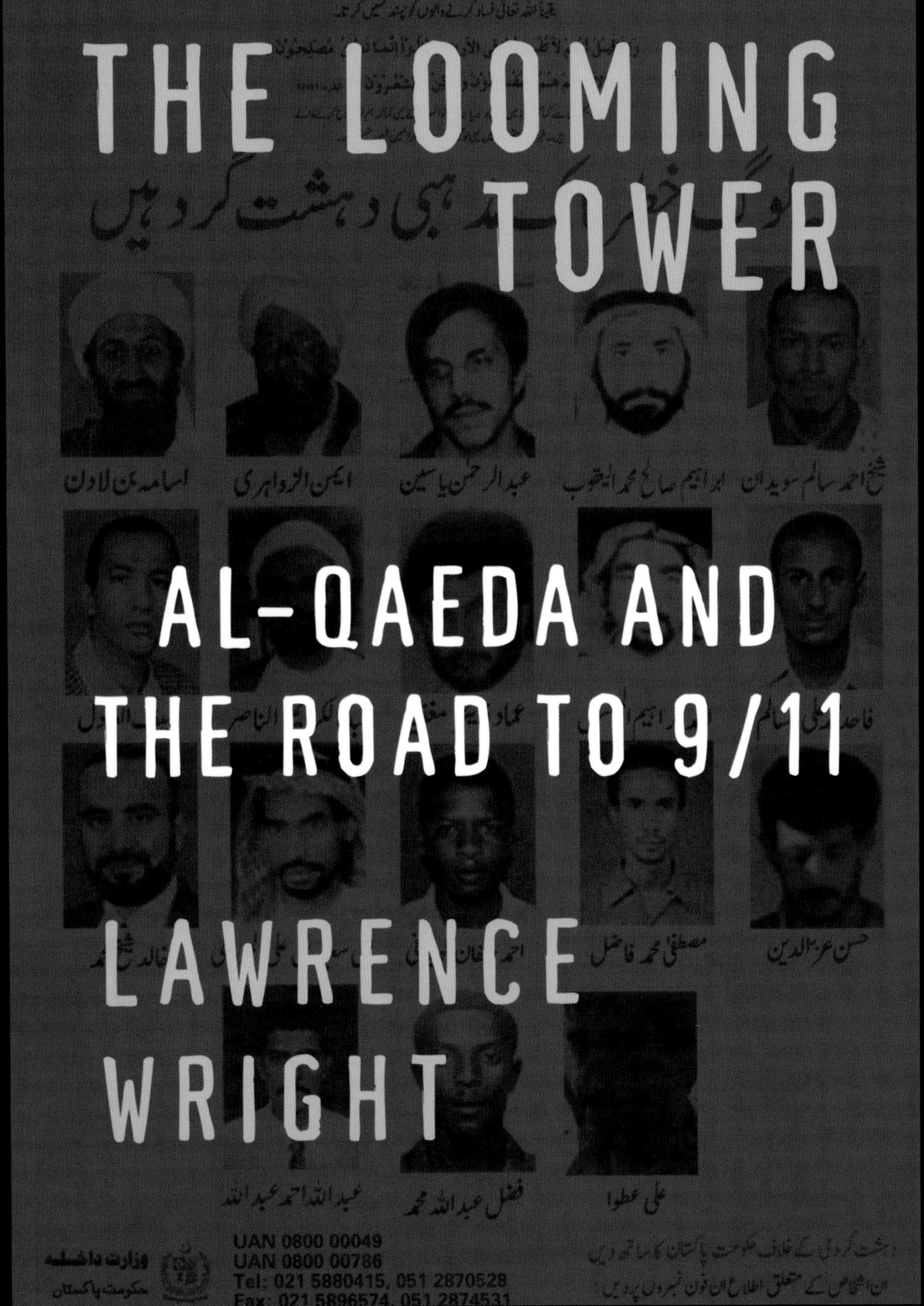
THE LOOMING TOWER
AL-QAEDA AND THE ROAD TO 9/11
LAWRENCE WRIGHT

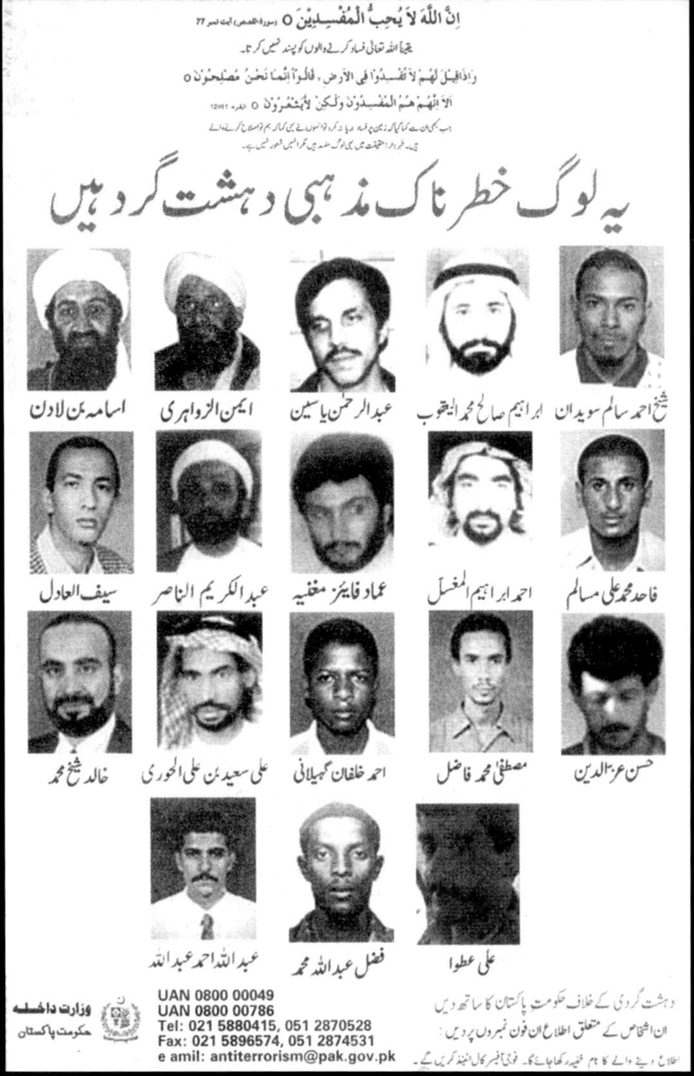
یہ لوگ خطرناک مذہبی دہشت گرد ہیں
UAN 0800 00049
UAN 0800 00786
Tel: 021 5880415, 051 2870528
Fax: 021 5896574, 051 2874531
e amil: antiterrorism@pak.gov.pk

## Never Forget

For Lawrence Wright's groundbreaking (and Pulitzer Prize–winning) account of the events leading up to September 11, 2001, *The Looming Tower*, the question became: what would best symbolize this event? Showing the World Trade Towers disintegrating was out of the question; that image had become too overexposed and heartbreaking (see pp. 50–51). The answer, after a lot of digging, became literally the world's ultimate "wanted" poster (above) for those involved.

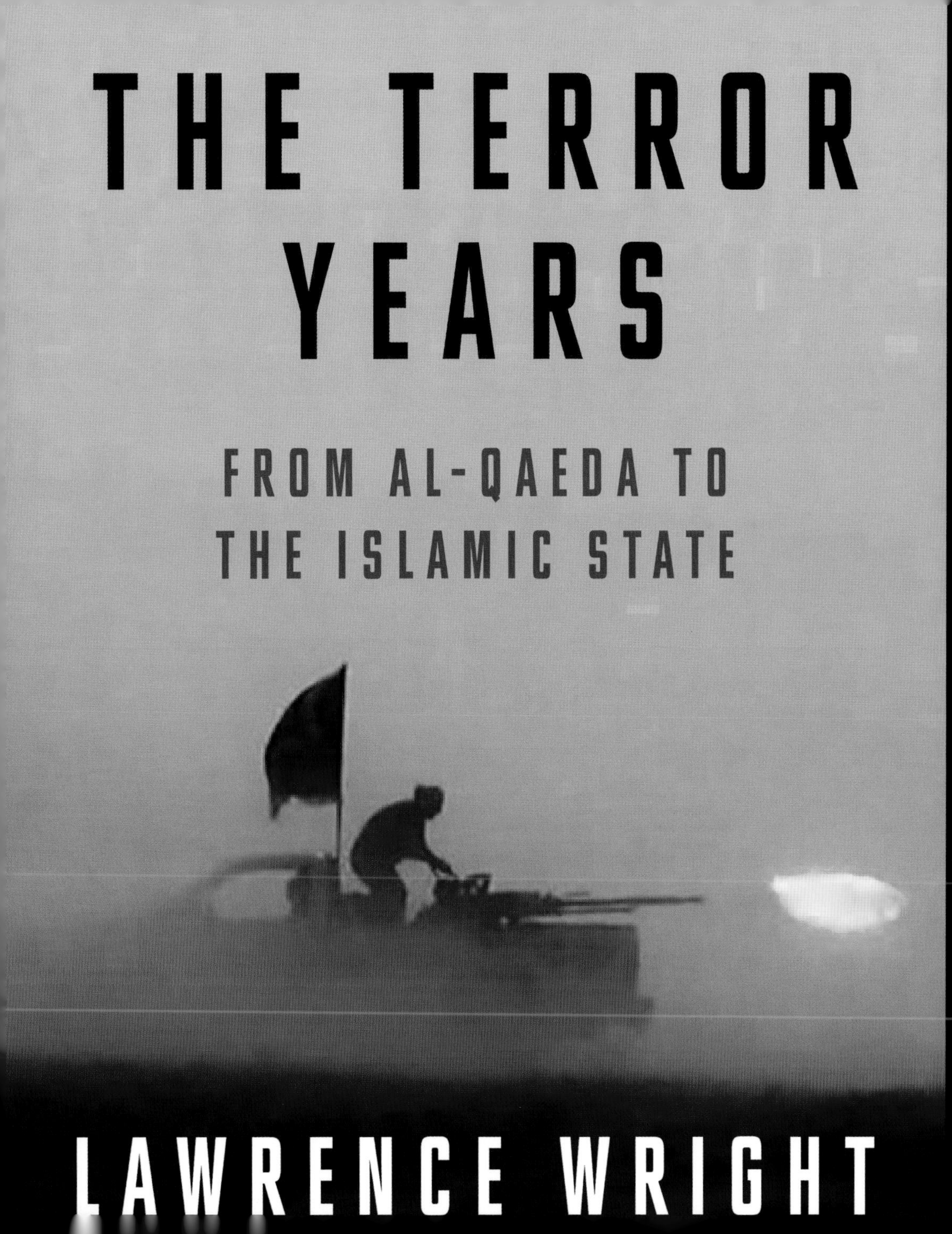
THE TERROR YEARS
FROM AL-QAEDA TO THE ISLAMIC STATE
LAWRENCE WRIGHT

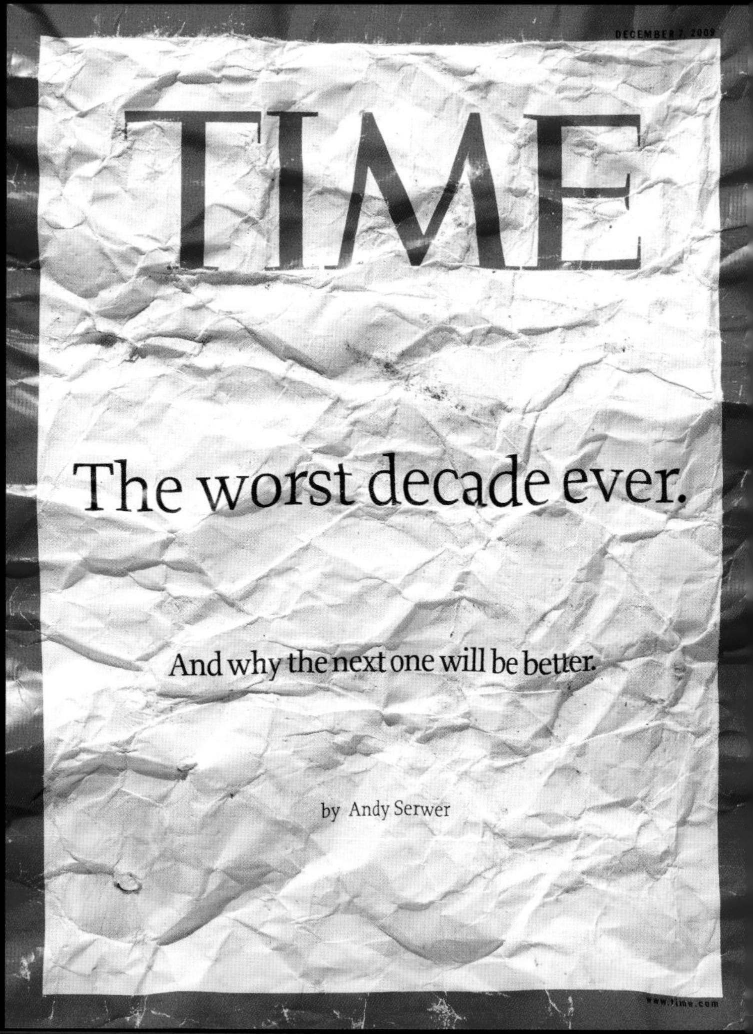
TIME
The worst decade ever.
And why the next one will be better.
by Andy Serwer

*The Terror Years* is a collection of Wright's recent pieces on how terrorism has evolved in the last two decades. The image is from a news telecast in the Middle East from 2016.

Above is an unused commission from *Time* magazine to close out the first decade of the 21st century. I'd wanted to execute this idea for years, but the right project hadn't come along. This almost made it except at the eleventh hour they got nervous that subscribers would think their copies had gotten ruined in the mail and complain. Wors

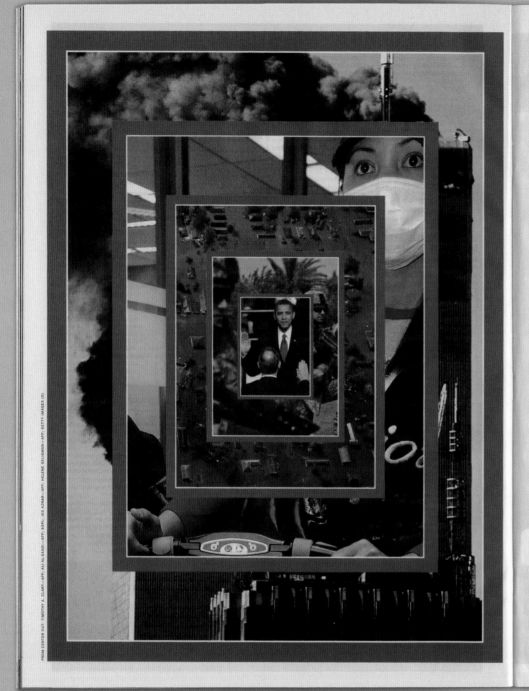

FROM CENTER OUT: TIMOTHY A. CLARY—AFP; ALI AL-SAADI—AFP; JES AZNAR—AFP; ESPL; JES AZNAR—AFP; HELENE SELIGMAN—AFP; GETTY IMAGES (5)

# TimeFrames

The end of history? More like the start. The 21st century runs on fast-forward, and the only way to keep up is to stop and figure out what really happened  By Nancy Gibbs

L IFE FELT FINE IN 1999. CRIME HAD FALLEN, stocks had soared, the Treasury was running a surplus, and we asked *Who Wants to Be a Millionaire* several nights a week. Our worries came down to this: Were there bugs in our computers that would bring our happy little worlds crashing down on us precisely at midnight on Dec. 31, 1999? "Millennium Countdown: Whole planet of apocalyptic possibilities—starting with Russian power stations," ran a headline in the London *Independent*.

We thought we got a reprieve. JUST Y2KIDDING, announced the Bergen County, New Jersey, paper, as the lights stayed on, banks didn't fail, planes didn't fall from the sky, cities didn't tumble into the sea. At least, not right away. It took more time for the bubbles to burst and markets to plunge and cities to drown, for faith in institutions to collapse—the banks, the court, the church, the intelligence community, the press and finally the government, which nearly 1 in 3 people now say they "almost never" trust to do the right thing.

But that is only half the story. As the mighty were falling, the lowly were able to rise, in the most immense devolution of power from institutions to individuals in all of human history. We're swapping careers as old industries die, retraining, networking, self-branding, writing apps. The constant hustle is less secure but more exhilarating: you want to be a crime fighter, a software engineer, a video star, a music sensation, a day trader, an entrepreneur, a journalist—the gatekeepers have had to hand over the keys.

The first decade of the 21st century moved so fast that it was easy, as the poet said, to have the experience but miss the meaning. It's hard to find the truth about the age of truthiness, of truthers and birthers and reality customized by ideology. So TimeFrames is our attempt to stop the clock, slow down, look back, see what comes into focus only from a distance. We know what happened in the past 10 years. But what really happened? Who gained power, and who lost it? Who's richer? Who's poorer? Who were the visionaries? Who were the rogues? And how do we find the music or the meaning in the noise of the news? ∎

**Artwork by Chip Kidd for TIME**

… But other *Time* projects have seen the light of day. The illustration above opened the lead story of the same issue, a summing up of the events of 2000–10. The "Time 100" (opposite) is a rethinking of the idea of the "Fortune 500," as it deals with influential news-making achievements rather than money-making. To me, the answer was obvious: 100 covers within a single cover, and I sent the basic schematic to get the idea approved (opposite, bottom). But I had another, far more interesting idea that I couldn't resist

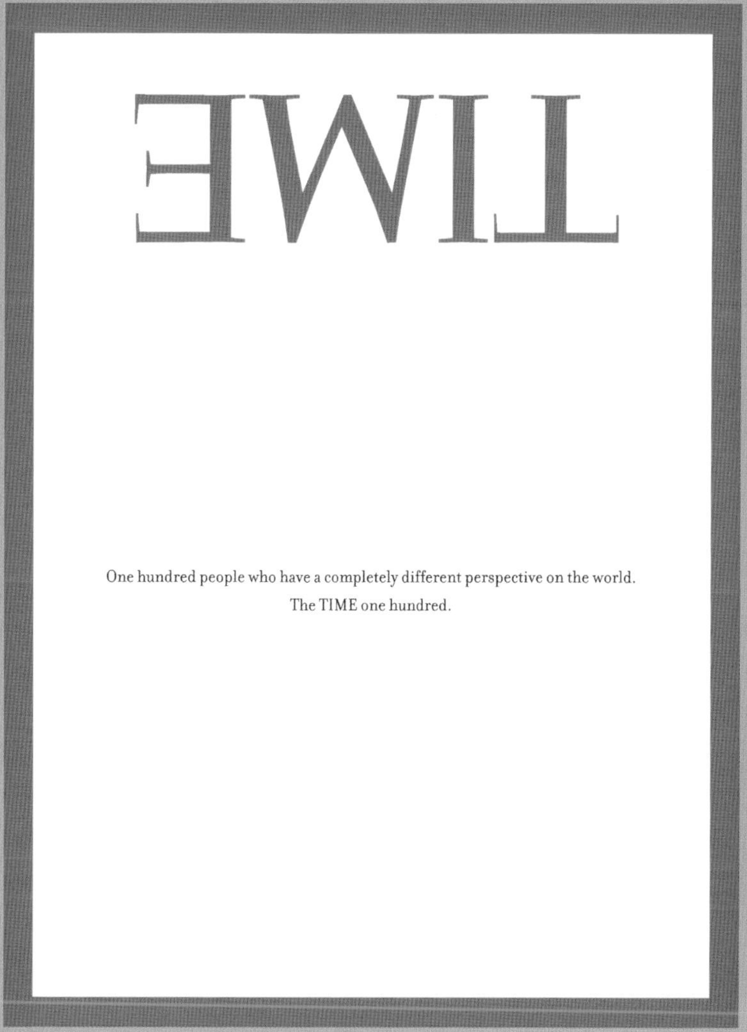
TIME
One hundred people who have a completely different perspective on the world.
The TIME one hundred.

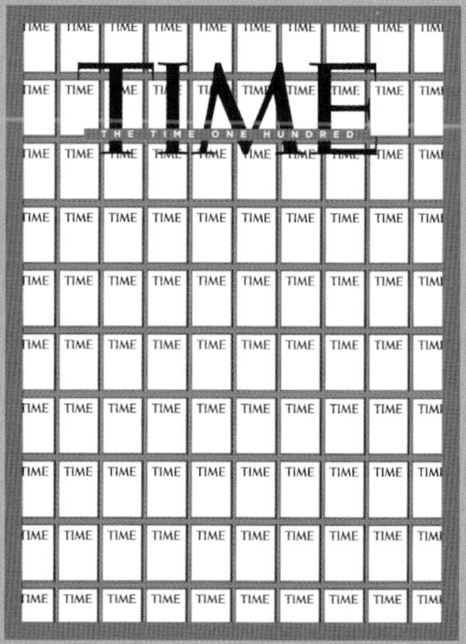
TIME
THE TIME ONE HUNDRED

sending to them, too (above). I wrote the copy to justify turning the logo upside-down. I knew this was a long shot, and indeed they went with the cover at right. But they appreciated the gesture and said the editorial staff was lobbying for the more radical one. It never hurts to give the client something to think about.

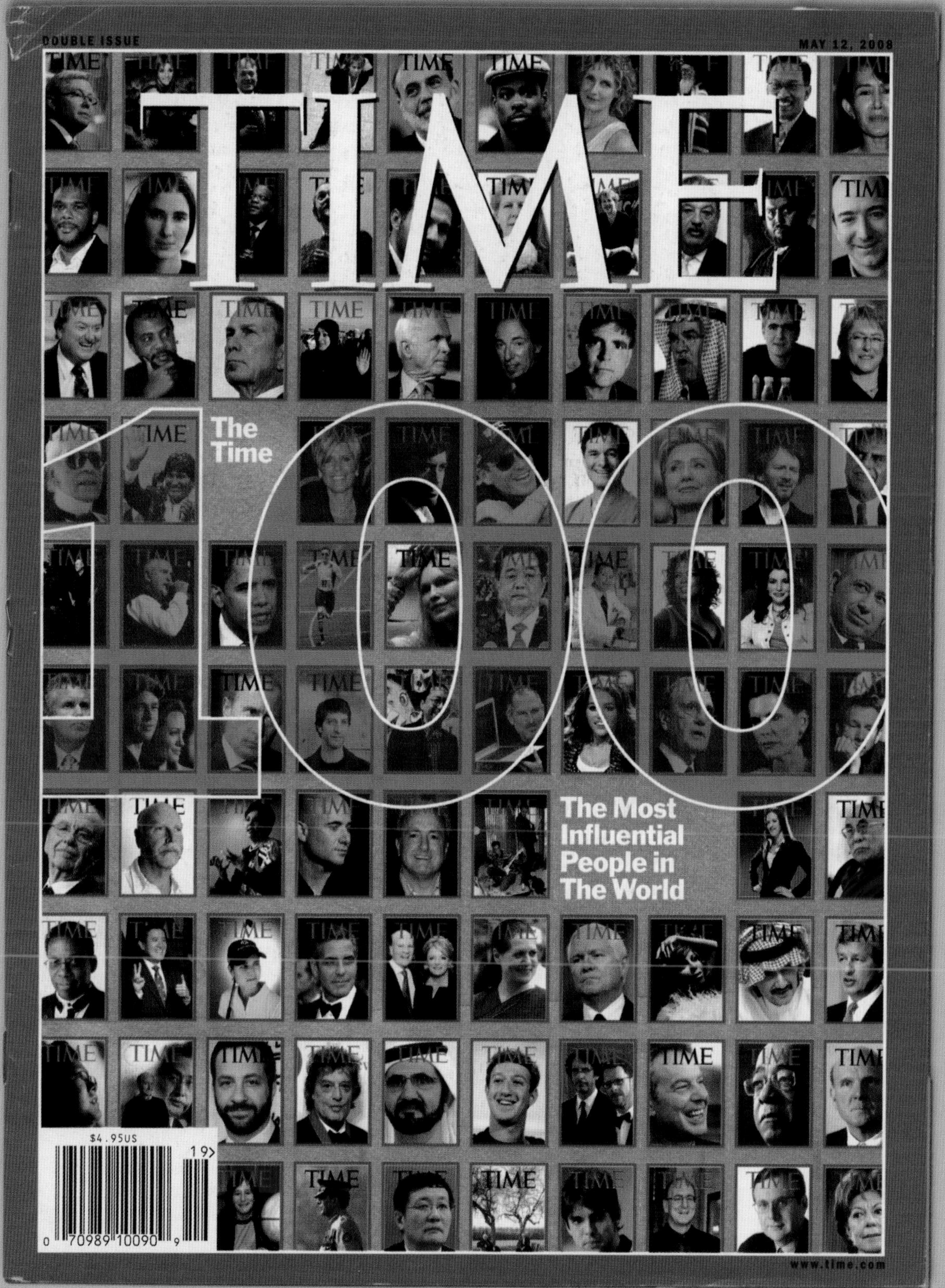
DOUBLE ISSUE
MAY 12, 2008
TIME
The Time
100
The Most Influential People in The World
$4.95US
www.time.com

# Divine Authors & Heavenly Prose

*Wired* magazine ran a science-fiction feature asking writers to create six-word stories along the line of Ernest Hemingway's classic "For sale: baby shoes, never worn." They managed to entice an amazing little group of talent and asked me to design the spread. My take on it was that a story that short would fit on the spine of a book, so I just designed a bunch of them, printed them out, wrapped them around books, and Geoff shot a stack of stories. Voilà! (The same basic concept was used for the Boston Book Festival poster, paired with maps, p. 146). Very cheekily, I slipped in one for me and one for Geoff underneath Alan Moore's.

The gist of both the review of Robert Wright's *The Evolution of God* and the book itself is that for a lot of worshipers, the concept of the wrath of the Almighty has eased up considerably. I mean, just look at the first sentence of the review.

Working with then-art director of the *New York Times Book Review* (and old friend) Nicholas Blechmann, initially I wanted to show a photograph of Our Father sending down a lightning bolt from the heavens made of stuffed yellow felt (opposite, center). This just wasn't working—it merely looked like exactly what it was: some guy in his backyard getting ready to hurl a jagged golden pillow like a Nerf ball.

The concept was right, the execution was wrong, time was running out, and I had to just take one for the team and—*gulp*—draw it myself (opposite, bottom & right), making the bolt into a balloon for good measure. This is yet another example of how illustration can work so differently from photography. You can take so many more liberties with it to get the right visual message across.

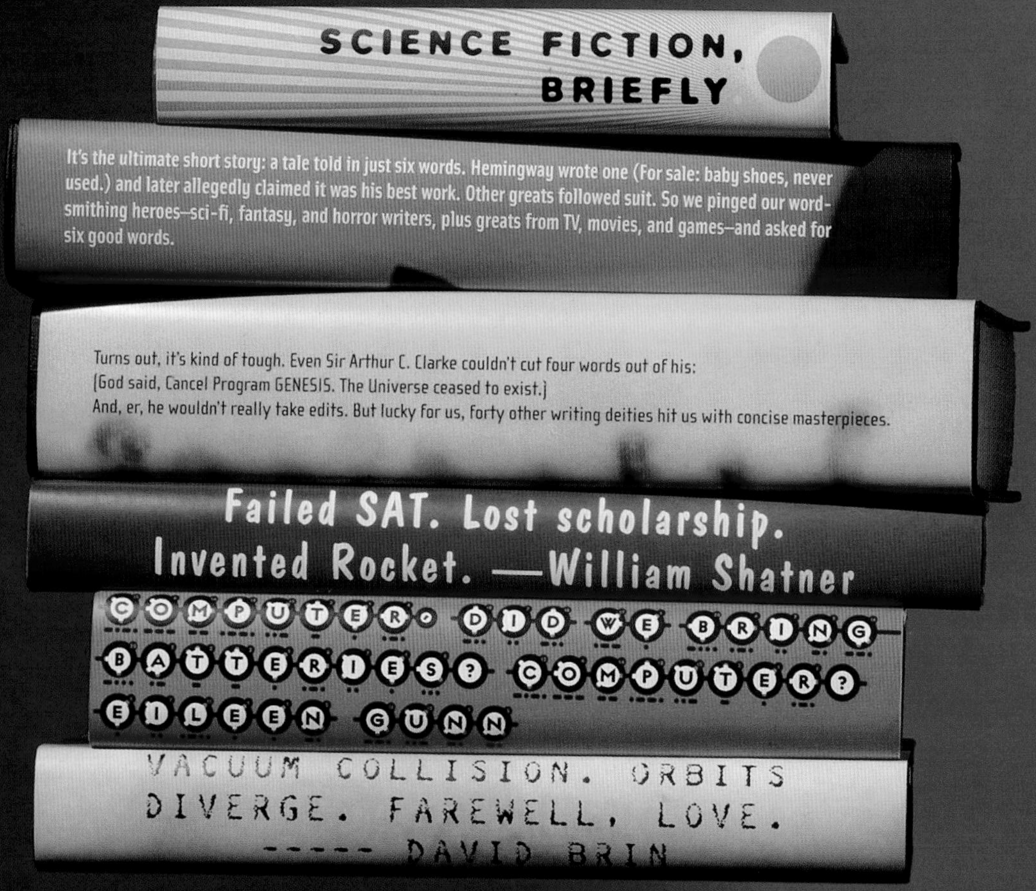
SCIENCE FICTION, BRIEFLY
It's the ultimate short story: a tale told in just six words. Hemingway wrote one (For sale: baby shoes, never used.) and later allegedly claimed it was his best work. Other greats followed suit. So we pinged our wordsmithing heroes—sci-fi, fantasy, and horror writers, plus greats from TV, movies, and games—and asked for six good words.
Turns out, it's kind of tough. Even Sir Arthur C. Clarke couldn't cut four words out of his: (God said, Cancel Program GENESIS. The Universe ceased to exist.) And, er, he wouldn't really take edits. But lucky for us, forty other writing deities hit us with concise masterpieces.
Failed SAT. Lost scholarship. Invented Rocket. —William Shatner
COMPUTER. DID WE BRING BATTERIES? COMPUTER? EILEEN GUNN
VACUUM COLLISION. ORBITS DIVERGE. FAREWELL, LOVE. ----- DAVID BRIN

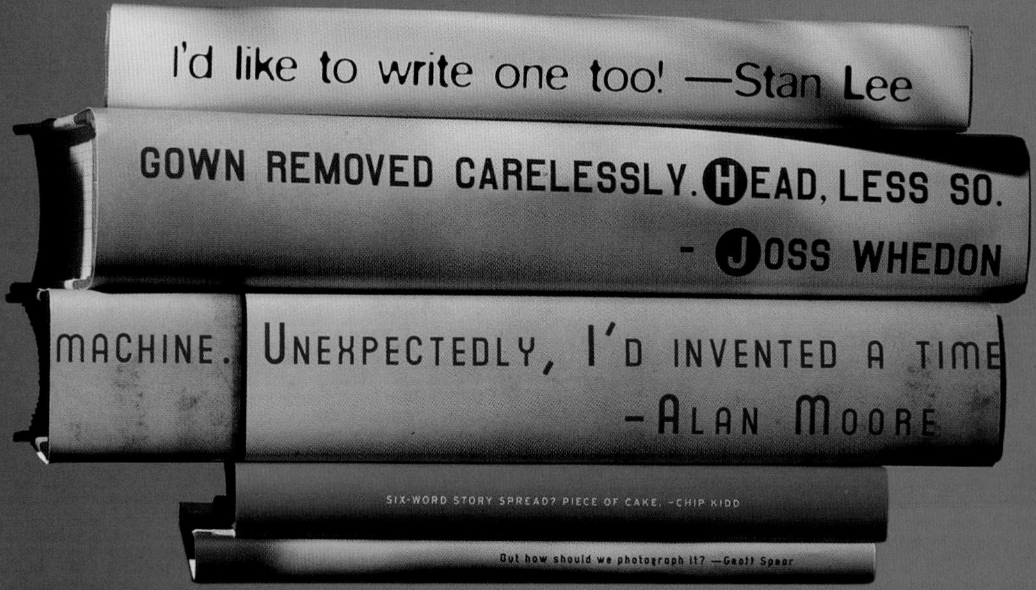
I'd like to write one too! —Stan Lee
GOWN REMOVED CARELESSLY. HEAD, LESS SO. - JOSS WHEDON
MACHINE.
UNEXPECTEDLY, I'D INVENTED A TIME -ALAN MOORE
SIX-WORD STORY SPREAD? PIECE OF CAKE. -CHIP KIDD
But how should we photograph it? —Geoff Spear

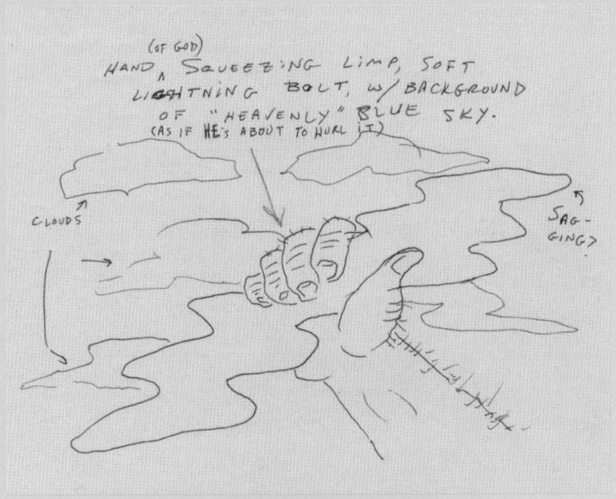
(OF GOD)
HAND, SQUEEZING LIMP, SOFT
LIGHTNING BOLT, W/ BACKGROUND
OF "HEAVENLY" BLUE SKY.
(AS IF HE'S ABOUT TO HURL IT)
CLOUDS
SAG-
GING?

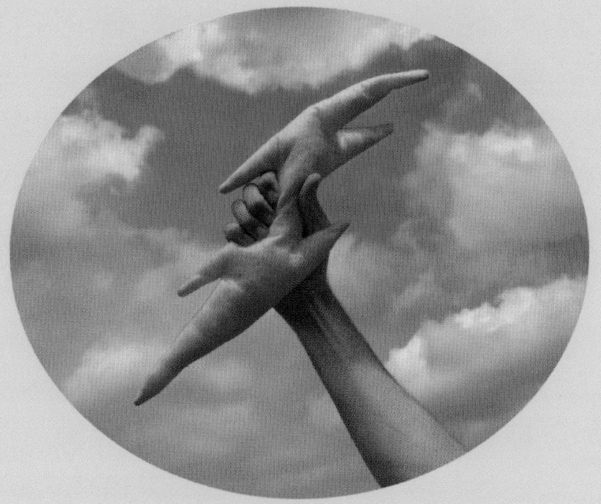

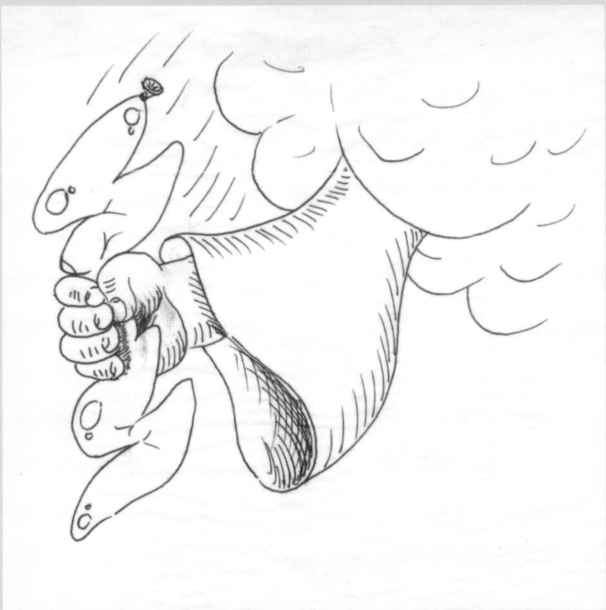

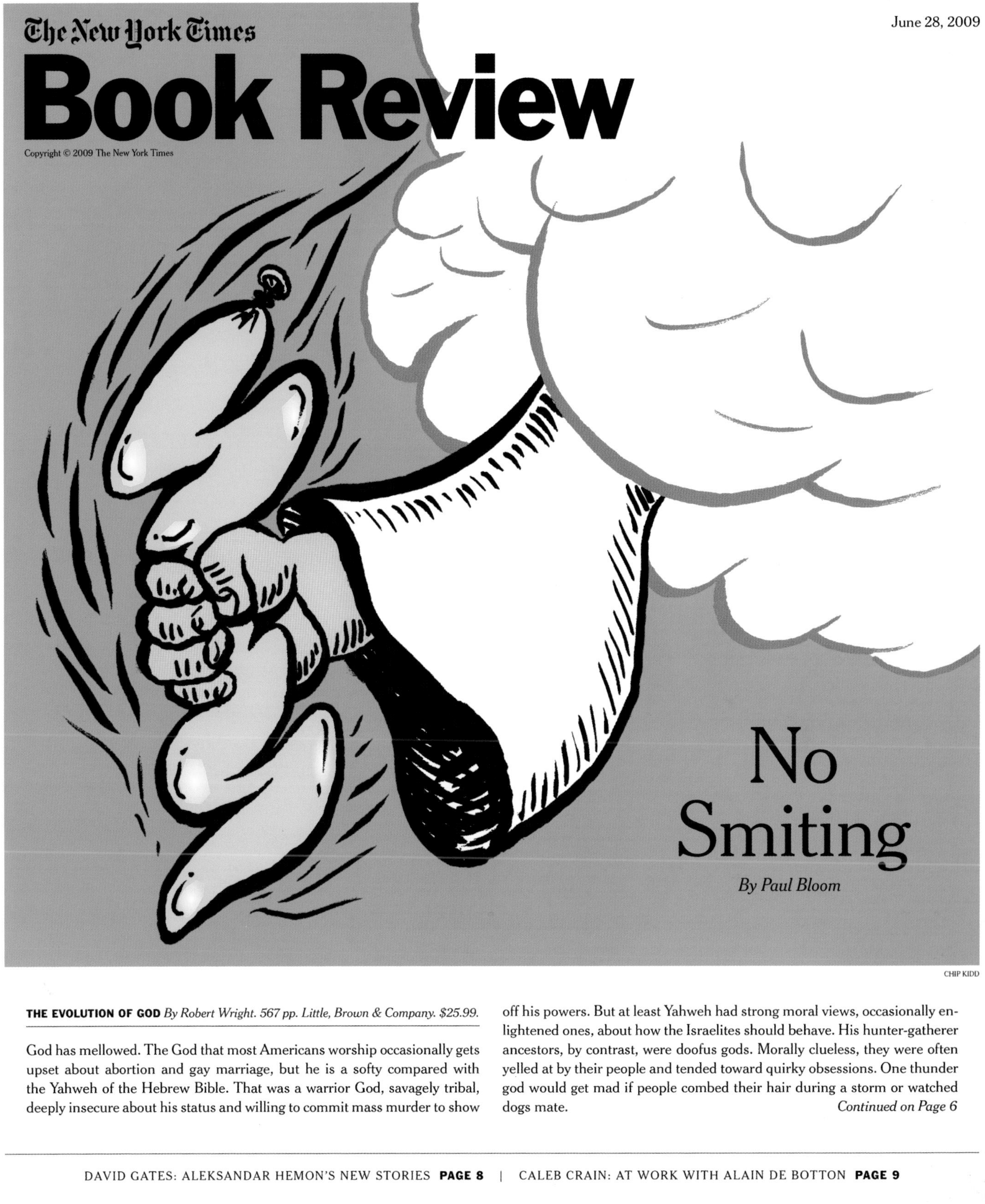

The New York Times

# Book Review

June 28, 2009

Copyright © 2009 The New York Times

## No Smiting

*By Paul Bloom*

CHIP KIDD

**THE EVOLUTION OF GOD** *By Robert Wright. 567 pp. Little, Brown & Company. $25.99.*

God has mellowed. The God that most Americans worship occasionally gets upset about abortion and gay marriage, but he is a softy compared with the Yahweh of the Hebrew Bible. That was a warrior God, savagely tribal, deeply insecure about his status and willing to commit mass murder to show off his powers. But at least Yahweh had strong moral views, occasionally enlightened ones, about how the Israelites should behave. His hunter-gatherer ancestors, by contrast, were doofus gods. Morally clueless, they were often yelled at by their people and tended toward quirky obsessions. One thunder god would get mad if people combed their hair during a storm or watched dogs mate.

*Continued on Page 6*

DAVID GATES: ALEKSANDAR HEMON'S NEW STORIES **PAGE 8** | CALEB CRAIN: AT WORK WITH ALAIN DE BOTTON **PAGE 9**

## Put Your Hands Up!

Another example of illustration saving the day is the commission I got in spring of 2008 to design the T-shirts for the farewell tour of one of my favorite bands of all time, The Police. This request came from no less than guitarist Andy Summers, who somehow thought I knew and/or had access to Robert Crumb. Alas, I wished I did, but such was not the case, and when Andy suggested his concept for the shirts I knew who the perfect illustrator would be: Tony Millionaire (see *Maakie's* and *Bizarro* in *Book One*). Basically, Andy wanted to goof on the classic album cover for *Ghost in the Machine* by Mick Haggerty. Since this was the final tour, it would now be *Toast in the Machine*: three pieces of bread popping out of a toaster, each emblazoned with the super-reduced digital "portraits" of Sting, drummer Stewart Copeland, and Andy. I knew Tony would knock this out of the park, and it just became an issue of staging, as it were. Andy was also fixated on the idea of the electrical cord of the appliance coiling and spilling onto the back of the shirt. Hey, fine by me.



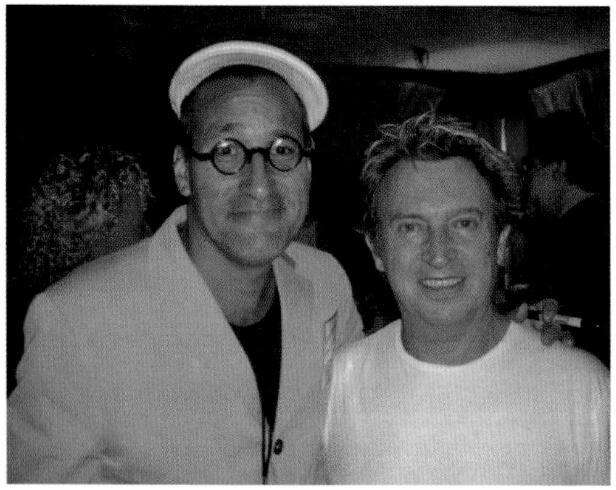

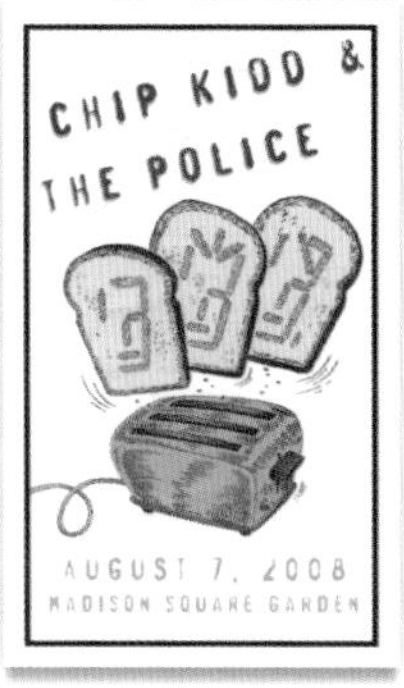
CHIP KIDD &
THE POLICE
AUGUST 7, 2008
MADISON SQUARE GARDEN

**ABOVE LEFT:** With Andy Summers backstage after the final show at Madison Square Garden. He was adorable and gracious. **ABOVE RIGHT:** A shameless self-promo "badge" I made for myself to give me an extra grain of credibility in case security tried to toss me out. Hey, I take no chances and have it plastered over my heart in the photo, though you really can't see it. **RIGHT & OPPOSITE:** The final design, which was applied to white, gray, and black T-shirts.

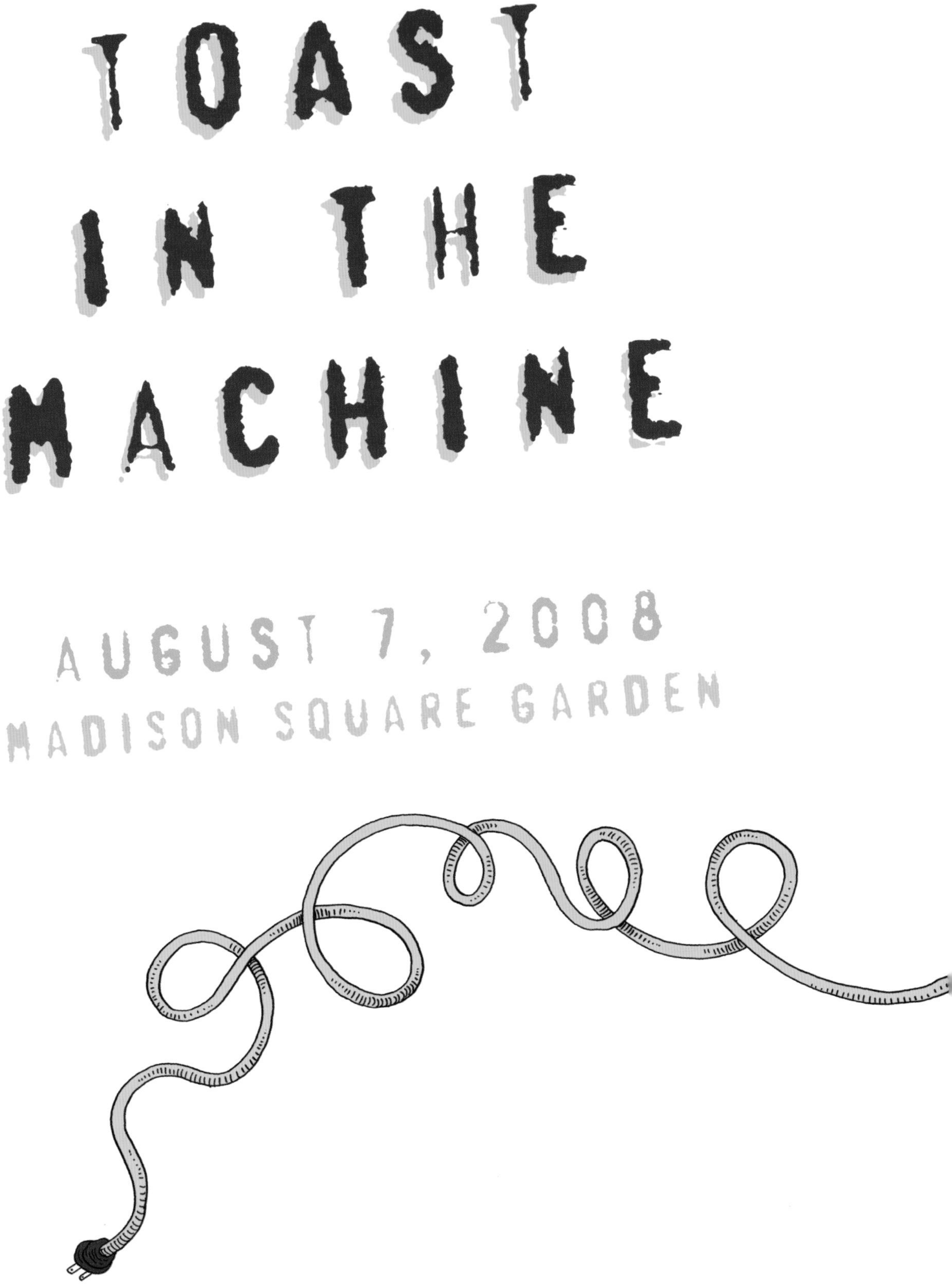
TOAST
IN THE
MACHINE
AUGUST 7, 2008
MADISON SQUARE GARDEN

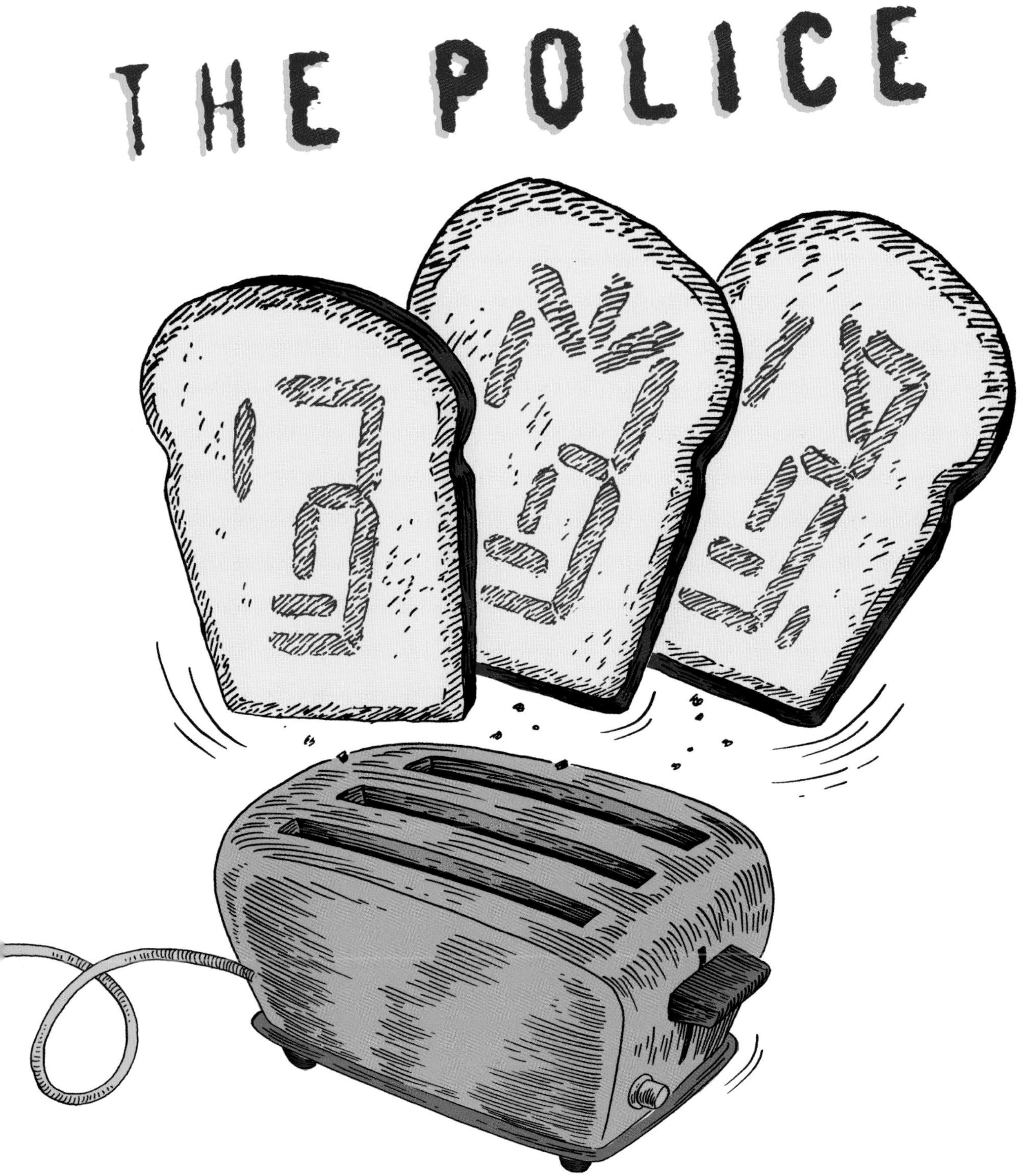
THE POLICE

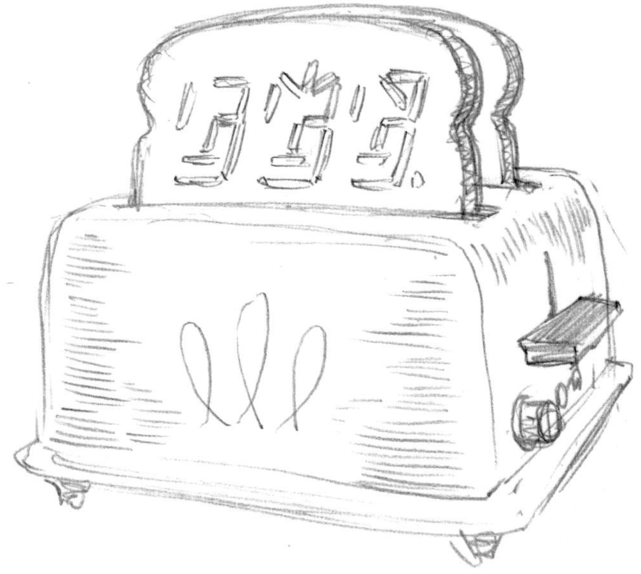

**ABOVE & BELOW:** Tony Millionaire's original sketches, which were good but didn't have the kinetic "zing" that was wanted—Andy really needed to see the pieces of toast launching from the machine, and I think he was right. Also, if it doesn't go without saying, Sting and Stewart had to approve these, too; I just didn't get to deal directly with them. *Wah.* But this was really Andy's idea and they followed his lead on it.

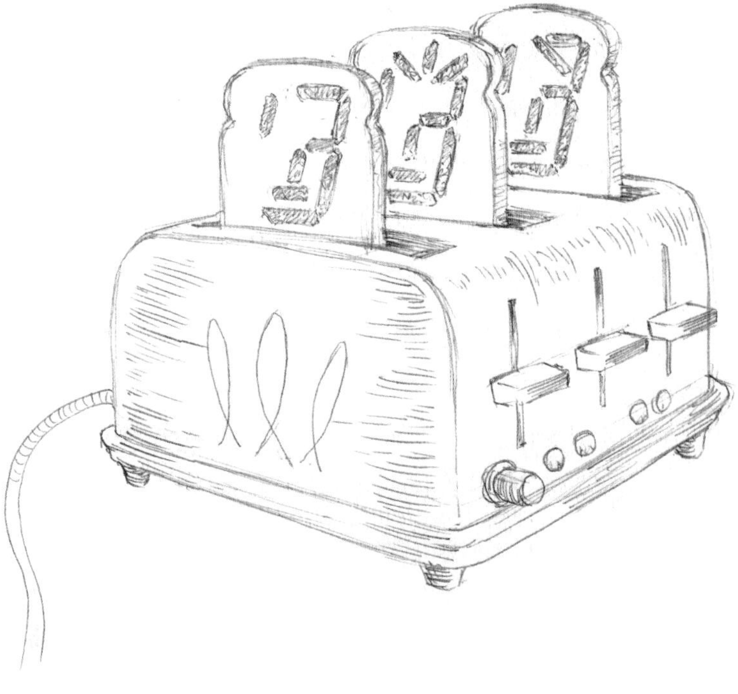

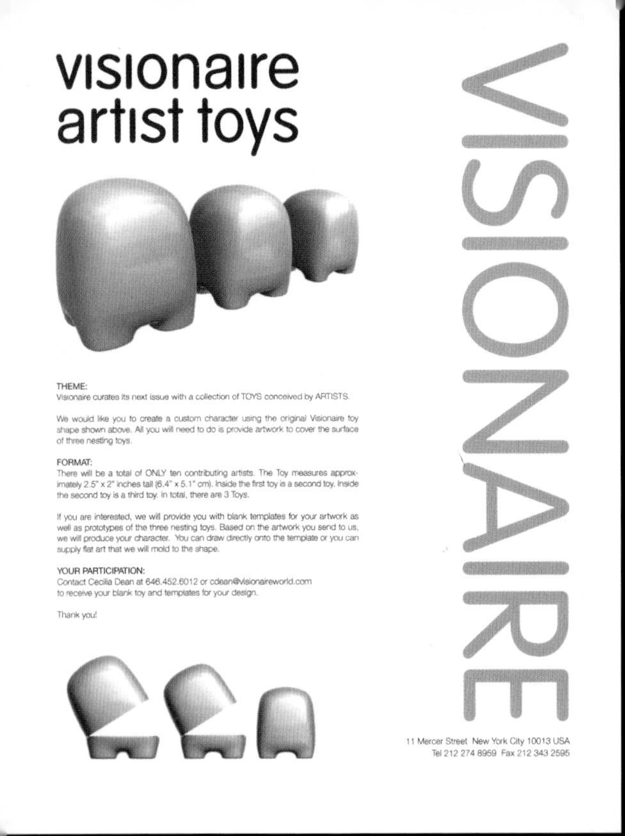

visionaire
artist toys

THEME:
Visionaire curates its next issue with a collection of TOYS conceived by ARTISTS.

We would like you to create a custom character using the original Visionaire toy shape shown above. All you will need to do is provide artwork to cover the surface of three nesting toys.

FORMAT:
There will be a total of ONLY ten contributing artists. The Toy measures approximately 2.5" x 2" inches tall (6.4" x 5.1" cm). Inside the first toy is a second toy. Inside the second toy is a third toy. In total, there are 3 Toys.

If you are interested, we will provide you with blank templates for your artwork as well as prototypes of the three nesting toys. Based on the artwork you send to us, we will produce your character. You can draw directly onto the template or you can supply flat art that we will mold to the shape.

YOUR PARTICIPATION:
Contact Cecilia Dean at 646.452.6012 or cdean@visionaireworld.com
to receive your blank toy and templates for your design.

Thank you!

VISIONAIRE

11 Mercer Street New York City 10013 USA
Tel 212 274 8959 Fax 212 343 2595

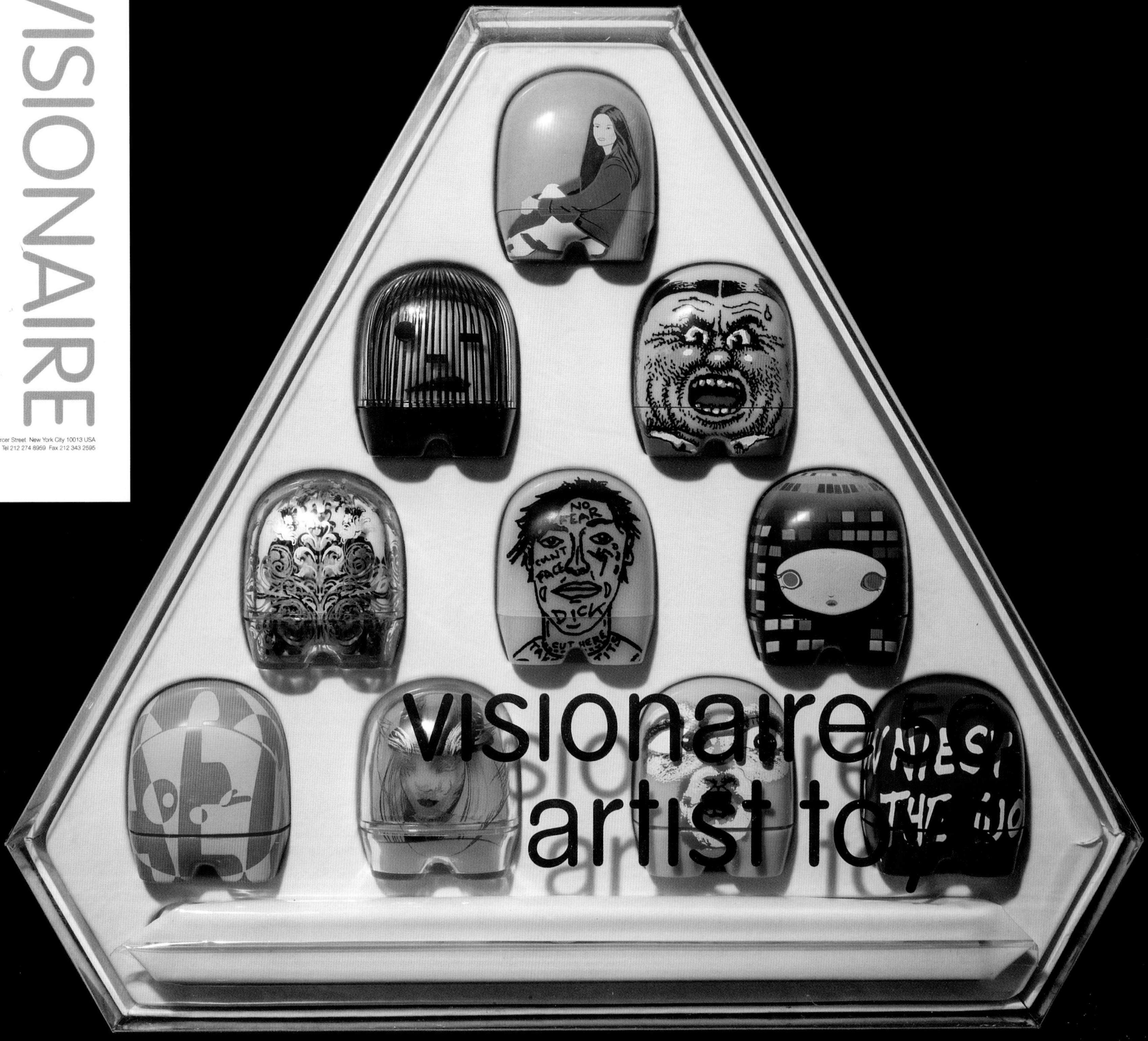
visionaire 50
artist toys
NO FEAR
CAN'T FACE
DICK
CUT HERE

# Kidd's Play

I'd been fascinated by *Visionaire* for years, just like everyone else in the art and design world. What Cecilia Dean, Stephen Gan, and James Kaliardos were able to create, starting in 1991, was an art and fashion magazine that evolved into so much more: it became art in itself, manifested in any number of forms including objects like a light box, a Louis Vuitton handbag, Lacoste polo shirts, vinyl records, films on DVD, and an issue on taste—as in the kind you have in your mouth—which featured dozens of dissolvable gel flavor strips.

For issue #50, Greg Foley on their creative staff invited me to join a group of artists, each of whom were asked to create a custom nesting-doll toy that would have five components—four layers and a base to rest on.

I wanted to play with the possibilities of transparency and moiré patterns, so I adapted a cover design I'd done for the Japanese author Koji Suzuki's novel *Birthday* (right), for Vertical Books. I was most excited by the prospect of my work appearing alongside that of legends such as Robert Crumb, Alex Katz, and the late, great writer Kurt Vonnegut. Only *Visionaire* could put together such a crazy, disparate group and make it look as if it all belonged together. I was thrilled by the opportunity to make a 3D object that wasn't a book and that entailed sixteen different surface combinations and three kinds of materials.

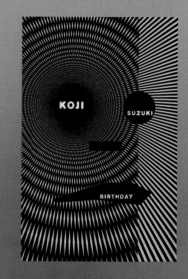

**BELOW:** The completed figure (one of four combinations), and its various components. It was sort of like making a book in toy form that could have multiple outcomes.

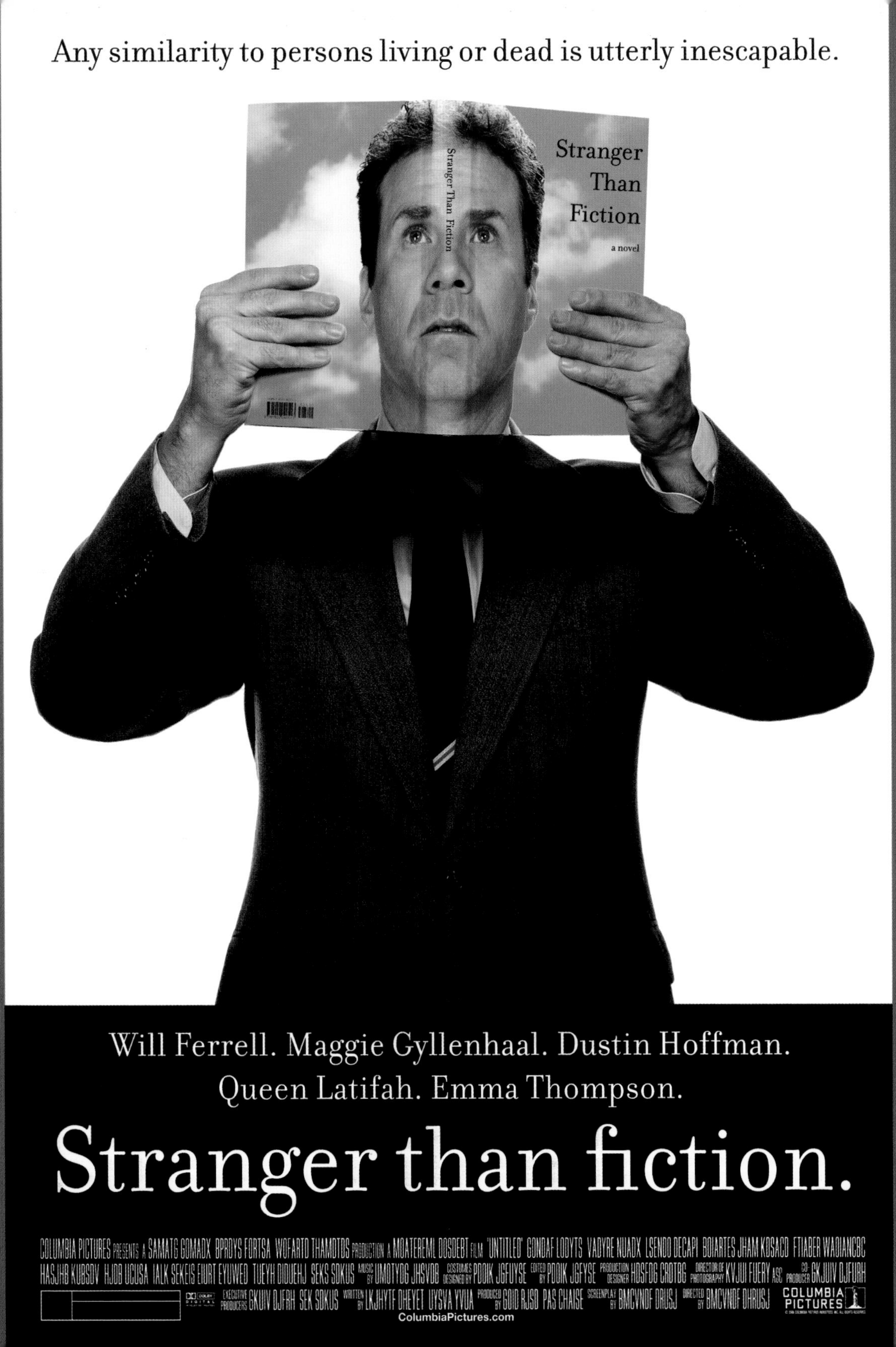
Any similarity to persons living or dead is utterly inescapable.
Stranger Than Fiction
a novel
Stranger Than Fiction
Will Ferrell. Maggie Gyllenhaal. Dustin Hoffman.
Queen Latifah. Emma Thompson.
Stranger than fiction.
ColumbiaPictures.com
COLUMBIA PICTURES

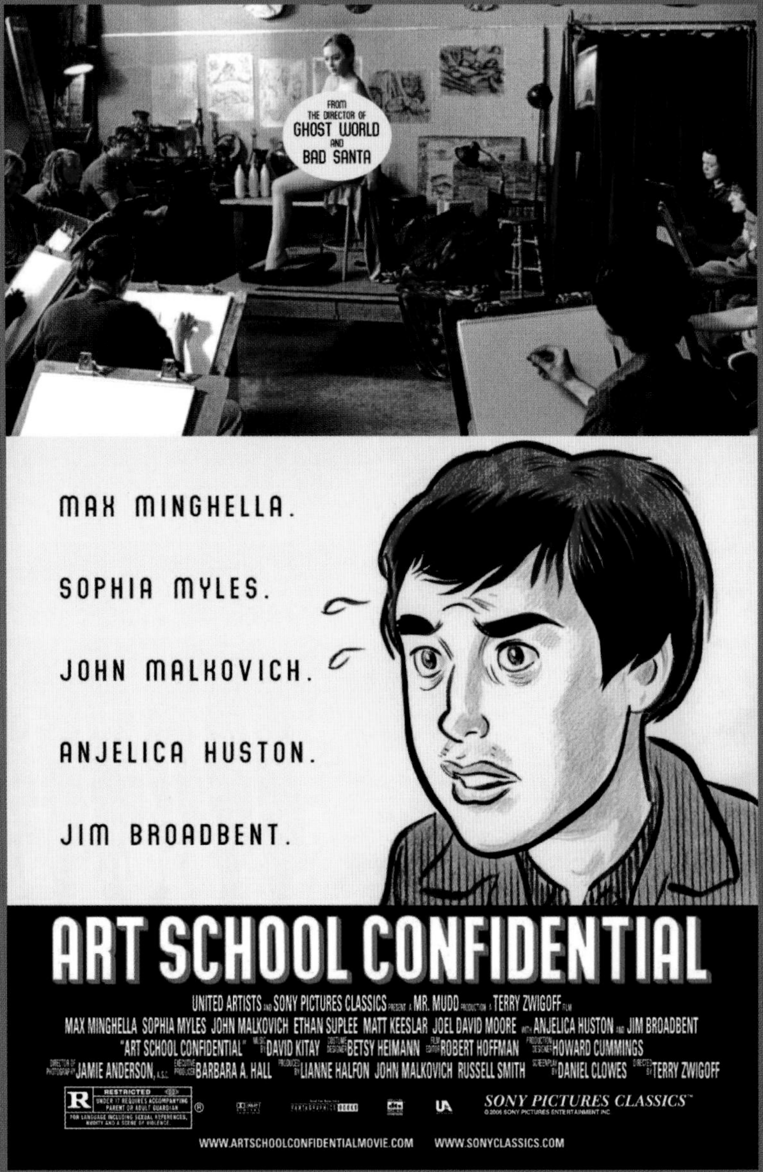
FROM THE DIRECTOR OF GHOST WORLD AND BAD SANTA
MAX MINGHELLA.
SOPHIA MYLES.
JOHN MALKOVICH.
ANJELICA HUSTON.
JIM BROADBENT.
ART SCHOOL CONFIDENTIAL
SONY PICTURES CLASSICS
WWW.ARTSCHOOLCONFIDENTIALMOVIE.COM WWW.SONYCLASSICS.COM

## Art and Commerce

At left is a concept for a 2006 Will Ferrell film poster in which his character slowly discovers he's fictitious, a fabrication created by a novelist (Emma Thompson), earmarked for death, and attempting to "wake up" out of it. This was a commission from Columbia Pictures, and that's a Geoff Spear shot of me holding up a book cover with Will Ferrell's face over mine. No one liked this. End of commission.

Dear friend Daniel Clowes's brilliant short story *Art School Confidential* (opposite, right), about his travails as an art student at Pratt, was turned into a movie in 2006. The challenge was to get the producers to allow Mr. Clowes to create the art featuring the star, Max Minghella. We prevailed! Dan also designed the lettering, and overall it really looks like a Dan Clowes film.

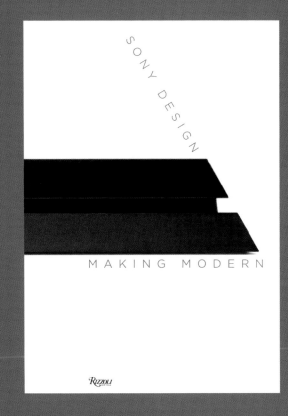

SONY DESIGN

MAKING MODERN

RIZZOLI

I have enjoyed working with Ian Luna—who just so happens to be the editor of this book—to design some of the widely diverse and fascinating projects he brings into Rizzoli. Among them are the cover for a book on the history of Sony design (above; 2015), using a detail of one of their latest gaming devices that looks utterly architectural, and a book on architecture and shopping (right; 2005), which looks like a miniature stage set (but is in fact the full-size Louis Vuitton flagship store in Tokyo).

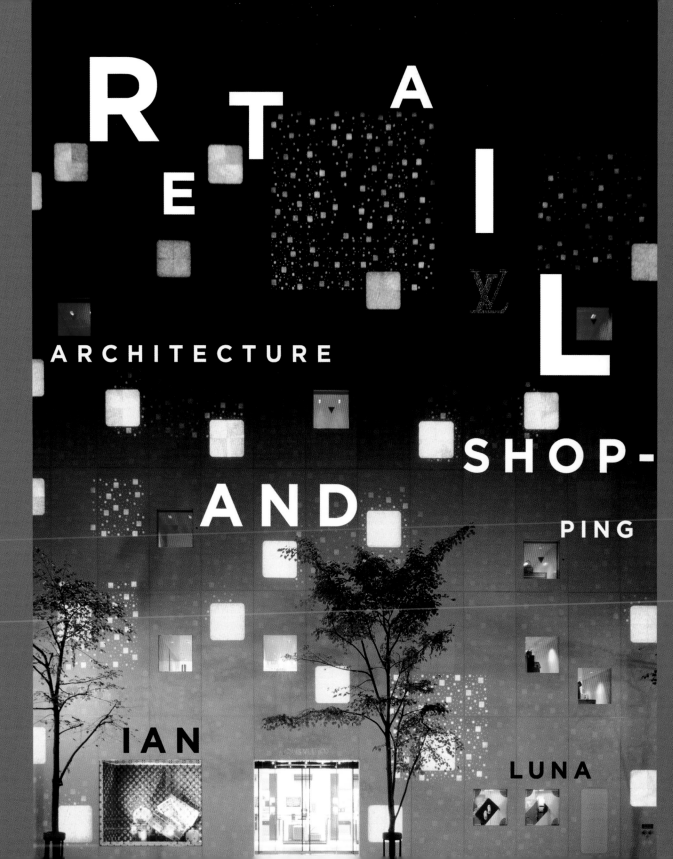

RETAIL

ARCHITECTURE

AND

SHOP-

PING

IAN

LUNA

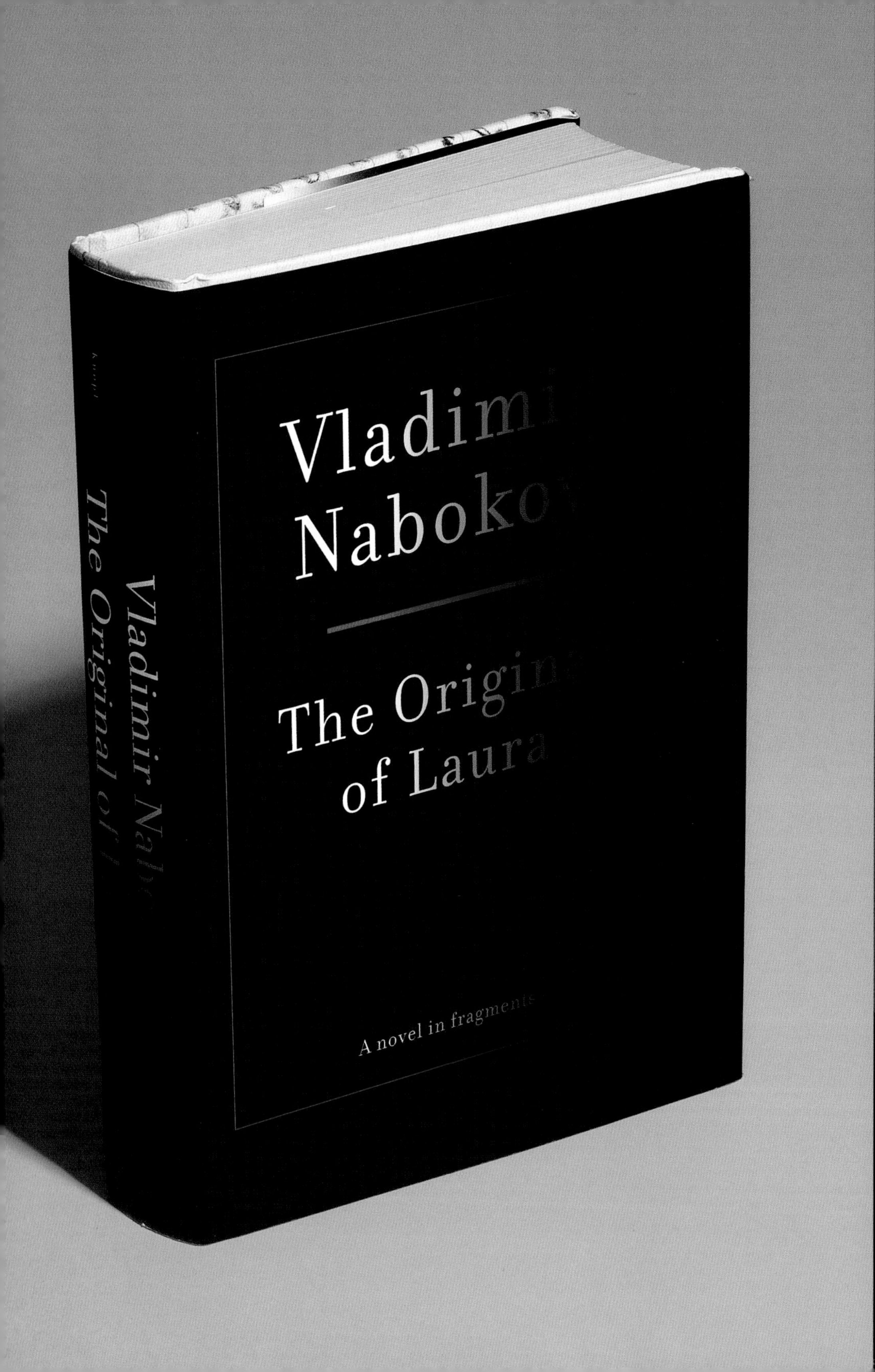
Vladimi
Nabokov
The Origin
of Laura
A novel in fragments
Vladimir Nab
The Original of

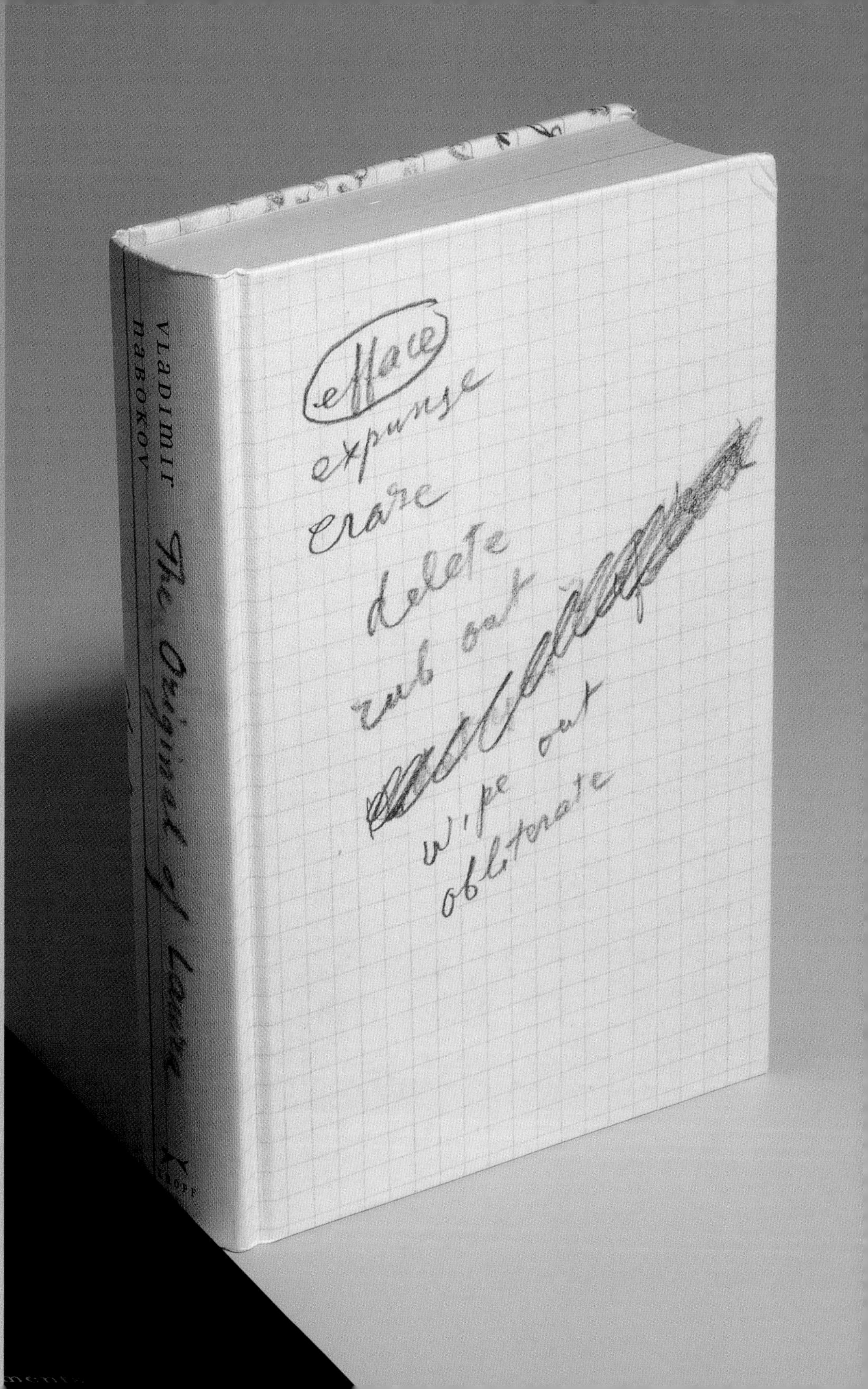
VLADIMIR
NABOKOV
The Original of Laura
efface
expunge
erase
delete
rub out
wipe out
obliterate

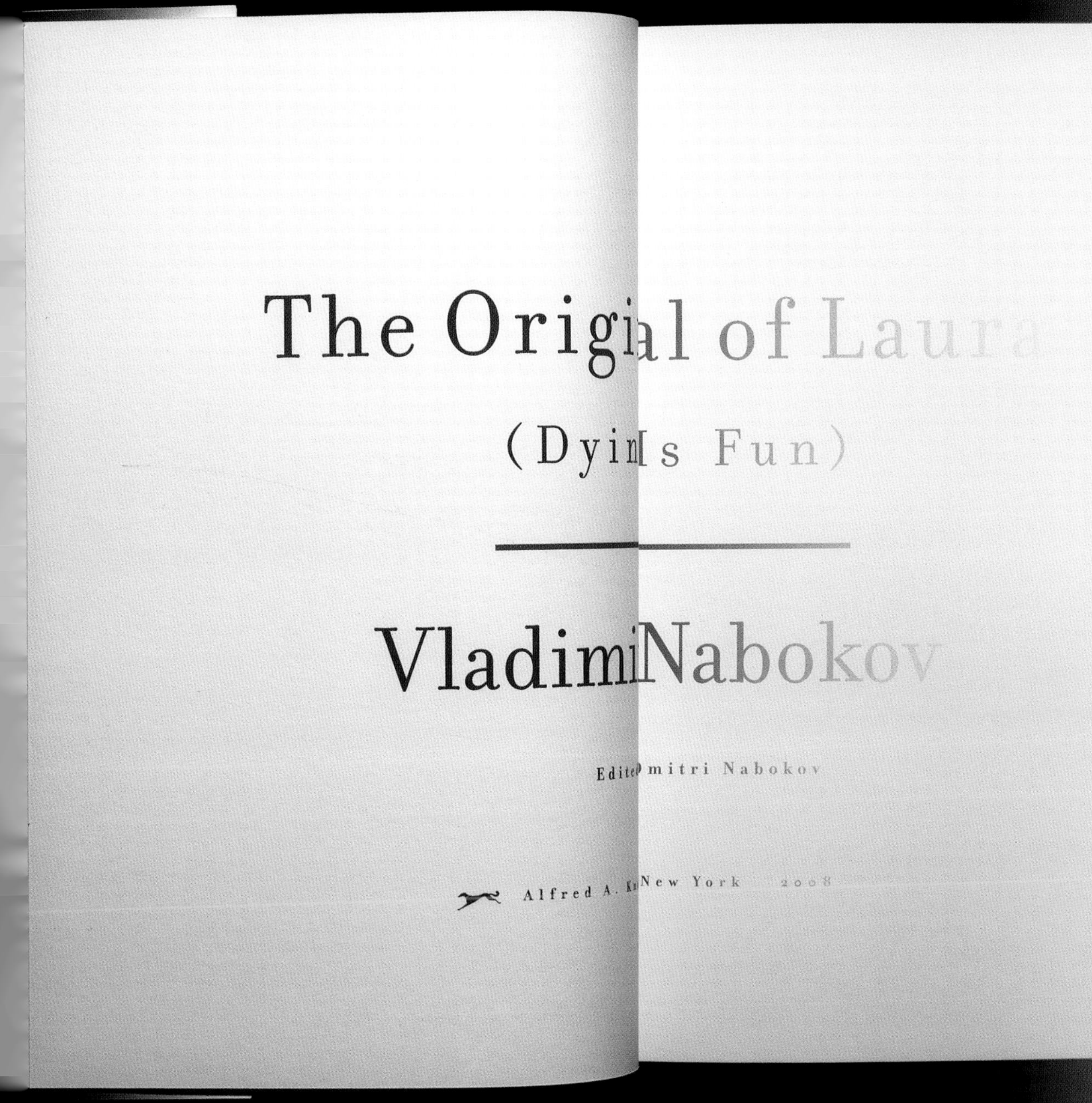

The Origial of Laura

(Dyins Fun)

VladimiNabokov

Edite mitri Nabokov

 Alfred A. KnNew York 2008

## Punching Out

It had been literary legend for years that the notes for Vladimir Nabokov's last novel (scribbled on 128 note cards)—to be titled *The Original of Laura*—survived his demise in 1977, despite his wishes that they be burned along with him. Instead, upon his death they were locked away in a vault in Switzerland by his son Dmitri.

By 2008 that vault had been reopened, with the intent to publish the cards as the last fiction that the great man had ever produced, in however raw a form they existed. There was a considerable groundswell among Nabokovian scholars to prevent this from happening. They argued that the author had asked for the material to be destroyed, and that the cards did not represent even an outline of a complete work. However, at that point the undeniable prospect of at last seeing what Nabokov was working on in his final days trumped any lingering propriety to cover it up. Plus, it is worth remembering that Nabokov had ordered his beloved wife, Vera, to burn the manuscript for *Lolita* because it was too sensational, but she famously refused him. And that turned out pretty well. (Thank you, Vera.)

So it was that Dmitri entrusted Knopf with figuring out how to publish this material with dignity, and that became my job. I was beyond thrilled—to design the very last Nabokov first edition in the best possible manner became this book designer's great dream and honor.

The question, as posed to me by Sonny Mehta, was: how do you make 128 note cards into a proper book and do it justice? For the cover and the title pages inside I wanted to play up the idea of "fading out." Not only was Nabokov dying as he wrote this, but the narrative itself—not surprisingly—is about an artist who is literally erasing himself out of existence. I had looked back on everything I'd done, and to my delight I was relieved to see that I had never made a cover that faded to black. So this would be a first, for me anyway, and was definitely what was needed. For contrast, the title pages faded to white, an entirely other kind of oblivion. Now, what to do with the rest of the interior?

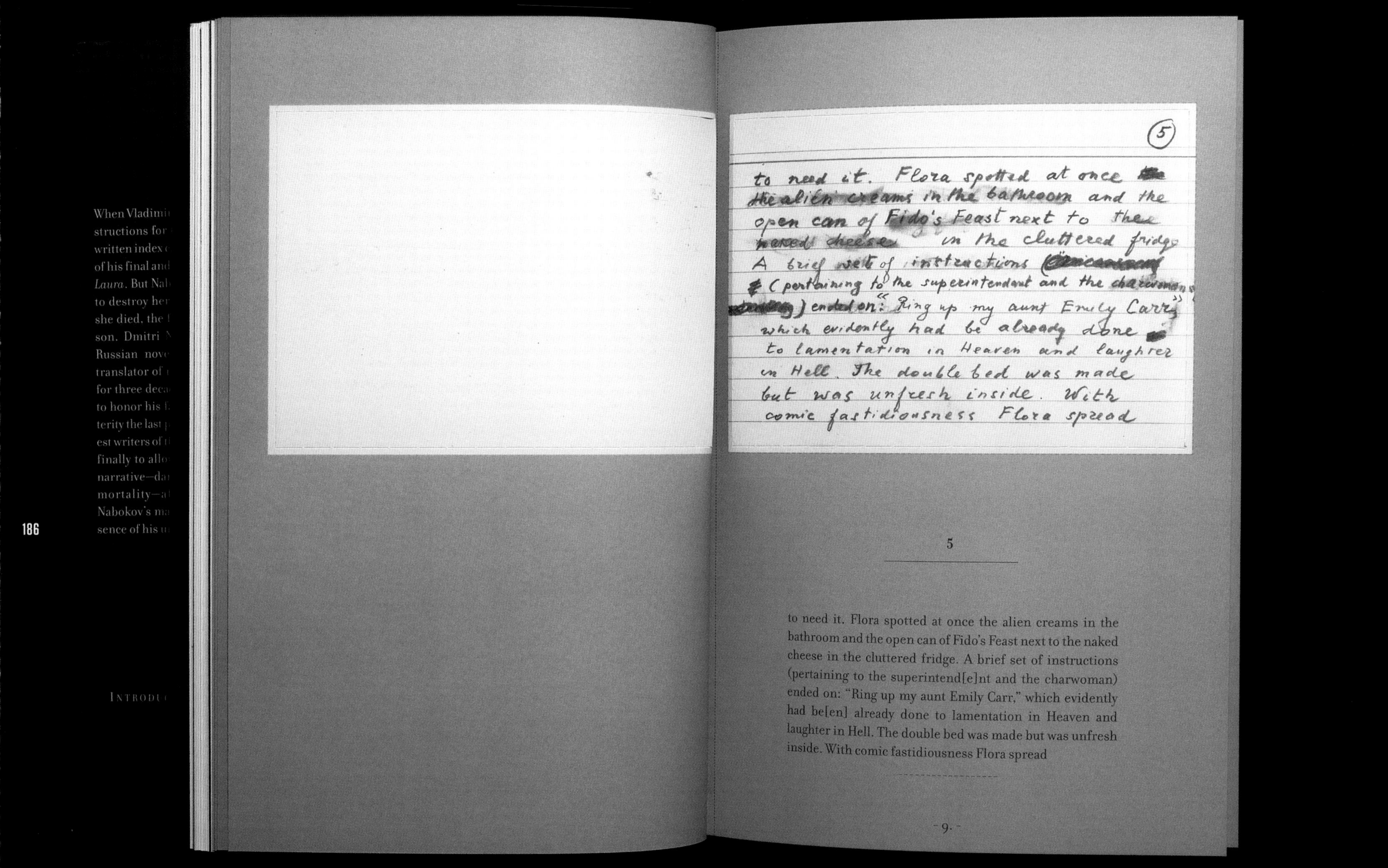

When Vladimi[r]
structions for
written index
of his final and
*Laura*. But Na[b]
to destroy her
she died, the
son. Dmitri
Russian nove
translator of
for three deca
to honor his f
terity the last
est writers of t
finally to allo
narrative—da
mortality—a
Nabokov's ma
sence of his u

INTRODU[C]

5

to need it. Flora spotted at once the alien creams in the
bathroom and the open can of Fido's Feast next to the naked
cheese in the cluttered fridge. A brief set of instructions
(pertaining to the superintend[e]nt and the charwoman)
ended on: "Ring up my aunt Emily Carr," which evidently
had be[en] already done to lamentation in Heaven and
laughter in Hell. The double bed was made but was unfresh
inside. With comic fastidiousness Flora spread

I concluded that the answer was to make the world's most literary punch-out book. What does that mean? It means that as a child I adored "activity books" featuring perforated shapes that you could separate or "punch out" of the page and otherwise repurpose.

Admittedly, these usually consisted of novelty workbooks for children. But this was going to be the ultimate novelty workbook for the literati. Some were amused. Many were not. But the fact was that the cards themselves were numbered … until they weren't, and at that point their intended order became pure speculation. What Sonny and I decided (and Dmitri approved) was that we'd let readers decide how, or if, they wanted to edit the text. I doubt that many did, but the idea that you could was what mattered. In that sense it was the novel as conceptual art.

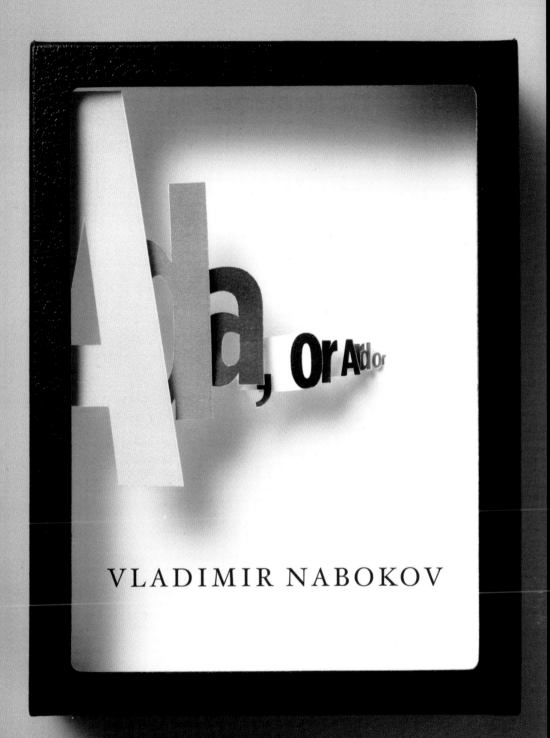

**VLADIMIR NABOKOV**

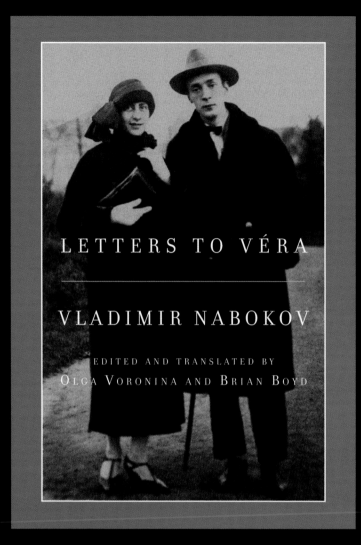

LETTERS TO VÉRA

VLADIMIR NABOKOV

EDITED AND TRANSLATED BY
OLGA VORONINA AND BRIAN BOYD

John Gall, the brilliant designer and then–art director of Vintage paper-backs, proposed a series redesign of Nabokov's backlist employing the idea of a shadow box in which the elements would be held in place via small pins, à la the butterfly specimens that so enthralled the great master. John enlisted a wonderful group of artists and designers to create these, and I was tapped for *Ada, or Ardor* (left). The pins are there, trust me; you just can't see them. The letters fade from gray to black to red, for reasons one would need to read the book in order to understand.

**ABOVE:** Knopf, 2016. There are many pictures of Vladimir and Vera, but this one shows them at the dawn of their partnership, still in Russia and ready to leave soon and take on the rest of the world. **LEFT:** Vintage, 2011.

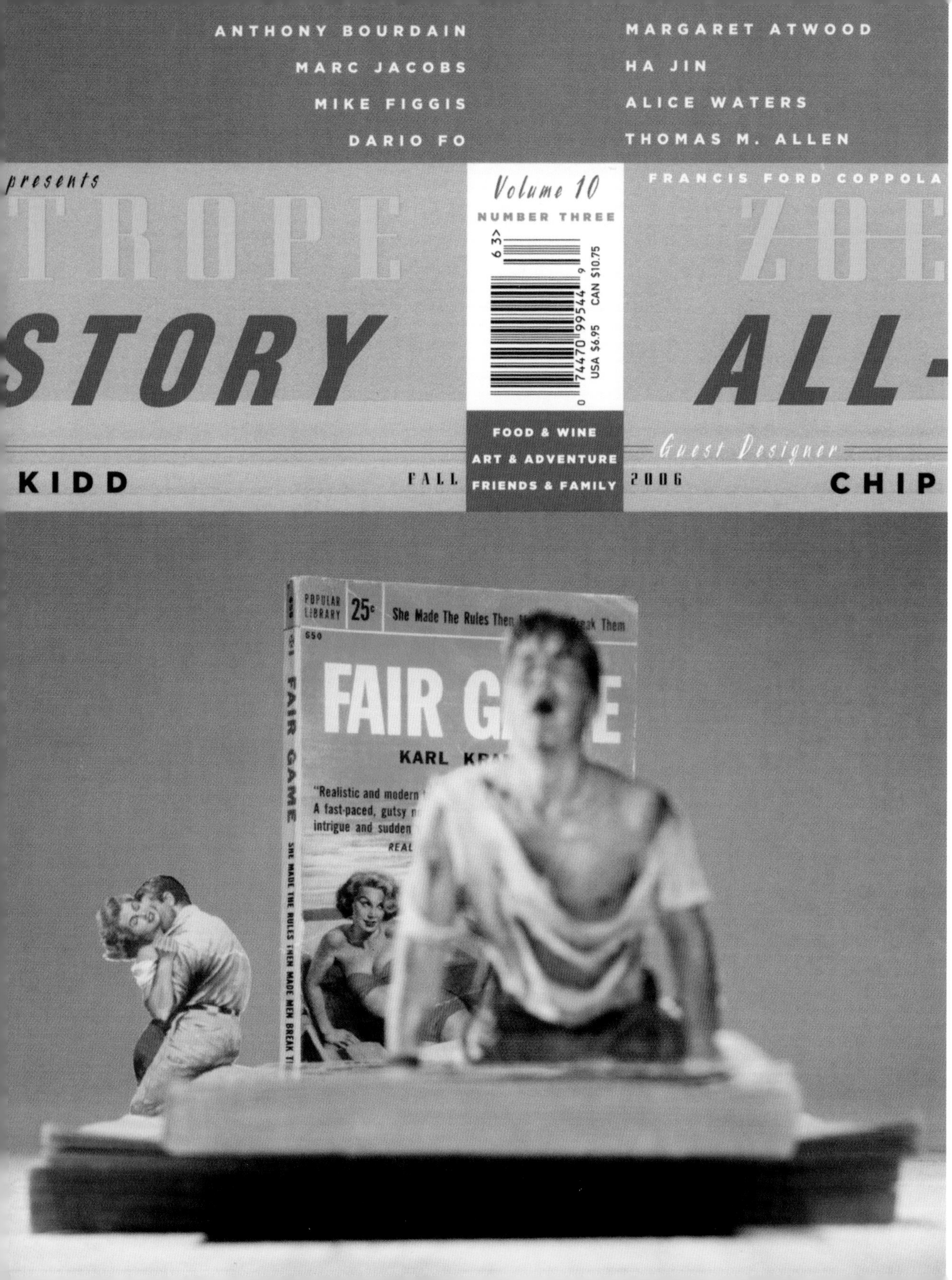
ANTHONY BOURDAIN
MARC JACOBS
MIKE FIGGIS
DARIO FO
MARGARET ATWOOD
HA JIN
ALICE WATERS
THOMAS M. ALLEN
FRANCIS FORD COPPOLA
presents
STORY
ALL-
Volume 10
NUMBER THREE
USA $6.95 CAN $10.75
FOOD & WINE
ART & ADVENTURE
FRIENDS & FAMILY
Guest Designer
KIDD
FALL
2006
CHIP
POPULAR LIBRARY
25¢
650
FAIR GAME
SHE MADE THE RULES THEN MADE MEN BREAK

# Round and Round

Francis Ford Coppola's literary quarterly *Zoetrope All-Story* surprised and delighted the publishing world when it debuted in the spring of 1997. A much-needed venue to showcase new short fiction and essays, *Zoetrope* also featured a truly ambitious idea that was unique in the history of magazines: every issue would be designed and art-directed by a different person. For the Fall 2006 issue, they chose me. I was thrilled but hesitant, only because I was still putting the finishing touches on *Book One* at the time. And yet how could I say no? Then the answer hit me: the photographer Thomas Allen, with whom I'd worked on a number of covers for James Ellroy. His still-life studies of paper-back cover dioramas could be perfect.

For this project to work, all the factors had to come together: Tom had to be keen on it (of course), as did the *Zoetrope* editors (ditto), and they would have to give me free rein with it—there would be no time in the schedule to submit multiple layouts or ideas. Amazingly, everyone involved was cool with all of this, and the results are what you see here.

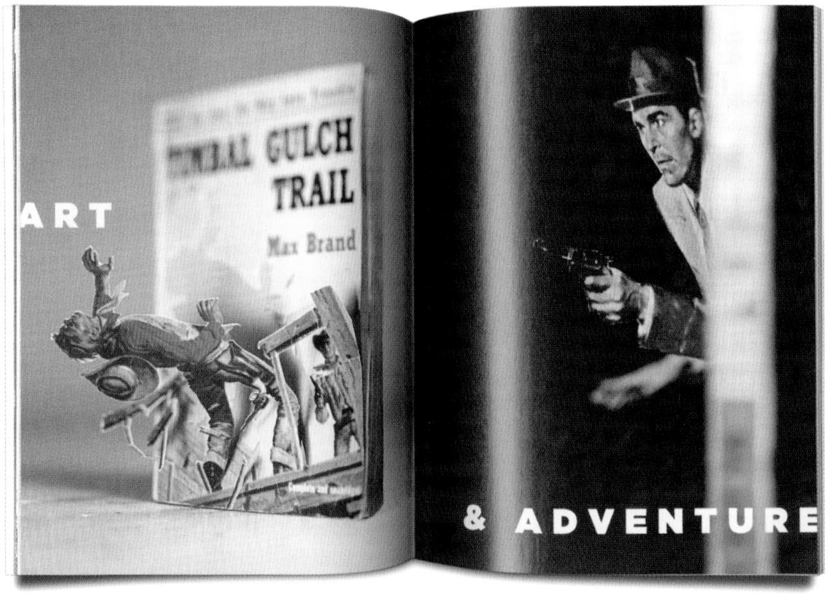
ART
GULCH
TRAIL
Max Brand
& ADVENTURE

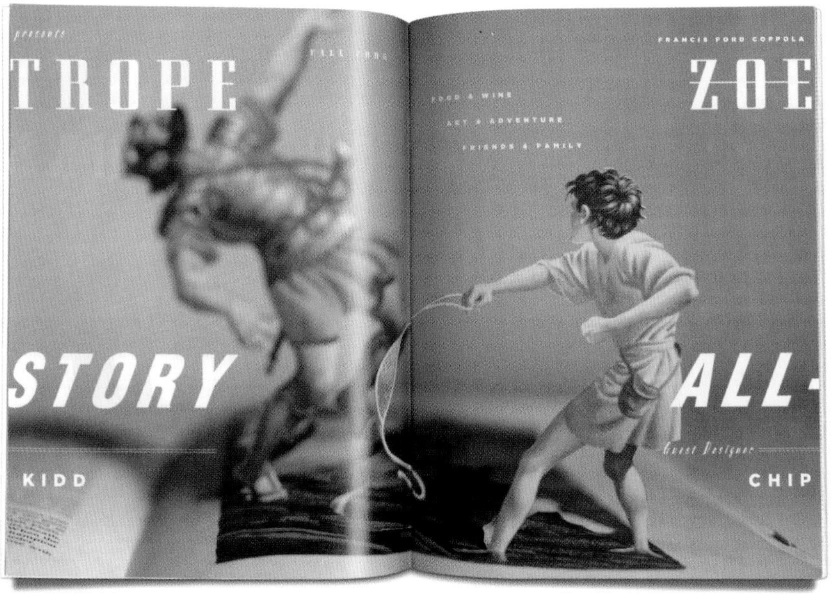
presents
TROPE
FRANCIS FORD COPPOLA
ZOE
FOOD & WINE
ART & ADVENTURE
FRIENDS & FAMILY
STORY
ALL-
Guest Designer
KIDD
CHIP

My main contribution as a designer was the idea that zoetropes spin, and so the cover (opposite, left) is set up to look like it's in the middle of a rotation; same with the title page spread (above) and back cover (right). All of the imagery throughout was preexisting, which is pretty amazing when you think about it—everything looks so tailor-made for the content.

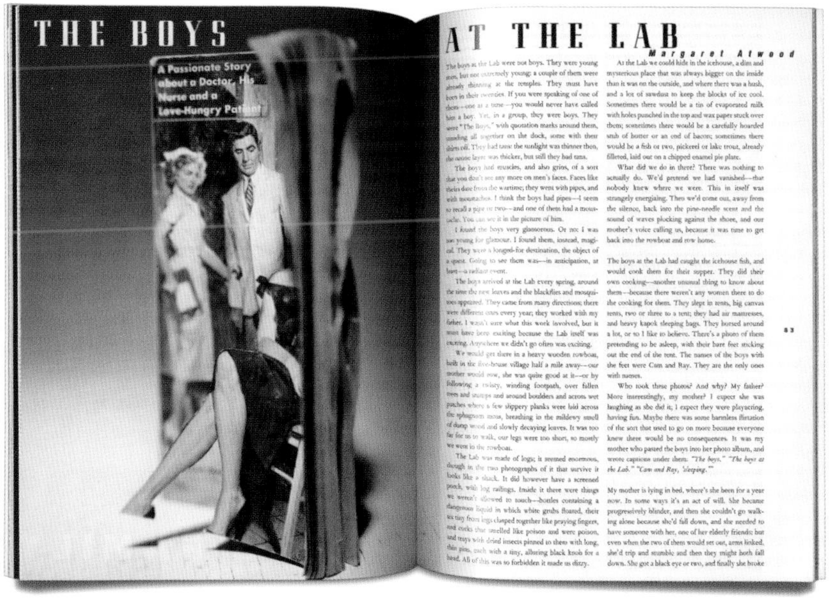
THE BOYS
AT THE LAB
Margaret Atwood
A Passionate Story about a Doctor, His Nurse and a Love-Hungry Patient

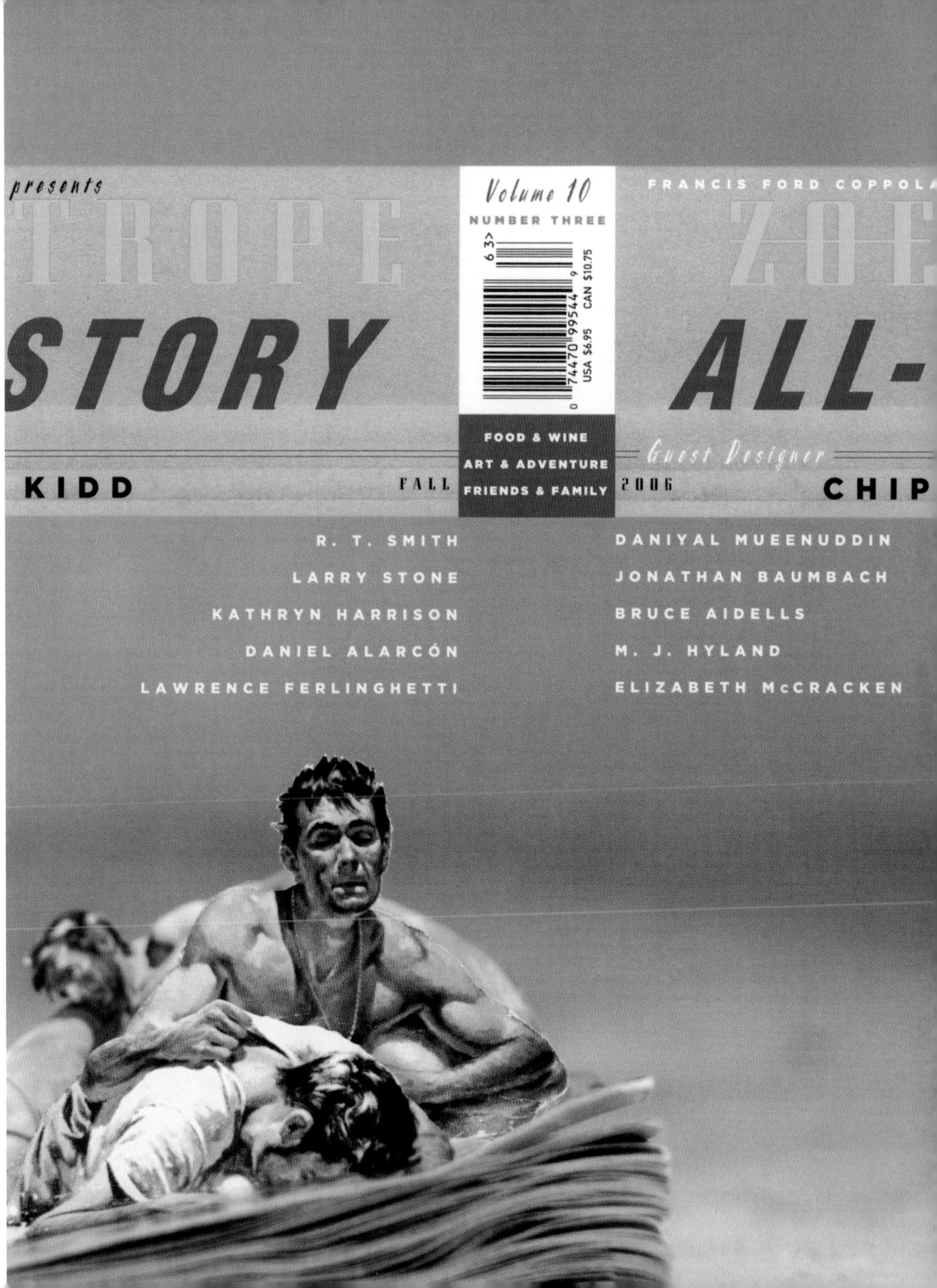
presents
TROPE
Volume 10
NUMBER THREE
USA $6.95 CAN $10.75
FRANCIS FORD COPPOLA
ZOE
STORY
ALL-
FOOD & WINE
ART & ADVENTURE
FRIENDS & FAMILY
Guest Designer
KIDD
FALL
2006
CHIP
R. T. SMITH
LARRY STONE
KATHRYN HARRISON
DANIEL ALARCÓN
LAWRENCE FERLINGHETTI
DANIYAL MUEENUDDIN
JONATHAN BAUMBACH
BRUCE AIDELLS
M. J. HYLAND
ELIZABETH McCRACKEN

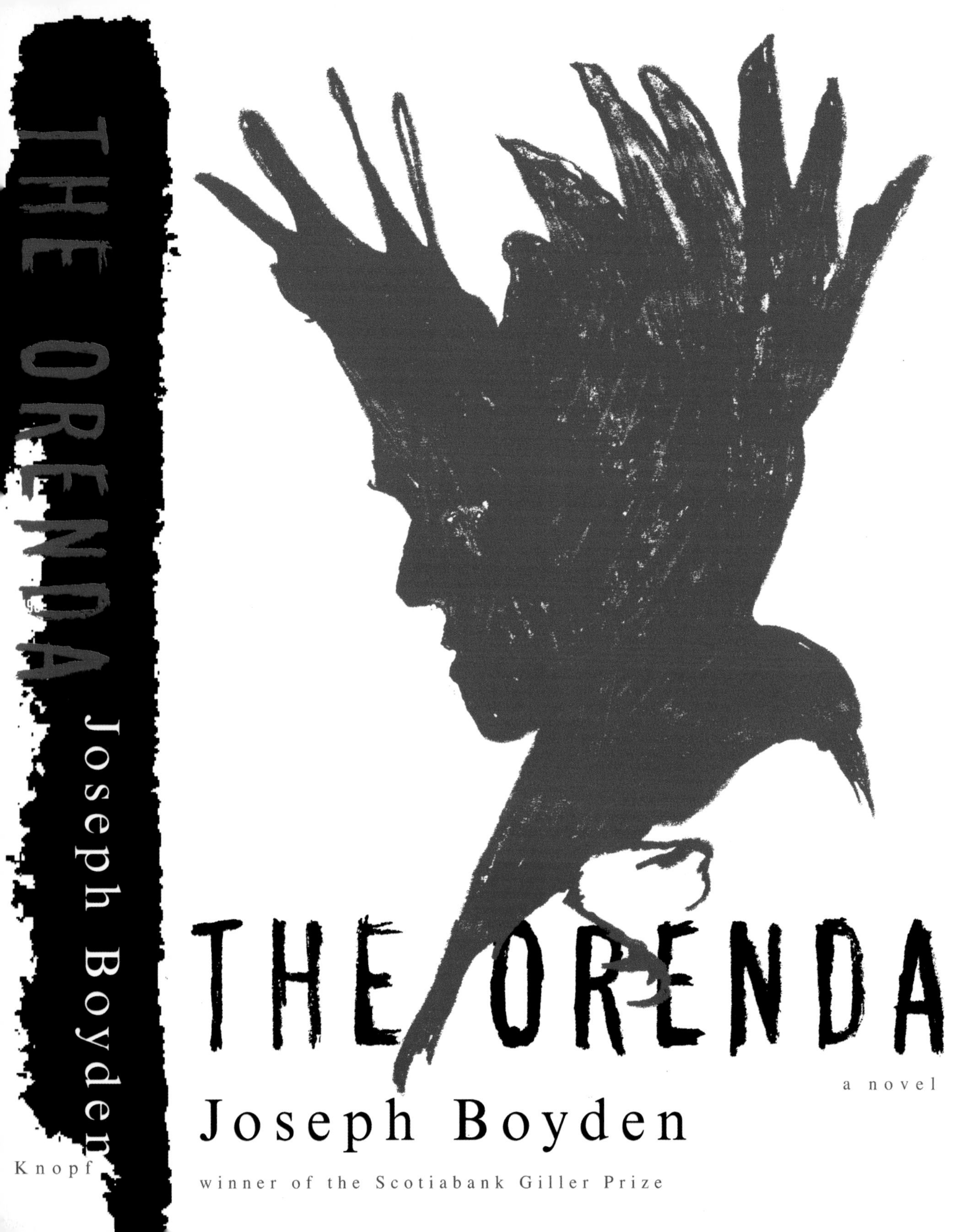
THE ORENDA
Joseph Boyden
Knopf
THE ORENDA
a novel
Joseph Boyden
winner of the Scotiabank Giller Prize

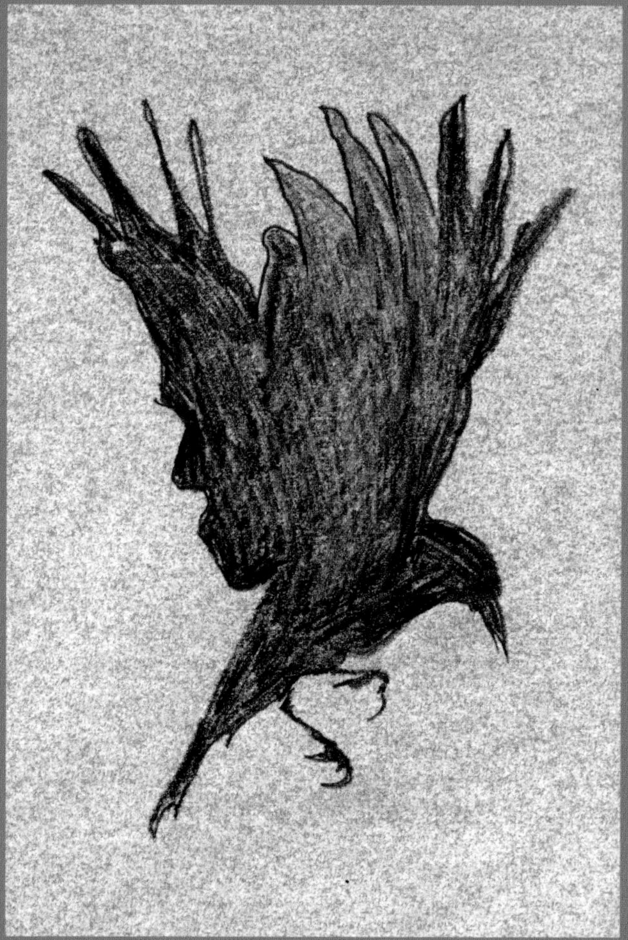

## Eat Like a Bird

Taking place in 17th-century Ontario, Joseph Byden's epic novel *The Orenda* is about a Jesuit missionary named Christophe who ventures into the wilderness to find converts and is captured by a chief of the Huron tribe named Bird. At first adversaries, they eventually unite to take on the threat of the rival Iroquois tribe. I started thinking about the idea of a tribal headdress of crow feathers that still had the crow attached. The theme of unity is strong in the narrative, and I worked to create a drawing (above) that would exemplify the concept of an amalgam of man and nature.

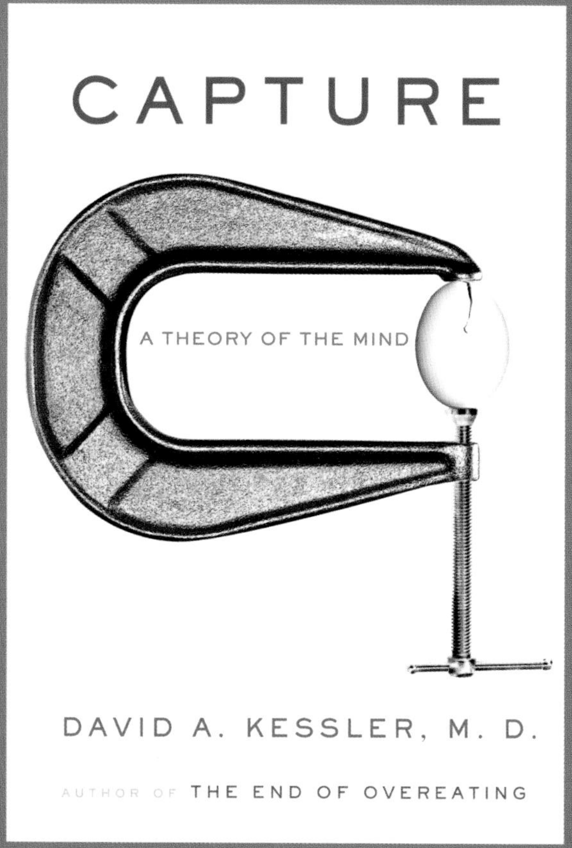
CAPTURE
A THEORY OF THE MIND
DAVID A. KESSLER, M. D.
AUTHOR OF THE END OF OVEREATING

The original title of the book at right, by David A. Kessler (the former commissioner of the Food and Drug Administration from 1990 to 1997), was *Sugar, Salt, Fat*. I was psyched; a title like that allowed for so many interesting possibilities. Then, a couple weeks later, he called to tell me he was changing it to *The End of Overeating*. Oops. How does one, um, show that? You can't just have someone sitting at the dinner table with nothing on the plate; that's just too weird. The solution arrived when I was ordering coffee at a deli one morning and saw slices of carrot cake on the display counter. They always cracked me up because the decoration of a carrot made of icing seemed to indicate that it was a healthy food. Not! It's the real carrots that are healthy. This juxtaposition exemplifies what the book is about: that the average American diet is filled with counterproductive ingredients.

**OPPOSITE, LEFT:** Knopf, 2014. **ABOVE:** *Captured* explored the idea of the tortured genius, and I thought the image of an egg cracking under the pressure of a vice grip conveyed that. Harper Wave, 2016. **RIGHT:** Rodale, 2009.

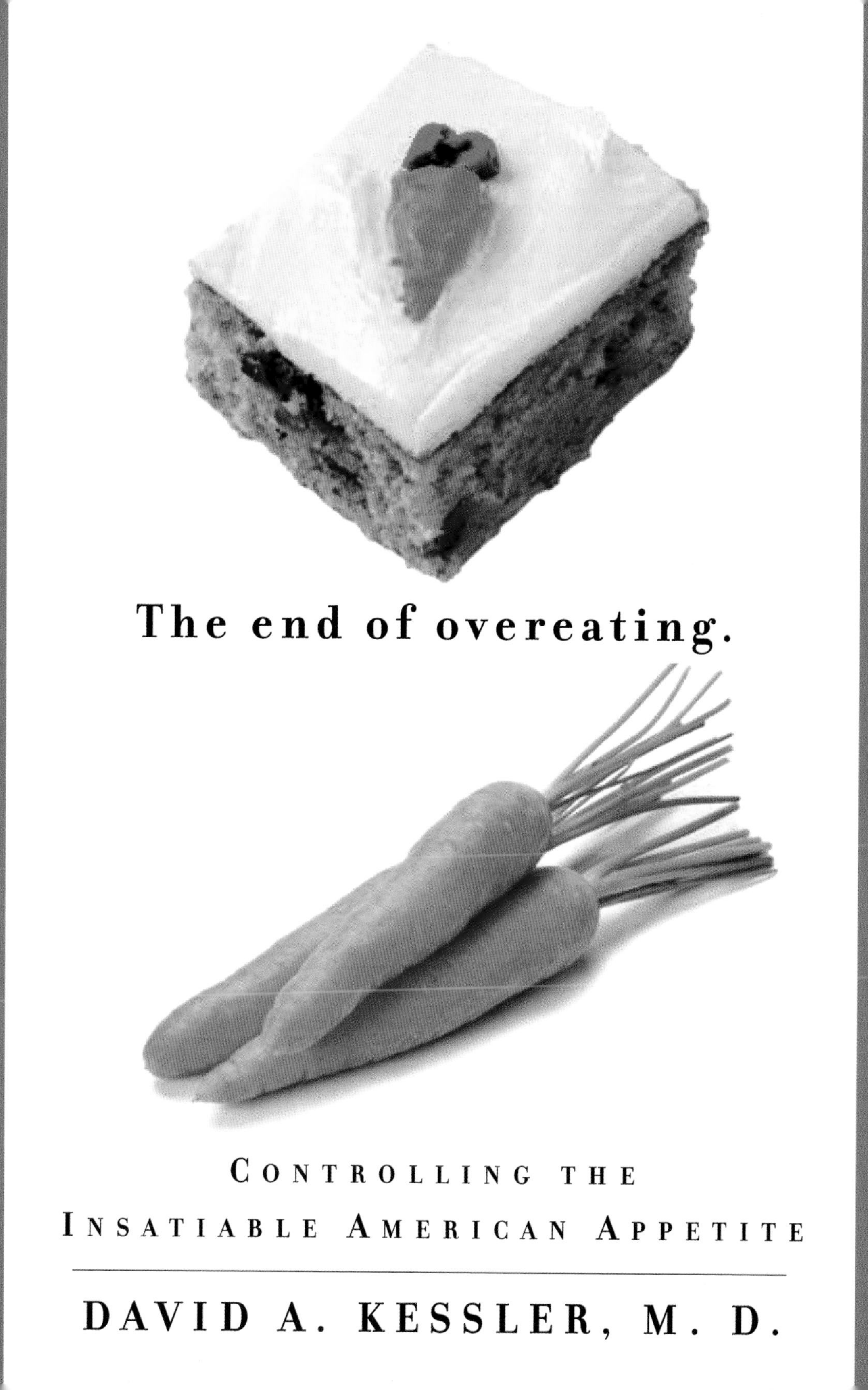
The end of overeating.
CONTROLLING THE
INSATIABLE AMERICAN APPETITE
DAVID A. KESSLER, M. D.

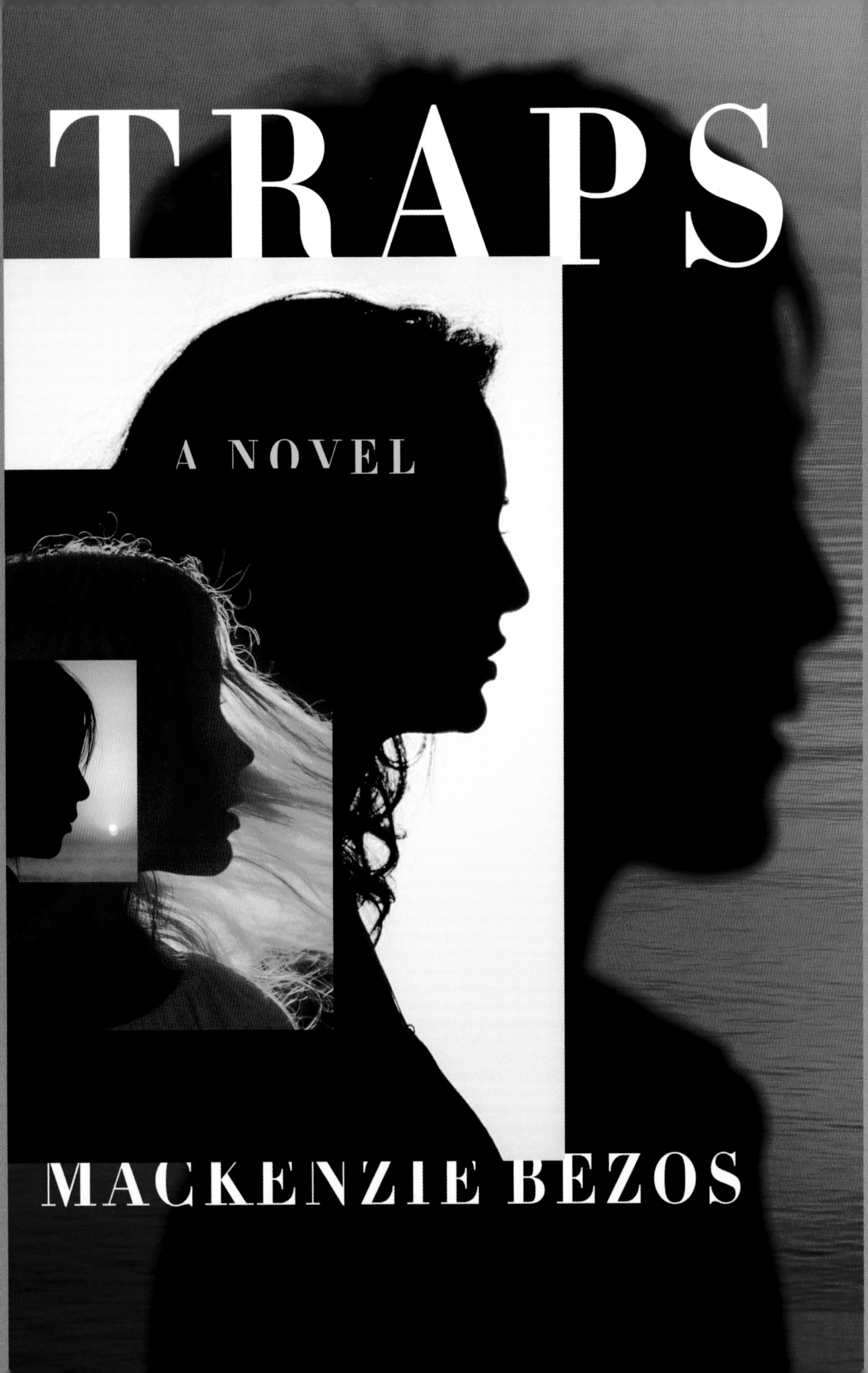
TRAPS
A NOVEL
MACKENZIE BEZOS



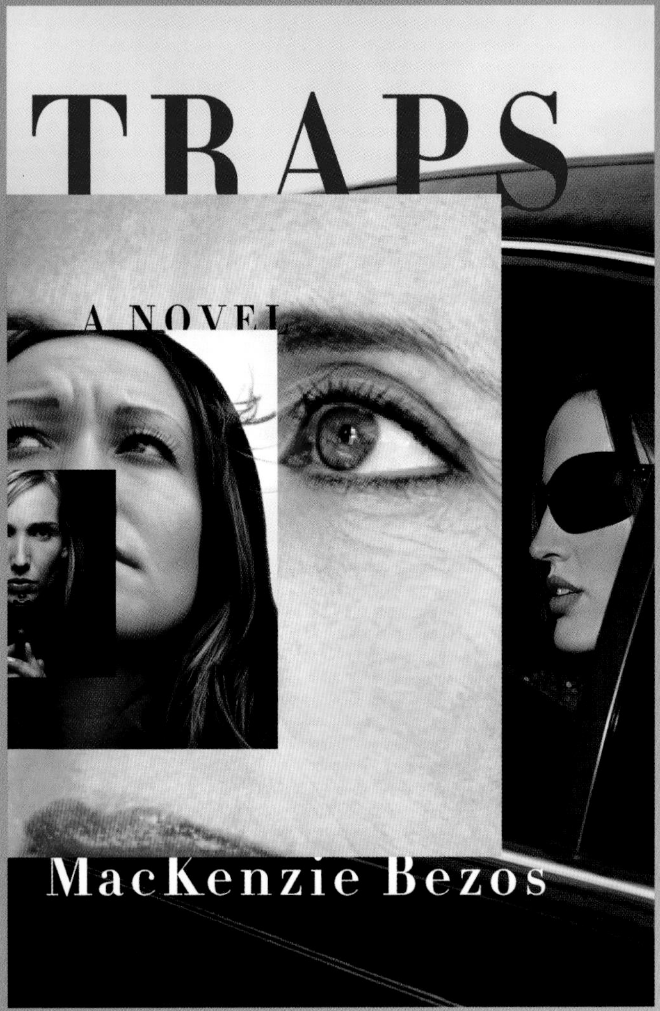
TRAPS
A NOVEL
MacKenzie Bezos

## Lives Within Lives

MacKenzie Bezos's novel *Traps* tracks the lives of four seemingly unconnected women in present-day California; as their stories progress, they gradually start to interweave with one another.

My first take is above . . . The author never saw this direction. It wasn't coming together, there wasn't enough sense of mystery to make it interesting. The faces are too clear and recognizable.

The final jacket (left) allows the reader to fill in the blanks, as it were. In a case like this, silhouettes work better than straightforward portraits.

**LEFT:** Knopf, 2013. **OPPOSITE, LEFT:** Knopf, 2009 **OPPOSITE, RIGHT:** Knopf, 2006.

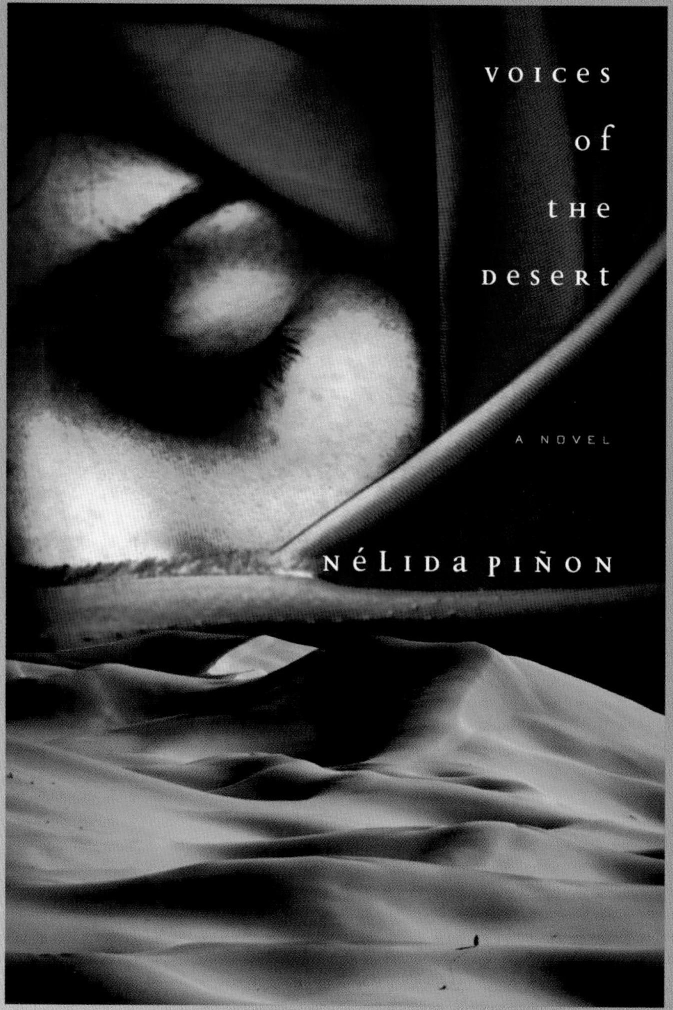
voices
of
the
desert
A NOVEL
nélida piñon

Nélida Piñon's *Voices of the Desert* (above) is a new interpretation of Scheherazade's *One Thousand and One Nights*, this time told from Scheherazade's point of view. I am playing with scale here: the extreme close-up of the woman's face juxtaposed with her dot-like size in the desert landscape. She looms large, yet is still a prisoner of her circumstances.

Anna Akhmatova was an anti-Stalinist modernist poet who became one of the most acclaimed writers in the Russian canon. I borrowed an autographed photo of her from my friend, Akhmatova collector and enthusiast Stephen Garmey, for this cover emblazoned with her own handwritten initial.

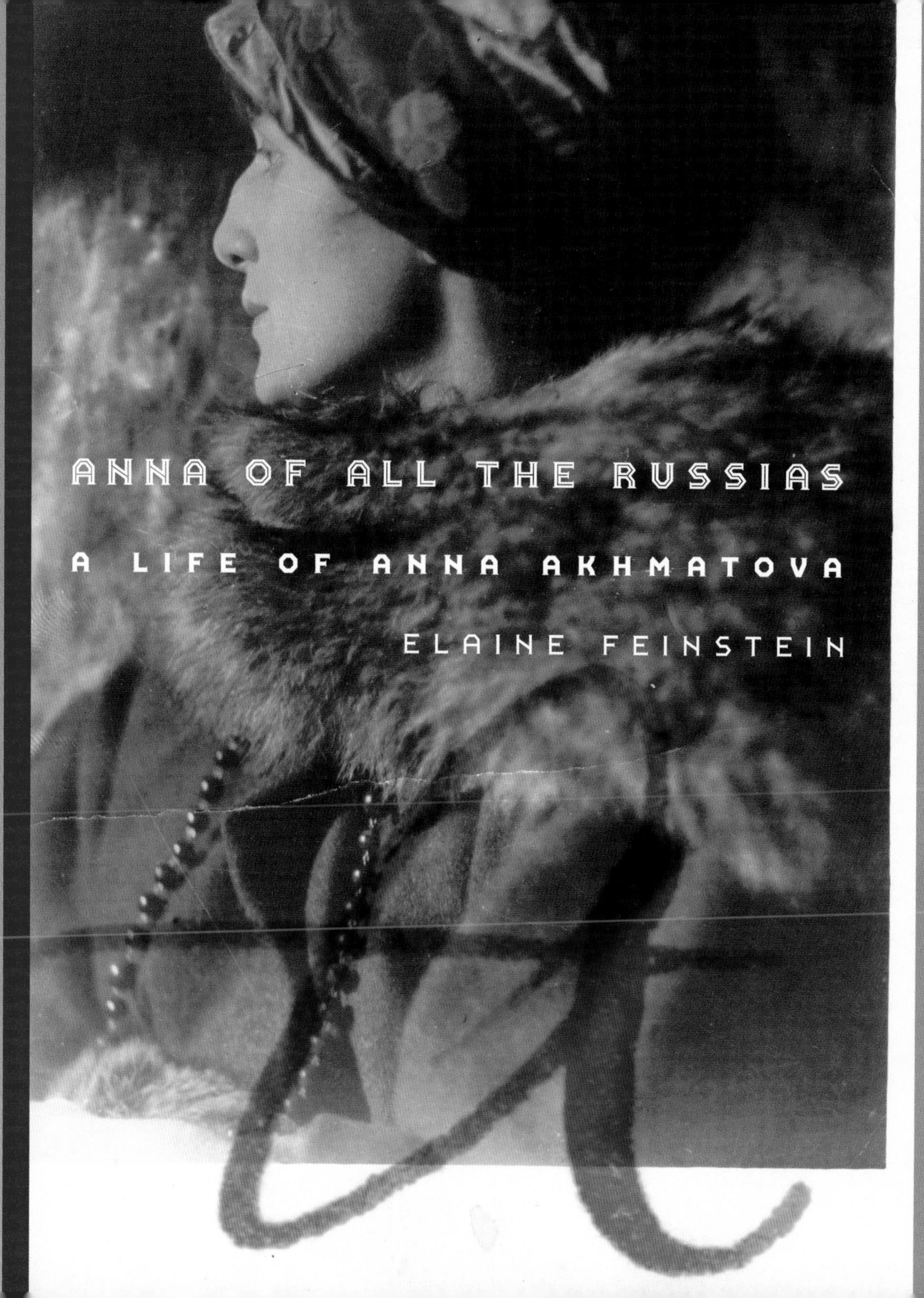
ANNA OF ALL THE RUSSIAS
A LIFE OF ANNA AKHMATOVA
ELAINE FEINSTEIN

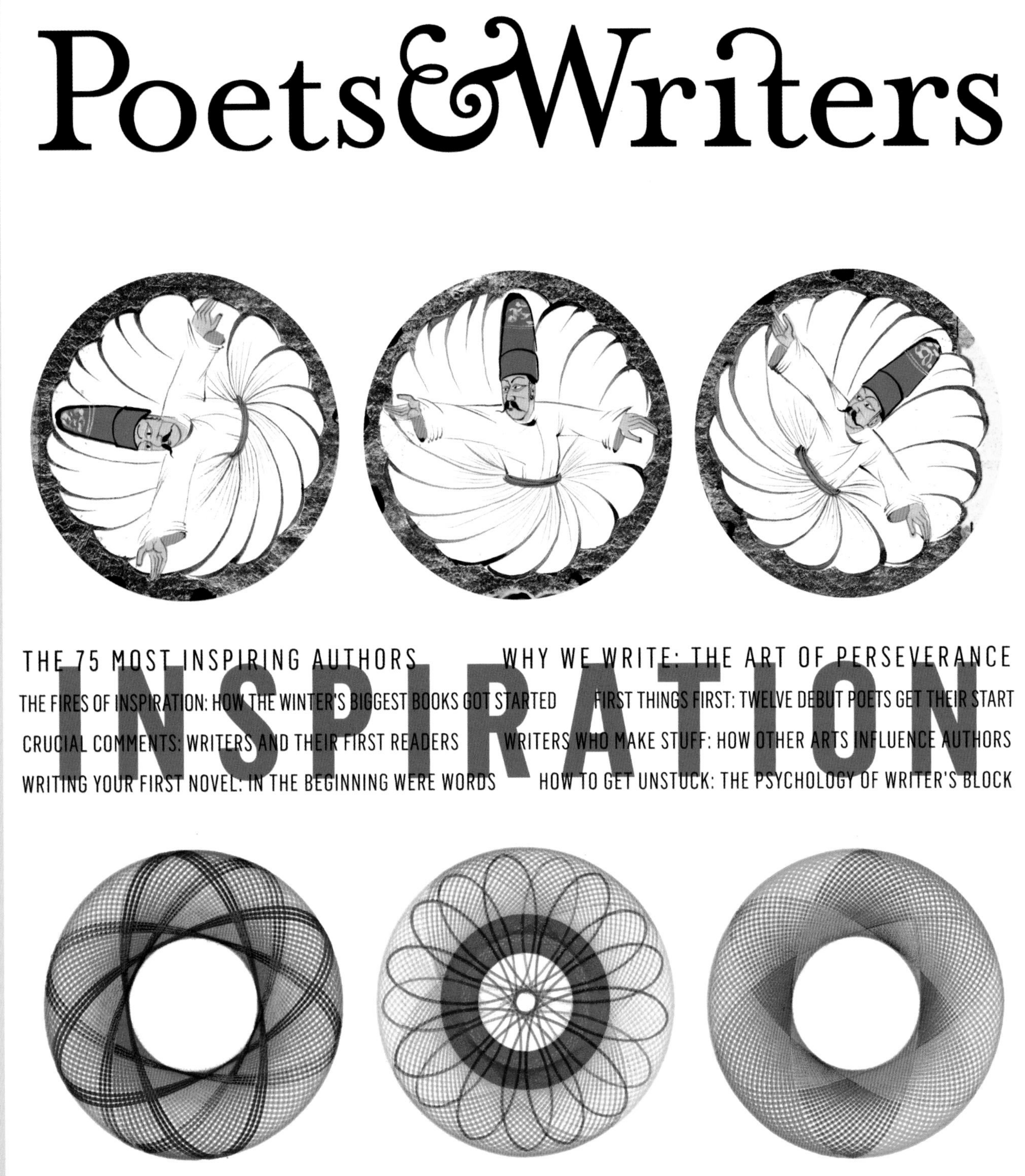
Poets&Writers
INSPIRATION
THE 75 MOST INSPIRING AUTHORS
WHY WE WRITE: THE ART OF PERSEVERANCE
THE FIRES OF INSPIRATION: HOW THE WINTER'S BIGGEST BOOKS GOT STARTED
FIRST THINGS FIRST: TWELVE DEBUT POETS GET THEIR START
CRUCIAL COMMENTS: WRITERS AND THEIR FIRST READERS
WRITERS WHO MAKE STUFF: HOW OTHER ARTS INFLUENCE AUTHORS
WRITING YOUR FIRST NOVEL: IN THE BEGINNING WERE WORDS
HOW TO GET UNSTUCK: THE PSYCHOLOGY OF WRITER'S BLOCK



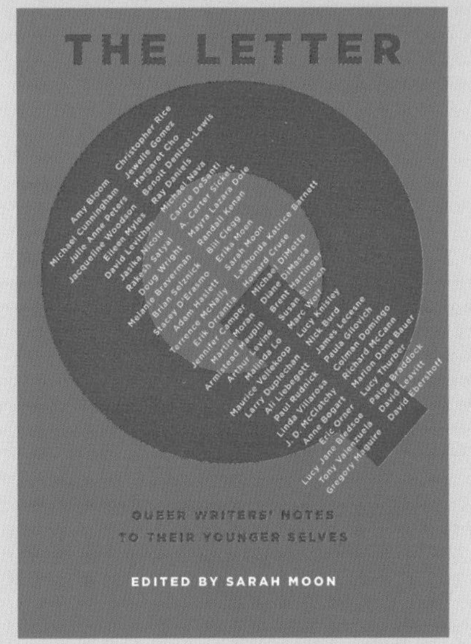
THE LETTER
QUEER WRITERS' NOTES
TO THEIR YOUNGER SELVES
EDITED BY SARAH MOON

## Letter Perfect

During a trip to Istanbul a few years ago, I was taken with vintage prints of whirling dervishes in the Grand Bazaar and bought a few (left, top). Oddly, soon after during the same trip, I came upon a teenaged kid selling Spirograph sets on the street outside the souk (left, bottom). I certainly didn't need another Spirograph (had one in my youth, loved it) but what really floored me were the drawings he was making to demonstrate what it could do. The thing was, he was selling the sets, not the drawings, and in negotiations typical to the culture, we bargained back and forth so that I could eventually buy them. When I returned to the States, I was asked to design a cover for the magazine *Poets & Writers* on the theme of "inspiration," and to me the link between spinning men and spinning pen lines was inescapable.

**ABOVE:** Pretty self-explanatory; I just wanted to make sure that it didn't look like I was ripping off the design of Broadway's *Avenue Q*. Arthur A. Levine Books, 2012.

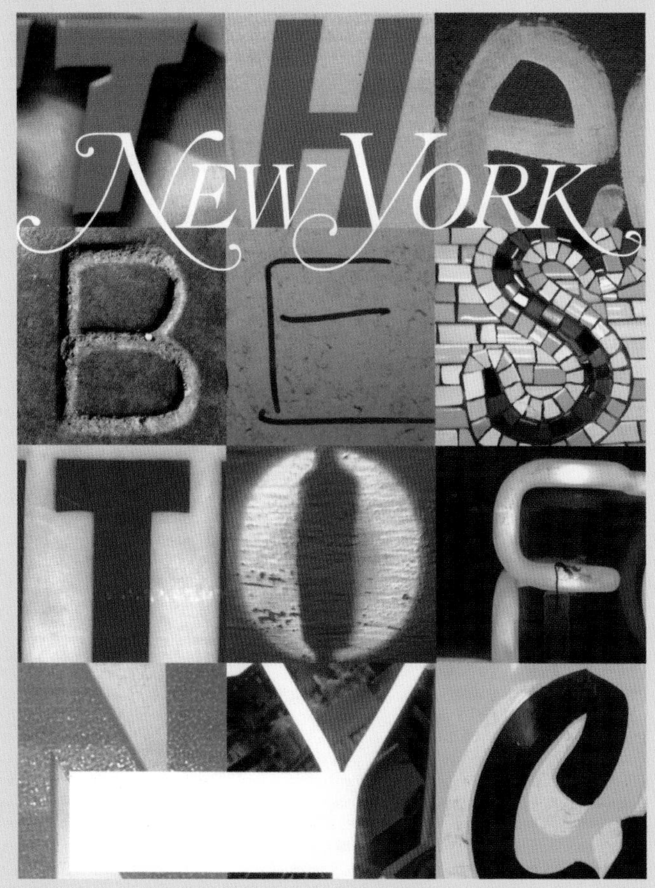
NEW YORK

Above is an unused sketch for the cover of *New York* magazine's "Best of NYC" issue for 2012. I took all the pictures myself on the street, and that was fun. I know by now that this idea is kind of obvious, and I suppose that's why they passed on it. But I love the magazine and pore over every issue. Hope to do a cover for them someday . . .

Whereas, Italian *GQ*? Who knew? Not on my radar, but they asked for something in honor of their tenth anniversary and I wasn't going to say no. I decided to do a montage of their logo and reading line in ten different colors and placements on the cover. I was just getting used to the "Multiply" effect in InDesign and how it blended the colors as if they were transparent.

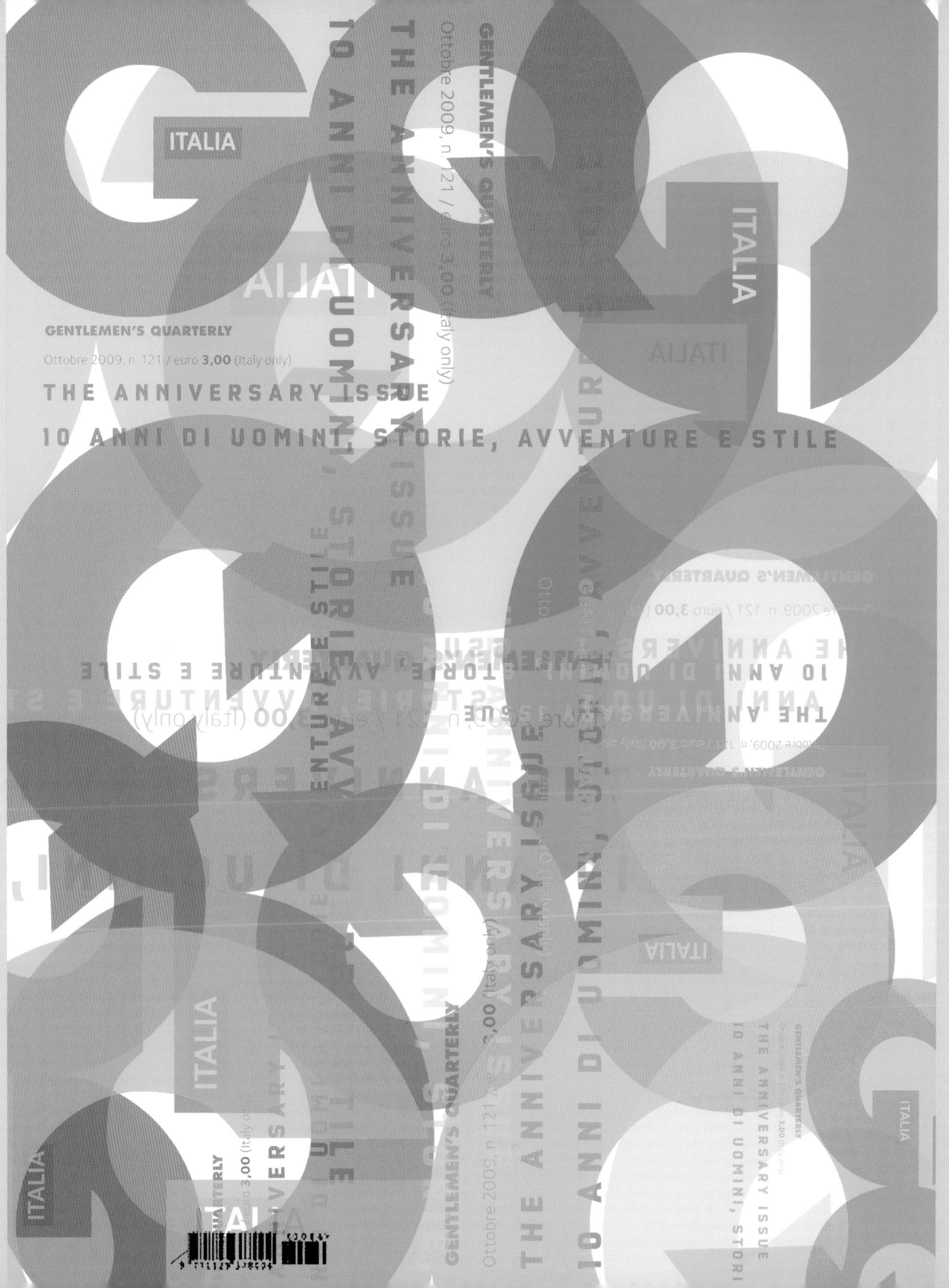
ITALIA
GENTLEMEN'S QUARTERLY
Ottobre 2009, n. 121 / euro 3,00 (Italy only)
THE ANNIVERSARY ISSUE
10 ANNI DI UOMINI, STORIE, AVVENTURE E STILE

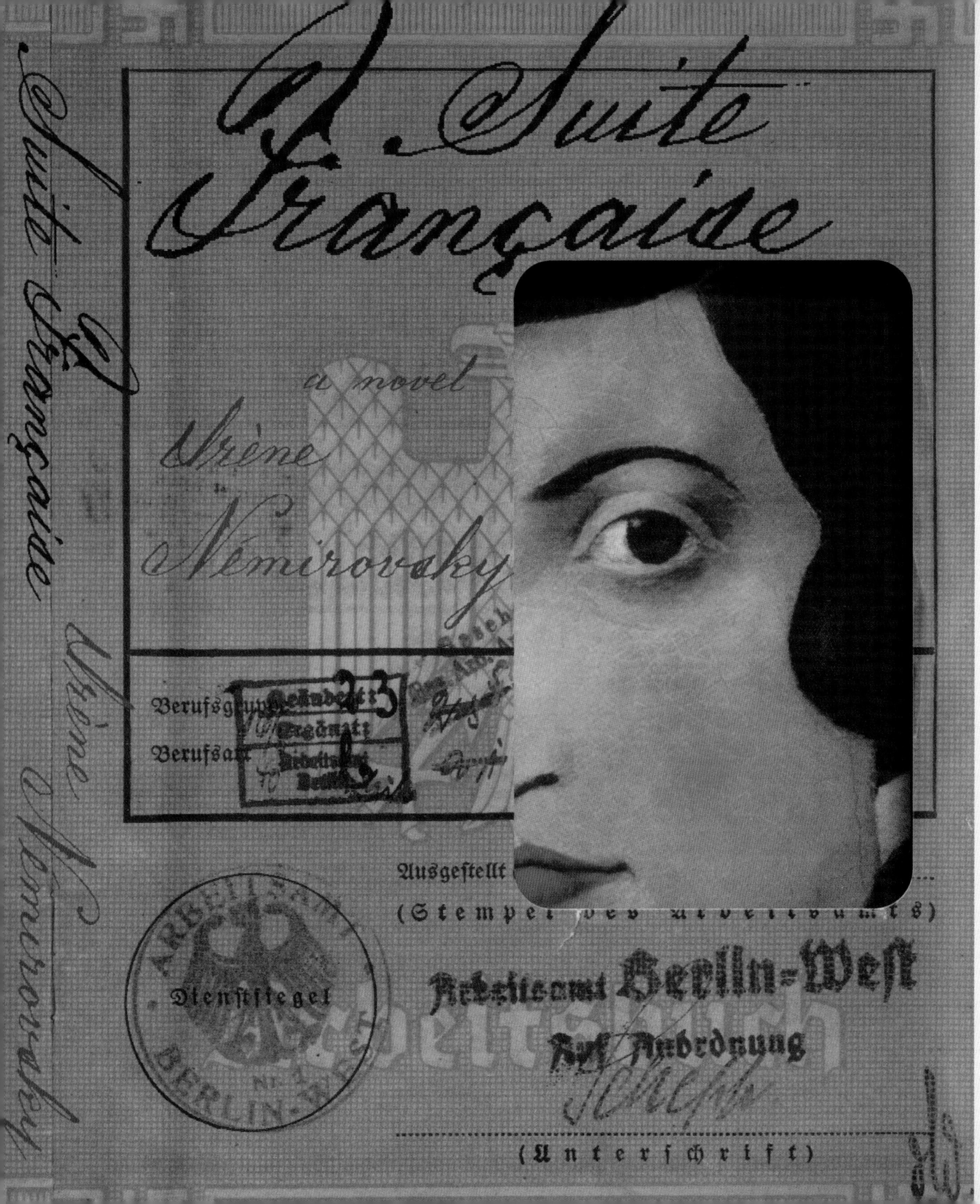
Suite Française
Suite Française
a novel
Irène Némirovsky
Irène Némirovsky
Berufsart
Ausgestellt
Dienstsiegel
Arbeitsamt Berlin-West
Auf Anordnung
(Unterschrift)

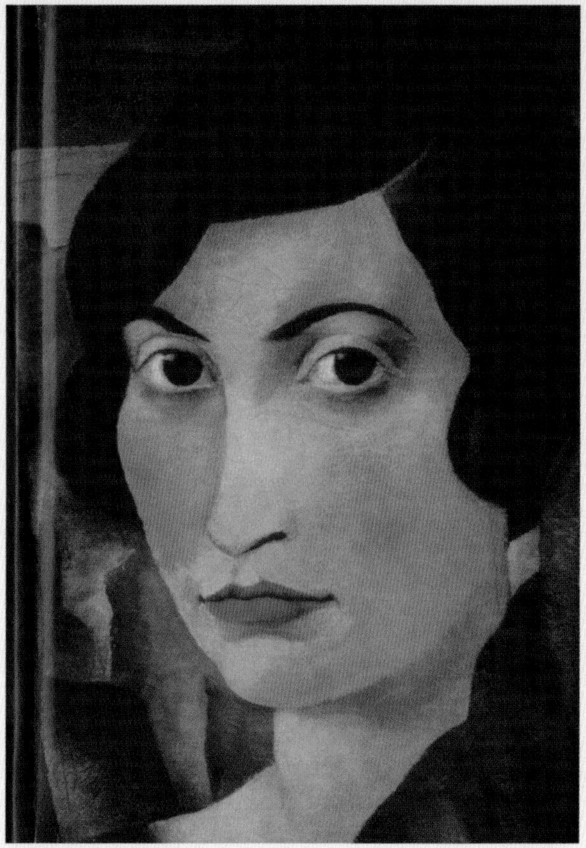

## Suite Series

I'll never forget listening to Sonny Mehta present *Suite Française* at the launch meeting for the Knopf Spring 2006 list. It was fascinating and heartbreaking; I hadn't heard of the novelist Irène Némirovsky and her tragic story—her daughter had only discovered the manuscript a full five decades after the author's death in Auschwitz in 1942. Sonny was convinced that this was going to be one of the great literary events of the year. Of course he was right.

My first design is at left, using a painting by Joseph Budko, an old German passport that I'd gotten at a Berlin flea market, and a die-cut hole. The hand lettering is by Elvis Swift. I was tremendously excited

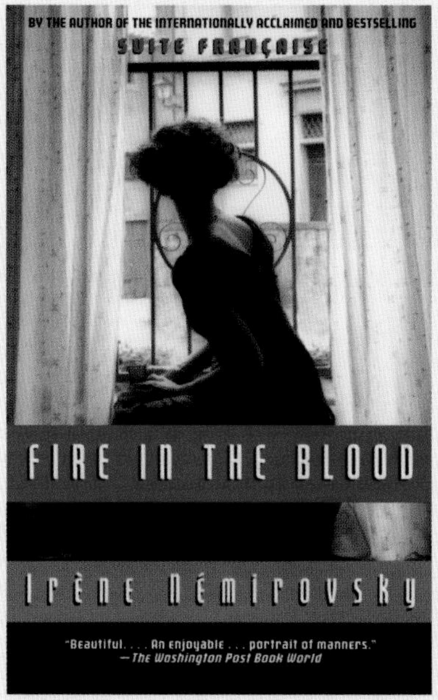
BY THE AUTHOR OF THE INTERNATIONALLY ACCLAIMED AND BESTSELLING
SUITE FRANÇAISE
FIRE IN THE BLOOD
Irène Némirovsky
"Beautiful. . . . An enjoyable . . . portrait of manners."
—The Washington Post Book World

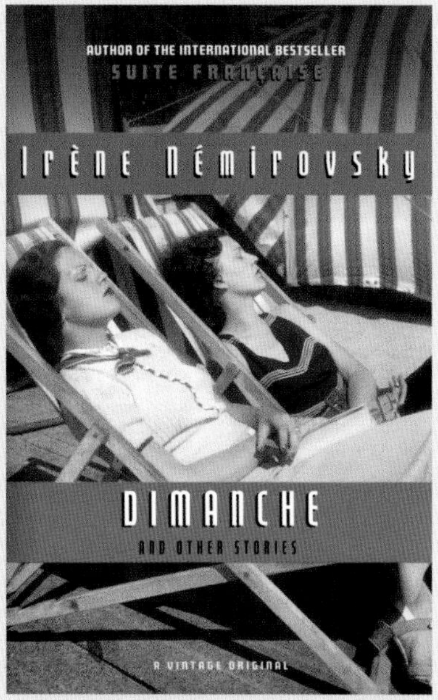
AUTHOR OF THE INTERNATIONAL BESTSELLER
SUITE FRANÇAISE
Irène Némirovsky
DIMANCHE
AND OTHER STORIES
A VINTAGE ORIGINAL

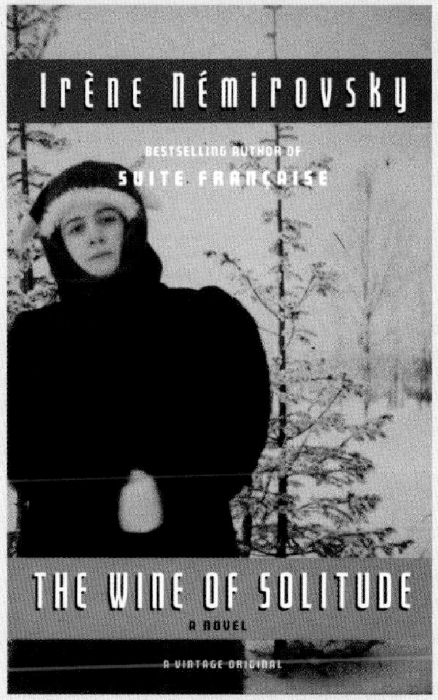
Irène Némirovsky
BESTSELLING AUTHOR OF
SUITE FRANÇAISE
THE WINE OF SOLITUDE
A NOVEL
A VINTAGE ORIGINAL

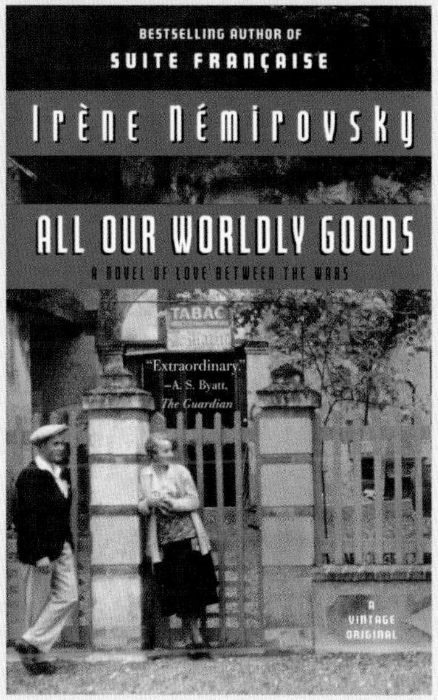
BESTSELLING AUTHOR OF
SUITE FRANÇAISE
Irène Némirovsky
ALL OUR WORLDLY GOODS
A NOVEL OF LOVE BETWEEN THE WARS
TABAC
"Extraordinary."
—A. S. Byatt,
The Guardian
A VINTAGE ORIGINAL

about this concept, but even I had to ultimately agree that it was too complicated and difficult to read.

The final jacket is at right, using art that the British publisher had found, paired with my typographic treatment. This look was so successful that it was adapted for Némirovsky's backlist in Vintage (above).

**RIGHT:** Knopf, 2006. **ABOVE:** Vintage, 2008–12.

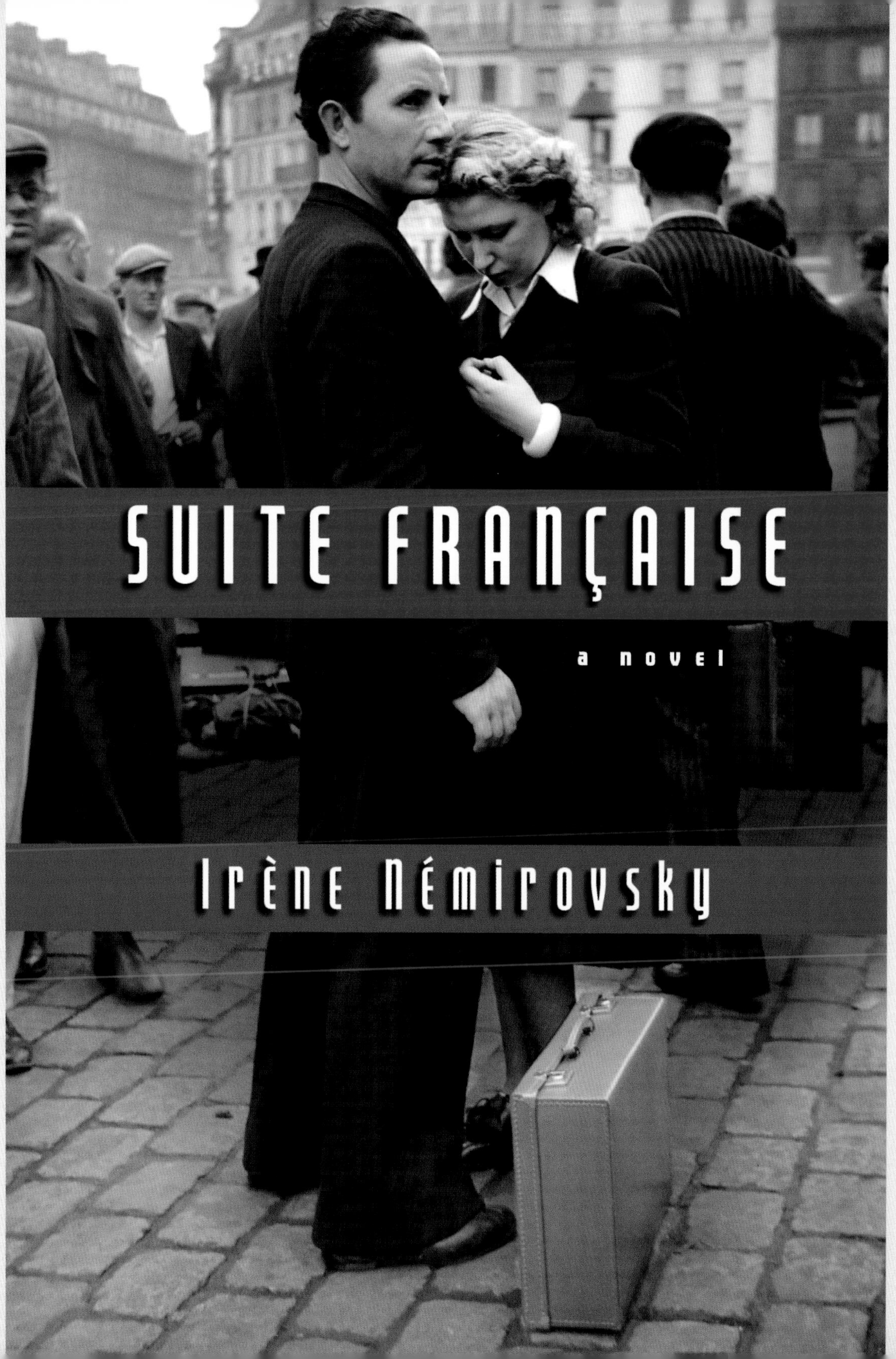
SUITE FRANÇAISE
a novel
Irène Némirovsky

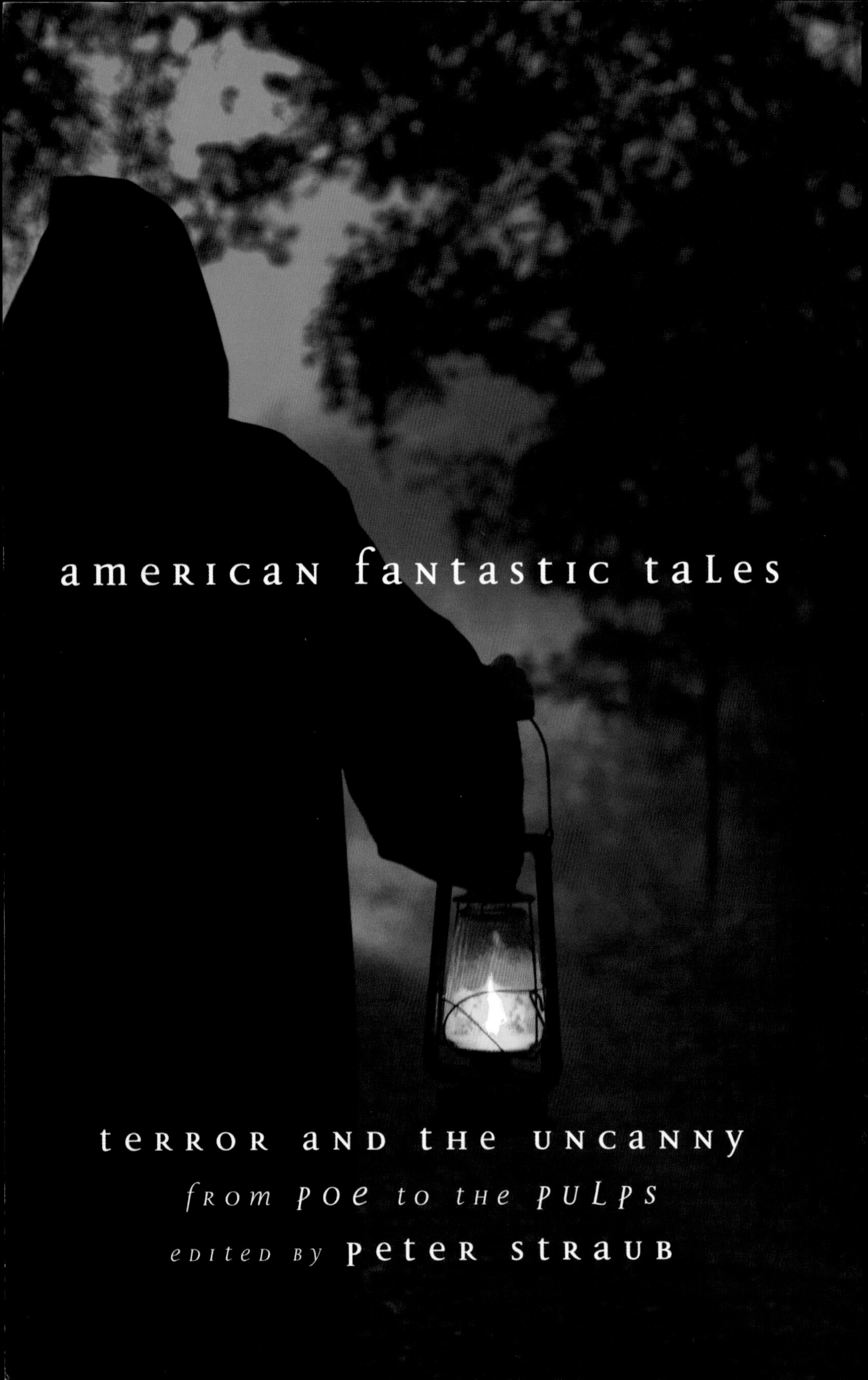
american fantastic tales
terror and the uncanny
from poe to the pulps
edited by peter straub

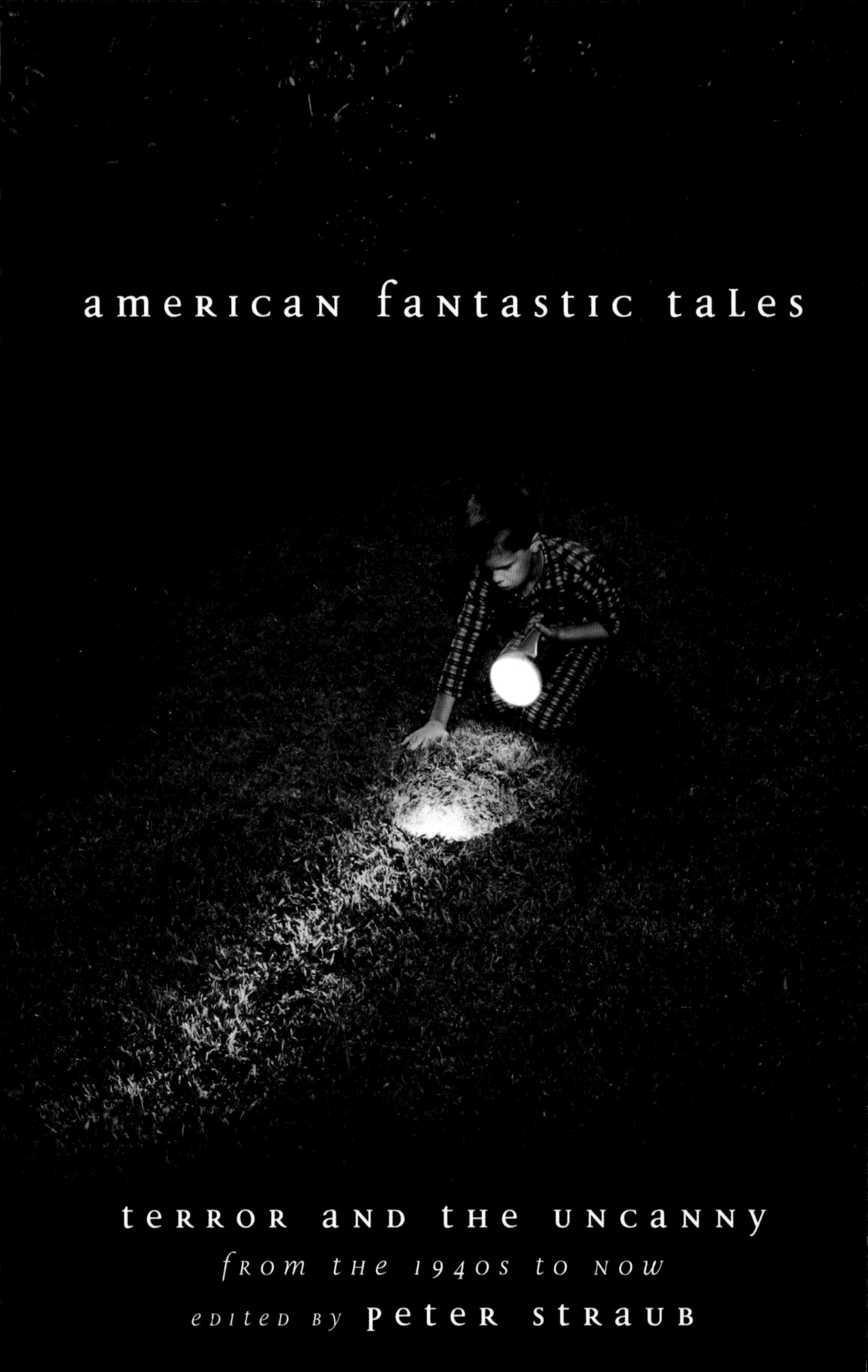
american fantastic tales
terror and the uncanny
from the 1940s to now
edited by peter straub

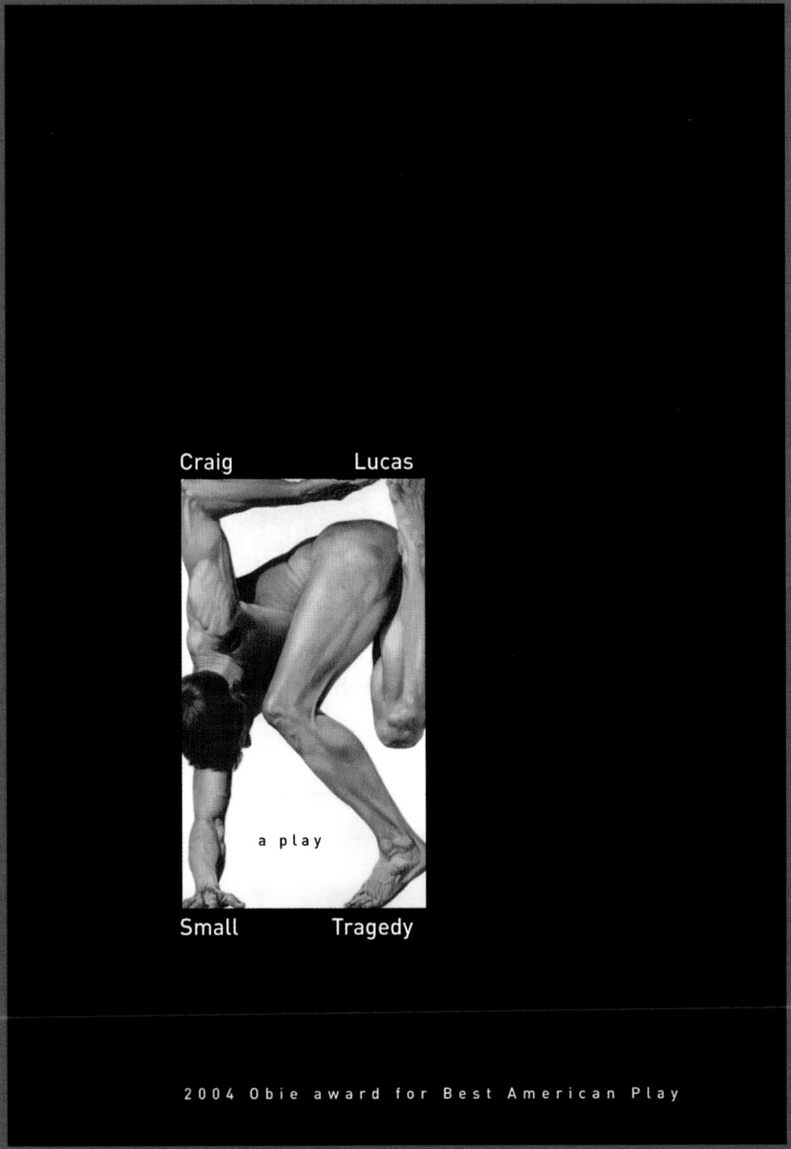
Craig Lucas
a play
Small Tragedy
2004 Obie award for Best American Play

**OPPOSITE:** For Peter Straub's two-volume anthology for the Library of America, *American Fantastic Tales* (2009), I needed to represent the idea of American spookiness past and present. The photograph on the left is by Andy and Michelle Kerry; the photograph on the right is by Frederik Broden.

**ABOVE:** I seem to remember that Craig found this art, and I just put it into an appropriate context. Theatre Communications Group, 2017.

**RIGHT:** This was rather uncanny—I was on a trip to Stockholm during the time I was to design a cover for this book by Henning Mankell about a Swedish woman in early 20th-century colonial Africa. During a random visit to an exhibit of photographs by Christer Strömholm (whom I had never heard of) I saw this picture and I knew it was perfect. We (Knopf) were able to obtain the rights to use it from the artist's estate.

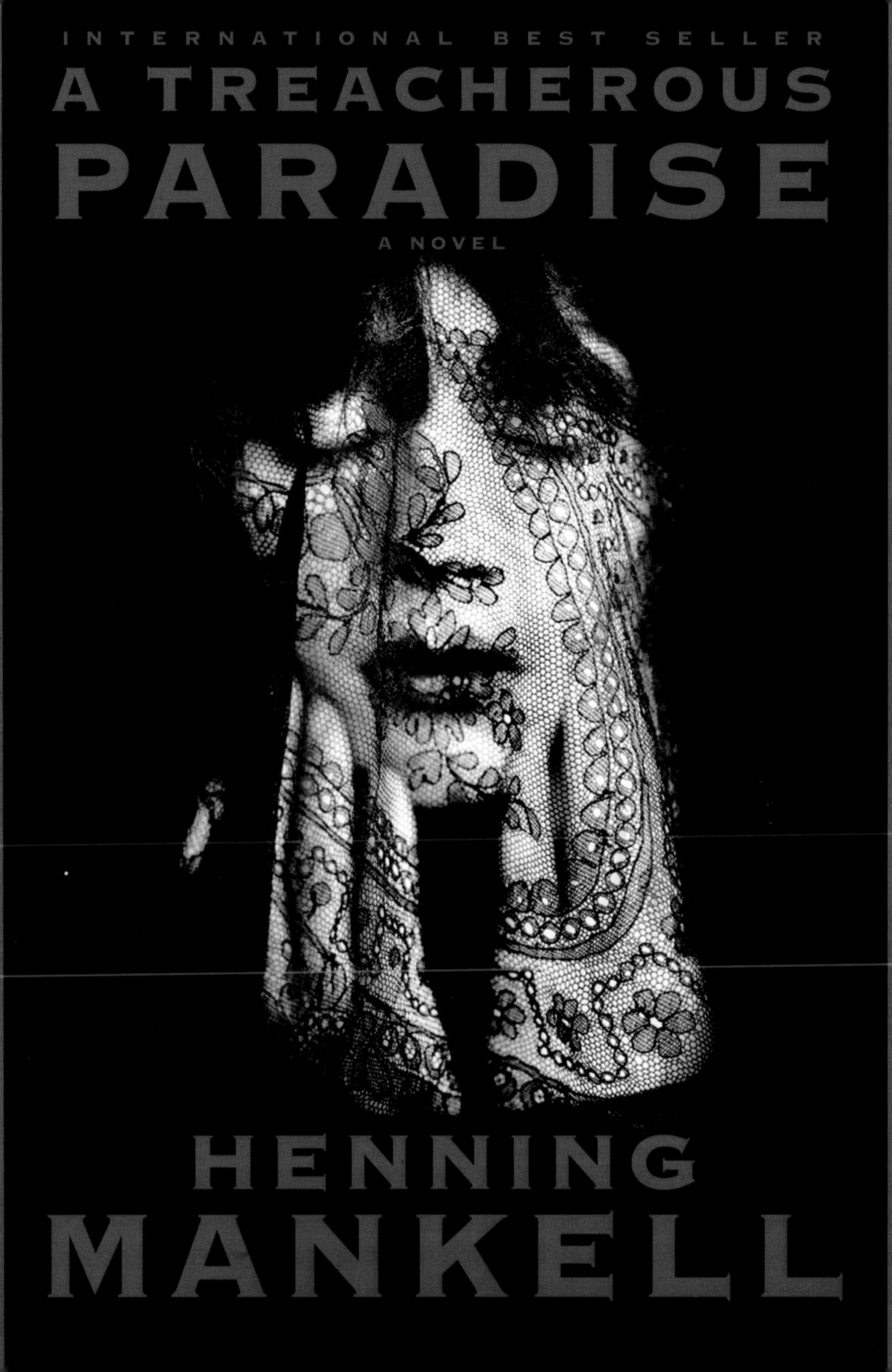
INTERNATIONAL BEST SELLER
A TREACHEROUS PARADISE
A NOVEL
HENNING MANKELL

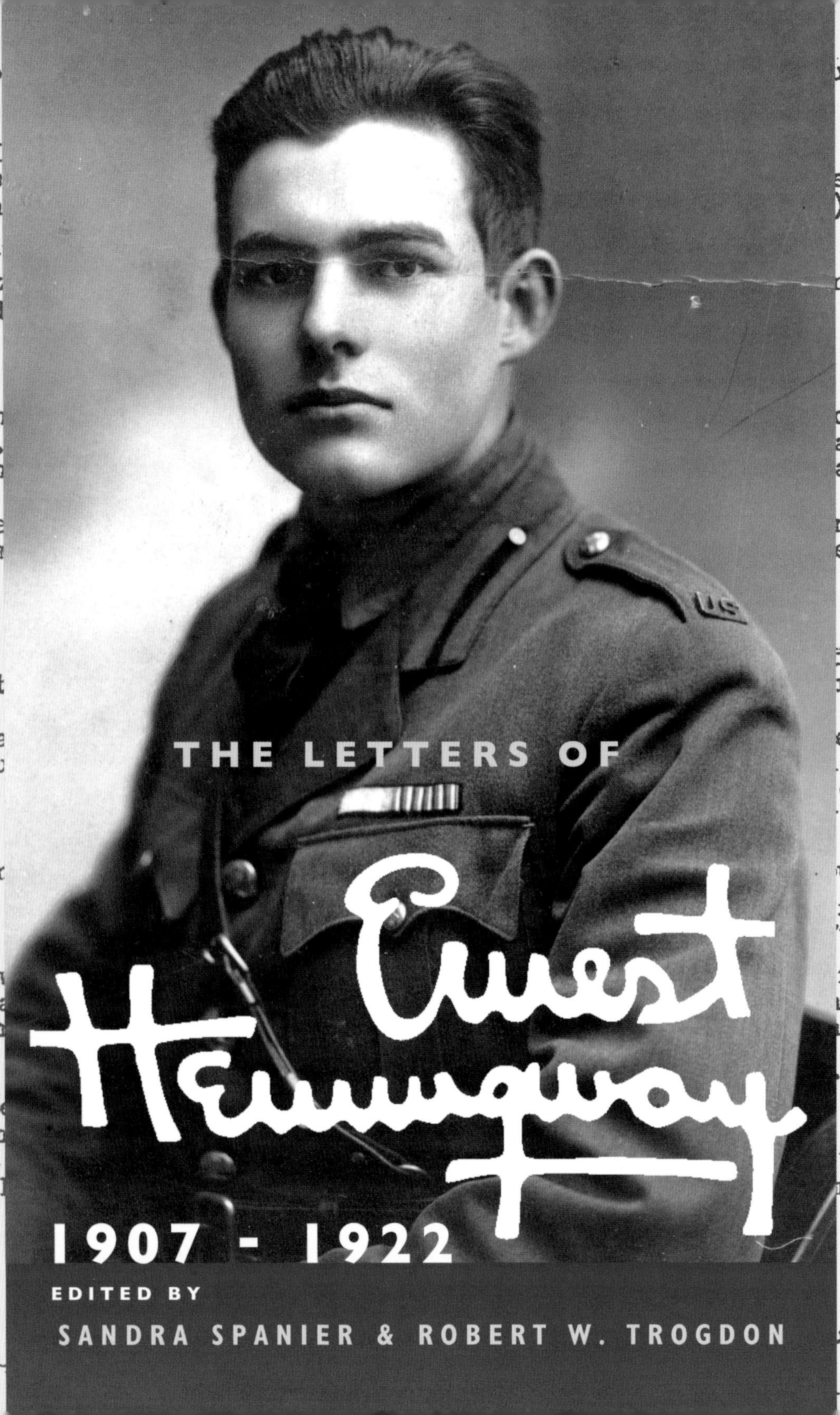
THE LETTERS OF
Ernest Hemingway
1907 - 1922
EDITED BY
SANDRA SPANIER & ROBERT W. TROGDON

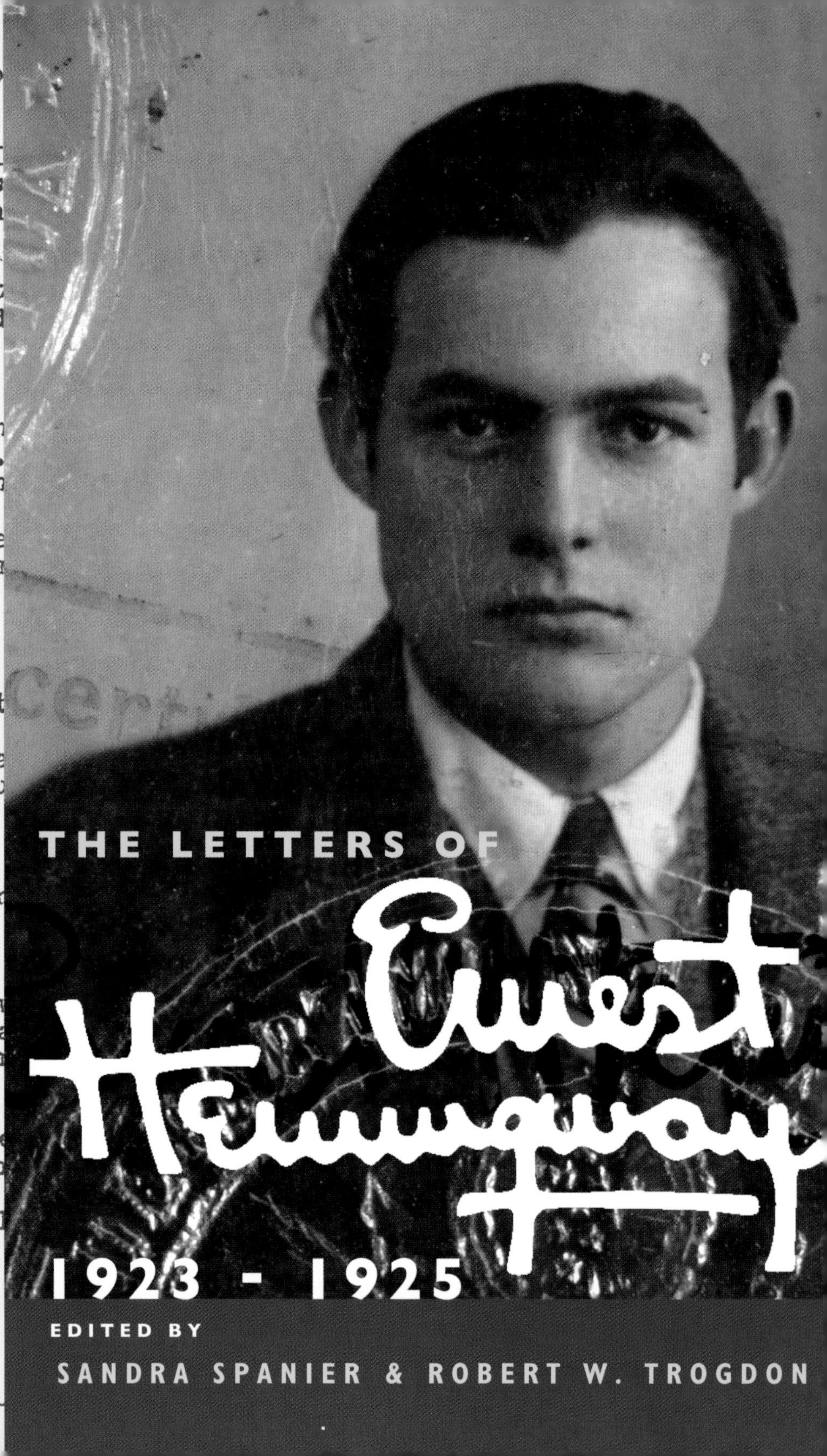
THE LETTERS OF
Ernest Hemingway
1923 - 1925
EDITED BY
SANDRA SPANIER & ROBERT W. TROGDON

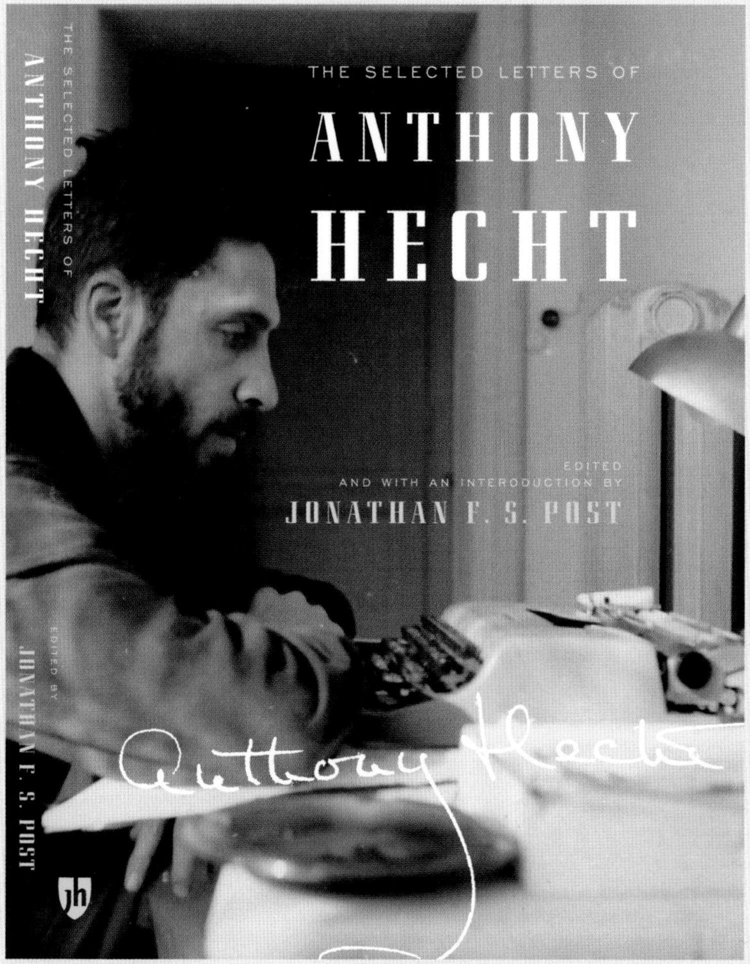
THE SELECTED LETTERS OF
ANTHONY HECHT
EDITED AND WITH AN INTRODUCTION BY
JONATHAN F. S. POST
THE SELECTED LETTERS OF
ANTHONY HECHT
EDITED BY
JONATHAN F. S. POST

# Letter Men

I honestly try not to use recognizable formulas for any given book category . . . except in this case. As in, collections of letters of distinguished authors. I want to see their signatures; I want terrific portraits that don't feel overly familiar. I want to either see them writing or glimpse a bit of manuscript. This doesn't mean that the covers need to look predictable; they just need to look interesting. In the case of Hemingway (opposite), this is quite an ambitious long-term, ongoing series that will cover a projected seventeen volumes.

**OPPOSITE, LEFT & RIGHT:** Cambridge University Press, 2011 & 2013. **ABOVE:** Johns Hopkins University Press, 2012. **RIGHT:** Harper, 2008.

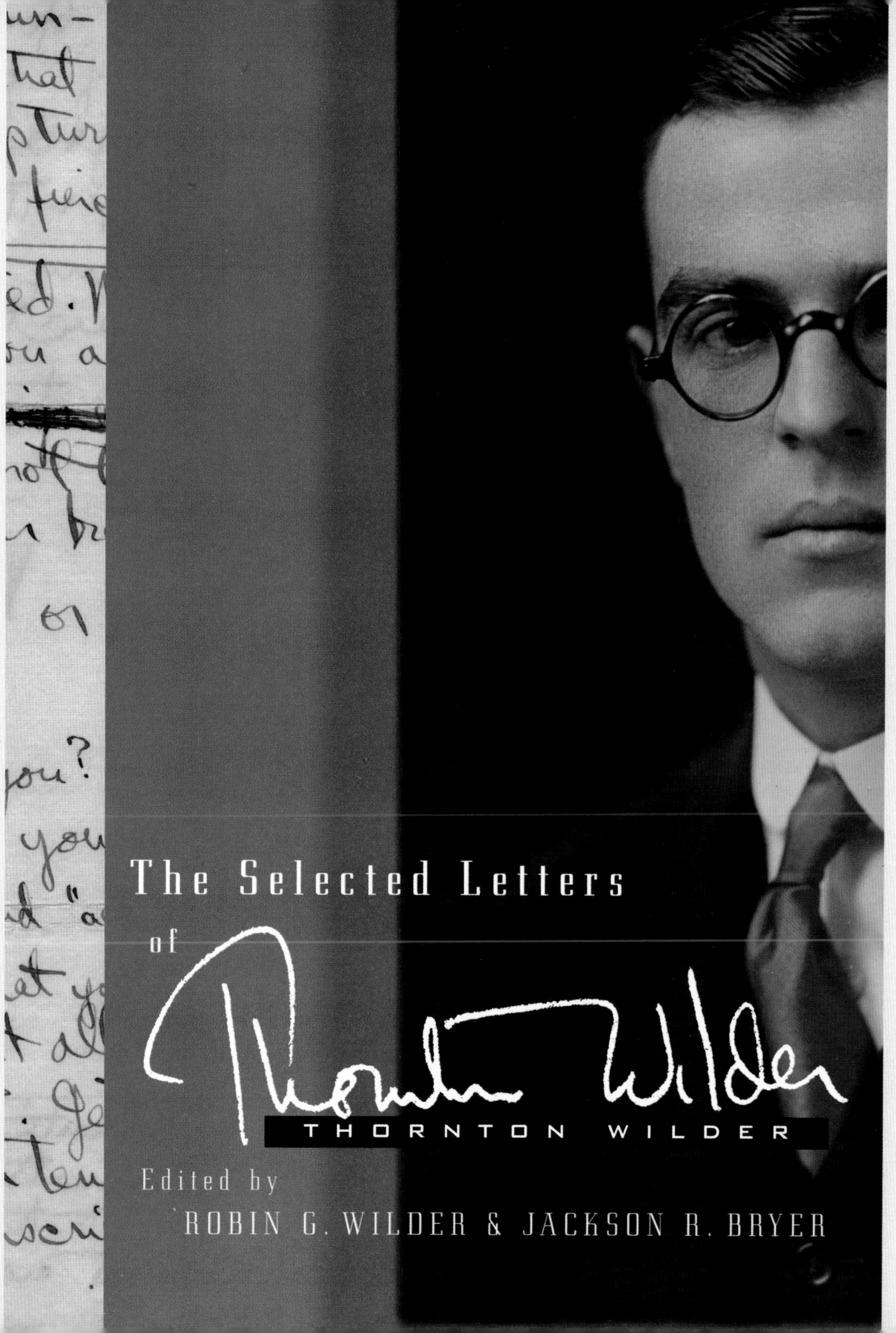
The Selected Letters
of
THORNTON WILDER
Edited by
ROBIN G. WILDER & JACKSON R. BRYER

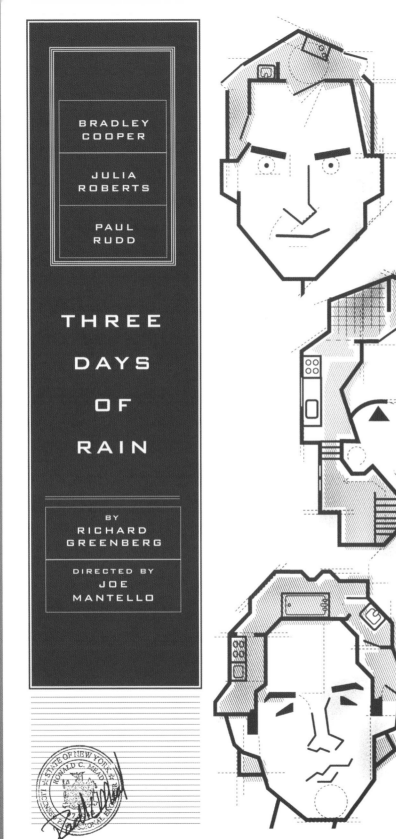

BRADLEY
COOPER

JULIA
ROBERTS

PAUL
RUDD

THREE
DAYS
OF
RAIN

BY
RICHARD
GREENBERG

DIRECTED BY
JOE
MANTELLO

# Three Months of Comps

I have known the theater director and actor Joe Mantello from the early '90s, when his partner was the playwright Jon Robin Baitz, for whom I've designed several covers (see *The Substance of Fire* in *Book One*, p. 38). In the fall of 2005, he asked the producer David Stone to bring me in to work with the Serino Coyne agency on the campaign for a Broadway revival of a play he was to direct called *Three Days of Rain* by Richard Greenberg. The opening date would be the following April. What made this a real event is that it would mark the Broadway debut of Julia Roberts. In retrospect, it was even more remarkable because her co-stars were then relative unknowns Bradley Cooper and Paul Rudd.

The plot revolves around a pair of young architects in 1960, the legendary modernist house they created, and the woman they both love. We also meet their children (played by the same actors), who meet up in 1995 in an apartment on New York's Lower East Side. There is a lot of emotional baggage, discussion, and argument about their parents' work and the nature of their relationship.

Because of the architectural design themes, my first thought was to render portraits of the actors as blueprint plans for apartment layouts. I reached out to my genius illustrator friend Christoph Niemann, who in turn enlisted the help of another illustrator named Stephen Savage for fine-tuning. I thought they totally, beautifully, nailed it (left).

Although this concept was met with initial enthusiasm, it was soon decided not to depict a specific image of any actor; some guessed that Julia didn't want to detract from her fellow cast members. Regardless, I had to start over. The title is literal, and they planned to stage a spectacular rainstorm on stage in Act II. So I went with New York in the rain, the idea of Before and After, the past and the present. I generated a lot of comps, and the final design appears on the opposite page, far right. I ultimately got way

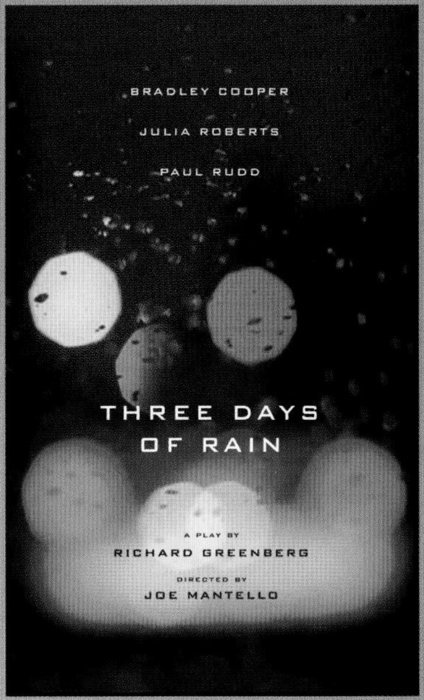
BRADLEY COOPER
JULIA ROBERTS
PAUL RUDD
THREE DAYS
OF RAIN
A PLAY BY
RICHARD GREENBERG
DIRECTED BY
JOE MANTELLO

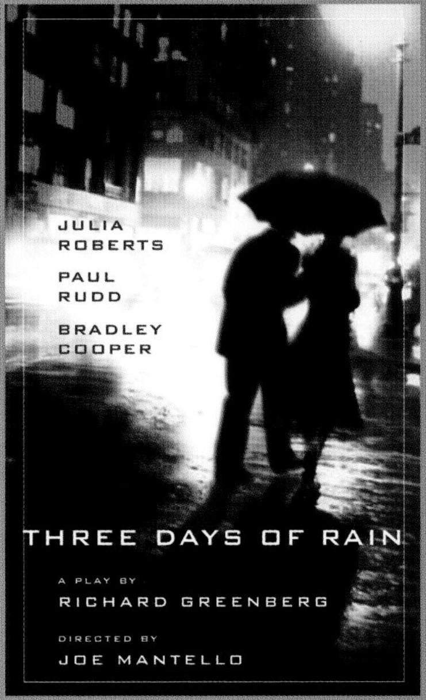
JULIA
ROBERTS
PAUL
RUDD
BRADLEY
COOPER
THREE DAYS OF RAIN
A PLAY BY
RICHARD GREENBERG
DIRECTED BY
JOE MANTELLO

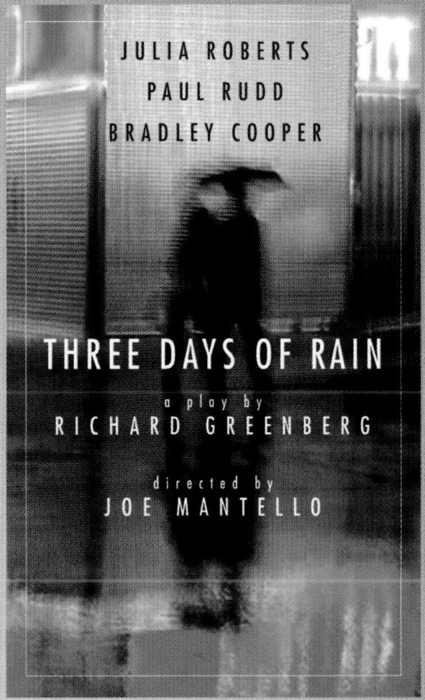
JULIA ROBERTS
PAUL RUDD
BRADLEY COOPER
THREE DAYS OF RAIN
a play by
RICHARD GREENBERG
directed by
JOE MANTELLO

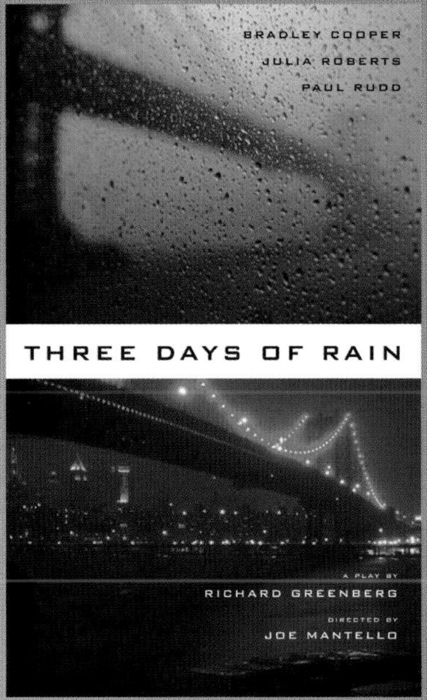
BRADLEY COOPER
JULIA ROBERTS
PAUL RUDD
THREE DAYS OF RAIN
A PLAY BY
RICHARD GREENBERG
DIRECTED BY
JOE MANTELLO

too much credit for it, my name appearing as the designer on all the ads and the materials covering the production. But the final image was created by the Serino Coyne staff, based on stock images I had provided. They were the ones who really made it work, and they did a beautiful job. It was a thrilling experience, but exhausting, and a reminder that the high-stakes theater world can be a lot more complicated than the book world.

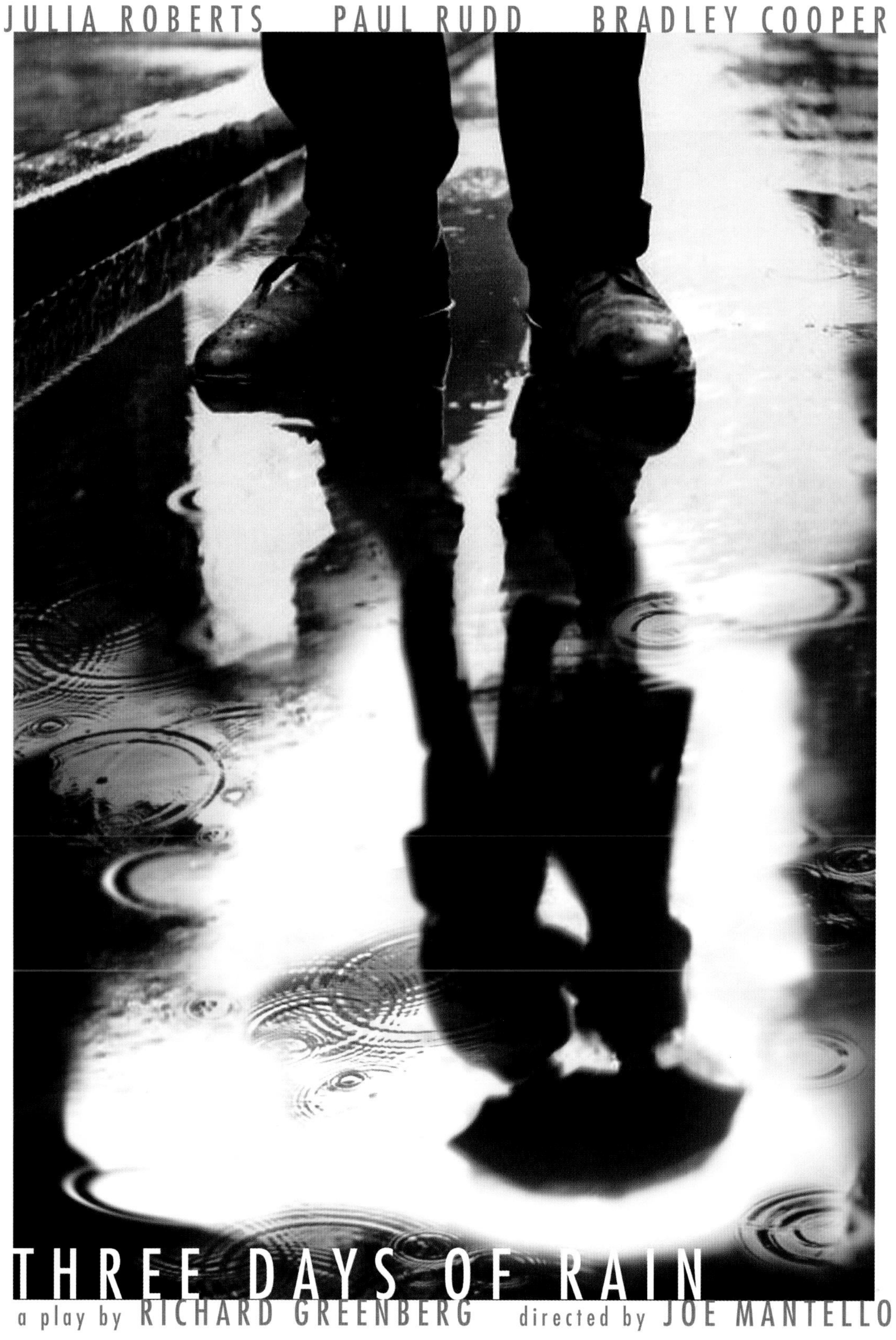
JULIA ROBERTS PAUL RUDD BRADLEY COOPER
THREE DAYS OF RAIN
a play by RICHARD GREENBERG directed by JOE MANTELLO

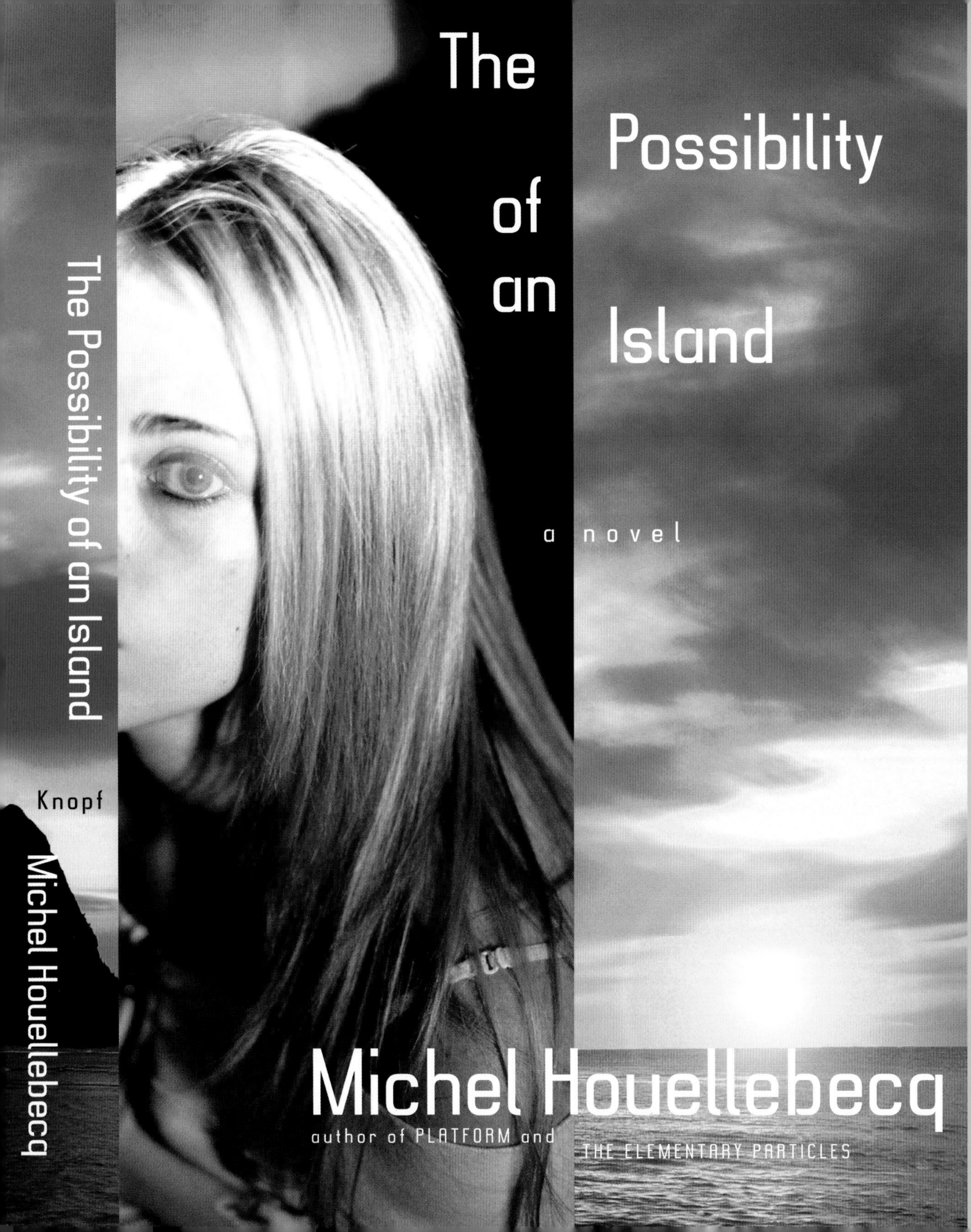
The Possibility of an Island
Knopf
Michel Houellebecq
The Possibility of an Island
a novel
Michel Houellebecq
author of PLATFORM and THE ELEMENTARY PARTICLES

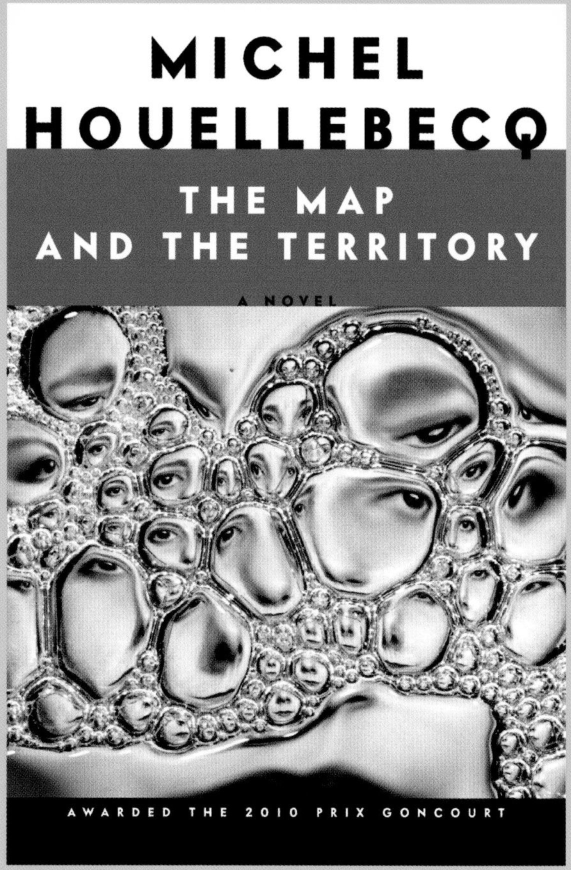
MICHEL HOUELLEBECQ
THE MAP AND THE TERRITORY
A NOVEL
AWARDED THE 2010 PRIX GONCOURT

## Permanent Vacations

Michel Houellebecq sort of baffles me (I am so lacking in French sensibilities. *Je m'excuse*!), but I love his ideas and his sheer contempt for (and articulation of) the idiocies of contemporary society. And it's fun to give them a face; or in the case of *The Map and the Territory*, many faces. Jagged juxtapositions seemed the best solution for his book *The Possibility of an Island*.

For filmmaker David Cronenberg's novel about cannibalism, *Consumed*, I was able to finally use a display font from 1958 called Calypso by French type designer Robert Excoffon, which I had been semi-obsessed with since I discovered it in college. I always thought it was cool in

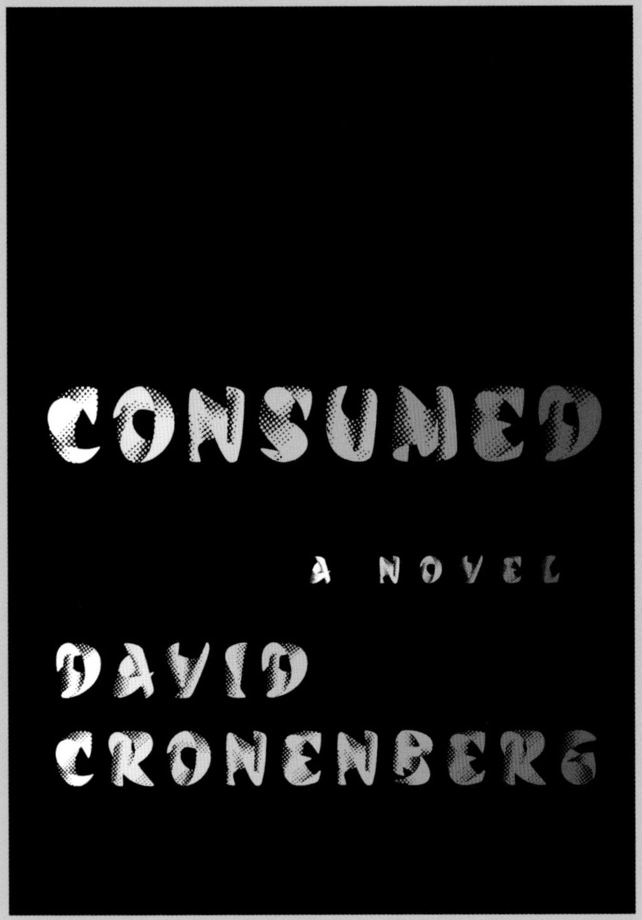
CONSUMED
A NOVEL
DAVID
CRONENBERG

and of itself, but what would you actually use it for? The answer: to suggest flayed flesh. Somehow I don't suspect that is what Mr. Excoffon had in mind, but such is the nature of using typography.

I have been a fan of photographer Francois Robert's work for years, but when I saw his "Stop the Violence" series using small compositions of bones to create images of weapons (some of them of mass destruction), I knew that his assemblage of a pistol was just right for Japanese author Shuichi Yoshida's novel *Villain*, about a serial killer in contemporary Tokyo. The image perfectly encapsulates all the facets of the story. Robert's combination of the intimate and detailed with the barbaric and reckless is eerily right-on.

**OPPOSITE, LEFT:** Knopf, 2006. **OPPOSITE, RIGHT:** Knopf, 2012.
**ABOVE:** Scribner, 2016. **RIGHT:** Pantheon, 2010.

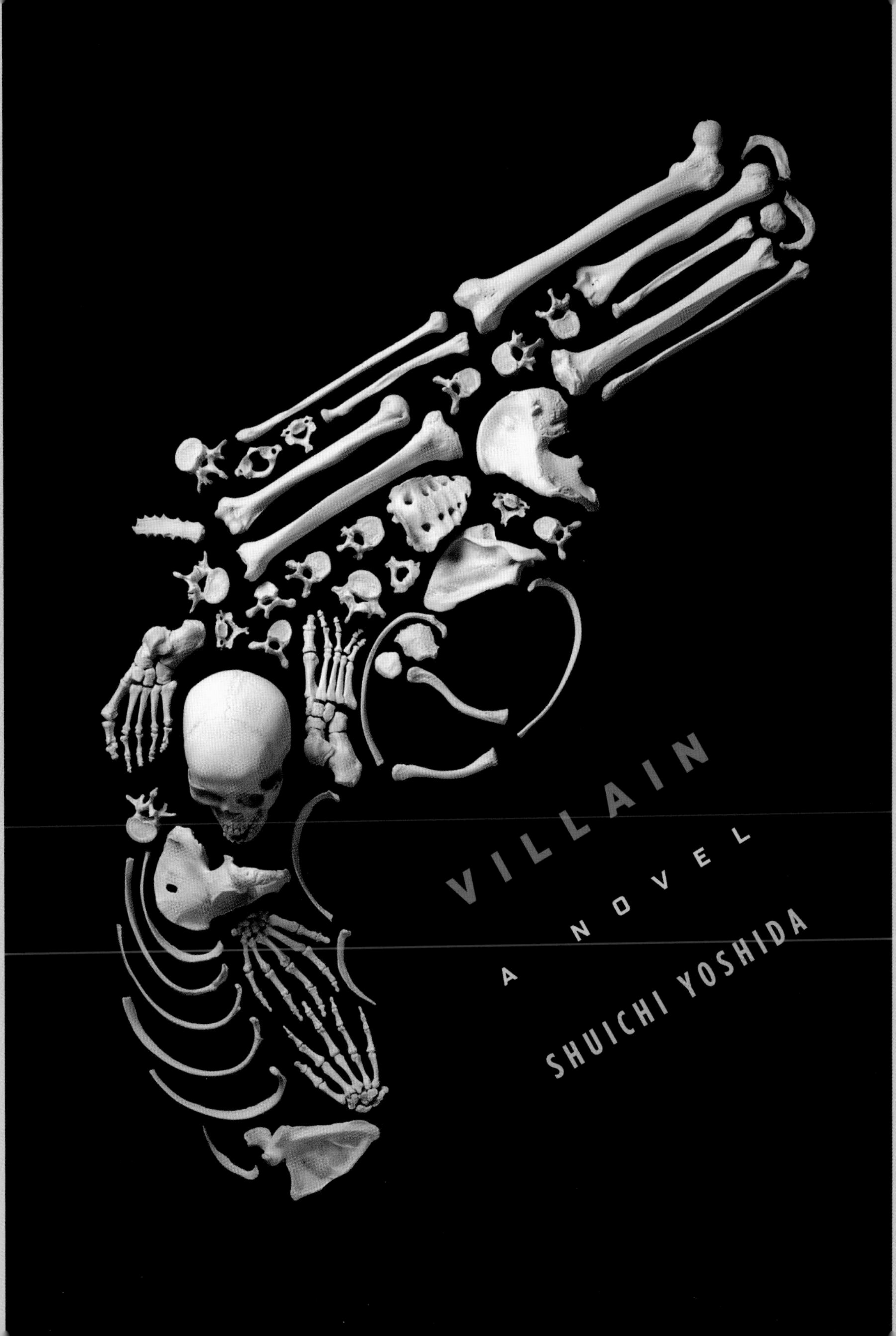
VILLAIN
A NOVEL
SHUICHI YOSHIDA

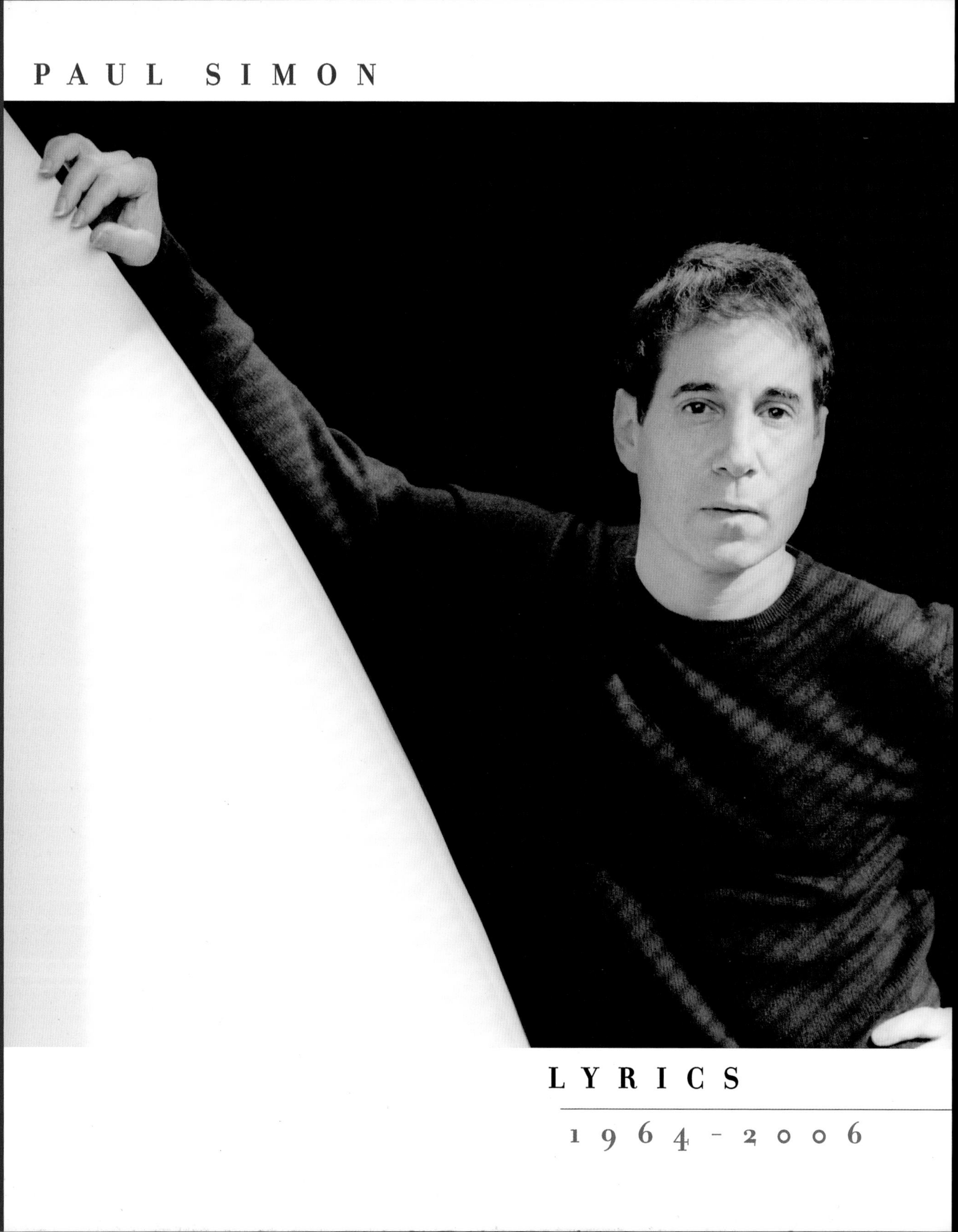
PAUL SIMON
LYRICS
1964-2006

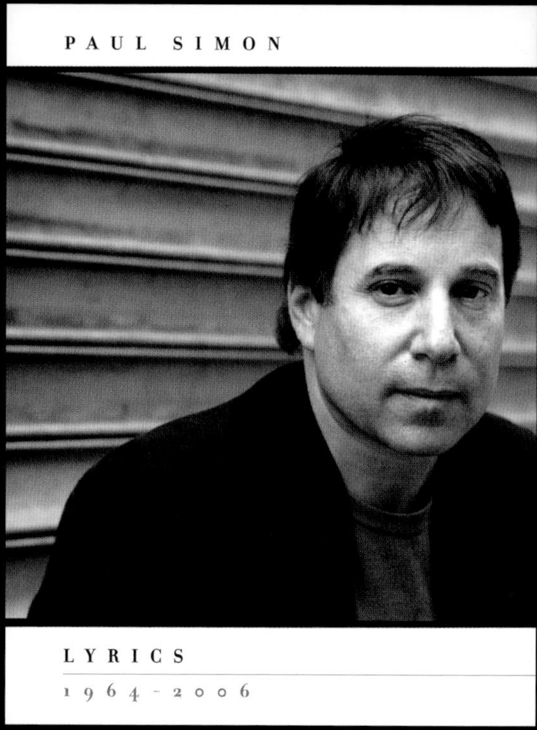
PAUL SIMON
LYRICS
1964-2006

**THIS PAGE:** Assorted comps (above & below) and final jacket (left). Simon & Schuster, 2008.

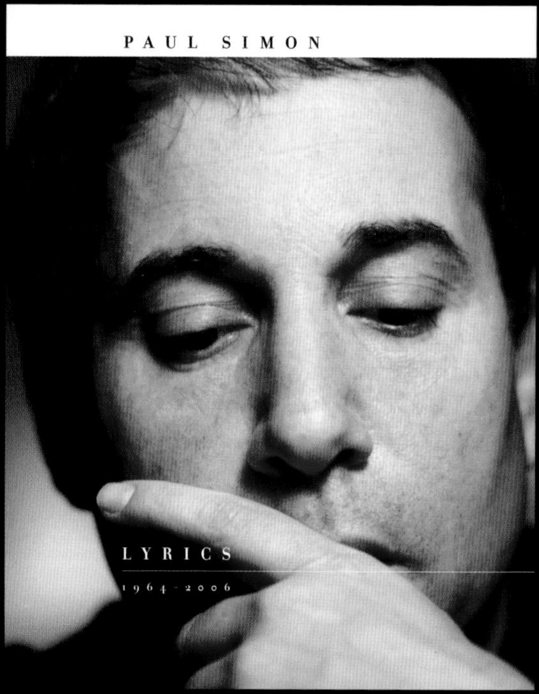
PAUL SIMON
LYRICS
1964-2006

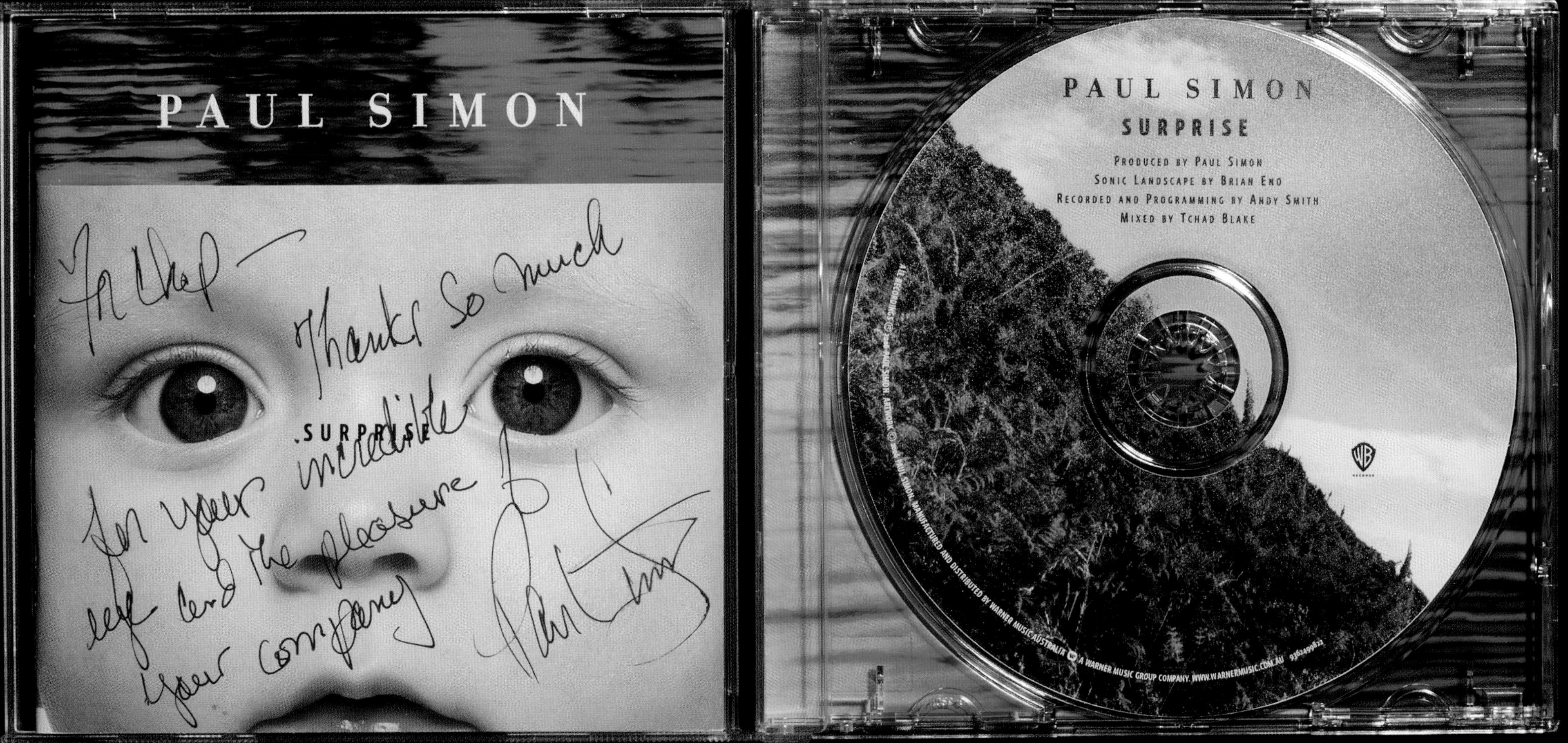
PAUL SIMON
SURPRISE
PAUL SIMON
SURPRISE
PRODUCED BY PAUL SIMON
SONIC LANDSCAPE BY BRIAN ENO
RECORDED AND PROGRAMMING BY ANDY SMITH
MIXED BY TCHAD BLAKE



## Surprise! A Living Legend Calls.

It was thanks to *Book One* that my work caught the attention of Paul Simon's brother and manager, Eddie, who passed my name on to the art director of Warner Bros. Records. Paul's new album was going to be called *Surprise*, and they asked if I would be interested in designing it. What ensued was one of the most fascinating and satisfying non-book projects I've ever had the privilege to work on. First, I was summoned to the famous Brill Building (which just happened to be five blocks south of my office) where Paul kept his base of operations. Ushered into a large receiving room overlooking Broadway just north of Times Square, I was asked to sit on a large sofa. On the other side of the room were two massive audiophile-grade stereo speakers. Paul came in and introduced himself, then asked, "Are you comfortable? You should be in the middle of the couch so you get the best sound balance. I want you to hear the new album." And with that, he sat himself on a chair catty-corner to my position, folded his arms in front of himself, and looked at me with focused intensity. Then the music started.

And we stayed like that, for the next forty-odd minutes, as the album played out. This was like winning some sort of bizarre radio contest: "Hey, the fifteenth caller gets a one-on-one audience with Paul Simon to listen to his new album while he stares intently at

**ABOVE:** The final cover, signed by Paul, and the label design. **FOLLOWING SPREAD:** My initial design proposal, including my transcription of the lyrics (note the words set in bold that relate to H2O). What I was determined to do (which took Paul by very pleasant, well, surprise) in the booklet was to treat the lyrics typographically as a collection of short stories and to render them as prose, with an accompanying image as visual commentary. And just for presumptuous fun I transcribed the lyrics myself, getting most of them right, but bits and pieces wrong. No matter, Paul appreciated the effort and made corrections.

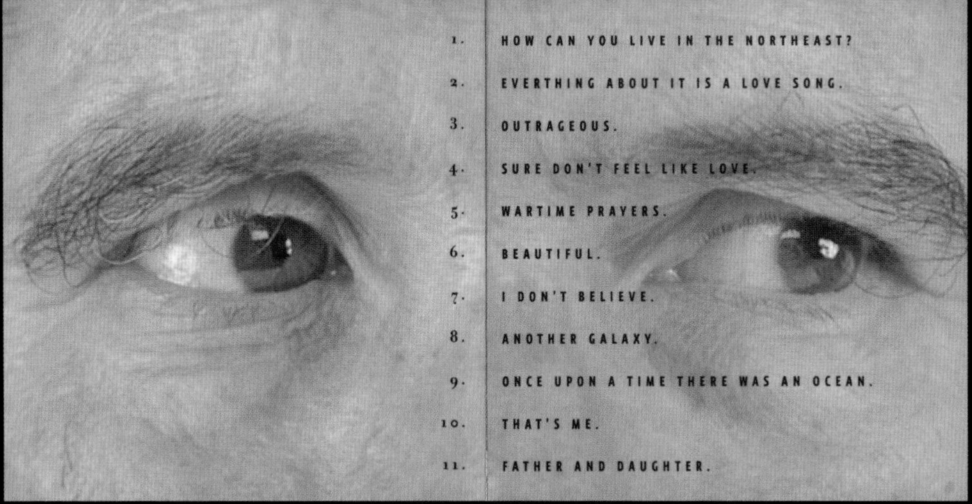

1. HOW CAN YOU LIVE IN THE NORTHEAST?
2. EVERTHING ABOUT IT IS A LOVE SONG.
3. OUTRAGEOUS.
4. SURE DON'T FEEL LIKE LOVE.
5. WARTIME PRAYERS.
6. BEAUTIFUL.
7. I DON'T BELIEVE.
8. ANOTHER GALAXY.
9. ONCE UPON A TIME THERE WAS AN OCEAN.
10. THAT'S ME.
11. FATHER AND DAUGHTER.

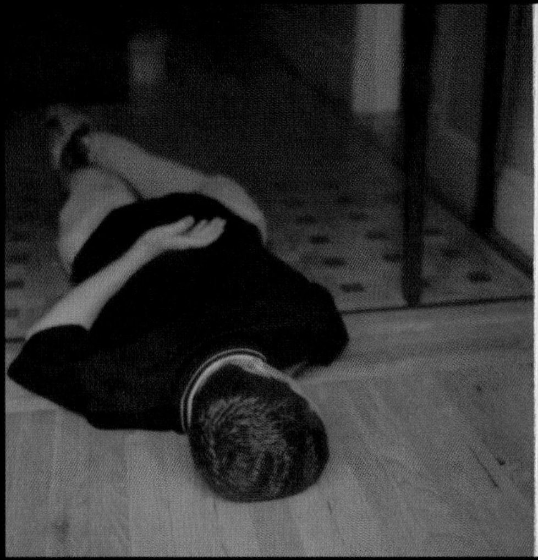

1.

## HOW CAN YOU LIVE IN THE NORTHEAST?

We heard the fireworks. Rushed out to watch the sky. Happy go lucky. Fourth of July.

How can you live in the Northeast? How can you live in the South? How can you live on the banks of a **river** when the **flood water** pours from the mouth?How can you be a Christian? How can you be a Jew? How can you be a Muslim, a Buddhist, a Hindu? How can you?

Weak as the winter sun, we enter life on earth. Names and religion come just after date of birth. Everybody gets a time to speak, and everyone has an inner voice. A day at the end of the week to wonder and rejoice. If the answer is infinite light, why do we sleep in the dark?

How can you live in the Northeast? How can you live in the South? How can you live on the banks of a **river** when the **flood water** pours from the mouth? How can you tattoo your body? Why do you cover your head? How can you eat from a rice bowl, ~~where~~ the holy man only bakes bread?

We watched the fireworks, til they were fireflies. Followed a path of stars, over the endless sky.

How can you live in the Northeast? How can you live in the South? How can you live on the banks of a **river** when the **flood water** pours from the mouth?

I've been given all I wanted. Only three generations off the boat. I've harvested and I've planted. I'm wearing my father's old coat.

1 TONGUE 3 BREAKS
2 HEARS

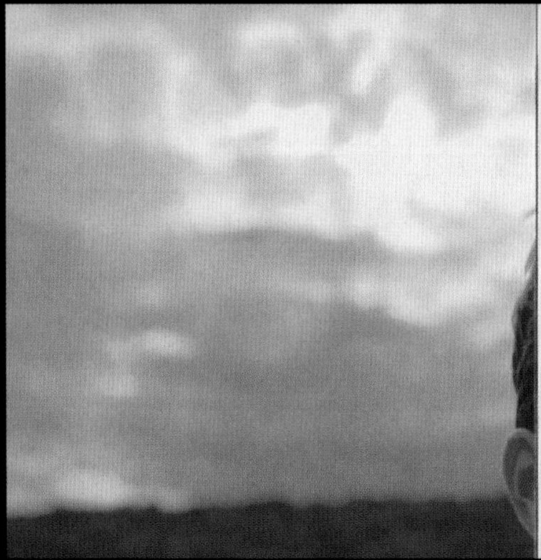

2.

## EVERYTHING ABOUT IT IS A LOVE SONG.

Locked in a struggle for the right combination—of words ~~and~~ IN a melody line, I took a walk along the **river**bank of my imagination. Golden **clouds** were shuffling the sunshine.

But if I ever get back to the twentieth century, guess I'll have to pay off some debts. Open the book of my vanishing memory, with its catologue of regrets. Stand up for the deeds I did, and those I didn't. Sit down, shut up, think about God, and wait for the hour of my rescue.

We don't mean to mess things up, but mess them up we do. And then it's "Oh, I'M sorry." Here's a smiling photograph of love when it was new. At a birthday party.

Make a wish and close your eyes: surprise, surprise, surprise.

Early ~~in~~ December, AND brown as a sparrow, **frost** creeping over the **pond**. I shoot a thought into the future, and it flies like an arrow, ~~from~~ my lifetime. And beyond.

If I ever come back as a tree or a crow, or even the wind-blown dust; find me on the ancient road ~~and~~ IN the song WHEN the wires ~~have~~ ARE hushed. Hurry on and remember me, as I 'M remember you. Far above the golden clouds, the darkness ~~beckons~~. VIBRATES ~~And~~ the earth is blue.

And everything about it is a love song. Everything about it. ~~And~~ everything about it is a love song. Everything about it. Everything about it is a looooooove song.

1. THROUGH

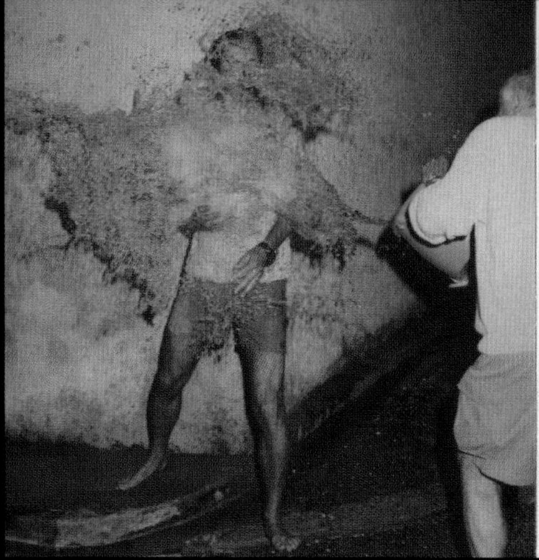

3.

## OUTRAGEOUS.

It's outrageous to line your pockets off the misery of the poor. Outrageous, the crimes some human beings must endure. It's a blessing to wash your face in the summer solstice **rain**. It's outrageous ~~for~~ a man like me ~~to~~ stand here and complain. But I'm tired. Nine hundred sit-ups a day. I'm painting my hair the color of mud, mud okay? I'm tired, tired. Anybody care what I say? No! I'm painting my hair the color of mud.

Who's gonna love you when your looks are gone? Tell me, who's gonna love you when your looks are gone? Aw, who's gonna love you when your looks are gone? Who's gonna love you when your looks are gone?

It's outrageous, the food they try to serve in a public school. Outrageous the way they talk to you like you're some kind of clinical fool. It's a blessing to rest my head in the circle of your love. It's outrageous: I can't stop thinking 'bout the things I'm thinking of. And I'm tired. Nine hundred sit-ups a day. I'm painting my hair the color of mud, mud okay? I'm tired, tired. Anybody care what I say? No! I'm painting my hair the color of mud.

Who's gonna love you when your looks are gone? Tell me, who's gonna love you when your looks are gone? Tell me, who's gonna love you when your looks are gone?

God will. Like he **waters** the flowers on your window sill. Take me. I'm an ordinary player in the key of C. And my will was broken by my pride and my vanity. Who's gonna love you when your looks are gone? God will. Like he **waters** the flowers on your window sill. Who's gonna love you when your looks are gone?

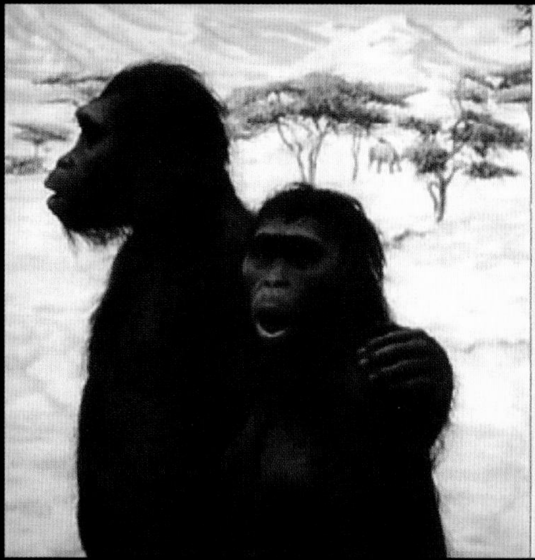

NO JOKE, NO JOKE. YOU GET SICK FROM THAT SURE DON'T FEEL LIKE LOVE. NO JOKE NO JOKE. SOME CHICKEN AND A CORN MUFFIN

4.

## SURE DON'T FEEL LIKE LOVE.

WELL THAT ~~FEELS~~ MORE LIKE LOVE

I registered to vote today. Felt like a fool. Had to do it anyway. Down at the high school. ~~Felt~~ about the second line. You know, felt like a fool. People say it all the time. Even when it's true. So, who's that conscience sticking on the sole of my shoe? Who's that consceince sticking on the sole of my shoe? Cause it sure don't feel like love.

A **tear drop** consists of electrolytes and salt. The chemistry of **crying** is not concerned with blame or fault. So, who's that consceince sticking on the sole of my shoe? Who's that consceince sticking on the sole of my shoe? Cause it sure don't feel like love. How does it feel? Feels like a threat. A voice in your head that you'd rather forget. ~~Sure don't feel like loooove. Corn muffin. That feels more like love.~~

Yay!
Boo!
Yay!
Boo!

Wrong again. Wrong again. Maybe I'm wrong again. Wrong again. Maybe I'm wrong again. Wrong again. I could be wrong again. I remember once in August 1993, I was wrong, and I could be wrong again. I remember one of my best friends turned enemy. So, I was wrong, and I could be wrong again. I remember once in a lowdown, down in Birminham. Yeah, but that didn't feel like love. Sure don't feel like, sure don't feel like, sure don't feel like love. Sure don't feel like, sure don't feel like, sure don't feel like love. It sure. Don't feel.

Like love.

1 THING
2 LOADOUT

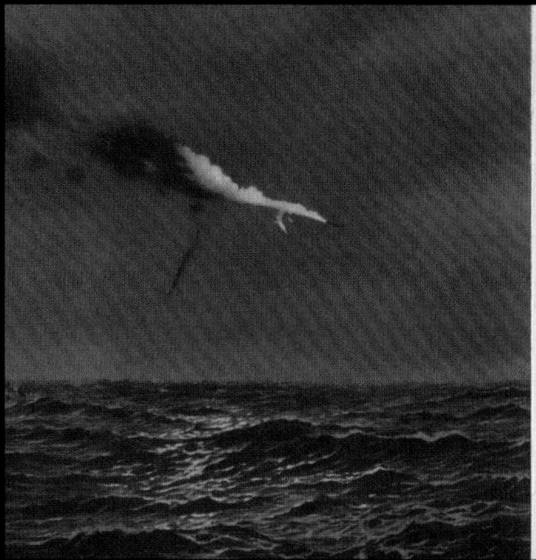

5.

## WARTIME PRAYERS.

Prayers offered IN in times of peace—are silent conversations. Appeals for love, or love's release. Private invocations. But all that is changed now. Gone like a memory form the day before the fires. People hungry for the voice of God hear lunatics and liars. Wartime prayers. Wartime prayers in every language spoken. For every family scattered and broken.

Because you cannot walk with the holy if you're just a halfway decent man. I don't pretend that I'm a mastermind with a genius marketing plan. I'm trying to tap into some wisdom. Even a little **drop** will do. I want to rid my heart of envy, and cleanse my soul of rage before I'm through.

Times are hard. It's a hard time, but everybody knows. ~~We~~ all about hard times, the thing is, what are you gonna do? Well, you cry and try to muscle through. ~~And~~ try to rearrange your stuff. But when the wounds are deep enough, and it's all that we can bare, we wrap ourselves. In prayer.

Because you cannot walk with the holy if you're just a halfway decent man. I don't pretend that I'm a mastermind with a genius marketing plan. I'm trying to tap into some wisdom. Even a little **drop** will do. I want to rid my heart of envy, and cleanse my soul of rage before I'm through. A mother murmurs in twilight space and draws her babies closer. With hush-a-byes for sleepy eyes, and kisses on the shoulder. To drive away despair she says a wartime prayer.

1. SLEEP

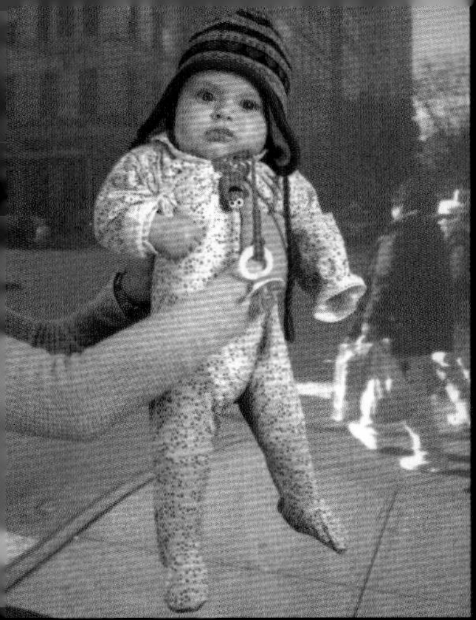

6.

# BEAUTIFUL.

SITTIN

Snowman sitt'in in the sun doesn't have time to waste. He had a little bit too much fun, now his head's erased. Back in the house, family of three: two do'in the laundry and one in the nursery.

DOIN'

We brought a brand new baby back from Bangledesh, thought we'd name her Emily. She's beautiful. Beautiful.

HURT SENSE OF

Yes sir, head's erased, body's a bowl of jelly. Hasn't learned to his taste, judging from his belly. But back in the house, family of four now: two doing the laundry and two on the kitchen floor.

We brought a brand new baby back from mainland China, sailed across the China Sea. She's beautiful. Beautiful.

Go-kart sitt'in in the shade: you don't need a ticket to ride, it's summertime, summertime, slip down a **water** slide. Little kid danc'in in the grass, legs like rubber bands. It's summertime, summertime. There's a line at the candy stand. Well keep an eye on them children, on them children in the **pool**. You better keep an eye on them children, on them children in the **pool**.

EYE

We brought a brand new baby back from Kosovo. That was nearly seven years ago. He cried all night. Could not sleep. His eyes were blind, dark and deep.

Beautiful.

1. BRAIN'S
2 EYE ON
3 BRIGHT

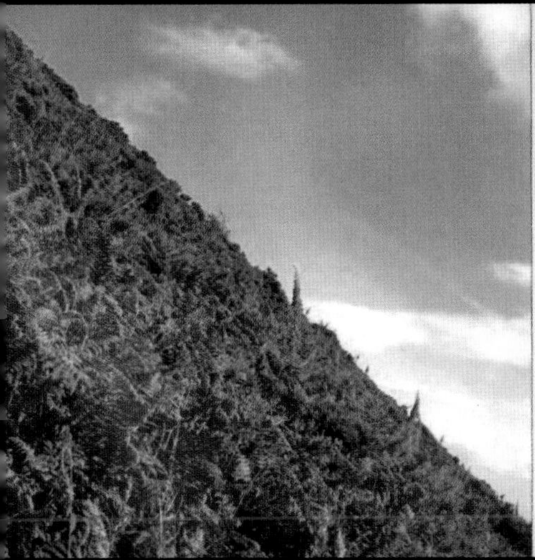

7.

# I DON'T BELIEVE.

Acts of kindness, like breadcrumbs in a fairytale forrest, lead us past dangers as light melts the darkness. But I don't believe, and I'm not consoled. I lean closer to the fire, but I'm cold.

The earth was born in a **storm**. The **waters** receded, the mountains were formed. The universe loves a drama, you know. And ladies and gentlemen this is the show.

I got a call from my broker. My broker informed me I'm broke. I was dealing my last hand of poker. My cards were as useless as smoke.

Oh, guardian angel. Don't taunt me like this, on a clear summer evening as soft as a kiss. My children are laughing, not a whisper of care. My love is brushing her long chestnut hair. I don't believe a heart can be filled to the brim and then vanish like **mist** as though life were a whim.

OR

Maybe the heart is part of the **mist**. And that's all that there is that could ever exist. Maybe and maybe and maybe some more. Maybe's the exit I'm looking for.

I got a call from my broker. My broker said he was mistaken. Maybe some virus software x had overtaken and he hopes that my faith isn't shaken.

Acts of kindness, like **rain** in a draught, release the spirit with a whoop and a shout. I don't believe we were born to be sheep in a flock. Two pantomime players with the hands of a clock.

1. OR BROKERAGE JOKE
2. PRAYERS

EB. SPOKEN AFTER 2004 PRES. ELECTION

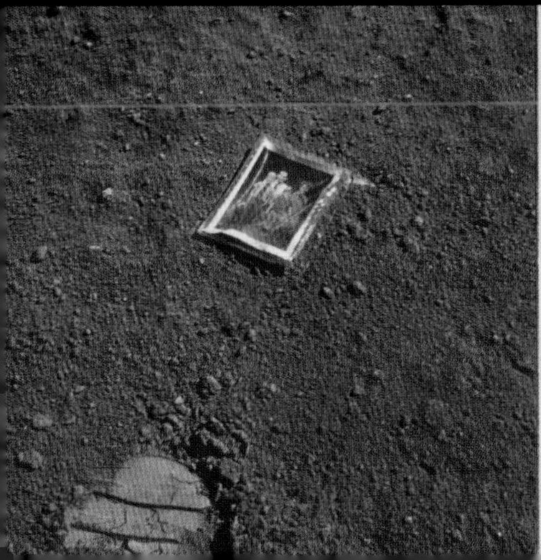

8.

# ANOTHER GALAXY.

On the morning of her wedding day, when no one was awake, she drove across the border. Leaving all the yellow roses on her wedding cake. Her mother's **tears**, her breakfast order.

She's gone, gone, gone.

There is a moment, a tip in time, when leaving home is the lesser crime.

When your eyes are blind with **tears**, but your heart can see: another life, another galaxy.

STORM

That night her dreams are stormy-tossed as a willow. She hears the **clouds**, she sees the eye of a hurricane, as it sweeps across her pillow.

But she's gone, gone, gone.

There is a moment, a tip in time, when leaving home is the lesser crime. When your eyes are blind with **tears**, but your heart can see:

Another life, another galaxy.

CHIP
CHIP

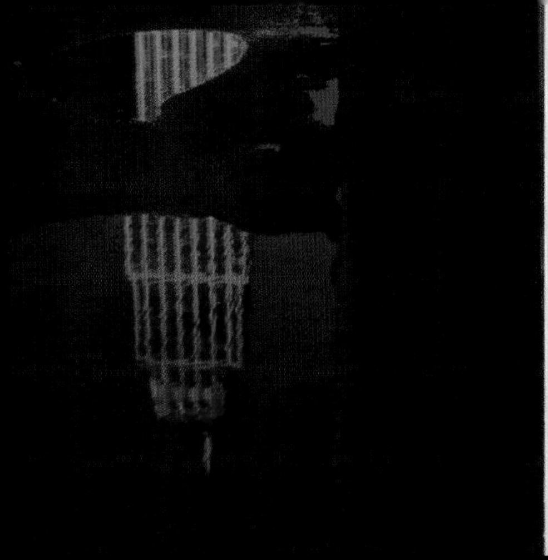

9.

# ONCE UPON A TIME THERE WAS AN OCEAN.

Once upon a time there was an **ocean**. But now it's a mountain range. Something unstoppable was set into motion. Nothing is different, but everything's changed.

It's a dead end job, and you get tired of sitt'in. And it's like a nicotine habit you're always thinking about quit'in. And I think about quit'in every day of the week. When I look out my window it's brown and it's bleak.

Outta here. How am I gonna get outta here? I'm thinking outta here. When am I gonna get outta here? And when will I cash in my lottery ticket, and bury my past with my burdens and strife? I want to shake every limb in the garden of Eden, and make every lover the love of my life.

I'm thinking that once upon a time I was an **ocean**. But now I'm a mountain range. Something unstoppable is set into motion. Nothing is different, but everything's changed.

HOT PLATE

Found a room in the heart of the city, down by the bridge. Card play and TV and beer in the fridge. But I'm easy, I'm open--that's my gift. I can flow with the traffic, I can drift with the drift. Home again? Naw, never going home again. Think about home again? I never think about home.

But then comes a letter from home, the handwriting's fragile and strange. Something unstoppable is set into motion. Nothing is different, but everything's changed.

The light through the stained glass was cobalt and red. And the frayed cuffs and collars were mended by halos of golden thread. The choir sang once upon a time there was an **ocean**. And all the old hymns and family names came fluttering down as leaves on an ocean. OF EMOTION

As nothing is different, but everything's changed.

HALOES?, BP

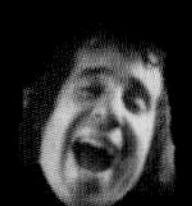

10.

# THAT'S ME.

Well I'll just skip the boring parts (chapters one, two, three) and get to the place where you can read my face and my biography.

Here I am, I'm eleven months old, dangling from my daddy's knee. There I go, it's my graduation. I'm picking up a bogus degree. That's me. Early me. That's me.

Well I never cared much for money, and money never cared for me. I was more like a land-locked sailor, searching for the emerald **sea**. Just seaching for the emerald **sea**, boys searching for the emerald **sea**.

Oh my God, the first love opens like a flower. A black bear running through the forest light holds me inside its power. But tricky skies, your eyes are true, the future is beauty and sorrow. Still, I wish that we could run away and live the life we used to. If just for tonight and tomorrow.

3 I'm walking up the face of the mountain. Counting every step I climb. Remembering the names of the constellations, forgotten for a long, long time. That's me.

4 Under the valley of twilight. That's me on the continental shelf. That's me--I'm answering a question I'm asking of myself.

NOW I'M

I AM

4 I'M IN THE

1. BOYS
2. IN HER SIGHT AND HER POWER
3 I AM

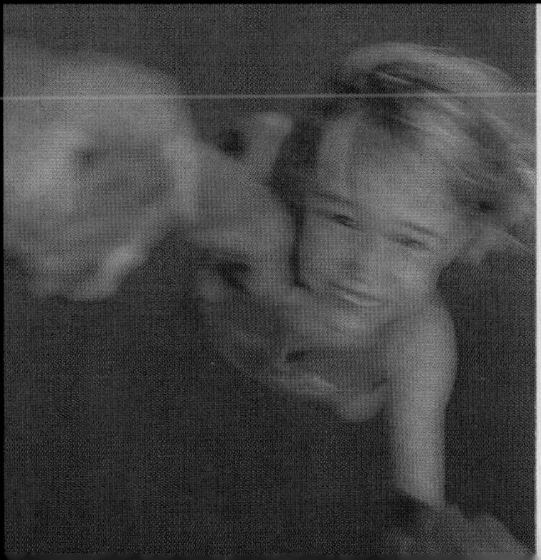

11.

# FATHER AND DAUGHTER.

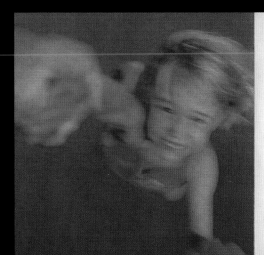

LEAP AWAKE

If you eyes awake in the mirror of a bad dream, and for a fraction of a second you can't remember where you are, just open your window and follow your memory up**stream**. To the meadow in the mountain where we counted every falling star.

I believe the light that shines on you will shine on you forever (forever). And though I can't guarantee there's nothing scary hiding under your bed, I'm gonna stand guard like a postcard of a golden retriever. And never leave til I leave you with a sweet dream in your head.

I'm gonna watch you shine, gonna watch you grow. Gonna paint the sign so you'll always know. As long as one and one is two.

There could never be a father who loved his daughter more than I love you.

Trust your intuition. It's just like go'in fish'in. You cast your line and hope you get a bite.

But you don't need to waste your time worrying about the marketplace, trying to help the human race, struggling to survive its harshest night.

I'm gonna watch you shine, gonna watch you grow. Gonna paint the sign so you'll always know. As long as one and one is two.

There could never be a father who loved his daughter more than I love you.

I'm gonna watch you shine, gonna watch you grow. Gonna paint the sign so you'll always know. As long as one and one is two.

There could never be a father who loved his daughter more than I love you.

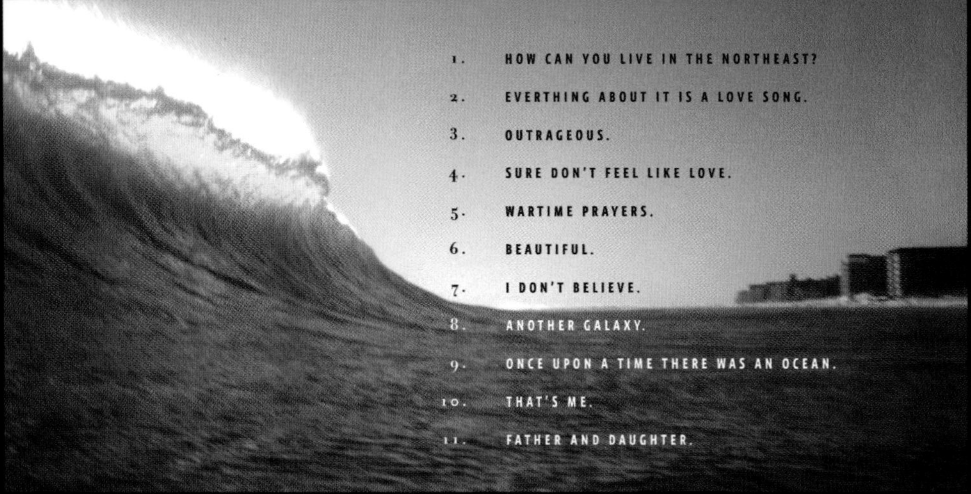
1. HOW CAN YOU LIVE IN THE NORTHEAST?
2. EVERYTHING ABOUT IT IS A LOVE SONG.
3. OUTRAGEOUS.
4. SURE DON'T FEEL LIKE LOVE.
5. WARTIME PRAYERS.
6. BEAUTIFUL.
7. I DON'T BELIEVE.
8. ANOTHER GALAXY.
9. ONCE UPON A TIME THERE WAS AN OCEAN.
10. THAT'S ME.
11. FATHER AND DAUGHTER.

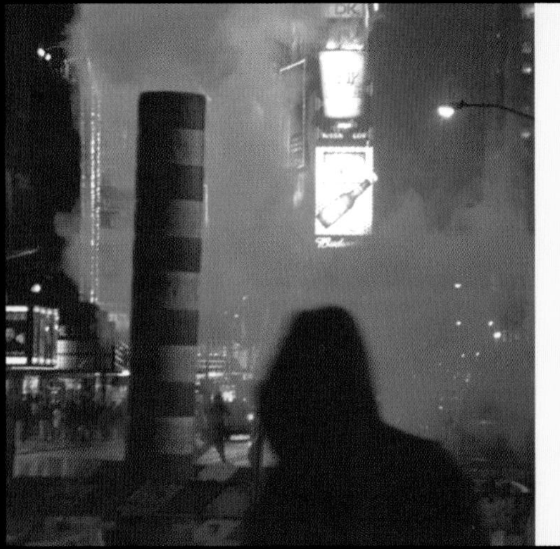

1.

## HOW CAN YOU LIVE IN THE NORTHEAST?

We heard the fireworks. Rushed out to watch the sky. Happy go lucky. Fourth of July.

How can you live in the Northeast? How can you live in the South? How can you build on the banks of a river when the flood water pours from the mouth?How can you be a Christian? How can you be a Jew? How can you be a Muslim, a Buddhist, a Hindu?

How can you?

Weak as the winter sun, we enter life on earth. Names and religion come just after date of birth. Then everybody gets a tongue to speak, and everyone hears an inner voice. A day at the end of the week to wonder and rejoice.

If the answer is infinite light, why do we sleep in the dark?

How can you live in the Northeast? How can you live in the South? How can you build on the banks of a river when the flood water pours from the mouth? How can you tattoo your body? Why do you cover your head? How can you eat from a rice bowl, the holy man only breaks bread?

We watched the fireworks, til they were fireflies. Followed a path of stars, over the endless skies.

How can you live in the Northeast? How can you live in the South? How can you build on the banks of a river when the flood water pours from the mouth?

I've been given all I wanted. Only three generations off the boat. I have harvested and I've planted. I am wearing my father's old coat.

Guitars: PAUL SIMON • Electronics: BRIAN ENO
Bass: PINO PALLADINO • Drums: STEVE GADD, ROBIN DIMAGGIO • Harmonium: GIL GOLDSTEIN

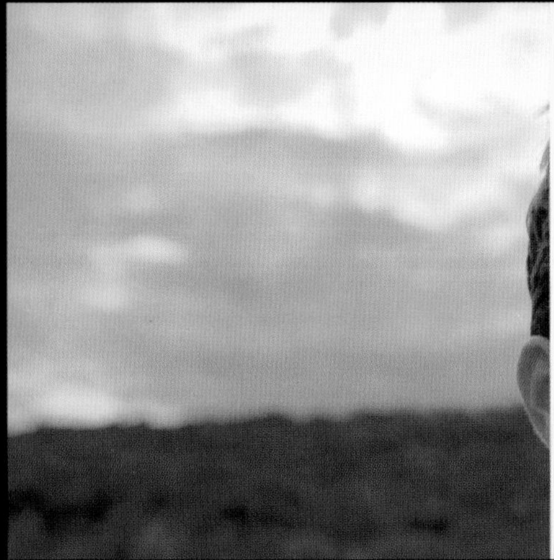

2.

## EVERYTHING ABOUT IT IS A LOVE SONG.

Locked in a struggle for the right combination—of words in a melody line. I took a walk along the riverbank of my imagination. Golden clouds were shuffling the sunshine.

But if I ever get back to the twentieth century, guess I'll have to pay off some debts. Open the book of my vanishing memory, with its catologue of regrets. Stand up for the deeds I did, and those I didn't do. Sit down, shut up, think about God, and wait for the hour of my rescue.

We don't mean to mess things up, but mess them up we do. And then it's "Oh, I'm sorry." Here's a smiling photograph of love when it was new. At a birthday party.

Make a wish and close your eyes: surprise, surprise, surprise.

Early December, and brown as a sparrow, frost creeping over the pond. I shoot a thought into the future, and it flies like an arrow, through my lifetime. And beyond.

If I ever come back as a tree or a crow, or even the wind-blown dust; find me on the ancient road in the song when the wires are hushed. Hurry on and remember me, as I'll remember you. Far above the golden clouds, the darkness vibrates.

The earth is blue.

And everything about it is a love song. Everything about it. Everything about it is a love song. Everything about it. Everything about it is a love song.

Electric and Acoustic Guitars: PAUL SIMON • Electric Guitar: BILL FRISELL • Electronics: BRIAN ENO
Bass: ABRAHAM LABORIEL • Drums: STEVE GADD

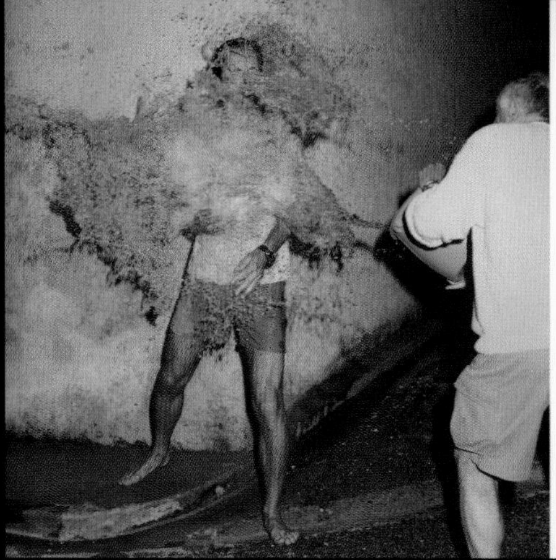

3.

## OUTRAGEOUS.

It's outrageous to line your pockets off the misery of the poor. Outrageous, the crimes some human beings must endure. It's a blessing to wash your face in the summer solstice rain. It's outrageous a man like me stand here and complain. But I'm tired. Nine hundred sit-ups a day. I'm painting my hair the color of mud, mud okay? I'm tired, tired. Anybody care what I say? No! I'm painting my hair the color of mud.

Who's gonna love you when your looks are gone? Tell me, who's gonna love you when your looks are gone? Aw, who's gonna love you when your looks are gone? Who's gonna love you when your looks are gone?

It's outrageous, the food they try to serve in a public school. Outrageous the way they talk to you like you're some kind of clinical fool. It's a blessing to rest my head in the circle of your love. It's outrageous: I can't stop thinking 'bout the things I'm thinking of. And I'm tired. Nine hundred sit-ups a day. I'm painting my hair the color of mud, mud okay? I'm tired, tired. Anybody care what I say? No! Painting my hair the color of mud.

Who's gonna love you when your looks are gone? Tell me, who's gonna love you when your looks are gone? Tell me, who's gonna love you when your looks are gone?

God will. Like he waters the flowers on your window sill. Take me. I'm an ordinary player in the key of C. And my will was broken by my pride and my vanity. Who's gonna love you when your looks are gone? God will. Like he waters the flowers on your window sill. Who's gonna love you when your looks are gone?

Guitars: PAUL SIMON • Electronics: BRIAN ENO • Bass: PINO PALLADINO • Drums: ROBIN DIMAGGIO

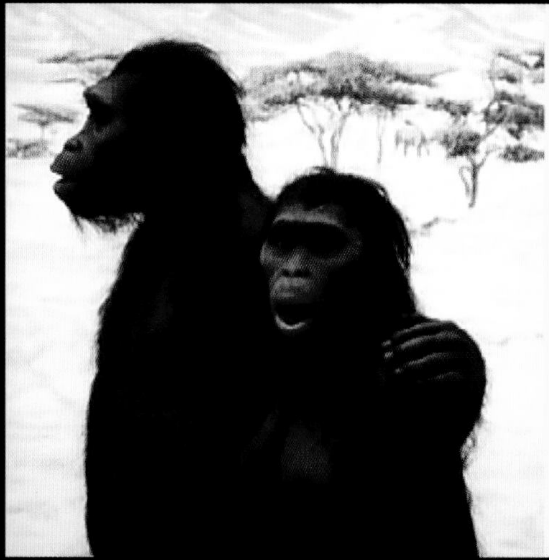

4.

## SURE DON'T FEEL LIKE LOVE.

I registered to vote today. Felt like a fool. Had to do it anyway. Down at the high school. Thing about the second line. You know, felt like a fool. People say it all the time. Even when it's true. So, who's that conscience sticking on the sole of my shoe? Who's that conscience sticking on the sole of my shoe? Cause it sure don't feel like love.

A tear drop consists of electrolytes and salt. The chemistry of crying is not concerned with blame or fault. So, who's that conscience sticking on the sole of my shoe? Who's that conscience sticking on the sole of my shoe? Cause it sure don't feel like love. How does it feel? Feels like a threat. A voice in your head that you'd rather forget. No joke, no joke. You get sick from that sure don't feel like love. No joke, no joke. Some chicken and a corn muffin well that feels more like love.

Yay! Boo!

Yay! Boo!

Wrong again. Wrong again. Maybe I'm wrong again. Wrong again. Maybe I'm wrong again. Wrong again. I could be wrong again. I remember once in August 1993, I was wrong, and I could be wrong again. I remember one of my best friends turned enemy. So, I was wrong, and I could be wrong again. I remember once in a load-out, down in Birminham. Yeah, but that didn't feel like love. Sure don't feel like, sure don't feel like, sure don't feel like love. Sure don't feel like, sure don't feel like, sure don't feel like love. It sure. Don't feel.

Like love.

Guitars: PAUL SIMON • Electronics: BRIAN ENO • Bass: ALEX AL • Drums: STEVE GADD

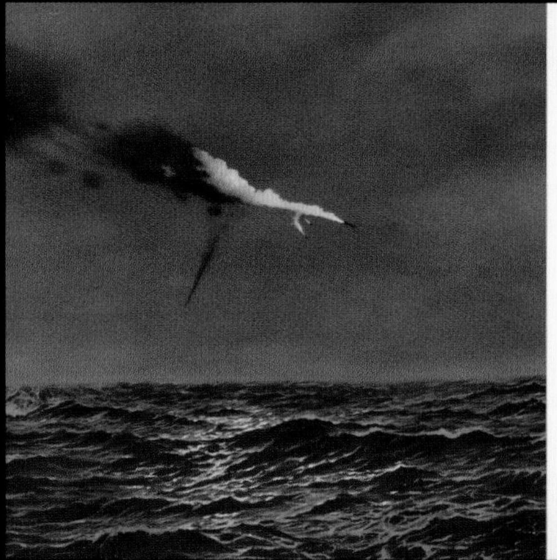

5.

## WARTIME PRAYERS.

Prayers offered in—in times of peace—are silent conversations. Appeals for love, or love's release. In private invocations. But all that is changed now. Gone like a memory form the day before the fires. People hungry for the voice of God hear lunatics and liars. Wartime prayers. Wartime prayers in every language spoken. For every family scattered and broken.

Because you cannot walk with the holy if you're just a halfway decent man. I don't pretend that I'm a mastermind with a genius marketing plan. I'm trying to tap into some wisdom. Even a little drop will do. I want to rid my heart of envy, and cleanse my soul of rage before I'm through.

Times are hard. It's a hard time, but everybody knows. All about hard times, the thing is, what are you gonna do? Well, you cry and try to muscle through. Try to rearrange your stuff. But when the wounds are deep enough, and it's all that we can bare, we wrap ourselves. In prayer.

Because you cannot walk with the holy if you're just a halfway decent man. I don't pretend that I'm a mastermind with a genius marketing plan. I'm trying to tap into some wisdom. Even a little drop will do. I want to rid my heart of envy, and cleanse my soul of rage before I'm through. A mother murmurs in twilight sleep and draws her babies closer. With hush-a-byes for sleepy eyes, and kisses on the shoulder. To drive away despair she says a wartime prayer.

Guitars: PAUL SIMON • Electronics: BRIAN ENO • Piano: HERBIE HANCOCK
Keyboards: GIL GOLDSTEIN • Bass: PINO PALLADINO • Drums: ROBIN DIMAGGIO, STEVE GADD • Choir: JESSE DIXON SINGERS

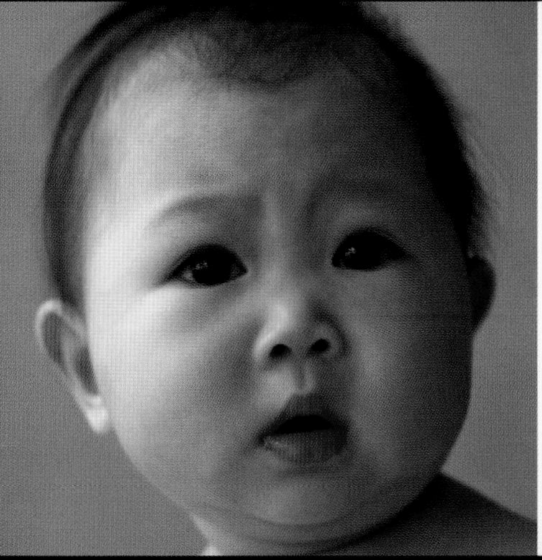

## 6.
## BEAUTIFUL.

Snowman sittin in the sun doesn't have time to waste. He had a little bit too much fun, now his head's erased. Back in the house, family of three: two doin the laundry and one in the nursery.

We brought a brand new baby back from Bangledesh, thought we'd name her Emily. She's beautiful. Beautiful.

Yes sir, head's erased, brain's a bowl of jelly. Hasn't hurt his sense of taste, judging from his belly. But back in the house, family of four now: two doing the laundry and two on the kitchen floor.

We brought a brand new baby back from mainland China, sailed across the China Sea. She's beautiful. Beautiful.

Go-kart sittin in the shade: you don't need a ticket to ride, it's summertime, summertime, slip down a water slide. Little kid danc'in in the grass, legs like rubber band. It's summertime, summertime. There's a line at the candy stand. Keep an eye on them children, eye on them children in the pool. You better keep an eye on them children, eye on them children in the pool.

We brought a brand new baby back from Kosovo. That was nearly seven years ago. He cried all night. Could not sleep. His eyes were bright, dark and deep.

Beautiful.

Guitars: PAUL SIMON • Electronics: BRIAN ENO • Bass: PINO PALLADINO • Drums: STEVE GADD

## 7.
## I DON'T BELIEVE.

Acts of kindness, like breadcrumbs in a fairytale forest, lead us past dangers as light melts the darkness. But I don't believe, and I'm not consoled. I lean closer to the fire, but I'm cold.

The earth was born in a storm. The waters receded, the mountains were formed. "The universe loves a drama,"* you know. And ladies and gentlemen this is the show.

I got a call from my broker. The broker informed me I'm broke. I was dealing my last hand of poker. My cards were useless as smoke.

Oh, guardian angel. Don't taunt me like this, on a clear summer evening as soft as a kiss. My children are laughing, not a whisper of care. My love is brushing her long chestnut hair. I don't believe a heart can be filled to the brim then vanish like mist as though life were a whim.

Maybe the heart is part of the mist. And that's all that there is or could ever exist. Maybe and maybe and maybe some more. Maybe's the exit that I'm looking for.

I got a call from my broker. The broker said he was mistaken. Maybe some virus or brokerage joke and he hopes that my faith isn't shaken.

Acts of kindness, like rain in a draught, release the spirit with a whoop and a shout. I don't believe we were born to be sheep in a flock. To pantomime prayers with the hands of a clock.

*Observation by E. B. after 2004 presidential election.

Guitars: PAUL SIMON • Electronics: BRIAN ENO
Bass: ABRAHAM LABORIEL • Drums: STEVE GADD, ROBIN DIMAGGIO • Harmonium: GIL GOLDSTEIN

## 8.
## ANOTHER GALAXY.

On the morning of her wedding day, when no one was awake, she drove across the border. Leaving all the yellow roses on her wedding cake. Her mother's tears, her breakfast order.

She's gone, gone, gone.

There is a moment, a chip in time, when leaving home is the lesser crime.

When your eyes are blind with tears, but your heart can see: another life, another galaxy.

That night her dreams are storm-tossed as a willow. She hears the clouds, she sees the eye of a hurricane, as it sweeps across her island pillow.

But she's gone, gone, gone.

There is a moment, a chip in time, when leaving home is the lesser crime. When your eyes are blind with tears, but your heart can see:

Another life, another galaxy.

Guitars: PAUL SIMON • Electronics: BRIAN ENO • Bass: PINO PALLADINO • Drums: STEVE GADD

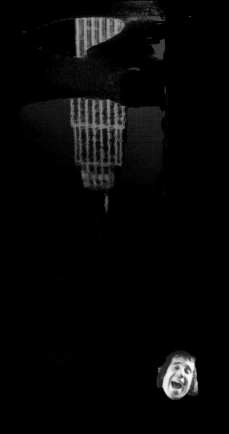

## 9.
## ONCE UPON A TIME THERE WAS AN OCEAN.

Once upon a time there was an ocean. But now it's a mountain range. Something unstoppable set into motion. Nothing is different, but everything's changed.

It's a dead end job, and you get tired of sittin. And it's like a nicotine habit you're always thinking about quitin. I think about quitin every day of the week. When I look out my window it's brown and it's bleak.

Outta here. How am I gonna get outta here? I'm thinking outta here. When am I gonna get outta here? And when will I cash in my lottery ticket, and bury my past with my burdens and strife? I want to shake every limb in the garden of Eden, and make every lover the love of my life.

I figure that once upon a time I was an ocean. But now I'm a mountain range. Something unstoppable set into motion. Nothing is different, but everything's changed.

Found a room in the heart of the city, down by the bridge. Hot plate and TV and beer in the fridge. But I'm easy, I'm open--that's my gift. I can flow with the traffic, I can drift with the drift. Home again? Naw, never going home again. Think about home again? I never think about home.

But then comes a letter from home, the handwriting's fragile and strange. Something unstoppable set into motion. Nothing is different, but everything's changed.

The light through the stained glass was cobalt and red. And the frayed cuffs and collars were mended by haloes of golden thread. The choir sang Once upon a time there was an ocean. And all the old hymns and family names came fluttering down as leaves of emotion.

As nothing is different, but everything's changed.

Guitars: PAUL SIMON • Electronics: BRIAN ENO
Fretless Bass: LEO ABRAHAMS • Drums: STEVE GADD • Percussion: JAMEY HADDAD

## 10.
## THAT'S ME.

Well I'll just skip the boring parts chapters one, two, three and get to the place where you can read my face and my biography.

Here I am, I'm eleven months old, dangling from my daddy's knee. There I go, it's my graduation, I'm picking up a bogus degree. That's me. Early me. That's me.

Well I never cared much for money, and money never cared for me. I was more like a land-locked sailor, searching for the emerald sea. Just seaching for the emerald sea, boys, searching for the sea.

Oh my God, First love opens like a flower. A black bear running through the forest light holds me in her sight and her power. But tricky skies, your eyes are true, the future is beauty and sorrow. Still, I wish that we could run away and live the life we used to. If just for tonight and tomorrow.

I am walking up the face of the mountain. Counting every step I climb. Remembering the names of the constellations. Forgotten is a long, long time. That's me. I'm in the valley of twilight. Now I'm on the continental shelf. That's me--I'm answering a question I am asking of myself.

Guitars: PAUL SIMON • Electronics: BRIAN ENO
Bass: PINO PALLADINO • Drums: STEVE GADD, ROBIN DIMAGGIO

## 11.
## FATHER AND DAUGHTER.

If you leap awake in the mirror of a bad dream, and for a fraction of a second you can't remember where you are, just open your window and follow your memory upstream. To the meadow in the mountain where we counted every falling star.

I believe the light that shines on you will shine on you forever (forever). And though I can't guarantee there's nothing scary hiding under your bed, I'm gonna stand guard like a postcard of a golden retriever. And never leave til I leave you with a sweet dream in your head.

I'm gonna watch you shine, gonna watch you grow. Gonna paint a sign so you'll always know. As long as one and one is two.

There could never be a father loved his daughter more than I love you.

Trust your intuition. It's just like go'in fish'in. You cast your line and hope you get a bite.

But you don't need to waste your time worrying about the marketplace, try to help the human race. Struggling to survive its harshest night.

I'm gonna watch you shine, gonna watch you grow. Gonna paint a sign so you'll always know. As long as one and one is two.

There could never be a father who loved his daughter more than I love you.

I'm gonna watch you shine, gonna watch you grow. Gonna paint a sign so you'll always know. As long as one and one is two.

There could never be a father loved his daughter more than I love you.

Guitars: Electric, Acoustic, Nylon String: PAUL SIMON • Acoustic Rhythm: VINCENT NGUINI
Drums: STEVE GADD • Bass: ABRAHAM LABORIEL • Additional Vocal: ADRIAN SIMON

**PREVIOUS SPREAD:** The final layout of the booklet. Only three pieces of art changed, but my boldface treatment of the water-related words didn't make the cut. Although Paul acknowledged the thread of these, he didn't really intend it to have that much emphasis. But I was allowed to use the water-based imagery on the front and the contents page.

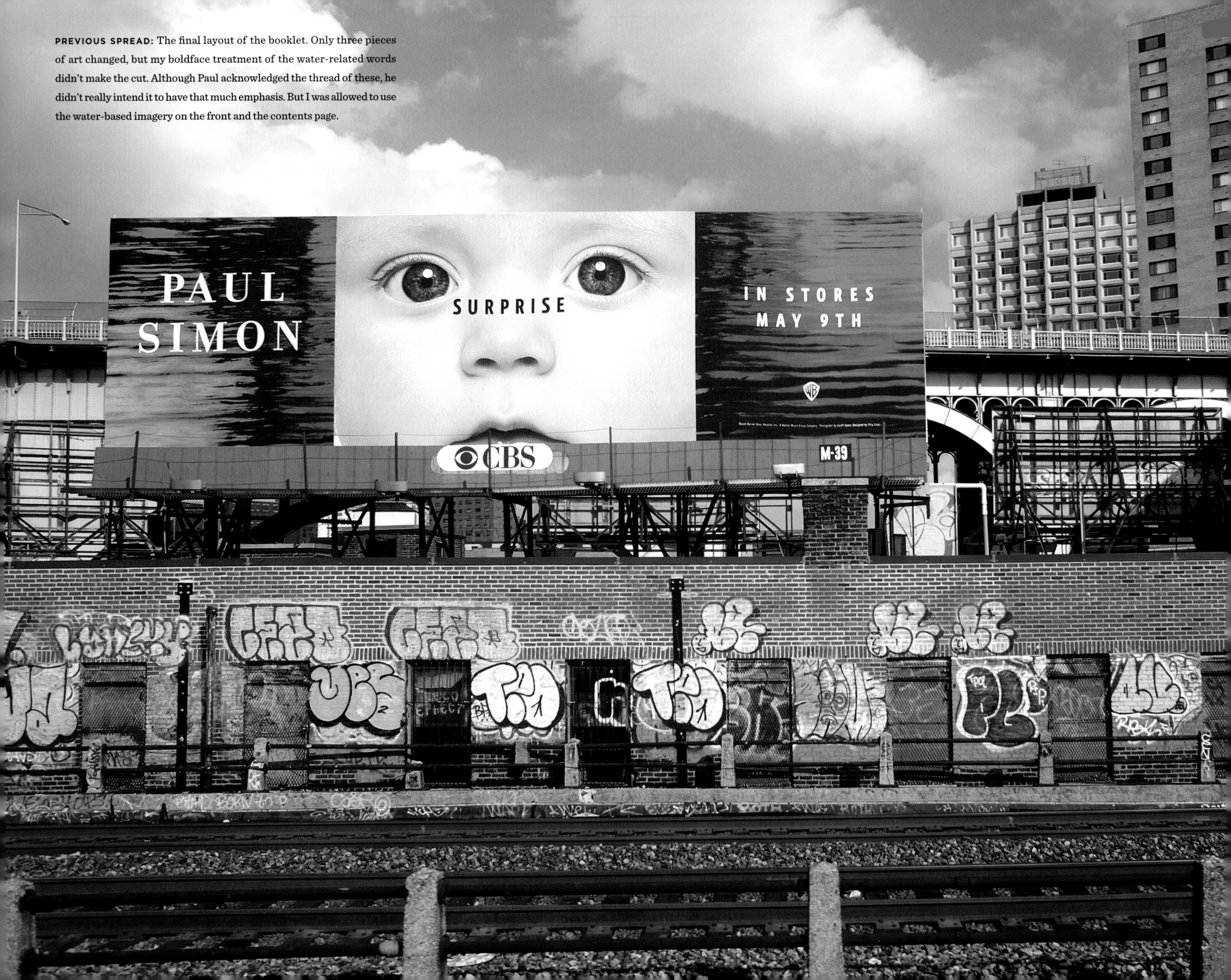
PAUL SIMON
SURPRISE
IN STORES MAY 9TH
CBS
M-39

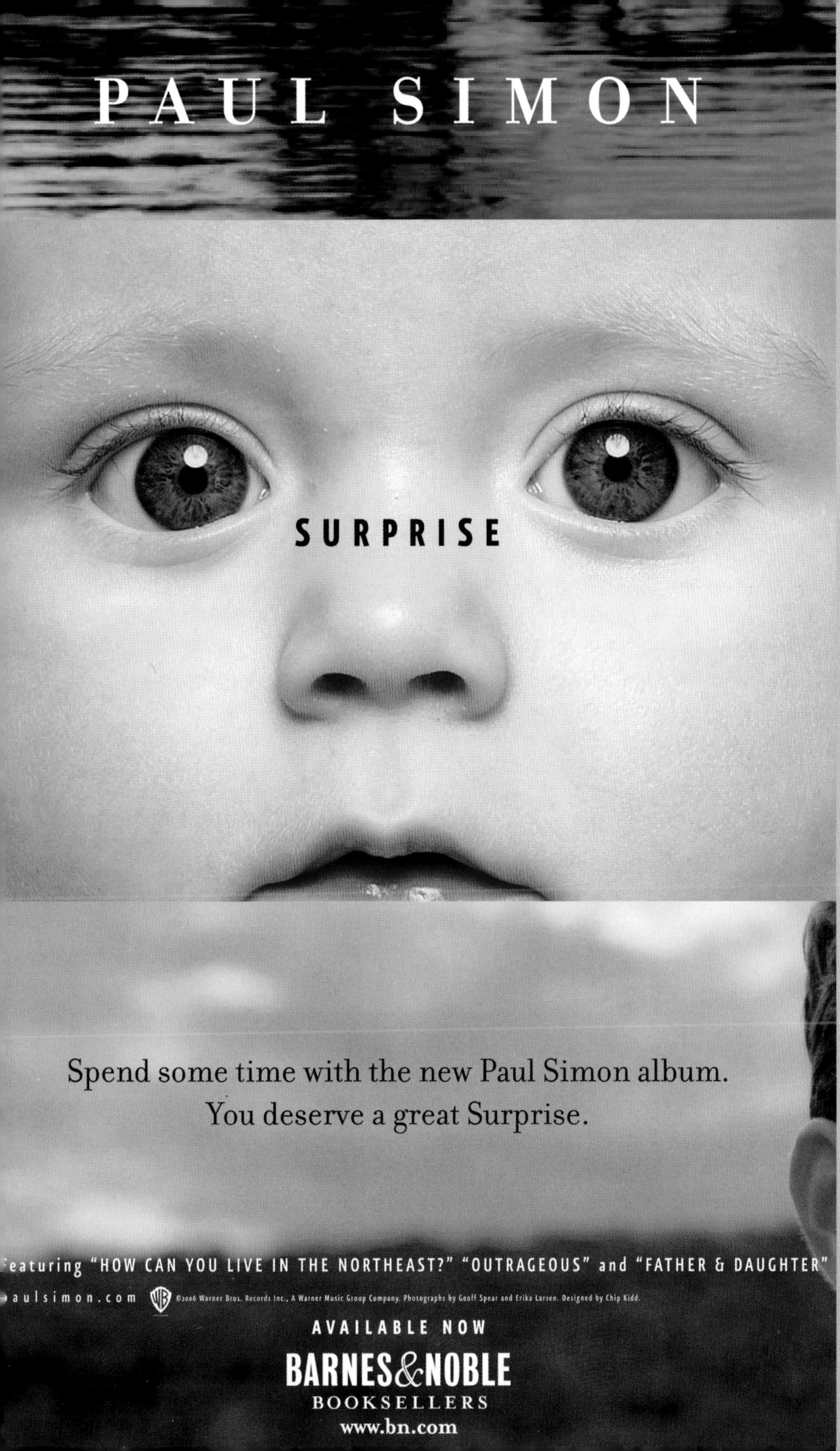
PAUL SIMON
SURPRISE
Spend some time with the new Paul Simon album.
You deserve a great Surprise.
eaturing "HOW CAN YOU LIVE IN THE NORTHEAST?" "OUTRAGEOUS" and "FATHER & DAUGHTER"
aulsimon.com
©2006 Warner Bros. Records Inc., A Warner Music Group Company. Photographs by Geoff Spear and Erika Larsen. Designed by Chip Kidd.
AVAILABLE NOW
BARNES&NOBLE
BOOKSELLERS
www.bn.com

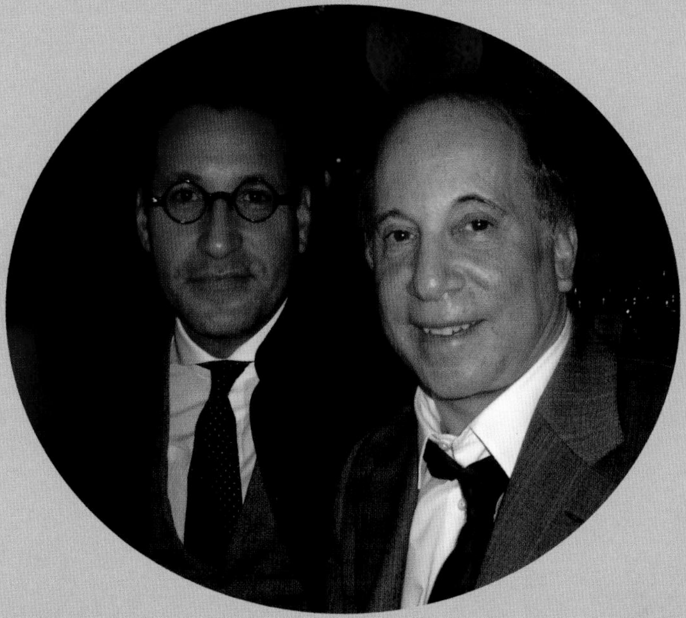

you the entire time to see if you like it!" I loved the songs (most were collaborations with Brian Eno, which was doubly thrilling for me), but I was on edge the entire time, afraid to even tap my toe, lest that betray a possible misinterpretation of the work. When it finally ended, with the glorious "Father and Daughter," I was utterly drained. Paul let the final notes ring out and then broke the silence by muttering quietly, "I'm not sure you liked it." To my credit, I did not burst into tears, but instead said, "I did very much, but I need to hear it at least ten more times." This seemed to be the right answer, and he entrusted me with a CD burnt with all the tracks. "Please don't put this on the web."



I had a Discman at the time, and I walked around New York City for the next month listening to the album constantly. Each time it was more endeared to me, and I started to notice a pattern, whether Paul intended it or not. Each of the songs had some reference to water, whether it was a cloud or a teardrop or a stream or an ocean or just the liquid itself.

For the front cover, I wanted to shoot Paul's eyes close up, but he balked because he didn't like the way that might look at his advancing age. So I thought about going the other direction—a baby's eyes—as babies are mentioned in the lyrics, especially in "Beautiful." Then I had an idea-gasm and asked Geoff Spear to shoot some studies of his one-year-old son (and my godson), Jet. I didn't tell Geoff what it might be for, just to go in close on Jet's face with various expressions. The results were divine, and the final image for the front marked the last piece of the puzzle for the package.

**ABOVE:** With Paul at the National Design Awards in Fall of 2008, which leads us to . . .

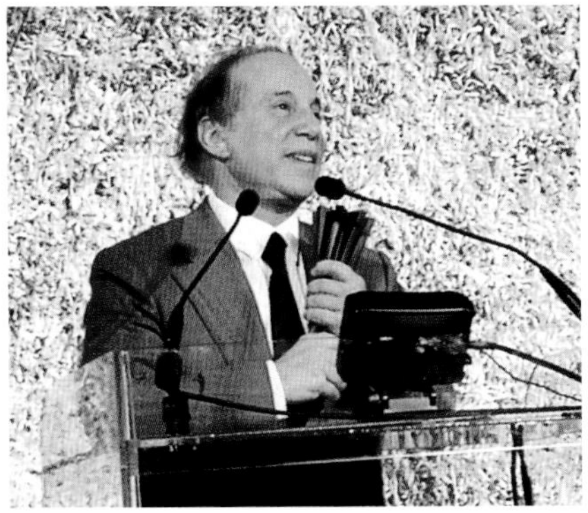

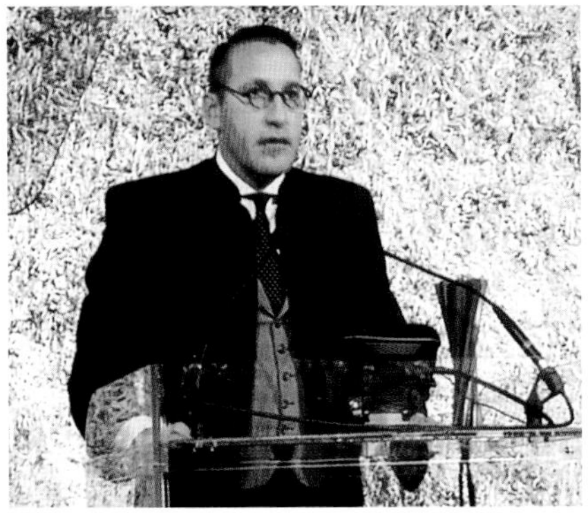

COOPER-HEWITT

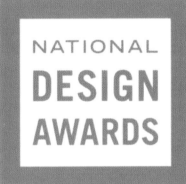

NATIONAL
DESIGN
AWARDS

To Chip!
Congratulations!
Laura Bush

The White House
July 10, 2006

The National Design Awards were conceived in 1997 by the Smithsonian's Cooper-Hewitt, National Design Museum to honor the best in American design.

First launched at the White House in 2000 as an official project of the White House Millennium Council, the annual Awards program celebrates design in various disciplines as a vital humanistic tool in shaping the world, and seeks to increase national awareness of design by educating the public and promoting excellence, innovation, and lasting achievement. The Awards are truly national in scope—nominations for the 2005 Awards were solicited from a committee of more than 800 leading designers, educators, journalists, cultural figures, and corporate leaders from every state in the nation. A suite of educational programs is offered every year in conjunction with the Awards, including a series of public programs, lectures, roundtables, and workshops based on the vision and work of the National Design Award winners.

The winners and finalists of the National Design Awards are chosen each year by a distinguished jury composed of design leaders:

**2005 JURY**

Ron Arad,
founder, Ron Arad Associates, London

Andrea Cochran,
principal and founder, Andrea Cochran Landscape Architects, San Francisco

Li Edelkoort,
chairwoman, Design Academy Eindhoven, The Netherlands

David Rockwell,
founder, The Rockwell Group

Jeff Speck,
director of design, National Endowment for the Arts

Frank Stephenson,
director of design, Fiat and Lancia

Nadja Swarovski,
vice president of international communications, Swarovski

Michael Vanderbyl,
founder, Vanderbyl Design

Michael Volkema,
chairman of the board, Herman Miller, Inc.

**2006 JURY**

Cindy Allen,
editor-in-chief, *Interior Design*

Yves Béhar,
founder, fuseproject, San Francisco

Michael Bierut,
partner, Pentagram

Roger Mandle,
president, Rhode Island School of Design

Enrique Norten,
principal, TEN Arquitectos

Janet Rosenberg,
principal and founder, Janet Rosenberg + Associates

Stefano Tonchi,
style editor, *The New York Times Magazine*

FINALIST **CHIP KIDD**

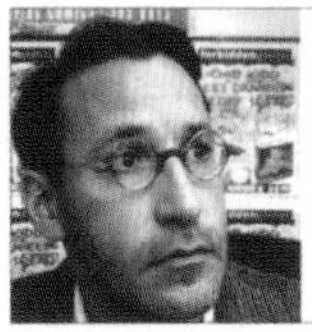

Chip Kidd

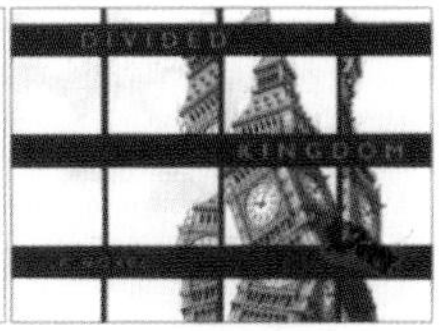
DIVIDED
KINGDOM

*Divided Kingdom* by Rupert Thomson, published by Knopf

Writer and graphic designer Chip Kidd has been designing book jackets for Alfred A. Knopf since 1986. His innovative work has helped spark a revolution in the art of American book packaging. Kidd has written about graphic design and popular culture and is an editor of comic books for Pantheon, a Knopf subsidiary. His work will be included in Cooper-Hewitt's 2006 *National Design Triennial*.

# Medal of Honor

The National Design Awards mark the pinnacle of achievement for the profession, especially in graphic design, which has no higher honor; in this case it falls under the category of "Communications." You can't apply for the award, you have to be nominated, and then you become a finalist, after which you may or may not win. I had the great fortune of being a finalist in 2006, not winning, and then named a finalist again the next year, and winning. Part of this process meant that I was invited to the White House to celebrate, not once but twice. Which was a very good thing because you're allowed only two guests, so the first time I was able to bring my parents, and the next year, my husband. The ceremony takes place over lunch in the East Wing and is overseen by the First Lady. In my case, for both years that was Laura Bush. She was fantastic and absolute graciousness itself, but in the weeks leading up to the event there was controversy in the design community about the awards. The war in Iraq was in full force, and some of the nominees were urging a boycott of the proceedings to protest it. I argued against that: the two events had nothing to do with each other, and this was the only occasion in which the US government—via the Smithsonian Institution—officially recognizes design achievement in America. I thought to spit in the face of that would be insane and ungrateful, and there was no way I would do so.

I will never forget Mrs. Bush saying to my mother, "I'll bet you took him to the library and grew his love of books that way." Which was exactly true. The next year I was able to bring Sandy as my out-and-proud partner, and she embraced us then as well.

*To Chip Kidd*
*With best wishes,*    Laura Bush

**OPPOSITE:** The National Design Awards program, signed by First Lady Laura Bush.

**OPPOSITE, TOP LEFT:** The following year, when I won, Paul Simon agreed to present me with the award. Unbelievable. He is my hero for doing so.

**ABOVE:** Group portrait of the nominees for 2006. I prided myself on not wearing black or gray (!!). It was actually a variation on a seersucker suit by Jil Sander. Hey, it was summer, and technically in the South!

**RIGHT:** Laura Bush with me and my mom and dad, Ann and Tom Kidd. I have no idea who or what we're looking at. Mrs. Bush is the absolute best, and her efforts promoting literacy in America are truly inspiring.

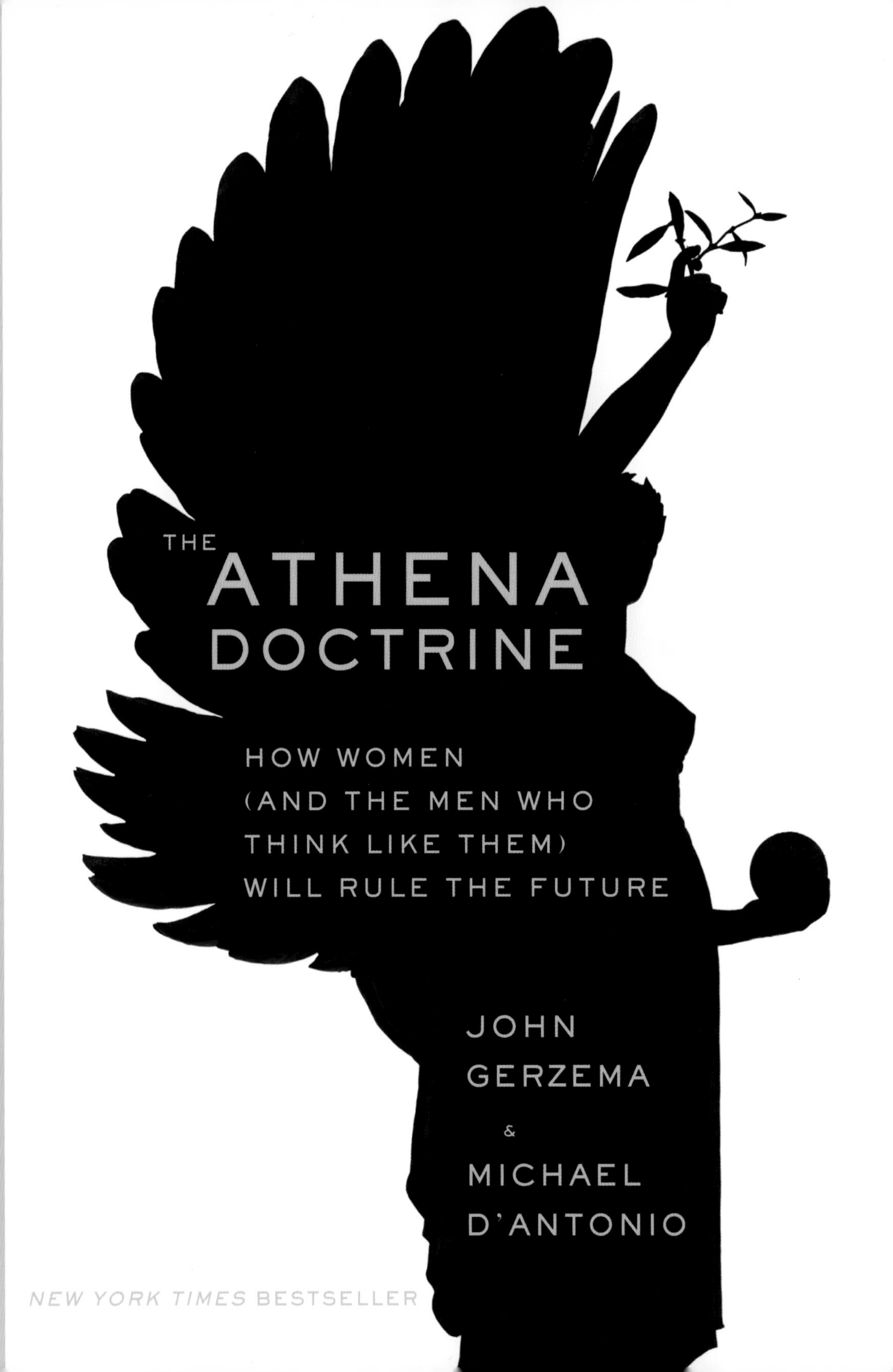
THE
ATHENA
DOCTRINE
HOW WOMEN
(AND THE MEN WHO
THINK LIKE THEM)
WILL RULE THE FUTURE
JOHN
GERZEMA
&
MICHAEL
D'ANTONIO
*NEW YORK TIMES* BESTSELLER

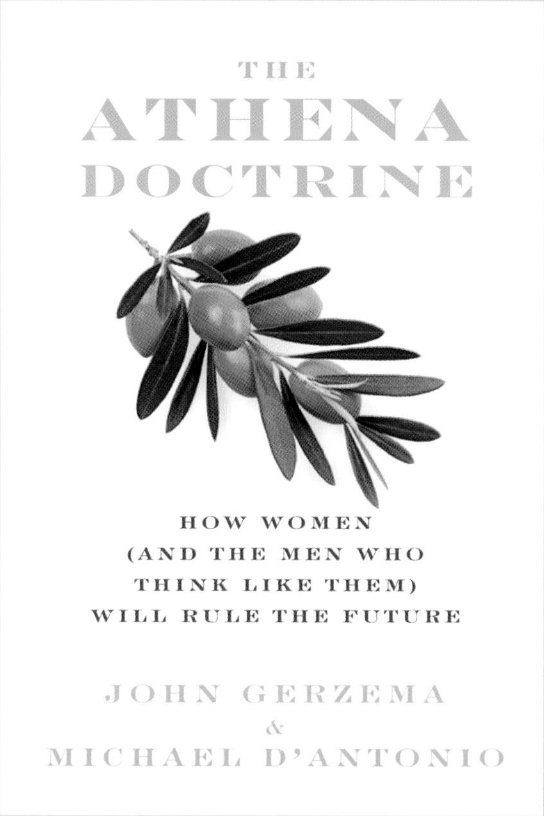
THE
ATHENA
DOCTRINE
HOW WOMEN
(AND THE MEN WHO
THINK LIKE THEM)
WILL RULE THE FUTURE
JOHN GERZEMA
&
MICHAEL D'ANTONIO

## The Body Politic

I first had the pleasure of working with John Gerzema and Michael D'Antonio on *Spend Shift* (p. 66), but their book *The Athena Doctrine* was entirely different. The simple yet challenging premise concerned the idea that women had better temperament and instincts to lead than men, and history had proved that to be correct.

I started with an olive branch (above), but that wasn't dramatic enough and was too gender neutral. My research led me to striking images of the Peace Statue of 1912 at the boundary of Brighton Hove in England (left). All the elements were there: an angel, wings ready for flight; an olive branch; and an orb symbolizing the Earth. Rendering it in silhouette allowed for typography to read within the shape, and the ultimate effect aims for heroism and hope.

**LEFT:** Jossey-Bass, 2013. **OPPOSITE, RIGHT:** Harvard Business Review Press, 2006.

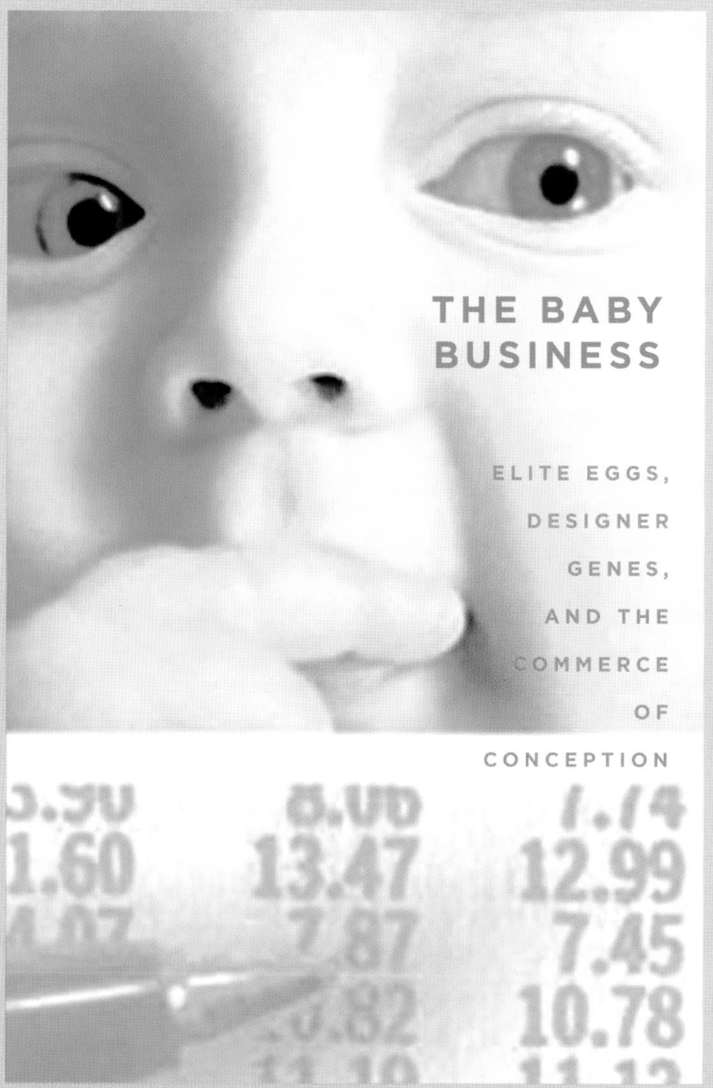
THE BABY BUSINESS
ELITE EGGS, DESIGNER GENES, AND THE COMMERCE OF CONCEPTION
1.60
13.47
12.99
7.45
10.78

My first thought for *The Baby Business* was something involving a bar code (maybe on his/her butt?), but that seemed too obvious and jokey. So I tried a baby's face montaged with a receipt (above), which seemed okay, but not dramatic enough. I did some more art research and found this stunning stock shot of a statue by no less than Michelangelo (right). Now the addition of the bar code didn't seem like a joke, but a juxtaposition of the old methods of creation and the new. The weirdly alien feel of the figure's eye and "skin" speak to the idea of creating life out of artificial means.

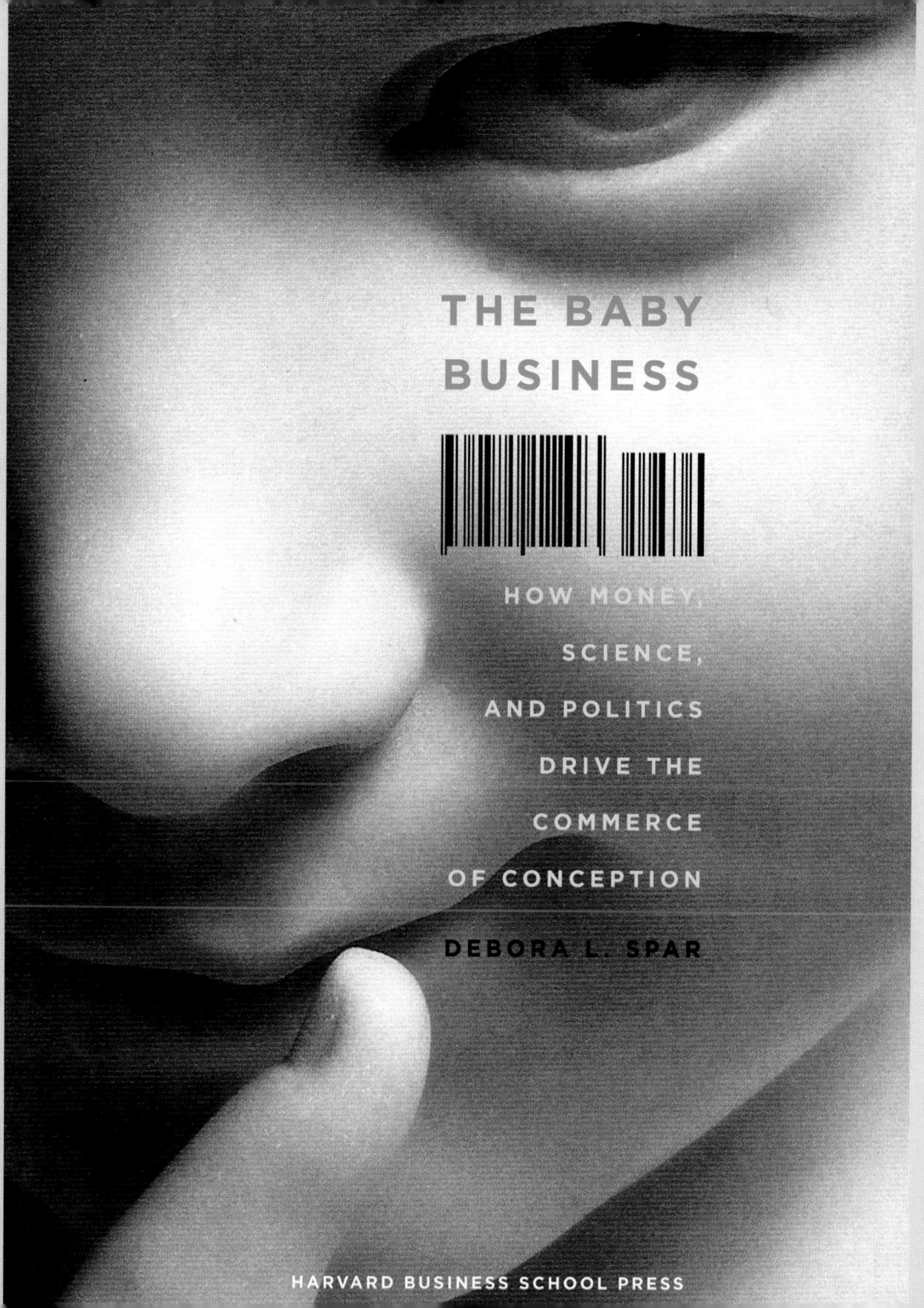
THE BABY BUSINESS
HOW MONEY, SCIENCE, AND POLITICS DRIVE THE COMMERCE OF CONCEPTION
DEBORA L. SPAR
HARVARD BUSINESS SCHOOL PRESS

ABRAMS COMICARTS

ABRAMS COMICARTS

ABRAMS COMICARTS

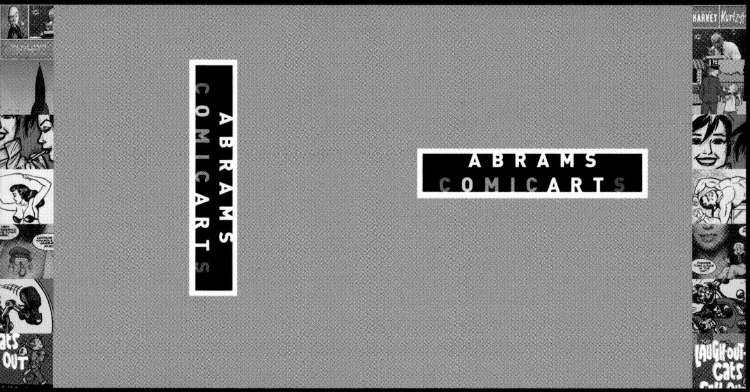
ABRAMS
COMICARTS

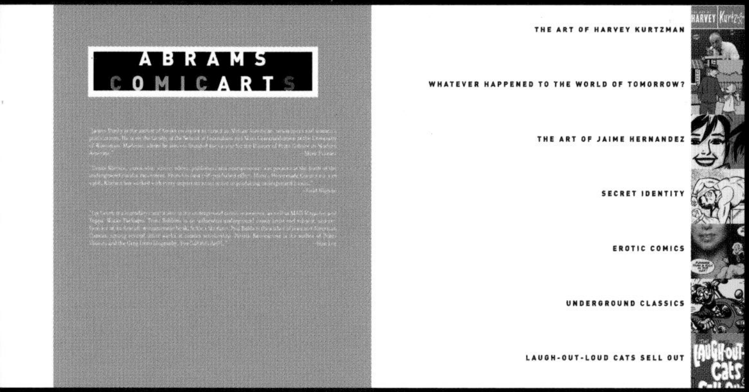
ABRAMS
COMICARTS
THE ART OF HARVEY KURTZMAN
WHATEVER HAPPENED TO THE WORLD OF TOMORROW?
THE ART OF JAIME HERNANDEZ
SECRET IDENTITY
EROTIC COMICS
UNDERGROUND CLASSICS
LAUGH-OUT-LOUD CATS SELL OUT

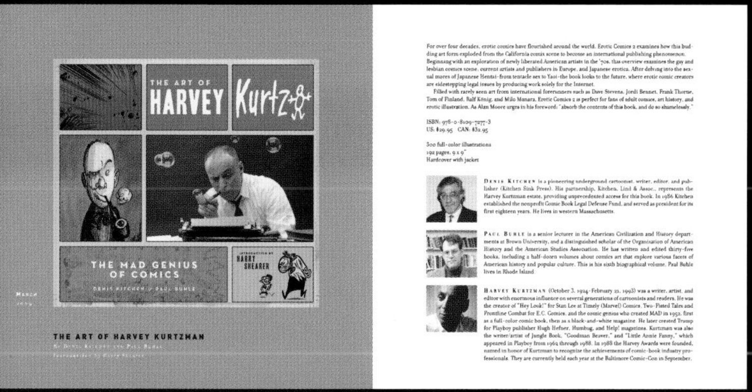
THE ART OF
HARVEY Kurtzman
THE MAD GENIUS OF COMICS
THE ART OF HARVEY KURTZMAN

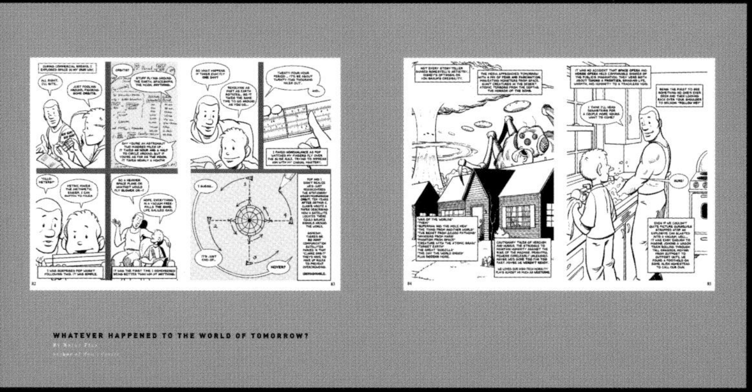
WHATEVER HAPPENED TO THE WORLD OF TOMORROW?

# Funny, Inc.

Charles Kochman, one of my best friends and a former colleague at DC Comics, moved to Abrams Books to serve as an acquiring editor in 2005. The following year he was conducting routine portfolio reviews at New York Comic Con when a young man approached him and asked, "Would you consider looking at a strip that started on the web?" At the time, web comics were not generally taken seriously, but Charlie said, "Sure." What he saw wasn't really a comic, and it wasn't really prose, but a fusion of the two—the story of a nerdy little boy and his manic travails coping with school and home. Charlie sort of liked it. He read more, then he really liked it—a lot. Long story short: he wanted to publish it as a book, but his higher-ups resisted, not understanding who the audience was or the work's eccentric combination of images and text. Charlie doubled down, fought for it, and ultimately won. And in April of 2007, *Diary of a Wimpy Kid* was released.

*Ahem.* (God, I love that story.) As a reward, Charlie was given his own imprint to run, and in 2008 Abrams ComicArts debuted. I was tapped to create the logo, and I had a ball doing it. Or a strip, rather. The idea is that the main components—Abrams, Comics, and Art—can be perceived as any combination of the three (opposite), depending on the use of the basic bright colors applied in the printing process. It also works in plain black and white and is perfectly legible when reduced and placed at the bottom of the spine of a book (see *Shazam!* p. 240). I also designed the introductory brochure (left) and the inevitable Comic Con lariat (right).

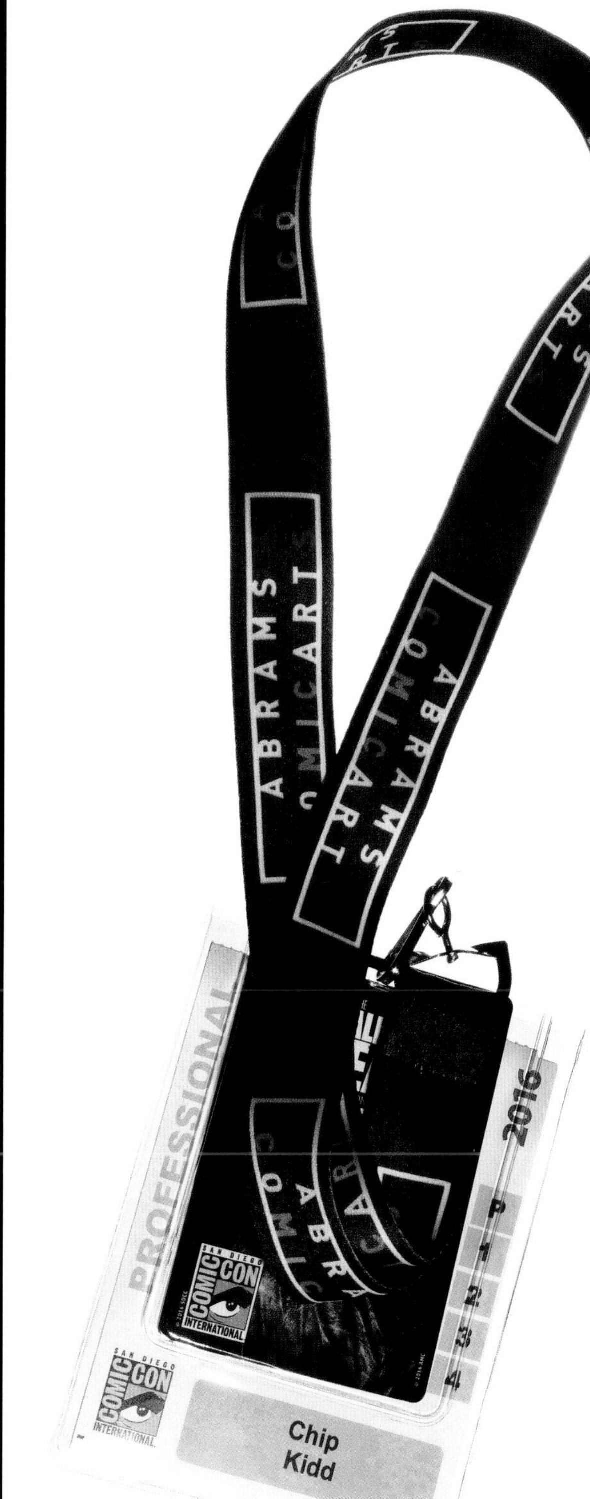
ABRAMS
COMICARTS
PROFESSIONAL
2016
COMIC CON INTERNATIONAL
SAN DIEGO
Chip
Kidd

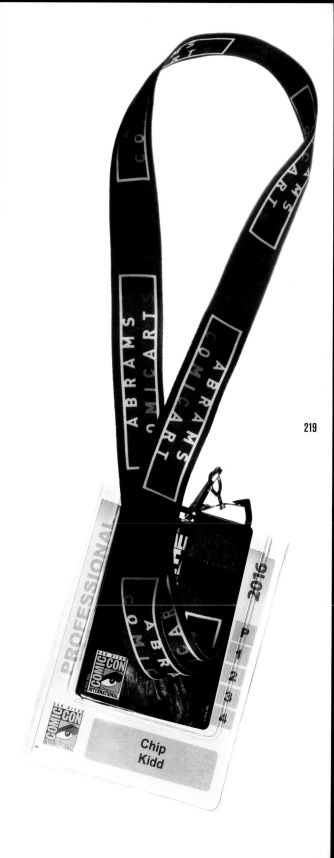

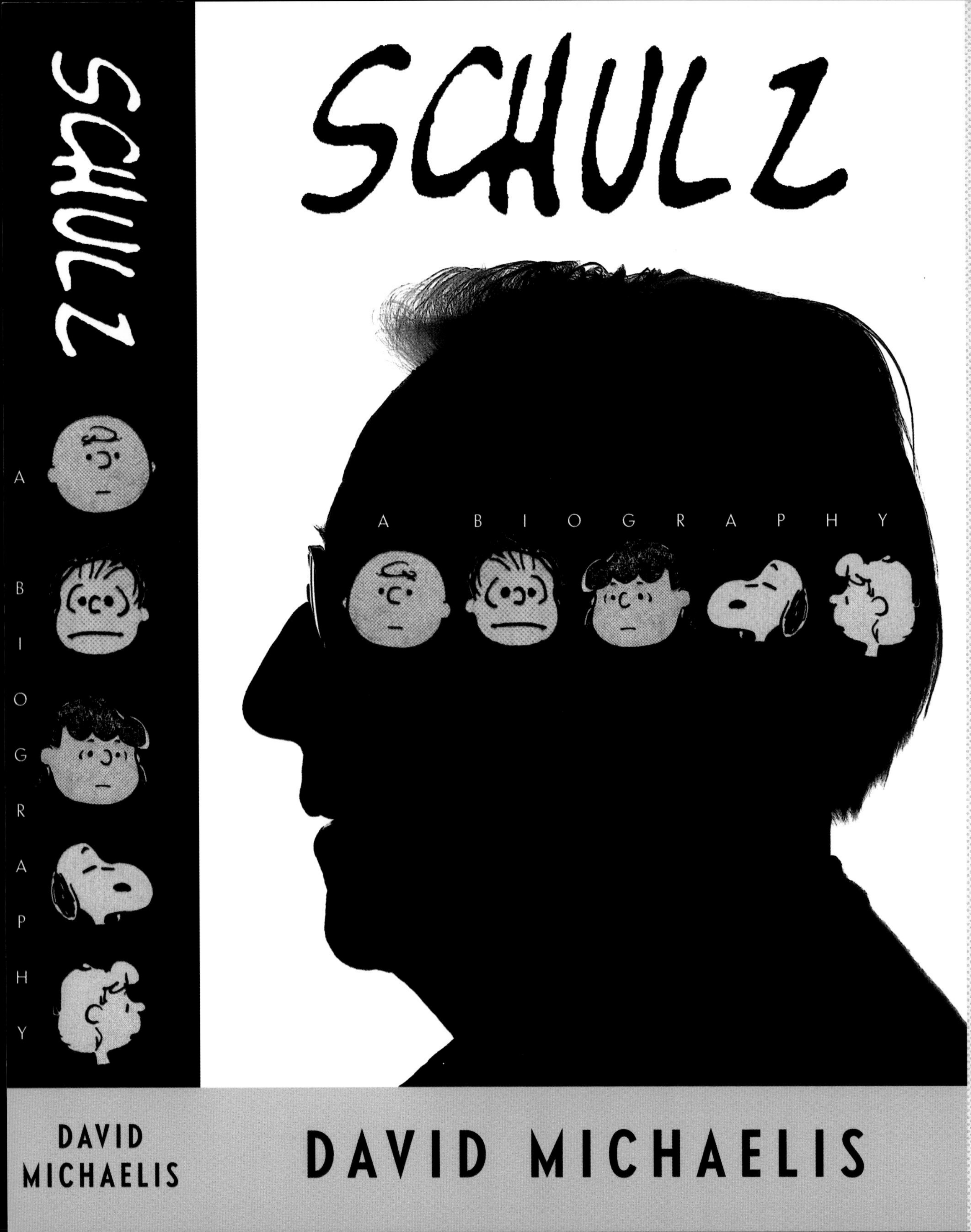
SCHULZ
A BIOGRAPHY
DAVID MICHAELIS
SCHULZ
A BIOGRAPHY
DAVID MICHAELIS

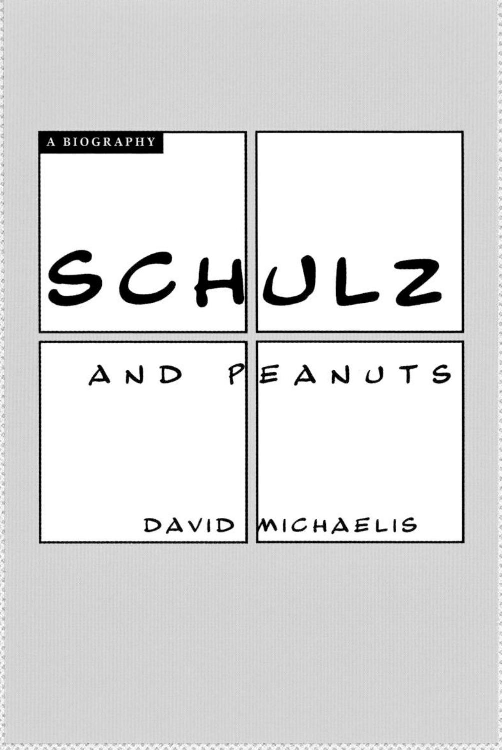
A BIOGRAPHY
SCHULZ
AND PEANUTS
DAVID MICHAELIS

## Sparky's Story

David Michaelis's remarkable and exhaustively researched biography of Charles M. Schulz proved to be a design challenge that neither he nor I was expecting. The project started out as a love-fest between the author and Schulz's surviving family and estate. David was hand-picked shortly after the subject's death to write the authorized life story because his previous work was the definitive and award-winning biography of N. C. Wyeth, the father of Andrew Wyeth, one of Schulz's greatest art heroes. All went well during the more than six years of work on the book, with everyone granting David extensive interviews and full access to archival material.

**LEFT:** My first idea before the trouble started, using a stunning silhouette image by Holgar Klopfel, from the last photo session that Schulz sat for.

**ABOVE:** A generic idea, not as good as the final.

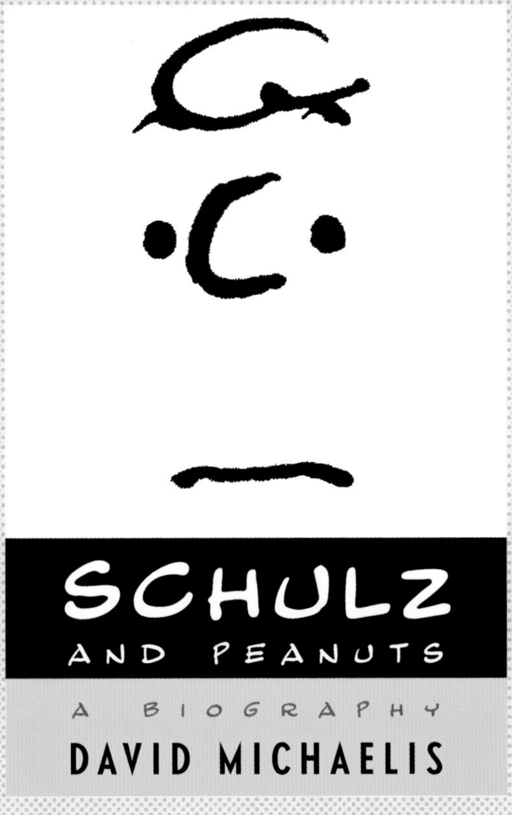
SCHULZ
AND PEANUTS
A BIOGRAPHY
DAVID MICHAELIS

But when the massive manuscript finally arrived and all who were intimately involved got a courtesy read, things changed. Dramatically. To say that disenchantment set in among the Schulz camp would be putting it mildly. They tried to halt publication of the book, but there was an iron-clad contract. When the legal smoke cleared, what was able to be withheld was the use of any of Schulz's imagery and his signature on the jacket. At that point an emotionally diminished Michaelis said that I was free to walk away from the project if I wished. But I didn't. I thought the book was truly great, but I also had a treasured relationship with Jeannie Schulz and Paige Braddock, Schulz's assistant at the time of his death and valued employee to this day. They did not discourage me from designing the jacket, but the lines were drawn, as it were.

**ABOVE:** A concept that I ultimately repurposed for the cover of *Only What's Necessary*.

**RIGHT:** The final cover, using a typeface that looked like Schulz's handwriting, but wasn't. And a black zig-zag on a yellow background that could only signify one thing, even in the most abstract of ways. Harper, 2007.

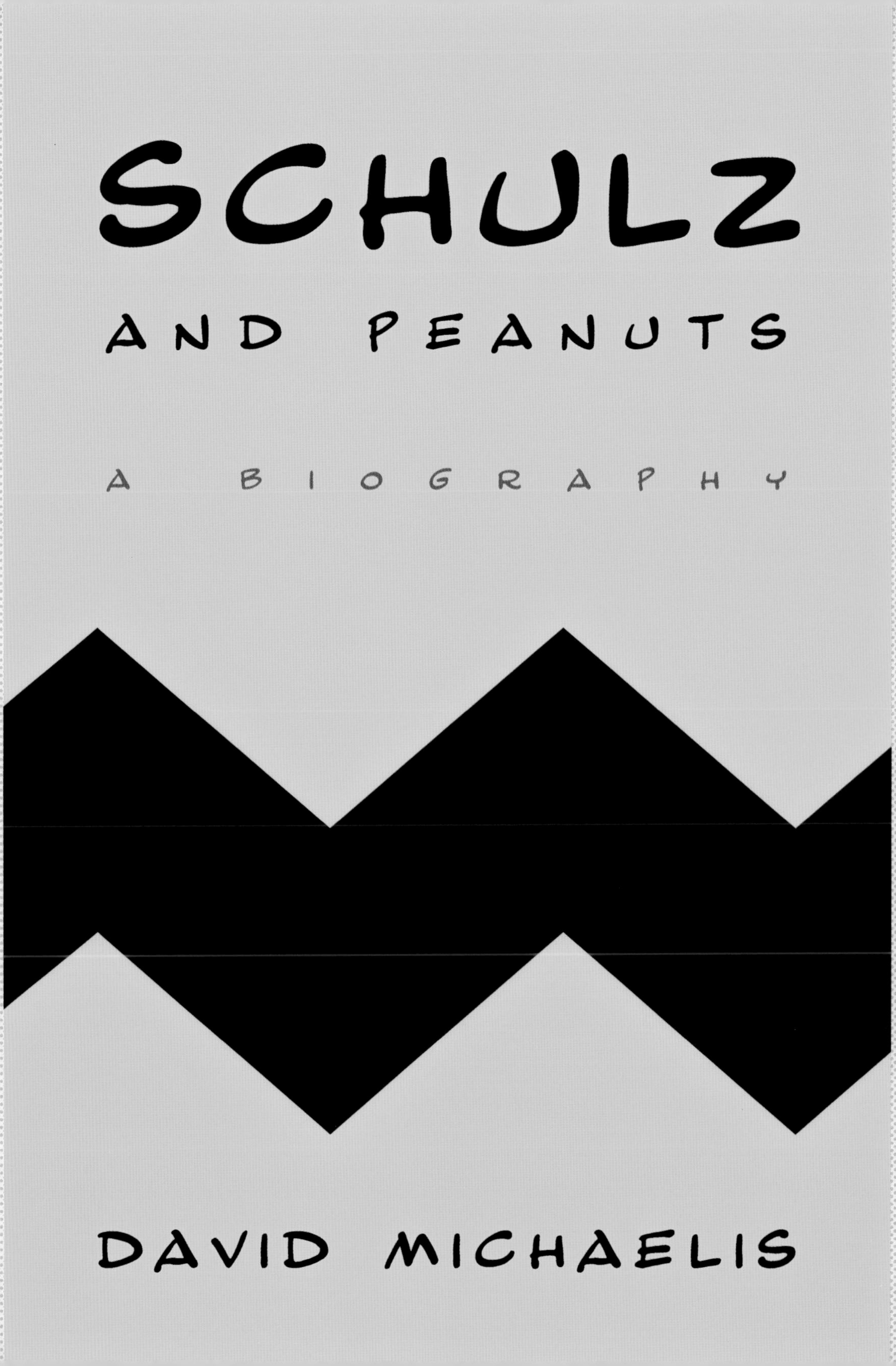
SCHULZ
AND PEANUTS
A BIOGRAPHY
DAVID MICHAELIS

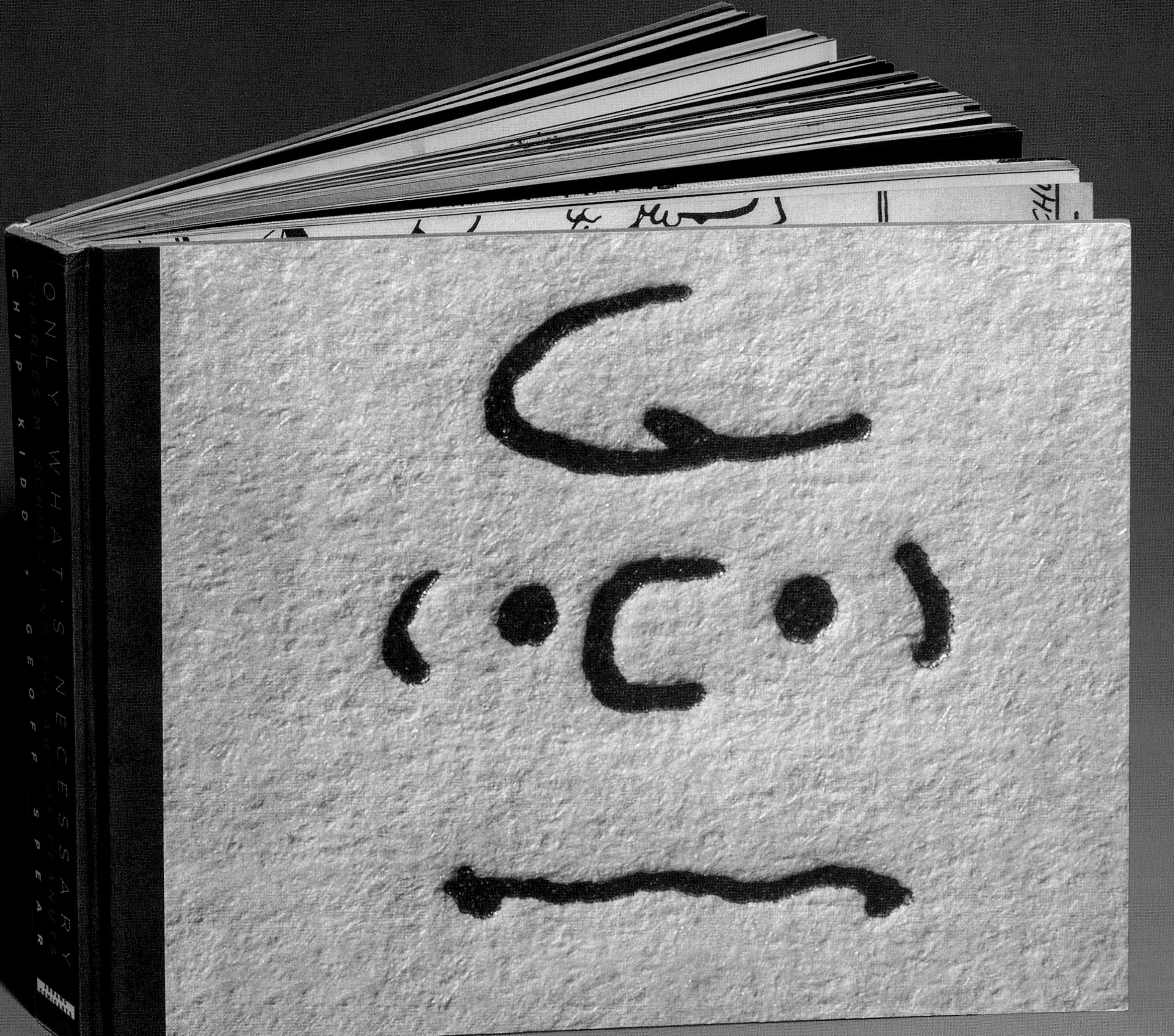
ONLY WHAT'S NECESSARY
CHARLES M. SCHULZ AND THE ART OF PEANUTS
CHIP KIDD . GEOFF SPEAR

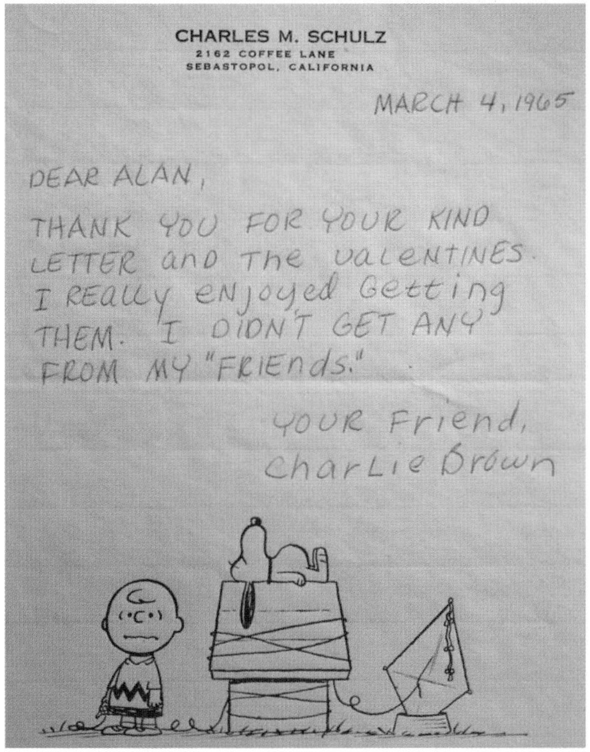
CHARLES M. SCHULZ
2162 COFFEE LANE
SEBASTOPOL, CALIFORNIA

MARCH 4, 1965

DEAR ALAN,

THANK YOU FOR YOUR KIND LETTER and THE VALENTINES. I REALLY ENJOYED GETTING THEM. I DIDN'T GET ANY FROM MY "FRIENDS."

YOUR Friend,
CHARLIE BROWN

# What a blockhead . . .

The situation with the book that became *Only What's Necessary* (opposite), nearly ten years later, could not have been more different from that of the biography. First, I was the author. More important, this was to be a visual history and appreciation of Schulz as an artist, drawing from the archives of the Charles M. Schulz Museum and Research Center in Santa Rosa, California, which opened in August 2002.

The project was initiated by conversations I'd had with Charlie Kochman at Abrams Books (pp. 218–19), as we talked about doing "the definitive original art book" for Schulz. Jeannie Schulz (his widow) and the curatorial staff had done such a spectacular job in the past decade building the archive of original drawings and ephemera at the museum, and yet there was no official catalogue. In fact, the closest thing available via their website was the first Peanuts book I worked on, *Peanuts and the Art of Charles M. Schulz.*

Jeannie, Schulz's children, Paige Braddock (dear friend and creative director of Schulz's licensing studio), the museum staff, and Peanuts Worldwide were all in favor of this project and gave us their full support. That may go without saying in light of the book's existence, but I never took it for granted and remain deeply grateful.

**OPPOSITE:** Abrams ComicArts, 2015. **ABOVE LEFT:** The original artwork used for the cover. **BELOW & FOLLOWING SPREAD:** An assortment of spreads from the book.



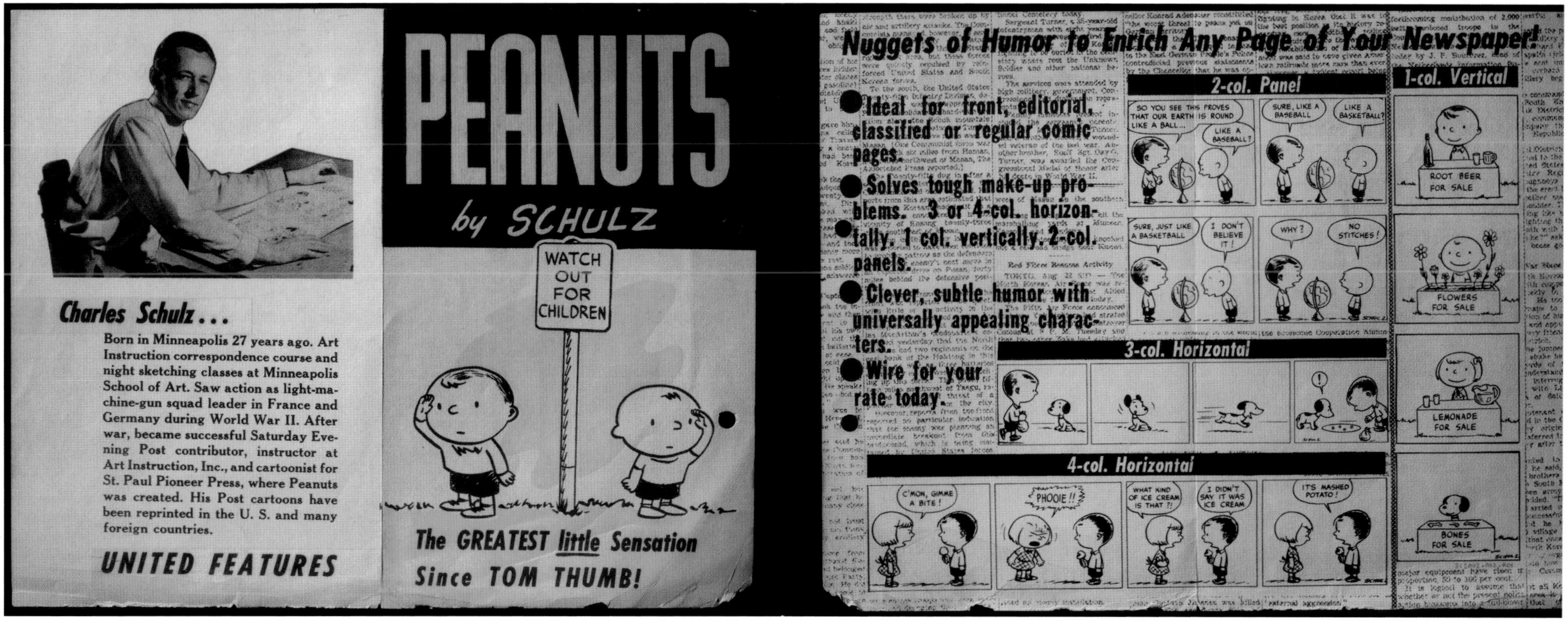
Charles Schulz . . .
Born in Minneapolis 27 years ago. Art Instruction correspondence course and night sketching classes at Minneapolis School of Art. Saw action as light-machine-gun squad leader in France and Germany during World War II. After war, became successful Saturday Evening Post contributor, instructor at Art Instruction, Inc., and cartoonist for St. Paul Pioneer Press, where Peanuts was created. His Post cartoons have been reprinted in the U. S. and many foreign countries.
UNITED FEATURES
PEANUTS
by SCHULZ
WATCH OUT FOR CHILDREN
The GREATEST little Sensation Since TOM THUMB!
Nuggets of Humor to Enrich Any Page of Your Newspaper!
Ideal for front, editorial, classified or regular comic pages.
Solves tough make-up problems. 3 or 4-col. horizontally, 1 col. vertically, 2-col. panels.
Clever, subtle humor with universally appealing characters.
Wire for your rate today.
2-col. Panel
SO YOU SEE THIS PROVES THAT OUR EARTH IS ROUND LIKE A BALL...
LIKE A BASEBALL?
SURE, LIKE A BASEBALL
LIKE A BASKETBALL?
SURE, JUST LIKE A BASKETBALL
I DON'T BELIEVE IT!
WHY?
NO STITCHES!
1-col. Vertical
ROOT BEER FOR SALE
FLOWERS FOR SALE
LEMONADE FOR SALE
BONES FOR SALE
3-col. Horizontal
4-col. Horizontal
C'MON, GIMME A BITE!
PHOOIE!!
WHAT KIND OF ICE CREAM IS THAT?!
I DIDN'T SAY IT WAS ICE CREAM
IT'S MASHED POTATO!

What I really wanted to see, first and foremost as a fan, was what they were able to find. And I wasn't disappointed. I was delighted and amazed, to say the least, because Schulz was notoriously cavalier about throwing away his sketches and giving away his originals to fans and friends. From the original drawing he did as a child that got published in *Ripley's Believe It or Not* when he was just fourteen to the last unpublished strips from late 1999, the museum's collection is fascinating, comprehensive, and heartbreaking in its scope and dedication to preserving every aspect of the artist's oeuvre. And wow, what a body of work! The man wrote and drew nonstop his entire life, while carefully raising a family of five children and slowly but steadily creating and growing a pop-cultural empire to rival that of Walt Disney. By himself, I might add; he never had or wanted an assistant to help write or draw the strip in all of its fifty years. He was determined that it was his responsibility, as an artist and a visionary.



During the time that Geoff, Charlie, and I were shooting the material, we started musing on what the title of the book should be. Charlie seemed to remember a quote from Schulz regarding his minimalist cartooning style as delineating "only what was necessary" to communicate what he needed to about the characters and their emotional states. We all liked this phrase and thought it was a unique and elegant way to describe something that had become so welcome and familiar. So we went with it, while still on the shoot, as well as firming up the design for the cover. Jeannie and Paige gave us their blessing on this approach right away, with all of the support that Linus gave the Great Pumpkin and with just as much factual basis to back it up. Which turned out to be none: we were never able to attribute an "only what's necessary" quote to any documented interview with Charles

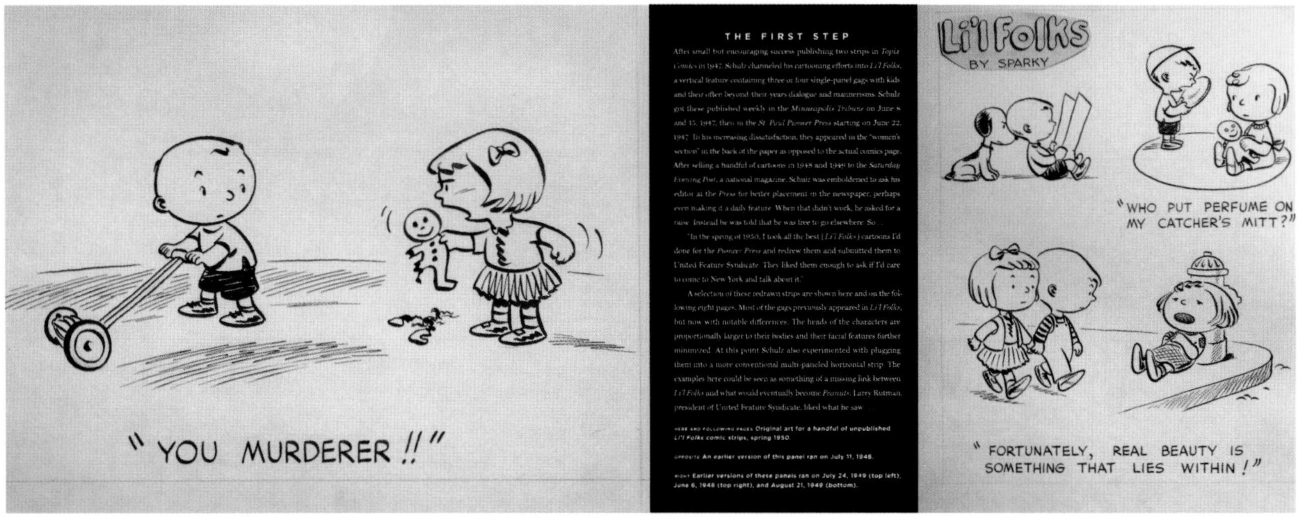
"YOU MURDERER!!"
THE FIRST STEP
Li'l Folks
BY SPARKY
"WHO PUT PERFUME ON MY CATCHER'S MITT?"
"FORTUNATELY, REAL BEAUTY IS SOMETHING THAT LIES WITHIN!"

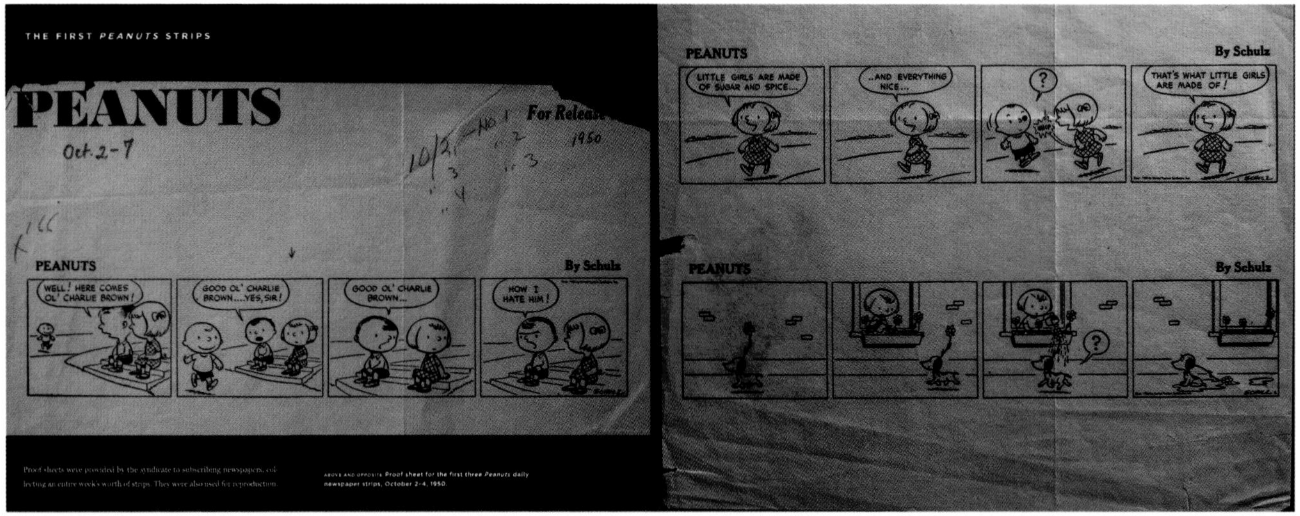
THE FIRST PEANUTS STRIPS
PEANUTS
For Release
Oct. 2-7
PEANUTS
By Schulz
WELL! HERE COMES OL' CHARLIE BROWN!
GOOD OL' CHARLIE BROWN....YES, SIR!
GOOD OL' CHARLIE BROWN...
HOW I HATE HIM!
PEANUTS
By Schulz
LITTLE GIRLS ARE MADE OF SUGAR AND SPICE...
...AND EVERYTHING NICE...
?
THAT'S WHAT LITTLE GIRLS ARE MADE OF!
PEANUTS
By Schulz
?

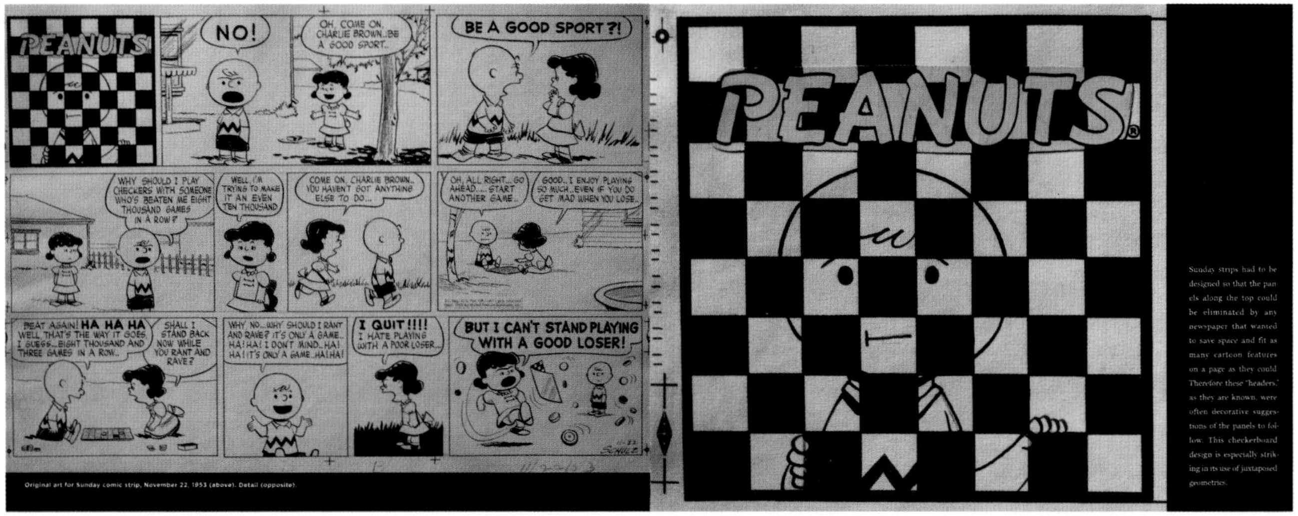
PEANUTS
NO!
OH, COME ON, CHARLIE BROWN..BE A GOOD SPORT...
BE A GOOD SPORT?!
WHY SHOULD I PLAY CHECKERS WITH SOMEONE WHO'S BEATEN ME EIGHT THOUSAND GAMES IN A ROW?
WELL, I'M TRYING TO MAKE IT AN EVEN TEN THOUSAND
COME ON, CHARLIE BROWN.. YOU HAVEN'T GOT ANYTHING ELSE TO DO...
OH, ALL RIGHT...GO AHEAD... START ANOTHER GAME...
GOOD...I ENJOY PLAYING SO MUCH...EVEN IF YOU DO GET MAD WHEN YOU LOSE..
BEAT AGAIN! HA HA HA WELL, THAT'S THE WAY IT GOES I GUESS...EIGHT THOUSAND AND THREE GAMES IN A ROW..
SHALL I STAND BACK NOW WHILE YOU RANT AND RAVE?
WHY, NO...WHY SHOULD I RANT AND RAVE? IT'S ONLY A GAME.. HA! HA! I DON'T MIND..HA! HA! IT'S ONLY A GAME..HA! HA!
I QUIT!!!! I HATE PLAYING WITH A POOR LOSER...
BUT I CAN'T STAND PLAYING WITH A GOOD LOSER!
PEANUTS
Original art for Sunday comic strip, November 22, 1953 (above). Detail (opposite).

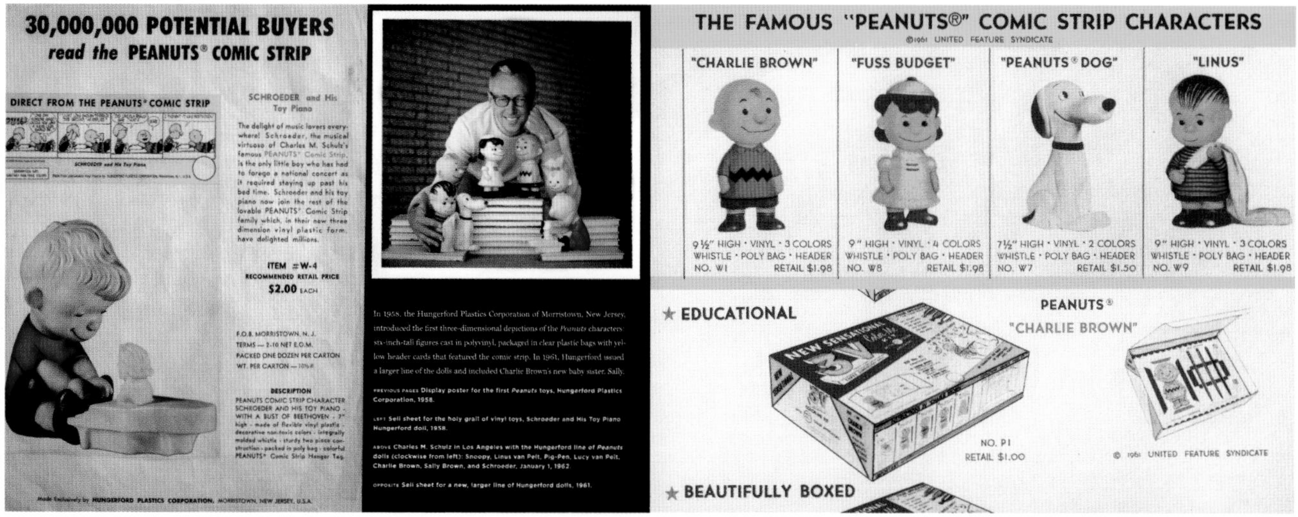
30,000,000 POTENTIAL BUYERS
read the PEANUTS® COMIC STRIP
DIRECT FROM THE PEANUTS® COMIC STRIP
ITEM #W-4
$2.00
THE FAMOUS "PEANUTS®" COMIC STRIP CHARACTERS
"CHARLIE BROWN"
"FUSS BUDGET"
"PEANUTS® DOG"
"LINUS"
★ EDUCATIONAL
PEANUTS®
"CHARLIE BROWN"
NO. P1
RETAIL $1.00
★ BEAUTIFULLY BOXED

Schulz. Moreover, the minimalist cover design, with no typography on the front and Charlie Brown's face reduced to seven squiggles, was a first for a Peanuts publication. But they believed in us and the way we wanted to champion the master's art, and we will always be grateful for their trust.

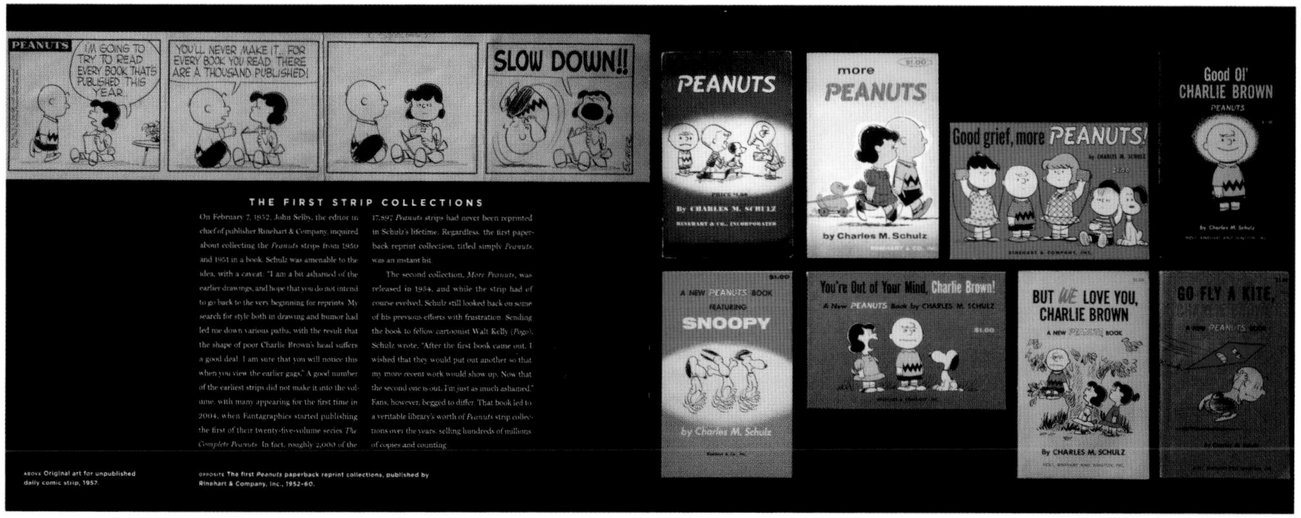
SLOW DOWN!!
THE FIRST STRIP COLLECTIONS
PEANUTS
more PEANUTS
Good grief, more PEANUTS!
Good Ol' CHARLIE BROWN
SNOOPY
You're Out of Your Mind, Charlie Brown!
BUT WE LOVE YOU, CHARLIE BROWN
GO FLY A KITE,

I was honored to appear in David Van Taylor's 2007 documentary, *Good Ol' Charles Schulz,* for the American Masters series on PBS. My commentary focused on the ingenious design of the Peanuts strip and how it stood out from everything else on the comics page when it first appeared.

They filmed my segment in my apartment, but we staged the shot so that a Hallmark "honeycomb" centerpiece of Snoopy can be seen in the background, out of focus, purposefully taped to the wall for the occasion. The film is brilliantly made (despite my inclusion in it), and the archival footage of Sparky, casual and impromptu at Art Instruction Inc. in the 1940s, is extraordinary.



**BELOW LEFT:** Title card for the documentary.

**BELOW RIGHT:** Discussing Charles Schulz, with a photobomb by Snoopy.

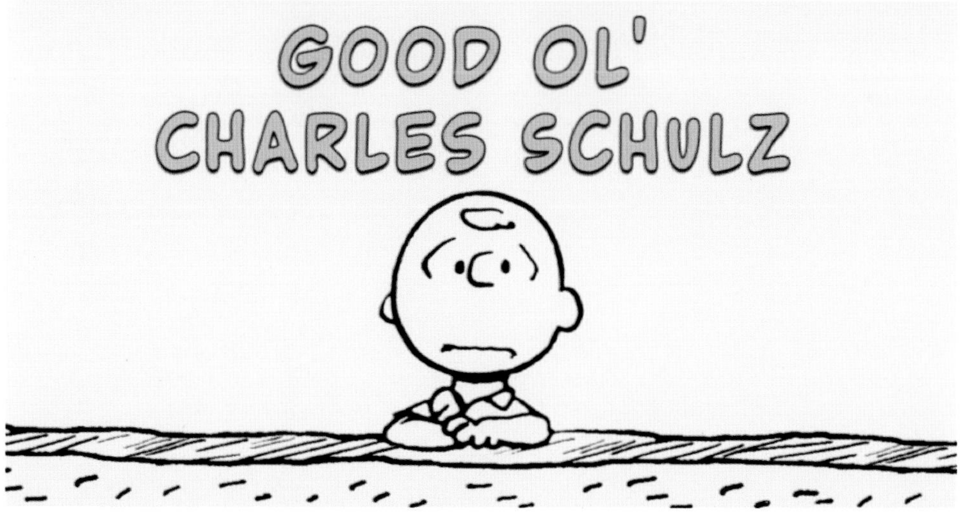
GOOD OL'
CHARLES SCHULZ

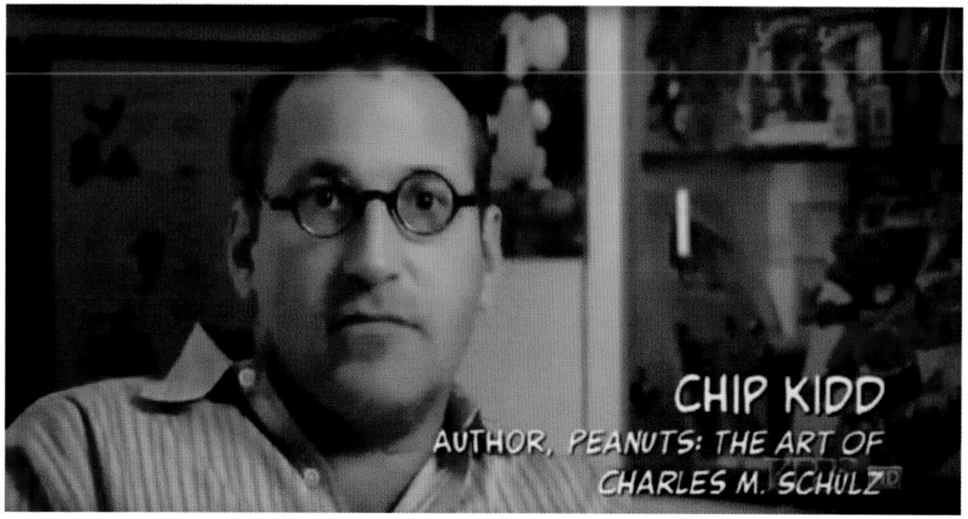
CHIP KIDD
AUTHOR, PEANUTS: THE ART OF
CHARLES M. SCHULZ

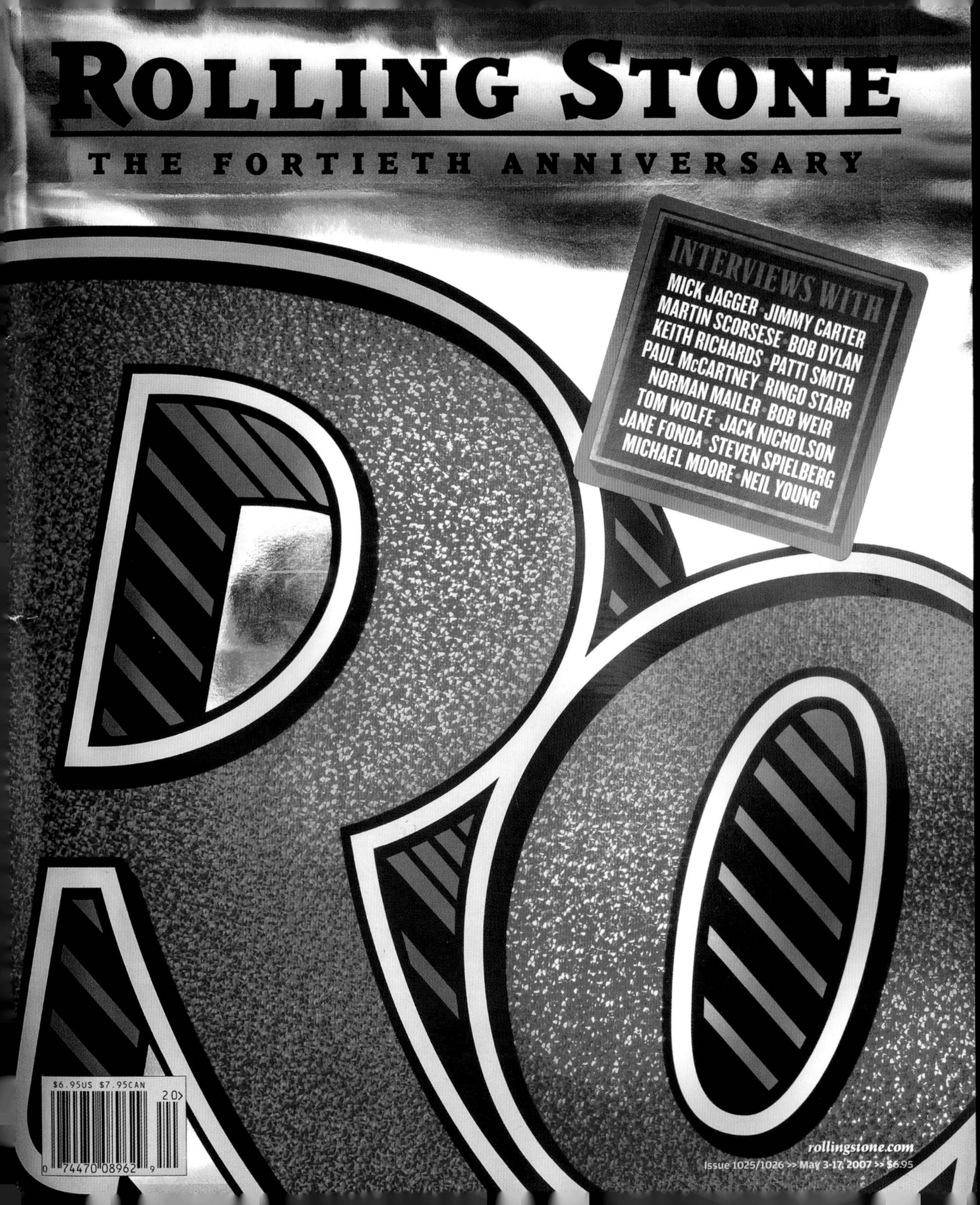
ROLLING STONE
THE FORTIETH ANNIVERSARY
INTERVIEWS WITH
MICK JAGGER · JIMMY CARTER
MARTIN SCORSESE · BOB DYLAN
KEITH RICHARDS · PATTI SMITH
PAUL McCARTNEY · RINGO STARR
NORMAN MAILER · BOB WEIR
TOM WOLFE · JACK NICHOLSON
JANE FONDA · STEVEN SPIELBERG
MICHAEL MOORE · NEIL YOUNG
$6.95US $7.95CAN
rollingstone.com
Issue 1025/1026 >> May 3-17, 2007 >> $6.95
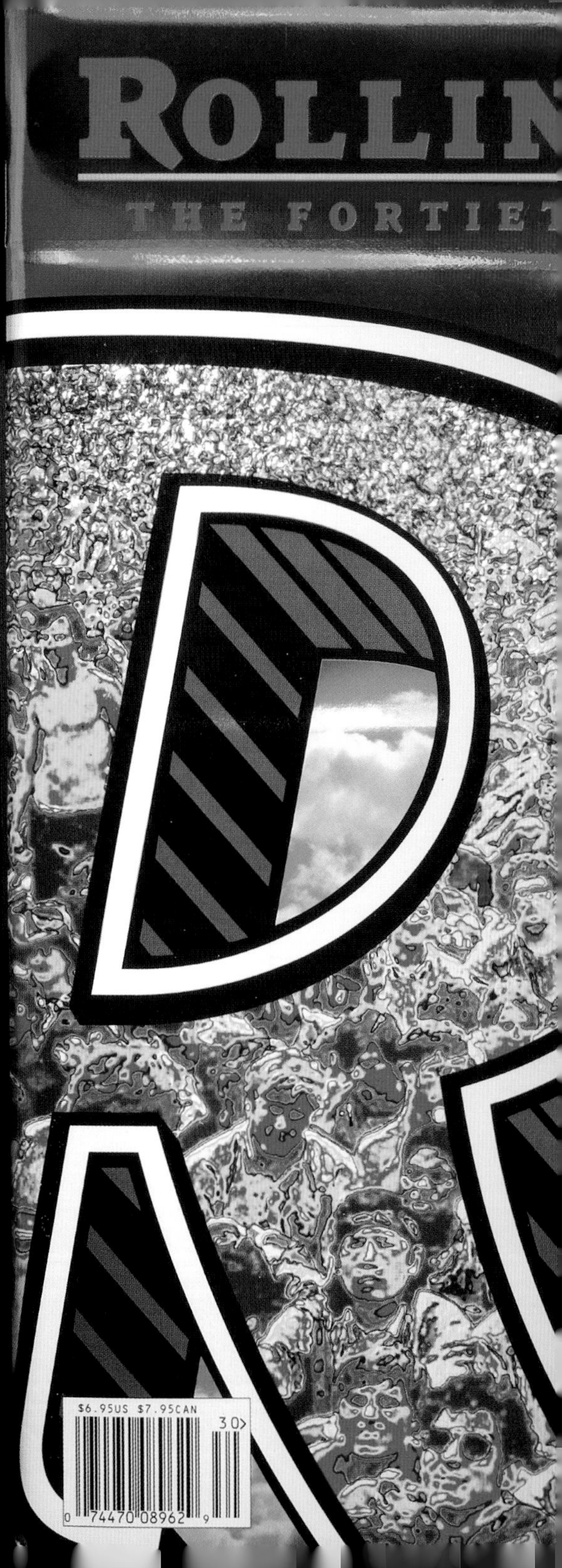
$6.95US $7.95CAN

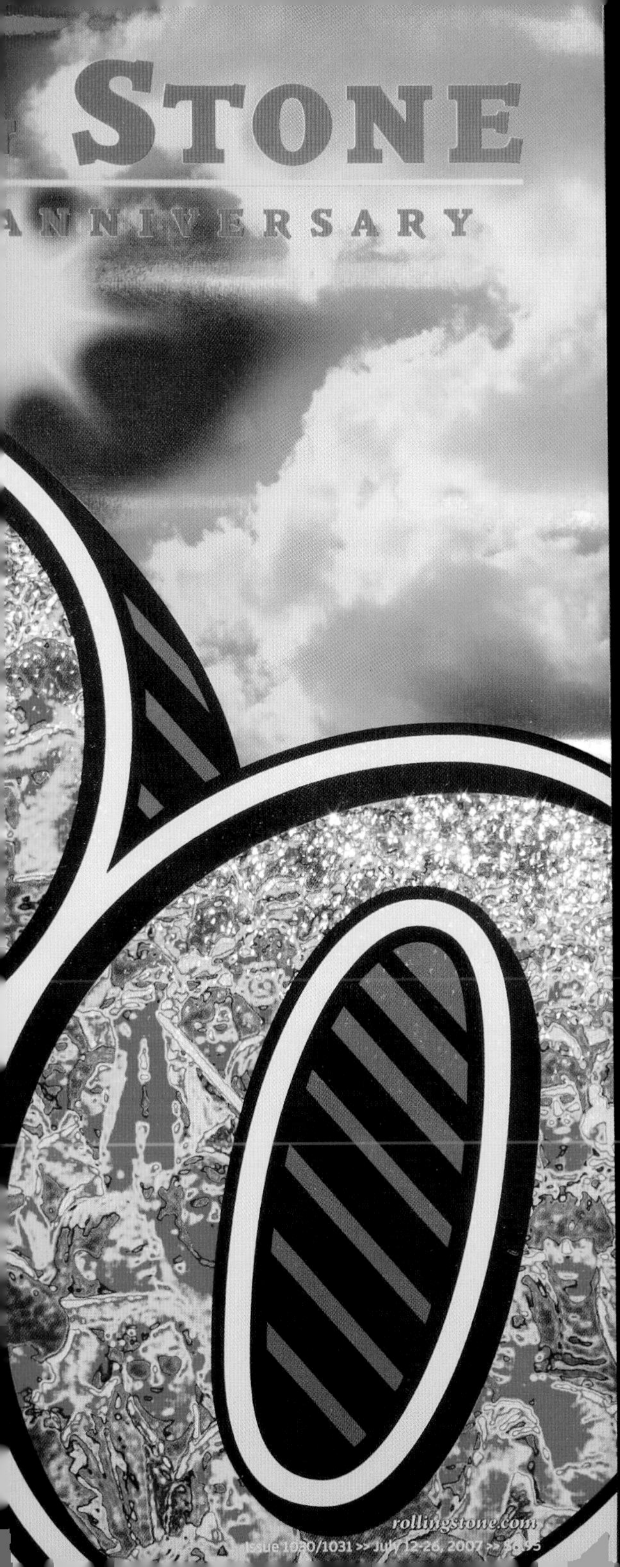
STONE
ANNIVERSARY
rollingstone.com
Issue 1030/1031 >> July 12-26, 2007 >> $6.95

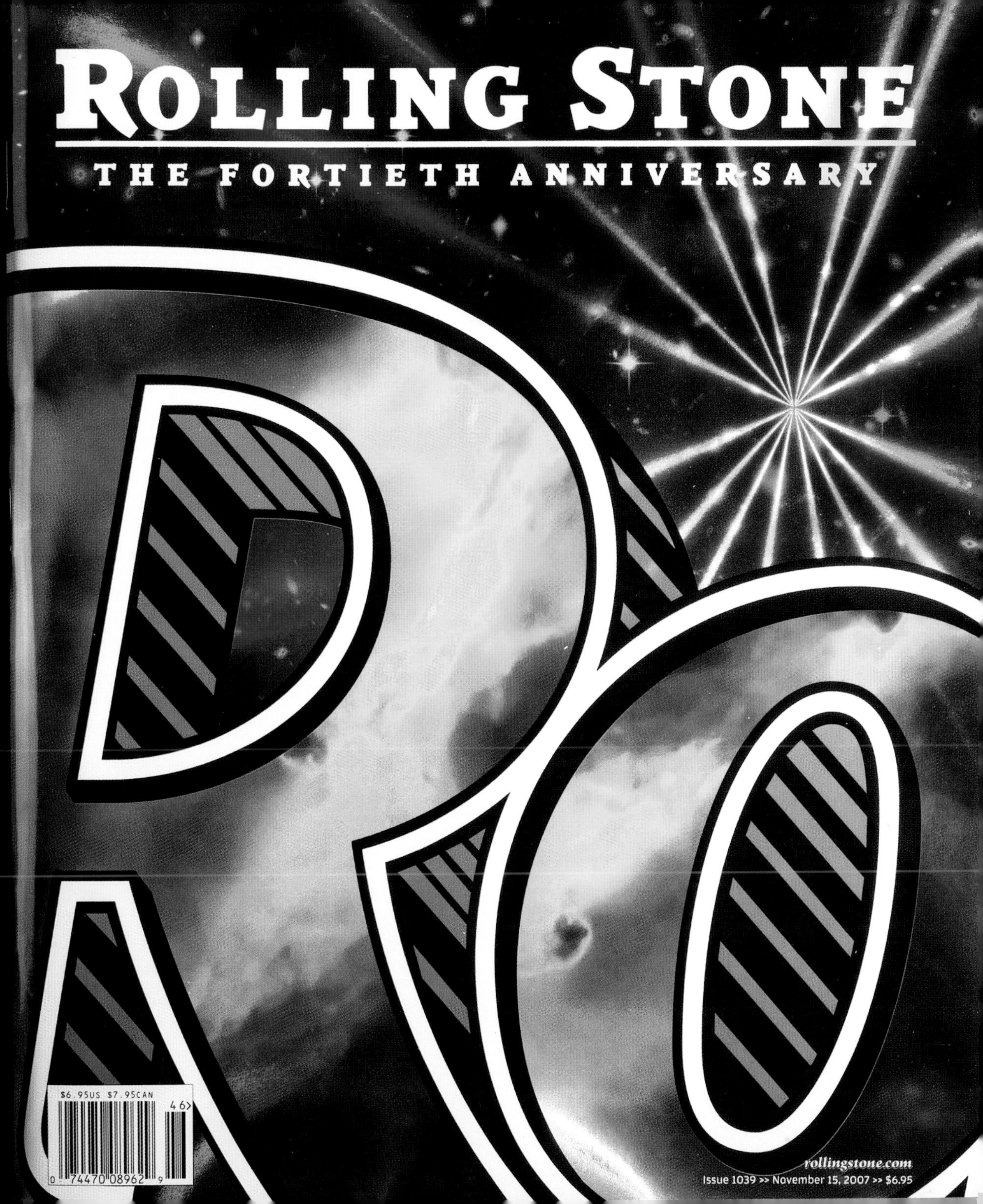
ROLLING STONE
THE FORTIETH ANNIVERSARY
$6.95US $7.95CAN
46>
0 74470 08962 9
rollingstone.com
Issue 1039 >> November 15, 2007 >> $6.95

**PREVIOUS SPREAD:** I was thrilled to be asked to design a trio of covers for the 40th anniversary of *Roll-ing Stone* magazine, under the art direction of Amid Capeci. I had been hoping that a zoom-in on the *Roll ing Stone* logo might resemble a 40, but it didn't; ye that didn't stop Jann Wenner from liking it. The trip tych is based on three concepts: 40th anniversary; th Summer of Love (1968); and the future. For the firs one, the red metal-flake pattern is a personal homage to the finish on the drum set of Chris Partridge fron *The Partridge Family* TV show.

New York Post, Wednesday, March 7, 2007 nypost

# Got it covered

## Wenner gets book-jacket big for RS birthday trilogy

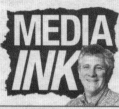

MEDIA INK

By KEITH J. KELLY

JANN **Wenner** solved at least one of his headaches in the art departments of Wenner Media. He's landed **Chip Kidd**, the noted book-cover designer, to do the magazine's three big 40th anniversary covers for Rolling Stone.

That still leaves him with only an interim art director working on most of the day-to-day covers. His last art director, **Amid Capeci**, split to go back to Newsweek late last year, and the replacement, **Matt Guemple**, was only hired on an interim basis while the search continues.

Kidd designed covers for books from **Michael Crichton**'s best-selling "Jurassic Park" to **John Updike**'s "Terrorist" and Noble Prize winner **Orhan Pamuk**'s "Snow."

While most publishers toot their own horns with anniversary issues from time to time, Wenner is one of the few to celebrate with three different anniversary issues over the course of one year. The first, which hits April 20, will be a long look backward with the theme "Where we've been."

"It will be on kind of prismatic foil that looks a lot like a guitar that T.Rex would have used in the '70s," said Kidd.

The cover will supersize the Rolling Stone logo to the point that the "R" and "o" dominate what is expected to be the highlight, to coincide with the 40th anniversary of the Summer of Love of 1967, hitting June 29. "That will be all psychedelic," said Kidd. The final, "Where we are going" cover, hits Nov. 3.

Last year RS did pretty well on newsstands, posting a 5.3 percent gain in single-copy sales to 135,344, while total circulation rose 12.12 percent to 1,462,095.

Wenner still has to search for a full-time art director. **Joe Hutchinson**, the Los Angeles Times art director, was offered the job but is said to have turned Wenner down.

"It's a tough gig working for the man," said one ex-Wennerite of the famously fastidious founder of Rolling Stone.

### Star role

You have to take your hat off to **Joe Dolce**.

While everyone else seems to be stampeding for the exits at Star — where up to eight editorial staffers have departed in the past week — the soon-to-be-deposed editor-in-chief brought his top staffers into his office yesterday with big news: He has just inked a two-day-a-week consulting gig, which effectively turns him into the Friday and Monday editor of the Star in New York.

With Dolce out of the big job and **Candace Trunzo**, the former National Enquirer executive editor, installed as the new editor-in-chief, there was a lot of uncertainty among staffers.

Some clearly didn't like the thought of working directly for Trunzo's boss, Editorial Director **Bonnie Fuller**. "She's constantly

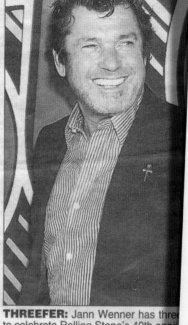

**THREEFER:** Jann Wenner has three
to celebrate Rolling Stone's 40th anniv

major editorial management change, some people get nervous and move on for their own reasons. It is the nature of the news

ries," said one insider.

Others, however, were clearly alarmed when all the rumors began flying that Star moving to Florida. Fuller did little to quell the unrest. As the rumors reached a fever pitch, embattled CEO **David Pecker** finally dragged himself to New York to tell staffers no move was planned.

But many had begun looking, and when Dolce's replacement was announced, many apparently took up their new offers. Aside from the beauty editors who left (see Page Six), Production Editor **Scott Ashwell** and Copy Chief **Edward Ekhbar** are also exiting.

The speculation is that

tor with
$1.5 milli
Star and
gated to
advertise
Last w
patched
Fla., to t
grance a
sociation
where a
and ma
swarm.
continue
was in c
itorial
was r
Trunzo
New Y
a week
time sh
of the
quarter
Of th
Fuller

RollingStone

1290 AVENUE *of the* AMERICAS NEW YORK NY 10104

JANN S. WENNER
*Editor & Publisher*

July 31, 2007

Chip Kidd
1745 Broadway, 19th floor
New York, NY 10019.

Dear Chip,

One of our best covers ever.

Many thanks,

Jann S. Wenner

JSW/np

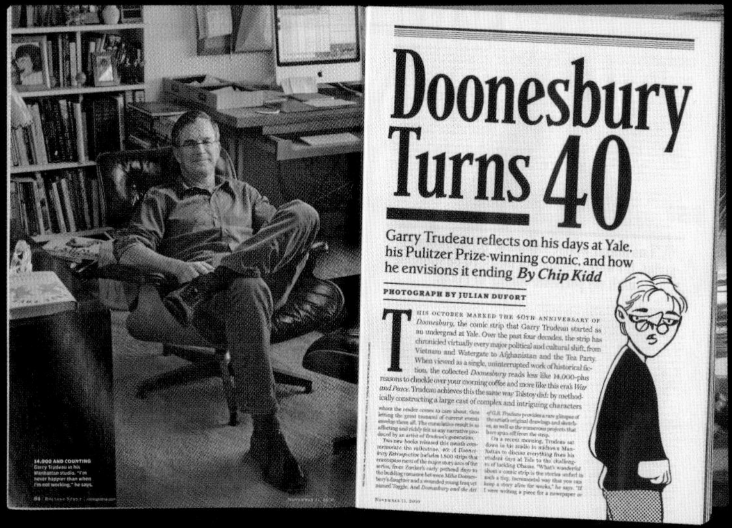
Doonesbury Turns 40
Garry Trudeau reflects on his days at Yale, his Pulitzer Prize-winning comic, and how he envisions it ending By Chip Kidd
PHOTOGRAPH BY JULIAN DUFORT
THIS OCTOBER MARKED THE 40TH ANNIVERSARY OF Doonesbury, the comic strip that Garry Trudeau started as an undergrad at Yale. Over the past four decades, the strip has chronicled virtually every major political and cultural shift, from Vietnam and Watergate to Afghanistan and the Tea Party. When viewed as a single, uninterrupted work of historical fiction, the collected Doonesbury reads less like 14,000-plus reasons to chuckle over your morning coffee and more like this era's War and Peace. Trudeau achieves this the same way Tolstoy did: by methodically constructing a large cast of complex and intriguing characters

## You Aught to Love It

After the 40th anniversary covers, I was given two more amazing assignments from *Rolling Stone*. The first was to interview one of my heroes, Garry Trudeau, on the 40th anniversary of his classic comic strip, Doonesbury (above). What an astonishing and delightful introduction to this man whom I'd admired since I was a kid.

The second was to design a cover for the magazine concerning the best music of the 2000s (right) with art director Joe Hutchinson. He wrote: "Chip came up with the concept of removing the two Os from the RS logo and dropped them to the center of the page to represent the aughts. Clever idea. Brilliant. At this stage the background was blank because we planned to use a collage of images of the artists of the decade. But as we started to think about it, it seemed that adding photos, not to mention cover lines, would dilute the concept. I called Jim Parkinson, who in 1981 designed the logo we currently use, and asked him to redraw it without the Os and asked him to draw new Os that could run large as display. Chip and I experimented with wild color combinations, but many of them didn't seem right. So I decided to go with the classic *Rolling Stone* palette: red, white, black and gray with yellow as an accent for the main cover headline. I also removed the secondary headlines, which made the cover less cluttered."

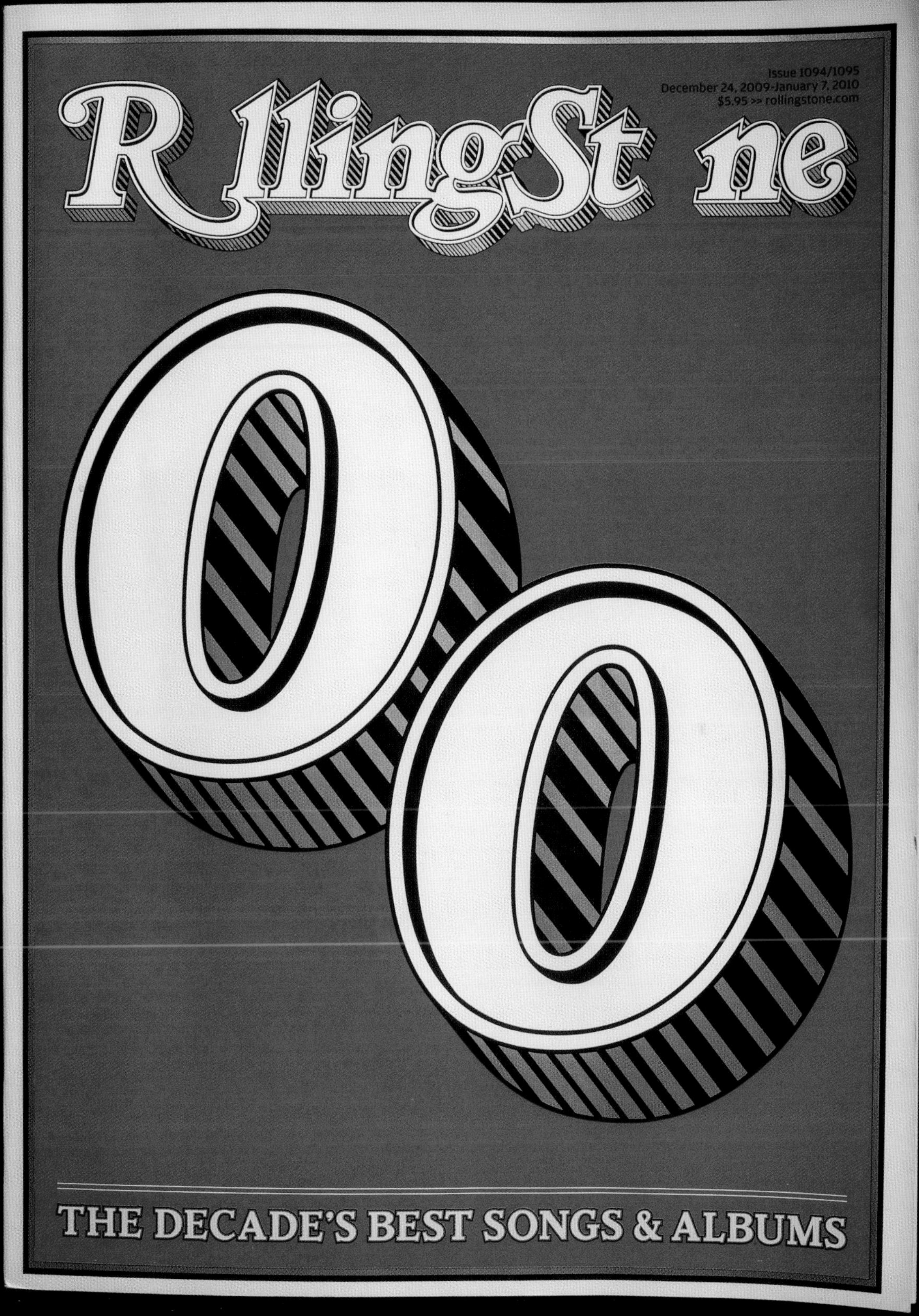
Issue 1094/1095
December 24, 2009-January 7, 2010
$5.95 >> rollingstone.com
THE DECADE'S BEST SONGS & ALBUMS

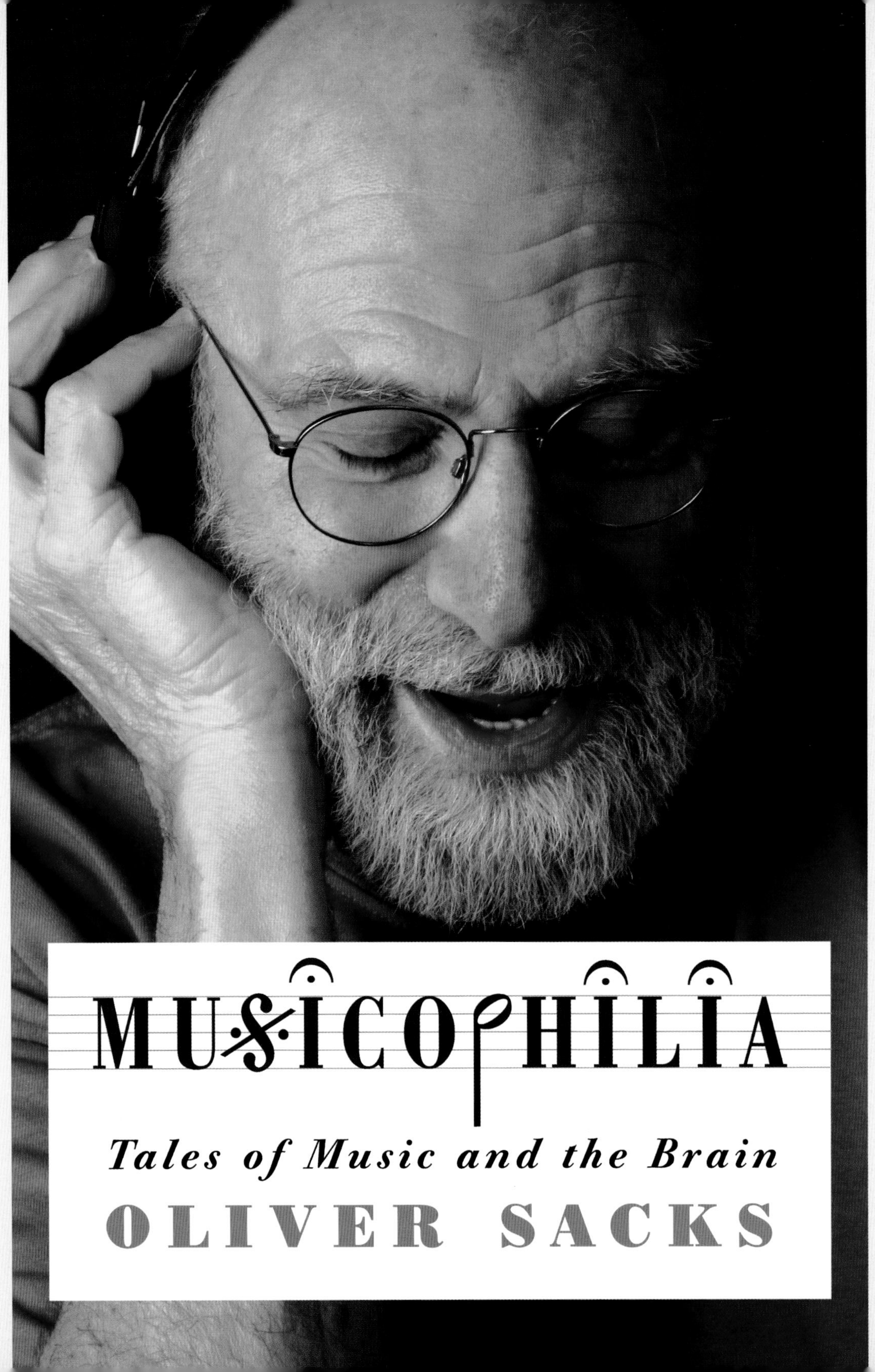
MUSICOPHILIA
Tales of Music and the Brain
OLIVER SACKS



# Sounds Great

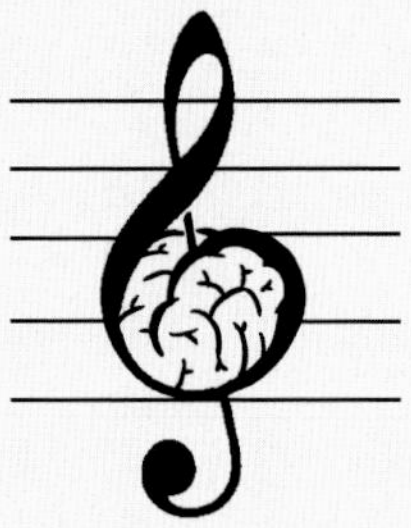

Oliver Sacks had been working on a book of essays and case studies about how music works in the brain, and he and his assistant, Kate Edgar, were having trouble coming up with what to call it. The problem was that at the time (2007) a book called *Music, Language and the Brain* by Aniruddh D. Patel had just been released to great reviews, including one by Oliver himself. So even though Sacks's book was quite different, to call it *Music and the Brain* would have been potentially too confusing. And yet that was what it was about. Eventually, Kate sent me a title of *Something, Something, Musicophilia, and Other Tales of Music and the Brain.* Normally, in my role as a designer, I work with whatever title I'm given, but I had known and associated with Oliver and Kate for so long, and this title sounded so clunky to me, that I felt compelled to respond with a suggestion. First, I asked Kate what "musicophilia" was. She laughed and said it was a term that Oliver had coined to mean "love of music." I thought that was perfect, and said that I thought it should be the title, and to let the subtitle explain what it meant. They agreed, and that was the first and only time I offered input on the title of a book that I had not written.

Reading the manuscript of *On the Move* was truly astounding because I had no idea that Oliver was going to be so candid and self-revealing. I had known for quite some time that he was gay, but he was also very discreet about it, and I totally respected that. Now it was all going to be out in the open, so to speak. Kate sent me dozens of personal photos to consider, and to me it was no contest (opposite, right). I mean, my God, how gorgeous. The typography of his name is from one of his medical ID badges from years past, as I had used on the redesign of his backlist for Vintage.

**LEFT:** Knopf, 2007. The first version was just the "musicalized" typography, but when the author photos by Elena Seibert came in, we all agreed that this one was too good not to use on the cover. **ABOVE:** I asked Christoph Niemann to explore a few ideas combining musical notes and brains, and this is one of them. Unused, but I loved them all. **OPPOSITE, RIGHT:** Knopf, 2015.

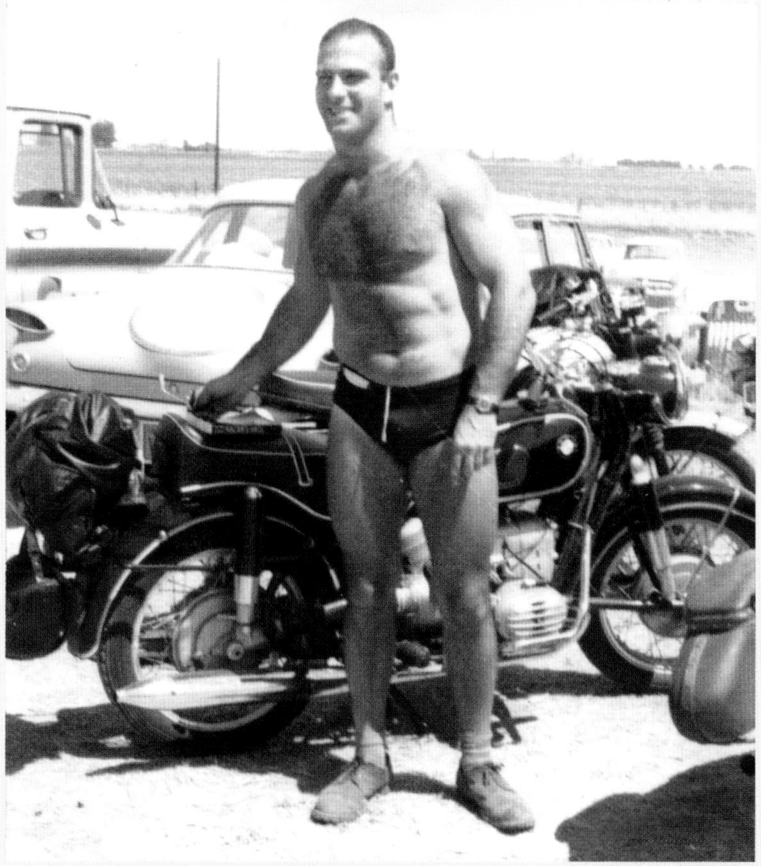

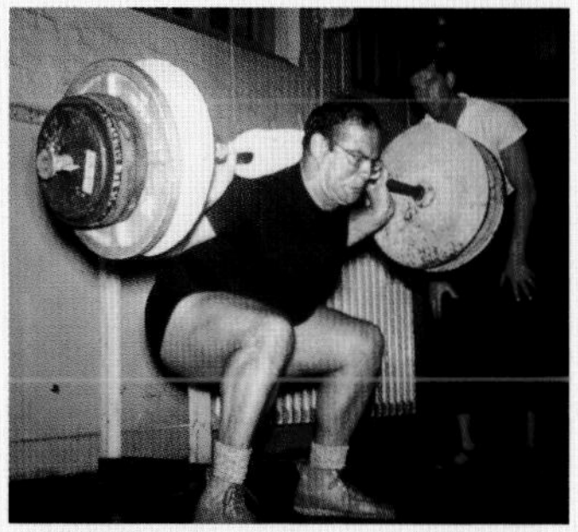

Then all of a sudden the book was moved from the Fall '15 list to the Spring '15 list. Very unusual, but at least the cover was done early and approved. I asked editor and friend Dan Frank why the schedule change, and the answer was devastating: Oliver had terminal cancer and was unlikely to live to the end of the year.

And indeed he did not, but not before inspiring his hundreds of thousands of readers and fans with an op-ed piece in the *New York Times* about how he was dealing with his diagnosis, and how grateful he was for the life he lived and the work he was able to do. Everyone was stunned by his bravery and candor.

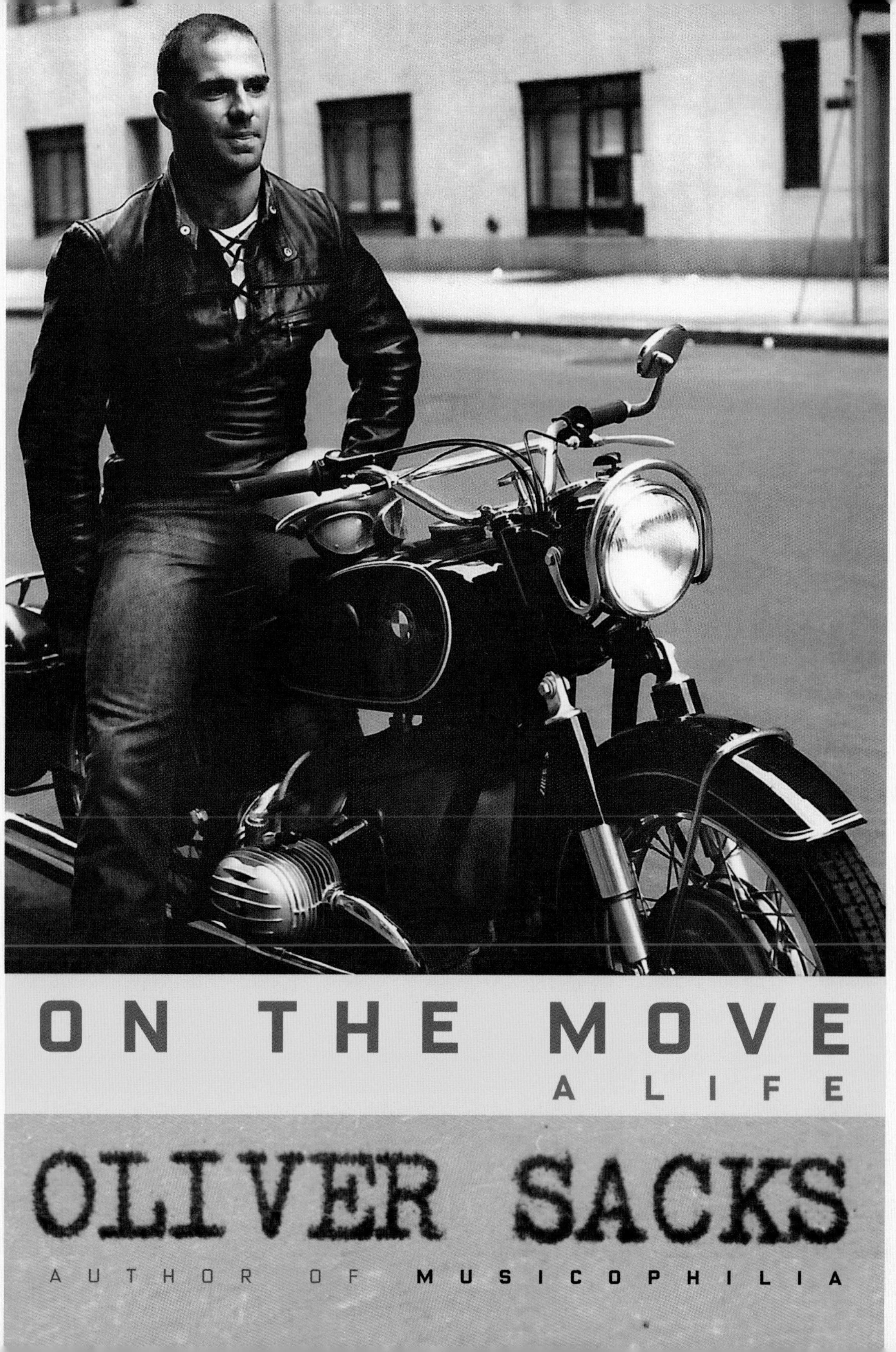
ON THE MOVE
A LIFE
OLIVER SACKS
AUTHOR OF MUSICOPHILIA

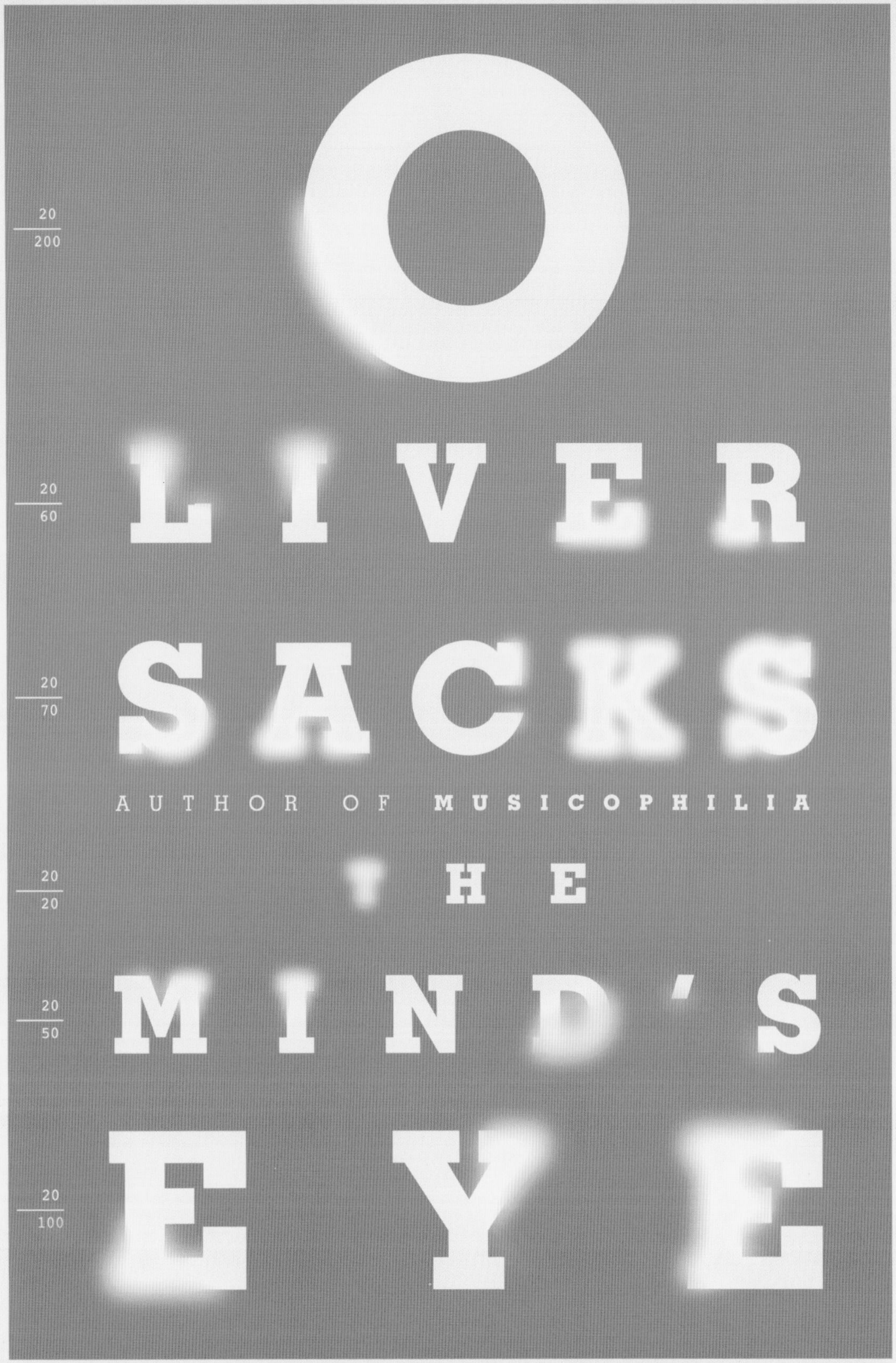
20
200
20
60
20
70
20
20
20
50
20
100
O
LIVER
SACKS
AUTHOR OF MUSICOPHILIA
THE
MIND'S
EYE

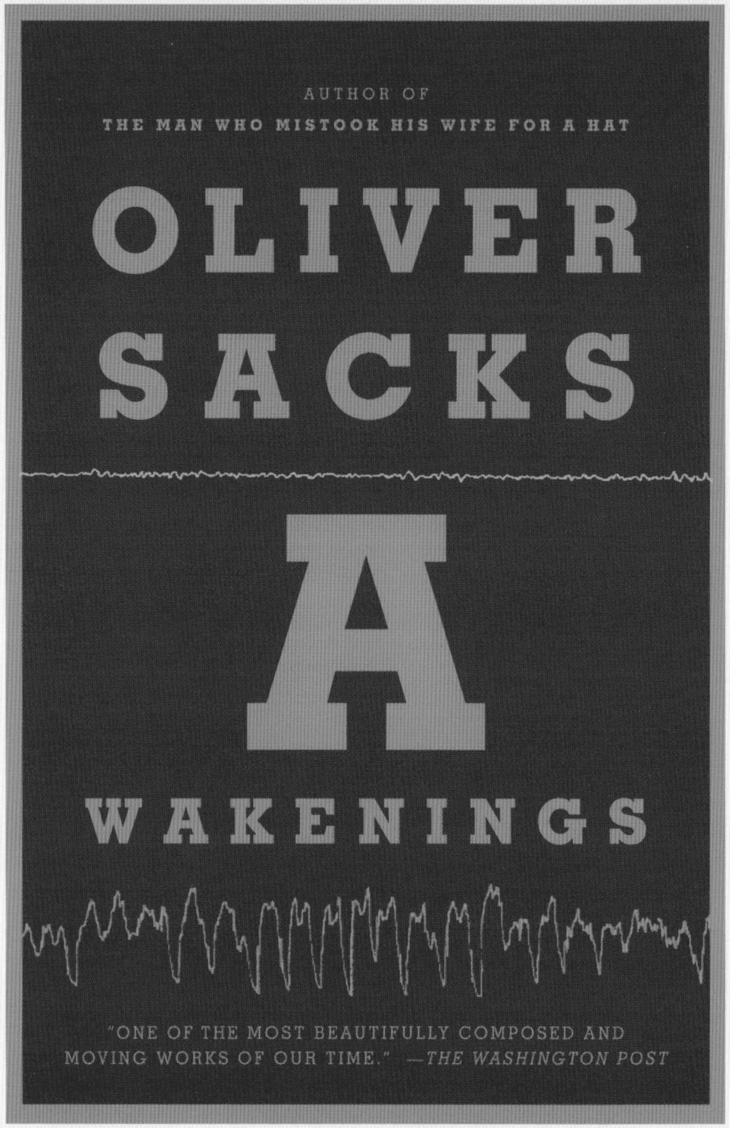
AUTHOR OF
THE MAN WHO MISTOOK HIS WIFE FOR A HAT
OLIVER
SACKS
A
WAKENINGS
"ONE OF THE MOST BEAUTIFULLY COMPOSED AND
MOVING WORKS OF OUR TIME." —THE WASHINGTON POST



The follow-up to *Musicophilia* was *The Mind's Eye* (left; Knopf, 2010), Oliver's exploration of how eyesight works in the brain. I used the visual trope of an eye-test chart, but juiced up the color (at Oliver's suggestion) and added just enough blurry spots to indicate there's a problem while still keeping the type legible. I was amazed and grateful that no one involved had a problem with the way I broke up his first name. Oliver loved this design—so much so that I was asked to adapt the approach to his backlist for Vintage paperbacks (above and opposite). This proposal was, alas, not used.

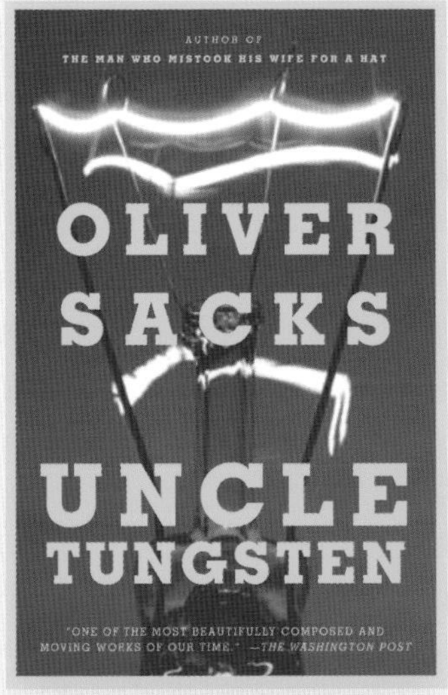
AUTHOR OF
THE MAN WHO MISTOOK HIS WIFE FOR A HAT
OLIVER
SACKS
UNCLE
TUNGSTEN
"ONE OF THE MOST BEAUTIFULLY COMPOSED AND MOVING WORKS OF OUR TIME." —THE WASHINGTON POST

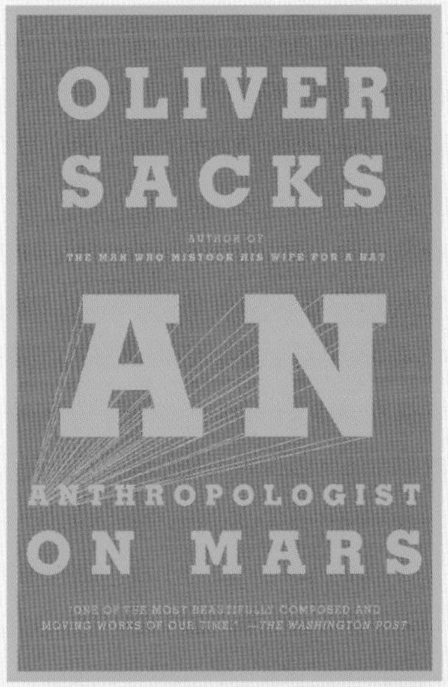
OLIVER
SACKS
AUTHOR OF
THE MAN WHO MISTOOK HIS WIFE FOR A HAT
AN
ANTHROPOLOGIST
ON MARS
"ONE OF THE MOST BEAUTIFULLY COMPOSED AND MOVING WORKS OF OUR TIME." —THE WASHINGTON POST

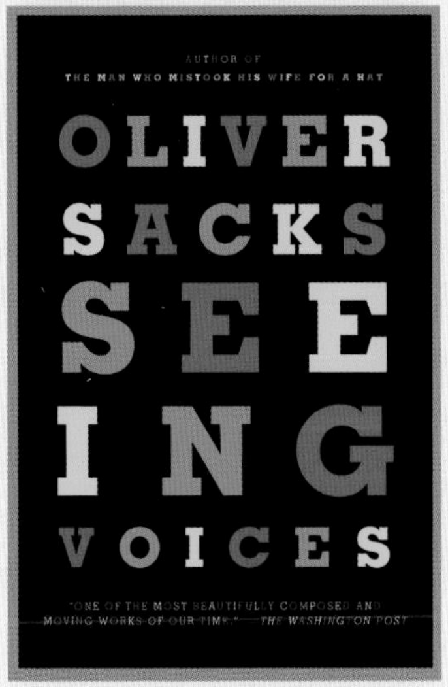
AUTHOR OF
THE MAN WHO MISTOOK HIS WIFE FOR A HAT
OLIVER
SACKS
SEE
ING
VOICES
"ONE OF THE MOST BEAUTIFULLY COMPOSED AND MOVING WORKS OF OUR TIME." —THE WASHINGTON POST

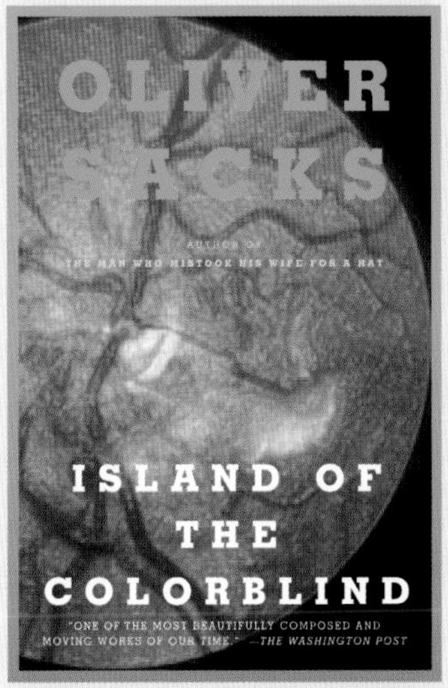
OLIVER
SACKS
AUTHOR OF
THE MAN WHO MISTOOK HIS WIFE FOR A HAT
ISLAND OF
THE
COLORBLIND
"ONE OF THE MOST BEAUTIFULLY COMPOSED AND MOVING WORKS OF OUR TIME." —THE WASHINGTON POST

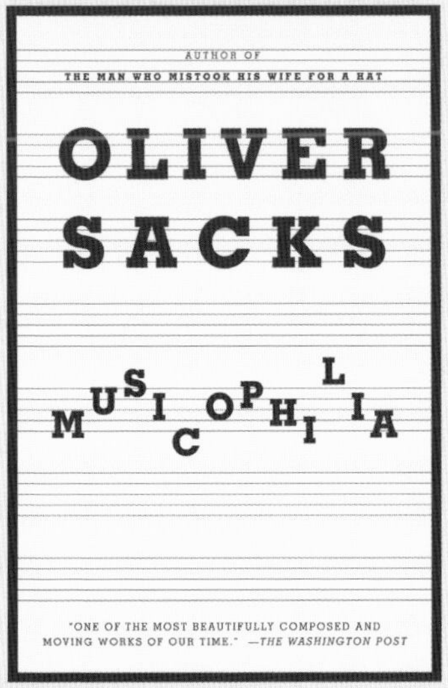
AUTHOR OF
THE MAN WHO MISTOOK HIS WIFE FOR A HAT
OLIVER
SACKS
MUSICOPHILIA
"ONE OF THE MOST BEAUTIFULLY COMPOSED AND MOVING WORKS OF OUR TIME." —THE WASHINGTON POST

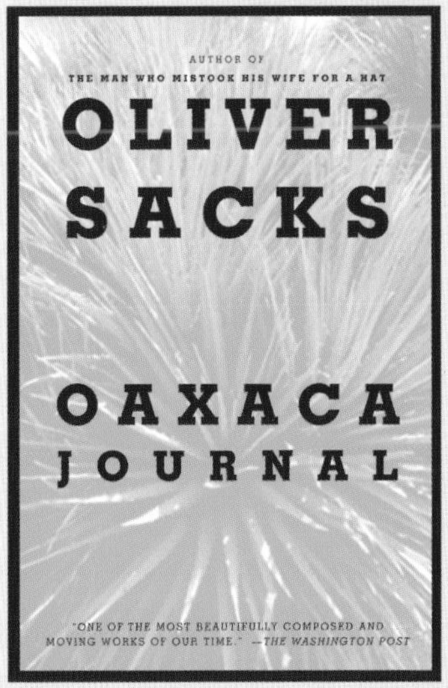
AUTHOR OF
THE MAN WHO MISTOOK HIS WIFE FOR A HAT
OLIVER
SACKS
OAXACA
JOURNAL
"ONE OF THE MOST BEAUTIFULLY COMPOSED AND MOVING WORKS OF OUR TIME." —THE WASHINGTON POST

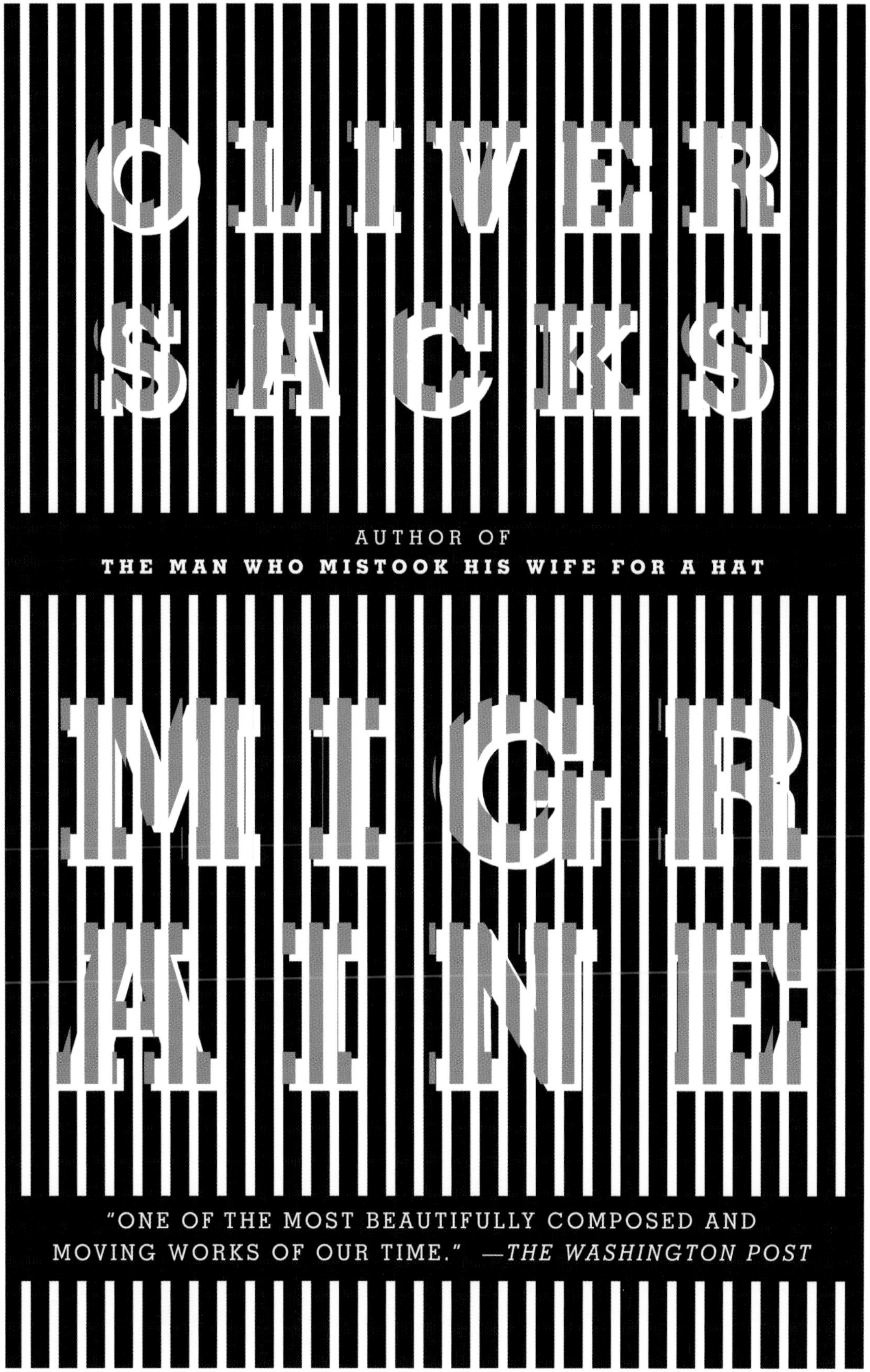
OLIVER
SACKS
AUTHOR OF
THE MAN WHO MISTOOK HIS WIFE FOR A HAT
MIGR
AINE
"ONE OF THE MOST BEAUTIFULLY COMPOSED AND MOVING WORKS OF OUR TIME." —THE WASHINGTON POST

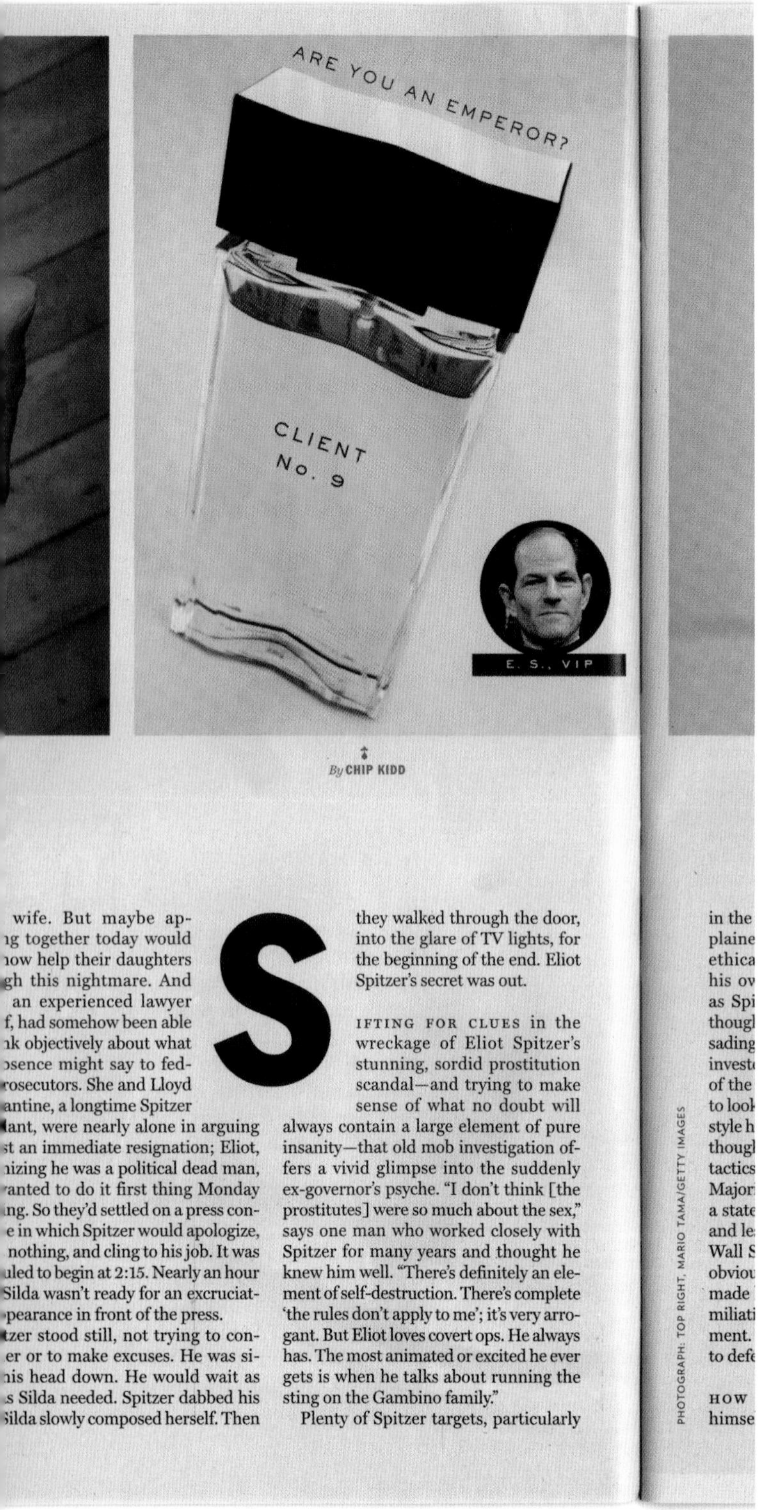

ARE YOU AN EMPEROR?
CLIENT No. 9
E. S., VIP


*By* CHIP KIDD

wife. But maybe ap-
ıg together today would
ıow help their daughters
gh this nightmare. And
an experienced lawyer
f, had somehow been able
ık objectively about what
ɔsence might say to fed-
rosecutors. She and Lloyd
antine, a longtime Spitzer
lant, were nearly alone in arguing
st an immediate resignation; Eliot,
ıizing he was a political dead man,
vanted to do it first thing Monday
ıng. So they'd settled on a press con-
e in which Spitzer would apologize,
nothing, and cling to his job. It was
uled to begin at 2:15. Nearly an hour
Silda wasn't ready for an excruciat-
pearance in front of the press.
tzer stood still, not trying to con-
er or to make excuses. He was si-
his head down. He would wait as
s Silda needed. Spitzer dabbed his
Silda slowly composed herself. Then

S

they walked through the door, into the glare of TV lights, for the beginning of the end. Eliot Spitzer's secret was out.

IFTING FOR CLUES in the wreckage of Eliot Spitzer's stunning, sordid prostitution scandal—and trying to make sense of what no doubt will always contain a large element of pure insanity—that old mob investigation offers a vivid glimpse into the suddenly ex-governor's psyche. "I don't think [the prostitutes] were so much about the sex," says one man who worked closely with Spitzer for many years and thought he knew him well. "There's definitely an element of self-destruction. There's complete 'the rules don't apply to me'; it's very arrogant. But Eliot loves covert ops. He always has. The most animated or excited he ever gets is when he talks about running the sting on the Gambino family."

Plenty of Spitzer targets, particularly

in the
plaine
ethica
his ov
as Spi
thoug
sading
invest
of the
to look
style h
thoug
tactics
Major
a state
and le
Wall S
obviou
made
miliati
ment.
to defe

HOW
himse

PHOTOGRAPH: TOP RIGHT, MARIO TAMA/GETTY IMAGES

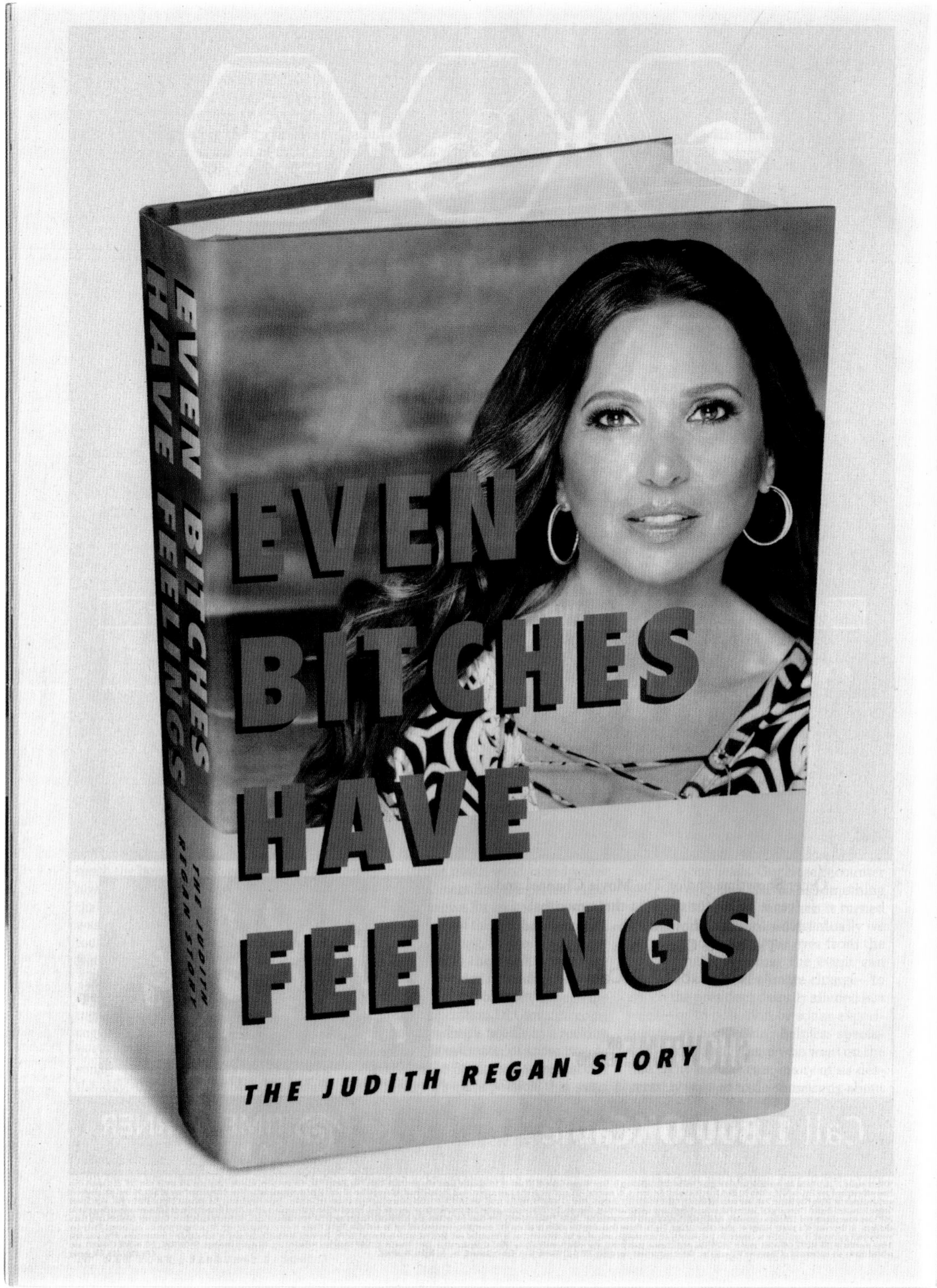

EVEN BITCHES HAVE FEELINGS
THE JUDITH REGAN STORY


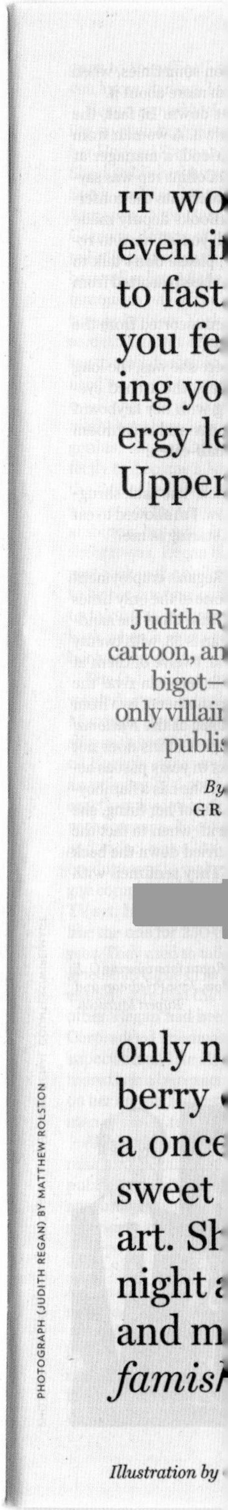

PHOTOGRAPH (JUDITH REGAN) BY MATTHEW ROLSTON

IT WO
even if
to fast
you fe
ing yo
ergy le
Upper

Judith R
cartoon, an
bigot—
only villain
publis

*By*
GR

only n
berry
a once
sweet
art. Sh
night a
and m
*famish*

*Illustration by*

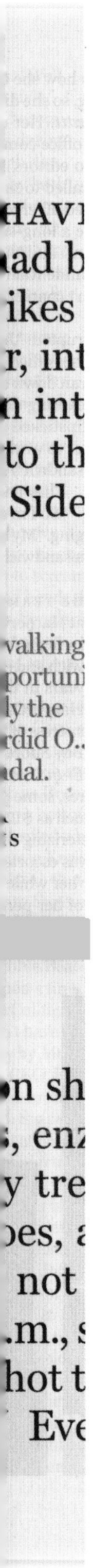

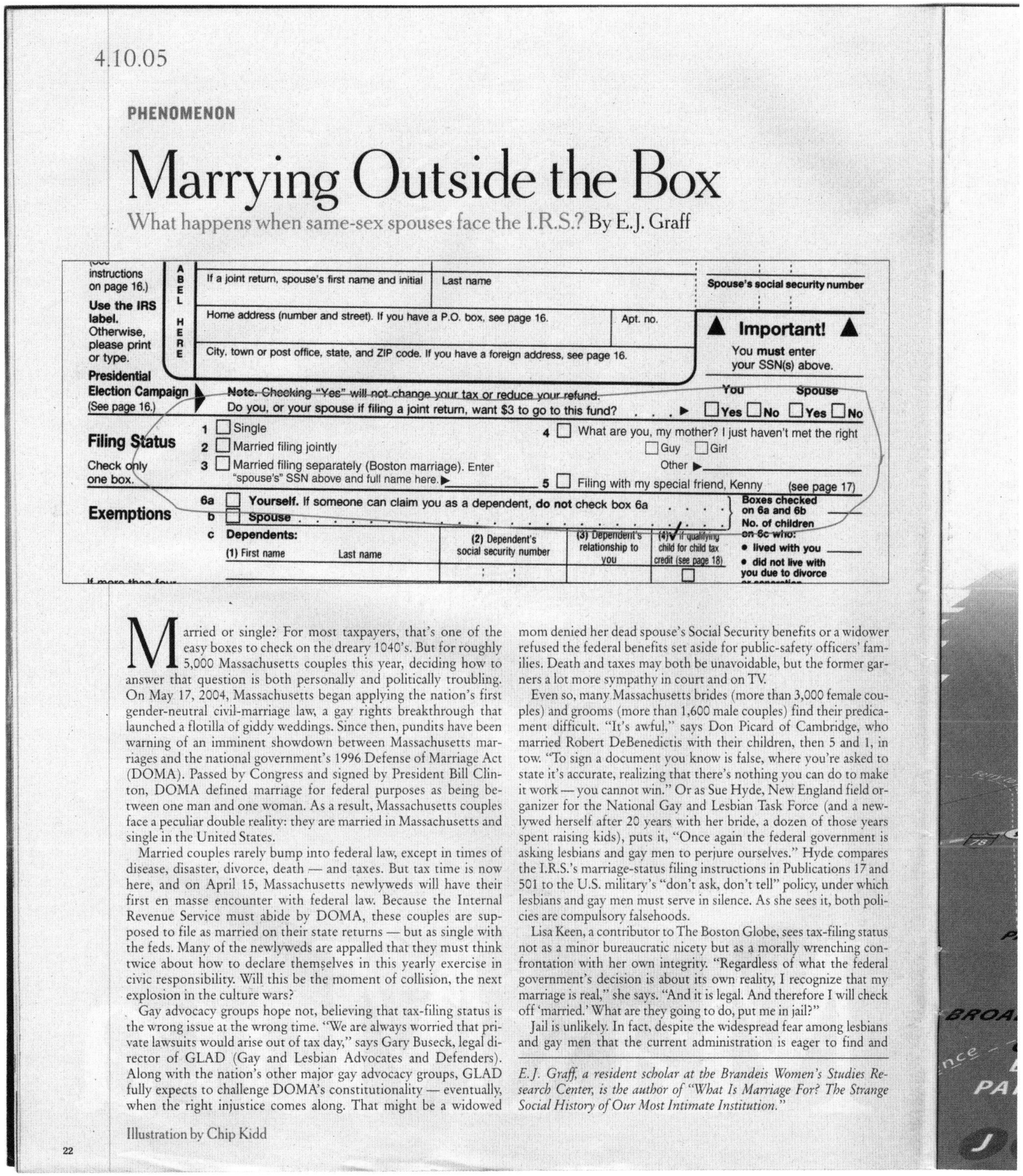

PHENOMENON

# Marrying Outside the Box

What happens when same-sex spouses face the I.R.S.? By E.J. Graff

| LABEL HERE | | |
|---|---|---|
| (See instructions on page 16.) Use the IRS label. Otherwise, please print or type. | If a joint return, spouse's first name and initial | Last name | Spouse's social security number |
| | Home address (number and street). If you have a P.O. box, see page 16. | Apt. no. | ▲ **Important!** ▲ You **must** enter your SSN(s) above. |
| | City, town or post office, state, and ZIP code. If you have a foreign address, see page 16. | | |

**Presidential Election Campaign** (See page 16.) ▶ Note. Checking "Yes" will not change your tax or reduce your refund. Do you, or your spouse if filing a joint return, want $3 to go to this fund? . . . ▶ You ☐Yes ☐No Spouse ☐Yes ☐No

**Filing Status**
Check only one box.

1 ☐ Single
2 ☐ Married filing jointly
3 ☐ Married filing separately (Boston marriage). Enter "spouse's" SSN above and full name here. ▶
4 ☐ What are you, my mother? I just haven't met the right ☐ Guy ☐ Girl Other ▶
5 ☐ Filing with my special friend, Kenny (see page 17)

**Exemptions**

6a ☐ Yourself. If someone can claim you as a dependent, **do not** check box 6a
b ☐ Spouse
c Dependents:
(1) First name  Last name
(2) Dependent's social security number
(3) Dependent's relationship to you
(4) ✓ if qualifying child for child tax credit (see page 18)

Boxes checked on 6a and 6b
No. of children on 6c who:
• lived with you
• did not live with you due to divorce

---

Married or single? For most taxpayers, that's one of the easy boxes to check on the dreary 1040's. But for roughly 5,000 Massachusetts couples this year, deciding how to answer that question is both personally and politically troubling. On May 17, 2004, Massachusetts began applying the nation's first gender-neutral civil-marriage law, a gay rights breakthrough that launched a flotilla of giddy weddings. Since then, pundits have been warning of an imminent showdown between Massachusetts marriages and the national government's 1996 Defense of Marriage Act (DOMA). Passed by Congress and signed by President Bill Clinton, DOMA defined marriage for federal purposes as being between one man and one woman. As a result, Massachusetts couples face a peculiar double reality: they are married in Massachusetts and single in the United States.

Married couples rarely bump into federal law, except in times of disease, disaster, divorce, death — and taxes. But tax time is now here, and on April 15, Massachusetts newlyweds will have their first en masse encounter with federal law. Because the Internal Revenue Service must abide by DOMA, these couples are supposed to file as married on their state returns — but as single with the feds. Many of the newlyweds are appalled that they must think twice about how to declare themselves in this yearly exercise in civic responsibility. Will this be the moment of collision, the next explosion in the culture wars?

Gay advocacy groups hope not, believing that tax-filing status is the wrong issue at the wrong time. "We are always worried that private lawsuits would arise out of tax day," says Gary Buseck, legal director of GLAD (Gay and Lesbian Advocates and Defenders). Along with the nation's other major gay advocacy groups, GLAD fully expects to challenge DOMA's constitutionality — eventually, when the right injustice comes along. That might be a widowed mom denied her dead spouse's Social Security benefits or a widower refused the federal benefits set aside for public-safety officers' families. Death and taxes may both be unavoidable, but the former garners a lot more sympathy in court and on TV.

Even so, many Massachusetts brides (more than 3,000 female couples) and grooms (more than 1,600 male couples) find their predicament difficult. "It's awful," says Don Picard of Cambridge, who married Robert DeBenedictis with their children, then 5 and 1, in tow. "To sign a document you know is false, where you're asked to state it's accurate, realizing that there's nothing you can do to make it work — you cannot win." Or as Sue Hyde, New England field organizer for the National Gay and Lesbian Task Force (and a newlywed herself after 20 years with her bride, a dozen of those years spent raising kids), puts it, "Once again the federal government is asking lesbians and gay men to perjure ourselves." Hyde compares the I.R.S.'s marriage-status filing instructions in Publications 17 and 501 to the U.S. military's "don't ask, don't tell" policy, under which lesbians and gay men must serve in silence. As she sees it, both policies are compulsory falsehoods.

Lisa Keen, a contributor to The Boston Globe, sees tax-filing status not as a minor bureaucratic nicety but as a morally wrenching confrontation with her own integrity. "Regardless of what the federal government's decision is about its own reality, I recognize that my marriage is real," she says. "And it is legal. And therefore I will check off 'married.' What are they going to do, put me in jail?"

Jail is unlikely. In fact, despite the widespread fear among lesbians and gay men that the current administration is eager to find and

---

*E.J. Graff, a resident scholar at the Brandeis Women's Studies Research Center, is the author of "What Is Marriage For? The Strange Social History of Our Most Intimate Institution."*

Illustration by Chip Kidd

22

---

# American Tabloid

Every time I am recruited to design or illustrate something for a magazine—especially a weekly—I am reminded how spoiled I am by the gently slow schedules of book publishing, where we work eight months ahead. If and when something needs to be changed (a lot, of course), there are weeks reserved to do it.

But for the Judith Regan piece I created for *New York* magazine (opposite, right) the headline of the "book" seemed to be changing every fifteen minutes for four days in a row, right up until the deadline. And they needed to see how it would look each time (not unreasonable, but still). That's okay once in a while, but I am not made for working on that kind of schedule all the time. I have much respect for those who do.

**FROM LEFT TO RIGHT:** Eliot Spitzer. Anyone remember him? Heh. *New York* magazine, 2008.

*New York* magazine, 2007.

Happily, this article and illustration would be rendered irrelevant in just ten years by the US Supreme Court. *The New York Times Magazine*, 2005.

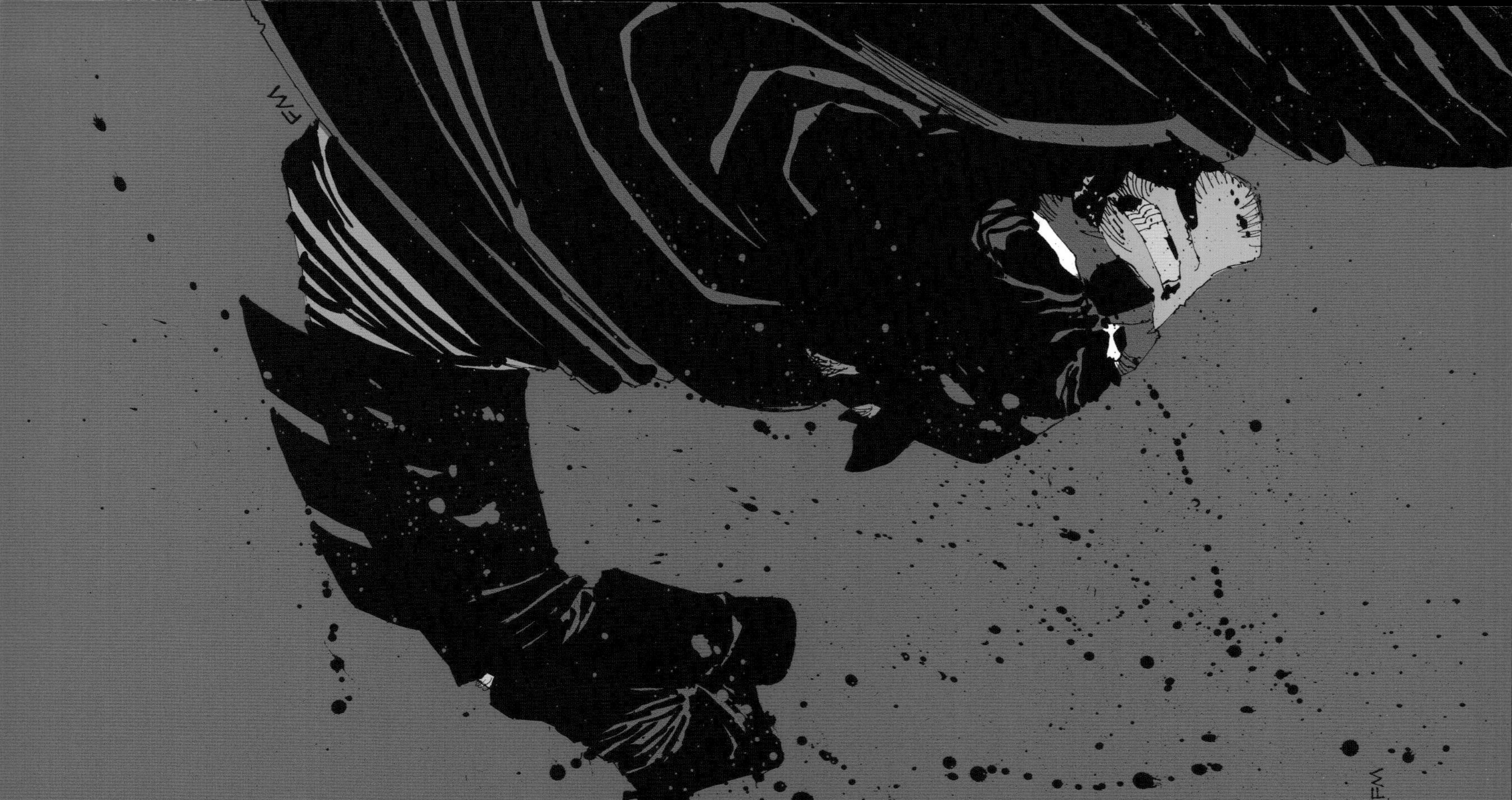

# ABSOLUTE DARK KNIGHT

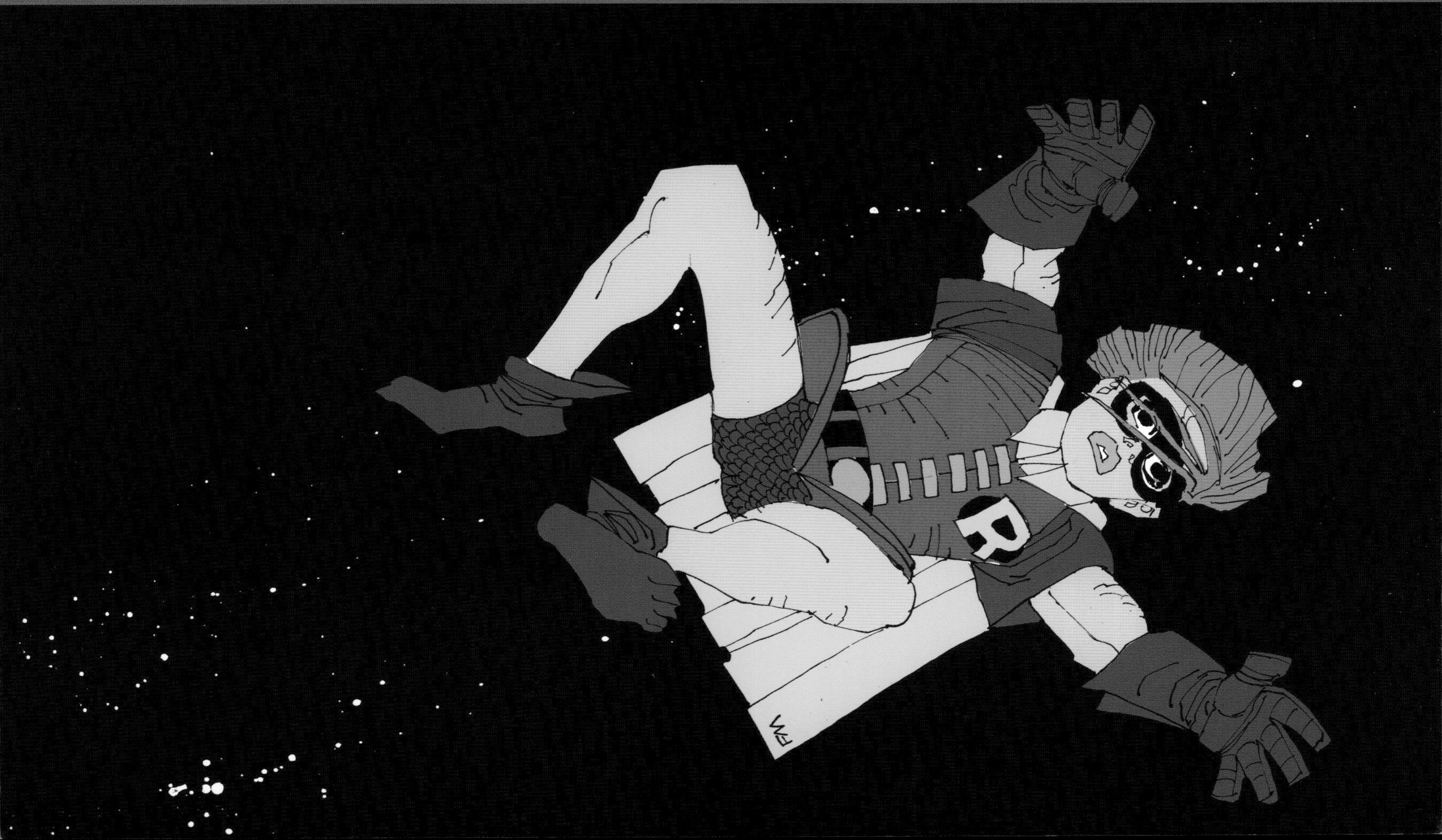

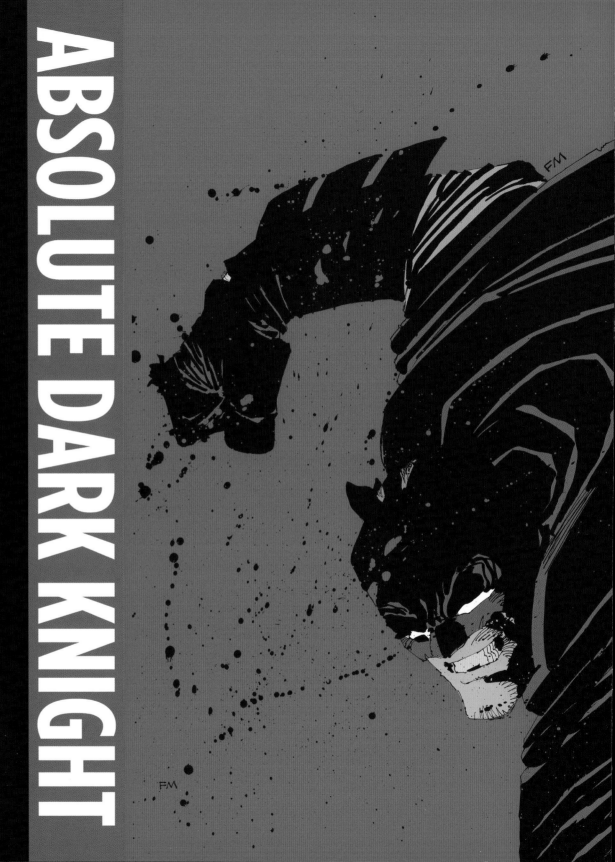

## Darkest before the . . .

Like most Batman comics fans, I worship at the feet of Frank Miller and hold his Dark Knight Returns series in the highest regard. I had the pleasure of redesigning a trade edition of it in 2003, and then again for DC's ultradeluxe Absolute line of oversized coffee-table editions in 2006, shown here. The format of the Absolute line is slipcased hardcovers, and for the book's binding I blew up the classic black-on-blue silhouette from the cover of issue #1 (right) to epic proportions. For the slipcase, Frank created new art (opposite) and my great thrill was that I did the coloring myself in Quark. Lots of red!

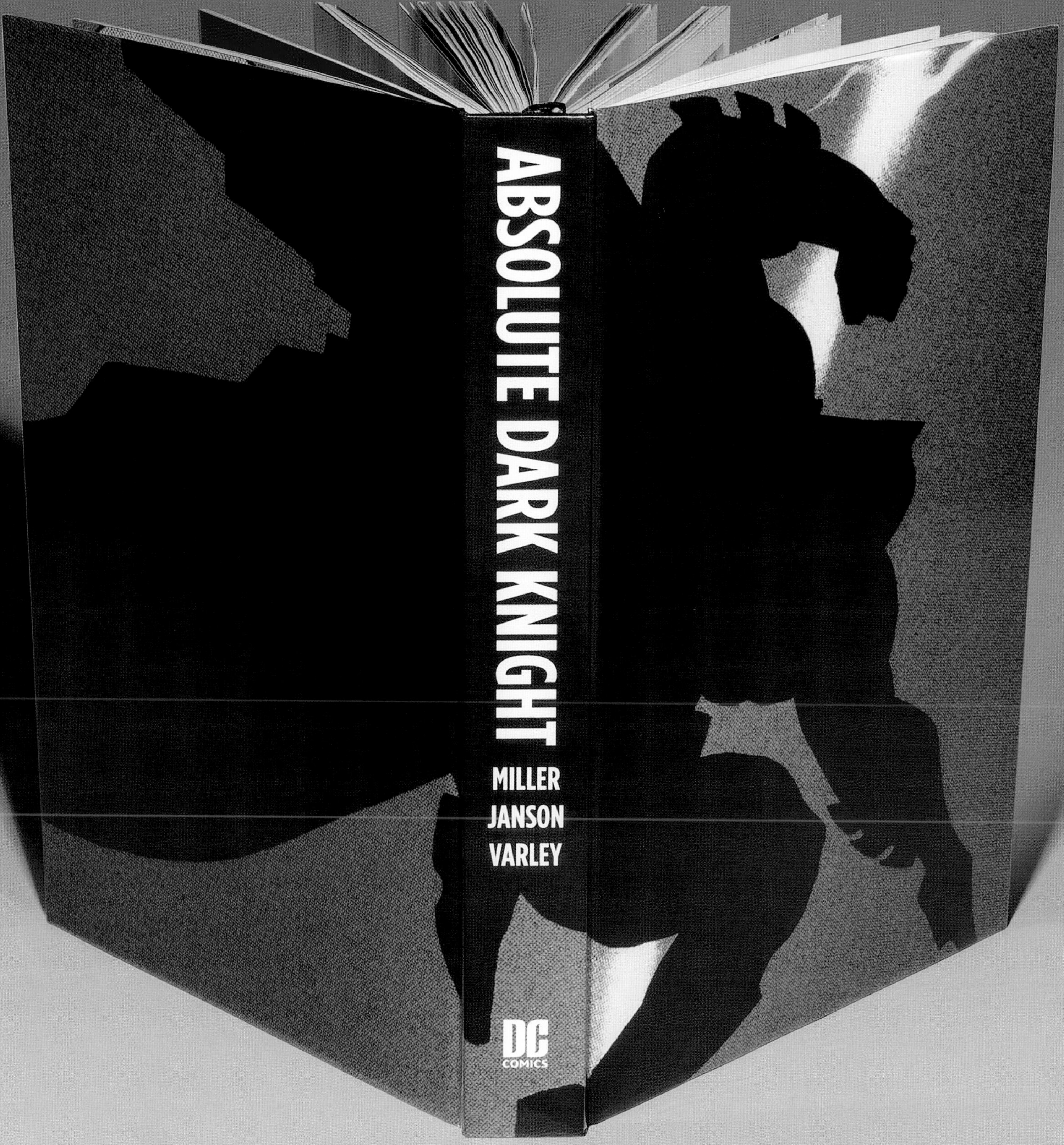
ABSOLUTE DARK KNIGHT
MILLER
JANSON
VARLEY
DC
COMICS

238

DAVID RAKOFF
LOVE
DISHONOR
MARRY
DIE
CHERISH
PERISH
A NOVEL


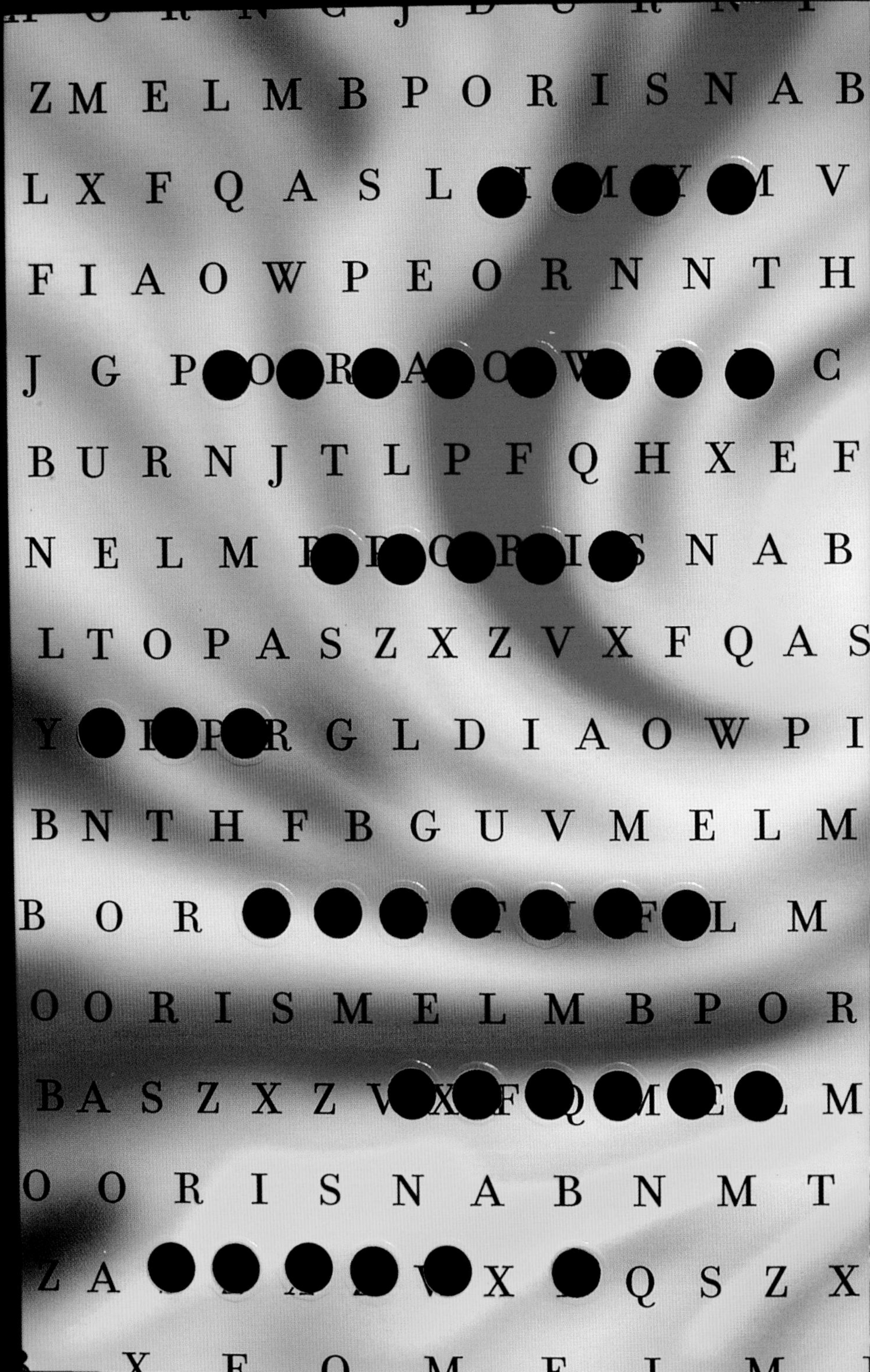

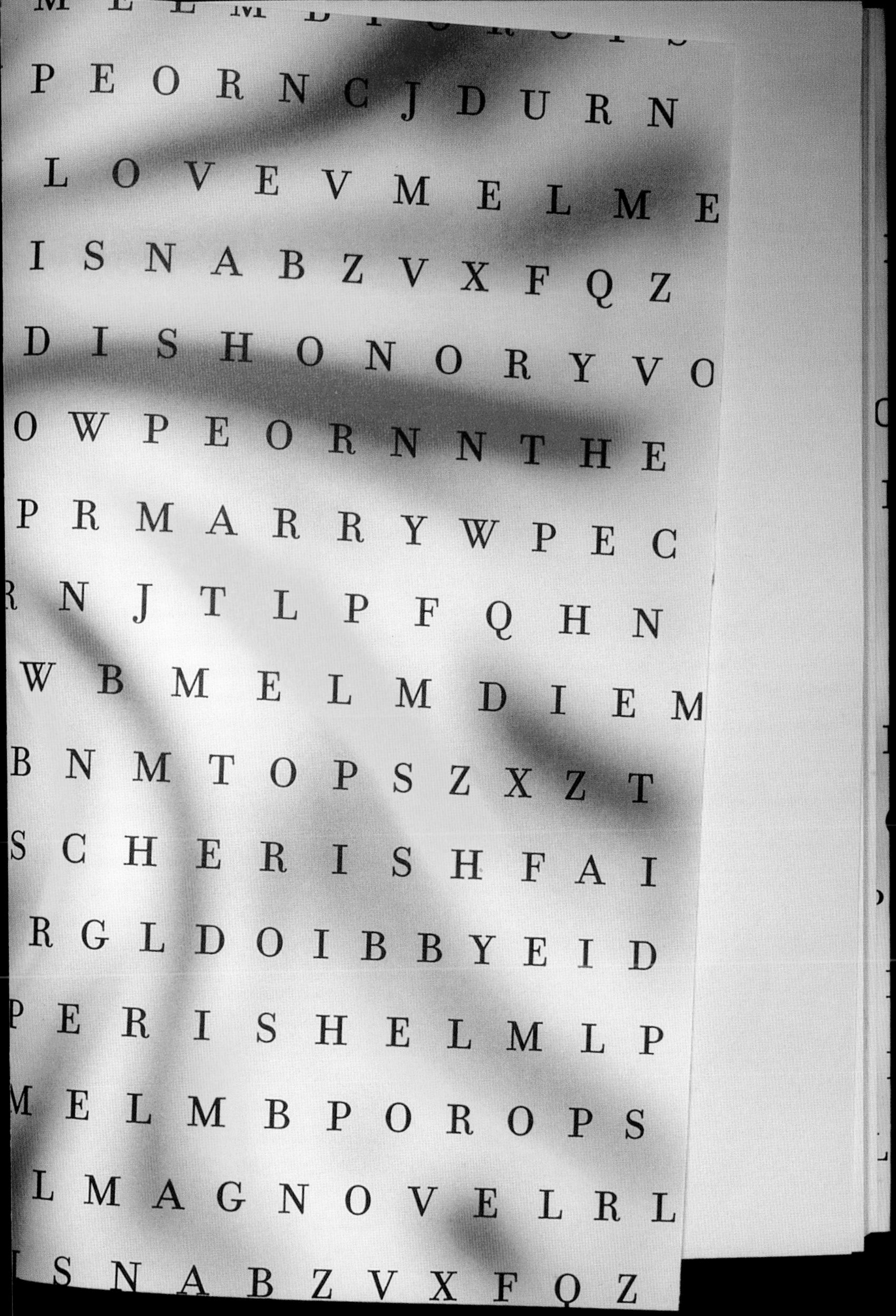
P E O R N C J D U R N
L O V E V M E L M E
I S N A B Z V X F Q Z
D I S H O N O R Y V O
O W P E O R N N T H E
P R M A R R Y W P E C
N J T L P F Q H N
W B M E L M D I E M
B N M T O P S Z X Z T
S C H E R I S H F A I
R G L D O I B B Y E I D
P E R I S H E L M L P
M E L M B P O R O P S
L M A G N O V E L R L
S N A B Z V X F Q Z

# Last Words

In late July of 2012, Doubleday editor-in-chief Bill Thomas called me into his office. He looked pained. Badly. "David [Rakoff] doesn't have much longer, and he wants you to design his book." I quietly burst into tears. All of us who knew him were expecting yet dreading this moment, and I hadn't heard from David for a couple of months, having last seen him the previous February when he came to dinner at Sandy's place in SoHo. Yes, his left arm was out of commission due to the returning cancer, but he said it was under control and otherwise he seemed okay (he was always, always trying to comfort his friends regarding his condition).

But now he was near the end and racing to finish his novel in verse, *Love, Dishonor, Marry, Die, Cherish, Perish.* He had intended to illustrate it himself, which was now out of the question, and I would have to figure out who was right for the job. My friend the acclaimed Toronto artist/cartoonist Seth seemed a natural fit (he had just done a cover for a Dorothy Parker collection, and David's verse style was not unlike hers), but I would have to see if he was available and willing. He didn't really have the time in his schedule, but he understood the gravity of the situation and basically dropped everything to make this happen. I will be forever grateful. The idea was to create a series of portraits of the characters, starting with flame-haired Margaret for the cover. I devised the conceit that the title would read through die-cut holes dotting her face, which when lifted would reveal a swirl of letters and language that was only decoded by closing the cover again. I was able to comp this by hand for presentation just in time for David to approve it before . . . he died.

Then we had to make the rest of the book. Michael Collica in the Doubleday interior art department worked extensively to ensure that my ideas were working for the cover and the text throughout, and Andy Hughes oversaw the logistics of the die-cut holes falling over the letters just right, so you could read the title properly. I would say it wasn't in vain—the book got great reviews and made the *New York Times* Best-Seller List for hardcover fiction. I think David would have been delighted.

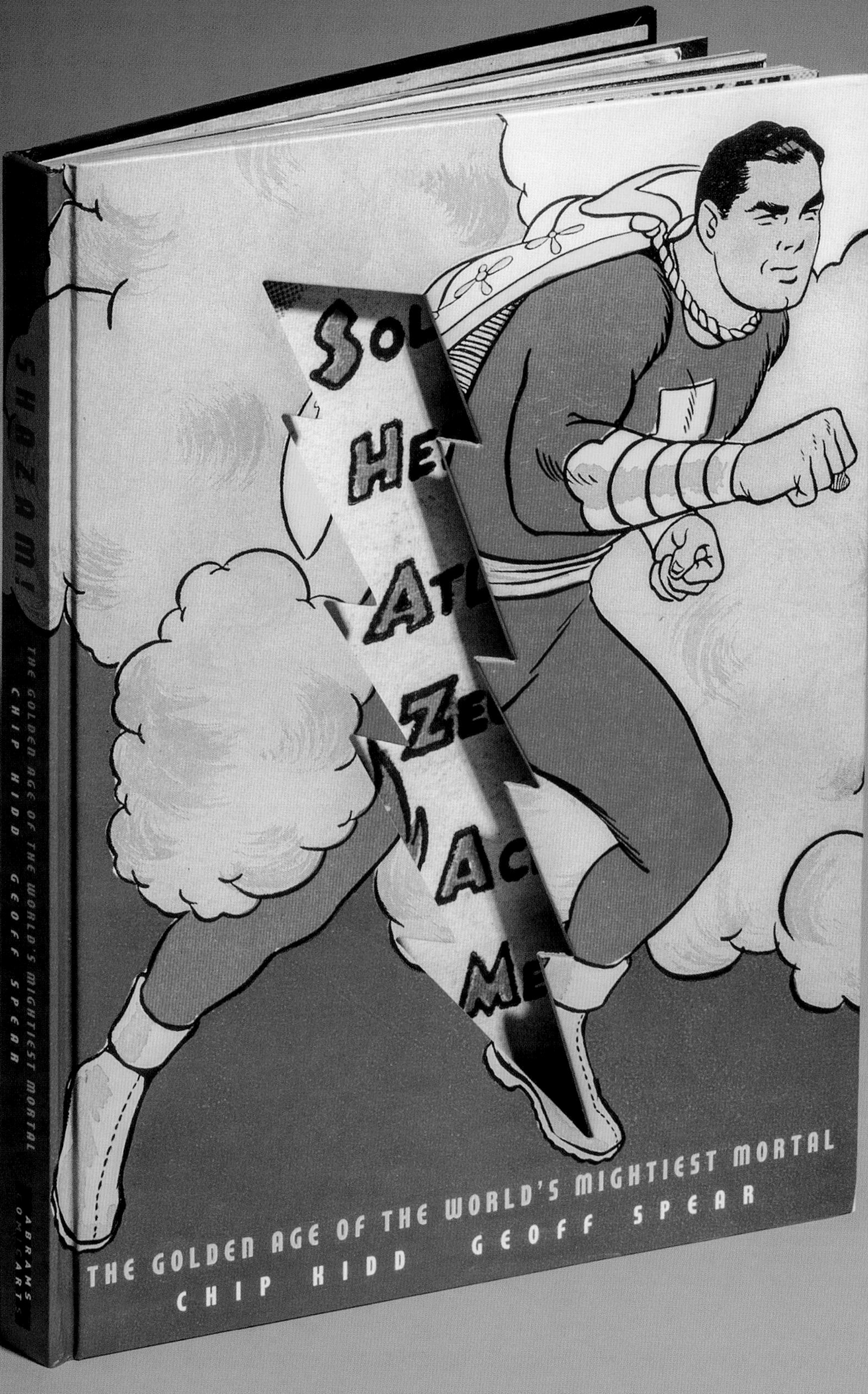
SHAZAM!
THE GOLDEN AGE OF THE WORLD'S MIGHTIEST MORTAL
CHIP KIDD GEOFF SPEAR
ABRAMS COMICARTS
THE GOLDEN AGE OF THE WORLD'S MIGHTIEST MORTAL
CHIP KIDD GEOFF SPEAR

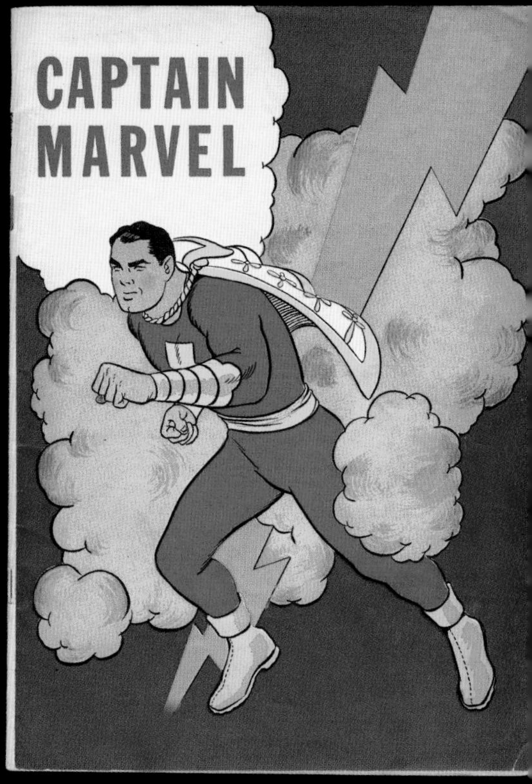
CAPTAIN MARVEL

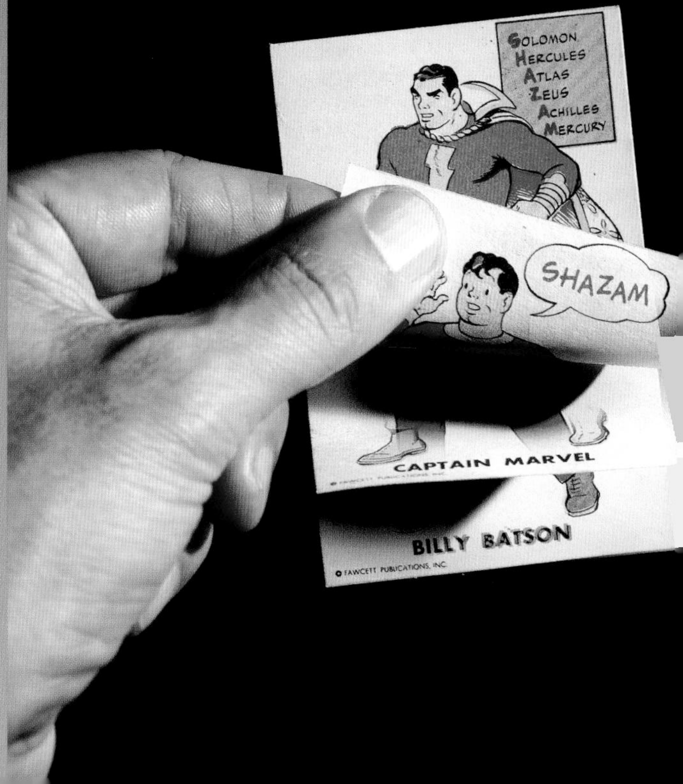
SOLOMON
HERCULES
ATLAS
ZEUS
ACHILLES
MERCURY
SHAZAM
CAPTAIN MARVEL
BILLY BATSON
© FAWCETT PUBLICATIONS, INC.

# Might Makes Light

I have been a fan of Captain Marvel since I was a kid, reading all of the reprinted adventures of "The World's Mightiest Mortal" from the 1940s and '50s; and again when DC Comics started producing new ones in the early 1970s. I later learned that the legal history of the character was complicated to say the least: Captain Marvel—deftly and charmingly drawn by artist C. C. Beck and based on actor Fred McMurray—was originally published by Fawcett in 1940 and quickly became the most popular superhero character in the business. Fawcett was then besieged by massive copyright lawsuits from DC, which claimed that Captain Marvel was too similar to Superman. This argument was baseless. What set Captain Marvel apart from all the other superheroes at the time was that his secret identity was as a young homeless boy named Billy Batson, who was chosen by the ancient wizard Shazam to take on the mantle of the Captain by shouting Shazam's name (accompanied by its attendant lightning bolt). This was a stroke of genius on the part of writers Bill Parker and Otto Binder, as millions of kids were thrilled by the concept. Young girls also became fans when the writers introduced Mary Marvel, Billy's long-lost sister, as an integral part of what became known as the Marvel Family, also a new idea in superhero comics. But DC eventually won out and acquired the rights to the characters by the end of the 1960s.

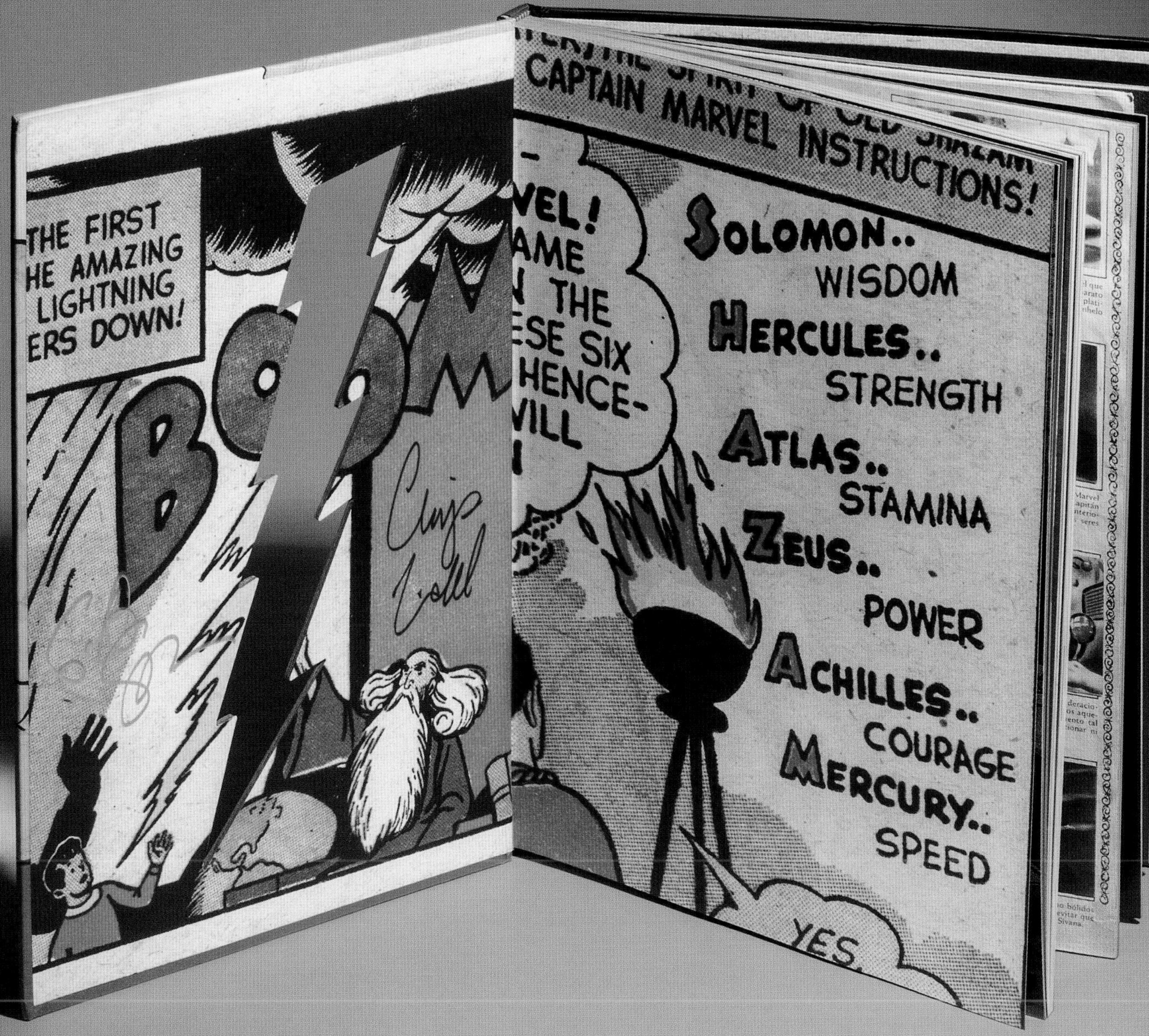
CAPTAIN MARVEL INSTRUCTIONS!
SOLOMON.. WISDOM
HERCULES.. STRENGTH
ATLAS.. STAMINA
ZEUS.. POWER
ACHILLES.. COURAGE
MERCURY.. SPEED
YES.

*Shazam! The Golden Age of the World's Mightiest Mortal* was made possible by the extensive Captain Marvel collection of Harry Matetsky, who generously allowed Geoff and me to photograph and publish it through Abrams ComicArts. The result is pure superhero comfort food, as sublimely good-natured and deliciously delineated as the 4-color comics genre ever got. Our book, while including an early Captain Marvel story by the legendary Jack Kirby and Joe Simon of Captain America fame, centers on all of the novelty ephemera for the Marvel Family that Fawcett created to connect so effectively with the fans: secret decoders to translate cryptogram messages in the comics and the fan-club notices; iron-on patches; novelty paper toys; rings; games; figurines. Fawcett, along with DC, really helped reinvent the way fans could connect with their favorite characters by sending personalized letters to readers asking for—and listening to—their feedback.

# Heartbreak Without the "He"

The story of the music project Artbreak stems from an unforeseen reunion with Marco Petrilli, an old Penn State dormmate of mine, in 2005. I was in my early 40s and had been thinking about playing music again, apropos of absolutely nothing, other than perhaps creative boredom. I wanted to hit drums like I did from the age of 11 to 22. And more than that: I wanted to sing and perform.

In 1982, at Penn State University, Marco and I lived on the same floor at Beaver Hall (I know, I know). We would often see each other in the hallway, and when he heard that I was in the marching Blue Band, we started to talk about music. That led to late-night booze-fueled jam sessions that were fun, but pretty much ended at that. I went on to pursue graphic design, while he studied finance. I didn't see him again until twenty-three years later.

In the spring of 2005, I was giving a reading at Housing Works bookstore in New York City. Marco waited in line at the signing afterwards and reintroduced himself. He asked if I was still playing. I said I was not, hadn't for some time, but was interested in trying to jump into it again.

Marco was living in the East Village with his wife and baby, doing freelance work in the local music industry. He knew of an inexpensive rehearsal studio, and we met there the following week. At first it was awkward, which was my fault—playing the drums again wasn't like riding a bicycle, more like trying to remember a foreign language that requires coordinating all four of your limbs. But Marco was great, strumming along, and we jammed away as I got my shit together. After a couple sessions, I said: "If I have a melody in mind, could you figure it out?" He was game, and we wrote a song called "Tracking Numb." More followed. Over the next several years we created an album's worth of original material and performed it at Joe's Pub in New York City. We filmed a video for our song "Asymmetrical Girl" with director Gary Nadeau (it's on YouTube, check it out). Eventually, Marco and his wife had another baby, and they moved to Fort Worth, Texas, which sort of cramped our style. But he also started a "school of rock" at a local high school there, and I came down and led a workshop where we performed with the kids at the Dallas Art Museum in the spring of 2012. We'll see where it goes from there . . .

## Asymmetrical Girl

She's wise to surmise
When it comes as no surprise

That the glints in her eyes
Are completely different-sized.

So what do you do
When your parts are all askew?

You take what you've got
And you make it new.

Look at all the plebes
sa-shaying with the sha-sha.
(You could baby-living-it-up
in that world)
All you really need
Is leaning with the La-La.
(You could be asymmetrical
girl)
Shredding the perceived
Of the raging social scene,
(You could baby-spinning-
it-up in a swirl)
All you really need is a new identity.
(You could be Asymmetrical Girl!)

It's time for sublime
To buck the trend to rhyme.

And go for the broke-en
jagged beauty line.
How smooth to pursue
A purview that's just for you.
So her ears don't align
And it looks just fine . . .

asymm
rl.
gi
etrical

CHIP KIDD MARS TRILLION
artbreak.
presents
wondergrounded.
LIMITED EDITION EP # 141 of 300

reak.
arb
NUMBER OF TIMES
PERCENTAGE OF ORIGINAL SIZE
SIZE OF ORIGINAL
REPRODUCTION SIZE

gi

rl.

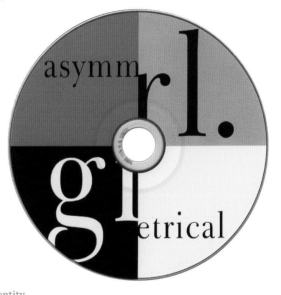

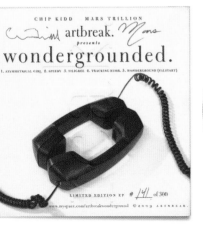

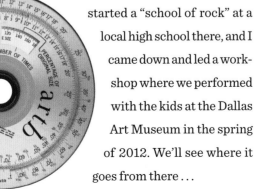

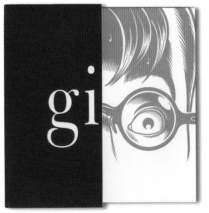

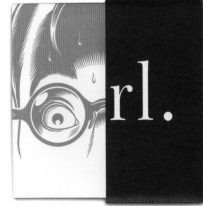

## Real headliners

ONE of The Post's famous headlines is now a rock band. Novelist and designer **Chip Kidd** was so taken by our Aug. 27, 2006, headline, "Artbreaking" — about famed quadriplegic artist **Chuck Close**'s battle with a condo project threatening to block his studio's sunlight — he adapted it for the name of his group. Artbreak — which Kidd and bandmate **Mars Trillion** describe as "Bowie crashing the Cars into Joy Division going 300 miles per hour at 4 a.m. on Abbey Road" — will play Joe's Pub on Aug. 4.

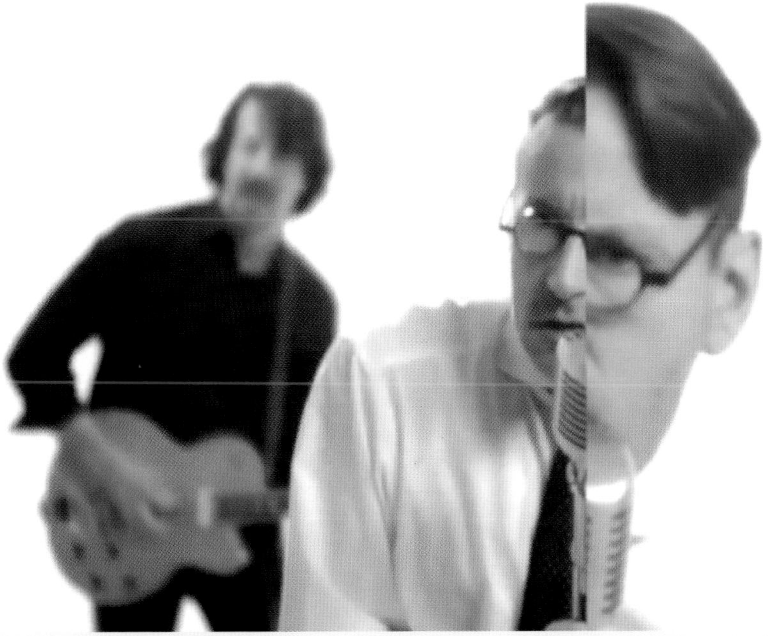

CHIP KIDD presents ARTBREAK "Asymmetrical Girl"

G.N. Gary Nadeau
Subscribe 66
19,273

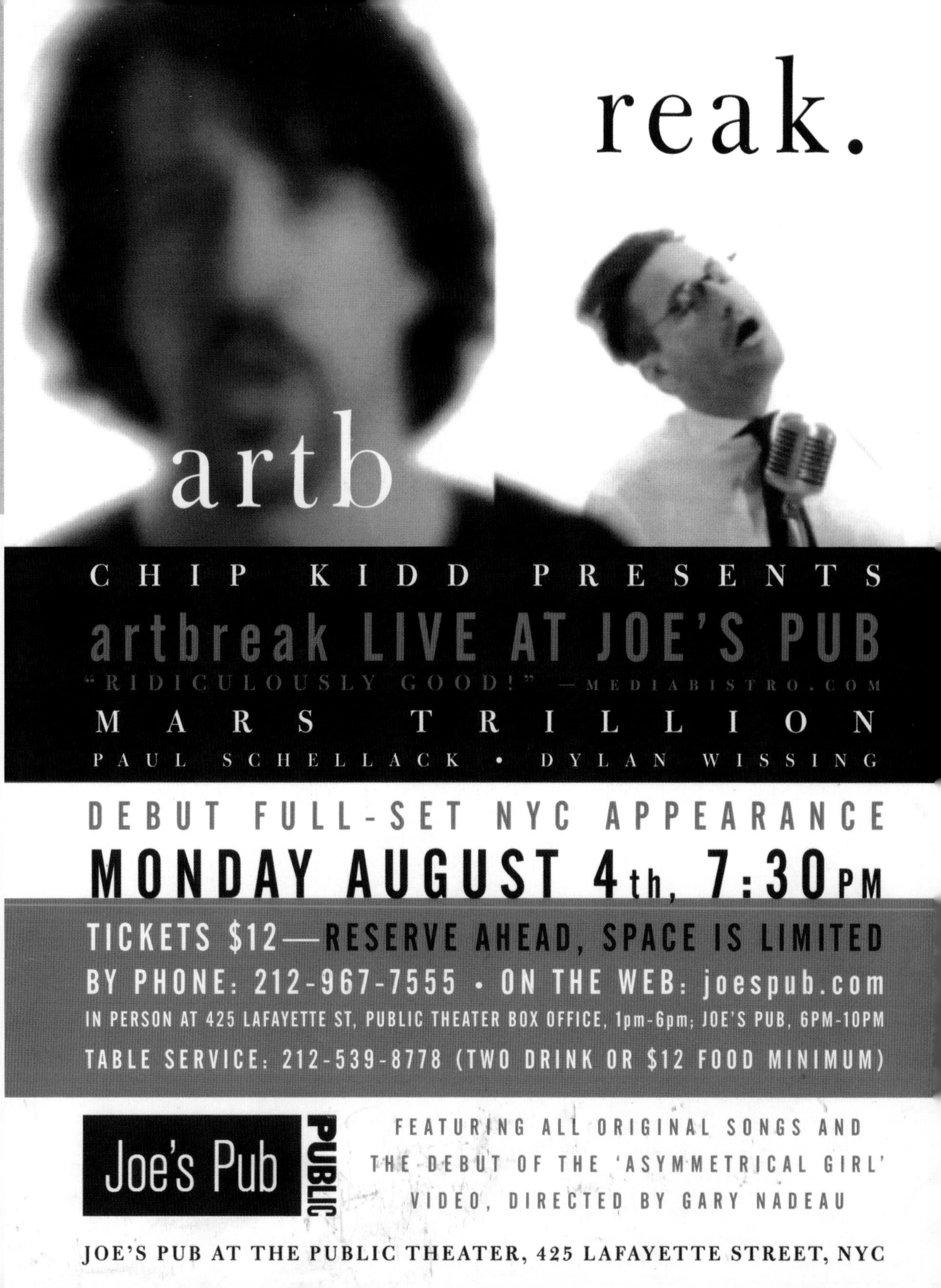
reak.
artb
CHIP KIDD PRESENTS
artbreak LIVE AT JOE'S PUB
"RIDICULOUSLY GOOD!" —MEDIABISTRO.COM
MARS TRILLION
PAUL SCHELLACK • DYLAN WISSING
DEBUT FULL-SET NYC APPEARANCE
MONDAY AUGUST 4th, 7:30PM
TICKETS $12—RESERVE AHEAD, SPACE IS LIMITED
BY PHONE: 212-967-7555 • ON THE WEB: joespub.com
IN PERSON AT 425 LAFAYETTE ST, PUBLIC THEATER BOX OFFICE, 1pm-6pm; JOE'S PUB, 6PM-10PM
TABLE SERVICE: 212-539-8778 (TWO DRINK OR $12 FOOD MINIMUM)
Joe's Pub
PUBLIC
FEATURING ALL ORIGINAL SONGS AND THE DEBUT OF THE 'ASYMMETRICAL GIRL' VIDEO, DIRECTED BY GARY NADEAU
JOE'S PUB AT THE PUBLIC THEATER, 425 LAFAYETTE STREET, NYC

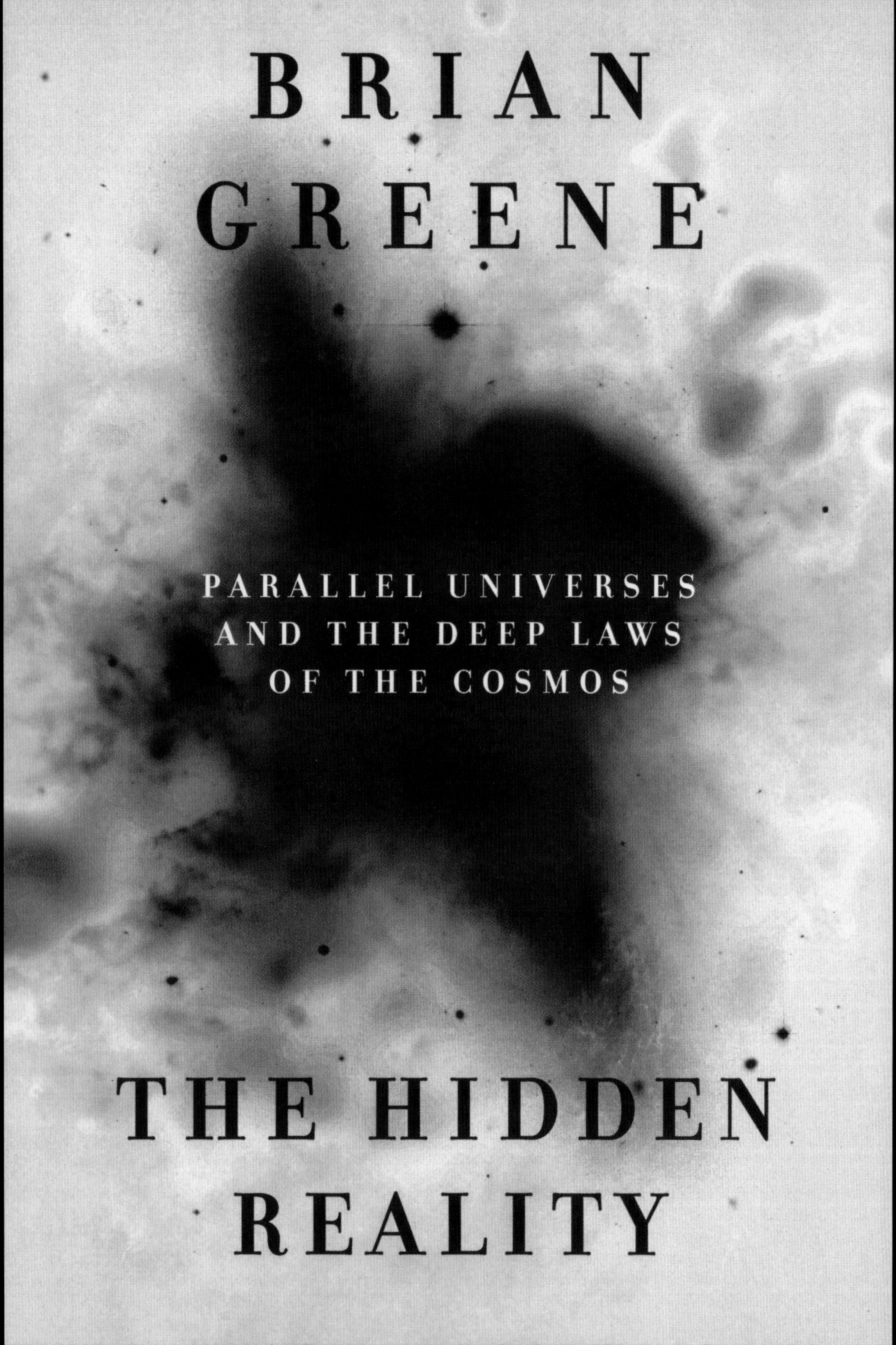
BRIAN
GREENE
PARALLEL UNIVERSES
AND THE DEEP LAWS
OF THE COSMOS
THE HIDDEN
REALITY

## Black Hole Son

Brian Greene is widely considered the Carl Sagan of his generation, and when he wrote a narrative for young adults called *Icarus at the Edge of Time* (opposite), about how black holes work, I was tapped to figure out how to turn it into an actual book. This was a very interesting problem: how should we illustrate it? The story is about a young boy (Icarus) on a spaceship in the not-too-distant future, bound on a years-long mission deep into the cosmos. He detects a black hole nearby, and against orders he boards a small craft, setting off to inspect this extraordinary and previously unexplored phenomenon.

I first wanted to confirm in my mind what outer space actually looks like, and that led me to images from the Hubble telescope. As it turns out, all of these pictures are in the public domain and available in high resolution via the NASA website to anyone who wants to download them. I was delighted and amazed to discover this. For the first time in years, I felt my tax dollars were being put to good use.

**LEFT:** An unused comp for Brian's 2011 book, *The Hidden Reality*.
**OPPOSITE & FOLLOWING SPREAD:** Knopf, 2008.

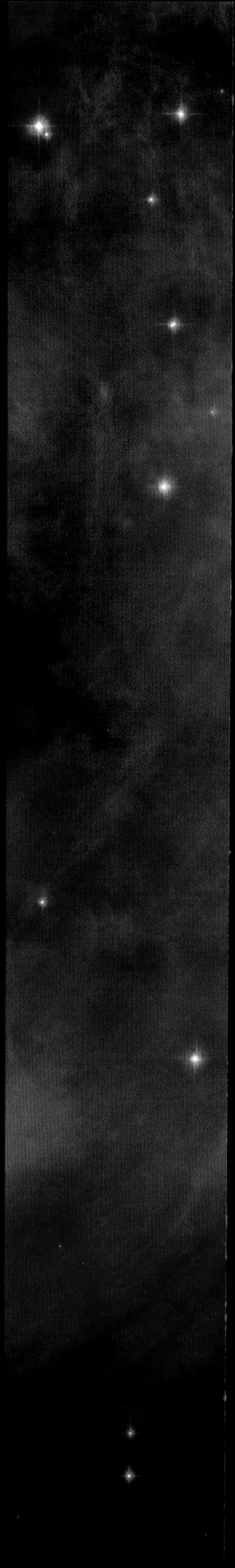

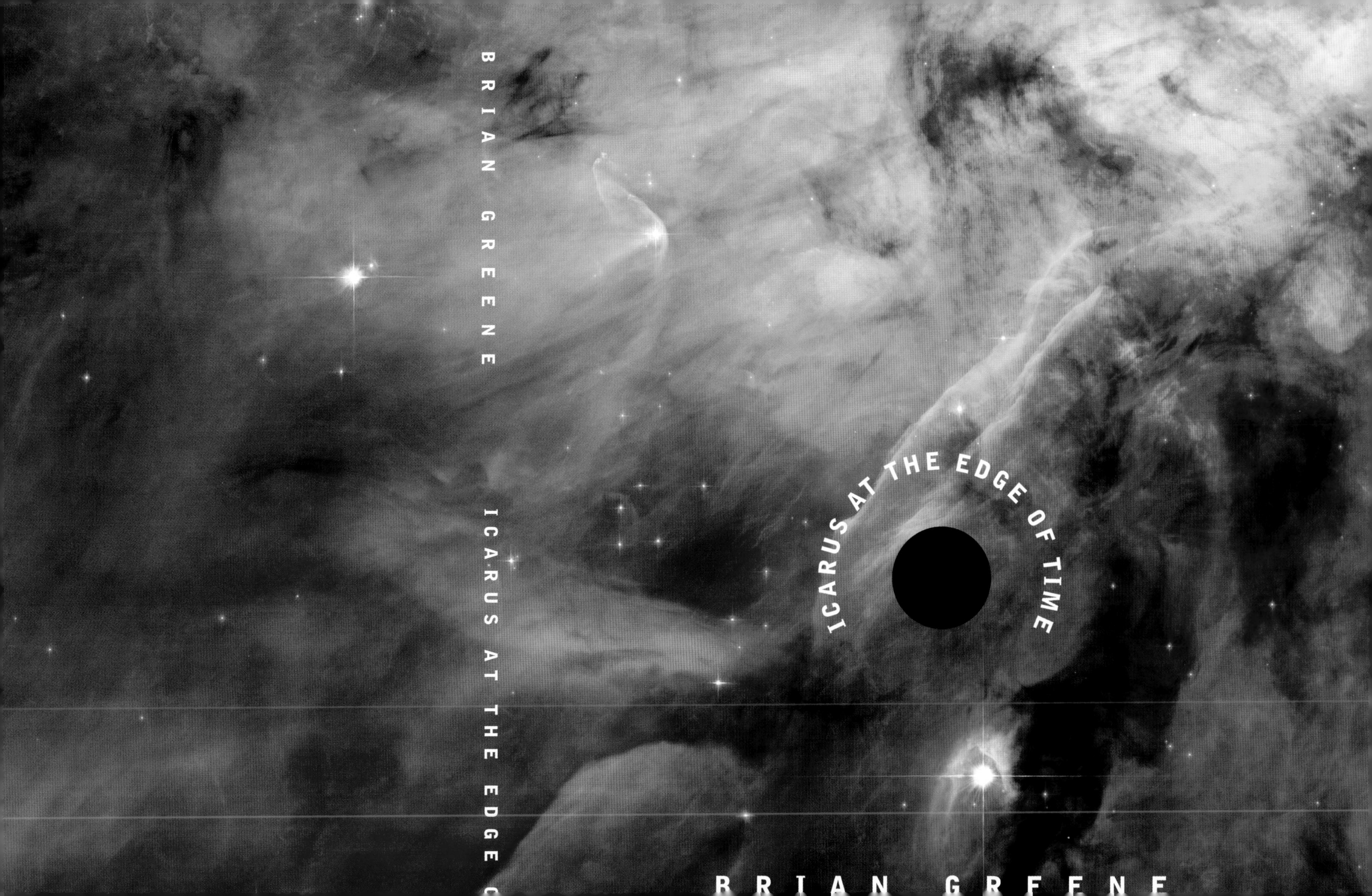
BRIAN GREENE
ICARUS AT THE EDGE
ICARUS AT THE EDGE OF TIME
BRIAN GREENE

The design concept is that the black hole is in the middle of the book and grows larger with each spread as Icarus gets nearer. Then, as he backs away from it, it gets smaller, until he's back on Earth. The payoff is that, by then, hundreds of years have passed because of the physics involved with black holes and time. Icarus has become a historic legend in space exploration, but he's still just a kid.

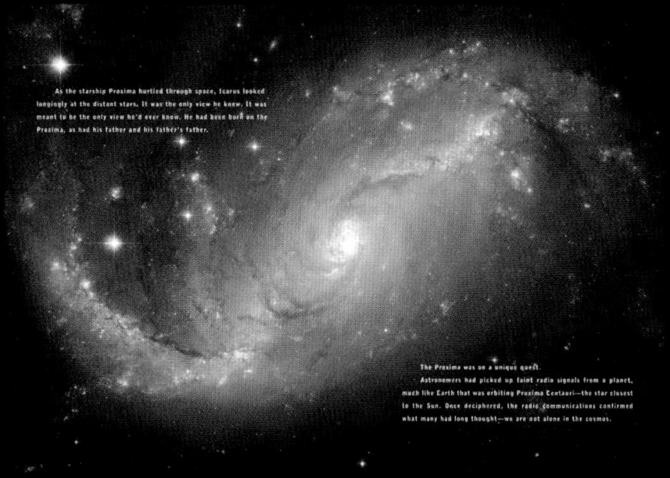

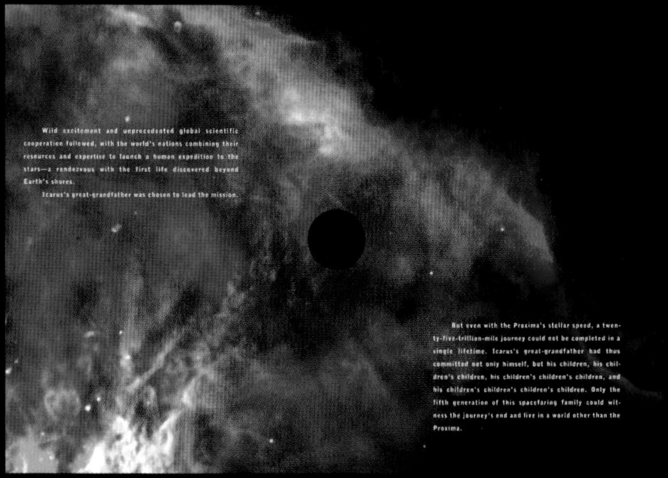

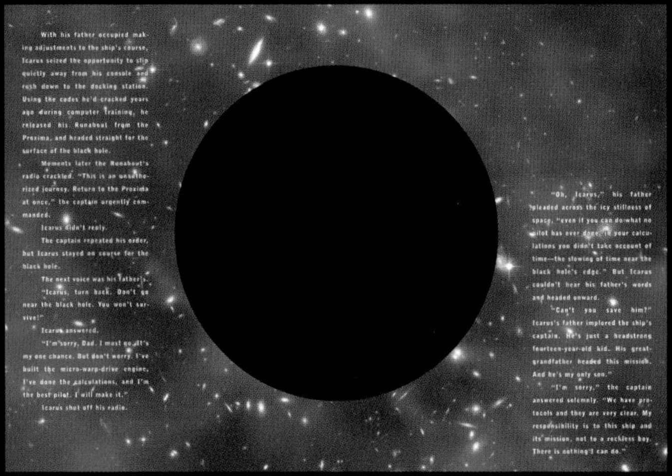

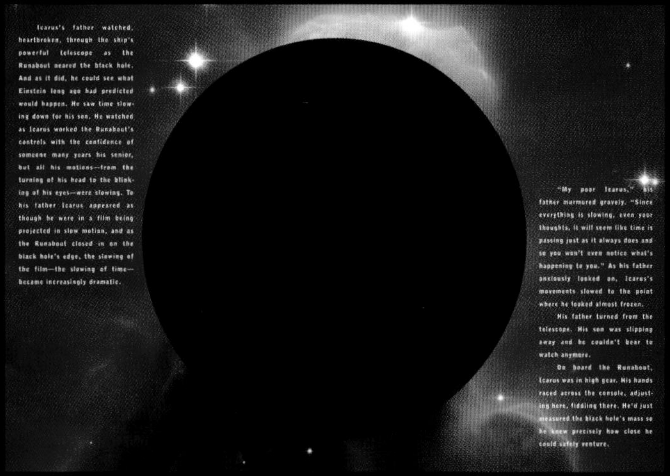

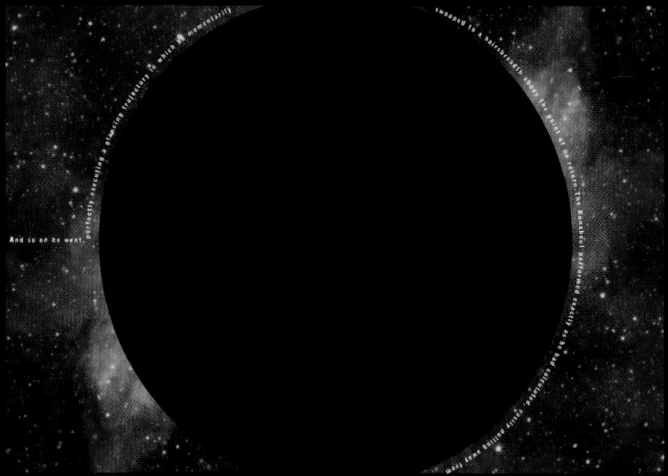

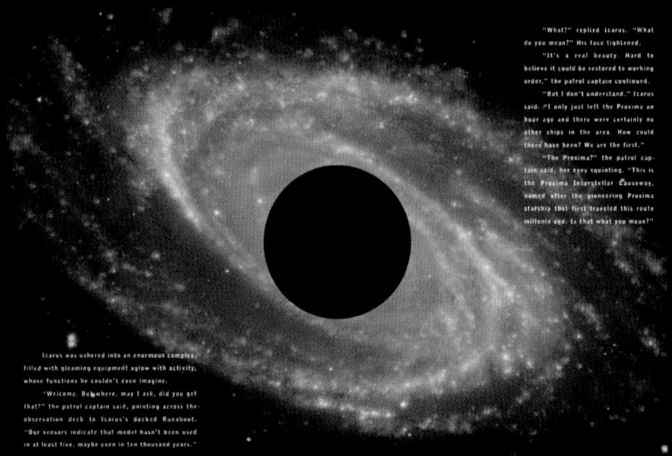

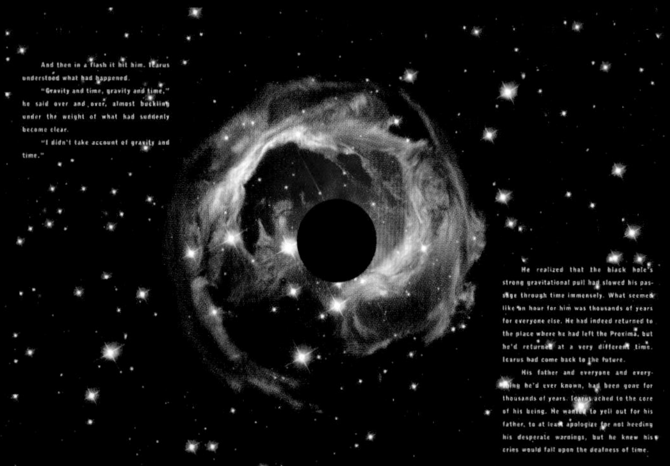

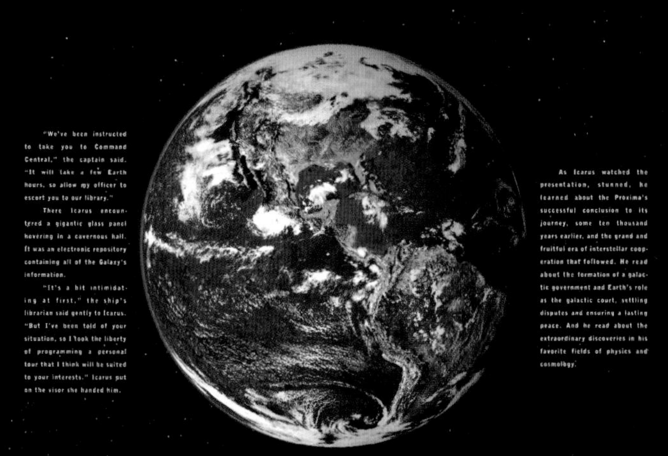

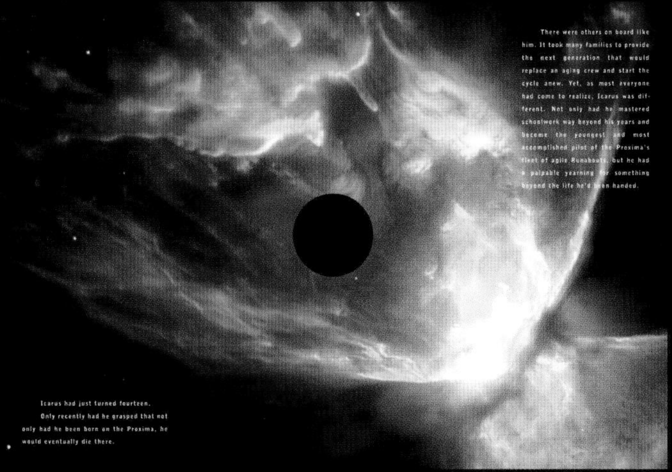

Icarus had just turned fourteen.

Only recently had he grasped that not only had he been born on the Proxima, he would eventually die there.

There were others on board like him. It took many families to provide the next generation that would replace an aging crew and start the cycle anew. Yet, as most everyone had come to realize, Icarus was different. Not only had he mastered schoolwork way beyond his years and become the youngest and most accomplished pilot of the Proxima's fleet of agile Runabouts, but he had a palpable yearning for something beyond the life he'd been handed.

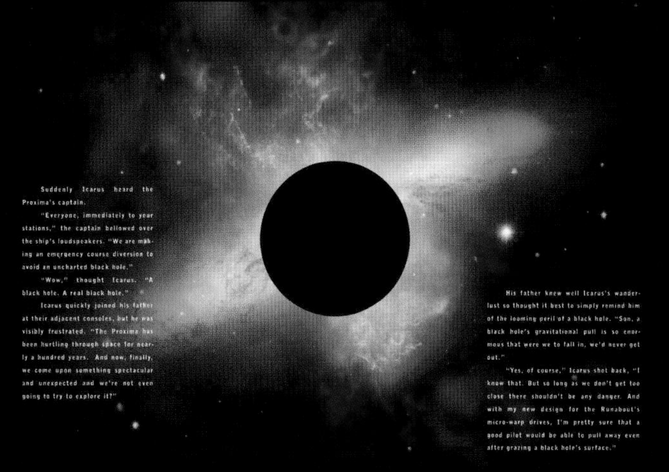

Suddenly Icarus heard the Proxima's captain.

"Everyone, immediately to your stations," the captain bellowed over the ship's loudspeakers. "We are making an emergency course diversion to avoid an uncharted black hole."

"Wow," thought Icarus. "A black hole. A real black hole."

Icarus quickly joined his father at their adjacent consoles, but he was visibly frustrated. "The Proxima has been hurtling through space for nearly a hundred years. And now, finally, we come upon something spectacular and unexpected and we're not even going to try to explore it?"

His father knew well Icarus's wanderlust so thought it best to simply remind him of the looming peril of a black hole. "Son, a black hole's gravitational pull is so enormous that were we to fall in, we'd never get out."

"Yes, of course," Icarus shot back, "I know that. But so long as we don't get too close there shouldn't be any danger. And with my new design for the Runabout's micro-warp drives, I'm pretty sure that a good pilot would be able to pull away even after grazing a black hole's surface."

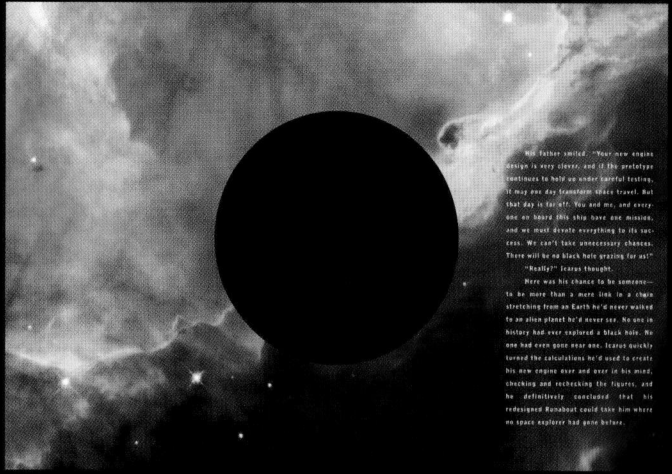

His father smiled. "Your new engine design is very clever, and if the prototype continues to hold up under careful testing, it may one day transform space travel. But that day is far off. You and me, and everyone on board this ship have one mission, and we must devote everything to its success. We can't take unnecessary chances. There will be no black hole grazing for us!"

"Really?" Icarus thought.

Here was his chance to be someone—to be more than a mere link in a chain stretching from an Earth he'd never walked to an alien planet he'd never see. No one in history had ever explored a black hole. No one had even gone near one. Icarus quickly turned the calculations he'd used to create his new engine over and over in his mind, checking and rechecking the figures, and he definitively concluded that his redesigned Runabout could take him where no space explorer had gone before.

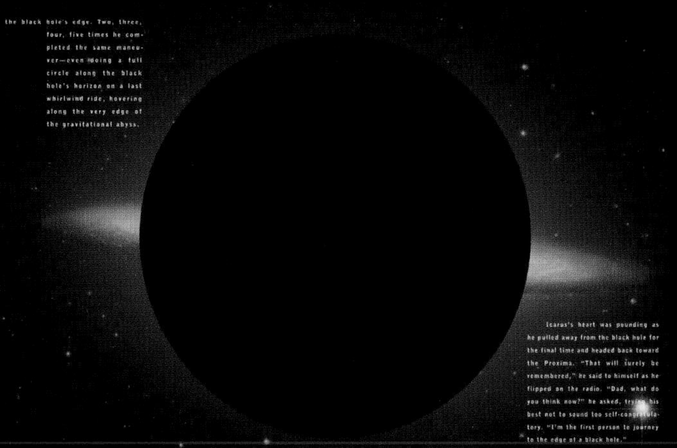

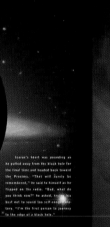

the black hole's edge. Two, three, four, five times he completed the same maneuver—even doing a full circle along the black hole's horizon on a last whirlwind ride, hovering along the very edge of the gravitational abyss.

Icarus's heart was pounding as he pulled away from the black hole for the final time and headed back toward the Proxima. "That will surely be remembered," he said to himself as he flipped on the radio. "Dad, what do you think now?" he asked, trying his best not to sound too self-congratulatory. "I'm the first person to journey to the edge of a black hole."

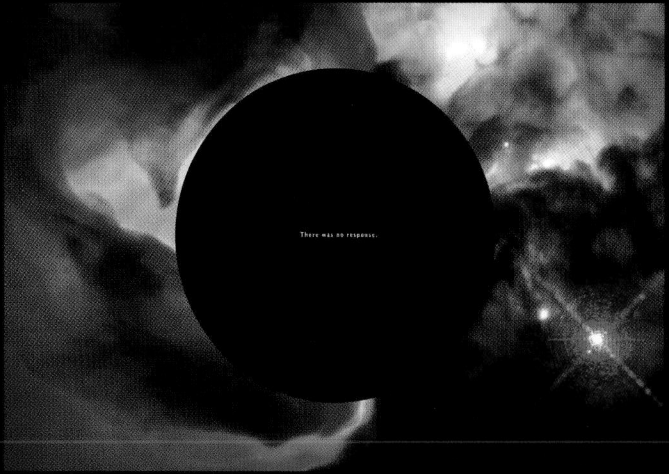

There was no response.

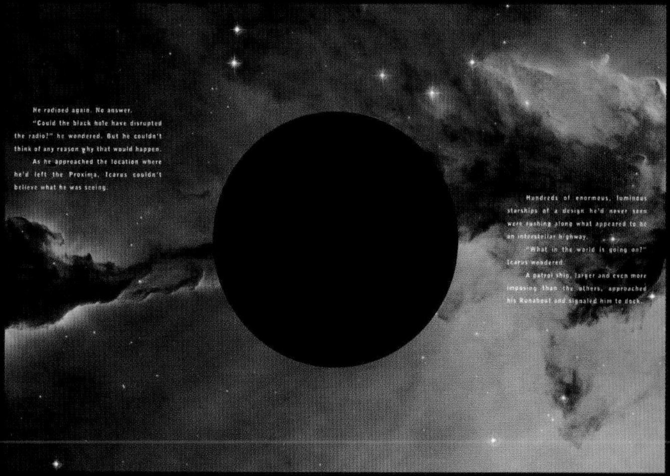

He radioed again. No answer.

"Could the black hole have disrupted the radio?" he wondered. But he couldn't think of any reason why that would happen.

As he approached the location where he'd left the Proxima, Icarus couldn't believe what he was seeing.

Hundreds of enormous, luminous starships of a design he'd never seen were rushing along what appeared to be an interstellar highway.

"What in the world is going on?" Icarus wondered.

A patrol ship, larger and even more imposing than the others, approached his Runabout and signaled him to dock.



And then he learned of a legend that parents had been telling their children for thousands of years. A cautionary tale that had been passed down from generation to generation. It told of a boy, who despite his father's warning, flew a small ship close to a black hole—a boy, as legend had it, who was never seen again.

THE END

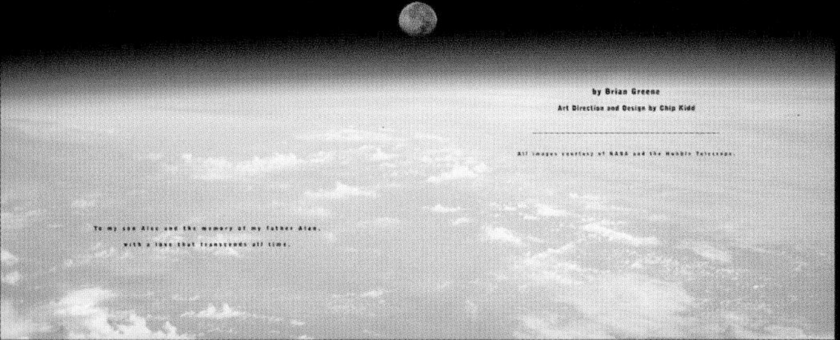

by Brian Greene

Art Direction and Design by Chip Kidd

All images courtesy of NASA and the Hubble Telescope.

To my son Alec and the memory of my father Alan,

with a love that transcends all time.

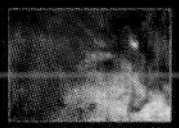

The Orion Nebula, about 1,500 light-years away, is the closest active star-forming region.

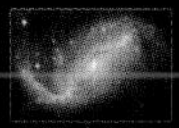

Known as NGC 1672, this "bar-spiral" shaped galaxy is about 60 million light-years away and likely harbors a giant black hole in its center.

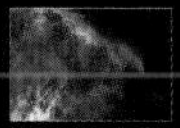

A close-up of a small portion of the Orion Nebula reveals bursts of gas surrounding newly formed stars.

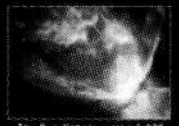

The Bug Nebula, some 4,000 light-years away, comprises two lobes emitted from an extraordinarily hot dying star.

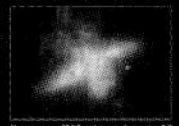

Known as M82, this galaxy is 12 million light-years away and harbors a black hole with a mass more than 500 times that of the Sun.

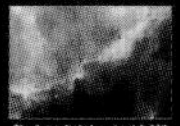

The Swan Nebula, about 5,500 light-years away, is mostly hydrogen gas intensely illuminated by nearby stars.

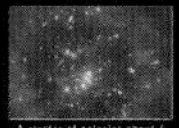

A cluster of galaxies about 5 billion light-years away, with a ring that may provide evidence for dark matter.

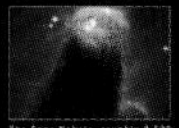

The Cone Nebula, roughly 2,500 light-years away, is a region of intense star formation.

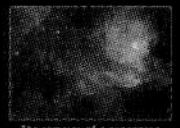

The remains of a supernova 50 times the mass of the Sun, at a distance of roughly 160,000 light years.

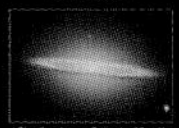

The Sombrero Galaxy, 28 million light-years away, likely has a central black hole with a mass a billion times that of the Sun.

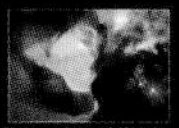

The Lagoon Nebula, 5,000 light years away, has two huge funnels of gas that may be cosmic tornadoes.

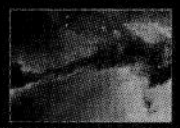

The Eagle Nebula, about 7,000 light-years away, lies in a neighboring spiral arm of our Milky Way Galaxy and is a region of active star formation.

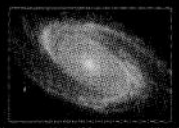

Known as M81, this galaxy is 12 million light-years away and harbors a supermassive black hole with a mass 70 million times that of the Sun.

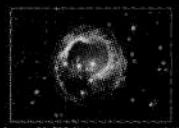

A star 20,000 light-years away that suddenly became more than half a million times brighter, vibrantly illuminating shells of surrounding dust.

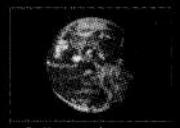

Earth as seen from space.

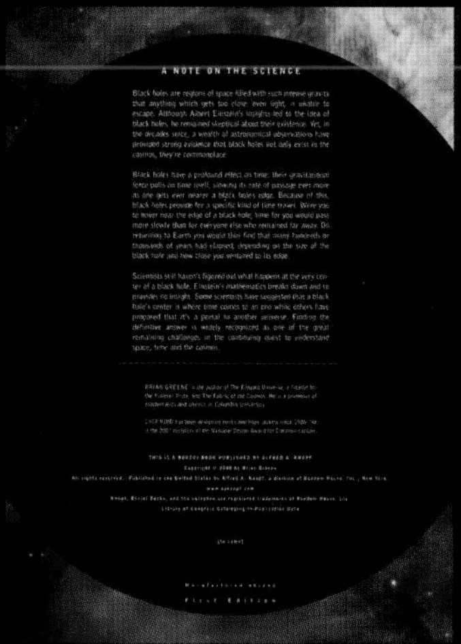

## A NOTE ON THE SCIENCE

Black holes are regions of space filled with such intense gravity that anything which gets too close, even light, is unable to escape. Although Albert Einstein's insights led to the idea of black holes, he remained skeptical about their existence. Yet, in the decades since, a wealth of astronomical observations have provided strong evidence that black holes not only exist in the cosmos, they're commonplace.

Black holes have a profound effect on time: their gravitational force pulls on time itself, slowing its rate of passage ever more as one gets ever nearer a black hole's edge. Because of this, black holes provide for a specific kind of time travel. Were you to hover near the edge of a black hole, time for you would pass more slowly than for everyone else who remained far away. On returning to Earth you would thus find that many hundreds or thousands of years had elapsed, depending on the size of the black hole and how close you ventured to its edge.

Scientists still haven't figured out what happens at the very center of a black hole. Einstein's mathematics breaks down and so provides no insight. Some scientists have suggested that a black hole's center is where time comes to an end while others have proposed that it's a portal to another universe. Finding the definitive answer is widely recognized as one of the great remaining challenges in the continuing quest to understand space, time and the cosmos.

First Edition

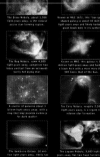

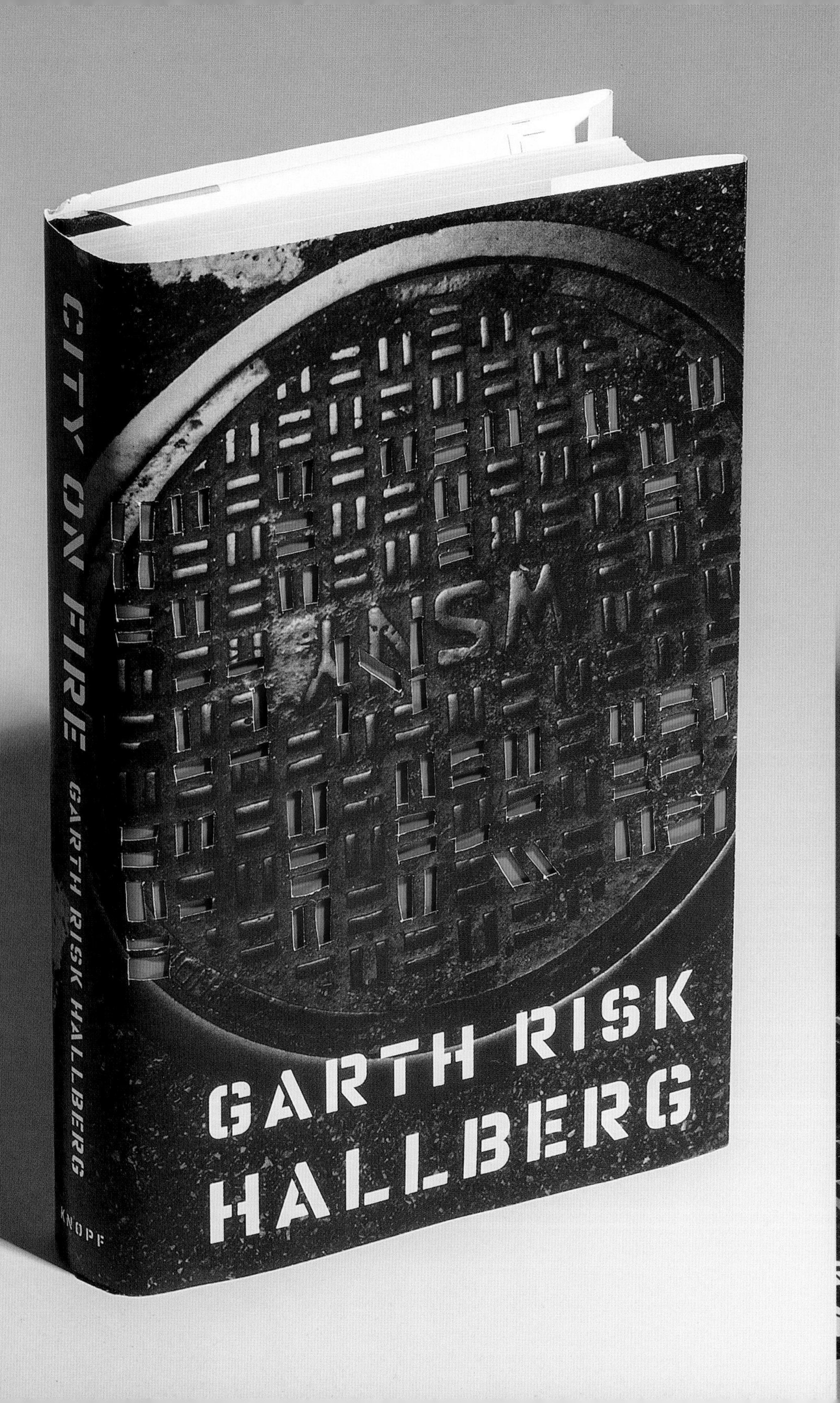
CITY ON FIRE
GARTH RISK HALLBERG
GARTH RISK
HALLBERG
KNOPF
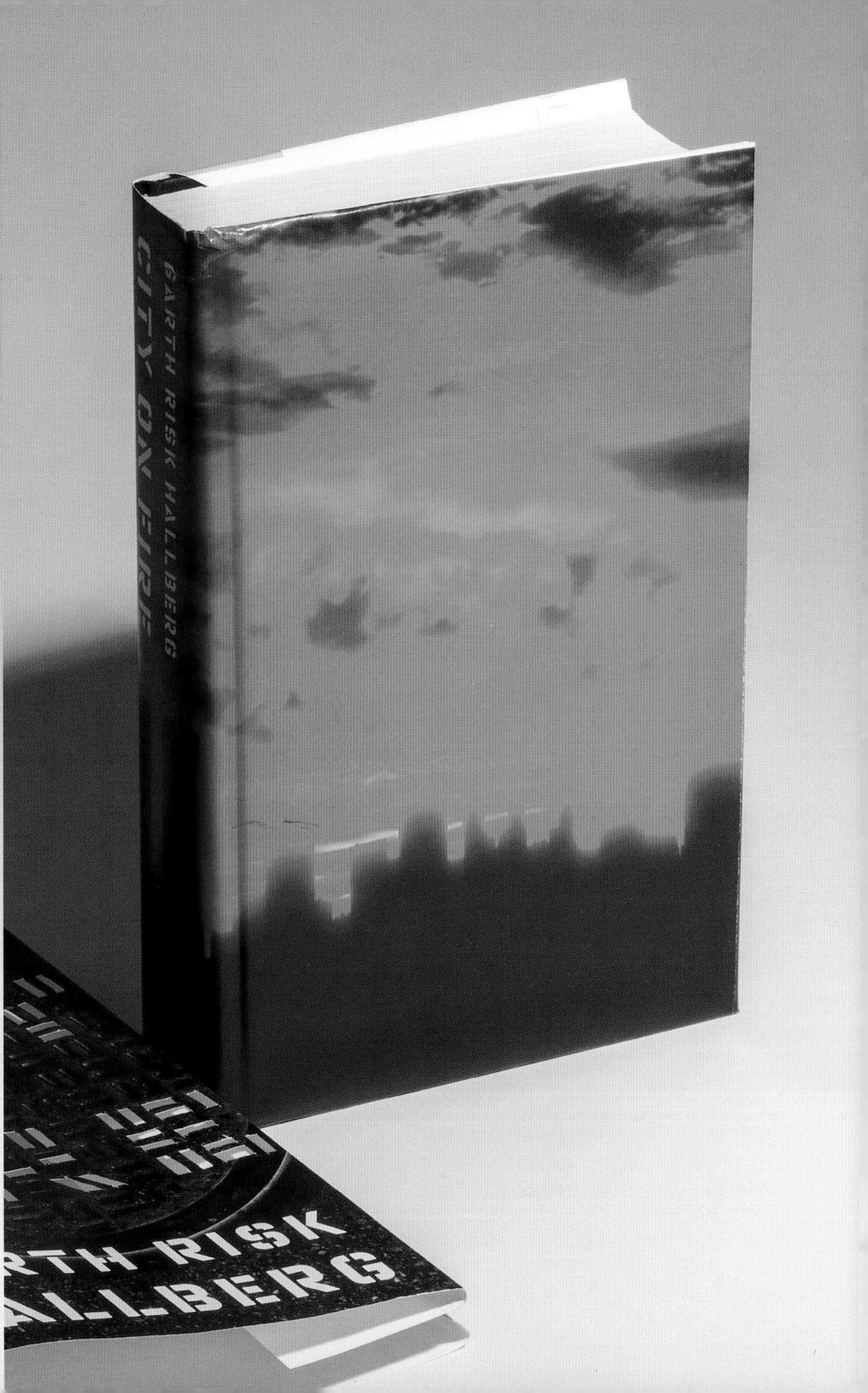
GARTH RISK HALLBERG
CITY ON FIRE
RTH RISK
ALLBERG

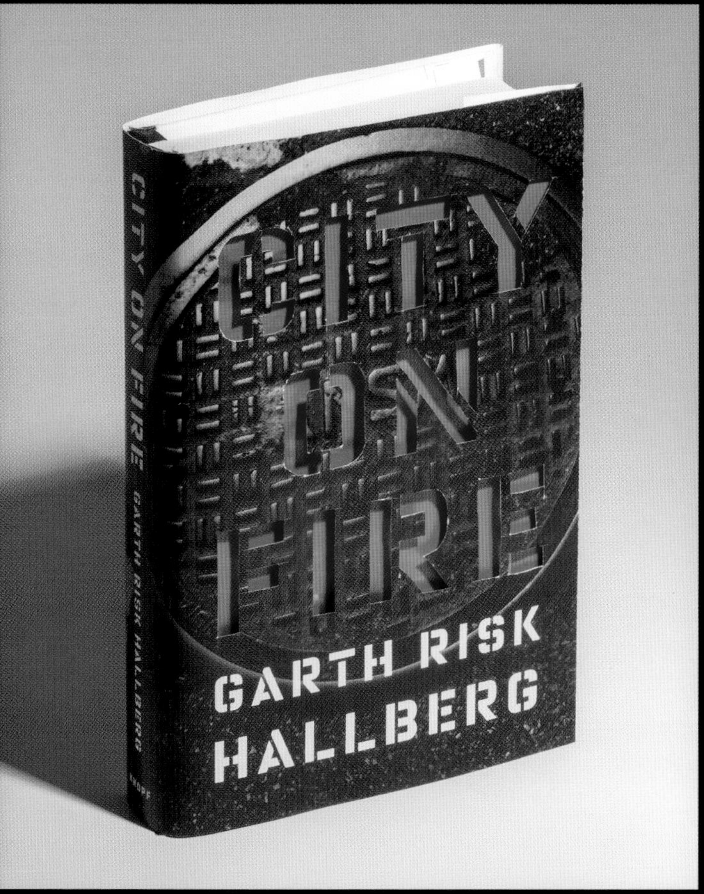
CITY ON FIRE
GARTH RISK HALLBERG
CITY ON FIRE GARTH RISK HALLBERG

## The Fire This Time

Garth Risk Hallberg's *City on Fire* was one of those New York publishing stories that we all thought didn't happen anymore: young wunderkind writes epic tale about the city, and then everyone in said city wants to publish it. It was like *Bonfire of the Vanities* with a whole new cast, both in front of and behind the scenes. The story is an epic tale of New York City in the mid-1970s, culminating in the blackout of 1977. I started with a manhole cover and pulled the title of the book out of the shapes therein (above & opposite). I frankly thought this was tremendously clever. The editor did not. On to the next idea . . .

**RIGHT:** This design was proposed for the hardcover, but was nixed. However, it was resurrected as the cover of the paperback edition. Neon title type by Terry Sanders.

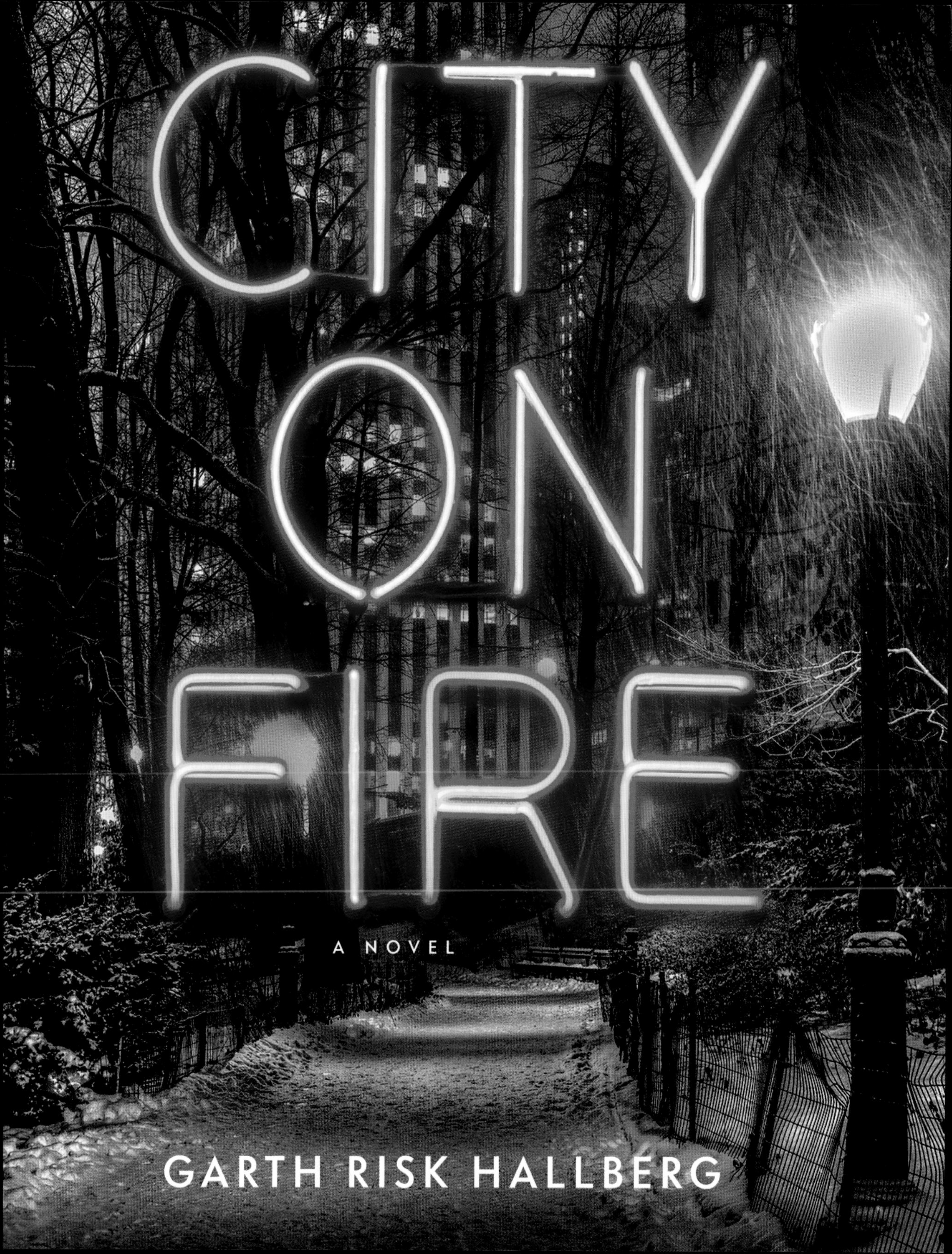
CITY ON FIRE
A NOVEL
GARTH RISK HALLBERG

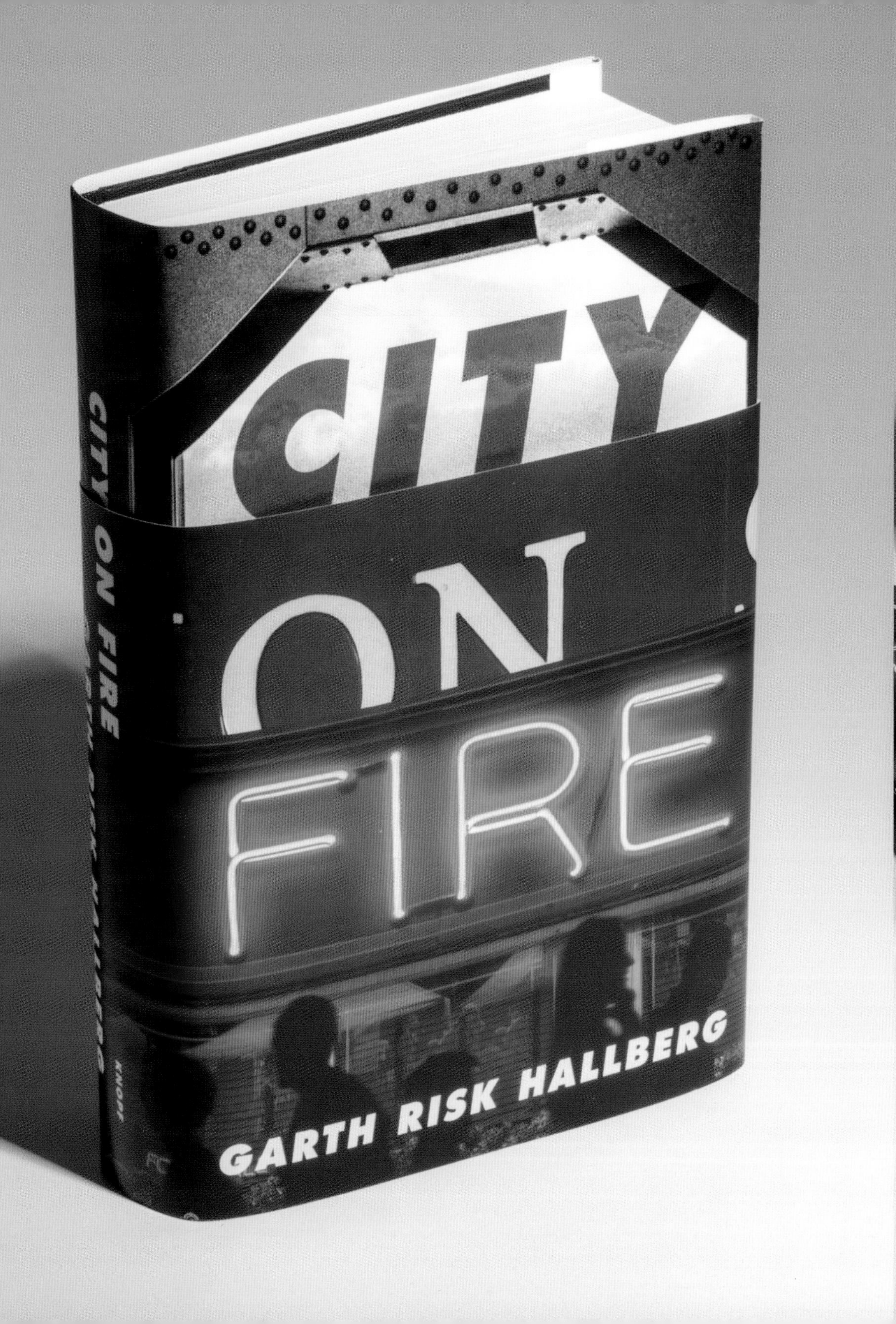
CITY
ON
FIRE
GARTH RISK HALLBERG
KNOPF

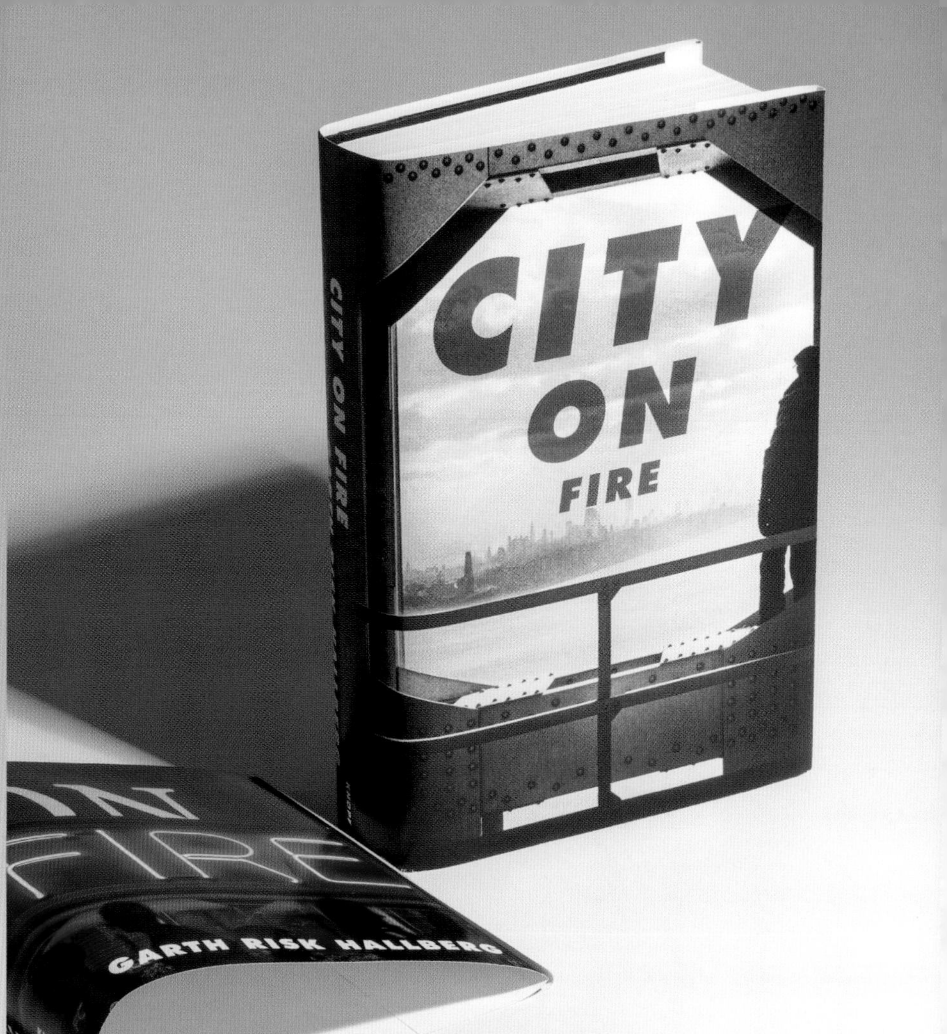
CITY
ON
FIRE
GARTH RISK HALLBERG

This book operates on so many levels that I thought an effective jacket approach could reflect that. The black-and-white image on the binding was suggested by Garth as a possibility and I added onto it (this page). The "ON" is a picture from ceramic tile subway signage in the Union Square station that I shot myself. Digital photographer and artist Terry Sanders (see *Bright, Precious Days*, p. 46) created the neon layer. This concept totally worked for me, but not so much for anyone else. Back to the drawing board.

On the opposite page is a romantic idea that I don't think Garth ever saw, replete with an oncoming subway train and kissing couple on the platform. I was trying to think of a package that would have multiple layers. This would ultimately prove unnecessary, but I had to work through the process for myself.

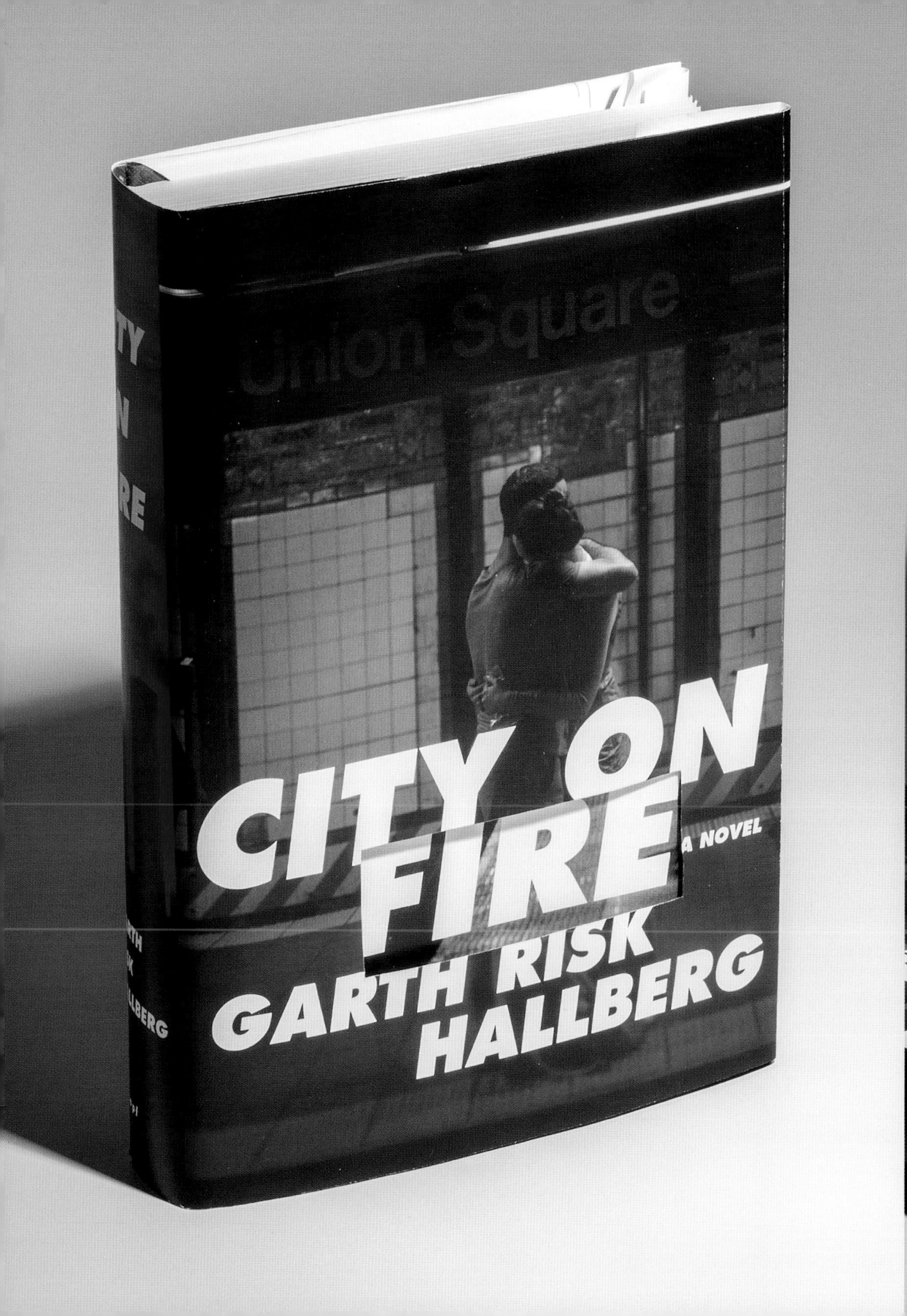
Union Square
CITY ON FIRE
A NOVEL
GARTH RISK HALLBERG

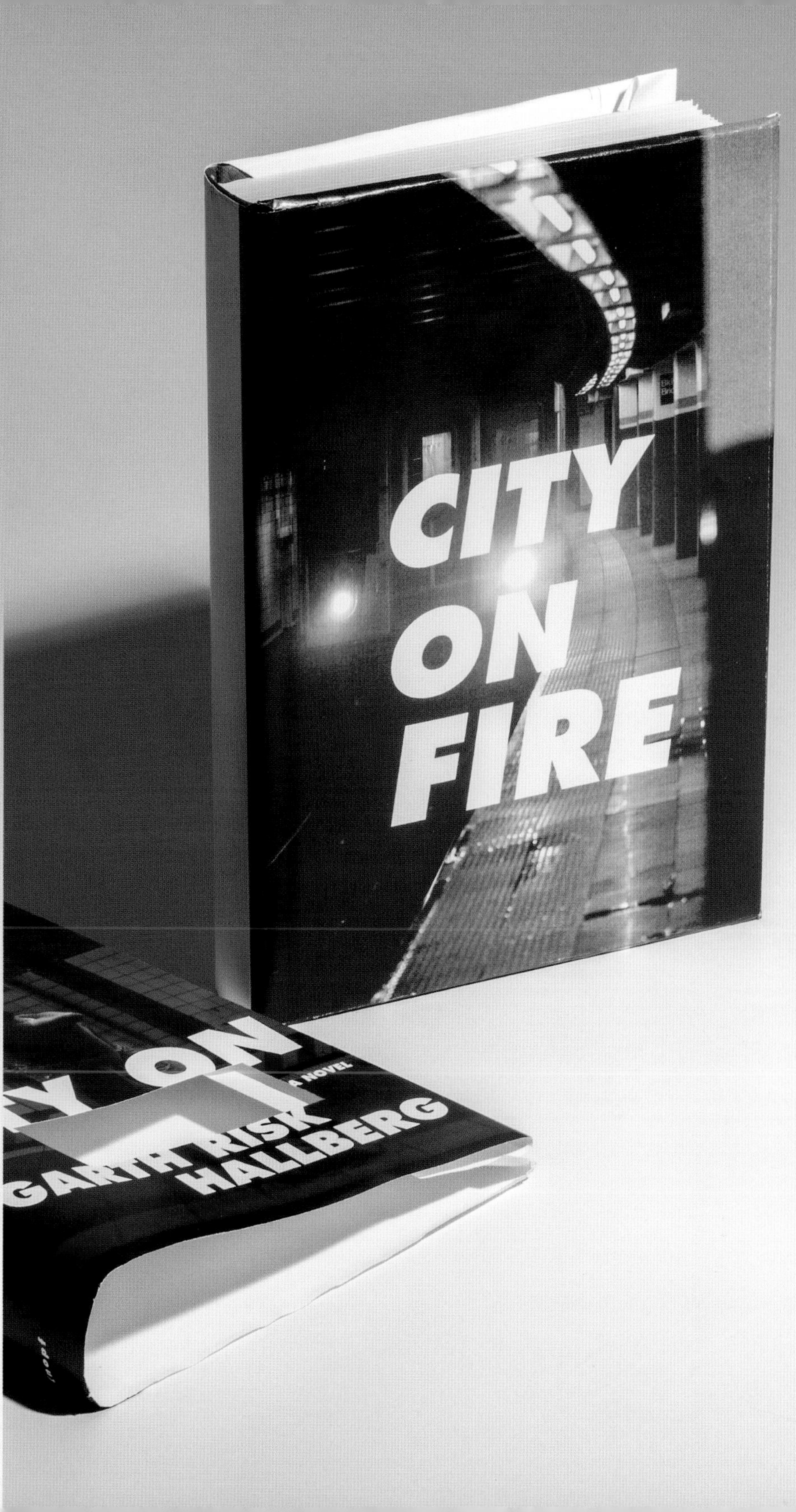
CITY ON FIRE
A NOVEL
GARTH RISK HALLBERG

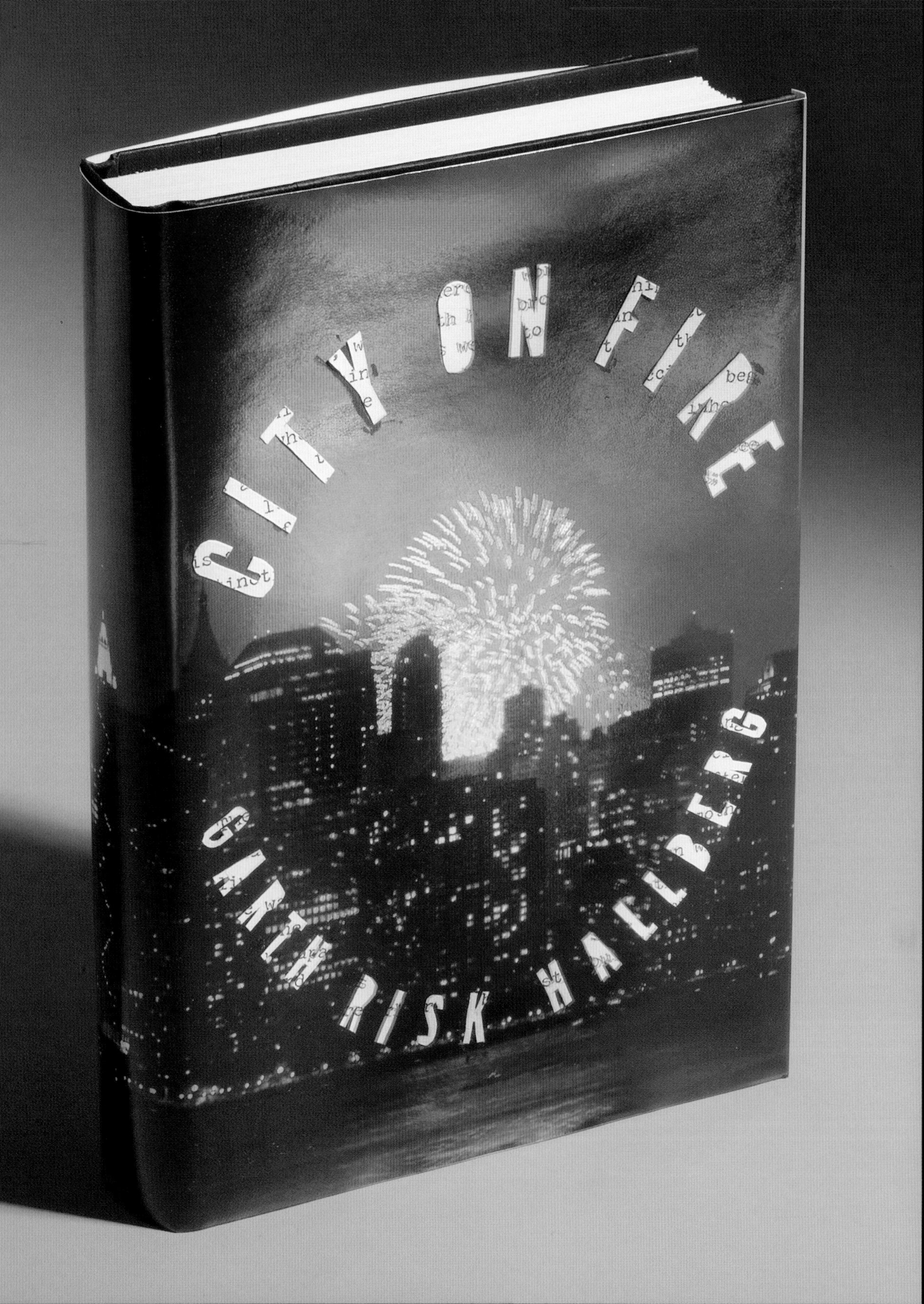
CITY ON FIRE
GARTH RISK HALLBERG

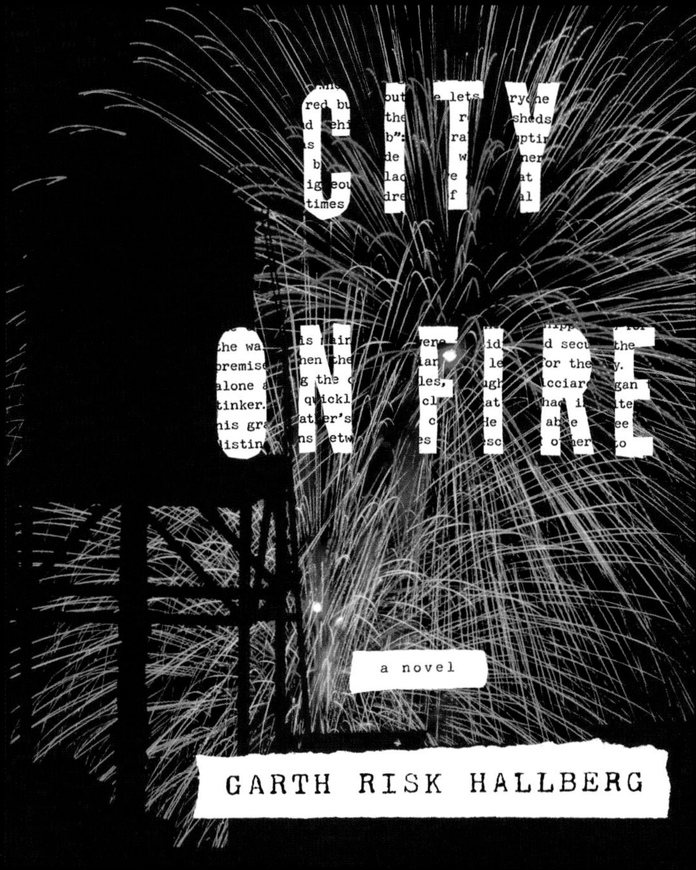
CITY
ON FIRE
a novel
GARTH RISK HALLBERG

Months of effort had gone by, and then the editor, Diana Miller, gave me a suggestion: "Why don't you try something crafty?" If that sounds a bit oblique, it certainly didn't to me. Some of the characters were constantly making things like punk fanzines, at a time when such an undertaking meant tremendous tactile handwork. That's what this cover needed to reflect. Part of the plot involves fireworks in New York and their history, so I printed out the passage in the manuscript discussing the Brooklyn-based manufacturer of the fireworks and how they achieve their color effects. I then cut out the letters of the title from those pages, and glued them onto photos of fireworks bursting over the city printed onto prismatic, metallic paper (above & left).

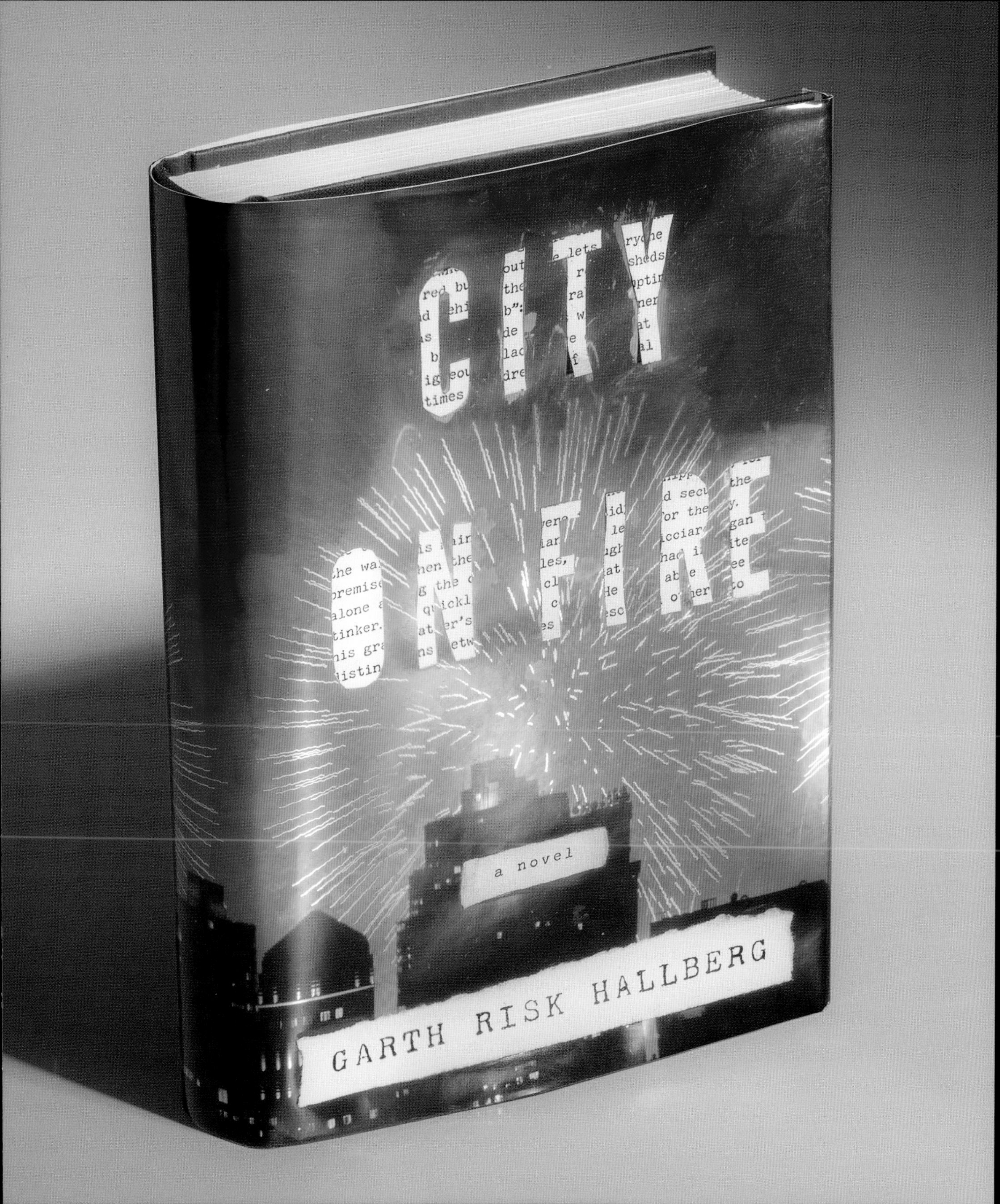
CITY
ON FIRE
a novel
GARTH RISK HALLBERG

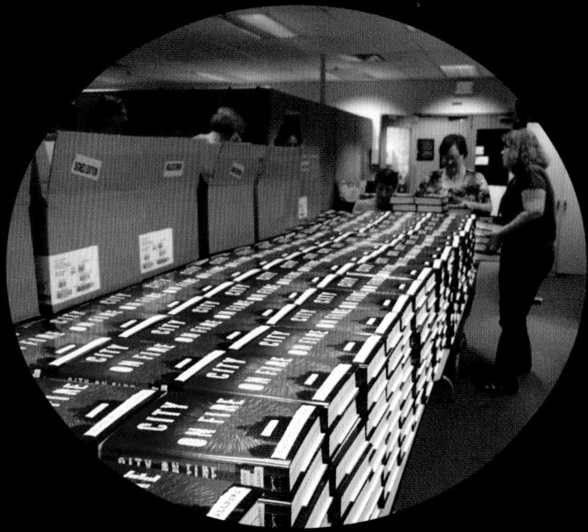

That worked (final jacket, left). We used embossing and spot-matte effects to make it look like someone hand-assembled each one, and Garth signed hundreds of the finished books (above).

**OVERLEAF, LEFT:** Cover illustration for the *New York Times Book Review*, May 5, 2013. This riff on the classic British WWII poster "Keep Calm and Carry On" seemed inevitable for master spy-writer John le Carré.

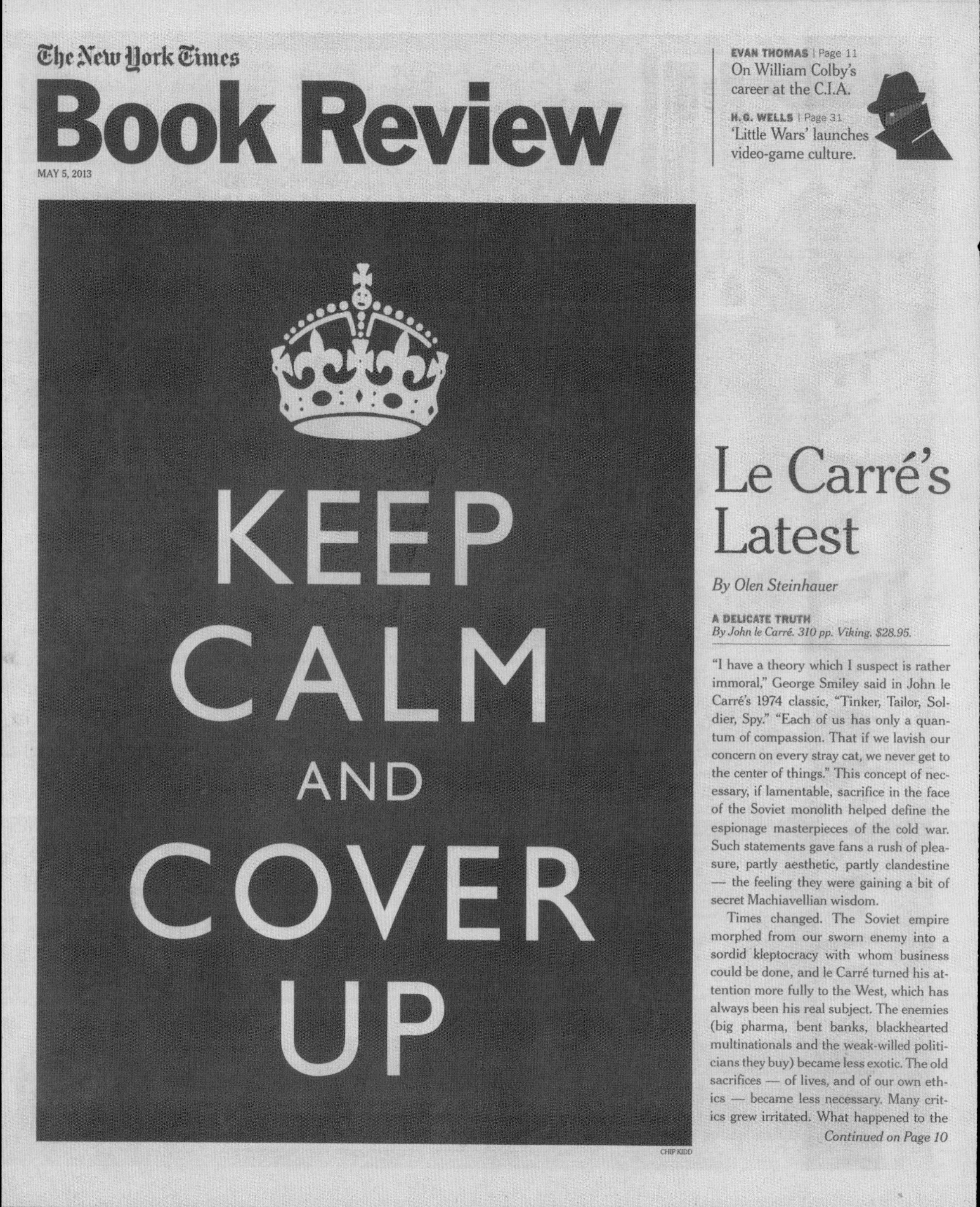
The New York Times

# Book Review

MAY 5, 2013

EVAN THOMAS | Page 11
On William Colby's career at the C.I.A.

H.G. WELLS | Page 31
'Little Wars' launches video-game culture.

KEEP CALM AND COVER UP

CHIP KIDD

## Le Carré's Latest

*By Olen Steinhauer*

**A DELICATE TRUTH**
*By John le Carré. 310 pp. Viking. $28.95.*

"I have a theory which I suspect is rather immoral," George Smiley said in John le Carré's 1974 classic, "Tinker, Tailor, Soldier, Spy." "Each of us has only a quantum of compassion. That if we lavish our concern on every stray cat, we never get to the center of things." This concept of necessary, if lamentable, sacrifice in the face of the Soviet monolith helped define the espionage masterpieces of the cold war. Such statements gave fans a rush of pleasure, partly aesthetic, partly clandestine — the feeling they were gaining a bit of secret Machiavellian wisdom.

Times changed. The Soviet empire morphed from our sworn enemy into a sordid kleptocracy with whom business could be done, and le Carré turned his attention more fully to the West, which has always been his real subject. The enemies (big pharma, bent banks, blackhearted multinationals and the weak-willed politicians they buy) became less exotic. The old sacrifices — of lives, and of our own ethics — became less necessary. Many critics grew irritated. What happened to the

*Continued on Page 10*

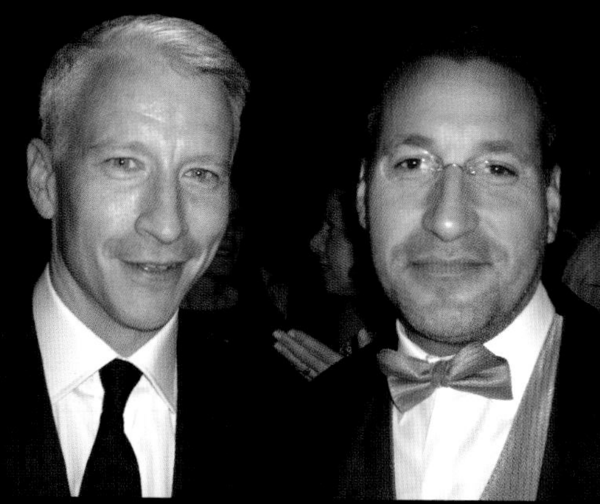

# Great Heir

I have designed books for Gloria Vanderbilt for over 27 years, start-ing with her novel *Never Say Goodbye* in 1989. We have been grea[t] friends ever since, and I've worked on many more projects with he[r] (see following spread). But I was especially thrilled when she sug-gested to her son, Anderson Cooper, that I design his 2007 memoi[r] of becoming a foreign news correspondent—a career he chose at a very early age—*Dispatches from the Edge*. Of course I was a fan, hav-ing been greatly moved by his coverage of Hurricane Katrina. His grilling of Louisiana Democratic senator Mary Landrieu during his reporting on that disaster was fearless, justifiably damning, and a landmark of broadcast journalism.

When we met at his office at CNN we bonded over—of all things—his SuperFriends Wonder Twins mouse pad. Oh my God, we were both geeks. He told me his favorite comics character as a kid was Jack Kirby's Kamandi—a gorgeous long-haired blond version of Charlton Heston's Taylor in *Planet of the Apes*, trapped in a dystopian future New York City and billed as the last boy on earth. Right. Anderson was not yet publicly out as a gay man at that time but totally opened up to me about this aspect of his life (without any prompting from me), and we shared a related connection over this, too.

**OPPOSITE:** The cover is a montage of images of his life covering these stories, but I think what makes it unique and specific to the content of the book is the use of a "crawl" across it for his name. There was some pushback from the publisher—HarperCollins—on this element, but Anderson convinced them it would work. And then of course there is the fire underneath him: not subtle on my part, but man, it's there.

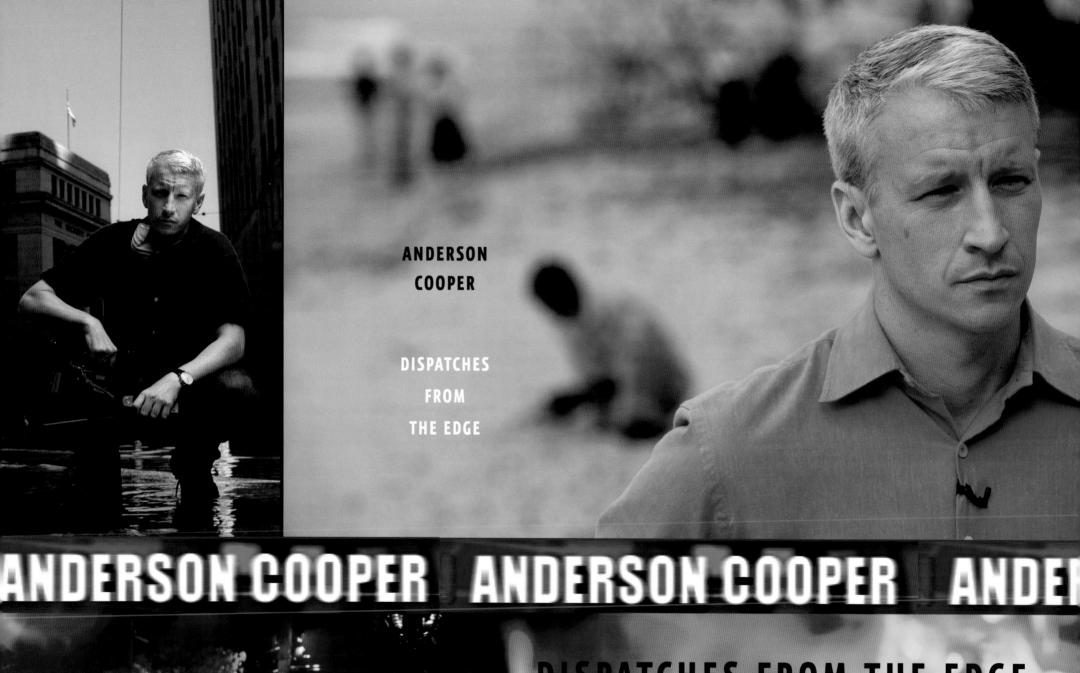

ANDERSON

COOPER

DISPATCHES

FROM

THE EDGE

ANDERSON COOPER  ANDERSON COOPER  ANDE

DISPATCHES FROM THE EDGE

A MEMOIR OF WAR, DISASTERS AND SURVIVAL

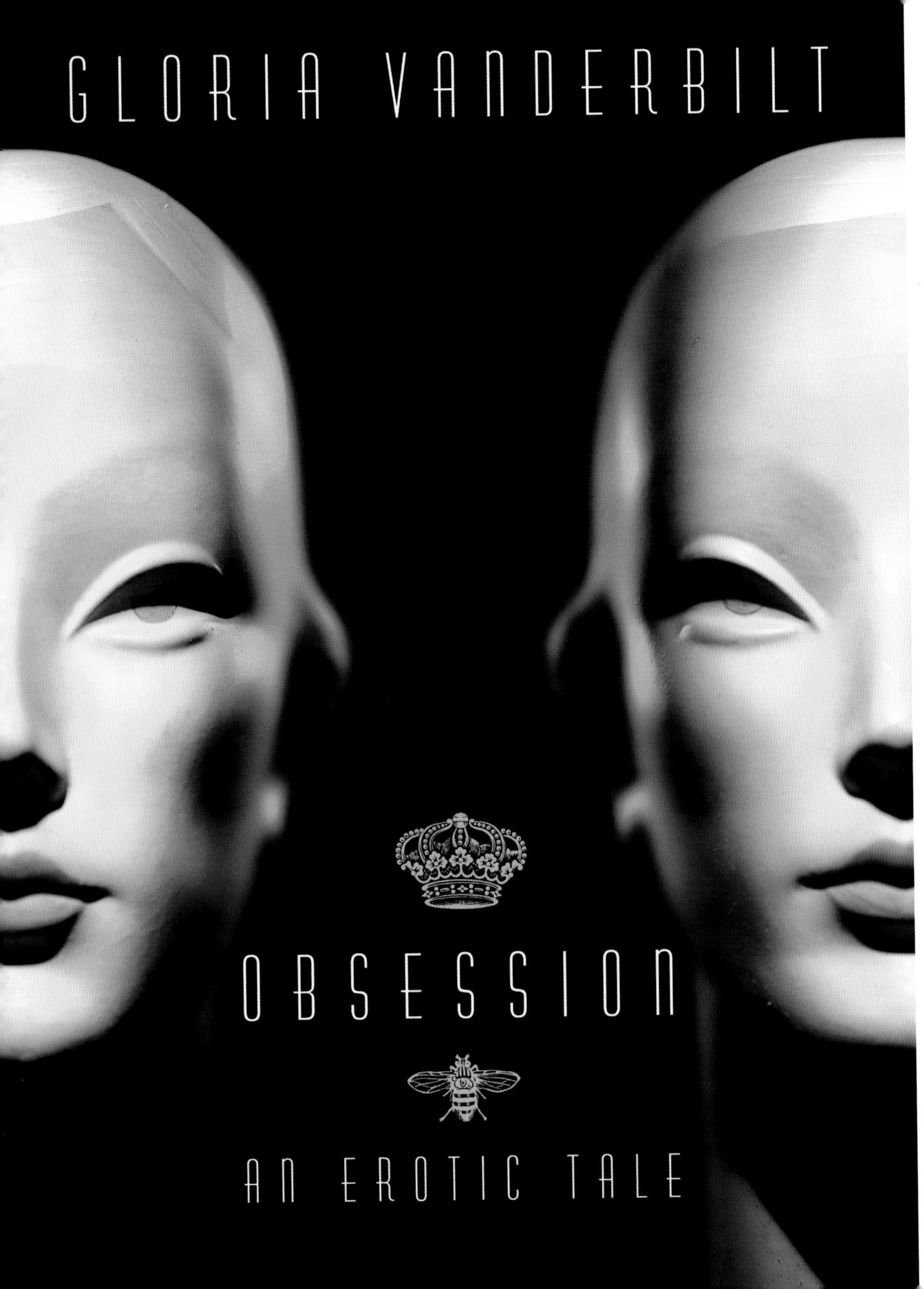
GLORIA VANDERBILT
OBSESSION
AN EROTIC TALE

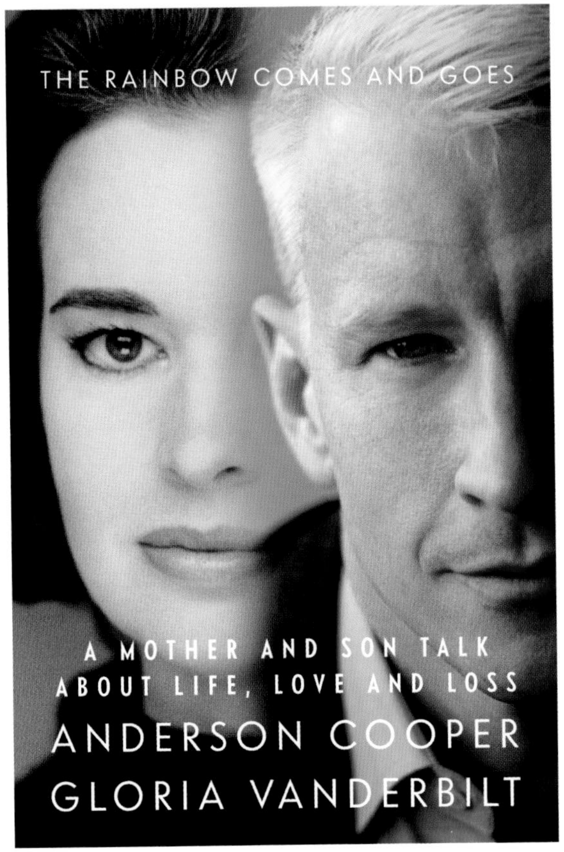
THE RAINBOW COMES AND GOES
A MOTHER AND SON TALK
ABOUT LIFE, LOVE AND LOSS
ANDERSON COOPER
GLORIA VANDERBILT

## Family Affair

Alas, HarperCollins could not be convinced regarding my design for 2016's *The Rainbow Comes and Goes* (above), the captivating chronicle of a year-long correspondence between Gloria and Anderson which opened up many subjects of their lives that had not been previously made public. It is ultimately a glimpse of the bond between an extraordinarily iconic mother and son and the many hard-fought triumphs and brutal tragedies they had shared over four-plus decades. I used a vintage black-and-white image of her, fading into a recent full-color image of him. I only later realized that this design echoed the cover I did for Gloria's 2009 novel *Obsession* (left), but that wasn't the issue. In fact I was never quite sure what the issue was, except that the publisher's sales force didn't like it; they wanted a custom contemporary photo of the two of them, and that was that.

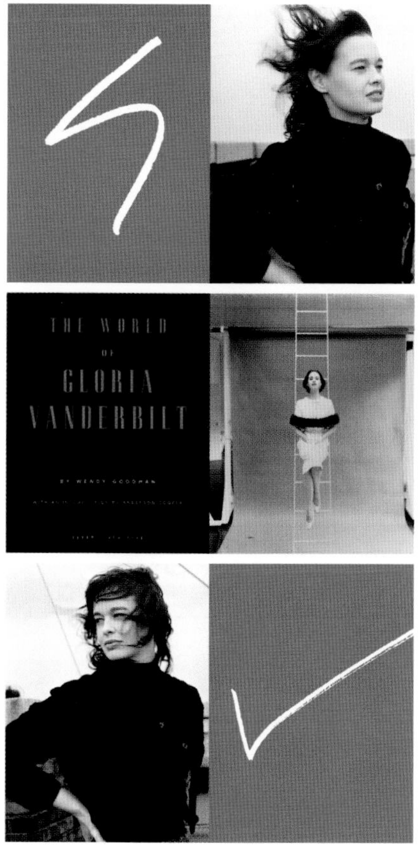
THE WORLD
OF
GLORIA
VANDERBILT

**RIGHT:** Front cover image by the legendary Richard Avedon, one of Gloria's best friends, as she was one of his favorite muses. The Avedon estate was very generous in allowing us to use many of his images inside the book, including previously unpublished outtakes and candid photos.

**LEFT:** Title page sequence of three spreads featuring two pictures by Inge Morath (top and bottom) book-ending an Avedon shot (middle) of Gloria on a ladder for *Harper's Bazaar*, March 1955.

So there I was, sitting in editor Michael Korda's office at Simon and Schuster in 2003, rummaging through several boxes of Gloria's pictures and photo albums. I was going to be designing the cover for her memoir about the men in her life to be called *It Seemed Important at the Time* (see *Book One*), and I wanted to find interesting and unexpected shots of her and all of them (Frank Sinatra, Gordon Parks, Marlon Brando, and then, of course, her four husbands). As I sat there amidst all of this amazing imagery, I couldn't help but think, "Wait, someone should really do a full-scale coffee-table book on Gloria and her astonishing life." And then, five years later, design writer Wendy Goodman was sitting in my office, asking me to design precisely that. The result was 2010's *The World of Gloria Vanderbilt* (Abrams), and what a world it is: an age of glamour, class, talent, and taste that we will never see again. I am so thankful to Wendy that she persevered and got this book done. For me it was a hectic double-duty because by then I was deep into working on *True Prep*, and there was considerable overlap. It was a lot of effort but totally worth it.

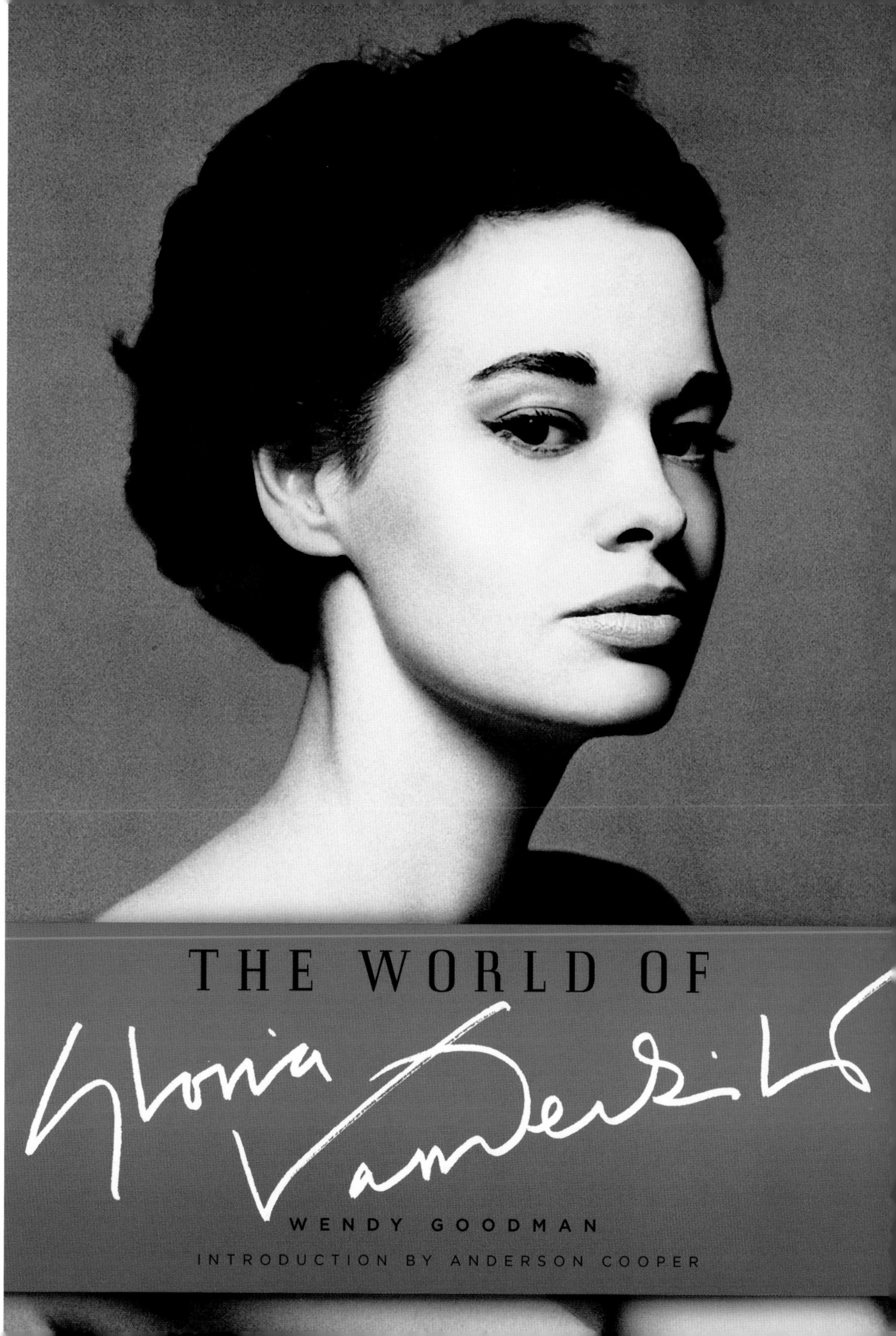
THE WORLD OF
Gloria Vanderbilt
WENDY GOODMAN
INTRODUCTION BY ANDERSON COOPER

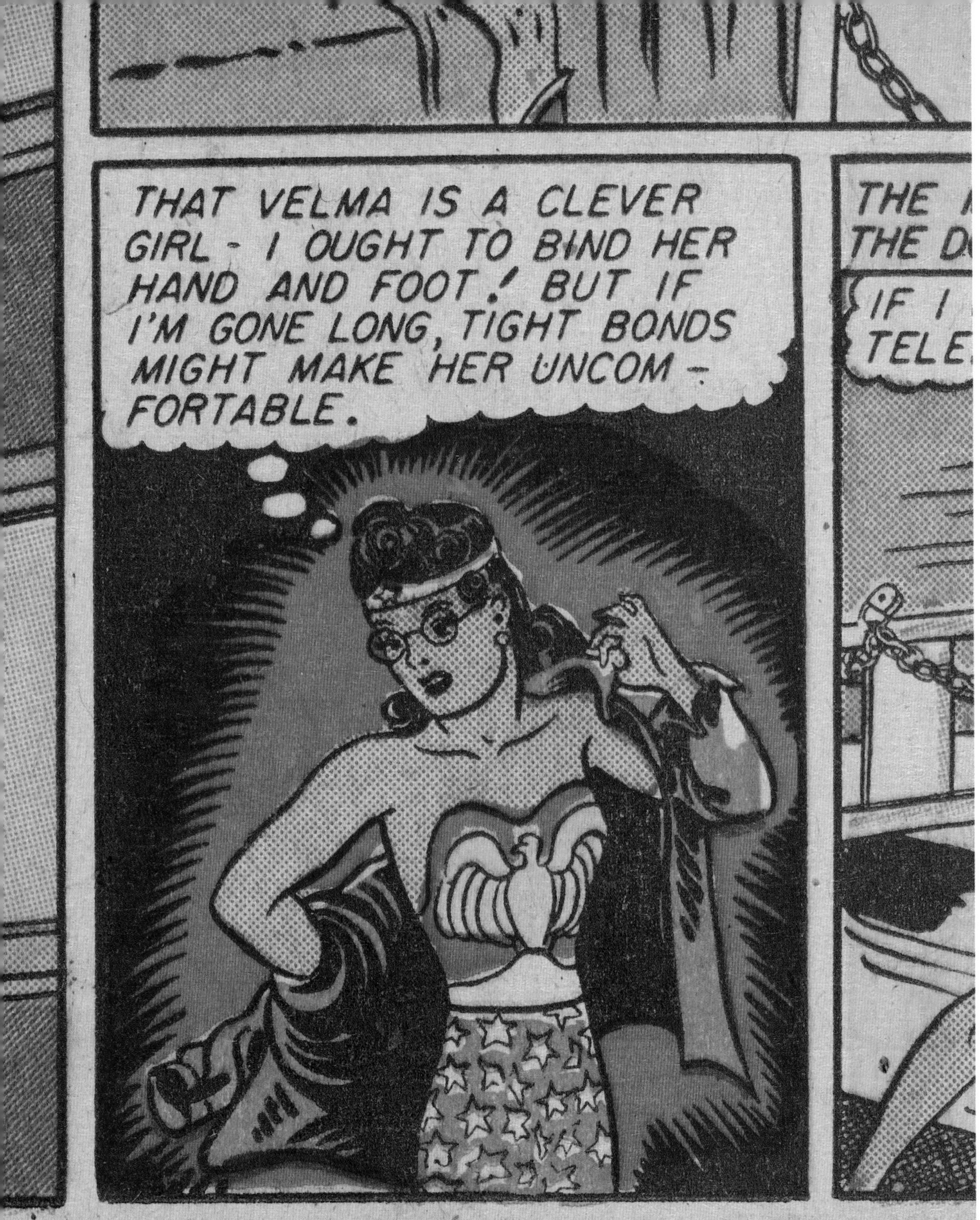
THAT VELMA IS A CLEVER GIRL - I OUGHT TO BIND HER HAND AND FOOT! BUT IF I'M GONE LONG, TIGHT BONDS MIGHT MAKE HER UNCOM-FORTABLE.

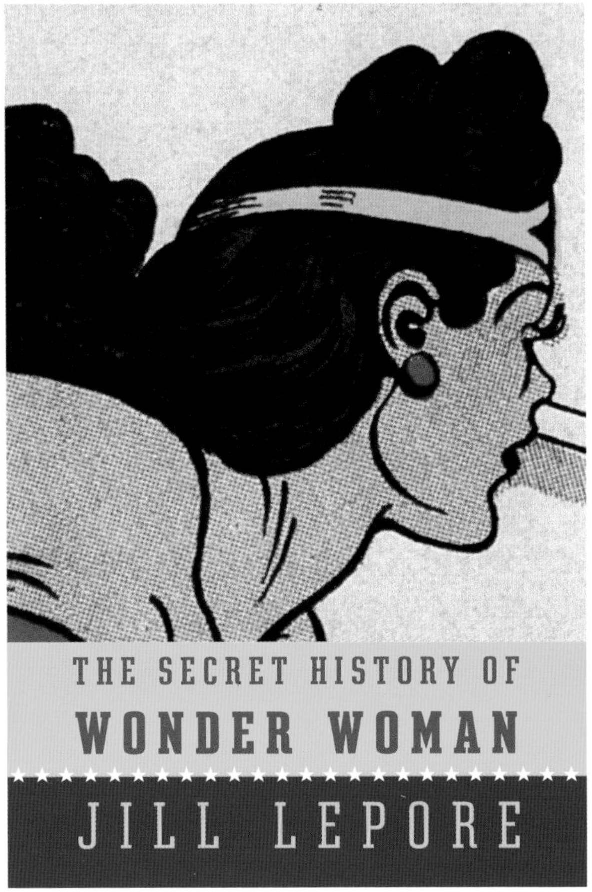
THE SECRET HISTORY OF
WONDER WOMAN
JILL LEPORE

## Hall of Femme

I knew that Jill Lepore was one of the premier investigative journalists working today (professor at Harvard, staff writer for *The New Yorker*); what I didn't know was that she was a Wonder Woman fan, and she had been channeling that interest into an intensive manuscript about the origins of the character and her fascinating and eccentric creator, William Moulton Marston. As the designer and art director of *Wonder Woman: The Complete History* (Chronicle, 2000), I already knew a lot of the weird stuff (Marston also invented the lie-detector test on which WW's golden lasso is based, fostered a major bondage fetish, and had a polygamous family situation). But Jill uncovered much more. As I sat with her to plan the cover, I came to understand how much art from the comics she intended to use in the book, a project that was not authorized by DC Comics. Um, uh-oh. But at the relative last minute DC approved everything, to my grateful amazement, and the CEO of DC Entertainment—Diane Nelson—gave everyone in her company a copy of the book for the holidays.

**RIGHT:** The final cover, using art from *Wonder Woman* #12 (opposite, left). Jill handpicked this panel, wanting to show Diana Prince changing into the Amazing Amazon. Knopf, 2014. **BELOW:** The "generic cover" I had in reserve in case we didn't get the art permissions from DC. **OPPOSITE, RIGHT:** An early cover idea using art with Wonder Woman looking away from the viewer, withholding her secrets.

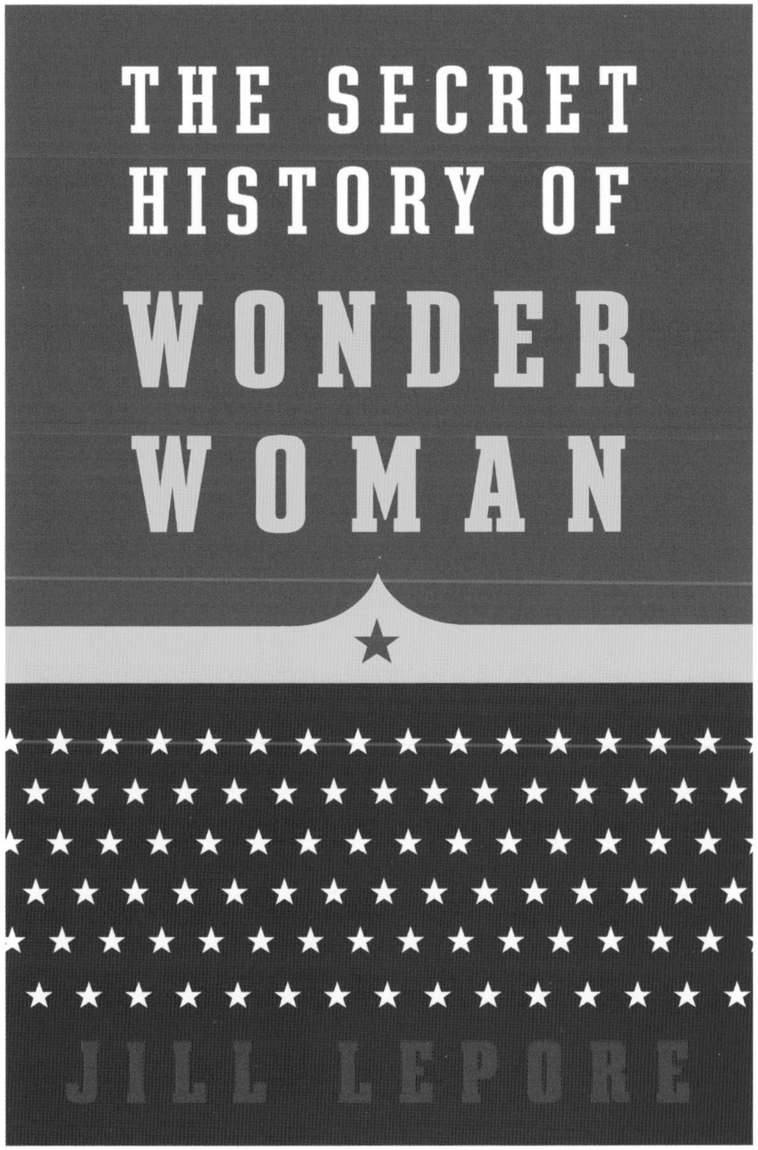
THE SECRET
HISTORY OF
WONDER
WOMAN
JILL LEPORE

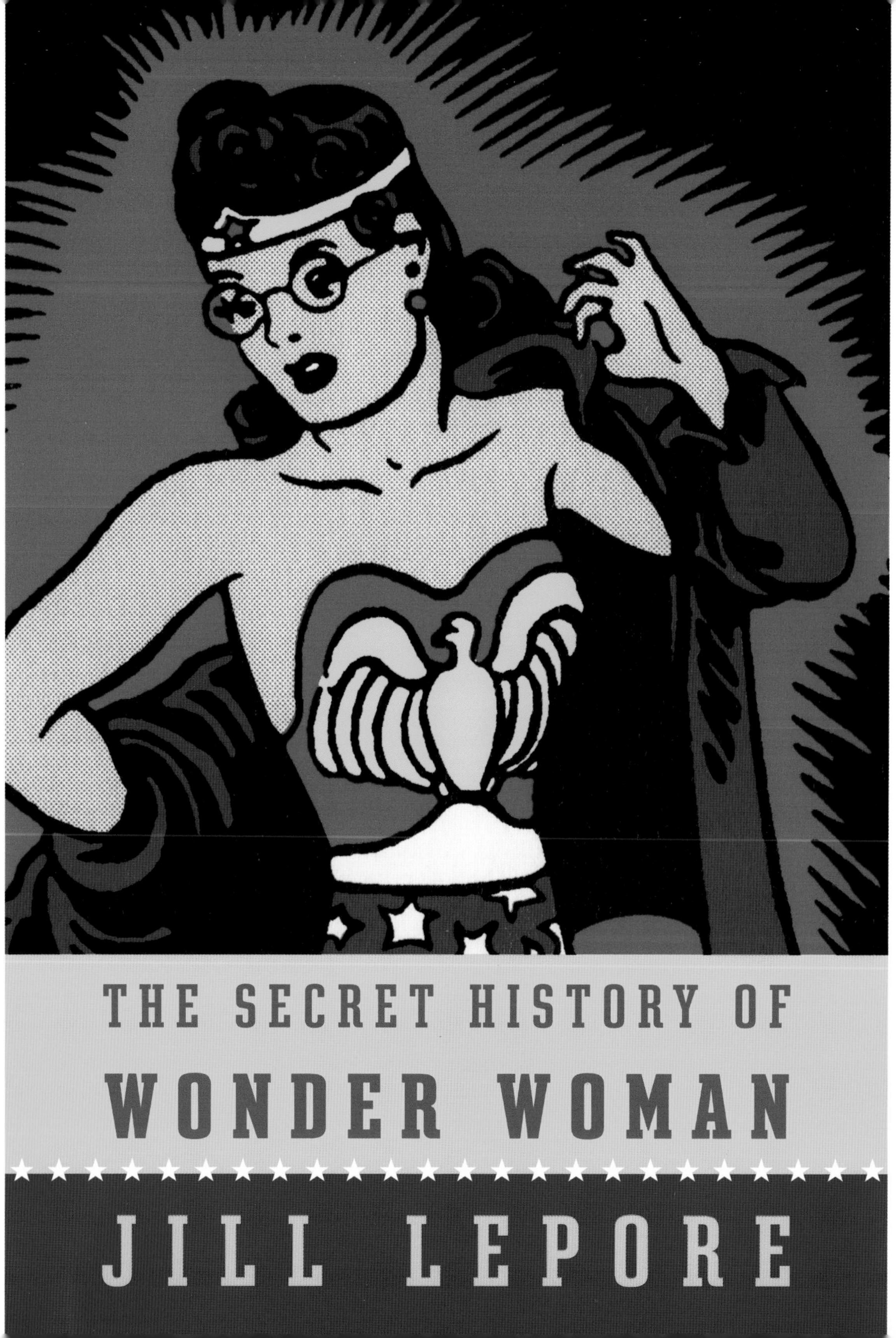
THE SECRET HISTORY OF
WONDER WOMAN
JILL LEPORE

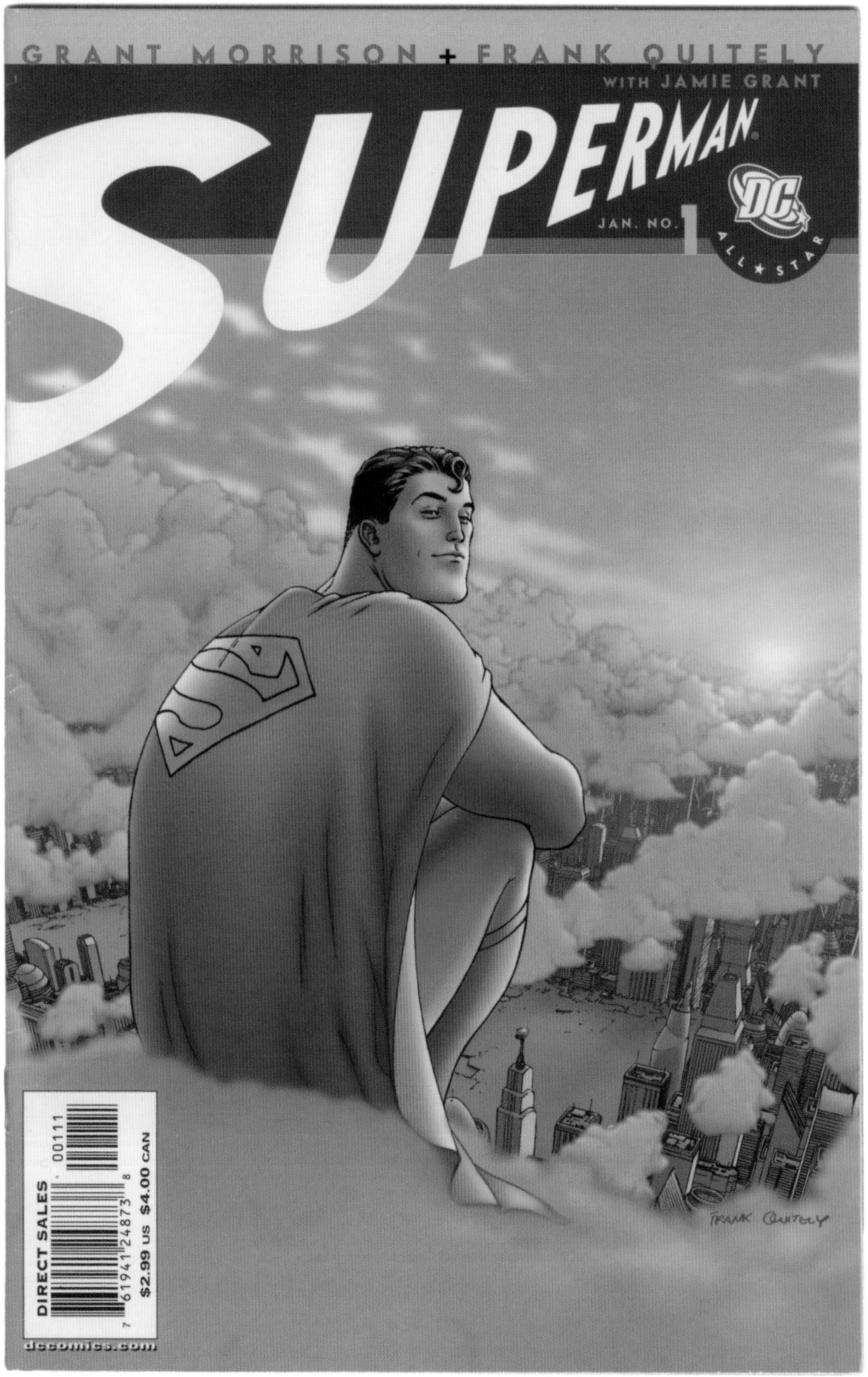
GRANT MORRISON + FRANK QUITELY
WITH JAMIE GRANT
SUPERMAN
JAN. NO. 1
DC
ALL STAR
FRANK QUITELY
DIRECT SALES
$2.99 US $4.00 CAN
dccomics.com
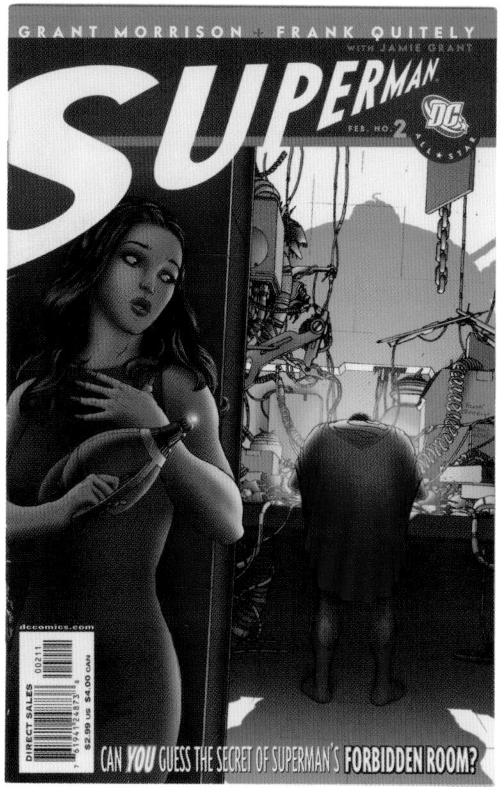
GRANT MORRISON + FRANK QUITELY
WITH JAMIE GRANT
SUPERMAN
FEB. NO. 2
DC
dccomics.com
CAN YOU GUESS THE SECRET OF SUPERMAN'S FORBIDDEN ROOM?
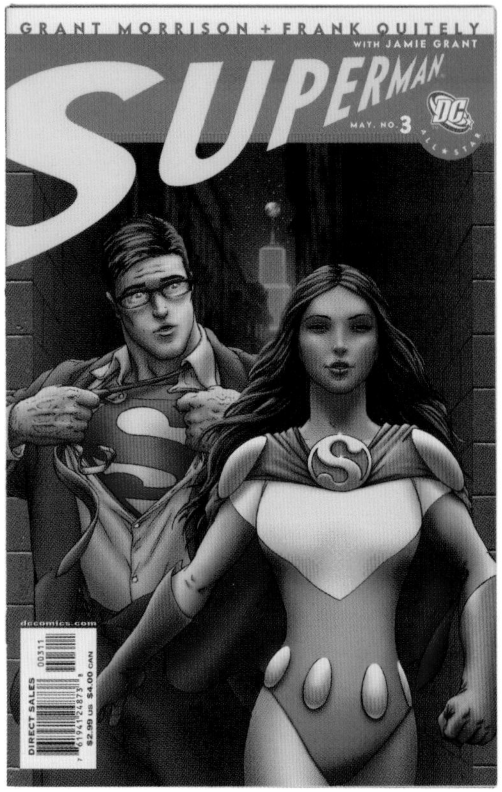
GRANT MORRISON + FRANK QUITELY
WITH JAMIE GRANT
SUPERMAN
MAY. NO. 3
DC
dccomics.com
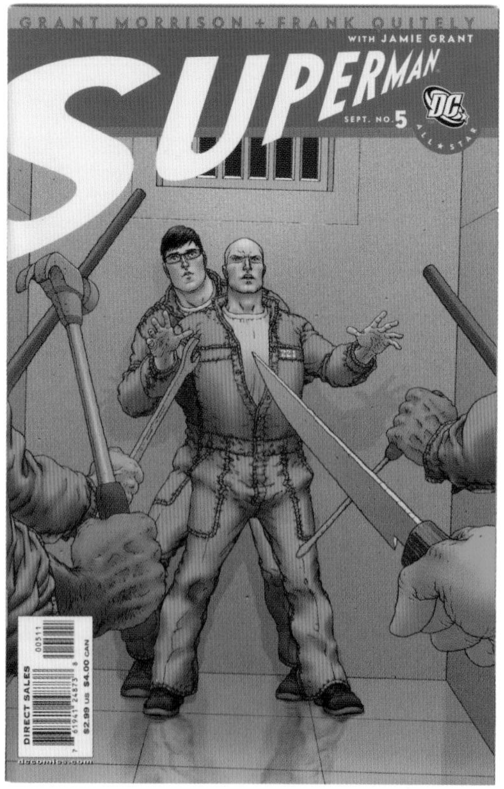
GRANT MORRISON + FRANK QUITELY
WITH JAMIE GRANT
SUPERMAN
SEPT. NO. 5
DC
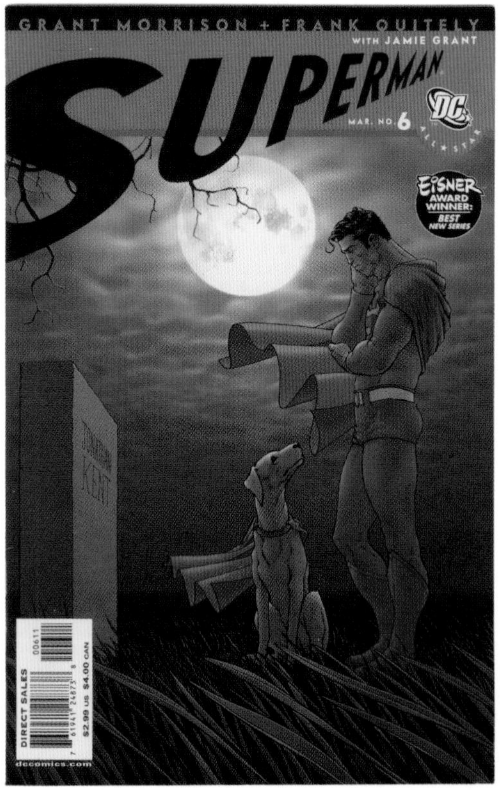
GRANT MORRISON + FRANK QUITELY
WITH JAMIE GRANT
SUPERMAN
MAR. NO. 6
DC
EISNER AWARD WINNER: BEST NEW SERIES
KENT
dccomics.com

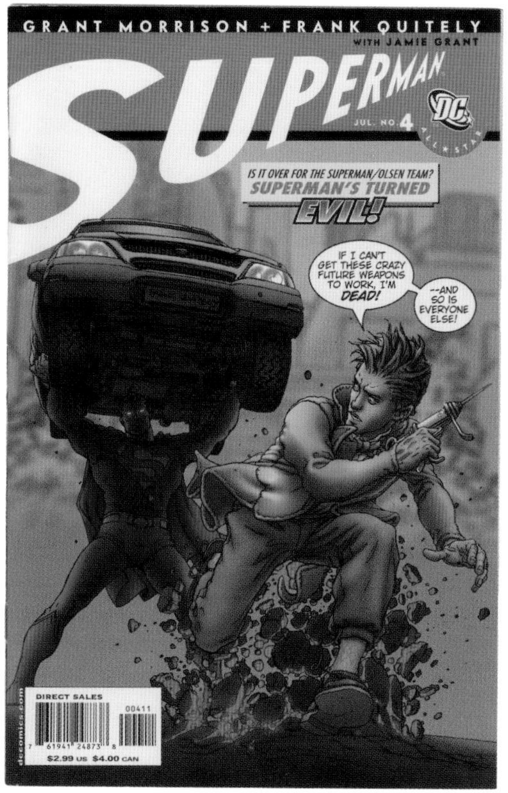
GRANT MORRISON + FRANK QUITELY
WITH JAMIE GRANT
SUPERMAN
JUL. NO. 4
ALL ★ STAR
IS IT OVER FOR THE SUPERMAN/OLSEN TEAM?
SUPERMAN'S TURNED
EVIL!
IF I CAN'T GET THESE CRAZY FUTURE WEAPONS TO WORK, I'M DEAD!
--AND SO IS EVERYONE ELSE!
DIRECT SALES
$2.99 US $4.00 CAN
dccomics.com

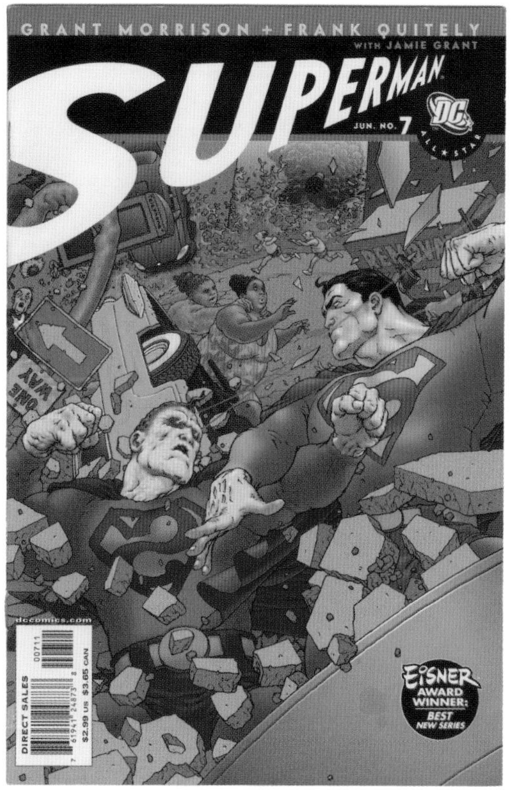
GRANT MORRISON + FRANK QUITELY
WITH JAMIE GRANT
SUPERMAN
JUN. NO. 7
ALL ★ STAR
ONE WAY
dccomics.com
DIRECT SALES
$2.99 US $3.65 CAN
EISNER AWARD WINNER: BEST NEW SERIES

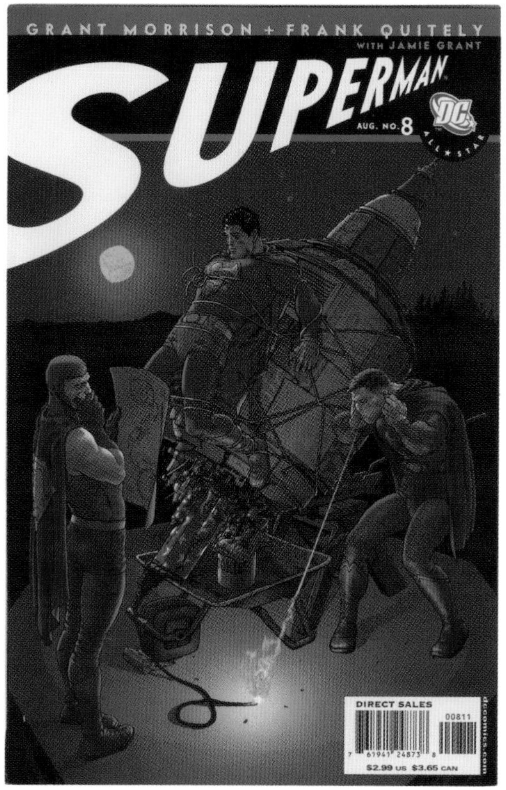
GRANT MORRISON + FRANK QUITELY
WITH JAMIE GRANT
SUPERMAN
AUG. NO. 8
ALL ★ STAR
DIRECT SALES
$2.99 US $3.65 CAN
dccomics.com

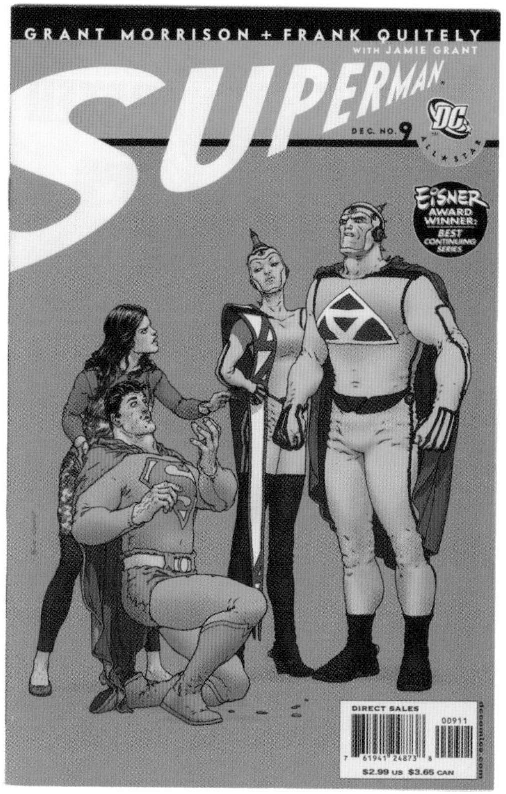
GRANT MORRISON + FRANK QUITELY
WITH JAMIE GRANT
SUPERMAN
DEC. NO. 9
ALL ★ STAR
EISNER AWARD WINNER: BEST CONTINUING SERIES
DIRECT SALES
$2.99 US $3.65 CAN
dccomics.com

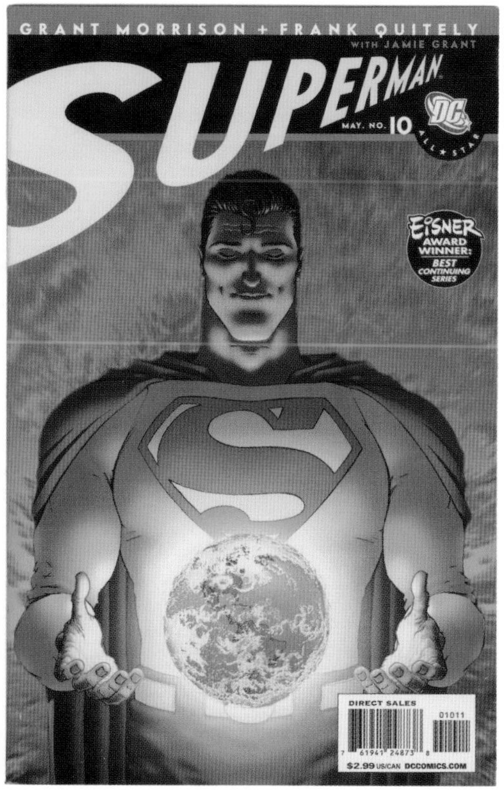
GRANT MORRISON + FRANK QUITELY
WITH JAMIE GRANT
SUPERMAN
MAY. NO. 10
ALL ★ STAR
EISNER AWARD WINNER: BEST CONTINUING SERIES
DIRECT SALES
$2.99 US/CAN DCCOMICS.COM

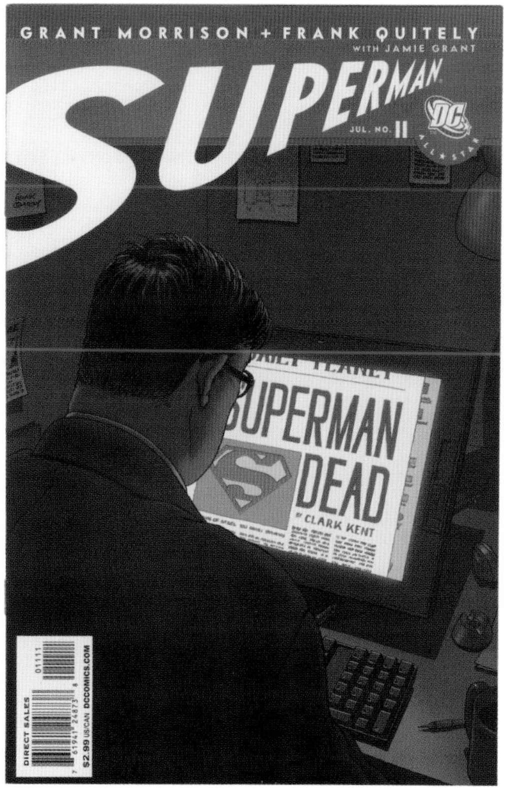
GRANT MORRISON + FRANK QUITELY
WITH JAMIE GRANT
SUPERMAN
JUL. NO. 11
ALL ★ STAR
SUPERMAN DEAD
BY CLARK KENT
DIRECT SALES
$2.99 US/CAN DCCOMICS.COM

# Up, Up & Away!

For the typographic treatment and basic cover design scheme of the All-Star Superman series, the general idea was to riff on the classic Superman logo (in use since 1939) and streamline it for a 21st-century fan base. This version would never replace the original, of course, and would be in use only for the twelve monthly issues you see here, but I wanted to convey a sense of movement that takes the reader up into the sky. Keeping the type just white, yellow, or black let all the other colors shine without having to compete for attention. For what it's worth, note how the barcode tends to jump around from cover to cover. I had no control over that—once the format was accepted by DC Comics, it was out of my hands and determined in-house, depending on the art that Frank Quitely came up with for each issue.

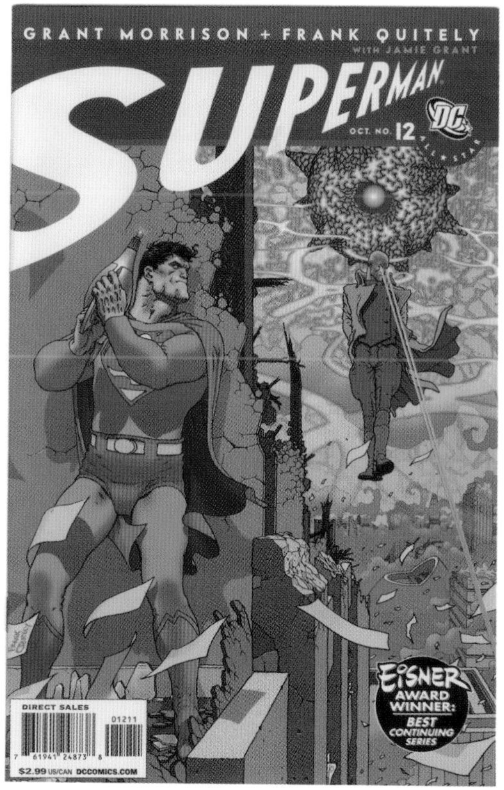
GRANT MORRISON + FRANK QUITELY
WITH JAMIE GRANT
SUPERMAN
OCT. NO. 12
ALL ★ STAR
EISNER AWARD WINNER: BEST CONTINUING SERIES
DIRECT SALES
$2.99 US/CAN DCCOMICS.COM

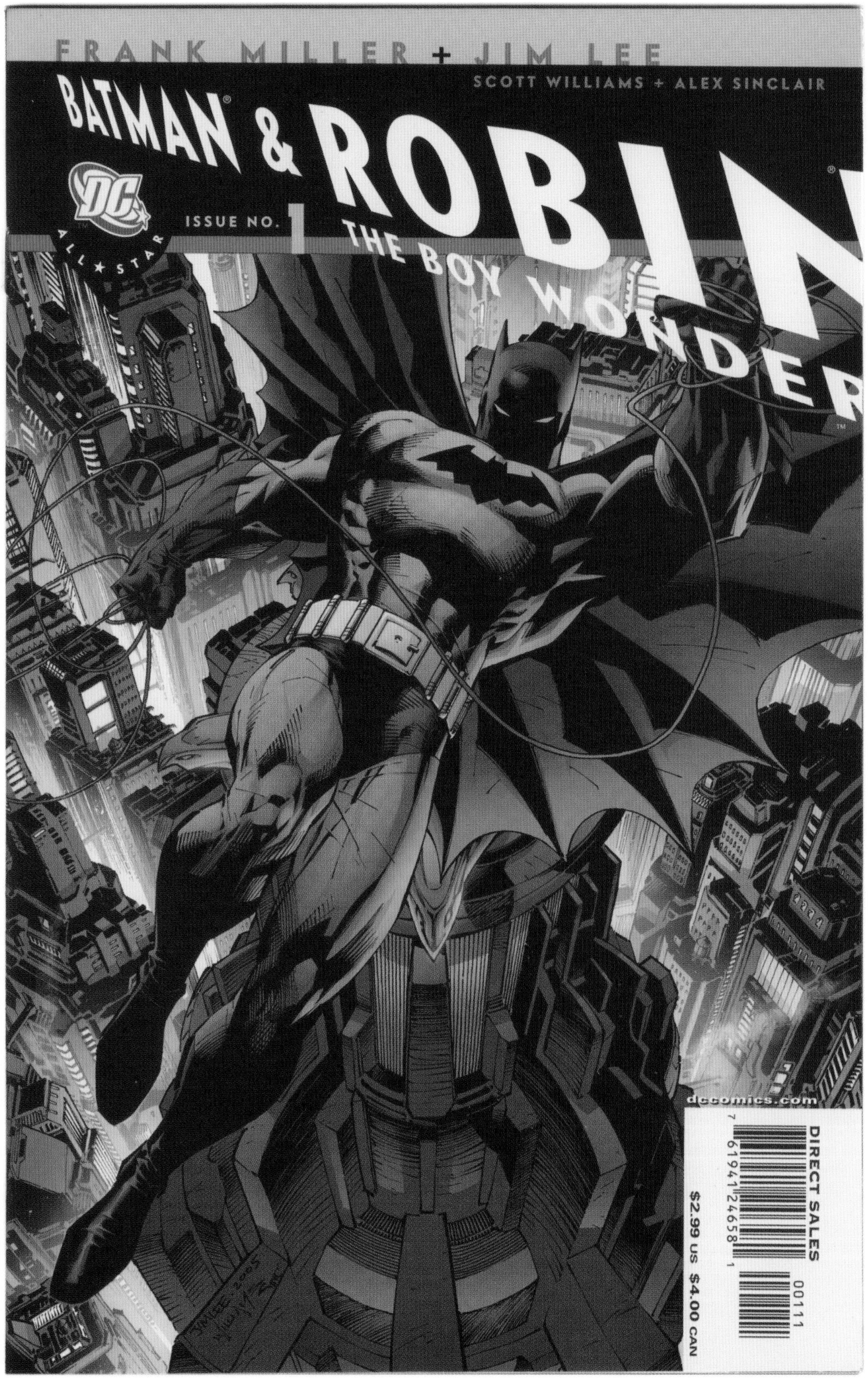
FRANK MILLER + JIM LEE
SCOTT WILLIAMS + ALEX SINCLAIR
BATMAN & ROBIN
THE BOY WONDER
ISSUE NO. 1
DC ALL STAR
dccomics.com
DIRECT SALES
$2.99 US $4.00 CAN

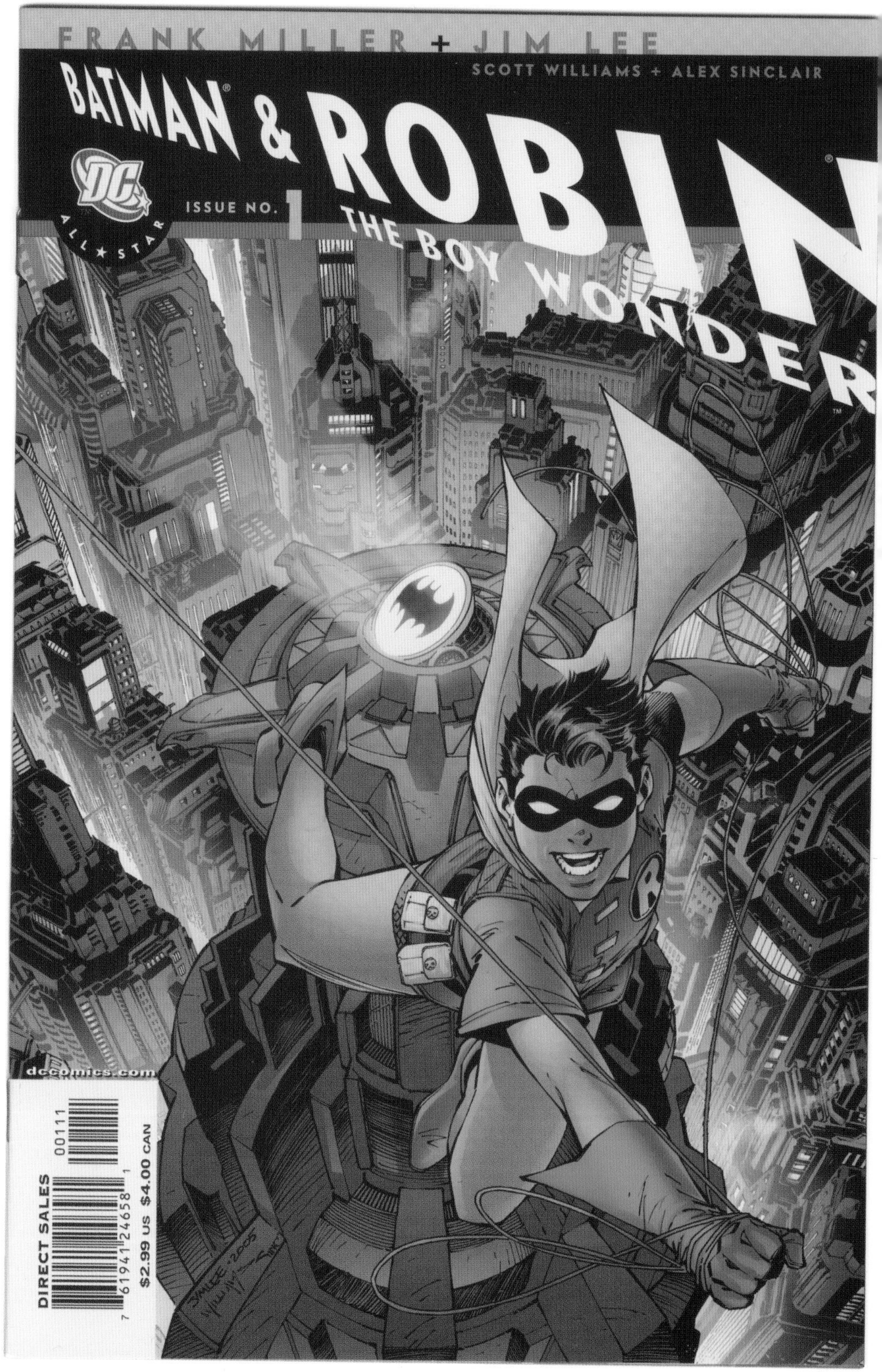
FRANK MILLER + JIM LEE
SCOTT WILLIAMS + ALEX SINCLAIR
BATMAN & ROBIN
THE BOY WONDER
ISSUE NO. 1
DC ALL STAR
dccomics.com
DIRECT SALES
$2.99 US $4.00 CAN

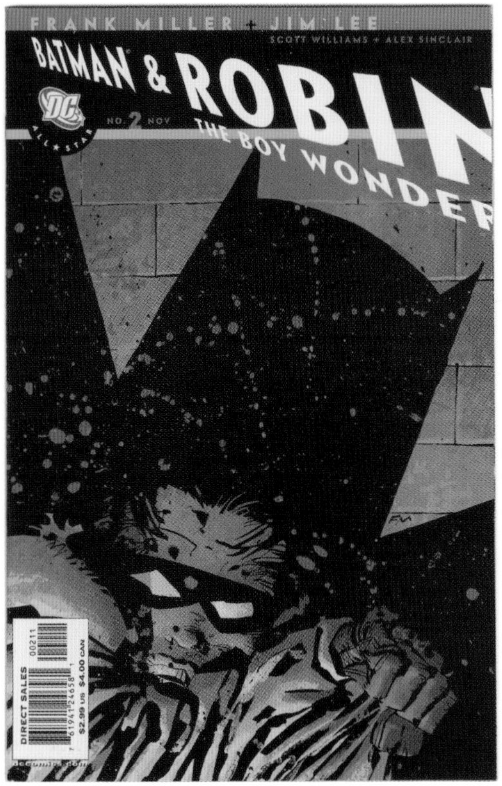
FRANK MILLER + JIM LEE
BATMAN & ROBIN
THE BOY WONDER
NO. 2 NOV
DIRECT SALES
$2.99 US $4.00 CAN
dccomics.com

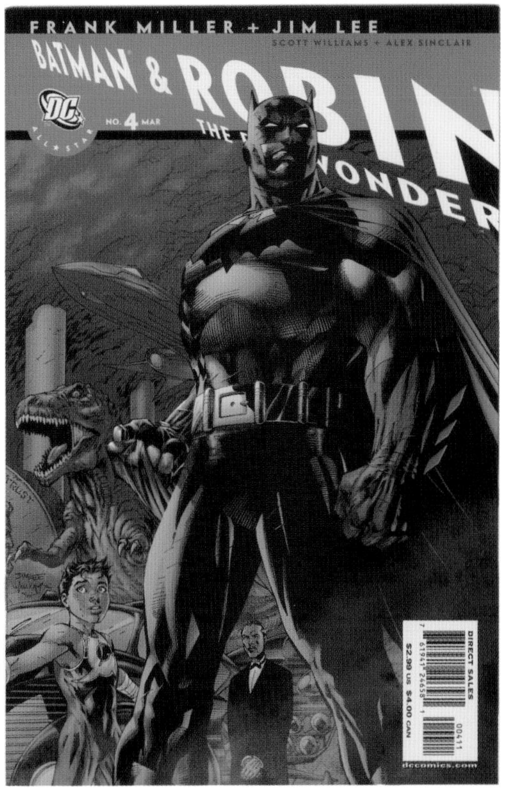
FRANK MILLER + JIM LEE
SCOTT WILLIAMS + ALEX SINCLAIR
BATMAN & ROBIN
THE BOY WONDER
NO. 4 MAR
DIRECT SALES
$2.99 US $4.00 CAN
dccomics.com

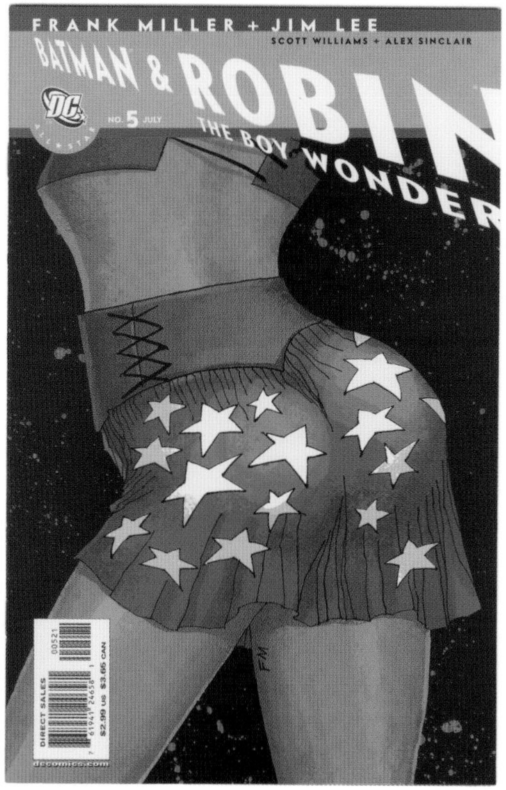
FRANK MILLER + JIM LEE
SCOTT WILLIAMS + ALEX SINCLAIR
BATMAN & ROBIN
THE BOY WONDER
NO. 5 JULY
DIRECT SALES
$2.99 US $3.65 CAN
dccomics.com

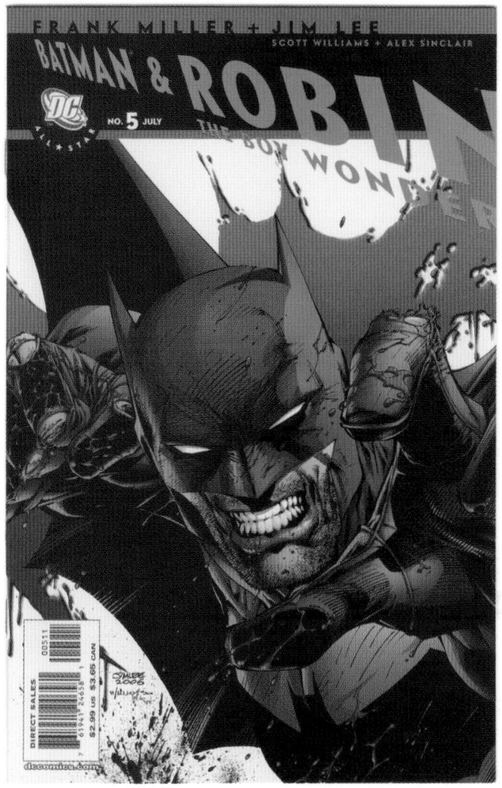
FRANK MILLER + JIM LEE
SCOTT WILLIAMS + ALEX SINCLAIR
BATMAN & ROBIN
THE BOY WONDER
NO. 5 JULY
DIRECT SALES
$2.99 US $3.65 CAN
dccomics.com

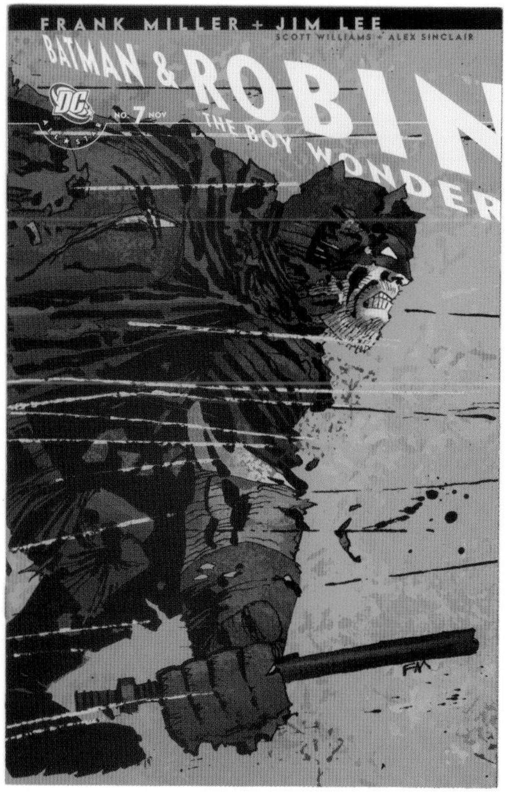
FRANK MILLER + JIM LEE
SCOTT WILLIAMS + ALEX SINCLAIR
BATMAN & ROBIN
THE BOY WONDER
NO. 7 NOV

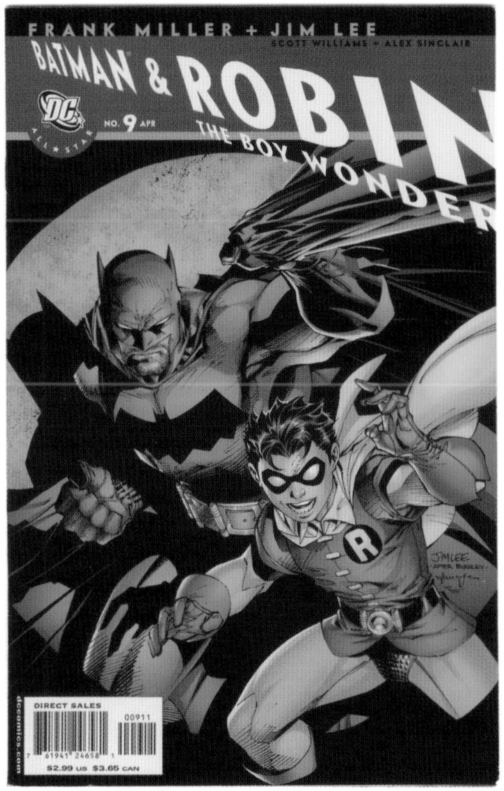
FRANK MILLER + JIM LEE
SCOTT WILLIAMS + ALEX SINCLAIR
BATMAN & ROBIN
THE BOY WONDER
NO. 9 APR
DIRECT SALES
$2.99 US $3.65 CAN
dccomics.com

## Boy, Wonder

Along with All-Star Superman, there was the concurrent All-Star Batman and Robin the Boy Wonder. If the effect of the logo for the former was to take you up into the ether, the goal of the latter was to have it come crashing down into your living room. Typographically it ultimately put a lot of the emphasis onto Robin, but that was okay because this series was really a focused retelling of his origin story by Frank Miller. Beautifully illustrated by Jim Lee, it never got beyond ten issues. But I loved working on both of these titles and relished the opportunity to design Superman and Batman comics by the very best creators in the field: Grant Morrison, Frank Quitely, Frank Miller, Jim Lee, Scott Williams, and Alex Sinclair.

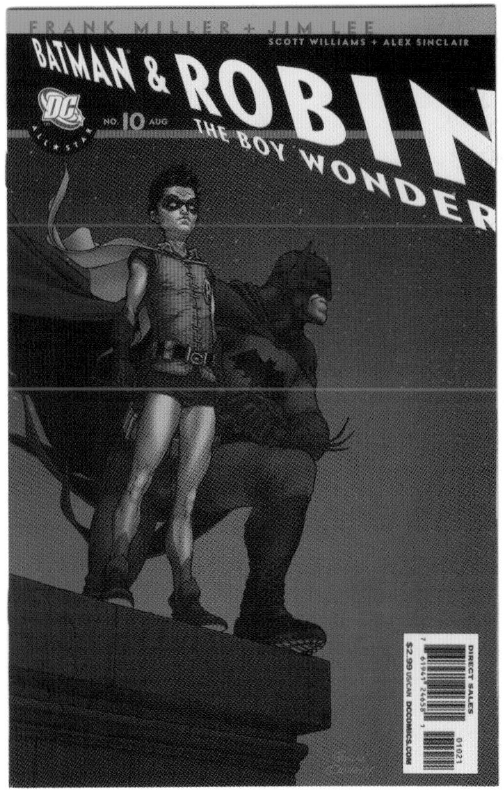
FRANK MILLER + JIM LEE
SCOTT WILLIAMS + ALEX SINCLAIR
BATMAN & ROBIN
THE BOY WONDER
NO. 10 AUG
DIRECT SALES
DCCOMICS.COM

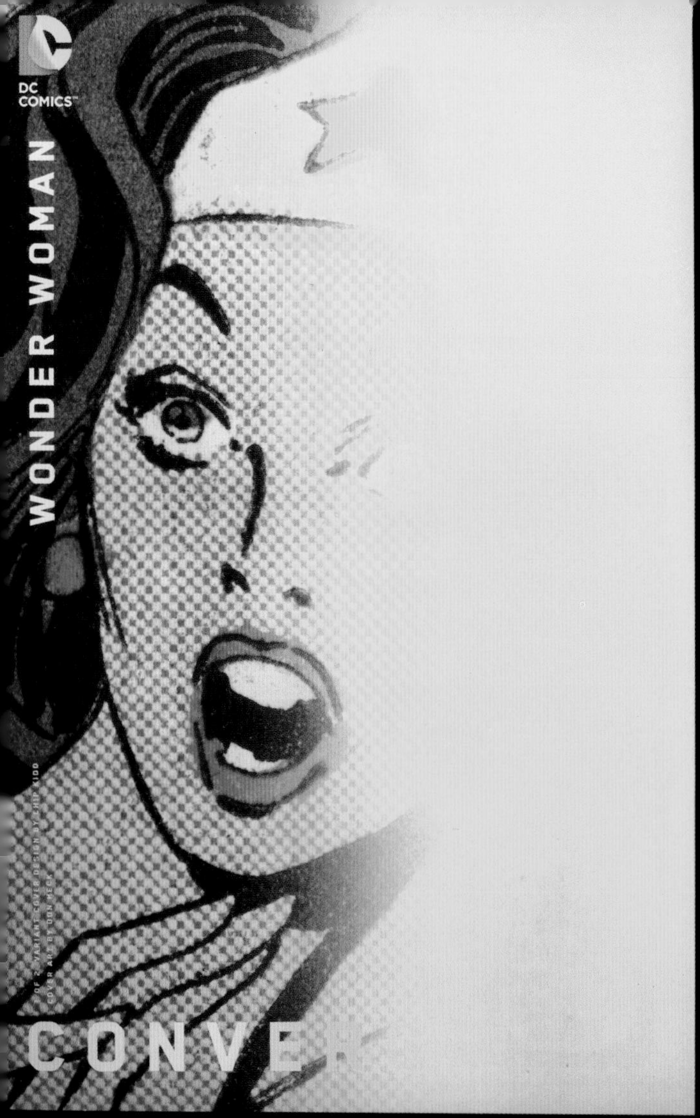
DC COMICS
WONDER WOMAN
CONVER
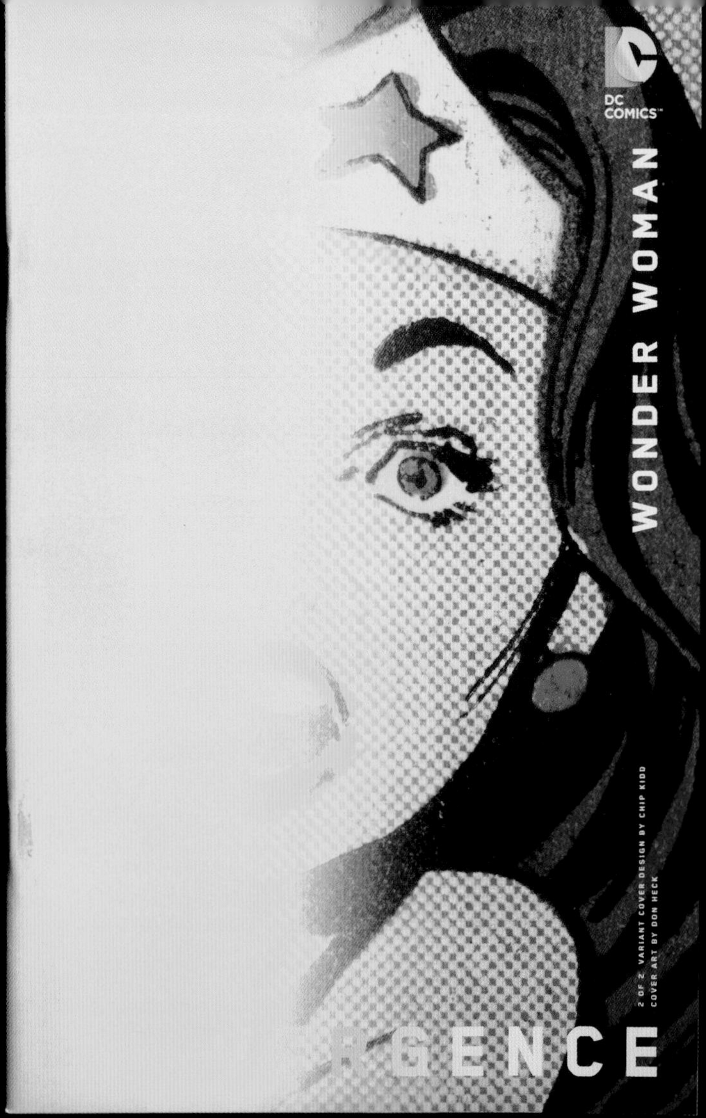
DC COMICS
WONDER WOMAN
2 OF 2 VARIANT COVER DESIGN BY CHIP KIDD
COVER ART BY DON HECK
GENCE

## The Urge to Converge

n the summer of 2014, DC editor-in-chief Dan Didio called me o see if I would be willing to take on a large commission; I prac- cally jumped through the phone to say "yes" without having any dea what it was. A week later, I was sitting in his office with art irector and friend Mark Chiarello to get the story: this was to be huge "event" called Convergence, spanning all of DC's monthly itles. The story arc was about the supervillain Brainiac warping time and space and corralling the hundreds of heroes and villains from the company's 75-year history into multiple arenas to fight one another to the death on a myriad of physical and astral planes. This was major. During the meeting, while everything was being explained, my brain started doing the math: 40 titles a month, four weeks each, twice for each title during the entire saga. The first month the characters are being dragged into the conflict. The second month they are working their way out of it. Dan wanted me to use vintage art from DC's publishing history—that made the project doable if no exactly easy. But I started thinking about them all phasing in and out in groups of two—the firs half and the second. Then you had four weeks in a month, and in my mind that invited the integration of the 4-color CMYK printing process, which has been a staple of comic book production since its inception in the late 1930s (see pp. 218–19). By the time I walked out of the meeting, I had the concept nailed in my mind; it would just be a matter of creating samples and seeing if Dan liked it.

He did. The concept was approved on the spot. To go to finish on the sprawling enterprise, I had the weeks-long help of old friend and then-current DC librarian Steve Korté, as well as editorial assistance on the project from Brittany Holzherr. However, to be fair to Dan as the mastermind of this narrative, I gave him two art options on each title. So I ended up designing 160 covers, twice the original 80. But I genuinely enjoyed it, and what I always had in mind was the experience of fans seeing these in comic book shops and being presented and confronted with the images of their favorite heroes in new and unexpected ways. Once the project was released, I took "field pics" in some of my favorite stores in Manhattan and Connecticut, to show how the resulting covers stood out amongst the competition. Also, I should clarify that the whole Convergence saga (as well as the visual scheme) was a metaphor for the bittersweet undertaking of DC moving its operations from its original New York City location to its new realities on the Warner Bros. lot and its film capabilities in Los Angeles.

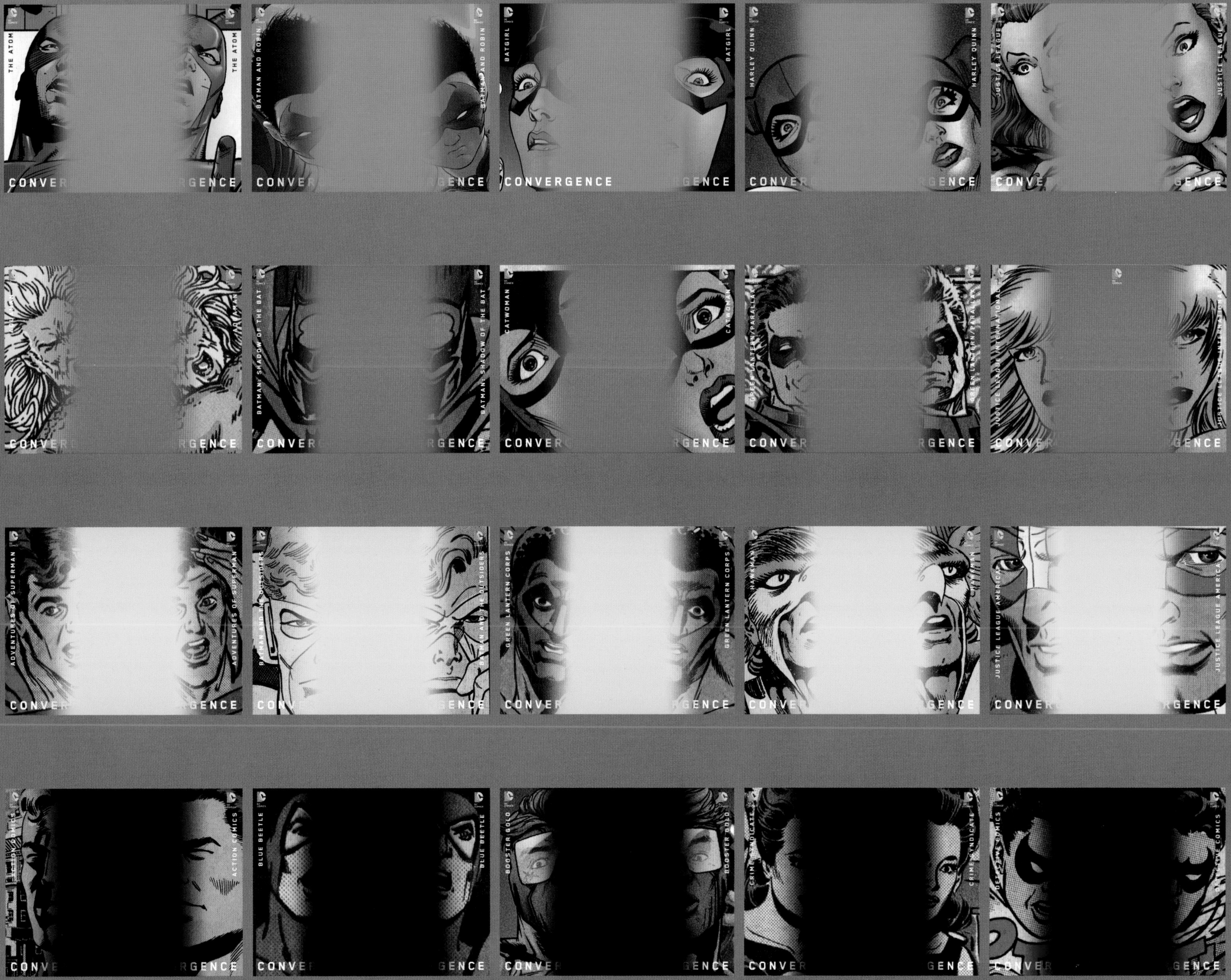
THE ATOM
CONVERGENCE
BATMAN AND ROBIN
CONVERGENCE
BATGIRL
CONVERGENCE
HARLEY QUINN
CONVERGENCE
JUSTICE LEAGUE
CONVERGENCE
BATMAN: SHADOW OF THE BAT
CATWOMAN
GREEN LANTERN/PARALLAX
JUSTICE LEAGUE INTERNATIONAL
ADVENTURES OF SUPERMAN
BATMAN AND THE OUTSIDERS
GREEN LANTERN CORPS
HAWKMAN
JUSTICE LEAGUE AMERICA
ACTION COMICS
BLUE BEETLE
BOOSTER GOLD
CRIME SYNDICATE
DETECTIVE COMICS

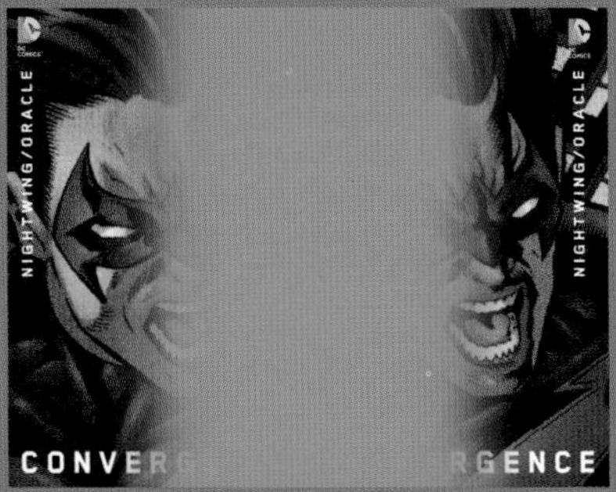
NIGHTWING/ORACLE
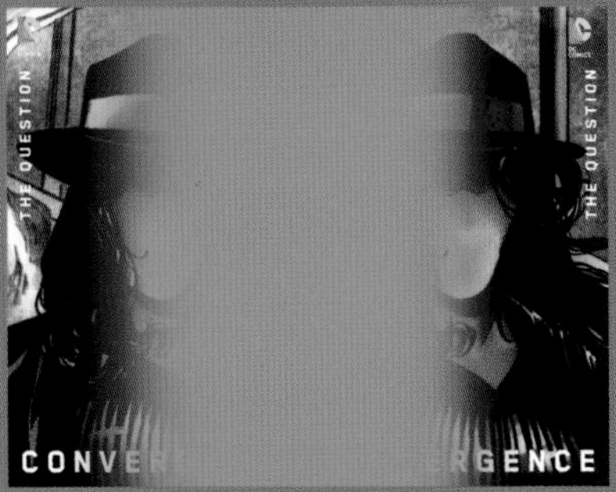
THE QUESTION
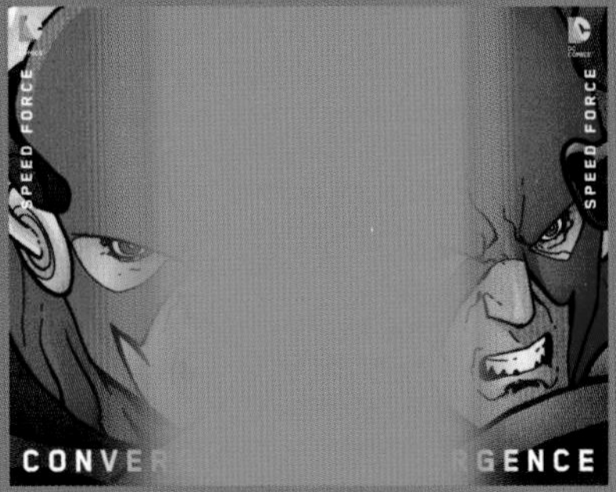
SPEED FORCE
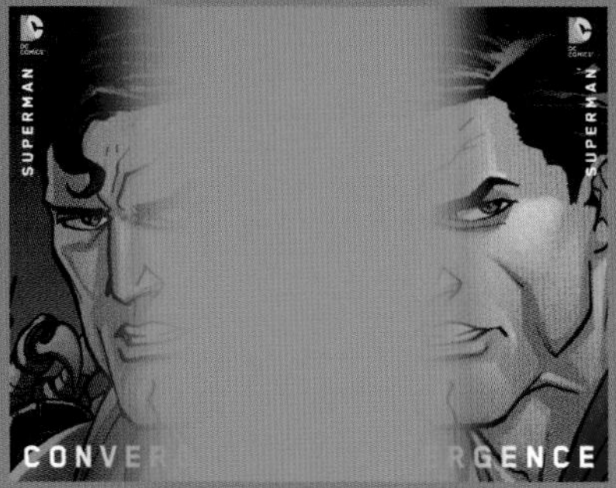
SUPERMAN
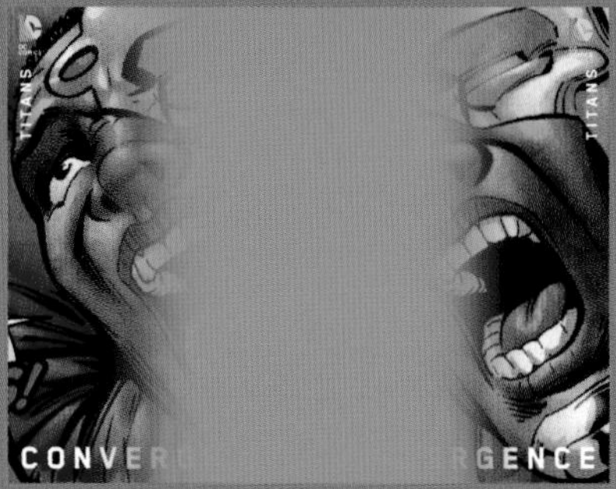
TITANS
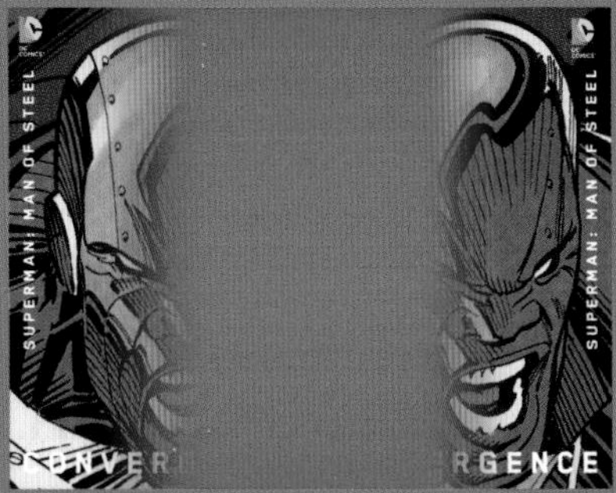
SUPERMAN: MAN OF STEEL
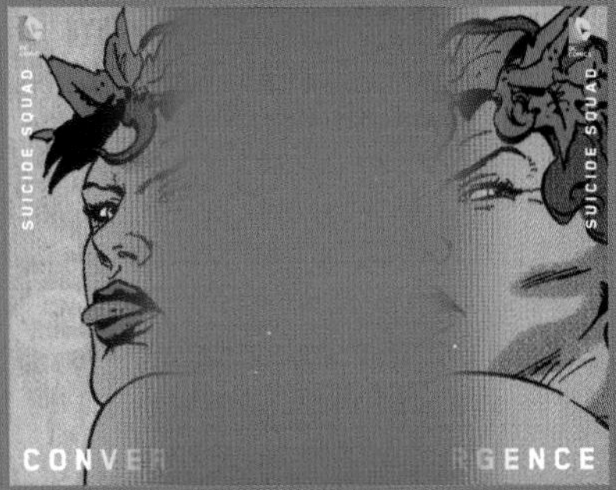
SUICIDE SQUAD
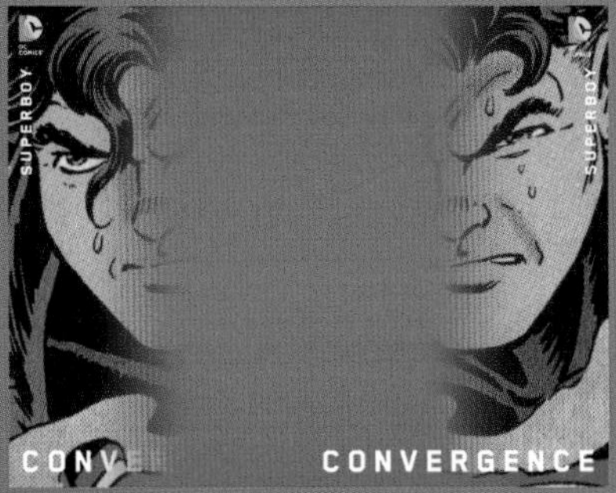
SUPERBOY
CONVERGENCE
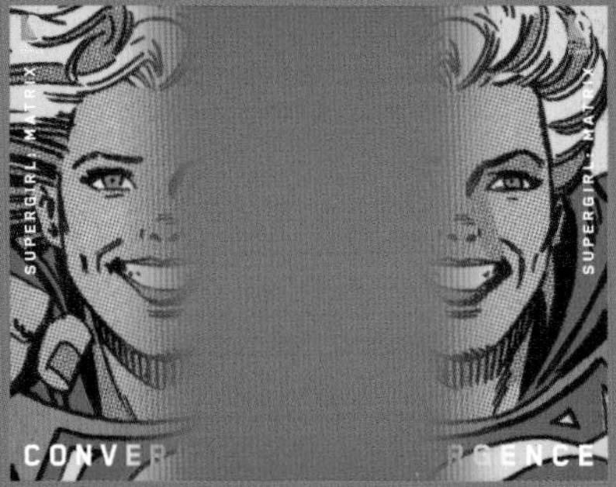
SUPERGIRL: MATRIX
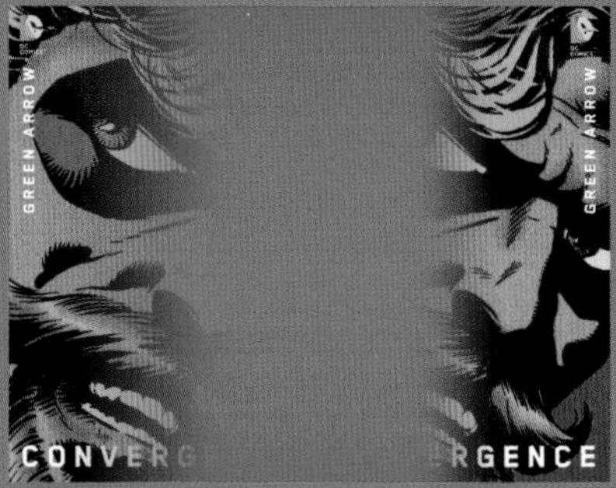
GREEN ARROW



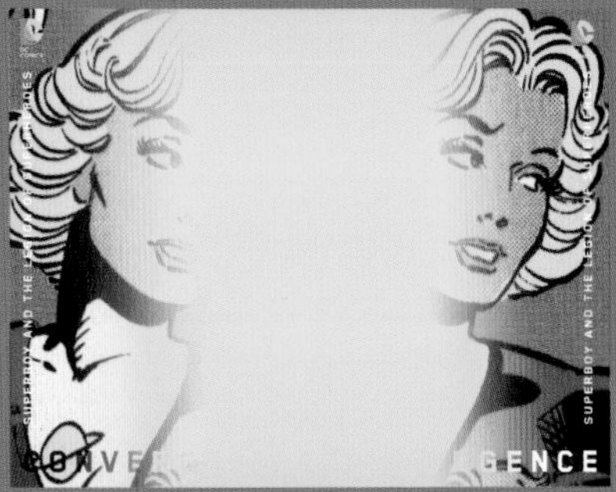
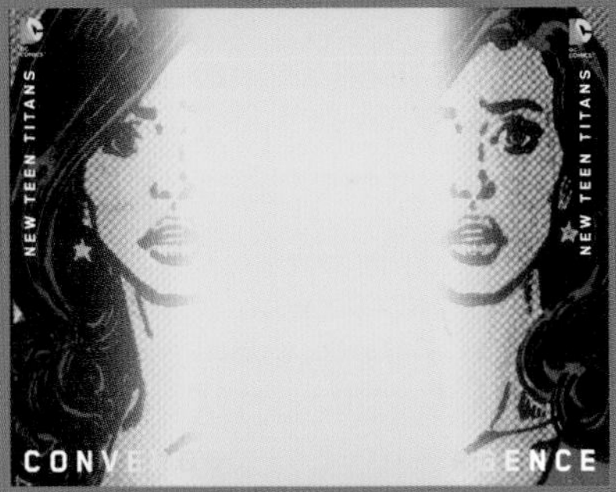
NEW TEEN TITANS
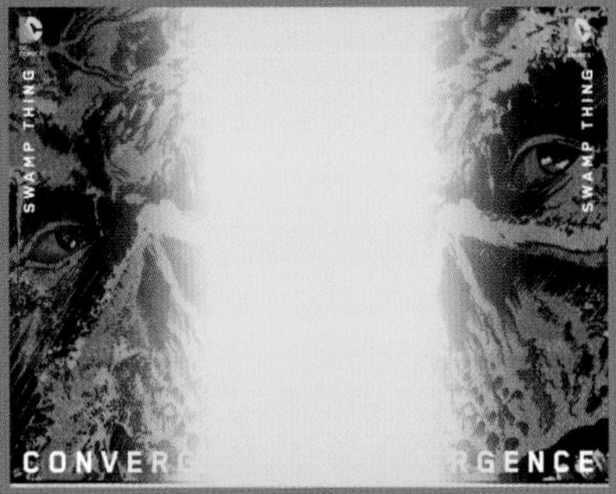
SWAMP THING
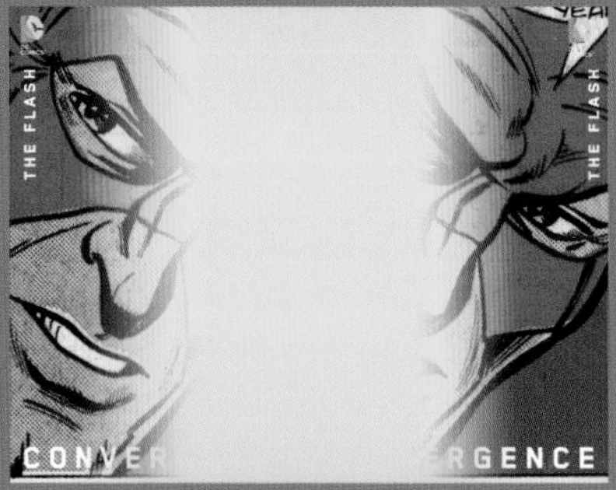
THE FLASH
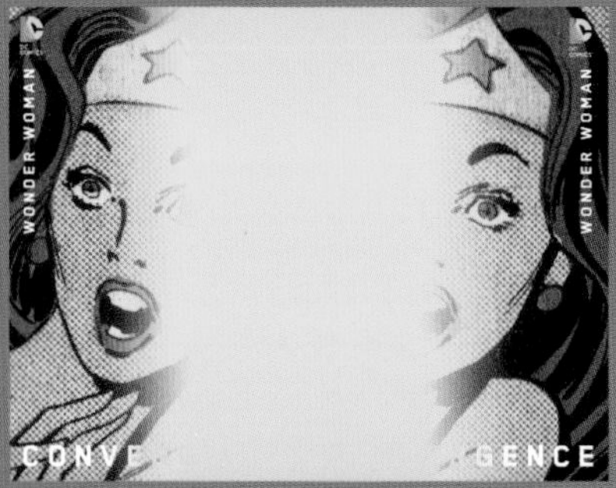
WONDER WOMAN
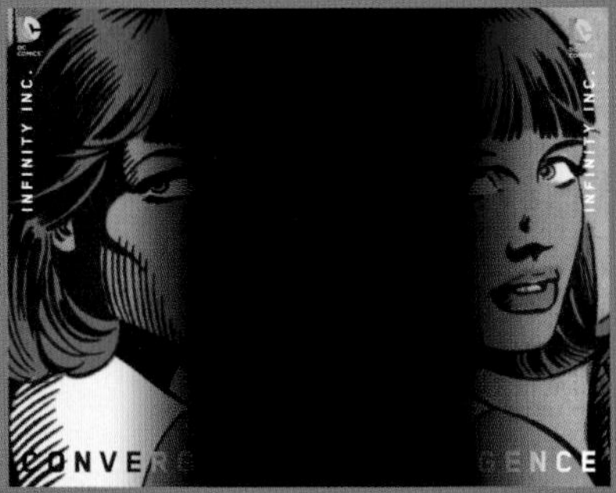
INFINITY INC.
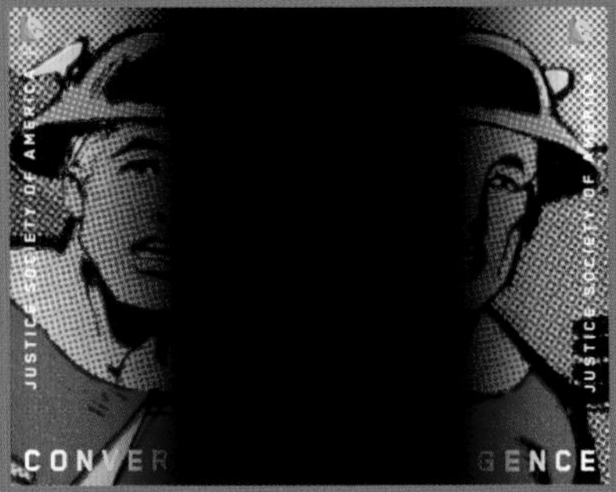
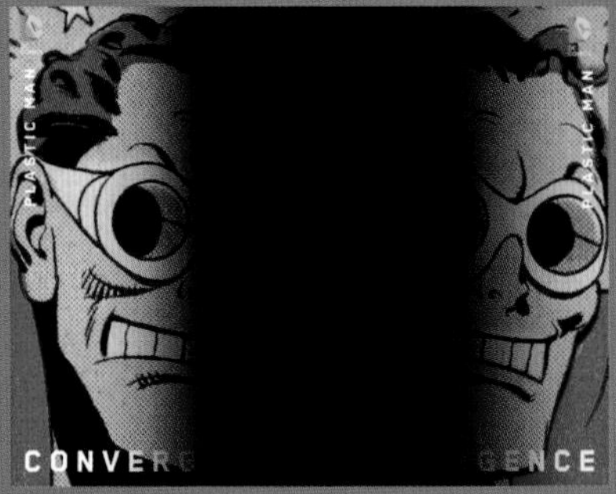
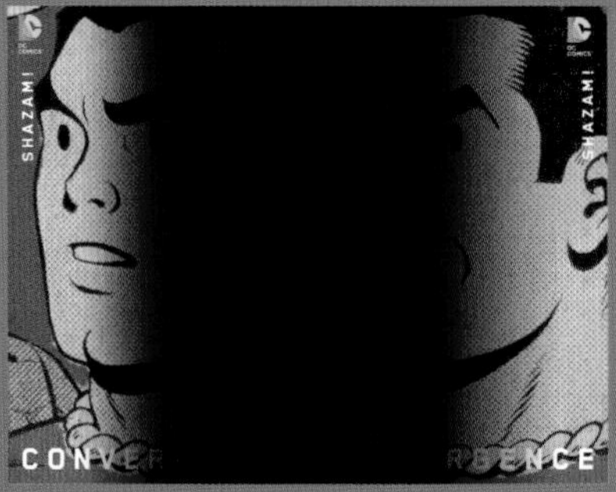
SHAZAM!
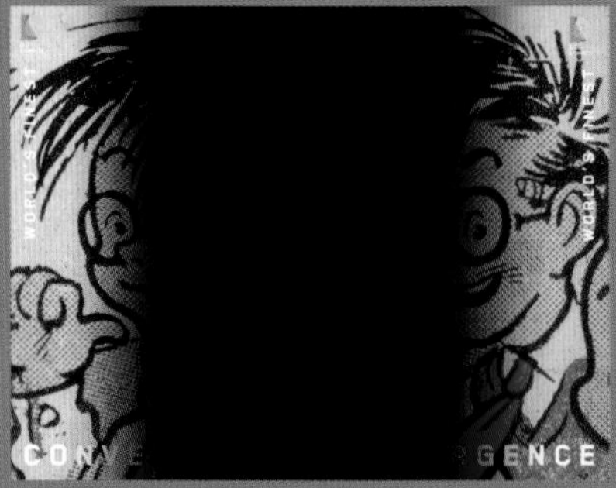

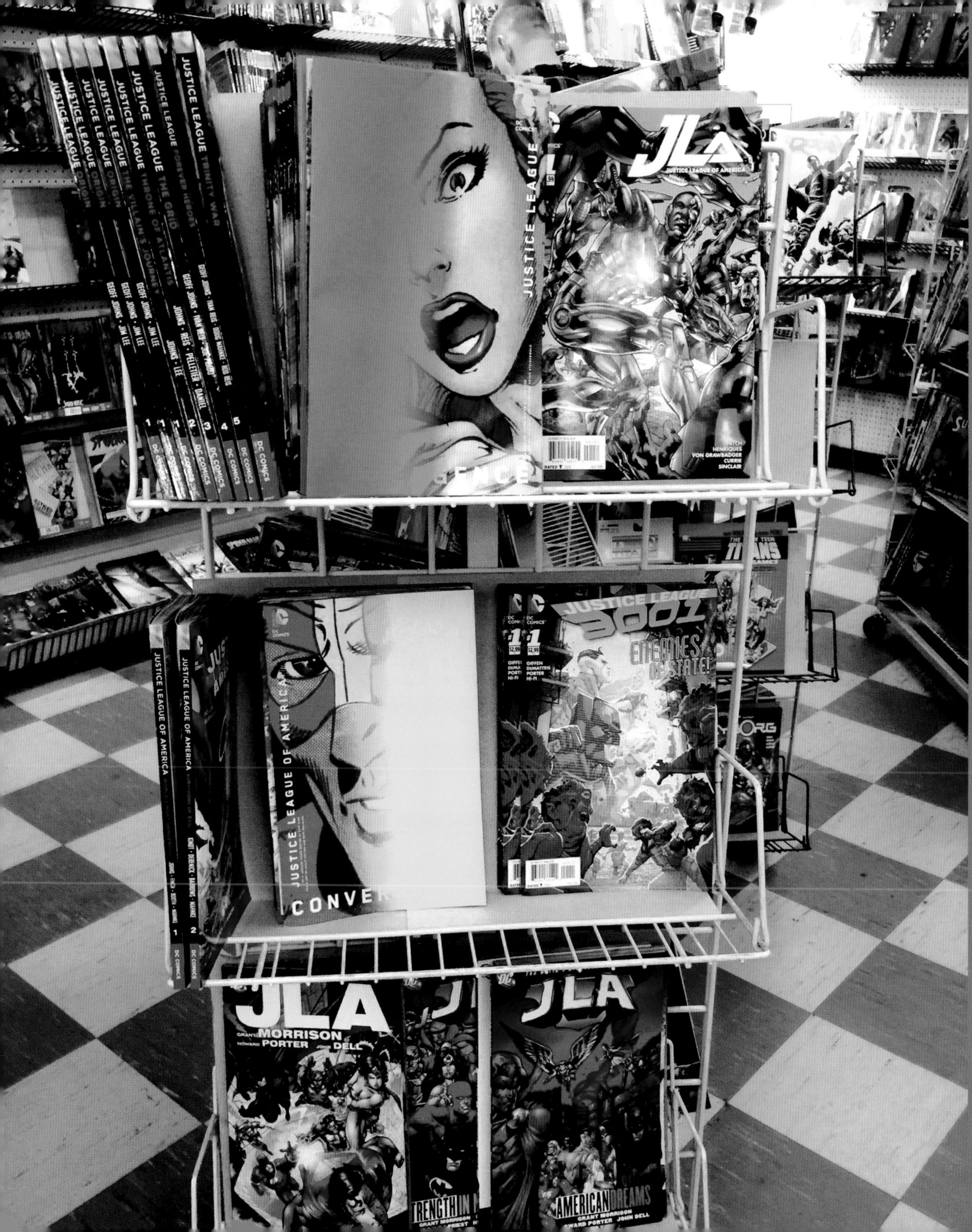
JUSTICE LEAGUE TRINITY WAR
JUSTICE LEAGUE FOREVER HEROES
JUSTICE LEAGUE THE GRID
JUSTICE LEAGUE THRONE OF ATLANTIS
JUSTICE LEAGUE THE VILLAIN'S JOURNEY
JUSTICE LEAGUE ORIGIN
DC COMICS
JLA
JUSTICE LEAGUE OF AMERICA
JUSTICE LEAGUE
CONVER
JUSTICE LEAGUE 3001
ENEMIES OF STATE!
JUSTICE LEAGUE OF AMERICA
JLA
GRANT MORRISON
HOWARD PORTER JOHN DELL
AMERICAN DREAMS
GRANT MORRISON
HOWARD PORTER JOHN DELL
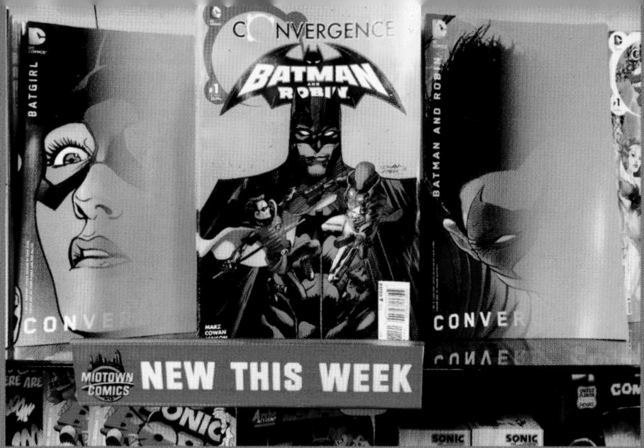
CONVERGENCE
BATMAN & ROBIN
BATGIRL
BATMAN AND ROBIN
CONVER
MIDTOWN COMICS
NEW THIS WEEK
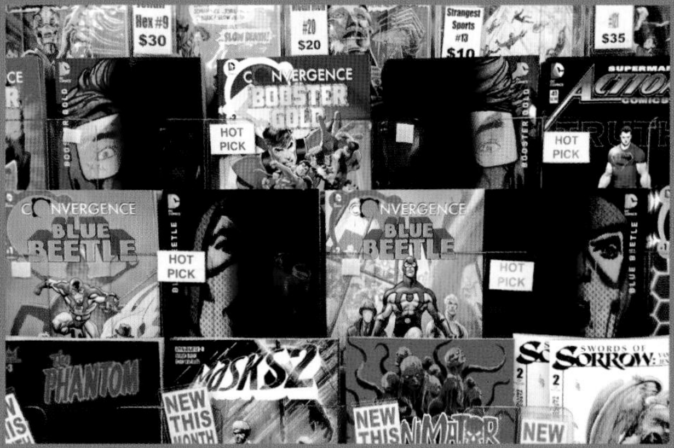
$30
$20
$35
CONVERGENCE
BOOSTER GOLD
HOT PICK
CONVERGENCE
BLUE BEETLE
HOT PICK
SWORDS OF SORROW
THE PHANTOM
NEW
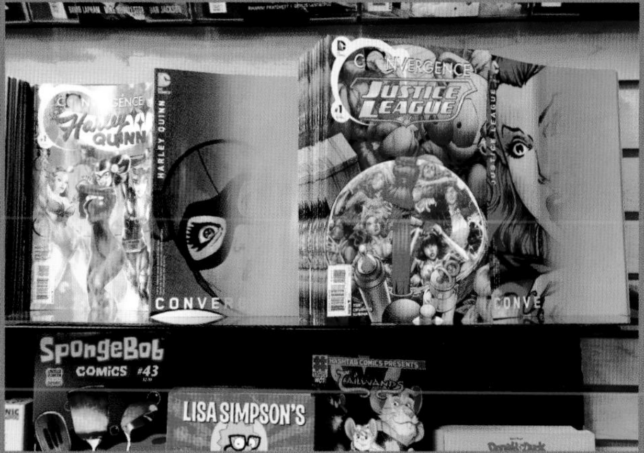
CONVERGENCE
HARLEY QUINN
CONVERGENCE
JUSTICE LEAGUE
CONVER
SpongeBob COMICS #43
LISA SIMPSON'S
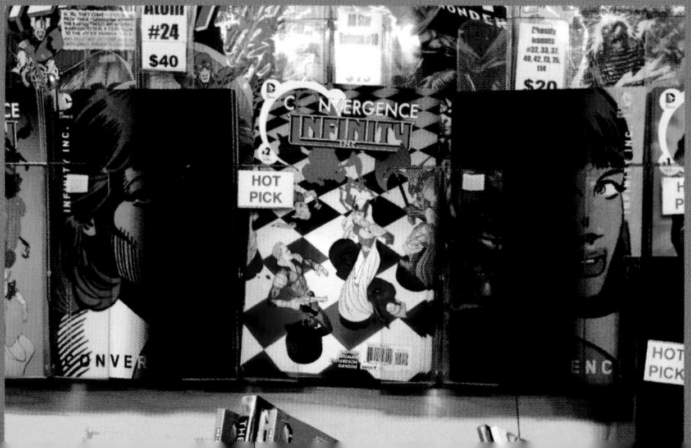
#24
$40
CONVERGENCE
INFINITY INC.
HOT PICK
CONVER

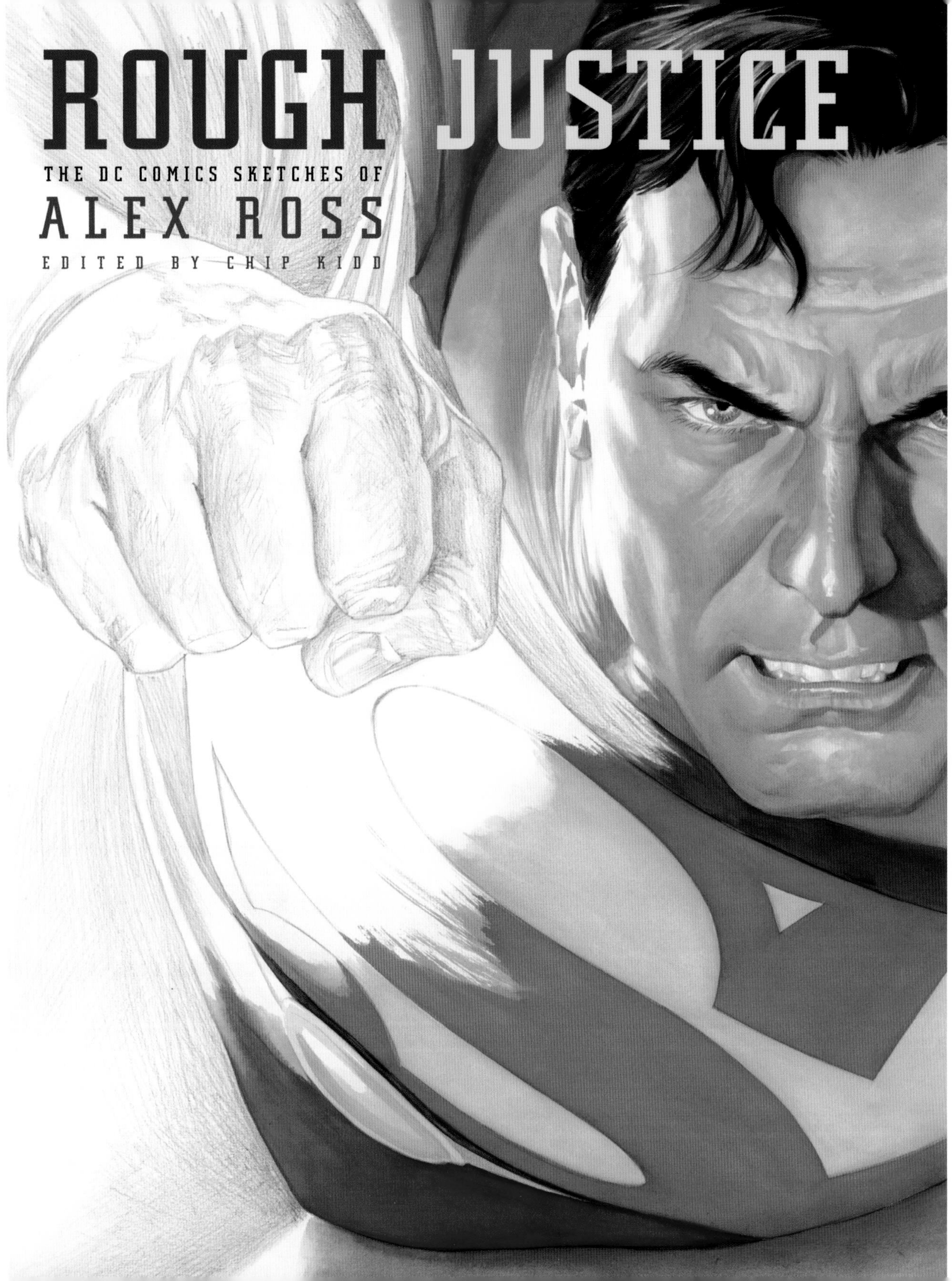
ROUGH JUSTICE
THE DC COMICS SKETCHES OF
ALEX ROSS
EDITED BY CHIP KIDD

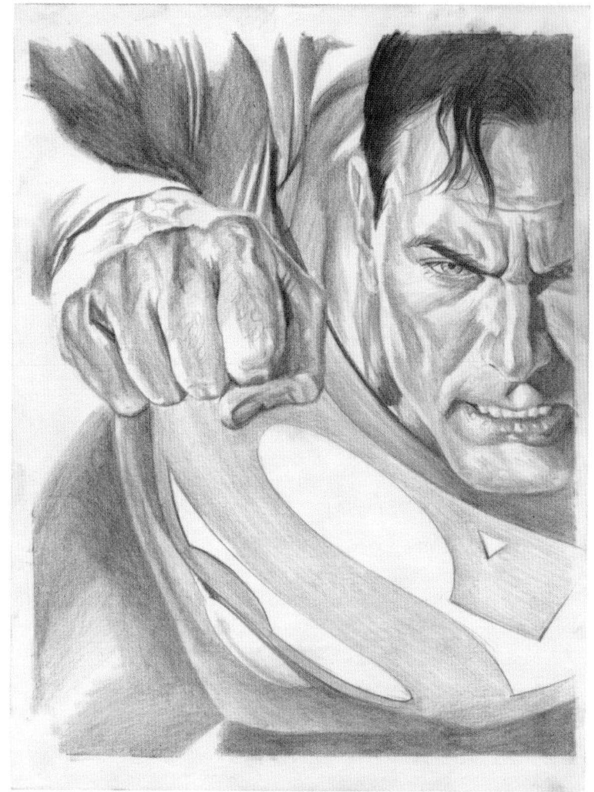

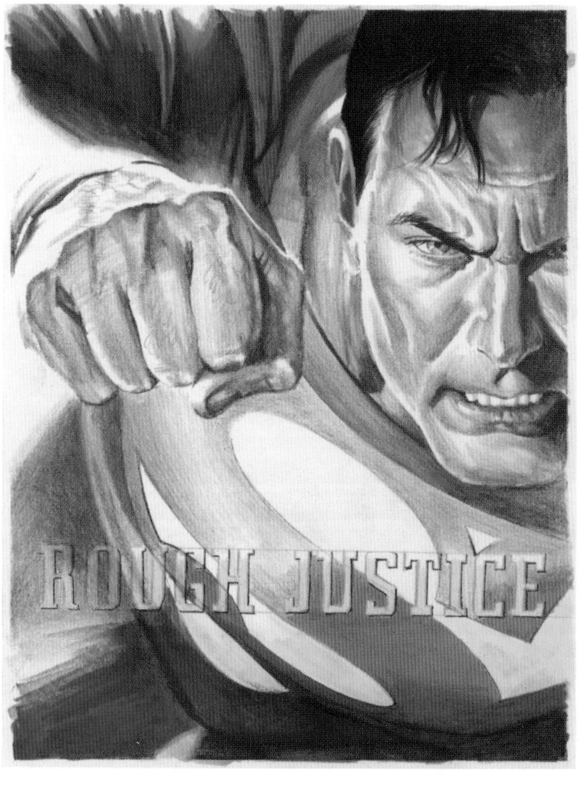
ROUGH JUSTICE

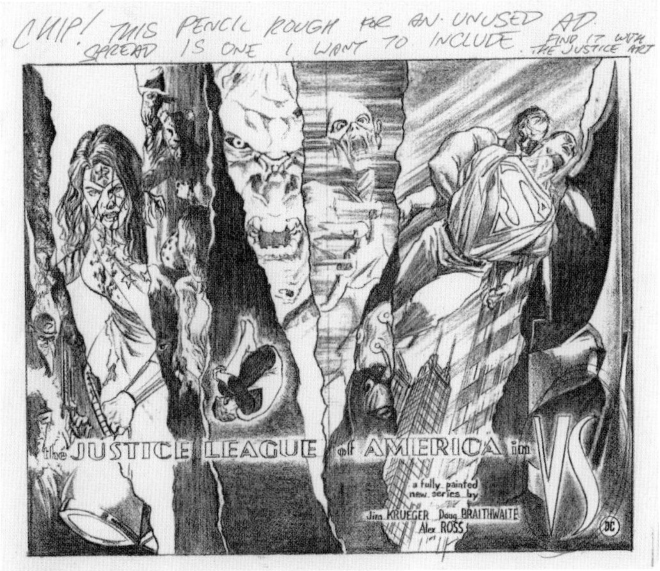
CHIP! THIS PENCIL ROUGH FOR AN UNUSED AD SPREAD IS ONE I WANT TO INCLUDE. FIND IT WITH THE JUSTICE ART
the JUSTICE LEAGUE of AMERICA in VS
a fully painted new series by
Jim KRUEGER Doug BRAITHWAITE
Alex ROSS
DC

## Unfinished Business

After the enormous critical and popular success of *Mythology: The DC Comics Art of Alex Ross,* Alex suggested publishing a sketchbook of his DC Comics–related pencil drawings. I was eagerly game and thought the obvious title had to be *Rough Justice*, referring of course to the preliminary nature of the drawings and the Justice League, which features prominently in the book. We wanted the cover to emphasize the process from pencils to finished paint, and the question was: should we show progress from the center out (opposite, lower right); or from left to right (opposite, far left), which made more visual sense. That was the final jacket for the hardcover edition. For the paperback cover (right), it seemed only natural to swap Superman with Batman, and to progress from finished art on the left to rough origins on the right.

**OPPOSITE, LEFT:** Pantheon, 2010. **RIGHT:** Pantheon, 2012.

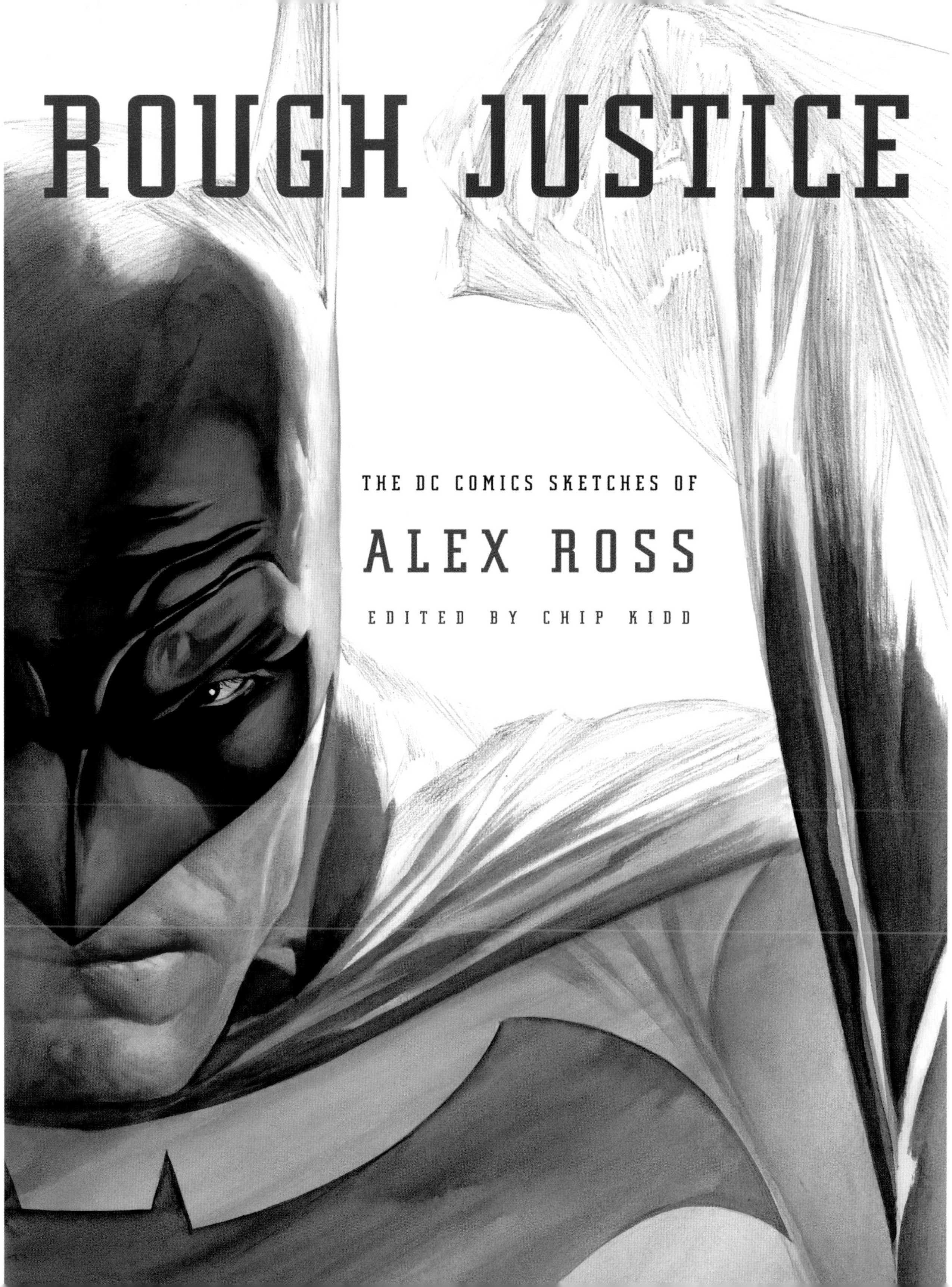
ROUGH JUSTICE
THE DC COMICS SKETCHES OF
ALEX ROSS
EDITED BY CHIP KIDD

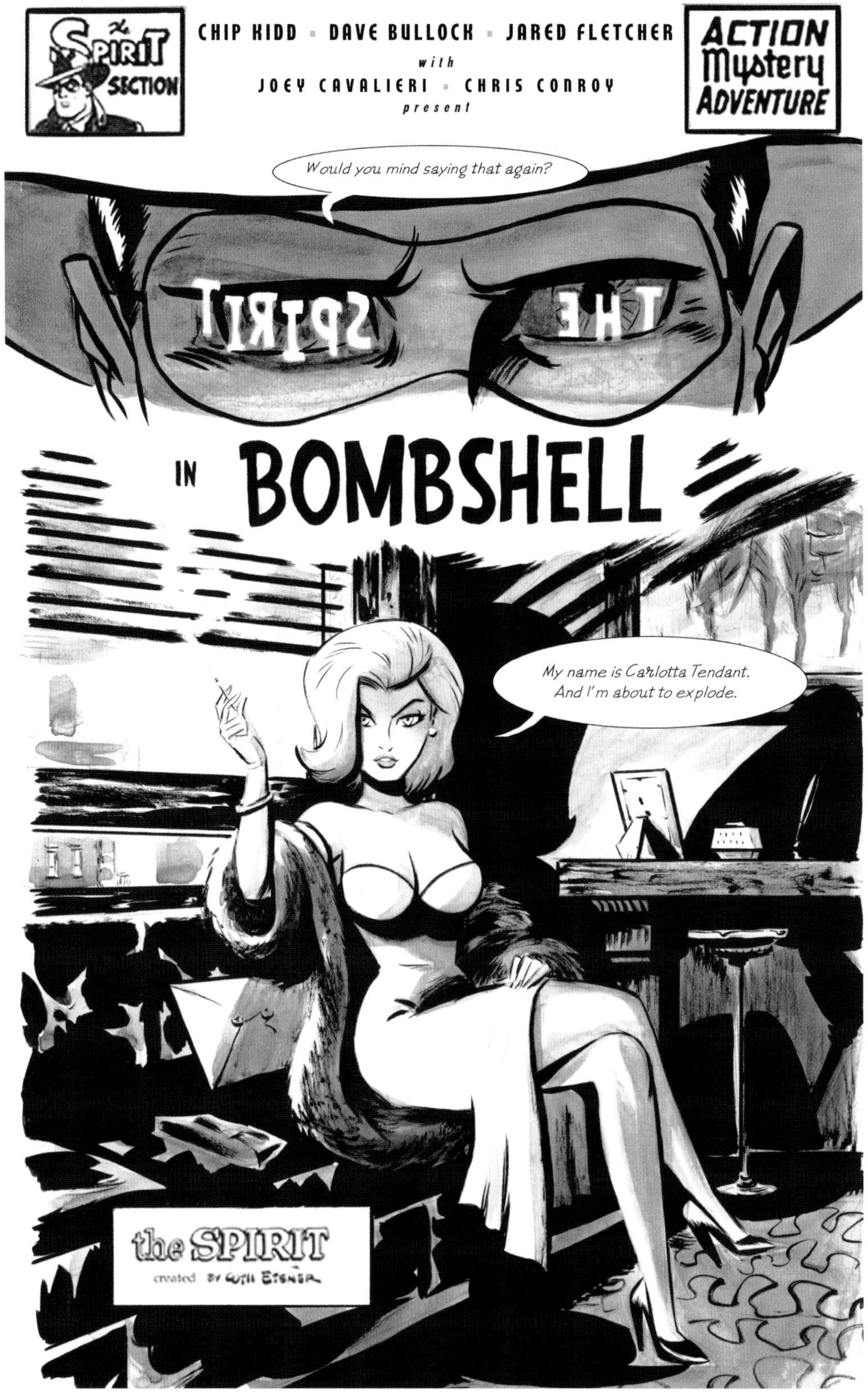
The Spirit Section
CHIP KIDD · DAVE BULLOCK · JARED FLETCHER
with
JOEY CAVALIERI · CHRIS CONROY
present
ACTION Mystery ADVENTURE
Would you mind saying that again?
THE SPIRIT
IN BOMBSHELL
My name is Carlotta Tendant. And I'm about to explode.
the SPIRIT
created by Will Eisner

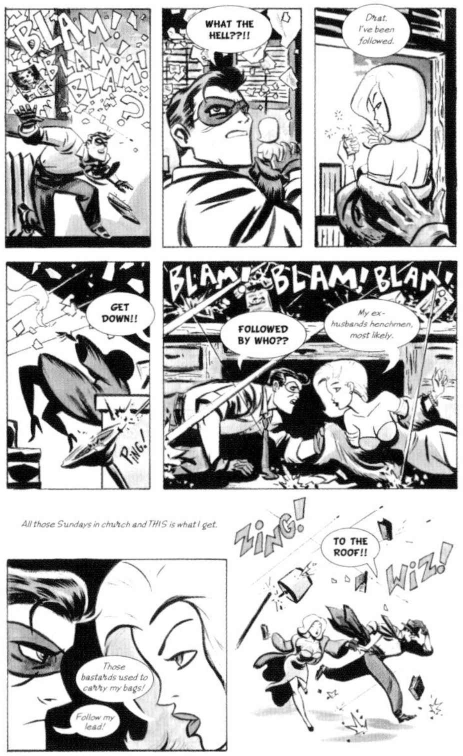
BLAM! BLAM! BLAM!
WHAT THE HELL??!!
Drat. I've been followed.
GET DOWN!!
PING!
BLAM! BLAM! BLAM!
FOLLOWED BY WHO??
My ex-husbands henchmen, most likely.
All those Sundays in church and THIS is what I get.
Those bastards used to carry my bags!
Follow my lead!
ZING!
TO THE ROOF!!
WIZ!

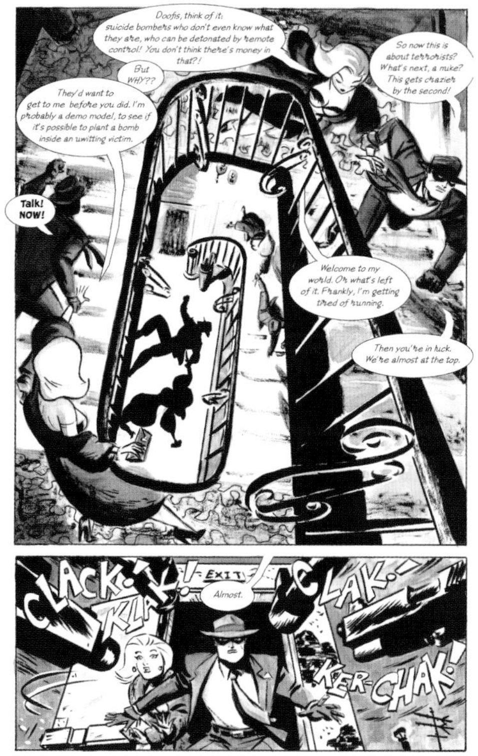
Doofis, think of it: suicide bombers who don't even know what they are, who can be detonated by remote control! You don't think there's money in that?!
So now this is about terrorists? What's next, a nuke? This gets crazier by the second!
But WHY??
They'd want to get to me before you did. I'm probably a demo model, to see if it's possible to plant a bomb inside an unwitting victim.
Talk! NOW!
Welcome to my world. Or what's left of it. Frankly, I'm getting tired of running.
Then you're in luck. We're almost at the top.
CLACK! KLAK!
EXIT
Almost.
CLAK!
KER-CHAK!

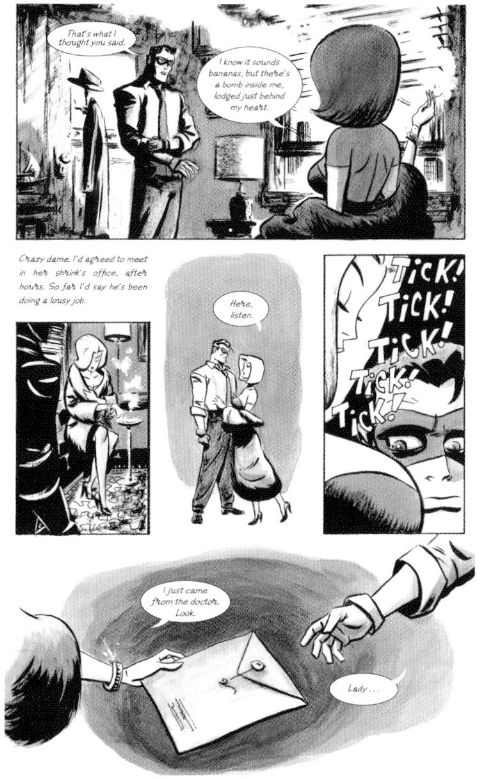
That's what I thought you said.
I know it sounds bananas, but there's a bomb inside me, lodged just behind my heart.
Crazy dame. I'd agreed to meet in her shrink's office, after hours. So far I'd say he's been doing a lousy job.
Here, listen.
TICK! TICK! TICK! TICK! TICK!
I just came from the doctor. Look.
Lady...

In 2010, DC Comics editor Joey Cavalieri enlisted me to write a ten-page story about Will Eisner's masked detective, The Spirit, as a backup feature for the character's monthly comics title. I had become obsessed with the idea that a human being could become an unwitting explosive device via ingested microcomponents, which could cohere within the body to become a bomb, and this opportunity seemed perfect to explore that. Alas, the monthly title was canceled before the fully completed story ran. Shown for the first time here, with art by the brilliantly talented Dave Bullock, it's sitting in a drawer somewhere at DC Entertainment. I hope it eventually sees the light of day.

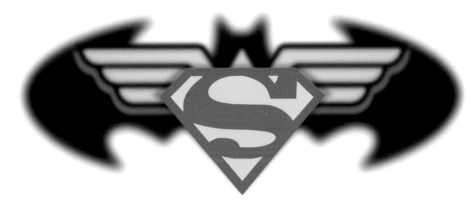

Mark Chiarello hired me to design a logo for Trinity (this page), a year-long weekly comics series featuring Superman, Batman, and Wonder Woman.

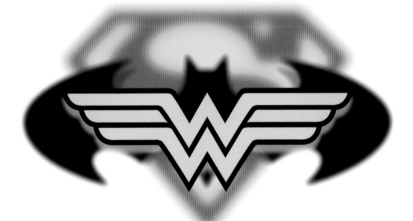

My idea was that the three characters' logos would be layered onto one another and switch prominence and levels of focus with each issue. Dozens of combinations were possible while still providing a unified series look for all 52 issues.

TRINITY
#38
FEB 18 2009
BUSIEK
BAGLEY
with NICIEZA NORTON THIBERT & WONG
TM & © DC COMICS
DIRECT SALES
$2.99 US
DCCOMICS.COM

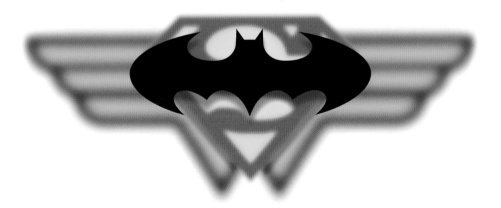

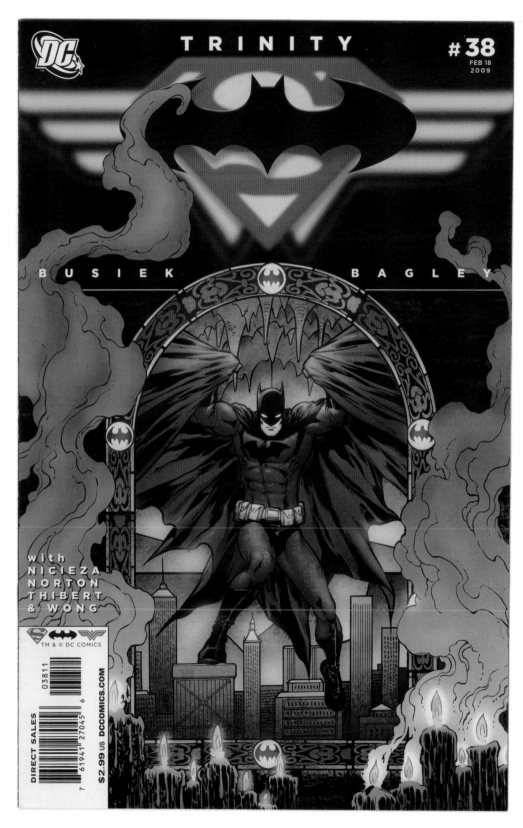

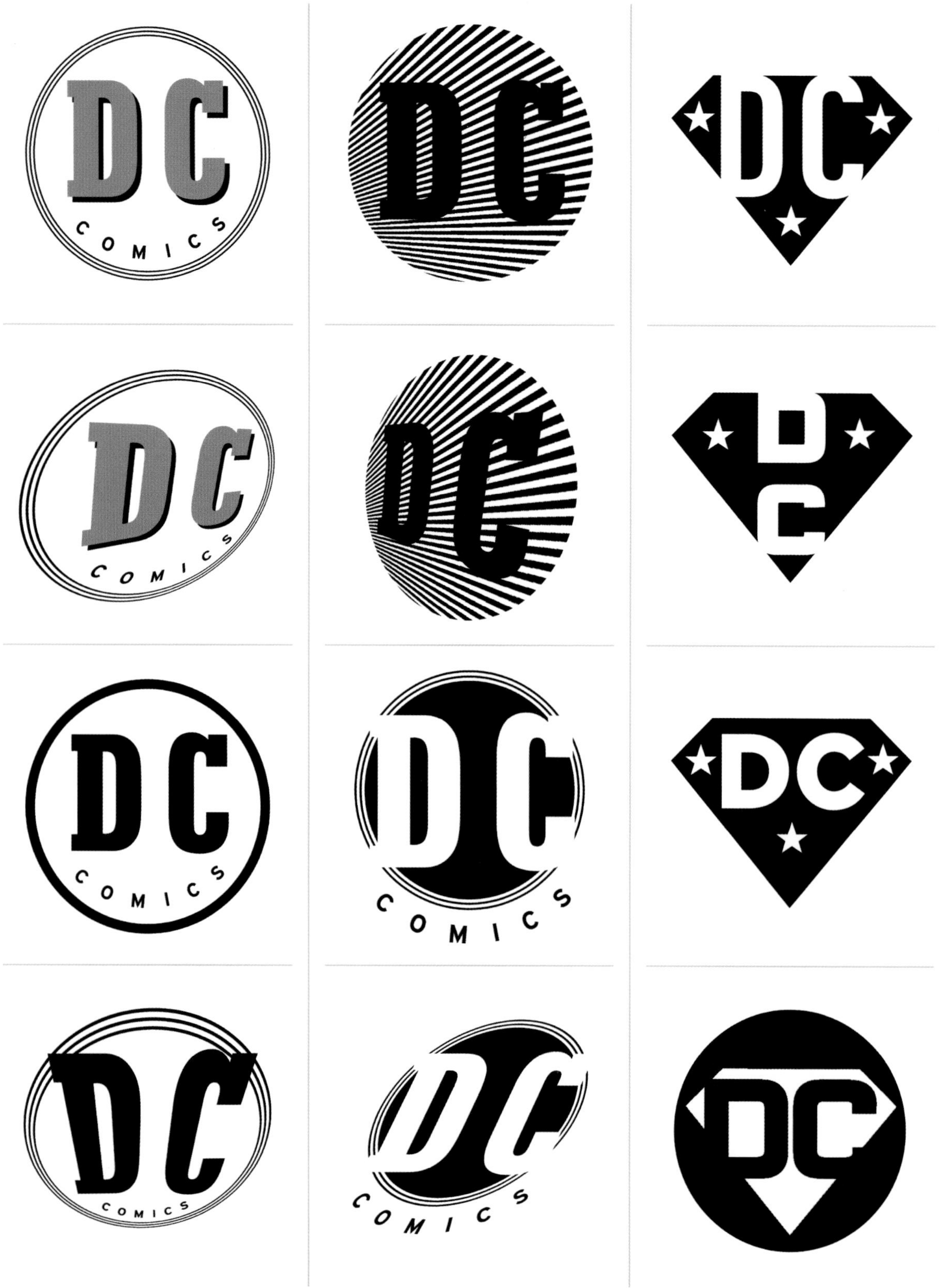

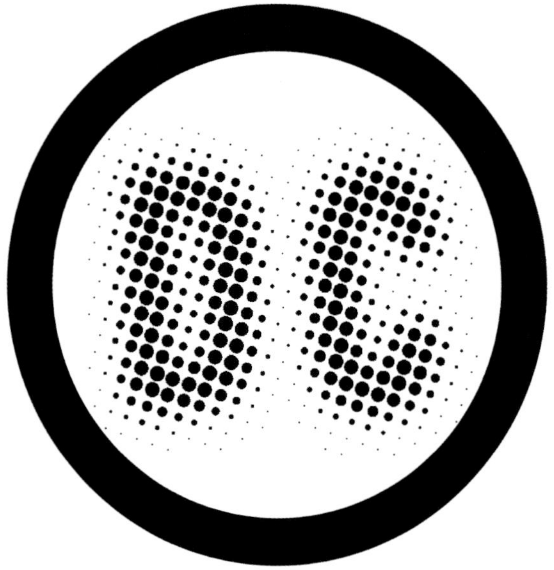

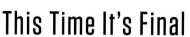

## This Time It's Final

I'll never forget the lunch I had with Mark Chiarello at San Diego Comic-Con 2013 when he all of a sudden declared, "I want you to think about redesigning this," and he placed on the table the current version of the DC Comics logo (see examples opposite on all eight covers). I was amazed and flattered. As a DC Comics fanboy graphic designer, this would be the assignment of a lifetime. I submitted everything you see at left, but nothing hit the mark. Oh well. Much fun to work on, though, regardless. I am pleased to say that an old friend and esteemed graphic design peer Emily Oberman, from the legendary design firm Pentagram, ultimately executed the handsome final mark, which I hope they stick with for the rest of eternity.

*Final Crisis* (opposite) was a 7-issue comics series by writer Grant Morrison (see *All-Star Superman*) set to shake up the entire DC Universe with all sorts of epic and cosmic goings-on. I presented the idea that with each issue the logotype would disintegrate—at first slightly and then dramatically, so that by the final issue (Superman!) it would be barely there. This was the first vertical and progressive/devolving series logo in the company's history.

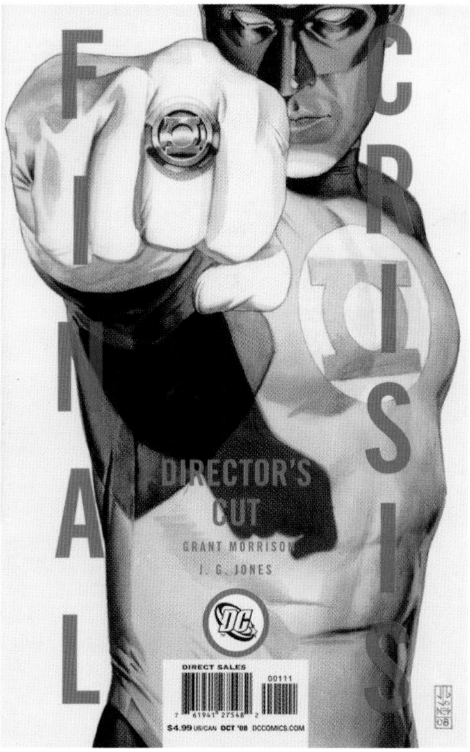
FINAL CRISIS
DIRECTOR'S CUT
GRANT MORRISON
J. G. JONES
DIRECT SALES
$4.99 US/CAN OCT '08 DCCOMICS.COM

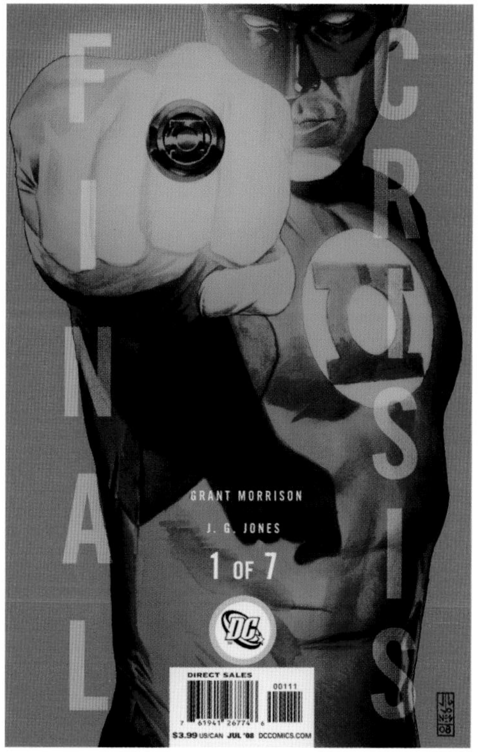
FINAL CRISIS
GRANT MORRISON
J. G. JONES
1 OF 7
DIRECT SALES
$3.99 US/CAN JUL '08 DCCOMICS.COM

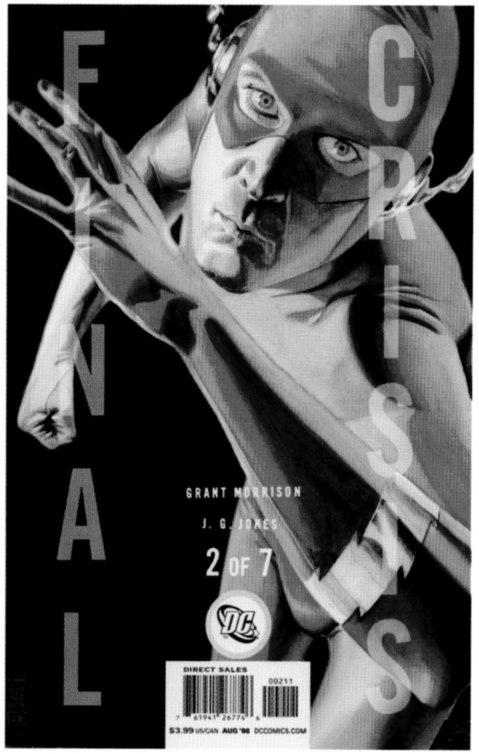
FINAL CRISIS
GRANT MORRISON
J. G. JONES
2 OF 7
DIRECT SALES
$3.99 US/CAN AUG '08 DCCOMICS.COM

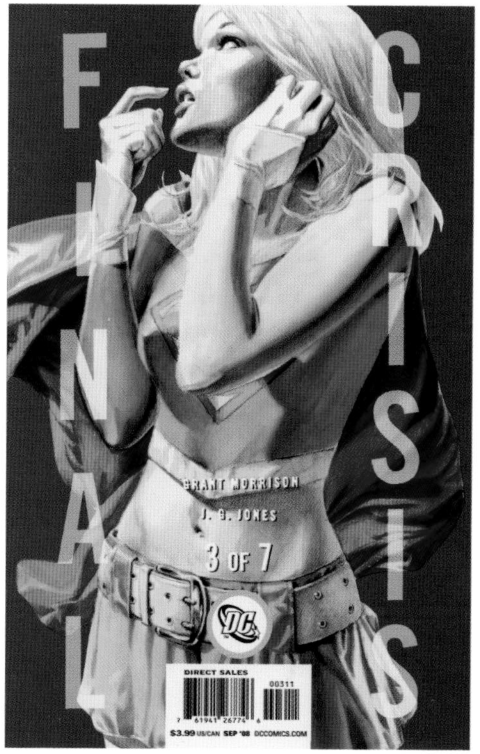
FINAL CRISIS
GRANT MORRISON
J. G. JONES
3 OF 7
DIRECT SALES
$3.99 US/CAN SEP '08 DCCOMICS.COM

THIS PAGE: The gorgeous character portraits are by artist J. G. Jones.



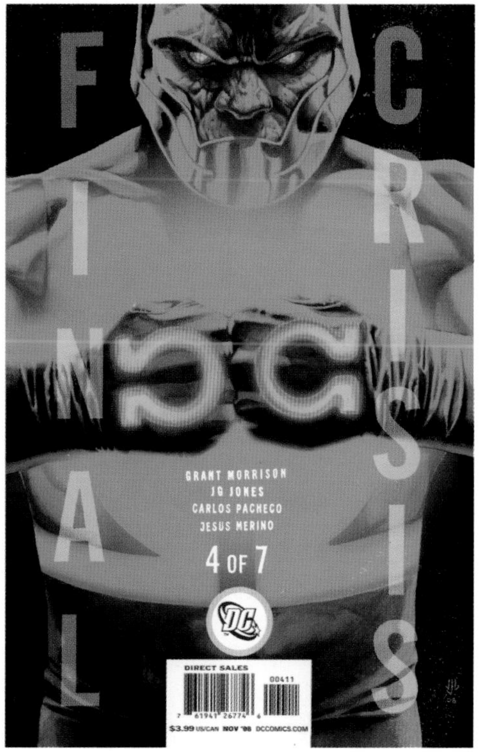
FINAL CRISIS
GRANT MORRISON
JG JONES
CARLOS PACHECO
JESUS MERINO
4 OF 7
DIRECT SALES
$3.99 US/CAN NOV '08 DCCOMICS.COM

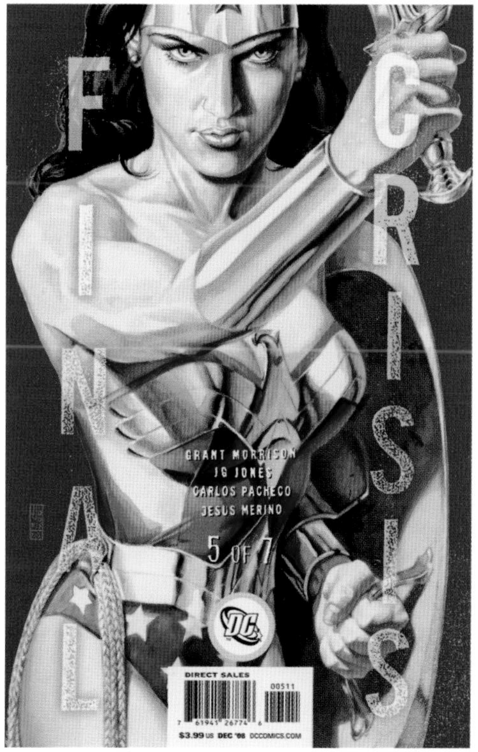
FINAL CRISIS
GRANT MORRISON
JG JONES
CARLOS PACHECO
JESUS MERINO
5 OF 7
DIRECT SALES
$3.99 US DEC '08 DCCOMICS.COM

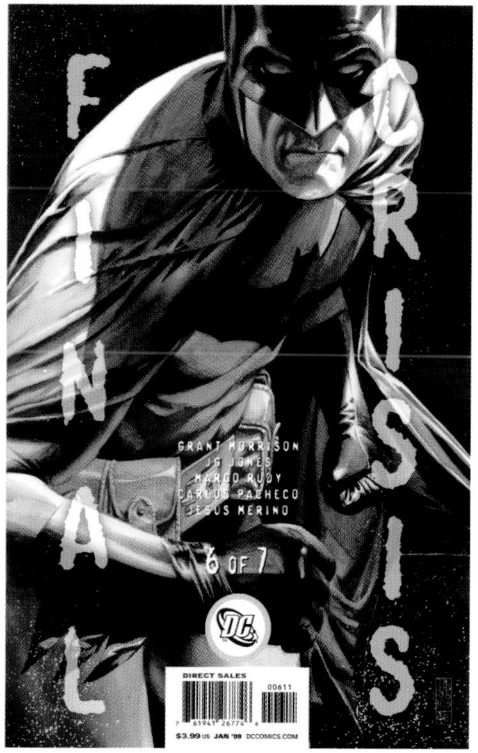
FINAL CRISIS
GRANT MORRISON
JG JONES
MARCO RUDY
CARLOS PACHECO
JESUS MERINO
6 OF 7
DIRECT SALES
$3.99 US JAN '09 DCCOMICS.COM

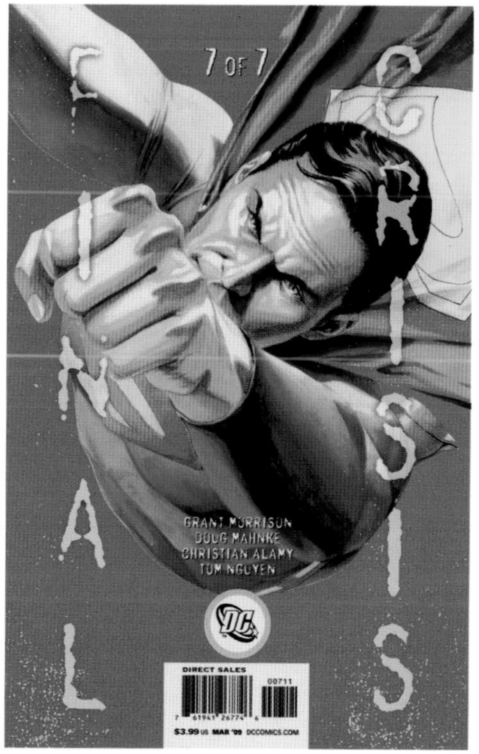
7 OF 7
FINAL CRISIS
GRANT MORRISON
DOUG MAHNKE
CHRISTIAN ALAMY
TOM NGUYEN
DIRECT SALES
$3.99 US MAR '09 DCCOMICS.COM

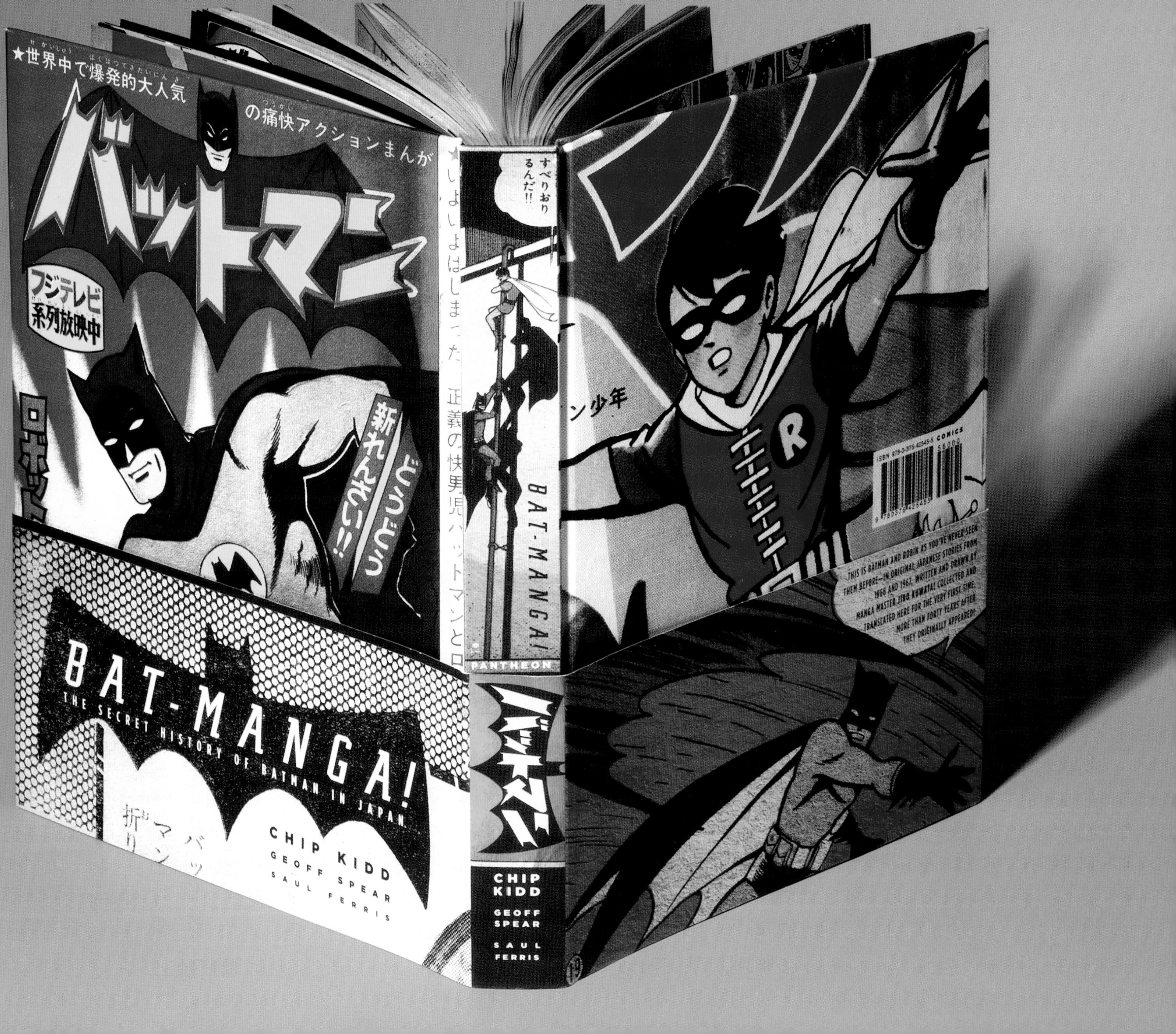
★世界中で爆発的大人気
の痛快アクションまんが
バットマン
フジテレビ系列放映中
新れんさい!!
どうどう
いよいよはじまった 正義の快男児バットマンとロ
すべりおりるんだ!!
BAT-MANGA!
PANTHEON
ン少年
BAT-MANGA!
THE SECRET HISTORY OF BATMAN IN JAPAN
CHIP KIDD
GEOFF SPEAR
SAUL FERRIS
CHIP KIDD
GEOFF SPEAR
SAUL FERRIS
THIS IS BATMAN AND ROBIN AS YOU'VE NEVER SEEN THEM BEFORE—IN ORIGINAL JAPANESE STORIES FROM 1966 AND 1967, WRITTEN AND DRAWN BY MANGA MASTER JIRO KUWATA! COLLECTED AND TRANSLATED HERE FOR THE VERY FIRST TIME, MORE THAN FORTY YEARS AFTER THEY ORIGINALLY APPEARED!

## M. Bat-terfly

The origins of what became *Bat-Manga!: The Secret History of Batman* in Japan (opposite) are explained in detail in that book's introduction and are well-chronicled on the web, but in short: in 1966 a Japanese comics publisher named Shonen Gahosha licensed the rights from DC Comics to create its own original Batman and Robin stories in its weekly manga anthology, and did so for the next year. The writer/artist they hired was Jiro Kuwata, a former child prodigy and co-creator of a popular early-1960s Japanese feature called 8th-Man. Kuwata was remarkably prolific, and for his Batman and Robin feature, he ultimately created 1,012 pages of comics in just under two years. All these stories appeared exactly once, in the *Shonen King* magazine during 1966 and 1967, and then disappeared—no collected anthology, no historical reprints, nothing. After that, gone.

I found out about these comics from artist David Mazzucchelli in the early 1990s, after he had returned from an artist's residence stint in Tokyo. He hadn't actually seen any of this work but had been told about it, and he said that the guy who did 8th-Man also did Batman. I had seen old 8th-Man cartoons on cable TV as a kid and loved them, so the idea that the same artist did Batman in Japan was beyond amazing. But also frustratingly out of sight or reach.

Then, in the mid-2000s, as I was bidding on a Japanese Batman tin toy on eBay, I received an extraordinary message from someone observing the sale (which you could do at the time; you can't now). This was my introduction to Saul Ferris, who was telling me I was about to be fleeced by the seller under false pretenses. He was right; I could see then that the toy wasn't authentic. I voided the sale, and one of my greatest geek friendships was launched. Over time, Saul (located just outside of Chicago) made it known that he had good connections to vintage manga dealers in Japan, and his goal was to build a library of Batman issues of Shonen King. He was eager to collaborate with me on a book of these stories, including lots of other related Japanese Batman toys and ephemera. Once we had enough material to make a substantial book, I put together a 40-page proposal and got an audience with then-president of DC Comics Paul Levitz. He was stunned; he had never before seen any of this material. Once it was all legally vetted that DC still had the

ROBIN - real name, Dick Grayson (sic)
Because even if I die, I will always come back to life
However, this will be the last time we see each other.
Batman and Robin! So you've uncovered my secret!
バットマン
★死神男の巻★
Shut up, Lord Death Man. You evaded the death penalty with your yoga secrets, but you will not do it again!!
But once you guys are buried in that grave, it's final.
He was then buried, but resurrected by his minions, and returned to his evil schemes.
My goons want to bury you two as soon as possible
Mwa ha ha ha, are those your last words?


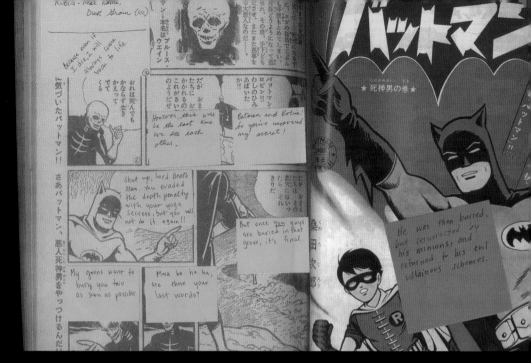

**ABOVE & BELOW:** Notes by the one and only Anne Ishii, who did all the heavy lifting as translator. This is four pages from the "Lord Death Man" saga, which gained particular traction in the media and resulted in a segment of the animated show "Batman: The Brave and the Bold."

Mwa ha ha ha. You didn't realize they were all around you?
Batman, I don't see any goons...
Gasp BATMAN!!
Agh!
JAPAN'S PREFECTURAL BIRDS: Tochigi Prefecture's bird is the blue-and-white flycatcher. It is a field bird about the size of a sparrow, but blue, and has a beautiful voice.
Ah! The tombstone!
He he he Batman isn't immortal. He takes a lead bullet and it's straight to the netherworld.
It's time for Batman's funeral.
Robin, you should take your time observing the

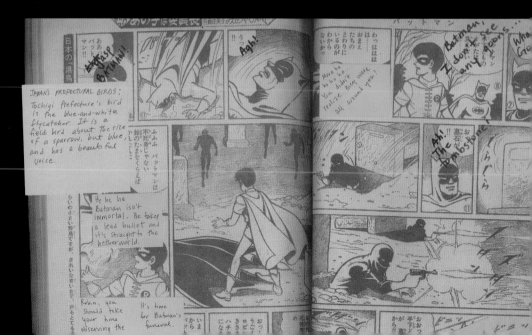

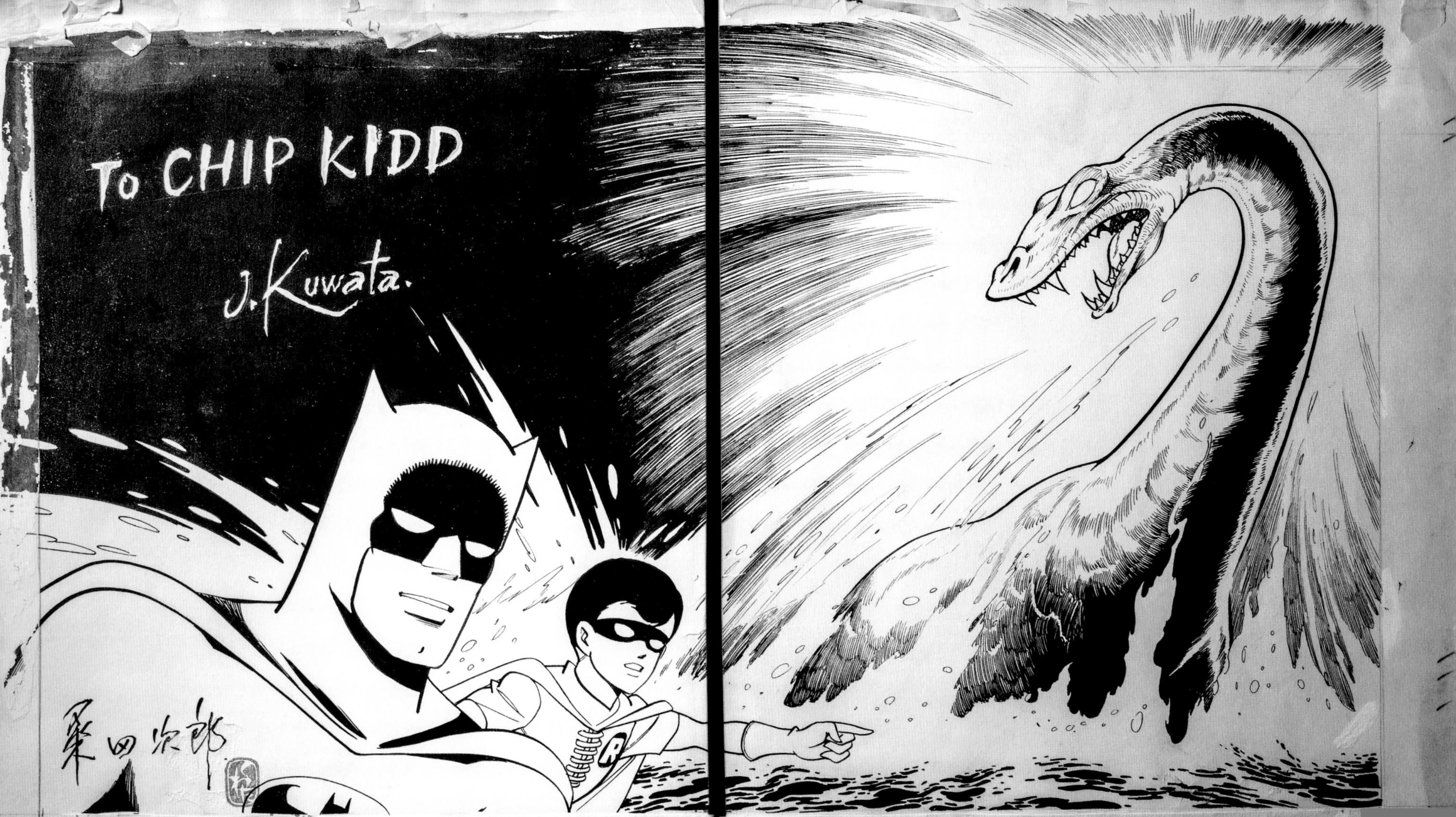
To CHIP KIDD
J. Kuwata.
桑田次郎

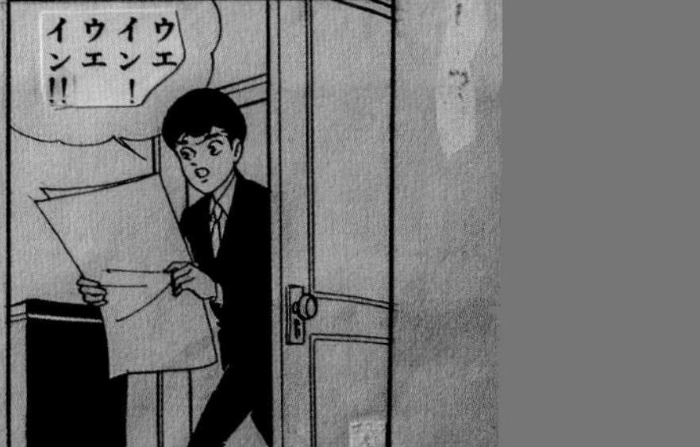
ウエイン！ウエイン!!

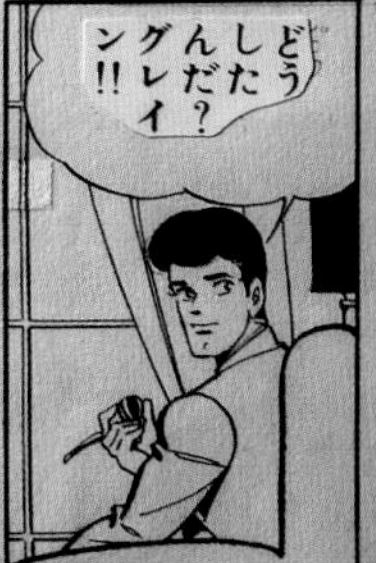
どうしたんだ？グレイン!!

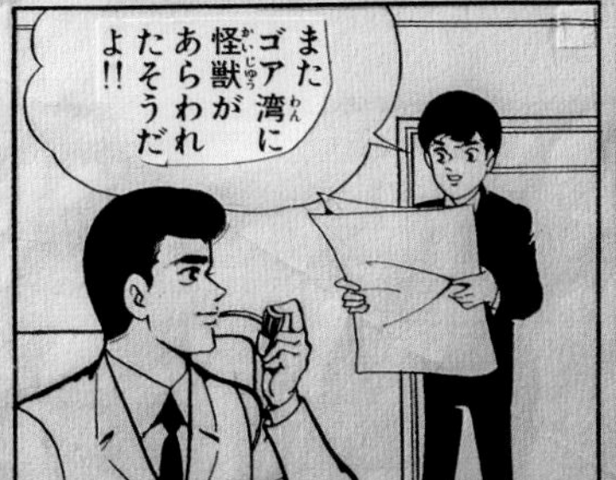
またゴア湾に怪獣があらわれたそうだよ!!

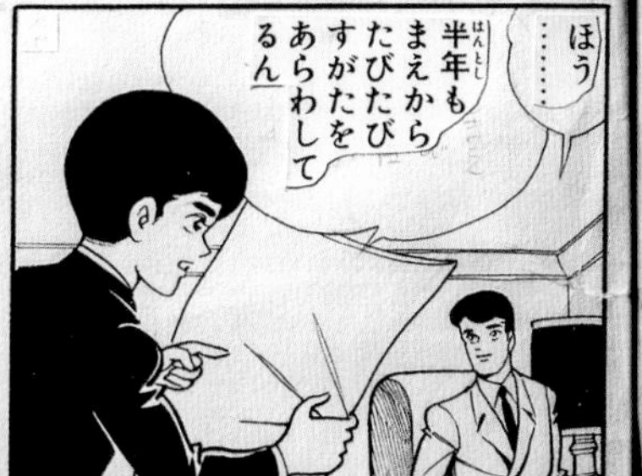
ほう……
半年もまえからたびたびすがたをあらわしてるん

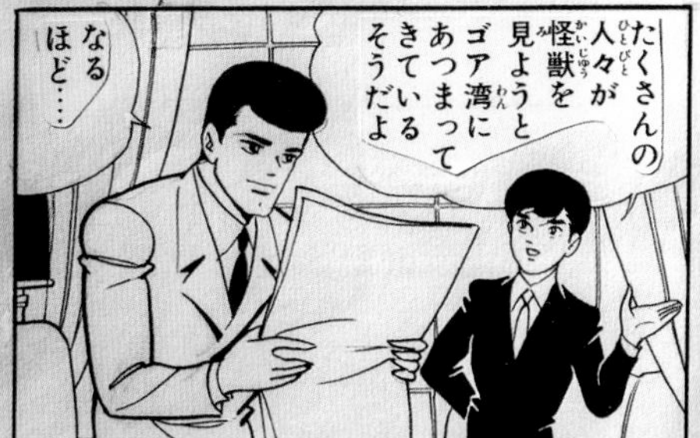
たくさんの人々が怪獣を見ようとゴア湾にあつまってきているそうだよ
なるほど……

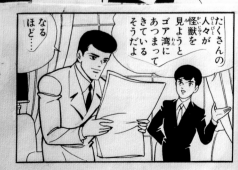

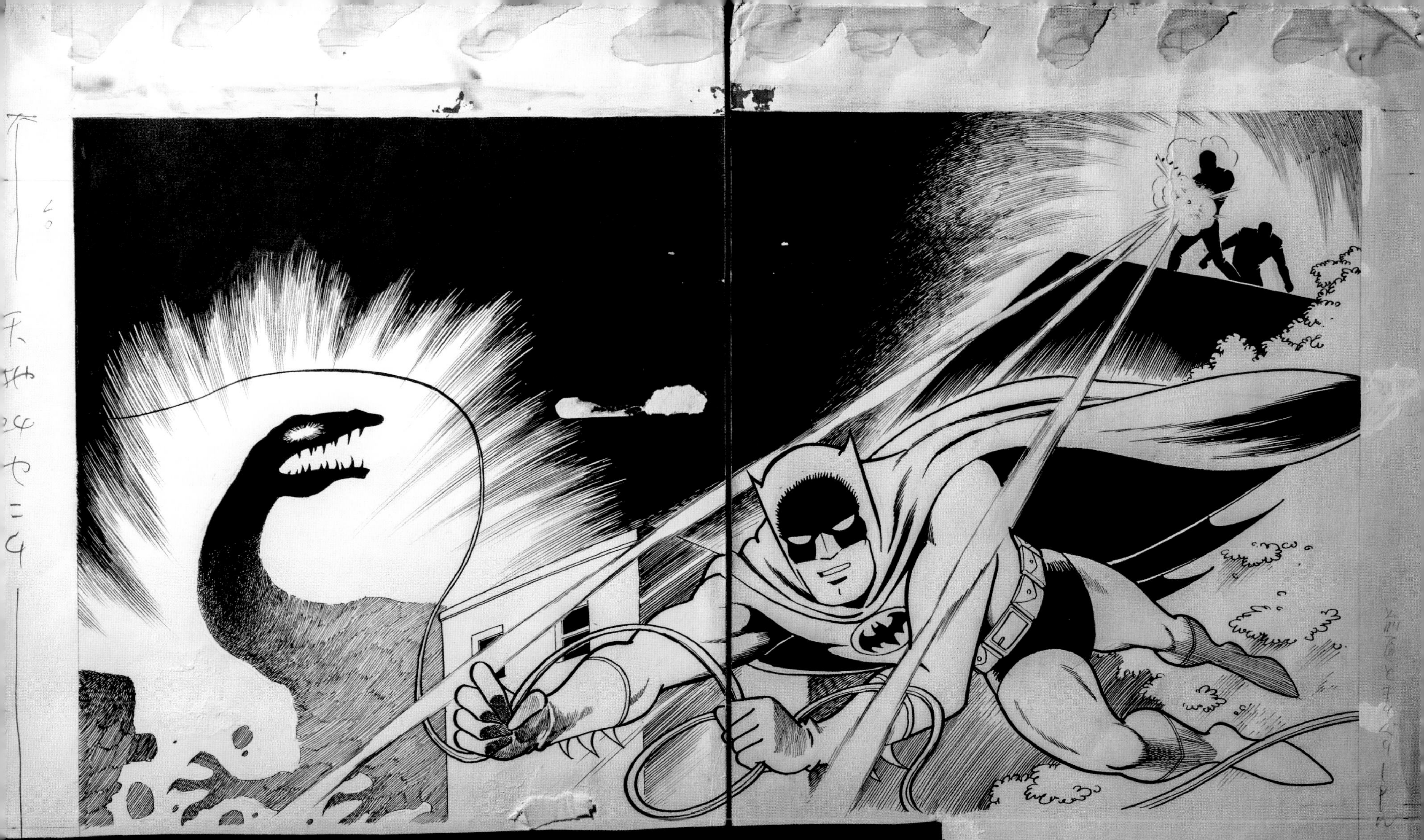

*Bat-Manga!* took a lot of people by surprise, and eventually it resulted in placing Kuwata-sensei in the official canon of significant Batman master artists, as he well deserves. It also led to his publisher returning a lot of his original artwork, 40 years after he submitted it. Which he then allowed me to purchase. The examples on this spread are double-splash pages from a story that was not included in *Bat-Manga!* called "The Sea Monster of Goa." Kuwata loves to draw animals, especially the fantastic kind. This is essentially "Batman and Robin vs. Godzilla," with some machine-gun-toting gangsters thrown in for good measure. But wow, how cool and cross-pop-cultural, so different from what

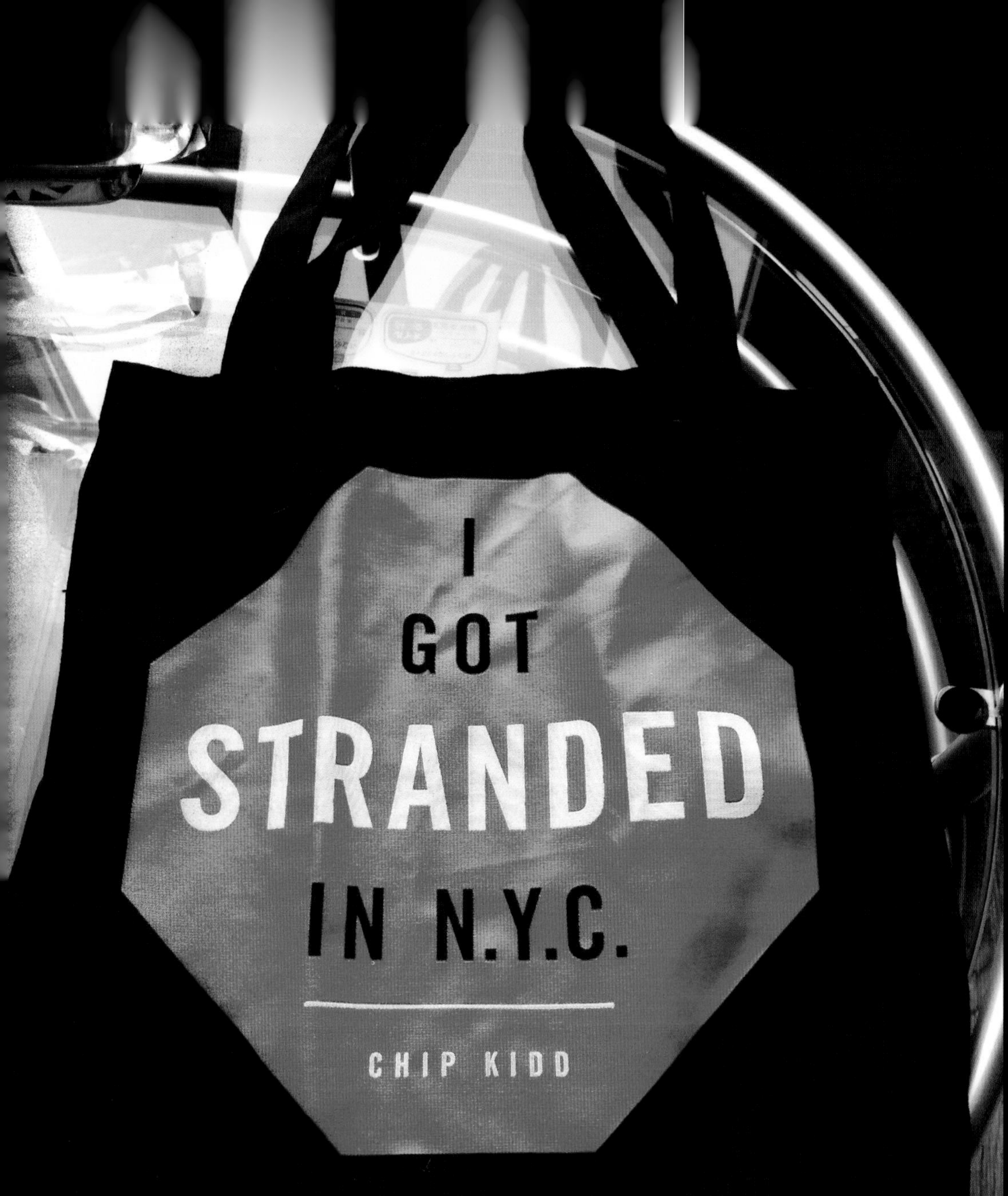
I
GOT
STRANDED
IN N.Y.C.
CHIP KIDD

**ABOVE:** A 2003 tote bag I designed for the mighty Strand bookstore in New York. This provided the starting point for what eventually became the cover of *GO*. For years I had been fixated on the shape of a Stop sign with contradictory information within it.

**OPPOSITE:** The initial cover proposal for *GO*. The graphic seemed perfect to me, I actually didn't think any additional information was necessary. Raquel gently suggested that we needed a subtitle, and of course she was right: "A Kidd's Guide to Graphic Design" was soon added, as well as a testimonial blurb at the top that I got from no less than Milton Glaser: "An excellent intro

I had thought for some time that Raquel Jaramillo and I had something like parallel careers in book design—she being the art director for Hol for many years, creating covers most notably for Sue Grafton, Salmar Rushdie, and Thomas Pynchon. I admired her work tremendously, we are the same age, and when she contacted me about doing a project I assumed she wanted to give me a freelance cover to design. But it wasn' that at all.

By that time (summer 2012) she had moved on to a new role as an acquiring children's book editor at Workman, and as we sat at lunch at Cognac—the bistro across the street from Random House, practically Knopf's cafeteria—she said, "You know, no one's ever created a book to teach graphic design to kids." As soon as she said it, I realized it was true There were many books to instruct kids about art, drawing, color, photography, and even typography. But not one that combined them all and explained how they can work together, especially in service to conceptua thinking and problem solving. She followed with, "And I think you should do it." This floored and thrilled me. I was totally out of my comfort zone I didn't have kids, I didn't really know any kids, I didn't relate to kids and most crucially (aside from my two godchildren): I didn't like kids.

So as a challenge, this was perfect. And the fact that it hadn't been done before really sealed the deal for me. "Wow," I replied, "I'm in."

That was the easy part. Then I had to figure out what this book was actually going to consist of. I drew upon a similar challenge in writing *The Cheese Monkeys*: if I was going to teach an introductory course in graphic design, regardless of the age group of students, how would I structure it?

The answer was: Start with Form—what things look like and how we perceive them; then Content—what things say and what they mean; then Letterforms—the origin of the written word and how to use the alphabe to get your point across, not just verbally but visually; then Concepts—

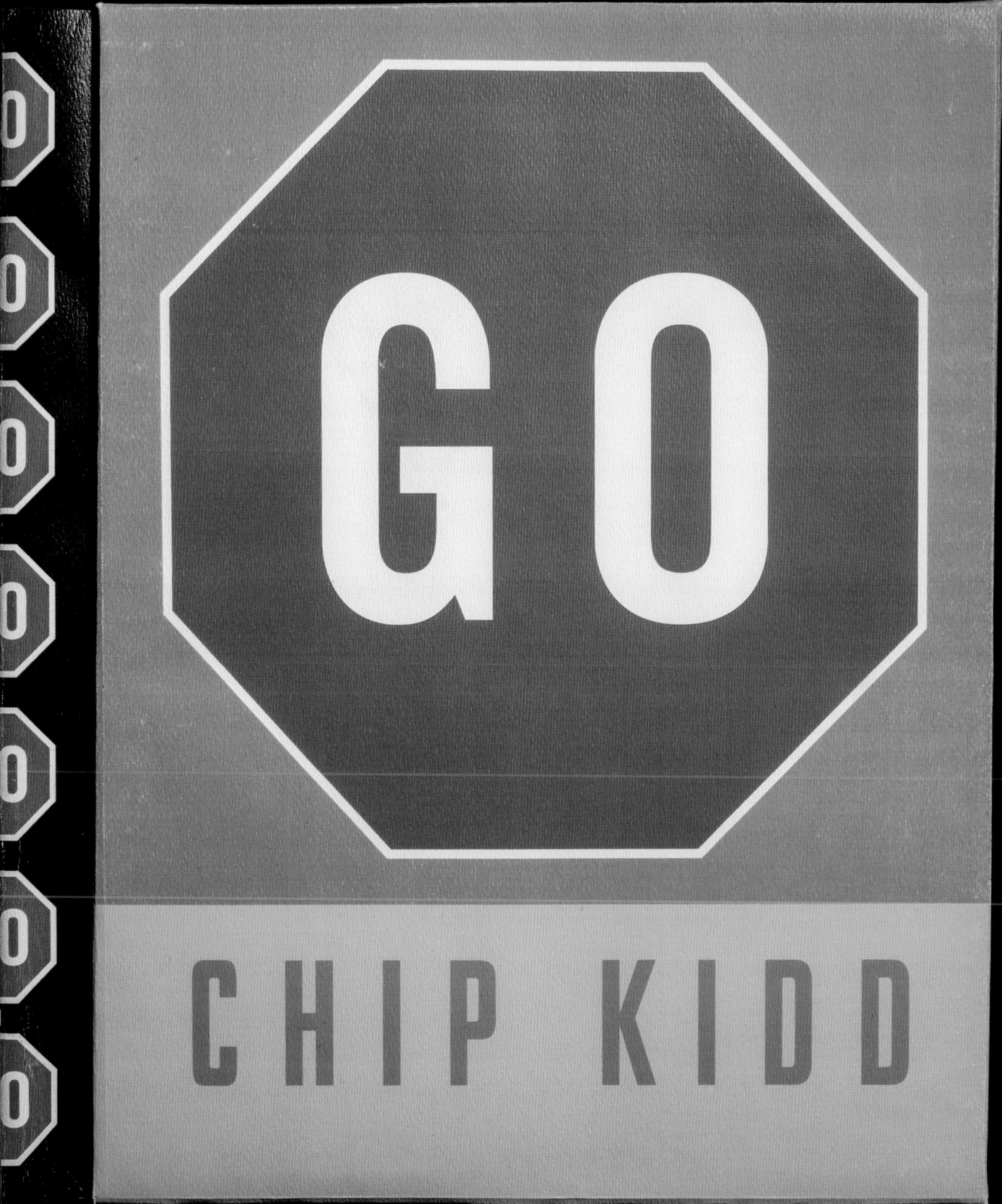
GO
CHIP KIDD

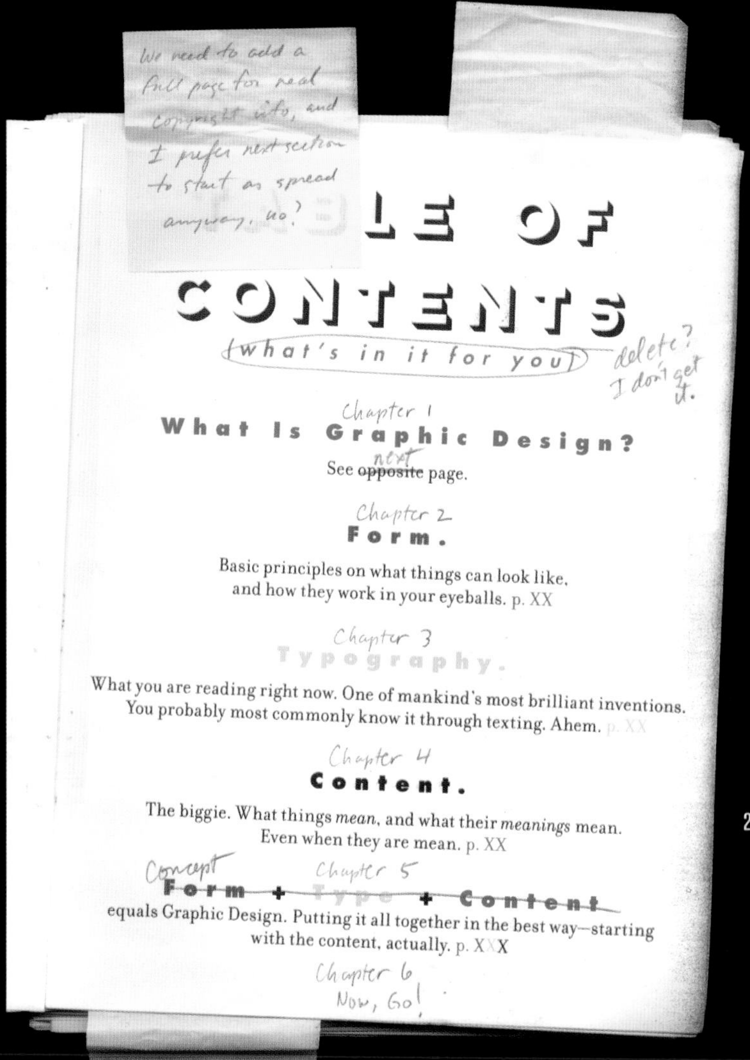
We need to add a full page for real copyright info, and I prefer next section to start as spread anyway, no?
LE OF
CONTENTS
(what's in it for you)
delete? I don't get it.
Chapter 1
What Is Graphic Design?
See ~~opposite~~ next page.
Chapter 2
Form.
Basic principles on what things can look like, and how they work in your eyeballs. p. XX
Chapter 3
Typography.
What you are reading right now. One of mankind's most brilliant inventions. You probably most commonly know it through texting. Ahem. p. XX
Chapter 4
Content.
The biggie. What things *mean*, and what their *meanings* mean. Even when they are mean. p. XX
Chapter 5
Concept
~~Form + Type + Content~~
equals Graphic Design. Putting it all together in the best way—starting with the content, actually. p. XXX
Chapter 6
Now, Go!

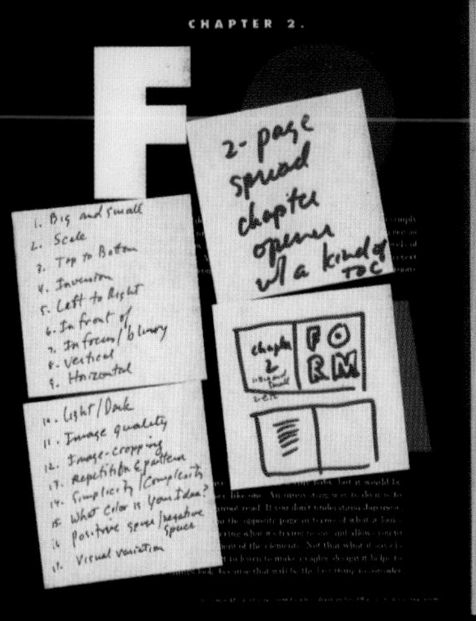
CHAPTER 2.
2-page spread chapter opener w/ a kind of TOC
FORM
1. Big and Small
2. Scale
3. Top to Bottom
4. Invention
5. Left to Right
6. In front of
7. In focus/blurry
8. Vertical
9. Horizontal
10. Light/Dark
11. Image quality
12. Image-cropping
13. Repetition & patterns
14. Simplicity/Complexity
15. What color is your idea?
16. Positive space/negative space
17. Visual variation

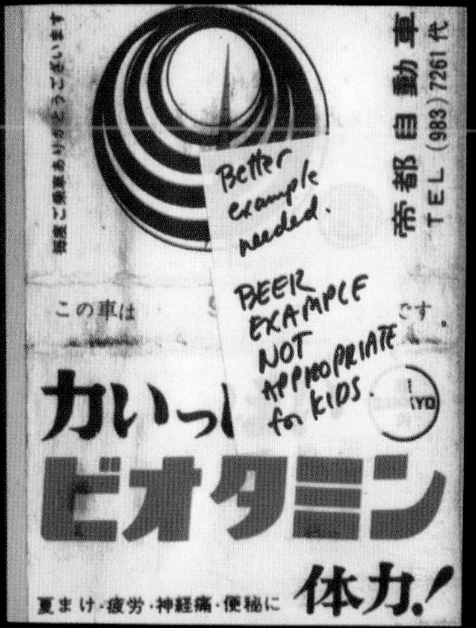
毎度ご乗車ありがとうございます
帝都自動車
TEL (983) 7261 代
この車は
です。
Better example needed.
BEER EXAMPLE NOT APPROPRIATE for KIDS.
力いっ
ビオタミン
夏まけ・疲労・神経痛・便秘に
体力!

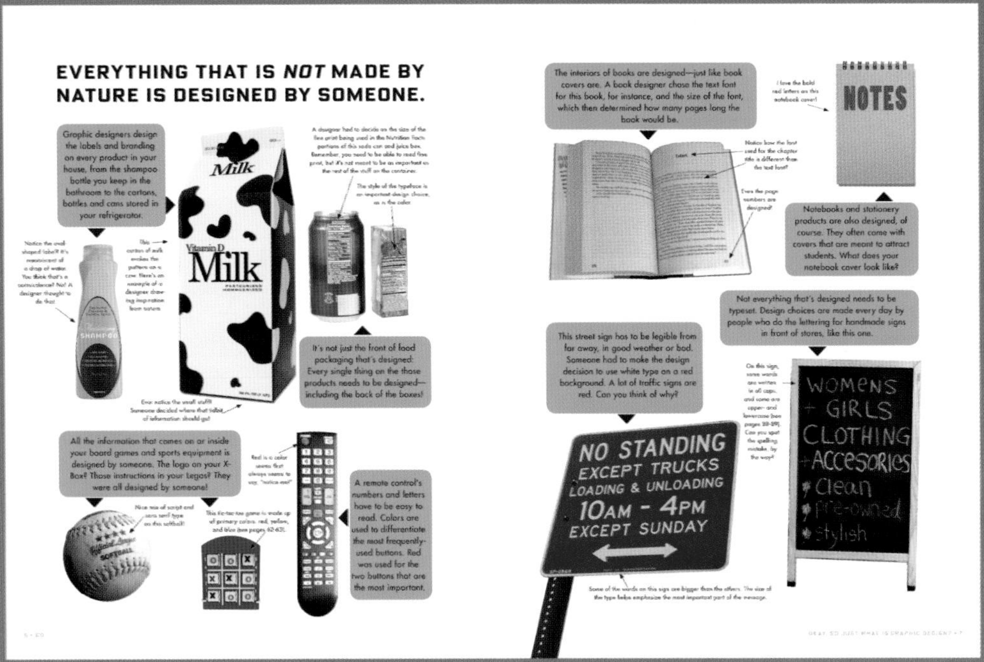
EVERYTHING THAT IS NOT MADE BY NATURE IS DESIGNED BY SOMEONE.
Graphic designers design the labels and branding on every product in your house, from the shampoo bottle you keep in the bathroom to the cartons, bottles and cans stored in your refrigerator.
Milk
Vitamin D Milk
It's not just the front of food packaging that's designed: Every single thing on the package needs to be designed—including the back of the boxes!
All the information that comes on or inside your board games and sports equipment is designed by someone. The logo on your X-Box? Those instructions in your Legos? They were all designed by someone!
A remote control's numbers and letters have to be easy to read. Colors are used to differentiate the most frequently-used buttons. Red was used for the two buttons that are the most important.
The interiors of books are designed—just like book covers are. A book designer chose the text font for this book, for instance, and the size of the font, which then determined how many pages long the book would be.
NOTES
Notebooks and stationery products are also designed, of course. They often come with covers that are meant to attract students. What does your notebook cover look like?
This street sign has to be legible from far away, in good weather or bad. Someone had to make the design decision to use white type on a red background. A lot of traffic signs are red. Can you think of why?
Not everything that's designed needs to be typeset. Design choices are made every day by people who do the lettering for handmade signs in front of stores, like this one.
NO STANDING
EXCEPT TRUCKS
LOADING & UNLOADING
10AM - 4PM
EXCEPT SUNDAY
WOMENS
+ GIRLS
CLOTHING
+ ACCESORIES
Clean
Pre-owned
Stylish

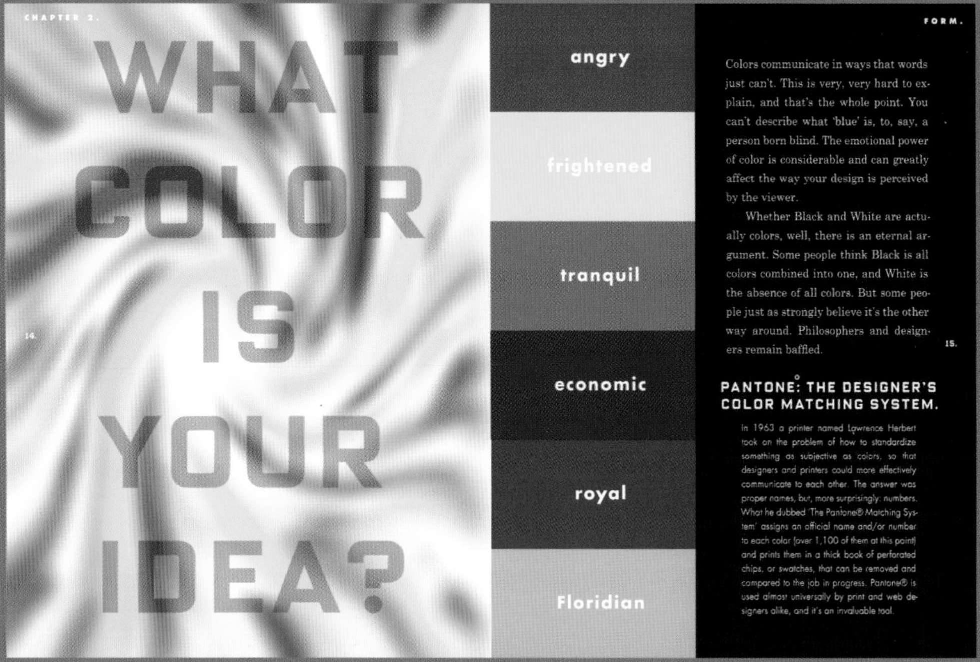
CHAPTER 2.
WHAT COLOR IS YOUR IDEA?
14.
angry
frightened
tranquil
economic
royal
Floridian
FORM.
Colors communicate in ways that words just can't. This is very, very hard to explain, and that's the whole point. You can't describe what 'blue' is, to, say, a person born blind. The emotional power of color is considerable and can greatly affect the way your design is perceived by the viewer.
Whether Black and White are actually colors, well, there is an eternal argument. Some people think Black is all colors combined into one, and White is the absence of all colors. But some people just as strongly believe it's the other way around. Philosophers and designers remain baffled.
15.
PANTONE: THE DESIGNER'S COLOR MATCHING SYSTEM.
In 1963 a printer named Lawrence Herbert took on the problem of how to standardize something as subjective as colors, so that designers and printers could more effectively communicate to each other. The answer was proper names, but, more surprisingly: numbers. What he dubbed The Pantone® Matching System assigns an official name and/or number to each color (over 1,100 of them at this point) and prints them in a thick book of perforated chips, or swatches, that can be removed and compared to the job in progress. Pantone® is used almost universally by print and web designers alike, and it's an invaluable tool.



The key here was NOT to talk down or condescend to the audience at all, but to write as if I was explaining these ideas and concepts to anyone who presumably had not seriously considered them, regardless of their age.

**ABOVE LEFT:** This spread appears in the beginning of the book, to show examples of graphic design that we all encounter in everyday life and the extent to which they are effective, or not. I just had to put the cable television remote in there, as I think it is one of the most egregious examples of unforgivably confusing design we deal with now and it is shameful (whoever figures out a way to simplify it will make a fortune). **BELOW:** Making the concepts like repetition and patterns immediately understandable with the visuals was very important—again, regardless of the age of the reader. That said, it was immediately clear that there were vital aspects of graphic design that I had studied in-depth in col-

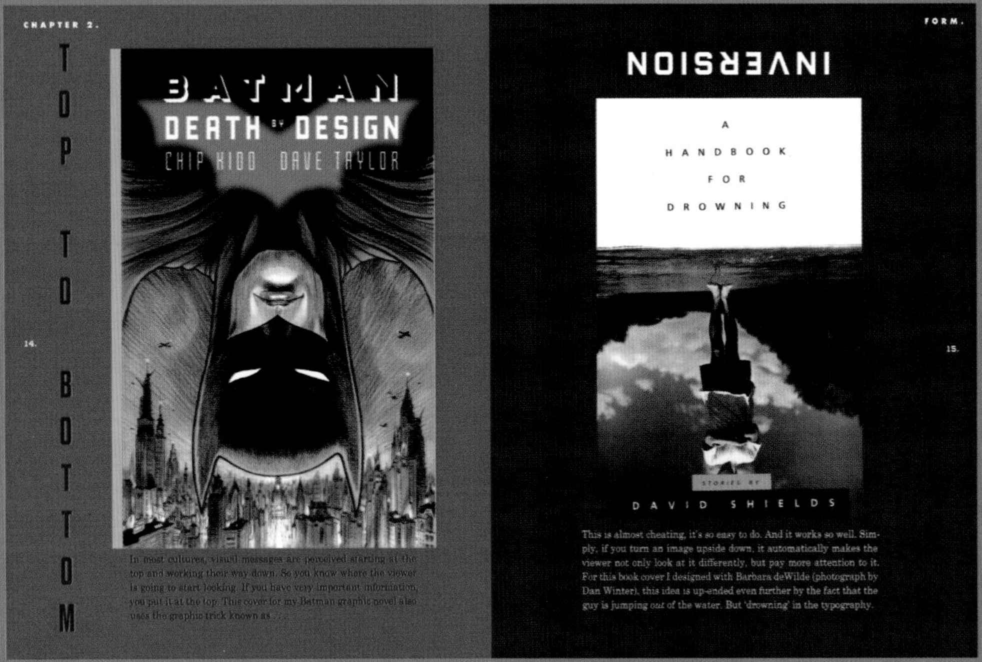
CHAPTER 2.
TOP TO BOTTOM
BATMAN
DEATH BY DESIGN
CHIP KIDD DAVE TAYLOR
14.
FORM.
INVERSION
A HANDBOOK FOR DROWNING
STORIES BY
DAVID SHIELDS
This is almost cheating, it's so easy to do. And it works so well. Simply, if you turn an image upside down, it automatically makes the viewer not only look at it differently, but pay more attention to it. For this book cover I designed with Barbara deWilde (photograph by Dan Winter), this idea is up-ended even further by the fact that the guy is jumping out of the water. But 'drowning' in the typography.
15.

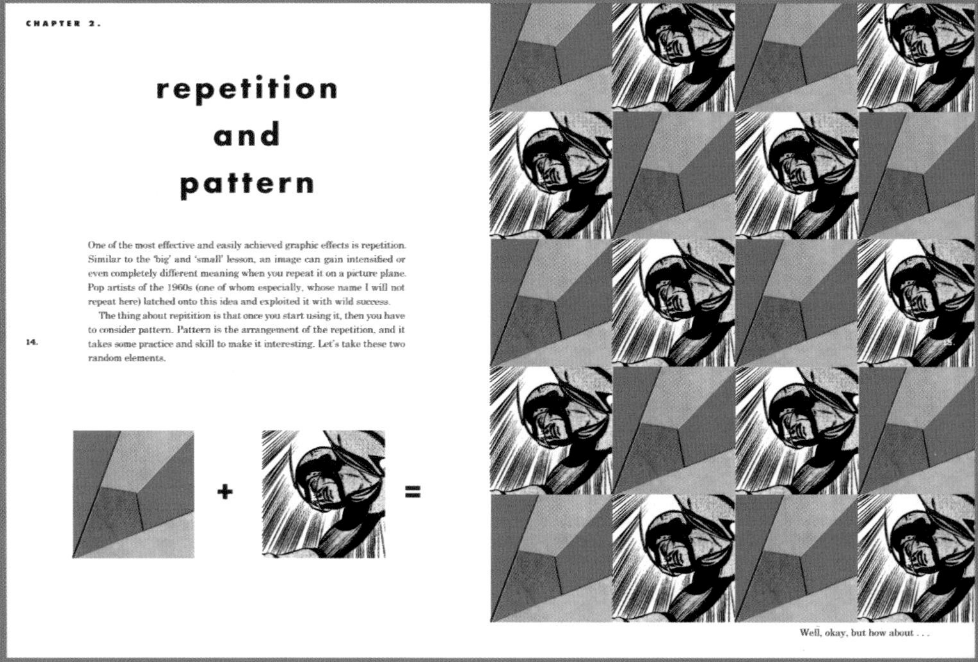
CHAPTER 2.
repetition and pattern
One of the most effective and easily achieved graphic effects is repetition. Similar to the 'big' and 'small' lesson, an image can gain intensified or even completely different meaning when you repeat it on a picture plane. Pop artists of the 1960s (one of whom especially, whose name I will not repeat here) latched onto this idea and exploited it with wild success.
The thing about repetition is that once you start using it, then you have to consider pattern. Pattern is the arrangement of the repetition, and it takes some practice and skill to make it interesting. Let's take these two random elements.
14.
+
=
Well, okay, but how about . . .

## Top-left spread (Chapter 5 / Concept)

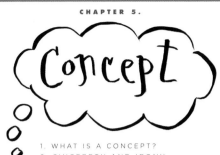

CHAPTER 5.

# Concept

1. WHAT IS A CONCEPT?
2. SINCERETY AND IRONY
3. ILLUSION 4. METAPHOR

14.

Your concept is your idea of what to do, based on what the problem is. It's the bridge between Content and Form, the means to get from the one to the other. Where do ideas come from? How can you create them? This is a very important question, one that designers ask themselves all the time.

The easy answer is that you let the problem itself give you ideas.

The harder answer is that ideas come from the world all around you, and you have to try and recognize them. An apple falls on Newton's head, and he starts to think about the concept of Gravity. Luck often plays a big part in how you generate ideas, but you have to meet it halfway.

On the opposite page is the cover for a book of poems I designed some years ago. The title, *Hazmat*, is short for 'Hazardous Material,' and though this usually refers to combustible things like gasoline, this time the author is applying it to human relationships. While I was trying to figure this out, I happened to see this amazing photograph by Erica Larson. Something clicked in my head: the door bell rings, you hear an explosion, and you open it. Poof! What happened?

**LUCK**
"I feel that luck is preparation meeting opportunity."
—Oprah Winfrey

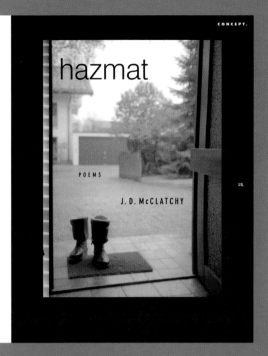

CONCEPT.

hazmat

POEMS

J. D. McCLATCHY

15.

## Top-right spread (Chapter 4 / Content)

CHAPTER 4.

So, basically, content is what you're trying to communicate. For any given design problem you have to ask: What is the content's purpose? What is it trying to do?

This purpose is called a function. And once you determine its function, then its form—or what it's going to look like—will follow. Always remember:

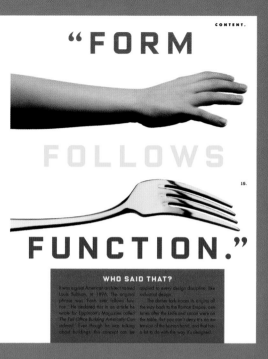

CONTENT.

# "FORM FOLLOWS FUNCTION."

**WHO SAID THAT?**

It was a great American architect named Louis Sullivan, in 1896. The original phrase was 'Form ever follows function.' He declared this in an article he wrote for *Lippincott's Magazine* called 'The Tall Office Building Artistically Considered.' Even though he was talking about buildings, this concept can be applied to every design discipline, like industrial design.

The dinner fork traces its origins all the way back to the Roman Empire, centuries after the knife and spoon were on the table. But you can't deny it's an extension of the human hand, and that has a lot to do with the way it's designed.

## Middle prose

lege which I wouldn't be able to touch in this context: sex, religion, politics, aggressive consumerism. I had to stick to the basic principles, applying them to problems that had nothing to do with adult themes and/or political stances. (Hey, let the kids figure all of that out for themselves later, as they may or may not see fit).

Once the foundation was established, I used examples of published pieces and explored how they came into being, what made them work. Raquel was tremendously helpful and suggested making the last section into a "workbook," a series of projects based on the lessons learned throughout. That tied it up very well, leaving the door open to seeing what readers might come up with and then post on the book's website.

281

**BELOW, LEFT:** Images of yours truly by photographer John Madere, illustrator Randy Glass, cartoonist Ivan Brunetti and . . . yours truly. **BELOW RIGHT:** My godson Jet Spear (see cover of Paul Simon's *Surprise*, p. 207) as he poses for the rebus "I, designer!" and on his favorite skateboard, which we staged with him lying on the ground (safety first!).

## Bottom-left spread (photography / illustration / cartoon / pict-o-gram)

CHAPTER 5.

GO!

14.

15.

### photography

Photographs show things as they really are, at least we are led to think so (remember about illusion), and this one of me was taken several years ago by a cameraman named John Madere. A picture like this is meant to be very sincere, with nothing to hide, and you use it when you want to be as honest as you can with your audience. I use this to promote my speaking gigs, because it makes me look totally unthreatening. Doesn't it?

### illustration

This drawing, by Randy Glass, is a literal 'translation' of the photograph to the left, in pen-and-ink on paper. He uses a technique that could be called 'stipple,' or in other words, lots of dots. It may look simple, but if you try it (and you should), you'll quickly find out that it is really, really hard to do it well.

What happens in our heads when we go from a photograph to a drawing like this, which is very realistic, but not real? Do we think about the subject in a different way? I used this as an 'author photo' on a book of satire I worked on called 'True Prep' (see p. xx). It is meant to convey an interpretation of reality.

### cartoon

The cartoonist Ivan Brunetti used ink and brush to create this portrait that is far simpler than Randy's, using fluid lines and a sense of whimsical mischief, but it's also a bit more complicated. Why? Because it seems to have a point of view, or opinion, about the subject. Cartooning can use exaggerated forms to get a stronger emotional reaction from you, and masters of the craft such as Charles Schulz have shown that making the body disproportionately smaller than the head gives even adults the look and feel of children or infants. Here the arched right eyebrow is also very important, suggesting disbelief and slight irritation.

### pict-o-gram

As we've gone from left to right on this spread we also have, in a way, gone back in time, in terms of how mankind has made pictures over many hundreds of years. Though I created this simple image on a computer, it is not all that different from the way a cave painting might have been made in prehistoric times. That is, showing your subject in as direct a way as possible, using as few lines or shapes as you need to get your point across, but also making it specific to your subject. Not like a generic emoticon, more like a logo.

## Bottom-right spread (Chapter 6)

CHAPTER 6.

, designer!

14.

1. YOUR IDENTITY
2. APPLICATION
3. RE-DESIGN
4. SCRAPBOOK
5. RE-CONTEXT
6. DON'T BUY IT
7. ARFS AND CRAFTS
8. BLOW IT UP
9. MAKE HISTORY
10. GIVE DESIGN BACK

or, Now,

GO!!

If you want to explore becoming a graphic designer, here are ten projects to get you started. As you can see, my friend Jet, here, has already done project number 2 by customizing his skateboard. GO, JET!!

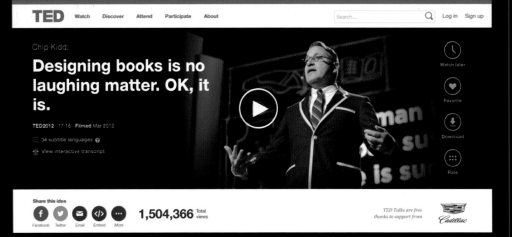

TED
Watch
Discover
Attend
Participate
About
Search...
Log in
Sign up
Chip Kidd:
Designing books is no laughing matter. OK, it is.
TED2012 · 17:16 · Filmed Mar 2012
34 subtitle languages
View interactive transcript
Watch later
Favorite
Download
Rate
Share this idea
Facebook
Twitter
Email
Embed
More
1,504,366 Total views
TED Talks are free thanks to support from
Cadillac

## Stage Presents

I had wanted to present at TED for many years, but it's not the sort of thing one can just decide to do—you have to be invited. In the late fall of 2011 that invitation finally came, from my old friend Chee Perlman, who was curating an afternoon of design-related talks for the main stage at the TED week-long conference (then in Long Beach, CA), with architectural designer David Rockwell. I of course said YES, but then we had to decide what exactly the talk was going to be about and how to meet the strict 18-minute limit—the clock is in the floor in front of you, counting down your time. If you go over, it's not a good thing. And watching countless TED talks online in preparation for my own, I came to understand why: at 15 minutes, no matter who you are, it just needs to wrap up soon. Live, it's a different story—you can keep an audience interested for much longer because you're right there and they feel a direct connection. But the vast majority of the simulcast and future audience will be watching on the web, at a remove. You need to have an interesting thing to say, in a unique way that will survive a tiny screen, and 18 minutes is already pushing it.

For months I rehearsed every Monday evening with Chee at Rockwell's spectacular studio on Union Square, just a twenty-minute subway ride from my office in Midtown West. There we slowly shaped it, and Chee contributed a lot of great ideas, but it was still clocking in at 30 minutes no matter what we did with the material—which was a combination of introducing who I was and what I did; showing some simple graphic design principles and how they related to my work; and then case studies that pleaded for the case of print editions versus e-books, although I knew that Jeff Bezos would likely be in the audience (no pressure!). The problem with this process was that instead of building my confidence, it was eroding it, and I was on the edge of a slow-motion nervous breakdown. The week before the conference, Chee suggested trying a session with a TED speaker-coach named Gina Barnett. I was skeptical but desperate (I had been doing public speaking for over twenty years and never needed a coach in my life), and I went to meet her fully believing that it would be a total waste of time. It was the opposite—she listened to the entire talk and said, "Okay, cut this, this, and this, you don't need it. Then you'll be fine." And she was right. I felt a weight lifted from my shoulders and I was reminded that when you're engaged in an intense project like this for months, you need a fresh pair of eyes and ears—hopefully connected to a cunning brain—to review it objectively. Gina totally saved my life, and I tried to return the favor by designing the cover for her subsequent book on body language in the workplace (right).

PLAY
HOW TO MASTER BODY SIGNALS TO CONNECT AND COMMUNICATE FOR BUSINESS SUCCESS
THE
GINA BARNETT
PART

The presentation went very well, despite being thrown off at the last minute by having to wear what I deemed the "Lady Gaga Skank Mic." It completely interfered with the delicate balance of my eyeglasses, which were only supported by the left temple at the time (due to my husband Sandy rolling onto them in bed and breaking off the right temple the week before. Thanks, Peach!). Other notes of note: TED in general frowns on men "dressing up" to give presentations; there is a strict "no ties" rule to bolster the "casual Friday" anti-corporate vibe. I had my outfit picked out months ahead of time as you see it, and Chee went to bat to tell them to lay off and let me be who I really am. Years later, Chris Anderson noted in his book *TED Talks* that I had "a wonderful sense of style."

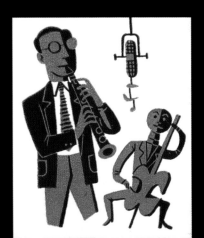

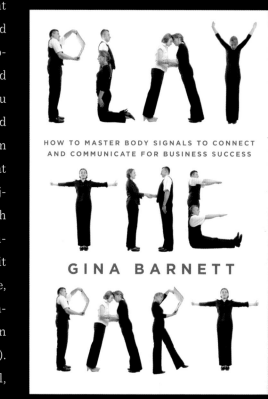

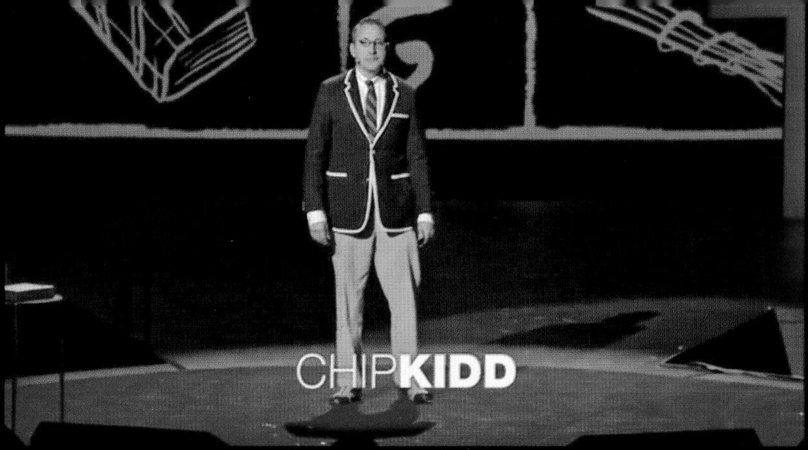
CHIPKIDD

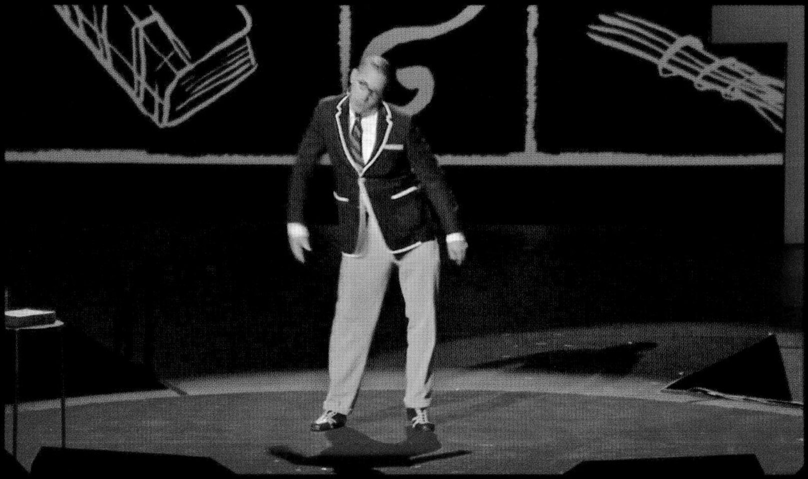

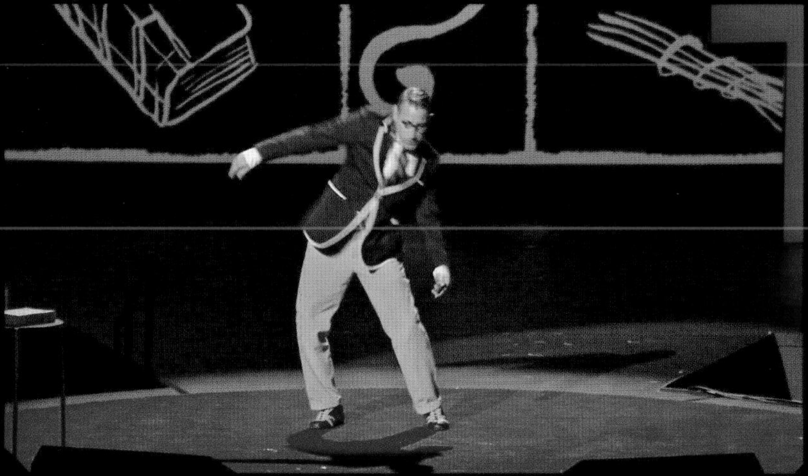

**OPPOSITE, BOTTOM RIGHT:** A fan sent me this 1950s illustration of Benny Goodman by Columbia Records artist Jim Flora, noting that he bears a striking resemblance to me in my TED outfit. I love Benny Goodman, and thus I love thinking that there was some psychic kinship at work!

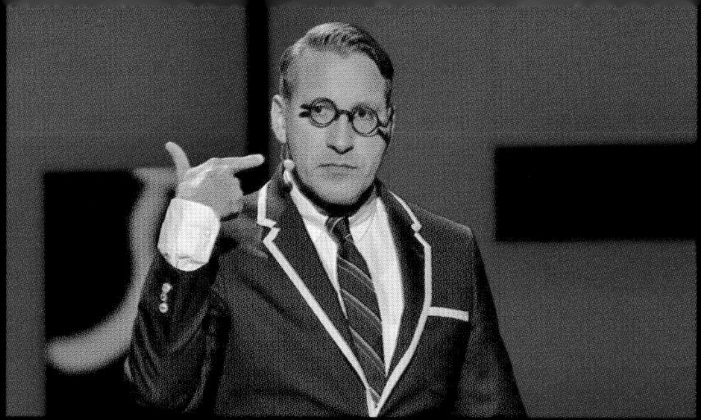

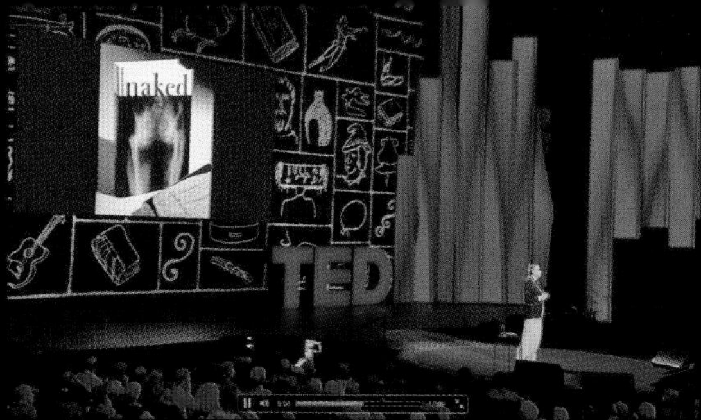
naked
TED

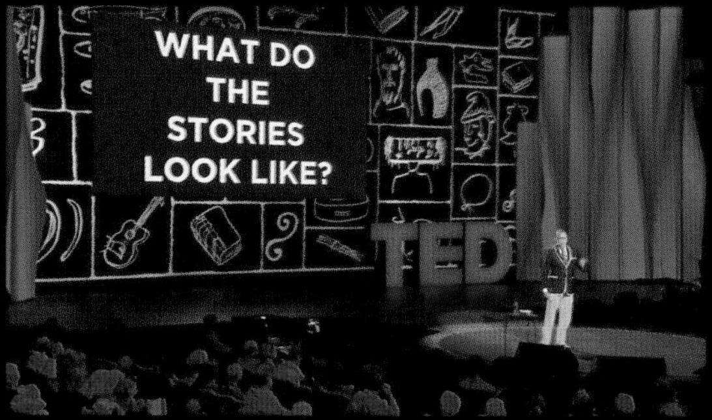
WHAT DO THE STORIES LOOK LIKE?
TED

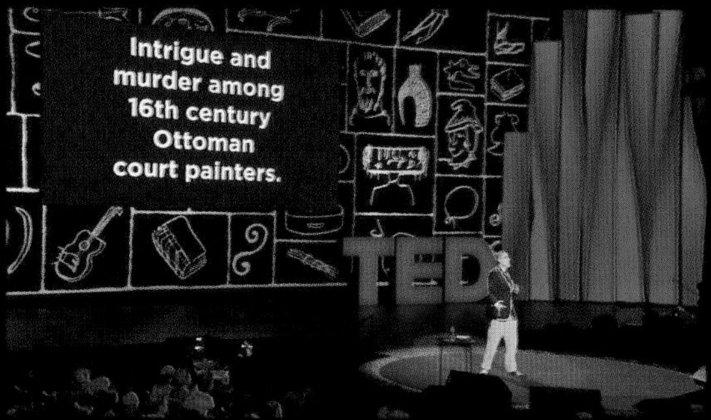
Intrigue and murder among 16th century Ottoman court painters.
TED

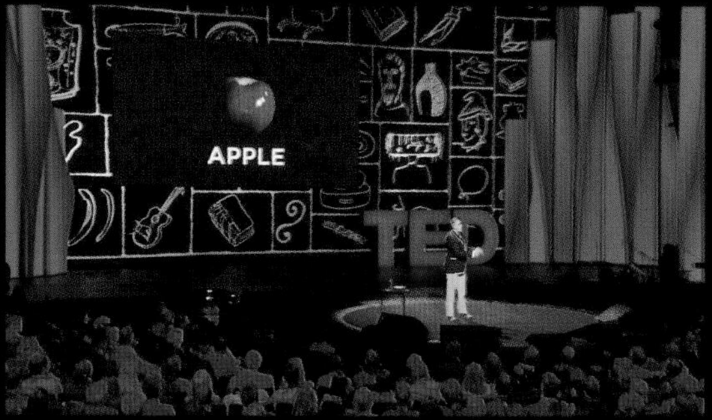
APPLE
TED

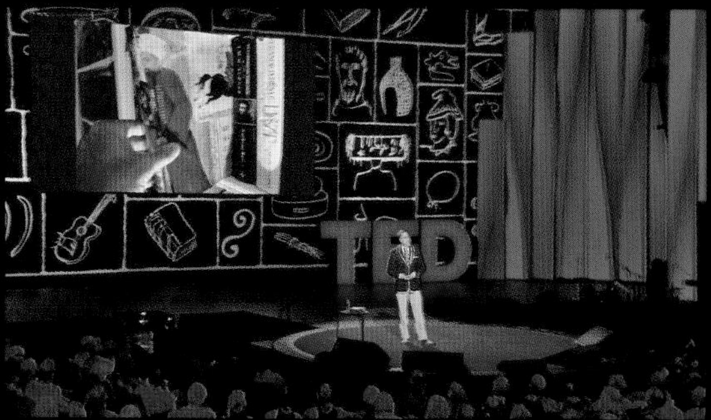
TED

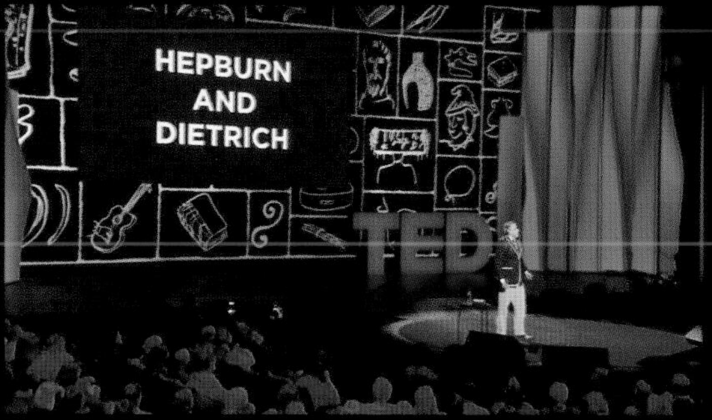
HEPBURN AND DIETRICH
TED

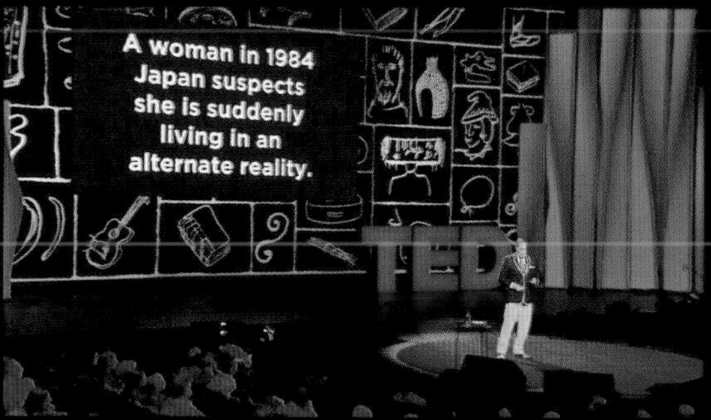
A woman in 1984 Japan suspects she is suddenly living in an alternate reality.
TED

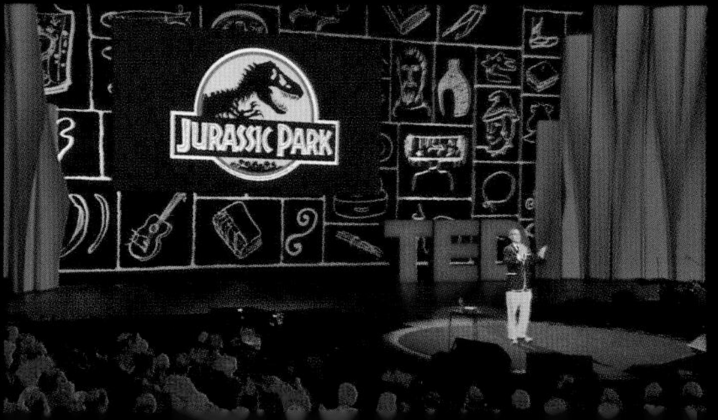
JURASSIC PARK
TED

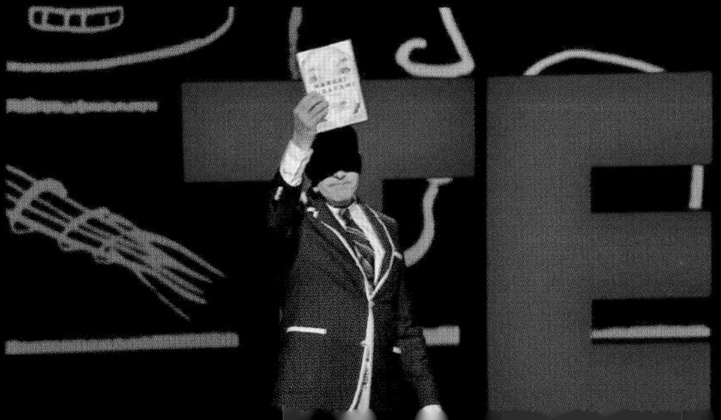

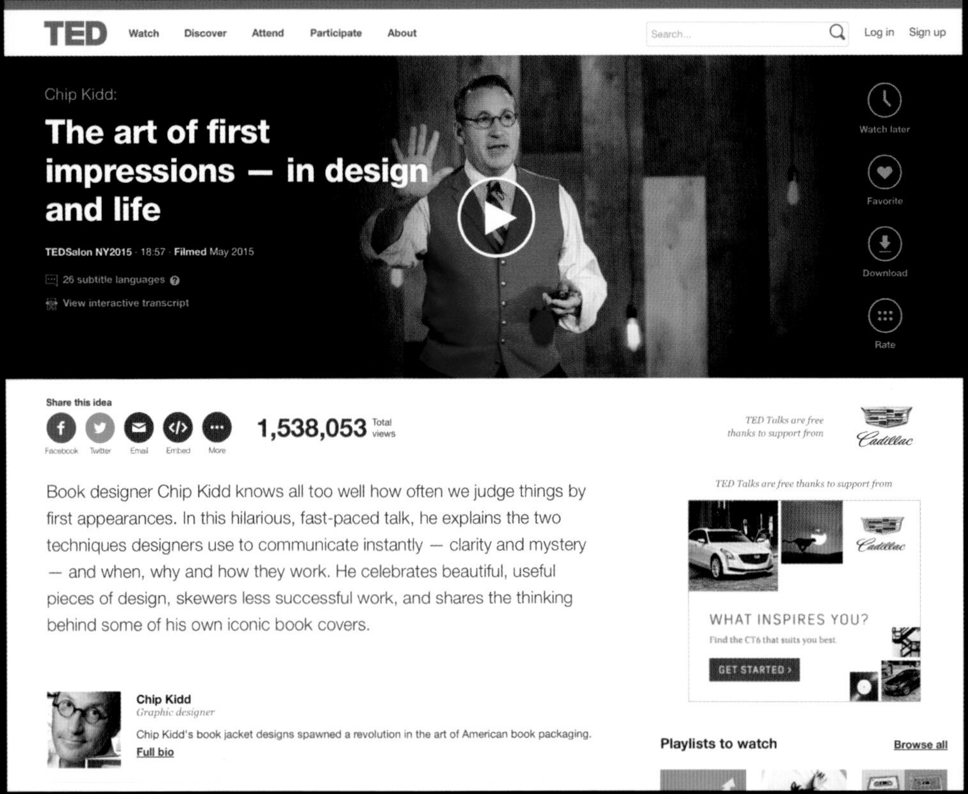
TED
Watch Discover Attend Participate About
Search...
Log in Sign up
Chip Kidd:
The art of first impressions — in design and life
TEDSalon NY2015 · 18:57 · Filmed May 2015
26 subtitle languages
View interactive transcript
Watch later
Favorite
Download
Rate
Share this idea
Facebook Twitter Email Embed More
1,538,053 Total views
TED Talks are free thanks to support from
Cadillac
Book designer Chip Kidd knows all too well how often we judge things by first appearances. In this hilarious, fast-paced talk, he explains the two techniques designers use to communicate instantly — clarity and mystery — and when, why and how they work. He celebrates beautiful, useful pieces of design, skewers less successful work, and shares the thinking behind some of his own iconic book covers.
TED Talks are free thanks to support from
WHAT INSPIRES YOU?
Find the CT6 that suits you best.
GET STARTED ›
Chip Kidd
Graphic designer
Chip Kidd's book jacket designs spawned a revolution in the art of American book packaging.
Full bio
Playlists to watch
Browse all



# Stage Presents, Again

My second TED talk, in May 2015, was a much more intimate affair. It was one of their informal salons, held regularly in a small amphitheater in the TED offices in New York City for about a hundred people. This was in conjunction with a book I had just created called *Judge This*, for their new imprint at Simon & Schuster.

*Judge This*, as relatively small scale as it is, proved to be an enormous challenge. When the TED folks announced that they would be creating a branded group of titles—essentially TED talks in book form—they asked me to be the art director for the series. Then they asked me to write one. This offer was too good to pass up, but soon the inevitable question became, "What exactly is this book, and how will it cover new ground?" I didn't want it to be *GO* for adults, but technically it was a follow-up and should be about graphic design. My editor, Michelle Quint, did what great editors do and helped me evolve the process and figure it out. We started with the idea of "A day in the life of a designer," and it morphed into "First impressions, and when should things be clear, and when should they be mysterious? And what happens when the two get mixed up?" As unwieldy as that may

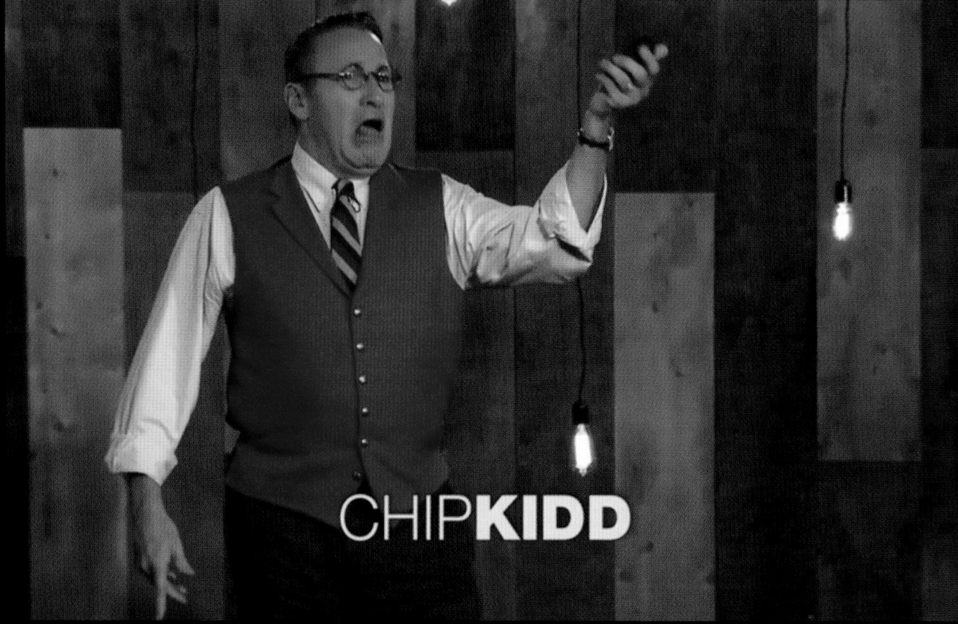
CHIPKIDD

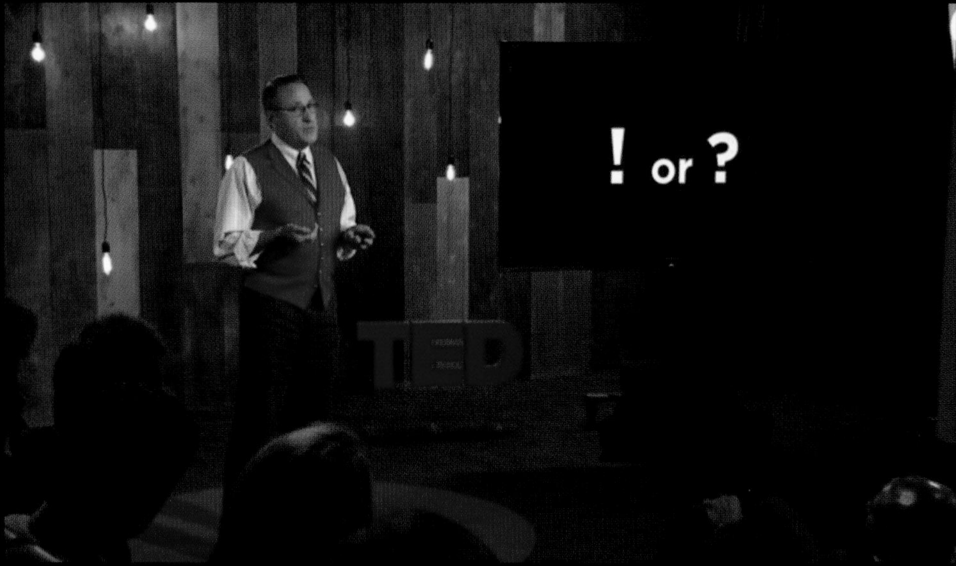
! or ?
TED

sound, it actually came together via a sliding scale I invented called the "mysteri-o-meter," which registered total Clarity (a "1") to total Mystery (a "10") and everything in between.

The book has been translated into a dozen languages (a record for one of my books, to be sure), and the talk has been viewed more than 1.6 million times as of this writing. Thanks again to Gina Barnett for once more helping me get the talk itself into shape, and to Michelle Quint for editing the text into coherency.

WHEN SHOULD YOU BE CLEAR?

MAKE IT LOOK LIKE SOMETHING ELSE.

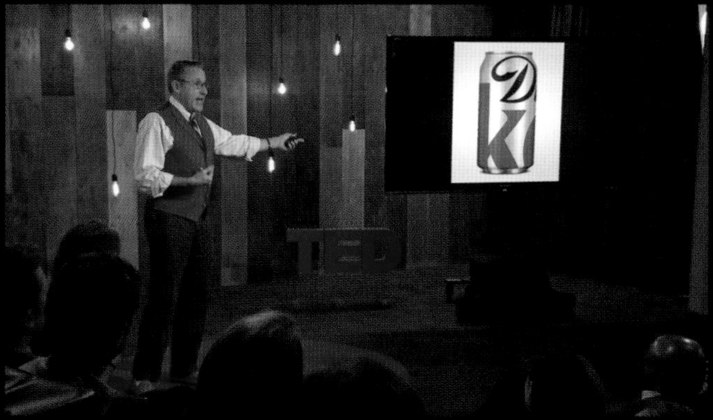

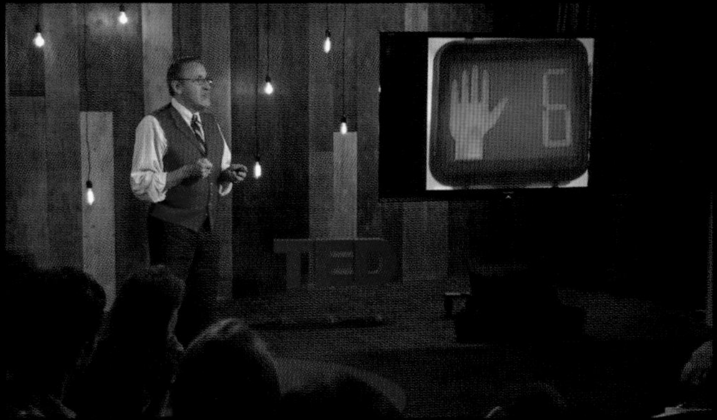

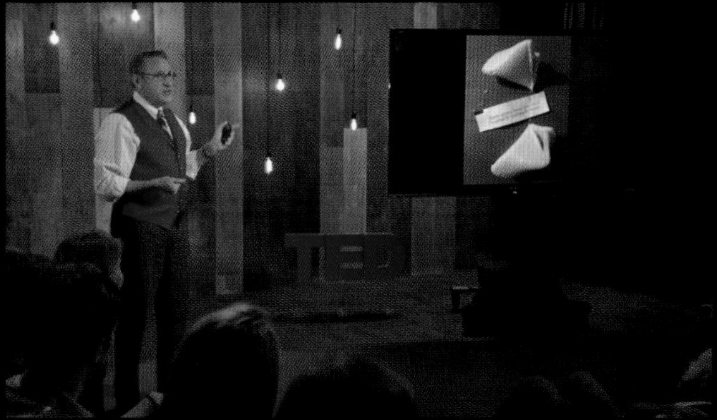

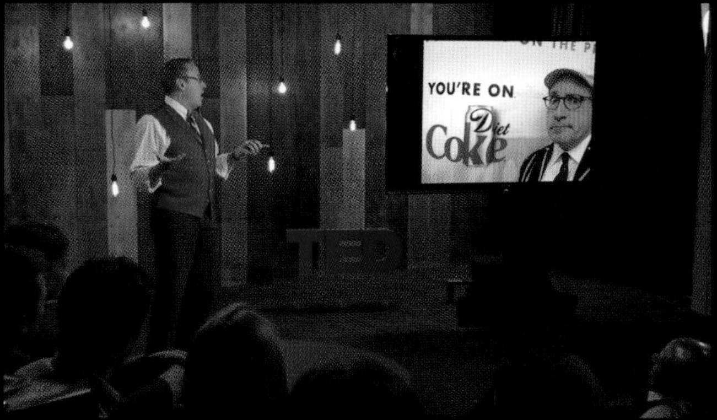
YOU'RE ON
Diet Coke



WHEN SHOULD YOU BE MYSTERIOUS?

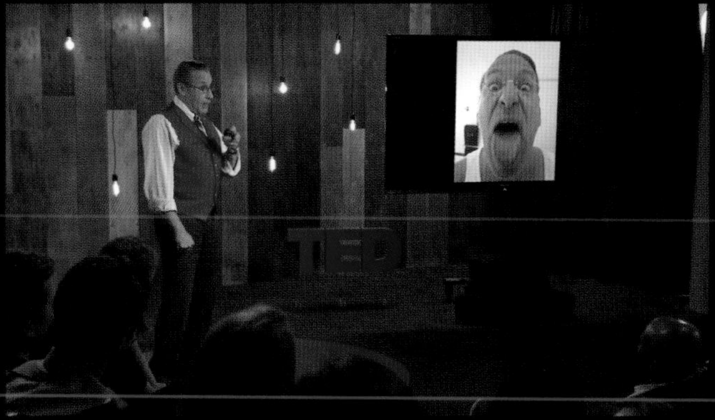

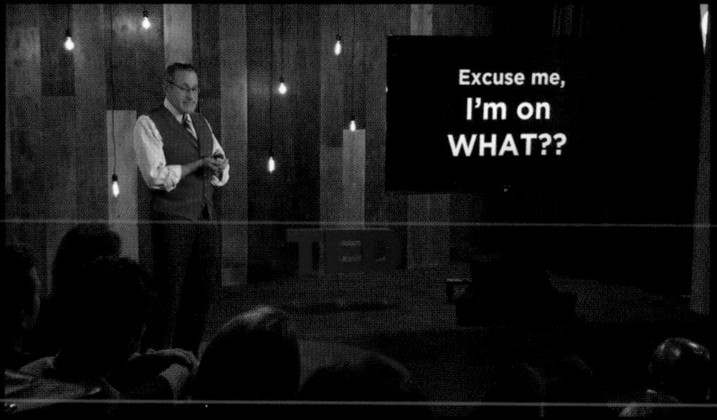
Excuse me,
I'm on
WHAT??

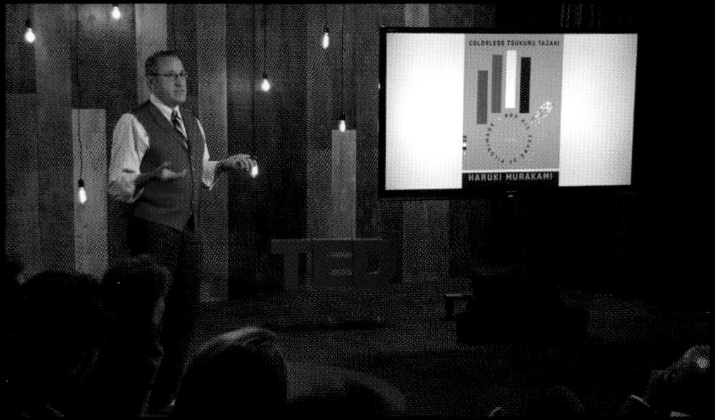
HARUKI MURAKAMI

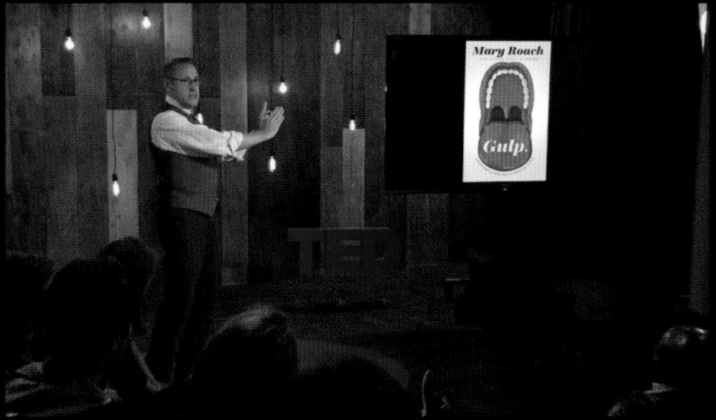
Mary Roach
Gulp.

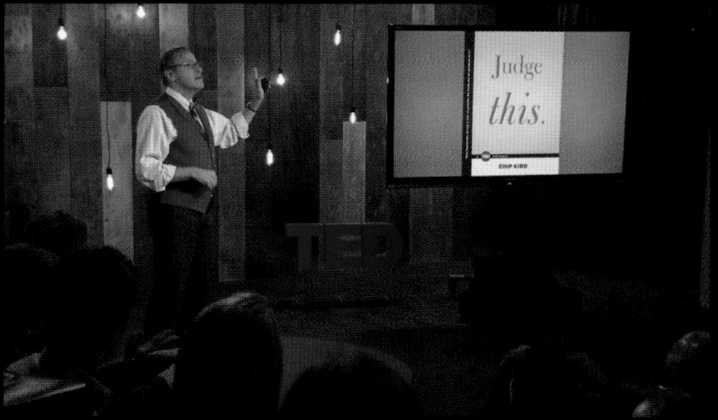
Judge
this.

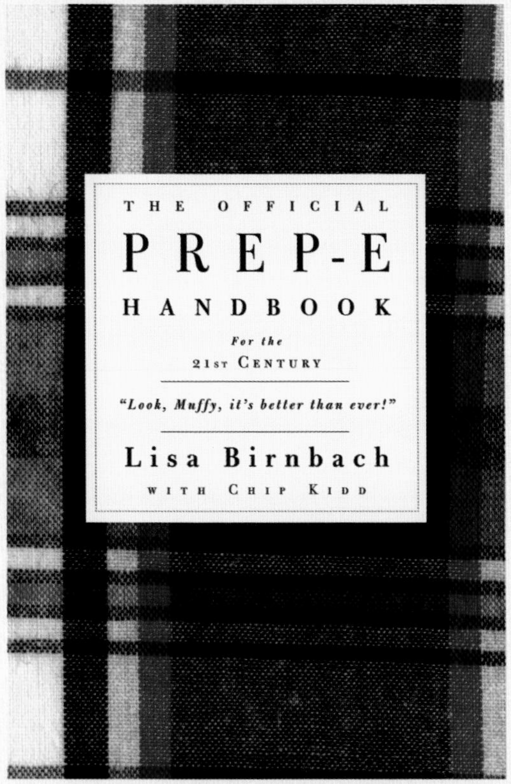
THE OFFICIAL
PREP-E
HANDBOOK
For the
21st CENTURY
"Look, Muffy, it's better than ever!"
Lisa Birnbach
WITH CHIP KIDD

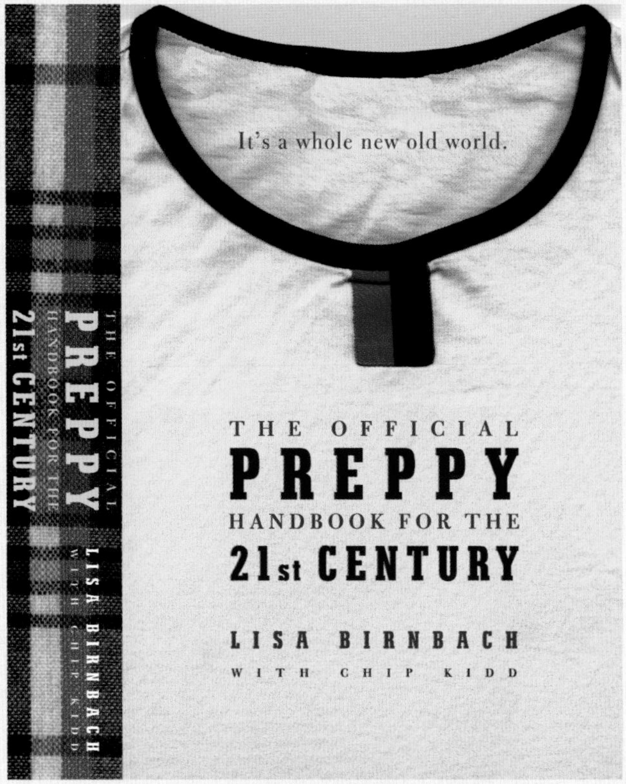
THE OFFICIAL PREPPY HANDBOOK FOR THE 21st CENTURY
LISA BIRNBACH WITH CHIP KIDD
It's a whole new old world.
THE OFFICIAL
PREPPY
HANDBOOK FOR THE
21st CENTURY
LISA BIRNBACH
WITH CHIP KIDD

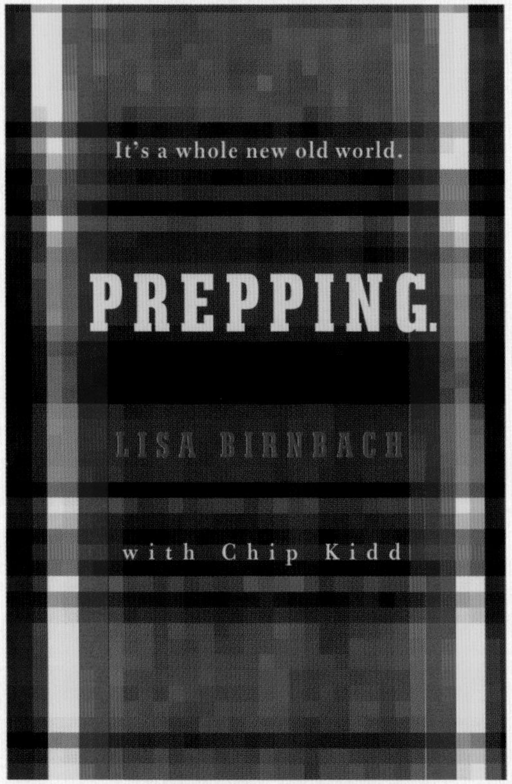
It's a whole new old world.
PREPPING.
LISA BIRNBACH
with Chip Kidd

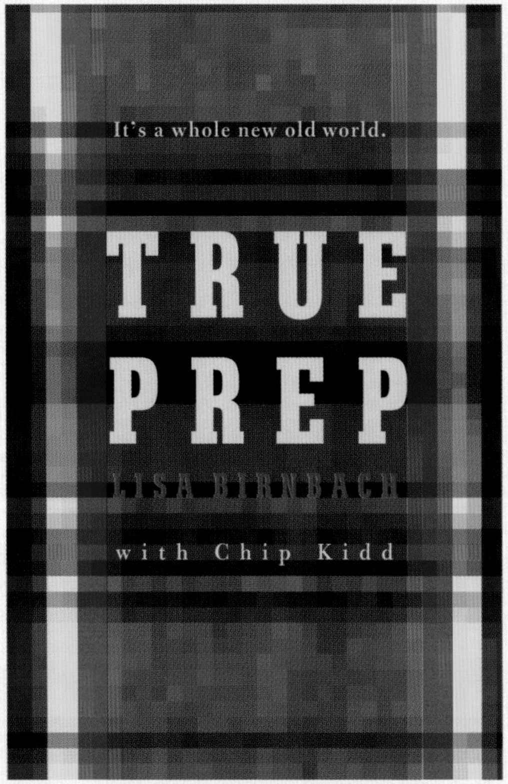
It's a whole new old world.
TRUE
PREP
LISA BIRNBACH
with Chip Kidd



# Prepare Yourself

I've said it in many interviews by now: *The Official Preppy Handbook* significantly changed my life when it first appeared in 1980, when I was in tenth grade at Wilson High School in West Lawn, Pennsylvania. As I told this to Sonny Mehta in his office some thirty years later, he stared at me incredulously across his desk and quietly implored, "How?" I thought carefully for a moment, then replied, "Because as a suburban kid in southeastern Pennsylvania, I finally learned how the class system works in America, even though there isn't supposed to be one. Plus, it was the Emily Post etiquette book of its day, only funnier and hipper."

All true, though let's back up: in April 2008, Facebook was still a novelty, but rapidly growing in popularity. I was okaying friend requests as they came, often from total strangers—hey, what did I care, the more the merrier. Then I got one from someone claiming to be Lisa Birnbach. I didn't believe it, but accepted and wrote back, "OMG, is that really YOU?" And she responded in kind, "OMG, is that really YOU?" So I said "OMG, is it really US?" This led to a lunch—at my urging—at Bouley Bakery in the spanking-new Time Warner Center on Columbus Circle. Sure enough, it was her, and WOW. She looked just like her pictures—very attractive, almond-shaped face, espresso-colored hair that caressed her shoulders, sparkling eyes that went half-mast just as she was about to emit a whiff of cheeky gossip, only to pop open as big as saucers upon hitting the punchline. I was entranced.

And then the conversation that eventually led to *True Prep* began.

"Preppy 2.0?" she asked. "It's come up a lot over the years, I just never found the right publisher, the right time . . ." I suggested as politely as possible that the right publisher was Knopf, and the right time was now (or rather two years from then, when it might actually exist). Plus, I could suggest the perfect editor within the house: Shelley Wanger. There was more back-and-forth over the next couple of weeks, but when Lisa and Shelley finally met, that clinched the deal. It was so perfect.

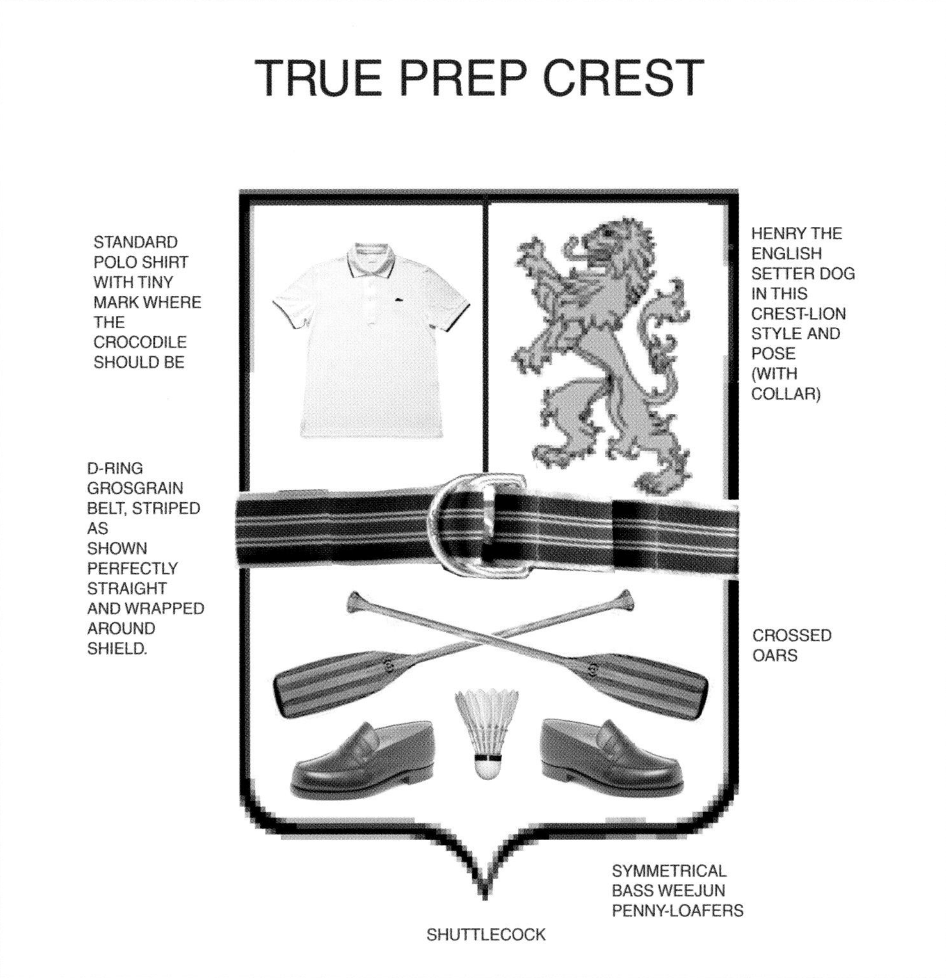
TRUE PREP CREST
STANDARD POLO SHIRT WITH TINY MARK WHERE THE CROCODILE SHOULD BE
HENRY THE ENGLISH SETTER DOG IN THIS CREST-LION STYLE AND POSE (WITH COLLAR)
D-RING GROSGRAIN BELT, STRIPED AS SHOWN PERFECTLY STRAIGHT AND WRAPPED AROUND SHIELD.
CROSSED OARS
SYMMETRICAL BASS WEEJUN PENNY-LOAFERS
SHUTTLECOCK

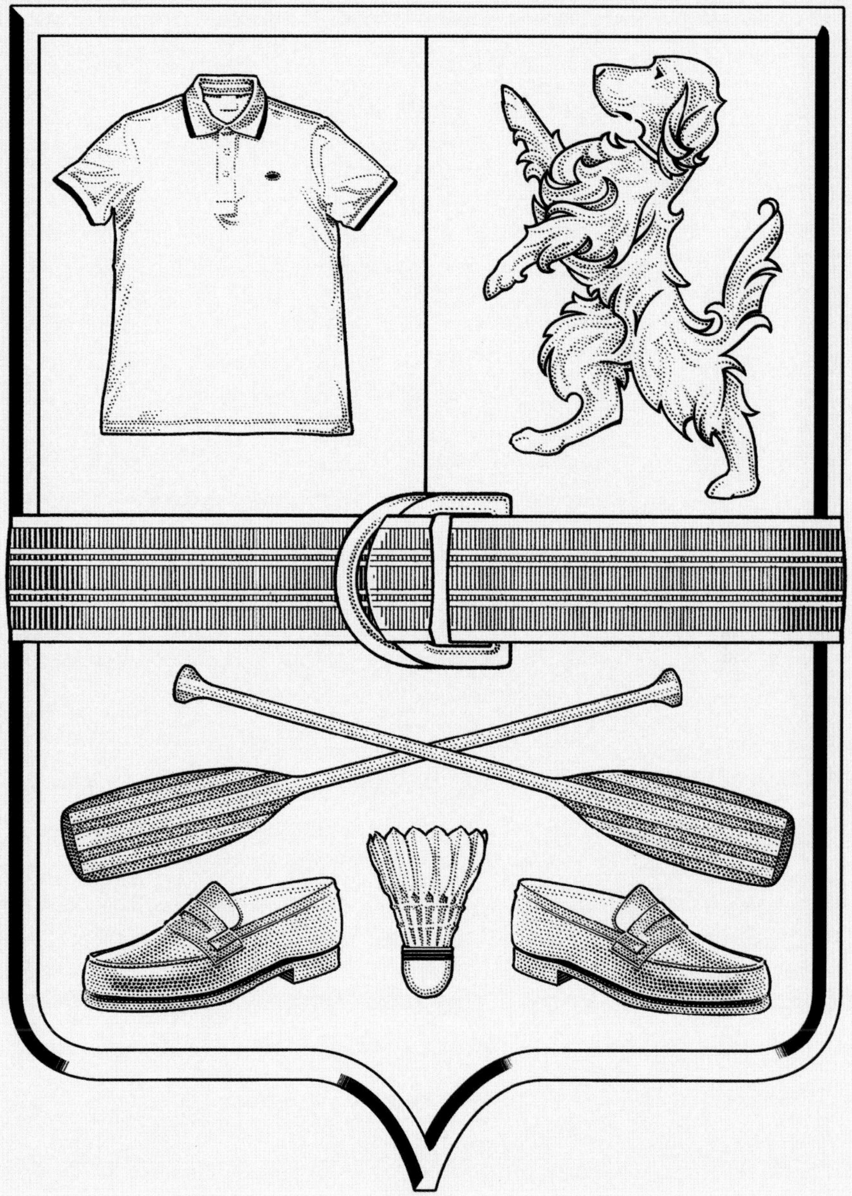

**ABOVE:** My photo reference for Randy, which he masterfully converted into a beautiful drawing. **RIGHT:** Randy's final crest, used throughout the book. When we saw this image, we knew we had the right guy. **OPPOSITE:** We struggled for months just to figure out what the book was going to be called. These early sketches for the cover show how the title evolved. Lisa came up with *True Prep*, and I coined the subtitle.

We all knew that to do the book right would take a lot of work, and that we didn't have a huge budget—hey, we were not *Vogue* or anything in that league. But the original *Preppy* book wasn't either—we could give this book better production values regarding art and photography, but what its success would really hinge on was how we articulated and presented this idea to a new generation, now known as Millennials. It helped that Lisa then had two daughters at Dalton and Shelley's daughter attended Spence. They had all the inside knowledge that I had no clue about; I was just there to make it look good. And that, I think, we did.

Early on we decided that the book would have both illustrations and photographs (as in the first book); the drawings would show things that could not be credibly photographed, and photos would be used for everything else. On this page is a good example of my art direction to the illustrator, Randy Glass, who regularly did stipple illustrations for the *Wall Street Journal*. There are many artists who also work in this style, but Lisa and I quickly figured out that Randy was far and away the best in artistry and technique. The downside was that it took him a good bit of time to finish each drawing, so we had to figure out early on what we needed him to do. We decided first on our own crest, shown above.

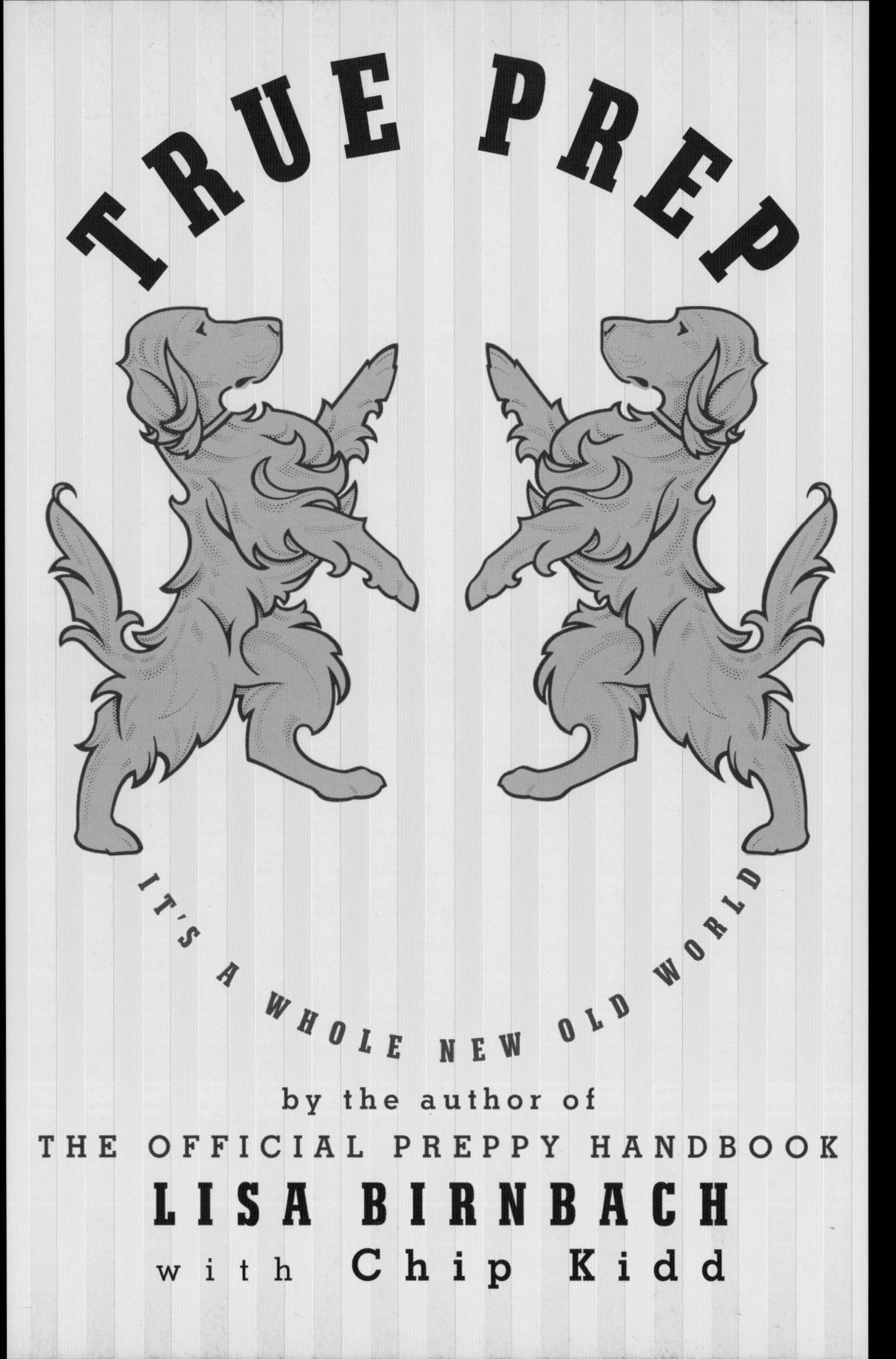

# TRUE PREP

### IT'S A WHOLE NEW OLD WORLD

by the author of

## THE OFFICIAL PREPPY HANDBOOK

# LISA BIRNBACH

## with Chip Kidd

---

**Late Edition**

Today, partly sunny, warm. High 75. Tonight, mostly clear. Low 53. Tomorrow, partly sunny, near-record warmth in afternoon. High 76. Details, SportsSunday Page 12.

# The New York Times

VOL. CLIX .. No. 55,000  © 2010 The New York Times  **NEW YORK, SUNDAY, APRIL 4, 2010**  $6 beyond the greater New York metropolitan area.  **$5.00**

## Contesting Jobless Claims Becomes a Boom Industry

### Errors and Delays by Agent for Employers Weaken Safety Net, Critics Charge

**By JASON DePARLE**

WASHINGTON — With a client list that reads like a roster of Fortune 500 firms, a little-known company with an odd name, the Talx Corporation, has come to dominate a thriving industry: helping employers process — and fight — unemployment claims.

Talx, which emerged from ob-

When fewer former workers get aid, a company pays lower unemployment taxes.

Wisconsin and Iowa passed laws to curtail procedural abuses that officials said were common in cases handled by Talx. Connecticut fined Talx (pronounced talks) and demanded an end to

*Continued on Page 10*

---

## Biff: The Preppy Primer Is Getting an Update

FRED R. CONRAD/THE NEW YORK TIMES

Chip Kidd, left, and Lisa Birnbach at a photo shoot last month for their new handbook on the preppy life, "True Prep."

to be good, it ended up being adopted as a kind of guidebook for those who wanted in.

book sold 1.3 million copies to aspiring prepsters wanted to know where to what to wear and how to appreciate what it called virtues of pink and green."

ong those buyers was Chip one of the industry's best-book designers, who loved iginal as a teenager growing near Reading, Pa., where ended public high school dored topsiders. The hand-e said, "changed my life."

he has teamed with the and one of the writers of iginal volume, Lisa Birn-or the follow-up, due out in

*Continued on Page 4*

---

## State Says Indian Point Plant Violates the Clean Water Act

**By DAVID M. HALBFINGER**

In a major victory for environmental advocates, New York State has ruled that outmoded cooling technology at the Indian Point nuclear power plant kills so many Hudson River fish, and consumes and contaminates so much water, that it violates the federal Clean Water Act.

The decision is a blow to the plant's owner, the Entergy Corporation, which now faces the prospect of having to spend hundreds of millions of dollars to build stadium-size cooling towers, or risk that Indian Point's two operating reactors — which

supply 30 percent of the electricity used by New York City and Westchester County — could be forced to shut down.

Entergy officials said that they were "disappointed" in the ruling and that they might fight it in court. The original federal licenses for the two 1970s-era reactors expire in 2013 and 2015, and a water quality certificate is a prerequisite for a 20-year renewal by the United States Nuclear Regulatory Commission. But a prolonged appeal in New York could delay a shutdown,

*Continued on Page 16*

## Rejoice, Muffy and Biff: The Preppy Primer Is Getting an Update

**By MOTOKO RICH**

Just when you thought it was safe to get back in your khakis.

Three decades after "The Official Preppy Handbook" was first unleashed into bookstores, a follow-up called "True Prep" is in the works — hoping to reignite preppy fervor, update the mindset and explain just what it means to be a Chip or a Muffy in a Barack world.

The original volume, a slim, plaid-covered paperback that poked fun at the gin-soaked polo-shirt and loafer-wearing set, started out as a piquant bit of mockery but, like "Liar's Poker," a bestseller about bond traders, and "Wall Street," the movie in which Michael Douglas declared

greed to be good, it ended up being adopted as a kind of guidebook for those who wanted in.

The book sold 1.3 million copies, many to aspiring prepsters who wanted to know where to shop, what to wear and how to fully appreciate what it called "the virtues of pink and green."

Among those buyers was Chip Kidd, one of the industry's best-known book designers, who loved the original as a teenager growing up near Reading, Pa., where he attended public high school and adored topsiders. The handbook, he said, "changed my life."

Now he has teamed with the editor and one of the writers of the original volume, Lisa Birnbach, for the follow-up, due out in

*Continued on Page 4*

Chip Kidd, left, and Lisa Birnbach at a photo shoot last month for their new handbook on the preppy life, "True Prep."

---

**INTERNATIONAL 6-10**

**25 in Iraqi Family Are Killed**
Men in uniforms resembling those of Americans killed 25 members of a family, but United States officials said their troops were not involved.  PAGE 6

**A Message for China**
Although it will delay a formal report on the issue, the Obama administration has vowed to press China to let its currency appreciate.  PAGE 10

**NATIONAL 12-21**

**Law Clinics Face a Backlash**
Legal clinics at law schools, which often take on powerful business interests, are facing attacks nationwide in courts and legislatures.  PAGE 12

**SPORTSSUNDAY**

**Duke vs. Butler in Final**
Butler, a small college in Indianapolis, will face Duke, a three-time champion, in the men's basketball title game. Duke reached its first final since 2001.  PAGE 1

**OP-ED IN WEEK IN REVIEW 8-11**

**Frank Rich**  PAGE 9

Geoff Spear photographed everything, which was fabulous but also a tremendous challenge. Most of what he and I had done over the years were still-life shots, and there would be many of those in this project, but the meat of the imagery was going to be live models in staged scenarios. And the models, by the way, weren't professionals; they were Lisa's friends and acquaintances (a bunch of mine, too)—which made the whole experience great fun and lent the end product an authenticity that you really can't fake.

We shot in Geoff's studio and on various locations, everywhere from Sandy's apartment in the famed Police Building in Soho to the offices at Knopf. Anyplace that looked right and yet didn't cost anything (oh, how preppy).

**OPPOSITE, RIGHT:** Once it was announced that the book was happening, there was media interest right away, but not even we could have anticipated that it would be front page news for the *New York Times* (!!). And on Easter Sunday, no less, a full six months before the book was set to release. My only regret was that this was no doubt the one and single time this would ever happen, and I looked utterly ridiculous. Oh well, at least I wasn't in the paper because I'd gotten arrested.

**OPPOSITE, LEFT:** The final jacket. Everyone kept asking me to make the title of the first book larger, and this was as big as it could get. Knopf, 2010.

**RIGHT:** The binding of the book. A wonderful chap named Greg D'Elia at the luxury footwear shop Stubbs & Wootton in Palm Beach had prototype slippers made with our logo on them in time to shoot for the cover.

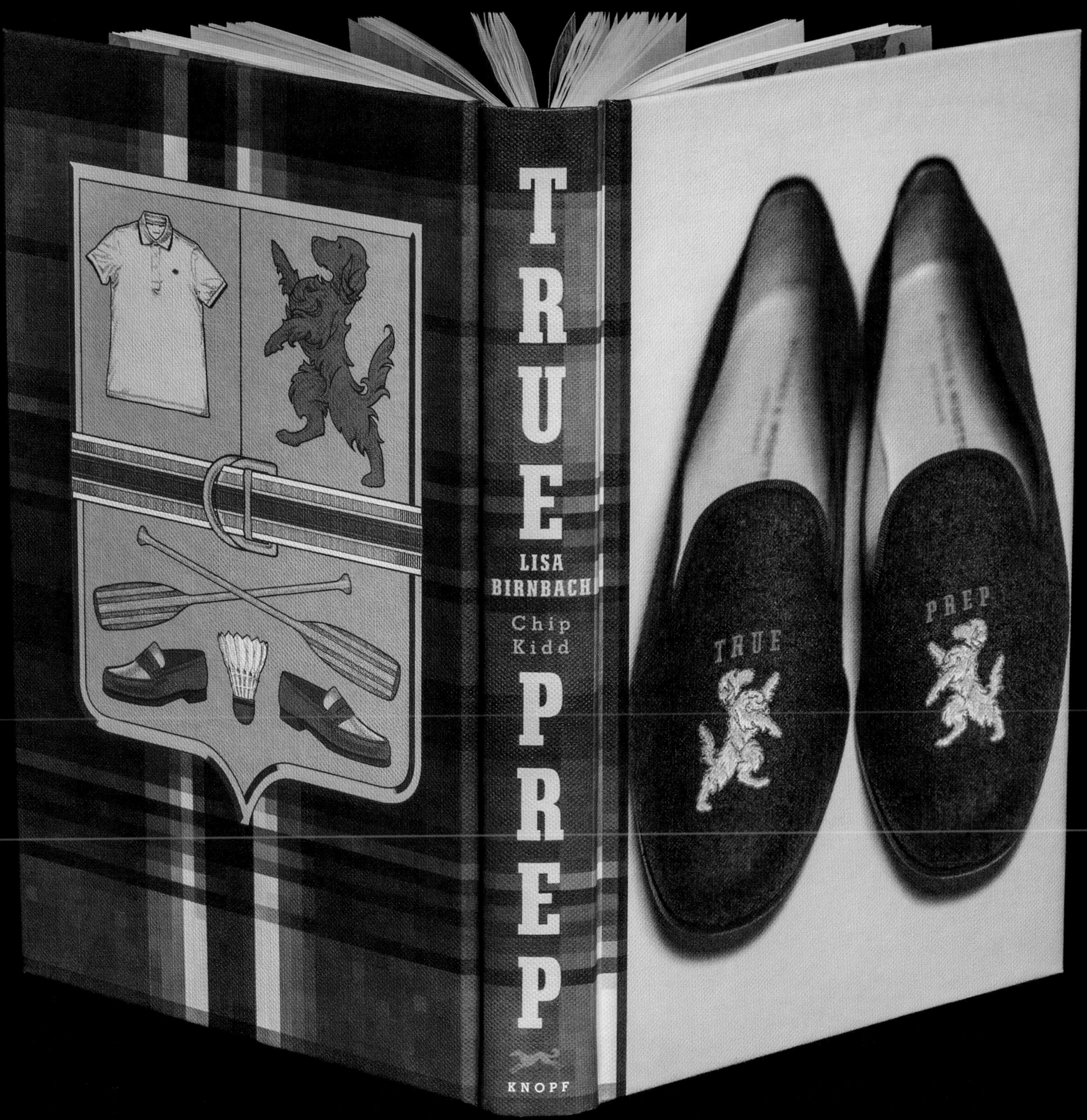
TRUE
LISA
BIRNBACH
Chip
Kidd
PREP
KNOPF
TRUE
PREP

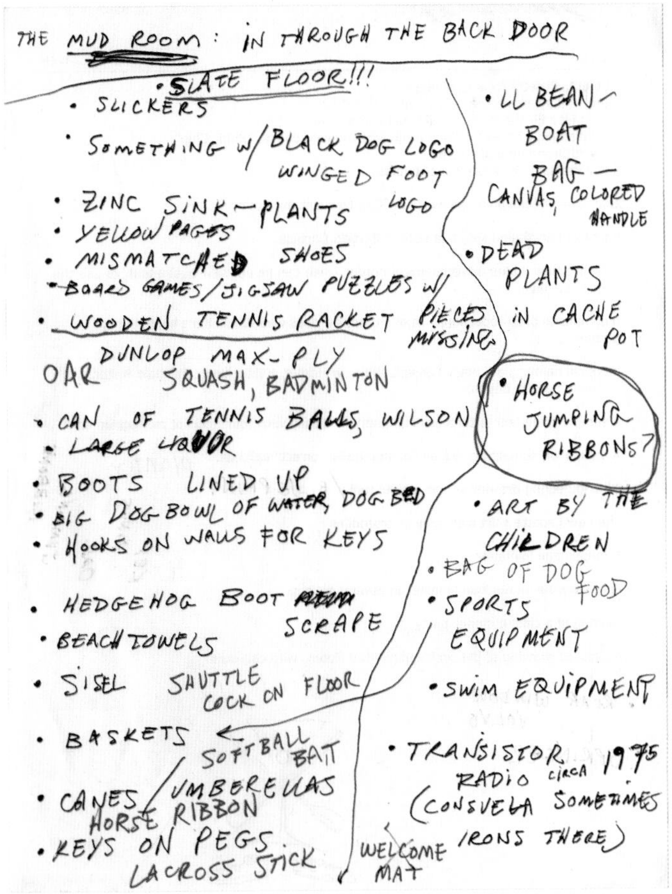

THE MUD ROOM: IN THROUGH THE BACK DOOR

- SLATE FLOOR!!!
- SLICKERS
- SOMETHING w/ BLACK DOG LOGO WINGED FOOT LOGO
- ZINC SINK — PLANTS
- YELLOW PAGES
- MISMATCHED SHOES
- BOARD GAMES / JIGSAW PUZZLES w/ PIECES MISSING
- WOODEN TENNIS RACKET DUNLOP MAX-PLY
- OAR SQUASH, BADMINTON
- CAN OF TENNIS BALLS, WILSON
- LARGE LIQUOR
- BOOTS LINED UP
- BIG DOG BOWL OF WATER, DOG BED
- HOOKS ON WALLS FOR KEYS
- HEDGEHOG BOOT SCRAPE
- BEACH TOWELS
- SISEL SHUTTLE COCK ON FLOOR
- BASKETS
- SOFTBALL BAT
- CANES / UMBERELLAS
- HORSE RIBBON
- KEYS ON PEGS
- LACROSS STICK
- LL BEAN — BOAT BAG — CANVAS, COLORED HANDLE
- DEAD PLANTS IN CACHE POT
- HORSE JUMPING RIBBONS?
- ART BY THE CHILDREN
- BAG OF DOG FOOD
- SPORTS EQUIPMENT
- SWIM EQUIPMENT
- TRANSISTOR RADIO CIRCA 1975 (CONSUELA SOMETIMES IRONS THERE)
- WELCOME MAT

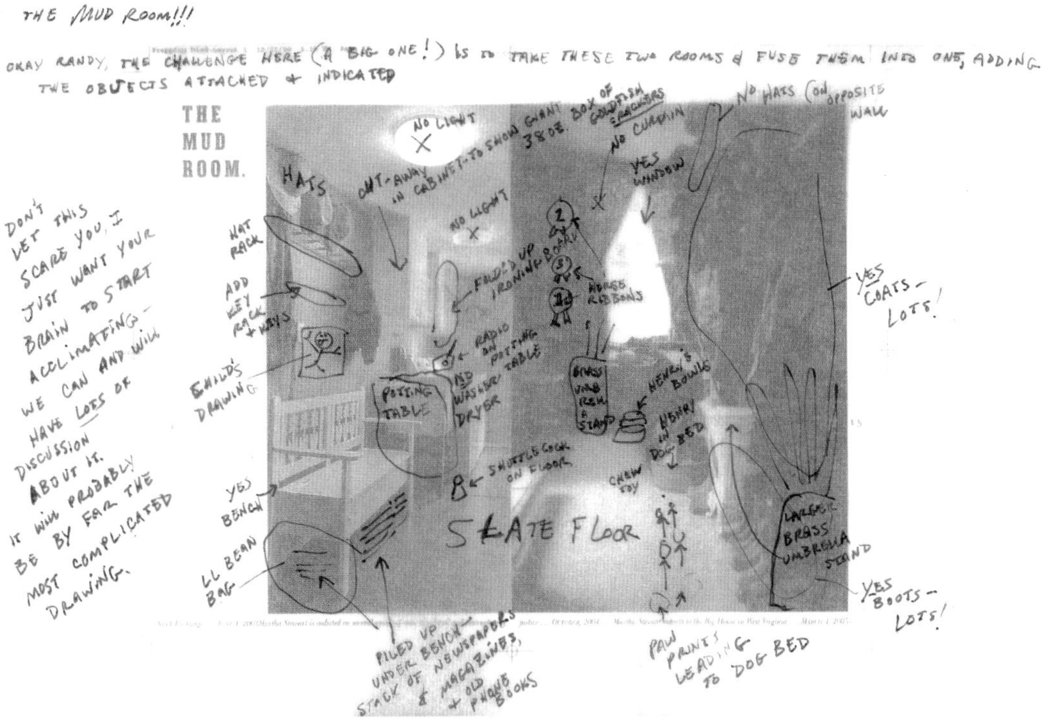
THE MUD ROOM!!!
OKAY RANDY, THE CHALLENGE HERE (A BIG ONE!) IS TO TAKE THESE TWO ROOMS & FUSE THEM INTO ONE, ADDING THE OBJECTS ATTACHED + INDICATED
THE MUD ROOM.
DON'T LET THIS SCARE YOU, I JUST WANT YOUR BRAIN TO START ACCLIMATING — WE CAN AND WILL HAVE LOTS OF DISCUSSION ABOUT IT. IT WILL PROBABLY BE BY FAR THE MOST COMPLICATED DRAWING.
HATS
HAT RACK
ADD KEY RACK + KEYS
CHILD'S DRAWING
POTTING TABLE
YES BENCH
LL BEAN BAG
NO LIGHT
NO CURTAIN
YES WINDOW
HORSE RIBBONS
SLATE FLOOR
YES COATS — LOTS!
LARGER BRASS UMBRELLA STAND
YES BOOTS — LOTS!
PAW PRINTS LEADING TO DOG BED
PILED UP UNDER BENCH — STACK OF NEWSPAPERS & MAGAZINES + OLD PHONE BOOKS

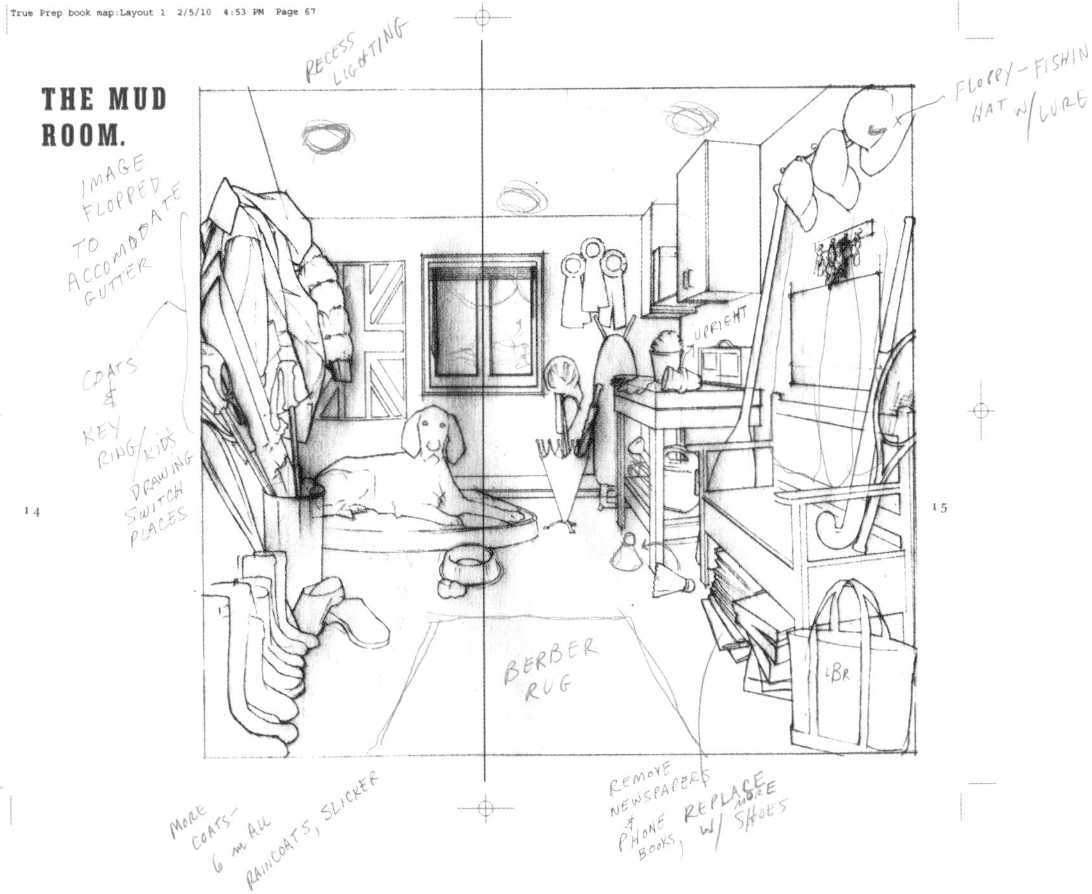
True Prep book map:Layout 1 2/5/10 4:53 PM Page 67
THE MUD ROOM.
RECESS LIGHTING
FLOPPY — FISHIN HAT w/ LURE
IMAGE FLOPPED TO ACCOMODATE GUTTER
COATS & KEY RING / KIDS DRAWING SWITCH PLACES
UPRIGHT
BERBER RUG
MORE COATS — 6 in ALL RAINCOATS, SLICKER
REMOVE NEWSPAPERS & PHONE BOOKS, REPLACE w/ MORE SHOES



This spread details the process of working with illustrator Randy Glass on one of the most complicated illustrations for the book, the Mudroom. As with so much else associated with this project, it was a real learning experience—I didn't even know what a mudroom was until Lisa brought it up. See definition at opposite, upper left.

There was no way we'd find or create the perfect photograph that would include everything we wanted, so it had to be drawn. I don't think there were two other pages in the book that we spent so much time on. Taking credit, it was I who made sure that Lisa's initials were on the monogrammed L.L.Bean boat and tote bag in the lower right of the drawing. (Details!)

*True Prep* debuted at No. 2 on the *New York Times* best-seller list in September 2010. I am immensely proud of it. Occasionally I open it up and what I see is a personal yearbook of wonderful memories about the time we spent creating it.

# THE MUDROOM.

*1. To the eat-in kitchen. More masterpieces from Prudence and Constance's lower school art classes awaits.*

*2. Daddy's boots. And an extra pair; no one seems to know where they came from.*

*3. Ski poles should be in the ski rack, too.*

*4. Who put the skis here? They belong in the ski rack.*

*5. Connie? Where are your ski boots? Did you leave them in the car again?*

*6. Every time the keys fall off, Mrs. Gibbs picks them up. Not because she's a stickler for neatness but because she's afraid Henry will eat them.*

*7. We bought this Union Jack banner when we were in India after grad school.*

*8. Ditto the Berber rug we haggled over in the souk in Marrakesh. Always reminds me of our first walk-up.*

*9. This paddle doesn't belong here at all. Tyler should put it back in the boathouse.*

*10. Henry in his "Sphinx" pose.*

*11. His water bowl and toy positioned to trip us.*

*12. Ernesto, the gardener, likes to sit on a swing and smoke a cigarette now and then. Not that we've noticed, but he's the only one around who uses it.*

*13. Umbrella stand from our old apartment on 74th between Park and Lexington. Doesn't really belong here, but where else do we put our golf umbrella and butterfly net?*

*14. The girls were so proud of winning their ribbons. Now they've forgotten what horses are.*

*15. Extra-large Goldfish box. Someone's been to Costco!*

*16. Potting table. For potting.*

*17. Old radio. Should bin it, but it works so well. Does anyone listen to it?*

*18. Drawing, untitled, circa 1994.*

*19. North Face, Pendleton, foul weather slicker by Carhartt, L.L.Bean barn jacket, Barbour quilted vest.*

*20. Bean duck boots and Prudence's Uggs. Ugh.*

*21. Assorted important hats.*

*22. Boat tote from L.L.Bean. One of seven in this family.*

English houses have long had mudrooms. Where else would you keep your Wellies after a tramp in the mud, Barbour and down jackets, walking sticks, racquets? Mudrooms can be wood-paneled and quite grand, depending. For us, where else would we find the keys to the twelve-year-old Land Rover? And where would Henry go for his REM sleep? Preppies are now focusing their domestic attentions on a room that was previously humble and misunderstood. This one is rather simple. But it will do fine.

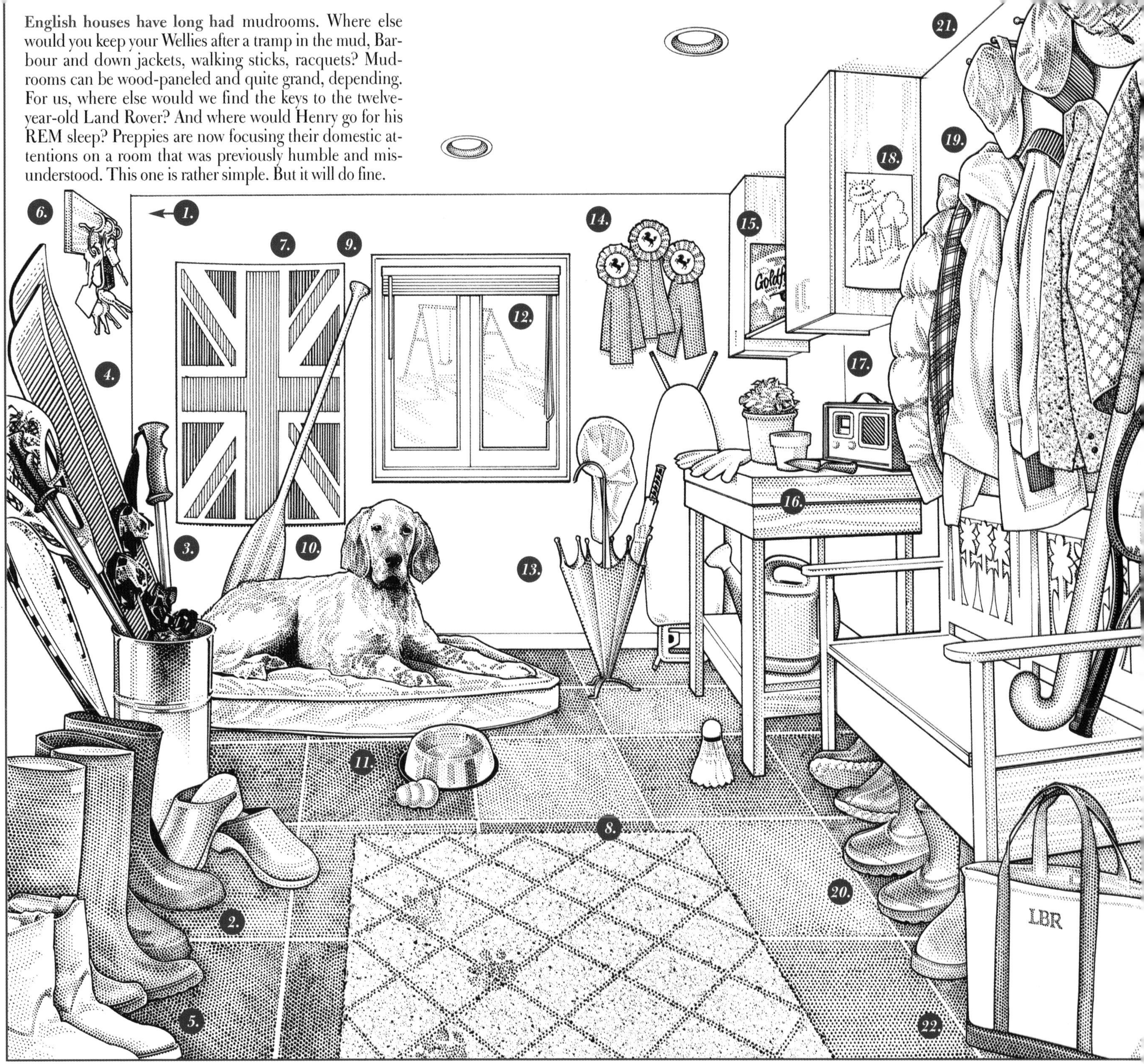

1.
2.
3.
4.
5.
6.
7.
8.
9.
10.
11.
12.
13.
14.
15.
16.
17.
18.
19.
20.
21.
22.
LBR

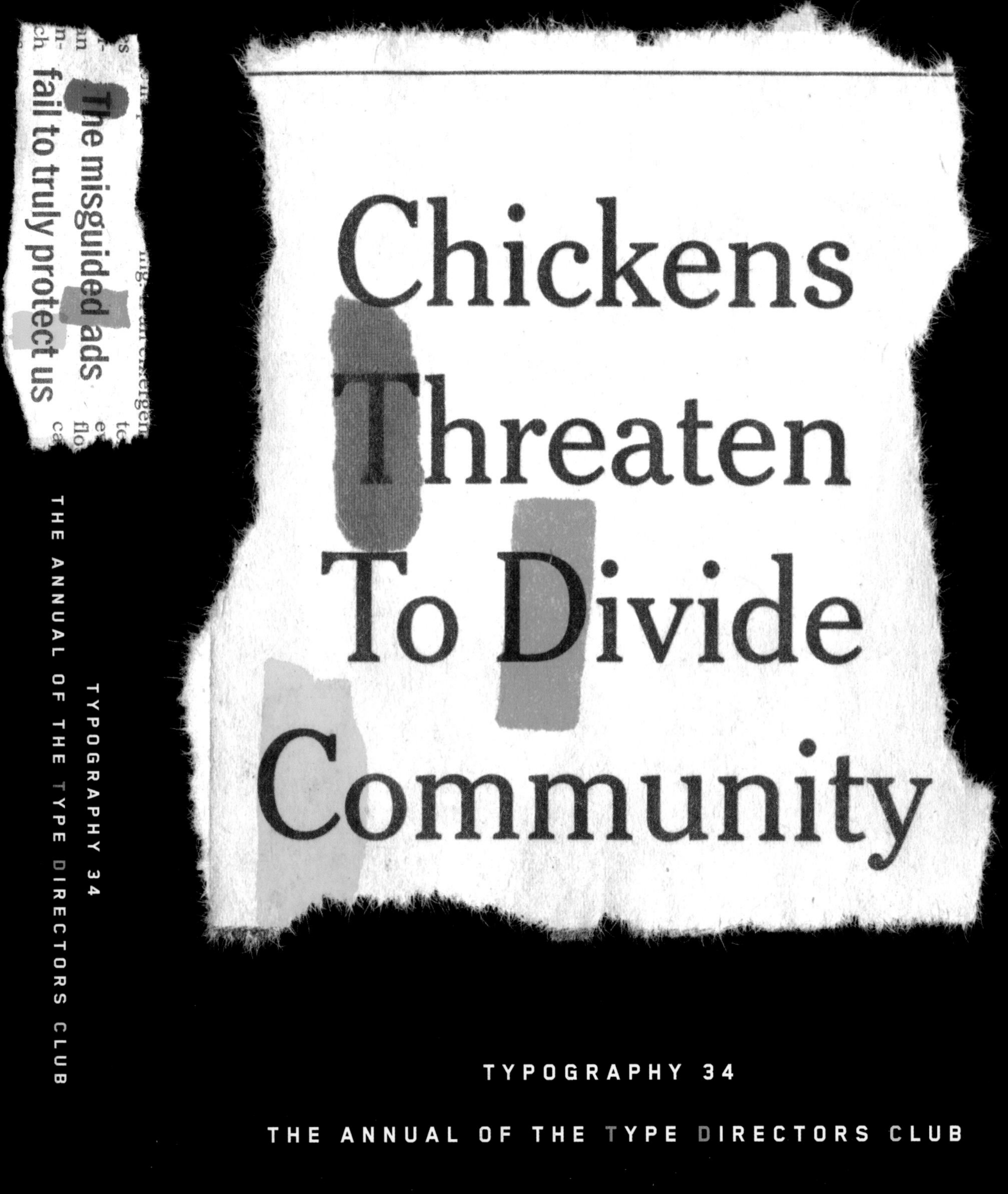
The misguided ads
fail to truly protect us
THE ANNUAL OF THE TYPE DIRECTORS CLUB
TYPOGRAPHY 34
Chickens Threaten To Divide Community
TYPOGRAPHY 34
THE ANNUAL OF THE TYPE DIRECTORS CLUB

# Read All about It

Designing the annual for the Type Directors Club is one of those bucket-list assignments that marks a highlight of any graphic designer's career. And it's utterly terrifying. The book is a collection of the winners in the annual competition to determine the best examples of typography for that year, and it has been ongoing since the 1920s. So to figure out how all of this information should be presented becomes a typographically conceptual problem, one that has been solved brilliantly by the best designers in the business, all before you get the chance. For example, the designer the year before me was Paula Scher. Thanks a lot.

I approached the problem by thinking about typography not as an aesthetic art form, but as a delivery system for something you actually read. I still subscribe to ink-on-paper newspapers and have them delivered to my door first thing in the morning, chief among them the *New York Times* and *New York Post*. To me they are the perfect yin and yang of journalism, and I have been obsessively clipping out headlines and pull-quotes from both papers for over a decade. Collecting them for what—other than my own amusement—I didn't know, until now. Here was the answer for this project. I had hundreds of these clippings, but for the Type Directors Club I whittled them down to those that contained a T, D, and C (in that order). And then I highlighted them in red, blue, and yellow (just like the Bauhaus!). My first idea for the cover image was the "Getting Ahead Can Be a Bitch" quote (above), about Martha Stewart going to jail, courtesy of the *Post*, but the publisher (HarperCollins) nixed it. So we went with a *Times* headline (left) about people raising artisanal poultry on the roof of their co-op in Brooklyn. All the other examples on this spread are totally genuine and I continue to collect them to this day.

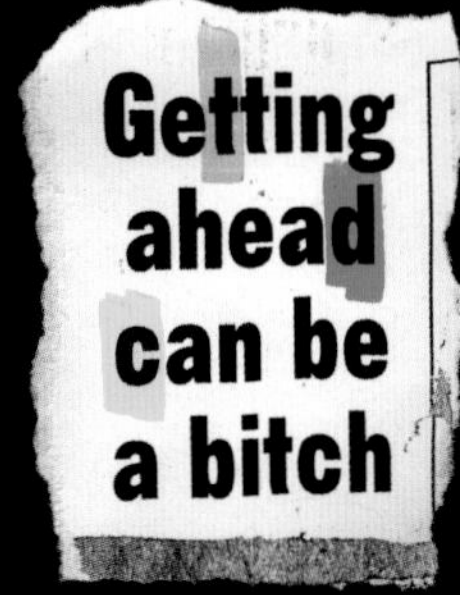
Getting ahead can be a bitch

jury that reached a
uilty verdict without
aving all of the facts.

A pet that
had to be fed
raw chickens
every day.

**'I thought he was kind of a dick yesterday.'**

'She's not a drug addict.
She wears clothes, she
wears underwear.'

A lactating
hooker
dressed as a
nun who
breast-feeds
diaper-clad
men

Body of Rat
Is Linked
To Blackout
At Atomic Site

**Dinosaurs got lucky**

Dinosaurs ended up ruling the Earth 200 million

"Life is very difficult and everything kills you," she once said. "The only thing you can do nowadays is sit fully clothed in the woods and eat fruit."

Unfulfilled at an Art Deco Bathhouse

A romantic tour
offers city views and
a lecture on how to
sterilize sludge.

"This world
will become
one giant
garbage can
one day."

Driver With Nixon Bobblehead
Has Encounters With Fame

"It all kind of happened
at once. Now I have
psoriasis."

**The vast majority falls into three categories: Wimps, Destroyers or Crazies.**

# Baby tossed from moving car

*Plastic garbage bags
containing body parts
were left along highways
in New Jersey.*

How to make a crisp crispy
and a crumble crumbly.

Live nude woman in
Times Square coffin.

'I'm supposed to
do this, and I can't
tell you why.'

Before the
Wonderbra, there
were falsies made
of elk hair and
boingy bustiers of
hard-coiled wire.

A choreographer, working with a team of scientists,
depicts a neurological illness onstage.

*The goal should not be to
create a population of
thin people, but those
who are less poor.*

*It has flying dentures, a
flatulent penguin and human testicles smeared with dog food.*

'If I followed my instincts,
I would be strangled by
some hairy sailor in a
public urinal.'

"I had no restraint. They
were crawling up
towards my face."

*A feat its engineer
likened to cutting the
legs off a table while
dinner is on it.*

"Life is very difficult and every-
hing kills you," she once said. "The
nly thing you can do nowadays is sit
ully clothed in the woods and eat
ruit."

*They're Tan
And Toned,
But They're
Not Very Nice*

The Naked Man Doesn't Dance

Hypothetically, donating
sperm so friends can have a
baby is a simple decision.

Top prizewinner: a
sand castle fountain
whose designers
spout water.

In Sly Tweets,
A Rich Lode
For Comedy

It was hard to be
counterculture and
give cellulite tips.

Divorce and all, sex change
and all, this would be a loving
family of three.

P. 1

# DON'T KNOW WHERE,

Okay, first off, this story takes place in the mid-1940s. Not that it has anything to do with WWII or that era in particular, I just love those versions of the characters. Michael need not emulate Dick Sprang or any of the other Golden Age artists in particular, he should do his own version thereof, which he has already ably demonstrated he's great at.

Opening splash page is bisected in half horizontally, two panels, one at top and one at bottom.
Top panel: Batman in a 3/4 pose, in full gear, from the waist up. He's hunched to the left a bit (our left), stern, concentrating on what he's saying. He is talking into the receiver of his utility belt buckle radio, which is in his right hand, held to his mouth, and connected to the belt buckle by a curly-cue wire. He is on a rooftop somewhere in Gotham.

B, dialogue: "Robin, come in."

R, dialogue, in jagged balloon coming out of radio: "Roger. Robin here."

B, dialogue: "I'm onto something. Meet me on the roof of the Sprang Building. Ten O'Clock."



# DON'T KNOW WHEN.

Robin in 3-Quarter pose to match Batman's above, though asymmetrically—hunched towards the right (our right), in the Batcave. He in turn is talking into his belt radio, with the receiver to his mouth in his left hand, also connected by a curly-cue wire to his belt buckle.

R, dialogue: "Got it. See you there and then."

B, dialogue, in jagged balloon, coming out of R's radio: "Avoid detection. Use the cloak on the Auto-gyro."

**ABOVE:** The title, of course, comes from that great British WWII torch song "We'll Meet Again," made famous by Vera Lynn. This is my first script page, which Michael totally nailed, as he did the rest of the story. Curiously, he works in black and red inks, though the final printing was rendered in black and gray. As we went on, we begged for more pages, but there was a strict limit. I could have stretched this story to a full-length graphic novel, an epic quest, but we were thrilled just to be able to do it at all; it's very old school. This collaboration went so well that I then worked as an editor with Michael to publish his first graphic novel, *Shoplifter*, at Pantheon a year later. There will be more to come.

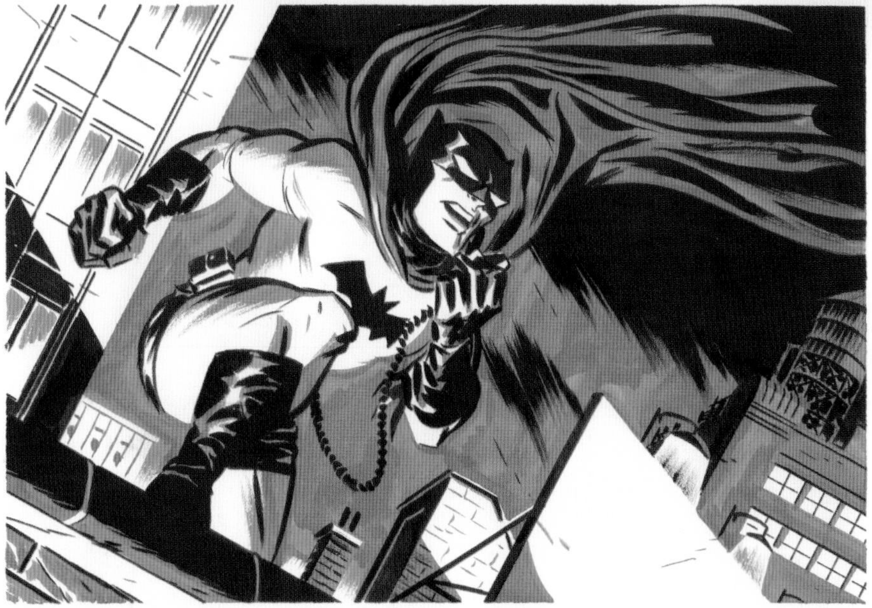

In 2012, DC Comics decided to do a new series of its beautifully conceived *Batman: Black and White* stories, an anthology project of short ten-page tales by a wide variety of writers and artists, and they asked me to kick off the first story in the first issue (there were to be six in all). I was given a free brief, and there was a young artist named Michael Cho in Toronto with whom I wanted to work. He had caught my eye with his extraordinary design sense that evoked a cross between Bruce Timm and Darwyn Cooke, yet he was unique from both of them. DC was aware of Michael but hadn't worked with him before, and we agreed that this

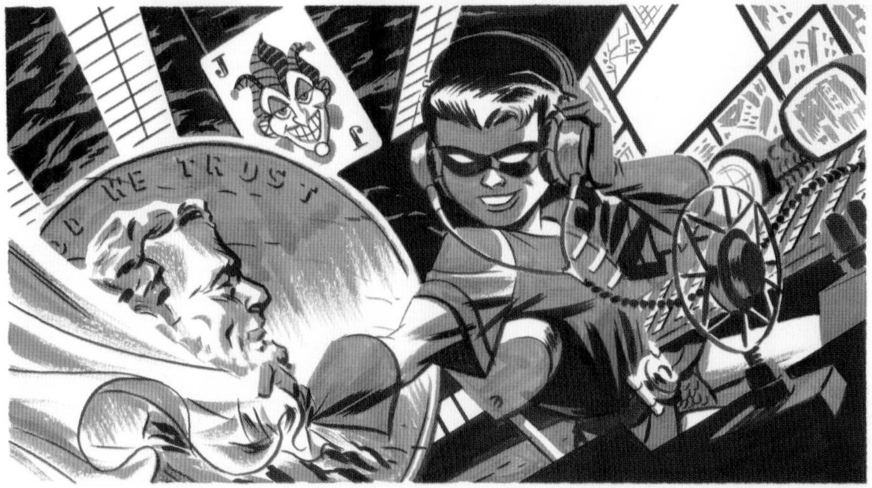

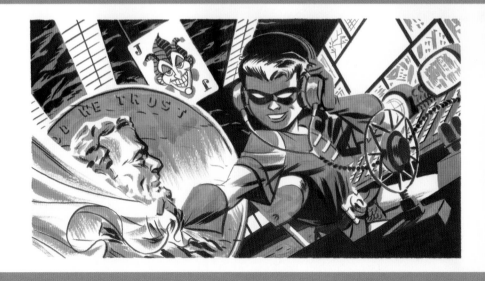

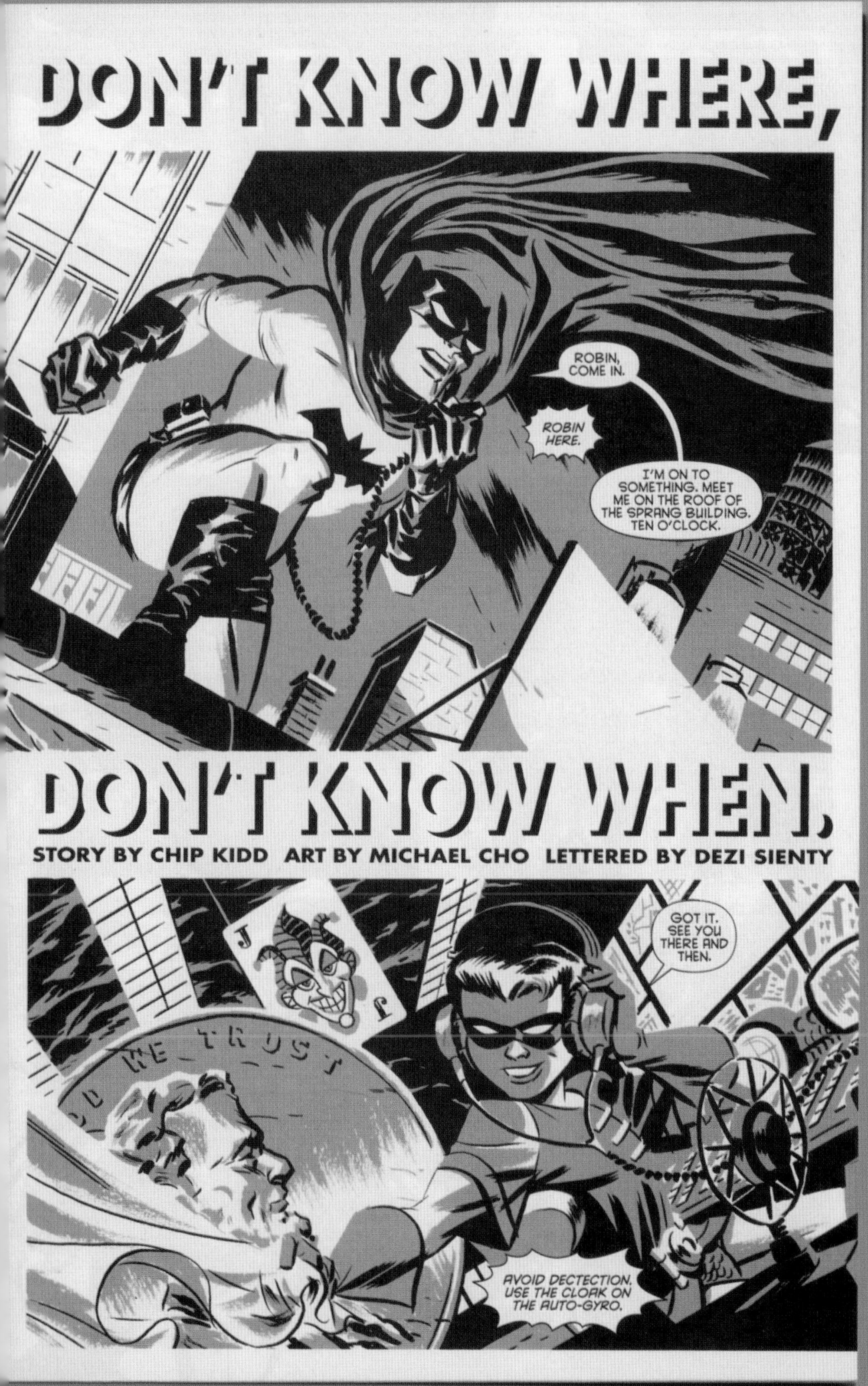
DON'T KNOW WHERE,
ROBIN, COME IN.
ROBIN HERE.
I'M ON TO SOMETHING. MEET ME ON THE ROOF OF THE SPRANG BUILDING. TEN O'CLOCK.
DON'T KNOW WHEN.
STORY BY CHIP KIDD ART BY MICHAEL CHO LETTERED BY DEZI SIENTY
GOT IT. SEE YOU THERE AND THEN.
WE TRUST
AVOID DECTECTION. USE THE CLOAK ON THE AUTO-GYRO.

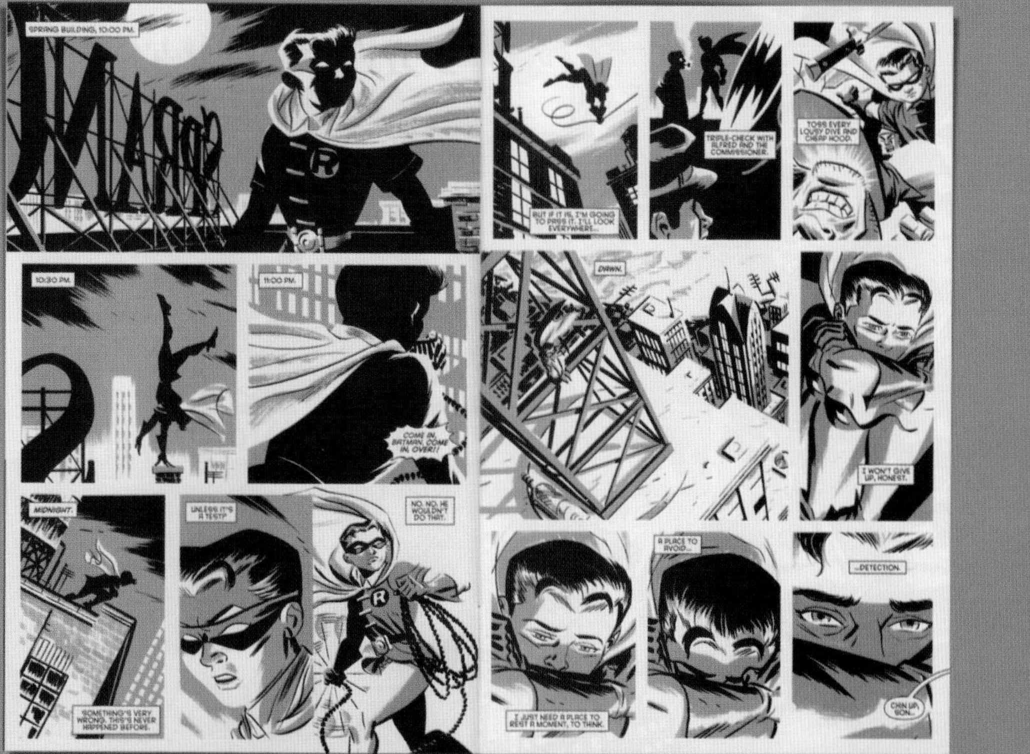
SPRING BUILDING, 10:00 PM.
10:30 PM.
11:00 PM.
COME IN, BATMAN, COME IN, OVER!!
MIDNIGHT.
SOMETHING'S VERY WRONG. THIS'S NEVER HAPPENED BEFORE.
UNLESS IT'S A TEST?
NO, NO, HE WOULDN'T DO THAT.
BUT IF IT IS, I'M GOING TO PASS IT. I'LL LOOK EVERYWHERE...
TRIPLE-CHECK WITH ALFRED AND THE COMMISSIONER.
TOSS EVERY LOUSY DIVE AND CHEAP HOOD.
DAWN.
I WON'T GIVE UP, HONEST.
I JUST NEED A PLACE TO REST A MOMENT, TO THINK.
A PLACE TO AVOID...
...DETECTION.
CHIN UP, SON...

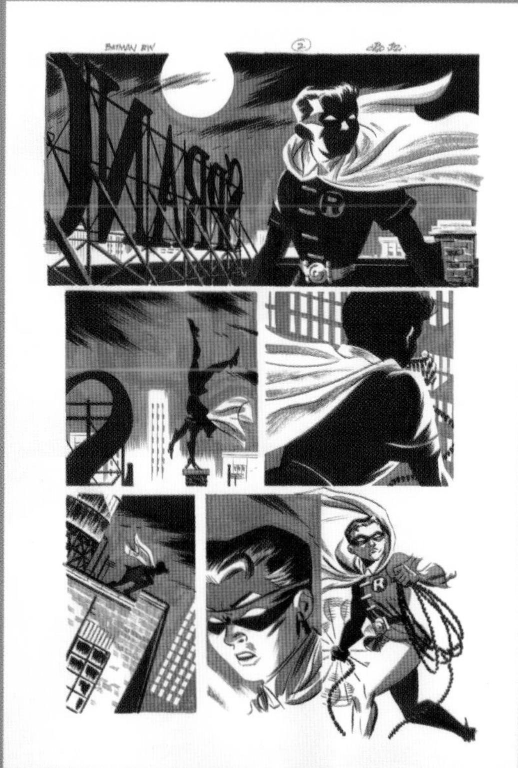



project would be the perfect introduction for all of us. He did a truly phenomenal job on a story idea that I had been harboring for quite some time: Batman goes missing, Robin has to find him, and in the process he meets and works with Superman for the first time. What I really liked about the dynamic between Robin and Superman is that Robin comes up with a brilliant idea about how to find Bruce that Superman never would have thought of, but the Man of Steel is the only being who could provide the means to pull it off.

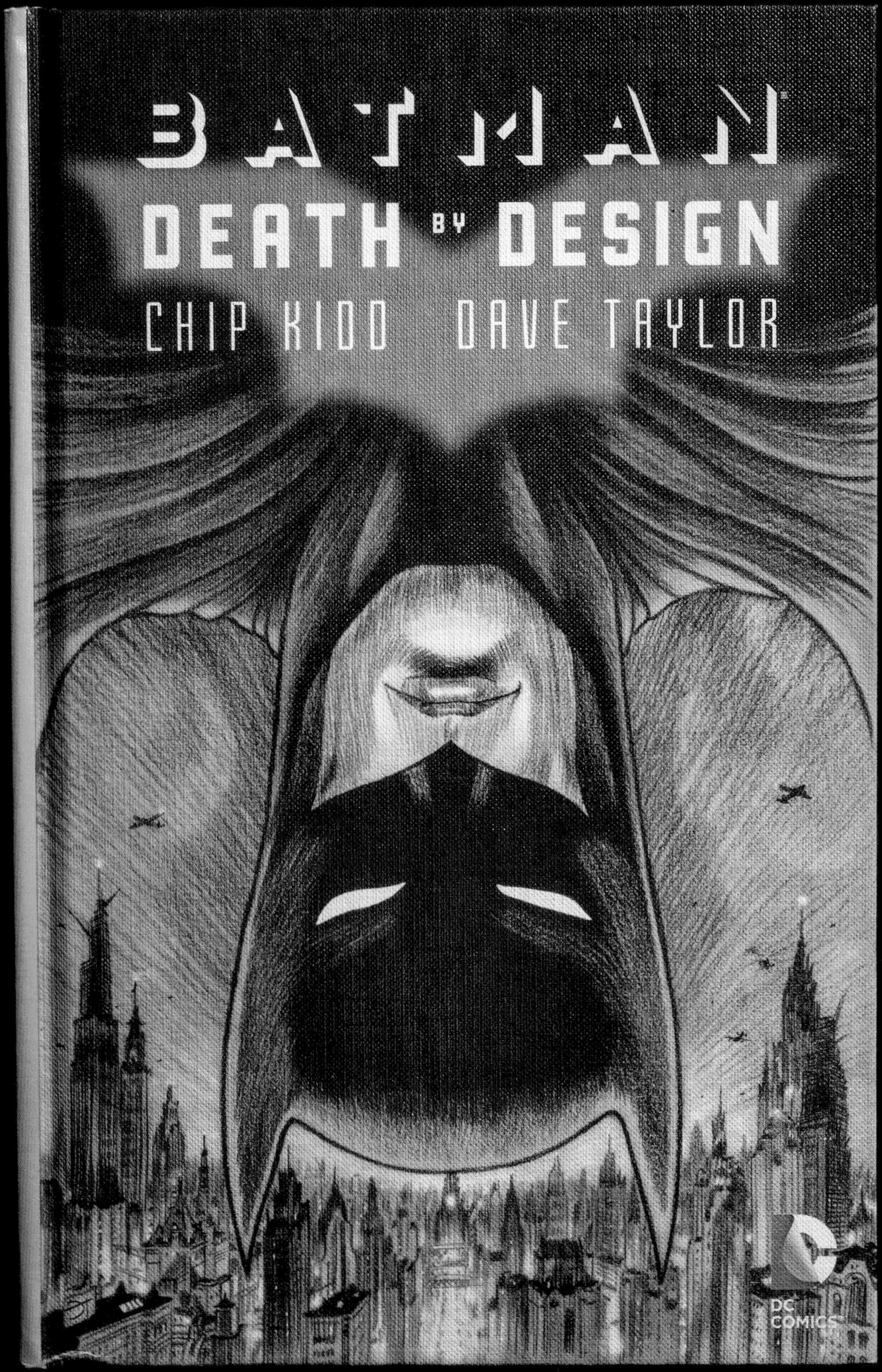
BATMAN
DEATH BY DESIGN
CHIP KIDD DAVE TAYLOR
DC COMICS



## My Bat Story

So, when I was on stage with Neil Gaiman at the 92nd Street Y in the spring of 2008 (see p. 29), we geeked out about Batman and the current issue of Detective Comics he was writing. I was quite public in my enthusiasm.

Afterwards, DC Comics editor-in-chief Dan DiDio arrived backstage, very pleased, and said to me, “Wow, I didn’t know you were such a Batman fan!” That struck me as odd because I had produced several books on the character over the years. He continued: “You should do a Batman graphic novel for us sometime!”

I was flabbergasted. “Please don’t say that if you don’t really mean it.”

“I mean it, just follow up with Chi,” meaning Mark Chiarello, VP and creative director of DC Comics, whom I had known and worked with for years on various design commissions for the company. We talked the following day, and the next step was for me to submit a proposal, the more details the better.

Even though I was a lifelong fan, and had thoroughly enjoyed creating the books about the history of Batman, I hadn’t been harboring an original Batman story in my gut all this time that I was dying to tell. But now I had to come up with one. I decided to approach it the way I would any design problem I set out to solve—first, define it. So, I posed the basic question: Why does Batman exist?

There are any number of ways to answer that, but I settled on this one: Batman exists because Gotham City is a mess, and the police alone cannot tackle the problem (hell, in a lot of Batman stories the police *are* the problem, or at least a big part of it). But following this thread further, Batman exists as a response to urban injustice. As someone who had been living and working in New York City for close to thirty years, I started thinking about examples of urban injustice that I encounter every day, things that might make good source material. I also considered what unique facets Batman fans might think I could bring to the table, and suddenly a title popped into my head—Batman: Death by Design. Now, normally, you don’t start with a title, you start with a story and then figure out what to call it later, but this seemed so right to me. Besides, as someone who had thoroughly studied the 70-plus years of Bat-lore, I knew that no one had ever used that title before. That was very important.

And then I opened the newspaper . . .

CHIP KIDD
DAVE TAYLOR
*PRESENT*

DEATH BY

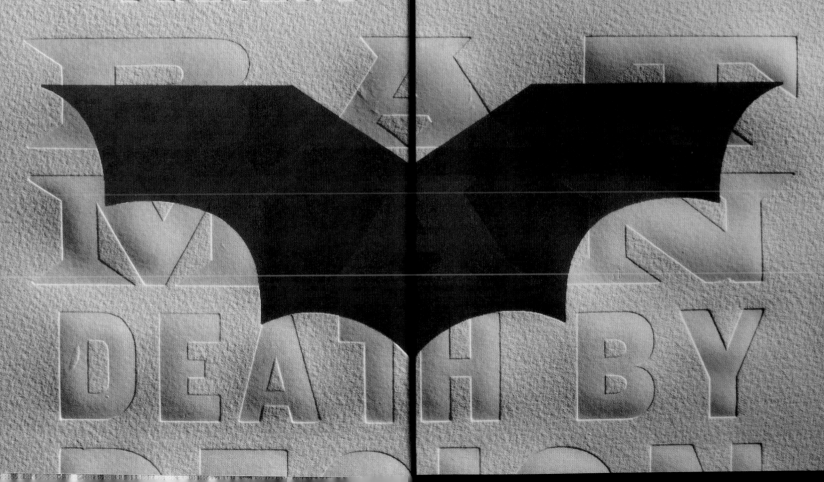

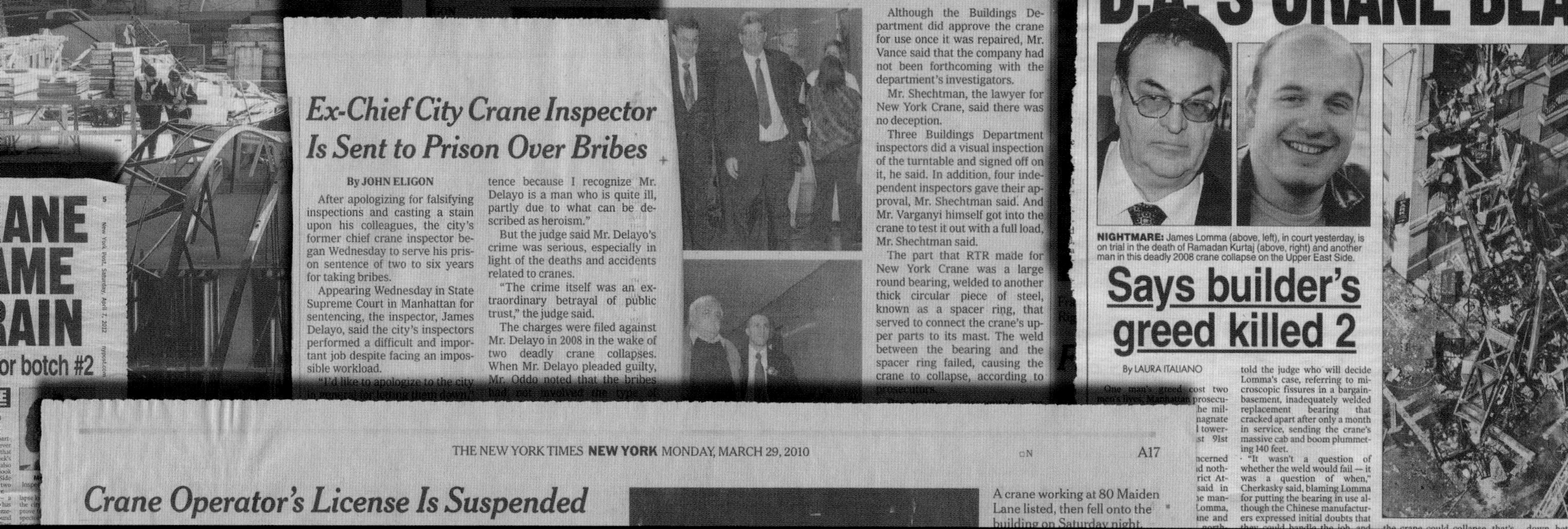


It was really quite astounding. In broad daylight on a sunny weekday afternoon, on New York's Upper East Side—one of the most affluent neighborhoods in the city and less than fifteen blocks south of my own apartment building—a massive construction crane came loose from its mooring and crashed headlong into the building across the street, killing two people. Headlines blared, fingers were pointed, the images were devastating, and for the longest time . . . no one was even indicted. I remember at the time thinking (as I so often do), "Damn, Batman would be so all over this."

So now I had a key piece of the story and the opening scene. But then another case of urban injustice started tapping me on the shoulder (or more accurately, bumping into me) as I waited one afternoon for a delayed Amtrak train to arrive at . . . Penn Station. By which I mean the airless, disorganized bastard child of what it used to be. The sudden demolition of the original magnificent Beaux Arts station in 1961 was one of the great American architectural crimes of the 20th century, and it eventually led to the creation of the Landmarks Commission in New York City that saved Grand Central Station a decade later. But the damage was done, and it has yet to be corrected in any acceptable way after more than fifty years. And there was the other part of my story. Now I just had to give it a time and some art direction, then fill it with characters. It was starting to become fun. I asked Mark Chiarello: "So who am I allowed to have?"

"What do you mean?"

"Cohorts, villains, who's off limits?" I knew character usage was an issue if one w working within the official ongoing narratives of the monthly comics. But he assure me that was not the case here; this was a self-contained story outside of that continui

"No one's off-limits. Who do you want?"

"Alfred, the Joker, a Penguin cameo." Hey, shoot for the moon.

"You got 'em."

Wow. "Also, I want to create a couple new characters—a female lead, a new antiher villain, an evil corrupt construction union boss, a pair of insufferable genius architec and an intrepid young reporter." That was all fine, but he reminded me that any cha acters I created who were published in the final story would be property of DC Comic That was fine with me, I thoroughly knew the rules.

What I was envisioning would look like a mythical great 1930s big-budget Batman fil by Fritz Lang, but thematically using a combination of *The Fountainhead* and *On t Waterfront*, with a little Busby Berkeley thrown in for a couple of dazzling set pieces submitted an outline and character summaries. Check. Now we needed an artist. C suggested Liverpudlian Dave Taylor, who perfectly fit the bill. He was an excellent draft man who did beautiful pencil work and whose father had been an architect. Dave kne how to draw buildings and channel Hugh Ferriss, another major influence to the loo of our Gotham City.

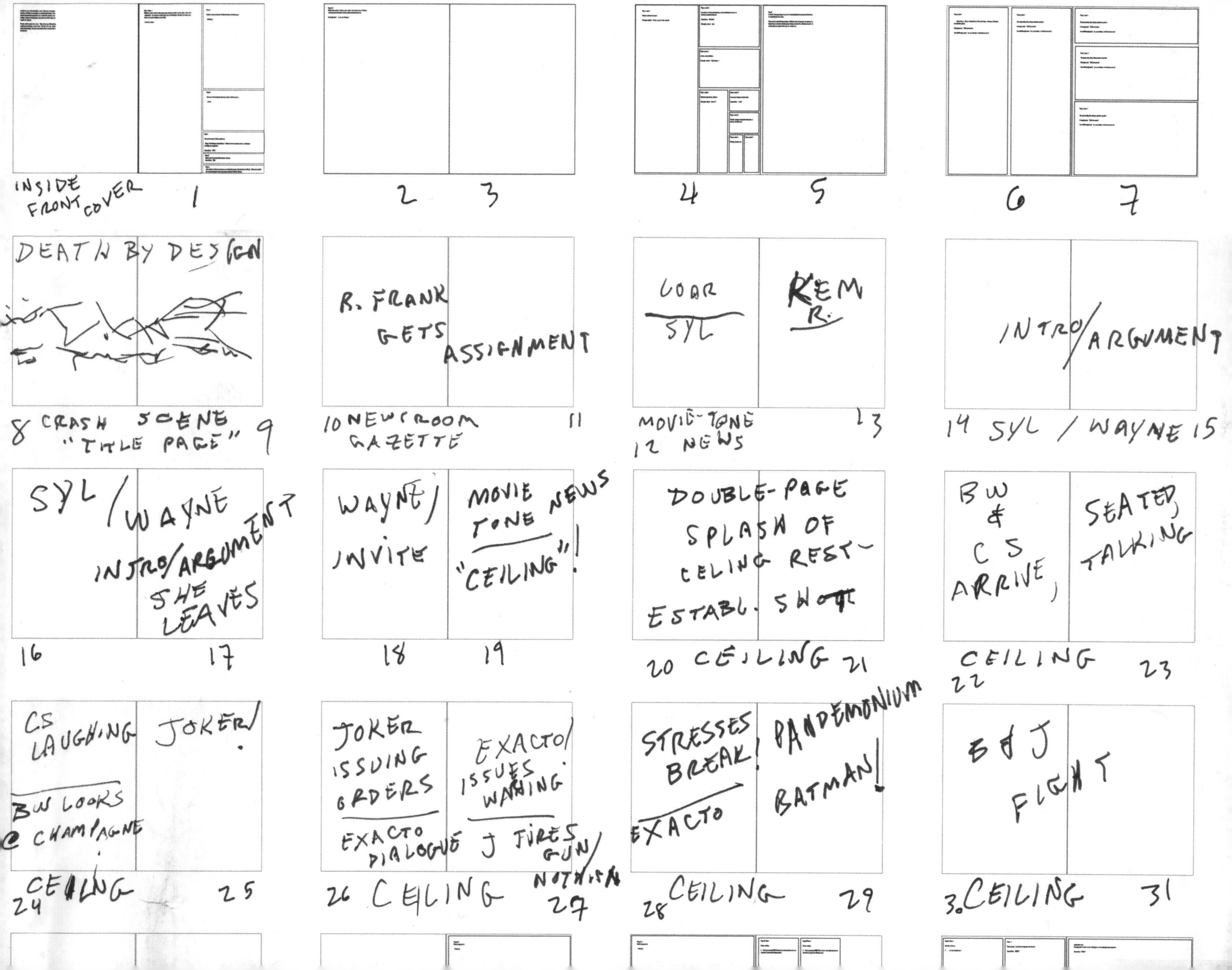
INSIDE FRONT COVER
1
2
3
4
5
6
7
DEATH BY DESIGN
8 CRASH SCENE "TITLE PAGE" 9
R. FRANK GETS ASSIGNMENT
10 NEWSROOM GAZETTE
11
LOAR
SYL
KEM
R.
MOVIE-TONE
12 NEWS
13
INTRO/ARGUMENT
14 SYL / WAYNE 15
SYL / WAYNE
INTRO/ARGUMENT
SHE LEAVES
16
17
WAYNE/ INVITE
MOVIE TONE NEWS
"CEILING"!
18
19
DOUBLE-PAGE SPLASH OF CEILING REST-
ESTABL. SHOT
20 CEILING 21
BW & CS ARRIVE,
SEATED, TALKING
CEILING
22
23
CS LAUGHING
JOKER!
BW LOOKS @ CHAMPAGNE
24 CEILING
25
JOKER ISSUING ORDERS
EXACTO DIALOGUE
EXACTO/ ISSUES WARNING
J FIRES GUN/ NOTHING
26 CEILING
27
STRESSES BREAK!
EXACTO
PANDEMONIUM
BATMAN!
28 CEILING
29
B & J FIGHT
30 CEILING
31

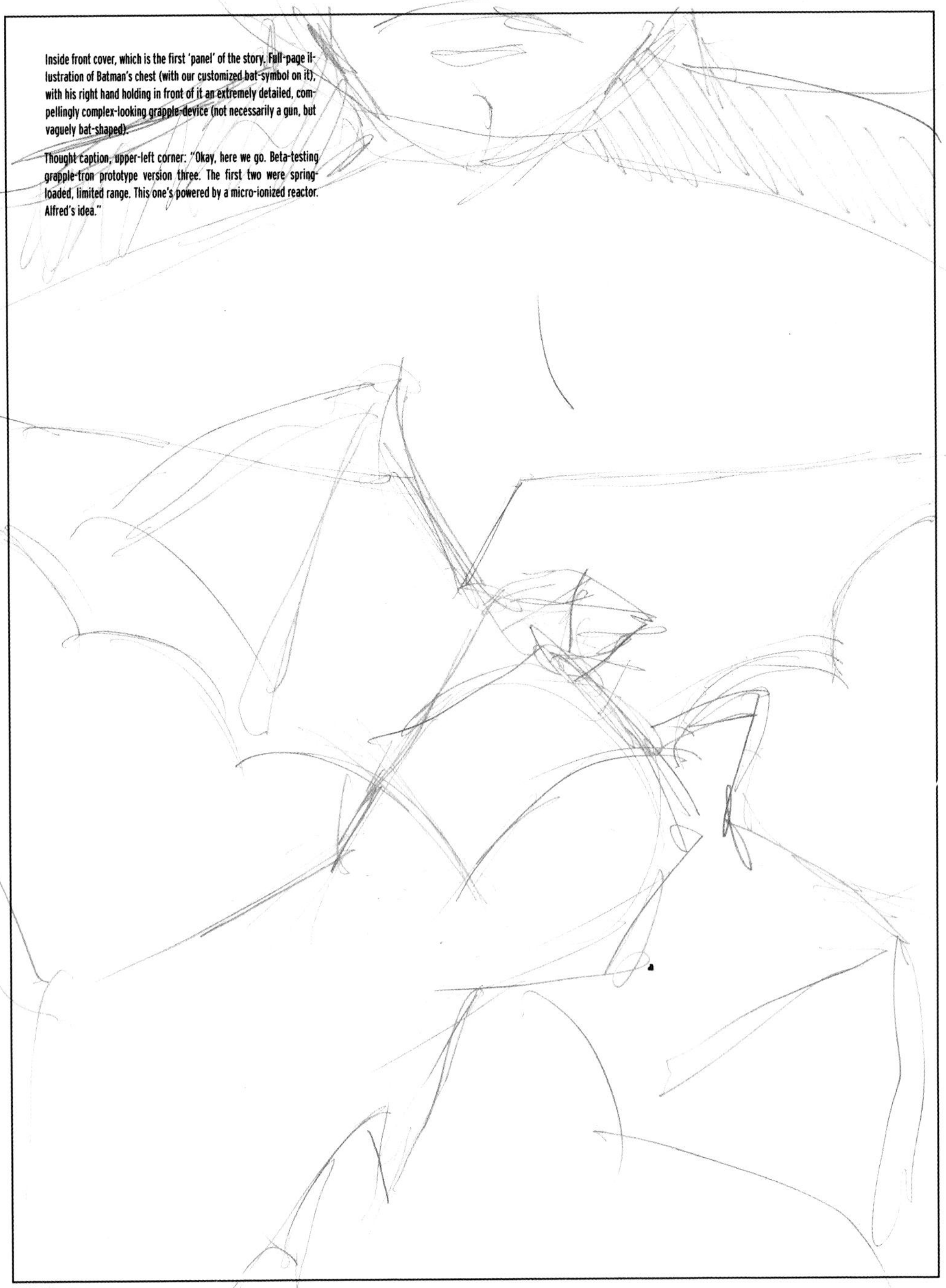
Inside front cover, which is the first 'panel' of the story. Full-page illustration of Batman's chest (with our customized bat-symbol on it), with his right hand holding in front of it an extremely detailed, compellingly complex-looking grapple-device (not necessarily a gun, but vaguely bat-shaped).
Thought caption, upper-left corner: "Okay, here we go. Beta-testing grapple-tron prototype version three. The first two were spring-loaded, limited range. This one's powered by a micro-ionized reactor. Alfred's idea."

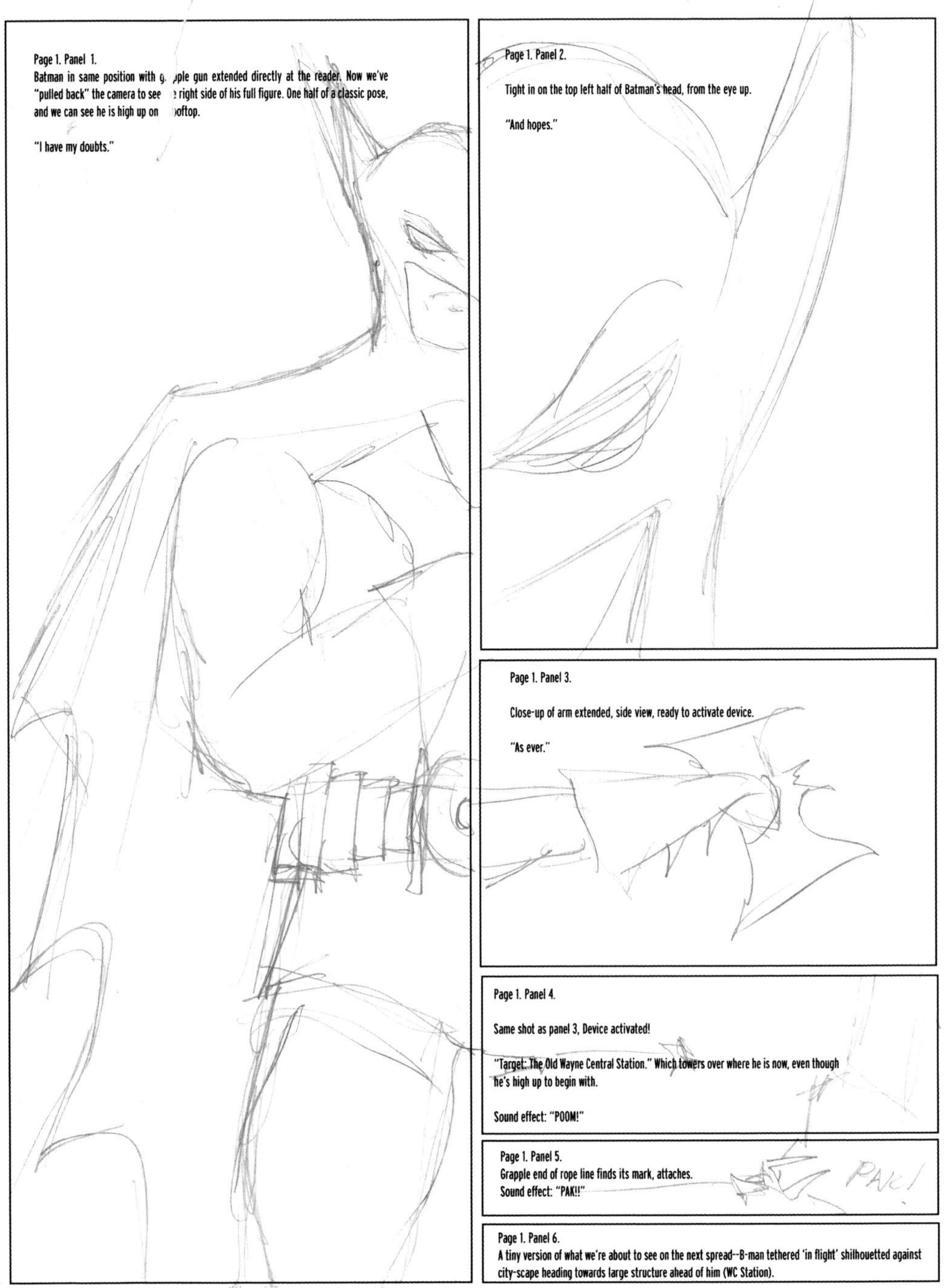
Page 1. Panel 1.
Batman in same position with g. ple gun extended directly at the reader. Now we've "pulled back" the camera to see e right side of his full figure. One half of a classic pose, and we can see he is high up on oftop.
"I have my doubts."
Page 1. Panel 2.
Tight in on the top left half of Batman's head, from the eye up.
"And hopes."
Page 1. Panel 3.
Close-up of arm extended, side view, ready to activate device.
"As ever."
Page 1. Panel 4.
Same shot as panel 3, Device activated!
"Target: The Old Wayne Central Station." Which towers over where he is now, even though he's high up to begin with.
Sound effect: "POOM!"
Page 1. Panel 5.
Grapple end of rope line finds its mark, attaches.
Sound effect: "PAK!!"
PAK!
Page 1. Panel 6.
A tiny version of what we're about to see on the next spread--B-man tethered 'in flight' shilhouetted against city-scape heading towards large structure ahead of him (WC Station).

**PREVIOUS PAGE:** An early "book map" I made of the working script in order to figure out the pacing of scenes and page breakdowns. We were limited to 96 pages, so once I figured out how the story was going to start and end (which I always do first when creating a narrative), it then became a logistical matter of how the events of the plot would move and fit in between the opener and the finale. **ABOVE:** My sketched-in first two pages of script. There are a variety of ways to write a comic book, and most people approach it like a screenplay, but I am most comfortable with figuring out the panel breakdowns and placing the captions, action, and dialogue within them. Dave really liked this method—as have the half-dozen other comics artists I've worked with—because it gave him more specific direction and fewer structural decisions to make. One thing he (politely) asked me to stop doing early on was making my own ham-fisted sketches; the panel diagrams and text would be enough. This was a relief, since I can't draw well, and it saved time. **OPPOSITE:** Dave's finished art for pages one and two. Magnificent. The whole process throughout was magic, the way he would make my words and ideas into glorious reality on the page. (These two pages are based on the Golden Mean, by the way.)

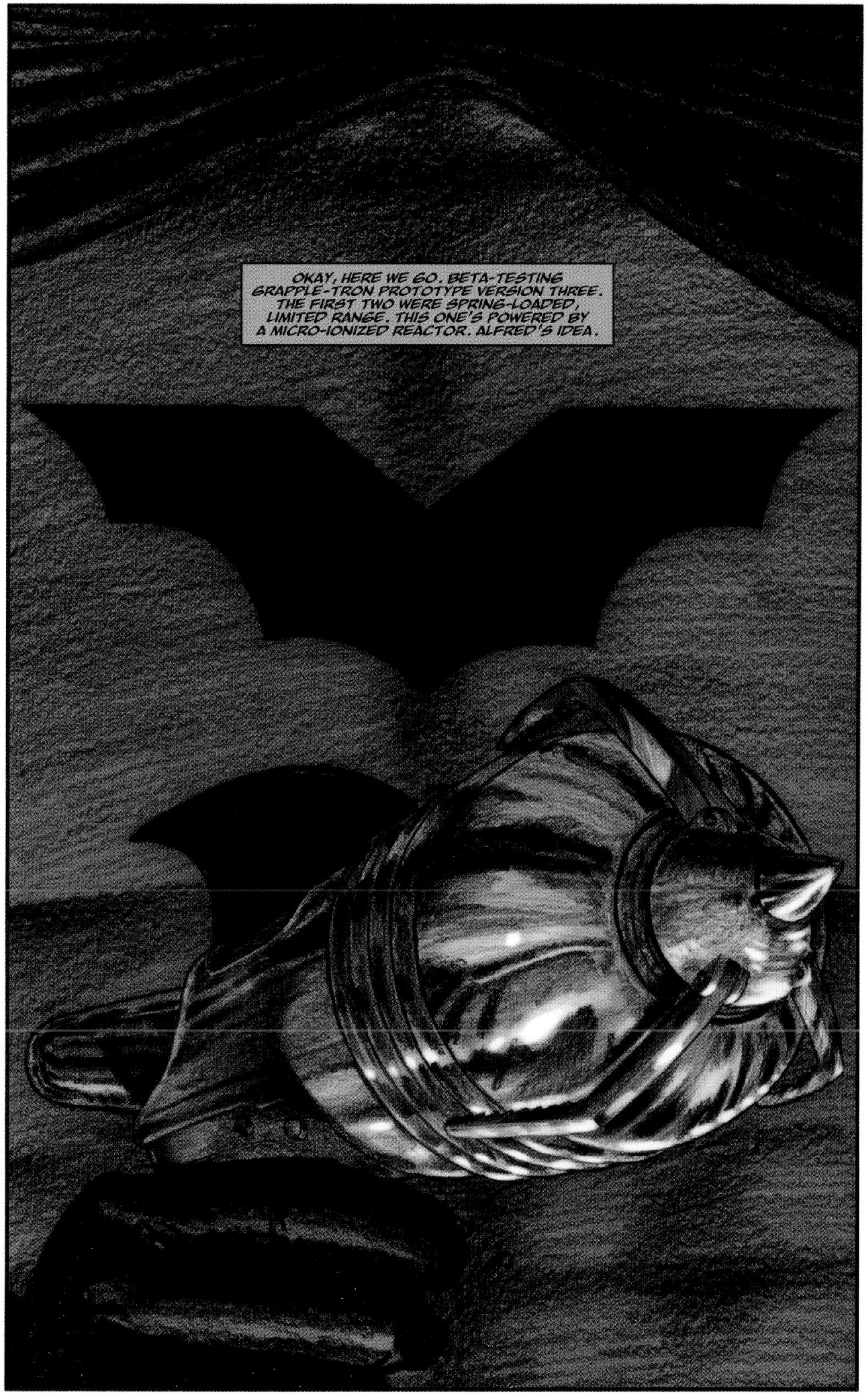
OKAY, HERE WE GO. BETA-TESTING GRAPPLE-TRON PROTOTYPE VERSION THREE. THE FIRST TWO WERE SPRING-LOADED, LIMITED RANGE. THIS ONE'S POWERED BY A MICRO-IONIZED REACTOR. ALFRED'S IDEA.
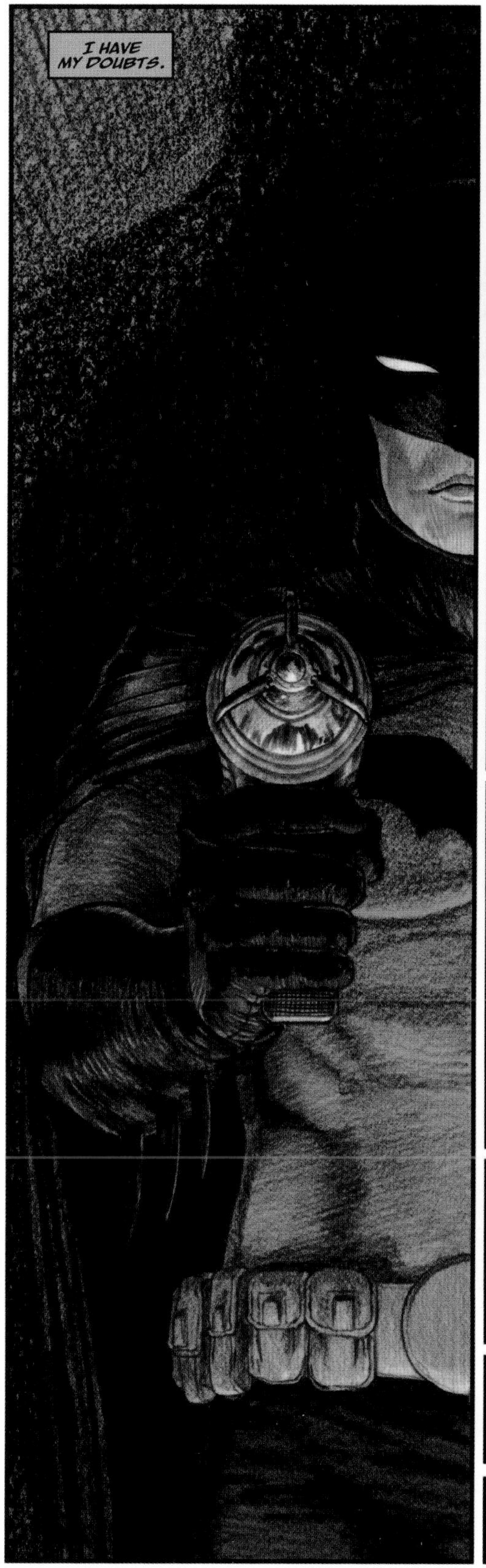
I HAVE MY DOUBTS.
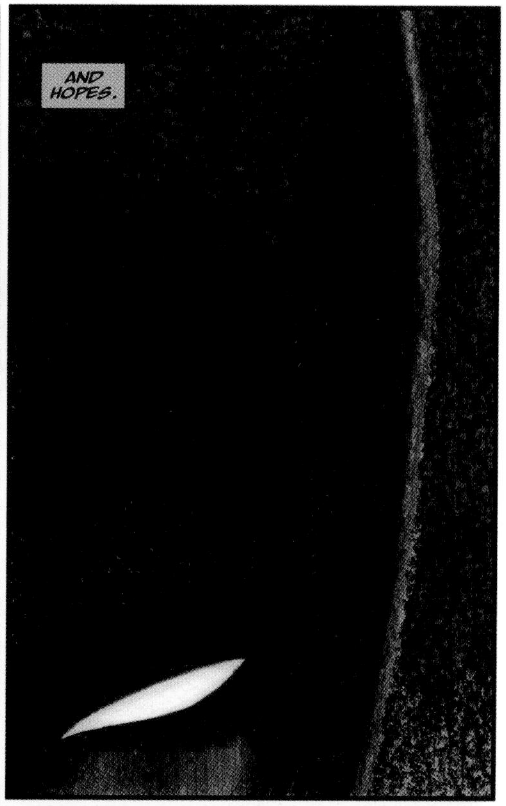
AND HOPES.
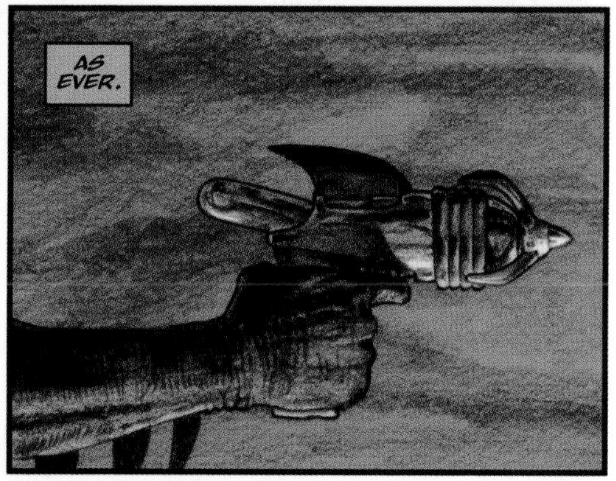
AS EVER.
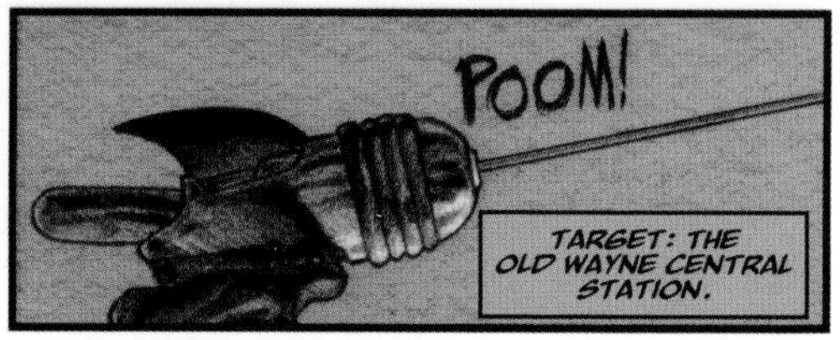
POOM!
TARGET: THE OLD WAYNE CENTRAL STATION.
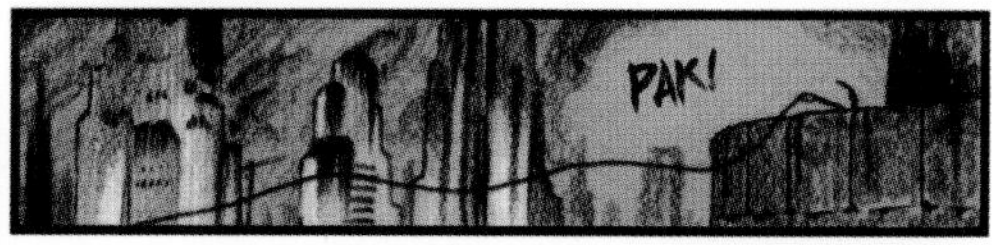
PAK!
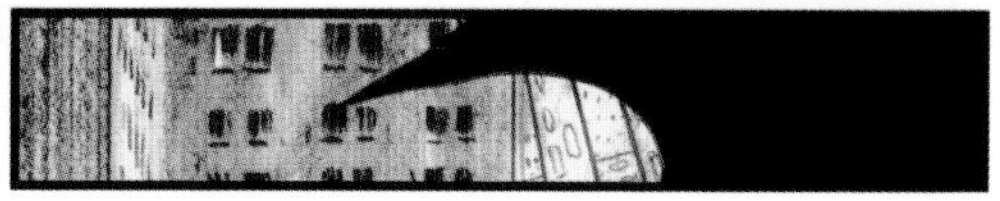

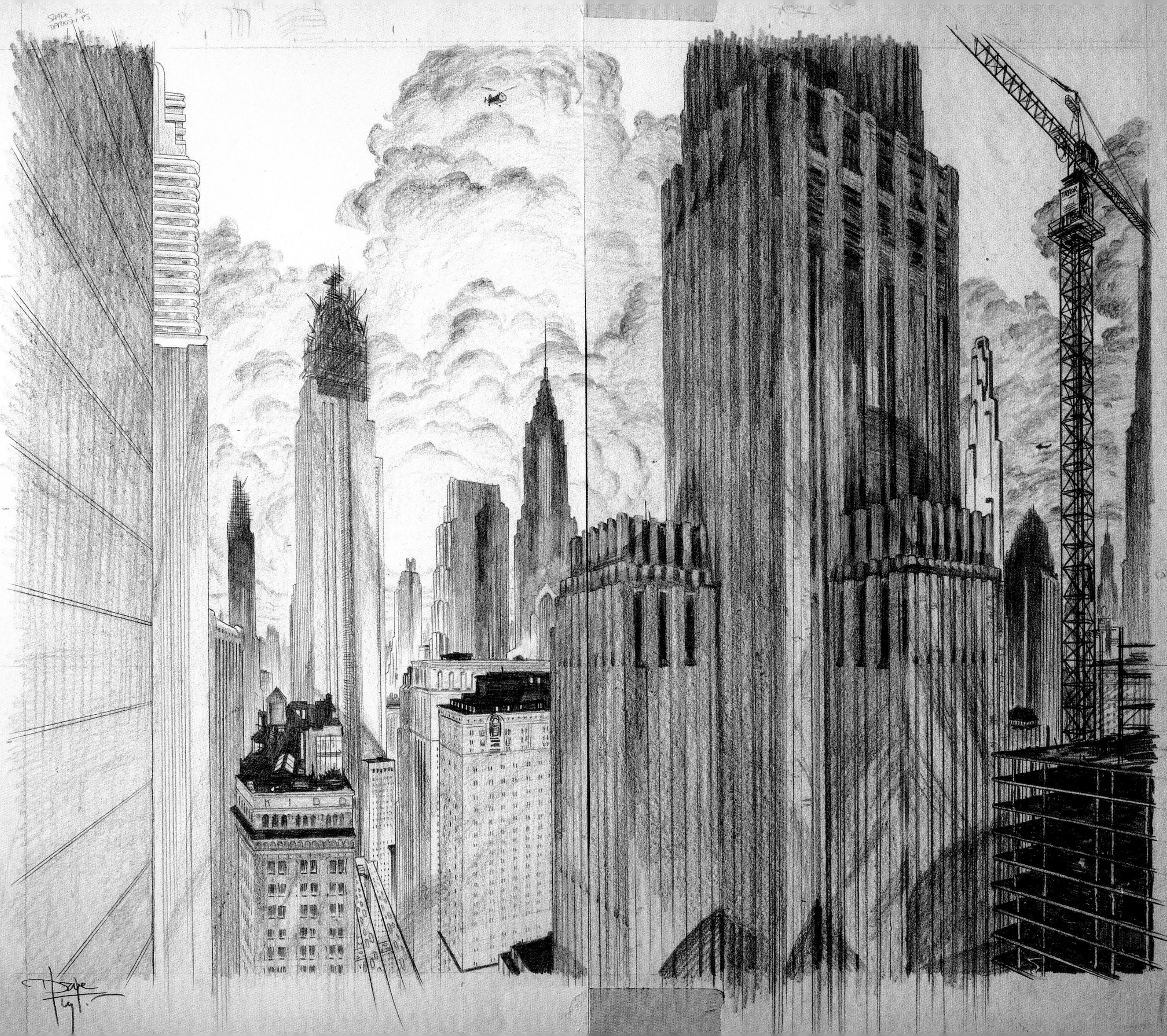
TAYLOR

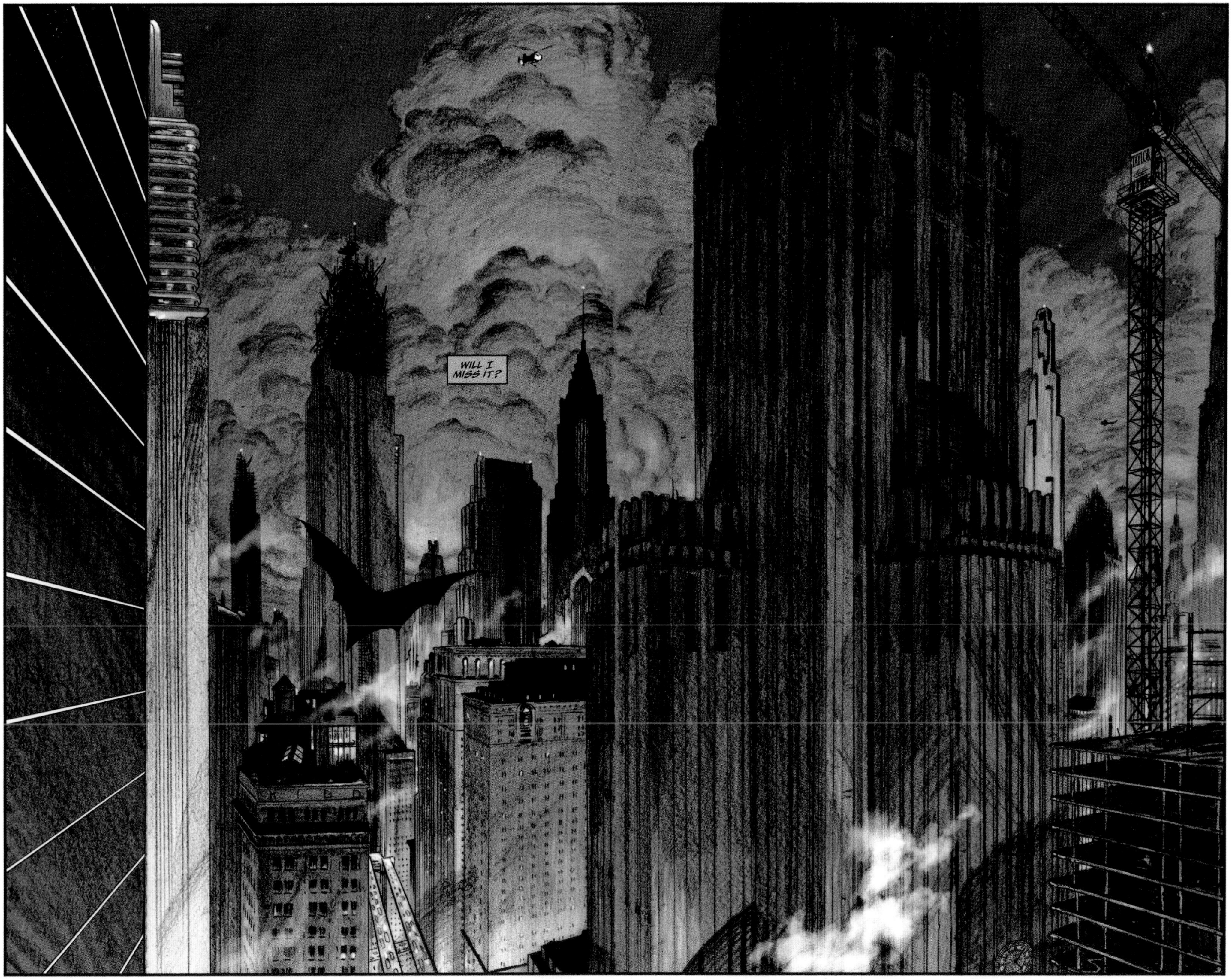
WILL I MISS IT?
TAYLOR

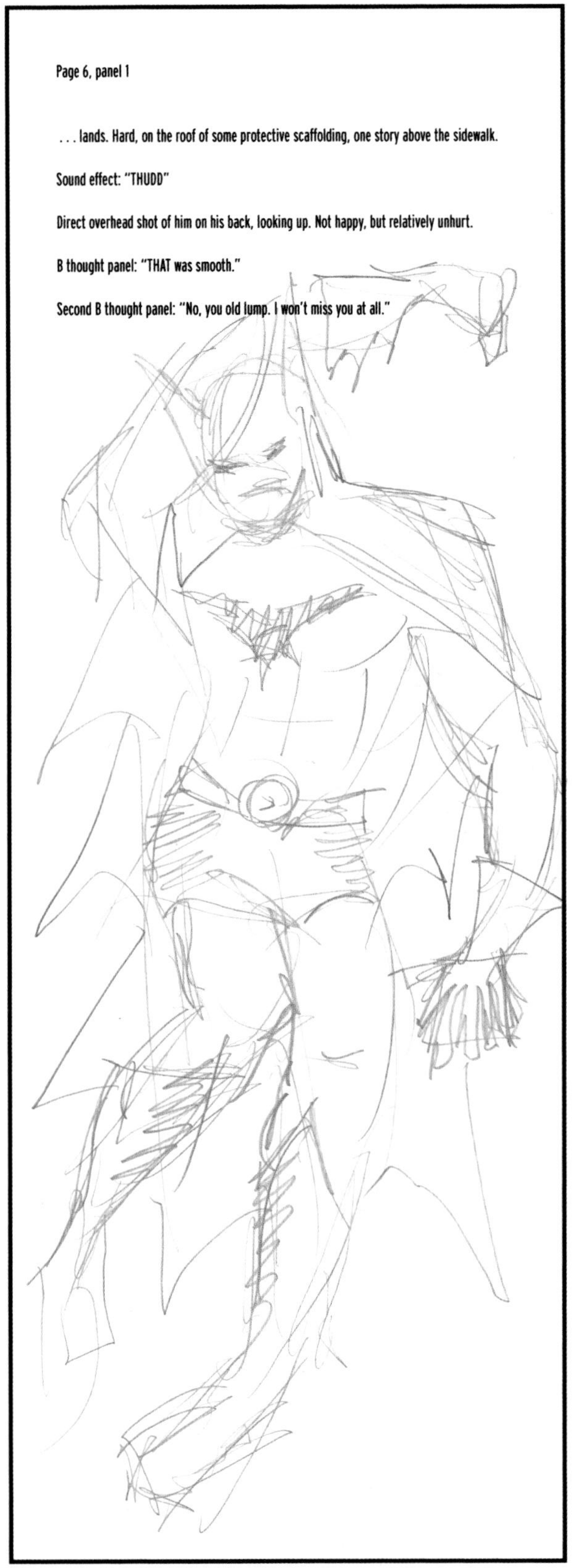

Page 6, panel 1

. . . lands. Hard, on the roof of some protective scaffolding, one story above the sidewalk.

Sound effect: "THUDD"

Direct overhead shot of him on his back, looking up. Not happy, but relatively unhurt.

B thought panel: "THAT was smooth."

Second B thought panel: "No, you old lump. I won't miss you at all."

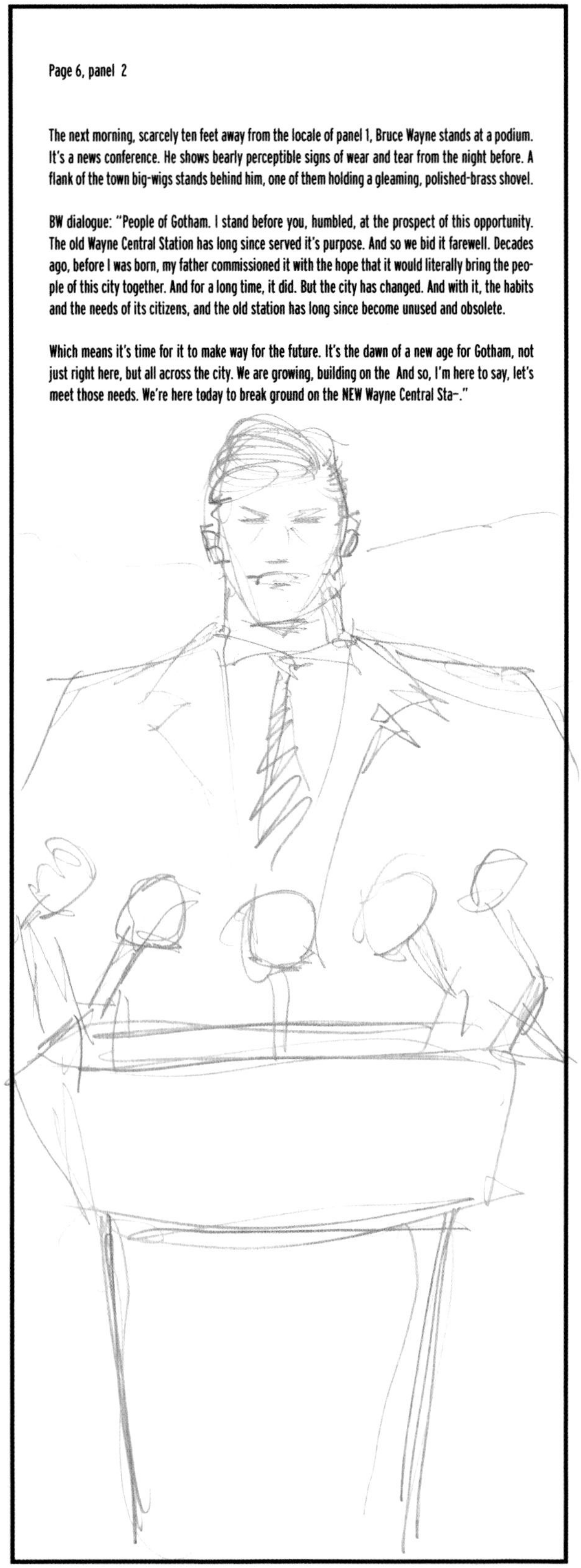

Page 6, panel 2

The next morning, scarcely ten feet away from the locale of panel 1, Bruce Wayne stands at a podium. It's a news conference. He shows bearly perceptible signs of wear and tear from the night before. A flank of the town big-wigs stands behind him, one of them holding a gleaming, polished-brass shovel.

BW dialogue: "People of Gotham. I stand before you, humbled, at the prospect of this opportunity. The old Wayne Central Station has long since served it's purpose. And so we bid it farewell. Decades ago, before I was born, my father commissioned it with the hope that it would literally bring the people of this city together. And for a long time, it did. But the city has changed. And with it, the habits and the needs of its citizens, and the old station has long since become unused and obsolete.

Which means it's time for it to make way for the future. It's the dawn of a new age for Gotham, not just right here, but all across the city. We are growing, building on the  And so, I'm here to say, let's meet those needs. We're here today to break ground on the NEW Wayne Central Sta–."



**PREVIOUS SPREAD:** My original script said something like, "We see Batman soaring over the Gotham cityscape at night, double-page spread." Well, I had pictured Batman front and center, splayed midflight with the city behind him. Dave gave me this composition instead (sketch, p. 302; final, p. 303), and that's why he was perfect for this project. Whenever he deviated from what I'd intended—and it wasn't that often—he was absolutely right, and I never contradicted him. He was bringing his A game and I knew it right away.

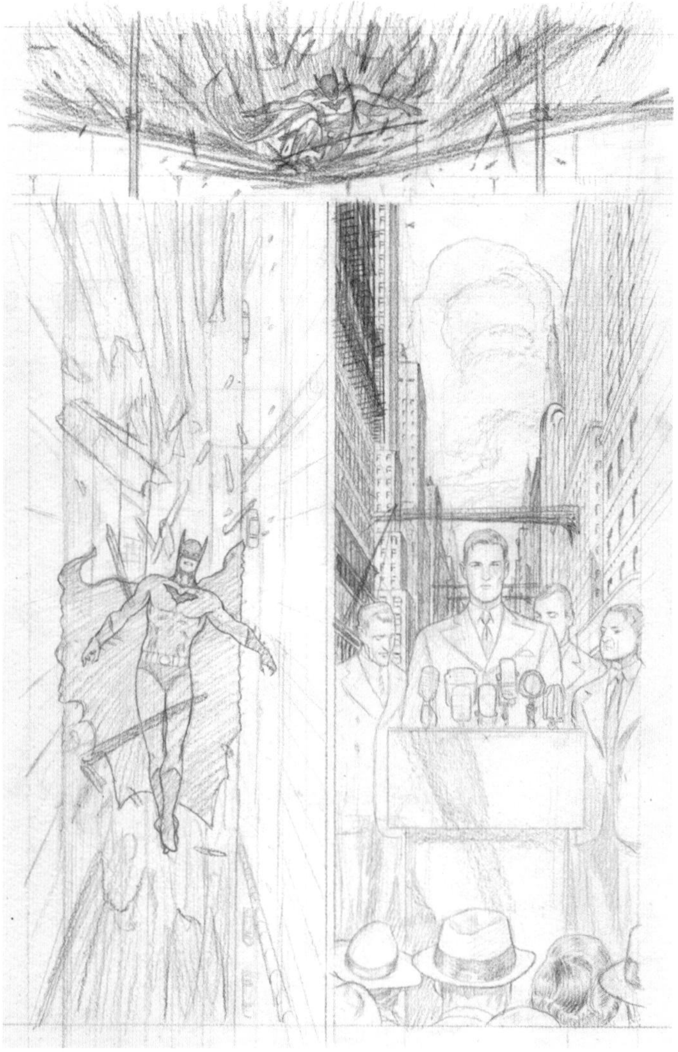

**LEFT:** I'm still sketching on my script, but that will stop soon. **ABOVE:** Dave drew everything in non-repro blue pencil first, for approval. In this pair of panels, at night Batman has fallen onto a scaffolding at the old Wayne Central Station; the following day Bruce Wayne is heralding the new era of what will be the next Wayne Central Station to take the old one's place. **OPPOSITE:** Final art. And then in the middle of the announcement a big-ass crane falls out of the sky. Heads up!!

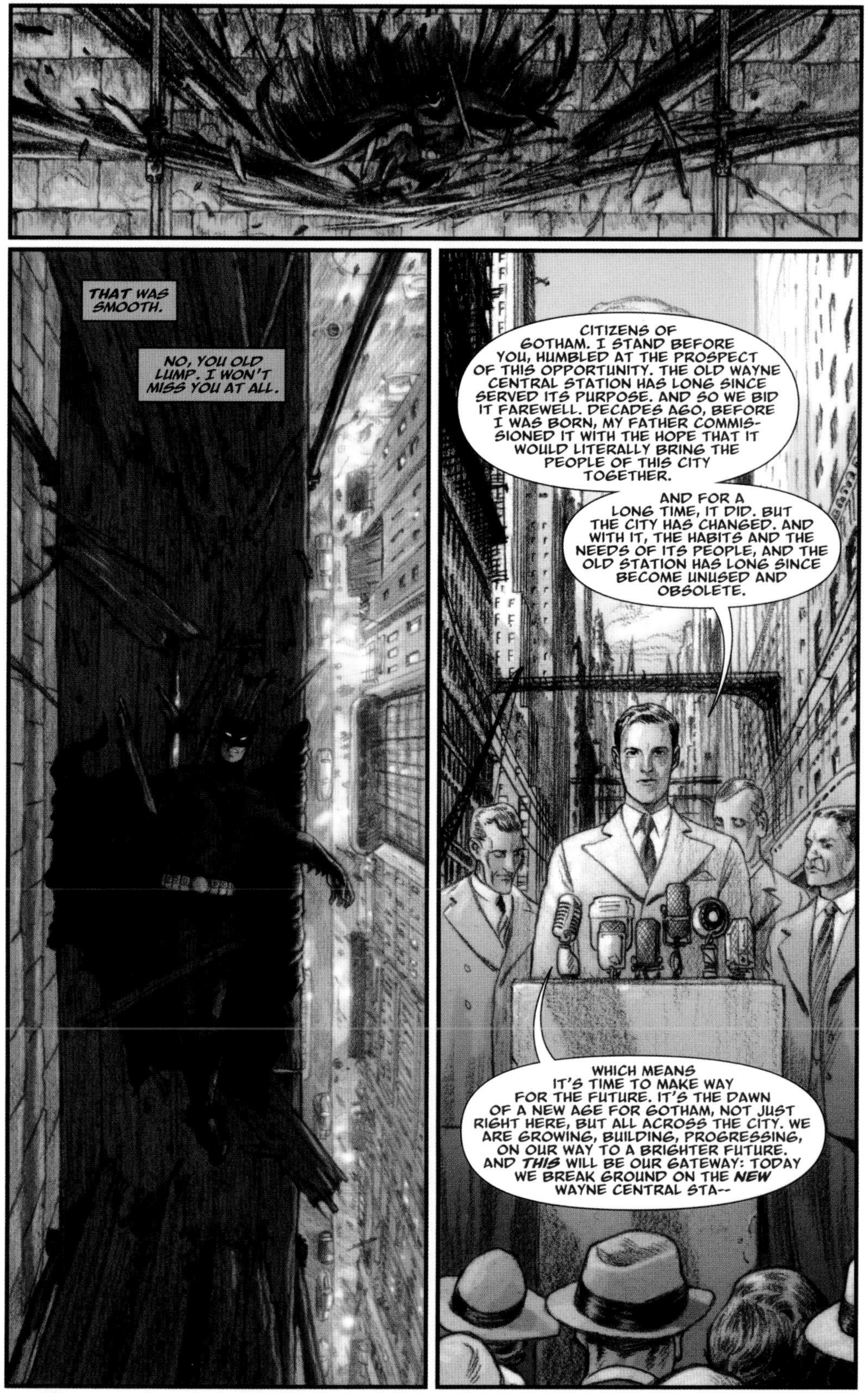
THAT WAS SMOOTH.
NO, YOU OLD LUMP. I WON'T MISS YOU AT ALL.
CITIZENS OF GOTHAM. I STAND BEFORE YOU, HUMBLED AT THE PROSPECT OF THIS OPPORTUNITY. THE OLD WAYNE CENTRAL STATION HAS LONG SINCE SERVED ITS PURPOSE. AND SO WE BID IT FAREWELL. DECADES AGO, BEFORE I WAS BORN, MY FATHER COMMIS-SIONED IT WITH THE HOPE THAT IT WOULD LITERALLY BRING THE PEOPLE OF THIS CITY TOGETHER.
AND FOR A LONG TIME, IT DID. BUT THE CITY HAS CHANGED. AND WITH IT, THE HABITS AND THE NEEDS OF ITS PEOPLE, AND THE OLD STATION HAS LONG SINCE BECOME UNUSED AND OBSOLETE.
WHICH MEANS IT'S TIME TO MAKE WAY FOR THE FUTURE. IT'S THE DAWN OF A NEW AGE FOR GOTHAM, NOT JUST RIGHT HERE, BUT ALL ACROSS THE CITY. WE ARE GROWING, BUILDING, PROGRESSING, ON OUR WAY TO A BRIGHTER FUTURE. AND ***THIS*** WILL BE OUR GATEWAY: TODAY WE BREAK GROUND ON THE ***NEW*** WAYNE CENTRAL STA--

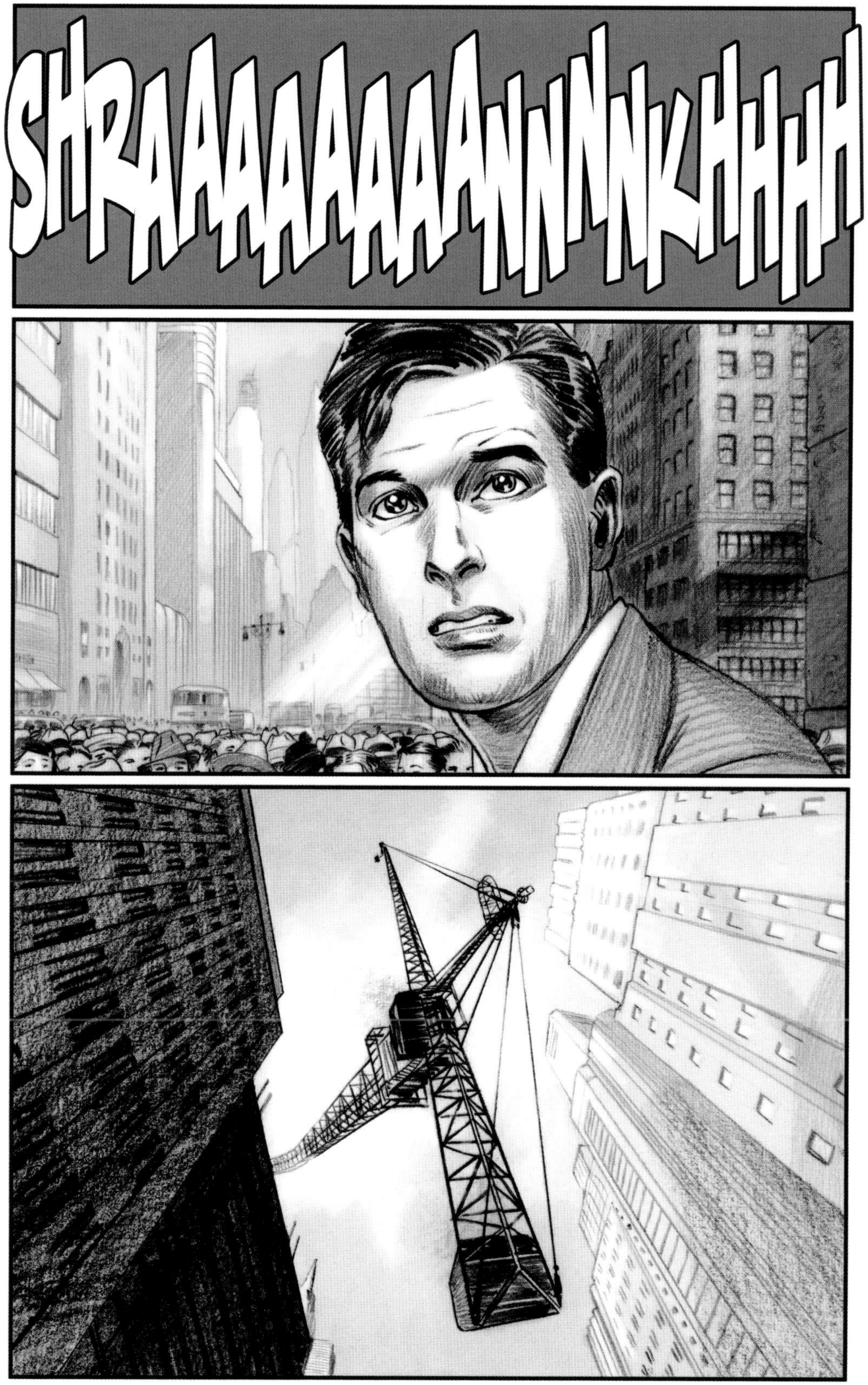
SHRAAAAAAAANNNNKHHHH

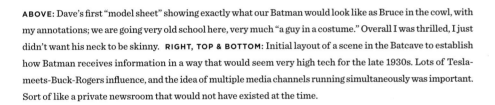

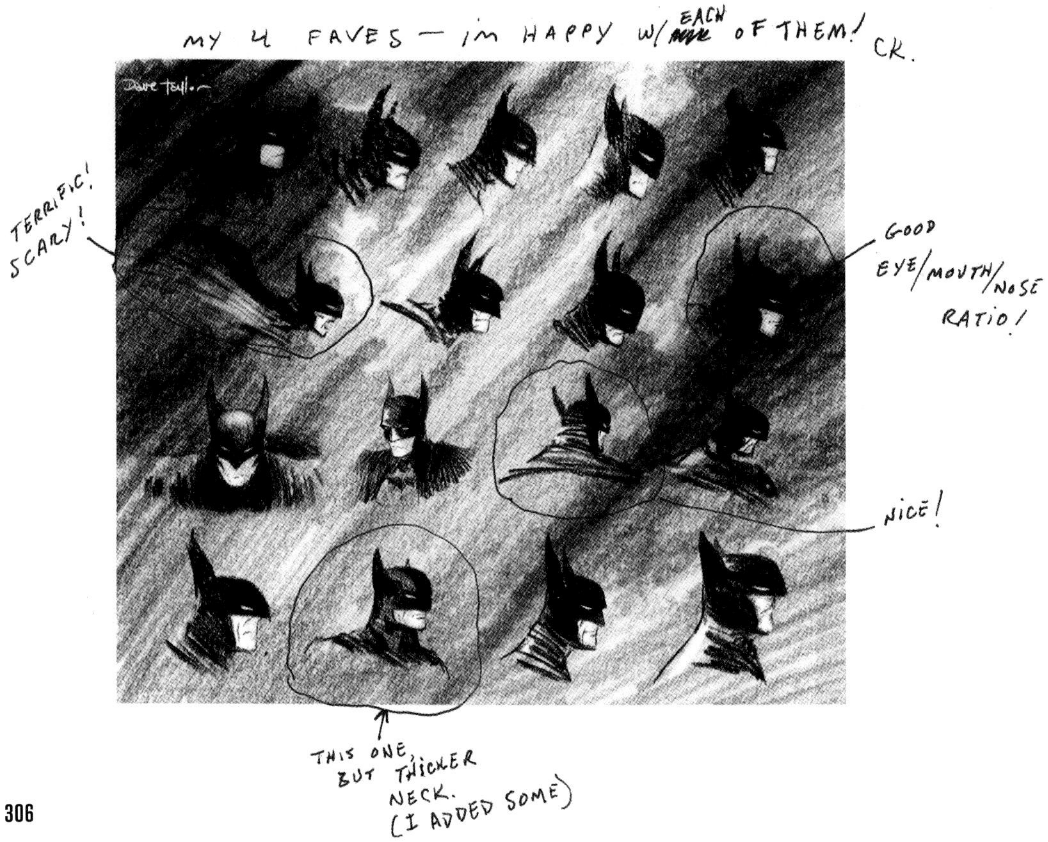
MY 4 FAVES — I'M HAPPY W/ EACH OF THEM! CK.
Dave Taylor
TERRIFIC! SCARY!
GOOD EYE/MOUTH/NOSE RATIO!
NICE!
THIS ONE, BUT THICKER NECK. (I ADDED SOME)



**ABOVE:** Dave's first "model sheet" showing exactly what our Batman would look like as Bruce in the cowl, with my annotations; we are going very old school here, very much "a guy in a costume." Overall I was thrilled, I just didn't want his neck to be skinny. **RIGHT, TOP & BOTTOM:** Initial layout of a scene in the Batcave to establish how Batman receives information in a way that would seem very high tech for the late 1930s. Lots of Tesla-meets-Buck-Rogers influence, and the idea of multiple media channels running simultaneously was important. Sort of like a private newsroom that would not have existed at the time.

The finished art (opposite), with subtle color touches. In most comics and graphic novels, you have a three-layered art process: non-photo-reproducible blue pencil for layout approval, then lead pencil onto that to finalize the drawings, then ink over that with the pencil erased afterwards for a "clean line" look. Of course there have been many variations on this process, especially once digital drawing, inking, and coloring came into common usage starting in the late 1990s. From the beginning Dave and I wanted to start in the traditional pencil-on-paper manner, but after that he deviated by scanning in his pencils and "digitally inking" them, adding the slightest bits of color onscreen. I thought the final effect was spot-on because you can still see the handwork in full, but the heightened contrast makes it look like stills from a movie. I thought we got the best of both mediums and genres.

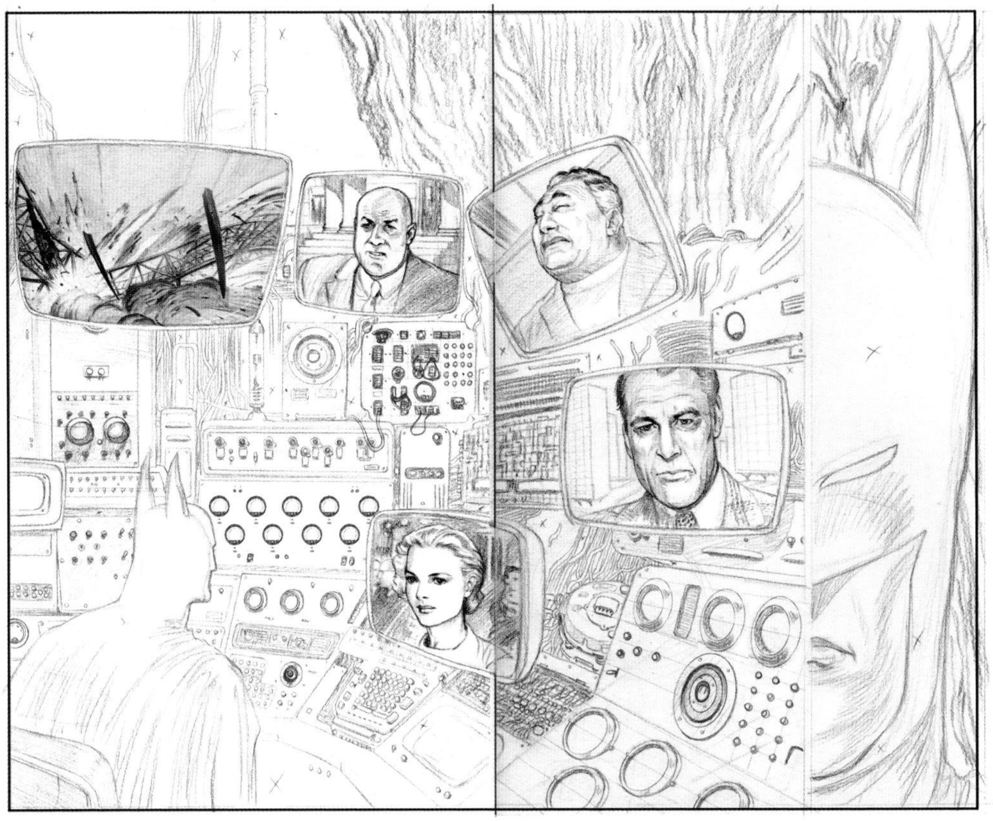

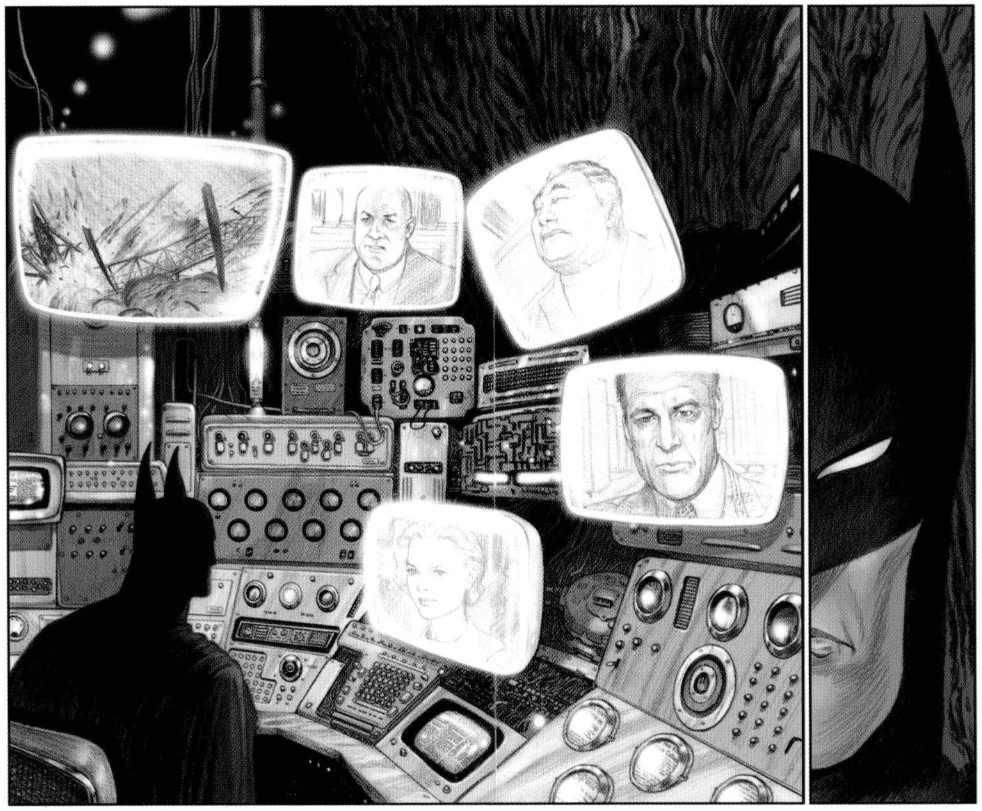

WHERE DO I START?
...THIS IS WGKO, GOTHAM. STILL NO WORD ON THE CAUSE OF MONDAY'S CATASTROPHIC CRANE COLLAPSE IN MIDTOWN, WHICH LEFT SCORES OF INJURED BUT NO REPORTED FATALITIES. THEY'RE CALLING IT A MIRACLE THAT PHILANTHROPIST BRUCE WAYNE, GIVING A SPEECH ACROSS THE STREET AT THE TIME, IN THE DIRECT PATH OF THE PLUMMETING MACHINE, ESCAPED WITH WHAT HE CALLED ONLY A FEW MINOR SCRAPES.
WHEN ASKED HOW THIS WILL AFFECT THE DEMOLITION AND REBUILDING OF THE ADJACENT WAYNE CENTRAL STATION, MR. WAYNE HAD NO COMMENT. BUT AUTHORITIES REPORTED THAT FOR NOW THE PROJECT IS ON HOLD, WHILE THE CONSIDERABLE JOB OF CLEANING UP THE AFTERMATH OF THE ACCIDENT WILL TAKE WEEKS, IF NOT MONTHS. INSPECTORS HAVE--
BRRRZZT
...IN A RELATED STORY, BART LOAR, UNION PRESIDENT OF CONSTRUCTION LOCAL 27, SAYS THAT THE CRANE COLLAPSE IS YET ANOTHER EXAMPLE OF MANAGERIAL OVERSIGHT, PUTTING HIS WORKERS IN AN UNACCEPTABLY DANGEROUS WORKPLACE.
LOAR, WHEN ASKED IF THE CAUSE COULD HAVE POSSIBLY BEEN DUE TO FAULTY OPERATION BY A UNION MEMBER, MADE A SUGGESTION TO THIS REPORTER THAT WOULD HAVE BEEN PHYSICALLY IMPOSSIBLE. THIS IS WXRT, GOTH--
BZZOOTT
...MOVIE-TONE NEWS. INTERNATIONALLY ACCLAIMED ARCHITECT KEM ROOMHAUS, WHO'S SET TO MAKE HIS GOTHAM DEBUT NEXT WEEK WITH THE SPECTACULAR CEILING NIGHT CLUB, UNVEILS A MODEL OF HIS WINNING DESIGN FOR THE NEW WAYNE CENTRAL STATION BUILDING, WHICH HE CALLS "THE FUTURE OF ARCHITECTURE."
THE NATIVE OF HOLLAND CLAIMS THAT HE IS OFTEN FRIGHTENED OF HIS OWN GENIUS; WHILE SEVERAL NOTABLE CRITICS HAVE CLAIMED THAT THERE'S ACTUALLY NOTHING TO BE SCARED OF. MOVING ON, WE--
ZZZRRRRP
...WGOG, WEST GOTHAM. THE MYSTERIOUS DISAPPEARANCE OF GREGOR GREENSIDE CONTINUES TO BAFFLE AUTHORITIES. THE ONCE-VENERATED ARCHITECT WAS REPORTED MISSING ON MONDAY BY HIS SON GARNETT, WHEN HE FAILED TO SHOW UP AT THE OFFICE THEY SHARE IN THE MARSHALL DISTRICT.
GREENSIDE, PRACTICALLY A HOUSEHOLD NAME AT THE HEIGHT OF HIS FAME, HAD LONG SINCE FALLEN INTO OBSCURITY. 87% OF GOTHAMITES POLLED ON THE STREET YESTERDAY BY THE GOTHAM GAZETTE RESPONDED THAT THEY THOUGHT HE HAD DIED AT LEAST TEN YEARS AGO. NEXT UP--
SZZRRRMM
. . . AN OPPORTUNITY BORN FROM TRAGEDY. THAT'S WHAT SELF-PROCLAIMED "URBAN PRESERVATIONIST" CYNDIA SYL CALLED MONDAY'S CRANE COLLAPSE, WHICH HAS FOR NOW HALTED PLANS TO DEMOLISH THE DERELICT WAYNE CENTRAL STATION.
SYL, A SOCIETY FIXTURE WHO HAS TAKEN UP THE CAUSE OF WHAT SHE SEES AS AN ARCHITECTURAL MASTERPIECE THAT'S BEEN NEARLY DESTROYED BY NEGLECT, MAINTAINS THAT IT'S NOT TOO LATE TO SAVE IT. WE GO NOW TO--
SPRRRRPPP
OH, GOD. CYNDIA SYL...

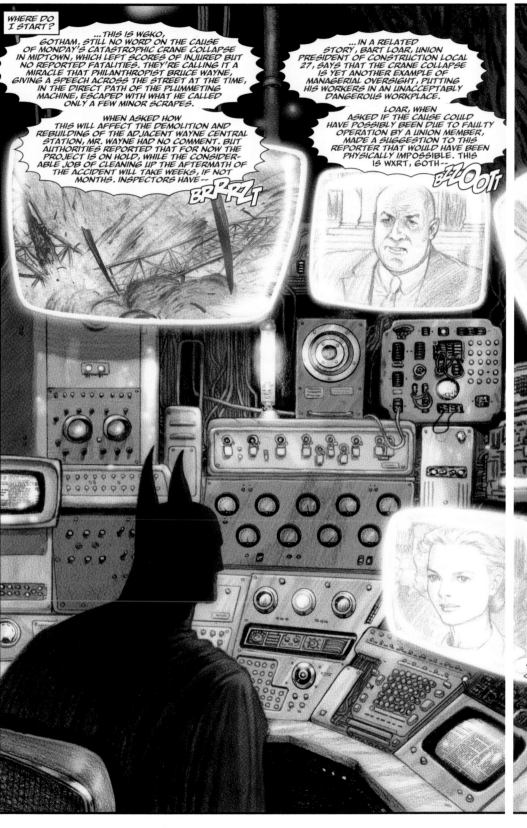

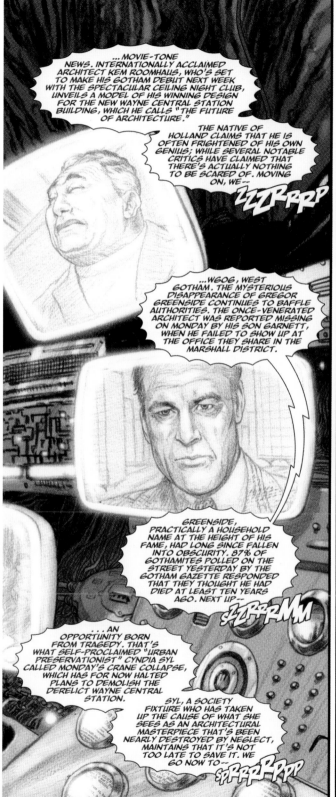

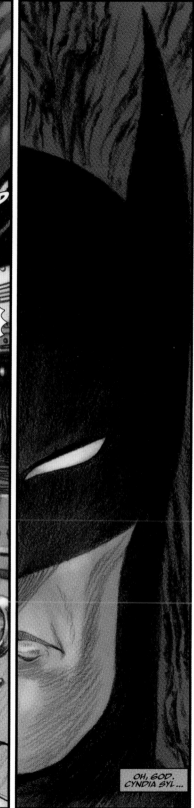

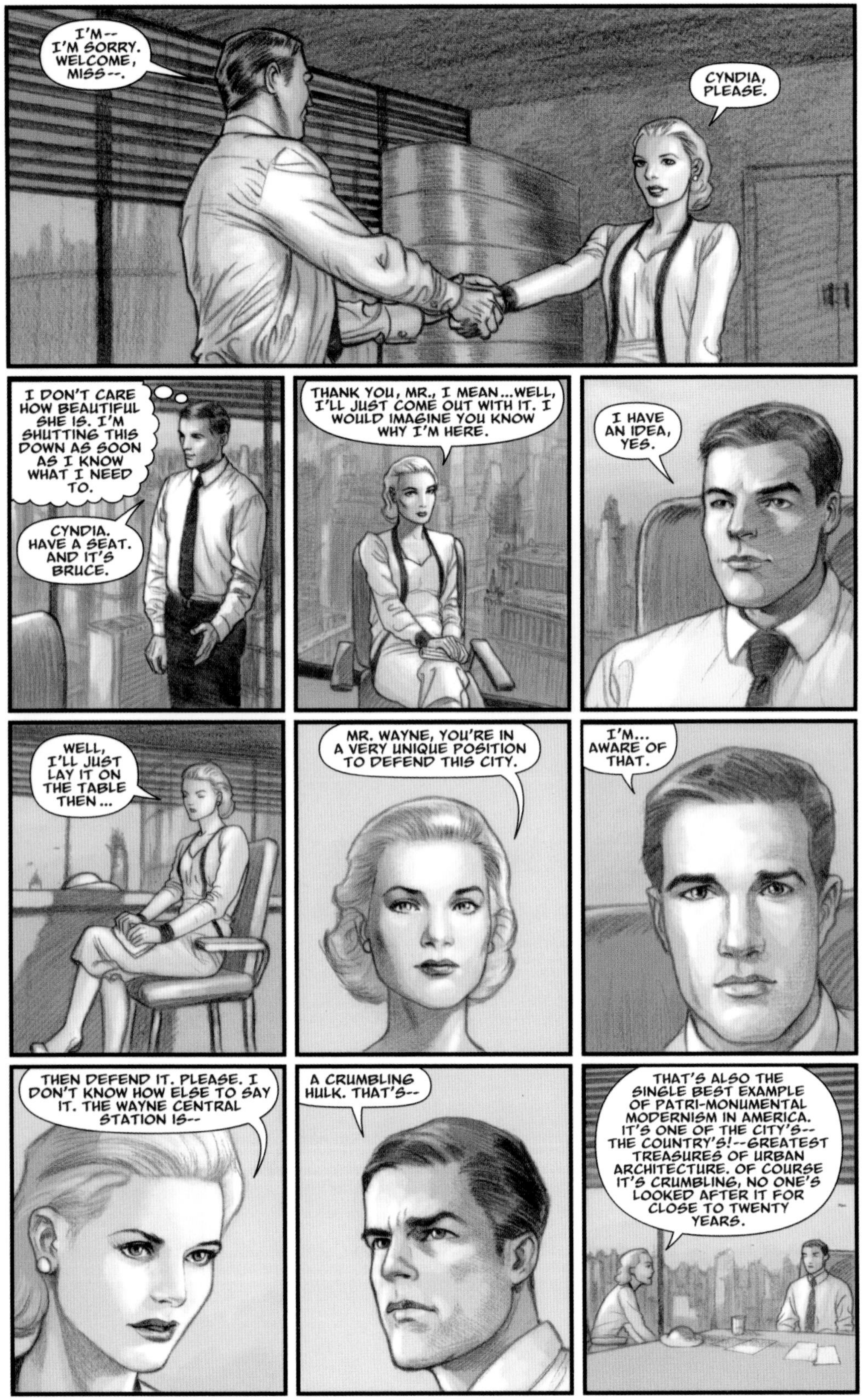
I'M-- I'M SORRY. WELCOME, MISS--.
CYNDIA, PLEASE.
I DON'T CARE HOW BEAUTIFUL SHE IS. I'M SHUTTING THIS DOWN AS SOON AS I KNOW WHAT I NEED TO.
CYNDIA. HAVE A SEAT. AND IT'S BRUCE.
THANK YOU, MR., I MEAN...WELL, I'LL JUST COME OUT WITH IT. I WOULD IMAGINE YOU KNOW WHY I'M HERE.
I HAVE AN IDEA, YES.
WELL, I'LL JUST LAY IT ON THE TABLE THEN...
MR. WAYNE, YOU'RE IN A VERY UNIQUE POSITION TO DEFEND THIS CITY.
I'M... AWARE OF THAT.
THEN DEFEND IT. PLEASE. I DON'T KNOW HOW ELSE TO SAY IT. THE WAYNE CENTRAL STATION IS--
A CRUMBLING HULK. THAT'S--
THAT'S ALSO THE SINGLE BEST EXAMPLE OF PATRI-MONUMENTAL MODERNISM IN AMERICA. IT'S ONE OF THE CITY'S-- THE COUNTRY'S!--GREATEST TREASURES OF URBAN ARCHITECTURE. OF COURSE IT'S CRUMBLING, NO ONE'S LOOKED AFTER IT FOR CLOSE TO TWENTY YEARS.

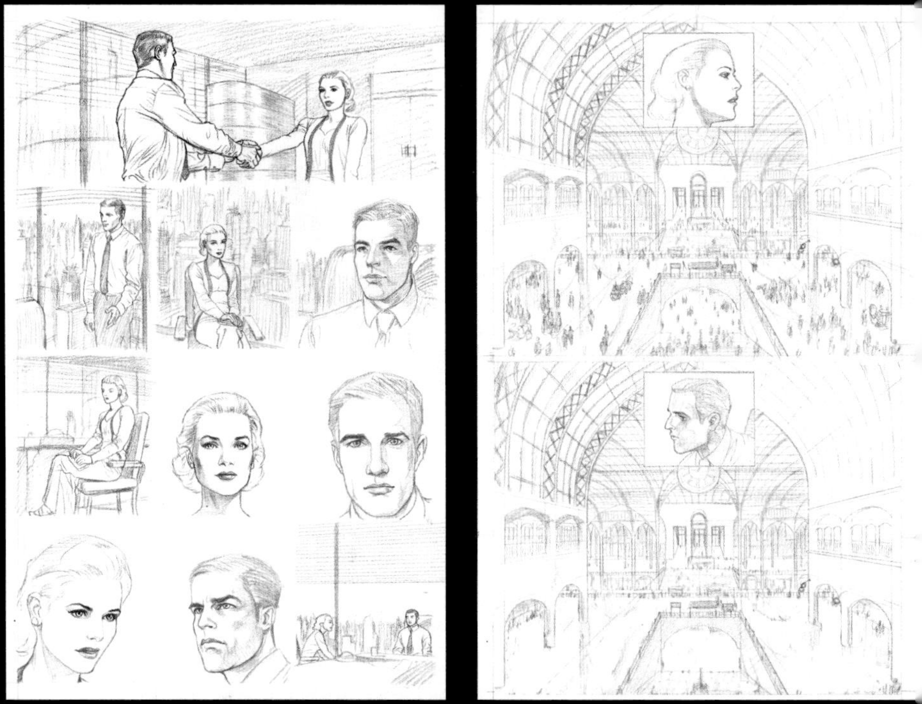

**ABOVE:** Physically, Cyndia is based on Grace Kelly, and Bruce on Montgomery Clift, because . . . why the hell wouldn't we?

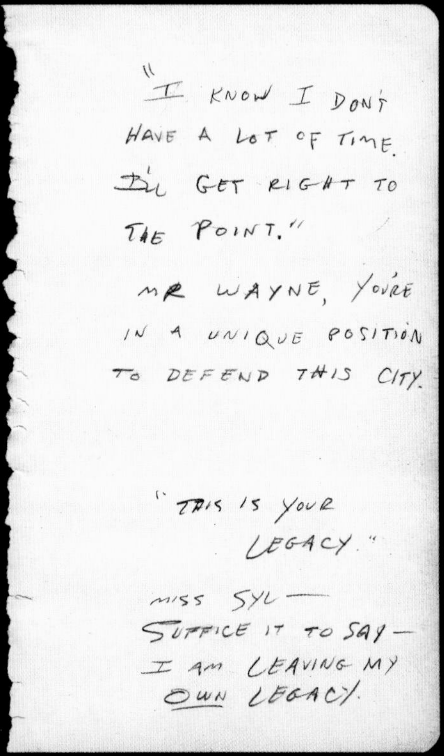
"I KNOW I DON'T HAVE A LOT OF TIME. I'LL GET RIGHT TO THE POINT."

MR WAYNE, YOU'RE IN A UNIQUE POSITION TO DEFEND THIS CITY.

"THIS IS YOUR LEGACY."

MISS SYL— SUFFICE IT TO SAY— I AM LEAVING MY OWN LEGACY.

I was determined to give Bruce Wayne a grea female costar for this story—so I created th character of Cyndia Syl, a passionate archi tectural historian who wants to save the crum bling-but-still-magnificent Wayne Centra Station, commissioned and overseen decade prior by Bruce's father. (Cyndia's quest is base on Jackie Onassis's successful campaign to save New York's Grand Central in the 1970s.)

Meanwhile, Bruce is in favor of the old Wayne Station demolition and rebuilding because a) it's falling apart due to faulty original con struction throughout, and b) he wants to build covert transit hub underneath that would allow the Batmobile to get anywhere in Gotham with out dealing with street traffic. But of cours he can't tell her that. Which is, I think, th stuff of great romantic dramedies.

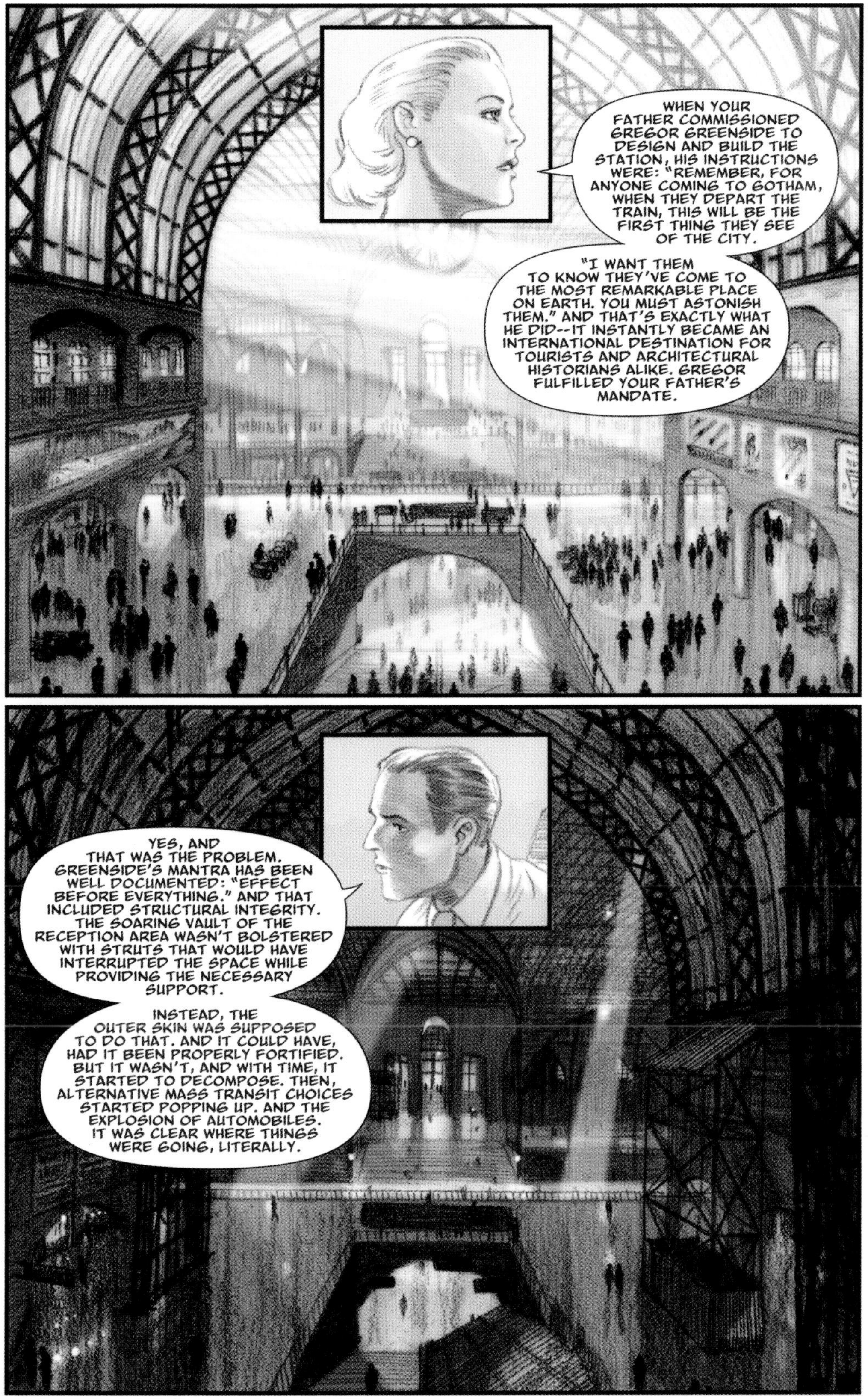
WHEN YOUR FATHER COMMISSIONED GREGOR GREENSIDE TO DESIGN AND BUILD THE STATION, HIS INSTRUCTIONS WERE: "REMEMBER, FOR ANYONE COMING TO GOTHAM, WHEN THEY DEPART THE TRAIN, THIS WILL BE THE FIRST THING THEY SEE OF THE CITY.
"I WANT THEM TO KNOW THEY'VE COME TO THE MOST REMARKABLE PLACE ON EARTH. YOU MUST ASTONISH THEM." AND THAT'S EXACTLY WHAT HE DID--IT INSTANTLY BECAME AN INTERNATIONAL DESTINATION FOR TOURISTS AND ARCHITECTURAL HISTORIANS ALIKE. GREGOR FULFILLED YOUR FATHER'S MANDATE.
YES, AND THAT WAS THE PROBLEM. GREENSIDE'S MANTRA HAS BEEN WELL DOCUMENTED: "EFFECT BEFORE EVERYTHING." AND THAT INCLUDED STRUCTURAL INTEGRITY. THE SOARING VAULT OF THE RECEPTION AREA WASN'T BOLSTERED WITH STRUTS THAT WOULD HAVE INTERRUPTED THE SPACE WHILE PROVIDING THE NECESSARY SUPPORT.
INSTEAD, THE OUTER SKIN WAS SUPPOSED TO DO THAT. AND IT COULD HAVE, HAD IT BEEN PROPERLY FORTIFIED. BUT IT WASN'T, AND WITH TIME, IT STARTED TO DECOMPOSE. THEN, ALTERNATIVE MASS TRANSIT CHOICES STARTED POPPING UP. AND THE EXPLOSION OF AUTOMOBILES. IT WAS CLEAR WHERE THINGS WERE GOING, LITERALLY.

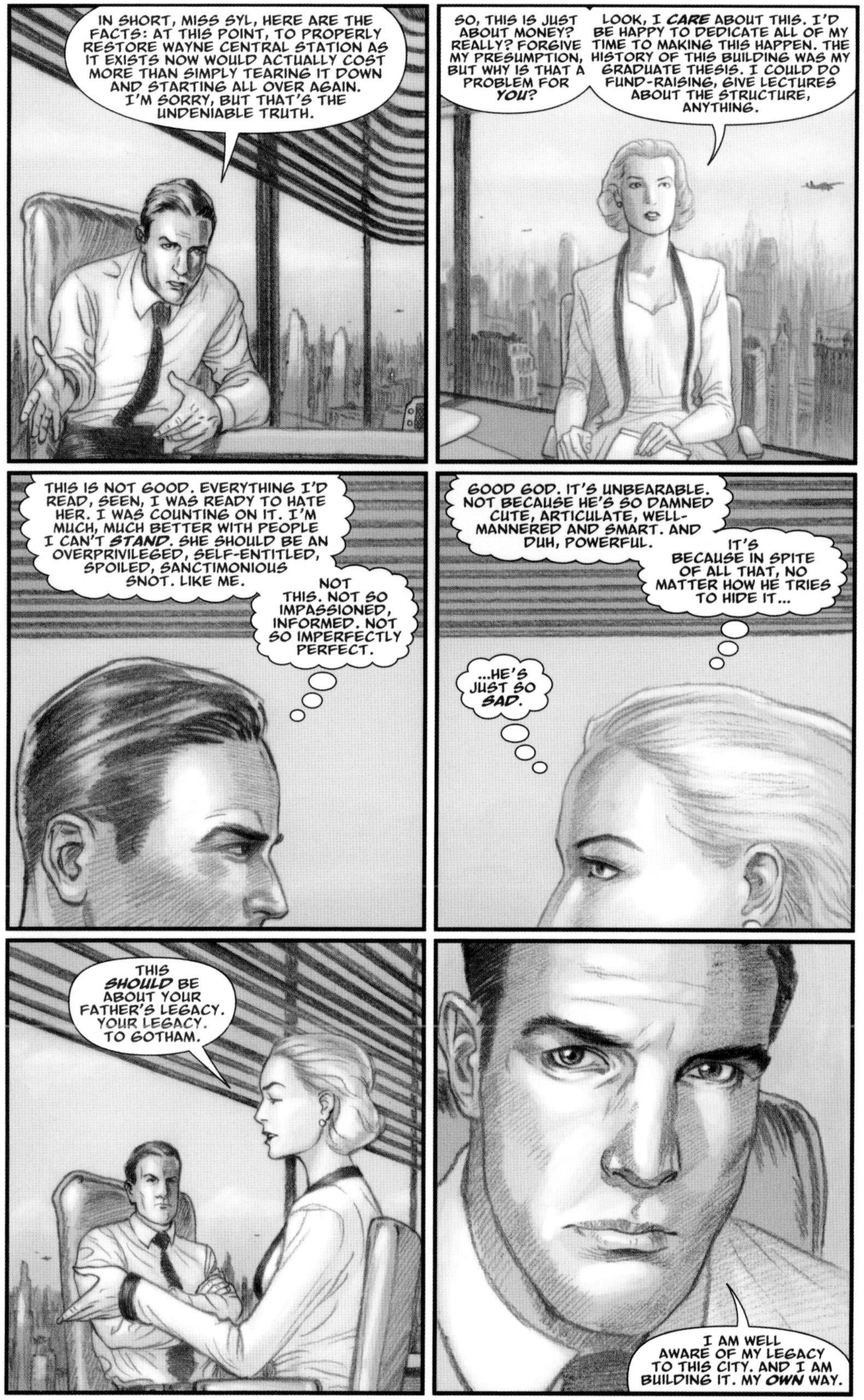
IN SHORT, MISS SYL, HERE ARE THE FACTS: AT THIS POINT, TO PROPERLY RESTORE WAYNE CENTRAL STATION AS IT EXISTS NOW WOULD ACTUALLY COST MORE THAN SIMPLY TEARING IT DOWN AND STARTING ALL OVER AGAIN. I'M SORRY, BUT THAT'S THE UNDENIABLE TRUTH.
SO, THIS IS JUST ABOUT MONEY? REALLY? FORGIVE MY PRESUMPTION, BUT WHY IS THAT A PROBLEM FOR YOU?
LOOK, I CARE ABOUT THIS. I'D BE HAPPY TO DEDICATE ALL OF MY TIME TO MAKING THIS HAPPEN. THE HISTORY OF THIS BUILDING WAS MY GRADUATE THESIS. I COULD DO FUND-RAISING, GIVE LECTURES ABOUT THE STRUCTURE, ANYTHING.
THIS IS NOT GOOD. EVERYTHING I'D READ, SEEN, I WAS READY TO HATE HER. I WAS COUNTING ON IT. I'M MUCH, MUCH BETTER WITH PEOPLE I CAN'T STAND. SHE SHOULD BE AN OVERPRIVILEGED, SELF-ENTITLED, SPOILED, SANCTIMONIOUS SNOT. LIKE ME.
NOT THIS. NOT SO IMPASSIONED, INFORMED. NOT SO IMPERFECTLY PERFECT.
GOOD GOD. IT'S UNBEARABLE. NOT BECAUSE HE'S SO DAMNED CUTE, ARTICULATE, WELL-MANNERED AND SMART. AND DUH, POWERFUL.
IT'S BECAUSE IN SPITE OF ALL THAT, NO MATTER HOW HE TRIES TO HIDE IT...
...HE'S JUST SO SAD.
THIS SHOULD BE ABOUT YOUR FATHER'S LEGACY. YOUR LEGACY. TO GOTHAM.
I AM WELL AWARE OF MY LEGACY TO THIS CITY. AND I AM BUILDING IT. MY OWN WAY.

**RIGHT:** I toyed with the idea of an "abbreviated" Batman costume, with a short poncho-like cape that would have logically fit into Bruce Wayne's briefcase more easily, but Dave pushed back against it as too wimpy, and I think he was right. One thing we did agree on was an altered, unique bat-chest-emblem for our story, which became a deco-streamlined version of the original that appeared only once, in the character's very first appearance in *Detective Comics* #27: just a pair of headless batwings.

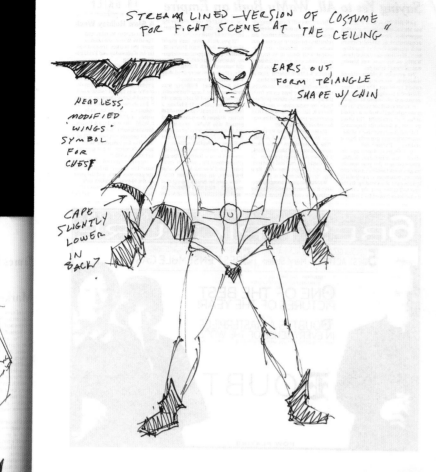

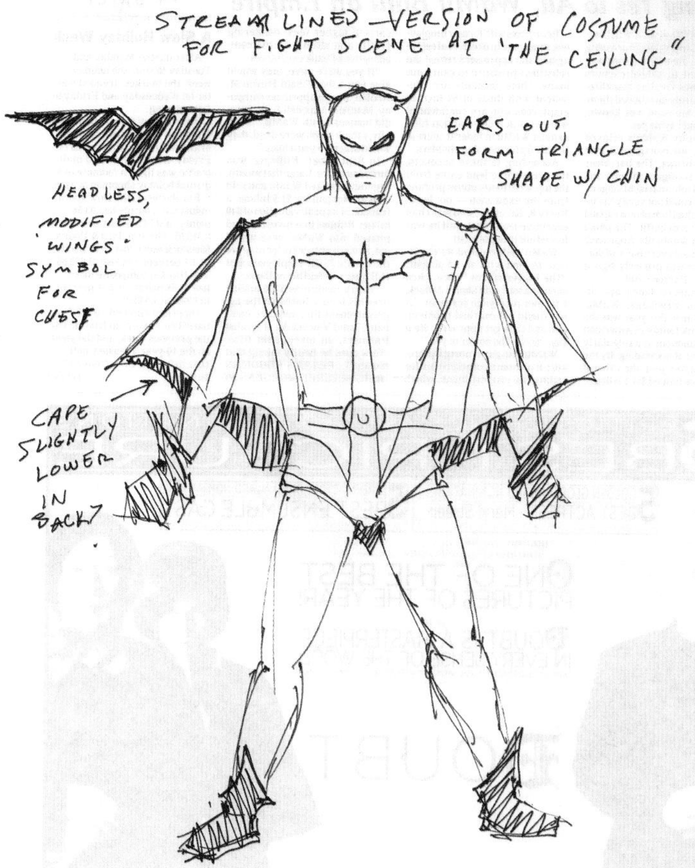
STREAMLINED VERSION OF COSTUME FOR FIGHT SCENE AT 'THE CEILING"
EARS OUT FORM TRIANGLE SHAPE W/ CHIN
HEADLESS, MODIFIED 'WINGS' SYMBOL FOR CHEST
CAPE SLIGHTLY LOWER IN BACK


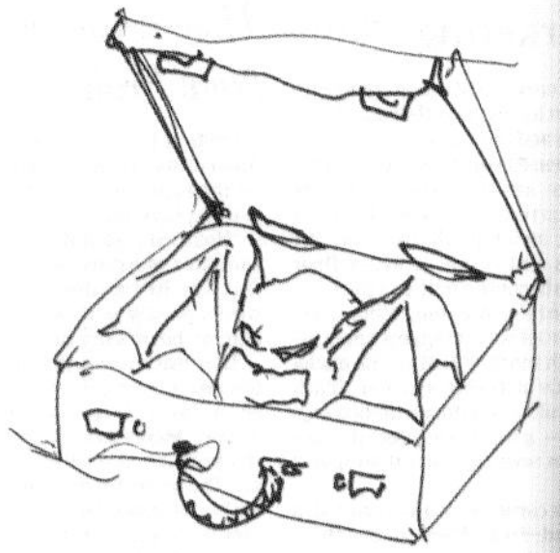

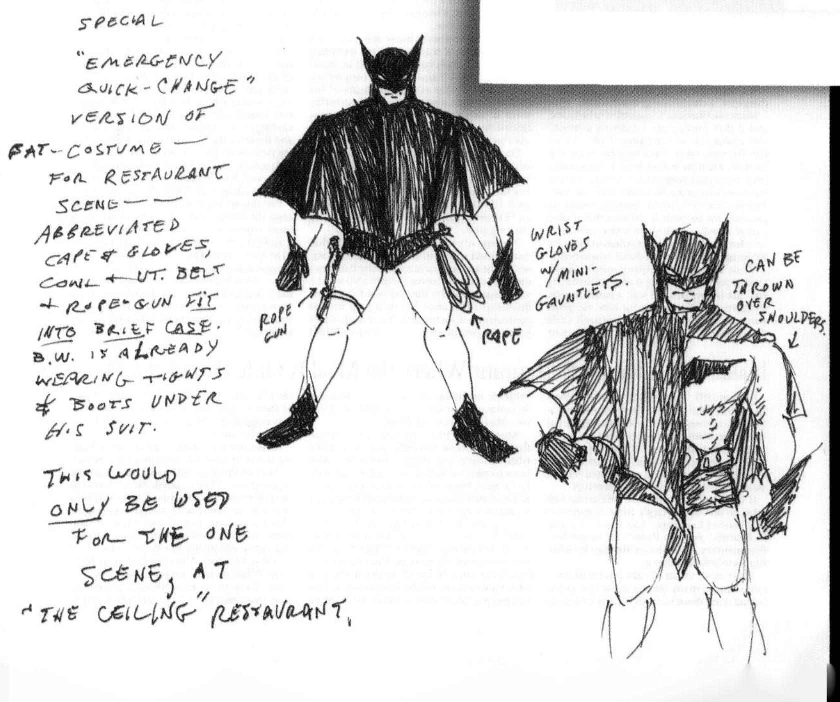
SPECIAL "EMERGENCY QUICK-CHANGE" VERSION OF BAT-COSTUME — FOR RESTAURANT SCENE — ABBREVIATED CAPE & GLOVES, COWL + UT. BELT + ROPE-GUN FIT INTO BRIEF CASE. B.W. IS ALREADY WEARING TIGHTS & BOOTS UNDER HIS SUIT.
THIS WOULD ONLY BE USED FOR THE ONE SCENE, AT "THE CEILING" RESTAURANT.
ROPE GUN
ROPE
WRIST GLOVES W/ MINI-GAUNTLETS.
CAN BE THROWN OVER SHOULDERS.


We also kept the circular belt buckle from the "The Case of the Chemical Syndicate." I always liked it, so why not?

In terms of a new villain, I had an idea for one, to be called "Exacto" (so perfect for a design-inclined bad guy, and legally spelled differently from the blades), who would be a Batman villain-as-architectural-critic. Like all great rogues of the Caped Crusader, he would have his own very good reasons for doing what he is doing. And, P.S., he was me. Heh.

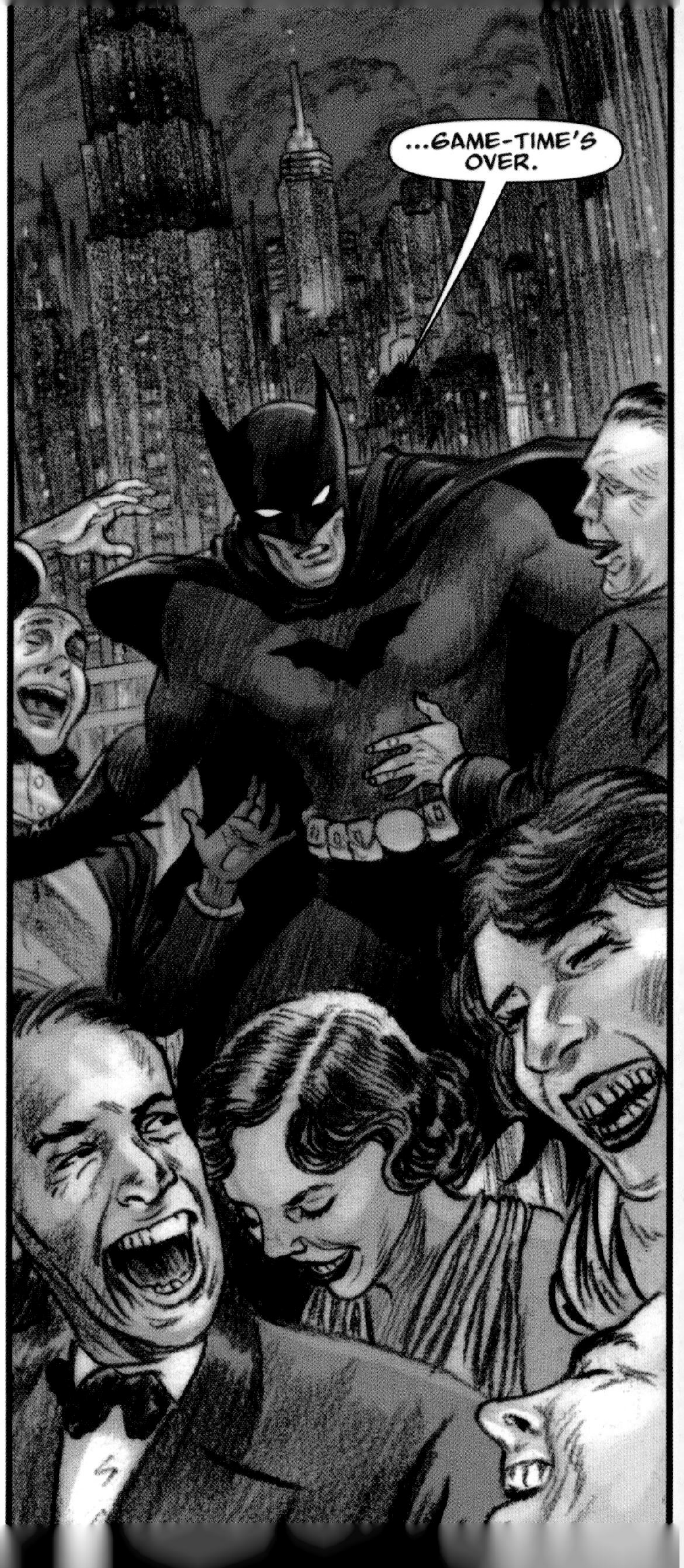
...GAME-TIME'S OVER.

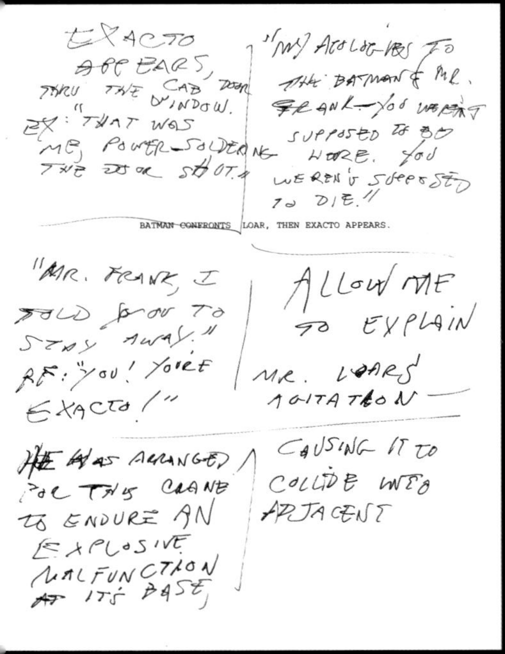
EXACTO APPEARS, THRU THE CAB DOOR WINDOW.
EX: "THAT WAS ME, POWER-SOLDERING THE DOOR SHUT."
"MY APOLOGIES TO THE BATMAN & MR. FRANK—YOU WEREN'T SUPPOSED TO BE HERE. YOU WEREN'T SUPPOSED TO DIE."
BATMAN CONFRONTS LOAR, THEN EXACTO APPEARS.
"MR. FRANK, I TOLD YOU TO STAY AWAY."
RF: "YOU! YOU'RE EXACTO!"
ALLOW ME TO EXPLAIN
MR. LOAR'S AGITATION
CAUSING IT TO COLLIDE INTO ADJACENT

**LEFT:** Notes for Exacto's dialogue in a key scene in the middle point of the story (right), in which Batman, Bart Loar (corrupt evil union boss), and Richard Frank (intrepid young reporter) are trapped high up in a construction crane cab that has been doomed to fall and crash to bits by Loar (who had planned to have escaped by now). Exacto looms mysteriously outside the cab, having suddenly sealed the men inside, and explains their fate. Batman responds by pointing out that Exacto is stuck up there with them, to which the villain replies, "Not really," and disappears by flicking a switch.

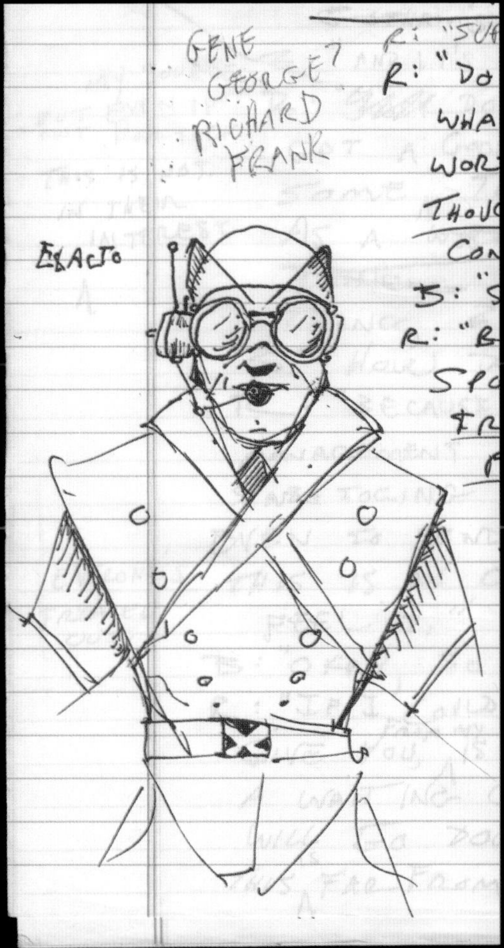
GENE
GEORGE?
RICHARD FRANK
EXACTO

**RIGHT:** My sketch for Exacto's costume. This was very much influenced by the eather flight jacket worn by Charles Lindbergh to cross the Atlantic. I always thought ts V-shaped cut was so elegant and unusual. have since asked several tailors to replicate it for me and they can't.

The goggles and retro headset with mouthpiece hearken to old hotel phone operators and complete the "mask," covering enough of Exacto's face so that he could be any number of men in the story. Dave managed to make all of this look cool and not completely ridiculous. (Especially the second panel on the page: Exacto looks totally n control, which must be driving Batman crazy.) I also love that we're seeing him through a haze of smudge and streaks on the thick glass, rendering him harder to read in the best possible way.

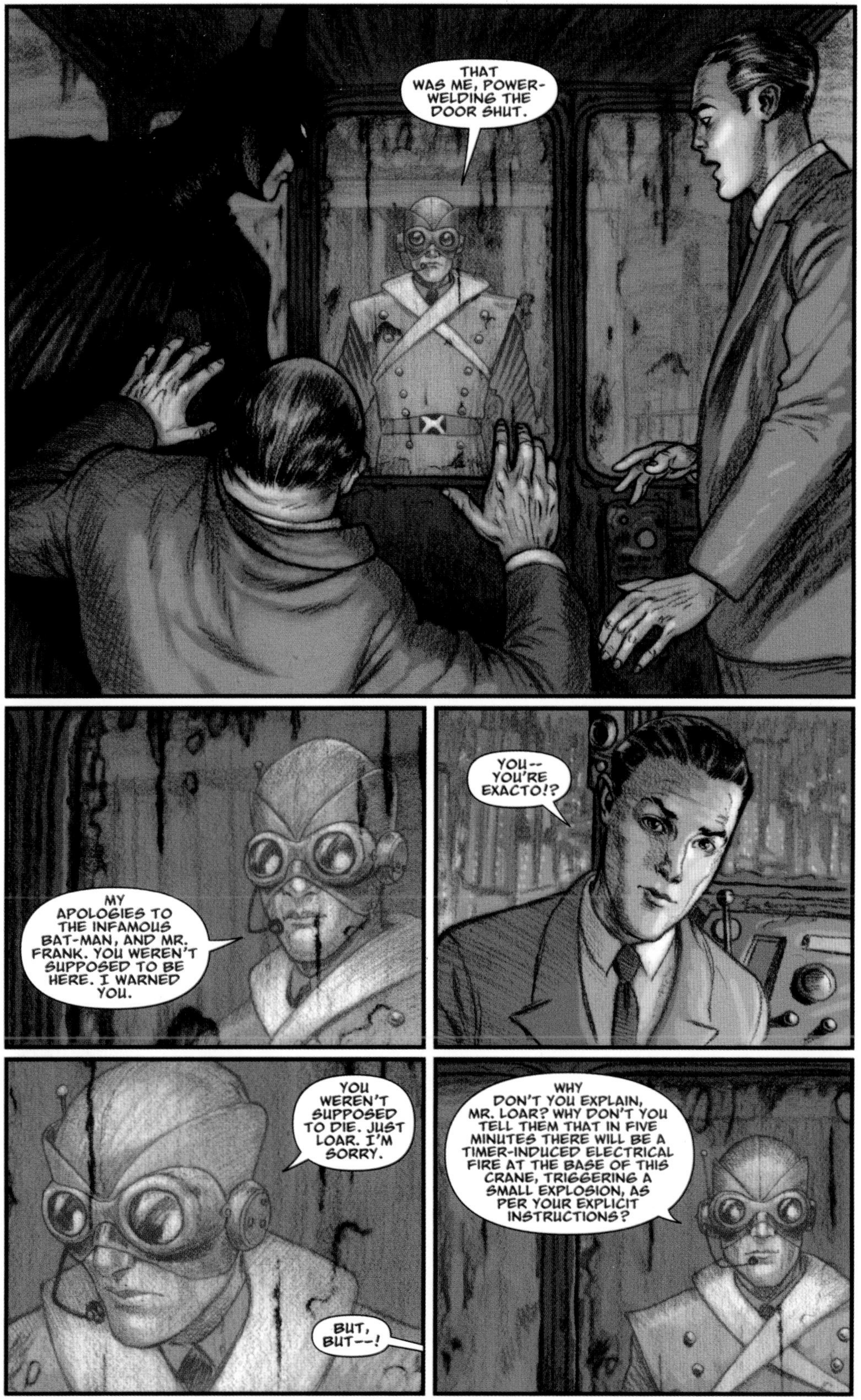
THAT WAS ME, POWER-WELDING THE DOOR SHUT.
MY APOLOGIES TO THE INFAMOUS BAT-MAN, AND MR. FRANK. YOU WEREN'T SUPPOSED TO BE HERE. I WARNED YOU.
YOU-- YOU'RE EXACTO!?
YOU WEREN'T SUPPOSED TO DIE. JUST LOAR. I'M SORRY.
BUT, BUT--!
WHY DON'T YOU EXPLAIN, MR. LOAR? WHY DON'T YOU TELL THEM THAT IN FIVE MINUTES THERE WILL BE A TIMER-INDUCED ELECTRICAL FIRE AT THE BASE OF THIS CRANE, TRIGGERING A SMALL EXPLOSION, AS PER YOUR EXPLICIT INSTRUCTIONS?

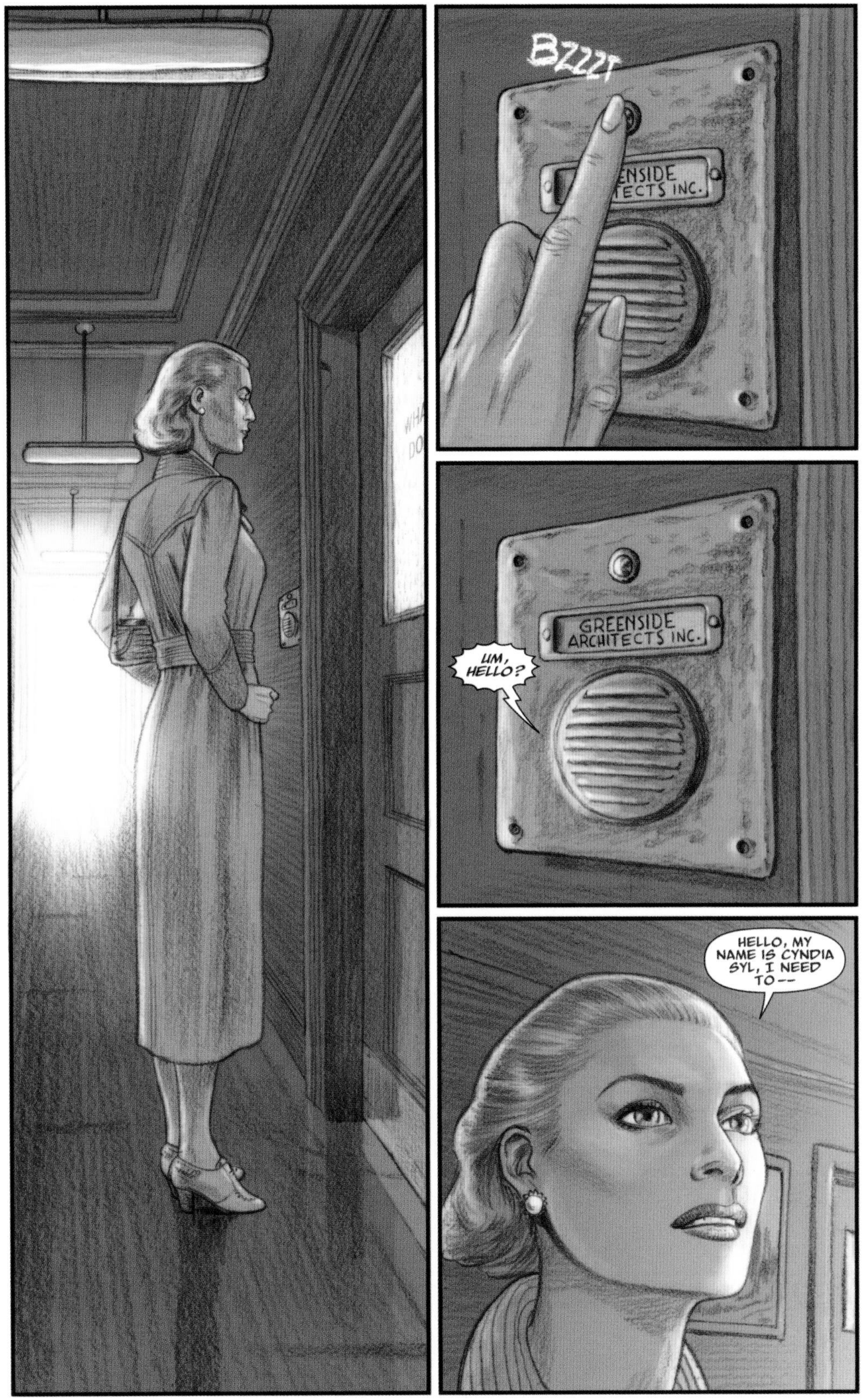
BZZZT
GREENSIDE ARCHITECTS INC.
UM, HELLO?
HELLO, MY NAME IS CYNDIA SYL, I NEED TO --



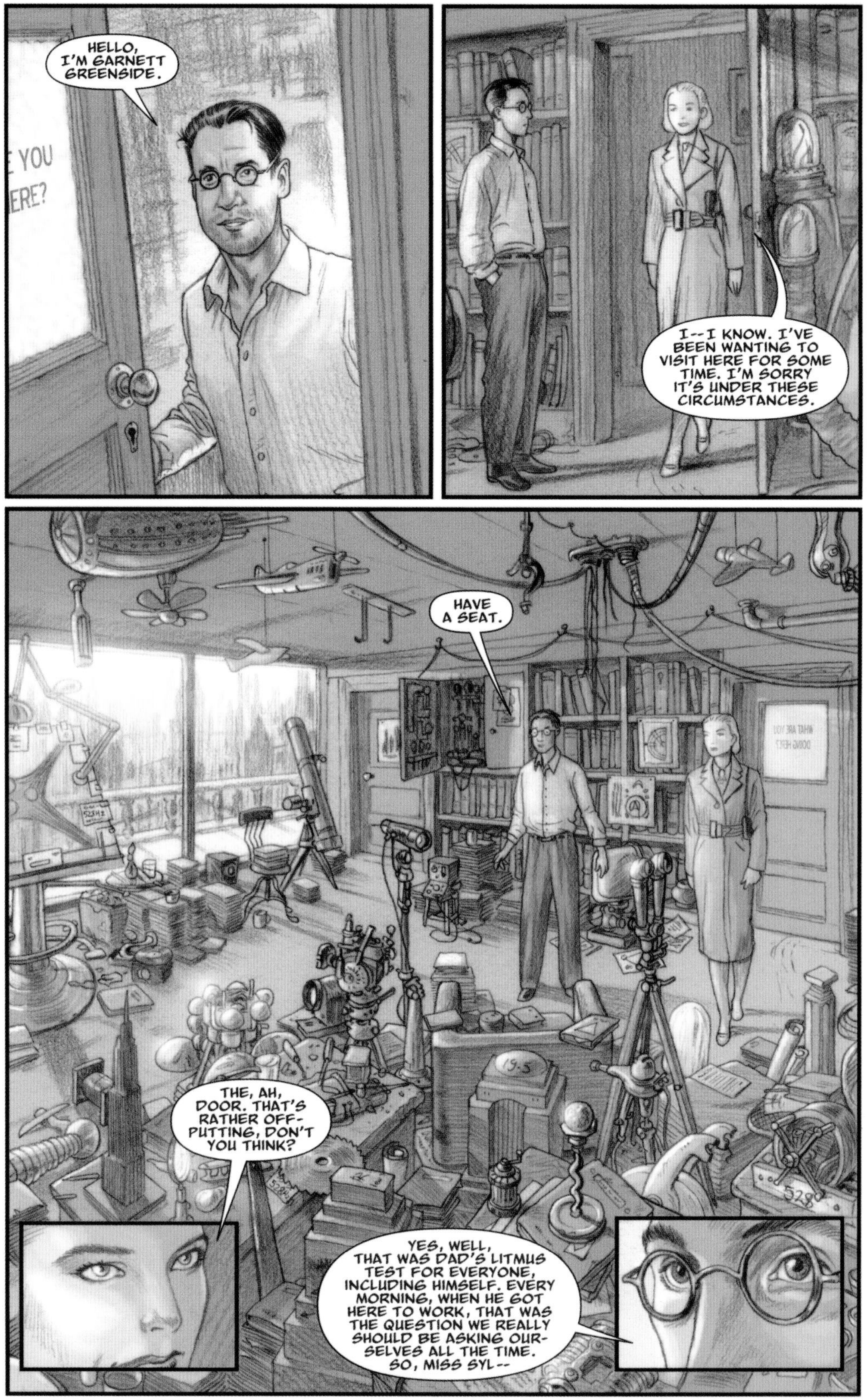
HELLO, I'M GARNETT GREENSIDE.
I--I KNOW. I'VE BEEN WANTING TO VISIT HERE FOR SOME TIME. I'M SORRY IT'S UNDER THESE CIRCUMSTANCES.
HAVE A SEAT.
THE, AH, DOOR. THAT'S RATHER OFF-PUTTING, DON'T YOU THINK?
YES, WELL, THAT WAS DAD'S LITMUS TEST FOR EVERYONE, INCLUDING HIMSELF. EVERY MORNING, WHEN HE GOT HERE TO WORK, THAT WAS THE QUESTION WE REALLY SHOULD BE ASKING OURSELVES ALL THE TIME. SO, MISS SYL --

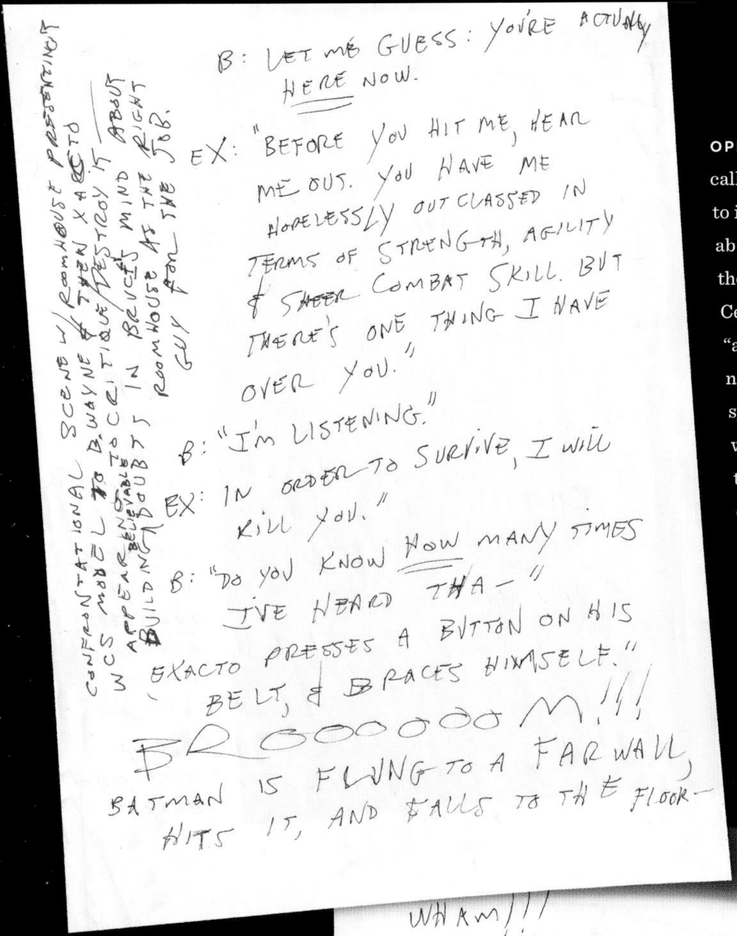
CONFRONTATIONAL SCENE W/ ROOMHOUSE PRESENTING WCS MODEL TO B. WAYNE & THEN EXACTO APPEARS ABLE TO CRITIQUE/DESTROY IT ABOUT BUILDING DOUBTS IN BRUCE'S MIND RIGHT ROOMHOUSE AS THE GUY FOR THE JOB.

B: LET ME GUESS: YOU'RE ACTUALLY HERE NOW.

EX: "BEFORE YOU HIT ME, HEAR ME OUT. YOU HAVE ME HOPELESSLY OUTCLASSED IN TERMS OF STRENGTH, AGILITY & ~~SHEER~~ COMBAT SKILL. BUT THERE'S ONE THING I HAVE OVER YOU."

B: "I'M LISTENING."

EX: IN ORDER TO SURVIVE, I WILL KILL YOU."

B: "DO YOU KNOW HOW MANY TIMES I'VE HEARD THA—"

EXACTO PRESSES A BUTTON ON HIS BELT, & BRACES HIMSELF."

BROOOOOOM!!!

BATMAN IS FLUNG TO A FAR WALL, HITS IT, AND FALLS TO THE FLOOR—

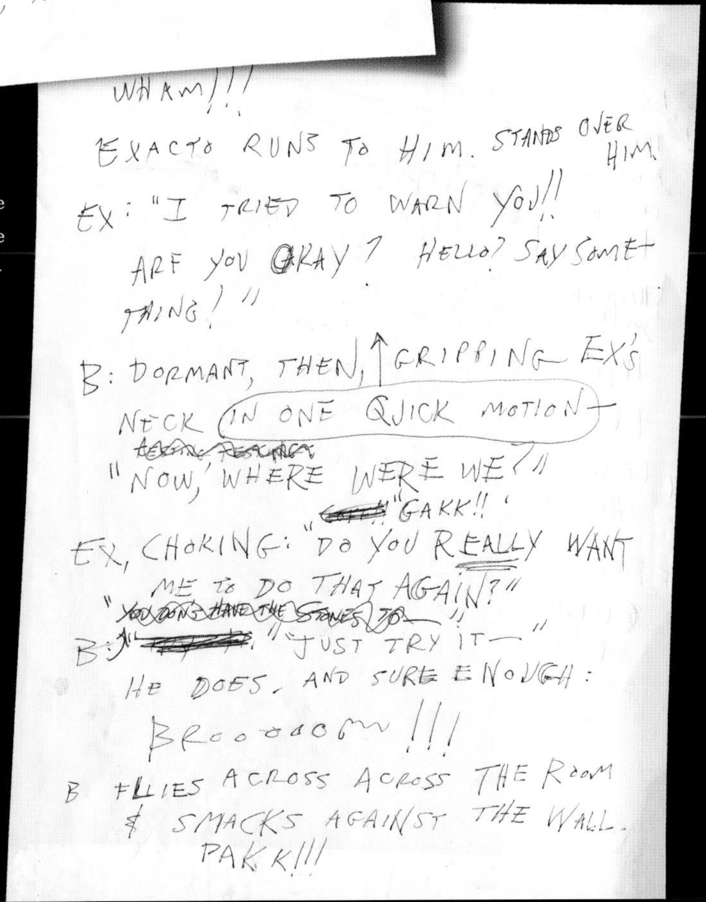
WHAM!!!

EXACTO RUNS TO HIM. STANDS OVER HIM.

EX: "I TRIED TO WARN YOU!! ARE YOU OKAY? HELLO? SAY SOMETHING!"

B: DORMANT, THEN, GRIPPING EX'S NECK (IN ONE QUICK MOTION)—

"NOW, WHERE WERE WE?"

"GAKK!!"

EX, CHOKING: "DO YOU REALLY WANT ME TO DO THAT AGAIN?"

~~"YOU DON'T HAVE THE STONES TO"~~

B: "JUST TRY IT—"

HE DOES. AND SURE ENOUGH:

BROOOOOOM!!!

B FLIES ACROSS ACROSS THE ROOM & SMACKS AGAINST THE WALL.

PAKK!!!

**OPPOSITE:** Cyndia Syl pays a call to Garnett Greenside (me) to inquire regarding the whereabouts of his father, Gregor, the original designer of Wayne Central Station. The Greenside "architectural design firm" by now is an apartment live/work space that is filled to bursting with various prototype furniture and gadgets. The glass on the front door, by the way, says, "What Are You Doing Here?"—as much an admonition to potential visitors as it is to the workers inside.

**ABOVE & RIGHT:** Dialogue notes for a climactic scene when Batman finally confronts Exacto in the flesh.

**FAR RIGHT:** By now Batman knows who he really is (Garnett Greenside), but he is more interested in figuring out how Exacto is able to pull off these crazy stunts. (Hint: a system he invented for something called "Smart Projections," which I suppose I wanted to be a metaphor of my goal for the book itself . . .)

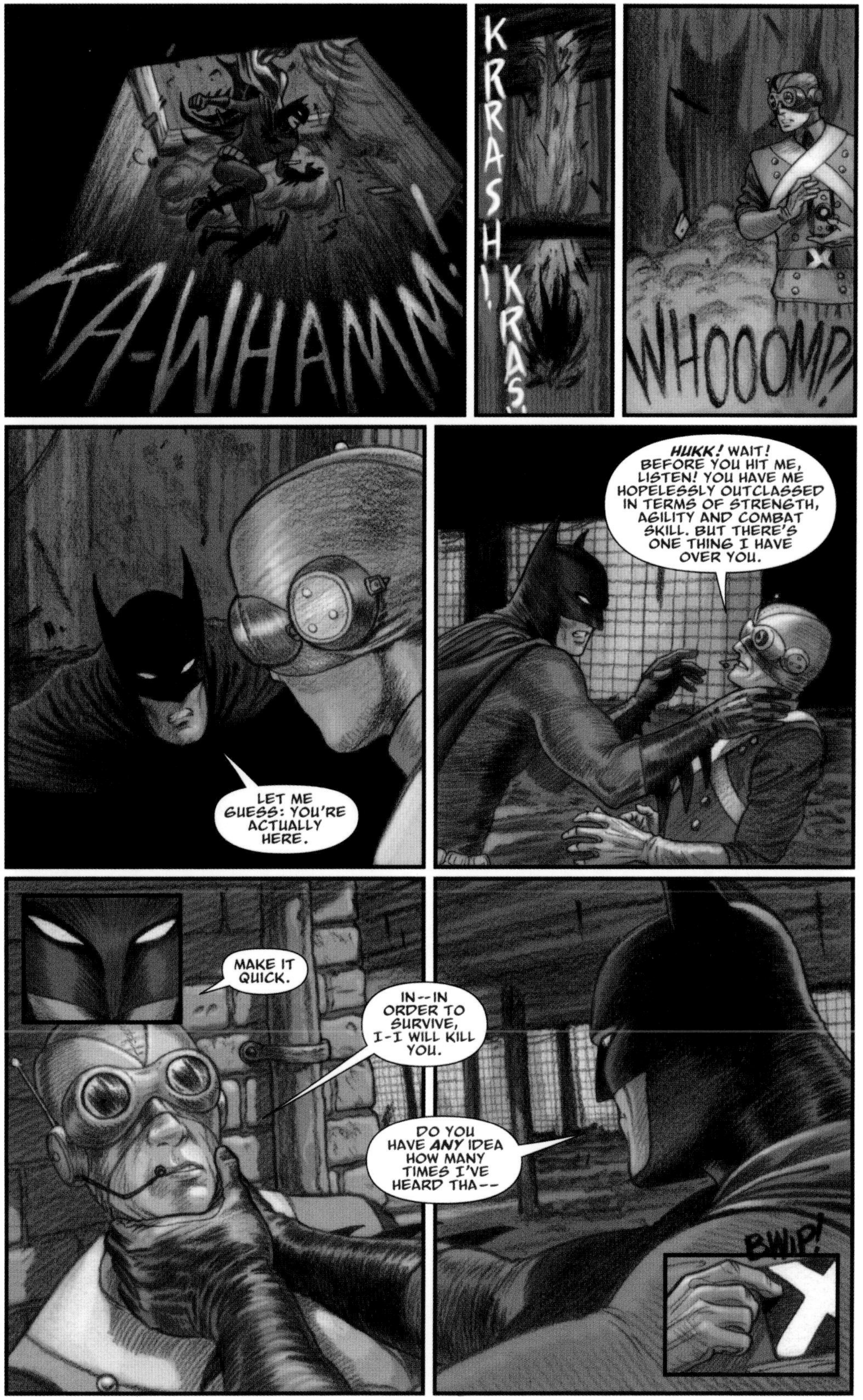
TA-WHAMM!
KRASH!
KRAS.
WHOOOMP!
LET ME GUESS: YOU'RE ACTUALLY HERE.
HUKK! WAIT! BEFORE YOU HIT ME, LISTEN! YOU HAVE ME HOPELESSLY OUTCLASSED IN TERMS OF STRENGTH, AGILITY AND COMBAT SKILL. BUT THERE'S ONE THING I HAVE OVER YOU.
MAKE IT QUICK.
IN--IN ORDER TO SURVIVE, I-I WILL KILL YOU.
DO YOU HAVE ANY IDEA HOW MANY TIMES I'VE HEARD THA--
BWIP!

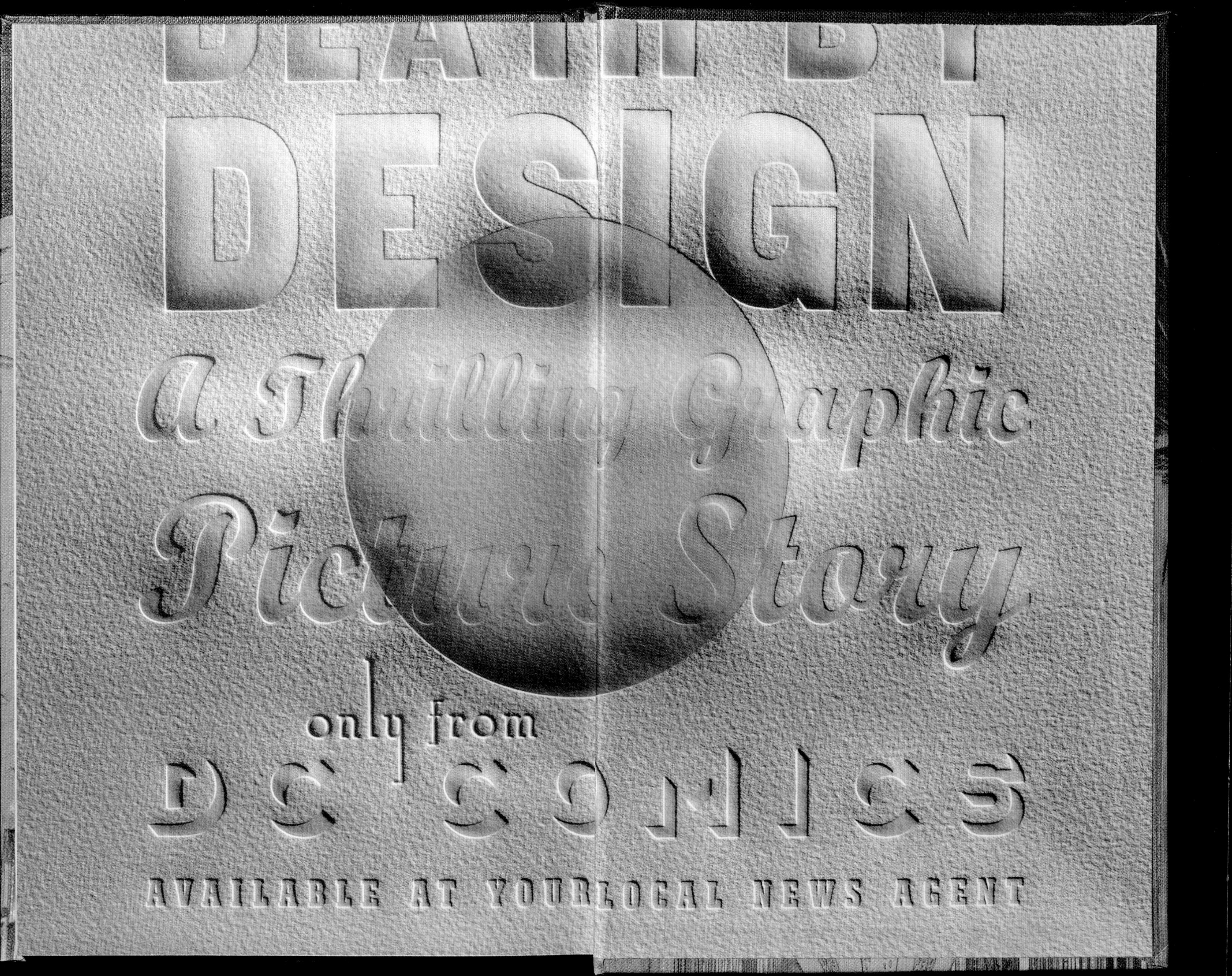

# DEATH BY DESIGN

## A Thrilling Graphic Picture Story

only from

DC SONICS

AVAILABLE AT YOUR LOCAL NEWS AGENT

# The Future Is Now

It was Thursday, June 25, 2009, and I was riding uptown to my office in a cab, psyched because I had just shot (with Geoff Spear, of course) my first *Newsweek* cover, which was about summer reading (right). Then the news came over the radio: Michael Jackson had died, at age 50. That was sad, but I had not connected the two events. Until my cellphone rang.

"Hey, it's Bonnie." As in Bonnie Siegler, at the time one-half of the legendary design duo Number 17 (with Emily Oberman). They were the current art directors of *Newsweek* and it was their idea to hire me for the job.

"Michael Jackson just died," she continued, very solemnly.

"Yes, I know, I just heard, so sad," I said, wondering why she was calling to tell me this. Yes, I was that thick.

"Um, we have to deal with this," she replied, and then I finally got it: duh, it's *Newsweek*, and this was news with a capital N, and the magazine wasn't due to go to the printer until the weekend to be available that Monday. Such was the nature of weekly news magazines, always at the mercy of late-breaking stories. I knew this from my friendship with Oz Elliott (another legend), who was editor-in-chief of the magazine in its glory days of the 1960s and '70s.

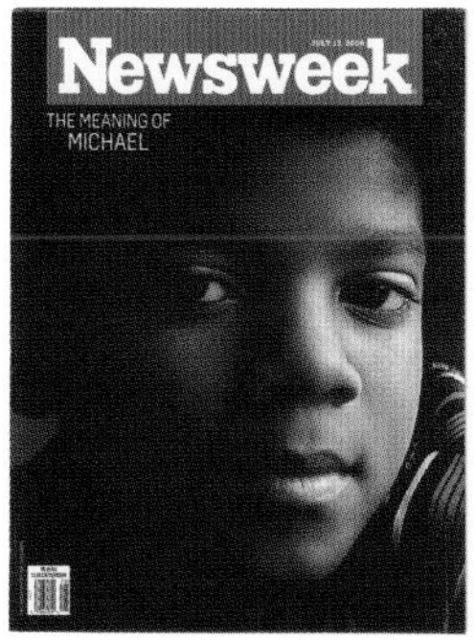
Newsweek
THE MEANING OF MICHAEL

Bye-bye, my summer reading cover. Or so I thought. Newsweek ultimately decided to print two versions: my cover would be sent to subscribers, whereas the Michael Jackson cover (left) appeared on newsstands. I was deeply, deeply grateful.

. . .

I can't help but marvel at how much our technology has advanced since that day in 2009, and how our media have changed in response to that technology. And we know it will continue to evolve: books, magazines, newspapers, movies, each industry will wrestle with new, perhaps even existential, challenges. And yet we the public crave stories—be they fiction or nonfiction—and always will. That simple fact gives me hope; and I am eager to help give a face and a voice to those tales yet to come.

**—C.K., New York City, 2016**

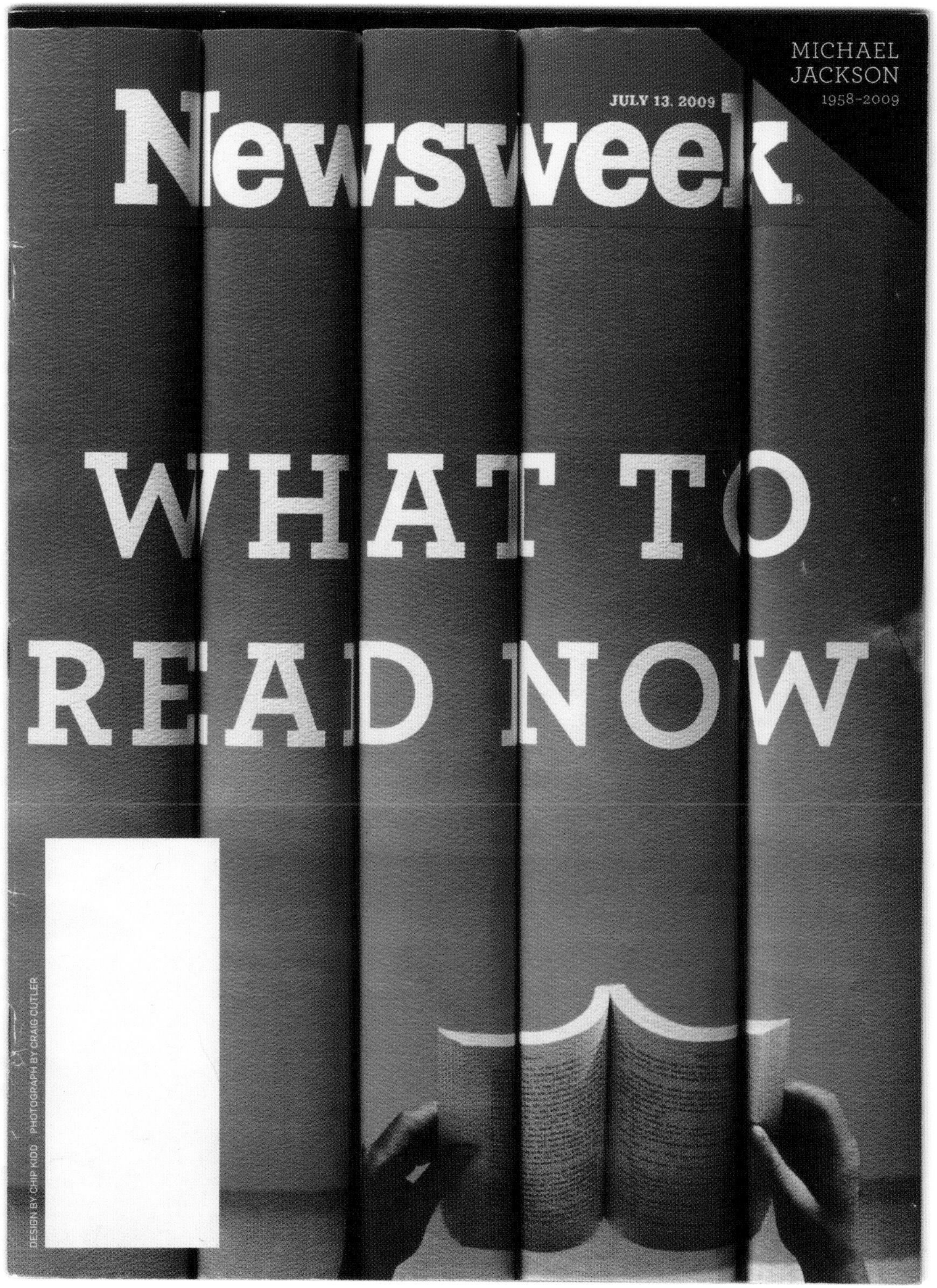
MICHAEL JACKSON
1958–2009
JULY 13, 2009
Newsweek
WHAT TO READ NOW
DESIGN BY CHIP KIDD PHOTOGRAPH BY CRAIG CUTLER

# Index

*Unless otherwise specified, all titles and projects listed in the index were designed by Chip Kidd.*

Abrams, Charles, 224
Abrams, J. J., 150, 154
Abrams Books, 219, 223
Abrams ComicArts, 71, 219, 223, 241
*Absolutely on Music: Conversations with Seiji Ozawa*, 15
Academy of American Poets, 110
ACT-UP, 47
*Ada, or Ardor*, 187
*After Dark*, 8–9
AIGA, 147
Akhmatova, Anna, 193
Aldrich, Nelson W., Jr., 107
Ali, Muhammad, 55
Allen, Thomas, 86, 188
Allen, Woody, 108–109
All-Star Batman and Robin the Boy Wonder, 262–263
All-Star Superman series, 260–261
*Almost Invisible*, 130
Amador, Paul, 156
*The Amalgamation Polka*, 126
*The Amazing Adventures of Kavalier and Clay*, 48–49
American Academy of Arts and Letters, 24
*American Fantastic Tales*, 198–199
*American Icon*, 72–73
*American Psycho*, 166
*The American People*, 111
*American Visions: The Epic History of Art in America*, 103
Amis, Martin, 50–51
*Amnesia*, 115
*Amphitryon*, 118
Amtrak, 52–53
Anderson, Chris, 282
Anderson, Christopher, 167
*And Then We Came to the End*, 66–67
Arbus, Diane, 136
*Artbreak*, 242–243
Art School Confidential, 182–183
"Asymmetrical Girl," 242
Atavist Books, 96
*The Athena Doctrine*, 216
Avedon, Richard, 257
*Awakenings*, 232

*The Baby Business*, 217
Bad Robot, 150
Baitz, Jon Robin, 202
Barnett, Gina, 282, 283
Bass, Gary J., 113
Batman, 7, 26, 29, 236–237, 262–263, 269, 271
*Batman: Black and White*, 294–295
*Batman: Death by Design*, 296–314
Batman and Robin, 275
*Batman Collected*, 122
*Bat-Manga: The Secret History of Batman*, 274–277
Beck, C. C., 241
*Before the Wind*, 134
*Before Watchmen*, 165
Bezos, Jeff, 282
Bezos, MacKenzie, 192
Binder, Otto, 241
*Bird in Space* (Brancusi), 57
Birnbaum, Lisa, 286–291
*Birthday*, 181
Bissell, Tom, 114
Blechmann, Nicholas, 176
*A Blessed Child*, 100
*Blind Willow, Sleeping Woman*, 8
Blitz, Jeffrey, 138–139
*Blood Meridian*, 85
*Blood's a Rover*, 171
*The Blood Telegram: Nixon, Kissinger, and a Forgotten Genocide*, 113
Bock, Dennis, 79
*Books for Living*, 40–41
*Border Songs*, 134–135
Boston Book Festival, 146–147, 176
Bowers, Kathryn, 58, 59
Boyden, Joseph, 190
Braddock, Paige, 223, 224
Brancusi, Constantin, 57
Brando, Marlon, 116–117, 257
Breyer, Stephen, 125
*Bridesmaids* (film), 71
*The Bridge*, 55
*Bright, Precious Days*, 46
*Bright Lights, Big City*, 46
*Brightness Falls*, 46
*Broadcast News* (film), 152
Broden, Frederik, 199
Brunetti, Ivan, 281
*Building Stories* (Chris Ware), 28
Bullock, Dave, 270
*The Bungler*, 118
Burns, Charles, 33, 34, 37, 71
Burns, Sarah, 144
Burroughs, Augusten, 86–89, 149
Bush, Laura, 215

Cantor, Jay, 113
Capeci, Amid, 228
Captain Marvel, 240–241
*Capture*, 191
Carey, Edith, 158–159
Carey, Peter, 115
Carroll, Lewis, 29
Carson, Carol Devine, 41, 77
Carver, Alyssa, 77
*A Case of Exploding Mangoes*, 78
Cavalieri, Joey, 270
*The Central Park Five: A Chronicle of a City Wilding*, 144–145
Chabon, Michael, 48–49
Charles M. Schulz Museum and Research Center, 223
*The Cheese Monkeys*, 33, 37, 39, 278
Chiarello, Mark, 264, 271, 272, 296, 298–299
*Chip Kidd: Book One*, 3, 75, 77, 178, 188, 202, 207, 257
Cho, Michael, 294–295
*Cities of the Plain*, 85
*City on Fire*, 13, 248–253
*The City of Devi*, 122
Clemens, Roger, 72–73
Clowes, Daniel, 182–183
Coady, Francis, 96
Collected Poems (Justice), 93
Collected Poems (Strand), 131
Collica, Michael, 239
*Colorless Tsukuru Tazaki and His Years of Pilgrimage*, 14–15
Columbia pictures, 182
*Consumed*, 204–205
Convergence, 264–267
*Conversations with Frank Gehry*, 56
*Conversations with Scorsese*, 116
*Conversations with Woody Allen*, 108
Cooke, Carolyn, 127
Cooke, Darwynne, 295
*Cool It*, 120–121
Cooper, Anderson, 254–255, 256
Cooper, Bradley, 202
Cooper-Hewitt, 168
Copeland, Stewart, 178, 179
Coppola, Francis Ford, 188–189
Costello, Elvis, 167
*The Court and the World*, 125
Cronenberg, David, 204–205
Crosley, Sloan, 148
Crumb, Robert, 178, 181
*Cuba Libre*, 60

D'Antonio, Michael, 66, 216
Dark Knight Returns series, 237
*Daughters of the Revolution*, 127

DC Comics, 28, 162, 219, 237, 241, 259, 261, 264–267, 268–273, 275, 294–295, 296, 298
DC Entertainment, 259, 270
Dean, Cecilia, 181
*Death of a Murderer*, 101
D'Elia, Greg, 289
Desiderio, Vincent, 156
Detective Comics, 29
deWilde, Barbara, 11
*Diary of a Wimpy Kid*, 219
Didio, Dan, 264, 296
Disney, Walt, 224
*Dispatches from the Edge*, 254–255
*Djibouti*, 60
Doonsbury, 229
Doubleday, 239
Downey, Robert, Jr., 136
*A Draft of Light*, 78
*Duty*, 99

*Easy*, 61
*Echo Hunt*, 114
Edgar, Kate, 230
*Edie*, 107
Ehrenhalt, Alan, 121
8th-Man, 275
Eisner, Will, 270
Eisner Awards, 28
Elliott, Oz, 315
Ellis, Bret Easton, 166–167
Ellison, Harlan, 29
Ellroy, James, 170–171, 188
*The End of Overeating*, 191
*The End of Your Life Book Club*, 41
Eno, Brian, 213
*The Essential Engineer*, 64
Essl, Mike, 163
*The Evolution of God*, 176–177
Excoffon, Robert, 204–205
*Extra Lives: Why Video Games Matter*, 114
*The Extraordinary Journey of the Fakir Who Got Trapped in an Ikea Wardrobe*, 63

*Faith Interrupted: A Spiritual Journey*, 109
*Famous* (music video), 157
*Fangland*, 96
Fawcett, 241
Feig, Paul, 71
Feinstein, Elaine, 193
Ferrell, Will, 182
Ferris, Hugh, 298
Ferris, Joshua, 66–67
Ferris, Saul, 275
*Final Crisis*, 272–273

Fixx, Jim, 10
Flora, Jim, 283
Foley, Greg, 181
*The Force Awakens* (film), 150
Ford, Harrison, 150, 152
Ford, Walton, 134
"Four Freedoms," 124
France, David, 47
Frank, Dan, 231
Frank, Ze, 110
Froelich, Paula, 143
Fulford, Jason, 81, 115
*Fur* (film), 136–137

Gabriel, Philip, 7
Gaiman, Neil, 26–31, 296
Galassi, Jonathan, 142
Gall, John, 187
Gan, Stephen, 181
García, Cristina, 79
Garmey, Stephen, 193
Garrisson, Deb, 128
Gates, Henry Louis, 145
Gates, Robert M., 98
Gehry, Frank, 56
*Geek Love*, 26
Gerzema, John, 66
*Get a Financial Life*, 67
*Ghost in the Machine* (Mick Haggerty), 178
Gibbons, Dave, 162–165
Gibson, Ralph, 42
Gilliam, Terry, 162
Glaser, Milton, 278
Glass, Randy, 281, 287, 290
*Go: A Kidd's Guide to Graphic Design*, 158, 278–281, 284
*Going Home Again*, 79
Goldblum, Jeff, 152
Goodman, Benny, 283
Goodman, Wendy, 257
*Good Ol' Charles Schulz* (documentary), 225
*The Good Life*, 46
Gowin, Elijah, 127
*GQ Italia*, 195
Grafton, Sue, 278
*The Great Inversion and the Future of the American City*, 41, 121
Greenberg, Jill, 148
Greenberg, Michael, 92–93
Greenberg, Richard, 202
Greene, Brian, 244–247
Grossman, Austin, 68–69
*Grunt*, 97, 98
*Gulp*, 97

*Half the Sky*, 123
Hallberg, Garth Risk, 248–253
Hammer, Langdon, 106
*A Handbook to Luck*, 79
*A Hand Reached Down to Guide Me*, 41
Hanif, Mohammed, 78
Hanson, Eric, 15
Harger, Nathan, 144
Harkaway, Nick, 94–95
Hattemer-Higgins, Ida, 62
Hecht, Anthony, 201
Hemingway, Ernest, 176, 200–201
*Hero*, 70–71
Heshka, Ryan, 94
*The Hidden Reality*, 244
Hinders, Maggie, 13
Hindley, Myra, 101
*The History of History*, 62
*Holidays on Ice*, 91
Hollander, John, 78
Hollinghurst, Alan, 132
*Hollywood Nocturnes*, 170–171
Holzherr, Brittany, 264
*Hostage*, 112
Houellebecq, Michel, 204
*How Did You Get This Number*, 148
*How It Ended*, 44–45
*How Literature Saved My Life*, 40–41
How to Survive a Plague, 47
Hubble telescope, 244
*Hub Fans Bid Kid Adieu*, 75
Hughes, Andy, 11, 239
Hughes, Robert, 102–104
*Hurry Down Sunshine*, 92–93
Hutchinson, Joe, 229

*Icarus at the Edge of Time*, 244–247
*The Illustrated Woody Allen Reader*, 109
*Imperial Bedrooms*, 167
Isenberg, Barbara, 56
*I Shudder: And Other Reactions to Life, Death, and New Jersey*, 149
*It Seemed Important at the Time*, 257

Jackson, Michael, 315
Jackson, Samuel L., 83
*James Merrill: Life and Art*, 106
Jaramillo, Raquel, 278, 281
Jen, Gish, 133
Jones, Tommy Lee, 83
*Judge This*, 284
*The Juice*, 42

*Jurassic Park*, 95
Justice, Donald, 93

Kafka, Franz, 113
Kaliardos, James, 181
Kammen, Michel, 57
Kanfer, Stefan, 116–117
Katz, Alex, 181
Keaton, Diane, 150, 152
*Keepers*, 116–117
Kendrick, Anna, 138
Kerry, Andy and Michelle, 199
Kessler, David A., 191
*The Hedonist in the Cellar*, 42–43
Kidd, Ann, 215
Kidd, Chip, 3–4, 6–7, 26, 32–37, 52–53, 158–161, 180–181, 214–215, 222–225, 240–241, 242–243, 274–277, 278–281, 282–283, 284–285, 286–289, 294–295, 296–313
Kidd, Thomas, 75, 215
Kidman, Nicole, 136
Kirby, Jack, 241
Kirkman, Robert, 80
Kissinger, Henry, 113
Klima, Martin, 61
Klopfel, Holgar, 220
Kluger, Richard, 144
Kobliner, Beth, 67
Kochman, Charles, 219, 223
Korda, Michael, 257
Korté, Steve, 264
Kramer, Larry, 111
Kristof, Nicholas, 123
Kunhardt, Peter W., 105
Kunhardt, Peter W., Jr., 105
Kunhardt, Philip B., III, 105
Kuwata, Jiro, 275, 277

Laforet, Vincent, 130
Landrieu, Mary, 254
Lang, Fritz, 298
Lasser, Scott, 100–101
*The Last Shift*, 106
Lax, Eric, 108–109
*The Learners*, 33–37
Lee, Jim, 262–263
*Left-Handed*, 142
Leonard, Elmore, 60
Lepore, Jill, 258–259
*Less Than Zero*, 166–167
*The Letter Q*, 194
*The Letters of Ernest Hemingway*, 200–201
*Letters to Véra*, 187
Levine, Philip, 106
Levitz, Paul, 275
Liebowitz, Annie, 140
*Life upon These Shores: Looking at African American History 1513–2008*, 145

316

Lindbergh, Charles, 311
Lindsay-Abaire, David, 100–101
*Lolita*, 185
Lomborg, Bjorn, 120–121
Longo, Robert, 44
*Looking for Lincoln: The Making of a Cultural Icon*, 105
*The Looming Tower*, 172
*Love, Dishonor, Marry, Die, Cherish, Perish*, 238–239
*Lovers' Quarrels*, 119
Lucas, Craig, 199
Luna, Ian, 183
Lynch, Jim, 134–135
*Lyrics: 1964–2006*, 206–207

McAdams, Rachel, 150, 152
McCarthy, Cormac, 80–85
McClatchy, J. D. "Sandy," 130, 132, 156–159, 161, 215, 239, 282, 289
McDougall, Christopher, 73
McInerney, Jay, 42–46
McKean, Dave, 28
McMullan, Patrick, 44
McMurray, Fred, 241
Madere, John, 281
*Make Good Art*, 26–27, 29–31
"Make Good Art" (Gaiman), 28
*Making Our Democracy Work*, 125
*Man and Camel*, 129–130
Mankell, Henning, 199
Mantello, Joe, 202
*The Map and the Territory*, 204
Marks, John, 96
Marston, William Moulton, 258
*The Mary Tyler Moore Show* (TV show), 152
Matcho, Mark, 60
Matetsky, Harry, 241
Mazzucchelli, David, 275
Medvedev, Dmitri, 62–63
Mehta, Sonny, 17, 64–65, 85, 99, 185, 186, 196, 286
Mendelsund, Peter, 51
*Men Without Women*, 7
*Mercury Dressing*, 156
*Mercury in Retrograde*, 143
Merrill, James, 106
Metropolitan Opera, 140–141
Michaelis, David, 220–221
Michelangelo, 217
*Migraine*, 233
Milgram, Stanley, 33–35, 37
Miller, Diana, 252
Miller, Frank, 49, 237, 262–263
Millionaire, Tony, 178–179
*The Mind's Eye*, 232
Minghella, Max, 183
MoCCA Arts Festival, 71

Molière, 118–119
Moore, Alan, 162–165
Moore, Andrew, 83
Moore, Perry, 70–71
Morath, Inge, 257
*Morning Glory* (film), 150–154
Morrison, Grant, 260–261, 272–273
Mould, Bob, 47
*Mr. Robot* (TV series), 114
Murakami, Haruki, 6–19
*The Museum of Innocence*, 22–23
*Museums and Women*, 77
*Musicophilia: Tales of Music and the Brain*, 230
*My Father's Tears* (Carol Devine Carson), 76–77
*My Name Is Red*, 23
*Mythology: The DC Comics Art of Alex Ross*, 268

Nabokov, Dmitri, 185, 186
Nabokov, Vera, 185
Nabokov, Vladimir, 47, 184–187
Nadeau, Gary, 242
NASA, 244
Nathan, Jean, 171
National Design Award for Communications, 168
National Design Awards, 214–215
National Design Museum, 108, 168
National Poetry Month, 110
Natterson-Horowitz, Barbara, 59
*Natural Born Heroes*, 73
Nelson, Diane, 259
Némirovsky, Irène, 196–197
*Never Say Goodbye*, 254
*Newsweek*, 315
*New York*, 144, 195, 235
New York ComicCon, 219
*New Yorker*, 127, 258
*New York Post*, 292
*New York Times*, 62–63, 121, 158, 231, 289, 292
*New York Times* Best-Seller List, 13, 15, 290
*New York Times* Book Review, 67, 99, 176
Niemann, Christoph, 98, 202, 230
*Night*, 112
Nixon, Cynthia, 101
Nixon, Richard M., 113
Nobel Prize for Literature, 23, 112
*Number 17*, 315

Obama, Barack, 55
Oberman, Emily, 272, 315

*Obsession*, 256
*The Official Preppy Handbook*, 286
Olds, Sharon, 128
Onassis, Jackie, 308
*1Q84*, 10–13, 15, 71
*One Woman Shoe*, 5
*Only What's Necessary*, 221–223
*On the Golden Porch*, 134
*On the Move: A Life*, 230–231
*Open Heart*, 112
*The Orenda*, 190
*The Original of Laura*, 47, 184–186
*Other Colors*, 21
Ozawa, Seiji, 15

Pamuk, Orhan, 20–25
Paramount, 150, 154
*Paris Review*, 107
Parker, Bill, 241
Parkinson, Jim, 229
Parks, Gordon, 257
*A Passion for Leadership*, 99
*A Path Appears*, 123
Peace Statue, 216
*Peanuts and the Art of Charles M. Schulz*, 223
Peanuts Worldwide, 223
Penn State University, 4, 33, 64, 77, 242
Pentagram, 272
*Perfidia*, 170
Perlman, Chee, 282
Petrilli, Marco, 242
Petroski, Henry, 64–65
Piñon, Nélida, 193
Platon, 99
*Play the Part*, 282
Plimpton, George, 107
*Plundered Hearts: New and Selected Poems*, 156–157
*Poets & Writers*, 194
Police, 178–179
Ponsot, Marie, 61
Pop Art, 33
Porter, Deborah, 147
*The Possibility of an Island*, 204
*Possible Side Effects*, 88–89
*Present Tense*, 143
Puércell, Phillip J., 67
Puértolas, Romain, 63
Pulitzer Prize for Poetry, 128
Purcell, Phillip J., 67
Pynchon, Thomas, 278

Quammen, David, 58
Quint, Michelle, 284
Quitely, Frank, 260–261

*Rabbit Hole*, 100–101
Rabinowitz, Anna, 92–93, 143

*The Rainbow Comes and Goes*, 256
Rakoff, David, 238–239
Rand, Ayn, 120–121
Reading Symphony Orchestra, 140
Reagan, Judith, 235
*Reality Hunger*, 39
Remnick, David, 54–55
*Remote* (Shields), 39
*Reporting*, 54
*Retail Architecture and Shopping*, 183
*Ripley's Believe It or Not*, 224
Rizzoli, 183
Roach, Mary, 97–98
*The Road*, 80–83, 85
Robert, Francois, 205
Roberts, Julia, 202
Roberts, Stone, 156
*Rocket Science* (film), 138–139, 150
Rockwell, David, 282
Rockwell, Norman, 124
Rodin, Auguste, 57
*Rolling Stone*, 226–229
*Rome: A Cultural, Visual, and Personal History*, 104
Roosevelt, Franklin D., 124
Ross, Alex, 268–269
Ross, Jonathan, 28
*Rough Justice*, 268–269
R. R. Donnelley, 11–12
Rudd, Paul, 202
Rudnick, Paul, 149
Rushdie, Salman, 278
Russell, Karen, 96–97
Ryan, Paul, 121

Sacks, Oliver, 230–233
Sagan, Carl, 244
Sander, Jil, 215
Sanders, Terry, 46, 250
San Diego ComicCon, 28, 71, 272
*Sandman*, 26, 28, 29
Savage, Stephen, 202
Scher, Paula, 292
Schickel, Richard, 116–117
*The School for Husbands and The Imaginary Cuckold*, 119
Schulz, Charles, 220–225
Schulz, Jeannie, 223, 224
*Schulz and Peanuts*, 220–221
Schwalbe, Will, 40–41
Schwarm, Larry, 85
*The Second Plane*, 50–51
*The Secret History*, 11
*The Secret History of Wonder Woman*, 258–259
Sedaris, Amy, 5
Sedaris, David, 5, 39, 90–91, 148

See a Little Light: The Trail of Rage and Melody, 47
Segal, Jonathan, 99
Seibert, Elena, 230
Seigler, Bonnie, 315
*The Selected Letters of Anthony Hecht*, 201
*The Selected Letters of Thornton Wilder*, 201
Serino Coyne, 203
Seth, 239
Shatner, William, 29
*Shazam! The Golden Age of the World's Mightiest Mortal*, 240–241
Shields, David, 38–40
*The Shock of the New*, 103
Shonen Gahosha, 275
*Silent House*, 23
Simon, Eddie, 207
Simon, Joe, 241
Simon, Paul, 149, 206–213, 215
*Simple Justice*, 144
Sinatra, Frank, 257
Sinclair, Alex, 263
Sklaroff, Sara, 158
*Sleep* (Vincent Desiderio), 156
*Sleep Donation*, 96–97
*Small Tragedy*, 199
Smithsonian Institution, 215, 168–169
*Snow*, 23
*Somebody: The Reckless Life and Remarkable Career of Marlon Brando*, 116–117
*Sony Design: Making Modern*, 183
*Soon I Will Be Invincible*, 68–69
Sorbeck, Winter, 39
Spar, Debora L., 217
Spear, Geoff, 15, 40, 41, 42, 65, 67, 68, 70, 88–89, 90, 96, 136, 138, 146, 149, 163, 165, 169, 176, 182, 213, 224, 241, 289, 315
Spear, Jet, 149, 213, 281
*The Spectacle of Skill*, 103
Speicher, Eugene, 132
*Spend Shift*, 66, 216
*Spillover*, 58
Spitzer, Eliot, 234, 235
*Springing* (Ponsot), 61
*Stag's Leap*, 128
Starn, Doug, 168
Starn, Mike, 168
Steinberg, Saul, 131
Stewart, Martha, 292
Sting, 178, 179
"Stop the Violence" series (Francois Robert), 205
Strand, Mark, 129–131

Strand bookstore, 278
*The Strange Library*, 16–19
*A Strangeness in My Mind*, 24–25
*The Stranger's Child*, 132
*Stranger Than Fiction*, 182
Straub, Peter, 199
Strömholm, Christer, 199
*The Substance of Fire*, 202
Suicide Squad (film), 68
Summers, Andy, 178
*The Sunset Limited*, 80
Superman, 70, 241, 260–261, 263, 268–269, 271, 272, 295
Suri, Manil, 122
*Surprise*, 149, 207–213
Suzuki, Koji, 181
*Sweet Theft: A Poet's Commonplace Book*, 157
Swift, Elvis, 197

Tartt, Donna, 11
Taylor, Dave, 296–314
Taylor, David Van, 225
TED, 282–283, 284–285
*Terrorist*, 74–75
*The Terror Years*, 173
*Theft*, 115
*The Thing about Life Is That One Day You'll Be Dead*, 38–39
*Things I Didn't Know*, 102–103
Thomas, Bill, 239
Thompson, Emma, 182
Thompson, Reece, 138
Thomson, Rubert, 101
*Thoughts on Democracy*, 124
*Three Days of Rain*, 202–203
Tigerman, 94–95
*Time*, 99, 116, 161, 173, 174–175
Timm, Bruce, 295
Tolstaya, Tatyana, 134
Tong, Kevin, 96
*The Toothpick*, 64–65
*The Toughest Show on Earth: My Rise and Reign at the Metropolitan Opera*, 140–141
*Traps*, 192
*A Treacherous Paradise*, 199
Trinity, 271
Troy, Marshall, 91
Trudeau, Gary, 229
*True Prep*, 257, 286–291
Type Directors Club, 292–293

Ullmann, Linn, 100
Updike, John, 10, 74–77
Updike, Martha, 75
Updike, Wesley, 75
*USA Today*, 33

Vanderbilt, Gloria, 254, 256–257
van Gogh, Vincent, 91
*Villain*, 205
Villarubia, José, 162
*Visionaire*, 181–182
*Visual Shock*, 57
*Voices of the Desert*, 193
Volpe, Joseph, 140–141
Vonnegut, Kurt, 181

*The Walking Dead* (Robert Kirkman), 80
*Wall Street Journal*, 79, 287
Wanger, Shelley, 140, 286
*The Wanton Sublime*, 92–93
Ware, Chris, 28, 34, 37, 76, 158, 160–161
Warner Brothers, 264
Warner Brothers Records, 207
*Watching the Watchmen*, 162–165
Watson, Albert, 112
Webster, Stephen, 91
Wenner, Jann, 228
West, Kanye, 157
*When You Are Engulfed in Flames*, 90–91
Whitman, Walt, 110
Wiesel, Elie, 112
Wilbur, Richard, 118–119
Wilder, Thornton, 201
Williams, Scott, 263
Williams, Ted, 10, 75
*Wind / Pinball*, 15
Winfrey, Oprah, 83
*Wired*, 176
*A Wolf at the Table*, 89
Wolfsonian Museum, 124
Wonder Woman, 258, 271
*Wonder Woman: The Complete History*, 258
*Working Girl* (film), 152
*World and Town*, 133
*The World of Gloria Vanderbilt*, 257
Wright, Lawrence, 172–173
Wright, Robert, 176–177
Wright, Stephen, 126
WuDunn, Sheryl, 123
Wyeth, Andrew, 220
Wyeth, N. C., 220

*The Yiddish Policemen's Union*, 48–49
Yoshida, Shuichi, 205
*You Better Not Cry*, 86–88

*Zoetrope All-Story*, 86, 188–189
*Zoobiquity*, 58–69

The International Design Magazine .... The New Androgyny in Products.... Outrageous at CES
.... Swedish Miracle Town .... Micro Dorms .... Proposals for North Korea .... Preparing for 2012
I.D.
"I am a very good dancer, by the way."
Chip Kidd
Interviewed by
Jonathan
Safran Foer

PRINT
PRINTMAG.COM 70.1 SPRING 2016
56
Inspiring
Designers
Shaping Our
World Today
(Like Chip Kidd!)

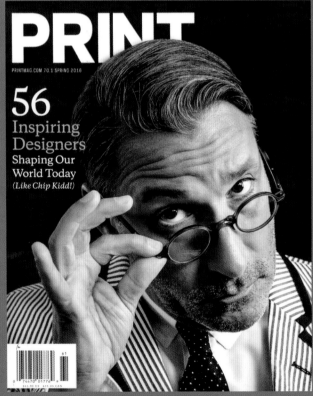

Try.

## Thank You!

Without the support for the last thirty years of Knopf Doubleday Group Art Director Carol Devine Carson and President and Editor-in-Chief Sonny Mehta, I would have no career. It's that simple. And to my other KDPG colleagues: Tony Chirico, Dan Frank, Gary Fisketjon, Lexy Bloom, Shelley Wanger, Anne Diaz, Andy Hughes, Altie Karper, Paul Bogaards, Deb Garrison, Claire Bradley, Robin Desser, Ann Close, Peggy Samedi, Jonathan Segal. Not only are they all the coolest people in the the world, they are also the best in the publishing business. Here's to the next three decades.

Mark Melnick made this book happen to an even greater extent and with more expertise than he did *Book One*, and that's saying something. He sifted through ten years' worth of work and made sense of it. I could not have done this without him.

Geoff Spear, one of my best friends in all the world, shot everything so beautifully. No one captures the moments better than he does.

Haruki Murakami, Neil Gaiman, and Orhan Pamuk. You wrote introductions for me. I am still pinching myself.

Alyssa Carver, Sandra Stelts, and Tim Pyatt at the Penn State Special Collections Library, for acquiring and presiding over my archives with such attention to detail. It's an honor to have the record of my existence at my alma mater.

At Rizzoli: editor Ian Luna, who has the best taste in the world and decided to do another book with me anyway; Charles Miers, who captains the mighty Rizzoli ship with grace and fortitude; and Monica A. Davis and Meaghan McGovern for editorial assistance and production.

Michael Cho, J. J. Abrams, Debbie Millman, Chris Ware, Edith Carey, Charlie Kochman, Anderson Cooper, Martin Parr, Maggie Appleton—you have all provided artwork, love, and guidance for this project—and best of all, friendship.

Mom and Dad, Ann and Tom Kidd, Aunt Syl, brother Walt and kids Lauren, Sam, Tommy, and Matthew: love and thanks for your continued support.

And to J. D. McClatchy, my husband of over 22 years, who kicks my ass out of bed every morning and reminds me to get something meaningful done before cocktail hour. I'm trying, Peach, I'm trying!!

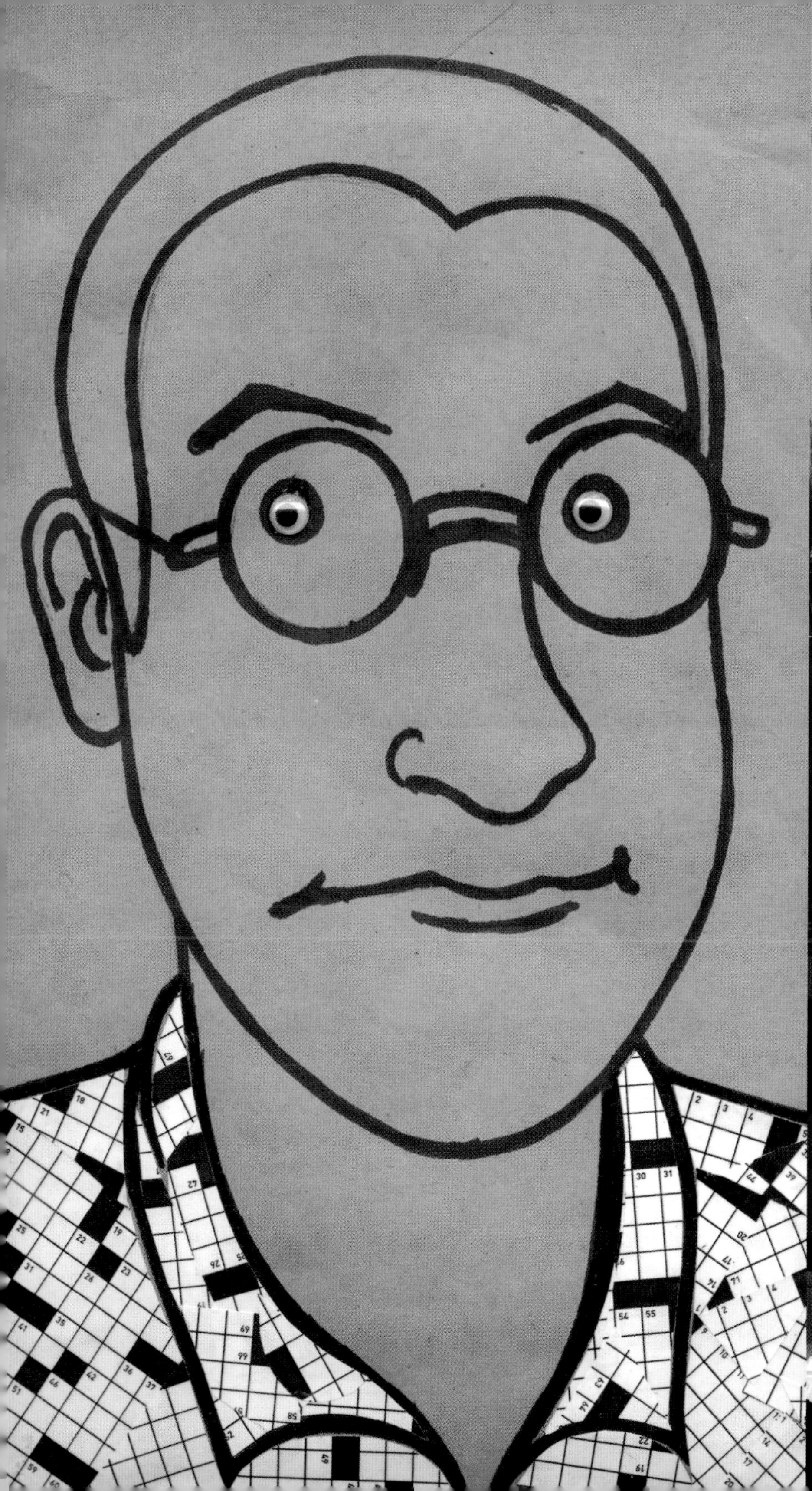

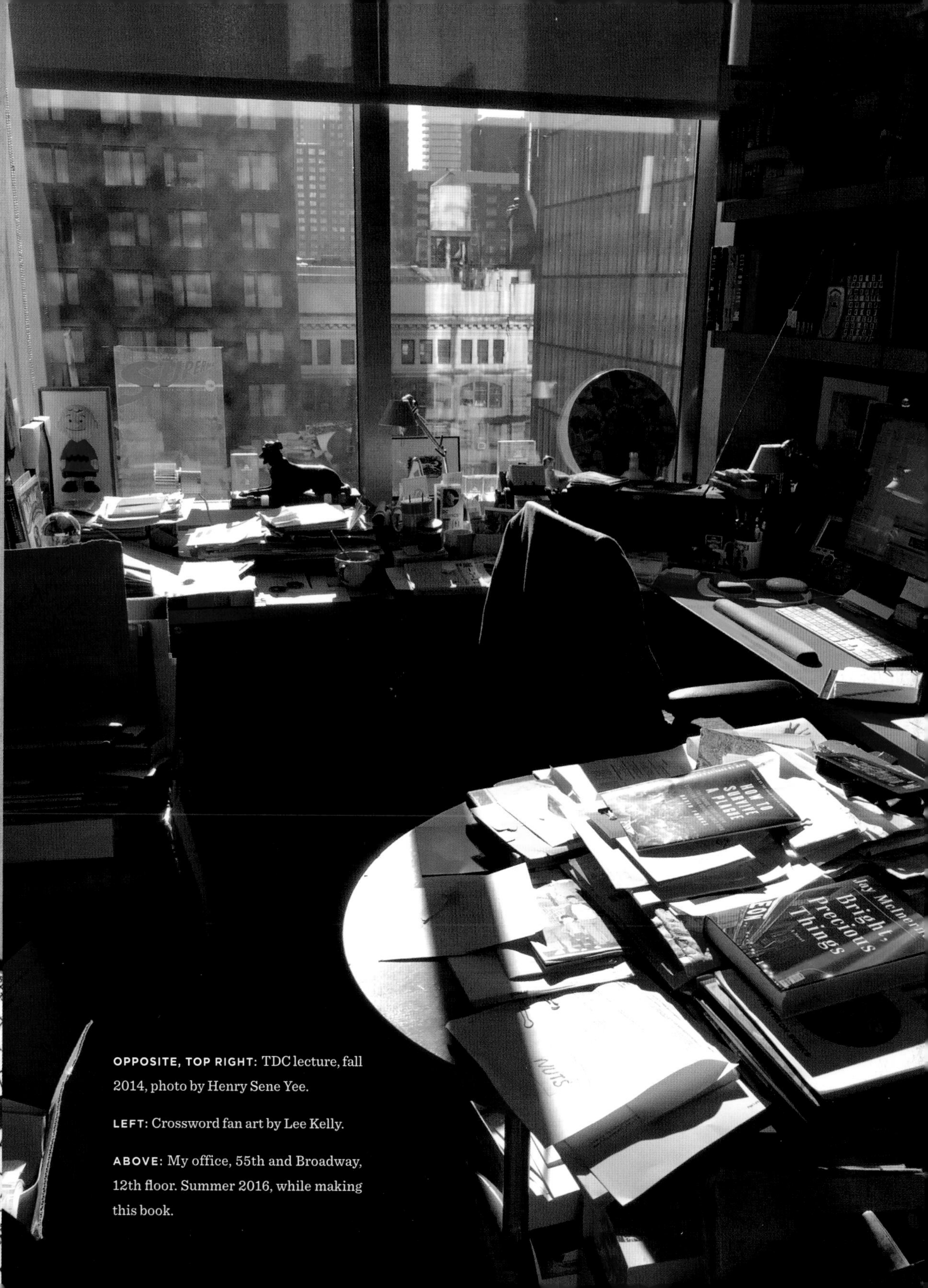
Bright, Precious Things

**OPPOSITE, TOP RIGHT:** TDC lecture, fall 2014, photo by Henry Sene Yee.

**LEFT:** Crossword fan art by Lee Kelly.

**ABOVE:** My office, 55th and Broadway, 12th floor. Summer 2016, while making this book.

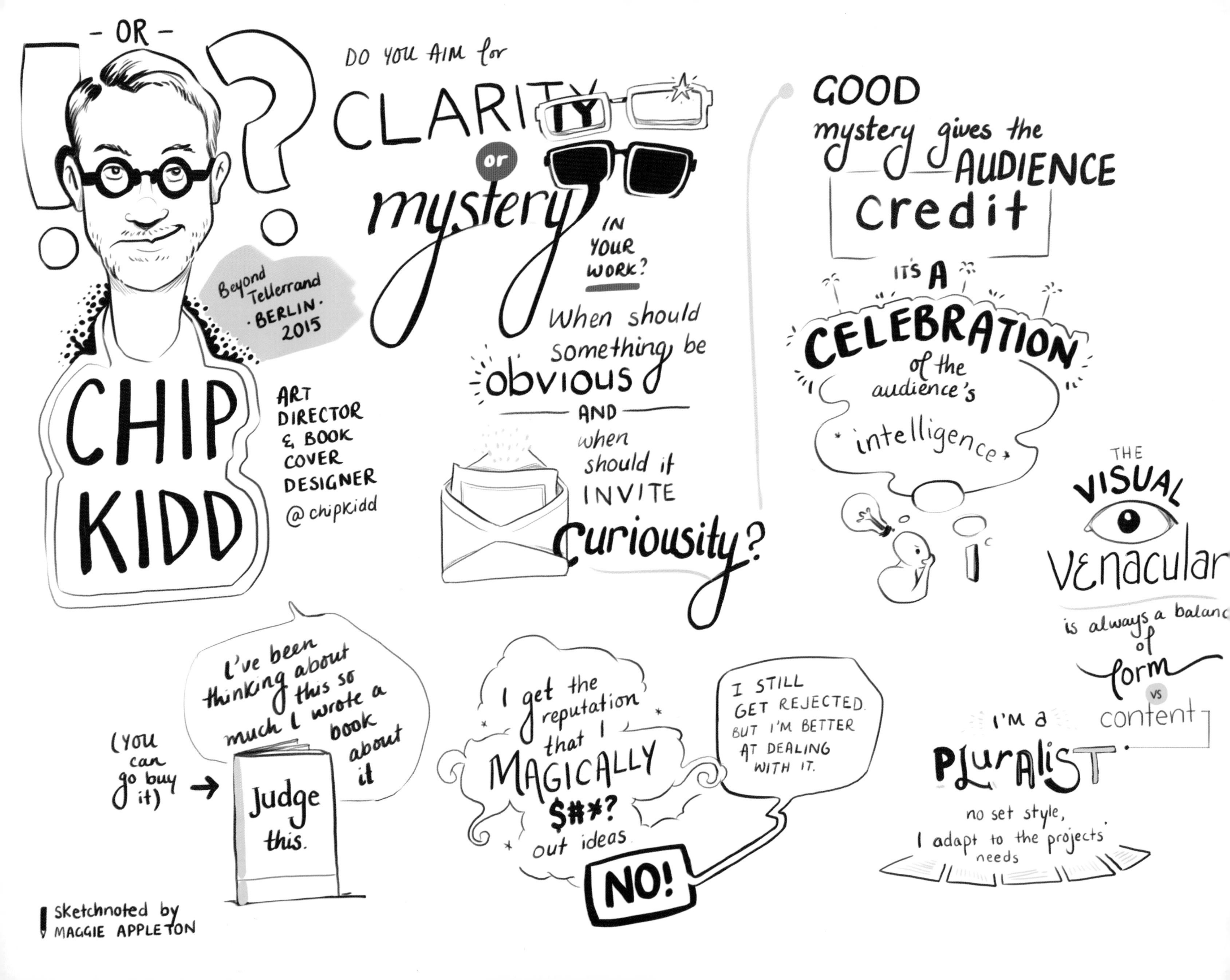
- OR -
DO YOU AIM for
CLARITY
or
mystery
IN YOUR WORK?
Beyond Tellerrand · BERLIN · 2015
CHIP KIDD
ART DIRECTOR & BOOK COVER DESIGNER
@chipkidd
When should something be obvious
AND
when should it INVITE curiousity?
GOOD mystery gives the AUDIENCE credit
IT'S A CELEBRATION of the audience's intelligence
THE VISUAL VENACULAR
is always a balanc of form vs content
I'M a PLURALIST
no set style, I adapt to the projects' needs
I've been thinking about this so much I wrote a book about it
(YOU can go buy it) →
Judge this.
I get the reputation that I MAGICALLY $#*? out ideas
NO!
I STILL GET REJECTED. BUT I'M BETTER AT DEALING WITH IT.
sketchnoted by MAGGIE APPLETON

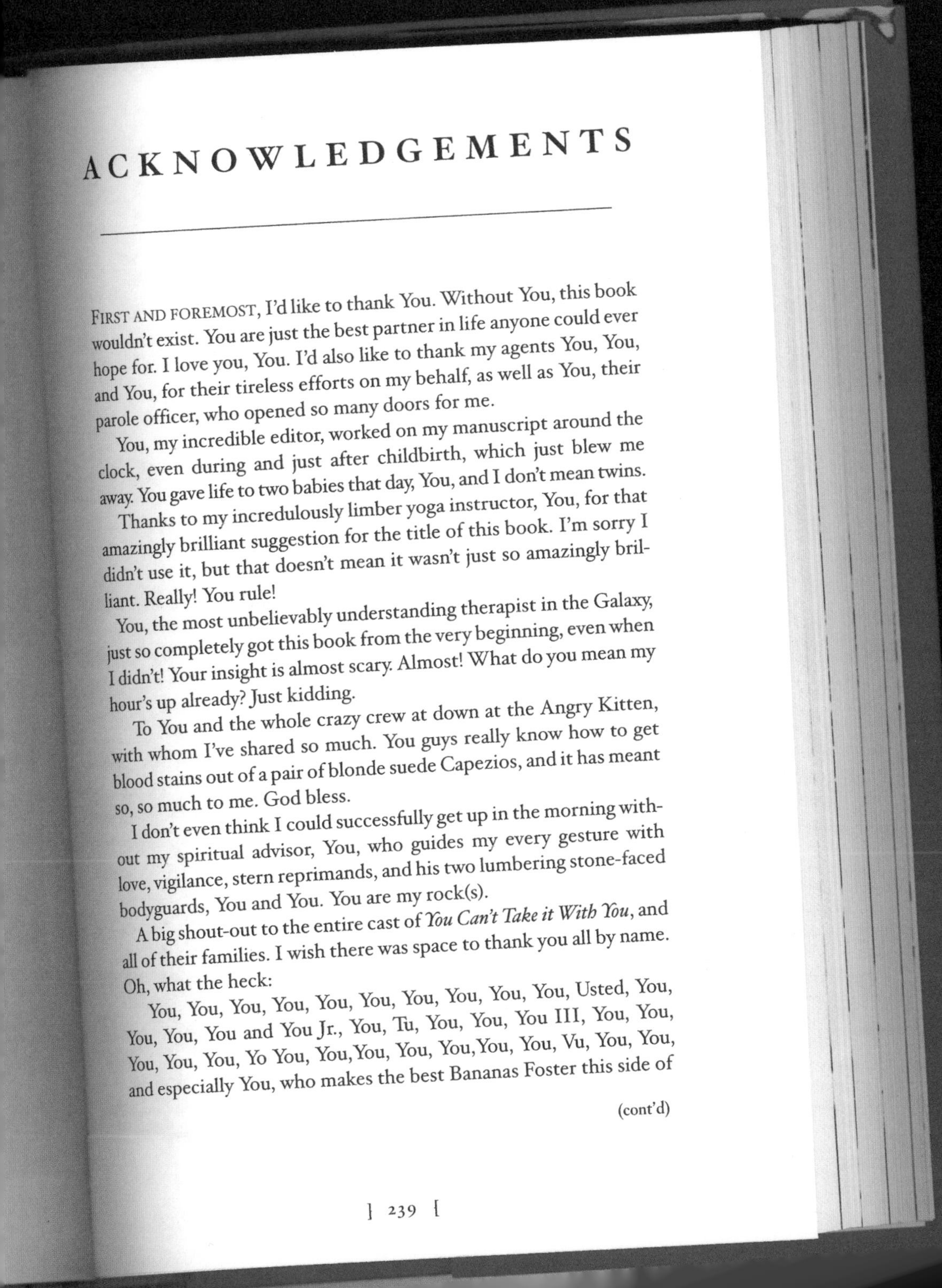

# ACKNOWLEDGEMENTS

FIRST AND FOREMOST, I'd like to thank You. Without You, this book wouldn't exist. You are just the best partner in life anyone could ever hope for. I love you, You. I'd also like to thank my agents You, You, and You, for their tireless efforts on my behalf, as well as You, their parole officer, who opened so many doors for me.

You, my incredible editor, worked on my manuscript around the clock, even during and just after childbirth, which just blew me away. You gave life to two babies that day, You, and I don't mean twins.

Thanks to my incredulously limber yoga instructor, You, for that amazingly brilliant suggestion for the title of this book. I'm sorry I didn't use it, but that doesn't mean it wasn't just so amazingly brilliant. Really! You rule!

You, the most unbelievably understanding therapist in the Galaxy, just so completely got this book from the very beginning, even when I didn't! Your insight is almost scary. Almost! What do you mean my hour's up already? Just kidding.

To You and the whole crazy crew at down at the Angry Kitten, with whom I've shared so much. You guys really know how to get blood stains out of a pair of blonde suede Capezios, and it has meant so, so much to me. God bless.

I don't even think I could successfully get up in the morning without my spiritual advisor, You, who guides my every gesture with love, vigilance, stern reprimands, and his two lumbering stone-faced bodyguards, You and You. You are my rock(s).

A big shout-out to the entire cast of *You Can't Take it With You*, and all of their families. I wish there was space to thank you all by name. Oh, what the heck:

You, You, You, You, You, You, You, You, You, You, Usted, You, You, You, You and You Jr., You, Tu, You, You, You III, You, You, You, You, You, Yo You, You,You, You, You,You, You, Vu, You, You, and especially You, who makes the best Bananas Foster this side of

(cont'd)

] 239 [

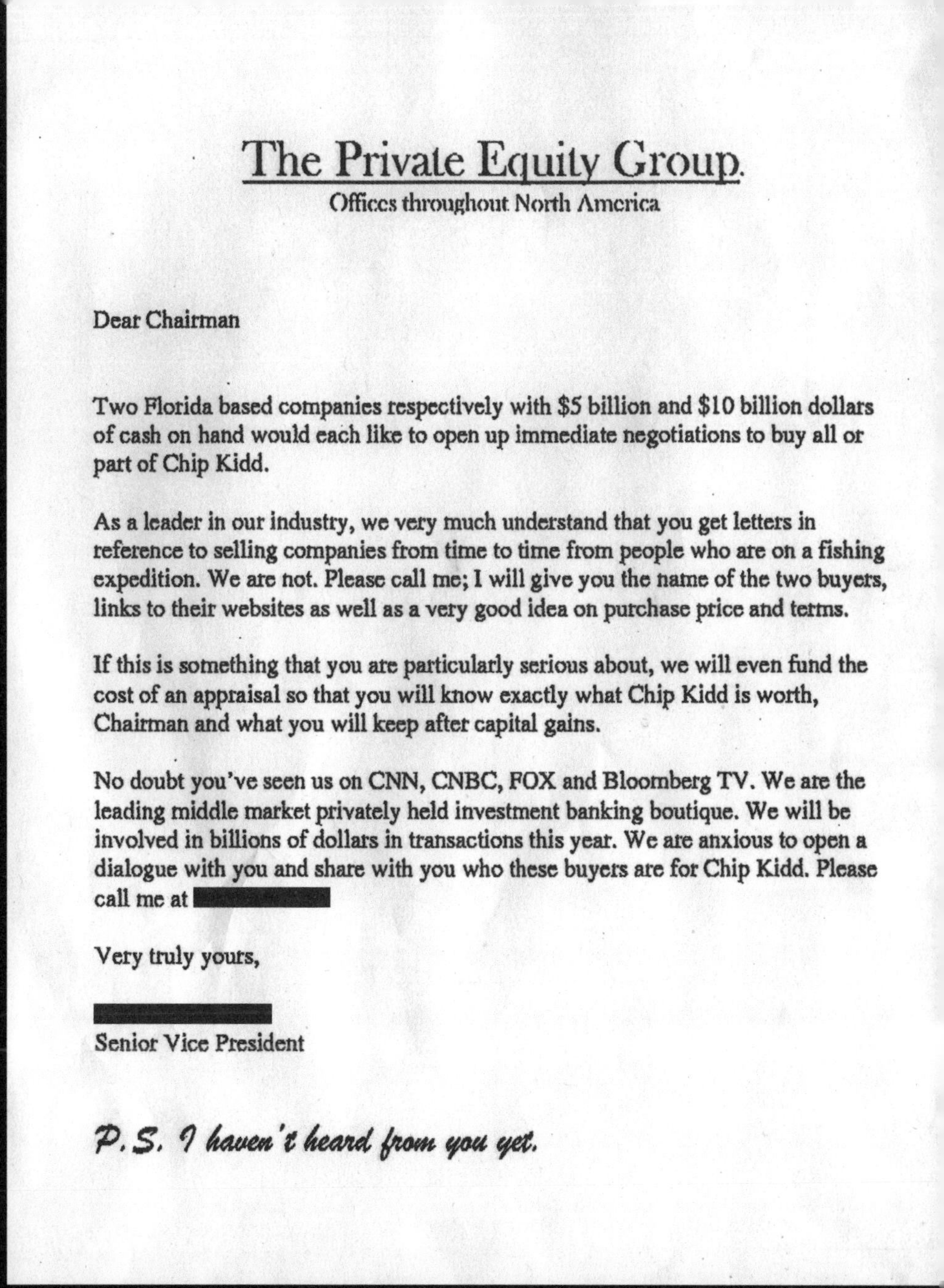

The Private Equity Group.
Offices throughout North America

Dear Chairman

Two Florida based companies respectively with $5 billion and $10 billion dollars of cash on hand would each like to open up immediate negotiations to buy all or part of Chip Kidd.

As a leader in our industry, we very much understand that you get letters in reference to selling companies from time to time from people who are on a fishing expedition. We are not. Please call me; I will give you the name of the two buyers, links to their websites as well as a very good idea on purchase price and terms.

If this is something that you are particularly serious about, we will even fund the cost of an appraisal so that you will know exactly what Chip Kidd is worth, Chairman and what you will keep after capital gains.

No doubt you've seen us on CNN, CNBC, FOX and Bloomberg TV. We are the leading middle market privately held investment banking boutique. We will be involved in billions of dollars in transactions this year. We are anxious to open a dialogue with you and share with you who these buyers are for Chip Kidd. Please call me at [redacted]

Very truly yours,

[redacted]

Senior Vice President

*P.S. I haven't heard from you yet.*

**OPPOSITE:** Visual notes taken by the artist Maggie Appleton, from my presentation at the Beyond Tellerrand design conference in Berlin, November 2015. **LEFT:** Illustration for *The New York Times Book Review* about excessive acknow

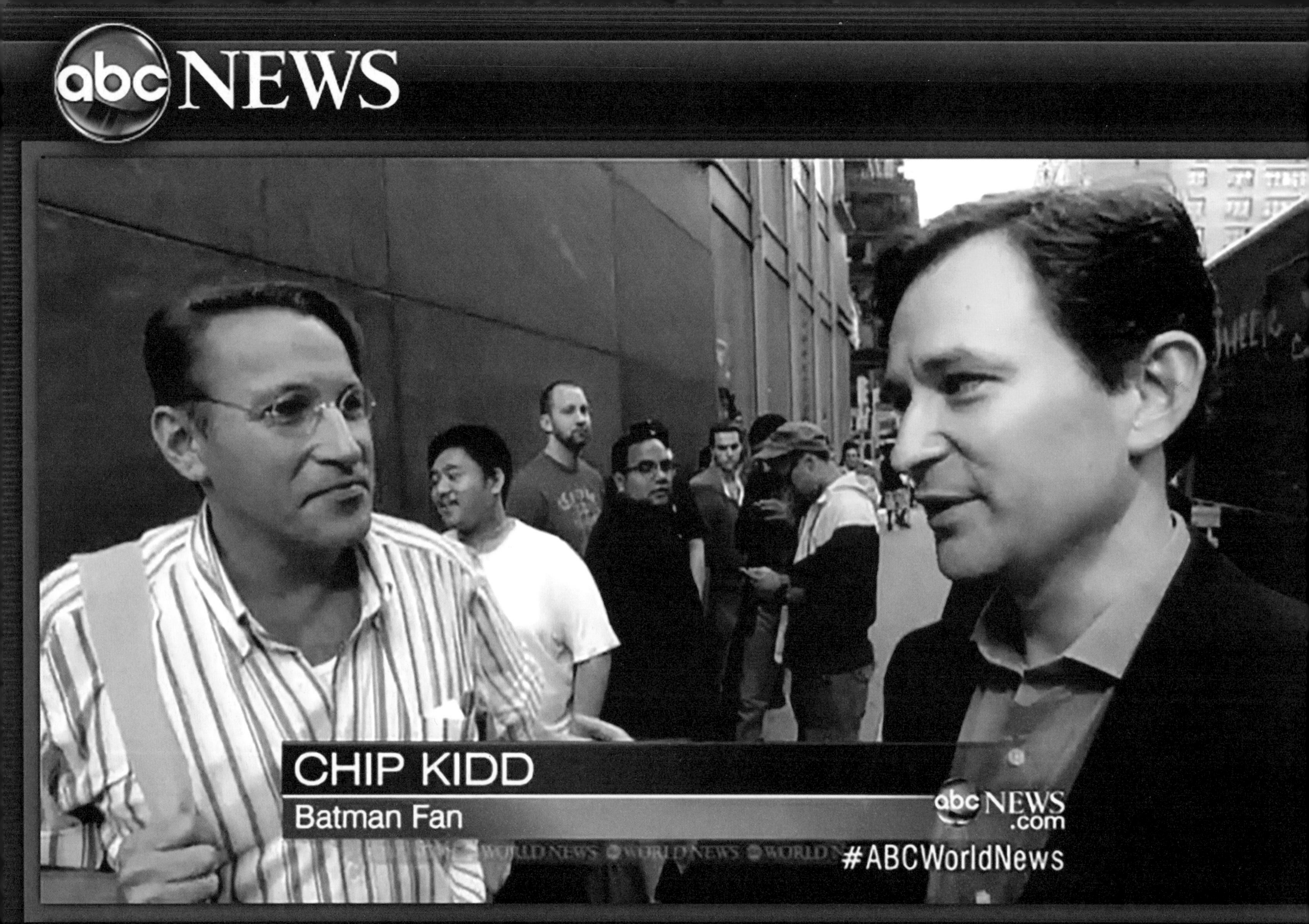
abc NEWS
CHIP KIDD
Batman Fan
abc NEWS .com
#ABCWorldNews

**ABOVE:** I was interviewed by ABC News while standing on line in New York City, before the premiere of *The Dark Knight Rises*, the morning after the horrific movie theater shooting in Aurora, Colorado. I repeatedly emphasized that it wasn't a Batman issue; it was a gun control issue. In fact, there is a rooftop fight scene in the film, in which an unarmed Batman and Catwoman take on a group of toughs. Catwoman wrestles a gun away from one of the bad guys and is about to use it against him, but Batman intervenes, shouting: "No guns, no killing!" And yet, despite my lengthy explanation, here is what ended up on air . . . Interviewer: "So, are you still going to see the movie?" Me: "Yes." End of interview. **OPPOSITE:** A custom Goyard travel bag I commissioned with the *Batman: Death by Design* logo along with my initials. And away we go!